Foundations of Property Law

Foundations of Property Law

Things as Objects of Property Rights

By

CHRISTIAN VON BAR DR JUR, DR JUR HC MULT, DR PHIL HC

University Professor and Director of the European Legal Studies Institute of the University of Osnabrück, Professor (Hon.) of the AJD Częstochowa, Bencher (Hon.) of Gray's Inn, FBA, MAE

Translated by

JASON GRANT ALLEN BA & LLB (HONS), LLM, GDLP, PHD

Associate Professor of Law, Singapore Management University Yong Pung How School of Law

OXFORD
UNIVERSITY PRESS

OXFORD
UNIVERSITY PRESS

Great Clarendon Street, Oxford, OX2 6DP,
United Kingdom

Oxford University Press is a department of the University of Oxford.
It furthers the University's objective of excellence in research, scholarship,
and education by publishing worldwide. Oxford is a registered trade mark of
Oxford University Press in the UK and in certain other countries

First Edition published in 2023

Published in the United States of America by Oxford University Press
198 Madison Avenue, New York, NY 10016, United States of America

British Library Cataloguing in Publication Data
Data available

Library of Congress Control Number: 2023937956

ISBN 978–0–19–888533–7

DOI: 10.1093/oso/9780198885337.001.0001

Printed and bound in the UK by
TJ Books Limited

Foreword

This book deals with 'things', i.e. with the objects of legal dealings in which peculiar rights can be held: the *erga omnes* rights of property law. In them, the answers to three questions constantly interact with each other: (i) in which objects can property rights arise? (ii) who can hold those rights? and (iii) which legal abilities do those rights give the person who holds them? Ever conscious of this reflexive dependence, we focus in this book on the first question. It has been more intensively discussed in the world of the Civilian tradition than in the jurisdictions of the common law world, in which the very title of this book might even sound a little audacious. As such, we cannot start a pan-European study *in medias res*. Instead, we set forth an analysis of the framework in which further discussion is made possible for a later time. This book is based on the first two sections of the first volume of my treatise *Gemeineuropäisches Sachenrecht*, which was published by C. H. Beck in Munich in 2015, which deals with all aspects of the property law of the European legal systems over six sections in two volumes. Dr Jason Grant Allen translated these first two sections, and I modified the English text to meet the requirements of a self-contained, separate publication. Works in the German language are accessible to a smaller audience than they once were. With a little luck, we can access readers not only in the British Isles and elsewhere in the Anglophone world but also in parts of the European Continent and abroad where English is more accessible than German. Property law is an aesthetically challenging, but also a very complex subject matter with many regional idiosyncrasies. Translations are thus a great challenge. We faced this challenge, but had to limit ourselves to tackling the 'Foundations of Property Law'.

The understanding of 'property law' and 'things' that we develop in the pages that follow rests on a huge body of data. Long footnotes are not necessarily to everybody's taste, but they are in this case unavoidable. They bear witness to the many paths by which we explored a dispersed, multi-lingual, and diverse body of material. Some parts of the book can be used as a reference text. Our actual focus, however, is on the understanding of connections and relations and on the internal logical structure of our material; it is ultimately a book about things. Where it fulfils our aspirations and affords new insights, it is usually as a result of a pan-European approach—i.e. of the ambition to bring together and present the property laws of the Member States of the European Union and the United Kingdom as part of a *single* picture. If this picture is drawn properly, it embraces every national legal order with its own conceptual and political preconceptions. Our system unfolds, to a certain extent, on its own. It must succeed in presenting this part of the property law of each Member State without the monotony of itemized, country-by-country reports, but instead decrypting a picture of the whole that evaluates, and values, each wealth of national knowledge and experience. To think through private law in a 'European' manner proceeds, in our view, with a constant shifting of focus from the whole to its parts and from the parts to their whole. It feeds on them, connects them, but also sets them on an equal footing in a marketplace of ideas. We have been guided by the conviction that property law is susceptible of truly European understanding, and that it is beneficial to analyse it in this European perspective. That goes for rights in land no less than rights in other things. The concentration on the legal systems of the European Union is justified above all by the fact that they have together created an area of freedom, security, and law that is unique in the world. This dynamic is tangible everywhere in private law, and private law cannot exist without a law of property.

I thank members of our Standing Seminar on Common European Property Law. They have done far more than I can express in a foreword. I thank them for their countless analyses and translations, for their encouragement, and for sharing the many insights which appeared in friendly but unflinchingly open discussions. I am also thankful for the constant flow of suggestions to improve the text, which at all times remained accessible to all participants. Every one of us impressed an accent on this book, even if I am the sole author.

The German manuscript was finalized as at January 2015. The English translation was finalized in January 2022.

Christian von Bar
Osnabrück
May 2023

The Standing Seminar on Common European Property Law

This book is based on the research of a Standing Seminar on Common European Property Law. I could not have gathered the material, which its members made available to me, by my own efforts alone. For that reason, this book is their book also:

Mateusz Badowski (Polish law)
Xavier Borremans (Belgian and French law)
Hinrich Doege (German law, from February 2013)
Robert Hammarstedt (Swedish law, until February 2011)
Galateia Tina Kalouta (Greek and Cypriot law)
Dr Geo Magri (Italian law, from February 2011)
Pádraic McCannon (English and Irish law, until December 2010)
Dr José Carlos de Medeiros Nóbrega (Portuguese law and, from February 2012, Spanish law)
Egil Nordqvist (Swedish law, from April 2011)
Dr Fabio Massimo Scaramuzzino (Italian law, until October 2010),
Dr Magda Schwandt (Czech law, law of the Baltic states)
Dr Christoph Karl Sliwka (Austrian law, from February 2014 also English law)
Dr Stephen Swann (English law, until January 2014)
Thorsten Tepaße (Netherlands law and, until December 2012, German law)
Laura Tomás Jiménez (Spanish law, until December 2011)
Information on Bulgarian law is thanks to Dimitar Stoimenov (Sofia), and information on Hungarian law is thanks to Dr Ferenc Szilágyi (Budapest).

Translator's Introduction

This book treats a cornerstone of private law in all legal traditions. Following the Civilian idiom, which derives often (though not exclusively) from Latin *res*, it uses the concept of 'things' to trace the conceptual foundations of 'property law' as a discipline concerned (in the first instance, at least) with *persons' rights in things*.

As Professor Christian von Bar's foreword explains, this is an abridged translation comprising § 1 and § 2 of the first volume of the original, *Gemeineuropäisches Sachenrecht*, published with the permission of C. H. Beck. The abridgement was, unfortunately, a function of limited time and other resources. However, there is at the present time a need for a book of accessible length that helps us to determine the province of 'property law', and that engages with its objects. This book does that by spelling out the relationship between things, persons, and rights (which are held by persons in things against other persons) in a compelling and useful way.

Its value is illustrated, for example, in the current debate about the legal treatment of digital objects, which is a site of activity in terms of both domestic legal development and harmonization efforts at the national, European, and international level. New (digital) 'objects' have arisen and now fall to be classified. Prominent examples include the Law Commission of England and Wales current work on digital assets (which broaches questions such as the reconceptualization of 'possession' for the digital era, and a 'third category' of personal property), the European Legal Institute's project on 'access to digital assets', and the UNIDROIT Study LXXXII on digital assets and private law. The concept of 'thing-ness' has become a matter of importance and urgency in the digital context—even in the common law world. There is open talk of structural renovation of property law's received categories, not just panel-beating. National responses to the question are proliferating, but coalescing around a number of different models, which underlines the importance of comparative study and harmonization work. The conceptual and comparative understanding of property law presented in this book provides an invaluable background for such work in commercial law, especially in the international context.

By setting out a conceptual scheme of property law as the *law of things*, this book will provide a fixed, universal point of reference for a very important discussion about the borders and foundations of property law itself. At its heart lies a conceptual schema that comprises three categories. 'Objects' (from the German *Gegenstände*) are everything that exists and is the case. 'Things' (from the German *Sachen*) are only the relevant legal system grants property rights. The concept of 'thing-ness' is an inherently legal one that turns on the reflexivity of 'rights' and 'things' rather than on physical (or other) characteristics of the object in question. Thus, von Bar presents sub-categories of 'things' that are partly or even wholly 'normative' as opposed to 'real'. Although the terminology is unfamiliar, in certain respects this concept of 'thing' comes closer to the English common law concept of an 'estate' than the Continental idea from which its terminology derives. The third category, 'objects of legal transaction', is perhaps the least idiomatic, being a translation of the German *Gegenstände des Rechtsverkehrs*. It comprises a set of objects that can be the object of dealings such as sale, but not the kind of monopoly rights that are quintessentially 'property rights'.

Not everyone will agree with this terminological scheme or the conceptual scheme on which it rests—after all, it challenges the dogmatic inheritance of all legal systems to some extent, at least. But that is the value of this book, and it will help to structure and discipline the debate it stimulates through the magisterial comparative frame of reference that is von Bar's legacy a legal scholar.

Indeed, this book is a pioneer work in its comparative ambition. The substantive theory of property law von Bar presents transcends the dogmatic conventions of any single legal tradition. His comparative scope is impressive—overwhelming, even. At times, his extensive reference to national law examples was exasperating for this translator! Yet, it will serve as an invaluable reference tool that is unparalleled in breadth and interwoven with von Bar's novel conceptual scheme. Without this kind of comprehensive survey, space would remain for the narcissism of small differences to creep in: one's received property law tradition often seems self-evidently the only logical or even possible way of doing things. In discussions about harmonization, or any sort of reform, it is tempting to grasp at the intricate details of that system and, perhaps unconsciously, defend its idiosyncratic responses to common problems. One virtue of this book's exhaustive reference to the doctrinal law of the European legal systems—including smaller ones generally ignored—is that no European legal scholar can feel that her legal system has been ignored (or spared) by its analysis. Von Bar's arguments simply must be faced head on.

Translating a text dealing with the common law jurisdictions of Europe in this project of 'common European law' was challenging. It was, for example, a fascinating exercise to describe English law 'easements' as 'servitudes' (the latter term being adopted as the most neutral from the pan-European comparative perspective). It was in these passages that I realized how ambitious the book—and therefore its translation by an outsider—was. I was able to refer to the original sources of (and on) English law, and reformulate sentences as necessary to reflect the substance of the argument as accurately and idiomatically as possible in English. I tried to do the same wherever I could with other languages—for example, French, Spanish, Italian, and Dutch statutes were partially accessible to me. Sources in languages such as Czech, Greek, or Estonian (to name but a few) were, on the other hand, utterly beyond reach. In many cases, I received help from my broader network—in particular my polyglot community of alumni from Cambridge, whom I thank. In many others, I simply did the best I could to translate from the German translation into English. I hope scholars from the relevant jurisdictions will judge these efforts kindly. The translation would serve its purpose well, I think, if it were to stimulate a debate directed towards a better (more commensurable?) set of definitions and concepts in European property law.

The quest for a 'common European property law' which includes the common law system of the British Isles is, in and of itself, enormously ambitious. Sometimes, the difficulty of this task was apparent in the act of translation itself. To take but one example, English law conceptualizes 'ownership' in land as a *freehold estate*, a bundle of rights that have some patch of the earth's surface as their reference point. The relevant object is the 'estate', not the 'land'. This is in many ways quite similar to von Bar's notion of 'land units' as 'normative objects with a physical substrate', but when it comes to the task of forging the common law and Continental approaches into a 'common' approach, there is evident strain. One discussion, for example, wrangles with the question whether a servitude (easement) forms part of the *right of ownership* in a land unit or forms part of the *land unit itself*. This is difficult enough to discuss over the common law–civil law divide; to translate that discussion back into English without presupposing common law modes of thought was even more challenging.

The idiom in which the enquiry is couched will be somewhat unfamiliar for Anglophone common lawyers. It rests on the basic orientation and approach of the enquiry. 'Thing' is a technical term in many European legal languages, but is not in English. It was thus necessary to avoid over-using 'thing' in its colloquial sense, in order to reserve it as a term of art, or at least disambiguate how it is being used in any given sentence. We common lawyers are not generally concerned with conceptual definitions of phenomena like 'things' or with axiomatic propositions (which are always, at base, tautological) such as 'a thing is an object in which a person can have all the rights a person can have in a thing' (or the inverse, 'a property right is a right a person can have in a thing which is effective against all other persons without a basis in the law of obligations'). We tend rather to ask: 'what is property?'—and we approach that question from the perspective of rights and remedies, not their objects. But this book is not only, or even primarily, for Anglophone common lawyers—it is also intended for other Civilian lawyers for whom English is the *lingua franca* through which they will access categories and conceptual approaches that are already familiar. Moreover—and more to the point—the unfamiliar language of 'things' may be of particular value for us common lawyers at the present time, as we grapple with the characteristics of fitting objects of property rights more directly than perhaps ever before.

Needless to say, this has not been an easy book to translate. Hence, a brief comment on practical matters is apposite. Awkward phrasing has generally been considered carefully and discussed between myself and von Bar. Not seldom, we have opted for a phrasing that is less idiomatic but more accurate, whether because truer to the original or less suggestive of a 'false friend'. Infelicities of course remain that reflect my limitations as a translator rather than conscious choice. Every bit of translation is a bit of treason, as the proverbial saying goes: *traduttore, traditore*. Through meetings in person, wherever possible, and on the telephone, we went over every line at least once. Terms that were difficult to translate, or otherwise better left in the original German, have sometimes been used in square brackets throughout the text and the footnotes. As an advanced text in comparative law, French text has generally been left in the original and original terms are used (especially in the Latinate languages) where the meaning is clear from the context and linguistic similarity to the English or a translated term in another, related language.

The civil law codifications of the European jurisdictions have different names. In the original German text, some were rendered in the original (where that is familiar or self-explanatory for German readers familiar with Latin, e.g. Italian *Codice civile*, Netherlands *Wetboek*). Others were referred to with their literal German translation (often *Zivilgesetzbuch* for 'civil code') or an abbreviation thereof. Others again were left in the original. I have taken a crude shorthand: I refer to them all as a 'Civil Code' (capitalized). This seemed the most straightforward solution to ensure consistency over the text. The original names of all the codes are set out at the start of the book. It seemed to me most important to distinguish, for an English-reading audience, whether it was a civil code or some subordinate statute under discussion. Other statutes in the German version were sometimes translated and sometimes left in the original language. In the English version, too, some appear in English and some appear in the original. Inevitably in a text of this length and complexity, stylistic gaffes will have been introduced by translation. I hope that these do not detract from the readability of the text or its usefulness as a point of reference.

I wish to acknowledge and thank our research assistant, Ms Eileen MacPherson, for her diligence in assisting me with the translation of the footnotes. In fact, a good part of the translation of the footnote text is her work. It deserves the highest credit, as it was instrumental in bringing this project to completion. Moreover, she worked independently—and for that reason often thanklessly—for several long months during the first COVID-19 lockdown in Berlin in early 2020 with utmost professionalism. Ms Stefanie Kämmerer was also instrumental in helping me to get the translated manuscript into presentable form, for which I am immensely grateful. For me, this translation ran in parallel to my own research—and therefore consumed weekends and evenings for some time. I thank my wife Stefanie for her patience over this time. Only she knows my reasons for doing so, to which I dedicate my efforts on our joint behalf.

Jason Grant Allen
Launceston
January 2022

Contents

Table of Abbreviated Literature

This table sets out the abbreviations (in the left-hand column) of texts cited frequently in the footnotes. They follow a system used in Professor von Bar's other publications on common European law, which is largely self-explanatory; the numbers in superscript refer to editions.

Advies van de Raad van State, Parl. Geschiedenis III	*Advies van de Raad van State, in: CJ Van Zeben and JW Du Pon in cooperation with MM Olthof* (eds), Parlementaire Geschiedenis van het Nieuwe Burgerlijk Wetboek. Parlementaire stukken. Book III: Vermogensrecht in het Algemeen (Deventer 1991)
Albaladejo, Derecho civil I(2)[14], II[13], III(1)[10]	*Manuel Albaladejo García*, Derecho civil. Volume I: Introducción y parte general, part 2: La relación, las cosas y los hechos jurídicos (14th edn, Barcelona 1996); Volume II: Derecho de obligaciones (13th edn, Madrid 2008); Volume III: Derecho de bienes (10th edn, Madrid 2004)
Albiges and Dumont-Lefrand, Droit des sûretés[3,4]	*Christophe Albiges and Marie-Pierre Dumont-Lefrand*, Droit des sûretés (4th edn, Paris 2013, 3rd edn, Paris 2011)
Aleksandrowicz, Komentarz do ustawy o dostępie do informacji publicznej[4]	*Tomasz Aleksandrowicz*, Komentarz do ustawy o dostępie do informacji publicznej (4th edn, Warsaw 2008)
Ancel, Droit des sûretés[6]	*Pascal Ancel*, Droit des sûretés (6th edn, Paris 2011)
Andrade da Silva, Código dos Contratos Públicos comentado e anotado[3]	*Jorge Andrade da Silva*, Código dos Contratos Públicos comentado e anotado (3rd edn, Coimbra 2010)
Asser (-*Hijma*), Bijzondere Overeenkomsten I[7]	*Carel Asser* (ed.), Carel Asser's handleiding tot de beoefening van het Nederlands burgerlijk recht. Volume V: Bijzondere overeenkomsten. Part 1: Koop en ruil; by *Jacob Hijma* (7th edn, Deventer 2007)
Asser (-*Mijnssen and de Haan*), Goederenrecht I[13]	*Carel Asser* (ed.), Carel Asser's handleidning tot de beoefening van het Nederlands burgerlijk recht. Volume III: Goederenrecht. Part 1: Algemeen goederenrecht; by *F.H.J Mijnssen and P. de Haan* (13th edn, Zwolle 1992)
Asser (-*Mijnssen/de Haan/van Dam/Ploeger*), Goederenrecht I[15]	*Carel Asser* (ed.), Carel Asser's handleidning tot de beoefening van het Nederlands burgerlijk recht. Volume III: Goederenrecht. Part 1: Algemeen goederenrecht; by *F.H.J Mijnssen, P. de Haan, C.C. van Dam and H.D. Ploeger* (15th edn, Zwolle 2006)
Asser (-*Mijnssen/van Velten/ Bartels*), Zakenrecht[15]	*Carel Asser* (ed.), Carel Asser's handleiding tot de beoefening van het Nederlands burgerlijk recht. Volume V: Zakenrecht. Eigendom en beperkte rechten; by *F.H.J. Mijnsen, A.A. van Velten and Steven Bartels* (15th edn, Deventer 2008)
Asser (-*Perrick*), Erfrecht[12]	*Carel Asser* (ed.), Carel Asser's handleidning tot de beoefening van het Nederlands burgerlijk recht. Volume VI: Erfrecht. Erfrecht en schenking; by *Steven Perrick* (12th edn, Deventer 1996)

Asser (-*van Mierlo und van Velten*), Vermogensrecht algemeen III[14]	*Carel Asser* (ed.), Carel Asser's handleidning tot de beoefening van het Nederlands burgerlijk recht. Volume III: Vermogensrecht algemeen. Part 3: Zekerheidsrechten; by *Antonius I.M. van Mirlo and Aart A. van Velten* (14th edn, Deventer 2010)
Atias, Les biens[8,10,11]	*Christian Atias*, Droit civil. Les biens (11th edn, Paris 2011, 10th edn, Paris 2009, 8th edn, Paris 2005)
Aynès and Crocq, Les sûretés[4,5,7]	*Laurent Aynès und Pierre Crocq*, Les sûretés. La publicité foncière (7th edn, Paris 2013, 5th edn, Paris 2011, 4th edn, Paris 2009)
Baker and Langan, Snell's Equity[29]	*Paul Vivian Baker and Peter St. John Langan*, Snell's Equity (29th edn, London 1990)
Bamberger and Roth (-*author*), BGB[3]	*Heinz Georg Bamberger and Herbert Roth*, Kommentar zum Bürgerlichen Gesetzbuch (3rd edn, Munich 2012)
von Bar, Gemeineuropäisches Deliktsrecht I, II	*Christian von Bar*, Gemeineuropäisches Deliktsrecht. Volume I: Die Kernbereiche des Deliktsrechts, seine Angleichung in Europa und seine Einbettung in die Gesamtrechtsordnungen (Munich 1996); Volume II: Schaden und Schadenersatz, Haftung für und ohne eigenes Fehlverhalten, Kausalität und Verteidigungsgründe (Munich 1999)
von Bar (-*author*), Sachenrecht in Europa I, III, IV	*Christian von Bar* (ed.), Sachenrecht in Europa. Systematische Einführung und Gesetzestexte. Volume I: Dänemark, England, Finnland, Schweden (Osnabrück 1999); Volume III: Griechenland, Portugal, Niederlande; Volume IV: Belgien, Spanien, Italien, Frankreich (Osnabrück 2001)
Barnsley (-*Thompson*), Conveyancing Law and Practice[4]	*Mark P. Thompson*, Barnsley's Conveyancing Law and Practice, (4th edn, London 1996)
Barta, Zivilrecht	*Heinz Barta* with collaboration of *Reinhold Beiser, Martin Binder et al.*, Zivilrecht. Grundriss und Einführung in das Rechtsdenken (Vienna 2004)
Baur and Stürner, Sachenrecht[18]	*Jürgen F. Baur and Rolf Stürner*, Sachenrecht (18th edn, Munich 2009)
Beckman, JB[2]	*Lars K Beckman et al.*, Jordabalken: en kommentar till JB och anslutande författningar (2nd edn, Stockholm 2012)
BeckOK (-*author*), BGB[20]	*Heinz Georg Bamberger and Herbert Roth* (eds), Beck'scher Online-Kommentar zum BGB (20th edn, Munich 2011)
BeckOK (-*author*), GBO[15]	*Stefan Hügel* (ed.), Beck'scher Online-Kommentar zur Grundbuchordnung (15th edn, Munich 2012)
Behrends/Knütel/Kupisch/Seiler (eds), Corpus Iuris Civilis I[2]	*Okko Behrends, Rolf Knütel, Berthold Kupisch and Hans Hermann Seiler* (eds), Corpus Iuris Civilis. Text und Übersetzung. Volume I: Institutionen (2nd edn, Heidelberg 1997)
Bell, Modern Law of Personal Property	*Andrew P. Bell*, Modern Law of Personal Property in England and Ireland (London 1989)
Bengtsson, Speciell Fastighetsrätt—Miljöbalken[7]	*Bertil Bengtsson*, Speciell Fastighetsrätt—Miljöbalken (7th edn, Uppsala 1999)
Bengtsson/Hager/Victorin, Hyra och annan nyttjanderätt till fast egendom[8]	*Bertil Bengtsson, Richard Hager, Anders Victorin*, Hyra och annan nyttjanderätt till fast egendom (8th edn, Stockholm 2013)
Benjamin (-*author*), Sale of Goods[7]	*Judah P. Benjamin*, Sale of Goods (7th edn, London 2008)
Bercovitz Rodríguez-Cano (-*Author*), Comentarios al Código Civil[2]	*Rodrigo Bercovitz Rodríguez-Cano*, Comentarios al Código Civil (2nd edn, Pamplona 2006)
Bergel/Bruschi/Cimamonti, Les biens[2]	*Jean-Louis Bergel, Marc Bruschi and Sylvie Cimamonti*, Les biens, in: Jacques Ghestin (ed.), Traité de droit civil (2nd edn, Paris 2010)

Berlioz, La notion de bien	*Pierre Berlioz*, La notion de bien (Paris 2007)
Bianca, Diritto civile VI, VII	*Cesare Massimo Bianca*, Diritto civile. Volume VI: La proprietà (Milan 1999); Volume VII: Le garanzie reali. La prescrizione (Milan 2012)
Bieniek and Rudnicki (*-author*), Nieruchomości. Problematyka prawna[5]	*Gerard Bieniek and Stanisław Rudnicki*, Nieruchomości. Problematyka prawna (5th edn, Warsaw 2009)
Bigliazzi Geri, Diritto civile I(1), II	*Lina Bigliazzi Geri*, Diritto civile. Volume I Part 1: Norme, soggetti e rapporto giuridico (Turin 1987, reprint 2001); Volume II: I diritti reali (Turin 1988)
Biondi, I beni	*Biondo Biondi*, I beni, in: Filippo Vassalli (ed.), Trattato di diritto civile italiano (Turin 1953)
Birks (*-author*), English Private Law I	*Peter Birks* (ed.), English Private Law. Volume I: Sources of law, law of persons, law of property (Oxford 2000)
Bourassin/Brémond/Jobard, Droit des sûretés[4]	*Manuella Bourassin, Vincent Brémond and Marie-Noëlle Jobard-Bachellier*, Droit des sûretés (4th edn, Paris 2014)
Brahn and Reehuis, Zwaartepunten van het vermogensrecht[9]	*O.K. Brahn and W.H.M. Reehuis*, Zwaartepunten van het vermogensrecht (9th edn, Deventer 2010)
Branca and Alpa, Istituzioni di diritto privato[7]	*Giuseppe Branca and Guido Alpa*, Istituzioni di diritto privato (7th edn, Bologna 1996)
Bridge, Personal Property Law[3]	*Michael G. Bridge*, Personal Property Law (3rd edn, Oxford 2002)
Brunet/Servais/Resteau (eds), Répertoire pratique de droit belge I	*Emile Brunet, Jean Servais and Charles Resteau (eds)*, Répertoire pratique de droit belge. Législation, Doctrine et Jurisprudence. Vol. 1 (Brussels 1928)
Bydlinski, Privatrecht[6]	*Peter Bydlinski*, Grundzüge des Privatrechts für Ausbildung und Praxis (6th edn, Vienna 2005)
Cabrillac/Mouly/Cabrillac/Pétel, Droit des sûretés[9]	*Michel Cabrillac, Christian Mouly, Séverine Cabrillac and Philippe Pétel*, Droit des sûretés (9th edn, Paris 2010)
Carbonnier, Droit civil II	*Jean Carbonnier*, Droit civil. Volume II: Les biens, Les obligations (Paris 2004)
Carrasco Perera/Cordero Lobato/Marín López, Tratado de los derechos de garantía I[2], II[2]	*Angel Carrasco Perera / Encarna Cordero Lobato / Manuel Jesús Marín López*, Tratado de los derechos de garantía, Volume I: Garantías personales. Hipoteca; Volume II: Garantías mobiliarias (2nd edn, Pamplona 2008)
Carvalho Fernandes, Lições de direitos reais[2]	*Luís A. Carvalho Fernandes*, Lições de direitos reais (2nd edn, Lisbon 1997)
Carvalho Fernandes, Teoria geral do direito civil I[2]	*Luís A. Carvalho Fernandes*, Teoria geral do direito civil. Volume I (2nd edn, Lisbon 1995)
Carvalho Fernandes and Brandão Proença (*-author*), Comentário ao Código Civil	*Luís Carvalho Fernandes and José Brandão Proença* (eds), Comentário ao Código Civil—Parte Geral
Castán Tobeñas, Derecho Civil Español II[14]	*José Castán Tobeñas*, Derecho Civil Español. Común y foral. Volume II (14th edn, Madrid 1992)
Caterina, Diritti reali III	*Raffaele Caterina*, I diritti reali. Volume III: Usufrutto, uso, abitazione, superficie, in: Rodolfo Sacco (ed.), Trattato di diritto civile (Turin 2009)
Cendon, Commentario al Codice Civile	*Paolo Cendon*, Commentario al Codice Civile (Milan 2010)
Cendon, Proprietà e diritti reali I, III	*Paolo Cendon*, Proprietà e diritti reali. Volume I: Proprietà, Beni, Multiproprietà, Superficie, Enfiteusi (Turin 2011); Volume III: Azioni petitorie. Servitù. Possesso. Usucapione. Azione possessorie (Turin 2012)

Cervelli, Diritti reali[2]	*Stefania Cervelli*, I diritti reali. Manuale e applicazioni pratiche dalle lezioni di Guido Capozzi (2nd edn, Milan 2007)
Cheshire and Burn (*-Burn und Cartwright*), Modern Law of Real Property[17]	*G.C. Cheshire, Edward Hector Burn and John Cartwright*, Modern Law of Real Property (17th edn, Oxford 2006)
Cian and Trabucchi (*-author*), Commentario breve[6,7,8]	*Giorgio Cian and Alberto Trabucchi* (eds), Commentario breve al codice civile (8th edn, Padua 2007, 7th edn, Padua 2004, 6th edn, Padua 2002)
Clarke and Kohler, Property Law	*Alison Clarke and Paul Kohler*, Property Law. Commentary and Materials (Cambridge 2005)
Clerk and Lindsell (*-author*), Torts[19]	*John Frederick Clerk, William Harry Barber Lindsell and Anthony M. Dugdale*, Clerk & Lindsell on Torts (19th edn, London 2006)
Coing, Europäisches Privatrecht I	*Helmut Coing*, Europäisches Privatrecht. Volume I: Älteres gemeines Recht (1500 bis 1800) (Munich 1985)
Coke on Liddleton	*Edward Coke*, The First Part of the Institutes of the Laws of England. A Commentary on Littleton (19th edn, London, 1st American edn, Philadelphia 1853)
Comporti, Diritti reali in generale[2]	*Marco Comporti*, Diritti reali in generale, in: Piero Schlesinger (ed.), Trattato di diritto civile e commerciale (2nd edn, Milan 2011)
Cornu, Droit civil[12,13]	*Gérard Cornu*, Droit civil. Introduction. Les personnes. Les biens (12th edn, Paris 2005; 13th edn, Paris 2007)
Cozian/Viandier/Deboissy, Droit des sociétés[20]	*Maurice Cozian, Alain Viandier, Florence Deboissy*, Droit des sociétés (20th edn, Paris 2007)
De Londras, Principles of Irish Property Law[2]	*Fiona de Londras*, Principles of Irish Property Law (2nd edn, Dublin 2011)
De Miguel, Instituciones de derecho privado II(2)	*Juan Francisco de Miguel*, Instituciones de derecho privado. Volume II: Reales (Part 2) (Madrid 2003)
De Page and Dekkers, Traité élémentaire V[2]	*Henri De Page and René Dekkers*, Traité élémentaire de droit civil belge. Principes—Doctrine—Jurisprudence. Tome cinquième. Les principaux contrats usuels (Deuxième partie). Les biens (Première partie) (2nd edn, Brussels 1975)
De Page, Traité élémentaire I[3]	*Henri De Page*, Traité élémentaire de droit civil belge. Principes, doctrine, jurisprudence. Volume I: Introduction, théorie générale des droits et des lois, les personnes, la famille (3rd edn, Brussels 1962)
de Ramón-Laca Clausen, Spanish Civil Code	*Sofía de Ramón-Laca Clausen*, Spanish Civil Code (Madrid 2009)
Dekkers, Précis I	*René Dekkers*, Précis de droit civil belge. Volume I: Introduction, les personnes, les biens, la transcription, la prescription (Brussels 1954)
Delgado de Miguel, Instituciones de Derecho Privado II(1)	*Juan Francisco Delgado de Miguel*, Instituciones de Derecho Privado. Volume II: Reales. Part 1 (Madrid 2002)
Díez-Picazo and Gullón, Sistema de Derecho Civil I[12], II(1)[10], II(2)[10], III(1)[8], III(2)[8]	*Luis Díez-Picazo and Antonio Gullón*, Sistema de Derecho civil. Volume I: Introducción, derecho de la persona, autonomía privada, persona jurídica (12th edn, Madrid 2012); Volume II, Part 1: El contrato en general, la relación obligatoria (10th edn, Madrid 2012); and Part 2: Contratos en especial, cuasi contratos, enriquecimiento sin causa, rasponsabilidad extracontractual (10th edn, Madrid 2012); Volume III, Part 1: Derechos Reales en general (8th edn, Madrid 2012); Volume III, Part 2: Derechos Reales en particular (8th edn, Madrid 2012)

Díez-Picazo, Fundamentos I^{6}, III^{5}, VI	*Luis Díez-Picazo*, Fundamentos del derecho civil patrimonial. Volume I: Introducción, teoria del contrato (6th edn, Madrid 2007); Volume III: Las relaciones jurídico-reales, el registro de la propiedad, la posesió (5th edn, Madrid 2008); Volume VI: Fundamentos del derecho civil patrimonial (Madrid 2012)
Dmowski and Rudnicki, Komentarz do kodeksu cywilnego I^{6,9}	*Stanisław Dmowski and Stanisław Rudnicki*, Komentarz do kodeksu cywilnego. Volume I: Część ogólna (6th edn, Warsaw 2004, 9th edn, Warsaw 2008)
Dross, Droit des biens	*William Dross*, Droit des biens (Paris 2012)
Dross, Les choses	*William Dross*, Droit civil. Les choses (Paris 2012)
Druffin-Bricca and Henry, Droit des biens^{3}	*Sophie Druffin-Bricca and Laurence-Caroline Henry*, Droit des biens (3rd edn, Paris 2009)
Eliáš et al., Nový občanský zákoník s aktualizovanou důvodovou zprávou a rejstříkem	*Karel Eliáš et al.*, Nový občanský zákoník s aktualizovanou důvodovou zprávou a rejstříkem (Ostrava 2012)
Eliáš et al., Občanský zákoník. Velký akademický komentář I	*Karel Eliáš et al.*, Občanský zákoník. Velký akademický komentář. Volume. I: §§1-487 (Prague 2008)
Erman (*-author*), BGB II^{13,14}	*Walter Erman, Harm Peter Westermann, Lutz Aderhold* (eds), Bürgerliches Gesetzbuch Handkommentar, Volume II (§§ 759–2385, ProdHaftG, ErbbauRG, VersAusglG, VBVG, LPartG, WEG, EGBGB) (14th edn, Cologne 2014, 13th edn, Cologne 2011)
Faber and Lurger (*-author*), National Reports I, III, IV, V, VI	*Wolfgang Faber and Brigitta Lurger* (eds), National Reports on the Transfer of Movables in Europe. Volume I: Estonia (*Kai Kullerkupp*), Slovenia (*Kai Kullerkupp*) (Munich 2008). Volume III: Hungary (*Ferenc Szilágyi*) (Munich 2011). Volume IV: Bulgaria (*Dimitar Stoimenov*); Portugal (*José Caramelo-Gomes and José Carlos de Medeiros Nóbrega*) (Munich 2010). Volume V: Schweden (*Martin Lilja*); (Munich 2011). Volume VI: Latvia (*Theis Klauberg and Julija Kolomijceva*) (Munich 2011)
Farré Alemán, Código civil comentado y concordado	*Josep M. Farré Alemán*, Código civil comentado y concordado (Barcelona 2001)
Feil/Marent/Preisl, Grundbuchsrecht^{2}	*Erich Feil, Karl-Heinz Marent and Gerhard Preisl*, Grundbuchsrecht (2nd edn, Vienna 2010)
Fekete, Občiansky zákonník I, II	*Imrich Fekete*, Občiansky zákonník: velký komentár Volume I (§§ 1–459) and Volume II (§§ 460–880) (Bratislava 2011)
Fiala and Kindl, Občanské právo hmotné^{2}	*Josef Fiala, Milan Kindl et alii*, Občanské právo hmotné (2nd edn, Pilsen 2009)
Fiala and Kindl, Občanský zákoník komentář I	*Josef Fiala, Milan Kindl et alii*, Občanský zákoník: komentář. Vol. I (§§ 1–487) (Prague 2009)
Filios, Emprágmato Díkaio^{3}	*Pavlos Chr. Filios*, Emprágmato Díkaio (3rd edn, Athens and Komotini 2009)
Franceschelli, Diritto privato^{5}	*Vincenzo Franceschelli*, Diritto privato (5th edn, Milan 2011)
Frank and Wächter (eds), Handbuch Immobiliarsachenrecht in Europa	*Susanne Frank and Thomas Wächter* (eds), Handbuch Immobiliarsachenrecht in Europa (Cologne 2015)
Gabrielli, Il pegno	*Enrico Gabrielli*, Diritti reali, Il pegno, in: Rodolfo Sacco (ed.), Trattato di diritto civile (Turin 2005)
Gabrielli, Il pegno anomalo	*Enrico Gabrielli*, Il pegno anomalo (Padua 1990)
Gabrielli, La pubblicità immobiliare	*Giovanni Gabrielli*, La pubblicità immobiliare, in: Rodolfo Sacco (ed.), Trattato di diritto civile (Turin 2012)

Galgano, Trattato di diritto civile I^2, II^2, III	*Francesco Galgano*, Trattato di diritto civile, Volume I (2nd edn, Padua 2010); Volume II (2nd edn, Padua 2010); Volume 3 (Padua 2010)
Galgano (-Gorla and Zanelli), Commentario del Codice Civile Scialoja-Branca, Pegno e Ipoteche, Art. 2784-2899	*Gino Gorla and Pietro Zanelli*, Pegno e Ipoteche (Arts 2784–2899), in: Franceso Galgano (ed.), Commentario del codice civile (4th edn, Bologna/Rome 1992)
Gambaro and Morello, Lezioni di diritto civile	*Antonio Gambaro and Umberto Morello*, Lezioni di diritto civile (Milan 2012)
Gambaro and Morello, Trattato dei diritti reali I	*Antonio Gambaro and Umberto Morello*, Trattato dei diritti reali, Volume I, Proprietà e possesso (Milan 2008)
Gambaro, Il diritto di proprietà	*Antonio Gambaro*, Il diritto di proprietà, in: Antonio Cicu, Francesco Messineo, Luigi Mengoni (eds), Trattato di diritto civile e commerciale (Milan 1995)
Gazzoni, Manuale di diritto privato^{13}	*Francesco Gazzoni*, Manuale di diritto privato (13th edn, Naples 2007)
Georgiades and Stathopoulos (-*author*), AK	*Apostolos Georgiades and Michael Stathopoulos*, Astikos Kodix. Kat' arthro ermineia (Athens 1982)
Georgiades, Emprágmato Díkaio I, II	*Apostolos Georgiades*, Emprágmato Díkaio. Volume I (Athens 1991) and Volume II (Athens 1993)
Georgiades, Genikés Archés Astikù Dikéu^2	*Apostolos Georgiades*, Genikés Archés Astikù Dikéu (2nd edn, Athens 1997)
Gloag and Henderson (-*author*), Introduction^{10}	*William Murray Gloag and R. Candlish Henderson*, Introduction to the Law of Scotland (10th edn, Edingburgh 1995)
Gniewek (-*author*), Kodeks cywilny I	*Edward Gniewek* (ed.), Kodeks cywilny. Volume I: Komentarz do artykułów 1-534 (Warsaw 2004)
Gniewek (-*author*), Kodeks cywilny^2	*Edward Gniewek* (ed.), Kodeks cywilny. Komentarz (2nd edn, Warsaw 2006)
Gniewek, Prawo rzeczowe^{7,8}	*Edward Gniewek*, Prawo rzeczowe (8th edn, Warsaw 2010, 7th edn, Warsaw 2008)
Gołaczyński and Leśniak (-*author*), Zastaw rejestrowy i rejestr zastawów	*Jacek Gołaczyński and Marek Leśniak*, Zastaw rejestrowy i rejestr zastawów. Kommentarz (Warsaw 2009)
González Poverda, Acciones protectoras del dominio	*Pedro González Poverda*, Acciones protectoras del dominio y de la posesion (Barcelona 2002)
González y Martínez, Estudios de Derecho Hipotecario y Derecho Civil I	*Jeronimo González y Martínez*, Estudios de Derecho Hipotecario y Derecho Civil. Volume I: Derecho Hipotecario (Madrid 2009)
Goode, Commercial law^3	*Roy Goode*, Commercial Law (3rd edn, London 2004)
Goode, Legal Problems of Credit and Security^3	*Roy Goode*, Legal Problems of Credit and Security (3rd edn, London 2004)
Gordon, Scottish Land Law I^3	*William M. Gordon*, Scottish Land Law Volume I (3rd edn, Edingburgh 2009)
Göransson, Traditionsprincipen	*Ulf Göransson*, Traditionsprincipen (Uppsala 1985)
Gray and Gray, Elements of Land Law^5	*Kevin Gray and Susan Francis Gray*, Elements of Land Law (5th edn, Oxford 2009)
Gray and Gray, Land Law^7	*Kevin Gray and Susan Francis Gray*, Land Law (7th edn, Oxford 2011)
Grégoire, Publicité foncière	*Michèle Grégoire*, Publicité foncière. Sûretés réelles et privilèges (Brussels 2006)
Grundmann and Zaccaria (-*author*), Einführung in das italienische Recht	*Stefan Grundmann and Alessio Zaccaria*, Einführung in das italienische Recht (Frankfurt am Main 2007)

Gschnitzer/Faistenberger/Barta/Call/Eccher, Sachenrecht^{2}	*Franz Gschnitzer, Christoph Faistenberger, Heinz Barta, Gottfried Call and Bernhard Eccher*, Österreichisches Sachenrecht (2nd edn, Vienna/New York 1985)
Gschnitzer/Faistenberger/Barta/Eccher, Österreichisches Schuldrecht Allgemeiner Teil^{2}	*Franz Gschnitzer, Christoph Faistenberger, Heinz Barta and Bernhard Eccher*, Österreichisches Schuldrecht Volume I, Allgemeiner Teil (2nd edn, Vienna 1985)
Gschnitzer/Faistenberger/Barta/Oberhofer/Schopper, Allgemeiner Teil des bürgerlichen Rechts^{2}	*Franz Gschnitzer, Christoph Faistenberger, Heinz Barta, Reinhold Oberhofer, Johanna Schopper*, Allgemeiner Teil des bürgerlichen Rechts (2nd edn, Vienna/New York 1992)
Hanbury and Martin (*-author*), Modern Equity^{18}	*Harold Greville Hanbury, Jill E. Martin*, Modern Equity (18th edn, London 2009)
Hansenne, Les biens	*Jacques Hansenne*, Les biens. Volume I and II (Liège 1996)
Håstad, Köprätt^{6}	*Torgny Håstad*, Köprätt och annan kontraktsrätt (6th edn, Uppsala 2009)
Håstad, Sakrätt^{6}	*Torgny Håstad*, Sakrätt. Avseende lös egendom (6th edn, Stockholm 2001, supplements 2003 and 2004)
Hellner, Metodproblem	*Jan Hellner*, Metodproblem i rättsvetenskapen. Studier i förmögenhetsrätt (Stockholm 2001)
Hessler, Allmän sakrätt	*Henrik Hessler*, Allmän sakrätt. Om det förmögenhetsrättsliga tredjemansskyddets principer (Stockholm 1973)
Hidasi/Horváth/Köszegi/Bedö (*-author*), Az ingatlanjog nagy kézikönyve	Gabor Hidasi, Gyula Horváth, Gabor Köszegi and Katalin Bedö, Az ingatlanjog nagy kézikönyve (Budapest 2010)
Hijma and Olthof, Compendium Nederlands Vermogensrecht^{9,10}	*Jacob Hijma and M.M. Olthof*, Compendium van het Nederlands Vermogensrecht (10th edn, Deventer 2008, 9th edn, Deventer 2005)
Holub, Sousedská práva^{2}	*Milan Holub, Jaroslav Bičovský, Jana Wurstová*, Sousedská práva podle současné úpravy občanského zákoníku a správního práva (2nd edn, Prague 1999)
Hörster, Parte geral	*Heinrich Ewald Hörster*, A parte geral do Código Civil português. Teoria geral do direito civil (Coimbra 1992)
Ignatowicz and Stefaniuk, Prawo rzeczowe^{2}	*Jerzy Ignatowicz and Krzysztof Stefaniuk*, Prawo rzeczowe (2nd edn, Warsaw 2006)
Iro, Sachenrecht^{4}	*Gerd Iro*, Bürgerliches Recht. Volume IV: Sachenrecht (4th edn, Vienna/New York 2010)
Jakobs and Schubert, Beratung des BGB II(1)	Horst Heinrich Jakobs and Werner Schubert, Die Beratung des Bürgerlichen Gesetzbuchs in systematischer Zusammenstellung der unveröffentlichten Quellen. Volume II: Allgemeiner Teil. Teilband 1: §§ 1–240 (Berlin 1985)
Jourdain, Les biens	*Patrice Jourdain*, Les biens (Paris 1995)
Kalaydjiev, Obligazionno pravo	*Angel Kalaydjiev*, Obligazionno pravo. Obshta chast (5th edn, Sofia 2010)
Kidyba (*-author*), Kodeks cywilny I	*Andrzej Kidyba*, Kodeks cywilny. Komentarz. Volume I: część ogólna (Warsaw 2009)
Klang (*-author*), ABGB II^{2}, IV(1)^{2}, IV(2)^{2}, V^{2}	*Heinrich Klang* (ed.), Kommentar zum Allgemeinen Bürgerlichen Gesetzbuch. Volume II: §§ 285–530 (2nd edn, Vienna 1950); Volume IV Part 1: §§ 859–1044 (2nd edn, Vienna 1968); Part 2: §§ 1045–1089 (2nd edn, Vienna 1978); Volume V: §§ 1090–1292 (2nd edn, Vienna 1954)
Klang (*-author*), ABGB^{3}	*Heinrich Klang, Attila Fenyves, Ferdinand Kerschner and Andreas Vonkilch* (eds), Kommentar zum Allgemeinen Bürgerlichen Gesetzbuch. §§ 285–352 (3rd edn, Vienna 2011); §§ 353–379 (3rd edn, Vienna 2011)

Kocher and Steppan, Grundzüge der Privatrechtsentwicklung und der Geschichte der Rechtswissenschaft in Österreich	*Gernot Kocher and Markus Steppan*, Grundzüge der Privatrechtsentwicklung und der Geschichte der Rechtswissenschaft in Österreich (2nd edn, Vienna 1997)
Koktvedgaard and Levin, Lärobok i Immaterialrätt[7]	*Mogens Koktvedgaard and Marianne Levin*, Lärobok i Immaterialrätt (7th edn, Stockholm 2003)
Kornilakis, Edikó enochikó dikaio I	*Panos Kornilakis*, Edikó enochikó díkaio. Volume I (Athens 2002)
Kousoulas, Emprágmato Díkaio	*Christos L. Kousoulas*, Emprágmato Díkaio (Athens and Thessaloniki 2004)
Koziol/Bydlinski/Bollenberger (-*author*), ABGB[4]	*Helmut Koziol, Peter Bydlinski and Raimund Bollenberger* (eds), Kurzkommentar zum ABGB. Allgemeines bürgerliches Gesetzbuch samt Ehegesetz und Konsumentenschutzgesetz (4th edn, Vienna 2014)
Koziol and Welser (-*author*), Bürgerliches Recht I[13]	*Helmut Koziol and Rudolf Welser*, Grundriss des bürgerlichen Rechts. Volume 1: Allgemeiner Teil, Sachenrecht, Familienrecht (13th edn, Vienna 2006)
Krimphove, Das europäische Sachenrecht	*Dieter Krimphove*, Das europäische Sachenrecht. Eine rechtsvergleichende Analyse nach der komparativen Institutionenökonomie (Cologne 2006)
Lábady, A magyar magánjog (polgári jog) általános része[3]	*Tamás Lábady*, A magyar magánjog (polgári jog) általános része (3rd edn, Budapest 2002)
Lacruz Berdejo, Elementos III(1)[3], III(2)[3]	*José Luis Lacruz Berdejo, Francisco de Asís Sancho Rebullida, Agustín Luna Serrano, Jesús Delgado Echeverría, Francisco Rivero Hernández, Joaquín Rams Albesa*, Elementos de derecho civil. Volume III: Derechos reales; Part 1: Posesión y propiedad (3rd edn, Madrid 2008); Part 2: Derechos reales limitados, situaciones de cotitularidad (3rd edn, Madrid 2009)
Larroumet, Les biens[3,5]	*Christian Larroumet*, Droit civil. Volume II: Les biens. Droits réels principaux (5th edn, Paris 2006, 3rd edn, Paris 1997)
Lasarte Álvarez, Principios I[3], IV[9], V[7,8]	*Carlos Lasarte Álvarez*, Principios de derecho civil. Volume I: Parte general y derecho de la persona (3th edn, Madrid 1992); Volume IV: Propiedad y derechos reales de goce (9th edn, Madrid 2009); Volume V: Derechos reales y derecho hipotecario (8th edn,, Madrid a.o. 2010, 7th edn, Madrid 2009)
Lawson and Rudden, The Law of Property[3]	*F.H. Lawson and Bernard Rudden*, The Law of Property (3rd edn, Oxford 2002)
Lazár, Občianske právo hmotné	*Ján Lazár*, Občianske právo hmotné, Závazkové právo. Právo duševného vlastníctva, Volume II (Bratislava 2010)
Lefebvre, Leçons de droit des biens	*José Lefebvre*, Leçons de droit des biens (Paris 2009)
Lenkovics, A dologi jog vázlata	*Barnabás Lenkovics*, A dologi jog vázlata (7th edn, Budapest 2006)
Lipari and Rescigno (-*author*), Diritto civile IV(2)	*Nicolò Lipari and Pietro Rescigno* (eds), Diritto civile, Volume IV, second part (L'attuazione dei diritti) (Milan 2009)
López y López and Montés Penadés (-*author*), Derechos reales	*Angel M. López y López and Vicente L. Montés Penadés* (coord.), Derechos reales y derecho inmobiliario registral (Valencia 1994)
Lüke, Sachenrecht[2]	*Wolfgang Lüke*, Sachenrecht (2nd edn, Munich 2010)
Lyall and Power, Land Law in Ireland[3]	*Andrew Lyall and Albert Power*, Land Law in Ireland (3rd edn, Dublin 2010)

M.v.A. II, Parl. Geschiedenis III	*Memorie van Antwoord, Tweede Kamer, in: C. J. Van Zeben and J. W. Du Pon* in Kooperation mit M. M. Olthof (ed.), Parlementaire Geschiedenis van het Nieuwe Burgerlijk Wetboek. Parlementaire stukken. Book III: Vermogensrecht in het Algemeen (Deventer 1991).
Makai, in: Vékás (ed.), Szakértői Javaslat az új Polgári Törvénykönyv tervezetéhez	*Katalin Makai*, Harmadik Könyv. Második rész VI. cím, in: Lajos Vékás (ed.), Szakértői Javaslat az új Polgári Törvénykönyv tervezetéhez (Budapest 2008)
Malaurie and Aynès, Les biens[3,4,5]	*Philippe Malaurie and Laurent Aynès*, Les biens (5th edn, Paris 2013, 4th edn, Paris 2010, 3rd edn, Paris 2007)
Malaurie/Aynès/Stoffel-Munck, Les obligations[4]	*Philippe Malaurie, Laurent Aynès, Philippe Stoffel-Munck*, Les obligations (4th edn, Paris 2009)
Martuccelli and Pescatore (-*author*), Dizionario di diritto civile	*Silvio Martuccelli and Valerio Pescatore* (eds), Dizionario del diritto privato. Diritto civile (Milan 2011)
Mathieu-Izorche, Les biens	*Marie-Laure Mathieu-Izorche*, Droit civil. Les biens (Paris 2006)
Mattei, La proprietà	*Ugo Mattei*, La proprietà, in: Rodolfo Sacco (ed.), Trattato di diritto civile (Turin 2001)
Mazeaud and Chabas, Biens[8]	*Henri Mazeaud, Léon Mazeaud, Jean Mazeaud and François Chabas*, Leçons de droit civil. Volume II Part 2: Biens. Droits de propriété et ses démembrements (8th edn, Paris 1994)
Mazeaud and Chabas, Introduction[12]	*Henri Mazeaud, Léon Mazeaud and François Chabas*, Leçons de droit civil. Volume I Part 1: Introduction à l'étude du droit (12th edn, Paris 2000)
Medicus and Petersen, Bürgerliches Recht[24]	*Dieter Medicus and Jens Petersen*, Bürgerliches Recht (24th edn, Cologne 2013)
Megarry and Wade (-*Harpum/Bridge/Dixon*), The Law of Real Property[8]	Robert Megarry and William Wade, *Charles Harpum, Stuart Bridge and Martin Dixon*, The Law of Real Property (8th edn, London 2012)
Mémeteau, Droit des biens[4]	*Gérard Mémeteau*, Droit des biens (4th edn, Orléans 2009)
Menéres Campos, Hipoteca	*Maria Isabel Helbling Menéres Campos*, Da hipoteca—caracterização, constituição e efeitos (Coimbra 2003)
Menezes Cordeiro, Tratado de direito civil I(1), I(2)[2], II(4), III[3], X	*António Menezes Cordeiro*, Tratado de direito civil. Volume I: Parte geral. Part 1: Introdução, doutrina geral, negócio juridico (Coimbra 1999). Part 2: Coisas (2nd edn, Coimbra 2002); Volume II: Direito das obrigações, Part IV: Cumprimento e não cumprimento, transmissão, modificação e extinção, garantias (Coimbra 2010); Volume III (3rd edn, Coimbra 2013); Volume X (Coimbra 2015)
Menezes Cordeiro, Direitos reais	*António Menezes Cordeiro*, Direitos reais (Lisbon 1979, reprint 1993)
Menezes Leitão, Direito das obrigações III[4]	*Luís Manuel Teles de Menezes Leitão*, Direito das obrigações. Volume III: Contratos em especial (4th edn, Coimbra 2006)
Menezes Leitão, Direitos reais[2]	*Luís Manuel Teles de Menezes Leitão*, Direitos reais (2nd edn, Coimbra 2011)
Menyhárd, Dologi jog[2]	*Attila Menyhárd*, Dologi jog (2nd edn, Budapest 2010)
Miller, Corporeal Moveables in Scots Law	*David L. Carey Miller*, Corporeal Movables in Scots Law (Edinburgh 1991)
Millqvist, Sakrättens grunder[5,6]	*Göran Millqvist*, Sakrättens grunder. En lärobok i sakrättens grundläggande frågeställningar avseende lös egendom (6th edn, Stockholm 2011, 5th edn, Stockholm 2009)

Mota Pinto, Teoria geral do direito civil[4]	*Carlos Alberto da Mota Pinto*, Teoria geral do direito civil (4th edn, Coimbra 2005)
MünchKomm (*-author*), BGB I(1)[5,6], II[6], VI[5,6]	*Kurt Rebmann and Franz Jürgen Säcker* (eds), Münchener Kommentar zum Bürgerlichen Gesetzbuch. Volume I Part 1: §§ 1-240 (5th edn, Munich 2006, 6th edn, Munich 2012); Volume II: §§ 241–432 (6th edn, Munich 2012); Volume VI: §§ 854–1296, WEG, ErbbauRG (6th edn, Munich 2013, 5th edn, Munich 2009)
Neocleous, Introduction to Cyprus Law	*Andeas Neocleous*, Introduction to Cyprus law (Cyprus 2010)
N.v.W., Parl. Geschiedenis V	Nota van wijzigingen, in: C. J. Van Zeben and J. W. Du Pon in cooperation with M. M. Olthof (ed.), Parlementaire Geschiedenis van het Nieuwe Burgerlijk Wetboek. Parlementaire stukken. Book V: Zakelijke rechten (Deventer 1981)
Nieuwenhuis/Stolker/Valk (-*author*), BW[6]	*J.H. Nieuwenhuis, C.J.J.M. Stolker and W.L. Valk* (eds), Burgerlijk Wetboek. Tekst & Commentaar. De tekst van de Boeken 1, 2, 3, 4, 5, 6, 7 en 8 van het BW voorzien van commentaar (6th edn, Deventer 2005)
O'Callaghan Muñoz, Código Civil[6]	*Xavier O'Callaghan Muñoz*, Código Civil. Comentado y con Jurisprudencia (6th edn, Madrid 2008)
O'Callaghan Muñoz, Compendio de derecho civil II(2)[2] and III[5]	*Xavier O'Callaghan Muñoz*, Compendio de derecho civil, Volume II: Derecho de Obligaciones, Part 2: Contratos en particular (2nd edn,, Madrid 1996); Volume III: Derechos reales e hipotecario (5th edn, Madrid 2007)
Oliveira Ascensão, Direito Civil—Reais[5]	*José de Oliveira Ascensão*, Direito civil reais (5th edn, Coimbra 1993, reprint 2000)
Oliveira Ascensão, Teoria Geral I[2]	*José de Oliveira Ascensão*, Teoria Geral do direito civil. Volume I: Introdução, As Pessoas, Os Bens (2nd edn, Coimbra 2000)
Pacilio, Proprietà e diritti reali	*Ciro Pacilio*, Proprietà e diritti reali (Turin 2008)
Pais de Vasconcelos, Contratos atípicos	*Pedro Pais de Vasconcelos*, Contratos atípicos (Coimbra 1995)
Palandt (*-author*), BGB[71,72,73,74]	*Otto Palandt*, Bürgerliches Gesetzbuch (74th edn, Munich 2015, 73th edn, Munich 2014, 72th edn, Munich 2013 and 71th edn, Munich 2012)
Palmer and Mc Kendrick (-*author*), Interests in Goods[2]	*Norman Palmer and Ewan Mc Kendrick* (eds), Interests in Goods (2nd edn, London 1998)
Papachristou, Astikí Nomothesía	*Athanasios Papachristou*, Astikí Nomothesía (Athens 2006)
Papasteriou, Emprágmato Díkaio I, II, III	*Demetrios Papasteriou*, Emprágmato Díkaio. Volume I, II and III (Athens and Thessaloniki 2008)
Pasquau Liaño (*-author*), Jurisprudencia civil comentada I[2]	*Miguel Pasquau Liaño* (ed.), Jurisprudencia civil comentada I—Código Civil (Arts 1–608) (2nd edn, Granada 2009)
Pélissier, Possession et meubles incorporels	*Anne Pélissier*, Possession et meubles incorporels (Paris 2001)
Petrik (*-author*), Polgári jog. Kommentár II	*Ferenc Petrik* (ed.), Polgári jog. Kommentár a gyakorlat számára. Harmadik kiadás (Budapest 2013)
Peuster, Código Civil. Das spanische Zivilgesetzbuch	*Witold Peuster*, Código Civil—Das spanische Zivilgesetzbuch. Spanisch-deutsche Textausgabe (Frankfurt am Main 2002)
Piasecki, Kodeks cywilny	*Kazimierz Piasecki*, Kodeks cywilny. Księga pierwsza. Część ogólna. Komentarz (Zakamycze 2003)
Picod, Droit des sûretés[2]	*Yves Picod*, Droit des sûretés (2nd edn, Paris 2008)

Piedelièvre, La publicité foncière	*Stéphane Piedelièvre*, La publicité foncière (Paris 2000)
Piédelièvre, in: Aspects de droit privé à la fin du XXe siècle	*Stéphane Piédelièvre*, Le matériel et l'immatériel. Essai d'approche de la notion de bien, in: Mélanges M. de Juglart, Aspects de droit privé à la fin du XXe siècle (Paris 1986)
Pietrzykowski (*-author*), Kodeks cywilny I^{4}	*Krzysztof Pietrzykowski*, Kodeks cywilny. Komentarz do artykułów 1-44911, Volume I (4th edn, Warsaw 2005)
Pinto Duarte, Direitos reais^{2}	*Rui Pinto Duarte*, Curso de Direitos reais (2nd edn, Cascais 2007)
Pires de Lima and Antunes Varela, Código Civil Anotado I^{4}, II^{4}, III^{2}	*Fernando Andrade Pires de Lima and João de Matos Antunes Varela*, Código Civil Anotado. Volume I: Artigos 1–761 (4th edn, Coimbra 1987, reprint 2011); Volume II: Artigos 762–1250 (4th edn, Coimbra 1997, reprint 2010); Volume III: Artigos 1251–1575 (2nd edn, Coimbra 1987, reprint 2010)
Pitlo (*-Reehuis and Heisterkamp*), Goederenrecht^{12}	*Adriaan Pitlo, Wim Reehuis and Antonius Heisterkamp*, Het Nederlands burgerlijk recht. Volume III: Goederenrecht (12th edn, Deventer 2006)
Planiol/Ripert/Picard, Les biens^{2}	*Marcel Planiol, Georges Ripert and Maurice Picard*, Traité pratique de droit civil Français. Volume III: Les biens (2nd edn, Paris 1952)
Prata, Dicionário jurídico I^{5}	*Ana Prata*, Dicionário jurídico. Part I: Direito civil, processo civil, organização judiciária (5th edn, Coimbra 2008)
Prchalová, Právní ochrana zvířat	*Jana Prchalová*, Právní ochrana zvířat (Prague 2009)
Prütting, Sachenrecht^{35}	*Hanns Prütting*, Sachenrecht (35th edn, Munich 2014)
Puig Brutau, Fundamentos III(1)^{4}, III(3)^{3}	*José Puig Brutau*, Fundamentos de Derecho Civil. Volume III Part 1: El derecho real, la posesión, la propiedad, sus límites, adquisición y pérdida, ejercicio de acciones (4th edn, Barcelona 1994); Volume III Part 3: Prenda, anticresis, hipoteca inmobiliaria y mobiliaria, reserva de dominio, venta fiduciaria, anotación preventiva, tanteo, retracto, opción censos (3rd edn, Barcelona 1983)
Puig i Ferriol and Roca i Trias, Institucions del dret civil de Catalunya IV	*Lluís Puig i Ferriol and Encarna Roca i Trias*, Institucions del dret civil de Catalunya, Volume IV: Drets reals (Valencia 2007)
Raaijmakers, Ondernemingsrecht	*M.J.G.C. Raaijmakers*, Ondernemingsrecht (Deventer 2006)
Radwański (*-author*), System Prawa Prywatnego II^{2}	*Zbigniew Radwański* (ed.), System Prawa Prywatnego. Volume II: Prawo cywilne—część ogólna (2nd edn, Warsaw 2008)
Radwański and Dybowski (*-author*), System Prawa Prywatnego III^{2}	*Zbigniew Radwański and Tomasz Dybowski* (eds), System Prawa Prywatnego. Volume III: Prawo rzeczowe (2nd edn, Warsaw 2007)
Radwański and Gniewek (*-author*), System Prawa Prywatnego III^{3}, IV^{2,3}	*Zbigniew Radwański and Edward Gniewek* (eds), System Prawa Prywatnego. Volume III: Praw rzeczowe (3rd edn, Warsaw 2013); Volume IV: Prawo rzeczowe (3rd edn, Warsaw 2012, 2nd edn, Warsaw 2007)
Radwański and Safjan (*-author*), System Prawa Prywatnego I	*Zbigniew Radwański and Marek Safjan* (eds), System Prawa Prywatnego. Volume I: Prawo cywilne—część ogólna (Warsaw 2007)
Ramos Alves, Penhor	*Hugo Ramos Alves*, Do penhor (Coimbra 2010)
Rassi, Grundbuchsrecht	*Jürgen C. T. Rassi*, Grundbuchsrecht (Vienna 2010)
Real Academia Española, Diccionario de la Lengua Española^{22}	*Real Academia Española*, Diccionario de la Lengua Española. Volume I: A/g; Volume II: H/z (Madrid 2001)
Reboul-Maupin, Droit des biens^{2,4}	*Nadège Reboul-Maupin*, Droit des biens (4th edn, Paris 2012, 2nd edn, Paris 2008)

Reid, The Law of Real Property in Scotland	*Kenneth G.C. Reid*, The Law of Real Property in Scotland (Edinburgh 1996)
Roca Sastre et al., Derecho hipotecario III[9], V[9], VIII[9], X[9]	*Ramón M. Roca Sastre, Luis Roca-Sastre Muncunill und Joan Bernà i Xirgo*, Derecho hipotecario. Volume III (9th edn, Barcelona 2008); Volume V (9th edn, Barcelona 2007); Volume VIII (9th edn, Barcelona 2009); Volume X (9th edn, Barcelona 2009)
Rudnicki and Rudnicki, Komentarz do kodeksu cywilnego II[9]	*Stanisław Rudnicki and Grzegorz Rudnicki*, Komentarz do kodeksu cywilnego. Volume II: Własność i inne prawa rzeczowe (9th edn, Warsaw 2008)
Rummel (*-author*), ABGB I[3],	*Peter Rummel (ed.)*, Kommentar zum Allgemeinen bürgerlichen Gesetzbuch. Volume I: §§ 1–1174 (3rd edn, Vienna 2000)
Ruscello, Istituzioni di diritto privato I, IV	*Francesco Ruscello*, Istituzioni di diritto privato. Volume I (Milan 2011), Volume IV (Milan 2007)
Sandstedt, Sakrätten, Norden och europeiseringen	*Johan Sandstedt*, Sakrätten, Norden och europeiseringen—Nordisk funktionalism möter kontinental substantialism (Stockholm 2013)
Santos Briz and Sierra Gil de la Cuesta, Tratado de derecho civil IV	*J. Santos Briz and I. Sierra Gil de la Cuesta* unter Mitarbeit von *P. González Poveda, J. M. Martínez-Pereda Rodríguez and J. M. Paz Rubio*, Tratado de derecho civil—Teoría y Práctica, Vol. IV Derecho de obligaciones. Los contratos en particular (Barcelona 2003)
Santos Justo, Direitos reais[2]	*A. Santos Justo*, Direitos reais (2nd edn, Coimbra 2010)
Schlesinger and Busnelli (-*author*), Codice civile	*Piero Schlesinger* (ed.), Il codice civile, commentario (now ed. by Francesco Donato Busnelli) (Milan 1998–2010)
Schwimann (*-author*), ABGB IV[3],V[3], VI[3]	*Michael Schwimann* (ed.), ABGB Praxiskommentar. Volume IV: §§ 859-1089 (3rd edn, Vienna 2006); Volume V: §§ 1090-1292 (3rd edn, Vienna 2006); Volume VI: §§ 1293-1502 (3rd edn, Vienna 2006)
Schwimann and Kodek (-author), ABGB II[4], III[4]	*Michael Schwimann and Georg Kodek* (eds), ABGB Praxiskommentar. Volume II: §§ 285–530 (4th edn, Vienna 2011); Volume III: §§ 531–858, AnerbG, Kärntner ErbhöfeG, Tiroler HöfeG (4th edn, Vienna 2013)
Schwimman (*-author*), Taschenkommentar[2]	*Michael Schwimann*, ABGB Taschenkommentar mit EheG, EPG, EKHG und KSchG (2nd edn, Vienna 2013)
Sheehan, Principles of Personal Property Law	*Duncan Sheehan*, The Principles of Personal Property Law (Oxford 2011)
Simler and Delebecque, Droit civil: les sûretés, la publicité foncière[5,6]	*Philippe Simler and Philippe Delebecque*, Droit civil: les sûretés, la publicité foncière (6th edn, Paris 2012, 5th edn, Paris 2009)
Smith, Assignment	*Marcus Smith*, The Law of Assignment (Oxford 2007)
Smith and Black (*-author*), Stair Memorial Encyclopedia XVIII: Property	*Thomas Smith and Robert Black* (eds), The Laws of Scotland: Stair Memorial Encyclopedia. Volume XVIII: Property (Edingburgh 1993)
Snijders and Rank-Berenschot, Goederenrecht[1,4]	*Henricus Josephus Snijders and Eline Beatrice Rank-Berenschot*, Goederenrecht, Studiereeks Burgerlijk Recht (1rst edn, Deventer 1994, 4th edn, Deventer 2007)
Soergel (*-author*), BGB I[13], XIV[13], XVI [13]	*Hans Theodor Soergel, Wolfgang Siebert* (eds), Bürgerliches Gesetzbuch. Mit Einführungsgesetz und Nebengesetzen. Volume I: §§ 1–103 (13th edn, Stuttgart 2000); Volume XIV: §§ 854–984 (13th edn, Stuttgart 2002); Volume XVI: §§ 1018–1296 (13th edn, Stuttgart 2001)

Spáčil and Spáčil, Přehled judikatury ve věcech občanskoprávních vztahů k pozemkům	*Jiří Spáčil and Michal Spáčil*, Přehled judikatury ve věcech občanskoprávních vztahů k pozemkům (Prague 2011)
Spáčil, Ochrana vlastnictví a držby v občanském zákoníku[2]	*Jiří Spáčil*, Ochrana vlastnictví a držby v občanském zákoníku (2nd edn, Prague 2005)
Spáčil (*-author*), Občanský zákoník III	*Jiří Spáčil et al.*, Občanský zákoník III. Věcná práva (§§ 976–1474). Komentář. (Prague 2013)
Sparkes, A New Land Law	*Peter Sparkes*, A New Land Law (Oxford 1999)
Spyridakis, Empragmato Dikaio I	*Ioannis Spyridakis*, Empragmato Dikaio. Volume I (Athens/Komotino 2001)
Staudinger (*-author*), BGB (2001), (2002), (2003), (2004), (2005), (2006), (2007), (2008), (2009), (2010), (2011), (2012)	Julius von Staudingers Kommentar zum Bürgerlichen Gesetzbuch mit Einführungsgesetz und Nebengesetzen. Buch 1: Allgemeiner Teil, Buch 2: Schuldrecht, Buch 3: Sachenrecht, Buch 5: Erbrecht (Berlin 2001–2012)
Stavrou, Veshtno pravo	*Stoyan Stavrou*, Vaprosi na balgarskoto veshtno pravo (Sofia 2008)
Strickler, Les biens	*Yves Strickler*, Les biens (Paris 2006)
v. Stubenrauch, Commentar zum ABGB I[8]	*Moritz von Stubenrauch*, edited by Maximilian Schuster von Bonnott, Commentar zum österreichischen allgemeinen bürgerlichen Gesetzbuche, Volume I (8th edn, Vienna 1902)
Švestka (*-author*), Občanský zákoník I[2]	*Jiří Švestka, Jiří Spáčil, Marta Škárová, Milan Humák et al.*, Občanský zákoník. Komentář. Volume I: §§ 1–459 (2nd edn, Prague 2009)
Švestka and Dvořák, Občanské právo hmotné[5]	*Jiří Švestka and Jan Dvořák et al.*, Občanské právo hmotné (5th edn, Prague 2009)
Švestka/Dvořák/Fiala (*-author*), Občanský zákoník I	*Jiří Švestka, Jan Dvořák, Josef Fiala*, Občanský zákoník I (§§ 1–654) (Prague 2014)
Synodinou, Κυπριακό Εμπράγματο Δίκαιο—Ακίνητη Ιδιοκτησία	*Tatiana-Eleni Synodinou*, Κυπριακό Εμπράγματο Δίκαιο—Ακίνητη Ιδιοκτησία (Kypriakó emprágmato Díkaio. Akínete Idioktesía) (Das zyprische Sachenrecht. Die Immobiliarinhaberschaft) (Athens and Thessaloniki 2011)
Szpor/Martysz/Wojsyk (*-author*), Ustawa o informatyzacji działalności podmiotów realizujących zadania publiczne	*Grażyna Szpor, Czesław Martysz and Kajetan Wojsyk*, Ustawa o informatyzacji działalności podmiotów realizujących zadania publiczne. Komentarz (Warsaw 2007)
T'Kint, Sûretés[4]	*François T'Kint*, Sûretés et principes généraux du droit de poursuite des créanciers (4th edn, Brussels 2004)
T.M., Parl. Geschiedenis III, V	*Toelichting-Meijers*, in: C. J. Van Zeben and J. W. Du Pon in cooperation with M. M. Olthof (ed.), Parlementaire Geschiedenis van het Nieuwe Burgerlijk Wetboek. Parlementaire stukken. Book III: Vermogensrecht in het Algemeen (Deventer 1991). Book V: Zakelijke rechten (Deventer 1981)
Tades/Hopf/Kathrein/Stabentheiner, ABGB I[37]	*Helmuth Tades, Gerhard Hopf, Georg Kathrein and Johannes Stabentheiner* (eds), Das Allgemeine bürgerliche Gesetzbuch. Volume I (37th edn, Vienna 2009)
Tepora, Inledning till grunderna för sakrätten	*Jarno Tepora*, Inledning till grunderna för sakrätten (Helsinki 2009)
Terré and Lequette, Grands arrêts de la jurisprudence civile[10]	*François Terré and Yves Lequette*, Les Grands arrêts de la jurisprudence civile (10th edn, Paris 1994)
Terré and Simler, Les biens[6,7,8,9]	*François Terré and Philippe Simler*, Droit civil. Les biens (9th edn, Paris 2014, 8th edn, Paris 2010, 6th and 7th edn, Paris 2002 and 2006)

Terré/Simler/Lequette, Les Obligations[9]	*François Terré, Philippe Simler and Yves Lequette*, Droit civil. Les Obligations (9th edn, Paris 2005)
Thompson, Modern Land Law[4]	*Mark P. Thompson*, Modern Land Law (4th edn, Oxford 2009)
Torrente and Schlesinger, Manuale di diritto privato[14,19,20,21]	*Andrea Torrente and Piero Schlesinger*, Manuale di diritto privato (14th edn, Milan 1995, 19th edn, Milan 2009, 20th edn, Milan 2011, 21th edn, Milan 2013)
Tousis, Empragmato Dikaio	*Andreas Tousis*, Empragmato Dikaio (Athens 1978)
Trabucchi, Istituzioni di diritto civile[44]	*Alberto Trabucchi*, Istituzioni di diritto civile (44th edn, Padua 2009)
Triantos, AK	*Nikolaos Triantos*, Astikós Kodikas. Ermineía kat' árthro (Athens 2009)
Trimarchi, Istituzioni[16/18]	*Pietro Trimarchi*, Istituzioni di diritto privato (18th edn, Milan 2009, 16th edn, Milan 2005)
Undén, Svensk sakrätt I[1/10], II[5]	*Bo Östen Undén*, Svensk sakrätt. Volume I: Lös egendom (10th edn, Lund 1976; reprint Lund 1995; 1st edn, Lund 1927); Volume II: Fast egendom (5th edn, Lund 1969)
Valentino (-*author*), Commentario al Codice Civile III	*Daniela Valentino (ed.)*, Commentario al Codice Civile III (dei singoli contratti) (Turin 2011)
Valette-Ercole, Fiches de droit des biens	*Vanessa Valette-Ercole*, Fiches de droit des biens. Rappels de cours et exercices corrigés (Paris 2007)
Van Neste, Zakenrecht I[2]	*Fernand Van Neste*, Beginselen van belgisch privaatrecht. Volume V: Zakenrecht. Book 1: Goederen, bezit en eigendom (2nd edn, Antwerpen 1990)
Vandenberghe, Goederenrecht	*Hugo Vandenberghe*, Goederenrecht (Leuven 2005)
Vassilev, Balgarsko veshtno pravo[2]	*Lyuben Vassilev*, Balgarsko veshtno pravo (2nd edn, Sofia 2001)
Vékás (-*author*), A Polgári Törvénykönyv magyarázatokkal	*Lajos Vékás* (ed.), A Polgári Törvénykönyv magyarázatokkal (Budapest 2013)
Venedikov, Novo veshtno pravo	*Petko Venedikov*, Novo veshtno pravo (Sofia 1995)
Victorin and Hager, Allmän fastighetsrätt[6]	*Anders Victorin, Richard Hager*, Allmän fastighetsrätt (6th edn, Uppsala 2011)
Vieira, Direitos reais	*José Alberto C. Vieira*, Direitos Reais (Coimbra 2008)
Vieweg and Werner, Sachenrecht[4]	*Klaus Vieweg and Almuth Werner*, Sachenrecht (4th edn, Cologne 2010)
Vinding Kruse, Ejendomsretten I[3]	*Frederik Vinding Kruse*, Ejendomsretten. Volume I (3rd edn, Copenhagen 1951)
Vojčík, Občianske právo hmotné	*Peter Vojčík* et alii, Občianske právo hmotné (Plzeň 2012)
Vojčík, Práva priemyselného vlastníctva	*Peter Vojčík*, Práva priemyselného vlastníctva (Bratislava 1998)
Vymazal, Zástavní právo	*Lukáš Vymazal*, Zástavní právo v novém občanském zákoníku (Prague 2014)
Watgen and Watgen, La propriété immobilière	*Monique Watgen, Raymond Watgen*, Droit civil. La propriété immobilière (Windhof 2013)
Wathrakokilis, AK	*Vasileios Wathrokokilis*, Astikos Kodikas (Athens 2004)
Weber, Sachenrecht I	*Ralph Weber*, Sachenrecht. Volume 1: Bewegliche Sachen (Baden-Baden 2005)
Westermann/Gursky/Eickmann, Sachenrecht[8]	*Harry Westermann, Harm Peter Westermann, Karl-Heinz Gursky* and *Dieter Eickmann*, Sachenrecht (8th edn, Heidelberg et al. 2011)
Wieling, Sachenrecht I[2]	*Hans Josef Wieling*, Sachenrecht. Volume I: Sachen, Besitz und Rechte an beweglichen Sachen (2nd edn, Berlin 2006)

Wilhelm, Sachenrecht[4]	*Jan Wilhelm*, Sachenrecht (4th edn, Berlin 2010)
Williams, Personal Property[18]	*Joshua Williams, Thomas Cyprian Williams and William J. Byrne*, Principles of the Law of Personal Property. Intended for the Use of Students in Conveyancing (18th edn, London 1926)
Wolf and Wellenhofer, Sachenrecht[28/29]	*Manfred Wolf and Marina Wellenhofer*, Sachenrecht (29th edn, Munich 2014, 28th edn, Munich 2013)
Worthington, Personal Property Law	*Sarah Worthington*, Personal Property Law. Text, Cases and Materials (Oxford 2000)
Wylie, Irish Land Law[3]	*J.C.W. Wylie*, Irish Land Law (3rd edn, Dublin 1997)
Zankl, Bürgerliches Recht[5]	*Wolfgang Zankl*, Bürgerliches Recht: Kurzlehrbuch (5th edn, Vienna 2010)
v. Zeiller, Commentar über das allgemeine bürgerliche Gesetzbuch für die gesammten Deutschen Erbländer der Österreichischen Monarchie, Vol. II/1	*Franz von Zeiller*, Commentar über das allgemeine bürgerliche Gesetzbuch für die gesammten Deutschen Erbländer der Österreichischen Monarchie, Vol. II/1 (1st edn, Vienna 1812)
Zenati-Castaing and Revet, Les biens[3]	*Frédéric Zenati-Castaing and Thierry Revet*, Les biens (3rd edn, Paris 2008)
Zetterström, Sakrättens fyra huvudfall[2]	*Stefan Zetterström*, Sakrättens fyra huvudfall (2nd edn, Uppsala 2008)

Abbreviations

A Crim R	*Australian Criminal Reports* (from 1980)
ABGB	*Allgemeines Bürgerliches Gesetzbuch*; Austrian Civil Code
AC	*The Law Reports. Appeal Cases, House of Lords* (from 1875)
AchN	*Achaiki Nomologia* (from 1985)
AcP	*Archiv für die civilistische Praxis* (from 1820) contains *Archiv für bürgerliches Recht* (1888–1917)
Ad & E;	Adolphus & Ellis *Reports of cases argued and determined in the Court of King's bench* (1835–1842)
AG	*Amtsgericht* (Germany)
AgrarR	*Zeitschrift für das gesamte Recht der Landwirtschaft, der Agrarmärkte und des ländlichen Raumes* (1971–2002)
AK	*Astikos Kodikas*; Greek Civil Code
AktG	*Aktiengesetz* (Germany)
ALJR	*Australian Law Journal Reports* (Sydney 1.1958 ff)
All ER	*All England Law Reports* (London 1.1936 ff)
AllgGAG	*Allgemeines Grundbuchsanlegungsgesetz* (Austria)
ALMD	*Australian Legal Monthly Digest* (Sydney 1.1967 ff)
ALR	*Australian Law Reports* (Chatswood 1.1973 ff)
AmEconRev	*The American Economic Review*, (Nashville, Tennessee 1.1911 ff)
AMN	*Anales de la Academia Matritense del Notariado* (Madrid 1.1942/1943 ff)
App.	*Corte d'Appello* (Court of Appeal, Italy)
App Cas	*Appeal Cases* (1875-1890)
Arch. Ass. Cost.	*Archivio assemblea costituente* (1946–48)
Arch. civ.	*Archivio civile* (1958–2004)
ArchN	*Archeio Nomologias* (from 1949)
Arm.; Harm.	*Armenopoulos* (Thessaloniki 1.1946/47 ff)
AUR	*Agrar- und Umweltrecht: Zeitschrift für das gesamte Recht der Landwirtschaft, der Agrarmärkte und des ländlichen Raumes*, (from 2003)
Banca Borsa e tit. cred.	*Banca, borsa e titoli di credito* (Milan 1.1934 ff)
BauGB	*Baugesetzbuch* (Germany)
BauR	*Baurecht. Zeitschrift für das gesamte öffentliche und zivile Baurecht* (from 1970)
BauRG	*Baurechtsgesetz* (Austria)
BayObLG	*Bayerisches Oberstes Landesgericht* (Germany)
BBergG	*Bundesberggesetz* (Germany)
BCC	*British Company Cases*; *British Company Law & Practice* (1983–89: *British Company Law Cases;* London 1983 ff)
BDT	*Bírósági Döntések Tára* (Compiled Hungarian court decisions)
BFH	*Bundesfinanzhof* (Germany)
BFHE	*Entscheidungen des Bundesfinanzhofs* (Germany)
BGB	*Bürgerliches Gesetzbuch* (Germany)

BGBl.	*Bundesgesetzblatt* (Germany)
BGH	*Bundesgerichtshof* (Germany)
BGHZ	*Amtliche Sammlung der Entscheidungen des Bundesgerichtshofes in Zivilsachen* (Cologne 1.1951 ff)
BH	*Bírósági Határozatok* (Hungary)
Bing	*Bingham's Common Pleas Reports* (ER 130–131) (London 1822–34) continued as *Bingham's New Cases. English Common Pleas* (ER 131–133) (London 1834–40)
Bing NC	*Bingham's New Cases. English Common Pleas* (ER 131–133) (London 1834–1840)
BISN	*Biuletyn Informacyjny Sądu Najwyższego* (Poland High Court Information Bulletin)
Biul.SN	*Biuletyn Sądu Najwyższego* (Warsaw 1.1995 ff)
BJagdG	*Bundesjagdgesetz* (Germany)
BKR	*Zeitschrift für Bank- und Kapitalmarktrecht* (Munich 2001 ff)
BLR	*Building Law Reports* (London 1.1975 ff)
BMJ	*Boletim do Ministério da Justiça* (Lisbon 1.1940/41–7.1947 = Nr. 1–40 published as *Boletim oficial do Ministério da Justiça*; 1.1947, 2.1947–499.2000 published as *Boletim do Ministério da Justiça*)
BMLR	*Butterworths Medico-Legal Reports* (London 1.1992 ff)
BPIR	*Bankruptcy and Personal Insolvency Reports* (London 1996 ff)
Bro CC	*Brown's Chancery Cases* (ER 28–29) (London 1778–94)
BTC	*British Tax Cases* (Kingston upon Thames 1.1982 ff)
BT-Drucks.	*Verhandlungen des Deutschen Bundestages. Drucksachen* (Bonn legislative period 1.1949–11.1987/90; Berlin legislative period 11.1987/90 ff) Proceedings of the German *Bundestag*
Buff. L. Rev.	*Buffalo Law Review* (Buffalo, New York 1951 ff)
Bull. Ass. Pl.	*Bulletin des arrêts de la Cour de cassation, assemblée plénière* (France)
Bull. civ.	*Bulletin des arrêts de la Cour de cassation. Chambres civiles* (Paris 1803 ff)
Bull. crim.	*Bulletin des arrêts de la Cour de cassation. Chambre criminelle* (Paris 1798 ff)
Bus LR	*Business Law Reports* (London 2007 ff)
BVerfG	*Bundesverfassungsgericht* (Germany)
BVerfGE	*Entscheidungen des Bundesverfassungsgerichts*
BW	*Nieuw Burgerlijk Wetboek* (Netherlands Civil Code)
C. propr. intell.	*Code de la propriété intellectuelle* (France)
CA	*Court of Appeal* (England), *Cour d'appel* (France)
Camp	*Campbell's Nisi Prius Cases* (ER 170–171) (London 1808–16)
Cass.	*Hof van Cassatie/Cour de cassation* (Belgium); *Cour de cassation* (France); *Corte Suprema di Cassazione* (Italy)
Cass. Ass. Pl.	*Cour de cassation, Assemblée plénière* (France)
Cass. civ.	*Cour de cassation. Chambre civile* (France), *Corte di Cassazione, civile* (Italy)
Cass. com.	*Cour de cassation. Chambre commerciale et financière* (France)
Cass. crim.	*Cour de cassation. Chambre criminelle* (France)
Cass. pen.	*Corte di Cassazione, penale* (Italian Court of Cassation Penal Division) and *Cassazione penale. Rivista mensile di giurisprudenza* (Milan 1961 ff)
Cass. req.	*Cour de cassation. Chambre des requêtes* (France, abolished 1947)

Cass. sez. un.	*Corte di Cassazione, sezioni unite* (Italy)
Cass. soc.	*Cour de cassation. Chambre sociale* (France)
CB NS	*Common Bench, New Series*, London 1857–66
CC	*Code civil* (Belgium, France, and Luxembourg), *Codi Civil/Código Civil* (Catalonia), *Codice civile* (Italy), *Codul Civil* (Romania), *Código Civil* (Portugal and Spain)
CCH	*Code de la construction et de l'habitation* (France)
CCom	*Code de commerce* (France), *Código Comercial* (Portugal)
CESL	*Common European Sales Law*
Ch	*The Law Reports. Chancery Cases* (from 1891)
Ch App	*The Law Reports. Chancery Appeal Cases* (London 1.1865/66–10.1874); continued as *The Law Reports. Chancery Division* (London 1.1875/76–45.1890, 1891 ff)
Ch D	*The Law Reports. Chancery Division* (1875/76–90; cf. LR)
CJ	*Colectânea de Jurisprudência* (Coimbra 1.1976 ff)
CJ(ST)	*Colectânea de Jurisprudência. Acórdãos do Supremo Tribunal de Justiça* (Coimbra 1.1993 ff)
CL	*Common Law* (Irish Reports, 3rd Series, Irish Reports, Common Law, 1866–78; Council of Law Reporting in Ireland); cf. IR
CLC	*CCH Commercial Law Cases* (Kingston upon Thames 1.1994 ff)
CLJ	*The Cambridge Law Journal* (Cambridge 1.1921/23 ff)
CLR	*Commonwealth Law Reports* (Melbourne 1.1903 ff)
COD	*Crown Official Digest* (London 1988–2000); continued as *Administrative Law Digest*
Cod. cons.	*Codice del consumo* (Italy); cf. Gesetzesregister for further information
Coll	*Collyer's Chancery Cases tempore Bruse V.C.* (London 1844–46)
Cons. Const.	*Conseil constitutionnel* (Constitutional Court, France)
Conv	*Conveyancer and Property Lawyer* (London 1936 ff)
Cornell LQ	*Cornell Law Quarterly* (Ithaca 1.1915–52.1966/67) continued as *Cornell Law Review* (Ithaca 53.167/68 ff)
Corr. giur.	*Corriere giuridico* (Mailand 1.1984 ff)
Cour const.	*Cour constitutionnelle* (Belgium)
CP	*Code pénal* (Penal Code, France), *Código Penal* (Penal Code, Portugal, Spain); *Codice penale* (Italy)
CPC	*Code de procédure civile* (France), *Código de Processo Civil* (Brazil/Portugal); *Codice di procedura civile* (Italy); cf. Gesetzesregister for further information
Cr App R	*Criminal Appeal Reports* (London 1.1908 ff)
Crim L Rev	*Criminal Law Review* (London 1954 ff)
CRP	*Código do Registo Predial* (Portugal)
CSOH	*Scotland Court of Session, Outer House*
CZK	*Czechoslovak/Czech koruna* (Kčs—Koruna česko-slovenská)
D	*Dike* (Athen 1970 ff)
	Recueil Dalloz de doctrine, de jurisprudence et de législation (Paris 179.2003, 29 ff). Published under various titles since 1791. Abbreviated to D. unless otherwise stated.
	- *Journal des audiences de la Cour de cassation ou Recueil des principaux arrêts rendus par cette cour en matière civile et mixte* (1791–1824)

	- *Recueil périodique et critique de jurisprudence, de législation et de doctrine en matière civile, commerciale, criminelle, administrative et de droit public* (1825–1940) [D.P.]
	- *Recueil hebdomadaire de jurisprudence en matière civile, commerciale, criminelle, administrative et de droit public* (1924–40) [D.H.]
	- *Recueil Dalloz. Recueil analytique de jurisprudence et de législation* (1941–44) [D.A.]
	- *Recueil Dalloz. Recueil critique de jurisprudence et de législation* (1941–44) [D.C.]
	- *Recueil Dalloz de doctrine, de jurisprudence et de législation. Hebdomadaire* (1945–1954, 1957–64)
	- *Recueil Dalloz et Recueil Sirey* (1955) [D.S.]
	- *Recueils Dalloz et Sirey* (1956) [D.S.]
	- *Recueil Dalloz Sirey* (1965–96)
	- *Recueil Dalloz de doctrine, de jurisprudence et de législation* (1997–1999, 2003 ff)
	- *Recueil le Dalloz* (1999–2003)
D.P.R.	*Decreto Presidente della Repubblica* (Decree of the President of the Republic, Italy)
DCFR	*Draft Common Frame of Reference*
De GJ & S	*De Gex, Jones & Smith's Chancery Reports*, London 1862–66
Defrénois	*Répertoire du notariat Defrénois* (Paris 86.1966 ff)
DGRN	*Dirección General de los Registros y del Notariado* (General Direction of Registers and Notaries, Spain)
DGVZ	*Deutsche Gerichtsvollzieher-Zeitung: Zeitschrift für Vollstreckungs-, Zustellungs- und Kostenrecht; Organ des Deutschen Gerichtsvollzieherbundes (DGVB)* (Berlin 1.1881–64.1944,8; 65.1950 ff)
DiDik	*Dioiketike Dike* (Athen-Thessaloniki 1.1989 ff)
Dikogr.	*Dikografia* (Lárisa 1.1993 ff)
Dir. trasporti	*Diritto dei trasporti* (Cagliari 1988 ff)
DJ	*Deutsche Justiz: Rechtspflege und Rechtspolitik* (1.1839–95.1933: *Justiz-Ministerialblatt für die preußische Gesetzgebung und Rechtspflege*; 95.1933,40–95.1933,46: *Preußische Justiz*; Berlin 1.1839–106.1945)
DL	*Decreto legge* (Italy); *Decreto-Lei* (Portugal); *Decreto ley* (Spain)
DNotZ	*Deutsche Notar-Zeitschrift* (1.1901–33.1933,5: *Zeitschrift des Deutschen Notarvereins*; Munich, 1.1901–44.1944; 1950 ff)
DodNom	*Dodekanisiakí Nomologia* (Rhodes 1994 ff)
DOGC	*Diari Oficial de la Generalitat de Catalunya*
DVBl	*Deutsches Verwaltungsblatt*; Cologne 1.1879–64.1943, 65.1950 ff)
Dz.U.	*Dziennik Ustaw Rzeczypospolitej Polskiej* (official Gazette, Poland)
E & B; El & B	*Ellis and Blackburn's Queen's Bench Reports* (ER 118–120) (London 1852–58)
E & E; El & El	*Ellis & Ellis' Queen's Bench Reports* (London 1858–61)
East	*East's Term Reports, King's Bench* (London 1800–1812)
EBH	*Elvi Bírósági Határozat* (cases decided in the Hungarian Supreme Court)
ECHR	*Convention for the Protection of Human Rights and Fundamental Freedoms (European Convention on Human Rights)*
ECLI	*European Case Law Identifier*

Ecolex	*Fachzeitschrift für Wirtschaftsrecht* (Wien 1.1990 ff)
EdinbLRev	*Edinburgh Law Review* (Edinburgh 1.1996 ff)
EEmpD	*Epitheoreses Emporikou Dikaiou* (Athens 1.1950 ff)
EEN	*Efemeris Ellenon Nomikon* (Athens 1.1934 ff)
EfAD	*Efarmogés Astikou Dikaiou* (Athens 2008 ff)
EG	*Estates Gazette* (London 1.1858 ff)
EGCS	*Estates Gazette Case Summaries* (London 1.1858 ff)
EGLR	*Estates Gazette Law Reports* (London, 1.1985 ff)
ECtHR	*European Court of Human Rights* (Strasbourg)
EGZGB	*Eisagogikos nomos* (Greece), Introductory statute
EJCL	*Electronic Journal of Comparative Law* (1.1997 ff)
EllDik; EllDni	*Ellenike Dikaiosyne* (Athens 1.1960 ff)
EMLR	*Entertainment and Media Law Reports* (London 1.1993 ff)
Enc. dir.	*Enciclopedia del diritto* (Mailand 1.1958 ff)
Enc. giur.	*Enciclopedia giuridica, Istituto della Enciclopedia italiana* (Rome 1988 ff)
Env LR	*Environmental Law Reports* (London 1.1992 ff)
EPolD	*Epitheorisi Politikes Dikonomias* (Athens—Thessaloniki 1.2003 ff)
ER	*The English Reports* (London 1.1900–178.1932)
ErbbauRG	*Erbbaurechtsgesetz* (Germany)
ERCL	*European Review of Contract Law* (Berlin, Boston 1.2005 ff)
EStG	*Einkommenssteuergesetz* (Germany)
Eu LR	*European Law Reports* (Oxford 1997–2012)
EuGRZ	*Europäische Grundrechte-Zeitschrift* (Strasbourg 1.1974 ff)
EvBl	*Evidenzblatt der Rechtsmittelentscheidungen* (Vienna 1.1934 ff; integrated into the ÖJZ since 1946)
EWCA Civ	*Approved Judgment of the Court of Appeal, Civil Division* (England and Wales)
EWCA Crim	*Approved Judgment of the Court of Appeal, Criminal Division* (England and Wales)
EWHC	*England & Wales High Court*
EWHC (Ch)	*England & Wales High Court (Chancery Division)*
EWHC (Comm)	*England & Wales High Court (Commercial Court)*
Ex Ch	*Exchequer Chamber* (United Kingdom)
Fam	*The Law Reports, Family Division* (London 1.1972 ff, previously: *The Law Reports, Probate, Divorce and Admiralty Division* 1.1865/1869 ff)
Fam Law	*Family Law* (London 1.1970 ff)
FamRZ	*Zeitschrift für das gesamte Familienrecht* (Bielefeld, 33.1986 ff)
FCAFC	*Federal Court of Australia. Full Court*
FCR	*Federal Court Reports* (Sydney 1.1984 ff)
FEK	*Fyllo Efemeridas tes Kyberneseos*, official Gazette Greece
FGPrax	*Praxis der freiwilligen Gerichtsbarkeit* (München 1.1995 ff)
FLR	*Family Law Reports* (London 1.1980 ff)
Foro amm.	*Foro amministrativo* (Milan 1925–1970); *Foro amministrativo TAR* (Milan 2002–13); *Foro amministrativo CdS* (Milan 2002–13)
Foro it.	*Il Foro italiano. Raccolta di giurisprudenza civile, commerciale, penale, amministrativa* (Rom 1.1876 ff)
ForstG	*Forstgesetz* (Austria)
FS	Festschrift

Gaz. Pal.	*La gazette du palais. Feuille officielle d'annonces légales* (Paris 1.1886 ff)
Gazz. Uff.	*Gazzetta ufficiale della Repubblica Italiana* (Rome 1860 ff)
GBG	*Allgemeines Grundbuchgesetz* (Austria)
(GBHG) UKWH	*Ustawa r. o księgach wieczystych i hipotece* (Poland)
Gbl. (SZ)	*Sbírka zákonů České republiky* (Prague 1993 ff), (*Gesetzblatt* of the Czech Republic)
GBO	*Grundbuchordnung* (Germany)
GG	*Grundgesetz* (Germany)
Giur. it.	*Giurisprudenza italiana* (Turin 1849 ff)
Giur. Merito	*Giurisprudenza di merito. Rivista bimestrale di giurisprudenza dei giudici di merito* (Milan 1.1969 ff)
Giust. civ.	*Giustizia civile. Rivista bimestrale di giurisprudenza* (Milan 1.1951 ff)
GKRG	*Prawo geodezyjne i kartograficzne* (Poland)
GlUNF	*Neue Folge der Sammlung von Civilrechtlichen Entscheidungen des k. k. Obersten Gerichtshofes, begründet von Julius Glaser und Joseph Unger* (Vienna 1=35.1900–18=52.1919)
GPCCA	*Tsiviilseadustiku üldosa seadus* (General Part of the Civil Code Act [Estonia])
Gruchot	*Beiträge zur Erläuterung des deutschen Rechts* (1.1857–10.1866: *Beiträge zur Erläuterung des preußischen Rechts durch Theorie und Praxis*; 11.1867–15.1871: *Beiträge zur Erläuterung des preußischen Rechts, des Handels- und Wechselrechts durch Theorie und Praxis*; Berlin 1.1857–73.1933)
GUG	*Grundbuchumstellungsgesetz* (Austria)
GuT	*Gewerbemiete und Teileigentum* (Bonn 1.2001 ff)
GVG	*Grundverkehrsgesetze der Länder* (Austria)
GWD	*Greens Weekly Digest* (Edinburgh 1.1986 ff)
H & C	*Hurlstone and Coltman's Exchequer Reports* (ER 158–159) (London 1862–66)
Hare	*Hare's Chancery Reports* (ER 66–68) (London 1841–53)
Harm.	Harmenopoulos (Thessaloniki 1.1946 ff)
Harv. L. Rev.	*Harvard Law Review* (Cambridge [Massachusetts] 1.1887/88 ff)
HD	*Högsta domstolen* (Supreme Court, Sweden)
HGB	*Handelsgesetzbuch* (Deutschland); *Obchodní zákoník* (Czech Republic)
HL	*House of Lords*
HLC	*Clark's House of Lords Cases* (ER 9–11) (London 1847–66)
HR	*Hoge Raad* (Supreme Court, Netherlands)
Hurl & N	*Hurlstone & Norman's Exchequer Reports*, London 1856–62
I contratti	*I Contratti, Rivista di dottrina e giurisprudenza* (Milan, 1993 ff)
ICCLR	*International Company and Commercial Law Review* (Oxford 1.1990 ff)
ICLQ	*International and Comparative Law Quarterly* (British Institute of International and Comparative Law) (Cambridge 1.1952 ff)
IEAG	*Ustawa z dnia 24 marca 1920 r. o nabywnianiu nieruchomości przez cudzoziemców* (Poland)
IL Pr	*International Litigation Procedure* (London 1.1990 ff)
IMF	*International Monetary Fund*
InDret	*InDret. Revista para el análisis del derecho* (Barcelona 1.2000 ff)
InsO	*Insolvenzordnung* (Germany)
IO	*Insolvenzordnung* (Austria)
IPD	*Intellectual Property Decisions* (London 1977 ff)

IR	*Irish Reports* (1838 ff); *Informations rapides du recueil Dalloz* (France), see D.
IRLR	*Industrial Relations Law Reports* (London 1.1972 ff)
Israel L Rev	*Israel Law Review* (Jerusalem 1966 ff)
ITELR	*International Trust & Estate Law Reports* (London 1.1997 ff)
J & H	Johnson & Hemming's Chancery Reports, (London 1860–62)
J.H.L.	*Journal of Housing Law* (Andover, 1.1997 ff)
J.T.	*Journal des tribunaux* (Brussels 1.1881 ff)
JB	*Jordabalken* (Sweden)
JBl	*Juristische Blätter* (Vienna 1.1872 ff)
JClCiv Code	*Collection des Juris-Classeurs. Juris-Classeur Civil Code* (Paris 1962 ff)
JCP	*La semaine juridique* (Juris Classeur Périodique, Paris 1.1927 ff)
JCP E	*La semaine juridique, édition Entreprise*
JCP G	*La semaine juridique, édition générale*
JCP N	*La semaine juridique, édition Notariale*
JhJb	*Jahrbücher für die Dogmatik des heutigen römischen und deutschen Privatrechts* (Jena 1857–1892, continued through *Jherings Jahrbücher für die Dogmatik des bürgerlichen Rechts* [Jena 1893–1943])
JO	*Journal officiel de la République française. Lois et Décrets* (Paris 1.1869 ff)
John & H	*Johnson & Hemming's Chancery Reports* (London 1859–62)
Journ. Leg. Stud.	*The Journal of Legal Studies* (Chicago 1.1972 ff)
Journ. Univ. Latvia: Law	*Journal of the University of Latvia: Law* (Juridiskā zinātne; Riga 2010 ff)
JP	*Justice of the Peace Reports* (1932–83: *Justice of the Peace and Local Government Review Reports;* London 1.1837 ff)
JPL	*Journal of Planning & Environment Law* (1948–53: *Journal of Planning Law*; 1954–72: *Journal of Planning & Property Law;* London 1948 ff)
JPN	*Justice of the Peace* (1837–1970/71: *Justice of the Peace and Local Government Review*; London 1837–2009) continued as: *Criminal Law and Justice Weekly* (London 2009 ff)
JRC	*Jurisprudence. Revue critique* (Paris 2010 ff)
Jur. Liège	*Jurisprudence de Liège* (Liège 83.1978–93.1986), continued as: *Revue de jurisprudence de Liège, Mons et Bruxelles* (Liège, 94.1987 ff)
Jura	*Juristische Ausbildung* (Berlin 1.1979 ff)
Jurid.Rev.	*The Juridical Review* (Edinburgh/London 1.1889 ff)
Juris Data DVD	*DVD Juris Data; giurisprudenza, legislazione, codici, sentenze della Cassazione civile e penale, sentenze della Corte costituzionale, sentenze di merito, sentenze UE, dottrina, prassi* (Italy)
JW	*Juristische Wochenschrift* (Organ des Deutschen Anwaltvereins) (Leipzig 1.1872–68.1939)
JZ	*Juristenzeitung* (Tübingen 6.1951 ff)
Katastrální zákon	*Zákon o katastru nemovitostí České republiky (katastrální zákon)* (Czechia)
Kay & J	*Kay & Johnson's Vice Chancellors Reports* (London 1855–59)
KB	*The Law Reports. King's Bench Division* (London 1.1875/76 ff)
Kh.	*Rechtbank van koophandel* (Commercial Court, Belgium)
KSchG	*Konsumentenschutzgesetz* (Austria)
KZS	*Krakowskie Zeszyty Sądowe* (Krakow 1.1991 ff)

Law Com Rep	*Law Commission Report* (Law Commission of England and Wales)
LC	*Lord Chancellor* (United Kingdom)
LCLRA	*Land and Conveyancing Law Reform Act 2009* (Ireland), cf. Gesetzesregister for further information
Legal Studies	*Legal Studies. The Journal of the Society of Legal Scholars* (London 1981 ff)
Legf. Bír.	*Legfelsőbb Bíróság* (Supreme Court, Hungary)
LexPolonica	*System informacji prawnej LexPolonica* (Online database, Poland)
LG	*Landgericht* (Germany)
LG Rev	*Local Government Review Reports* (1971–93: *Local Government Review*; London 1971–96) merged into: *Justice of the Peace*, siehe JP
LGERA	*Local Government and Environmental Reports of Australia* (Sydney 1993 ff)
LGR	*Local Government Reports* (1.1903–98: *Knight's Local Government Reports;* London 1.1903 ff)
LH	*Ley Hipotecaria* (Spain)
LHMPSD	*Ley sobre hipoteca mobiliaria y prenda sin desplazamiento de posesión* (Spain)
LiegTeilG	*Liegenschaftsteilungsgesetz* (Austria)
LJ Ch	*Law Journal Reports, Chancery New Series* (London 1831–1946)
LJ KB	*Law Journal Reports, King's Bench New Series* (London 1831–37, 1901–46)
LJN	*Landelijk Jurisprudentie Nummer* (Netherlands)
Lloyd's Rep	*Lloyd's Law Reports* (London 1.1968 ff)
LLR	*London Law Review* (London 1.2005 ff)
LM	*Lindenmaier-Möhring. Nachschlagwerk des Bundesgerichtshofs* (Munich 1.1951 ff)
LMCLQ	*Lloyd's Maritime and Commercial Law Quarterly* (London 1.1974 ff)
LOA	*Law of Obligations Act* (Estonia)
LPA	*Law of Property Act* (England), *Asjaõigusseadus* (Law of Property Act, Estonia)
LPAP	*Ley de Patrimonio de las Administraciones Públicas 33/2003 de 3 de noviembre* (Spain)
LPHE	Ley del Patrimonio Histórico Español (Spain)
LQR	*The Law Quarterly Review* (London 1.1885 ff)
LR	*The Law Reports, the Incorporated Council of Law Reporting for England and Wales.* 11 subdivisions (London 1865–75); Subdivisions cited here: CP (Court of Common Pleas), Eq (Equity Cases), Ex (Exchequer Cases), QB (Court of Queen's Bench),
LRA	*Land Registration Act 2002* (England and Wales)
LRDA	*Ley de Reforma y Desarollo Agrario* (Spain)
LS Law Medical	*LS Law Medical* (1998–2006: *Lloyd's Law Reports Medical;* London 1.1998 ff)
LSG	*Law Society's Gazette* (London 1903–93; also: *Law Society's Guardian Gazette*); continued as: *Gazette*
LT	*Law Times Reports* (London 1859–1947)
LTR	*Landlord & Tenant Review* (London 1.1996 ff)
Lux.	*Tribunal d'arrondissement* (Landgericht of the city of Luxembourg)
M & W	*Meeson and Welsby's Exchequer Reports* (ER 150–153) (London 1836–47)

M.v.A.	*Memorie van Antwoord*, in: Parl. Geschiedenis van het Nieuwe Burgerlijk Wetboek
Macq	*Macqueen's Scotch Appeal Cases* (cases from the years 1851–65)
Mass. giur. it.	*Massimario della giurisprudenza italiana* (Turin 1.1931 ff)
Mass. giust. civ.	*Giustizia civile. Massimario annotato della Cassazione* (Milan 5.1955 ff)
MDR	*Monatsschrift für deutsches Recht. Zeitschrift für die Zivilrechts-Praxis* (Cologne and others 1.1947 ff)
Med LR	*Medical Law Reports* (London 1989–97) continued as: *Lloyd's Law Reports Medical*
MedR	*Medizinrecht* (Munich 1983 ff)
MinroG	*Mineralrohstoffgesetz* (Austria)
MittBayNot	*Mitteilungen des Bayerischen Notarvereins, der Notarkasse und der Landesnotarkammer Bayern* (Munich 1949 ff)
MittRhNotK	*Mitteilungen Rheinische Notarkammer* (Cologne 1.1961–2000); continued through Rheinische Notar-Zeitschrift (RNotZ) (Cologne 2001 ff)
MLR	*The Modern Law Review* (London 1.1937/38 ff)
MMR	*Multimedia und Recht. Zeitschrift für Informations-, Telekommunikations- und Medienrecht* (Munich 1.1998 ff)
Motive	*Motive zu dem Entwurfe eines Bürgerlichen Gesetzbuches für das Deutsche Reich* (Berlin 1888)
MP	*Monitor Prawniczy* (Warsaw 1.1993 ff)
MTJ	*Számú törvényjavaslat „Magyarország Magánjogi Törvénykönyve"* (1928. évi 500)
My & K; M & K	*Mylne & Keen's Chancery Reports* (London 1832–35)
N.v.W.	*Nota van Wijzigingen*, in: Parl. Geschiedenis van het Nieuwe Burgerlijk Wetboek
NCC	*Noul Cod civil* (Romania)
NCPC	*Nouveau Code de procédure civile* (France)
Nds. BauO	*Niedersächsische Bauordnung* (Germany)
NedJur	*Nederlandse Jurisprudentie—Uitspraken in burgerlijke en strafzaken* (Deventer 1.1976 ff)
NGCC	*La nuova giurisprudenza civile commentata* (Padua 1.1985 ff)
NI	*Northern Ireland Law Reports* (London 1925 ff)
NJA	*Nytt Juridiskt Arkiv* (Stockholm 1.1874 ff; divided into two sections since 1876: Section 1: *Rättsfall från högsta domstolen*; Section 2: *Tidskrift för lagstiftning*)
NJB	*Nederlands Juristenblad* (Zwolle, Deventer 1.1926 ff)
NJW	*Neue Juristische Wochenschrift* (Munich/Frankfurt am Main 1.1947 ff)
NJW-RR	*NJW-Rechtsprechungs-Report Zivilrecht* (Munich, Frankfurt am Main 1.1986 ff)
NLJ; NLJ Rep	*New Law Journal* (London 1.1965 ff)
NoB	Nomiko Bima (Athens 1.1953 ff)
NOMOS	*NOMOS* (legal database, Greece)
NordÖR	*Zeitschrift für öffentliches Recht in Norddeutschland* (Baden-Baden 1.1998 ff)
NotBZ	*Zeitschrift für die notarielle Beratungs- und Beurkundungspraxis* (Cologne 1.1997 ff)
NPC	*New Property Cases* (London 1986 ff)

NSWCA	*New South Wales Court of Appeal*
NTBR	*Nederlands Tijdschrift voor Burgerlijk Recht* (Deventer 1.1984 ff)
NZ Recent L. Rev.	*New Zealand Recent Law Review* (Auckland 1989–94)
NZG	*Neue Zeitschrift für Gesellschaftsrecht* (Munich/Frankfurt am Main 1.1998 ff)
NZLR	*New Zealand Law Reports* (Wellington 1.1883 ff)
NZM	*Neue Zeitschrift für Miet- und Wohnungsrecht* (Munich/Frankfurt am Main 1.1998 ff)
O Direito	*O Direito. Revista de jurisprudência* (Lisbon 1868 ff)
OGH	*Oberster Gerichtshof* (Austria)
ÖJZ	*Österreichische Juristenzeitung* (Vienna 1.1946 ff)
OLGR	*OLG-Report Celle, Hamburg, Schleswig, Oldenburg, Braunschweig, Bremen. Schnelldienst zur Zivilrechtsprechung der Oberlandesgerichte* (Saarbrücken, Cologne 1.1994–15.2009)
OSNC	*Orzecznictwo Sądu Najwyższego. Izba Cywilna* (Compiled Supreme Court judgements Civil Chamber) (Warsaw 1918 ff)
OSNCP	*Zbiór Orzeczeń Sądu Najwyższego. Orzeczenia Izby Cywilnej i Administracyjnej oraz Izby Pracy i Ubezpieczeń Społecznych* (Compiled Supreme Court judgements, Poland)
OSNP	*Orzecznictwo Sądu Najwyższego Izba Pracy, Ubezpieczeń Społecznych i Spraw Publicznych* (Warsaw 1.1994 ff)
OSNPG	*Orzecznictwo Sądu Najwyższego, Wydawnictwo Prokuratury Generalnej* (Warsaw)
OSP	*Orzecznictwo Sądów Polskich* (Warsaw 1.1957 ff)
OSPiKA	*Orzecznictwo Sądów Polskich i Komisji Arbitrażowych*
OxJLegStud	*Oxford Journal of Legal Studies* (London 1.1981 ff)
OZ	*Obligacijski zakonik* (Slovenia)
P	*The Law Reports. Probate Division* (1876–1941); continued as *The Law Reports. Probate, divorce and admiralty division* (1942–71) and *The Law Reports. Family Division* (from 1972)
P & CR	*Property, Planning and Compensation Reports* (London 1986 ff)
Parl. Geschiedenis	*Parlementaire Geschiedenis van het Nieuwe Burgerlijk Wetboek.* Parlementaire stukken; edited by C. J. Van Zeben and J. W. Du Pon in cooperation with M. M. Olthof
Pas. belge	*Pasicrisie belge. Recueil général de la jurisprudence des cours et tribunaux de Belgique* (Brussels 1865 ff)
Pas. luxemb.	*Pasicrisie luxembourgeoise. Recueil de la jurisprudence luxembourgeoise* (Luxembourg 1.1881 ff)
PEL	*Principles of European Law*
PEL Liab.Dam.	*Principles of European Law: Non-Contractual Liability Arising out of Damage Caused to Another*
PEL Unj.Enr.	*Principles of European Law: Unjustified Enrichment*
PIQR	*Personal Injuries and Quantum Reports* (London 1.1992 ff)
PLR	*Planning Law Reports* (London 1.1988 ff; also: *Estates Gazette Planning Law Reports*)
PoinChr.	*Poinika Chronika* (Greece)
Právní rozhledy	*Právní rozhledy* (Prague 1993 ff)
Prop.	*Proposition* (Draft Legislation, Sweden)

PTSR	*The Public and Third Sector Law Reports* (London 1.2009 ff)
QB	*The Law Reports. Queen's Bench Division* (London 1.1876 ff)
Quaderni fiorentini	*Quaderni fiorentini per la storia del pensiero giuridico moderno* (Milan 1.1972 ff)
R.I.D.C.	*Revue internationale de droit comparé* (Paris 1.1949 ff, Continuation of: *Bulletin de la Société de législation comparée* [Paris 1.1869–71.1947/48])
R.J.D.A.	*Revue de jurisprudence du droit des affaires* (Paris 1.1991 ff)
R.M. Themis	*Rechtsgeleerd magazijn Themis. Tijdschrift voor publiek- en privaatrecht* (Zwolle 1.1939 ff)
R.W.	*Rechtskundig Weekblad* (Antwerp 1.1931/32 ff)
RAJ	*Repertorio Aranzadi de Jurisprudencia* (Pamplona 1.1930/31, 2.1934 ff)
Rb.	*Arrondissementsrechtbank* (Court of first instance, Belgium, Netherlands)
RC	*Tribunal da Relação de Coimbra* (Court of appeal of Coimbra, Portugal)
RCDI	*Revista Crítica de Derecho Inmobiliario* (Madrid 1.1925 ff)
RCJB	*Revue critique de jurisprudence belge* (Brussels 1.1947 ff)
RDACM	*Revista Doctrinal Aranzadi Civil-Mercantil* (Cizur Menor 2011 ff)
RDC	*Revue des contrats* (Paris 2003 ff)
RdE	*Recht der Energiewirtschaft* (Cologne 1992 ff)
RDL	*Real decreto legislativo* (Spain)
Recht	*Das Recht. Übersicht über Schrifttum und Rechtsprechung* (Berlin and Munich 1897–1944)
Redur	*Revista Electrónica del Departamento de Derecho de la Universidad de la Rioja* (Logroño Juni 2002 ff, http://www.unirioja.es/dptos/dd/redur/home.htm)
Rép. civ. Dalloz	*Répertoire de droit civil Dalloz* (Paris 1970 ff)
Rep. Giur. it	*Repertorio generale della giurisprudenza italiana* (Turin 71.1969 ff; Continued by *Repertorio generale annuale della Giurisprudenza italiana* [Turin 1.1899–70.1969])
Rev. crit. dr. int. priv.	*Revue critique de droit international privé* (Paris 1.1905 ff)
RG	*Reichsgericht* (Supreme Court of the German Reich)
RGBl.	*Reichsgesetzblatt* (Berlin 1871–1945, divided into Part I and Part II since 1922 (Vienna 1848–1918)
RGZ	*Amtliche Sammlung der Entscheidungen des Reichsgerichtes in Zivilsachen* (Berlin 1.1872–172.1945)
RH	*Reglamento Hipotecario* (Spain)
RhNotZ	*Rheinische Notar-Zeitschrift* (Cologne 2001 ff)
Riv. dir. civ.	*Rivista di diritto civile* (Padua 1.1955 ff)
Riv. dir. ind.	*Rivista di diritto industriale* (Milan 1.1952 ff)
Riv. giur. edilizia	*Rivista giuridica dell' edilizia* (Milan 1958 ff)
Riv. giur. sarda	*Rivista giuridica sarda* (Cagliari 1986 ff)
Riv. it. per le scienze giur.	*Rivista italiana per le scienze giuridiche* (Rome 1886–1974; 2010 ff)
Riv. notariato	*Rivista del notariato. Rassegna di diritto e pratica notarile* (Milan 1.1947 ff)
Riv. pen.	*Rivista penale* (Rome 1930 ff)
Riv.trim.dir. e proc.civ.	*Rivista trimestrale di diritto e procedura civile* (Milan 1.1947 ff)

ROA	*Revista da Ordem dos Advogados* (Lisbon 1.1941 ff)
ROJ	*Repertorio Oficial de Jurisprudencia* (Centro de Documentación Oficial, Consejo General del Poder Judicial)
RP	*Tribunal da Relação do Porto* (Court of appeal of Porto, Portugal)
RPfleger	*Rechtspfleger* (1.1889–110.2002: *Der deutsche Rechtspfleger*; Bielefeld 111.2003 ff)
RTD civ.	*Revue trimestrielle de droit civil* (Paris 1.1902 ff)
RvdW	*Rechtspraak van de Week* (Zwolle/Deventer 1.1939 ff)
RVR	*Rating & Valuation Reporter* (London 1.1961 ff)
S.	*Recueil Sirey. Pandectes françaises périodiques. Journal du palais. Jurisprudence, législation* (Paris 1791–1954, 1957–64, combined with Recueil Dalloz since 1965 [see D.])
S.I.	*Statutory Instrument* (Ireland and United Kingdom)
Sbírka nálezů a usnesení	*Sbírka nálezů a usnesení Ústavního soudu České republiky* (Decisions of the Czech Constitutional Court) (Prague 1.1993/94(1994/95) ff)
Sbírka rozhodnutí Nejvyššího správního soudu	*Sbírka rozhodnutí Nejvyššího správního soudu* (Prague 1. 2003 ff)
Sbírka soudních rozhodnutí a stanovisek	*Sbírka soudních rozhodnutí a stanovisek* (Prague 1. 1971 ff)
Scand.Stud.L.	*Scandinavian Studies in Law* (Stockholm 1.1957 ff)
SFS	*Svensk författningssamling* (Stockholm 1.1825 ff)
SGA	*Sale of Goods Act* (England and Wales)
Sing L Rev	*Singapore Law Review* (Singapore 1969–72, 1983 ff)
SJ; SJLB	*Solicitors Journal; Solicitors Journal Law Brief* (London 1.1857 ff)
SN	Sąd Najwyższy (Supreme Court, Poland)
Soubor rozhodnutí NS	*Soubor rozhodnutí Nejvyššího soudu* (Prague 2001 ff), cited according to reference number (Volumes 27–31 were published as *Soubor civilních rozhodnutí Nejvyššího soudu)*
Soudní rozhledy	*Soudní rozhledy* (Prague 1. 1996 ff)
SPZ	*Stvarnopravni zakonik* (Slovenia)
Sr	*Wetboek van Strafrecht* (Penal Code, Netherlands)
SR (NSW)	*New South Wales State Reports* (Sydney 1901–70); *New South Wales Law Reports*
Stark	*Starkie's Nisi Prius Reports* (Reports of cases, determined at Nisi Prius, in the Courts of King's Bench and Common Pleas) (1814–23 in three volumes)
STC	*Simon's Tax Cases* (London 1973 ff; also: *Simon's Weekly Tax Service*)
StE	*Symboulio tes Epikrateias* (Regional Council Athens)
StGB	*Strafgesetzbuch* (Germany); *Poinikos Kodikas* (Greece); *Trestní zákoník* (Czechia); *Brottsbalk* (Sweden)
STJ	*Supremo Tribunal de Justiça* (Portugal)
Suppl. Ord.	*Supplemento ordinario* (Italy)
SvJT	*Svensk Juristtidning* (Stockholm 1.1916 ff)
SZ	*Entscheidungen des österreichischen Obersten Gerichtshof in Zivilsachen* (Vienna 1.1919 (1922) ff)

T.M.	*Toelichting-Meijers*, in: Parl. Geschiedenis van het Nieuwe Burgerlijk Wetboek; cf. Schrifttumsverzeichnis for further information
TAR	*Tribunale amministrativo regionale* (Italy)
TCLR	*Technology and Construction Law Reports* (London 1.1999 ff)
TGI; Trib. gr. inst.	*Tribunal de grande instance* (France)
Themis; Th	*Themis* (Athens 1.1890/91–65.1954/55)
TKG	*Telekommunikationsgesetz* (Austria)
TLR	*Times Law Reports* (London 1884–1952)
TR	*Durnford & East's Term Reports, King's Bench* (ER 99–101) (London 1785–1800)
Trib. civ.	*Tribunal civil* (France), *Tribunale civile* (Italy)
Trib. prem. inst.	*Tribunal de première instance* (Belgium)
Trustees Act 1996	*Trusts of Land and Appointment of Trustees Act 1996* (England)
Trusts e attività fiduciarie	*Trusts e attività fiduciarie* (Milan 2000 ff)
TS	*Tribunal Supremo* (Spain)
UGN	*Ustawa o gospodarce nieruchomościami* (Poland)
UKHL	*Approved judgment of the House of Lords*
UKSC	*United Kingdom Supreme Court*
UKVAT	*United Kingdom VAT & Duties Tribunal*
UNTS	*United Nations Treaty Series. Treaties and international agreements registered or filed and recorded with the Secretariat of the United Nations* (Washington D.C. 1.1946/47 ff)
Ur.l. SRS	*Zakon o poslovnih stavbah in poslovnih prostorih 18/1974 of 18.05.1974* (Slovenia)
UrhG	*Urhebergesetz* (Austria)
VermG	*Vermessungsgesetz* (Austria)
VersR	*Versicherungsrecht. Zeitschrift für Versicherungsrecht, Haftungs- und Schadensrecht* (Karlsruhe 1.1950 ff)
VfGH	*Verfassungsgerichtshof* (Czechia) (Ústavní soud České republiky)
W	*Weekblad van het Recht* (Zwolle, 1.1839–105.1943)
WEG	*Wohnungseigentumsgesetz* (Germany, Austria)
WGO-MfOR	*WGO Monatshefte für osteuropäisches Recht. Die wichtigsten Gesetzgebungsakte in den Ländern Ost- und Südeuropas* (Münster, Berlin, Hamburg 1958–2011)
Wils KB	*Wilson's King's Bench and Common Pleas Reports* (London 1742–74)
WiRO	*Wirtschaft und Recht in Osteuropa. Zeitschrift zur Rechts- und Wirtschaftsentwicklung in den Staaten Mittel- und Osteuropas* (Munich, Frankfurt a.M. 1.1992 ff)
WL	*Westlaw* (http://legalsearch.westlaw.co.uk)
WLR	*The Weekly Law Reports* (London 1.1953 ff)
WM	*Wertpapier-Mitteilungen. Zeitschrift für Wirtschafts- und Bankrecht* (Frankfurt am Main et. al. 1.1947 ff)
WN	*Weekly Notes of Cases* (London 1.1866–1952)
WN (NSW)	*Weekly Notes, New South Wales* (Sydney 1884–1970)
WPNR	*Weekblad voor privaatrecht, notariaat en registratie* (The Hague 1.1870 ff)

WR	*Weekly Reporter* (London 1853–1906)
WRG	*Wasserrechtsgesetz* (Austria)
WTLR	*Wills & Trusts Law Reports* (London 1.2000 ff)
WWSG	*Wald- und Weideservitutengesetz des Bundes* (Austria)
Y & J	*Young & Jervis's Exchequer Reports* (London 1826–30)
Yale LJ	*The Yale Law Journal* (New Haven 1.1891/92 ff)
Zak	*Zivilrecht aktuell* (Austria)
Zdravotnictví a právo	*Zdravotnictví a právo* (Prague 1997 ff)
ZGB	*Zivilgesetzbuch*; *Astikos Kodikas* (Greece), *Civillikums* (Latvia), *Kodeks cywilny* (Poland), *Zivilgesetzbuch* (Switzerland), *Polgári Törvényköny* [Ptk] (Hungary); cf. Gesetzesregister for further information
ZInsO	*Zeitschrift für das gesamte Insolvenzrecht* (Cologne, 1.1998 ff)
ZIP	*Zeitschrift für Wirtschaftsrecht* (Cologne 1.1980 ff)
ZPO	*Zivilprozessordnung* (Germany)
ZRG GA	*Zeitschrift der Savigny-Stiftung für Rechtsgeschichte. Germanistische Abteilung* (Vienna, Cologne, Weimar 1.1880 ff)
ZVG	*Gesetz über die Zwangsversteigerung und die Zwangsverwaltung* (Germany)

I

Property Law and Property Rights

1. 'Property Law' and 'Property Rights'

The rules of what we call 'property law'[1] (*asjaõigus, derecho de cosas/derechos reales, direito das coisas, diritto delle cose,*[2] *dologi jog, droit des biens, εμπράγματο δίκαιο, вещно право, goederenrecht,*[3] *prawo rzeczowe,*[4] *Sachenrecht, sakrätt, stvarno pravo, věcná práva, vecné práva*, etc.) belong to that part of a legal order which governs relationships between private subjects in relation to their entitlement to make use[5] of **things**. Objective property law creates rights and powers to occupy and to use things,[6] as well as to encumber them (e.g. through the creation of a security interest)[7] and to acquire[8] rights in them. The special feature of the property rights, i.e. the rights which property law creates for this purpose (*derechos reales, direitos reais, diritti reali, dologi jogok, droits réels, εμπράγματα δικαιώματα, praw rzeczowych, Sachenrechte, sakrätter, věcná práva, goederenrechtelijke rechten,*[9] etc.), is that they operate against every person who purports to use an object in a manner reserved to the one who holds them.[10] Legal remedies (claims, rights to sue) that are rooted in property law attach only to the holder 1.1

[1] The need to make a terminological distinction between 'objective' law (as the sum of legal norms binding on all subjects) and 'subjective' rights (as the rights and powers guaranteed to individuals by the objective law) arises in languages which only have one word for the two concepts—unlike English, for example, which has two (namely 'law' and 'right'). In this translation, the distinction between objective law and subjective rights is an artefact of the original language but will be used from time to time for additional precision.

[2] There does not appear to be an established term for expressing 'property law' as the sum of norms binding on third parties in Italian. The third book of the *Codice civile* is headed with the title '*Della proprieta*' ('of ownership'). The German-language version of the bi-lingual Italian Civil Code translates this heading as '*Sachenrecht*' (lit. 'the law of things').

[3] In the Netherlands, one traditionally spoke of '*zakenrecht*' (lit. 'law of things') until the passage of the new Civil Code. However, this term already included not only physical objects but rights in assets of all types that were effective against third parties. Since 1992 the whole area of law has been called '*goedenrecht*' (lit. 'law of the goods') (see Pitlo [*-Reehuis and Heisterkamp*], Goederenrecht[12], no. 1 p. 1). *Zakenrecht* is only a part of the *goederenrecht*, which concerns only corporeal objects (or 'goods').

[4] The Polish literature speaks expressly of a 'law of things ('*pravo rzecowe*'); the title, however, to the second book of the Polish Civil Code refers to 'Ownership and other real rights'.

[5] In the sense of 'enjoyment', i.e. *aproveitamento, gebruik, korzystanie, Nutznießung, požívání, ωφέλεια*, etc.

[6] In the sense of 'use and profit', i.e. *genot, Genuss, godimento, goze, gozo, jouissance, use and profit, užívání, używanie*, etc.

[7] *Garantía, garantia, garanzia, προστασία, security, sûreté, zabezpieczenie, zajišťení, zekerheid*, etc.

[8] *Acquisto, adquisición, aquisição, acquisition, κτήση και απώλεια, nabycie, nabytí, verkrijging*, etc.

[9] A sub-group of these rights are organized in the fifth book of the Netherlands Civil Code under *zakelijke rechten* (lit. 'thingly rights'). These are the rights of ownership and all rights, that are split ('*afgesplitst*') from them: see *Brahn and Reehuis*, Zwaartepunten van het vermogensrecht[9], no 37 p 17.

[10] So argues *Sjef van Erp* in Reiner Schulze and Hans Schulte-Nölke (eds), *European Private Law: Current Status and Perspectives*, 227, 231: 'The broad notion of property law which I propose is: relations between subjects, concerning objects with effect against a substantial group of other subjects.' Statutory definitions of subjective property rights are, incidentally, infrequent. An exception is observable for example in Art. 973 of the Greek Civil Code, according to which property rights ('rights on things') are defined as such rights 'which guarantee a direct right effective against every other person to control of the thing.' § 307 of the Austrian Civil Code defines real rights

Foundations of Property Law. Christian von Bar and Jason Grant Allen, Oxford University Press. © Christian von Bar 2023.
DOI: 10.1093/oso/9780198885337.003.0001

of the relevant property rights (the relevant 'title'). In contrast to subjective rights based in the law of obligations, the rights of property law reveal their unique nature not in bi-lateral, but rather in tri-lateral relations.

2. Legal Relationships in Relation to Things

1.2 Property law is concerned with the legal relationships between persons in relation to *things*. The construction of a strict logical system would also require the inversion of this proposition, i.e. that legal relationships which do not relate to 'things' are not part of property law. Not all extant legal systems make this inversion systematically,[11] but this fact need not trouble us. It only shows that we lack, at present, a coherent European terminology. To put it differently: the foundational question of what should be called a 'thing' is answered differently from legal system to legal system.[12] On the other hand, some codifications deal with rights under the 'law of things', although the

('*dingliche Rechte*') as rights over things 'which inure to the benefit of a person without reference to certain other persons' ('[*Rechte, die*] *einer Person über eine Sache ohne Rücksicht auf gewisse Personen zustehen*').

[11] Although, in principle, they only define corporeal objects as 'things', the German, Greek, Hungarian, and Polish Civil Codes organize the rules governing pledges over outstanding claims in the relevant section on the law of things (§ 1273(1) of the German Civil Code; Art. 1247 of the Greek Civil Code; Art. 327 of the Polish Civil Code; § 5:101(1) of the Hungarian Civil Code. Likewise, the rules governing rights of usufruct over rights and company shares are placed in the property law section of each code (see § 1068(1) of the German Civil Code; Art. 265 § 1 of the Polish Civil Code; § 5:156 of the Hungarian Civil Code. Polish law also recognizes a hypothec on perpetual usufruct and on outstanding claims secured with a hypothec: see Art. 65(2) of the Polish Civil Code. Such rights to rights are often said to be, in fact, 'obligational' and not 'real' (e.g. Staudinger [-*Wiegand*], BGB [2001], Vorbem. zu §§ 1273 ff no. 5), but to create 'proprietary consequences', like security rights in things, particularly in the case of a debtor's insolvency (Canaris, *FS Flume I*, pp. 371, 375). The Portuguese Civil Code, however, deals with security rights in things (Art. 66) *and* in outstanding claims (Art. 679) in exactly the opposite order, i.e. in the sixth chapter of the second book entitled 'law of obligations' [*direito das obrigações*] together with security deposits, guarantees, and hypothecs. Portuguese law recognizes hypothecs not only over land, but also over moveable objects that are subject to registration and deemed equal to land (vehicles, ships, and aeroplanes) and over certain specified rights, e.g. the rights under a public permit or franchise (Art. 688 of the Portuguese Civil Code). Differently, again, the Italian Civil Code distinguishes, under the rubric of limited real rights [*diritti reali limitati*], between real rights of enjoyment and real rights of security (pledges and hypothecs). The former are set out in the third book of the Civil Code on the law of property [*Della proprietà*] and the latter under the sixth book on the protection of rights [*Della tutela dei diritti*]. A pledge [*pegno*] can be imposed on things, aggregated assets, claims and rights over moveable things (Art. 2784 of the Italian Civil Code), and a hypothec can have as its subject matter the ownership and enjoyment of land, certain servitudes, heritable building rights, public bonds, and registered moveable objects (Art. 2810 of the Italian Civil Code). The Spanish Civil Code, on the other hand, regulates pledges over outstanding claims in Art. 1861, which stands in the fourth book ('On obligations and contracts').

[12] The broader definition of the 'law of things' ('*sakrätt*') in Sweden is, by way of contrast, internally consistent. It includes all rights that are effective against all the world. 'Property law' is concerned, on this view, with a problem that can arise with all subjective rights in assets (*Håstad*, Sakrätt[6], p. 16). It is concerned with legal relationships between persons in relation to objects of value: a 'thing' is anything that can be transferred and therefore be used as security (that means, e.g. that company shares can be 'things', but labour potential cannot: *Hessler*, Allmän Sakrätt, pp. 6 and 19). The word *sakrätt* (lit. 'thing law') is a loan-word from the German (i.e. '*Sachenrecht*'), but it has acquired its own meaning in the laws of the Nordic countries (*Millqvist*, Sakrättens grunder, p. 16). So, too, the law of the Netherlands has avoided a definition of 'pledge and 'hypothec' as *either* obligational *or* real rights. It has instead positioned them in the general part of its law of property (Book 3 of the Netherlands Civil Code). A pledge is, accordingly, a 'real' right when it is attached to a 'thing', and not when it is attached to something which is not a 'thing', such as a claim (Pitlo [-*Reehuis and Heisterkamp*] op. cit. no. 754 pp. 573–4; Brahn and Reehuis, *Zwaartepunten van het vermogensrecht*[9], nos 38–40, pp. 18–19). The Austrian Civil Code also proceeds from a very broad definition of 'thing', however it only applies the rules of property law to corporeal objects (Schwimann and Kodek [-*Hofmann*], ABGB II[4], § 285 no. 1; *Iro*, Sachenrecht[4], no. 1/1; *Bydlinski*, AcP 198 [1998] p. 287, 291; Klang [-*Klang*],

point of reference of these rights might lack corporeality and cannot be considered a 'thing' at all on the terms of the codification itself. Take, for example, a pledge over an outstanding claim or a right of usufruct over a company share. These codifications must admit to a lack of systematic coherence.[13] It is, however, generally beyond question that (i) neither human beings[14] nor their actions are 'things'[15] (one cannot, without the institution of slavery, 'own' either another human being or his labour potential);[16] and that (ii) at least parcels of land and other corporeal objects belong to the category of 'things'.[17] Rights in parcels of land and moveable physical objects are

ABGB II², § 285 no. 1). In the Austrian law of pledges, however, we again find an exception; a pledge can attach under § 448 Austrian Civil Code to outstanding claims.

[13] They are rightly criticized by Professor Menyhárd, among others. He argues that the border between the law of things and the law of obligations is only the result of a theoretical construct, and is not necessarily a condition of the correct understanding of private law (*Menyhárd*, Dologi jog, p. 42). On this view, the conceptualization of a 'law of things' is only sensible if rights in things—and their creation and destruction—reveal characteristics that make a self-sufficient regulation necessary or at least possible. The determination of property law's sphere of application depends, for this reason, on the definition of the concept of 'thing' (*Menyhárd* loc. cit.).

[14] Problematic, however, is the formulation in Art. 202 of the Portuguese Civil Code, by which everything that can be the subject matter of a legal relationship is defined as a 'thing'. If one took this definition literally, then even human beings could belong to the category of 'things' in, e.g. Art. 202(1) in the context of family law. The Portuguese literature has, therefore, been very critical of the text and has resoundingly rejected the (linguistically possible) implications of this formulation (see e.g. *Carvalho*, Direito das coisas, pp. 79–82; *Menezes Cordeiro*, Direitos reais, p. 189; *Mota Pinto*, Teoria geral do direito civil⁴, pp. 333 and 343; *Carvalho Fernandes*, Teoria geral do direito civil I², p. 545, and *Hörster*, Parte geral, p. 177).

[15] Although it is comparatively broad in other respects, the conceptual definition in Austrian law makes this point very clearly. § 285 Austrian Civil Code provides that 'everything which is distinct from the person, and which can be used by human beings, is called a "thing" in the legal sense'. Labour potential per se is not a thing, on this definition, because it is a part of the person (*Gschnitzer/Faistenberger/Barta*, Allgemeiner Teil des bürgerlichen Rechts², pp. 396–7). On the other hand, the individual performance of a service is. That follows from § 303 Austrian Civil Code, which assigns physical and mental labour that has an objectively calculable economic value to the category of 'quantifiable things' (see e.g. OGH 29 April 1925, SZ 7/155 holding that services were incorporeal things and could be the subject matter of a gift; OGH 20 October 1985, SZ 55/155 holding that the unsatisfactory qualifications of employees left by one business for another were to be handled according to the contract law provisions governing defects in moveable goods).

[16] Equally, a father with sole rights of parental custody cannot use property law to compel the mother to hand over children who want to stay with her: OGH 11 May 1966, SZ 39/89. Such claims for delivery of custody must be provided by family law, not property law.

[17] See, in the first instance, § 90 of the German Civil Code (only corporeal objects are 'things'), Art. 947 of the Greek Civil Code (corporeal objects, but under certain conditions also energy), Art. 3:2 of the Netherlands Civil Code (the human control of accessible, material objects), Art. 45 of the Polish Civil Code (only corporeal objects), § 5:14(1) of the Hungarian Civil Code, 'corporeal object which can be taken into possession' and Art. 202 of the Portuguese Civil Code (a 'thing' is anything which can be the object of legal relations). Art. 810 of the Italian Civil Code, on the other hand, counts as 'goods' ('*beni*') all 'things' ('*cosi*') which can be the object of rights. The term *cosa* is, however, not defined in the text. According to the prevailing view, *beni* can be both corporeal things (*beni materiali*, i.e. things apprehensible in the external world with the senses) and non-corporeal things (*beni immateriali*, i.e. inventions and intellectual works) (*Bianca*, Diritto civile VI, p. 51). In certain cases, however (e.g. in Art. 274), the Italian Civil Code uses a broader definition of the concept of thing; this concept embraces rights in assets of all kinds. For this reason, it is often said that all legally relevant material or immaterial goods fall under the definition of *beni* (e.g. *Biondi*, I beni, p. 9; Grundmann and Zaccaria [-*Troiano*], *Einführung in das italienische Recht*, pp. 265–7; *Bianca* op. cit. p. 49 fn. 1; Cian and Trabucchi [-*Pellegrini*], Commentario breve⁸, sub Art. 813 p. 779 no. I, 1). The Spanish Civil Code also puts the concept of 'goods' (*bienes*) front and centre. Goods, whether moveable or immoveable, are defined in Art. 333 as 'all things, which are or can be the object of an acquisition'. Swedish law has not defined its broad concept of 'things' (see above, n. 12) by statute. It distinguishes between real property (*fast egendom*, lit. 'fixed property' defined in Ch 1 § 1 of the Swedish land law code or *Jordabalken*) and moveable property (*lös egendom*, lit. 'loose property'). Everything, which is not real property, is *lös egendom*. To the latter belong corporeal things. *Lös egendom* embraces *lösören* (goods capable of being transported), ships and aeroplanes, *byggnad på ofri grund* (houses on another person's land), debentures and other securities (including company shares), liquidated claims for money ('*enkla skuldebref och fordringar*'), electronically registered claims (under the relevant financial instruments statute), claims for the delivery of goods, intellectual property rights, and options granted under a statute ('*syntetiska tillgångar*') (*Millqvist*, Sakrättens grunder⁵, p. 32).

always property rights, when they satisfy the other requirements of such objects of legal transactions. In the understanding of this book, a 'thing' is anything in which a property right can arise. Only such a wide definition enables us to free ourselves from the particularities of individual jurisdictions and to perceive the reflexive relationship between property rights and their objects. The right of ownership, for example, is not directed to the same purposes as rights such as usufruct, hypothec, or pledge. The definition is not, however, just circular. The number of possible property rights is limited. The so-called *numerus clausus* of property rights is thus integral to understanding the concept of things.

1.3 In some European legal systems, it is common to describe property law as the sum of norms that 'govern the relation of persons to things', i.e. which govern the relationship 'between subjects recognised by the legal system as having legal capacity and things'.[18] While one can live with this description, it is not wholly unproblematic.[19] Not everyone has the necessary force of imagination to imagine how a true 'legal relationship'—or indeed any 'relationship' capable of being governed by law—can subsist between a human being and an object.[20] The image of a 'relationship' of a person to a thing must not lead to the misunderstanding, however, that property law only creates powers of control

[18] This view is particularly influential in Germany (see e.g. *Vieweg and Werner*, Sachenrecht[4], no. 1; *Lüke*, Sachenrecht, no. 1; *Prütting*, Sachenrecht[35], no. 1; *Weber*, Sachenrecht *I*, § 2 no. 1; *Wieling*, Sachenrecht I[2], § 1 I 1 a; MünchKomm [-*Gaier*], *BGB VI*[5], Einl. no. 1; Staudinger [-*Seiler*], *BGB* [2007], Einl. zum Sachenrecht no. 5) (somewhat more nuanced *Baur and Stürner*, Sachenrecht[18], § 2 no. 2: subjective property rights are 'the legal position which accrues to a certain person over a certain thing'). It is also influential in Greece (e.g. *Georgiades*, Empragmato Dikaio I, no. 1: *Εμπράγματο δίκαιο* means literally right 'on' goods, *εμπράγματα δικαιώματα* are accordingly 'rights on goods') and in the Czech Republic (e.g. *Švestka and Dvořák*, Občanské právo hmotné[5], p. 272: property rights create legal relationships to things, obligational relationships create legal relationships between persons). In French law, *Atias*, Les biens[8], p. 46 no. 69, argues that a property right is every direct control over a thing that is due to a person. For *Larroumet*, Les biens[3], p. 6 '*le droit des biens se définit par opposition au droit des obligations, c'est-à-dire qu'il faut considérer que relève de l'étude du droit des biens tout ce qui, en ce qui concerne le patrimoine, ne relève pas du droit des obligations*'. In Portugal, property rights are even defined as the legal attribute of an object, which is aimed at the satisfaction of the interests of one or more persons (*Oliveira Ascensão*, Direitos Civil—Reais[5], p. 44; see also Faber and Lurger [-*Caramelo-Gomes and Nóbrega*], National Reports IV, Portugal, p. 602). *Vieira*, Direitos reais, pp. 90 and 97, on the other hand, stipulate that a 'property right is a right that confers [on a person] a certain use of a corporeal thing'). In Poland, most definitions of property law and property rights lay emphasis on the fact that they concern the use of things (e.g. Radwański and Dybowski [-*Machnikowski*], System Prawa Prywatnego III[2], p. 3 no. 2). *Gniewek*, Prawo rzeczowe[7], p. 2 no. 3 opines that a property right is a civil, absolute right over assets, that has a thing as its object.

[19] In Hungary, criticism of the thesis that property law is concerned with the relationship between a person and a thing was already articulated before the revision of the current Civil Code and has recently been strengthened: *Lábady*, A magyar magánjog (polgári jog) általános része[3], p. 285; *Lenkovics*, A dologi jog vázlata[7], p. 24, and *Menyhárd*, Dologi jog, p. 15.

[20] Handwörterbuch des Europäischen Privatrechts I (-*Michaels*), Eigentum, p. 358 suggests, in the Continental European context: 'Earlier, one saw the relation to the thing as central, and the relation to third parties as reflexive; later, and contrariwise, one limited legal relations to relations between persons and held the supposition of relation to a thing as conceptually wrong. On the correct view, one can connect both: Property is the complete ascription of a thing to the owner in relation to all others.' In a very similar vein, *Georgiades*, Empragmato Dikaio I, p. 32 no. 2 emphasizes that every real right has a positive (or internal) and a negative (or external) aspect. The positive aspect of a real right consists of direct control over a thing and the power to use it; the negative aspect consists of its effect against third parties, i.e. against all the world. For *Díez-Picazo*, Fundamentos III[5], p. 81, a property right is a subjective right which protects the interests of a person in a thing in an absolute manner, in the sense that it guarantees that person at once a direct and immediate power over the thing, and rights against third parties, such as the thing's potential aquirers and all other persons that find themselves in a relation to it ('*que se encuentren en relación con ella*').

'on' or 'over' things, *actiones in rem*,[21] but not rights 'against persons'.[22] The opposite is the case. Subjective rights create *legal effects against persons*, and this is entirely independent of whether one uses the term 'right' to denote only the primary right (e.g. of ownership, possession, security, etc., according to the legal system) or also to denote the legal remedies that help to protect it (which occurs wherever, as in § 194 of the German Civil Code, legal remedies are conceptualized as 'claims', i.e. as the material 'right to demand that another does or refrains from an act). When one speaks of 'real claims'[23] in the context of such a legal system, however, one's language is imprecise. This is because a claim is always against a *certain* person,[24] and cannot have the property of being effective against *all the world*, which is characteristic of property rights; in other words, cannot here show the properties of an absolute right over an asset. A claim to a legal remedy arises, with the content given to it by the relevant legal order necessary to protect the property rights it recognizes, only when the adversary (i.e. the one who has violated or threatened to violate the property right through his actions) is already identified. In other words, only the primary right which the remedy helps to realize has a 'real' nature, not the remedy itself.[25]

[21] The habit, still well established in the common law world, of speaking of rights or actions '*in rem*' (see also para. 4) apparently has its historical basis in the linguistic formula of the Roman *legis actio* process. True, the judgment given on an *actio in rem* declared ownership of the thing in question to vest in one of the parties, but the judgment did not compel the one possessing it in the meantime to deliver it to the prevailing party. The losing party did not, therefore, have any personal liability. The *legis actio in rem* only determined a right to the thing, not a right against the possessor (for more information, with more evidence, see *Sliwka*, Herausgabeansprüche als Teil des zivilrechtlichen Eigentumsrechts? p. 41).

[22] *Lüke* op. cit. for this reason immediately adds to this definition of 'property law' [*Sachenrecht*] that it does not exclude the creation of 'claim relationships'. In addition, of course property law also recognizes contracts over property law rights, and in some countries even party autonomy in private international law. This would all be unthinkable if we were just concerned with the relationship between a person and a thing. One cannot make an agreement with a thing! It is also remarkable that the formulation in § 307 of the Austrian Civil Code (already mentioned in n 10), which speaks of rights which inure to the benefit of a person *without reference to certain other persons*. In this manner, the absolute character of real rights is very adroitly circumvented; the statute does not say that other persons generally play no role in the law of property. In the Austrian literature, however, § 307 is not generally understood in this sense; it is rather thought that the provision equates property rights with control over things (e.g. Koziol/Bydlinski/Bollenberger [*-Eccher and Riss*], ABGB^4, § 307 no. 1).

[23] The expression 'real claim' [*dinglicher Anspruch*] is, however, apart from very few exceptions, not a statutory term but rather, insofar as it is used at all, part of the general legal parlance of some Continental European states. In Hungary, neither the Civil Code [2014] nor its predecessor [1959] uses the term. See Vékás, *Magyar Jog* 7/2003 p. 385, 386 (the author equates the 'real claim' with the *rei vindicatio*), and the older literature Almási, *Dologi jog I*, p. 11 (a claim is 'real' when it enables the claimant to bring an end to the position in which his right is impinged and demand the restoration of one consistent with his right). In the Netherlands, 'real claim' is mostly used to refer to claims arising from a real right, including the claim of vindication, i.e. for delivery of the thing. See Hijma and Olthof, *Compendium Nederlands Vermogensrecht*^{10}, no. 104 pp. 74–5 and no. 212 p. 141–2 and Asser (-Mijnssen and de Haan), *Goederenrecht I*^{13}, no. 235 p. 146. For the Czech Republic, see Spáčil, *Ochrana vlastnictví a držby v občanském zákoníku*^{2}, p. 84 (the claim for the delivery of the thing and its fruits is 'real' insofar as those fruits are also 'things'). One only finds the term used directly in the statutory text in the German Civil Code. § 198 reads: 'If a thing in respect of which a real claim exists comes into the possession of a third party by succession of title, the part of the limitation period that passed during the possession of his predecessor-in-title is deemed to accrue to the benefit of the successor-in-title.' (See in relation to the identical wording of the predecessor provision *Finkenauer*, *JZ* 2000 pp. 241–7.) This is intended to prevent the thirty-year limitations period for the claim of *vindicatio* [*Vindikationsanspruch*] in § 985 to begin running anew following a change of possession. The provision weakens a property right in this manner, however, rather than strengthening it. Besides, it uses the expression 'real claim' not for the purpose of furnishing the right with effect against third parties, but for the purpose of subordinating a group of proprietary claims for delivery to the statute of limitations.

[24] The same counts for judgments (unless one speaks of a judgment which changes, rather than declares, the legal position [*Gestaltungsurteil*]). There are, accordingly, no 'real judgments'.

[25] It would be nonsensical for this reason to argue over whether a claim such as that arising from Art. 491 of the Spanish Civil Code (by which a usufruct holder is obligated *vis-à-vis* the owner to produce an inventory sheet) has

1.4 One might see things differently where an *actio in rem* is accepted as a claim against a thing itself (e.g. against a ship or its cargo). In such a case, one would be confronted with a substantive claim against a thing which one could, for that reason, call 'real'. The United Kingdom Senior Courts Act 1981 envisages in section 21(2) that 'an action in rem may be brought in the High Court against the ship or property in connection with which the claim or question arises' under certain conditions, and subsection (3) provides that 'in any case in which there is a maritime lien or other charge on any ship, aircraft or other property for the amount claimed, an action in rem may be brought in the High Court against that ship, aircraft or property'. The text seems to proceed on the basis that it is concerned with the ship, i.e. that it provides for a claim against a thing itself.[26] On this basis, and on the basis of older sources, the maritime law of the common law has developed the apparently logical thesis that, in the context of an admiralty action in rem, the ship is 'personified' (thus the 'personification theory'),[27] and certain legal systems derived from the English common law still maintain this position.[28] In English law, the House of Lords abandoned this theory in a devastating[29] judgment in *Republic of India and Others v India Steamship Co. Ltd. (No. 2)*.[30] Lord Steyn there opined that this type of *actio in rem* had served the purpose of extending the limited jurisdiction of the High Court of Admiralty, and that this purpose had been rendered otiose by the passage of the Judicature Acts 1873–1875. The personification theory had become, in the meantime, a superfluous procedural fiction. Following this—by no means universally welcomed[31]—decision of the House of Lords, the view is now, correctly, that claims against ships are finally abolished.[32] Traditionalists, however, interpret the decision as a single instance with limited application: as a real claim, the admiralty action *in rem* still performs a number of functions and retains importance.[33]

an 'obligational' or a 'real' nature. It does not allow itself to be pressed into either of these categories. For this reason, the formulation in the German Civil Code § 197(1) no. 1 and § 438(1) no. 1a appears better than that chosen in § 198 (see n 23). The statute here speaks of 'claims for delivery arising from ownership [and] other proprietary rights', not of 'proprietary claims for delivery'. The term 'real right' [*dingliches Recht*] is not, however, defined anywhere in the German Civil Code.

[26] See also *Derrington*, 123 (2007) LQR 358. There is no comparable rule in any legal system outside the common law systems—not even in Sweden, where Ch. 3 § 1 of the Sea Law (Sjölagen [1994:1009]) provides for attachment of a ship only.

[27] E.g. *Fletcher Moulton LJ* in The Burns [1907] p. 137, 149: 'The action in rem is an action against the ship itself'; see also *The Nordglimt* [1988] QB 183 (per *Hobhouse J*).

[28] See, e.g. for South Africa *Hare*, Shipping Law & Admiralty Jurisdiction in South Africa, § 1-9.1 (p. 32) and for Australia *Cremean and Thompson*, in White, Australian Maritime Law^2, 2.1, p. 26, and *Allsop J* in *Comandate Marine Corp v Pan Australia Shipping Pty Ltd* [2006] FCAFC 192, para. 128: '[T]he law of Australia is that an action in rem, at least prior to the unconditional appearance of a relevant person, is an action against the ship, not the owner or demise charterer of the ship.'

[29] *Davenport*, LQR 114 (1998) 169, 171.

[30] [1998] AC 878.

[31] For critique see e.g. *Teare* [1998] LMCLQ 33; *Derrington and Turner*, The Law and Practice of Admiralty Matters, ch. 2; *Kuo Fen Ching v Dauphin Offshore Engineering & Trading Pte Ltd* [1999] 3 Sing. L. Rev. 721; *The Irina Zharkikh and the Ksenia Zharkikh* [2001] 2 NZLR 801; [2001] Lloyd's Rep. 319.

[32] *Davenport* op. cit. 169.

[33] *Derrington* op. cit. 359.

On the proper view, then, modern English maritime procedural law no longer recognizes the right to bring a suit against a thing. Rather, claims and rights to sue that arise from property rights are, here as elsewhere (and irrespective of the problematic turn of speech 'actions *in rem*'), always against persons.[34] They are, indeed, legal remedies which serve to realize property rights properly so called,[35] and for this reason they belong to 'property law'.[36] For example, the right of the owner to demand delivery of a thing by the possessor (or destrainor) is treated, in every legal system that recognizes this *rei vindicatio*,[37] either as the expression and content of the basic property right of 'ownership', or at least as a legal remedy[38] which serves its protection; in this sense, it is conceived as a part of 'property law'.[39] This appears to be correct, because the right to delivery arises anew in the person of the new owner on the transfer of ownership. In other words, the right to vindication is part of property law because it is reserved exclusively to the owner *at the relevant time*,[40] and because it is automatically extinguished 1.5

[34] In Sweden, it is often taught that the rights in or even against things follow the 'Germanic conceptualization', where rights against persons follow the 'Romanistic conceptualization'. In so doing, it is emphasized that the latter approach has gained unequivocally the upper hand (*Hellner*, Metodproblem, p. 162; *Hessler*, Allmän sakrätt, pp. 3–4).

[35] The right to choose whether or not one will purchase a parcel of land, for example, is no property right. Nothing changes when this right can be entered into the register of property titles and made, as a result, enforceable against third parties. Accordingly, Art. 14 of the Spanish title register regulation (lit. 'hypothec regulation', *Decreto de 14 de febrero de 1947 por el que se aprueba el Reglamento Hipotecario*, abbreviated as *Reglamento Hipotecario*) which creates registrable options (*contrato de opción de compra*) only creates an 'obligational' right; registration does not transform the option into a property right (*Díez-Picazo*, Fundamentos III^5, p. 120).

[36] See e.g. *Menyhárd*, Dologi jog, p. 40: The right of ownership is absolute in its effect, but relative in the reality of its existence. This is because even the right to possession has to be enforced *inter partes*.

[37] e.g. Art. 108 of the Bulgarian Property Statute, § 985 of the German Civil Code, Art. 5:2 of the Netherlands Civil Code, Art. 1094 of the Greek Civil Code, Art. 948 of the Italian Civil Code, § 366 of the Austrian Civil Code, Art. 222 § 1 of the Polish Civil Code, Art. 1311 of the Portuguese Civil Code, § 126(1) of the Slovakian Civil Code, Art. 348(2) of the Spanish Civil Code, § 1040(1) of the Czech Civil Code). The *action en revendication* is also known in French law, however it is not provided for expressly in the French Civil Code (see *Carbonnier*, Droit civil II, p. 1834 no. 867; *Terré and Simler*, Les biens^6, p. 382 no. 520). On the common law position see below paras 29–31. The DCFR deals with the claim for possession in VIII.-6:101(1) ('The owner is entitled to obtain or recover possession of the goods from any person exercising physical control over these goods, unless this person has a right to possess the goods in the sense of VIII.-1:207 (Possession by limited-right-possessor) in relation to the owner').

[38] On the history of this remedy see *Sliwka*, Herausgabeansprüche als Teil des zivilrechtlichen Eigentumsrechts? p. 19.

[39] Caution must be exercised regarding the expression *vindicatio* (and in particular with the anglicized term 'to vindicate'). In some jurisdictions, this term can be understood to connote a restitutionary remedy that is triggered when the object of property rights has ceased to exist or has ceased to be in the possession of the defendant. In such cases, we are concerned with a claim for payment of money; *such* a claim's proprietary nature is doubtful, as has been noted in the context of Scottish law: *Stewart*, The Law of Restitution in Scotland, p. 94; *Schneiderhan*, Der Quasi-Contract im schottischen und englischen Recht, p. 19; *Miller*, Corporeal Moveables in Scots Law, p. 176 and *Birks*, Jurid. Rev. 1985 pp. 227, 236–7. On the English law of conversion, which affords priority to the judgment debtor in the case of insolvency, see below para. 29. The *azione di rivendicazione* in Art. 948 of the Italian Civil Code allows the owner not only to demand possession from any third party, but also to prosecute the claim when the defendant has, by his own conduct, ceased to possess the thing. In such a case, the defendant is obliged to reproduce the thing for the claimant, or to compensate him to the value of the thing and any other losses that have arisen. *Gallo*, Arricchimento senza causa e quasi contratti, p. 3 speaks, for this reason, of *rimedi restitutori*, by which is meant both *azione di rivendica* and purely obligational claims for possession arising from *ripetizione di indebito* and *arricchimento senza causa*. In Austrian law, on the other hand, the 'claim for vindication' relates only to physical goods despite Austrian law's broad definition of 'things'. As such, questions such as who owns a claim for deposits held by a bank and the passbook associated with the account cannot be settled by means of the *Vindikationsklage* in § 366 of the Austrian Civil Code (OGH 7 April 1970, SZ 43/67).

[40] On the inalienability of the claim of vindication see below para. 33. *How* ownership is transferred (whether already through the contract of sale, through some subsequent transfer of possession, or even through an additional contract of transfer) does not affect this conclusion.

with the extinction of the thing. The same counts for every other legal remedy which serves the realization of a property right, e.g. those directed towards acquiescence in a certain state of affairs or cessation of a certain kind of dealing. As all private law, property law operates not between persons and things but between persons. It concerns the *relationship between persons* in relation to the use of things, not the relationship between persons and things.

3. Protection in Tri-Partite Relationships

1.6 Property rights are intended and designed to reveal their specific effects in tri-partite and multi-lateral relationships. Only the entry of a third party allows the distinction to be made between rights based in the law of obligations and property rights (or, as it is often expressed, between 'relative' and 'absolute' or 'contractual' and 'real' rights). As G.L. Gretton puts it, Robinson Crusoe needs no law on his island so long as he is alone. Once Friday enters the scene, the two castaways have need for a system of law on their island, but the rules of that system could not be distinguished as 'obligations' or 'property law'. This distinction would only arise with the arrival of a third castaway.[41] Indeed, property rights are calibrated for effect against third parties; they are designed to put the one who holds them in a position to prevail against all the world in conflicts over the control of a thing, not only against a contractual partner or other obligee (the 'second party').[42] Were Robinson Crusoe and Friday to divide the island between themselves, it would be insignificant whether their respective right to insist on the proper division arose from an obligational relationship between them or from the property rights assigned to each. The categorization of these rights other only becomes an issue when it is necessary to determine whether the arrangement between the two of them is also enforceable against a new inhabitant of the island. (A contemporary example of this basic question is whether administrative agreements between co-owners are effective against third parties; Art. 221 of the Polish Civil Code expressly confirms such effect against the acquirer of a share in community property.) Likewise, someone who has booked a numbered seat in the opera (or cinema, aeroplane, etc.) has a property right in the seat only if he is able to defend it against an intruder of his own right. If he has, rather, to call upon the usher to banish the intruder from the field, then he has only a contractual

[41] *Gretton*, 'Trusts Without Equity', 607 fn. 44.

[42] This is also the position in the Scandinavian literature. Admittedly, many Scandinavian legal systems do not distinguish clearly between obligations and real objects; however, e.g. in Sweden, there is a great level of agreement that all questions of third party legal relationships are of a 'proprietary' nature—and that *only* such questions concern property law. It is accepted, for example, that the consequences of a contract on the relationship of the contracting parties to third parties is a matter governed by property law (*Hellner*, Metodproblem i rättsvetenskapen, p. 164; *Rodhe*, Handbok i sakrätt, p. 323). 'Proprietary' protection is therefore enjoyed above all by the one who has priority over the other creditors of an insolvent creditor, or the one who can successfully assert his right of succession to a particular object of property over a (general) successor-in-title. *Håstad*, Sakrätt[6], p. 25 speaks, in the first case, of a 'right of separation', and opines in the second case that the 'better right' prevails.

right against the opera house to require *it* to take action. In such a case, only the opera house has an effective property right against the intruder. If it is the opera house that contests the booked seat, on the other hand, and if no-one else were interested in the seat, then it would be irrelevant whether the opera-goer could marshal (for the duration of the show) a contractual or (also) a proprietary right against the opera house.

The situation is similar where a buyer makes a claim against the seller for the delivery of a good that has been purchased but not yet delivered, or where a seller demands the return of the good from the buyer with the argument that the contract of sale was invalid. In both cases it is without consequence, in the first instance, whether the claimant relies on an obligation (i.e. the claim for delivery based in the contract of sale, the claim for the return of goods based in 'unjust enrichment')[43] or whether, independently of any such rights, he relies on a right of property in the contracted-for good.[44] This question only becomes important when a third party enters the contest, when for example another creditor or one of the parties claims an interest.[45] Consider the case where a loan is secured by a mortgage on a unit of land owned by the borrower. The mortgage may give the lender possibilities to access the assets of the borrower more quickly and easily in the case that he cannot or will not pay, but it does not fundamentally change the creditor–debtor relationship as such. The mortgage's purpose as security, and therefore its proprietary character, first comes into play when a third party, e.g. a purchaser of the encumbered parcel of land, claims the right to block the mortgagee's rights in the land: the property right of the lender sets the limits of the rights of the purchaser, and has priority over them within these limits. It is to this extent, in the situation just described, a 'better right' than that of the encumbered property the purchaser has acquired. In contrast, although one might try to bolster the position of a leaseholder who has paid the landlord a security deposit by analogizing from the proprietary nature of a pledge, one nevertheless remains in the law of obligations to the extent that the position of the leaseholder *vis-à-vis* third parties remains unaffected. 1.7

[43] On the ambiguous meaning of the expression 'law of unjustified enrichment' in contemporary Europe, see *von Bar and Swann*, Principles of European Law. Unjustified Enrichment [*von Bar and Swann*, PEL Unj.Enr.], Introduction, B8–C132.

[44] It is only conceivable that *other* areas of law (e.g. international private law, the law of limitations periods, or the law of civil procedure) regard the characterization of obligations or property law as important for their own purposes; from a pure, private law perspective in such a two-person constellation, however, nothing depends on it.

[45] e.g. in TS 30 March 2000, RAJ 2000 no. 2431 p. 3772. The Spanish Ministry of Education purchased historically valuable tiles from the owner of a private palace, which were attached to the wall of the room in question. The owner was meant to keep the tiles until further notice for the Ministry, which planned first to open a museum for the artist who had created them. The owner, however, sold the palace. The Ministry prevailed in its claim for delivery of the tiles against the purchaser. The sale was a sale of a future object; the tiles would become, upon their separation from the wall of the palace, moveable goods. The justification is, however, circular. It does not explain why ownership of a future object can require that the object be separated from the main object; only through this separation do the tiles become independent things capable of 'vindication'. However, one finds in this decision an impressive example of the difference between bilaterally effective obligations and trilaterally effective property rights. Another fine example is found in STJ 15 December 2011, www.dgsi.pt, Processo 3037/05.0TBVLG.P1.S1 (Parents gifted their daughter a unit of land. She later prohibited their access to the garage, contrary to an agreed arrangement; the court granted the mother possession. Whether the mother's right to use the garage was obligational or proprietary played no role as long as no other party—for example a bank financing the construction of a house—came into the picture. Against such a bank a property right such as a usufruct would prevail, but not a mere life-long license.)

1.8 Impressive examples of the difference between bi-lateral obligations and tri-laterally effective property rights are found in the common law systems of the British Isles (albeit, of course, couched in the local terminology). The English case of *Hill v Tupper* concerned a right to hire out boats on a canal.[46] The Basingstoke Navigation Canal Co had leased a parcel of land on a canal to the plaintiff Hill. The lease agreement guaranteed Hill the sole and exclusive right to hire out pleasure boats. The publican Tupper, however, provided his guests with pleasure boats for use on the same canal. The outcome of Hill's claim against Tupper turned solely on the question whether Hill had a proprietary or a mere contractual right (i.e. against the Basingstoke Canal Navigation Co).[47] The court held the latter:

> This grant is perfectly valid as between the plaintiff and the canal Company; but in order to support this action, the plaintiff must establish that such an estate or interest vested in him such that the act of the defendant amounted to an eviction. None of the cases cited are at all analogous to this, and some authority must be produced before we can hold that such a right can be created. To admit the right would lead to the creation of an infinite variety of interests in land, and an indefinite increase of possible estates. The only consequence is that, as between the plaintiff and the canal Company, he has a perfect right to enjoy the advantage of the covenant or contract; and, if he has been disturbed in the enjoyment of it, he must obtain the permission of the canal Company to sue in their name.[48]

In *King v David Allen & Sons (Billposting) Ltd*, the defendant King had entered into an agreement with the plaintiff David Allen & Sons (Billposting) Ltd, which gave the latter an exclusive licence to affix billboards to the walls of a cinema building yet to be constructed on King's land.[49] King then entered into a contract with one Farell, who was dealing as the promoter for Phibsboro' Picture House Ltd. This company was meant to take an assignment of King's contractual obligations towards David Allen & Sons Ltd, but this was not done, and the lease agreement made over the land contained no reference to the right to erect billboards. Phibsboro' Picture House Ltd took possession of the property and then denied the right to David Allen & Sons Ltd, who in consequence sued King for breach of contract. King denied that there was a breach of contract on the grounds that the plaintiff had acquired a proprietary rather than a contractual right, i.e. a right in the nature of an easement or a restrictive covenant.[50] The House of Lords did not accept this argument. The licence agreement had only created a personal obligation in relation to the use of the cinema walls. The four-year term of the licence agreement did not change this fact; no right in the land had been created which could be effective against the new leaseholder.[51]

[46] (1863) 2 H & C 122; 159 ER 51 (Court of Exchequer).
[47] *Pollock* CB, ibid., p. 126 resp. p. 53.
[48] *Martin* B, ibid., p. 128 resp. p. 53.
[49] *King v David Allen & Sons (Billposting) Ltd* [1916] 2 AC 54 (HL).
[50] [1916] 2 AC 54, 57.
[51] [1916] 2 AC 54, 60 and 61 (*Lord Buckmaster LC*). A comparable example is found in Netherlands law in HR 3 March 1905, W 8191 (A purchased a parcel of land from B, who promised to create a path on an adjacent parcel

The assignment of any given right into one or the other category is naturally contested in other places, as well; on the whole, however, every legal system regards it as important to keep the number of doubtful cases to a minimum.[52] Each legal system uses for this purpose a variety of techniques, of which the most common is to limit the number and types of property right recognized in that legal system.[53] The fact that grey zones subsist does undermine the fundamental approach. Examples of such hybrid constructions appear *inter alia* where a legal system treats some right of the owner, especially the right to the enjoyment of a thing, as effective only relative to a certain person. One has in mind examples such as retention of title in the context of payment by instalment in Italian law.[54] 1.9

In the case of a purchase by instalment with retention of title, the buyer first acquires ownership upon payment of the final instalment (Art. 1523 sentence 1 of the Italian Civil Code); risk, however, passes to the buyer at the time of delivery (Art. 1523 sentence 2).[55] But the seller can only enforce his property rights against the buyer's creditors (as under Art. 589 and Art. 590 of the Polish Civil Code) when the retention of title is evidenced in a certificate which bears a precise date that precedes the date of

which also belonged to him. B however but did not keep his promise, and later sold the latter parcel to another. B was liable to compensate A for non-fulfilment. His obligation to build the path did not pass to the purchaser of the latter parcel; A had a contractual, not a proprietary, right against B).

[52] Perhaps overstating the case, *Ginossar* (1979) 14(3) Israel Law Review 286, 288 opines that 'there is practically no type of legal relationship which has been successfully allocated to its proper category with complete certainty' and to support this thesis refers to the dualism of common law and 'equitable ownership' as well as to the contested nature of the leaseholder's interest as either contractual or proprietary ('a hybrid, a mixture of this and that'). It is certainly correct that this disagreement plays out in many legal systems. (A nice example is the discussion in the Netherlands concerning the scope of the rule that sale of a property does not break a lease [see Art. 7:226 of the Netherlands Civil Code]. The case HR 26 March 2010, LJN BK9632 for example overruled the judgment of the court Den Bosch 29 June 2006, LJN AY9629, which had held that a tenant's option to purchase agreed between the landlord and tenant was effective against the new owner. This judgment was approved by *van Oostrom-Streep*, WPNR 2010 p. 469. The Den Bosch court neglected the principle of the relativity of contractual obligations; the Hoge Raad fortunately corrected the mistake.) On the whole, there are only a few particular situations in which the obligational or proprietary nature of a subjective right remains uncertain. Difficulties, however, attend those legal institutions which were meant to replace private property in the communist period and which survived (and in some cases survive) beyond the collapse of the communist system. The Czech Nejvyšší soud České republiky 12 January 2006, 22 Cdo 44/2005, for example, characterized the 'right to personal use' of state property as a property right on the basis that it was temporally unlimited, could not be withdrawn unilaterally by the state, and could even be entered into the land registry. (The right to personal use of a dwelling was transformed into tenancy, and the right to personal use of a parcel of land into ownership, in 1992.) The right of an individual to exercise the state's power of administration over state property was also considered a 'property right' (Czech Nejvyšší soud České republiky 27 February 2003, 33 Odo 23/2002; for further details *Havlan*, Veřejné vlastnictví v právu a společnosti, pp. 123–4).

[53] Scepticism regarding this technique prevails, outside the United Kingdom, above all in Sweden where a holistic picture of 'obligations' and 'property rights' and a functional, case-based analysis of conflicts with 'third parties' is preferred.

[54] The position in Italy reflects, to a large extent, the position in Belgium. There, too, compliance with the formal requirements is necessary for a retention of title to have effect against third parties. A retention of title agreed after the delivery of a good is likewise only effective relatively, i.e. against the buyer: Rechtbank van koophandel Tongeren 6 April 1998, R.W. 1997–1998 p. 338; Hof van beroep Gent 17 November 2003, R.W. 2004–2005 p. 704; Cass. 25 September 2006, C050554F, N-20060925-2, juridat.be.

[55] We are here concerned with a derogation from the general rule in Art. 1465(1); cf. Cass. 13 August 1996, no. 7555, Giur. it. 1997, I, 1, 1086; Cass. 20 May 1994, no. 4976, *Foro Italiano* 1995, I, 893 and Enciclopedia del diritto XLVI (*-Lipari*), Vendita con riserva di proprietà, p. 526.

attachment by those other creditors (Art. 1524(1)). Without such a certificate, the retention of title has only relative effect, i.e. *vis-à-vis* the buyer. That could lend support for the idea of characterizing purchase by instalment with retention of title (in the absence of a certificate) as a purely obligational phenomenon.[56] Characterization is, however, problematic. One may argue (along the lines of: even a toothless tiger is a 'tiger') that the characterization of reserved ownership as *diritto assoluto* should not falter on the fact that its *opponibilità erga omnes* is limited in particular cases; characterization as 'absolute' requires only an 'abstract' capability of effect against third parties. Further, it is emphasized that while the proprietary consequences of sale may be temporarily limited, all other incidents of sale occur immediately upon execution of the contract.[57] The buyer does not acquire possession only, but an expectant property right.[58] Sale by instalment, according to a minority opinion, is properly seen as a full transfer of ownership to the buyer with a contemporaneous reassignment of (proprietary) security rights back to the seller.[59]

1.10 The question arises whether the numerous provisions giving the owner power to use a thing according to his own wishes—often placed in the middle of the codified law of property—contradict the thesis that property rights are, in fact, directed at third parties. The mere use of a thing (for example hanging a picture in one's own home) has little or nothing to do with any third parties in the ordinary case; the owner does nothing 'against them'. For example, similar to the law of many other European jurisdictions,[60]

[56] Sale by instalment with retention of title is characterized as a 'sale' under the law of obligations, albeit for different reasons, by *Greco and Cottino*, Della vendita: Arts 1470–1547, p. 366.

[57] See further *Torrente and Schlesinger*, Manuale di diritto privato[21], p. 705; cf. *Rubino*, La compravendita, p. 430.

[58] *Cattaneo*, Riv.trim.dir. e proc.civ. 1965 p. 945, 980.

[59] *Bianca*, La vendita e la permuta[2], pp. 584–91. In this context the German case BGH 2 February 1966, BGHZ 45 p. 95 = NJW 1966 p. 879 is also worthy of mention. This case turned on the question whether and how a relative retention of title under Italian law worked in German law over a sewing machine exported to Germany. The *Bundesgerichtshof* opined (at p. 880) that, while German law recognizes no retention of title with relative effect, 'it does however recognise relatively ineffective legal transactions ... A retention of title that was only relatively effective would, then, not be wholly incompatible with the German law of property... and it would not mount any insuperable difficulties to recognise, on the basis of a retention of title with relative effect in Italian law, the seller as owner as between seller and buyer and to see the buyer as owner as between the buyer and his creditors.' The *Bundesgerichtshof* also accepted that, as a consequence of the change in jurisdiction, the relative retention of title would not be transformed *ex lege* into an absolute retention of title under German law, but that the parties' agreement had to be interpreted in light of the fact that they intended from the outset to assign absolute ownership to the seller by way of a (re)assignment of security rights once the machine was on German soil. The *Bundesgerichtshof* regarded this agreement as possible and effective under German law.

[60] Estonian law defines ownership as the control of a person over a thing. The owner has the right to possess the thing, use it, and dispose of it; further, to demand that any violation of these rights cease and that any consequences of violation be unwound (§ 68(1) Estonian Asjaõigusseadus). One finds very similar formulations in Art. 927 of the Latvian Civil Code. § 354 of the Austrian Civil Code provides that 'Considered as a right, ownership is the power to control the substance and the use of a thing according to will, and to exclude every other from it.' § 362 complements this provision: the owner can 'generally use his things or leave them unused according to his will; he can destroy them, wholly or partly dispose of them, or disclaim them unconditionally, that is, abandon them.' Under Art. 37 of the Slovenian Civil Code, ownership is defined as the right to possess, use, and enjoy a thing. It affords the most extensive right in a thing and subsists, when no law expressly provides otherwise, for an unlimited amount of time. It cannot be bound to any condition. § 123 of the Slovakian Civil Code considers the owner, within the constraints of the law, to be 'entitled to possess the object of property, to enjoy its fruits and uses, and to dispose of it'. Under § 1012 of the Czech Civil Code the owner has 'the right to deal with his property, within the framework of the legal system, according to his will and to exclude other persons from it'. Art. 5:1 of the Netherlands Civil Code describes ownership as the most comprehensive right that a person can have in a thing. Under Art. 544 of the French Civil Code, '*[l]a propriété est le droit de jouir et disposer des choses de la manière la plus absolue, pourvu*

§ 903 of the German Civil Code, gives the owner of a thing (insofar as no other law or third party's right stands in the way) not only the express right 'to exclude others from every interference' but also the right to 'deal with the thing at his discretion'. This latter right embraces every kind of factual dealing up to and including the destruction of the thing.[61] Accordingly, it is often said, in the Continental literature at least, that property rights guarantee the right-holder legal powers in two directions: on the one hand, he is, with regards to the direct object, empowered to act in a manner reflective of the right that gives him the right to possession, use, and disposition (the 'positive' content of property rights). On the other hand, he is empowered to remove obstacles that stand in the way of the exercise of his rights (the 'negative' content of property rights).[62] It is not, however, necessary to interpret the power to deal with a thing at will as the content and necessary hallmark of a property right. True, it describes the position for those who view property rights as the expression of a relationship between a person and a thing. But those who do not share this view should prefer to see the right to deal freely with one's own things as a consequence of the general freedom of action of the person. That only the owner, and no-one else, has a right that could hinder the destruction, damage, or alteration of a thing simply means, on this view, that the rights of ownership preserve (or, in the case of acquisition, restore) what was taken away from everybody else when the property rights were first created. When, for example, someone wants to remove a tree growing on his land, his neighbours may not take any actions to prevent him from doing so unless and to the extent that his act of felling the tree would interfere in some way with their respective property rights.[63] The freedom to deal with one's own things

qu'on n'en fasse pas un usage prohibé par les lois ou par les règlements'. In Sweden, a statutory definition of ownership is lacking, but even here it is said that ownership is the most comprehensive right that one can have in a thing. It is further said that ownership can only be defined negatively, as the owner can make use of his right in any way he wishes insofar as no statutory or contractual limitations stand in his way (*Håstad*, Sakrätt[6], pp. 23–4). The position is similar in Bulgaria. The Property Act does not define the content of ownership. The literature describes ownership as the most extensive right, that one can have in a thing within the confines of the law and the rights of others (*Venedikov*, Novo veshtno pravo, p. 76 no. 66).

[61] e.g. Staudinger (*-Seiler*), BGB (2007), § 903 no. 10. DCFR VIII.-1:202 (Ownership) even states this point expressly: '"Ownership" is the most comprehensive right a person, the "owner", can have over property, including the exclusive right, so far as consistent with applicable laws or rights granted by the owner, to use, enjoy, modify, *destroy*, dispose of and recover the property' (emphasis added).

[62] *Menyhárd*, in Vékás (ed.), Szakértői Javaslat az új Polgári Törvénykönyv tervezetéhez, p. 585. This 'dualistic' view of the content of property relations seems to be especially marked in Portugal. Leading authors attribute to proprietary rights a *conteúdo positivo ou negativo* (e.g. *Vieira*, Direitos reais, p. 318 and *Carvalho Fernandes*, Lições de direitos reais[2], p. 181). Both active and passive legal positions are said to belong to the content of a proprietary right (*situações jurídicas activas e passivas*) (*Vieira* op. cit.; *Menezes Cordeiro*, Tratado de direito civil I(1), p. 103). 'Active' legal positions flow from permissive norms or from norms that confer a legal power; 'passive' legal positions flow from prohibitive norms and norm that require agents to do an action or make something the case ('impositive' norms). Active legal positions create advantages; passive legal positions create burdens. In the end, however, we are always dealing with the two sides of a single coin. The value of recognizing a distinction between the positive and negative content of a proprietary right does not, therefore, seem particularly high.

[63] Besides this restriction it is of course possible that felling a tree might be prohibited under a provision of public law (e.g. environmental regulations), which gives the neighbours the possibility to turn to the authorities and cause *them* to prevent the intended action. Such public law restrictions on the use of property are, of themselves, not relevant restrictions or encumbrances of private property on the present analysis. No-one is allowed to cut the tree in question—it is not just the owner that is restricted from doing so. In its logical structure, this problem is no different to the speed limit imposed on street traffic: no-one is allowed to exceed the stipulated speed limit—not just the automobile owner, but also the thief.

according to one's own list can therefore also be explained as a simple reflex of the state of affairs that no-one else has a competing right. 'My' property right *guarantees* my general freedom of action and at the same time derogates, in relation to the things I own, the freedom of action of everybody else. The merit of this conceptual approach reveals itself not only in analysing the differences between private property law and constitutional rights and freedoms (which, admittedly, often sail under the flag of 'property'), but also in explaining particular rules within property law. Take, for example, the acquisition of ownerless goods. As long as they remain unappropriated, *everyone* is allowed to deal with them as they see fit. Even the right to appropriation arises, typically, not from a property right (or even property law), but from the general freedom of action possessed by every person.[64] The right claimed (the way its acquisition is enforced) follows the property law regime. This limits the freedom, which at first everyone possessed equally, to a single person.[65]

1.11 Property rights unfold in an active manner only against other persons. On the 'passive' side of a legal relationship no distinction can be made between obligations and property rights. Duties are neither *goederen*,[66] nor *biens*, nor *Sachen*, nor *property*—duties are duties. One can distinguish between duties to bring about a state of affairs and duties to discharge a standard of care, or between duties that are independently

[64] That is, unless the appropriator holds throughout a private property right to the appropriation (not one resting only on a concession of the state). In that case, of course, only he may appropriate the thing to himself, and no-one else. The Austrian theory of radical title [*Obereigentum*, lit. 'superior ownership'] presents a particular variant of such a right of appropriation. § 287 of the Austrian Civil Code defines things which are left open for the appropriation of all members of the state as free-standing. 'Free-standing' things are ownerless (Koziol/Bydlinski/Bollenberger [-*Eccher and Riss*], ABGB^4, §§ 287–288 no. 2); no property in them exists in the sense of a current and comprehensive right of control (Rummel [-*Spielbüchler*], ABGB I^3, § 381 no. 1). However, a public superior ownership should be recognized over such things, which leads to the situation that anyone who appropriates such a thing against any given law does not become owner himself but acquires ownership of the thing for the state (e.g. OGH 15 November 1990, GZ 7Ob637/90, *obiter* on the question of who becomes owner of wild birds' eggs collected illegally). It appears to state the case too narrowly to say that the relevance of the state's radical title provides only the individual's right to appropriate ownerless things and then exhausts itself (cf. *Eccher and Riss* op. cit.).

[65] The situation is comparable with the use of airspace above a land unit in private ownership or possession: in the heights above, to which no rights of the owner reach, the air can be used by everyone; below a certain height, only by the holder of the property rights in the land unit. Accordingly, the common law distinguishes in a pragmatic fashion between the 'upper' and 'lower' strata of the airspace. Ownership in airspace exists only in the lower stratum (see e.g. *Gifford v Dent* [1926] W.N. 336 and *Kelsen v Imperial Tobacco Co. (of Great Britain and Ireland) Ltd.* [1957] 2 QB 334). The maxim *cuius est solum, eius est usque ad coelum et ad inferos* is not based in any authority (*Bernstein of Leigh (Baron) v Skyviews & General Ltd.* [1978] QB 479 per Griffiths J: 'I can find no support in authority for the view that a landowner's rights in the air space above his property extend to an unlimited height'). Other European legal systems aim for a similar result; only the technique by which this is achieved differs. e.g. Art. 202(2) of the Portuguese Civil Code excludes things in public ownership from the definition of property in private law. According to Art. 84 of the Portuguese constitution, the upper strata of the atmosphere above private land units are public property. § 905 of the German Civil Code and Art. 1001 of the Greek Civil Code, on the other hand, confirm that the rights of ownership extent 'into the space above the surface and into the body of the earth beneath the surface', but add that 'the owner can, however, not prohibit actions at such heights or such depths where he has no interest in their exclusion'. The legal position in Bulgaria is that the rights of owner reach up to such a height as allows the owner to use the parcel of land, but do not extend beyond the permitted building height under the relevant planning provisions (*Stavrou*, Veshtno pravo, p. 80).

[66] So much is confirmed in the structure of the Netherlands Civil Code. In the third book ('General Property Law') is found the rule that, fundamentally, all goods can be transferred (Art. 3:84). The transfer of debts, on the other hand, is found in the sixth book of the Civil Code. The transfer of rights and the transfer of debts are, indeed, both forms of 'transfer', but a debt does not simply pass without more. The transfer of a debt requires another (purely 'obligational') legal transaction between the first debtor and the third party assuming the debt, as well as the consent of the creditor (Art. 6:155).

enforceable and duties protected by claims other than specific performance (e.g. damages). But one cannot distinguish between duties arising from the law of obligations and duties arising from the law of property.[67]

For this reason, the attempt to capture the special features of a license over intellectual property within the concept of a 'real obligation' in reliance on the common rule that sale does not break a subsisting lease[68] is doomed to fail—although the rights of a licensee against the new owner of intellectual property rights may be protected.[69] This attempt is wrong because, as argued, it is not possible to distinguish sensibly between 'obligational' and 'real' duties on the side of the debtor. The duty to do or refrain from doing something is never 'directed at third parties'. A duty can, of course, be owed towards several parties, but it cannot be enforced against more than one party. The fact that a tenant retains her rights as such against the new owner of land (or that a licensee can enforce her rights as such against the new holder of the intellectual property rights) can thus be understood (from some legal-dogmatic points of view) as a 'reification' of the *rights* ('upgrading'), but not as a reification of the *obligations*, i.e. the contractual relationship of tenant and landlord and the duties that arise from it.[70] For the same reason, the common habit of speaking in Italy of *obbligazioni reali* is infelicitous. This expression refers to a particular kind of statutory obligational relationship, namely one in which the creditor and debtor 'automatically' changes according to the position of a thing in property law.[71] An *obligazione reale* arises, for example, from Art. 1104 of the Italian Civil Code, which provides that every co-owner is obliged, by force of statute, towards every other co-owner to contribute to the maintenance and amenity of common

[67] See *contra* Ginossar op. cit. 302: 'Our notion of real obligation, conceived as indissolubly linked to some determinate *res*, gives us the key to the mysterious structure of *iura in re aliena*... Indeed, a real right may be defined as a right that correlates a real obligation.' A debt can, however, not have any effect against third parties, and for this reason alone cannot have the nature of a 'proprietary debt'.

[68] According to the 'sale does not break lease' rule, the acquirer of a leased apartment or parcel of land (sometimes the acquirer of any leased object generally) would step, by force of statute, into the rights and duties incumbent on the previous owner by virtue of the latter's tenancy agreement with the tenant. See e.g. § 566 of the German Civil Code, Art. 7:226 of the Netherlands Civil Code (which applies to moveable things as well, but is only mandatory in the case of dwellings: Art. 7:226(4)), Art. 1743 of the French Civil Code, Arts 614 and 615 of the Greek Civil Code, § 1120 of the Austrian Civil Code (whose narrow formulation has been construed generously in favour of tenants in possession, but not necessarily registered in the land register: OGH 21 June 2000, SZ 73/102), Arts 678 § 1 und 680 of the Polish Civil Code, Art. 1057 of the Portuguese Civil Code, § 680(2) of the Slovakian Civil Code, Art. 13 of the Spanish statute of 29/1994 on the rental of urban dwellings (*Ley de Arrendamientos Urbanos* 29/1994), § 2221(1) of the Czech Civil Code, and § 6:340(2) of the Hungarian Civil Code.

[69] *McGuire*, Die Lizenz, § 9. Insofar as the author relies on *Dulckeit*, Verdinglichung obligatorischer Rechte, for her choice of language, the reference is unclear. Dulckeit in fact always spoke only of the reification [*Verdinglichung*] of rights, not the reification of obligations. More precise in this respect is *Hauck*, AcP 211 (2011) p. 626.

[70] The language is particularly unclear where, as provided in Austrian law, particular obligational rights are to be recorded in the land register. § 1095 of the Austrian Civil Code, which allows the entry of a tenancy agreement in the land register, provides that the right of a tenant so registered in the 'public books' is to be considered 'as a real right'. Here, too, the point is that the tenant should be able to enforce his rights against a subsequent owner. 'Not the legal relationship as such, only particular... claims are potentially effective against all the world. In this limited context the right assumes the characteristics of a 'real' right' (Rummel [-*Spielbüchler*], ABGB I^3, § 308 no. 4). On the conceptual definition of the term 'obligation' in European private law, see DCFR III.-1:101(1) ('An obligation is a duty to perform which one party to a legal relationship, the debtor, owes to another party, the creditor').

[71] See e.g. *Bigliazzi Geri*, Oneri reali e obbligazioni propter rem; *Fusaro*, Oneri reali e obbligazioni «propter rem», p. 390; *Gazzoni*, La trascrizione immobiliare I^2, p. 632; Enciclopedia del diritto XXX (-*Gandolfi*), Onere reale, p. 127.

property. This is, indeed, a duty that arises out of the position of ownership, but is no 'real' duty.

From the principle that property rights only manifest in their active (rights-strengthening) aspect *vis-à-vis* third parties, it follows that limitations of liability for the benefit of third parties have nothing to do with property law. For example, when (and insofar as) the liability of a bailee towards the bailor is successfully excluded in a contract for the carriage of goods, and it is argued that the bailor cannot proceed against an employee of the bailee personally for damage to the goods,[72] one is concerned with a contractual waiver for the benefit of a third party (according to the relevant national law), but not with the reification [*Verdinglichung*] of an obligation. In such a case, the contractual right of the bailor is excluded or limited in its enforcement, but it is not the case that some absolute, i.e. third party directed, right against being sued is created in favour of the employee. Equally, the rules of the law of assignment, which protect a bona fides debtor from additional claims by the assignee following performance toward the assignor, do not belong to property law.[73] Even though payment by the debtor to the assignor extinguishes the claim of the assignee, this is not because a right to the termination of the claim is created in the debtor effective *erga omnes*. A connection to the law of property is only established when the assignor encounters liquidity problems after receipt of the money, his creditors begin to quarrel over the money paid by the debtor, and (for example) the assignee is given a better right to satisfaction on the basis that the assignor is deemed to have received payment by the debtor on trust for the assignee.[74]

[72] The classical example of such a situation is *Adler v Dickson (The Himalaya)* [1955] 1 QB 158; [1954] 2 Lloyd's Rep. 267; [1954] 3 WLR 696; [1954] 3 All ER 397. An injured passenger of the *SS Himalaya* brought a claim in damages against the captain and the boatswain, who brought a defence based on an exclusion clause printed on the rear side of the passenger ticket issued by the shipping company. The Court of Appeal considered such an exclusion of liability to be capable in principle of protecting servants of the shipping company, but denied in the circumstances that the clause in question was valid for this purpose. Later, a so-called 'Himalaya clause' was drafted to cover harbour workers and other servants of the company and this was included in the bill of lading. Today, this Himalaya clause is the subject of a whole line of special rules in the law pertaining to maritime commercial law. Another example is found in § 607a(2) of the German Commercial Code, which provides: 'If a claim in damages for loss or damage to goods, which are the subject matter of a contract of carriage, is brought against one of the persons of the carriers or one of the members of the ship's personnel, this person can rely on the exclusions and limitations of liability provided in this part for the carrier.' Compare the English case of *Enviroco Ltd v Farstad Supply AS* [2011] UKSC 16; [2011] 1 WLR 921 (an exclusion of liability clause was held in principle to extend to other companies in a corporate group; in this case, however, the defence failed on the exact terms of the clause).

[73] This could not be held otherwise in Sweden. One is not dealing with a situation in which different persons bring claims to one legal object, only one of which can be satisfied—and that is the decisive factor from the point of view of Swedish law (see e.g. *Millqvist*, Sakrättens grunder[5], pp. 13–14). In the case of full satisfaction of a debt by payment in instalments to the wrong creditor the legal object itself is extinguished.

[74] For the English common law see *Smith*, The Law of Assignment, no. 13.20 and for the Australian common law see *G E Crane Sales Pty Ltd* v *Federal Commissioner of Taxation* (1971) 126 CLR 177, 183–4 (*Menzies J*). The contract of assignment between assignee and assignor creates for the latter a trust in relation to the claim; after repayment of the principal the trust over receipts subsists as a surrogate for the claim. In the context of factoring, the customary general business terms expressly envisage such a situation. This is because a trust arises when the debtor, despite knowledge of the assignment, nevertheless pays the assignor (*International Factors Ltd* v *Rodriguez* [1979] 1 QB 351 (CA)).

4. Connection Only to Title in the Right

Proprietary remedies are tied only to one's holding of the relevant property right. They react to impingements (or threatened impingements) of the entitlement of the holder of a property right; they do not react, however, to either encumbrance with debt or enrichment of a defendant, or to loss or any particular status of the claimant. For this reason, for example, the rules governing liability for inducing breach of contract belong to the law of obligations (and to tort law in particular), not to the law of property—independently of how one defines a 'thing' for the purposes of property law. This result would not change even if one should count claims to the category of 'things' capable of constituting an object of property rights. True, one could characterize the rules governing liability for inducing breach of contract (which, properly seen, do not even concern breaches 'by' third parties, but only breaches 'induced' by third parties) as claims with a certain protection against third party interference;[75] however, these rules by their nature can only operate in a tripartite relationship. Some level of culpability, usually specific intention, is an element of the claim against the inducer.[76] The promisee affected by the promisor's breach has, then, no claim against a third party when that third party received performance 'actually' due to the promisee from the unfaithful promisor innocently. So long as the latter acted of his own volition and made the agreement without the third party's inducement, the rights of the promisee remain limited to his rights against the promisor for breach. For this reason, the law of liability for inducing breach of contract stands outside the law of property. The same applies to the law governing liability for loss of maintenance as a result of the killing of someone's provider. The delictual claim to damages against the tortfeasor does not transform into an absolute property right, not even when the tortfeasor who caused the accident is held responsible under a regime of strict liability. Even then, the liability of the tortfeasor is tied not to his interference with the right to maintenance, but by an additional element, for instance his position as the keeper (or *gardien*) of the thing that caused the accident. **1.12**

The so-called *ius ad rem* found in Art. 59 Polish Civil Code presents,[77] in our view, an important and nuanced counter-example. This provision gives a promisee (the 'third **1.13**

[75] For a more recent example from the Netherlands jurisprudence, see HR 8 January 2010, RvdW 2010 no. 125, NedJur 2010 Nr. 187 with note *Mok* (violation of an arrangement consistent with competition law between Fiat and Alfa Romeo by a related, but unidentified trader; further alienation of the automobile by a middle-man to a Dutch parallel importer, who must have at least had knowledge of the breach of contract; injunction sought by Fiat against the Dutch defendant granted with reference to the delictual nature of the conduct). In *OBG Ltd v Allen* [2007] UKHL 21; [2008] 1 AC 1, 27 Lord Hoffmann opined that the tort of inducing breach of contract, which protects the legal position of a contractual creditor, was concerned with a 'species of property'. That may be, but it does not lead to the conclusion that the law concerning liability for inducing breach of contract is concerned with a problem of property law; it remains a part of tort law and therefore a part of the law of obligations. For this reason, *Lee*, OxJLegStud 29 (2009) pp. 511, 513, and 519 is not very convincing in the argument that the characteristic function of 'property' (understood as a bundle of rights) to exclude even contractual rights is immanent and therefore that the traditional dichotomy between contractual rights and property rights rests on a fallacy.

[76] For a comparative overview see *von Bar*, PEL Liab.Dam., Ch. 2, notes to Article 2:211.

[77] This expression, too—*ius ad rem*—is ambiguous and is often given very different meanings. It has been frequently debated, e.g. in the context of Art. 1005 of the old Netherlands Civil Code, which conferred the right of a legatee of a specific bequest to demand a thing of the testator's heirs. The authorities interpreted this *ius ad rem* inconsistently, but in most cases as a real right—i.e. as a legacy that confers a proprietary right [*Vindikationslegat*]

party') the right to have a contract between his promisor (the 'first party') and another person (the 'second party') declared ineffective relative to his own legal position, where the fulfilment of this contract would prejudice his claim against the promisor—provided that the parties to the impugned contract had knowledge of the third party's rights, or that the impugned contract was formed without consideration. The impugned contract remains binding on the parties to it, but is deprived of any legal effect *vis-à-vis* the third party. As a result, the third party's contractual rights work not only against the promisor, but also against the promisor's (subsequent) contractual partners. The *ius ad rem* would, therefore, be a 'property right' if Polish law counted incorporeal assets as 'things' capable of being objects of property rights in their own right (Art. 45 Polish Civil Code). That is to say, characterization of this right as a 'property right' only falters on the fact that claims to performance are not 'things' in Polish law, not on the fact that the *ius ad rem* would arise in connection with anything other than holding the relevant right. This is evident in the fact that the *ius ad rem* is always effective against gratuitous contracts, and is effective against contracts for value when both parties had knowledge of the third party's rights and acted in bad faith. This latter is a criterion stemming from the realm of good faith acquisition of (unencumbered) title, not from the realm of delict (i.e. inducement of breach of contract). The peculiar nature of the rule in Art. 59 is underlined in the Polish literature, and it is stressed that although the provision embraces all kinds of claim (including statutory and family law claims), it must yield to special regimes governing conflicts of interest (for example in the provisions of the *actio Pauliana* in Art. 527 Polish Civil Code). It is also emphasized that Art. 59 is a subsidiary rule, i.e. that it is subordinate to specific proprietary defences which give the third party broader and more effective protection.[78]

1.14 The list of examples can of course be extended. One might also consider the concept, much discussed in French law, of *opposabilité du contrat*. According to the principle of the relative effect of contracts, contracts only operate between their parties.[79] This *relativité des conventions* does not, however, mean that contracts have no impact on third parties in the French legal conception. Rather, contracts and the legal relationships that they create are considered as factual states of affairs (albeit concerning *legal facts*) that are important for third parties, too.[80] Although not bound to any kind of performance, a stranger to a contract is not free simply to ignore it. Thus, although the *Cour*

and not as one that confers only an obligational claim against the heirs [*Damnationslegat*] (HR 4 March 1881, W 4622 and HR 19 April 1861, W 2268). In the literature, however, the exact opposite position has always held sway—it has even been said that the formulation of the provision is based on a mistake in translation from French (Asser [-*Perrick*], Erfrecht^{12}, no. 519).

[78] See further Kidyba (-*Janiak*), Kodeks cywilny I, Art. 59; Radwański (-*Radwański*), System Prawa Prywatnego II^{2}, p. 455; *Gniewek*, Kodeks cywilny I, p. 209; *Dmowski and Rudnicki*, Komentarz do kodeksu cywilnego I^{6}, p. 245.

[79] *Terré/Simler/Lequette*, Les Obligations^{9}, p. 487 no. 483: '*Le contrat ne crée, en principe, de liens d'obligations qu'entre les parties contractantes.*'

[80] Ibid. p. 492 no. 490: '*Et de fait le contrat crée une situation juridique dont les tiers, même s'ils ne sont pas personnellement liés par elle, ne peuvent méconnaître l'existence. Le contrat et la situation juridique qu'il a fait naître sont, dit-on, opposables aux tiers en tant que fait.*'

de cassation opined in a decision of 1954 that '*les conventions ne sont pas opposables à ceux qui n'y ont pas été parties*',[81] it recognized in 1972 that

> *si, en principe, les conventions n'ont d'effet qu'à l'égard des parties, il ne s'ensuit pas que les juges ne puissent rechercher, dans des actes étrangers à l'une des parties en cause, des renseignements de nature a éclairer leur décision, ni ne puissent considérer comme créant une situation de fait à l'égard des tiers les stipulations d'un contrat.*[82]

The following year, the court added that '*un même fait, susceptible de constituer un manquement à une obligation existant entre deux parties liées par un contrat, peut être au regard des tiers étrangers au contrat, une faute quasi-délictuelle engageant la responsabilité de son auteur*',[83] and in a judgment given on 22 October 1991 that '*s'ils ne peuvent être constitués ni débiteurs ni créanciers, les tiers à un contrat peuvent invoquer à leur profit, comme un fait juridique, la situation créée par ce contrat*'.[84] Insofar as the subject matter of the contract is an obligational right, the doctrine of the *opposabilité du contrat aux tiers par les parties* overlaps in part at least with the delictural principles of liability for inducing breach of contract. However, it does not change the delictual characterization of this legal institution that a third party who has been harmed through the malperformance of a contract (the seller delivers a faulty good to the buyer, which fault leads to the injury of the stranger to the contract) can point to a breach of contract *vis-à-vis* the buyer as evidence of the defendant's *faute*.[85]

In our view, it is necessary clearly to distinguish the influence of the rule, understood in France also to flow from the doctrine of the *opposabilité du contrat*, that contracts whose subject matter is a real right (*contrats translatifs de droits réels*) have to be respected by *all the world*. In this case we are concerned with a (basically self-evident) rule of property law. Naturally, one who acquires a thing can enforce the property right that emerges from the contract of sale against everyone;[86] if not, it would be no property right. Already in 1864, the *Cour de cassation* had decided correctly that a *contrat translatif de propriété* created a title by which the acquiring party could demand delivery from a third party.[87] Consistently with this precedent, the *Cour de cassation*

[81] Cass. civ. 6 February 1952, Bull. civ. 1952, I, no. 55 p. 44.

[82] Cass. civ. 21 March 1972, Bull. civ. 1973, III, no. 193 p. 137.

[83] Cass. com. 16 January 1973, Bull .civ. 1973, IV, no. 28 p. 22.

[84] Cass. com. 22 October 1991, Bull. civ. 1991, IV, no. 302 p. 309; D. 1993 p. 181, note *Ghestin*; JCP 1992, I, 3570, p. 148, note *Billiau*.

[85] Cass. soc. 21 March 1972, JCP 1972, II, 17236, note *Saint-Jours*; RTD civ. 1973 p. 128, note *Durry* ('*Toute faute contractuelle est délictuelle au regard des tiers étrangers au contrat*'); Cass. com. 16 January 1973, Bull. civ. 1973, IV, no. 28 p. 22 ('*un même fait susceptible de constituer un manquement à une obligation existant entre deux parties liées à un contrat, peut être, au regard des tiers étrangers au contrat, une faute quasi délictuelle engageant la responsabilité de son auteur*'); Cass. civ. 15 December 1998, Defrénois 1999 p. 745, note *Denis Mazeaud*; RTD civ. 1999 S. 625, note *Mestre*; Cass. civ. 18 July 2000, Bull. civ. 2000, I, no. 221; JCP 2000, II, 10415, note *Sargos*; JCP 2001, I, 338, no. 9, note *Viney*; RTD civ. 2001 p. 146, note *Jourdain*; Cass. civ. 13 February 2001, Bull. civ. 2001, I, no. 35; Defrénois 2001 p. 712, note *Savaux*; JCP 2002, II, 10099, note *Lisanti-Kalczynski*.

[86] *Terré/Simler/Lequette* op. cit. p. 493 no. 492.

[87] Cass. civ. 22 June 1864, D.P. 1864.1.142; p. 1864.1.349: '*Les contrats qui servent de titre et de preuve (à la propriété) sont ceux qui sont passés entre l'acquéreur et le vendeur; le droit de propriété serait perpétuellement ébranlé si les contrats destinés à l'établir n'avaient de valeur qu'à l'égard des personnes qui y auraient été parties*'. See also Cass. req. 15 November 1897, D.P. 1898.1.38.

reminded the *Cour d'appel* in 1982 that someone who claims to be owner of a real estate could rely on his *titres translatifs* or *déclaratifs de propriété* against third parties.[88] The *contrat translatif de droit réels* must be effective against third parties because otherwise one's creditors could attach things sold long ago.[89] Indeed, without the (auxiliary) institution of *opposabilité* no real transfer of ownership would be possible at all; one would only be 'owner' *vis-à-vis* the previous owner in the chain of acquisition. We might interpret the doctrine of *opposabilité* with Billiau as a complement to the *force obligatoire du contrat* and say that the *opposabilité* of a contract for the sale of property makes it possible to make strangers to the contract to recognize the legal position created by the transaction.[90] It seems more straightforward, however, simply to recognize the characteristic feature of property rights and to concede that there is an obvious contradiction between the principle of relativity of contract and the rule that transfer of ownership occurs, without more, upon contracting.

1.15 Rules of law which have effect against third parties in relation to the use of things, but which take a certain personal status or other personal attribute of the holder of the right as a point of reference (and therefore not solely the fact that they hold the right) do not, in contrast, belong to property law. They should, rather, be understood as a component of that body of law which grants the relevant status. Take § 2032 of the German Civil Code as an example. Under this rule, when a testator leaves more than one heir, his estate becomes the common property of the joint heirs [*Miterben*]. Under § 2033, every *Miterbe* can make use of his part of the estate, but under § 2034 the other *Miterben* have a right of pre-emption if one wishes to sell his share, and they can even exercise this right of pre-emption against a third party to recover assets after ownership has passed. The right of pre-emption is clearly effective against third parties, which makes it 'real'. It is, however, not a rule of property law but a rule of succession. Quite apart from the dubious characterization of the estate as a 'thing' to which the right of pre-emption attaches, this right of pre-emption is reserved to the *Miterben* and is not transferable, not even through the disposal of one's own share in the inheritance to (another) third party.[91] The right 'sticks' to the status of belonging to the group of heirs; the claim that flows from the right is, therefore, not connected only with the individual heir's title in the right of pre-emption.

1.16 The numerous rules that limit an owner's normal powers of disposition over the family home or other objects of importance to the life of a family are, accordingly, not matters of property law but of family law, and the same applies to the right of the *other* marital partner that accompany these restrictions, such as the right to demand

[88] Cass. civ. 5 May 1982, Bull. civ. 1982, III, no. 116 p. 82. So too Cass. civ. 2 July 1997, Bull. civ. 1997, III, no. 161 p.108; Defrénois 1997 Art. 36703 no. 154 S. 1420, note *Atias*.

[89] *Ghestin/Jamin/Billiau* op. cit. p. 767; *Billiau*, L'opposabilité des contrats ayant pour objet un droit réel, p. 190.

[90] *Billiau* op. cit. p. 191.

[91] So held, correctly, in BGH 22 April 1971, BGHZ 56 p. 116 and BGH 16 December 1992, NJW 1993 p. 726. The question is contested in the literature, however—see the overview in Staudinger (-*Werner*), BGB (2002), § 2034 no. 9.

the rescission of a sale. Under § 1365 and § 1368 of the German Civil Code, for example, when a married couple live in the statutory property regime and one spouse (without the consent of the other) disposes of his or her property as a whole, 'the other spouse is entitled to enforce the rights accruing from the invalidity of the disposition against a third party'. Under Art. 1687 of the Portuguese Civil Code, the rules 'applicable to the disposition of another's property' are applicable to invalid dispositions or encumbrances of the personal property of a spouse, in this case Arts 892 to 904. According to these rules, the disposition of another's property is fundamentally null and void (Art. 892).[92] Section 3:51 of the Expert Report on the Draft of a New Hungarian Civil Code envisaged that spouse A could regard a contract made between spouse B and a third party without A's consent as relatively invalid from A's own legal position, according to the rules of the *actio Pauliana* (§ 5:94(1) of the Expert Report), so long as the third party acted in bad faith or the transaction was not for value. § 4:50 of the Hungarian Civil Code essentially maintained this position, but now the legal consequences (i.e. relative invalidity of the contract in case of bad faith or lack of consideration) are expressly and independently set out.[93] Pursuant to Art. 1393 of the Greek Civil Code, the court can make an order for the exclusive use of a family home by one spouse, in whole or in part, on grounds of fairness and the best interests of the children, without reference to the property relations between the spouses. If the spouse who owns the family home is in control of the property at this time, then, according to the balance of opinion, the rule that sale does not break a lease operates in favour of the spouse who does not own, but is entitled (under such an order) to use the property by analogical application of Art. 614.[94] A disposition is even considered null and void in the case that it was made for the purpose of prejudicing the spouse entitled to use the property. In this case, that spouse can rely on the invalidity of the disposition against the third-party purchaser. Art. 1433 of the Spanish Civil Code gives a marital partner the right to challenge all gratuitous dispositions and, beyond this, all of his or her spouse's dispositions made with the purpose of deception. Finally, Art. 3:233 of the Netherlands Civil Code protects spouses through two peculiar personal rights restricted in their content to the use of goods and dwellings. This provision is concerned with property [*zakelijke*] rights. True, they are applied as appropriate to the rules of usufruct, but they are bound to the person of the relevant spouse; they cannot be assigned and they cannot be exercised by anybody else (Art. 3:226(4)).[95]

[92] For details (including how the principle interacts with the rules governing good faith acquisition) see *Nóbrega*, Der rechtsgeschäftliche Eigentumserwerb an beweglichen Sachen in Deutschland und Portugal[2], pp. 45–6.

[93] See further *Makai*, in Vékás (ed.), Szakértői Javaslat az új Polgári Törvénykönyv tervezetéhez, p. 441 resp. Vékás (*-Kőrös/Makai/Szeibert*), A Polgári Törvénykönyv magyarázatokkal, p. 274.

[94] See *Wathrakokilis*, AK, Art. 1393 no. 15; *Pouliadis*, Arm. 1995 S. 589, 596; *Deliyiannis*, Oikogeneiako Dikaio II, p. 197 and Georgiades and Stathopoulos (*-Koumantos*), AK, Art. 1393 no. 20. The legal position is, however, contentious.

[95] See further *Hijma and Olthof*, Compendium Nederlands Vermogensrecht[10], no. 254 p. 167; Pitlo (*-Reehuis and Heisterkamp*), Goederenrecht[12], no. 703 pp. 534–5.

All of the above rules attach to the status of being married, not to the position of being entitled as the holder of a particular property right. The legal systems mentioned have thus, quite properly, organized these provisions in the family law (and not in the property law) sections of their codifications. One exception to this technique, and from the systematic basis for it, was for a time observable in Czech law. The Czech Civil Code [1964] (now out of force) took rules governing marital community property which had been contained (since 1951) in a statute on family law and, in a modified form, put them in the property law section of the codification (§ 143 of the Civil Code [1964]). These rules were then, in the same place, revised and extended in 1998 (§§ 143–151). The new, Civil Code [2014] has, however, removed the relevant sections from the property law part, in our view correctly, back into the family law (§§ 708–753). This was always the case in the Italian law governing statutory rights of usufruct which accrued to the parents of minors over assets of their children under Art. 324 and following of the Italian Civil Code: this section is seen to belong, in the structure of the Italian Civil Code, not with property law but with family law.

1.17 These observations are confirmed by the jurisprudence of the English courts on the so-called 'deserted wife's equity' and the legislative interventions in this area of law. Take, for example, *National Provincial Bank v Ainsworth*.[96] Mr Ainsworth left his wife in 1957. She continued to live with the children after she was given custody, in her husband's house with their four children, without paying rent. One year later, he took out a loan and gave the bank a charge over the house to secure the loan. The bank called in the loan some years later and brought an action for possession in order to realize the security interest for a reasonable price. Mrs Ainsworth defended the action with the argument that she, as wife, had the right to dwell in her husband's house, and that this right was not merely a personal right against her husband but also (in equity) a property right that was effective against all the world with the exception of a good faith purchaser for value without notice. The House of Lords confirmed the existence of the right of occupation in equity, but denied its character as a property right.[97] A right that depended on one's status as a wife was, by its nature, not a property right, because it did not flow from a contract or the grant of a license.[98] Besides, the wife's right of occupation was much too vague and uncertain. It could, for example, be terminated at any time by the husband's provision of alternative accommodation, so it did not relate to any particular object, and it could be lost by the wife by her own conduct (for example if she refused to follow the husband to a new house or if she chose to live with another man). A right can only have real effects (can only acquire the character of a *property* right) if it is definable,

[96] [1965] AC 1175 (HL).

[97] [1965] AC 1175, 1226E (Lord Hodson) and 1233G (Lord Upjohn). Remarkable in this context, though decided in a different family law regime, is OLG Celle 2 May 2011, NJW 2011 p. 2062. Since their separation, the (meanwhile divorced) husband had left the house, which he owned in his sole name, for the exclusive use of his wife under § 1361b(1) of the German Civil Code. He later sold the house. The court held that her license did not create any right of possession enforceable against the purchaser of the property, so long as no tenancy relationship (limited in time) was created expressly beyond the license.

[98] [1965] AC 1175 (HL), 1220 (Lord Hodson). See also Lord Cohen at 1228B-D and Lord Upjohn at 1232.

recognizable for third parties, and is capable by its nature of being perceived by them. It must possess a certain degree of persistence or stability. All of these characteristics were lacking here.[99] The policy of this result, however, did not reflect the sense of justice of the times.[100] The legislature intervened with the Matrimonial Homes Act 1967, the provisions of which (relevant for present purposes) were incorporated in sections 30 and 31 of the Family Law Act 1996. The Family Law Act 1996 grants 'rights to the marital home' which guarantee the non-owning spouse certain protections against third parties, providing that the marital right of abode is entered in the correct register.[101] The registered right has the character of a charge based in family law binding on the estate of the spouse. It enjoys the same priority as the equitable interest acquired in a family home through the act of marriage.

5. Regulatory Objectives of Property Law

Like contract law, property law is understood as an instrument of optimal resource allocation in states with a market-based economic order. Property law promotes this objective by guaranteeing rights of exclusion and rights of control over things. It does this, in turn, by furnishing property rights effective against third parties. This helps to define relationships between persons by reference to their entitlement to use things. Property law can only operate fairly, efficiently, and independently when it accepts the following objectives and adopts a suitable approach to achieving them in the context of the relevant legal system. Property law worthy of the name must (i) recognize rights over assets with effect against third parties as building blocks of private law, and provide appropriate legal remedies; (ii) determine which of such rights it accepts in its territory, on what basis, and determine their reach; (iii) determine to which objects such rights should be allowed to attach; (iv) provide rules governing the acquisition, transfer, and extinction of property rights, and (v) answer the question whether competing titles to the same thing or good are possible, and, if so, what the consequences are. In every one of the named areas, the main priority is to find a reasonable balance between the interests of the holder of the property rights and the rights of third parties. **1.18**

[99] Ibid., 1248–9; [1965] 2 All ER 472, 494 (Lord Wilberforce).

[100] See further *Sparkes*, A New Land Law, p. 327.

[101] On the limits of this protection, see *Ansari v Ansari* [2008] EWCA Civ 1456; [2009] 3 WLR 1092. The case dealt with the question whether the wife (whose right was registered and who could therefore regard the contract of sale made by the husband as an avoidable transaction in the sense of § 37(2)(b) Matrimonial Causes Act 1973) could also avoid the creation of a security interest in favour of the purchaser's bank. The question was answered in the negative by the Court of Appeal (Longmore LJ).

II

Absolute Rights in Assets

1. National and Fundamental Principles of Property Law

The legal literature of many European countries stereotypically begins the exposition of property law with a catalogue of the main concepts that characterize that country's law of property. These are then distilled into 'fundamental principles of property law', or some similar formulation.[1] Such principles are comparable to the brightly coloured trans-regional transport routes marked on a road atlas. They provide an overview for quick orientation. Because they are so remarkable and easy to remember, they contribute powerfully to the continuity of many national property law regimes. But what seems desirable from a domestic point of view presents considerable difficulties for European private law. This is because these so-called fundamental principles of property law create strong, nationally inflected patterns of argumentation and identification. Some of them do not even say anything about the necessary characteristics of property law as a discipline; instead, they exhaust themselves with a definition of certain regional particularities.[2] Other so-called fundamental principles concern themselves only with contingent details, such as regulating the transfer of property rights or answering the question how precisely an object of legal transaction must be capable of description in order for property rights to arise in it.[3] At the fundamental level, however, property law is not concerned with such details, but with the meaning of the concept of efficacy against third parties and, in light of that, with how property law takes account of third party interests. **2.1**

[1] For Greece see *inter alia Triantos*, AK, pp. 584 and 1185; *Georgiades*, Empragmato Dikaio I, § 2, particularly nos 8, 26, and 37–42, and *Spyridakis*, Empragmato Dikaio, p. 19.

[2] *Schreiber*, Jura 2010 p. 272 provides a nice example designed for German law students, which presents 'the fundamental principles of property law' and gives first rank(!) within this category to the principle that those acts-in-the-law [*Rechtsgeschäfte*] that create obligations [*Kausalgeschäfte*], and those that affect property rights [*Verfügungsgeschäfte*] are separate under the principle of separation and abstraction [*Trennungs- und Abstraktionsprinzip*]. Even *Stadler*, JZ 2010 pp. 380, 388 notices in its critique of the VIII Book of the DCFR that 'one would have wished, for the defence of the *Abstraktionsprinzip*, a more self-confident appearance by the representatives of German law in the working group'. Quite apart from the fact that the *Abstraktionsprinzip* is only known in a very few European legal systems at all, it is not even a principle exclusive to property law as such. For example, the assignment of claims does not belong to property law according to the German view; however, assignment is subject to the fundamental *Abstraktionsprinzip*. Thus Staudinger (-*Seiler*), BGB (2007), Einl. zum Sachenrecht no. 61 is correct that: 'Abstraction is a general principle of patrimonial law, which establishes the independence of obligation and the transfer of rights.'

[3] Even for the national (in this case Hungarian) law, Menyhárd, *Dologi jog* p. 18 'Fundamental Principles of Property Law' places no special importance here and abstains from presenting these principles as a whole. He even suggests that property law possesses no fundamental principles in a normative sense independent from, or going further than, the general principles of private law. The so-called 'fundamental principles of property law' merely reflect the necessities that emerge from the internal logic of this area of law.

Foundations of Property Law. Christian von Bar and Jason Grant Allen, Oxford University Press. © Christian von Bar 2023.
DOI: 10.1093/oso/9780198885337.003.0002

2. Absolute Rights in Assets as Building Blocks of Private Law

a. The Concept of an 'Absolute Right'

2.2 Rights protected against all the world are called 'absolute' in many legal systems. Consistent with this approach, property rights are also counted as 'absolute' rights.[4] *Absolutus* is the past participle of Latin *absolvere* (to free or separate). In one of its first meanings, therefore, a right is 'absolute' when it does not correspond to any specific duty in another person. That is, it exists separate from any such duty. While a 'relative' right can always be formulated simultaneously as the concrete duty of another, and cannot exist without such duty because it consists in demanding something specific of him, an 'absolute' right corresponds only with the *non-specific* duty of all the world to refrain from violating the right. This peculiarity characterizes a raft of personality rights in many legal systems (e.g. the right to protection of bodily integrity or freedom of movement). But it also reflects an important aspect of all property rights. Austin already viewed the property rights of the common law in this manner in the nineteenth century. The most comprehensive right, that of ownership, was a general right that did not correspond to any specific duty.[5] Only a relative duty, according to Austin, could be incumbent on a person and correspond to the relative right of another. The duty answered, in this case, to a right of the counter-party. The expression 'absolute' was, in contrast, a negative or privative expression. It signified that no antipode was referred to, for want of an appropriate object.[6] With the exception of the Austin's attempt to introduce the concept of an 'absolute duty', his approach to conceptualizing 'absolute rights' reflects the understanding of the civilian legal systems to the present.[7] The new Czech Civil Code [2014] goes so far as to elevate this conceptual definition to one of the fundamental criteria for its systemic organization. It distinguishes expressly between 'absolute' and 'relative' rights at the level of the headings of its individual books. Real rights of all kinds belong in the first category, and obligational rights belong in the second.[8]

[4] See only *Lenkovics*, A dologi jog vázlata, p. 14, who defines property law as that part of a legal system which gives persons legal control, in a framework of absolute rights, over the available goods and things of value, and thereby establishes the basic structure of the society's economic order. Art. 5 Slovenian Civil Code provides that the holder of a property right can enforce his rights against every other person.

[5] *Austin*, Lectures on Jurisprudence[5], p. 382.

[6] Ibid. p. 357: 'A relative obligation is incumbent on one party, and correlates with a right residing in another party. Changing the expression, a relative obligation corresponds or answers to a right; or implies, and is implied by, a right. Where an obligation is absolute, there is no right with which it correlates ... It neither implies, nor is implied by a right. Here, as elsewhere, the term "absolute" is a negative or privative expression. Here, as elsewhere, it denotes the *absence* of an object to which the speaker or writer expressly or tacitly refers.'

[7] *Spáčil*, Ochrana vlastnictví a držby v občanském zákoníku[2], pp. 8–9 e.g. observes appositely that absolute rights are rights that exist outside of a concrete legal relationship. Their holders do not require a cooperative partner. Only as a result of an unjustified interference with an absolute right do relative legal relations arise. On this view, everyone is obligated not to impinge on the property rights of others; if he does it anyway, this gives rise to a new concrete duty, e.g. the duty to deliver a thing to its owner.

[8] The Czech Civil Code is structured as follows: General Provisions (Part I), Family Law (Part II), Absolute Rights in Assets (Part III), Relative Rights in Assets (Part IV), and Concluding Provisions (Part V). The attempt by the author of this legislation to define, at least indirectly, which rights over assets have the character of absolute rights has already been rejected by some critics as problematic. They opine that some limited property rights could be mere relative rights, and that some obligational rights have an absolute element: Švestka [-*Spáčil*], Občanský zákoník I[2], p. 678.

In sharp contrast to this position is that taken, for example, by Gray (again in the context of the common law) who opines that 'property is a relative concept' because 'the physical, legal and moral conditions of excludability may vary according to time and circumstance'.[9] Practically the whole of English jurisprudence adopts this doctrine of the relativity of title. What the doctrine actually concerns, however, becomes evident to the Continental jurist only at second glance. The habit of speaking of the relativity of property rights does not demolish the distinction between obligational and real rights, but rather defines a phenomenon *within property law itself*—namely, that the core question of property law in the British Isles is whether one can defend his right to the use of a thing of value against persons who have, or claim to have, a conflicting right to the use of the same thing. In legal proceedings, one asks (and for this reason one asks *only*) whether the claimant has a better right (or title) to the relevant object than the defendant. This, however, does not change anything about the 'absoluteness' (effectiveness against third parties, excludability) of title in property law; if rights had no *erga omnes* effect, they would not have the status of property rights at all. *Every* title is, in other words, absolute. That is to say, title is effective against every person—but not against persons with an even better title. English jurists do not thereby refer, as many jurists schooled in the Continental tradition of ownership might think, to conflicts between those holding different absolute rights. The notion of relativity of title does not serve to describe the relationship between, for example, the owner ('general owner') of property and the holder of a pledge (the 'pledgee' as owner of 'special property') in a moveable thing, and thereby to express the fact that the pledgee has a 'better' title in or to the thing when the pledge reaches maturity or that the pledgor has 'better' title when the debt has been repaid in full. (The details of this relationship would be, in any case, a matter of contract and not of property law.) The concept of relativity of title is, for the most part,[10] rather concerned with rights of the *same type*, and the word 'right' in this context refers without differentiation to the claim made good on the basis of the primary right from which it flows. Even when both rights (or titles) exist independently of specific duties in third parties (and therefore have an 'absolute' character), the logic of the common law demands determination, in the individual case (and only for that individual case), which of the conflicting rights prevails 'relative to the other'. The reason for this conceptual approach is historical. The property law of the common law did not develop on the model of the protection of ownership, but rather on the model of the 2.3

[9] *Gray* [1991] CLJ 252, 295.

[10] Conflicts between the holders of rights of *different* kinds are often solved be reference to the doctrine of relativity of title where one or the other parties to the conflict derive their right from another person, e.g. where someone (P) is the possessor and pledgee of a moveable thing which both A and B claim as their property. Where P derives his rights of security as pledgee from A, P has a better title against B if and only if A's title is better than B's. If, on the other hand, B's title is better than A's, then B's claim in conversion against P would succeed (assuming P had made use of the thing). Relativity of title, however, often plays a role (albeit in a slightly different sense) when a bailee (e.g. the lessee of a moveable thing) issues proceedings against a tortfeasor who has destroyed the thing and thereby has actually caused harm over and above the limited interests of the bailee to use the thing. The bailee may, in such cases, enforce the full rights of the owner. In his internal relationship with the bailor, however, he remains liable to account. One can thus say that the bailee is 'owner' of the thing relative to the tortfeasor, but not relative to the bailor: *Curwen*, Legal Studies 20 (2000) 181, 182.

protection of possession of a thing. Whoever possesses a thing is allowed to keep it unless another has the positive right to disturb or deprive him of possession. Title (albeit a weak form of title) flows already from mere possession. Possession establishes of itself a property right, the strength of which is determined by the manner in which possession was acquired (theft, finding, loan, hire, purchase, etc.). The property right whose content is concretized in this way is, by nature, effective against all the world, and appears in the Continental idiom as 'absolute'. In the English understanding, however, the title is of *relative* quality because one places less emphasis on the substantive legal position and more emphasis on the procedural legal position. Person A, (e.g. the erstwhile lessee of an automobile following the termination of a lease) can, from the point of view of the substantive law, have a better right to possession than B (e.g. a thief) but a weaker right to possession than C (e.g. the lessor) at the same time. C's right plays no role in a legal proceeding between A and B under the common law.[11] This phenomenon would be captured equally well if one would speak not of the 'relativity of title' but instead of the 'priority of absolute titles', but the terminology seems too well entrenched to be toppled now. Relativity of title has, besides this, other facets, too. The expression reflects not only the notion that ownership and possession are seen as being more closely related than on the Continent, and eventually merge into each other. Rather, it expresses the belief that one can, by taking this approach, reduce the scope of legal argument required. This is because the doctrine of the relativity of title expresses not just the banal point that, at the end of the day, one of the two parties before the court has to win (namely, he with the relatively better title). It also relieves the burden of answering the question of who has the *most* comprehensive right ('ownership', the 'best' title) in the thing: if a thing has been taken from its purchaser, that purchaser need not, *vis-à-vis* its thief, establish that he was already the true owner at the time. Determination of the matter between the purchaser and the thief appears, in the eyes of an English jurist, to be simply beside the point. It would appear the same in the law of possession on the Continent,[12] but not in the law of the vindication of property rights. What occurs on two tracks in the latter occurs in the course of a single enquiry under the common law.

2.4 A subjective right can, however, also be described as an 'absolute' right to the extent it is all-embracing, i.e. *freed from all limitations of content*. A right is absolute in this sense not because it is independent of any specific duty (although this can certainly be said of such a right), but rather because it affords its owner all powers over the thing such that he must never, in any concrete relationship, yield to a competitor in his use of it. The right exists 'free' (or 'freed') from all encumbrances; it has not (yet) been the object of

[11] At this point, however, the legislature intervened. B can, under the Torts (Interference with Goods) Act 1977 sec. 8(1), point to C's better right in partial or complete defence against A's claim. Rule 19.5A of the Civil Procedure Rules 1998 governs the procedural aspects of such a referral.

[12] German law affords a thief who himself falls victim to theft the claim for possession in §§ 861 and 862 of the German Civil Code (the legal protection of possession does not expressly require a legal right to possession: MünchKomm [-*Joost*], BGB VI^5, § 861 no. 5 and § 862 no. 8; Staudinger [-*Bund*], BGB (2007), § 861 no. 6); further, the claims in § 1007(1) and (2) might also operate to his benefit. While bad faith precludes a claim (§ 1007(3)), this relates not to a general lack of a right of possession but only a wanting right of possession *vis-à-vis the current possessor*: MünchKomm [-*Baldus*], BGB VI^5, § 1007 no. 15.

any process of hiving or spinning off. An 'absolute' right in this sense does not appear as the counterpart of the 'relative' rights of the law of obligations, but rather as the counterpart of 'limited' rights to that which belongs to another, and especially of the limited real rights recognized by the relevant national law of property.[13] Italian and Spanish jurists, for example, associate the expressions *diritto assoluto* and *derecho absoluto* first and foremost with ownership, as the most extensive property right of all (in their view),[14] and contrast it with the *diritti reali limitati* and *derechos reales limitados*.[15] That is linguistically and conceptually quite plausible, but can lead to misunderstandings if one does not pay attention to the shift in accent. Where necessary, one should construct sentences which expressly stipulate whether the term 'absolute right' is being used in contradistinction to (i) a *relative obligational right* or (ii) a *limited real right*, as the case may be.

Two further reasons why English and Irish jurists are reluctant to speak of 'absolute rights' are related to this ambiguity. While 'ownership' [*Eigentum*] is the paradigmatic absolute right in assets on the Continent, little depends on ownership for common lawyers. The 'owner' is simply he who, in all the circumstances, has the most comprehensive set of property rights or the best title.[16] *Ownership* is a descriptive word; it is not something from which rights flow, but rather, according to this view, a label for a bundle of rights that one has in some object.[17] Further, it is more important in the British Isles than elsewhere to distinguish between 'land' and other objects of value. This is because land was subject to the law of feudal tenure following the Norman conquest, whereas chattels (from 'cattle'; generally moveable assets) were not. The law of feudal tenure (and only this law) took its point of departure in the politically useful doctrine that the ultimate ownership in all land was exclusively in the Crown. From this followed (and follows, at least linguistically, to this day) that no subject could be the 'absolute owner' of land; this position was (or is) exclusive to the Crown.[18] Private persons have, at most, 2.5

[13] It is not typical, but it would be in this sense linguistically possible, to distinguish between 'absolute' and 'conditional' obligational rights. An unencumbered claim would belong to the first group, a security interest in the claim of a third party would belong to the second group.

[14] The latter idea—the notion that ownership is the most comprehensive right that a person can have in an asset—is common to all Continental legal systems. It has precipitated into an express legislative expression in Art. 5:1(1) of the Netherlands Civil Code.

[15] See *Stanzione*, Manuale di Diritto Privato[3], pp. 43 and 449; see further *Lacruz Berdejo*, Elementos III(1)[3], p. 16.

[16] See *Honoré*, Oxford Essays in Jurisprudence 1961, pp. 107–46.

[17] *Bridge* op. cit. p. 30. For an especially incisive expression, see Lord Judge CJ in *Yearworth v North Bristol NHS Trust* [2009] EWCA Civ 37 para. 28; [2010] QB 1, 12 (CA): 'The concept of ownership is no more than a convenient global description of different collections of rights held by persons over physical and other things.'

[18] Surprising parallels appear when one compares the ancient feudal system of the British Isles with (now abolished) constructions in former socialist legal systems of Central and Eastern Europe. In Bulgaria, for example, Art. 63 of the Property Act of 1951 lifted the *superficies solo cedit* principle, and thus separated ownership of buildings from ownership of land, in order to insulate the state ownership of land by creating a private right to the building only (*Venedikov*, Novo veshtno pravo, p. 128 no. 108). A further example is provided by the right to the personal use of land in § 198 to § 192 of the former Czech Civil Code [1964]. The provisions, which were in operation until 1 January 1991, guaranteed citizens the possibility to have real (*Spáčil*, Ochrana vlastnictví a držby v občanském zákoníku[2], pp. 109–11) right capable of inheritance in land units, although ownership in land was 'socialist' property, which is to say state property. (Rights to the personal use of a land unit were, following the end of socialism, transmuted into rights to the personal use of a dwelling in tenancy law). The ideological motives behind such rules were (and are) naturally fundamentally different, and the English concept of ownership also lacks the Roman influence which was assumed in the legal systems reformed by socialism—indeed, it was such a concept that socialism

estates (so-called 'freeholds' or 'estates in fee simple').[19] One is, in the framework of these different types of tenure, only a holder of land belonging to the Crown, and one's estate determines the duration of this legal position.[20] The feudal obligations of tenants belong now to legal history,[21] but they continue to inform the English and Irish legal terminology. Not only does the Crown (in contemporary Ireland, the 'State')[22] figure (or posture) as the only 'absolute' owner of land units. The inherited terminology of the feudal law of status is still used to describe the legal position that most closely reflects the Continental institution of land ownership.[23] This is the 'freehold estate' or 'fee simple absolute in possession'. An estate (whether freehold or leasehold) is, in this context, absolute if it is not granted to end in terms and is not otherwise limited. A fee simple absolute subsists without a fixed end date and unconditionally. For this reason, it is properly understood as 'absolute ownership'.

The fact that English and Irish jurists use the word 'ownership' in connection with land in a contextual sense, but not as a *terminus technicus*,[24] has a double reason. This reason also relates to the notion that there exist only derivative rights in land (i.e. rights deriving from the Crown or the state). Disputes between private subjects in the law of real property are, then, disputes about title. The question of who has the 'best' right in a parcel of land is (i) clear as a matter of fundamental principle, and (ii) without any

fought. However, both the law of feudal tenures and socialist land law served exaggerated claims of state power, and produced some juristic constructions that were, viewed from this perspective, not altogether dissimilar.

[19] *Williams*, Personal Property[18], p. 1.

[20] Megarry and Wade (-*Harpum/Bridge/Dixon*), *The Law of Real Property*[8], no. 2-005.

[21] The fact that the rights of an intestate estate lapses to the Crown in English law also has its basis in the feudal concept of escheat (i.e. reversion). This was a characteristic feature of the tenure system and ensured that land without an owner would fall back to the Crown (or in some cases the Duchy of Lancaster or the Duchy of Cornwall) (*Harpum/Bridge/Dixon* op. cit. p. 31). Already sec. 45(1)(d) of the Administration of Estates Act 1925 abolished the mechanism of escheat. Since then, under sec. 46(1)(vi) of that Act, the simple rule operates that an estate without heirs falls to the Crown, the Duchy of Lancaster, or the Duchy of Cornwall. This reflects the legal position on the Continent; there too, intestate estates go to the state (see e.g. Arts 723 and 768 Belgian Civil Code; Art. § 1936 German Civil Code; Art. 724(3) French Civil Code; Arts 972 and 1824 Greek Civil Code; Arts 565 and 586 Italian Civil Code; Art. 768 Luxembourg Civil Code; Art. 4:189 Netherlands Civil Code; Art. 2152 Portuguese Civil Code; Art. 956 Spanish Civil Code; § 462 Slovakan Civil Code, § 1634 Czech Civil Code). The legal position in Ireland is also worthy of note. The feudal law of escheat was abolished there (on the basis of the Law Reform Commission Consultation Paper on Reform and Modernisation of Land Law and Conveyancing Law 34-2004, 37) (see sec. 9(2) of the Land and Conveyancing Law Reform Act 2009). Only the terminology (e.g. 'estate' and 'fee simple') has survived these reforms. Under sec. 73(1) of the Succession Act 1965 an intestate estate of land reverts to the Irish State as the 'ultimate intestate successor'.

[22] Art. 11 Constitution of the Irish Free State (Saorstát Éireann) 1922 (the first Irish constitution) envisaged the following: 'All the lands and waters, mines and minerals, within the territory of the Irish Free State hitherto vested in the State, or any department thereof, or held for the public use or benefit, and also all the natural resources of the same territory (including the air and all forms of potential energy), and also all royalties and franchises within that territory shall, from and after the date of the coming into operation of this Constitution, belong to the Irish Free State'. Art. 10.2 Bunreacht na hÉireann (the current Irish constitution of 1972) adopted this formulation in its substantive features: 'All land and all mines, minerals and waters which belonged to Saorstát Éireann immediately before the coming into operation of this Constitution belong to the State to the same extent as they then belonged to Saorstát Éireann.'

[23] Nonetheless the proprietorship register expresses the holder of a registered estate as 'registered proprietor' (see *Sparkes*, A New Land Law, p. 9).

[24] On 'ownership' in the common law and equity see *Goode*, Commercial law[3], p. 31. Statute law uses the term only occasionally, for example in the title to sec. 7 and in sec. 58(1) of the Settled Land Act 1925, in the (English) Law of Property Act 1925, Schedule 1 paras 1–2, and in the (Irish) Land and Conveyancing Reform Act 2009, Part 2 ('Ownership of Land') in sec. 9.

substantive importance anyway. The important question is who has the better right of possession in the land, and that is, according to the English understanding, even in this context the disputant with the better title *relative* to the other.[25]

The point of departure is different for things which did not fall under the feudal system, in particular 'choses in possession'. These are moveable corporeal objects of all kinds, and as such the most important category of chattels.[26] They can certainly be the object of an 'absolute' (i.e. an exclusive and unconditional) right of use. This includes the right to possession of the thing against all the world and, at least in principle, the right to demand possession from another in the case it is lost; it further includes the right to deal with the thing as one wishes, to enjoy its affordances, to alienate and to destroy it. 'Property' in a chose in possession is, in other words, 'absolute' in a different sense than property in an estate in fee simple (i.e. the most comprehensive interest that a subject of the Crown can have in land). This is because every estate in fee is derivative of the estate of another, who granted it; property in a chose in possession, by way of contrast, does not have its source in the feudal pyramid, i.e. in the rights of one's immediate feudal lord and ultimately in the rights of the Crown. One is, rather, lord of one's own moveable property. One's right therein has, in consequence, never been conceived of as a temporally limited right. One has never held choses in possession as (or in the framework of) an 'estate'. Where a common law estate in fee simple in land could fragment and cascade down to a plurality of subordinate estates—most of them spatially smaller—and where these subordinate estates could even be legally divided in later periods,[27] property in personal chattels is and has always been in one hand. It knows neither a future interest ('remainder') nor a lapse ('reversion') to another with a higher-ranking entitlement; subordinate interests in choses in possession could only be created in equity.[28] A further consequence of the fact that choses in possession did not fall under the rules of feudal tenure is that (until the end of 1925) succession to intestate choses in possession was governed by different rules to those governing real property. Finally, very different causes of action were available to recover possession of real property and 'chattels personal' (i.e. choses in possession as well as choses in action)[29], respectively. Until the present day, the 'owner' of moveable property (more precisely: the person with the better right to possession) has a cause of action in the law of delict, 2.6

[25] *Clarke and Kohler*, Property Law, p. 386: '[I]n property disputes, the question at issue tends to be whether one party has a better claim to the property interest than another, not whether either of them is the absolute or "true" owner of it. What each party has to prove is that he has a better title than the other, not that he has a better title than anyone else in the whole world.' Similarly, see Cockburn CJ in *Asher v Whitlock* (1865) LR 1 QB 1, 5 ('I take it as clearly established, that possession is good against all the world except the person who can shew a good title').

[26] *Harpum/Bridge/Dixon* op. cit. p. 3.

[27] When the Law of Property Act 1925 came into force, this common law hierarchy (or, seen in economic terms, fragmentation) was abolished. The statute, however, left the corresponding mechanisms of equity largely unaffected.

[28] *Williams*, Personal Property[18] p. 47.

[29] These are 'things' ('choses') which are only realized in the course of a legal claim (i.e. 'in action'). They are, at core, rights to bring an action, or, in other words, points of reference for rights of ownership that owe their very existence to the legal system alone. They are, therefore, 'intangible property', or, as we will argue in this book, 'incorporeal normative things'.

while the holder of land has legal remedies specific to the law of real property (directed to the termination of another's unlawful possession).

b. *Erga Omnes* Effect

2.7 The expression 'absolute right' is connected, wherever it is used as a counterpart to the 'relative rights' of the law of obligations, with the idea that property rights are effective against all the world.[30] But this effect against third parties belongs to the defining characteristics of property law in all the legal systems of Europe;[31] even between common law and civil law systems only terminological differences appear, not substantive ones.[32] The *erga omnes* effect (or, in English, 'enforceability') counts as a paradigmatic, constitutive element of property law itself. Without effect against third parties there is no law of property, or, as the Scandinavians put it, no 'protection of [the sort offered by] property law'. This proposition can also be reversed. Although not every legal system automatically characterizes every *erga omnes* (or 'absolute') right as a property right without exception,[33] neither difficult cases in the penumbra nor varying definitions of

[30] See, e.g. in relation to Belgium *Vandenberghe*, Goederenrecht, p. 4; Bulgaria *Vassilev*, Balgarsko veshtno pravo, p. 14; Germany *Baur and Stürner*, Sachenrecht[18], § 2 no. 2, and MünchKomm (*-Gaier*), BGB VI[5], introduction no. 4; France *Malaurie and Aynès*, Les biens[3], p. 95 no. 368 as well as *Atias*, Les biens[10], p. 56 no. 77; Greece (where absoluteness is seen as one of the defining characteristics of real rights; according to Art. 973 of the Greek Civil Code, real rights are to be respected by all the world and are protected against all the world) *Triantos*, AK, p. 1185 and *Filios*, Empragmato Dikaio[3], p. 44; Italy *Torrente and Schlesinger*, Manuale di diritto privato[21], p. 257, *Gazzoni*, Manuale di diritto privato[10], p. 247, *Bianca*, Diritto civile VI, p. 121 fn. 1, and *Trabucchi*, Istituzioni di diritto civile[44], pp. 77 and 540–50; Netherlands Asser (*-Mijnsen/van Velten/Bartels*), Zakenrecht[15], no. 18, Pitlo (*-Reehuis and Heisterkamp*), and Goederenrecht[12], p. 13 no. 22; Austria *Barta*, Zivilrecht, p. 484 and *Gschnitzer/Faistenberger/Barta/Call/Eccher*, Sachenrecht[2], p. 1; Poland Art. 140 and Art. 251 of the Polish Civil Code and *Liebscher and Zoll*, Einführung in das polnische Recht, p. 163, as well as *Gniewek*, Prawo rzeczowe[8], p. 12 no. 31; Portugal *inter alia* Art. 1311 of the Portuguese Civil Code and *Vieira*, Direitos reais, pp. 229–30; Czech Republic *Švestka and Dvořák*, Občanské právo hmotné[5], p. 272 and *Eliáš et al.*, Občanský zákoník. Velký akademický komentář I, p. 511; Hungary *Menyhárd*, Dologi jog, p. 18 and *Lenkovics*, A dologi jog vázlata[7], pp. 23–4; Sweden *Håstad*, Sakrätt[6], p. 15. The DCFR brings the fundamental principle of the absolute quality of real rights to expression in VIII.-6:101.

[31] See, e.g. for Spain *Lasarte Álvarez*, Principios IV[9a], p. 7 and *Díez-Picazo*, Fundamentos III[5], p. 81, and for Poland *Gniewek* op. cit.

[32] Instead of speaking of 'relative' and 'absolute' rights, common lawyers tend to speak of 'personal' and 'property' rights; substantively, this does not change matters. *Bell*, Modern Law of Personal Property, p. 6 ('The distinction between personal and property rights is commonly said to be that a personal right, for example a contractual right, is a one against a specific person, whereas a property right is a right against the world'); *Clarke and Kohler*, Property Law, p. 18 ('What distinguishes a property right in a thing from other rights in the same thing is the breadth of enforceability of the right. We designate as property rights those rights that the law will uphold against people in general (either the whole world, or everyone except a specified class of exceptions)'), and *Worthington*, Personal Property Law, p. 19 ('At root there is a policy decision at stake: which rights ought to be enforceable against the world, rather than simply between consenting parties? Much of the debate over whether certain assets are property, or, in legal terms, whether certain rights are proprietary, is concerned to answer this policy question').

[33] That this is so is demonstrated by the fact that there are security rights and rights of use in the law of obligations that are effective against third parties (liens over a cause of action; rights of usufruct over company shares etc), by the fact that some absolute moral rights display 'proprietary' elements (the right to one's own name, the right to one's own voice, etc.), and by the fact that some legal systems recognize certain obligational rights as being capable of registration in the real property register. In Austria we encounter the opinion that the registration of certain obligational rights, such as claims of transfer for use arising from a lease agreement (see § 1095 Austrian Civil Code, further examples in §§ 1073 and 1079) lends these rights an absolute character, but that the corresponding rights do not have a real nature (Klang [*-Klang*], ABGB II[2], § 308 no. 3). In the narrower sense, 'real' or 'property' rights in Austrian jurisprudence are only rights that guarantee direct control of a thing (Koziol/Bydlinski/

'property' change this fact: there is a law of property wherever *erga omnes* rights in assets exist. And because all European legal systems give their subjects the possibility to acquire such absolute rights, it is plausible to claim that property law is ubiquitous.

How it is *labelled* in each legal system is, of course, a different matter; but it should not bother us, in the first instance, whether and how the European legal systems present the self-sufficiency of property law in their legislation,[34] current literature,[35] and university curricula.[36] That occurs, in fact, in very different ways, but this diversity does not affect the common, fundamental conviction. The recognition of rights in assets directed at third parties flows from the concept of freedom; such rights are meant to allow subjects to structure their own lives with respect to their legal interest in objects of value.[37]

The corresponding picture of the 'absoluteness' of legal positions guaranteed by real rights is conceived from the perspective of the bearer of the right. It rests on the notion that the holder of a real right can enforce his legal position against every other person. Of course, one can express this essential idea from the opposite perspective, too. For a right that is absolute in this sense can not only be enforced against every other person, but it can also (in theory at least) be *violated* by every other person. Precisely this aspect differs in the case of a relative, obligational right: an obligation to pay a debt can only be breached by the debtor, and by no-one else. Property rights are thus stronger, but 2.8

Bollenberger [*-Eccher and Riss*], ABGB I[4], § 307 no. 1). Even registered obligational rights do not belong to this category.

[34] There is no law of property bundled together in a separate part in, e.g. the Spanish, Belgian, French, and Luxembourgish Civil Codes. Although the second book of these codes contains many property-related provisions, the third book also contains provisions relating to the manners of acquiring property. (In the case of the Belgian code, this book contains provisions relating to security rights in property, which are barely mentioned in the textbooks on property law and are usually treated separately in texts on the law of *sûretés*, which also treat personal securities; in France, on the other hand, both real and personal securities are the subject of a new, fourth book of the code: see *Simler*, JCP 2006, I, 13, no. 124 p. 597.) The manner of regulation of the Romanic codifications is, however, not inconsistent with the hypothesis that property law is amenable to an independent systematic categorization. The same goes for Sweden, which (at least in the statute law) consciously refrains from distinguishing between a law of obligations and a law of things. For example, statutes on competition law (*Kommissionslagen*, SFS 2009:865), on consumer sales (*Konsumentköplagen*, SFS 1990:932), and debt securities (*Lag (SFS 1936:81) om skuldebrev*) all have real as well as obligational significance. In contrast, the statute on sales law (*Köplagen*, SFS 1990:931) deals only with obligational matters.

[35] The Portuguese Civil Code of 1966 contained a second book with the title 'Property Law', but left many questions related to property law to the law of obligations (e.g. transfer of ownership, hypothecs). Many principles which, in our view, are relevant to questions of property law are dealt with in Portuguese texts on the law of obligations (e.g. *Menezes Leitão*, Direito das obrigações III[4], p. 20) as well as in texts on property law (e.g. *Carvalho*, BFD 87 [2011] pp. 1–20), for example the consensus principle, the causality principle, and the publicity principle. The categorization of real security rights [*direitos reais de garantia*] and other security rights [*garantias*] is especially problematic. *Pestana de Vasconcelos*, Direito das garantias, pp. 15–30 thus suggests that no distinction should be made between the law of obligations and property law, and that the law of security should be considered as its own, autonomous discipline within legal studies.

[36] In English and Irish universities, 'land law' and 'equity' is often taught but not 'property law' as an independent subject. *Worthington*, Personal Property Law, p. v thus complains that personal property law is one of the most neglected and least understood aspects of English law. *Lawson and Rudden*, The Law of Property[3], p. 192 concur: 'The law of property remains very complicated and not entirely free from confusion. Too many kinds of people have had a hand in producing it to admit of a simple orderly system, consistent in all its parts.' Swedish jurisprudence accords the law of obligations the leading, system-defining role, but does not negate the difference between the law of obligations and property law: *Hellner*, Metodproblem i rättsvetenskapen, p. 153.

[37] *Mijnsen/van Velten/Bartels* op. cit. no. 14; Staudinger (*-Seiler*), Eckpfeiler Zivilrecht, III.2.a. p 959.

also more vulnerable than obligational rights. They therefore require a different form of protection.

c. The 'Absoluteness' of the Best Conceivable Property Right

(1) General

2.9 The precise content of this protection depends, in turn, on the content of the relevant property rights. In other words, *erga omnes* effectiveness (or 'absoluteness') can change from right to right and, accordingly, from legal system to legal system. The principle that property rights are protected against all the world does not, in and of itself, say anything conclusive about *how* they are protected, that is, which remedies or causes of action protect individual property rights in a concrete sense. This counts even for the strongest right conceivable in a legal system, which is most often (though, as mentioned, not always) called 'ownership'. We will confine our present discussion to this right. Ownership is naturally effective against all the world, and is the prototype of an absolute right. At the same time, even this best conceivable property right is subject to inherent constraints. These derogate from ownership's claim to absoluteness in parts, without undermining it in principle. The problem is that these exceptions and countermeasures, viewed from a pan-European perspective, restrict the protection afforded the right of ownership by property law in very different aspects in different legal systems. Ownership bears different 'dents' from country to country.

2.10 From a Continental legal perspective, the claim for delivery (for example) of an owner against a person in possession of a thing but with no right in it [*Detentor*] appears as the content and expression of his 'absolute' legal position.[38] He who cannot decide who is allowed to have possession of the thing does not deserve, from the perspective of these legal systems, to be called its 'owner' at all. But that is just the consequence of a certain definitional concretization of the meaning of ownership.[39] Just because the common law (in particular) does not recognize a right of vindication over moveable things (i.e. the claim for delivery of possession) does not mean that the common law equips an 'owner' (or holder of a right of ownership) with less rights, in sum, than the Civilian legal systems. In individual cases, in fact, the opposite may be true; for example, where an owner loses his right of possession simply through the effluxion of time or, through the interventions of third parties, to a bona fide acquirer. Ownership remains, in other words, an absolute right everywhere; that different content and powers fall in the penumbra of ownership from country to country does not change this fact.

[38] This can be observed in the systematic structure of many codifications, perhaps especially in the structure of the Netherlands Civil Code. Art. 5:1 defines ownership as the most comprehensive right that a person can have in a thing, and Art. 5:2 adds to this immediately that the owner of a thing is entitled to demand its delivery from every person who 'holds' it without right. The common description of the *vindicatio* claim in Austrian law as the 'claim of ownership' or even as the 'real claim of ownership' (Koziol and Welser [-*Kletečka*], Bürgerliches Recht I^{13}, p. 345) also gives a clear impression. This claim is derived immediately from the right of the owner to exclude every other person from the use of his things (§ 366 Austrian Civil Code).

[39] For more detail see *Sliwka*, Herausgabeansprüche als Teil des zivilrechtlichen Eigentumsrechts? pp. 365–9.

(2) Compensation In Lieu of Delivery: 'Conversion'

The common law, as indicated, illustrates that not even the best conceivable property right in a legal system must always, in every relationship, be protected in the strongest (or, if a play on words be allowed once more, the 'most absolute') manner, i.e. with a remedy directed towards re-establishing control over the thing. Here we arrive, from the European point of view, at a *chiasmus* (a criss-crossing rhetorical structure). While the holder of a common law estate in land (for which 'absolute' ownership lies with the Crown) can always vindicate his right to possession,[40] the proprietor of a moveable thing who seeks to vindicate his sole and unlimited right cannot. It is, in other words, specifically the holder of an estate in land, not the holder of the 'best relative title' in a moveable thing, who most resembles the Continental owner. The reason is, again, historical. The common law never developed a property right to delivery of possession for chattels (physical moveable things). In its place served (and still generally serves today) a right to compensation for damages. The interests of an owner of chattels were protected by the so-called property torts, that is by the law of delict rather than by property law itself. **2.11**

Originally the torts of *trespass de bonis asportatis*, *detinue*, and *conversion* were the three most important property torts, and each could be considered discretely from the others. Trespass reacted to unauthorized taking or taking away (*asportatio*), detinue to unauthorized detention (e.g. by retaining a thing after the end of a lease), and conversion to unauthorized alienation of chattels. Later, conversion clearly became the most important cause of action. This is because elements of *asportatio* and, as a result of the Interference with Goods Act 1977, elements of detinue were incorporated into it.[41] Trespass, on the other hand, was placed on another basis of harm, e.g. putting scratches in another's carriage,[42] or shooting another's pigeons.[43]

> Unauthorized user of goods is a trespass; unauthorized acts of riding a horse, driving a motor car, using a bottle, are all equally trespasses, even though the horse may be returned unharmed or the motor car unwrecked or the bottle unbroken.[44]

Only the person in possession of the chattel at the time of the trespass (or entitled to immediate possession) is however, entitled to sue.[45]

The tort of conversion evolved from the writ of trover, which was in turn derived from the writ of trespass on the case. In its original form, the writ of trover had four elements: the plaintiff had (i) to have had the chattel (a physical, moveable thing) in **2.12**

[40] This flows, in England, from Part 5 of the Civil Procedure Rules. Under this Part every person, who has a right of possession over real property, can sue for possession.
[41] See *Bridge*, Personal Property Law[3], pp. 47–8.
[42] *Fouldes v Willoughby* (1841) 8 M & W 540; 151 ER 1153 (Alderson B).
[43] *Hamps v Darby* [1948] 2 KB 311.
[44] Latham C in *Penfolds Wines Pty Ltd v Elliott* (1946) 74 CLR 204.
[45] *Bridge*, Personal Property Law[3], p. 51 (with the addition, that in this context the distinction between factual possession and the right to possession practically vanishes).

possession and (ii) had to have lost it *causaliter et per infortunatem*. The defendant had to have (iii) found the chattel (thus 'trover' from Anglo-Norman French 'to find') and (iv) had to have integrated it into his own property, i.e. converted it to his own use.

The second and third elements were, in the first instance, assumed or even irrebuttably presumed; later, they were abandoned altogether. At the same time, the first element was relaxed, in that standing in the cause of action was extended to persons who only had a right to the immediate possession of a chattel. Finally (in 1977), as mentioned above, the common law tort of conversion along with detinue and some forms of trespass was replaced by statute. The 1977 Act, however, did not adopt all the recommendations of the Law Reform Commission on which it was based;[46] in particular, it did not endorse the recommendation to replace trespass, detinue, and conversion *in toto* with a new tort, the 'tort of unlawful interference with goods'. The statute retains conversion as an independent cause of action and has only modified some of its legal consequences.[47] Conversion thus lies, according to Lord Atkin's formulation (which still enjoys wide approval), whenever one deals with the moveable property of another in a manner that is inconsistent with his rights of ownership, provided only that this occurs with the intention to challenge or deny the rights of the true owner.[48] Conversion is actionable per se, i.e. does not require any actual damage.[49] It is concerned, at core, with protection of possession, or more exactly with the protection of possession of one's property. The common law did not adopt the conceptual definition of ownership of the Enlightenment for personal property, either. The right to possession (or rights flowing from possession) stood in its place, and for this reason one felt no impetus to develop a cause of action in the nature of *vindicatio*.

> The Common Law never had any adequate process in the case of land, or any process at all in the case of goods, for the vindication of ownership pure and simple. So feeble and precarious was property without possession, or rather without possessory remedies, in the eyes of medieval lawyers, that Possession largely usurped not only the substance but the name of Property.[50]

In other words, 'a person possessed of goods as his property has a good title as against every stranger'.[51] Even one who is actually 'owner', but at the time of tortfeasance has neither possession nor the right to immediate possession,[52] cannot sue in conversion;[53] he can, at most, join the suit of a plaintiff with standing in virtue of possession.[54]

[46] 18th Report on Conversion and Detinue 1971, Cmnd. 4774.

[47] For further details *Bridge* op. cit. p. 52.

[48] *Lancashire and Yorkshire Railway Co v MacNicoll* (1918) 88 LJ KB 601; confirmed by Scrutton LJ in *Oakley v Lyster* [1931] 1 KB 418.

[49] *Bridge* op. cit. p. 53 makes clear that a certain intensity of interference is required before it can be said to deny the plaintiff's title.

[50] *Pollock and Wright*, An Essay on Possession in the Common Law, p. 5.

[51] Lord Campbell CJ in *Jeffries v Great Western Railway Co* (1856) 5 E & B 802; 119 ER 680.

[52] *Bridge* op. cit. p. 62.

[53] *Gordon v Harper* (1796) 7 TR 9; 10 ER 828.

[54] *Bridge* op. cit. p. 63 (with the example of an owner who has given possession of a chattel to another on a term bailment, i.e. for a limited period of time).

The effect of conversion was thus (and is still in certain cases) a 'forced judicial sale' of the thing to the defendant.[55] For this reason, the quantum of damages is measured by the price which the defendant would have had to pay if he had purchased title from the plaintiff.[56] Title passes, in consequence, not at the date of the judgment but first when the damages are actually paid.[57] A remedy to demand delivery of the actual thing did not exist at all until passage of the Common Law Procedure Act 1854. In the period between 1854 and 1977 the court could, within the framework of detinue, make an order for delivery of chattels or give the plaintiff the choice between damages and delivery.[58] Orders for delivery were, however, seldom made; the rules were applied in such a manner as to enable an exceptional right to specific performance in contract.[59] Simultaneous with the abolition of detinue in the 1977 Act,[60] the rules that had applied to detinue were carried over to the more widespread tort of conversion.[61] This Act, however, limited itself to giving the courts competence to make an order for specific relief for delivery of chattels (in sec. 3(3)(b)); the statute is silent as to *how* this competence is to be used, even to this day. The necessary decisions thus remained within the discretion of the court.[62] **2.13**

(3) Lasting Divergence of Legal Title and *De Facto* Control

The paradox that one may never be able to demand his property back from another who has it in his possession or custody is also observable in the Civilian jurisdictions. It appears first in certain provisions of national law designed to transpose Art. 9 of the so-called Distance Selling Directive.[63] These national instruments have answered the question whether an undertaking which sends a consumer unsolicited goods loses ownership in those goods, or whether the undertaking remains the owner but 'only' loses his claim to demand the goods back.[64] Where the latter is the case, from the point **2.14**

[55] *Prosser* (1957) 42 Cornell LQ 168.

[56] The yardstick is the value of the chattel at the time of its conversion (*General & Finance Facilities v Cooks Cars (Romford) Ltd* [1963] 1 WLR 644, per Diplock LJ).

[57] *Brinsmead v Harrison* (1872) LR 7 CP 547; sec. 5(1) of the Torts (Interference with Goods) Act 1977.

[58] *General & Finance Facilities v Cooks Cars (Romford) Ltd* [1963] 1 WLR 644.

[59] Specific performance, like specific relief, is not guaranteed when damages would provide an adequate remedy, which is typically safe to assume in the case with common items of trade (*Cohen v Roche* [1927] 1 KB 169).

[60] sec. 2(1) of the Torts (Interference with Goods) Act 1977.

[61] sec. 3 of the Torts (Interference with Goods) Act 1977.

[62] *Bridge* op. cit. p. 76.

[63] Directive 97/7/EC of the European Parliament and of the Council of 20 May 1997 on the protection of consumers in respect of distance contracts (Official Journal L 144, 4 June 1997).

[64] See, e.g. Art. 76 of the Belgian *Loi du 14 juillet 1991 sur les pratiques du commerce et sur l'information et la protection du consommateur*) (meanwhile abolished by Art. VI.108 *Code de droit économique*); Art. 62(2) of the Bulgarian Consumer Protection Law; § 241a German Civil Code; Art. L 122-3(1) of the French *Code de la consommation*; Art. 4 of the Greek Consumer Protection Law (Statute 2251/1994, renewed through the joint ministerial order KYA Z1-496/7-18 December 2000, FEK B' 1545/18 December 2006); Arts 26 lit. f and 66 *quinquies* Italian *Codice del consume*; Art. 8 of the Luxembourg Art. L. 213-7 *Code de la consommation*; Art. 7:7 Netherlands Civil Code; § 864(2) Austrian Civil Code; Art. 5 of the Polish Statute of 30 May 2014 on consumer rights; Art. 13(1) Portuguese DL 57/2008 of 26 March 2008; § 53(8) Slovakian Civil Code; § 1838 Czech Civil Code (according to which the consumer is to be seen as one entitled to possession), and § 8 Hungarian Regulation 45/2014 (*Korm. rendelet a fogyasztó és a vállalkozás közötti szerződések részletes szabályairól*). The Spanish Statute 47/2002 amending the Statute 7/1996 (*Ley de Ordenación del Comercio Minorista*) reserves the decision about the return of

of view of the Continental legal systems one is dealing with no less an exception to the principle of 'absoluteness' than in the case of a 'forced judicial sale' in the law of conversion. Indeed, we come to another (rather unexpected) *chiasmus* in the interpretation of the law of unsolicited goods. While English and Irish law treat the delivery of unsolicited goods as a gift, and thereby apportion all rights in the goods to the consumer,[65] French,[66] Bulgarian, Austrian,[67] and German law takes exactly the opposite approach. For example, § 241a of the German Civil Code provides that 'through the delivery of unsolicited goods ... by an undertaking to a consumer... no claim against the latter arises'. That is, although there occurs no change of ownership because the requirements of § 929 are not fulfilled ('Transfer of ownership through agreement and delivery'), § 241a cuts across all the rights of the sender including the claim of vindication [*Vindikationsanspruch*] (§ 985); the owner remains indefinitely cut off from his right to possession of the things.[68] This is a noteworthy exception from the fundamental principle of the absoluteness of ownership—an exception which neither English, nor Portuguese (which affirms a transfer of ownership),[69] nor Hungarian law (which appears to permit a claim of vindication)[70] accept.[71]

goods to the consumer. If he gives them back, he remains free of any liability. This reflects the legal position under Art. 66-4 (2) of the Italian *Real decreto legislativo* 1/2007 of 16 November 2007.

[65] For the United Kingdom, see the Consumer Protection from Unfair Trading Regulations 2008(a), reg. 27A(4) ('The consumer may, as between the consumer and the trader, use, deal with or dispose of the [unsolicited] goods as if they were an unconditional gift to the consumer') and for Ireland see the Sale of Goods and Supply of Services Act 1980, sec. 47(1). Similarly, for Cyprus see the Law on Consumer Contracts Concluded Away from Business Premises of 2000 (L.13(I)/2000), sec. 11(7).

[66] Matters are similar in Belgium and Luxembourg. The rules of these three Romanic legal systems are clear, in harmony with the Directive, that silence is not to be taken as consent by the consumer. As a result, there is no contract of sale and therefore there is no change of ownership from the undertaking to the consumer.

[67] Art. 62(2) of the Bulgarian Consumer Protection Statute. The literal meaning of § 864(2) Austrian Civil Code is, on the other hand, not wholly unambiguous. Sentence 2 says only: 'The receiver is not obliged to store or return the thing, he may also dispose of it.' However, the Austrian literature seems to tend towards the position that a claim in ownership (§ 366 Austrian Civil Code) is excluded by this provision. This is implied *inter alia* from the fact that the consumer is allowed to 'dispose of the thing', which encompasses the right to pass the thing on without giving notice of any third-party property rights (Koziol/Bydlinski/Bollenberger [-*Bollenberger*], ABGB^4, § 864 no. 5). The consumer is permitted, in other words, to ignore any property rights held by the undertaking.

[68] That § 241a German Civil Code also excludes the *Vindikationsanspruch* reflects the intention of the legislature (BT-Drucks. 14/2658 p. 46). The legislature justified its solution on the one hand with the punitive function of the norm and on the other with the argument that a lasting divergence between ownership and control already appears in the case were the *Vindikationsanspruch* is time barred (BT-Drucks. 14/2658 op. cit.; BT-Drucks. 14/2920 p. 14.

[69] The thesis that this leads to a transfer of ownership rests on Art. 13(1) DL 57/2008 (by which the receiver of unsolicited goods may keep them without payment) and on Art. 1316 Portuguese Civil Code (by which the right of ownership can be acquired not only by contract but also by statutory means). One conceivable alternative is a gift which, although invalid, may only be impugned by the consumer (Arts 940 and 287 Portuguese Civil Code; Art. 14(1) DL 57/2008).

[70] The Hungarian rule only excludes counter-performance and agreement by silence by the consumer. From this, one would be permitted to draw the conclusion that vindication subsists. There appears, however, to be no decided cases on this question.

[71] Practical consequences, however, do not seem to flow from these interpretative differences. It is conceivable that the German system would leave the sender of goods the possibility of vindicating his property rights against third parties, to the extent that these acquired the goods from the first receiver and did not acquire ownership in good faith (see Staudinger [-*Gursky*], BGB [2006], § 985 no. 129); the legal position on this question is, however, contentious.

The law of the Netherlands also takes this approach. Art. 7:7(1) of the Netherlands Civil Code envisages that, when goods are sent to a person (not necessarily a consumer) and that person can assume that the goods' delivery is meant to induce him to purchase them, he is entitled to ignore any contrary notice from the sender and to keep them without payment, save only if the delivery took place on some basis attributable to himself. Art. 7:7(2) prohibits the act of sending unsolicited goods to a consumer connected with a demand for payment. The sanction for doing so is that the consumer is allowed to keep the goods.[72] Art. 7:7, however, leaves open the question whether the consumer becomes owner of the goods.[73] The preponderance of the literature tends towards an affirmative answer.[74] The fact that the sender loses any and all claim to delivery of possession can only lead to a loss of ownership.[75] The consumer, on this view, acquires ownership (according to the general rules) through physical transmission [*overdracht*] (Art. 3:84), whereby Art. 7:7 not only stands in as title, but also replaces the real agreement necessary for legal delivery [*levering*].

A second category of exceptions to the fundamental principle of absolute ownership, which rests on the fact that ownership and possession can diverge over long periods of time, is provided by statutes of limitations. True, all Continental legal systems share the view that the claim of vindication (the claim of the owner for delivery of possession against another who holds his property without a legal basis) cannot be separated from ownership—in other words, that this right cannot be alienated by an owner without also alienating the right of ownership. For the Continental jurist, the *action en revendication* is, as noticed above, the expression and content of ownership itself; it is impossible to have one without the other.[76] However, opinions divide on the question whether one must push this manifestation of 'absoluteness' so far that *vindicatio* becomes a right free of any limitations period, which extinguishes only on loss of ownership (especially through acquisitive prescription). German law answers this question in the negative (§ 197(1) No. 1 German Civil Code: time bar after thirty years), as does Greek law (Arts 249 and 251 Greek Civil Code: twenty years). The expiry of the limitations period does not affect ownership relations as such,[77] but enables the possessor to keep the thing. In Sweden, too, where vindication was only introduced by statute in § 3 *Lag (1986:796) om godtrosförvärv av lösöre*, vindication is subject to a statute of limitations with quite a short limitations period of just ten years. 2.15

72 Nieuwenhuis/Stolker/Valk (-*Castermans and Krans*), BW[6], Art. 7:7 no. 3 p. 2591.
73 Asser (-*Hijma*), Bijzondere Overeenkomsten I[7], no. 155.
74 *Castermans and Krans* op. cit. no. 1 p. 2591.
75 *Hijma* op. cit.
76 *Terré and Simler*, Les biens[7], p. 406 no. 520 and *Mazeaud and Chabas*, Biens[8], p. 362 no. 1627. The disposition of the claim for delivery of possession without a contemporaneous transfer of ownership is, besides, impossible for the reason that the claim for delivery of possession accrues expressly, in all legal systems that recognize it, to the owner, that is, the owner *at the relevant time* (e.g. *Carvalho Fernandes*, Lições de direitos reais[2], p. 252). That a claim of vindication might be made only by someone other than the owner (e.g. by an insolvency administrator or an executor) does not change its non-disposability (*Georgiades*, Empragmato Dikaio I, p. 557 no. 4; *Papasteriou*, Empragmato Dikaio II, p. 451 no. 14).
77 See further *Georgiades*, Empragmato Dikaio I, pp. 570–72.

Spanish law distinguishes between moveable and immoveable things. In the case of the former, the *acción reivindicatoria* is subject to a limitations period of just six years (Art. 1962 Spanish Civil Code); this period drops in cases of an uninterrupted possession in good faith to just three years (Art. 1955 Spanish Civil Code). If the claim of vindication is directed towards a unit of land, the general limitations period of thirty years applies (Art. 1963 Spanish Civil Code). Art. 1957 Spanish Civil Code docks this period in certain cases to ten or twenty years, as appropriate.[78] Spanish legal opinion tends heavily towards the view that the limitation of a claim of vindication is to be distinguished clearly from acquisitive prescription and has an autonomous, parallel role.[79] Under Art. 223 Polish Civil Code, a limitations period applies to causes of action regarding moveable, but not immoveable, things.

2.16 In the Netherlands, on the other hand, the principle of 'acquisition through extinctive lapse of time' [*verkrijging door extinctieve verjaring*] governs. The claim of vindication is extinguished through the passage of time; the right of ownership passes to the possessor (Art. 3:105 Netherlands Civil Code).[80] This regime applies to all goods (i.e. goods [*goederen*], which includes all 'rights in assets' [*vermogensrechten*] and 'things' [*zaken*]); the limitations period is, generally, twenty years (Art. 3:306 Netherlands Civil Code).[81] A lasting divergence of ownership and possession is also prevented by Portuguese law—albeit via another interpretative approach. Under Art. 1313 Portuguese Civil Code 'vindication expires through the passage of time'. This is viewed in Portugal as a 'logical' consequence of the fact that the right of ownership itself (the basic right from which the claim for delivery of possession flows) is not subject to any temporal limitations. Therefore, an extinction of ownership and vindication comes about, as Art. 1313 Portuguese Civil Code itself provides, only in the case of prescriptive acquisition.[82] In Hungary, Austria,[83] and Italy, the prevailing opininon is that the concept of ownership is incapable of temporal limitation and that, as a result, vindication must be free of any

[78] The law distinguishes between 'absent' and 'present' persons; 'a person is absent who lives for more than one year abroad' (see *O'Callaghan Muñoz*, Código Civil^{6}, p. 2116 (Art. 1958 Spanish Civil Code)).

[79] For an overview of the state of the literature, see *González Poverda*, Acciones protectoras del dominio, p. 40. It is, however, not contentious that in the jurisdiction of Navarra only prescriptive acquisition is possible through the passage of time: Compilation of Navarra (Ley 1/1973, de 1 de Marzo, Fuero Nuevo de Navarra), ley 39.

[80] In the end result, things fall out the same way in England and Ireland. Under sec. 2 of the English Limitation Act 1980 and sec. 11 of the Irish Statute of Limitations 1957, claims of action in tort (including claims in conversion) are time barred after six years. Section 3(2) of the English Act and sec. 12 of the Irish Act make clear that, in case of conversion, the title of the claimant is extinguished after the passage of six years. Claims for the possession of land expire after twelve years (under sec. 15(1) of the Limitation Act 1980 and sec. 13(2) of the Statute of Limitations 1957, respectively).

[81] Prescriptive acquisition does not depend on the good faith of the acquirer. Limited property rights remain unaffected under Art. 3:105 Netherlands Civil Code. They are subject to their own respective limitations periods, after which they expire (Nieuwenhuis/Stolker/Valk [-*Rank-Berenschot*] BW^{6}, Art. 3:105 no. 4; *Brahn and Reehuis*, Zwaartepunten van het vermogensrecht^{9}, nos 245–254 pp. 127–30).

[82] The Portuguese law is built on the model of Art. 948(3) Italian Civil Code (*Pires de Lima and Antunes Varela*, Código Civil Anotado III^{2}, p. 117, Comments 2 and 3 to Art. 1313).

[83] Here, the absence of a limitations period for claims of vindication are derived from the absence of temporal limitations to the right of ownership (§ 1459 Austrian Civil Code) (Schwimann [-*Mader and Janisch*], ABGB VI^{3}, § 1479 no. 2). Prescription is only possible for moveable goods through *de facto* possession in good faith (§§ 1455, 160 Austrian Civil Code) after thirty years of uninterrupted possession (§§ 1468, 1470, 1477 Austrian Civil Code) or, when the possession also has some valid title, after three years (§ 1466 Austrian Civil Code).

limitations period—albeit without prejudice to the acquisition of ownership through others in consequence of prescriptive possession (§ 5:35 Hungarian Civil Code; Art. 948(3) Italian Civil Code). In contradistinction to all other claims, which expire at the latest after thirty years (Art. 2262 Belgian Civil Code, Art. 2262 Luxembourg Civil Code), the *action en revendication* is also unlimited in Belgium, Bulgaria, and France; again, this rule is justified by the ever-present character of ownership.[84] § 100(2) Czech Civil Code [1964] and § 100(2) Slovakian Civil Code (which use identical wording) finally say that all property rights with the exception of ownership expire after a limitations period. So long as the right of ownership subsists, the owner is not in danger of losing the ability to use or protect his right.[85] The drafters of the Czech Civil Code [2014] have retained this position.[86] The Supreme Court has, however, answered the question whether a claim for damages connected with the claim of vindication also partakes of this non-extinguishability in cases where the defendant no longer has the thing in his possession and, for this reason, is unable to give it back. Such a claim in damages is subject to the normal limitations rules.[87]

(4) Loss of Right as a Result of Good Faith Acquisition

Another problem area is the law governing good faith acquisition of another's property. **2.17**
This is the subject of many divergent opinions across the European legal systems, both as regards the fundamental principles and as regards the details. Some of these differences have their origin again in the struggle correctly to understand the principle of absoluteness (effect against all the world) of property rights. The possibility of the good faith acquisition of another's property (in some cases free of encumbrances) results, effectively, in a limitation of the *erga omnes* effect of property rights. The legal policy decision for or against a regime of good faith acquisition is thus always, at the same time, a decision about the content and scope of the principle of absoluteness.

A legal system only maintains the principle of absoluteness without compromise when **2.18**
it insists that no-one can assign more rights than he himself has. Insofar as it permits exceptions to this proposition, it sets limits to the principle of absoluteness. Whether such an exception is accepted openly (in the sense that good faith acquisition is said to flow from a private dealing and therefore as 'derivative') or whether it is hidden by the device of an 'originary' (statutory) acquisition makes a difference in a theoretical, but not

[84] *Mazeaud and Chabas* op. cit. p. 362 no. 1628, also Bulgarian OG 31 December 1966, First Chamber in civil matters, case no. 2704.

[85] *Spáčil*, Ochrana vlastnictví a držy v občanském zákoníku², p. 10. The owner can, however, of course lose his right through prescriptive possession (Švestka [-*Švestka*], Občanský zákoník I², p. 590).

[86] Under § 614 Czech Civil Code [2014] a number of other rights, along with ownership (op. cit. lit. (a)), are removed from the statute of limitations, including the right to the distribution of common property, the right to the removal of a real encumbrance, and the right to an emergency access way. There are special rules for the law of pledges (§ 615 Czech Civil Code [2014]).

[87] Nejvyšší soud České republiky 11 April 2001, 33 Cdo 1221/99, Soubor rozhodnutí NS, C 405.

in any practical sense. In the latter case, it appears—from the postulate of *erga omnes* effect—as if everything were 'in order'. It is, after all, the law (and not a contract) which extinguishes the rights of the person originally entitled and creates new, original rights (free of the rights of third parties) in the person newly entitled,[88] like a phoenix from the ashes. In a derivative acquisition of title, by contrast, all the 'old' property rights are transferred from the erstwhile owner to the new owner. This transfer of rights occurs by an autonomous private act, i.e. by means of a contract. This contract, however, is concluded between the acquirer of title and a person who, as a matter of legal fact, has no authority to deal with the property rights in the thing at all. These rights therefore travel with all the encumbrances they carried at the time of the transfer of title.[89] But, even in a system of derivative acquisition, one who acquires a thing in good faith takes it free of encumbrances only when he acts in good faith—with regards to the rights of the erstwhile owner and with regards to the more limited property rights of others.[90] Whether one construes good faith acquisition as 'derivative' or 'originary' has theoretical relevance but no practical consequences.[91] What is decisive is rather that both systems accept that dealings by a third party, who has control of a thing but no authority over it, can result in the loss of property rights in that thing without the consent of the true rights-holder. In all systems which have developed a law of good faith acquisition, third parties can, at least in the end result, successfully usurp the control of a thing from the true owner and then create a legal position which must, in turn, be respected by all the world (even the erstwhile owner).[92] That, however, is a clear departure from the

[88] *Lasarte Álvarez*, Principios IV[9], p. 24. The term 'originary' acquisition of title does not seem to be used in an identical sense in all European jurisdictions. Staudinger (-*Wiegand*), BGB (2004), § 937 no. 17 thus rightly observes that the terms (in German) '*derivativ*' and '*originär*' are not clearly defined. In Sweden, for example, an acquisition of title is understood to be 'originary' when the thing has not previously belonged to anybody (was ownerless): *Håstad*, Sakrätt[6], p. 43 and *Millqvist*, Sakrättens grunder[5], p. 23.

[89] *Lasarte Álvarez* op. cit. p. 25.

[90] See, e.g. § 936(1) Sentence 1 German Civil Code; Art. 1040 Greek Civil Code and Art. 3:86(2) Netherlands Civil Code.

[91] Conceivable exceptions in Germany include, depending on one's point of view, cases of re-acquisition of a thing through the unentitled person (cf. the following footnote and MünchKomm (-*Oechsler*), BGB VI[5], § 932 no. 69) as well as those provisions of the civil procedure law which refer to a 'successor in title' [*Rechtsnachfolger*] (e.g. § 325 German civil procedure code); cf. Staudinger (-*Wiegand*), BGB (2004), § 932 no. 108 as well as § 937 no. 17. Aside from this, only a system of originary acquisition can 'afford' to treat contracts of sale over things owned by third parties as null and void (e.g. Art. 1599 French Civil Code: '*La vente de la chose d'autrui est nulle*'). And it is only systems that work on a principle of originary acquisition that allow a temporal extension of certain procedures of acquisition. A system of derivative acquisition would, e.g. typically prohibit the good faith acquisition of stolen goods (e.g. § 935(1) German Civil Code). That, however, does not exclude a good faith 'originary' acquisition through prescriptive possession of stolen goods following the passage of the prescriptive period (e.g. under Art. 2276(2) French Civil Code and Art. 78(2) of the Bulgarian Property Act Law [vindication of stolen property subsists only during a period of three years following the time of the theft] and under § 937 German Civil Code [prescriptive acquisition of third party property after ten years of good faith possession [*Eigenbesitz*]; no exception for the prescriptive acquisition of stolen property]).

[92] It is, however, contentious (particularly in Germany) whether the first owner has to accept the legal consequences of the dealings of a third-party interloper, including the acquisition of title in good faith by a new owner, if the latter disposes of the thing *back* to the interloper. This is considered by some authors to be an unsatisfactory situation, particularly when the interloper knew from the beginning that he was unauthorized to deal with the things, or when he became aware in the meantime of his defective title (for an overview of the status of the debate, see *Musielak*, JuS 2010 pp. 377–82). This problem exists, however, independently of the question whether one considers this as a derivative (as in Germany) or as an originary (as under § 367 Austrian Civil Code) acquisition of title. It is debated in Austria, too, whether or not the good faith of the interloper who acquires title back from the good faith acquirer is relevant (against OGH 22 April 1999, SZ 72/72; for *inter alia* Schwimann and Kodek [-Klicka and Reidlinger], *ABGB II*[4], § 367 no. 5).

fundamental principle of the absolute effect of property rights.[93] The law of good faith acquisition necessarily entails that the acquirer, although he contributes to the destruction of the rights of the one originally entitled, acts lawfully.[94] Where one acting lawfully destroys the right of ownership of another,[95] that right is not effective against him.

One could argue that property is, in light of the realities of life, never really protected absolutely. Property rights do nothing to help accidental destruction of the things they protect, for example. This argument, however, falls wide of the mark. The law that permits one to acquire, in good faith, something protected by the property rights of another occasions a loss of right, although the thing itself continues to exist without harm. Property law is distinguished from the law of delict in precisely this point. In cases where the thing is destroyed, the loss of one's rights rests only on factual circumstances. The law of good faith acquisition, in contrast, deprives the 'actual' owner (or holder of some other property right) conclusively of any right to possess the thing, and it does so by fortifying the right of possession in the person acquiring the thing to a right of ownership.[96] This, in turn, occurs to protect the concourse of legal transactions—that is, on a legal policy, and not on a natural, basis.

Against this background it is possible to see how differently the European legal systems position themselves, even in the fundamentals, in relation to the concept of good faith acquisition of title. This legal institution is rejected in relation to moveable things, for example, in Portugal. The exclusion of good faith acquisition of title in moveable goods under Art. 892 and following Portuguese Civil Code[97] is based in the intention to guard the principle of absoluteness,[98] and the possibility of acquiring immoveable property from a third party without good title under Art. 5, Art. 7, and Art. 17(2) of the Portuguese land registry statute is characterized as an exception to this general **2.19**

[93] *Albaladejo*, Derecho civil III(1)[8], p.16; *Georgiades*, Empragmato Dikaio I, pp. 483–4 nos 1–3; *Kousoulas*, Empragmato Dikaio, p. 311; *Papasteriou*, Empragmato Dikaio II, pp. 281–2 nos 4–5; *Vieira*, Direitos reais, p. 311; *Wieling*, Sachenrecht I[2], § 10 p. 358.

[94] Thus it is said, for example in German law, that the rule in § 932 German Civil Code (good faith acquisition of a moveable thing from an unauthorized third-party) excludes the illegality of the conduct of the one acquiring title (Schulze/Dörner/Ebert [-*Schulte-Nölke*] BGB[6], § 932 no. 2; similar *Baur and Stürner*, Sachenrecht[18], § 13 no. 6). If that were different, the acquirer would, even in the case of minor negligence under § 823(1) German Civil Code, be liable in damages for delict, with the result that the newly acquired property would have to be transferred right back *via* § 249 German Civil Code by way of restitution in kind.

[95] As, for example, in the case of damage or destruction of another's property in an emergency situation (e.g. Art 142 Polish Civil Code, § 1037 Czech Civil Code or § 904 German Civil Code; for a comparative overview see *von Bar*, PEL Liab.Dam., Notes III 19–31 under Article 5:202).

[96] The legal history of how the lasting deprivation of an owner's right of possession transformed into an acquisition of title in the person of a good faith possessor is described exactly and very instructively in *Coing*, Europäisches Privatrecht I, p. 296. This development is still recognizable in § 367 Austrian Civil Code. This provision formulates good faith acquisition of title (in the first sentence) primarily as an exclusion of the claim of ownership (i.e. of *Vindikation*) against the *bona fides* acquirer. Only in the second sentence does it provide that the *bona fides* possessor acquires ownership himself.

[97] Under Art. 467 of the Portuguese *Código Comercial*, the sale of another's goods is possible as a matter of the law of obligations, but ownership is not transferred by such a sale; see further *Nóbrega*, Der rechtsgeschäftliche Eigentumserwerb an beweglichen Sachen in Deutschland und Portugal[2], pp. 40–47 and *Menezes Leitão*, Direito das obrigações III[4], p. 92.

[98] On the nullity of a sale of another's goods under Art. 892 Portuguese Civil Code see *Bártolo*, FS Galvão Telles IV, pp. 383, 394, *Hörster*, Zum Erwerb vom Nichtberechtigten im System des Portugiesischen Bürgerlichen Gesetzbuches, pp. 94–7, and *Pietrek*, Konsens über Tradition? chap. 3, A, II.

principle.[99] Latvian law, too, proceeds from the principle that a thing cannot be acquired in good faith through a contract of sale with someone other than its owner (Art. 2010 Latvian Civil Code); the good faith acquisition of title in stolen things is excluded completely (Art. 1003 Latvian Civil Code). Good faith acquisition of title is only possible in an exceptional case, where someone sells and delivers a thing that was given to him on loan, for safe-keeping, as a pledge, or was otherwise entrusted to him; in this case, the true owner can sue the seller, but cannot demand delivery from the purchaser (Art. 1065 Latvian Civil Code). The Czech Civil Code[100] also based its approach historically[101] on the principle that *nemo ad alium plus iuris transferre potest, quam ipse haberet* (i.e. that no-one can transfer a greater right than he himself has). One could not acquire ownership from one who was not the owner. In a legal transaction with a person without title one could only obtain possession. This legal status, however, only entitled one to the hope that it would (by way of prescription) one day be fortified into ownership.[102]

2.20 The common law does not allow good faith acquisition of title as a matter of fundamental principle, either. Though the common law generally considers talk of 'absolute property rights' unfitting, in *this* context it actually comes much closer to the substantive content of the principle of absoluteness than many Continental legal systems.

The details are relatively complicated. One must, in the first instance, distinguish between good faith unencumbered acquisition and 'real' good faith acquisition of property rights. The primary rule—that so-called 'equitable encumbrances' (i.e. encumbrances on estates in land grounded in the law of equity) are ineffective against a good faith purchaser for value of a 'legal estate'[103]—is not understood as a proposition of the law of good faith acquisition of title. In this constellation, the purchaser is rather seen as getting good title to *land*, in virtue of which both an exception to the *nemo dat*

[99] von Bar (*-de Seabra and Xavier*), Sachenrecht in Europa III, Portugal, p. 347. The possibility of acquiring property rights in immoveable property from someone without title (*aquisição tabular*) is justified as a matter of legal policy in the first instance, however, by the public faith in the Register (*fé pública registal*), not in the good faith (*boa fé*) of the acquirer. It is not concerned so much with the protection of good faith of third parties as with the reliability of the register: *Vieira*, Direitos reais, p. 309; *Oliveira Ascensão*, Direito Civil—Reais[5], p. 376; *Carvalho*, BFD 87 [2011] pp. 1, 3: '*protecção que, independentemente da boa ou da má fé, gozam os terceiros por força do registo*.'

[100] § 446 of the Czech Commercial Code, however, differs (a good faith purchaser can acquire ownership from a non-owner: see further *Švestka and Dvořák*, Občanské právo hmotné[5], p. 313). It must also be noticed that the parties can by agreement make their obligational relationship subject to the commercial code (§ 262 Czech commercial code). (The earlier commercial code was repealed with the passage into force of the new Civil Code).

[101] Under the new civil code the legal situation has changed fundamentally. (§§ 1109–1113 Czech Civil Code [2014]). The new law tends towards the German system.

[102] The law in force until 2014 recognized two exceptions to the general principle that good faith acquisition of title was impossible. They were found in § 161(1) (pledge of a thing by one without title) and § 486 Czech Civil Code [1964] (good faith acquisition of something part of a testamentary estate by an apparent heir). The Czech literature sees in the brief (one year) period of Latvian law (Art. 1023 Latvian Civil Code) an adequate counterpoint to the highly restrictive rules of good faith acquisition (*Krimphove*, Das europäische Sachenrecht, p. 260).

[103] Further, and with reference to *Pilcher v Rawlins* (1872) LR 7 Ch. App. 259, 269 (James LJ), see Megarry and Wade (*-Harpum/Bridge/Dixon*), The Law of Real Property[8], no. 8-005: 'It is a fundamental rule that a purchaser of a legal estate for value without notice is "an absolute, unqualified, unanswerable defence" against the claims of any prior equitable owner or incumbrancer.'

principle and a good faith rule become superfluous. A doctrine of good faith acquisition in the strict sense is therefore only known in the common law systems in some peripheral areas of the law of choses in possession, but not at all in the law of real property (land and property rights bound up with land) nor in the law of choses in action (claims and other assets which can only be realized in the course of a legal action). As a matter of legal policy and legal history, as Lord Denning once observed in *Bishopsgate Motor Finance Corpn v Transport Brakes Ltd*, it has always been a contest between protecting property and protecting certainty of transactions—in the common law, too. The rule that no-one can *give* a better title than he *has* serves the protection of property. The inverse rule (that he who acquires a thing in good faith for value without knowledge of the seller's defective title gets good title) serves the protection of commerce.[104] The common law decides, in most cases, for the protection of property. *Nemo dat quod non habet*. One can only transfer a *property interest* when one has such an interest. However, the common law has sought a pragmatic settlement with the market's need for legal certainty,[105] and in the law of moveable things it has permitted five exceptions to this rule.[106] The first of these is the fundamental principle of ostensible authority under sec. 21 of the Sale of Goods Act 1979 (England and Wales) and sec. 21 of the Sale of Goods Act 1893 (Ireland). If the true owner has created the impression through his own conduct that he has authorized a third party to sell his goods, then one who purchases them from that third party in good faith gets good title to them. This is, according to the statutory formulation, a derivative acquisition; the question does not, however, seem very important given the doctrine of the relativity of title.[107] A further exception from the so-called *nemo dat* principle is found in sec. 2 of the Factors Act 1889 (applicable in England, Wales, and Ireland): someone who gives his goods to a mercantile agent (e.g. as security for a debt) loses his title to a purchaser who takes it from the mercantile agent in the ordinary course of business in ignorance of the true position. The disposition of the goods is valid as if the mercantile agent were expressly authorized to sell them. The purchaser acquires title in a derivative manner. Under sec. 23 of the Sale of Goods Act 1979 (in Ireland sec. 23 of the Sale of Goods Act 1893) 'good title' is transferred when one sells a voidable, but not yet voided, title to a good faith purchaser.[108] Here, too, we are dealing with a derivative acquisition. Another category of cases includes the double sale of the same goods. Under sec. 24 of the Sale of Goods Act 1979 (in Ireland sec. 25(1) of the Sale of Goods Act 1893) in connection with sec. 8 of the Factors Act 1889, the second purchaser of goods (which have already been sold) that

[104] *Bishopsgate Motor Finance Corpn v Transport Brakes Ltd* [1949] 1 KB 322, 336–7: 'In the development of our law, two principles have striven for mastery. The first is for the protection of property: no one can give a better title than he himself possesses. The second is for the protection of commercial transactions: the person who takes in good faith and for value without notice should get a good title.'

[105] *Bridge*, Personal Property Law^3, pp. 166–7.

[106] See further *Worthington*, Personal Property Law, pp. 223–4.

[107] A statutory provision, under which a purchaser acquires 'a good title' is, according *Curtis v Maloney* [1951] 1 KB 736 (CA), to be read such that this title is effective against all the world, which includes the former owner. (The case, however, concerned not s. 21 of the Sale of Goods Act 1979 but sec. 15 of the Bankruptcy and Deed of Arrangements Act 1913.)

[108] See further *Bridge*, Personal Property Law^3, p. 124.

are still in possession of the seller gets good title to them on delivery, provided that he had no notice of the first sale at the time. The disposition has the effect it would have had, had the seller acted on the authority of the owner. Again, we are here concerned with a derivative acquisition of title. Finally, sec. 25(1) of the Sale of Goods Act 1979 (in Ireland, sec. 25(2) of the Sale of Goods Act 1893) in connection with sec. 9 of the Factors Act 1889 deals with the scenario where a purchaser who acquires possession of goods with the consent of the seller has sold them on to other purchasers. If they are unaware of the ownership of the (first) seller, the latter acquire good title in the goods. The disposition has the effect that it would have had, had the seller without title been a mercantile agent who sold the goods with the consent of the true owner. This, again, effects a derivative acquisition of title.

2.21 Most European legal systems, on the other hand, place the interests of commerce noticeably higher. Among them is German law, which, however, resembles English (and e.g. Netherlands[109] and Hungarian[110]) law in following the model of derivative good faith acquisition (at least according to the prevailing view in the literature).[111] One acting in good faith acquires ownership by a private juridical act and not by operation of law, as in the case of prescription, confusion, fixture, or processing. Some authors have found it irritating that the good faith of the acquirer displaces the authority of the disponor under § 932 German Civil Code, that the code itself in §§ 135(2), 161(3) speaks of one 'whose rights derive from an unauthorised person', and that, under § 816(1) Sentence 1, such a disposition is 'effective against the authorised person'.[112] The acquisition unfolds, on the one hand, as the consequence of a juridical act (and to this extent '*derivativ*'). On the other hand, it appears that the right of the new owner does *not* flow from the right of the old owner, but rather from the unauthorized possessor and therefore perhaps *ex lege* and '*originär*'.[113] That, however, does not change the fact that German law stresses not the owner's loss of right against (or irrespective of) his will, but the fact that one acting in good faith acquires his right as the result of an effective juridical act.[114] Other legal systems differ on precisely this point, namely those systems which treat good faith acquisition as the acquisition of a right by operation of law. Where they remain strictly consistent, they stick to the rule that a contract of sale

[109] The national literature suggests that Art. 3:86(1) Netherlands Civil Code (protection against inadequate authority of the disponor) only applies in the case of 'transfer' of rights in things (Pitlo [-*Reehuis and Heisterkamp*], Goederenrecht[12], no. 94 p. 64, fn. 5). Art. 3:86(2) Netherlands Civil Code (extinction of third party rights) speaks for a derivative acquisition of title.

[110] Arguing for derivative acquisition see EBH 1999/13 (Legf. Bír. 1999/1, Pfv.V.23.728/1996. sz). Arguing for originary acquisition see *Menyhárd*, Dologi jog, p. 300 and Faber and Lurger (-*Szilágyi*), National Reports III, Hungary, pp. 614–18.

[111] In this sense see e.g. *Prütting*, Sachenrecht[35], § 35 VIII no. 441.

[112] See e.g. *Hübner*, Der Rechtsverlust im Mobiliarsachenrecht, p. 46 and *Sohm Hölder/Strohal*, Drei Beiträge zum bürgerlichen Recht, p. 51.

[113] For an overview of the debate see Staudinger (-*Wiegand*), BGB (2004), commentary to §§ 932–936 no. 40.

[114] Staudinger (-*Gursky*), BGB (2008), § 892 no. 11 rightly opines that characterization as derivative or originary depends, in the last instance, on which aspect one chooses to emphasize (i.e. 'expropriation' of the old owner *versus* acquisition by the new owner as a consequence of a private juridical act).

(which is generally effective to transfer ownership) concluded over the goods of another is simply null and void.[115]

Finally, those legal systems in Europe that treat the good faith acquisition of title as a combination of statutory loss of ownership and statutory acquisition of ownership can claim to have stipulated the content of ownership only, and to have left the absoluteness principle *per se* unaffected. This does not, however, change anything of the actual point—that an owner, even in a system that provides for the good faith acquisition of 'originary' title, loses his property without his consent. **2.22**

Greek legal doctrine interprets Arts 1036–1039 Greek Civil Code (acquisition of a moveable thing by a non-owner) as a stipulation of the content of ownership, along with numerous other provisions which enable the good faith acquisition of another's rights.[116] Good faith acquisition is said to be a 'primary' acquisition just like cases of processing (Art. 1061 Greek Civil Code) or prescription (Art. 1041 and following Greek Civil Code).[117] The former owner loses his right without his consent, the good faith acquirer gets a new one by force of law. Czech legal doctrine interprets good faith acquisition as a primary acquisition of title, too, insofar as Czech law permits it at all.[118] Things are viewed the same way in Bulgaria, in Poland,[119] and in Austria. The good faith acquisition of things belonging to third parties, it is said, is only comprehensible as an originary acquisition of title because the non-owning disponor cannot transfer any right of ownership at all.[120] The central rule governing good faith acquisition of title in moveable physical goods (§ 367 Austrian Civil Code) formulates, on the face

[115] This is the legal position under Art. 892 Portuguese Civil Code; Art. 1599 of the French, Belgian, and Luxembourgish Civil Codes, and under § 39 Slovakian Civil Code (nullity because the juridical act is substantively inconsistent with the law). The Spanish cases, however—an express statutory provision is lacking—accept that a contract of sale over a thing owned by a third party can be valid as a matter of the law of obligations, insofar as the thing has not been lost by its true owner (TS 14 April 2000, RAJ 2000 no. 3356 p. 5313; TS 11 October 2006, RAJ 2006 no. 6693 p. 14649). Under Art. 1478 Italian Civil Code, too, the sale of a thing belonging to another is obligationally valid as a matter of basic principle (*Bianca*, La vendita e la permuta[2], pp. 718–23). A purchaser who does not know that he is purchasing the property of a third party can, however (as in Spain) demand the immediate termination of the contract of sale (Cass. 21 March 1987, no. 2827, Mass. Giur. it. 1987, Vendita, no. 47 p. 4217; Cass. 18 February 1986, no. 960, Mass. Giur. it. 1986, Vendita, no. 44 p. 4087; Cass. 12 March 1984, no. 1694, Arch. civ. 1985 p. 366) (Art. 1479(1) Italian Civil Code; *risoluzione*). In both legal systems, the contract can be avoided by the seller to the extent that only the buyer knows that it is concerned with the property of a third party (TS 11 October 2006 op. cit.; Art. 1429 no. 2 Italian Civil Code; *errore sulle qualità giuridiche della prestazione*). The highest court in Hungary now deems the sale of another's property as obligationally valid: EBH 1999/96, Legf. Bír. 1999/2; EBH 2003/867, Legf. Bír. 2003/1; see *Kisfaludi*, in Vékás (ed.), Szakértői Javaslat az új Polgári Törvénykönyv tervezetéhez, p. 869. The position in the old law of Romania reflected that in Italy and Spain; Art. 1599 French Civil Code was not adopted in Romanian law (see further *Stănciulescu*, Drept Civil, pp. 41-43). In Art. 1683(1) of the new Romanian Civil Code it is now expressly provided that a contract of sale over the property of another is valid. That also reflects the legal position in Bulgaria (Art. 189(1) Sentence 1 of the Bulgarian statute on obligational relationships and contracts. In Poland, the purchase of a thing from one without title is treated as valid when the purchaser acts in good faith.

[116] *Triantos*, AK, p. 1212 no. 3; *Papasteriou*, Empragmato Dikaio II, pp. 27–9; *Georgiades*, Empragmato Dikaio I, pp. 271–2 no. 8; CFI Florina 98/2002, Arm. 2003 p. 1593; Areopag 289/1974, NoB 22 (1974) p. 1279; CA Thessaloniki 235/2000, Arm. 2001 p. 476. *Contra* (derivative acquisition) *Filios*, Empragmato Dikaio[3], p. 146.

[117] *Georgiades* op. cit. p. 56 no. 4; *Papasteriou* op. cit. pp. 176–7 nos 2–3.

[118] *Švestka and Dvořák*, Občanské právo hmotné[5], p. 309.

[119] *Stavrou*, Veshtno pravo, p. 662; Radwański and Dybowski (-*Stelmachowski*), System Prawa Prywatnego III[2], p. 318 no. 7.

[120] *Iro*, Sachenrecht[4], no. 6/45; Koziol and Welser (-*Kletečka*), Bürgerliches Recht I[13], p. 332.

of it, a limitation of *Vindikation* ('The claim of ownership … is to be rejected when …') and with this a clear exception to the principle of absoluteness; only in the second sentence of this provision is it said that the acquirer also becomes owner of the thing. In France (Art. 2276 French Civil Code) and Belgium (Art. 2279 Belgian Civil Code), '*en fait de meubles, la possession vaut titre*'. Possession stands in place of a void contract of sale (Art. 1599 French Civil Code) from which title would have followed in any other case (i.e. when the seller had sold his own property instead of someone else's). Both provisions apply only for those physical objects in which ownership can be transferred without formality or publicity.[121] They bring about the state of affairs that ownership passes *a non domino* immediately one obtains good faith possession. Possession grants the possessor a *new* title, which has nothing to do with the title of the old owner and therefore is not affected by its *vices* (defects).[122] In Italy, too, *possesso di buona fede vale titolo*:

> The disponee of moveable things, to whom the things have been alienated by one who is not their owner, acquires ownership by means of possession insofar as he is *bona fide* at the time of hand-over and a legal title appropriate for the transfer of ownership is presented.' (Art. 1153 Italian Civil Code)

The good faith possessor of a non-registered moveable thing becomes owner, in the case of a formally valid process of acquisition (such as sale), immediately upon obtaining possession.[123] This is not a case of prescriptive possession, but rather an independent form of *acquisto a titolo originario* (in contrast to an *acquisto a titolo derivativo*).[124] Art. 464(1) of the Spanish Civil Code, finally, deems 'possession of moveable goods acquired in good faith' to be 'equal to title'. Special rules apply to things stolen or otherwise lost.[125] They can be acquired by a good faith possessor only *ex lege* (through prescription); that 'normal' good faith acquisition under Art. 464(1) Spanish Civil Code is *ex lege* is, apparently, not discussed but would seem to follow. Some special rules apply, however, in the law of immoveable property. One who acquires immoveable property in good faith and for value, from a person authorized to deal with it in the land registry, is protected in case that title does not actually belong to that person (Art. 34 of the Spanish *Ley Hipotecaria*). The Spanish system of good faith acquisition of title, therefore, approaches the French model in the case of moveable property and, to a certain extent at least,[126] the German model in the case of immoveable property.[127]

[121] So, for e.g. not for ships and aeroplanes: *Carbonnier*, Droit civil II, p. 1869 no. 889.

[122] *Terré and Simler*, Les biens[7], p. 339 no. 425; *Carbonnier* op. cit. p. 1873 no. 892.

[123] *Mengoni*, Gli acquisti «a non domino»[3], pp. 128–30; Schlesinger (-*Argiroffi*), Codice civile, Arts 1153–1157 pp. 53 and 57–62.

[124] *Relazione ministeriale* al codice civile no. 543; Grundmann and Zaccaria (-*Troiano*), Einführung in das italienische Recht, pp. 294–5.

[125] See further *Díez-Picazo and Gullón*, Sistema de Derecho Civil III(1)[8], p. 191.

[126] Art. 32 *Ley Hipotecaria*, which concerns the double sale of immoveable property, stands however again in the tradition of French law: *Saborido Sánchez*, Reflexiones sobre el tercero hipotecario, p. 97.

[127] *Saborido Sánchez* op. cit.

(5) Relativity of Title, Relative Possession, and Relative Ownership

The Continental systems express 'their' conceptual definition of ownership such that an owner can deal with his property as he will (within the limits set by the law and without prejudice to the rights of others); he can therefore exclude every other person from every type of interference with his things. Ownership is not only an everlasting right and a right that is fundamentally the same regardless of its object; it also exists against *everyone*, and ownership means the same to everyone. To speak of 'relative ownership' appears, in the system of the civil law, as a contradiction in terms. The civilian definition of ownership has no (or nearly no) room for the idea that one and the same thing belongs to A *vis-à-vis* X and to B *vis-à-vis* Y. One is either 'owner' of a thing against all the world, with the same rights and powers, or one is not its owner at all;[128] the same applies to all the other property rights besides ownership, as well.[129] The property laws of England and Ireland, on the other hand, choose a different point of departure (and with it another emphasis for their definition of 'ownership'). Their lynchpin is not an all-encompassing and therefore 'absolute' right of ownership, but rather the best 'relative' right of ownership between the parties to a dispute. The question of 'absolute' ownership (and thus of the absolute owner) remains, to a certain extent, external to the solution of concrete cases; one rather verifies *who between the parties* is to be regarded as the owner in any given case. Everything else is supposed to be an academic, practically irrelevant, problem. This conceptual approach is in turn possible because the preponderance of property law analysis[130] centres instead on the right of possession of the thing.[131] Such a right of possession is called 'title'. Possession already grants a kind of title.[132] That is the control of things exercised in *animo domini*.[133] Who possesses a thing as his own, that is with the will to possess it and to exclude all others from controlling it, has a title which ranks already as a property right.[134] Conversely, a **2.23**

[128] e.g. *Baur and Stürner*, Sachenrecht[18], § 4 no. 7.

[129] One can observe a (very rare) division of the right of usufruct in, for example, § 157 Hungarian Civil Code [1959] under which the holder of the right of usufruct 'can hold, use, and take the fruits of the thing' (Sentence 1) but the owner can, nevertheless, during the subsistence of the usufruct, 'exercise the rights of possession, use, and taking of fruits … insofar as the holder of the usufruct does not make use of these rights'. Relative to the owner, the right of usufruct has a different content to that which it has against 'the rest of the world'. See *Menyhárd*, Dologi jog[2], pp. 342–3. The Hungarian Civil Code [2014] has abolished this peculiarity of its predecessor.

[130] Incorporeal hereditaments, in particular, belong to the category of legal relationships of a proprietary nature which do no rest on possession, according to the common law. Incorporeal hereditaments are rights in incorporeal objects which originally fell under the rules of succession governing land.

[131] *Clarke and Kohler*, Property Law, pp. 259–60.

[132] Admittedly, English law has 'never worked out a completely logical and exhaustive definition of possession': Earl Jowitt in *United States of America* v *Dollfus Mieg et Cie SA* [1952] AC 582.

[133] Lord Campbell CJ in *Jeffries v Great Western Railway Co* (1856) 5 E & B 802, 805; 119 ER 680 ('against a wrongdoer possession is title'). See further *Bell*, Modern Law of Personal Property, p. 77 and *Clarke and Kohler* op. cit. p. 260 (Possession provides a *prima facie* evidence of title. Who can establish possession is presumed to be owner).

[134] A certain circularity reposes in this notion. The question who is a thing's 'owner' is, ultimately, answered with the proposition that *everyone* who wants to be its owner (even a thief!) can, by obtaining possession with a pretention of ownership, become its owner 'a little bit', albeit a worse or weaker 'owner'.

thing is not 'property' (or, what is the same, is not an object of property rights) so long as it has not been possessed (with intent). For this, the thing only need have stood in the possession of some person under a claim of ownership at the beginning of its life as an object of legal transactions. From that point, non-possessory titles can arise as well. One can, in other words, not only possess a thing without title (in the case of possession of a thing with recognition of the right of another in it), but one can also have title without possession[135] (factual control of the object) without derogating from the characterization of that right as one of 'property'. One who has been sold or gifted a thing thus also has a title in it, even when it is not yet[136] (or is no longer) in his possession. Different persons can thus have categorically similar titles in one and the same thing. This, in turn, gives rise to the problem of weighing the respective titles[137]—which explains the manner of speaking of relativity of title. He who can establish a longer claim of title has the better title. The further an unbroken chain of title can be followed into the past, the better is the current title that rests on it.[138] The title of the purchaser of a thing (or of the recipient of a gift) extends to the spans of time for which the immediate and the previous sellers each held the title, which they finally passed to him.[139] However, the purchaser cannot generally, by reason of the general exclusion of good faith acquisition of title, acquire a better title than the seller had. A thief has a particularly weak or 'bad' title; his title has no chain, it only rests on his usurpation of control without any claim of right.

2.24 The practical relevance of the doctrine of the relativity of title and, with it, the relativity of 'property' itself, appears most clearly when possession and contractually-derived title diverge. Take the following example. Assume that A is the 'owner' of a painting (i.e. the person acknowledged to have possession and the best title in the relevant bilateral relationship). A gifts and delivers it to B. B sells the painting to C, but does not deliver it to him, instead giving it back to A for the purposes of an art exhibition. After A receives the painting, he sells it of his own account to X. X sells the painting to Y, but before X can deliver it, it is stolen from him by Z. If one now asks in which relationship the parties' titles stand to each other, a complex, many-layered picture emerges. A has no title at all anymore. His original title (acquired some time from an earlier possessor) was transferred to B. By taking possession of the painting for the exhibition,

[135] The absence of a property law title, however, does not mean that the lessor or borrower of a moveable thing cannot claim in the torts of trespass and conversion as the bailees of a thing. Rather the opposite is the case; see e.g. *Lawson and Rudden*, The Law of Property^3, p. 116 and *Bridge*, Personal Property Law^3, p. 52.

[136] Delivery of the thing is not required. Under sec. 18, rule 1 Sale of Goods Act 1979, the basic rule provides that, so long as the parties have not otherwise agreed, the title to specific goods passes to the purchaser upon execution of the contract—even when the parties have postponed the date of payment or delivery (or both) to a later date.

[137] See (among others) *Goode*, Commercial Law^3, pp. 52–4 (A person's 'interest' in an object of value traces the scope of the rights which he can enforce against others, but not necessarily against *all* others. The intensity of one's interest *vis-à-vis* others is measured according to their respective titles).

[138] *Clarke and Kohler*, Property Law, p. 391.

[139] Ibid. p. 384.

A got only bare possession without any title. Only by disposing of the painting to X did A, of his own motion as it were, stake a (new) claim to possession-as-owner—which title he gave, in the same instant, to X. In a traditional common law claim against Z, however, A would have prevailed: Z would not have been able to rely, in his defence, on the fact that another (the buyer X) had a better title than A, and that Z would have had to yield to A's original title (the one gifted to B).[140] The intervention of the legislature with sec. 8 of the Torts (Interference with Goods) Act 1977, however, changed this position; in a dispute between A and Z, only the latter would have a title (based on his own possession-as-owner). Z has a right, and A has no right anymore. In a dispute with X and Y, however, Z would have a weaker title. X and Y derive their title from a longer chain of possession. This chain reaches to the point in time where A (whether in good faith or bad) founded possession-as-owner through disposition to X. If it came to a dispute over the painting between X and Y, Y would have the better right; his chain of title is one link longer. Y's title is, however, weaker than that of B and C. Both B and C could trace their title back through a longer chain because they derived it by way of sale or gift from A, that is from A's original title and not from A's later title created by his usurpation of possession-as-owner from bailment. In the relationship between B and C, C would of course have the better title; he did, after all, purchase the thing from B. Indeed C, of all people in this scenario, would have the relative best title, so long as the transaction between A and X did not, by way of exception, fall under the protection of a good faith acquisition rule. Equally, the question remains open whether there is another person altogether who holds the 'absolutely' best title (for example because A was only ever a thief or a finder); this question is relegated to the periphery of the relations between the six people in our example.[141] That helps, it is said, to purge the subject matter of the legal process. On the other hand, however, legal proceedings are also burdened with additional complications insofar as not everyone who has a title automatically has a cause of action in the relevant property tort. Y, C, and B, for example, would have no claim in trespass against Z;[142] A, B, and X would not be able to

[140] *Clarke and Kohler* op. cit. p. 383.

[141] *Waverley Borough Council v Fletcher* [1996] QB 334 (Auld LJ) at 345 ('[T]he English law of ownership and possession, unlike that of Roman Law, is not a system of identifying absolute entitlement but of priority of entitlement'). See also *Clarke and Kohler* op. cit. (When someone claims to have a certain right in a thing, it is generally sufficient for him to show that his title is better than the title of the person actually contesting the claimed right. It is only seldom necessary to prove an absolute entitlement to the thing.) See further *Gablesfarm Dogs and Cats Home v HMRC* [2008] UKVAT V20519; [2008] STI 1070 (Animal shelter took in free-roaming dogs and cats that citizens delivered to it; for tax purposes this lead to the question whether the later sale of the creatures by the shelter fell under the so-called 0% VAT rules [which provide tax relief for vendors and purchasers] because non-owners, as the tax authority determined, were not in the position to 'donate' ownerless animals or animals owned by unknown third parties. The Tribunal confirmed the tax privilege: the finders of the animals had acquired a title in them; for this reason, they could be gifted to the shelter and for this reason they could be sold free of VAT to families).

[142] Clerk and Lindsell (*-Tettenborn*), Torts[19], no. 17-128 (a claim in trespass requires that the claimant is in possession of the thing at the time of the interference).

enforce their claim in conversion once the fact that they disposed of their titles was adduced.[143]

2.25 Unlike the English and Irish concept of ownership, the Continental approach distinguishes strictly between ownership and possession, and also between ownership and possession-as-owner.[144] That someone 'has' a thing and wants to have it *as his own* does not make him, in this part of the world at least, an owner. But that does not prevent the Continental European legal systems from giving possession a special kind of legal protection[145]—and this, already, demands explanation. Even when one follows the bulk of the Continental legal systems in limiting the concept of possession to possession-as-owner (hiving off possession of another's property [*Detention*]), the question remains what possession in contrast to ownership actually 'is'. Is possession a mere fact, a right, or a combination of both?[146] On the one hand, if possession is conceptualized

[143] sec. 8 Torts (Interference with Goods) Act 1977 provides that the possession of a wrongdoer is only equiparated with title when it cannot be shown that a particular third party has a better right than the party in possession (*Tettenborn* op. cit. no. 17-79).

[144] It does, however, occasionally happen that *Eigenbesitz* assumes the role of *Eigentum*, so to speak. An example is the liability for damages caused by defective buildings. The old codifications tend to burden the owner, while the newer generation of codifications tend to place this burden on occupiers. For a comparative overview see *von Bar*, Common European Law of Torts I, nos 234–235.

[145] See DCFR VIII.-6:201-6:204 ('Protection of mere possession') and VIII.-6:301-6:302 ('Protection of better possession') and the comparative commentary to these Articles.

[146] The legal nature of possession remains contentious in nearly all Continental jurisdictions. For example, in Greece (where Art. 974 Greek Civil Code sets out the distinction between mere possession and possession-as-owner in detail), possession used to be interpreted as a special right (*Georgiades*, Empragmato Dikaio I, p. 141 no. 29), but is now conceived as a legal relationship *sui generis* (*Kousoulas*, Empragmato Dikaio, pp. 183–92; *Papasteriou*, Empragmato Dikaio I, pp. 347–8 no. 75, *Filios*, Empragmato Dikaio^3, pp. 93–4; see further *Spyridakis*, Epitomo nomiko lexiko, p. 248). In Germany (where the term 'possession' [*Besitz*] embraces both possession-as-owner [*Eigenbesitz*] and mere possession of things owned by another [*Fremdbesitz*]) an almost overwhelming literature is concerned with describing its legal nature. To some, *Besitz* appears as a mere fact (e.g. *Wieling*, Sachenrecht I^2, § 3 III a), while most call for it to be categorized as neither a subjective property right, nor as a purely factual circumstance, but instead as a special legal position of its own kind (e.g. Soergel [*-Stadler*], BGB XIV^{13}, Vor § 854 no. 6; for a good overview see Staudinger [*-Bund*], BGB (2007) Vorbem. zu §§ 854 ff no. 36). One cannot surpass Savigny's aphorism that possession is a 'fact and a right' at once (*Stadler* op. cit.). So held the case BGH 21 April 1960, NJW 1960 pp. 1201, 1204, which formulates the proposition that, although possession is admittedly not a right, it is protected against all the world the same as a right. In the Netherlands, possession [*bezit*] is exercised through the creation of a situation of factual control over a thing (Art. 3:113 Netherlands Civil Code). In Italy many opine, in the end result, that 'possession' describes a factual circumstance as well as a right, namely the *ius possessionis*, which guarantees protection from deprivation or disturbance of possession (*Bianca*, Diritto civile VI, p. 715). For France (Art. 2255 French Civil Code) and Belgium (Art. 2228 Belgian Civil Code), possession has been defined as '*la détention ou la jouissance d'une chose ou d'un droit*'. *Possession* is said to be the factual (physical) control (*maîtrise de fait*) of a thing (*Carbonnier*, Droit civil II, p. 1713 no. 780; *Zenati-Castaing and Revet*, Les biens^3, p. 648 no. 441 ['*la possession n'est pas une prérogative juridique mais un pouvoir de fait sur un bien*']; *Cornu*, Droit civil^{12}, p. 477 no. 1126). One distinguishes, however, between *possession pour autrui* and *detention précaire*. Bulgarian law has adopted this system (Art. 68(1) of the Bulgarian Property Act). Possession of another's property (i.e. 'detention') consists of physical control over a thing; the detentor holds it not as his own (Art. 68(2) op. cit.). According to Art. 1252(1) Portuguese Civil Code, possession can be exercised personally or through another. The legal nature of possession is unclear. According to the prevailing opinion, possession is understood as a right, but there is a lack of consensus on the question whether this right is a *direito real* or only a non-proprietary right of use (a *direito de gozo sem natureza real*) (see, e.g. *Oliveira Ascensão*, Direito Civil—Reais^5, pp. 77, 128–32, *Menezes Cordeiro*, Posse^3, pp. 159–64, and *Menezes Leitão*, Direitos reais, pp. 169–71; for the contrary [that possession is a property right] *Vieira*, Direitos reais, pp. 641–56, and *Carvalho Fernandes*, Lições de direitos reais^2, pp. 259–62). The disagreement continues in Spain. The conceptual definition of possession in Spanish law embraces possession of both one's own and others' property (Arts 431 and 432 Spanish Civil Code). For some authors, possession is a mere fact (*de Miguel*, Instituciones de derecho privado II(2), p. 38), for others a provisional (transitory) right (*Díez-Picazo and Gullón*, Sistema de Derecho Civil III(1)^8, p. 89) and for others again a mixture of both (*Lacruz Berdejo*, Elementos III(1)^3, p. 45). § 308 Austrian Civil Code counts possession as a 'real property right' [*dingliches Sachenrecht*]. But, at the same time, it stipulates in § 309 Austrian Civil Code: 'Who has a thing in his power or

as the mere holding of a thing, it is difficult to explain why possession should enjoy independent protection under property law[147] (and not only under delict or criminal law);[148] on the other hand, if possession is characterized as a right, then one (partially) abandons the distinction between ownership and possession as soon as it is established. Every system makes, so to speak, its dogmatic concessions. One system has to live with the strange thesis that a person can acquire a 'piece of ownership'—however small—through theft or fraud; the other has to live with the problem that the legal nature of possession cannot be described coherently in every relationship. Considered functionally, there are many overlaps between the civil law and the common law simply in virtue of the fact that many[149] Civilian legal systems expressly provide a (rebuttable) presumption that the possessor of a thing is also its owner.[150] In the Scandinavian legal systems,

custody is called holder [*Inhaber*]. If the holder of a thing has the will to keep it as his own, he is its possessor [*Besitzer*].' Possession is thus often described as having a double nature, between right and fact, in the Austrian literature (e.g. *Gschnitzer/Faistenberger/Barta/Call/Eccher*, Sachenrecht², p. 6).

147 Matters are even more confusing where so-called 'possessory protection' is expressly provided in the property law section of the relevant codification, but is only guaranteed as against certain persons (namely 'disturbers' subject to special definitions) and not really against all the world. This, and the rule in Art. 1267(1)(d) Portuguese Civil Code, has even led to the development of a doctrinal opinion that possession is a non-proprietary right of use. Under Art. 1267(1)(d), the possessor loses possession through the assumption of possession by another even when this assumption takes place against the will of the first possessor, as long as the new possession persists for at least one year.

148 § 130(2) Slovakian Civil Code, which in turn reflects § 996 Czech Civil Code, goes as far as saying that one entitled to possession 'has the same rights as an owner' in the absence of express statutory provision; 'in particular, he has during the time of his legal possession rights to the fruits and use of the thing'. This spares some owners the difficult burden of proving their ownership and allows them to be satisfied with proving their right to possession. (Švestka [-*Spáčil*], Občanský zákoník I², p. 734).

149 But not in all, and especially not in all Central-Eastern European, legal systems (on the *Code Napoléon* see below n 150). e.g. in the Sloviakian and Czech statute law, one searches in vain for an express provision for a presumption of ownership in favour of the possessor. Such a provision exists neither in the [1964] nor in the [2014] codification. In § 130(2) Slovakian Civil Code one finds a functional equivalent to the extent that the provision affords the possessor basically the same rights as an owner has. *Švestka and Dvořák*, Občanské právo hmotné⁵, p. 273 comment in this that one can 'derive the existence of a property right (above all the right of ownership) in moveable things from their possession (so-called legitimating function of possession). From the factual circumstance of possession, one can conclude a certain subjective right of the possessor in the thing, or, to put it differently: with the factual circumstance [of possession] is traditionally associated a presumption that the possessor has a right in the thing.' Support for this approach is found, at least indirectly, in § 1043(1) Czech Civil Code. There is no express rule in the Polish Civil Code, either, which sets up a presumption of ownership in favour of one in possession. However, Art. 339 Polish Civil Code does presume that he who exercises control over a thing possesses 'as owner'. Possessor-as-owner is, in turn, he who exercises control of the thing as an owner (Art. 336 Polish Civil Code). In Hungary it is said that a presumption of ownership connected with possession is not needed because (i) the procedural legal protection of ownership follows the rules protecting possession anyway, (*Menyhárd*, Dologi jog, p. 294) and (ii) though the courts determine questions on the basis of legal entitlement to possession, the entitlement of a party disturbed in the peaceful possession is presumed (at least in the older literature, in particular *Nizsalovszky*, Magyar magánjog mai érvényében II, p. 145). In the end result, then, a right to possession but not ownership is presumed (*Lenkovics*, A dologi jog vázlata⁷, p. 264; *Menyhárd*, in Vékás (ed.), Szakértői Javaslat az új Polgári Törvénykönyv tervezetéhez, pp. 593–4).

150 See *inter alia* § 1006 German Civil Code; Art. 1153 Italian Civil Code; Arts 3:109 and 3:119(1) Netherlands Civil Code (double presumption: factual control speaks for possession-as-owner, possession-as-owner speaks for ownership, see further Asser [-*Mijnssen/van Velten/Bartels*], Zakenrecht¹⁵, no. 115, p. 154); Art. 1268(1) Portuguese Civil Code; Arts 448 and 466 Spanish Civil Code. Under Art. 69 of the Bulgarian Property Act, having factual control gives rise to a rebuttable presumption of possession-as-owner. § 309 Australian Civil Code distinguishes between the holder [*Inhaber*] and possessor [*Besitzer*] of a thing. The 'possessor' is the one who possesses the thing as his own [*Eigenbesitzer*]; a presumption in § 323 operates in his favour, that his possession rests on a valid title. The presumption of ownership in favour of one who possesses a thing as his own is, however, ruptured by the so-called *acto Publiciana* (§ 372 Austrian Civil Code), because in some cases it presumes the ownership of a claimant without possession, which takes priority over the possession of the defendant. It is contentious in France whether a possession-based presumption of ownership can be read from the text of the *Code Napoléon*. e.g.

this presumption has grown to become the lynchpin of their dogmatic understanding of ownership itself.[151]

2.26 The concept of relativity of title thus allows itself to be placed in relation to several doctrines of the civil law. None of these relations is, however, direct. For example, the discussion in Germany of the possibility of 'relative possession' [*relativer Besitz*] is at most only peripherally related to relativity of title. This discussion is restricted to the question whether two different persons should be considered as possessing the same thing, in exceptional cases, *vis-à-vis* individual third parties.[152] This is argued in situations such as the case where the owner of a shop assigns the business to his employee, and thereby switches social roles with him, such that the erstwhile owner becomes an employee, and thereby an agent with control but no possession, while the erstwhile agent in possession becomes the boss and thereby a genuine possessor *animo domini*. Some authors suggest that, as against third parties who could not perceive this changing of places, the former owner should still be treated as the one in possession, with the consequence that in certain cases debtors of the business should be able to satisfy their obligations (insofar as they pertain to possession) by delivery to him.[153] This result could be achieved on the basis of general principles of ostensible authority; a manipulation of the conceptual definition of possession is unnecessary.[154] Clearer parallels to the doctrine of relativity of title are therefore first encountered in Continental European legal systems that

Carbonnier, Droit civil II, p. 1721 no. 784 denies that such a presumption can be derived from Art. 2276 French Civil Code. It follows, however, from the nature of the matter ('*La présomption n'est pas inscrite dans la loi encore que les tribunaux invoquent parfois à l'appui, en matière mobilière, l'article 2279, al.1* [now Art. 2276]. *Mais elle résulte de la nature des choses*'). Other authors interpret Art. 2276, however, as the basis for such a presumption (e.g. *Bergel/Bruschi/Cimamonti*, Les Biens^2, p. 158 no. 148 and *Reboul-Maupin*, Droit des biens^2, p. 176 no. 299 ['*Selon l'article 2276 al. 1er du Code civil, ladite possession fait présumer... qu'il y a un titre et donc qu'il y a eu un contrat translatif de propriété entre les parties. Il en résulte que le possesseur est présumé propriétaire*']). The situation in Belgium and Luxembourg is different. Art. 2230 Belgian Civil Code (identical to Art. 2256 French Civil Code) gives rise for e.g. for *Hansenne*, Les Biens, p. 167 no. 148 a general presumption that the possessor of a right is also its owner. This is clearly the case in Luxembourg, too, since Tribunal d'arrondissement de Luxembourg 18 March 1931, Pas. luxemb. 13, 1931, p. 531.

[151] See further *Håstad*, Sakrätt^6, p. 51. In Swedish law, things such as agency in possession, necessity, poaching, and retention of ownership fall into a single category. What appears at first blush to be a highly heterogenous collection of legal rules reveals itself, on closer examination, to belong together because in each case we are concerned with a restriction on the presumptive effect of ownership (the presumption of ownership operates neither in favour of an agent in possession of his principal's thing, nor for a thief caught in the deed, nor for the poacher of protected wild animals, nor for someone who has acquired possession of a thing under a reservation of the owner's rights).

[152] Another special problem is presented by § 866 German Civil Code, according to which several persons who possess a thing jointly do not benefit from any protection of possession with respect to the limits of their respective use of the common property. In a case concerning a commercial elevator leased and used in common by the claimant and the defendant, BGH 26 March 1974, BGHZ 62 S. 243, 248, the court confirmed the defendant's liability in delict *vis-à-vis* the claimant. It was thus said that the legal protection of possession is 'relativized' only in the case of a full deprivation of possession, but not in the case of a mere disturbance of possession.

[153] Proponents of the theory of the 'relativity of the concept of possession' (*Schmelzeisen*, AcP 136 [1932] p. 38; *Ernst*, Eigenbesitz und Mobiliarerwerb, pp. 31–2) point in this context to the rule in § 851 German Civil Code ('If the person liable to pay damages for the deprivation of a person or for damage to a moveable thing pays compensation to the person in whose possession the thing was at the time when the deprivation or damage occurred, then by this payment of compensation he is released, even if a third party was the owner of the thing or had another right in the thing, unless he knows of the right of the third party or his lack of knowledge results from gross negligence') and attempt, through a relativization of the concept of possession, to achieve an appropriate level of protection for the obligee.

[154] See, correctly, Staudinger (-*Bund*), BGB (2007), Vorbem. zu §§ 854 ff no. 40.

contain rules governing the so-called 'petitory protection' of possession. The expressed goal of this doctrine is to restore a former possessor into possession of a thing, where his right to possession is better than the person in whose possession the thing currently finds itself.[155] One must, however, reckon with the fact that this legal protection does not necessarily accrue only to the possessor-as-owner, but also to detentors.[156]

An example of such a rule is found in § 1007 German Civil Code. Under § 1007(1) the earlier possessor of a thing can demand delivery from its current possessor, insofar as the latter acted *mala fides* when he acquired possession. Under § 1007(2), the earlier possessor has the same right against the current possessor, even when the latter acted *bona fides* at the time he acquired possession, provided the thing was stolen or otherwise wrongly taken from him. Both claims, however, require under § 1007(3) that the earlier possessor was *bona fides* at the time he acquired possession of the thing, that he did not voluntarily surrender possession at any subsequent point in time, and that the current possessor has no claim (as against the earlier possessor) to possession of the thing. Greek law contains no exact equivalent of § 1007 German Civil Code, but comes to very similar results in the application of Arts 1098, 1110, and 1111 Greek Civil Code. Under Art. 1267(1)(d) Portuguese Civil Code, a possessor loses possession, even against his will, one year after possession is seized in fact by another. This prescriptive period, however, only begins to run when the new possession was seized patently or on notice. Before the prescriptive period expires, the *conflito possessório* between the earlier and the current possessor is decided by reference to the criteria of better possession.[157] Under Art. 1278(3) Portuguese Civil Code, the better possession (*melhor posse*) is the one which rests on a title. If a title is wanting, then the older possession is the better one; if this criterion also fails to decide the matter, then the current possession is the better one. § 5:5(3) Hungarian Civil Code also provides expressly that the possessor enjoys legal protection 'according to his title' against a person from whom he derives his title and, in turn, against a person to whom he surrendered possession for a limited time. To this rule we can add the cases covered by petitionary protection of possession (the so-called action in possession, *birtokper*). § 5:9(3) Hungarian Civil Code sets the rule up that the court should decide on the basis of the better possessory title. The action in possession for this reason is only successful when the claimant has a stronger title than the person who has disturbed his possession.[158] The competing titles are compared to each other.[159] Under Art. 3:125 Netherlands Civil Code, the possessor *animo domini* can, within one year, enforce the same rights of delivery and forbearance from interference as the owner. The claim will be dismissed when the defendant **2.27**

[155] *Vieweg and Werner*, Sachenrecht[4], p. 54; *Sosnitza*, Besitz und Besitzschutz, p. 175.

[156] This is the case, e.g. under § 1007 German Civil Code (*Bund* op. cit. § 861 no. 28); on the basis of English terminology one would also have to say that a non-owner possessor also has a 'title'.

[157] *Vieira*, Direitos reais, p. 631.

[158] *Lenkovics*, A dologi jog vázlata[7], p. 265.

[159] See further *Petrik*, Tulajdonjogunk ma—A dologi jog mai érvényében, p. 311. See also BH 1984/149 (in an action for possession concerning the use of an apartment, a decision could only be made on the basis of a right to possession. For that reason, it was necessary under § 192 Hungarian Civil Code to investigate who had the strongest right and on the basis of which title).

has a better right than the claimant to possession of the good. Art. 76 of the Bulgarian Property Act empowers the detentor and the possessor *animo domini* who has lost factual control of a moveable thing through deception or force to demand the thing back from the one who took it within six months; in the case of land units only the possessor *animo domini* has standing to claim (Art. 75). Austrian law has adopted the Roman law and *ius commune*-based *actio Publiciana*. Someone who cannot not prove their title, but is a lawful, good faith, and true (§ 345 Austrian Civil Code) possessor *animo domini*,[160] is 'deemed to be the true owner in relation to any possessor who can purport no, or only a weaker, title for his possession' (§ 372 clause 2 Austrian Civil Code). The question whether (and if so, to what extent) a one in possession of another's things [*Fremdbesitzer*] may also be pulled into this statutory fiction is contested, but is generally answered positively in the case law.[161] The *actio Publiciana* of § 372 Austrian Civil Code guarantees a 'claim of right from better possession',[162] 'from legal presumed ownership';[163] this is the claim that protects 'better relative right to possession'.[164] It exists, however, despite the fact that possession is actually defined in the Austrian Civil Code as factual and not as a right.[165] Under § 373 Austrian Civil Code, possession is 'weaker' when it is either not in good faith or not lawful. The position of a possessor who cannot identify from whom he acquired possession, or who can only point to a suspicious source, is also weaker. Further, possession acquired for value is generally stronger than possession acquired gratuitously.[166] If these criteria do not provide the answer who has the stronger possession, then the thing remains in the possession of the defendant (§ 374 Austrian Civil Code).[167] The claim under § 372 Austrian Civil Code is, however, never successful against the owner.[168] Whether the *acción publiciana* remains part of the modern Spanish law is sometimes disputed,[169] but is confirmed in the preponderance of the literature.[170] Besides this, a sophisticated protection is found in Art. 464 Spanish Civil Code for an earlier possessor. According to this provision, possession

[160] Austrian law identifies the owner-possessor [*Eigenbesitzer*] as '*Sachbesitzer*' and the non-owner possessor [*Fremdbesitzer*] as '*Rechtbesitzer*' (Koziol and Welser [-*Kletečka*], Bürgerliches Recht I[13], p. 279).

[161] Evidence in Koziol/Bydlinski/Bollenberger (-*Eccher and Riss*), ABGB[4], § 372 no. 3, and *Kletečka* op. cit. p. 280. See in particular OGH 31 January 2006, JBl 2006 p. 790 and OGH 26 January 1949, SZ 22/13 (where the tenant in possession prevails on the sole basis of § 374 Austrian Civil Code).

[162] Rummel (-*Spielbüchler*), ABGB I[3], § 372 no. 1.

[163] Schwimann and Kodek (-*Klicka and Reidlinger*), ABGB II[4], § 372 no. 1, which draws attention to the fact that this presumption cannot be used to determine ownership in court, but is only usable in the course of a claim for delivery or injunction against interference.

[164] *Kletečka* op. cit. p. 278. *Gschnitzer/Faistenberger/Barta/Call/Eccher*, Sachenrecht[2], p. 146 points correctly to the similarities with § 1007 German Civil Code and Arts 934–936 Swiss Civil Code.

[165] *Gschnitzer/Faistenberger/Barta/Call/Eccher* op. cit. p. 4.

[166] This can play a role, in particular, in case of a double sale of land parcels, see OGH 13 December 1990, SZ 63/221 (A first disposed of his land parcel for value to B, then gifted it to C, who was also entered into the land registry (was '*verbüchert*'). B could claim possession from C, as he had acquired it for value and C gratuitously. The claim for delivery includes a claim for correction of the land register; see further *Klicka* op. cit. § 372 no. 1).

[167] One example is the double rental of two good faith tenants (OGH 26 January 1949, SZ 22/13: the tenants' right to possession had the same rank, therefore the tenant who had first taken possession of the thing prevailed).

[168] Not even when the (still) owner had already contracted to sell the thing to the purchaser (*Klicka* op. cit.).

[169] e.g. by *Albaladejo*, Derecho Civil III(1)[8], p. 100. For an overview of the discussion, see *González Poveda*, Acciones protectoras del dominio y de la posesion, p. 296.

[170] e.g. by *Díez-Picazo and Gullón*, Sistema de Derecho Civil III(1)[8], p. 114, who bases his position *inter alia* upon Art. 445 Spanish Civil Code.

of moveable goods acquired in good faith is equal to title. However, one who has lost a moveable thing or has had it taken from him in an unlawful manner, can demand delivery of it from the one in possession. Here, too, we are dealing with an instrument for the recovery of a thing from its present, but less entitled, possessor. This stands on its own feet next to 'possessory claims' (i.e. claims arising out of the infringement of possession only), which must be brought within a year (Art. 460(4) Spanish Civil Code), but which are available to every person in possession (including detentors)[171] and operate independently of title.

The position is different in French, Belgian, and Luxembourgish law. Under Art. 2278 French Civil Code (formerly Art. 2282 French Civil Code), *possession* is '*protégée sans avoir égard au fond du droit, contre le trouble qui l'affecte ou la menace*'. Only this *action possessoire* exists for the protection of (mere) possession or *détention précaire*; the French law of possession does not admit of any *action pétitoire* directed at the recognition of a right and the restitution of the relevant object.[172] The *action possessoire*, which is directed at the reestablishment of *detention* does not depend on any right in the thing,[173] and is limited to immoveable things.[174] The principle in Art. 2278 French Civil Code is confirmed again in Art. 1265 *Nouveau Code de procédure civile* with the words that '*la protection possessoire et le fond du droit ne sont jamais cumulés*[175] [...], *les mesures d'instruction ne peuvent porter sur le fond du droit*.' The judge is only permitted to '*examiner les titres à l'effet de vérifier si les conditions de la protection possessoire sont réunies*.'

As soon as one moves from the plane of *possession* back onto the plane of *ownership*, it becomes even more difficult to find parallels to the notion of relativity of title in the Continental legal systems. Their concept of ownership does not allow that someone can only be a 'bit of an owner'. A non-owner is not even able to claim against a third party for delivery of the thing to the owner; only a joint owner can demand delivery to all joint owners.[176] However, even the doctrine of 'absolute' ownership hits limits here and there. This doctrine has to accommodate the fact that a person can, exceptionally, **2.28**

171 *González Poveda* op. cit. p. 203.

172 *Malaurie and Aynès*, Les biens[3], p. 149 no. 504.

173 Ibid: '*[Les actions possessoires] ont pour seul objet le rétablissement de la possession ou de la détention; elles s'opposent ainsi à l'action pétitoire, par laquelle est réclamée en justice la reconnaissance d'un droit et la restitution de son objet. C'est pourquoi l'action possessoire peut être exercée par une personne dépourvue de droit sur la chose*.'

174 *Terré and Simler*, Les biens[7], p. 172 no. 197.

175 The same rule is found in Art. 1371 of the Belgian *Code judiciare* and in Art. 119 of the Luxembourgish *Nouveau Code de Procédure Civile*.

176 e.g. Art. 209 Polish Civil Code and Arts 1094 and 1116 Greek Civil Code. On the latter see Areopag 8/2001, EllDni 43 (2001) p. 382 and Protodikeio Larissa 187/2004, Arm. 2005 p. 24. It is not, however, as a rule possible for one joint owner to bring a claim for delivery of ownership against the other joint owners. For a nice example see Arrondissementsrechtbank Utrecht 5 February 2003, LJN AF4007. The claimant municipal authority was the owner of a land parcel on which an excavator operator of a contracting firm found a Roman helmet. Under Art. 5:13 Netherlands Civil Code, ownership of such a treasure trove is shared equally between the finder and the owner of the land. The finder sold his share to the defendant. The municipal authority's claim failed. A joint owner not in possession could not proceed by way of vindication against a joint owner in possession. Bulgarian law, on the other hand, permits a claim of vindication between joint owners when the defendant extends his possession *animo domini* over the claimants share without permission (OG 4th Chamber in Civil Matters, 2048/1995; see also Art. 31(1) and (2) of the Bulgarian Property Act).

be seen as an owner relative to another only. Such relative ownership should not, strictly speaking, be permitted as a matter of doctrine, but the reality is always more complicated.

2.29 A first example was already encountered earlier, in the context of the Italian law purchase by instalment with retention of title. A second is found in the law of dispositions with relative invalidity.[177] In German law, §§ 135, 136, and 883(1) German Civil Code contain rules under which a legal dealing, in particular a disposition of property, effects a transfer of the right in question *vis-à-vis* the world at large but not *vis-à-vis* particular individuals. Under §§ 135 and 136, dispositions made against a statutory or administrative prohibition for the protection of certain persons 'is invalid against these persons only'. Under § 883(1), a 'priority notice can be made in the Land Registry to secure a claim to the grant or cancellation of a right in a land unit'. Such an entry has the consequence under § 883(2) that a 'disposition made, after the registration of the priority notice, is ineffective to the extent that it would defeat or adversely affect the claim'. If a transfer of ownership occurs against the terms of the priority notice, an extraordinary ownership position necessarily arises.[178] For example, if V sells a land parcel to K and a priority notice is entered in favour of K to secure his right to the transfer of ownership, then according to the literal meaning of the statutory text a transfer of the land unit (against the terms of the notice) by V to X would be invalid relative to K (and only relative to K) insofar (and *only* insofar) as it would defeat V's claim to the transfer for ownership. V is, accordingly, still 'owner' relative to K as far as the legal ability to give K ownership in the land unit is concerned. That is, however, all that V still has. He could not, for example, answer either Z or K's demand to grant a mortgage over their land unit to their (i.e. either Z or K's) benefit. This right is, in relation to K, already gone over to X, and conversely X, not V, would be liable if K were harmed by a defect with the building on the land unit.[179] Effectively, the ownership position in which V remains in relation to K is not a comprehensive or 'absolute' one any more, rather it consists only in a residue (which does not really deserve the name 'ownership' anymore), being the power to transfer the full rights to a single person—namely K.[180]

177 A peculiar property law situation can also arise in this context under the rules governing so-called simulation, or sham transactions. Under Art. 138(2) Greek Civil Code, an act-in-the-law hidden by a sham transaction is valid when it was willed by the parties and reflects all the requirements for formal validity of such a transaction. Art. 139 adds, however, immediately: that someone who did not know the sham nature of the transaction, and took part in it on this basis, cannot have the invalidity of the transaction used against them. Insofar as Art. 139 applies to property transactions under the principle of abstraction in Greek law, it is conceivable that the *hidden* transaction (e.g. the creation of a pledge) is operative between the parties to the sham, whereas the *sham* transaction is operative with regards to third parties (e.g. a transfer of ownership), such that (e.g.) different people are to be regarded as the owner *vis-à-vis* the creditors of the disponee and the creditors of the disponor respectively.

178 See the extensive presentation, with an overview of a large number of different opinions, in Staudinger (-*Gursky*), BGB (2008), § 883 nos 239–242.

179 Under German law (§ 836(3) German Civil Code), liability for harm caused by the building [*Gebäudehaftung*] applies only to the *Eigenbesitzer*, not the owner [*Eigentümer*].

180 So too *Wieling*, Sachenrecht I^2, § 1 III 5 b and *Gursky* op. cit.; similar MünchKomm (-*Armbrüster*), BGB I(1)^5, § 135 no. 36 and *Mehrtens*, Das gesetzliche Veräußerungsverbot, p. 25. For the case of a disposition with relative invalidity under §§ 135 or 136 German Civil Code, BGH 7 June 1990, NJW 1990 pp. 2459, 2460 opined that the disponor remains vested with the legal power for the purposes of fulfilling his obligations towards the protected person, and to deal with the thing for their benefit. The protected person does not, therefore, have a direct claim

An interesting construction, by which some dogmatic problems associated with priority notices of the German type are avoided, is found in Hungary. In principle, the act of registering a right in the land register is constitutive. The entry (for example) of the right of ownership, however, is effective *ex tunc*, which is to say that it operates from the time that the *application* for registration was made.[181] This flows from § 5:178(4) Hungarian Civil Code. Under this provision, the number of the application is to be entered as a margin note on the date it is submitted. The date of the margin note determines the time of the changed legal position, rather than the date of the registration itself, which might be much later.[182] The notion of relative ownership, however created, is therefore not necessary. The priority notice in Austrian law (§ 438 Austrian Civil Code) is also distinct from the priority notice in German law in certain respects. A person may have a priority notice registered where, although he can produce documentation to show that a transfer of ownership [*Auflassung*] was declared, he cannot produce documentation to show that all the other requirements for registration [*Verbücherung*] have been satisfied, for example because of notarizations, or sufficiently accurate details of the land parcel, or the so-called 'conveyance declaration' [*Aufsandungserklärung*[183]] (§ 32(1)(b) Austrian Land Book Statute) are missing.[184] In Austria, the priority notice is understood as a conditional registration of a change of legal position; similar to Hungary, the (final) registration of the legal change is effective from the time of the priority notice (§ 49 Austrian Land Book Law);[185] this procedure is called *Rechtfertigung* ('legal completion').[186] Until this procedure is complete, all the rights and powers of the erstwhile owner are effective without limitation; from completion, they become ineffective with retrospective effect.[187] Conversely, the beneficiary of the priority notice can only act within the conditions of the *Rechtfertigung*; his acts-in-the-law are only effective from the date of completion, but then with retrospective effect.[188] 2.30

against the disponee for transfer of ownership. Rather, the disponor must first transfer his residual legal powers to the protected person. Only after this has occurred does the protected person have a claim for delivery against the disponee under § 985 German Civil Code.

181 See further Hidasi/Horváth/Köszegi/Bedö (-*Horváth*), Az ingatlanjog nagy kézikönyve, p. 214 and Vékás (-*Menyhárd*), A Polgári Törvénykönyv magyarázatokkal, p. 500.

182 Confirmed *inter alia* in EBH 2006/1508, also published as BH 2007/231, Legf. Bír. Pfv. VI. 21.900/2006, BH 2007/7. In terms of substantive law, this situation also entails that the disponee acquires a kind of expectancy of ownership as a result of the notice (CFI Csongrád, BDT 2000/273).

183 Different from the *Auflassung*, the *Aufsandungserklärung* is an express, formal declaration of intention by the previous registered owner regarding the transfer of rights. It is necessary in order to inscribe the transfer in the land register [*Grundbuch*]. The word '*Aufsandserklärung*' derives from Old German *aufsenden* (lit. sending off, in the sense of giving a thing up or leaving it over, and thus transferring it with a symbolic gesture; see *Gschnitzer/Faistenberger/Barta/Call/Eccher*, Sachenrecht, 7 B III, p. 53).

184 See further Schwimann and Kodek (-*Hinteregger*), ABGB II^4, § 438 no. 3.

185 To be precise, what is decisive is not the time of the entry of the priority notice in the register, but rather the receipt of the application for its entry (this flows from the general rule in §§ 29, 128 of the Austrian Land Book Statute: OGH 22 June 1955, SZ 28/170; Rummel [-*Spielbüchler*], ABGB I^3, § 438 nos 8 and 11).

186 See OGH 22 June 1955 op. cit. and Koziol/Bydlinski/Bollenberger (-*Eccher and Riss*), ABGB^4, § 439 no. 1.

187 *Spielbüchler* op. cit. no. 8.

188 Ibid. § 49(1). Austrian Land Book Statute also puts it succinctly: 'When a priority notice of a right of ownership is entered against a person who has been previously registered as the owner of land, further priority notices can be approved against both the previous owner and the future owner marked in the priority notice, but its legal import depends on whether the priority notice of the right of ownership is justified or not.'

2.31 The German law governing dealings with land units against the terms of a priority notice leads to surprisingly complicated questions of ownership parallel to those raised by the Belgian and French law on the double sale of land parcels.[189] Under Art. 1141 of the Belgian, French, and Luxembourgish Civil Codes,[190] the *bona fides* second purchaser (P2) of a *moveable* thing becomes owner when the seller (S) places him in factual possession of it. The first purchaser (P1) in such a case loses his already-acquired (but non-possessory) ownership;[191] P2 acquires ownership *a non domino.*[192] Art. 1141 follows the principle in Art. 2276 French Civil Code,[193] and is sometimes understood as merely an application of the latter provision.[194] Under Art. 2276, every person who acquires possession of a thing with *animus domini* and in good faith but *a non domino* (i.e. in reliance only on a disposition in his favour as evidence of title) becomes its owner—even when, as in our example, the thing no longer belonged to S at the time when the contract of sale was concluded.[195] P1 was owner for a time, in virtue of an executed contract of sale with S (Art. 1138), but the ownership acquired by P2 through good faith acquisition of possession destroys that of P1. This does not, however, result in an exception to the general principle of the absoluteness of ownership; P1 and P2 are never owner of the thing contemporaneously.[196] Things are more complicated in the case of *land units.* Their disposition is governed by the principle of register publicity. Only when the requirements of registration in a public register have been fulfilled is the transfer of real rights in immoveable property effective against third parties,[197] or more precisely: against such third parties as can claim a competing real right in the immoveable property ('*ceux pouvant prétendre avoir un droit réel concurrent sur l'immeuble*').[198] Thus, if S sells a land parcel to P1 without the contract of sale being registered, P1 becomes owner *vis-à-vis* S (Art. 1138): S cannot rely on the lack of registration in the public register against P1. But if S sells the land parcel later to a *bona fides* P2 and the

[189] For a comparative and historical examination see *Ernst*, in Jakab and Ernst (eds.), Kaufen nach römischem Recht, pp. 83–103.

[190] Similar rules exist in numerous other statutes, e.g. Art. 113 of the Bulgarian Property Law Statute and Art. 1473 Spanish Civil Code (if one and the same thing has been sold to different purchasers, ownership, when it is a moveable thing, is transferred to the person who took possession in good faith. If it is an immoveable thing, ownership goes to the person who was first entered into the land register. If no-one has been so entered, then ownership goes to the person who first took possession of the land parcel in good faith. If no-one has taken possession, then whoever can show the oldest title, so long as that title was given in good faith).

[191] As the *traditio* is not required for the transfer of ownership under French law, V's creditors could not attach the thing already after execution of the contract with K1—not even if the thing was still in V's possession (fundamentally see Cass. civ. 24 June 1845, D.P. 1845 p. 309). K1's creditors, on the other hand, would have priority in the case that they took a pledge on the from V before it was handed over to K2 (*Terré and Simler*, Les biens^7, p. 326 fn. 3).

[192] *Larroumet*, Les biens^5, p. 228 no. 402.

[193] Earlier Art. 2279 French Civil Code (and still in the Civil Codes of Belgium and Luxembourg).

[194] See further *Jourdain*, Les biens, p. 504, who, however, also opines that the question (whether Art. 1141 French Civil Code is a case for the application of Art. 2276 or whether both provisions as resting on the same principle) is of only academic interest.

[195] *Jourdain* op. cit.

[196] *Terré and Simler* op. cit. p. 326 no. 409.

[197] *Larroumet* op. cit. p. 222 no. 389 ('*La publicité foncière, qui ne produit aucun effet dans les rapports des parties à un contrat translatif ou constitutif de droit réel immobilier, est indispensable pour permettre à celui auquel un droit réel a été transféré ou constitué de l'opposer aux tiers, c'est-à-dire à tous ceux pouvant prétendre avoir un droit réel concurrent sur l'immeuble*').

[198] Cass. civ. 8 April 1999, R.J.D.A. 1999 no. 739.

latter registers 'his' contract of sale, then P2 acquires ownership on registration. The transfer of ownership from S to P1 thus only gives rise to rights of ownership *inter partes* in relation to S,[199] but does not cause that P1 should also be seen as owner *vis-à-vis* P2. Ownership of land parcels that only rests on the basis of Art. 1138 (i.e. without publicity), thus appears as merely relative ownership.[200] Such ownership cannot, under Art. 30(1) of the French *Décret n° 55-22 du 4 janvier 1955 portant réforme de la publicité foncière* be enforced against third parties who have acquired ownership in the same land parcel from the same seller on the basis of publicly registerable and duly registered legal processes. The right first publicly registered has priority over the right later registered, even if the latter right rest on an older title. This is, however, only superficially parallel to the rule for moveable things under Art. 1141. One could argue that publicity (registration in a public register and possession, respectively) is a prerequisite for *erga omnes* effect. But Art. 1141 (together with Art. 2276) has the task of curing the defects of *a non domino* acquisition. P2 is not only secure against claims by P1 for delivery of possession, but himself becomes owner against all the world—even when S himself never was.[201] In matters concerning land parcels, on the other hand, publicity is only designed to give *erga omnes* effect to transfers of real rights, *not* to cure the defective authority of a disponor. Under Art. 3 of the *Décret n° 55-22 du 4 janvier 1955 portant réforme de la publicité foncière*, in fact, publicly registerable legal processes are only allowed to be registered if the title of the previous holder was already publicly registered.

(6) Split Ownership: Trust

Ultimately, absolute property means that, while *all* the rights of ownership can, as a unit, be allocated jointly to multiple people at the same point in time, it is not possible to separate the *content* of an owner's legal position and distribute it between more than one person.[202] Under Continental European laws one cannot split ownership—neither temporally, nor by object, nor by content. Exceptions to the congruence of thing and ownership require express statutory provision and a justification in special rights that **2.32**

[199] That does not, however, exclude the *delictual liability* towards third parties of the purchaser of a house whose contract with the seller has not yet been registered: see Cass. civ. 3 March 1964, D. 1964 Jur. 245. The purchaser had just acquired a house in an auction. As the group moved to the living room to effect the sale, the floor collapsed, and the newly minted owner was liable towards those injured. (The fact that the transfer of ownership in this case followed an auction rather than an ordinary contract of sale did not make any difference for the purposes of the law governing compensation for injuries.)

[200] *Planiol/Ripert/Picard*, Les biens[2], p. 653 no. 640 explain: '*Le système de la transcription laisse subsister le principe de la transmission de la propriété par le seul consentement: l'article 1138 n'a pas été abrogé par la loi . . . et la vente est encore, en principe, translative de propriété par elle-même; seulement l'application de cet article, au lieu d'être absolue, n'est plus que partielle: il ne régit plus toutes les personnes que la vente intéresse. Il y a certaines personnes . . . qui auront le droit de méconnaître la vente si elle n'a pas été rendue publique et à l'égard desquelles le vendeur n'aura pas cessé d'être propriétaire. . . . Pour ces personnes, mais pour elles seulement, les choses doivent se passer comme si cet acte tenu secret n'avait pas été fait. En d'autres termes, le défaut de transcription entraîne une inefficacité simplement relative du titre non transcrit.*'

[201] *Jourdain* op. cit. p. 505.

[202] See *Mijnsen/van Velten/Bartels* op. cit. no. 19; *Baur and Stürner*, Sachenrecht[18], § 4 no. 7; *Lenkovics*, A dologi jog vázlata[7], p. 23; *Terré and Simler*, Les biens[7], p. 138 no. 144, and *Hansenne*, Les Biens, pp. 584–5 no. 632.

are, for their part, personal and non-separable, such as apartment ownership or a customary law of heritable leases. Outside of such special regimes, there is no ownership in part of a thing or ownership limited to certain dealings with a thing.[203] In this part of the world, ownership is, by definition, the most comprehensive right that a person can have in a thing. For this reason, it is not possible to appoint, *uno actu*, A as the permanent owner of a thing from 0:00 to 12:00 and B as the permanent owner from 12:00 to 24:00; A and B could only approximate this relationship by transferring full ownership back and forth between each other every day. Likewise, A cannot own all of the olive trees on an agricultural holding and B own the fruit trees on it;[204] nor can A be given the exclusive power to grant pledges over a thing and B the exclusive power to grant rights of way over it; the owner can only authorise one other person to undertake certain actions

[203] One cannot, e.g. hive off from ownership the right of disposal, or dispose of a thing on conditions effective against third parties (such as that the disponee must keep the thing for himself and not dispose of it further). Exceptions to this fundamental principle are extremely seldom outside the context of the law of gifts, inheritance law, and family law. One example is found in *Ley 482 Compilación de Navarra* (*Ley 1/1973, de 1 de marzo, por la que se aprueba la Compilación del Derecho Civil Foral de Navarra*). Under this law, prohibitions on disposition can be entered into the land register for a fee, which gives them real effect for four years. A somewhat concerning special form of ownership has, however, developed within the German-influenced legal conceptions of property in security interests. BGH 26 September 2006, BKR 2007 p. 72 opines that ownership as security [*Sicherungseigentum*] is 'not full, unencumbered ownership'. 'Dealings other than outright alienation, for example granting of usufruct, destruction of the security, or taking control of the security by the security holder, are not encompassed by the general power of disposition without special agreement.' This is neither consistent with the *numerus clausus* principle of property law nor with the general concept of ownership in Continental legal systems. The case concerned a bowling alley, which had been transferred to a claimant bank as security for a loan. The borrower installed the bowling alley in restaurant premises leased from the defendant. After the borrower became unable to pay, the defendant exercised its lessor's lien and leased the restaurant, including the bowling alley, to a third party. The unjustified enrichment claim of the bank for a sum of money, based on the defendant's use of the bowling alley, failed on the stated grounds. Although the claimant was owner of the bowling alley, it did not have the right of its use.

[204] This is because, according to all Continental legal systems, such trees are part of the land unit on which they stand. In consequence, it is impossible to alienate a parcel of forest but to retain ownership in the standing trees. Only an obligational right could arise to fell trees, not a property right effective against third parties (OGH 1 October 1980, EvBl 1981/48 [ÖJZ 1981 p. 160]). Only in exceptional cases is it thinkable that property in the plants and property in the land unit in which they are planted could diverge. The textbook example is that of trees ready for sale in a nursery, in which the trees are only sitting on the ground of leased land for a temporally limited reason (waiting for a buyer); see, e.g. § 95(1) Sentence 1 German Civil Code and Art. 955(1) Sentence 1 Greek Civil Code and, on the latter, Thessaloniki Court of Appeal 734/1973, Arm. 27 (1973) p. 686, and Areopag 1376/1978, NoB 26 (1978) p. 1063 (a simple time factor is not dispositive of the question whether a purpose is 'temporally limited', rather, this depends on whether the nature of the purpose is temporally limited; the connection with the land unit could even last for several years). It must also be considered that some European legal systems have created the possibility through special legislative enactments to grant pledges over the fruits of agricultural land parcels, including pledges in the fruits of olive trees, and granting such a security interest is possible even at a time far earlier than the time of harvest; see, again for Greece, Statute 2184/1920 on Agricultural Bonds and the commentary in *Georgiades*, Empragmato Dikaio I, p. 106 no. 27. Greek law recognized, besides this, several property rights before the introduction of the Civil Code which have subsisted, to the extent they had already validly arisen, even though they cannot be created under the new law (old rights under Arts 58–59 of the Introductory Statute to the Greek Civil Code; see further *Georgiades* op. cit. pp. 53–4 nos 20–24). To these also belongs the special property right ('*emphyteuse*') in a plantation, tree, or building which is found on another's land parcel. The separate right of ownership was found in the Civil Code of Crete (Art. 248), of the Ionian Islands (Art. 441), and in that of the island Samos (Art. 512). Besides this, local customary laws also apply. Under Arts 60–63 of the Introductory Statute to the Greek Civil Code, the owner of a land unit has the right to purchase these separate rights for market value (see further Athens Court of Appeal 6811/1985, NoB 34 [1985] p. 230, Areopag 1251/1997, NoB 26 [1997] p. 1039, and Protodikeio Nàfplio 199/1988, NoB 37 [1988] p. 463). On *emphyteuse* see, besides Art. 58 Introductory Statute to the Greek Civil Code (whereby rights of *emphyteuse* on others' land that existed at the time of coming into force would subsist for the future and be governed according to the previous law) and also Areopag 451/2001, NOMOS 304228 (the old separate ownership of a tree would not lead through prescription to the acquisition of ownership of the soil. This is because the possessive intention of the owner of the tree is not directed towards the soil, but towards the tree).

over the thing on his behalf. Even attempts to distinguish, not only for tax law but for property law purposes, between a 'legal' and an 'economic' owner are bound to fail.[205] Ownership in the Latin tradition operates *omnes alios excludendi; duorum vel plurium in solidum esse non potest.*[206]

It is doubtful whether the same could be said of ownership in the English tradition. This has to do with the various possibilities to encumber so-called 'common law property' with 'equitable property', i.e. with rights which have their roots in the law of equity. The most important (but by no means the only)[207] example is provided by the trust. If the agricultural holding in the example above were held by the 'trustee' A 'on trust' for the 'beneficiaries' B and C, then A would hold all of the rights of ownership at common law in the plantation (namely the rights of a 'freeholder'). A could, however, be obliged according to the terms of the trust to manage and harvest the olive trees exclusively in B's interests and the fruit trees exclusively in C's interests. In this way, B would have an 'equitable interest' (only) in the olive trees, and C would have an equitable interest (only) in the fruit trees. Because these equitable interests manifest, for their part, legal consequences for third parties very similar to those of ownership, it can be said (subject to conditions described in more detail presently) that B and C have 'equitable ownership' (or, alternatively, equitable or beneficial 'property') in the relevant class of trees. In this sense, ownership would be horizontally 'stapled' (i.e. between A on the one side and between B and C on the other) and vertically 'divided' (i.e. between B and C). **2.33**

[205] This has been suggested in the Netherlands literature (see *Mijnsen/van Velten/Bartels* op. cit. no. 16; *van Straaten*, WPNR 2011 Nr. 6908 pp. 980–84), but has remained without any palpable success in property law (*Mijnsen/van Velten/Bartels* op. cit. no. 19). HR 5 March 2004, NedJur 2004, no. 316 p. 2705 concerned a case in which a municipal authority had invested a building contractor with so many powers, that it could be described as the 'economic' owner even though the municipal authority remained the 'legal' owner. The contractor developed the land parcel and leased it to G; later, it sold the land parcel to the family V, to whom the municipal authority later transferred ownership. The case turned *inter alia* on the question whether V could rely on Art. 7:226 Netherlands Civil Code (the rule that a sale does not break a lease, but that the lease contract binds the purchaser) against G. The *Hoge Raad* answered in the negative, because 'legal' ownership had been transferred to V only from the municipal authority but not from the landlord. The *economische eigendom* first acquired by V was not 'ownership'. The term 'economic ownership' merely stood for a bundle of obligational rights and duties (HR op. cit. p. 2706). 'By economic ownership' (according to *Stein* in the commentary to the decision at p. 2707) 'is to be understood the position of one who is not, in fact, an owner, but has been given so many powers by way of contractual arrangements with the owner in relation to a particular item of property, that the interests of ownership accrue to him rather than to the owner in relation to increases or decreases in the property's value'.

[206] von Bar (-*Plancker and Pfeifer*), Sachenrecht in Europa IV, Italien, p. 335. See also Czech Nejvyšší soud České republiky 21 May 2003, 22 Cdo 382/2002, Soudní rozhledy 3/2004 (several persons can only own a thing as co-owners in shares. Outside of the regime of co-ownership in shares, it is impossible to acquire ownership of an extant thing without extinguishing the ownership of the previous owner. Two equally valid legal titles in one piece of real property is only conceivable in the form of co-ownership in shares).

[207] Rights under a trust are only one example among many because, as *Bridge* op. cit. p. 11 rightly explains, all property rights recognized by the common law can also be subject to this splitting of ownership, by which one person has mere legal ownership and another the beneficial (or equitable) ownership, such that the latter receives all the material benefits of the object. *Lawson and Rudden*, The Law of Property[3], p. 83 add to this: 'Before the Common Law will enforce rights it often insists that they be created by some particular formality. . . . Equity, however, is wider in its acknowledgement of property rights . . . [I]t will not refuse to recognize transactions simply because they do not comply with strict formality.' In other words, all property rights of the common law could also arise in the system of equity, but not all equitable property rights could arise under the common law system. Only equity 'looks on that as done which ought to be done'.

2.34 The modern trust of the common law jurisdictions developed from the medieval concept of the *use*. To summarize, subordinate land 'owners' in the middle ages developed a particular technique of transferring estates in land to third parties, so as to circumvent laws of escheat and rents due to those higher in the feudal pyramid, but also to remove capital from the reach of creditors. The transferee would receive 'ownership', but only in order to possess it for the transferor. The land unit would go 'to A in the interests of B'. B retained no 'legal estate', and thus no 'property' in the common law conception (according to which custom property was held only by A). But the Court of Chancery recognized in B an equitable or beneficial property in the land B had given away. What began as a merely moral obligation on A towards B transformed into a real legal duty; it would be, so it was said, 'unconscionable' not to respect the mechanism of the *use*. Statutory measures intended to put an end to *uses* in the sixteenth and seventeenth centuries foundered,[208] ironically, on the fact that they did not encompasses a *use* on a *use*. A transfer of freehold land 'unto A and his heirs to the use of B and his heirs to the use of C and his heirs', was not enforceable at common law and under the new statute law, but the Court of Chancery accepted its enforceability *de novo*, as it were, in equity. The nomenclature of 'trust' established itself for this 'second' *use*, and it became common to transfer property 'unto and to the use of B (the trustee) in trust for C (the beneficiary)'.[209] The figure of the trust has remained a fixture of English and Irish law since then, and can now be created ('settled') over legal objects of all kinds (i.e. not only over land). This entails the differentiation of a 'legal' and an 'equitable' estate[210] and is perhaps best defined by Keeton and Sheridan as follows:

> A trust is the relationship which arises wherever a person (called the trustee) is compelled in equity to hold property, whether real or personal, and whether by legal or equitable title, for the benefit of some persons (of whom he may be one and who are termed beneficiaries) for some object permitted by law, in such a way that the real benefit accrues, not to the trustee, but to the beneficiaries or other objects of the trust.[211]

In the modern law, a trust can even arise in certain cases *ex lege*. Such 'constructive trusts' are particularly difficult to define in property law terms. Above all, they overlap with another figure of equity, namely the so-called 'proprietary estoppel'. Both are aimed at the prevention or removal of an unjustified enrichment. Important cases of application include (express or implied) consent by an owner of land which are not binding in virtue of non-compliance with formal requirements. The constructive trust, however, applies in numerous other situations, including enrichment in case of a breach of fiduciary duty (so-called 'secret

[208] The English Statute of Uses 1535 and the Irish Statute of Uses 1634.

[209] On the history of the trust in England and Ireland, see *inter alia Delany*, Equity and the Law of Trusts in Ireland[4], pp. 53 ff.

[210] *Abdul Hameed Sitti Kadija v De Saram* [1946] AC 208 (Ceylon), 217.

[211] *Keeton and Sheridan*, The Law of Trusts[12], p. 3.

profits'), while proprietary estoppel extends the judicial toolkit in the remedial sphere.[212]

Whether one can really argue that 'personally split' ownership arises through the creation of a trust—namely property in the person of the trustee as well as in the person of the beneficiary—depends on how one classifies the latter's rights. At their point of origin, they were (and are) obligational rights, directed towards ensuring that the trustee fulfils his duties, based in the trust relationship, in the administration of the assets in which the common law gives him property. The rights of the beneficiary, however, are bolstered by equity with certain *erga omnes* effects. They, in turn, lend to the beneficiary's rights the character of property rights—but only of *equitable* property rights. Property rights can, namely, not only be transferred 'horizontally' from one person to another, but can also be distinguished 'vertically': every common law property right can also exist or be established as an equitable property right. Such a downstream property right, encumbering the common law right of the trustee, has the beneficiary of a trust. The beneficiary can dispose of his equitable interest *inter vivos* and by testament; he can sell it, pledge it, encumber it, even make it subject to a trust. A beneficiary can, however, only ever enforce his rights against a current or previous trustee. The beneficiary does not become *ex lege* 'owner' of the fruits and other income of the trust; rather, he remains limited to claims for payment against the trustee. The latter first deducts all necessary expenditures and his own fees. The beneficiary has, in other words, no claim to the trust property in kind, but only a claim to an account and payment of the excess. Further, the fact that the beneficiary cannot initiate proceedings against third parties for interference with the trust property (for example through violation of the right of possession or damage to the trust property), but can only act with the involvement of the trustee, speaks against the qualification of the beneficiary's legal position as that of an owner. It is the trustee that must bring the relevant claim;[213] if he refuses to do so, the beneficiary must proceed against the trust assets and join the trustee in the action.[214] At the same time, however, the rights of the beneficiary are never classified only as obligational rights (rights *in personam*). Maitland, for example, could say that the equitable right of the beneficiary 'in ultimate analysis appears to be *ius in personam* (the benefit of an obligation)'; however, it was treated such that 'for practical purposes it has become equivalent to *ius in rem* and is habitually thought of as a kind of ownership'.[215] This equiparation with a true property right is expressed in 2.35

[212] On the relationship between constructive trusts and proprietary estoppel, see further *Pawlowski* (2006) 12 Trusts & Trustees 10.

[213] Who only has equitable ownership of goods cannot make a claim in negligence against another who has, in breach of a duty of care, caused the loss of or damage to the thing, unless he also involves the legal owner as a claimant: *Leigh & Sullivan Ltd v Aliakmon Shipping Co. Ltd (The Aliakmon)* [1986] AC 785 (HL).

[214] Only the legal owner (the trustee) has standing at common law to claim (Parker and Mellows [-*Oakley*], The Modern Law of Trusts[8], p. 802, with reference to *MCivil Code Proceeds v Lehman Brothers International (Europe)* [1998] 4 All ER 675 (CA); see also *Fletcher v Fletcher* (1844) 4 Hare 67; 67 ER 564). The court can instruct the trustee to bring a claim or give the beneficiary leave to proceed for the benefit of the trust and in the name of the trustee (see further *Oakley* op. cit. p. 717 with reference to *Foley v Burnell* (1783) 1 Bro Civil Code 274; 28 ER 1125).

[215] *Maitland*, Selected Essays, pp. 128, 129.

numerous legal provisions. According to recent, but not unproblematic, case law, we should count to these the protection of equitable interests by the tort of negligence.[216] Above all, however, equitable interests are enforceable against every *mala fides* successor in title[217] to a trustee acting in breach of his duties, and against every successor in title who receives trust property gratuitously (even in good faith).

2.36 Some Continental European systems are now making efforts to approach the trust law of the common law tradition in an almost 'experimental' manner. The new Czech Civil Code names, in its catalogue of real rights, both fideicommissary funds (§§ 1448–1474) and the 'administration of others' property' (§§ 1400–1447). Both unite, within themselves, obligational and property rights.[218] Portuguese law recognizes, since the entry into force of DL 352-A/88, a 'trust', or rather *gestão fiduciária*, within the free trade zone of Madeira. The literature speaks of *propriedade fiduciária*, of fiduciary ownership. By this term is meant the legal position of an owner who (usually by agreement rather than *ex lege*) is duty-bound to exercise his rights for a certain purpose in the interests of a third party and, in case that certain conditions occur, to transfer the assets back to that person.[219] Besides this special rule for Madeira, the law of the mainland remains with the general rules of Arts 406(2) and 1306 Portuguese Civil Code, which in effect make it impossible to give *contratos fiduciários* real effects by acts of contractual autonomy.[220] Private autonomy can achieve obligational constructions which imitate the rules of trust law closely,[221] but they do not permit the rights of the beneficiary [*fiduciante*] to be furnished with *erga omnes* effect. They remain limited to their (obligational) effects *vis-à-vis* the fiduciary administrator [*fiduciário*].[222] The situation is the same in Bulgaria, also; the *fiducia cum amico* has only obligational effects.[223] The *fiducia cum creditore*, by

[216] *Shell UK Ltd v Total UK Ltd* [2010] EWCA Civ 180, [2011] QB 86 para. 142 ('[A] duty of care is owed to a beneficial owner of property (just as much as to a legal owner of property) by a defendant, such as Total, who can reasonably foresee that his negligent actions will damage that property'). The justification for this decision stands, however, in apparent tension (which is difficult to resolve) with *Leigh & Sullivan Ltd v Aliakmon Shipping Co Ltd (The Aliakmon)* op. cit. (n 213). *Shell* would presumably have been decided more coherently if the court had used the concept of transferred loss and had said that the trustee could also claim in his own name for the damage suffered by the beneficiaries (see amongst the literature *Turner* (2010) 69 CLJ p. 445 and *Low* (2010) 126 LQR p. 507). The matter was settled out of court after permission to appeal was granted by the UK Supreme Court (http://ukscblog.com/in-the-supreme-court-wc-4-april-2011).

[217] In the case of real estate, the situation is much more complicated. The beneficiaries' position does not 'technically' depend on the *mala fides* of the acquirer, but rather on protective mechanisms specific to land such as the registration of (registerable) rights of beneficiaries (sec. 29 Land Registration Act 2002 in connection with [especially] Schedule 3, para. 2 ['Interests of persons in actual occupation']). The acquirer's position, in turn, depends on the number of trustees making the disposition (sec. 27 Law of Property Act 1925: the purchaser of a legal estate from trustees of land is 'not to be concerned' with the trusts when he makes payment to two or more trustees).

[218] See further Spáčil (*-Pihera*), Občanský zákoník III, p. 1153 and *Švestka/Spáčil/Škárová/Hulmák*, Občanský zákoník I^2, p. 678.

[219] *Pinto Duarte*, Direitos reais^2, p. 161.

[220] *Vaz Tomé and Leite de Campos*, Propriedade fiduciária (trust), p. 280.

[221] *Pais de Vasconcelos*, Contratos atípicos, pp. 272–3.

[222] *Pinto Duarte* op. cit. p. 165. Critical of the view, which they perceive as orthodox in the Portuguese Civil Code, is *Barreto Menezes Cordeiro*, Do trust no direito civil, pp. 1143–4, and *Vaz Tomé and Leite de Campos* op. cit. p. 281. They appeal for the recognition of the trust (they mean, however, the legal position of the beneficiary) on the mainland as an 'atypical' real right.

[223] See further *Stavrou*, Veshtno pravo, p. 563.

which a debtor transfers ownership to his creditor by way of security, is actually invalid (Art. 152 Bulgarian Statute on Obligations and Contracts).

3. The Basis and Limits of Property Rights

Like the law of obligations, the law of property follows its own internal logic. Each area of law rests on different fundamental evaluative judgments. They therefore work with different methods, and only within a delimited frame of reference can their relationship be stated without being forced. It can be said that the law of obligations creates the possibility for private subjects to bind *themselves* to act or forbear from action. It utilizes contracts and factual dealings as the source of these duties. The law of property, on the other hand, creates the possibility for private subjects to bind others to act or forbear from action. It utilizes monopoly rights as the source of this legal ability, that is: property rights. These are 'stem' rights in the sense that they lay the basis for various legal remedies. Both the law of obligations and the law of property limit the duties they create according to their basis, content, and scope, and they both make this step in the interests of the individual concerned as well as the interests of the community in which he lives. In the law of obligations, in the interests of the individual the general rule is that he must only shoulder those burdens to whose creation he (through contractual dealings or delictual behaviour) has contributed, or when he has received a benefit which he should not be allowed to retain without compensation (e.g. because the benefit arose in the course of an unsolicited but beneficial service or because it would constitute an unjustified enrichment). Property law, on the other hand, channels the duty of action or forbearance incumbent on 'the others' towards particular resources specified by property law itself; it limits the (i) types and (ii) contents of the monopoly and 'stem' rights which are possible in relation to these resources, and it also limits the duties that it imposes on third parties. One is not, generally, obliged to perform or forbear from a certain action (i.e. in fulfilment of a promise); one is burdened with a non-specific duty to respect the property rights of one's contemporaries. Even this (relatively moderate) impingement on third parties, however, requires justification according to a higher principle. This is provided by the notion of a common interest in the efficient allocation of resources. Individual subjects are given exclusive rights in specified objects for the benefit, ultimately, of all. 2.37

It follows from the basic principle of the law of obligations that no contract can be accepted which burdens third parties,[224] and it also follows that the law has no reason 2.38

[224] This does not, however, exclude the fact that some rights have a double nature or that they can arise, under the same name, as either obligational or real rights. One example of the first type is the position of a residential tenant in certain legal systems. This is fundamentally of an obligational nature (and embraces, e.g. the obligation to pay rental instalments and to maintain the leased object, which corresponds to the right to use it) but also bears defining characteristics of a property right when the tenant, for example in Czech law (Švestka [-*Spáčil*], Občanský zákoník I^2, p. 677) can enforce his right not only against the landlord but also every other person or (as

to circumscribe the parameters within which obligors and obligees must confine their actions. There is no basis to prohibit hotel contracts only because they do not fit neatly into the categories of contractual relationships recognized by the relevant national law. A hotel contract is not ineffective because it cannot be characterized as a pure lease, as a pure contract for services, or as a pure contract of sale. Property law, on the other hand, allows contracts that burden third parties, namely contracts that in substance transfer or grant rights in a thing. When ownership, for example, is transferred or pledge is made over a thing, someone somewhere has to take cognisance of the new rights-holder and respect his position just as he respected that of the previous rights-holder. The third party, who is not involved in the legal transaction, has no other choice. This, in turn, generally only appears tolerable because (and to the extent) that no-one can, of his own motion or in cooperation with a contractual partner, create new property rights with a greater reach. Everyone must, instead, basically satisfy himself with the tools provided to him by the relevant legal system. When, for example, the applicable law does not recognize hypothecs over automobiles, subjects of that legal system must come to terms with the fact and decide between a pledge and security arrangement involving the transfer of ownership in the collateral to meet their needs, where these are the only alternatives. Two people can bind themselves as they like, as between themselves, because it does not affect anyone else; but they must, in respect of third parties, generally use the instruments prescribed by the legal system. The fact that occasional exceptions to this rule can be found does not change the general principle. If national law abolishes hereditary leases,[225] for example, this legal instrument cannot be revived by anyone within the jurisdiction—at least not with any claim to effect against third parties.

2.39 Obligational duties, especially those created through an intentional act-in-the-law in fulfilment of a promise, do not bind (according to the legal system) when they are based on an improper motive, when they are perceived as disproportionate for want of counter-performance, or when they are prohibited by statute on the basis of a supervening public interest. Property law, on the other hand, underscores the protection of legal transactions. The duty to respect others' property rights is particularly limited in the interests of private legal transactions, for example through rules governing the prohibition of misuse of rights (e.g. in Art. 334 Portuguese Civil Code), through the *ad hoc* 'relativization' of absolute rights, or through the possibility of acquiring the rights of third parties in good faith (i.e. through innocent ignorance, not having to allow them

in Poland: Art: 16(2) Polish UKWH) can even enter it in the land registry. For the same reason, the legal nature of a lease over real property is disputed in Portugal, where the *arrendamento* has been attributed a 'mixed nature' (STJ 27 March 2007, CJ XV (2007-1) p. 146; see further *Garcia*, O arrendamento plural—quadro normativo e natureza jurídica, esp. pp. 362–97). An example of the second type in many legal systems is the right of pre-emption, which, despite an identical name, can be established as either an obligational or a real right. Matters are the same with time sharing; see, e.g. § 481 German Civil Code, which provides that the relevant right of use 'can ... be a real right or another right'.

[225] e.g. Portugal, where it was formerly governed by Arts 1491–1523 Portuguese Civil Code. These provisions have been repealed by DL no. 195-A/76 of 16 March 1976 and DL no. 233/76 of 2 April 1976.

to operate against oneself). The key word in the protection of legal dealings is *publicity*. Rights designed to be enforceable *erga omnes*, especially rights in real estate, should be possible for everyone to recognize. The rights-holder needs more than an instrument that signals the creation of a property right to the general public. In addition, one can often only expect affected 'third parties' to behave consistent with those rights when they have had a reasonable chance to learn which rights they actually have to accommodate. If a spouse, for example, neglects to enter his interest in the land register, he bears the risk that his share of the property will be lost to the creditors of his spouse in the course of a statutory auction.[226] The creditors, for their part, could not know of the co-ownership share and, in consequence, would not have to respect it as they took steps to realize their claim. As opposed to the public interest in the protection of transactions, however, public interests manifest as propositions of private property law relatively infrequently. Limitations of the powers of an owner (or the holder of any other property right) based in the public interest are generally effected through public law norms rather than norms of property law.[227] These are norms that either grant a public authority the competence to compel or forbid a certain type of action, or norms which directly compel or forbid a type of action and prescribe sovereign sanctions for their violation, for example through criminal punishment. Such norms only become the subject matter of property law when they derogate from the duty owed by private subjects to the holder of the relevant right. That is the case, for example, where permission is granted to fly over land unit, to hunt[228] (or at least use rights of way) in private forests, where certain forms of surface water use can be prevented or compelled by neighbouring property owners,[229] where land owned by others can be

[226] Swedish HD 19 November 1984, NJA 1984 p. 772. Compare Cass. Civ. 16 March 2011, RTD civ. 2011 p. 373, note *Revet*; D. 2011 p. 2304, note *Mallet-Bricout and Reboul-Maupin* (A right of way over a land unit was not registered, but if it was positively known to the purchaser, it was as good as registration; the right of way was enforceable against him).

[227] The border between private law and public law can become difficult to distinguish, particularly in the context of property law. They come particularly close when states grant rights in land units in a manner similar to licenses. One example from Polish law is the so-called 'heritable usufruct' (or 'perpetual usufruct') which only the state and its agencies (the '*fiscus*') is competent to grant and distribute, under Art. 232 Polish Civil Code. English law provides an example with exploration rights for oil. Property in subterranean oil reserves is, by force of law, in the Crown rather than the owner of the surface land parcel under which the oil rests. The Crown grants real exploration rights to companies under sec. 3 Petroleum Act 1998, Schedule 3, para. 4 (earlier sec. 2 Petroleum (Production) Act 1934). These rights even grant the power to drill diagonally from a land unit under which no oil is found into the earth below the neighbouring land unit, in order to reach the tip of the oil well, tap it, and transport pressurized water there (see further *Bocardo SA v Star Energy UK Onshore Ltd* [2010] UKSC 35; [2011] 1 AC 380). The granting of such a licence must be an act of sovereign authority, but the rights bestowed on the grantee are property rights subject to private law. It is similar, in our view, in the case of the Polish heritable usufruct.

[228] See first ECtHR of 20 January 2011, *Herrmann v. Germany*, Application no. 9300/07 (the Chamber decided with a majority of 4:3 that it was consistent with the European Convention on Human Rights that owners of smaller forests and fields could become compulsory members of so-called 'hunting associations' [*Jagdgenossenschaften*] under German law, as a result of which they had to tolerate hunting activities by others on their property when they objected to hunting) and then the reversal of this decision by the Grand Chamber of the ECtHR of 26 June 2012, NJW 2012 p. 3629, JZ 2013 p. 519 (the obligation to allow hunting on their property against their will was a disproportionate burden on the landowners and violated Art. 1 of the First Protocol to the Convention (the protection of property); for critical commentary, see *Meyer-Ravenstein*, AUR 2013 p. 124).

[229] A nice example is found in Art. 1388 Portuguese Civil Code, which allows a demand for water in the case of a fire emergency. The administrative agencies can, without prior compensation or legal process, order the immediate use of private waters for the purpose of firefighting. The owner has, in such a case, a claim for damages against those who benefited from the use of the water.

used for domestic[230] or commercial[231] purposes, where noises or vibrations have to be tolerated for the excavation of resources, or where (as under Art. 13(1) of the Spanish *Ley del Patrimonio Histórico Español*) the owner of cultural goods has to permit the examination of objects (without charging fees) by researchers. Such cases concern not just individual interests, but also the public weal, because the modern state has an independent interest in the mobility of its people, in the guarantee of living space, in opportunities for recreation, in research, in the protection of natural resources and in the promotion of commerce.[232]

4. Content and Dissemination of the *Numerus Clausus* Principle

a. Predominance of *Typenzwang* and *Typenfixierung*

2.40 Property rights thus find their counterpoint in provisions for the protection of legal certainty. The most widespread rule for the protection of legal dealings, albeit it one that has come increasingly under pressure in some regions of Europe,[233] stipulates that

[230] The legal position was particularly dramatic for a time in the Netherlands. The Netherlands were, until 1 October 2010, one of the few countries on earth in which it was legal, under certain circumstances, to squat in unoccupied buildings. This practice was called *kraken*. Until the named date, under Art. 429^{sexies} of the Netherlands Penal Code it was only an offence to refuse to leave an occupied house following the order of the owner. Besides this, *kraken* was only an offence if the building had not been empty for a period of at least twelve months prior to the start of the occupation. The civil law situation was, however, somewhat unclear. It was certain that civil proceedings were possible against actions that were also punishable under the criminal law. That proposition, however, could not be stated in the reverse; civil proceedings against non-criminal behaviour followed their own criteria. The Hof Leeuwarden 24 January 2007, LJN AZ7475 required, for e.g. evidence of particular urgency for an expedited proceeding for vacation of premises. This was present in the case, because the *kraken* had extinguished the owner's insurance. Further, the courts undertook a balancing of the competing interests. This embraced questions such as whether the owner wanted to vacate in order to lease the building (and so fill it), but also whether the *kraker* could establish any legally cognizable interest in the building. The courts generally ruled in a manner friendly to squatters: e.g. Arrondissementsrechtbank Dordrecht 10 July 2008, LJN BD6843 refused to make a vacation order over apartments in an apartment complex on the basis that concerns of waste, fire, over-occupancy, insurance were insufficient to create a justified interest in vacation and that the stated intention to lease the premises to others was insufficient because other apartments in the complex were empty; the insurance problems, for their part, could have been resolved by entering into a lease agreement with squatters. The interests of the *kraker*, on the other hand, took priority because of the prevailing accommodation crisis and the lack of affordable housing. In a similar vein see Arrondissementsrechtbank Leeuwarden 12 February 2007, LJN AZ8682. Since 1 October 2010, Art. 429^{sexies} has been replaced by Art. 138a; *kraken* is now generally an offence. Full civil legal protection is thereby restored.

[231] e.g. Art. 1309 Portuguese Civil Code and in particular § 5:43(1) Hungarian Civil Code, § 128(2) Slovakian Civil Code, §§ 1037–1039 Czech Civil Code, according to which things can not only be appropriated from their owners in the public interest, but the right of ownership in them can be (permanently or temporarily) limited. The concept of public interest is interpreted broadly. It concerns not only governmental interests (including municipal and regional governmental) interests, but also the interests of larger groups of private subjects. However, difficult border questions arise from time to time in this context, to the extent that not every 'collective' interest is also a 'public' interest; group interests can also run counter to the public interest (*Eliáš et al.*, Občanský zákoník. Velký akademický komentář I, p. 559. Czech Constitutional Court 28 March 1996, I. ÚS 198/95, Sbírka nálezů a usnesení 5 (1997) no. 23 p. 193 concerned a private parking lot built on municipal land. It was meant to help ease access to a holiday park. However, the municipal authority then decided to lease the larger part of the parking lot to a company for the purposes of an 'auto bazaar'. This was held to be not in the public interest).

[232] For a detailed enquiry into the constitutional framework for the pursuit of these goals (environmental protection and the promotion of commerce) through rules of property law, see BverfG 24 November 2010, EuGRZ 2010 pp. 755–80.

[233] *Vieira*, Direitos reais, p. 210 comments rather pointedly that the *numerus clausus* principle 'is one of the reasons for the scientific backwardness of property law and for the low levels of interest that property law has

property rights can only arise and subsist in the forms, and with the contours, provided by the legal system. This notion is usually expressed in the shorthand formula of a *numerus clausus* (a 'closed catalogue') of property rights, and is elaborated with the concepts of type-determinacy [*Typenzwang*] and determinacy of content [*Typenfixierung*] of those recognized types. *Typenzwang* means that one can only utilize the types of property rights provided for by the legal system; *Typenfixierung* means that these types have a concrete content determined by the legal system. A statutory enactment of *Typenfixierung* is found, for example, in Art. Art. 525 Spanish Civil Code, according to which real rights of use and habitation (Art. 524) cannot be demised or transferred to another with any kind of title. But the concept of *Typenfixierung* also entails, for example, that the rule in § 1018 German Civil Code (which allows another's land parcel to be encumbered with a servitude in virtue of which 'certain dealings'[234] concerning the land are prohibited) is not allowed to be misused so as to prevent dealings which have nothing to do with the ownership of the land.[235] The principle of *Typenfixierung* is, on the other hand, softened when rights of disposition (or of granting security) can be transformed, by private autonomous acts, into rights of use. Art. 1221 Greek Civil Code, for example, provides that it can be 'agreed that the (pledgee) creditor can make use of the thing. In the case of a thing that produces fruits by its nature, it is to be presumed in cases of doubt that the creditor has this right.' Art. 1222 provides that, if 'the creditor is entitled to make use [of the thing], he is responsible for procuring its use and has to render account for it. The net yield of the use is to be, unless otherwise agreed,

aroused in scholars of civil law in the last decades'. In Portugal, however, this critique has not made a mark; few legal systems hold so strictly to the *numerus clausus* principle.

[234] The formulation of what can be the object of a servitude presents considerable difficulties in many legal systems. e.g. Art. 1119 Greek Civil Code gives the owner of the servient land unit the option to permit a certain use or to forbear from certain actions which he would otherwise be entitled in virtue of his right of ownership. This formulation appears to be clearer than that found in § 1018 German Civil Code. But it is even said that Art. 1119 Greek Civil Code relaxes the *numerus clausus* principle because it gives the parties such a broad framework within which to shape their relations (*Georgiades*, Empragmato Dikaio I, pp. 19–20 no. 13). This view is prevalent in Portugal, too. Under Art. 1544 Portuguese Civil Code, objects of land servitudes can be any kind of use [*quaisquer utilidades*], even future or contingent uses, through which the dominant land unit can be enjoyed, even when they do not increase its value. As the statutory text does not define the term 'use', it makes possible private autonomous agreements concerning uses of every kind; it is then open to the parties to determine the content of the use [*conteúdo de aproveitamento*]. The land servitude [*servidão predial*] is therefore seen as an 'open' type of property right (*Vieira*, Direitos reais, p. 209). Art. 5:71 Netherlands Civil Code formulates that the burden, which is imposed by a land servitude on the servient land unit, manifests as a duty to allow an action or to forbear from an action on, over, or under one of the two land unit concerned. § 151n Slovakian Civil Code (and § 151n Czech Civil Code [1964]) burdens the owner of a moveable thing such that he must permit an action, forbear from an action, or perform an action. The new § 1257(1) Czech Civil Code [2014] uses the formulation that a thing subject to a servitude can be burdened such that the owner 'must permit or abstain from something'. Under § 1258 the servitude embraces everything that is necessary for its exercise. 'If the content and scope of the servitude are not determined, then they will be judged according to the local custom; if such is lacking, it will be presumed that the content or scope is smaller rather than larger.'

[235] BGH 3 May 1985, NJW 1985 p. 2474 uses, with reference to BGH 30 January 1959, BGHZ 29 pp. 244, 249 the example of an exclusive supply contract, i.e. the obligation of a landowner not to deal with the wares of any other manufacturer or supplier on his land unit. The right freely to choose from the available suppliers of wares is not a consequence of the right of ownership of a land unit. Matters are very similar in Austria under § 472 Austrian Civil Code. The servitude [in Austria, *Servitut*; the German Civil Code terminology is *Dienstbarkeit*] must show some connection to the thing it burdens; see *inter alia* OGH 18 August 1996, SZ 69/180 and on the distinction between servitudes related to land parcels and those not related to land parcels, see further OGH 2 February 1955, SZ 29/27 and OGH 2 March 1972, SZ 45/26.

to be used first in payment of the costs, then repayment of interest, and finally repayment of the capital of the claim.' The right of the pledgee, conceived as a right of disposal or a security right, takes on the properties of a right of use (a servitude) in the context of such an agreement; the law tolerates these blurry edges, despite inherently only recognizing concrete, determinate property rights 'in principle'. Such penumbral cases, however, are already inherent in the distinction between *Typenzwang* and *Typenfixierung*. For example, a legal system which limits the possibility of creating a pledge over another's property to the case in which the pledgee acquires factual possession of the thing, prevents the parties from creating a non-possessory pledge (an instance of *Typenzwang*).[236] It thereby hinders the parties from creating a pledge in such a manner that both parties waive the requirement for the delivery of the thing pledged (an instance of *Typenfixierung*). An agreement that purported this effect would be ineffective against third parties (effecting a *numerus clausus*).

2.41 For the vast majority of European legal systems, the principle of *numerus clausus* is almost self-evident. It is, however, relatively seldom fixed in statutory language. Art. 1306(1) Portuguese Civil Code is one example. This provision says that it is

> not permitted to create limitations on the right of ownership of a real nature, or to create parcelled forms of this right, except in the cases expressly provided for in statute; all limitations that arise on the basis of an act-in-the-law that do not satisfy the requirements of these provisions are of an obligational nature.

This is complemented by Art. 406(2) Portuguese Civil Code, which provides that a contract manifests 'effects against third parties only in cases and provisions specially provided for by statute'. Ownership is, on this view, the 'mother right' of all absolute property rights; only that which derives from ownership, and unfolds into an independent 'daughter right' within the parameters defined by the statute, bears the nature of an absolute property right. This entails, in the first instance, that Portuguese law does not allow the creation of a trust with real effects.[237] But, moreover, judicial decisions

[236] e.g. under § 1205(1) German Civil Code things behave similarly. Art. 1214 Greek Civil Code, on the other hand, recognizes non-possessory pledges as well; such pledges must be publicly registered in order to be valid (details in Art. 1 of the Statute 2844/2000 on Contracts over Movable Things and Claims Subject to Publicity Requirements, and Other Contracts over Security Rights). Spanish law also provides the possibility (in Arts 52–66 *Ley de 16 de diciembre de 1954 sobre hipoteca mobiliaria y prenda sin desplazamiento de posesión* [LHMPSD]) to agree to a pledge without transferring possession (so-called 'pledge without displacement' [*prenda sin desplazamiento*]). This security interest, too, requires registration for effect against third parties; besides this, it can also only be created over goods expressly classified in the statute.

[237] *Vaz Tomé and Leite de Campos*, Propriedade fiduciária (trust), pp. 277–90, esp 287–9, prefer to have the *propriedade fiduciária* of Portuguese law and with it also the trust recognized as an atypical property right [*direito real atípico*]. Legal doctrine must be capable of giving such a *direito real atípico* priority over the *numerus clausus* principle, as the latter has no practical value and harks from the museum of *Begriffsjurisprudenz*. It should at least expand the number of existing property rights, but better would be to allow the private creation of new kinds of rights. In fact, Portuguese law presents only three forms of *propriedade fiduciária* (see further *Pinto Duarte*, Direitos reais^2, pp. 161, 164), namely the *fideicomisso* (a kind of testamentary power of appointment), the *trust da Zona Franca da Madeira*, and the *contratos fiduciários*. The *fideicomisso* (Arts 2286–2296 Portuguese Civil Code), however, is a matter of the law of succession. The 'trust' in the law of Madeira does not create any 'ownership' in the sense of Art. 1305 Portuguese Civil Code. A *pactum fiduciae* brings about, in the end, only obligational effects (*Pais de Vasconcelos*, Contratos atípicos, p. 273). Besides, Arts 694 and 678 expressly prohibit forfeiture agreements (the

have declined, for example on the basis of Art. 1306(1) Portuguese Civil Code, to find real rights of use or security in agreements for a retention of title in favour of the seller. A retention of title does not have the legal nature of a property right. In consequence, a finance company must suffer its retention of title in an automobile to be removed from the register[238] if it wishes to dispose of the automobile to a third party. The appearance of a real encumbrance has to be removed by the company itself. A deletion by administrative act *sua sponte* (Art. 888 Portuguese Civil Procedure Code (now out of force) in connection with Art. 824(2) Portuguese Civil Code) does not come into consideration because dispositions made in the course of enforcement proceedings only relate to property rights. An enforcement proceeding concerning an automobile subject to a pledge, for which a retention of title clause in favour of the creditor bringing the enforcement proceedings, could thus only proceed once the creditor had applied for its removal himself.[239] On the basis of the *numerus clausus* principle, the Supreme Court also denied that the conditions of sale imposed by a municipal authority could have real effect. The authority had disposed of land units in its ownership by way of public auctions to various different purchasers. The latter had undertaken to the authority only to develop the land parcels in certain, limited ways, but not all of the purchasers subsequently honoured these undertakings. A claim brought by the purchasers who did honour their undertakings, and who feared a loss in the value of their properties as a result of these building activities, was rejected; the claimants had acquired no land servitudes, no other property right could have arisen in virtue of Art. 1307(1) Portuguese Civil Code.[240]

Art. 973 Greek Civil Code orients itself even more directly according to the principle of type-determinacy of property rights (*'αρχή του κλειστού αριθμού των εμπράγματων δικαιωμάτων'*): it stipulates that 'rights, which guarantee direct control in a thing effective against every other person (property rights), are ownership, the servitudes, the pledge, and the hypothec'. The Greek Civil Code does not recognize other property rights, and subjects cannot 'invent' any new ones either. The creation and determination of the content of real legal positions are, according to the Greek legal view, tasks **2.42**

so-called *pacto comissório*). An agreement under which a creditor obtains the right to appropriate the thing in case of default is ineffective against hypothec and pledge creditors (see further *Pinto Duarte* op. cit. p. 165).

238 Under Portuguese law, retention of title in immoveable property and forms of moveable property deemed to be equal to it (including automobiles) require registration in order to have effect against third parties (Art. 409(2) Portuguese Civil Code in connection with Art. 5 DL 54/75 of 12 February 1975 [*Registo da Propriedade Automóvel*], and Art. 94 lit. a DL 224/84 of 6 July 1984 [*Código do Registo Predial*]).

239 STJ 2 November 2004, CJ(ST) XII (2004-3) pp. 102, 103 and STJ 9 October 2008, Processo 07A3965 (reconciliation of the authorities to the effect that a registered retention of title cannot be deleted by an administrative act, as it is not of a real nature). The old Art. 888 Portuguese Civil Procedure Code, however, has no counterpart in the new Civil Procedure Code (Statute 41/2013 of 26 June 2013, in force since 1 September 2013); the provision concerning deletion by administrative act was dropped without replacement.

240 STJ 29 June 1989, BMJ 388 (1989) p. 520. On the *numerus clausus* principle see further STJ 27 September 2011, Processo 360/005.7TBODM.E1.S1 (no analogue application of the preference regime in construction law to other property rights) and STJ 16 April 2013, Processo 230/08.7TBPNH.P1.S1 (temporally unlimited clause providing that the purchaser was not permitted to dispose of his real estate violated the concept of ownership).

for the legislature.[241] They may not be left to the parties,[242] because to do so would adversely affect the clarity and certainty of legal dealings.[243] The cases, for example, consistently conclude from the *numerus clausus* principle that possession is not a property right. Possession is, after all, not mentioned Art. 973.[244] This further entails that the transfer of possession in an immoveable thing does not require writing, let alone notarization.[245] On this view, the possession of a right of way (whether used in good or bad faith) is not a property right.[246] This is because possession of rights is not named in Art. 973.[247]

2.43 The Italian legislature has only expressly confirmed the *numerus clausus* principle for rights of security (i.e. not for rights of use) in Art. 2741(2) Italian Civil Code,[248] but the cases[249] and the literature[250] agree that it is a general principle of property

[241] The Greek legislature has, however, not always provided the necessary certainty. e.g. it is not completely clear whether 'time sharing', introduced in Statute 1652/1986 (FEK A' 167/30 October 1986) is a real right or merely an obligational right. The same goes for the 'leasing' of land units introduced in Statute 1665/1986 (FEK A' 194/4 December 1986) and modified in Statute 2367/1995 (FEK A' 261/29 December 1995). Both dealings are, on the one hand, subject to notarization and registration requirements, but on the other hand are, at core, only obligational dealings. The same could be observed for the 'floating charge' introduced in Arts 16–18 of the Statute 2844/2000 on non-possessory pledges. CFI Athens in Chamber 6624 and 6625/2008, www.dsanet.gr made clear that the floating charge is a security interest in a collection of moveable things and/or rights as a whole. It is characterized by the feature that the chargor of the pledged things is permitted to dispose of them free of encumbrances, but is obligated to replace them with objects of a similar value within a reasonable time. Because the chargee does not have factual control over the things, the provisions of the civil code governing hypothecation do not apply. The floating charge does show similarities to the non-possessory pledge, but is not a limited property right because it does not encumber a specific object of property rights. In the literature, too, the floating charge is characterized as an obligational arrangement *sui generis* (*Stefanaki*, EempD 2001 p. 831).

[242] *Georgiades*, Empragmato Dikaio I, § 2 no. 8, *Triantos*, AK, p. 1185.

[243] *Triantos* op. cit.; *Spyridakis*, Empragmato Dikaio, p. 19; von Bar (-*Eleftheriadou*), Sachenrecht in Europa III, Griechenland, p. 20; *Georgiades* op. cit. p. 16; *Papasteriou*, Empragmato Dikaio I, p. 29.

[244] See Areopag 1593/1979, NoB 28 (1979) p. 1120; Areopag 291/1989, EEN 34 (1990) p. 70; Areopag 826/1991, www.dsanet.gr; Areopag 650/1995, EEN 63 (1996) p. 563; Areopag 220/2000, EllDik 41 (2000) p. 762; Areopag 1082/2000, EllDik 42 (2001) p. 429; Areopag 1561/2001, EllDik 44 (2003) p. 1630; Areopag 1417/2002, EllDik 44 (2003) p. 183; Areopag 621/2004, www.dsanet.gr; Areopag 504/2009, NoB 57 (2009) p. 1704 and NoB 58 (2010) p. 681; Areopag 2029/2009, www.dsanet.gr; Areopag 275/2010, NoB 58 (2010) p. 1747, and Areopag 818/2010, www.dsanet.gr.

[245] Areopag 220/2000 op. cit. Areopag in Chamber 1593/1979 and Areopag 1082/2000 op. cit. explain that the legal position was different before the entry into force of the Greek Civil Code.

[246] Greece belongs to the numerous European jurisdictions which recognize the possession of rights as well as the possession of things (Art. 975 Greek Civil Code: 'In the case of pledges and servitudes, possession consists in the exercise of these rights with the consent of one thereto entitled'). Comparable concepts are found, e.g. in Slovakia and the Czech Republic (§ 129(1) Slovakian Civil Code and § 129(1) Czech Civil Code [1964]), in Poland (Art. 352 Polish Civil Code), and in the common law (still impressive is Bracton: 'The possession of a right is acquired by use, as where an owner, being present and cognizant of the matter, by acquiescence permits a neighbour, who has no right to do so, to use some servitude in his unencumbered estate': Bracton Online, English & Latin II, p. 158, http://hlsl5.law.harvard.edu/bracton/Framed/mframe.htm). That Portuguese law recognizes the possession of rights is evident from Art. 1287 Portuguese Civil Code, which speaks of 'possession of the right of ownership or another real right of use' in the context of prescriptive acquisition. The Czech Civil Code [2014] has gone so far as to shift its whole law of possession to the possession of rights (see § 987). The possession of things is construed as the possession of the right of ownership (§ 989).

[247] CA Athens 6099/2000, EllDik 46 (2005) p. 498; CFI Patmos 4/1997, www.dsanet.gr.

[248] See further *Bigliazzi Geri*, Diritto civile I(1), p. 311 and vol. II, p. 37; *Gazzoni*, Manuale di diritto privato[13], p. 252.

[249] Consistent decisions, including Cass. 29 February 1960, no. 392, Rep. Giur. It. 1960 p. 2502; Cass. 23 August 1978, no. 3931, Mass. Giust. Civ. 1978 p. 1642; Cass. 8 July 1981, no. 4477, *Foro Italiano* 1982, I, p. 152; Cass. 2 January 1997, no. 8, Corr. Giur. 1997, 5, p. 556; Corte d'Appello Milano 28 September 1998, I contratti 1999 p. 555; Cass. 26 September 2000, no. 12765, Rep. Giur. It. 2000 p. 3365; Cass. 19 September 2005, no. 18476, Giur. It. 2006 p. 2277; Cass. 4 December 2007, no. 25289, Mass. Giur. It. 2007 p. 3974, and Cass. 26 February 2008, no. 5034, NGCivil Code 2008, I, p. 1272.

[250] See the overview in Grundmann and Zaccaria (-*Troiano*), Einführung in das italienische Recht, pp. 270–71.

law.[251] Rights not provided for by statute cannot be created by acts of private autonomy. This is a consequence of the fact that legal transactions would be rendered unreasonably difficult if private subjects had the possibility of subdividing property rights according to their whim, with effects for all third parties.[252] Further, this would be irreconcilable with the general principle of the relativity of contractual relationships (Art. 1372 Italian Civil Code).[253] In the context of property rights in immoveable property, reference is often made to Art. 2643 and the following provisions of the Civil Code governing registration (*trascrizione*, lit. 'transcription') in the land register. This is said to entail that only an exhaustive catalogue of real rights in land units exists, and that this in turn underscores the general principle.[254] Sections 1(1) and 1(2) of the Law of Property Act 1925 establish the same principle for the real property law of the Common Law. Estonia has established the *numerus clausus* principle in § 5(1) of its Law of Property Act ('*Asjaõigusseadus*'). Property rights are listed as: ownership, servitudes and land charges, heritable building rights, options, and pledges. § 5(2) of this Act adds that the legislature can create further property rights. Finally, § 308 Austrian Civil Code creates a kind of statutory cataloguing of real rights. According to this provision, 'Real rights in things are the right of possession, of ownership, of pledge, of servitude, and of inheritance.' This list, however, is not very happy. Today, subjective inheritance rights are not seen as property rights at all any more,[255] and possession is only seen as a property right in a limited sense; on the other hand, many property rights that have been created over time in specific statutes are not yet mentioned in § 308 at all.[256]

Although the principle of a *numerus clausus* of property rights has not been expressly provided for in statute in Germany, the Netherlands, or (with the exception of Art. 2 Slovenian Property Law Statute) any of the Central and Eastern Member States of **2.44**

[251] Counter-opinions, which deny the predominance of the *numerus clausus* principle in Italian law have remained isolated (see in particular *Costanza*, Studi in onore di Grassetti I, p. 421 and Corte d'Appello Genova 29 September 2000, NGCivil Code 2001, I, p. 532). One should not interpret Cass. 9 October 2014 no. 21356 as representative of such a counter-opinion. The decision only leaves it open to the parties to elect whether to create a right of way as an obligational or a property right; what must have been intended by the parties at the time has to be determined by construction of their contractual language.

[252] This principle is, according to prevailing opinion, a matter *d'ordre public* (*Comporti*, Diritti reali in generale, p. 5; *Bianca*, Diritto civile VI, p. 134.)

[253] *Comporti*, Contributo allo studio del diritto reale, p. 287; *Natucci*, La tipicità dei diritti reali I, p. 160; *Gazzoni*, Manuale di diritto privato[13], p. 212.

[254] *Gambaro*, Il diritto di proprietà, p. 67; *Gazzoni* op. cit. p. 252. Conversely, this provision is regarded by some as a basis for a deduction in the opposite direction; from the provision of *trascrizione* it follows that real rights of use in moveable goods, which are not capable of being registered, are *not* subject to the *numerus clausus* principle (however see *Gambaro*, La proprietà, p. 73).

[255] OGH 22 October 2003, SZ 2003/134 ('According to orthodox opinion, the right of inheritance is not a property right because it does not give a right of immediate control over a thing').

[256] Including the so-called *Baurecht* (the real right to construct a building on a land parcel for a limited period of time [between ten and 100 years] (§§ 1, 3 *Baurechtgesetz*), mining permission (§§ 22, 40 *Mineralrohstoffgesetz*), the right of ownership in an apartment (*Wohnungeigentumgesetz*) and, insofar as they are (partially) seen as property right, also land charges (the Austrian literature is not, however, unified on the question of their real or obligational nature; an intermediate position between real and obligational rights is argued *inter alia* by Koziol and Welser [-*Kletečka*], Bürgerliches Recht I[13], p. 433). Besides this, the right of retention provided in § 472 Austrian Civil Code is another possible candidate for a real right (*Iro*, Sachenrecht[3], no. 1/5).

the European Union, it is also part of the law in these jurisdictions. Both the literature and judicial opinions derive it from the overall system of the relevant codification[257] and give it some importance.[258] It is consistently emphasized that *Typenzwang* and *Typenfixierung* are necessary in the interests of legal certainty and legal clarity.[259] Legal relations in relation to things must be recognizable to outsiders; indeterminate criteria (such as the common limitation on obligations based on good faith) are to be restricted to a minimum sphere of operation in property law.[260] Private subjects must not be given the right to create new property rights outside of the positive law; property law is, in contrast to the law of obligations, mandatory law.[261] In the context of Czech law, Eliáš goes so far as to opine that the *numerus clausus* principle is a logically necessary consequence of the absolute character of property rights.[262] This, however, goes too far. The *numerus clausus* principle operates in other areas of law (e.g. in the company law and in the law of marital property in many European legal systems). Besides, moral rights could also be considered absolute rights, but they certainly do not, for this reason, have to be subject to the principle. Eliáš' thesis does, however, illustrate the importance that *Typenzwang* and *Typenfixierung* are still given in this part of the world, despite the fact that subjects had anything but a positive experience with it during the period of communist rule.[263] In Poland, the applicability of the *numerus*

[257] Sometimes provisions on private acts-in the-law and their limits contain an (indirect) reference to the fundamentally different bases of the law of obligations and property law. Art. 353[1] Polish Civil Code is one example. This provision says that 'the contracting parties ... can form their legal relationship at will, insofar as the content of that will and the nature of the relationship is not inconsistent with law and with the fundamental principles of society'.

[258] e.g. Asser (*-Mijnssen/van Velten/Bartels*), Zakenrecht[15], no. 2 p. 2; *Bydlinski*, Grundzüge des Privatrechts[6], no. 286; Faber and Lurger (*-Szilágyi*), National Reports III, Hungary, pp. 458–9; *Gniewek*, Prawo rzeczowe[7], p. 14 no. 35 and pp. 20–21 nos 49–50, Polish Sąd Najwyższy 13 January 2011, III CSK 85/10, Lex-No. 686143, G.Prawna TPwF 2011/16/8 (no 'real obligations' beyond those which the law expressly recognizes); *Menyhárd*, Dologi jog, p. 18; BGH 13 September 2013, NZM 2013 pp. 733, 734 (the procedural priority of condominium owners to reserves of accumulated fees not a property right; the legislature did not intend to introduce a hitherto unknown type of real encumbrance); Soergel (*-Stadler*), BGB XIV[13], Einl. Sachenrecht no. 41; Staudinger (*-Seiler*), BGB (2007), Einl. Zum Sachenrecht no. 39 and *Švestka and Dvořák*, Občanské právo hmotné, p. 273; *Venedikov*, Novo veshtno pravo, p. 33 no. 19.

[259] e.g. *Schapp and Schur*, Sachenrecht[4], no. 6; *Stadler* op. cit. no. 41; *Seiler* op. cit. no. 38. *Typenzwang* and *Typenfixierung* are also understood in Belgium to be self-evident instantiations of the *numerus clausus* principle. The principle of *Typenfixierung*, however, comes under more pressure where the positive law gives the parties more autonomy to shape their legal relationship. e.g. Art. 64 of the Bulgarian Property Act gives a person who has constructed building on land belonging to another the right to take actions that are necessary for the use of the building, but also to make certain contractual arrangements that affect the use of the entire land unit (*Stavrou*, Veshtno pravo, p. 583). This extends beyond a type of usufruct, and for this reason derogates from the *numerus clausus* principle.

[260] *Mijnssen/van Velten/Bartels* op. cit. no. 2a p. 3.

[261] *Menyhárd* op. cit. p. 137; HR 3 March 1905, W 8191 (Blauboer/Berlips). The thesis of property law's mandatory nature, however, requires closer examination for some other legal systems. It is possible that the rules governing the transfer of ownership are subject to the parties' disposition in so-called 'causal' transfer systems.

[262] *Eliáš et al.* op. cit. p. 511.

[263] The *numerus clausus* principle has caused some problems in the formerly communist countries of Central and Eastern Europe, whose property law was, for political reasons, generally not well developed. e.g. the Czech Civil Code of 1951 (Statute No. 141/1951) recognized neither servitudes nor land charges; instead, it used only a category of 'real encumbrances'. At least parties were free to create these by agreement. Communist legal doctrine stipulated that, in the future, the law could operate properly without any such real encumbrances, and for this reason the code of 1964 only dedicated two paragraphs to them. Under this codification, real encumbrances could only be created by statute or by an administrative act. In practice, one dealt with this situation by creating servitudes by agreement with reference to § 51 Czech Civil Code [1964] (which provided that the parties could form 'such a contract' as was not otherwise regulated, provided it did not contravene the 'content or purpose of the statue'). Encumbrances on land created in this manner, however, had only obligational and not real effects. The

clausus principle seems so reflexive that the textbooks there tend simply to state that the *erga omnes* effect of property rights can only be properly regulated by statute and that property rights cannot be altered without some statutory basis.[264] *Typenzwang* and *Typenfixierung* are, as Menyhárd[265] has made clear in the Hungarian context, a consequence of the abstract conception of ownership. Without the *numerus clausus* principle it is impossible, on this view, to prevent a lasting divergence of the power to use land and to dispose of land, in the interests of a free commerce in land units.[266]

That said, the application of the same principle does not always produce the same results. This is illustrated well by the example of security arrangements in which ownership in moveable things is transferred. German judicial decisions recognized this right quite early, on the basis that it was concerned with the property right of ownership, not with a possessory pledge (which would be against the German moveable property law), and that no violation of the *numerus clausus* principle arose, i.e. through the creation of a 'new' kind of pledge through a private act-in-the-law.[267] The prevailing opinion in Greece is similar,[268] as is that in **2.45**

duties they created passed to the party's heirs, but not to any other successor-in-title; the legal relationship was, for this reason, unstable and worthless. Only in 1982 was the situation rectified with Statute No. 131/1982 SZ (for further details *Bradáč*, Věcná břemena od A do Z[4], pp. 31–8). Possession shared a similar fate. The code of 1964 did not engage with possession at all; rules governing possession were introduced into the new code through the same statute of 1982 (*Spáčil*, Ochrana vlastnictví a držby v občanském zákoníku[2], p. 215).

264 *Ignatowicz and Stefaniuk*, Prawo rzeczowe[2], p. 35; *Gniewek*, Prawo rzeczowe[8], pp. 19–22 nos 49–53. Polish Sąd Najwyższy 15 February 2011, III CZP 90/10, http://www.sn.pl/orzecznictwo/uzasadnienia/ic/III-CZP-0090_10.pdf decided (with a panel of seven judges, departing from some previous decisions of the same court) that public faith in the land register under Art. 5 of the Polish Land Register Statute also protected the good faith acquirer of a perpetual usufruct, even when the *fiscus* or the municipal authority had been unlawfully registered because the land parcel in question in truth belonged to a private person and not the state. This, however, threatened to lead to a derogation of the *numerus clausus* principle, because it appeared that a perpetual usufruct was available over a privately owned land unit. The court (somewhat inventively) extricated itself from this difficulty by assuming that the 'naked' ownership of the land had passed, as a result of the good faith purchase, *ipso jure* to the state. The perpetual usufruct could only be acquired in this way, as provide for in the statute, namely as a right in a land parcel in public ownership. The acquisition of ownership by the *fiscus* was, according to the court, a side-effect of the protection of the good faith third party (see p. 8 of the judgment).

265 The *numerus clausus* principle was considered to be self-evident in traditional Hungarian private law. 'Property rights', according to the definition in § 608 MTJ of 1928 'can only be encumbered with the limited real rights defined by statute'. The justification was that 'the contractual freedom of the parties has no importance in the creation of property rights. Accordingly, the intention to perform an act-in-the-law is insufficient to create a property right, rather it is necessary that the right is capable of enforcement against all the world. Which rights are capable of such enforcement must be determined by statute. Only the law can qualify certain rights as property rights' (text from explanatory documentation of 1928, here cited as in *Menyhárd*, Dologi jog[2], p. 138).

266 *Menyhárd* op. cit. p. 142.

267 See the seminal case RG 8 November 1904, RGZ 59 pp. 146, 148. The principle that the subject matter of a pledge has to be given over (physically) to the pledgee (called the '*Faustpfandprinzip*'), however, only counts for pledges over moveable things created by agreement, not for those that arise by operation of law. In German law, even immoveable things can be given over as security (by use of the general formality requirements); however, because of the hostility of the conveyancing process [*Auflassung*] to the imposition of conditions, this cannot occur in the form of a conditional transfer that is dissolved on the satisfaction of the secured claim. It is, however, possible to secure the obligation claim to the return of the property on satisfaction of the secured debt through the entry of a priority notice in the land register, with quasi-real effects (see, e.g. *Wilhelm*, Sachenrecht[4], p. 935 no. 2404). Whether this form of security does not actually create a new form of property right outside the statutory catalogue is, however, questionable.

268 The opinion dominant in the judicial decisions (e.g. Areopag 1307/1994, NoB 44 [1994] p. 419; CA Thessaloniki 2642/1992, EllDik 35 [1992] p. 629; CA Athens 6395/1976, NoB 25 [1976] p. 406 and 236/1976, NoB 24 [1976] p. 638) and literature (e.g. *Vouzikas*, EEN 18 [1951] p. 657; NoB 6 [1957] p. 557; *Kornilakis*, Katapisteftikí ekhórisi ton apetiseon, p. 62; *Tousis*, Empragmato Dikaio, § 251 p. 770 fn. 1) takes the position that the pledge and

Hungary.[269] In French law, on the other hand, until the reforms of 2006 and 2007 (which introduced a registered pledge as well as the *fiducie* into French law), judges took the exact opposite approach in their decisions. Proprietary security interests could not be recognized by the courts during this time because the French law of moveable property only recognized the pledge [*gage*] and the idea of a proprietary security interest was merely seen as an attempt to circumvent this legal position.[270] For the same reasons, in Austria a transfer of ownership for security is only allowed when it is in fact accompanied with a (lasting) transfer of possession on the proprietary charge; to hold otherwise would allow a circumvention of the provisions governing possessory pledges.[271] Besides this, certain other provisions relating to pledges (e.g. § 1371 Austrian Civil Code) apply to transfer for ownership for security.[272] Art. 3:84(3) Netherlands Civil Code expressly excludes the creation of such security interests. The fact that the *numerus clausus* principle does not bring about the same practical consequences wherever it is applied of course relates to the fact that the number and variety of property rights is different in every legal system. The smaller the number of property rights, the more pointed are the consequences of the *numerus clausus* principle and the stronger

the hypothec are not the only real security rights, and that a fiduciary transfer of ownership of moveable things must be recognized as valid once it is accepted that the *numerus clausus* principle is violated by these rights. Art. 1213 Greek Civil Code (which excludes an arrangement whereby ownership is passed to the secured creditor but the debtor remains in possession on obligationally defined terms) only affects the creation of a pledge. Further, the *numerus clausus* principle is not really violated by an arrangement whereby the debtor remains in possession after the transfer of ownership, because the fiduciary transfer of ownership also rests on the right of ownership. The contrary position relies on the principle of *Typenzwang*. The *numerus clausus* principle, it is argued, is not just about the listing of all property rights, but also about the conviction that their content is pre-determined by the legislature in a binding manner for the parties. The *numerus clausus* principle is *ius cogens* (Art. 3 Greek Civil Code); every act-in-the-law that violates it is null and void for being contrary to a statutory prohibition (Art. 174 Greek Civil Code). The legislature has only provided the hypothec and the pledge as real security rights (*Spyridakis*, Empragmato Dikaio I, p. 71; Genikes Arches I, p. 21 and II p. 489; NoB 24 [1976] pp. 638, 639; similar in effect *Doris*, Emprágmati Asfália, p. 115). The authorities also distinguish strictly between moveable and immoveable things on the basis that the transfer of ownership only follows the so-called causal system of transfer in the case of immoveable things. Fiduciary transfer of ownership is said to be prohibited in consequence (Areopag 1315/1989, NoB 41 [1989] p. 87; Areopag 91/1984, NoB 33 [1984] p. 241; Areopag 1154/1980, NoB 29 [1980] p. 529).

269 The situation is currently somewhat unclear. For a long time, security arrangements by which ownership was transferred to the creditor but the debtor remained in possession were seen as void (*Menyhárd*, Dologi jog^2, p. 396). That was, at least in the case of immoveable things, also the view taken in BH 2006/118 Legf. Bír. Pfv. IX. 21.703/2005 (the court ordered the deletion of the right of ownership of the creditor in the land register, and ordered the entry of a hypothec). BH 2009/300, Legf. Bír. Gfv. X.30.384/2008, on the other hand, held that a contract of sale for the purposes of granting security (in this case, the transfer of shares in a limited company) to be valid and, by so doing, bolstered an alternative, early line of authorities (e.g. EBH 2003/857, Legf. Bír. Pfv. VI.22404/2001, published in *A Legfelsőbb Bíróság határozatainak hivatalos gyűjteménye* 2003/1). CA Debrecen, Pf. II. 20337/2007/3, BDT 2007/173 p. 12, concerned the transfer of two pieces of real estate. The contract of sale included a purchase-back option for the seller. The court refused to characterise the contract as a sham transaction. From the principle of contractual freedom, it held that it followed that the parties could form a second contract to secure the first and, in this process, choose a construction that went beyond the means of granting security provided for in the Civil Code. Hungarian practice often used such contracts of sale with a re-purchase clause. The alternative would be that the debtor (and owner) grant the creditor a mere purchase option (*Menyhárd* op. cit.), which, however, would have nothing to do with a transfer of ownership. There is no suggestion that the validity of security interests of this kind depends on the nature of the object itself (i.e. land unit, moveable thing, right).

270 Cass. Civ. 8 July 1969, Rev. crit. Dr. int. priv. 1971 p. 75, note *Fouchard*. See also *Graham-Siegenthaler*, Kreditsicherungsrechte, p. 100 and also Cass. Civ. 3 May 1973, Rev. crit. Dr. int. priv. 1974 p. 100. The validity of such a contract *in personam* was accepted, but its validity *in rem* was rejected, as *Fouchard* correctly notes in his case comment.

271 See the foundational case OGH 22 June 1926, SZ 8/200.

272 Koziol/Bydlinski/Bollenberger (-*Eccher and Riss*), ABGB^4, § 358 no. 4.

the pressure, in turn, on the legislature, the courts, and the legal academy to create remedies. This is observable not only in the legal systems of France, Spain, and Sweden, which will be dealt with below; it is also observable in the jurisdictions that comprise the heartland of the *numerus clausus* principle.

Without doubt, Germany is among these jurisdictions. Especially in Germany, however, extensions of the sphere of property rights provided for in the original text of the code have been created, which are contrary to that code's systemic structure. Insofar as these extensions have been achieved in the course of legislative measures, they remain formally within the framework of the *numerus clausus* principle. The creation of a right of residential apartment ownership [*Wohnungseigentum*] in the eponymous statute (*Gesetz über das Wohnungseigentum und das Dauerwohnrecht* of 15 March 1951)[273] provides an example. This right deviates from the fundamental principle set out in §§ 93 and 94 German Civil Code that a land unit and all buildings on it form one entity. The *Wohnungseigentumgesetz* provides a right of ownership in individual parts of buildings, that is, in individual dwellings. Another new property right is the *Sicherungsgrundschuld*, created in § 1192(1a) German Civil Code in 2008. In this case, the defences of the land unit owner remain effective even against a good faith (third party) purchaser of the land charge [*Grundschuld*]. The proprietary security interest [*Sicherungseigentum*] mentioned above, however, is a purely judicial creation in response to the conceptual weaknesses of the German law of pledges over moveable things.[274] While the law of pledges requires the delivery of possession at the time of creation (§ 1205 German Civil Code), it is said that the pledgor can remain in possession of the thing when he creates a *Sicherungseigentum* under §§ 929, 930 German Civil Code. The violation of the publicity principle that this entails is accepted, with reference to §§ 930, 931 German Civil Code. The consequence of all this has been the substantial increase in the importance of the *Sicherungseigentum* as a means of obtaining security in goods transactions.[275] A further derogation from the *numerus clausus* principle is found in the recognition of so-called 'expectancy rights' [*Anwartschaftsrechte*]. These are, for the most part, an alternative version of ownership, a kind of 'junior' ownership (not dissimilar in this respect to the *Sicherungseigentum*) that is not to be found either in the Civil Code or in any special purpose statute. An expectancy right is the right to acquire a statutory property right in the future (typically, but not necessarily the right of ownership), subject to the rules governing the acquisition and protection of the expected right. Such a right arises, according to the prevailing opinion, when the 'facts giving rise to an absolute right have not yet been completed, but the legal position of the disponee is already so secure that it can no longer be defeated by any unilateral action of the disponor'.[276] It is therefore concerned to protect the position of a disponee; such a position consists of more than just a hope of acquiring the 'full' or 'main' right, but less 2.46

[273] Bundesgesetzblatt Teil I, p. 175, corrected at p. 209.
[274] Staudinger (-*Seiler*), BGB (2007), Einl. Zum Sachenrecht no. 44.
[275] Soergel (-*Stadler*), BGB XIV[13], Einl. No. 40.
[276] *Seiler* op. cit. no. 46.

than that of the right that it secures.[277] The real nature of this right, which bears the same nature of its corresponding full right 'minus' something,[278] remains questionable until this day.[279] However, the *Anwartschaftsrecht* is subject to the same principles that govern the full right the acquisition of which it secures; the same rules governing transfer, collateralization, and protection apply as to the full right.[280] Finally, it is difficult to reconcile the *numerus clausus* principle with the recognition of rights in one's own property [*Rechte an eigenen Sachen*] beyond the sphere of subjective property rights expressly provided by statute. § 1196 German Civil Code recognizes, for example, the so-called 'owner's land charge' [*Eigentümersgrundschuld*]. This is meant to prevent subordinate creditors from automatically moving up the ladder when a claim is extinguished through payment. The owner of the land parcel keeps the priority position in the land register so that he can use it, if needed, to access a new line of credit. Rights in one's own property therefore influence the priority between several limited property rights. For this reason, rights in one's own property that are not expressly provided by statute are 'actually' (from the perspective of the *numerus clausus* principle) unacceptable. Nevertheless, according to the majority of opinion, *Eigentümerrechte* are also said to be possible for servitudes and usufructs by way of analogy to § 1196.[281]

b. France and Spain: *Numerus Apertus* Not *Numerus Clausus*?

2.47 The situation appears less straightforward in two other Continental legal systems, namely France and Spain. French orthodoxy contests the validity of the *numerus clausus* principle in property law. Only a portion of the French scholarship today sticks to the principle and to the opinion that it is impossible to create new property rights with *erga omnes* effect through an act of private autonomy.[282] Traditionalists often refer to Art. 543 French Civil Code, which provides that '*On peut avoir sur les biens, ou un droit de propriété, ou un simple droit de jouissance, ou seulement des services fonciers à*

[277] *Baur and Stürner*, Sachenrecht[18], § 3 no. 46.

[278] This uses the oft-cited formulation of the *Bundesgerichtshof* (BGH 24 June 1958, NJW 1958 pp. 1133, 1134).

[279] See *Seiler* op. cit. Greece has followed the German 'special path' in recognizing the supposedly real nature of these expectancy rights expressly (Areopag 1316/2010, NoB 59 [2011] p. 388; Areopag 1491/2006, www.dsanet.gr; Areopag 187/1998, EllDik 39 [1998] p. 843 and CA Piräus 2/2008, EempD 14 [2009] p. 127).

[280] RG 4 April 1933, RGZ 140 pp. 223, 228–9, a leading decision in this area, which the post-war authorities have returned to time and again (e.g. BGH 24 June 1958, NJW 1958 pp. 1133, 1134), rather irritatingly justified this rule with no less than the *numerus clausus* principle itself—against which the notion of expectancy rights offends. 'Expectancy as such does not create any property right. The existing legal system only recognises a fixed number of property rights of limited content; the expectation of acquiring ownership of a moveable thing does not belong to these. The creation of a property right through granting the expectancy of acquiring ownership can therefore only proceed in the manner proscribed for the transfer of the property right itself (§§ 929 and following German Civil Code).'

[281] BGH 11 March 1964, NJW 1964 p. 1226 and BGH 14 July 2011, NJW 2011 p. 3517 ('A usufruct can be created in one's own land parcel; proof of a justified interest in its creation is not required'). See further *Seiler* op. cit. no. 47; *Baur and Stürner* op. cit. § 33 no. 34. We are here concerned with a further exception from the principle of *nemini res sua servit*.

[282] See especially *Carbonnier*, Droit civil II, p. 1588 no. 706; *Mazeaud and Chabas*, Introduction[12], p. 273 no. 163 and *Zenati-Castaing and Revet*, Les biens[3], p. 458 no. 296, p. 473 no. 313; see also *Zenati*, RTD civ. 1992 p. 791, 793.

prétendre'. This list, they say, is exhaustive. In particular, the regulation of property in land is a matter *d'ordre public* in the sense of Art. 6, as it is a matter of the highest importance for third parties, for the possible forms for transferring ownership, and for legal certainty.[283] Besides this, many 'younger' statutes (i.e. post-dating the enactment of the civil code) expressly emphasize the real nature of the rights they create. This is the case, for example, with the *Loi de 25 June 1902 sur le bail emphytéotique* (whose provisions concerning heritable leases are now found in Arts L 451-1 and following of the *Code rural et de la pêche maritime*),[284] and with the Arts L 251-1 and following of the *Code de la construction et de l'habitation* (based on the *Loi de 16 December 1964*), which concern the *bail à construction*.[285] According to the defenders of the *numerus clausus* principle, if it is necessary to enact a new statute in order to create a new property right, then the converse is true, and it is not within the powers of private parties to create such a right; further, a statute that does not expressly emphasize the real nature of a new right creates only obligational, *in personam* building blocks for parties to form their dealings. An uncontrolled proliferation of real rights would inexorably lead, on this view, to an unacceptable hollowing out of the concept of ownership.[286] Not everyone, however, finds this type of argument convincing.[287] Against such views, it is argued that not even the heritable building right (the '*droit de superficie*') is expressly named in any statutory text as a property right, and yet it was from early on accepted as having a real nature in judicial decisions, and its real nature is now totally uncontroversial.[288] Besides this, nothing in the text of Art. 543 supports the thesis that the list enumerated there is exhaustive. Rather, it follows from the principle of freedom of contract, that the parties can create any and all rights that are not prohibited by statute, even including rights that

[283] See especially *Terré and Lequette*, Grands arrêts de la jurisprudence civile[10], p. 267; also *Terré and Simler*, Les biens[6], p. 60 no. 52.

[284] Art. 451-1 *Code rural* provides: '*Le bail emphytéotique de biens immeubles confère au preneur* un droit réel *susceptible d'hypothèque; ce droit peut être cédé et saisi dans les formes prescrites pour la saisie immobilière. Ce bail doit être consenti pour plus de dix-huit années et ne peut dépasser quatre-vingt-dix-neuf ans; il ne peut se prolonger par tacite reconduction*' (emphasis added).

[285] According to Art. L 251-1 *Code de la construction et de l'habitation*, '*constitue un bail à construction le bail par lequel le preneur s'engage, à titre principal, à édifier des constructions sur le terrain du bailleur et à les conserver en bon état d'entretien pendant toute la durée du bail*'. A *bail à construction* is thus a form of tenancy, in which the tenant commits himself to construct a building on the land parcel and to keep it in good repair. According to Art. L 251-1(1), a *bail à construction* can be created by agreement for a period of eighteen to ninety-nine years. The *bail emphythéotique* guarantees a similar right of use. The tenant is obligated to work the land in a certain way (but not, as in the *bail à construction*, to construct a building which passes into his ownership during the period of the arrangement). It is said to be a provisional *droit de superficie* (heritable building right). In default of agreement to the contrary, it is extinguished at the end of the relevant period (*Jourdain*, Les biens, p. 233 no. 175-1). Art. 251-3 makes clear that the one entitled to a *bail à construction* has a property right in an immoveable thing ('*Le bail à construction confère au preneur* un droit réel immobilier. *Ce droit peut être hypothéqué, de même que les constructions édifiées sur le terrain loué; il peut être saisi dans les formes prescrites pour la saisie immobilière*' (emphasis added)).

[286] See (albeit rather critical of the *numerus clausus* principle) *Malaurie and Aynès*, Les biens[3], p. 89 no. 358.

[287] Against the pre-eminence of the *numerus clausus* principle see, e.g. *Planiol/Ripert/Picard*, Les biens[2], p. 54 no. 48 and *Larroumet*, Les biens[5], p. 33 no. 51. See further *Atias*, Les biens[10], no. 74, p. 51 and *Jourdain*, Les biens, p. 10 no. 8.

[288] The *droit de superifice* is, since Cass. 16 December 1873, D.P. 1874, I, S. 249, generally seen as a *variété de droit de propriété*. It is not extinguished through non-use, exists in perpetuity insofar as the parties have not agreed otherwise, can be burdened with a hypothec and can even be acquired by prescriptive possession. The holder of a *droit de superificie* has all the prerogatives of ownership: *usus*, *fructus*, and *abusus* (*Malaurie and Aynès* op. cit. p. 284 no. 904; *Jourdain* op. cit. p. 238 no. 177).

give their holders direct rights of control over things—even when such rights are not incorporated into any statutory list of property rights.[289]

2.48 Decisive for practice was the fact that the *Cour de cassation* held quite early, namely in a decision of 1834, against the application of a strict *numerus clausus* principle and for the freedom of parties to create property rights: '*Les articles 544, 546, 552 du Code civil*', it said:

> *sont déclaratifs du droit commun relativement à la nature et aux effets de la propriété, mais ne sont pas prohibitifs; ni ces articles, ni aucune autre loi, n'excluent les diverses modifications et décompositions dont le droit ordinaire de propriété est susceptible.*[290]

Neither Arts 544, 546, and 552 nor any other statutory provisions excluded the modification of the right of ownership. As a result, new rights could be created, in particular real rights of use, through contract and by unliteral acts-in-the-law. Judicial recognition of such privately created property rights has not, however, been very frequent. The case of 1834 was concerned with a form of joint ownership of the fruits and products of a riverbank, which deviated from the general rules of the civil code. A case of 1873 was concerned with the recognition of heritable building rights,[291] a case of 1984 with the implicit acceptance of a right to place advertising as a *sui generis* property right,[292] a case of 1992 with a sole and exclusive right of use ('*droit de jouissance exclusif et privatif*') of the parts of the surface of a courtyard which the owners of apartments in a building owned as joint owners,[293], and in the same year with a right to pasture (namely the '*droit de seconde herbe*').[294]

Two inhabitants of the municipality of Saint-Nervin, Mssrs. Fraud and Bouvier, had claimed to be the owners of a real right to pasture their herds on a moor (after the first cut of the grass) in virtue of an agreement with a former owner. Certain Mssrs.

[289] *Malaurie and Aynès* op. cit. p. 90 no. 358.

[290] Cass. req. 13 February 1834, p. 1834, 1, p. 205; D. 1834, 1, p. 218; see *Jourdain* op. cit. p. 11 and *Atias* op. cit. p. 51.

[291] Cass. 16 December 1873, D.P. 1874, I, p. 249.

[292] Cass. civ. 18 January 1984, D. 1985 p. 504, note *Zenati*, and JCP G, 1986, II, 20547, note *Barbieri*. The owner of real estate intended to be subdivided and sold in parcels retained a perpetual right to attach billboards on the wall of a building and the possibility of disposing of this right to third parties. The condominium regulations characterized this right as a servitude. The Court of Appeal of Aix-en-Provence characterized it as a *usufruit*. The *Cour de cassation* quashed this appellate decision. The right was unlimited in time and could not, for this reason, be a *usufruit* (which could only be created for a lifetime). Because the right was not created in favour of the owner of another land parcel, it could only be considered as a property right *sui generis*. Zenati (op. cit.) thus comes to the conclusion that this decision speaks against the principle of a limited number of property rights.

[293] Cass. 4 March 1992, D. 1992 p. 386, note *Atias*. The *Cour de cassation* confirmed the existence of this property right ('*que le droit de jouissance exclusif et privatif sur une fraction de la cour, partie commune, attribué par le règlement de copropriété aux lots n° 2 et 3, dont il constituait l'accessoire, avait un caractère réel et perpétuel, que l'usage de ce droit était sans incidence sur sa pérennité et que ce droit ne pouvait être mis en cause sans le consentement de son bénéficiaire*'). But it was not a heritable building right, because the beneficiary of the *droit de jouissance exclusif* could neither build nor dispose of his right separately. Equally, it could not be a run of the mill servitude, as a servitude could not be granted in favour of co-owners and this right only concerned one, not two, land units (see further *Malaurie and Aynès*, Les biens^3, p. 91 no. 361, fn. 20 and *Zenati*, RTD civ. 1993 pp. 162, 163). See further Cass. 24 October 2007, Bull. civ. 2007, III, no. 183 (the *droit d'usage privatif* of the joint owners of a residential complex in a garden belonging to the complex was a perpetual, real right, which could be acquired by prescriptive occupation).

[294] Cass. 25 March 1992, D. 1993 p. 65, note *de la Marnierre*.

Rousselot brought an action for declaratory relief to the effect that no such right existed. The appellate court had indeed refused to characterize the putative right as a servitude, as the moor was said to be burdened not in favour of a dominant land unit but in favour of the inhabitants of the town of Saint-Nervin. The *droit de seconde herbe* nevertheless constituted '*un droit réel immobilier d'une nature particulière*'. A similar position is occupied by the apparently 'rediscovered' *droit de crû et à croître* (the 'right to what has grown and what is to grow') in a forest which, not subject to a limitations period, displays *erga omnes* effects.[295] Finally, a case of 2012 concerned a foundation that had sold a stately townhouse to a corporation. The notarized certification of the sale excluded *la jouissance ou l'occupation* of the foundation's rooms in the contract; the purchaser could get these rooms at any time, provided only that it constructed premises on the land of the same type and made it available to the foundation in perpetuity. An action for vacant possession brought in 2007 against the foundation was rejected. The case concerned not a right of use in a legal person, which would normally expire after thirty years, but rather with a *sui generis* property right of special use which the owner could create under Arts 544 and 1134 insofar as it did not violate any public order provisions—which was not the case.[296]

On the whole, then, there are certainly derogations of the *numerus clausus* principle to be found in French law, but they are few in number and generally quite mundane. The *Cour de cassation* has accepted modifications of property rights which already existed according to their kind, but has not sanctioned the creation of new property rights 'out of thin air'.[297]

In Belgium on the other hand, neither judicial nor scholarly opinion appear willing to take even these modest steps; they hold fast to the pre-eminence of the *numerus clausus* principle. The prevailing opinion (albeit not completely uncontested)[298] again accepts, at least since a decision of the *Cour de cassation* of 1966,[299] that property rights comprise a closed statutory catalogue.[300] In this decision, the court confirmed the rule that new property rights could only be introduced by the legislature. The claimant's predecessor-in-title had sold a land parcel to a company in 1927, on which a casino had **2.49**

[295] Cass. civ. 23 May 2012, D. 2012 p. 1934, note *d'Avout*.

[296] Cass. civ. 31 October 2012, Bull. civ. 2012, III, no. 159, p. 149; analysis of the decision in *Tardos*, D. 2012 p. 2596; *Testu*, JCP G 2012, 1400, p. 2352; *d'Avout and Mallet-Bricout*, D. 2013 p. 53 and *Dross*, RTD civ. 2013 p. 141.

[297] *Larroumet*, Les biens^5, p. 33 no. 51.

[298] For *Hansenne*, Les biens, p. 36 no. 30, the statutory list of property rights was only indicative ('*On ne voit point, il est vrai, quelle raison impérieuse pourrait conduire à l'interdiction absolue pour les particuliers de donner naissance à des droits réels nouveaux,* sui generis. *Encore faut-il que ces innovations ne conduisent pas à consacrer l'existence de relations juridiques dont la seule raison d'être serait le souci, conscient ou volontaire, apparent ou caché; d'échapper aux contraintes résultant des dispositions légales impératives en vigueur*') and the same can be said of *Dekkers*, Précis I, p. 511 no. 842 (he maintained that the private autonomous creation of new security rights was impossible, but not the creation of new *droits réels d'usage et de jouissance*).

[299] Cass. 16 September 1966, Pas. belge 1967, I, p. 63; J.T. 1967 p. 59.

[300] In this vein, see, e.g. *Van Neste*, Zakenrecht I^2, p. 59 no. 30; *Vandenberghe*, Goederenrecht, p. 4 no. 13; *Glansdorff*, J.T. 1968 p. 1 no. 1 and also *De Page*, Traité élémentaire I^3, p. 195 no. 130. The latter considers the practical importance of this controversy to be low, because one can think of hardly any other property rights to be provided for in statute. In the case of security rights, it is in any case given that they can only be created by the legislature.

later been built, and also granted the company a temporally unlimited right of use in another land parcel (called a 'park'). In 1928 the company was dissolved and disposed of the land parcel and the right of use to a newly created second company. The appellate court had decided that the usage right was not extinguished by the dissolution of the first company nor through the expiry of any statutory time period.[301] The owner, it had said, had the freedom to grant rights other than those named in Art. 543 Belgian Civil Code. It was also not important whether the contested right of use was a property right *sui generis* or a servitude. The *Cour de cassation*, however, held that Art. 543 did not allow the creation of property rights outside of those listed in it and defined in Arts 544, 578, and 628 (apart from communal servitudes, heritable leases, heritable building rights, and certain statutory rights of security). Property rights outside of these were 'outside contemplation'. The *Cour de cassation* also refused to characterize the right of use as a servitude and decided that it was concerned with a license in the sense of Art. 628. As such, it was extinguished in 1957 in accordance with Arts 619 and 625. These provisions were *d'ordre public* and therefore mandatory.

2.50 In Spain, too, the *numerus clausus* principle has not remained uncontested. Leading voices there are even of the opinion that Spanish law does not operate with such a principle at all, but rather with its exact opposite—a *numerus apertus* principle (the doctrine of an 'open catalogue' of property rights).[302] In support of this thesis, reference is made to the fact that the civil code (i) lacks a textual basis for the *numerus clausus* principle, and that (ii) Art. 2(2) of the *Ley Hipotecaria*[303] (in conjunction with Art. 7 of *Reglamento Hipotecario*) expressly envisages the possibility of registering not only those rights named in the civil code, but 'every other property right'.[304] It is, however, questionable whether that provision and the lived experience of the law in practice over the past century really bear out the argument that Spanish law operates on a *numerus apertus* principle. In any case, it again boils down to a question of determining the limits of party autonomy by reference to statutory property rights, both existing and not (yet) statutorily defined.[305] With regards to the first group, Díez-Picazo considers the Spanish statutory law of property[306] to be adequately flexible to adapt the content of

[301] In particular Art. 625 Belgian Civil Code in connection with Art. 617 (by which usage rights are extinguished by the death of their beneficiary) and in connection with Art. 619 (by which licenses expire after thirty years).

[302] In this vein see *inter alia Albaladejo*, Derecho civil III(1)[10], p. 30; *Lasarte Álvarez*, Principios IV[9], p. 14 and *O´Callaghan Muñoz*, Compendio de derecho civil III[5], p. 36.

[303] 'In the Registers listed in the previous article, the following shall be registered: . . . (2) The titles in which rights of usufruct, use, habitation, leasehold, mortgage, census, easements *and any other real right* is constituted, recognized, transmitted, modified or extinguished' (emphasis added).

[304] The meaning of this formulation is not uncontentious. One could also read it in such a manner that, as *Díez-Picazo*, Fundamentos III[5], p. 137 points out, this expression means nothing more than that such 'other rights' are allowed to be registered; the fact that some rights are registerable provides no basis for the proposition that all registerable rights automatically assume the character of absolute property rights. This is confirmed to a certain extent by TS 27 May 2009, RAJ 2009 no. 3047 p. 7497. The builder (and original owner of the building) could retain certain rights in the first title (in a new chain of titles) in a residential apartment, which would otherwise belong to all co-owners. This included the right to undertake construction underneath or above (i.e. adding additional stories to the building). This right, however, would only take on a real character under Art. 16(2) *Reglamento Hipotecario* if it was described in precise terms, which meant satisfying the fundamental principle of legal certainty.

[305] See (correctly) *Díez-Picazo* op. cit. p. 141.

[306] This law embraces more than just the civil code and the hypothec statute; it also includes a raft of special purpose instruments including statutes on hypothecs in moveable things (*Ley de 16 de diciembre de 1954 sobre*

its rights to the needs of the case by interpretative means.[307] A statutory framework for the creation of completely new rights, however, is missing. The law authorizes parties to adapt property rights already provided for and defined by statute, but that does not mean that it allows private persons to create new property rights outside the statutory types.[308]

A review of the Spanish registration practice confirms this view. The most important exception to the general proscription of privately created property rights relates to the introduction of heritable building rights (which have now long been governed by statute).[309] A more recent example is provided by timesharing, which was recognized as having the character of a property right long before there was a statutory explanation[310] for this status.[311] For the most part, however, development has proceeded in modest steps. The *Dirección General de los Registros y del Notariado* has, for example, recognized the right to erect billboards on someone else's land as a property right capable of registration.[312] Besides this, it has recognized a raft of extensions to the sphere of application of pre-emption rights (*derechos de adquisición preferente*[313]).[314] Such rights, although **2.51**

hipoteca mobiliaria y prenda sin desplazamiento de posesión) and on timesharing (*Ley 42/1998, sobre derechos de aprovechamiento por turno de bienes inmuebles de uso turístico y normas tributarias*).

[307] *Díez-Picazo* op. cit. p. 136.

[308] Ibid. p. 137.

[309] The heritable building right was already recognized as an atypical property right before its statutory provision in Art. 16 *Reglamento Hipotecario* and in the (often amended) *Ley del Suelo* (lit. 'Soil Law') (*Díez-Picazo*, RCDI 1976 pp. 299, 321).

[310] The real character of this right was first recognized by statute in the 1998 *Ley* 42/1998.

[311] *Dirección General de los Registros y del Notariado* 4 March 1993, RAJ 1993 no. 2471 p. 3176.

[312] *Dirección General de los Registros y del Notariado* 25 November 1992, RAJ 1992 no. 9494 p. 12432.

[313] The term *derechos de adquisición preferente* (which does not appear in the civil code) is understood to mean heritable obligational and property rights broadly construed. Most importantly, these include *derechos de tanteo*, *derechos de retracto*, and *derechos de opción*. The common attribute of all *derechos de adquisición preferente* is that they give a person priority in the right to inherit ownership of a thing. The definition and classification of this set of rights is the result of a theoretical effort which has, in the meantime, been recognized and adopted in judicial opinion (see further *Lasarte Álvarez*, Derechos reales y derecho hipotecario[7], p. 166). Real *derechos de adquisición preferente* limit the dispositionary powers of the owner. The real right of pre-emption (*derecho de tanteo*) gives its holder the right to demand the acquisition of an as yet unsold thing. The real right of repurchase (*derecho de retracto*) gives a seller the right to buy a thing he has sold back from the (erstwhile) buyer. Whether these are really different kinds of property rights, or just different manifestations of a single right, is not entirely clear but not particularly important (see further *Lacruz Berdejo*, Elementos III(2)[3], p. 343). Spanish law recognized a whole raft of real repurchase rights before the introduction of the Civil Code; these were abolished in 1889 (*Lasarte Álvarez* op. cit. p. 168). An example is the *retracto gentilicio*, which gives the members of a family the priority right to acquire certain goods. It is today (under various aliases) only found in certain foral legal systems (*retracto gentilicio* ley 452–ley 459 Compilación del derecho civil foral de Navarra, Ley 1/1973 of 1 March 1973; *derecho de abolorio o de la saca* Arts 588–598 Código del derecho foral de Aragón, Decreto Legislativo 1/2011 of 22 March 2011; *derecho de tornería del Valle de Arán* Arts 568-21 to 568-26 Catalonian Civil Code). Certain pre-emption rights (*derechos de opción de compra)* and the pre-emptive right to sell (*derecho de opción de venta*) must, under Art. 14 *Reglamento Hipotecario* be registered in certain cases. According to the prevailing view, they acquire the status of property rights upon registration (see however *Díez-Picazo*, Fundamentos III[5], pp. 118–20 with the modification, that *derechos de tanteo, derechos de retracto, derechos de opción de compra* and the *derecho de opción de venta* enjoy *erga omnes* effect, but are not real rights).

[314] It is particularly important that such rights can also be created by party autonomy without any express statutory basis (e.g. Arts 1507 ff. Spanish Civil Code for the real right of repurchase). This is also true for the *derecho de tanteo* and the *derecho de opción de compra*, among others (*Puig Brutau*, Fundamentos III(3)[3], p. 395). They must, however, meet the requirements in Art. 14 *Reglamento Hipotecario* in order to acquire real character.

of a purely obligational nature, can be furnished with real effects by the parties.[315] In other words, the parties seem be able to impress a *derecho de adquisición preferente* with a real character, but have to agree on this expressly; in the absence of such a clear agreement the right only has *in personam* effect.[316] This view is shared by the *Tribunal Supremo*.[317] Reciprocal rights of first refusal have been registered, which in effect gave a swap agreement real effect.[318] An agreement giving a prospective purchaser the right to build an underground garage extending under the soil into the neighbouring land parcel can also be furnished with a real character.[319] An administrative decision giving a company the right to encumber a palatial estate with a hypothec has also been entered into the land register. The administrative decision included the right to run a hotel in the palace for a period of fifty-five years.[320]

c. The *Numerus Clausus* Principle in England and Ireland

2.52 In the system of the common law of England and Ireland, too, the fundamental principle applies that interests in objects only constitute property rights when the law provides an appropriate framework. That is only guaranteed in a limited number of cases.[321] 'Incidents of a novel kind' cannot, according to the principle in *Keppell v Bailey*, 'be devised and attached to property at the fancy or caprice of any owner'.[322] This fundamental principle applies, however, only to the common law, not for equity. Equity is, proverbially, 'not past the age of childbearing'.[323] For rights in land units, secs 1(1) and 1(2) of the English Law of Property Act 1925[324] provide (to formulate it in a Continental idiom) an express statutory confirmation of the *numerus clausus* principle in the common law,[325] and sec. 1(3) of the same Act adds that rights in land, which are

[315] The further requirements for the 'elevation' of an obligational right into a property right were set out by the *Dirección General de los Registros y del Notariado* in *Resolución* 20 September 1966, RAJ 1966 Nr. 4020 p. 4020.

[316] *Dirección General de los Registros y del Notariado* 6 March 2001, RAJ 2002 no. 2172 p. 2172.

[317] TS 3 March 1995, RAJ 1995 no. 1776 p. 2303. The parties had called their contract *contrato de derecho de adquisición preferente*, but in the opinion of the court they only drafted it as an obligational instrument. In order to grant a *derecho de adquisición preferente* of real character, they would have had to agree to it expressly.

[318] *Dirección General de los Registros y del Notariado* 20 September 1966, RAJ 1966 no. 4020 p. 4020.

[319] *Dirección General de los Registros y del Notariado* 14 May 1984, RAJ 1984 no. 2588 p. 1993.

[320] *Dirección General de los Registros y del Notariado* 16 July 2002, RAJ 2002 no. 9317 p. 17179.

[321] *Merrill and Smith*, 110 Yale L.J. 2000–2001 pp. 1, 3.

[322] *Keppell v Bailey* (1834) 2 My & K 517; 39 ER 1042, 1049.

[323] *Baker and Langan*, Snell's Equity^{29}, p. 11.

[324] 1925, ch. 20.

[325] sec. 1(1) stipulates that 'the only estates in land which are capable of subsisting or of being conveyed or created at law are (a) an estate in fee simple absolute in possession; (b) a term of years absolute'. sec. 1(2) lists 'the only interests or charges in or over land which are capable of subsisting or of being conveyed or created at law'. (This is reflected in Ireland by sec. 11 Land and Conveyancing Law Reform Act 2009.) Some entries in this list are, however, so broad and uncertain, that the scope of the parties' freedom goes far beyond that which is typical of many Continental legal systems. Besides this, one also encounters quasi-proprietary 'fortifications' of obligational rights. *Finnamore t/a Hanbridge Storage Services v HMRC* [2011] UKFTT 216 (TC) concerned a question in the context of tax law, namely whether the lessees of containers resting on a land unit, which provided a kind of self-service storage, had a license to occupy land in the sense of Sched. 9, Group 1, Item 1 Value Added Tax Act 1994, in virtue of which they would not have to pay VAT. The court answered this question in the affirmative, because the containers were set up on a certain and delineated portion of the land unit. In fact, an obligational right has crept in the direction of a property right here, albeit only for the purpose of tax law.

not named in this list, can only arise as *equitable property rights in land*.[326] *Keppell v Bailey* also concerned rights in land, but the decision is now taken as the expression of an overarching principle, namely a kind of *numerus clausus* that also applies to property rights in moveable things.[327] There is no statutory basis for this principle, and it does not rank as a strict principle of property law as it does in many legal systems on the Continent. However, the decision reflects a common posture, and expresses a generally restrictive attitude towards the recognition of new property rights. Although the courts are not generally barred from accepting new property rights in chattels, generally they refuse to do so. In the law of chattels, the common law recognizes only a handful of rights connected to (or derived from) possession alongside legal ownership, for example the so-called *special property* of a pledgee or other bailee. Except in case of an inducement to breach of contract, the one who has merely rented a chattel has no rights against a purchaser, when the owner of the chattel still has possession and refuses to deliver it to the renter. The rental agreement alone gives the renter no property right in the chattel before he acquires possession. He remains limited to obligational claims against the owner.[328]

The fundamental principle that owners cannot create novel property rights at will is, **2.53**
however, not usually emphasized in the textbooks nor discussed under the moniker of a '*numerus clausus* principle'.[329] In fact, the term is only rarely mentioned, even in specialist analyses;[330] neither the cases nor the literature have established an independent term for the rule that property law is concerned with only a fixed number of property rights. In substance, however, the common law courts deal with property rights in a manner that resembles the Continental practice; they too accept that the forms of property rights accepted today form a closed list which only the legislature can extend or truncate.[331] Outside of the law of real property this is a matter of a general principle of interpretation, which acts as a kind of norm of judicial self control.[332] However, one must immediately qualify this statement, as the common law (to use the Continental idiom) mitigates its strict *Typenzwang* with a relatively weak form of *Typenfixierung*. Within the pre-existing types of property rights there remains some leeway for judicial development of sub-types. This can be seen among other things in the law of easements (encumbrances that bind the landowner to suffer some activity on his land, similar to

326 sec. 1(3): 'All other estates, interests, and charges in or over land take effect as equitable interests.'

327 We are concerned with an 'almost closed' list of property rights in 'pure personalty': Birks (*-Swadling*), English Private Law I, no. 4-186.

328 See further *Goode*, Commercial Law^3, pp. 34–5.

329 The keyword '*numerus clausus*' appears, for example, neither in the table of contents nor in the glossary of the more than 1600 page work Megarry and Wade (*-Harpum/Bridge/Dixon*), The Law of Real Property,^{8} nor in the somewhat shorter textbook Cheshire and Burn (*-Burn and Cartwright*), Modern Law of Real Property^{17}. A significant exception, however, is *Clarke and Kohler*, Property Law, pp. 159–60 and Ch. 9 (which the authors place under the title 'Recognition of new property interests').

330 Exceptions are found in *Merrill and Smith*, 110 Yale L.J. 2000–2001 pp. 1, 3, and in *Rudden*, in Oxford Essays in Jurisprudence. Third series (1987) p. 239 (critical of this, see *Sparkes*, ERPL 2012 pp. 769–804).

331 *Merrill and Smith* op. cit. p. 10.

332 Ibid. *Clarke and Kohler* op. cit. point to a 'general reluctance' of the legal system towards the recognition of new property rights.

servitudes). The judges' readiness to innovate is perhaps more modest in the case of so-called 'negative' easements (which bind the land owner to forebear from certain actions on his own land) than in the case of 'positive' easements (which grant the *dominant owner* the right to take certain actions on the land of the *servient owner*).[333] But there seems to be a general desire to preserve the possibility, for both categories of easements, to adapt continually with changes in living conditions in the community.[334]

2.54 The right to use another's land for the purposes of rambling (that is, with a changing destination and for the purpose of recreation) cannot, under the rules of the common law, generally be secured with real rights as an easement, as such an easement would in substance be concerned with a so-called *jus spatiandi*.[335] However, exceptions to this rule have been allowed, for example in favour of the respective owners of dwellings around a park and garden.[336] In *Middleton v Clarence*, an Irish court even recognized the right to remove quarry leftovers from the land of another as the content of an easement.[337] Another development in property law concerns the position of a tenant (i.e. one renting a thing and in possession of it). The common law has always recognized a real aspect to tenants' legal position. The courts, however, have only recently recognized the property rights of a person who is given the possession and use of a thing gratuitously.[338] An example for the maintenance of a *numerus clausus* and *Typenzwang*, on the other hand, is the case of *Hill v Tupper*, the case of the pleasure boats on a canal discussed above at paragraph 8. The claimant failed in his attempt to show that he had an estate or interest. The cases cited to the court by the claimant did not appear to be analogous: 'some authority must be produced before we can hold that such a right can be created.'[339] At the same time, however, the case illustrates that the question of a right's 'real' nature can always be posed anew, where in the Continental legal systems it is answered with a mere glance in the codification. The question answered in *Hill v Tupper* would, in principle, not arise in these jurisdictions in the first place.

2.55 All property rights at common law can also arise, as already mentioned, in equity. But this proposition does not hold in reverse. The list of equitable property rights is not closed—neither in respect of land nor moveable possessions. There are, accordingly, equitable property rights with no counterpart in the domain of common law property rights. However, 'new' property rights are only created in equity when they bear a sufficient resemblance to a previously recognized right. There remains

333 *Wylie*, Irish Land Law^3, p. 364.

334 'The category of servitudes and easements must alter and expand with the changes that take place in the circumstances of mankind': *Dyce v Lady James Hay* (1852) 1 Macq 305, 312–13 (Lord St Leonards), here cited as in *Wylie* op. cit.

335 *Henry Ltd v McGlade* [1926] NI 144.

336 *Re Ellenborough Park* [1956] Ch 131.

337 *Middleton v Clarence* (1877) IR 11 CL 499.

338 *Skipton Building Society v Clayton* (1993) 66 P & CR 223, 230 (Sir Christopher Slade).

339 (1863) 2 H & C 122, 128; 159 ER 51, 53 (Martin B: 'None of the cases cited are at all analogous to this, and some authority must be produced before we can hold that such a right can be created. To admit the right would lead to the creation of an infinite variety of interests in land, and an indefinite increase of possible estates').

room for new developments, but equity, too, generally moves in small steps. The most important innovation that the law has made in the area of property law *via* equity in the last 150 years is the so-called restrictive covenant (i.e. 'equitable (negative) servitude').

The number of possible easements and *profits à prendre* under the common law was strictly limited. Whoever had a right over another's land that fell outside the list of recognized easements and profits generally held only an obligational, *in personam* right. Even if B, for example, had a right to use A's land (or to have A refrain from certain actions on that land) as the result of covenant made by A to B and his successors, A's transfer of his 'property' to C left B without any property rights against C. This differed only in certain cases, for example where a landlord–tenant relationship existed between A and B ('sale does not break a lease'). In this case, C would step into A's legal position. The common law rule is, accordingly, that burdens of this kind, which are created contractually in respect of land, only bind the acquirer of a land parcel in the framework of a landlord-tenant relationship.[340] *Tulk v Moxhay*,[341] however, took an important step beyond this rule. The case turned on the question whether a contract of sale of part of a land unit could secure, with real effects, that one of the parties refrain from certain actions on their part of the land (for example construction). This became relevant when one of the parties sold his land unit to a third party and it became a question of whether the agreement between the vendor and the (first) purchaser could be binding on third parties. The Court of Chancery affirmed that this was the case with the creation of a new right in equity, the *equitable servitude* (or *restrictive covenant*). This step was, however, rather difficult to square with the general rule in *Keppell v Bailey*. *Keppell v Bailey* concerned a common law property right, and was therefore not directly binding, but was generally interpreted as a warning against the too-hasty transformation of mere contractual rights into new forms of property right. In consequence, this new creation of Chancery was quickly made subject to substantial limitations. In equity, too, a right created by a private act-in-the-law in this manner can only be made into a property right against third parties when (i) the covenant is intended to benefit a neighbouring land unit and does in fact benefit it,[342] (ii) the person against whom the covenant is meant to be enforced had notice of the covenant at the time he acquired the tenement,[343] and (iii) the covenant does in fact 'concern and touch' the land.[344] In Ireland, on the other hand, the restrictive covenant has been (in a directly opposite legal policy decision) 'upgraded' from a mere equitable interest to a common law right.[345]

[340] Cheshire and Burn (-*Burn and Cartwright*), Modern Law of Real Property[17], p. 662.
[341] (1848) 18 LJ Ch 83; 41 ER 1143.
[342] *London County Council v Allen* [1914] 3 KB 642; *Kelly v Barrett* [1924] 2 Ch 379.
[343] More precisely: the protection of third parties was traditionally dependent on ignorance and payment of value; today, *erga omnes* effect depends on registration in the land register.
[344] *Merrill and Smith* op. cit. p. 16 f; *Rogers v Hosegood* [1900] 2 Ch 388 (Farwell J).
[345] s. 49 Land and Conveyancing Law Reform Act 2009.

d. Property Rights and the Rights of Third Parties: Sweden

2.56 The concept of property law has shifted in recent decades in Sweden. A dramatic change in the self-conception of Swedish legal doctrine has precipitated, among other things, an extension of the catalogue of legal objects protected by property law. This change is both an element and a consequence of the thesis that the distinction between obligations and property law should no longer be given much importance. In the end, every legal position *vis-à-vis* an object of value boils down to whether, and to what extent, a right is effective against a particular third party. Where that is the case, it is said that the legal position enjoys 'property law protection' (or 'protection against third parties'). At the same time, it is considered important to emphasize that a 'property right' does not mean the same thing in the context of Swedish law as it means in the context of German law (for example). 'The law of things' [*sakrätt*] was, originally, a strictly defined discipline in Swedish law as elsewhere. It was concerned with only a few property rights that were clearly defined in their content from the outset. They, in turn, were anchored in only such objects as were, through their spatial extension, clearly defined from all other objects of legal commerce.[346] In the category of *lös egendom* (moveable, lit. 'loose' property), for example, property rights were listed as the rights of ownership, pledge, and retention, and a few other rights derived from them. These were the sole objects of the leading pronouncements of Swedish property law in the first half of the twentieth century.[347] New property rights could not be created by private parties; property law was (and is, in principle, today) mandatory law. The strict division between obligations and property law—or, more precisely, this form of strict separation between obligations and property law—has increasingly been seen as unsatisfactory since mid-century. It is considered better to analyse obligations and property law as a coherent whole and to develop them as such in a manner driven by practical interests. The necessary nuance, according to this view, is impossible to achieve so long as one remained limited to property rights (namely ownership [*äganderätt*], security rights [*säkerhetsrätter*], and, in relation to land parcels, rights of use [*nyttjanderätter*]) and was thereby forced to categorize every other right as a mere *in personam* obligation. This led to a fundamental change of perspective. One began to emphasize the distinction between legally cognizable interests which were only meant to be achievable *inter partes* through a private act-in-the-law, and interests which were meant to be enforceable against third parties. There were good reasons for the recognition of such effect against third parties even when the relevant interest could not be dressed in the guise of a recognized property right. Although the traditional Swedish

[346] *Hessler*, Allmän sakrätt, p. 4.

[347] We are concerned with *Östen Undén*'s Svensk sakrätt, the first volume of which (*Lös egendom*) was published in 1927 (10th edn, 1976) and the second volume of which (*Fast egendom*) was published in 1936 (5th edn, 1969). This book dealt with, in the law of moveables, ownership (*äganderätt*), pledges (*panträtt*), and certain other security rights (*säkerhetsrätter*); in the law of immoveables, it dealt with ownership and usufruct (*nyttjanderätt*). It counts today as the classic among the older property law textbooks in Sweden (*Håstad*, Sakrätt[6], p. 18, and *Hessler* op. cit.).

law recognized no rights of use in moveable property, it was seen as necessary to make contractual rights of use enforceable against *mala fides* successors-in-title, at least exceptionally. The flexibility necessary was not, however, to be found either in the law of sale nor in the law of property; one had to look beyond these categories to the legal consequences that an act-in-the-law had for third parties.[348] However, whether the border between obligations and property law has been completely levelled out remains an open question. One could also describe these developments with the proposition that Swedish law has simply recognized more property rights over the years than the traditional law used to recognize.

These developments were, however, only possible by reason of the fact that Swedish law **2.57**
never fixed the *numerus clausus* principle in any statute; perhaps it is even necessary to say that, formally, this principle never applied in Sweden. In any case, the silence of the legislature gave the courts sufficient room to distance themselves from the original concept of a closely circumscribed number of absolute rights with fixed content in physical objects; in its place, the Swedish courts have used the 'functional' question, which admits of different answers in different cases, of what kind of third party effects a given legal position should have.[349] Sweden and the remaining Scandinavian legal systems thus elude a general categorization of countries with and without the *numerus clausus* principle. So-called 'Scandinavian functionalism' often proceeds on the basis of sweeping interest-balancing exercises, with the aid of which conflicts with third persons are resolved. Rights and powers, too, which did not fall in the once-closed list of property rights, can thus be given 'real protection' in the individual case; or, to put it in other words: the borders of the once-tightly circumscribed law of 'moveable property' have been erased.[350] Conversely, however, the conceptual figure of ownership has been demoted from its formerly pre-eminent position as the means of resolving questions of property law. The modern law considers a property law conflict to be, typically, a situation in which two persons claim an object for their own, which object is in the possession of a third person, where only one of their claims can be validated by the law. The task of property law is to decide which claim is to be given priority. The expression 'property law' (*sakrätt*, lit. 'thing law') has, in this manner, come to embrace more than one meaning. In the narrower—static or substantial—sense, *sakrätt* embraces the 'classical' rights in physical objects; in the broader—dynamic or functional—sense, it embraces all powers effective against third parties in whatever objects of legal commerce, i.e. in physical objects, but not only in physical objects.

The guarantee of 'property law protection' beyond rights of use has been discussed, for example in the context of option rights, limitations on the manner of using an object,

[348] *Hessler* op. cit. pp. 11–12.
[349] *Håstad* op. cit. p. 16; Faber and Lurger (-*Lilja*), National Reports V, Sweden, pp. 13–16. For an example from the cases, see HD 25 May 1988, NJA 1988 p. 257 (A had sold a restaurant to B and had transferred to him the right to use the rooms of the premises; the right of use manifested *erga omnes* effects, because A informed his landlord of the transfer in a timely fashion).
[350] *Millqvist* op. cit. pp. 13–14.

and restrictions on disposition or transfer. None of these private law models can be said for once and for all to bear an *in personam* or an *in rem* character; the true results of the acts-in-the-law that created them can only be determined on the facts of the case. Prohibitions on disposition and transfer, for example, began as a unique phenomenon in family law and the law of succession, but are described in the contemporary literature as having third party effects when they are the subject of a formally constituted gift,[351] though not when they are agreed in a contract of sale. If a third person acquires the thing, he is not bound by the agreement between the disponer and the first disponee.[352] Option rights do not enjoy the protection of property law as a rule. Exceptionally, however, they are said to be enforceable against a pledgee.[353] Matters are similar in the case of rights of use in moveable things. Again, they do not in principle enjoy the status or legal protection of property rights.[354] But exceptions exist, as the registration of aeroplanes already illustrates. The limited legal effect of rights of use in moveable things is said to be explained by historical relations in production, namely the use of short-term supply contracts. The present situation has completely changed, and for this reason it is said that the courts must be able to review and extend the protection of rights of use as a matter of urgency. On the whole, this conceptual approach has not only shifted the meaning of 'property law' but has also entailed a change in the meaning of 'ownership', which is now understood, much as it is in England, as a mere bundle of rights.[355] Sandstedt has aptly described the situation thus:

> For a substantialist [he means a jurist in the Continental school], creditor protection can normally be derived from the concept of ownership, whereas the Nordic approach in particular treats the transfer situation as a legal fact legal effect scenario, i.e., *without using the concept of ownership.*[356]

This notwithstanding, one remains true to the *numerus clausus* principle to the extent that one accepts that the objective law (i.e. the legal system as such, and not the parties themselves) determines whether or not a given right over a given asset is effective against third parties.[357]

351 Ibid. p. 19. Certain statutory provisions (e.g. § 2 *Preskriptionslag* (1981:130)), however, still distinguish now as before between a real right (*sakrätt*) and a mere obligational right (*fordringsrätt*).

352 HD 10 March 1998, NJA 1998 p. 135.

353 *Millqvist* op. cit.

354 HD 2 October 1975, NJA 1975 p. 528.

355 *Lilja* op. cit. (n 349 above) pp. 16–20.

356 *Sandstedt*, Sakrätten, Norden och europeiseringen, p. IX. The correctness of this analysis is confirmed by an endless line of authorities. An early example is found in HD 16 February 1960, NJA 1960 p. 9. B had purchased a truck from A and, later, had purchased new tires for it from C. Both transactions were subject to a retention of title (mostly, in order to avoid using the word 'ownership', couched as a 'right to claim delivery of possession') in favour of the respective supplier. As B defaulted in payment, A took possession of the truck; C demanded possession of the tires. The court did not ask whether the tires had become a part of the truck through fixture and therefore had become part of A's property; the word 'ownership' did not appear in its analysis. Instead, all the circumstances of the case and the interests of the parties were enquired into in the context of the question, whether C's retention of title was effective against A. That was answered in the negative 3:2. The result (no remedy for C) could, however, have been different if the truck had still found itself in B's possession and if A had not yet exercised his right. Had that been so, *Håstad*, Sakrätt[6], pp. 188–9 opines that the situation could have been dealt with as a simple bilateral relationship with the consequence that C would have been able to get 'his' tires back from B.

357 *Hessler* op. cit. p. 84; *Millqvist* op. cit. pp. 17–18.

III

Object, Holder, and Content of Property Rights

Even more so than for the internal study of a single national legal system, it is helpful for a European survey of the current state of legal developments to be aware of three matters. One must consider (i) in which *objects* property rights can arise, (ii) *who* can hold (or acquire) such property rights, and (iii) which *powers* property rights give their holder.[1] The laws of the European Union are not uniform on any of these three (interrelated) aspects of property law. Property rights arise in a different, broader or narrower set of objects from jurisdiction to jurisdiction, they are not always available to every person, and they do not have the same substantive content—not even when they are called by the same name. Terminologically, we are traversing difficult terrain. **3.1**

The question who may occupy a legal position based in property law sometimes raises questions of public law, because it may be the case that certain rights in land units (up to and including the right of ownership)[2] can only be held or acquired by the state[3] or by citizens of a certain state[4] (or even, in certain cases, **3.2**

[1] For a similar argument, see *inter alia Bianca*, Diritto civile VI, p. 121; *Vieira*, Direitos reais, p. 133 (mainly, however, with the plea to characterize rights in rights as rights in things or 'goods' on the basis that it is not the encumbered right, but the object to which it relates, that is the relevant legal object) and *Wieling*, Sachenrecht I^2, § 1 I 1 a ('Property law governs the legal relations of a human being to a physical object ['thing', German *Sache*]. This relationship to a thing manifests as a property right [right in the thing, real right, *ius in re*], for example as ownership or the right of a pledgee'): *Papasteriou*, Emprágmato Díkaio I, pp. 50–52 nos 7–10 distinguishes between the subject as the bearer of the proprietary relationship, the object of the property rights, and the duration of the proprietary relationship.

[2] The notion that only the Crown or the State can be an absolute owner of land informs the theoretical concept of English and Irish real property law to this day.

[3] In most European legal systems, the rights in certain mineral resources are bracketed out of the ownership of the private subject by statute and given to the state, which then passes them on to enterprises by way of concession which allows those enterprises to acquire the resources for themselves.

[4] Under the influence of European Union law, however, limitations on the acquisition of property by foreigners have visibly diminished. In the Czech Republic, for example, foreigners were subject to limitations on the acquisition of dwellings under the so-called Foreign Exchange Statute (Statute No. 219/1995) up to 1 May 2010; thereafter, foreigners were 'only' restricted in the acquisition of agricultural land and forests. Even these restrictions have fallen away since 1 May 2011. Under Art. 1(1) Sentence 1 of the *Polish Ustawa z dnia 24 marca 1920 r. o nabywnianiu nieruchomości przez cudzoziemców*, foreigners have required the approval of the ministry for the interior to purchase real estate, and the approval of the ministry for agriculture to purchase agricultural land. For EU citizens, the purchase of land should have been made easier within twelve years of the country's accession to the Union (Radwański and Dybowski [*-Stelmachowski*], System Prawa Prywatnego III^2, pp. 329–31 nos 37–43). Similar regimes are found in Schedule 6 of the Accession Treaty of 2005 for Bulgaria and Romania. The deadlines for limitations and prohibitions for non-resident EU citizens has, however, expired. In Greece, real property in certain border areas may only be acquired by Greeks (natural and juristic persons) and by persons of Greek heritage (often persons resident in the USA or Australia). However, all EU citizens are placed on an equal status with Greeks under Art. 28 of the Greek Constitution, such that they are not subject to restrictions any more (CA Dodecanese 227/2009, EfAD 11/2009 p. 1201, note by Boulgaris). Insofar as the limitations still apply for non-EU citizens, they also embrace acquisition in the course of enforcement of legal claims (CA Dodecanese 23/2002, Dodekanisiakí Nomologia 7 (2003) p. 168), and the same applies to the acquisition of shares in a Greek company which owns such real estate (see *Vrellis*, Díkeo Allodapón, p. 27). Art. 30 of the Spanish *Ley Orgánica 5/2005 de 17 de noviembre, de la Defensa Nacional* creates a legal basis on which to exclude foreigners from acquiring land units that are of significance for the national defence. Under Art. 10 no. 6 (in connection with Art. 15) of the Austrian Constitution,

Foundations of Property Law. Christian von Bar and Jason Grant Allen, Oxford University Press. © Christian von Bar 2023.
DOI: 10.1093/oso/9780198885337.003.0003

the residents of a certain area within the state).[5] The same is sometimes true of churches,[6] and monastic institutions.[7] The issue, however, goes deeper and demands investigation above all because property rights are also to be found that can only be created or acquired by traders,[8] farmers,[9] banks,[10] or (other) juristic

the federal states have the power to limit the acquisition of land by foreigners; all states have established an approval regime on this basis, from which EU citizens are, however, exempt.

[5] A decree of the Flemish Regional Government of 27 March 2009 on land development policy (Belgian Official Gazette, 15 May 2009), for example, empowered local government authorities in 69 communes in Flanders to prevent persons without a 'sufficient connection' with the commune, as defined in Art. 5.2.1 § 2 from purchasing real estate. The francophone population of Belgium (and not least a large part of the population of Brussels) felt that the decree was directed towards them. The provision was worded in French as follows: '§ 2. *Pour l'application du § 1er, deuxième alinéa, une personne a un lien suffisant avec la commune si elle satisfait à une ou plusieurs des conditions suivantes: 1° avoir était domicilié dans la commune ou dans une commune avoisinante pendant au moins six ans de manière ininterrompue, à condition que cette commune soit également reprise sur la liste, stipulée à l'article 5.1.1; 2° à la date du transfert, réaliser des activités dans la commune, pour autant que ces activités occupent en moyenne au moins la moitié d'une semaine de travail; 3° avoir construit avec la commune un lien professionnel, familial, social ou économique en raison d'une circonstance importante et de longue durée*.' The CJEU held in *Eric Libert and Others vs Flämische Regierung* und *All Projects & Developments NV v Flämische Regierung*, C-197/11 and C-203/11 (8 May 2013) para. [60] that 'Articles 21 TFEU, 45 TFEU, 49 TFEU, 56 TFEU and 63 TFEU and Articles 22 and 24 of Directive 2004/38 preclude legislation, such as Book 5 of the Flemish Decree, which makes the transfer of immoveable property in the target communes subject to verification, by a provincial assessment committee, that there exists a "sufficient connection" between the prospective buyer or tenant and those communes.' Accordingly, the Belgian Constitutional Court declared the discriminatory sections of the decree, including its Book 5, to be null and void in its judgment of 7 November 2013 (no. 144/2013).

[6] e.g. Arts 23 and 24 of Concordat Between the Portuguese Republic and the Holy See of 18 May 2004 which governs the state's powers over the property of the Catholic Church.

[7] The privileges of the monasteries on the Greek peninsular of Athos are particular impressive, not only in relation to property situated on the peninsular but also in relation to property scattered throughout the rest of the country. Art. 105 of the Greek Constitution guarantees these privileges, which are concretized through the Order of the Holy Mountain (statutory decree of 16 September 1926). No person can have ownership of any land on the peninsular except for the monasteries (Art. 2, confirmed in numerous recent statutes and in the Presidential Directive 227/1998). Every monastery keeps its own land register; land units may be swapped, but never alienated by sale (Art. 100).

[8] Under Greek law, for example, non-possessory pledges and floating charges can only be created and acquired by merchants, commercial undertakings, and members of certain professions (Art. 1 of Statute 2844/2000). German law confines numerous security rights to commercial people (e.g. the commission merchant's pledge in § 397 German Commercial Code, the carrier's pledge in § 441 German Commercial Code, the shipping agent's pledge in § 464 German Civil Code, and the warehouser's pledge in § 475b German Commercial Code). This position is substantially the same in the Czech Republic (see e.g. §§ 2429, 2481, and 2571 Czech Civil Code). Bulgarian law takes the mercantile characteristics of the debtor (not the creditor) as dispositive for the permissibility of a non-possessory pledge (Art. 3(1) of the Bulgarian Statute on Special Security Rights). Non-commercial people can only pledge company shares and rights in immaterial goods; besides this, the spouse of a sole trader can take non-possessory security interests (Art. 3 subs. 2).

[9] The so-called milk quota presents a kind of special right for primary producers in England, i.e. the right under European law to market milk free of levies. It is treated effectively as a property right (see *Swift v Dairywise Farms Ltd* [2000] 1 WLR 1177, Jacob J holding that the milk quota could be the subject matter of a trust). The Swedish Supreme Court, on the other hand, has made more cautious pronouncements and has decided that the milk quota cannot form part of a joint liability arrangement in the context of a hypothec: HD 5 February 2001, NJA 2001, 46. In Poland, agricultural knowledge was a prerequisite to acquiring agricultural land until 1990 (Arts 160–165 of the old Polish Civil Code). Today, such knowledge only plays a role in the context of various pre-emptive purchase rights (see Radwański and Gniewek [-*Gniewek*], System Prawa Prywatnego III[3], p. 589 nos 282–285).

[10] Here belong, among other things, the financial collateral arrangements created in Directive 2002/47/EC of 6 June 2002. Portugal, for example, transposed the Directive through DL 105/2004 of 8 May 2004. The financial collateral arrangement that resulted, and the fiduciary transfer of ownership in the security interests are characterized as real security rights in Portuguese law (STJ 9 October 2008, Processo 07A3965). Parties to such a financial collateral arrangement can, under Art. 3(1) DL 105/2004, only be public bodies, state-owned banks, the ECB, the IMF, corporations, and certain institutions, but not natural persons (Art. 3(1)(e)). This reflects the position under Art. 1(2) no. 5 and Art. 5 of the Greek Statute 3301/2004 (FEK 263/A of 23 December 2004). Spain transposed the Directive with the Royal Decree 5/2005 of 11 March 2005 *de reformas urgentes para el impulso de la productividad y para la mejora de la productividad pública*, Chapter II of which creates new security rights for credit and financial institutions. Art. 4 lists more than 30 different types of entity which can create such security rights. Only credit institutes and lawyers can be *fiduciaires* of a French *fiducie* (introduced by Loi n°. 2007-211 de 19 February 2007 into Arts 2011–2031 French Civil

persons.[11] If we are precise about it, the separation of one's legal position and one's holding of a right is both necessary and possible, even in the case of ownership. Where one speaks of the 'owner of a thing', one is in truth using a shorthand; what is meant by this is the current 'holder of the right of ownership in a thing'. If this were not the case, no-one could ever 'transfer ownership'; the right of ownership of the first owner would have to extinguish, and a right of ownership of the new owner would have to arise *ex lege* and *de novo*. This is not how matters work according to the literal meaning of the relevant statutory provisions.[12] Some doubts remain here and there about the categorization; such ambiguities are unavoidable. One need only think of the phenomenon of statutory pledges or their functional equivalents, the *privilèges*. The fact that a whole raft of legal systems recognize, by statute, a security interest in favour of a landlord over things brought to the premises by a tenant (as a statutory non-possessory pledge limited to corporeal moveable property),[13] could be interpreted either as a peculiarity of the law of security interests or as a special property right of the landlord.[14] The question whether narcotics can be the object of property rights presents similar issues, to

Code) under Art. 2015 French Civil Code. A *fiduciaire* is a natural or juristic person to whom 'fiduciary ownership' is transferred. Under Art. L-314-1 of the French *Code de consommation*, hypothecary loans during one's lifetime (*prêt viager hypothécaire*, also called *hypothèque inversée*) can only be granted by a banking or financial institution. Art. 2 of the Spanish Ley 41/2007 stipulates that only banks, mutual savings banks, building societies, and the Spanish union of building societies have the right to create an *hipoteca de máximos* or a *hipoteca inversa*.

[11] e.g. the one providing security by way of a Spanish law *hipoteca de máximos* or an English law floating charge must be a juristic person (secs 4 und 5 Bills of Sale Act (1878) Amendment Act 1882); the charge itself, however, attaches to chattels that are not specifically named in the contract and did not belong to the debtor at the time execution—the charge is, accordingly, only effective against the debtor and not against third parties. Exceptions to this general rule apply in the case of the working stock of an agriculturalist (sec. 5 Agricultural Credits Act 1928). Besides, the Bills of Sale Acts do not apply to charges created by unincorporated associations: *Online Catering Ltd v Acton* [2010] EWCA Civ 58; [2011] QB 204; sec. 17 Bills of Sale Act (1878) and Amendment Act (1882). That is not the case for a floating charge in Greek law. However, Greek law also limits so-called *kymenómeni asfália* in Art. 1 no. 1 of Statute 2844/2000 to commercial undertakings. As in the case of non-possessory pledges, both parties must be entrepreneurs or merchants and the secured debt must be of a commercial nature. In Art. 515 Spanish Civil Code is the rule that a usufruct in favour of a village, an association, or a company cannot be created for a period of more than thirty years. The usufruct of a juristic person can, however, also differ from the usufruct of a natural person in other respects as well, e.g. in matters of transferability (see e.g. § 1059a German Civil Code).

[12] e.g. Art. 711 Belgian, French, and Luxembourgish Civil Codes ('*La propriété des biens s'acquiert et se transmet par succession, par donation entre vifs ou testamentaire, et par l'effet des obligations*'); § 929 German Civil Code ('For the transfer of ownership in a moveable thing, it is necessary that ...'); Arts 1033 and 1034 Greek Civil Code (similar words); Arts 1350 and 1376 Italian Civil Code ('Contracts, which transfer ownership'; see also Art. 1470); Art. 3:83(1) Netherlands Civil Code ('Ownership, limited rights, and claims are transferable, except ...'); Art. 879(a) Portuguese Civil Code ('The contract of sale has the following relevant consequences: (a) The transfer of ownership in the thing ... ') (cf. Art. 874 Portuguese Civil Code); Art. 155 § 1 Polish Civil Code ('Through a contract of sale, exchange, gift, or conveyance of land or another contract which obliges the transfer of ownership in a certain thing, ownership is transferred to the acquirer, except ...') and Art. 609(2) Spanish Civil Code ('Ownership and the remaining rights in goods are acquired and transferred by statute, gift, testamentary or statutory inheritance, and as a consequence of certain contracts').

[13] This type of pledge can be found in § 562 German Civil Code, § 1101 Austrian Civil Code, Art. 670 § 1 Polish Civil Code, § 672 Slovakian Civil Code, and § 2234 Czech Civil Code. Regarding Belgium and France see previous note (12); regarding Italy see the *privilegio* of landlords in Art. 2764 Italian Civil Code. In turn, the common law does not technically operate with pledges or with privileges; rather, it uses special remedies of landlords and tenants. One may consider 'distress' in particular, the right to take possession and to auction any of the tenant's (or even a third party's) chattels, which are located in his home or on his land unit without the intervention of a court (for details see Cheshire and Burn [-*Burn and Cartwright*], Modern Law of Real Property[17], p. 267, and *Lyall and Power*, Land Law in Ireland[3], pp. 232, 647, and 661–2 [with detailed reference to multiple Irish characteristics]). Additionally, Arts 733 and following Portuguese Civil Code concerning *privilégios creditórios* do not contain reference to a preferential right of landlords.

[14] One would have to say that the question of whether such rights arise systematically belongs to contract law. However, it is not contract law but property law which decides the scope of protection and transferability of these

the extent that a legal system answers it in the positive for some (i.e. pharmacies and hospitals) and in the negative for others (i.e. for ordinary private persons).

3.3 In a similar vein, certain property rights are common in some European legal systems (or perhaps only in one), but unknown in others. This is because regional differences have a further, and different, basis. All Continental legal systems operate, for example, with the institution of the usufruct. English law, in contrast, does not recognize the *usufructus* of the Roman law tradition as a stand-alone property right. The common law allowed the establishment of a so-called 'life estate in realty' until 1925. Since 1926, however, an estate in land for life can only arise in equity (through the creation of a trust).[15] Such is the position for personalty, too. A usufruct-like result can today only be achieved through the creation of a life estate under the rules governing trusts in the law of equity.[16] The legal institution of a perpetual usufruct in immoveable property, on the other hand, is only found in Poland.[17] Expectancy rights [*Anwartschaftsrechte*] are a special creature of (not only, but mainly) German and Greek law.[18] Bulgarian, Greek, Swedish, Spanish, and Cypriot law—but not Austrian, Polish, Czech, Portuguese, or German law—recognize a property right modelled on the English floating charge (a non-possessory real security right in a pool of assets of changing composition[19]).[20]

rights *once they have arisen*. This corresponds to, e.g. the legal usufruct over the assets of minors, to which their parents are entitled under Arts 324 and following Italian Civil Code.

[15] This follows from sec. 1 of the Law of Property Act 1925.

[16] This follows from limiting the idea of estates to real estate; personality was not governed by the feudal system. It is for this reason that a life interest concerning moveable property can only be established in the context of a trust (Birks [-*Swadling*], English Private Law I, nos 4.187–4.191; *Swadling* also denies the possibility of establishing rights concerning moveable properties for a lifetime by will.

[17] While the abolition of a perpetual usufruct has been considered for some time, circumstances pertaining to tax law have so far prevented its' realization (for further details see *Skwarło*, Ustawa o przekształceniu prawa użytkowania wieczystego w prawo własności nieruchomości, p. 11). Perpetual usufruct can, however, be converted into full ownership.

[18] Both legal systems are especially concerned with strengthening the position of a buyer who buys goods (not land units) under retention of ownership; see (for Greece) *Georgiades*, E exasfálisi ton pistóseon, p. 537 and *Kornilakis*, Edikó enochikó díkeo I, p. 350. This construct is closely connected to the so-called separation principle [*Trennungsprinzip*] (unconditional obligation, conditional disposition) in both countries. While Portugal, which follows the unity principle [*Einheitsprinzip*], has real acquisition expectancy rights, these are limited to certain narrow legal matters, such as rights of finding and *superficies* (for further details see von Bar [-*de Seabra and Xavier*], Sachenrecht in Europa III, Portugal, pp. 360, 382, 395).

[19] A statutory definition of the floating charge does not yet exist, not even in the Companies Act 2006, which uses the term a number of times. The definition in sec. 251 Insolvency Act 1986 is not particularly helpful (a '"floating charge" means a charge which, as created, was a floating charge'!). The legislature simply adopted the definition with which the authorities work (*National Westminster Bank Plc v Spectrum Plus Ltd* (*Re Spectrum Plus Ltd*) [2005] UKHL 41, [98]; [2005] 2 AC 680, 717, Lord Scott). With the proviso that he was not, in fact, advancing a definition, Romer LJ in *Illingworth v Houldsworth (Re Yorkshire Woolcombers Association Ltd*) [1903] 2 Ch 284, 295 explained that a floating charge was (i) a charge on a class of assets of a company, present and future, (ii) that class was one which, in the ordinary course of the business of the company, would be changing from time to time; and (iii) until some future step is taken by or on behalf of the chargee, the company could carry on its business in the ordinary way and deal with the assets within the particular class of assets. Much importance has been put on this *dictum* in the later authorities, with the qualification that the floating charge is only distinguished from the fixed charge in relation to the third of Romer LJ's points (*National Westminster Bank Plc v Spectrum Plus Ltd* (*Re Spectrum Plus Ltd*) [2005] UKHL 41, 107; [2005] 2 AC 680, 720, Lord Scott). In any case, a floating charge can also embrace the entire assets of a company (this is also implied in sec. 876(1)(b) Companies Act 2006, which speaks of a 'floating charge on the whole or part of the company's property or undertaking'; see also sec. 1 Industrial and Provident Societies Act 1967).

[20] The floating charge (*κυμαινόμενη ασφάλεια*) was introduced to Greek law by Arts 16-18 of the Statute of 2844/2000 concerning non-possessory pledges as a real security right, which grants the debtor possession and

French law attempts to achieve a somewhat similar result with the institution of a pledge over intangible objects (*nantissement*, Art. 2355 French Civil Code), in this case relying on the construction of a *nantissement* in a *fonds de commerce*.[21] In contrast to German law, legal systems including Belgian, Bulgarian, Estonian, French, Greek, Italian, Austrian, Polish, Portuguese, Spanish, Czech, and Hungarian law do not recognize the non-accessory land charge [*Grundschuld*]; security rights in immoveable property are always accessory rights in these legal systems.[22] Equally, limited property rights in one's own things are only accepted to exist in a few jurisdictions.[23] Spanish law, for example, denies them on the basis that an encumbrance extinguishes 'as soon as the creditor and debtor unite in one and the same person' (Art. 1192 Spanish Civil Code).[24] The so-called abstraction principle that governs the disposal of rights does not apply in Spanish law. The 'minor' *droit d'usage et d'habitation* of French, Belgian,

disposition of the pledged good. He must, however, provide appropriate security according to the agreement made with the secured creditor (Art. 16(2)). For Swedish law see HD 5 February 2001, NJA 2001 p. 46; for Portugal *Menezes Leitão*, Garantias das obrigações, pp. 303–8 (a *garantia flutuante* is not known in Portuguese law) and for Austria Koziol/Bydlinski/Bollenberger (*-Koch*), ABGB[4], § 448 no. 4 (a floating charge would violate the principle of specialty [*Spezialitätsprinzip*] of pledges). The non-possessory pledge of Bulgarian law is interpreted as an absolute real right (*Kalaydjiev*, Obligazionno pravo, p. 658). It can be created for individual things, for claims, and for the whole undertaking of a sole trader as a going concern.

21 *Terré and Simler*, Les biens[7], p. 696 no. 788; *Reboul-Maupin*, Droit des biens[2], p. 300 no. 500; *Malaurie and Aynès*, Les biens[3], p. 261 no. 814; *Larroumet*, Les biens[5], p. 265–9 nos 466–470.

22 See Art. 150(1) Bulgarian Code of Obligations and Contracts; § 276(1) Estonian LPA; Arts 2387 (antichrese), 2393 (hypothec) and Art. 2488-1 French Civil Code (security ownership; *Propriété cédée à titre de garantie*); Art. 2701 Belgian Civil Code (*antichrese*) and Art. 41 Belgian Code of Hypothecs, 16 December 1851 (*hypothec*); Art. 1265 Greek Civil Code; Art. 2080 Italian Civil Code; § 447 Austrian Civil Code; Arts 666 and 686 Portuguese Civil Code; Art. 1857 Spanish Civil Code, and § 1309 Czech Civil Code. It is similar under §§ 5:86(1) and 5:142(1)(d) and (e) Hungarian Civil Code.

23 This is the case, e.g. under § 1196(1) German Civil Code ('A *Grundschuld* may also be created for the owner'). BGH 14 July 2011, NJW 2011, p. 3517 even states that a usufruct may be created for one's own land unit; it is not even necessary to provide evidence of a justified interest for this. In Austria, the holder of the hypothec and the owner of the burdened land unit can be one and the same (for further detail see *Zankl*, Bürgerliches Recht[5], no. 360). If the originally secured claim is extinguished, the hypothec falls to the owner of the land unit. He can then use it to secure a further claim (§ 469 Austrian Civil Code). The legal status in England is especially complicated. With estates, mergers usually take place; the smaller of the rights burdening the land unit merges into the larger as soon as they are united in one person (*Burn and Cartwright*, Real Property[17], p. 1005). If a tenant purchases the freehold estate from his landlord (or if a subtenant purchases the leasehold estate from his landlord) the estate of the (sub-)tenant is generally extinguished. It does not come to a merger if the holder of the rights holds them in different roles, e.g. the landlord becomes the executor of his tenant. In equity, mergers could always be prevented by a simple declaration of intent to the effect of keeping the limited right; if this meets the interests involved even an implied (assumed) declaration of intent was sufficient (*Burn and Cartwright* op. cit. p. 1006). This principle was assumed into common law through sec. 185 Law of Property Act 1925. The same applies to charges. If a mortgage debt is repaid and if the security right is transferred to the paying party, the security right is not extinguished if the paying party has a corresponding intent (*Thorne v Cann* [1895] AC 11 [HL]). The latter is in turn generally assumed (for further details see Megarry and Wade [*-Harpum/Bridge/Dixon*], The Law of Real Property[8], nos 25–104). However, the paying debtor himself cannot invoke priority *vis-à-vis* the other mortgagees (*Harpum/Bridge/Dixon* op. cit. nos 25–103; see also sec. 115(3) Law of Property Act 1925). On the other hand, repayment by a person other than the debtor usually results in a transfer of the security to him (sec. 115(2) and 115(3)(2) op. cit.). Mergers also occur with moveable properties (for further detail see *Watts* (1994) NZ Recent L. Rev. pp. 336, 339–42).

24 For further detail see *Díez-Picazo and Gullón*, Sistema de Derecho Civil III(2)[8], p. 19. Art. 1192 Spanish Civil Code is substantiated by Arts 513(3) and 546 Spanish Civil Code ('Servitudes are extinguished by coincidence in the same person of ownership of the dominant tenement and the servient tenement'). Provisions with the same content of course exist in many countries, e.g. Art. 1014 Italian Civil Code.

and Luxembourgish law (Art. 625 in each of the Civil Codes), which is also found in the Italian (Arts 1021 and 1022 Italian Civil Code), Spanish (Arts 523–539 Spanish Civil Code),[25] Portuguese (Arts 1484–1490 Portuguese Civil Code), and Hungarian (§ 5:159 Hungarian Civil Code) legal systems; they the form of a limited personal servitude in German (§§ 1091 and 1093 German Civil Code), Greek (Arts 1189 and 1183 Greek Civil Code), and Austrian (§ 521 Austrian Civil Code)[26] law. Limited personal servitudes are, conversely, not recognized in the Romanic jurisdictions first listed; they (and Swedish law) accept only servitudes in favour of the owner from time to time of the dominant land unit, not *in personam* servitudes.[27]

3.4 Significant differences, however, sometimes arise even between property rights of the same name and function. The reason for this is that they are attached to different *objects* in different legal systems. Italy, for example, recognizes hypothecs not only in immoveable property, but also in moveable property that is registerable (automobiles, airplanes, ships), and even in state pensions (Art. 2810 Sentence 2 Italian Civil Code). Matters are similar in Spain (Art. 107 *Ley Hypotecaria*) and Portugal. Under Art. 688 Portuguese Civil Code, not only immoveable property and moveable property deemed equivalent (automobiles, airplanes, ships: Art. 205(2) Portuguese Civil Code), but also rights can be encumbered with a hypothec. This includes *inter alia* rights derived from concessions over public goods and usufructs over things as well as over rights.

The *antichrese*—a pledge in which the pledgee is entitled to use of the thing—is found in French law (as a *gage immobilier*: Arts 2387–2393 French Civil Code), Belgian and Luxembourgish law (Arts 2085–2091 of the relevant civil code), Spanish law (Art. 1881–1886 Spanish Civil Code), Greek law (Arts 1221 and 1222 Greek Civil Code), and in German law (§ 1213 German Civil Code); however, French law permits such a pledge only over land units, while German and Greek law take the exact opposite position and allow it as matter of basic principle only over moveable things.[28] Art. 1960

[25] See especially Art. 524 Spanish Civil Code ('Use entitles a person to receive out of the fruits of a thing belonging to another, those which are sufficient for the needs of usuary and his family, even if the latter should increase in size. Habitation entitles a person to occupy in another's house the necessary rooms for himself and the persons in his family').

[26] For further detail see *Gschnitzer/Faistenberger/Barta/Call/Eccher*, Sachenrecht[2], p. 170.

[27] Arts 637 Belgian and French Civil Code; Art. 1027 Italian Civil Code; Art. 1543 Portuguese Civil Code. It therefore does not make sense to speak of predial servitudes in these countries, as correctly observed in the case of Portugal (*servidões prediais* or *servitù prediali*); there exist only servitudes (*servidões*) (von Bar [*-de Seabra und Xavier*], Sachenrecht in Europa III, Portugal, p. 383 fn. 115 and fn. 116). Personal servitudes can only be created out of a law of obligations, meaning without an *erga omnes* effect; a contract focused on real effect would violate Art. 1306 Portuguese Civil Code and thus be void (*Carvalho Fernandes*, Lições de direitos reais[2], p. 79). While the Spanish *Código Civil* generally follows the French model, it acknowledges, to the benefit of one or more persons (e.g. a collective of holders of a right) and by way of exception, the possibility to grant personal servitudes (Art. 531 Spanish Civil Code). However, only the servitudes of grazing communities (Art. 600 Spanish Civil Code) are regulated explicitly. Spain also acknowledges a difference between *servidumbres personales* and *servidumbres prediales*. However, here also the latter are the rule, and the personal servitudes are rare exceptions (*Lasarte Alvarez*, Principios IV[9], p. 298, 322). Sweden also only acknowledges predial servitudes (*servitut*) (*Hillert*, Servitut[3], p. 29). It can only be transferred together with the dominant land unit (Ch. 14 § 3 JB); however, it is possible to entrust the exercise of it to another within certain limitations (Svea hovrätt 25 September 2001, Nr. T7703-99).

[28] § 1213 German Civil Code only provides an *antichrese* for moveable things. There is no corresponding provision for land units. However, as early as RG 3 February 1908, RGZ 67 p. 378, 379 the *Reichsgericht* accepted that

Italian Civil Code also restricts the *anticresi* to land units—but characterizes it as a mere obligational right.[29] Statutory pledges (as the pledge in favour of a landlord or contractor mentioned by way of illustration earlier) are generally limited to moveable objects; Czech law, however, has also developed a statutory pledge over immoveable property.[30] § 447 Austrian Civil Code goes so far as to recognize a general rule for statutory pledges of all kinds, regardless of whether they apply to moveable or immoveable property.

Even the concept of 'ownership' is capable of a unified definition—one that applies in all legal systems and captures all of the concept's manifestations—only at a very high level of abstraction, in which it is almost empty of concrete meaning (e.g. the proposition that 'the right of ownership is the most comprehensive right that a person can have in an object',[31] or that 'ownership is the right to grant real rights in a thing and to prevail over merely obligational rights in the same object'). Such a definition implies that not everyone who holds a right of 'ownership' will have the same remedies against an intruder, or enjoy the same scope of protection, in every legal system. But it blurs the fact that 'ownership' (or 'the right of ownership') can mean something different from legal system to legal system[32] because it is limited in some jurisdictions to **3.5**

'a usufruct for a land unit [is created] as a means to repay personal debts'. However, the *antichrese*, which was considered an outdated and defunct legal institution (*Motive zu dem Entwurfe eines bürgerlichen Gesetzbuches für das deutsche Reich Vol. 3*, p. 628), was not included in the civil code; this does not prevent other legal institutions being used to attain the same or a similar result provided that is compatible with their nature. Greek law also understands *antichrese* as a type of pledge and for this reason only allows it for moveable things. It is subject to Art. 1209 Greek Civil Code (according to which a pledge can only be created for a moveable thing belonging to a third party). Concerning fruit-bearing moveable things, there even exists the rebuttable presumption that the creditor has the right to *antichrese* (Art. 1221(2) Greek Civil Code).

[29] In Portugal, the *anticrese* was replaced by the so-called *consignação de rendimentos* (Arts 656–665 Portuguese Civil Code) (*Prata*, Dicionário jurídico I[5], p. 134). This 'consignment of income' applies to immoveables and such moveables that can be equated to immoveables. It is considered a real security right which must usually be registered in order to be legally effective (Art. 660(2) Portuguese Civil Code).

[30] For example, § 13(2) of the Czech Statute No. 72/1994 Coll on Apartment Ownership gave the community of owners a right against any one of their number in default of his obligations. This took the form of a pledge right not only over the moveable property but also over the apartment of the offending owner. This right arose at the point in time of a judgment for damages. That statute, however, was repealed by the passage of the new civil code. Under § 15(1) of Statute No. 503/2012 Coll on the Public Land Office, the state retains a pledge right to secure its claim for the purchase price of any alienated agricultural land unit. This approach is also found in §§ 30–32 of the Hungarian Statute CXXXIII of 2003 on the Law of Condominiums. If the apartment owner is at least three months in arrears, the owners' meeting can resolve the entry of a registered pledge.

[31] See, in this sense, DCFR Art. VIII.-1:202 ('"Ownership" is the most comprehensive right a person, the "owner", can have over property, including the exclusive right, so far as consistent with applicable laws or rights granted by the owner, to use, enjoy, modify, destroy, dispose of and recover the property') and, e.g. Art. 5:1 Netherlands Civil Code (according to which ownership is the most comprehensive right a person can have over a thing). Similar to this are the many different definitions of ownership in the European literature (e.g. Radwański and Dybowski [-*Stelmachowski*], System Prawa Prywatnego III[2], p. 340 no. 1: ownership comprises 'the full extent of all possible rights').

[32] This can occasionally apply to one and the same country. In some European countries, the constitutionally defined concept of ownership far exceeds the same concept in private law. In these cases, 'ownership' in the civil law sense frequently only refers to corporeal objects. In the constitutional sense, 'ownership' can also refer to claims and other rights. This is the case in Germany (ownership in the sense of § 903 German Civil Code only applies to things, i.e. corporeal objects. In Art. 14 of the German Constitution [*Grundgesetz*], ownership also applies to rights [e.g. BVerfG 26 May 1993, NJW 1993 pp. 2035, 2036: a tenant's obligational right of possession is 'ownership' within the meaning of Art. 14 GG]). In Greece, the constitutional definition of ownership (Art. 17 Greek Constitution) also far exceeds the definition of ownership in private law. The constitution even makes this clear in its terminology by terming it *idioktesía* (which refers to holding a right), instead of *kyrióteta* (which refers

tangible objects, and is applied to rights in others.[33] In lived reality, at least, 'ownership' of (or in) a right cannot give one the same concrete benefits as 'ownership' of (or in) a physical good.[34] No human being can physically destroy a claim, for example, or paint it blue. Even ownership in an apartment differs, in its concrete content, from ownership in a detached house or in a parcel of agricultural land. The same applies for the many 'lesser' property rights, and indeed for possession. A pledge over a right gives its holder different incidents to a pledge over a tangible object; a usufruct in consumable goods[35] gives its holder different incidents to a usufruct over land. Beneath the word 'possession', moreover, may lie a different concept depending on whether one thinks of possession as a right, as a factual circumstance, or as a mixture of the two. The meaning of the word 'possession' differs between legal systems not only because it denotes possession *animo domini* only and sometimes embraces possession for another (bailment, *possession précaire*) as well.[36] 'Possession' can also stand for something qualitatively different

to control) in the manner of the Greek Civil Code. Art. 11(1) of the Czech Charter of Fundamental Rights clarifies that 'everyone has the right to own property'. There can be no doubt that 'property' is by no means limited to corporeal objects, but equally encompasses claims, as well as intellectual and industrial property. In this respect, it reaches beyond the definition of ownership in conventional private law (*Eliáš et al.*, Občanský zákoník. Velký akademický komentář I, pp. 521–2). Art. 20(1) of the Slovakian Constitution (no. 460/1992 Gbl.) corresponds to this. Differences in the definitions of ownership can also be seen between domestic and European constitutional texts (for further details see Comporti, *Riv. dir. civ. 2011*, I, pp. 189–206). The concept of ownership in Swedish constitutional law comprises every type of property right under Kap. 2 § 15 Regeringsformen, including profit expectation from a business (*utövande av näringsverksamhet*). According to the reform commission tasked with revising the constitution, the constitutional concept of ownership is *självständig och vidsträckt innebörd* (autonomous and wide-ranging) (Proposition 2009/10:80, pp. 164–5).

[33] e.g. the private law definition of ownership is not limited to corporeal objects in Belgium, France and Luxembourg. While Art. 544 of their respective civil codes only refers to *propriété* with regard to *choses*, it is the dominant (but not quite uncontroversial) view that the term *chose* encompasses incorporeal things.

[34] With regard to Italy, *Caterina*, Il possesso, p. 388, states that while ownership, possession and property rights can be held over incorporeal things, it must be conceded that these are not the same as those rights which can be held over corporeal objects. In the Spanish Civil Code, the distinction between ownership in general and ownership over certain specific objects has been made (Arts 407–425 Spanish Civil Code: water; Arts 426–427 Spanish Civil Code: mines; Arts 428–429 Spanish Civil Code: intellectual property). These, strictly speaking, are different varieties of ownership. In other words, the general definition of ownership in Art. 348 Spanish Civil Code merely provides a framework which has been amended and filled in over the course of history. It has, moreover, been removed from its original interpretation by constitutional and administrative developments (*Díez-Picazo and Gullón*, Sistema de Derecho Civil III(1)^{8}, pp. 142–3).

[35] This exists in German (§ 1067 German Civil Code), French (and Belgian and Luxembourgish) law (Art. 587 French Civil Code, the so-called quasi-usufruct), as well as Greek (Arts 1174 and 1175 Greek Civil Code), Italian (Art. 995 Italian Civil Code), Polish (Art. 264 Polish Civil Code), Portuguese (Art. 1451 Portuguese Civil Code), and Hungarian (§ 5:151 Hungarian Civil Code) law. The wording of § 1067 German Civil Code is considered imprecise. As the usage of a thing necessitates its preservation, a 'usufruct in consumable goods' is technically a contradiction. It is, as it is called in most of the aforementioned legal systems, an improper usufruct. Therefore, § 1067 German Civil Code provides that the usufructuary becomes the owner of the consumable goods. § 510 Austrian Civil Code speaks of the 'enjoyment of fruits' [*Fruchtgenuss*], which is then termed 'improper enjoyment of fruits'. It is assumed, just as in Germany, that the ownership of the thing transfers to the usufructuary. He is given a kind of loan of the thing (without interest) (Koziol/Bydlinski/Bollenberger [-*Koch*], ABGB^{4}, § 510 no. 1).

[36] Possession is synonymous with possession for oneself with intent [*Eigenbesitz*] in common law systems [*supra* no. 41], in Belgium (Arts 2228, 2230 Belgian Civil Code), Bulgaria (Art. 68 Property Law Statute), France (Arts 2255, 2256 French Civil Code: *possession* is '*la détention ou la jouissance d'une chose ou d'un droit que nous tenons ou que nous exerçons par nous-mêmes, ou par un autre qui la tient ou qui l'exerce en notre nom*') and Luxembourg (Arts 2228, 2230 Luxembourg Civil Code), in Greece (Art. 974 Greek Civil Code distinguishes explicitly between detention and possession), in Italy (Art. 1140 Italian Civil Code), in the Netherlands (Art. 3:107(1) Netherlands Civil Code: 'Possession is the legal status in which a person holds an asset for himself'; possession [*bezit*] is a special form of keepership [*houderschap*]; in the same manner as the detentor, a *bezitter* is a *houder*), Portugal (Art. 1251 Portuguese Civil Code) and in Slovakia (§ 129 Slovak Civil Code). Equally, possession of a thing only exists as possession with intent in Austria. Possession for another [*Fremdbesitz*] is constructed as a possession of

because some national legal systems only regard possession of corporeal objects as possible, while others regard possession of rights as possible, and some go so far as to posit that *only* possession of rights is possible.[37]

In light of such considerations, the habit of speaking of 'limited real rights'—which is encountered in the judicial *dicta*, scholarly writing, and even in the statutory language[38] of various jurisdictions[39]—appears problematic. Granted, it is generally better to speak of 'limited real rights' in the sense of rights that are truly real, but limited, 3.6

rights: the use right is possessed, and control over the thing is exercised on this basis (§§ 311, 312, 313 as well as § 327 Austrian Civil Code; OGH 22 February 1929, SZ 11/50; Koziol and Welser [-*Kletečka*], Bürgerliches Recht I[13], p. 259). The term 'possession' encompasses possession *animus domini* e.g. in Germany (§ 868 German Civil Code), Poland (Art. 336 Polish Civil Code), Spain (Art. 432 Spanish Civil Code) and Hungary (§ 5:1(1) Hungarian Civil Code). In Art. 432 Spanish Civil Code, Spain has differentiated between possession with intent and possession *animo domini*, which arguably corresponds to the difference between 'legal' and 'natural' possession (*O'Callaghan Muñoz*, Código Civil[6], Art. 432 Civil Code p. 487). While French law acknowledges *possession pour autrui* (or *détention précaire*), it is not possession in a legal sense. It is, however, possible for one and the same person to be *détenteur précaire* and possessor of the same object. This is true for the usufructuary (for example), who exercises his right for himself but remains *détenteur précaire* with regard to the – uncontested – ownership of a third party (*Terré and Simler*, Les biens[7], p. 154 no. 164).

[37] Possession of rights is acknowledged, *inter alia*, by Austrian, Greek (Art. 975 Greek Civil Code), Spanish (Arts 430 and 431 Spanish Civil Code), Italian (Arts 1066 and 1170 Italian Civil Code), French (Art. 2255 French Civil Code '*[l]a possession est la détention ou la jouissance d'une chose ou d'un droit*') and Belgian law (Art. 2228 Belgian Civil Code). In the words *of Malaurie and Aynès*, Les biens[3], p. 138 no. 482, possession of rights represents the exercise of the right in question. '*Posséder un droit c'est l'exercer effectivement. On peut être titulaire d'un droit et ne pas en faire usage; ou inversement se comporter comme si l'on en était titulaire, alors qu'il n'en est rien. La possession est l'exercice de fait d'un droit qu'on en soit ou non titulaire.*' Equally, § 129(2) Slovakian Civil Code enables possession of every kind of right, not only intellectual property rights (Švestka [-*Spáčil*], Občanský zákoník I[2], p. 736), but also ownership itself. According to § 987 Czech Civil Code, an owner must be described as someone who possesses an ownership right (*Eliáš et al.*, Občanský zákoník. Velký akademický komentář I, pp. 567–8). Indeed, this can be identified in § 989(1) Czech Civil Code. In consequence, one must say that a thief possesses the right of ownership. However, as he is in unlawful possession of the right of ownership, he must pay compensation for use and damages under § 1000 Czech Civil Code. Art. 1251 Portuguese Civil Code (which is based on Art. 1140 Italian Civil Code) states that possession is equivalent to the exercise of the ownership right or any other real right. The provisions regarding acquisition and loss of possession (Art 1263 and 1267 Portuguese Civil Code) suggest that only corporeal objects can be object of possession. While ownership rights and 'other real rights of use' can be acquired by prescription (for further details see *Pinto Duarte*, Direitos reais[2], p. 293), the Portuguese literature makes little mention of *posse de direitos*, not even, as in Italy, of *possesso delle servitù*. In Sweden, the question of whether possession of rights is possible appears to be open (generally *Göransson*, Traditionsprincipen, p. 471 and *Bengtsson*, FS Thornstedt, pp. 75–122). The Supreme Court of Sweden twice answered this question in the negative, both judgments concerning pledges over claims (HD 17 February 1984, NJA 1984 p. 73 and HD 18 September 1984, NJA 1984 p. 656). Besides possession of moveable objects and immoveables (Art. 352 Polish Civil Code), Poland only acknowledges the possession of servitudes (Art. 352 Polish Civil Code). However, the possession of servitudes should not be understood as a possession of rights in itself, rather as a particular form of partial possession of an immoveable (Radwański and Gniewek [-*Gołaczyński*], System Prawa Prywatnego IV[2], p. 11 no. 27). Bulgaria recognizes the concept of quasi-possession, under which limited real rights (such as servitudes) can be possessed (*Vassilev*, Balgarsko veshtno pravo, p. 30).

[38] Such as Art. 3:8 Netherlands Civil Code and Art. 244 § 1 Polish Civil Code.

[39] The term is particularly common in German (e.g. *Vieweg and Werner*, Sachenrecht[4], p. 576 defines in its glossary 'limited real rights' as 'real rights that, in comparison to the right of ownership, only guarantee rights in things to a limited extent'; these are, namely, rights of use, security rights, and inheritance rights; Spanish (e.g. *Díez-Picazo and Gullón*, Sistema de Derecho Civil III(2)[8], p. 19) and Greek literature (in Greek law, all property rights except for ownership are described as limited real rights [*periorisména emprágmata dikeómata*] [*Georgiades*, Empragmato Dikaio I, p. 48 nos 2–3; limited real rights are always contrasted with ownership; see e.g. *Georgiades* op. cit.; *Kousoulas*, Empragmato Dikaio, p. 76; *Papasteriou*, Empragmato Dikaio I, pp. 76–7, nos 3–4]). In Sweden, the terms 'specific rights' (*särskilda rättigheter*) or 'limited rights' (*begränsade rättigheter*) are used. This refers to all patrimonial rights (*förmögenhetsrättsliga rättigheter*) which can be charged (*belastad*). Recently, the term 'specific rights' appears to be preferred, as ownership rights can also be limited (*Håstad*, Sakrätt[6], p. 26; *Hessler*, Allmän sakrätt, p. 25).

than rights that are supposedly limited in their real character. Such rights are, after all, not limited in their *erga omnes* effectiveness. But this does not change the fact that the picture of limited real rights derives from the so-called 'split-off theory' of property rights. According to this theory, a real right is 'limited' (in its scope) when it accords its holder fewer incidents than the most comprehensive right that is possible in the relevant type of object. This image can, however, only be correct when the most comprehensive right—ownership—can arise in every conceivable object (and not just corporeal objects). Rights in rights (for example pledges over claims) can, on the other hand, be described (in comparison to ownership) as 'limited', but cannot easily be described as 'real'. The implicit comparison with the right of ownership is, in other words, terminologically troublesome wherever the legal system limits 'ownership' (the right of ownership) to corporeal objects. Such legal systems produce illogically 'limited real rights' in legal objects that cannot, according to the system's axioms, be the objects of the right of ownership. Moreover, the notion that limited real rights are always fragments of another's right of ownership[40] cannot explain the fact that, in some legal systems, an owner can *also* have certain limited real rights in his own property.[41] Further still, it can also be the case that someone retains a limited real right in a thing that has no owner at all in consequence of his abstention [*Dereliktion*].[42] Above all, however, the 'split-off theory' sets itself on an unavoidable collision course with its own concept of ownership. That which remains (after limited real rights are 'split off') is, in truth, not 'ownership' anymore, at least in the sense the theory demands; this residual position *cannot* be the best conceivable right in the relevant object.

3.7 The result of this is that, for example, the usual classification of real rights in France (and Belgium) is by no means beyond question. One distinguishes traditionally between *droits réels principaux* and *droits réels accessoires*. *Droits réels principaux* are said to have an autonomous, independent existence. They are grounded in the *utilité* of the goods to which they are connected. The right of ownership is said to accord its holder the full utility of the thing [*chose*] in question. The 'fragmentation' or 'dismemberment' of ownership is said to create the so-called *droits réels démembrés de la propriété*.[43]

[40] This is the case in Poland, see Radwański and Gniewek (-*Gniewek*), System Prawa Prywatnego IV², pp. 340–41 no. 2 (all property rights besides ownership are derived from the right of ownership; the extent of these limited property rights is always smaller than ownership). In this sense and with far-reaching consequences OGH 21 January 2011, JBl 2011 p. 503. The plaintiff's land unit had been damaged due to a burst wastewater pipe on a neighbouring land unit. The wastewater pipe had been laid pursuant to a servitude to the benefit of a third party. This raised the question of who was responsible for its maintenance. According to the OGH, this responsibility lay with the third party, not the neighbour. The neighbour was deemed to have a 'largely empty' ownership(!) right, meaning he was no longer able to specify how his land unit was handled. This included the maintenance of the wastewater pipe. In other words, the owner had renounced his most important ownership rights and obligations upon creation of the servitude.

[41] For Greek law, *Georgiades*, Empragmato Dikaio I, p. 48 opines that the terminology of *iura in re aliena* is nothing other than a synonym for real rights of limited scope.

[42] Spanish law, for example, does not recognize any (other) rights in one's own property. The scholarship, however, accepts that real rights of limited scope can arise in ownerless goods (*Díez-Picazo and Gullón*, Sistema de Derecho Civil III(2)⁸, pp. 19–20). It is important to remember than ownerless land units, however, often revert to the state (e.g. under Art. 972 Greek Civil Code), such that they are never technically ownerless at all.

[43] e.g. Bergel/Bruschi/Cimamonti, *Les biens*², p. 41 no. 46. See also *Larroumet*, Les biens⁵, pp. 22–4 nos 30–33 and *Carbonnier*, Droit civil II, p. 1580.

'Ownership' embraces and includes all classical trifecta of prerogatives over the object (*usus, fructus, abusus*); only the holder of the right of ownership can 'extract the entire utility' of the thing.[44] A property right 'hived off' of ownership, a *droit réel 'démembré'*, gives its holder, by way of contrast, only a part of the rights of the owner (e.g. the holder of a usufruct holds the *usus* and the *fructus*, but not the *abusus*—the latter remains with the owner, now called the 'bare owner' or *nu-propriétaire*). These *droits réels principaux*, including the *droits réels démembrés*, are then defined in opposition with the *droits réels accessoires*. The latter are said to secure only a claim for their holder, but not to guarantee him any possibility of using the thing.[45] They are said to connect not to the utility of the object, but rather to its value. As such, rights such as the *hypothèque*, the *antichrèse*, and the *gage* are said not to be *droits réels démembrés*, but rather mere *droits réels accessoires*. Granted, speaking of *droits réels démembrés*, and categorizing them with *droits réels principaux*, has the advantage of avoiding the need to distinguish between rights in different kinds of objects (i.e. because incorporeal objects can also have 'utility'). It would only cause moderate problems, even, that, since the reform of the law of real security interests, ownership itself has to be considered as a security right in certain cases.[46] The picture of 'dismembered' rights, however, is fundamentally problematic. If the rights of an owner really were dismembered and distributed in this way, there would not remain any owner at all, according to the definition of 'ownership' in Art. 544 French Civil Code (i.e. the most comprehensive right in a thing).[47] With every *démembrement* ends—as a matter of logical necessity—the situation that one person holds *all* the prerogatives over the thing in question; if one maintains the premise, this in turn means the end of the right of ownership, at least in the interim. The thing would perhaps not be 'masterless', but it would certainly be 'ownerless' for the time being. It would thus be better to speak of an *encumbrance* of the right of ownership rather than its *dismemberment*.[48] This is evident also in the fact that, when the 'piece' supposedly excised from the right of ownership defaults, the owner returns *ipso facto* and *ex lege*, i.e. without any bilateral act-in-the-law, to his erstwhile, unencumbered legal position. *All* the 'minor' property rights are, in other words, encumbrances on the right of ownership; their differentiation into *droits réels démembrés* and *droits réels accessoires* suggests a categorical difference which is difficult to maintain.

[44] *Bergel/Bruschi/Cimamonti* op. cit. p. 41 no. 47 ('*Parce qu'il confère l'ensemble des prérogatives (usus, fructus, abusus) que l'on est susceptible d'exercer sur une chose, le droit de propriété met seul son titulaire à même de retirer la pleine utilité du bien*').

[45] *Reboul-Maupin*, Droit des biens[2], p. 109 no. 197.

[46] Ibid. p. 109 no. 199 correctly adverts to this point.

[47] *Georgiades*, Empragmato Dikaio I, p. 49 no. 4, says of Greek law that the 'general' and 'abstract' control of the owner remains intact, despite these limited real rights. An 'abstract' control of a thing is, however, not what the drafters of Art. 544 French Civil Code had in mind. They intended, as it was then expressed, *un hommage rendu au droit sacré de la propriété* (Cass. 22 April 1823, pp. 1822–4, 1, p. 234, cited in *Terré and Lequette*, Grands arrêts de la jurisprudence civile[10], p. 279). The right of ownership encumbered by all the various limited rights of third parties is not really something that could be described as a 'sacred right'.

[48] More accurately, *Gniewek*, Prawo rzeczowe[8], p. 176 no. 532 says of Polish law: 'The limited real rights are encumbrances on the right of ownership.'

IV
Objects, Not Persons

1. Preliminary Terminological Observations

Hardly any other area of European private law presents one with such grave terminological difficulties as property law. Whatever terms one chooses, it is simply impossible to find words that are not already used in some national legal system with a different meaning. We are thus compelled to make suggestions for the formation of a European terminology, and to satisfy ourselves with showing how they relate to the current terminology of the Member States. It would be impossible in the European context, for example, to take the definitions of the various codifications at face value. Let us take the German Civil Code as an example, which names a systemically relevant book 'the law of things',[1] but then, in the same instant, stipulates that 'only' 'corporeal objects' are 'things in the sense of the statute'.[2] This would give a false impression of property law: namely, that property rights can only exist in corporeal (i.e. spatial) objects. If one measures it on its own terms, this is not even true of German law or the legal systems that have followed it in this respect.[3] Such an approach, therefore, would be totally impossible in 4.1

[1] See the title of the third book of the German Civil Code beginning with § 854.

[2] Thus, § 90 German Civil Code and § 49(1) Estonian Civil Code General Part. The Greek Civil Code defines the concept of a 'thing' in Art. 947 in the same way, but (i) only introduces this definition in the part on property law and not in the General Part, and (ii) adds in Art. 947(2) the following: 'The natural forces or energies also count as things, especially electrical current and heat, insofar as they are subject to control in a certain place.' This does not remove the problem completely, however, because Greek law recognizes property rights in rights (e.g. Art. 1247 Greek Civil Code: Pledge). The position is similar in Portugal. The third book of *Código Civil* (*Direito das coisas*) follows the Pandectist model of the German Civil Code. The definition of 'thing' is, however, different insofar as Art. 202(1) Portuguese Civil Code provides: '"Thing" means everything that can be the object of legal relations.' The problem is not, however, completely avoided in this manner, either. Art. 1302 Portuguese Civil Code makes clear, that 'only the corporeal things, moveables or immoveables, can be the object of the right of ownership'. Thus, electrical current is a 'thing', but not a thing suitable for the right of ownership. In the literature one finds the opinion that Art. 1302 Portuguese Civil Code is applicable to all property rights (*Vieira*, Direitos reais, p. 131), but Portuguese law also recognizes property rights (e.g. the *penhor de direitos*, Arts 679–685 Portuguese Civil Code) in rights. Matters are similar in Polish law, where the general definition of ownership (Art. 140 Polish Civil Code) is again limited to things. Although the Slovakian Civil Code does not contain a definition of 'thing', it is said to be a general rule that real rights are only possible in corporeal objects. This general principle, it is said, is subject to exceptions specially provided for, typically in the law of pledges (*Švestka and Dvořák*, Občanské právo hmotné[5], p. 276). Under § 489 Czech Civil Code, on the other hand, a thing is defined legally as 'anything that is distinguishable from a person and is useful to human beings'. Art. 841 Latvian Civil Code provides that things can be corporeal or incorporeal; the latter include various personal and real rights and some forms of claim. Art. 929 Latvian Civil Code then provides that everything, which is not excluded from ordinary commerce by statute can be the object of the right of ownership. A claim for delivery of possession is, however, only possible for such things and combinations of things that are composed of corporeal objects (Art. 1050 Latvian Civil Code). The drafters of the Latvian Civil Code did, however, avoid using the term 'ownership' for incorporeal objects consistently. One gets the impression, therefore, that only corporeal objects can be objects of the right of ownership.

[3] See e.g. *Menyhárd*, Dologi jog[2], p. 13 on Hungarian law (in contrast to ownership, many important property rights including the pledge and the usufruct can be held in rights that are capable of transfer and in claims).

Foundations of Property Law. Christian von Bar and Jason Grant Allen, Oxford University Press. © Christian von Bar 2023.
DOI: 10.1093/oso/9780198885337.003.0004

respect of Europe as a whole. If one takes all the Member States together, one is compelled to accept that property rights in the European Union relate to a much broader class of objects, according to statute, judicial decisions, and scholarly opinion: property rights exist in corporeal and incorporeal objects, in living and non-living objects, in both real objects in the external world and mere credit card numbers, in electricity and heat, in aggregations of changing composition, in parts of land and buildings, and in integrated components of moveable goods. Nearly everything that is not a *subject* (i.e. a person) can slip, for better or worse, into the role of an (apparently functional) *object* of property rights.[4] The challenge is to capture the nearly endless range of national variations on this theme in a single picture. The fact that almost everything that is an object of commerce is recognized as an object of property rights *somewhere* in Europe has the entails, conversely, that there are innumerable objects that are excluded from the catalogue of 'property' in some *other* part of the Union. Moreover, it is sometimes even the case that, in order to preserve flexibility and keep potential avenues of development open, some legal systems consciously avoid any systematic categorization of the possible objects of 'property rights'.[5]

4.2 Accordingly, it seems at least possible to draw a fundamental tri-partite distinction between (i) 'objects', (ii) 'objects of legal transaction' ('goods' in the sense of commodities), and (iii) 'things'. One proceeds, in this scheme, from the general to the specific. Anything of which a rule-set is willing and able to take notice of for private law purposes is an 'object'. Anything, which can be sold or gifted is an object of legal transaction and therefore a 'good'. A good is an object of some utility to human beings, and whatever is of utility to human beings can generally be incorporated in legal transactions. Finally, 'things' are, in our account, such objects of legal transaction in which *erga omnes* rights can be created—namely, property rights. But because not all things can be the object of all property rights in any given legal system, it is advisable to further divide the category of things into (i) 'real things', (ii) 'land units', and (iii) 'other (incorporeal) normative things'. The word 'thing' certainly denotes moveable corporeal objects. They form one group of 'real' things. Land units share with them the property of corporeality, but, because they comprise a portion of the earth inseparable from the rest of the earth, they are only 'objects', 'objects of legal transaction', and

[4] § 285 Austrian Civil Code is particularly rigorous in its terminology, but sometimes overshoots the mark ('Everything, that is different to a person, and serves the needs of human beings, is called a thing in the legal sense'). Such a broad conceptual definition of 'thing' [*Sachbegriff*] leads again, in the end, to the situation in which it is necessary to distinguish between types of 'things' according to the different purposes they serve and according to the context of the regulation.

[5] This is the approach advocated by some authors in Sweden, for example. There, all rights are counted as 'property' rights—including rights of use and claims—so long as one can say that they are, in the facts of the case, protected against the competing claims of others. Property law, on this view, does not relate to specific rights, but rather to a problem that can arise in the context of *every* right (*Håstad*, Sakrätt[6], p. 16). This broad understanding of property law or the 'law of ownership', however, also entails that the question of the possible objects of property rights is hardly ever asked—neither in the literature nor in the cases. In the latter, however, one does encounter (in virtue of the relevant statutory provisions) distinctions between immoveable and moveable property and between sub-categories of moveable property such as that between corporeal and incorporeal moveable property (*lösöre*), intellectual property and *sui generis* manifestations of limited property rights.

indeed 'things' at all in virtue of the *normative framework* provided by a legal system. The earth is, ultimately, not an 'object' of private law at all. Land units are, accordingly, normative things. Land units generally share with moveable corporeal things, however, the ability to be the object of a broader spectrum of property rights. This distinguishes them from mere rights and other incorporeal objects. The latter—the other (or purely normative) things—are generally only fitting as objects of special property rights. Normative things are placed on an equal footing with real things for *specific purposes* within a legal system; in this manner, they can slip into the role of a thing, without really being one.

2. Objects

For the purposes of this book, we understand 'objects' (or 'goods') to include everything which (i) is not a person and (ii) is an entity that appears sufficiently ascertainable that it can be successfully incorporated into a legal system's complex of private law rules. All things and all objects of legal transaction are *objects*, but the opposite is not true; not all objects are *things* or even *objects of legal transaction*. The concept of an 'object' itself excludes not only persons, but also whatever by its nature cannot be controlled by human beings. Something that human beings are incapable of controlling cannot function as an object of (relative or absolute) private rights. One can neither sell such a phenomenon nor acquire ownership it in. Familiar examples include, *inter alia*, single atoms or their sub-atomic components, the celestial bodies,[6] the air of the atmosphere, the wind, the oceans,[7] and the flowing water of rivers.[8] Only when sea water or spring water is bottled, when small meteorites land on earth and are found,[9] or when a state hands out tradeable concessions for the emission of greenhouse gases,[10] is one (again) speaking of 'objects'. **4.3**

Something that is beyond human control is not considered as an object of private law in any legal system. That is no different in legal systems that categorize such entities as *res extra commercium*. The latter appear linguistically unhappy, because such *res* fall **4.4**

[6] This refers to the celestial bodies as such, meaning Earth, the Moon, or Mars. 'Separated' parts of Earth (land units) can be objects in the sense of property law. However, it is impossible to own a separated part of the Moon, as international treaties prohibit such an acquisition (Staudinger [-*Jickeli and Stieper*], BGB [2004], preface to §§ 90–103 no. 50).

[7] As early as 1625, *Hugo Grotius* (*Grotius*, De jure belli ac pacis, 1625 [cited according to the German translation by *Schätzel*, Drei Bücher vom Recht des Krieges und des Friedens, p. 148]) gave two reasons why the ocean could not be private property, one 'moral' (it is large enough to suffice both for all peoples and for every use) and one 'natural': 'One can only take possession of limited things.' This is self-evident in Member States of the European Union; however, other regions of the world treat this matter differently. Art. 169 of the Uzbek Civil Code states that the air can be an object in the sense of property law (*Knieper/Chanturia/Schramm*, Das Privatrecht im Kaukasus und in Zentralasien, p. 336).

[8] One can specifically not acquire ownership of surface water or groundwater under Art. 967 Greek Civil Code and § 3(1) Czech Water Act (Statute No. 254/2001 Gbl.).

[9] See *Süß*, Jura 2011, pp. 332–5 with reference to LG Augsburg 6 July 2007, 8 O 1758/06.

[10] Such as under § 2 lit. t Czech Statute No. 383/2012 Gbl. These concessions are treated as tradeable assets, not as a reference for a property right.

outside of the category of 'things' (objects) for natural rather than normative reasons, but this changes nothing in the end result.

The Italian idiom, for example, distinguishes between *cose* and *beni*. All objects are *cose*, moveable and immoveable, corporeal and incorporeal, *in commercium* and *extra commercium*. In contrast, only those *cose* which can be the object of rights are counted as *beni* (Art. 810 Italian Civil Code). The sun, the oceanic waters, and the air of the atmosphere belong to the *cose*. But because they are *res communes omnium*, they are also *res extra commercium* and for this reason not *beni*. There exist, however, *cose* as well as *beni* which can be categorized as *extra commercium*. The things just mentioned are 'mere' *cose*. Objects which belong to the state and are for this reason *extra commercium*,[11] on the other hand, are counted as *beni* (because they are the object of rights, albeit only of rights vested in the state).[12] In daily usage, however, the words *bene* and *cosa* are often used synonymously. One speaks of *cose mobile* and *immobili* as well as of *beni mobile* and *immobili*, for example, as well as of *cose generiche, specifiche, fungibili, infungibili, consumabili, inconsumabili*, and so on. 'Technically', however, all of these *cose* are actually *beni* in the sense of Art. 810 Italian Civil Code. It appears that Italian law has adopted usage from the Roman law, in which the word *res* is thought also to have had a good number of different meanings.[13] Arts 348, 467, 530, 1628, 1864, and 1874 Spanish Civil Code speak,[14] in like manner, of *cosa* and of *bien*, but seem to use these two words to mean (to the confusion of translators)[15] the same thing, namely objects in which a property right can be created.[16] The literature, however, seeks to elaborate nuances with the help of which distinctions could be made between the two. *Díez-Picazo*, for example, would prefer to use *cosa* to refer only to objects which have some corporeal reality in the external world.[17] For incorporeal objects of legal transaction, he uses only the word *bien*, and argues *bienes incorporeales* to be artificial creatures of the law.[18] However, he concedes that this distinction has no basis in the codification; in the civil code, *cosa* and *bien* have the same meaning.[19] *Lasarte* also opines that the term *bien* is wider than *cosa*. *Bienes* are all valuable assets, *cosa* on the other hand only

[11] This follows from Art. 823 Italian Civil Code. For details see *Bianca*, Diritto civile VI, pp. 103 and 107.

[12] That objects in state ownership are *beni* follows from the formulation of Arts 826 and 828 Italian Civil Code. Both provisions speak of *beni* that belong to the state, the provinces, and the municipalities.

[13] *Grosso*, Corso di diritto romano. Le cose, p. 1.

[14] In the older *Partidas* (Titulo XII, Partida 2), a brigher distinction was found akin to that of the contemporary Italian Civil Code (*'Bienes son llamadas aquellas cosas de que los omes se sirven o ayudan'*, i.e. '*bienes* are those *cosas* that are useful or helpful to human beings').

[15] The German translation of the *Código Civil* by *Peuster*, Código Civil. Das spanische Zivilgesetzbuch, p. 227 correctly translates *bienes* to *Güter* [goods]; the official English translation by *de Ramón-Laca Clausen*, Spanish Civil Code, p. 51 equally correctly to *property*. The Real Academia Española, entrusted with the care of the Spanish language, defines *cosa* in a similar manner to 'object' in the above text. It is defined as any unit, be it corporeal or incorporeal, natural or artificial, tangible, abstract, or virtual. A second meaning of the word is every non-living object, meaning the opposite of a life form. However, *bien* is defined as a commercial object, something which has a positive value (*Real Academia Española*, Diccionario de la Lengua Española[22], entries for '*bien*' and '*cosa*').

[16] Bercovitz Rodríguez-Cano (*-Badenas Carpio*), Comentarios al Código Civil[2], pp. 495–6; *Delgado de Miguel*, Instituciones de Derecho Privado II(1), p. 41.

[17] *Díez-Picazo*, Fundamentos III[5], p. 184.

[18] Ibid. pp. 186–7.

[19] *Díez-Picazo and Gullón*, Sistema de Derecho Civil I[12], p. 384.

corporeal objects.[20] German law makes clear that *Sachen* are only 'corporeal objects' (§ 90 German Civil Code), however the civil code does not make clear what is meant when it speaks of an 'object' [*Gegenstand*]. The literature explains that a 'legal object' [*Rechtsgegenstand*] is 'the single substantive point of reference for all dealings which are, in virtue of [some person's] subjective rights, "allowed", "prohibited", or "obligatory"'.[21] The Polish term *przedmiot* is more ambiguous. A German dictionary translates it as '*Gegenstand, Objekt*',[22] an English dictionary as 'object, subject, matter', and a Polish dictionary as 'thing, material element of the world'.[23] Art. 45 Polish Civil Code, however, defines 'things' (as does § 90 German Civil Code) by reference to 'objects'; 'things' are, on this approach, corporeal [*materialne*] 'objects' [*przedmioty*]. So much is uncontested; however, there is no legal definition of *przedmiot* to be found.

3. Persons

a. Natural and Legal Persons

Fundamentally, a person is not an object. A person is not, therefore, either an object of legal transaction (as we have defined it) or the point of reference for any kind of property right: no person 'belongs'—either to himself or to another person.[24] One can neither sell nor gift a legal subject, nor can one have a right of ownership or any other property right in him; one cannot even possess another person.[25] This counts for 4.5

[20] See *Lasarte Álvarez*, Principios I[3], pp. 394–5. See also *González y Martínez*, Estudios de Derecho Hipotecario y Derecho Civil I, p. 43. This approach is also found in Art. 511-1 Catalonian Civil Code.

[21] See, in connection with *Zitelmann*'s Schriften zum Internationalen Privatrecht (1897), Staudinger (*-Jickeli and Stieper*), BGB (2004), preface to §§ 90–103 no. 3.

[22] *Kilian*, Wörterbuch der Rechts- und Wirtschaftssprache, Band II: Deutsch-Polnisch, p. 250.

[23] See http://sjp.pwn.pl/szukaj/przedmiot.

[24] *Yearworth v North Bristol NHS Trust* [2009] EWCA Civ 37 [2010] QB 1, 13 (Judge CJ) with reference to Ulpian, Edict 9.2.13 pr. ('*Dominus membrorum suorum nemo videtur*') with the addition: 'The common law has always adopted the same principle: a living human body is incapable of being owned. … One consequence is that, if our bodies cannot be our own property, it follows that they cannot be the property of other persons; and that therefore we cannot sell ourselves, or be sold, to others.' See also JClCiv Code (*-Labbée*), Respect et protection du corps humain, Art. 16 à 16-13, Fasc. 50, no. 18 (the contemporary French doctrine considers the human body as a thing in the service of a person, such that, from birth to death, the human body is to be considered a person under the rule *accesorium sequitur principale*), Austrian OGH 11 June 1966, SZ 39/89 (a father with sole custody could not claim for delivery of the children by the mother under property law provisions; the children were legal subjects and could not be seen as legal objects at the same time) and Asser (*-Mijnssen/de Haan/van Dam/Ploeger*), Goederenrecht I[15], no. 58 (as a subject of law, a human being cannot be an object). An embryo is not a thing, but a part of the mother's body (see correctly *Zenati-Castaing and Revet*, Les biens[3], p. 31 no. 8d, and *Berlioz*, La notion de bien, p. 522 no. 1683). In the case of fertilization outside the body the legal position is often unsettled (for an in-depth introduction to the current state of affairs in France, see *Berlioz* op. cit. pp. 511 ff nos 1648 ff). Cass. crim. 30 June 1999, D. 1999 Jur. 710, note by *Vigneau* refused to treat factors leading to the death of an embryo as a homicide; an embryo is not a person. Art. L 2141-4 of the *Code de la santé publique* corresponds, which provides that a couple that has no further wish of fertility can assent to the transfer of the embryo to another couple. This indeed bears resemblance to a transfer of ownership. For a summary of the legal position in Germany, see *Busch*, Eigentum und Verfügungsbefugnisse am menschlichen Körper und seinen Teilen.

[25] *R v Bentham* [2005] UKHL 18, [2005] 1 WLR 1057; confirmed in *Yearworth v North Bristol NHS Trust* op. cit. An example that is correct in its outcome, if unhappy in its formulation, is OGH 11 May 1966, SZ 39/89 (no enforcement of a French title, with which a father sought the delivery of children against the Austrian mother, under the property-related procedural norms of Austrian law). 'According to Austrian jurisprudence, minor children in their 18th and 14th year are not to be dealt with as things, the delivery of which can be forced, but rather legal

juristic persons as well as natural persons. Company shares and company assets can be bought and sold, but not the company itself.[26] Equally, ownership and subordinated property rights are only conceivable in the membership[27] or assets of a juristic person, but not directly in the legal person itself. The floating charge, for example, is not a right in a company, but rather in its assets. If the case were otherwise, the chargee (the bank) would have priority in every constellation over all other creditors of the company. The fact that a human being (more precisely: the body of a living human being) cannot be the object of either a contract of sale nor of a property right[28] flows from the prohibition of slavery, which in turn flows from the state duty to protect the dignity of the human being; the habit of speaking of the 'sale' of a professional football player, for example, is rather cynical and false. Human abilities and capabilities are indivisible from the person; they fall outside the concept of the legal object, and therefore outside property law.[29] So, too, the thoughts and secrets that one carries in one's mind form a part of one's own person. It is necessary, however, to distinguish the intellectual capacity and labour of a person from their product, even when the latter is immaterial. At an appropriate

subjects in their own right. They are not, as such, an object for enforcement proceedings but rather parties to which the claim of the initiating party is, in the first instance, directed.'

[26] Sales of businesses are usually distinguished between so-called 'share deals' and 'asset deals'. In the first case, the buyer acquires the shares in the corporation; the juristic person that runs the business subsists and only the registered ownership changes. In an asset deal, the buyer acquires the assets of the enterprise. The enterprise subsists with the same shareholding structure (who can of course liquidate the juristic person); the purchase price stands in place of the previous assets of the company. In neither case, however, is the company as a juristic person *itself* sold (see further on German law BGH 28 November 2001, NZG 2002 pp. 298, 299, and Staudinger [-*Beckmann*], BGB [2004]), § 453 no. 25). The notion that one can sell the 'enterprise' as a whole (as e.g. expressly provided in Art. 55^2 and Art. 75^1 Polish Civil Code, § 476(1) Slovakian Civil Code and § 2175 Czech Civil Code) does not, on the proper view, affect the principle that a juristic person cannot be sold, nor the thesis (which is not uncontroversial in Poland) that one can be the owner of a whole enterprise (see e.g. Radwański and Dybowski [-*Stelmachowski*], System Prawa Prywatengo III^2, pp. 216–17 no. 8).

[27] German company law speaks, when so considered, of a strict principle that the majority of the shareholding of a legally independent enterprise 'belongs' to another enterprise, and it uses the noun 'majority possession' [*Mehrheitsbesitz*] (§ 16(1) German Public Company Statute). From the perspective of the property law of the German Civil Code, however, a terminological problem arises: in the schematic of German property law, 'possession' and 'ownership' only exist in *physical* objects.

[28] It is only conceivable to treat the body of a living human being as if it were a thing in other legal contexts, for example the law of delict, when the point is that the human body is, like all other 'bodies', the object of physical forces such as gravity. In TS 12 March 1975, RAJ 1975 Nr. 1798 p. 1355, for example, a patient suffering with depression fell from the window of the defendant hospital, killing one passer-by and injuring another. The *Tribunal Supremo* gave judgment against the hospital on the basis of Art. 1910 Spanish Civil Code (the *actio de effusis vel ejectis*), although this provision is expressly limited in application to objects that fall or are thrown.

[29] This may be viewed differently in Austria due to the extremely far-reaching definition of things in § 285 Austrian Civil Code. OGH 29 April 1925, SZ 7/155 decided in the context of a restitution that even the provision of a service can be a thing [*Sache*]. A child of unmarried parents was unable to enforce alimony payments from their father. They therefore filed a claim against the father's mother, citing that their father had performed agricultural services for her free of charge. The success of this claim under §§ 938 and 950 depended on whether or not services are 'things' and can be gifted. The court answered in the affirmative and allowed the child to claim alimony from their grandmother. OGH 28 July 1982, SZ 55/155 was the case of a defendant who refused to pay the plaintiff the agreed sum for temporary workers [*Leiharbeitnehmer*] with whom he had been entrusted as he alleged they were unqualified. The question to decide was whether the objection had lapsed. The court applied a provision for mobile corporeal objects (§ 933 Austrian Civil Code). 'With regard to the performance object [*Leistungsgegenstand*] (provision of workers for the purpose of performing labour), only the six-month warranty for mobile corporeal objects can be considered.' See also OGH 20 October 1982, SZ 55/155. All three cases are clearly only dealt with obligational issues; there were no inherent questions pertaining to property law. Once a question of property law arises, the Austrian judiciary appears to tacitly reduce the far-reaching definition of a thing. For example, a claim can therefore not be acquired by prescription OGH 28 October 1959, EvBl 1959/405.

creative level, the externally apprehensible conception of a sequence of sounds, for example, can, under certain further conditions, be made *ex lege* to the object of a copyright, and this can in turn be interpreted as a manifestation of 'ownership'. The question then becomes whether the legal system in question distinguishes intellectual property from the ordinary civil law of property, or treats them as one and the same.

b. Bodies, Body Parts, and Body Products

The legal position concerning organs, body parts, body products, corpses, and prosthetics is more complicated (and often quite ambiguous). Special rules are necessary for material with human DNA, which reflect the latter's implications in terms of personality rights and morality. The same applies to prostheses and other aids. They are placed, in some relationships, on the same level as the biological components of the human body. On the whole, we are here concerned with a part of property law that is overlaid by the law governing the personality and dignity of human persons, in which sometimes the one (personality rights [*Persönlichkeitsrechte*]) and sometimes the other (property rights) wins the upper hand, and in which sometimes both play a role simultaneously.[30] Think, for example, of the question of who owns cut (human) hair. The correct answer (that it is not only an 'object', and an 'object of legal transaction', but also a 'thing' capable of ownership belonging not to the hairdresser but to the human on whose head it grew)[31] cannot be categorized, either linguistically or substantively, as purely a question of property law (e.g. as an application of the rule that the fruits of a thing belong to its owner). Before the separation of the hair from the head, there was neither an owner nor, in truth, an object; the hair of a human being is not easily qualified as the 'product' of a person (much less, the organs of a living human taken for the purposes of an organ transplant).[32] Attempts to analogize with plants and animals are **4.6**

[30] Similar interactions between property and personality rights can arise regarding graves and tombs. For example, Polish Sąd Najwyższy 29 September 1978, III CZP 56/78, OSNC 1979 Nr. 4 Pos. 68, OSNPG 1979 Nr. 2 Pos. 13 str. 36 (LexPolonica-No. 301283, Lex-No. 2309) considered a stonewalled family plot with space for four coffins a part of the land unit. It was therefore not an object over which one could exercise an ownership or property right in itself. Nevertheless, cemetery regulations created a *Detention*-like relationship, under which the family would have special rights with regard to occupancy and care of the tomb. Austrian OGH 17 December 2003, SZ 2003/176 was the case of a family dispute over a tombstone. According to the court, while a tombstone was *res religiosa*, this did not mean all disposition over it was prohibited.

[31] This is the sense in Germany BGH 1 November 1993, BGHZ 124 pp. 51, 55; in England *Yearworth v North Bristol NHS Trust* op. cit.; in France JClCiv Code (-*Loiseau*), Biens, Art. 527–532, Fasc. 10, no. 25 (hair, nails, and breast milk have been considered things for a long time); in Greece Kousoulas, *Empragmato Dikaio*, p. 35 (similar); in Sweden Proposition 2005/06:64, p. 210 (the prohibition to sell parts of the human body does not extend to blood, hair, breast milk, and teeth. It is therefore possible to acquire ownership of them once they have been separated from the body); in Austria OGH 6 November 1907, GlUNF 3965 (The inebriated plaintiff's beard had been cut off during Carnival celebrations. The beard became a worthless thing in the moment it was cut off. While the court at the time ruled that the actions did not constitute bodily harm, this decision was revised in OGH 12 December 1974, SZ 47/147) see also Koziol and Welser (-*Kletečka*), Bürgerliches Recht I^{13}, p. 242 and Schwimann and Kodek (-*Hofmann*), ABGB II^{4}, § 285 no. 8; and in the Czech Republic § 112 Czech Civil Code. The cases usually concern special types of hair, such as a young woman selling her long hair to a doll manufacturer, or (more realistically) 'Indian temple hair'. In most cases in daily life, cut hair will simply be ownerless rubbish, as neither the customer nor the hairdresser will have any material interest in it.

[32] However, this appears to be the majority opinion in Germany. See e.g. Staudinger (-*Jickeli and Stieper*), BGB (2004), § 90 no. 21 and MünchKomm (-*Holch*), BGB I(1)5, § 90a no. 29 (natural parts of the body such as arms,

prohibited, in our view, by the imperative to protect the dignity of the human being, including in and through property law.

(1) Material with Human DNA

4.7 Components of the living body of a human being are transformed on their separation into objects, but do not—despite the widely held view to the contrary[33]—automatically become objects of legal transaction or things (as we have defined them). In the latter case, we are concerned with a mere rule of thumb. It does not mean that the whole canon of contract and property law[34] would be applicable to material with human DNA without limitations. Trade in organs with human DNA is basically prohibited;[35] we are rather concerned with objects that can be *gifted*, and in this way become objects of legal transaction. Further, it is important to note that many questions that seem like questions of property law actually reveal themselves to be questions of delict; they become relevant in the framework of property law when the law of delict itself places importance on the distinction between an act as a violation of property rights and as a violation of bodily integrity or personality rights. The latter are protected with a right to damages for pain and suffering in all European legal systems, the former only in certain ones.

4.8 The impact of personality rights [*Persönlichkeitsrechte*] on the law applicable to human body parts manifests in various ways. Some legal systems give these rights expression

hair, a kidney, pulled teeth, semen, or egg cells become things in the sense of § 90 German Civil Code upon their separation from the body; upon separation the erstwhile carrier obtains ownership in accordance with § 953 German Civil Code (separated products)).

[33] For Germany, England, France, and Austria see the references in the previous footnotes; see also for France JCLCiv Code (*-Binet*), Protection de la personne, Art. 16 à 16-13, Fasc. 12, no. 90 and *Berlioz*, La notion de bien, p. 514 no. 1661; for Austria see *Kopetzki*, FS Burgstaller, p. 609; for Greece, see inter alia *Georgiades*, Empragmato Dikaio I, p. 79 no. 10, and *Kourtis*, Astikó Díkeo metamoschéfseon, símfona me ton N. 2737/1999, pp. 90–94; for Hungary *Menyhárd*, Dologi jog, pp. 45–6, and for Italy, see *Torrente and Schlesinger*, Manuale di diritto privato[19], p. 132 (human hair, nails, and teeth are autonomous goods, which become saleable things upon legal separation from the body). This is different in § 493 Czech Civil Code: 'The human body and its parts, even if they are separated from the body [are] not things.' §§ 489 and 493 Czech Civil Code appear to exclude the provisions concerning things to the application to human body parts.

[34] Preliminary questions of property law can also arise outside private law, e.g. in cases of criminal liability for theft. See *R v Kelly* [1999] QB 621. The defendant had taken preserved organs and body parts from the Royal College of Surgeons, which are displayed and used for educational purposes. He objected that, as body parts cannot be owned, they could therefore not be stolen. This objection was refused. (Another point, which will not be discussed here, is the question of whether there is a distinction to be made between private and public law. The Australian case of *Doodeward v Spence* (1908) 6 CLR 406, which was controversial in England, concerned a stillborn baby with two heads. The doctor who had cared for the mother preserved the baby in a liquid. The baby's body was sold upon the doctor's death. It came into the possession of the plaintiff, who exhibited the baby against payment. The body was then seized by a policeman for burial. Seeking to prevent this, the plaintiff successfully brought an action for detinue. From a Continental European perspective, this would have been an act of public law. Detinue, however, was a 'normal' common law tort until it was converted.)

[35] See in particular Art. 3(2) Charter of Fundamental Rights of the European Union. This is followed both in Art. 12(1) of the Directive 2004/23/EG of the European Parliament and the Council of 31 March 2004 on setting standards of quality and safety for the donation, procurement, testing, processing, preservation, storage, and distribution of human tissues and cells (HOJ L 102/48 of 7 April 2004) and in the corresponding national implementation.

by assigning dealings with the body to the law of persons, or by making them subject to the general limits of morality;[36] others give them expression by imposing appropriate conditions on the characterization of body parts as objects or things,[37] or by answering this question in the affirmative but treating them where necessary as *res extra commercium*.[38] Human tissue and cell material, which is taken from a patient's body in order to be placed back into it (so-called autotransplantations), is particularly delicate. One is meant to believe that such material still belongs to the person from whom it was taken, but that it be neither an object of legal transaction nor a thing.[39] If blood is taken before or during an operation in order to be transfused back into the patient's body in the course of the operation, the correct view is that it remains part of the patient. The situation is the same when a piece of skin, bone, or vascular tissue is taken from one part of the body to be put into another part of the body, or when the egg cell of a woman is fertilized *in vitro* in order to be transplanted later.[40]

Matters are different, however, when an organ or other DNA material is taken from one living human being in order to be transplanted into another. The prevailing European view tends, in this context, to see the material not only as an object, but also fundamentally as an object of property rights. With the final separation from the body, such material does indeed cease to be a part of the person. It therefore becomes an object. That does not, however, preclude exceptions. Blood that has been donated and prepared so as to be capable of transfusion can generally be classified,[41] without problems, **4.9**

[36] e.g. Art. 5 Italian Civil Code.

[37] This is the approach of the majority opinion in Netherlands law, which states that the respect for the person demands a restrictive definition of 'thing' (*Mijnssen/de Haan/van Dam/Ploeger*, op. cit.). There is still the possibility that human body parts do not attain the character of a thing. Body parts can only be subject to patrimonial rights once enough distance to the 'personality sphere' has been established. For example, an anonymous blood or semen donation, which is given to the disposition of a third party according to the will of the donor, is considered to be sufficiently distant from the person of the donor and is thus a thing within the meaning of Art. 3:2 Netherlands Civil Code. This must be regarded differently when the donation is stored with the intention of personal use. In this case the donation does not (yet) reach the quality of a thing (*Mijnssen /de Haan/van Dam/Ploeger* op. cit.).

[38] This is the case in Portuguese law, where the prevailing view sees the human body and its parts as *res extra commercium* within the meaning of Art. 202(2) Potuguese Civil Code (see above, para. 2 n 14; a different position is assumed by Carvalho Fernandes and Brandão Proença [*-Sottomayor and Ribeiro*], Comentário ao Código Civil, note 4.IV to Art. 202, p. 454). In Polish law, it is said that there exist objects which may fulfil the common criteria to be a thing, but which, for moral and legal reasons, must be considered *res extra commercium* and therefore not a potential object of ownership. This group includes human embryos and transplants. The principle of *in dubio pro res extra commercium* applies here (Radwański and Dybowski [*-Stelmachowski*], System Prawa Prywatnego III^2, pp. 219–20 no. 13).

[39] The privileged position of these body parts is indirectly confirmed by Art. 2(2) of the Directive 2004/23/EG.

[40] See correctly BGH 9 November 1993, BGHZ 124 pp. 52, 55. The same conclusion follows from Art. 1456(2) Greek Civil Code. The situation is different under Art. 1457 Greek Civil Code, which regards cryo-conserved egg cells of a married woman or a woman in a long-term relationship. In this case, a man may obtain permission from a court to access the fertilized and cryoconserved egg cells of his deceased partner if he wishes to have a child by a surrogate mother.

[41] Human blood, blood products, and similar cell material (e.g. umbilical cords) can, as a rule, only be processed in expressly authorized transfusion centres (see e.g. Art. 3 of the Italian Statute of 21 October 2005, no. 219). Whether blood, biological implants, and cell material sourced from the human placenta are capable of being owned prior to a lawful manufacturing process—or whether they remain *res nullius* that belong to no-one—is answered differently. Sweden has multiple statutes which provide a detailed and complex regime for this problematic (e.g. *Lag (1995:831) om transplantation* and *Lag (2002:97) om biobanker i hälso- och sjukvården*). The position in the Czech Republic is that blood only becomes a thing, i.e. something capable of being sold and owned, through being processed into a pharmaceutical product. Blood, on this view, undergoes a legal transformation process much like moveable property. The value added by processing exceeds the value of the raw material; as the latter

as a 'thing' capable of being owned.[42] The same would count for breast milk. Where the milk is pumped for a child in intensive care, who cannot drink and requires a naso-gastric tube, the accent shifts a little. The problem is even clearer in the case where someone wishes to donate a kidney for their spouse or child,[43] and the harvested (but not yet transplanted) organ is handled inappropriately. A claim by the donor based on immaterial loss could not be denied on the basis that the only wrong was damage to a physical object!

A comparable, but differently nuanced, problem has come before the European courts in relation to frozen sperm. The German *Bundesgerichtshof*[44] has qualified the negligent destruction of frozen sperm as a bodily injury giving rise to damages for pain and suffering. The sperm was from a man who had had it stored in anticipation of an operation that would leave him infertile. The English Court of Appeal, on the other hand, has held in a very similar case that the destruction of frozen sperm is a property tort (albeit one giving rise to damages for pain and suffering, as well).[45] Claimants whose sperm were unusable because of inadequate cooling, it was held, retained a sufficient right of control over the sperm to accord them a central prerogative of ownership. The court did not wish to base its reasoning on the *Doodeward* test,[46] which asks whether 'work and skill' have been applied to a body or a body part, despite the fact that it would have been fulfilled *in casu* (the technically complicated freezing process 'conferred on [the sperm] a substantially different attribute, namely the arrest of its swift perishability').[47] The approaches of the *Bundesgerichtshof* and the Court of Appeal respectively have been followed in other places.[48] The difference may, however, be smaller than

starts with a 'null' value, the manufacturer does not even owe the original 'owner' any payment in money (*Dostál*, Zdravotnictví a právo 10 [2003] pp. 8–14).

[42] JClCiv Code (*-Binet*), Protection de la personne, Art. 16 à 16-13, Fasc. 12, no. 75; Tribunal de grande instance Toulouse 16 July 1992, JCP G 1992 no. 50, 21965 p. 437, note by *Labbée* (*'L'unité de sang ne peut être, en droit, qu'une chose dans le commerce, susceptible d'une vent'*). The Swedish statutes mentioned in the previous footnote contain specific exceptions for blood products under the general definition of *förmögenhetsobjekt* (i.e. objects that can, under normal circumstances, be transferred, used, or used as security: Hessler, *Allmän sakrätt*, p. 6) which leads, without more, to the result that such cell material (in contrast to most other types) is capable of being owned.

[43] Whether, and under which circumstances, organ donations are permitted is the subject of a special legislative regime in many legal systems. See e.g. the Italian Statutes of 26 June 1967, no. 458 (kidneys) and 16 December 1999, no. 483 (liver parts); see the Greek Statute 3984/2011 of 16 June 2011 on the donation and transplantation of organs (FEK 150 A΄/27 June 2011).

[44] BGH 9 November 1993 op. cit. p. 52. Critical of this decision are *Laufs and Reiling*, NJW 1994 pp. 775–6 and Staudinger (*-Jickeli and Stieper*), BGB (2004), § 90 no. 22.

[45] *Yearworth v North Bristol NHS Trust* op. cit. In *R v Human Fertilisation and Embryology Authority, ex parte Blood* [1999] Fam. 151 it had been decided that sperm, which the husband of the claimant had collected and (unlawfully) stored just hours before his death, had to be delivered to the claimant in Belgium, where she wanted to undergo fertility treatment with this sperm. The hesitation of the British authorities to hand over the frozen gametes was against European Community law.

[46] *Doodeward v Spence* (1908) 6 CLR 406 (High Court of the Commonwealth of Australia).

[47] [2010] QB 1, 20 B.

[48] e.g. for France see JClCiv Code (*-Loiseau*), Biens, Art. 527 à 532, Fasc. 10, no. 25 (thing-ness of sperm affirmed) and for Greece *Kounougeri-Manoledaki*, Techniti gonimopoiisi kai Oikogeneiako Dikaio, pp. 38–40 and Arm. 53 (1999) pp. 465–79 (advancing the thesis that sperm and egg cells have a double nature; they are to be seen as things and as parts of the person). For an emphatic thesis that they are things only, see *Papachristou*, FS Manoledaki III, pp. 915 and 919. The OLG Rostock 7 May 2010, MedR 2010 p. 874 considered the frozen egg cells of a woman to be her property. The woman could, as such, vindicate them under the provisions of § 985 German

appears at first blush. Not only did the German court have to consider the fact that harm to property does not, as a matter of German delictual law, sound in damages for non-pecuniary loss (§ 253 German Civil Code). The court also had to recognize that, at least for 'donated organs, that are destined by the intention of the donor to be implanted in another person, or for blood donations destined for others', it seemed proper that 'the ownership of things ... [could be] overlaid by the law governing personality rights'.[49] This being so, however, damages for immaterial harm (i.e. pain and suffering) would be available again.

Corpses are indeed objects, but on the proper (albeit contested) view,[50] they are neither objects of legal transaction nor things so long as one can recognize a certain person in them, i.e. so long as they retain their individual characteristics.[51] For this reason, the 4.10

Civil Code (OLG Rostock op. cit. p. 877). In Scots law, Lord Stewart tended in *Holdich v Lothian Health Board* [2014] SLT 495, 499 towards the position of the German Federal Court (*in obiter*).

[49] BGH 9 November 1993 op. cit. p. 55.

[50] In France the predominant view is that every corpse is a thing. However, it is contested whether the corpse is a *chose commune* in the sense of Art. 714 Civil Code ('*Il est des choses qui n'appartiennent à personne et dont l'usage est commun à tous. Des lois de police règlent la manière d'en jouir*') or a *chose sacrée*, as argued in Tribunal de grande instance Lille 5 December 1996, *D.* 1997 Jur. 376, note by *Labbée* and Tribunal de grande instance Lille 10 Novrmber 2004, *D.* 2005 Jur. 930, note by *Labbée*. From this categorization flows the range of property rights which could conceivably be had in a corpse. *Berlioz*, La notion de bien, pp. 524–5 no. 1693 treats corpses generally as *res extra commercium*. This is said to show appropriate respect for the departed. Tribunal de grande instance Lille 10 November 2004 op. cit. opines that the mortal remains of a human being who has not left testamentary instructions is the property of the family.

[51] See Czech Nejvyšší soud České republiky 15 December 2005, Az. 22 Cdo 2773/2004 and Czech Nejvyšší soud České republiky 9 March 2006, Az. 22 Cdo 685/2005 (*Švestka*, Ochrana osobnosti, p. 173 in agreement). The position is the same in Greek law (corpses are in principle not things, in virtue of the human personality that subsists in them even after death; the position only differs in the case of mummies and corpses prepared for research and teaching purposes—they have ceased to represent any personality and can, for this reason, be the object of legal transactions: *Georgiades*, Empragmato Dikaio I, pp. 79–80 nos 10–12; *Kousoulas*, Empragmato Dikaio, p. 35 and *Papasteriou*, Empragmato Dikaio I, pp. 172–4 nos 17–21; see also Court of Appeal of Athens 5316/1990, EllDik 32 [1991] p. 1043: no vindication for the corpse and bones of a human being, so long as they represent the personality of a human being; during this time they are objects *extra commercium*), and in Austria (as long as the human corpse is still properly seen as the remains of a certain, individually identifiable person it is generally not said to be a thing: OGH 5 December 1972, SZ 45/133; Schwimann and Kodek [-*Hofmann*], ABGB II[3], § 285 no. 2 [with the reasoning that a corpse does not serve the uses of a human being]; *Tades/Hopf/Kathrein/Stabentheiner*, ABGB I[37], § 285 no. E 2; see however Rummel [-*Spielbüchler*], ABGB I[3], § 285 no. 3 [corpses are always things] and *Peichl*, ÖJZ 2003 pp. 581, 584). OGH 13 December 2012, JBl 2013 p. 166 accordingly denied an executor the competence to give the deceased's corpse to the University of Vienna for research purposes in accordance with the deceased's wishes. In Germany, it is often said that the corpse is by definition a thing (e.g. *Baur and Stürner*, Sachenrecht[18], § 3 I 2 a and MünchKomm [-*Holch*], BGB I(1)[5], § 96 no. 32), but it is simultaneously recognized that the transactability of this class of thing is severely restricted on the basis of the law protecting the personality of the deceased even after death. The protection of 'post-mortem personality rights' is said to be strongest during the period of respect following a person's death; it is said to abate continually and to extinguish when 'the image of the deceased fades and his memory expires' (OLG München 26 January 1994, NJW-RR 1994 p. 925). Corpses and parts of corpses that are no longer to be seen as the mortal coil of an individual become things capable of being dealt with free of limitations in the sense of § 90 German Civil Code (Schulze/Dörner/Ebert [-*Dörner*], BGB[6], § 93 no. 3). In English law, *Dobson v North Tyneside Health Authority* [1997] 1 WLR 596 decided that everyone entrusted with the burial of a corpse has a right to possession of the corpse for this purpose. The rule that there is no property in a corpse is displaced when a corpse has been 'processed' (e.g. embalmed). The same principle applies, as for body parts that are used as anatomical preparations; they can at least be stolen (*R v Kelly* [1999] QB 621 (CA, Criminal Division)). In Sweden it is emphasized that the human body is not a fitting object of the right of ownership. For this reason, it does not form part of a deceased estate (*kvarlåtenskap*). This extends for example to gold teeth (which fact was pointed out in the preparatory works to the statute on burial, Begravningslag (1990:1144): Proposition 1990/91:10, p. 53). Bones of those long dead, on the other hand, belong to their finder, to the extent that the state does not exercise its right to take them with compensation (§§ 3 and 4 *Lag om kulturminnen m.m.* (1988:950)); see further *Adlercreutz*, SvJT 2004 pp. 809–17. For Hungarian law, see *Menyhárd*, Dologi jog, p. 46.

law of personality rights continues to operate even in the context of organ harvesting after the death of the person, i.e. over the dead body. Human beings can determine, during their lifetime, whether or not they wish to make their organs available for transplantations.[52] The fact that certain European legal systems have taken the approach of imputing consent to organ donation as the default position in order to overcome medical shortages does not change this basic principle.[53] The remains of a human body only assume the quality of things when they are no longer the expression of the uniqueness of the human person. This is the case when they are prepared for scientific purposes or when they are otherwise removed from the natural process of decomposition (such as mummies or preserved scalps in a museum).[54] Bodies and body parts of archaeological or anthropological value are, in any case, objects; whether they are objects of legal transaction and/or things depends only on whether the relevant legal system counts them to the *res extra commercium* or not.[55]

(2) Prostheses and Medical Aids

4.11 Prosthetics, artificial joints, pace-makers, and similar technical medical aids are saleable and capable of ownership so long as they are not a fixed component of the body of a living human being; from this point onwards, their quality as an object and a thing lapses, and therewith their capacity to be owned.[56] This line is drawn in principle where the medical aid can be removed without compromising the bodily integrity of its user. Spectacles remain, unproblematically, things, as do wigs; hip replacements in place are just as unproblematically neither things nor objects of legal transaction. Dental

[52] Accordingly, it is said in Italy that every person has an *ius eligendi sepulchrum* and can therefore decide what happens with their body by testamentary disposition (e.g. to decide between burial or cremation, or whether to donate their organs for transplantation): *Torrente and Schlesinger*, Manuale di diritto privato[19], p. 132. See for Austria OGH 13 December 2012, JBl 2013 p. 166 (donation for medical and scientific purposes is a highly personal decision of the deceased. The deceased cannot therefore authorize an agent to make this decision. Consequently, an administrator may not dispose over the corpse of the deceased). Under Art. 20(1) of the Bulgarian Law on organ transplants, every legally competent natural person has the right to oppose the taking of organs from their body after death. This must be declared to a doctor, who must in turn register the declaration with the relevant health insurer. Otherwise, the taking of organs can only be prevented by a written statement from the deceased's next of kin.

[53] This system is followed *inter alia* by Belgium (Art. 10 § 1 of the Statute of 13 June 1981 on the Removal and Transplantation of Organs), France (Art. L1232-1 *Code de la santé publique*), Austria (§ 5 Abs. 1 *Organtransplantationsgesetz*), Sweden (Preparatory Works to *Lag (1995:831) om transplantation m.m.* [Proposition 2005/06:64, p. 210]) and to the *Begravningslag (1990:1144)* [Proposition 1990/91:10, p. 53]), and Spain (Art. 5 of *Ley 30/1979, de 27 de octubre, sobre extracción y trasplante de órganos*).

[54] This should also apply to the bodies of stillborn children. In other words, they are to be treated as corpses. This is not changed by the fact that they were never persons. The equality with the bodies of people who were born living follows from the fundamental concept of the protection of human dignity.

[55] Schwimann and Kodek (*-Hofmann*), ABGB II[4], § 285 no. 4; *Gschnitzer/Faistenberger/Barta/Call/Eccher*, Sachenrecht[2], p. 395. See also Art. 1(2) span. Ley del Patrimonio Histórico Español.

[56] Equally e.g. *Dostál*, Zdravotnictví a právo 10 (2003) pp. 8–14; *Georgiades*, Empragmato Díkaio I, p. 79 no. 10; *Kourtis*, Astikó Díkaio metamoschéfseon, símfona me ton N. 2737/1999, pp. 90–94; *Kousoulas*, Empragmato Díkaio, p. 35; *Menyhárd*, Dologi jog, p. 46; MünchKomm (*-Holch*), BGB I(1)[5], § 90 no. 31; *Papasteriou*, Empragmato Díkaio I, p. 173 no. 20 (Artificial body parts which are permanently and organically fixed to the body, as well as objects which are added to the body to permanently aid it, are not things. The author gives the example of dental implants), and Staudinger (*-Jickeli and Stieper*), BGB (2004), § 90 no. 25. Art. 4(12) ital. Decreto Ministeriale of 27 August 1992, Nr. 332 states more generally that the prosthetics belong to the patient ('*i dispositivi protesici . . . si intendono ceduti in proprietà all'assistito*').

prosthetics, on the other hand, are the subject matter of divergent opinions.[57] Cass. civ. 11 December 1985[58] concerned a dentist who removed a dental prosthesis from a patient during a later visit, and then retained it pending payment of all fees in full. *Cour d'appel de Douai* held for the dentist on the basis of the then-current Art. 592-2 CPC (which allowed a pledge over objects for non-payment, even an object relied on by a disabled person). The *Cour de cassation*, however, held that '*ce texte ne concerne pas les objets qui font partie intégrante de la personne humaine*' and allowed the patient's appeal. A dental prosthesis was, on this view, an integral part of the human person.

By way of contrast, it no longer seems plausible to consider seeing eye dogs legally as tantamount to a prosthesis bound to the person. The *Tribunal de grande instance Lille* had so held in two decisions from the years 1999 and 2000.[59] The tribunal held that a seeing eye dog was a '*prothèse vivante au service de la personne non-voyante*'. The killing of such a dog therefore sounded in damages for bodily damages. The award of 10,000 francs was meant to compensate the victim for the 'special incapacity' suffered during five months owing to the death of the dog. *Labbée* went so far as to draw the conclusion that the dog, as a 'living prosthesis', was a part of the human body itself. A prosthesis was a moveable thing in the service of a person and ought therefore to follow the statutory provisions relating to persons.[60]

[57] For Greek law, *Georgiades*, Empragmato Dikaio I, p. 79 no. 10 or *Kousoulas*, Empragmato Dikaio, p. 35 argues that all artificial body parts (dental prosthetics, artificial legs and hips, pacemakers, etc.) permanently integrated into a human body are not things.

[58] Bull. civ. 1985 no. 348 p. 313.

[59] The first decision was the accelerated and simplified proceedings before a single judge (*Tribunal de grande instance Lille* 23 March 1999, *D.* 1999 p. 350, note by *Labbée*), the second the main proceedings before the chamber (*Tribunal de grande instance Lille* 7 June 2000, *D.* 2000 p. 750, note by *Labbée*).

[60] Ibid. p. 750 (*Labbée*): '*La prothèse est donc un objet mobilier au service de la personne, qui suivra le régime juridique de la personne. C'est un élément du corps humain.*'

V

A Tri-Partite Conceptual Framework: Objects of Legal Transaction, Goods, and Things

1. Objects Within and Outwith the Scope of 'Legal Transaction'

a. Objects of Legal Transaction

With the technical term 'objects of legal transaction', we understand all objects that one person can oblige another to alienate; in other words, all objects that can be sold, swapped, or gifted, even if by a limited number of authorized persons. For example, one's private sphere would be a 'mere' object, i.e. not an object of legal transaction. One's right to a private sphere is inalienable. The same applies to most of the other incorporeal 'personality rights', from marriage to the moral rights of an author. One can consent to their violation, but one cannot validly obligate oneself to alienate them for good. In some legal systems, the 'future assets' of a person or a part of their 'future assets' are not objects of legal transaction, either. Under German law (§ 311b(2) German Civil Code), contracts that attempt to do so (in either variation) are void; in Czech law, attempts to dispose of more than half of a person's future assets are void (§ 2058 Czech Civil Code). The claim to delivery of possession which flows from the right of ownership (i.e. *vindicatio*) cannot be sold separately in a so-called causal transfer system,[1] and in an abstract transfer system this claim cannot be ceded separately. The claim for delivery is indeed an object, but in the systems first mentioned it is no 'object of legal transaction', and in the latter systems it is no 'thing'. Claims [*Forderungen*], company shares, wares, and land units are, in contrast, not only objects, but also objects of legal transaction *and* things. One can sell or gift all of these things. When (and to the extent that) one can transfer property rights in these phenomena or encumber them with a pledge, usufruct, or another right (which is usually transferable and encumberable itself) they become things. Cumulative double qualifications are thus unavoidable, but do not detract from the explanatory power of the distinctions we have drawn: there exists a multitude of 'objects' which (either categorically or according to the positive law of some legal system) are 'objects of legal transaction' but are not 'things'. **5.1**

[1] See, for Poland only Radwański and Dybowski (-*Gniewek*), System Prawa Prywatnego III^2, p. 490 no. 42 and p. 499 no. 74.1 (vindication claims cannot be object of an independent legal transaction, because they are fixed to the rights of the owner).

Foundations of Property Law. Christian von Bar and Jason Grant Allen, Oxford University Press. © Christian von Bar 2023.
DOI: 10.1093/oso/9780198885337.003.0005

5.2 Such a proposition, however, presupposes that 'things' and 'objects of legal transaction' are not synonymous—as they so often appear in the Portuguese Civil Code. Art. 202(1) provides the following definition: 'Everything is called a thing [*coisa*] that may be the object of legal relationships'.[2] *Coisa*, the literature explains, comprise every part of reality that is distinguished from the person which can be controlled and used.[3] This is largely isomorphic with our concept of 'objects of legal transaction', however it also implies a critique of the literal meaning of Art. 202(1). *Menezes Leitão*, for example, considers the definition both over- and under-inclusive. It is too broad because (theoretically) persons can be the object of legal relationships (for example relationships based in family law) and also because under Art. 202(1) rights and claims are 'things', too. The definition is too narrow because there are 'things' which, as *res extra commercium*, cannot be the object of a private law legal relationship.[4] Others criticize the definition in Art. 202(1) on the grounds that it embraces not only human beings but also their efforts, character, and commercial expressions of their personality.[5] The much-criticized definition in Art. 202(1) must, however, be read together with the definition in Art. 1302.[6] According to this provision, only 'corporeal things' can be the object of the right of ownership, where *coisas corpóreas* serves as an umbrella term for moveable and immoveable property. Art. 1302 is found in the part of the civil code that deals with the law of things, while Art. 202(1) is found in the General Part, Chapter II (on legal relationships), Sub-Chapter II (on things). The narrow definition of 'things' adopted from German law has thus become part of the Portuguese law of property, but not part of the legal system as a whole, which uses a definition more like 'object of legal transaction'.[7]

b. *Res Extra Commercium*

5.3 From the range of possible objects of private law protection, and of property law protection in particular, some codifications take certain objects aside and declare them to be *res extra commercium*. Under these civil codes, a private subject cannot sell, gift, acquire, or grant ownership or any other property right in these objects; they are 'outside of commerce'.[8] As long as the list includes objects that are already removed from

[2] '*(Noção) Diz-se coisa tudo aquilo que pode ser objecto de relações jurídicas*.' This in turn corresponds almost verbatim to the definition of *beni* under Art. 810 Italian Civil Code.

[3] *Carvalho Fernandes*, Teoria geral do direito civil I², p. 547 ('*Coisa é toda realidade autónoma, que não sendo pessoa em sentido jurídico, é dotada de utilidade e susceptível de dominação pelo homem*').

[4] *Menezes Leitão*, Direitos reais, p. 59.

[5] *Mota Pinto*, Teoria geral do direito civil⁴, pp. 333 and 343. See also *inter alia Santos Justo*, Direitos reais², p. 121; *Carvalho Fernandes* op. cit. p. 545; *Hörster*, Parte geral, p. 177, and *Menezes Cordeiro*, Direitos reais, pp. 189–90.

[6] *Vieira*, Direitos reais, p. 131.

[7] From a comparative law perspective (Germany, Italy, and Portugal) in detail *Müller*, Der Allgemeine Teil im portugiesischen Zivilgesetzbuch, pp. 88–9.

[8] The Portuguese literature emphasizes that the more appropriate expression is *coisas fora do comércio privado*, not merely *coisas fora do comércio*. What is meant by this expression is that all legal transactions are excluded, not just mercantile transactions (*Carvalho Fernandes* op. cit. p. 552). This is confirmed in Art. 1267(1)(b) Portuguese Civil Code, according to which the possessor loses possession of a thing 'if it is removed from commerce'.

human control in virtue of their nature, the category does little to further the purpose of putting *res extra commercium* outside the sphere of legal transactions. These are, in truth, not even 'objects', at least as we have defined them. The same criticism applies when human bodies and their components are counted to the 'objects outside of commerce'. The category only becomes important when it is used to pursue some policy or another through the positive law. In most cases, this is in the context of so-called public goods. They are meant, through categorization as *res extra commercium*, to be removed from the reach of private actors and so preserved for public purposes.

Greek and Portuguese law is particularly complex in this regard. Art. 966 Greek Civil Code provides a list of *res extra commercium* that includes (i) things common to all, (ii) things dedicated to common usage, and (iii) things specified for public, municipal, regional, or religious purposes.[9] To the first category belong the atmospheric air and the high seas; in truth, however, they already fall outside Greek law's definition of 'things' because they are by nature uncontrollable. To the second category belong a number of both natural and artificial things that the law makes available for public use. These objects are, in principle, capable of being objects of property rights, but their use is confined in keeping with their public dedication.[10] For example, Art. 967 Greek Civil Code lists free flowing (above ground)[11] waters, streets[12] and squares,[13] beaches,[14] harbours,[15] bays and banks of navigable rivers,[16] and large natural lakes with their banks. Other things can be dedicated to public use by statute.[17] The authorities can, under Art. 970 Greek Civil Code, grant specific concessions of usage rights to private persons (e.g. the right to erect a kiosk or the right to place tables and chairs before a café[18]). Whether such concessions are of an obligational or real character, however, is contested; in any case, their beneficiaries enjoy a degree of legal protection against third parties (Art. 997 Greek Civil Code). What is important is that all things removed from ordinary dealings in this way are not subject to acquisitive possession (Art. 1054 Greek Civil Code). As 5.4

[9] In this and the following regard in detail *Georgiades*, Empragmato Dikaio I, pp. 120–31; *Kousoulas*, Empragmato Dikaio, pp. 59–72; *Papasteriou*, Empragmato Dikaio I, pp. 56–8 and 203–25, as well as *Filios*, Empragmato Dikaio[3], pp. 84–7.

[10] CA Larissa 666/2004, Dikografia 2005 p. 266; CA Korfu 117/2006, ArchN 57 (2006) p. 610.

[11] CA Crete 115/1960, ArchN 12 (1961) p. 505.

[12] For the definition of streets, see Areopag 98/2010, EfAD 2010 p. 537 and Areopag 800/2006, EllDik 47 (2006) p. 1081.

[13] For this also, see Areopag 98/2010 op. cit.

[14] Established case law dictates that it depends on how the beach is formed in the winter, when the sea retreats by several metres (e.g. Areopag 931/2000, EllDik 42 [2001] p. 76 and Areopag 1398/2003, EllDik 46 [2005] p. 738).

[15] For further details, see Areopag 1677/2005, NoB 54 (2006) p. 670.

[16] See Areopag 1483/1983, NoB 32 (1984) p. 1208 and Areopag 207/1993, EllDik 35 (1994) p. 1067.

[17] e.g. cemeteries are things *extra commercium* under Art. 3 Law 582/1968. It is possible to obtain certain private rights over them under an administrative concession and following the requirements of the law (Art. 970 Greek Civil Code). The right of use is exclusive but cannot be sold. Coasts are also *res extra commercium*; regarding the legal status of land units within the coastline see Areopag 33/2008, NOMOS 450754 and Areopag 573/2008, NOMOS 453091, NoB 56 [2008] p. 2178. In certain regions of Greece, the so-called *Vakufia* (areas which originally belonged to Muslim cloisters) are still subject to Ottoman property law. They are permanently dedicated to charitable causes, *res divini juris* and are as such *res extra commercium* (Areopag 331/1995 and Areopag 447/2005; both only published by the Isokrates-database of the bar association in Athens).

[18] For further detail see Areopag 950/2009, NoB 57 (2009) p. 2179 and (regarding the rights of use of a fishing company in a lagoon) the reports of the state legal council (*Nomikó Symbúlio tou Krátous*) 330/2001.

such, state and church property are also outside the regime of acquisitive possession. *Res extra commercium* are made subject to private law transactions only on the deconsecration, as it were, of the thing (Art. 971 Greek Civil Code).

5.5 The public sector is also large in Bulgaria and Portugal. In Bulgaria, 'public property of the state' encompasses, according to Art. 18 of the Constitution, mineral resources, sea coasts, federal streets, waters, forests, natural and archaeological parks, and the buildings of state institutions. In addition, there is the exclusively public property of the municipal authorities. These assets are removed from private law; they cannot be transferred, encumbered, nor acquired by possession; for private subjects only the possibility of acquiring a concession remains (Art. 7 of the Bulgarian Statute on State Property). Art. 202(2) Portuguese Civil Code stipulates that all things which cannot be the object of private rights are outside legal commerce. This refers to Art. 202(2) Portuguese Civil Code, according to which a thing is 'everything that can be an object of legal relationships'. *Coisas fora do comércio (privado)* can neither be sold, nor can private ownership or any other private property right arise in them. Art. 202(2) Portuguese Civil Code lists *coisas* in public ownership[19] and 'things' that by their nature are not appropriate for individual appropriation.[20] *Coisas* which must by their nature be in public ownership include, according to Art. 84 of the Portuguese Constitution, the territorial waters, lakes, lagunes, and navigable waterways (each with its bed), the upper strata of the atmosphere, mineral deposits, streets and railway tracks, vital telecommunications and energy infrastructure, objects of cultural and historical significance, military facilities, and cemeteries. In contrast to the Greek Civil Code (and in contrast to Art. 381 of the old Portuguese Civil Code of 1867), the current code of 1966 does not recognize *coisa comum* anymore;[21] that which is placed beyond private law transactions is, in consequence, in public ownership (*domínio público*). Special statutory provisions can, however (as in Greece) extend the already long list. All *coisas* in public ownership are owned by juristic persons created by public law, and never by a natural person or a private law juristic person. The latter can, however, acquire a *concessão*.[22]

[19] What is meant are things over which the state exercises its *ius imperii*, not things that are in the private ownership of an organ of the state. The latter are subject to the normal provisions of civil law. (Art. 1304 Portuguese Civil Code provides that the provisions of the civil code are to apply equally to the ownership of things that belong to the state or any other collective person of public law insofar as no special provisions exist to the contrary and the nature of the rights in question are consistent therewith.) See further *Carvalho Fernandes* op. cit. pp. 20–21.

[20] Things which are by their nature not suitable for individual appropriation include, as previously mentioned, the human body and its parts, as well as objects such as the air, the oceans, planets and the stars, which cannot be controlled by humans (*Menezes Leitão*, Direitos reais, p. 63). However, the term 'appropriation' has multiple meanings. What is meant is an appropriation within the meaning of *apropriação*, meaning an act which is aimed towards acquiring a right, especially ownership, over a good either by *ocupação* or by acquisition of actual control. Appropriation within the meaning of *ocupação* is by contrast a form of acquiring ownership over mobile things which are ownerless (Arts 1318 and 1319 Portuguese Civil Code) or have been lost or hidden (Arts 1323 and 1324 Portuguese Civil Code).

[21] *Carvalho Fernandes* op. cit. p. 554 attempted to revitalize the former division into three parts, *coisa comun* (common or charitable things), things which are not appropriate for individual appropriation, and things over which private ownership is not possible. However, this was not widely followed and does not have a basis in law. Portuguese law only acknowledges *baldios*, rural areas which are assigned to a local community for agricultural use by customary law. STJ 20 January 1999, Processo 98B1030 confirms, that a *baldio* is land that cannot be appropriated individually.

[22] In some cases, this is only granted in exchange for a fee: *Menezes Leitão*, Direitos reais^2, p. 63.

The Spanish Civil Code has neither defined *cosas fuera del comercio de los hombres* nor even collated them into a list. Art. 1271 Spanish Civil Code only stipulates that 'all *cosas* that are not *fuera del comercio* can be the subject matter of a contract'. They stand outside of commerce, so they are not capable of transaction; they cannot be alienated (sold, gifted, or conveyed). The Spanish term is, however, much narrower than its Portuguese cognate. According to Díez-Picazo, it embraces (i) objects of public property, public use, public services, or sovereign wealth that have not been de-commissioned,[23] (ii) objects by their nature incapable of appropriation (air, light, etc.), and (iii) goods, which on some other legal basis are not to be treated as mere assets (personality rights, family status, etc.). Objects that are *fuero del comercio* only count to the category of *res extra commercium* proper, however, when they cannot be transferred for value under any circumstances (e.g. embryos, but not 'drugs' for licit medical use).[24] The Italian Civil Code does not define its concept of *res extra commercium*, either. Art. 1145 Italian Civil Code provides some rules governing the particularities of possessory rights under the heading *possesso di cose fuori commercio*. Besides this, Art. 823(1) Italian Civil Code stipulates public goods to be fundamentally inalienable. These include, according to Art. 822 Italian Civil Code, the sea coasts, beaches, estuaries and harbours, rivers, streams, lakes, and all other waters listed in statute,[25] and certain installations dedicated to the national defence. The *demanio pubblico* also includes, to the extent that they are owned by the state, streets, highways, railways, airports, water pipes, real estate of historical, archaeological, or cultural value, collections in museums, galleries, archives, and libraries.[26] 5.6

Under Art. 1(1) of the Greek Statute 5351/1932 and Art. 826(2) Italian Civil Code, all 'things of historical, archaeological, paleoethnological, paleontological, and artistic interest' are the property of the state, regardless of where in the earth's surface they are found. The finder must register such a find with the authority responsible for heritage. The state's ownership arises *ex lege* and *ipso jure*; it lasts as long as it takes to determine whether or not the object is of interest for research and art. They, accordingly, *res extra commercium*. The finder has, under Art. 92 Italian Civil Code, only a claim to payment for *beni culturali*; he does not acquire ownership. The Italian Statute No. 364 of 1909 establishes a presumption of ownership in favour of the state; it is simultaneously presumed that the private possession of such an object is illegal. The consequences of this

[23] See e.g. for beach areas TS 23 June 1981, RAJ 1981 Nr. 2613 p. 2174 and TS 13 October 1981, RAJ 1981 Nr. 3737 p. 3021.

[24] *Díez-Picazo*, Fundamentos I^6, p. 250.

[25] This also includes the Laguna di Venezia, whose peculiarities have led to a number of laws and higher court judgments. Art. 1 Law of 5 March 1963, no. 366, *Nuove norme relative alle lagune di Venezia e di Marano—Grado* states that the Laguna di Venezia is a public brackish-water basin, and describes its geographical extent. The lagoon was already state owned in Austrian times (Corte Appello Venezia 10 June 2008, Dir. trasporti 2010, 1, p. 191). For further details, see Cass. sez. un. 14 February 2011, no. 3665, Juris Data DVD.

[26] For further details, see Cian and Trabucchi (*-Bullo and Fochesato*), Commentario breve^6, sub Art. 822; *Torrente and Schlesinger*, Manuale di diritto privato^{19}, p. 189; *Bianca*, Diritto civile VI, p. 103 and *Gazzoni*, Manuale di diritto privato^{10}, p. 203. 'Public things' in this sense refer only to 'Italian' things. A 'French' cultural asset brought into Italy (*in casu* a historical tapestry stolen from a French court building) is not *extra commercium* in Italy (Cass. 24 November 1995, Nr. 12166, Foro it. 1996, I, p. 907).

rule are illustrated in Cass. 10 February 2005.[27] In this case, the court held that a private person in possession of an object of historical, archaeological, paleoethnological, paleontological, or artistic value found in the ground had to prove that the object was private property before 1909. The claimant, who sought for the return of a confiscated vase, had argued that it must have been of no cultural interest because the administrative body, which had known of his possession, had never given him any notification. Besides this, the claimant relied on Art. 2697(1) Italian Civil Code, which places the burden of proof onto the party asserting the existence of a right—in this case the state. The Court of Cassation rejected these arguments. The general rules on appropriation, finding, and treasure trove (Art. 923, Art. 927, and Art. 932 Italian Civil Code respectively) found no application; the state's right of ownership arose upon the discovery of the object in the ground, independently of whether it was actually of cultural or artistic value, and independently of any action (or inaction) by the relevant authorities. In consequence, the state could demand delivery of the vase with the claim of vindication, which was not subject to any statute of limitations (Art. 948 Italian Civil Code). Because the named objects are *res extra commercium*, they could not be acquired through acquisitive possession, either. In consequence, the state did not need to prove its ownership under Art. 2697(1) Italian Civil Code, but the citizen did need to prove the legality of his possession under Art. 2607(2) Italian Civil Code.[28]

5.7 The predecessor of the Spanish and Italian civil codes, the French, Belgian, and Luxembourgish *Code civil*, makes reference in a number of provisions to *choses hors du commerce*. They cannot be the subject matter of a contract (Art. 1128 in all three versions), cannot be sold (Art. 1598 in all three versions), and cannot be acquired by prescriptive possession (Art. 2260 French Civil Code, Art. 2226 Belgian and Luxembourgish Civil Codes). The term *choses hors du commerce* is, however, not defined further in these provisions. Judicial decisions and the academic literature warn of conflating *appropriation* (in the sense of forming ownership) with being *dans le commerce* (Art. 1128 in all three versions). A thing *extra commercium* remains a thing capable of *appropriation*.[29] Art. 1128 only means that the thing is not transactable in the ordinary sense, not that it cannot have a single owner at all.[30] Theft of certain *choses hors du commerce* is possible, for example of narcotics.[31] The *choses hors du commerce*

[27] Cass. 10 February 2005, Nr. 2995, Giust. civ. 2007 p. 2231. See in this regard *Magri*, Riv. crit. dir. priv. 2009 p. 73.

[28] This applies only to private law, not to criminal proceedings, owing to the presumption of innocence (thus Cass. pen. 16 March 2000, Nr. 5714, Cass. pen. 2001 p. 973 and Cass. pen. 4 May 1999, Nr. 7131, Cass. pen. 2000 p. 151; however, Cass. pen. 1 February 2005, Nr. 12618, Cass. pen. 2006 p. 2928 approved the same distribution of the burden of proof as used by the civil courts).

[29] *Terré and Simler*, Les biens[7], p. 18 no. 14; Cass. 24 September 2003, *D.* 2003 p. 2683, note by *Caron*; RTD civ. 2003 p. 703 note by *Mestre and Fages*; RTD civ. 2004 p. 117, note by *Revet*. Similarly, but with nuanced differences, for Belgium *de Page and Dekkers*, Traité élémentaire V[2], p. 539 no. 542 ('*Au sens étroit, [l'expression "choses hors du commerce"] désigne les choses susceptibles d'appropriation qui échappent au droit de propriété en raison d'un obstacle légal. Il résulte de cette interdiction que ces choses ne peuvent faire l'objet d'une convention (art. 1128 et 1598), ni de la prescription (art. 2226)*').

[30] *Libchaber*, in Le Code civil 1804–2004. Livre du bicentenaire, p. 297, 346 no. 43.

[31] Cass. 5 November 1985, Bull. crim. 1985 no. 340 ('*Que la circonstance que la chose qui aurait été soustraite serait une marchandise illicite et hors commerce, est sans influence sur la qualification de vol*').

therefore have to be at least *biens*, when they are by nature capable of appropriation and it is only in consequence of a legislative policy that they cannot be alienated in the normal course.

Hungarian law resembles French law in this respect. The case of an underground parking lot in Sopron has been much discussed in recent times.[32] The defendant developer had built a multi-level garage beneath a land unit forming part of the so-called 'stock assets' of the Sopron municipal body, along with some above-ground pedestrian access. It was agreed between the authority and the defendant that the garage would be entered as a standalone title in the land register once permission to commission the garage was granted and that the developer would be registered as owner. The rules in § 137 Hungarian Civil Code [1959] (ownership arrangements in the case of building on another's land) were not meant to apply. The authority later took the position (apparently after a change in the party balance of power in the council) that the contract was null and void and that the defendant had acquired no property in the garage. The Supreme Court took the same position. Land unit and underground garage could, according to § 97(2) Hungarian Civil Code [1959] have different owners in principle. And under the conditions listed in that provision, ownership arose *ex lege* with the first building measures. In this case, however, the land unit in question before the separation was public property and was therefore (under § 173(1) Hungarian Civil Code [1959] and § 79 of the Statute on Local Government) an object belonging to the *res extra commercium*. Objects which cannot be transacted cannot be transferred or encumbered; contractual agreements to the contrary are void according to §§ 114(1) and 173(2) Hungarian Civil Code [1959]. Being incapable of forming the subject matter of a transaction even excluded statutory acquisition of the right of ownership. The rules governing objects outside of commerce had priority even over § 97(2) Hungarian Civil Code [1959] (according to which ownership in a construction project can remain with the developer pursuant to an appropriate agreement). The Statute on National Assets of 2012 has, meanwhile, created an independent regime for the *res extra commercium*; § 172 Hungarian Civil Code [1959] has been repealed. 5.8

In those systems which adhere to the concept of *res extra commercium* without an express statutory basis, the substance of the category changes. Moreover, the concept also loses some of its dogmatic importance; though it retains a descriptive function, it loses its normative character. Such is the case, for example, in the Czech Republic and Poland. Neither the Czech Civil Code [1964] nor [2014] mentions *res extra commercium*. Scholars are still striving for a definition, namely for one that defines them as 'things' that cannot be disposed of by the act of a private party, or cannot be 5.9

[32] BH 2009/175, Legf. Bír. Pfv. I.21.446/2008. See in this regard especially *Menyhárd*, Jogesetek Magyarázata 4/2010 p. 19; *Lábady*, BDT 2009 p. 83 and *Pomeisl*, Gazdaság és Jog 2009/5 p. 14. BH 2012/34, Legf. Bír. Pfv. I. 21.379/2010, Bírósági Határozatok 60 (2012) p. 107 follows the same line: in a public space—here a public parking lot owned by a municipality—the acquisition of a basic servitude by prescription (§ 168(2) Hungarian Civil Code) is impossible. A public space can only be charged by a law-based basic servitude to secure access to a land unit (§ 167 Hungarian Civil Code 1959).

so disposed of except within strictly defined parameters. Private acts-in-the-law concerning the things in question are only possible according to the provisions of special public law regulations; named objects include weapons, explosives, poisons, and narcotics.[33] Representative scholars of Polish law also subscribe to the doctrine of *res extra commercium*.[34] Some things (in the sense of corporeal objects) are said to be unfit objects of ownership on the basis of moral and legal considerations. Whether one can derive from this principle that pharmacists (but not drug dealers) and banks (but not counterfeiters) can be the owners of objects prohibited for private individuals remains uncertain. Such opinions are found in the literature,[35] but find no support in the text of the Polish Civil Code.

5.10 Legal systems that operate without the concept of *res extra commercium* include English,[36] German, Swedish,[37] and Netherlands law.[38] German and Netherlands law do not even recognize the term. German law rather takes its point of departure (in § 137 German Civil Code, among other places) from the fundamental principle of the transactability of all corporeal objects, i.e. all 'things' as defined in § 90 German Civil Code.[39] Rules are found in the overlaps between public and private law which bring the theory of *res extra commercium* to mind. In § 928(2) German Civil Code, for

[33] *Švestka and Dvořák*, Občanské právo hmotné[5], p. 241; Švestka (-*Švestka*), Občanský zákoník I[2], p. 640.

[34] Radwański and Dybowski (-*Stelmachowski*), System Prawa Prywatengo III[2], pp. 219–20 no. 12. In the former Polish People's Republic, the distinction between *res extra* and *res in commercio* was regarded as 'completely outdated'. The term *res extra commercium*, which was regarded as 'capitalist', was only used because no other term existed. To this term were assigned things which belonged to the state and were designated for its administration, as well as fixed assets of the state and such things as agricultural real estate, which fell under a special regimentation. By contrast, rivers, streets, squares, parks, etc. were termed *res omnium communes*, things which serve the public (Radwański and Safjan [-*Katner*], System Prawa Prywatnego I, p. 1197 no. 51).

[35] For example, *Stelmachowski* op. cit. does not consider *res extra commercium* (he gives the example of counterfeit money) ownable things.

[36] A kind of connection to the Continental theory of *res extra commercium* is found in the criminal law jurisprudence on the question whether 'property in prohibited goods' is possible, i.e. whether such goods can be stolen in the meaning of the Theft Act 1968. This was answered in the affirmative, without reservation, in *R v Smith* [2011] EWCA Crim 66; [2011] 1 Cr App R 379. The case concerned the theft of drugs from a drug dealer. Whether private law would provide the drug dealer with a claim in damages for loss of his goods was said to be totally irrelevant for the criminal law, and was said to be a purely academic exercise because no drug dealer would pursue such an action by reason of the fact that the judge would be bound to refer the matter to the Crown Prosecution Service. Of little assistance, but cited in *Smith*, is *R v Turner (No. 2)* [1971] 1 WLR 901 (CA). This case turned on the question whether someone could commit the crime of theft over a car that he possessed in the course of a hire purchase agreement. He took the car to an auto mechanic, without consulting the car's owner, and then drove it away from the parking lot on which the mechanic parked it without permission and without paying the bill. The possibility of theft was also affirmed in these circumstances. *Turner* decided, in other words, that the criminal law is not concerned with the private law regularity of possession (there, possession by the auto mechanic); *Smith* decided that it is also irrelevant whether the act depriving a party of possession is, of itself, a criminal act.

[37] Sweden does not use the concept of *res extra commercium* in a legal context, at least not explicitly. Limits on the disposition of certain objects are regulated by specific legal provisions. For example, illegally held drugs are forfeit to the state (§ 6 *Narkotikastrafflag* (1968:64); see also e.g. Kap. 8 § 7 *Lag om genetisk integritet m.m.* (2006:351). In the absence of any monetary damage, it is not possible to steal them (Kap. 8 § 1 *Brottsbalk* (1962:700)). The owner's authority is reduced to a minimum in the case of other assets (nature reserves, streets etc.) by authorization of use by the general public. Rights of commons [*Allemansrätten*] over nature are even guaranteed in the Constitution (Kap. 2 § 15(4) *Regeringsformen*).

[38] This is not changed by the fact that Art. 3:86a Netherlands Civil Code implements the requirements of the Directive 93/7/EEC by excluding the possibility of good faith acquisition of certain cultural assets. To qualify these as *res extra commercium* merely for this reason (such as *Weidner*, Kulturgüter als res extra commercium im internationalen Sachenrecht) misses the point of the term.

[39] MünchKomm (-*Holch*), BGB I(1)[5], § 90 no. 37.

example, the right to appropriate an ownerless land unit is ascribed solely to the state; the transactability of such land units is, accordingly, circumscribed. Further, the laws of some federal states [*Länder*] stand in stark contrast to the civil law of the Federal Republic. The Federal Constitutional Court has, however, held that certain lands (the case concerned flood levies in Hamburg) that were 'public property' according only to the laws of the one of the *Länder* were completely removed from the regime of (private) property law.[40]

Commentary that states that the air, sea water, and the rivers are non-transactable by their very nature is correct,[41] but is actually no reference to the concept of *res extra commercium* in German law. These objects are not 'things' [*Sachen*] in the sense of § 90 German Civil Code in the first place. The same applies to the sea floor and the celestial bodies.[42]

2. Goods

The term 'good' is another ambiguous term. Goods are definitely objects of legal transaction. When the English term 'goods' is used, what is usually meant are corporeal objects that can be bought and sold that are not 'land'. At the risk of oversimplification, one is dealing with 'wares' [*Waren*] in the sense of German,[43] Greek,[44] and Czech law,[45] with *merchandises* in the sense of French law, *mercadorias* in the sense of Portuguese law,[46] *merci* in the sense of Italian law, and *mercaderías* (oder *mercancías*) in the sense 5.11

[40] BVerfG 18 December 1968, NJW 1969 p. 309. The court explicitly left the question open, whether control over the flood levies in question even constituted ownership within the meaning of applicable law and if, were this the case, it would be public ownership as opposed to private ownership. Were the latter the case, it would be a matter of 'normal' ownership on the basis of civil law, which would be limited in its usability and saleability by public law regulations.

[41] MünchKomm (*-Holch*), BGB I(1)^5, § 90 no. 38.

[42] The sea floor cannot be owned (Staudinger [*-Jickeli and Stieper*], BGB [2004], preface to §§ 90–103 no. 48; also BGH 31 May 1965, NJW 1965 pp. 1712, 1713). Meteorites that have impacted the Earth and been found can be owned under German law (*Süß*, Jura 2011 pp. 332–5).

[43] The former § 1(2) No. 1 German Commercial Code, which defined 'wares' as moveable things, was abolished when the Commercial Code was reformed; however, this does not change the meaning of this term. Paper securities are not 'wares'. This follows *e contrario* from § 383(1) German Commercial Code. The German Commercial Code also acknowledges the term 'good' [*Gut*], but does not apply a uniform definition. In a commission contract, 'goods' is a generic term for wares and securities, which the commissioner receives with the commission contract (Ebenroth/Boujong/Joost/Strohn [*-Krüger*], HGB II^2, § 390 no. 2). In § 407 German Commercial Code (contract of carriage) 'good' refers only to corporeal objects, therefore to 'wares' (MünchKomm HGB [*-Czerwenka*], VII^2, § 407 no. 50).

[44] In Greece, the term 'wares' (*εμπορεύματα*) refers to moveable objects and thus excludes rights and land units (Georgiades, *Empragmato Dikaio I*, p. 94 nos 23–24). Georgiades ibid. p. 94 fn. 15 cites Areopag 412/1937, Themis 1939 p. 14, according to which electricity can also be considered a 'ware'.

[45] § 2079 Czech Civil Code (formerly § 409(1) Czech Commercial Code).

[46] Throughout the French version of the CISG, goods are translated as *marchandises* (e.g. Art. 1 CISG: '*La présente Convention s'applique aux contrats de vente de marchandises entre des parties ayant leur établissement ...*' This term does not appear in the French property law literature. In this, only the terms *biens*, *meubles*, or *meubles corporels* appear, not *marchandises*. The Civil Code only uses the latter term in Arts 1585, 1586, and 1779. The English translation in turn consistently refers to 'goods'). Portugal used to differentiate between *produtos* (wares destined for the consumer) and *mercadorias* (wares destined for intermediate trade), but has since given up this distinction, which is meaningless in practice (Schmidt-Kessel and Schubmehl [*-Pinto Monteiro*], Lauterkeitsrecht in Europa, p. 542 fn. 57.

of Spanish law. We are not here concerned with the property of solidity; butane gas, for example, belongs (unproblematically) to the category of goods.[47] Section 62 of the Irish Sale of Goods Act 1893 defines *goods* as 'including all chattels personal other than things in action and money'. 'Chattels personal' in this provision means all moveable objects capable of ownership, but excludes (besides land) *inter alia* company shares and patents. Included, however, are 'emblements' (agricultural harvests) and all other objects connected with land but which can be separated from it in the course of the enforcement of a contract (or which should be separated from it according to the terms of a contract). The English Sale of Goods Act 1979 has left this definition largely, but not entirely, unchanged. Section 61(1) has replaced the term 'chattels personal' with 'personal chattels', which is only a linguistic modernization. The Sale of Goods Act 1979 was amended by sec. 2(c) of the Sale of Goods (Amendment) Act 1995 such that the expression 'goods' only includes a portion of 'wares'. What was thereby intended was to include a quantity of goods not yet separated from a mass. The Vienna Convention on the International Sale of Goods does not define its concept of 'goods' (German *Ware*, French *merchandises*); it is unclear whether it includes more than moveable corporeal goods.[48] European sales law defines 'wares' for its purposes as 'moveable corporeal goods' excluding, (i) electricity and natural gas, and (ii) water and other forms of gas, unless they are offered for sale in limited volumes or in certain quantities'.[49]

5.12 English 'goods' are not, however, identical to the *gods* of Swedish law,[50] nor to the *biens* of Belgian or French law. In the Belgian context, de Page and Dekkers explain that everything that exists is a *chose* except for human beings[51] (which largely reflects the definition of Italian *cose* and German *Gegenstand* or 'object'). A *chose* is said to become a *bien* when the *chose* reveals itself to be useful and capable of appropriation. Most *choses* have, in the course of the development of civilization, become *biens*, which explains why so many jurists use the words as synonyms. The utility of a thing in turn

[47] *Borealis AB v Geogas Trading SA* [2010] EWHC 2789 (Comm); [2011] 1 Lloyd's Rep. 482.

[48] Schlechtriem and Schwenzer (*-Ferrari*), Kommentar zum Einheitlichen UN-Kaufrecht[5], Art. 1 no. 34 and OLG Köln 26 August 1994, CISG-online no. 132 interpret the term 'wares' in the German translation of the CISG in this way (as moveable corporeal goods). However, the English version of the same commentary defines 'goods' as 'moveable tangible objects' which are not necessarily corporeal (Schlechtriem and Schwenzer (*-Schwenzer and Hachem*), Commentary of the UN Convention on the International Sale of Goods (CISG)[3], Art. 1 nos 16, 17). Software would also be a 'good' in the sense of the CISG by this definition. This would moreover not depend on whether the software is contained on a digital storage device, or merely available for download online (see *Schwenzer and Hachem* op. cit. no. 18). RB Arnhem 28 June 2006, CISG-online no. 1265 likewise judges the sale of software by the regulations in the CISG.

[49] Proposal for a Regulation of the European Parliament and of the Council on a Common European Sales Law, COM(2011) 635 final.

[50] The previous Swedish sale of goods statute (*Lag om köp och byte av lös egendom* (1905:38), § 1), which was in effect until 31 December 1990, differentiated between species goods and genus goods [*specieköp* and *genusköp*] calling the former *gods*. The same definition is used for the term in the current *Lag om handel med lösören, som köparen later i säljarens vård kvarbliva* (1845:50 p. 1) (law of legal protection of third parties through registration of rights over moveable goods [*sak* or *lösöre*], which remain with the seller). The new sale of goods law (*Köplag* (1990:931)) has given up the distinction between species goods and genus goods; the object of sale is now called *vara* ('ware'). 'Goods' in UN sales law was also translated into 'wares' [*vara*] (*Lag om internationella köp* (1987:822)). The preparatory work clarified that the Swedish transformation law would not only refer to moveable goods (*sak* and *lösöre*) (*Proposition* 1986:87:128, p. 96).

[51] *De Page and Dekkers*, Traité élémentaire de droit civil belge V[2], p. 535 no. 531.

reveals itself in the fact that someone has appropriated it to himself.[52] Similarly (and in the end equally circular, as we are here concerned with the question of what can be appropriated) Hansenne opines that a *bien* is an asset that belongs to a legal subject, such that he can control it. It includes both substantive and economic goods, i.e. corporeal objects and rights. The latter, in turn, are traditionally divided into property rights, obligations, and intellectual property rights.[53] The French literature posits a relation between *biens* and *choses*; however, it often does so with a different emphasis. One often reads that '*tous les biens ne sont pas des choses et toutes les choses ne sont pas des biens*'.[54] Not all *biens* in the sense of the second book of the civil code are, however, *choses* because *biens* include incorporeal objects as well. That implies a terminological understanding of *chose* as an umbrella term that is by no means consistent for objects and land units. Numerous closer definitions of *biens* are proffered. It is said that 'goods' are economically valuable rights,[55] all things worth money, which can be appropriated and serve the needs of human beings,[56] all things which can be useful to a human being,[57] all rights which entitle one to make use of a thing,[58] or all rights which one can acquire in a thing with some kind of value.[59] The decisive criterion is thus always utility; the *chose* (here, that term obviously embraces corporeal *and* incorporeal 'things') becomes a *bien* when it proves itself to be useful.[60] (Thus: *toutes les choses ne sont pas des biens.*) 'Things' in the sense of *choses* only acquire the status of 'goods' when they are capable of appropriation, have economic value, and can be the object of rights.[61] *Choses communes* in the sense of Art. 714 French Civil Code, that is *res extra commercium*, are not *biens*.[62] Cornu thus offers the definition that a *bien* is '*toute chose susceptible d'une appropriation et constituant une partie du patrimoine du sujet de droit*'.[63] Rights, too, are therefore 'goods'.[64] The Association Capitant sees matters the same. It suggests in

[52] Ibid.

[53] *Hansenne*, Les biens, p. 11.

[54] *Carbonnier*, Droit civil II, p. 1595; *Druffin-Bricca and Henry*, Droit des biens[3], p. 19; *Mathieu-Izorche*, Les biens, p. 9 no. 27. *Carbonnier* gives the following examples of (incorporeal) goods: court actions, subjective rights, shares and stakes in finance companies (Art. 529 French Civil Code), intellectual property over works of literature, science and art, the customer base of *fonds de commerce*, designations of origin, energies, and progress in technology.

[55] *Druffin-Bricca and Henry* op. cit.; see also *Belloir-Caux*, Dictionnaire de droit des biens, p.65.

[56] *Reboul-Maupin*, Droit des biens[2], pp. 5 and 21 ('*chose susceptible d'appropriation répondant aux besoins de l'homme*' and '*choses évaluables en argent susceptibles de conférer des droits ayant une valeur économique aux personnes*').

[57] *Atias*, Les Biens[10], p. 1 no. 1 ('*toutes les choses, qui pouvant procurer à l'homme une certaine utilité, sont susceptibles d'appropriation privée*') and *Zenati-Castaing and Revet*, Les biens[3]. p. 18 no. 1 ('*choses dont l'utilité justifie l'appropriation*').

[58] Argued by *Terré*, Introduction générale au droit, no. 338; cited with approval by *Mathieu-Izorche* op. cit. p. 9 no. 29 ('*Les biens, ce sont les droits divers permettant de se procurer le bénéfice des choses [droit de propriété, droit de créance]*').

[59] *Valette-Ercole*, Fiches de droit des biens, p. 5 ('*droit sur une chose ayant une valeur patrimoniale et susceptible d'appropriation*').

[60] *Carbonnier* op. cit. p. 1596.

[61] *Mémeteau*, Droit des biens[4], p. 3.

[62] *Reboul-Maupin* op. cit. p. 9 no. 14.

[63] *Cornu*, Vocabulaire juridique[8], 'Bien', p. 10.

[64] *Lefebvre*, Leçons de droit des biens, p. 10. The situation is similar in Spanish law. Art. 334(10) Spanish Civil Code counts, *inter alia*, concessions from public authorities over public buildings as 'immoveable goods', as well as servitudes and all real rights in land units.

Art. 520 of its proposal for the reform of the French *Code civil* to consider as *biens* all corporeal or incorporeal(!) *choses* that can be appropriated, as well as all *droits reels* (property rights) and all *droits personnels* (obligational rights).[65]

5.13 Art. 333 Spanish Civil Code, placed in the chapter titled 'Categorization of Goods', provides that every 'thing' (*cosa*) which is (or can be) the object of appropriation should be considered as a moveable or immoveable 'good' (*bien*). 'Immoveable goods' are for the most part land units, their components and fixtures (Art. 334 Spanish Civil Code). Goods are considered moveable if they are 'capable of appropriation' and are not counted as immoveable, and generally include 'all those [goods] which can be brought from one place to another without damage to the immoveable thing with which they are connected' (Art. 335 Spanish Civil Code). No bright distinction between *cosa* and *bien* is posited. The text uses both terms synonymously,[66] as does the academic literature for the most part.[67] The Portuguese usage is the same; the terms *coisa* and *bem* (plural *bens*) are generally used without differentiation. Some opine that the concept of *coisa* is central and the concept of *bem* is peripheral,[68] but that view finds no statutory support;[69] the law of sales contracts already uses a different language (e.g. Art. 880 [*bens futuros*] and Art. 882 [*entrega de coisa*] Portuguese Civil Code). This is also true of the transposition of European Directives.[70] Basically, the exchangeability of the terms *coisas* and *bens* was established from the beginning. In the course of contemporary discussions of its draft (the text of which was adopted as Art. 202(1) in the Portuguese Civil Code unchanged), a 'novel problem' appeared to the drafters, namely that the Italian Civil Code (which was used as a model) defined neither its concept of 'things' nor 'goods'. Pires de Lima came, however, to the conclusion that there was no practical need for any amendment of the terminology in the draft text. Both words, it was said, referred to the same 'juristic reality' (*realidade jurídica*).[71]

[65] '*Sont des biens au sens de l'article précédent, les choses corporelles ou incorporelles faisant l'objet d'une appropriation, ainsi que les droits réels ou personnels tels que définis aux articles 522 et 523*': *Périnet-Marquet*, Propositions de l'Association Henri Capitant pour une réforme du droit des biens, p. 116.

[66] See above, para. 86. The Catalan Civil Code strives for greater terminological precision in Art. 511-1(1) by interpreting 'goods' as the general term and 'things' as a sub-class of goods ('*Se consideran bienes las cosas y los derechos patrimoniales*'). '*Se consideran cosas los objetos corporales susceptibles de apropiación, así como las energías, en la medida en que permita su naturaleza*' (Art. 511-1(2) op. cit.)

[67] See e.g. Bercovitz Rodríguez-Cano (-*Badenas Carpio*), Comentarios al Código Civil², pp. 495–6 and *Delgado de Miguel*, Instituciones de Derecho Privado II(1), p. 41. These authors readily consider the term 'thing' to include incorporeal objects and energies. By contrast, *Díez-Picazo and Gullón*, Sistema de Derecho Civil I¹², p. 385 propose a differentiation between corporeal and incorporeal.

[68] *Menezes Cordeiro*, Direito civil português I(2)², pp. 24–5. (*Bens* is a more common term in family law and inheritance law. It is less frequently used in general civil law.)

[69] *Carvalho Fernandes* op. cit. p. 539, correctly notes that *bem* and *coisa* are frequently used synonymously in legislation. This corresponds to colloquial language, in which *coisa móvel* and *bem móvel* mean the same.

[70] For example, Art. 13 DL 57/2008 of 26 March 2008 ('*Envio de bens ou serviços não solicitados*') refers to *bens*, Arts 123 and 130 DL 72/2008 of 16 April 2008 (concerning the legal regime of liability contracts) refers to *coisas* (the object of a liability contract [*seguro de danos*] is a *coisa*, *bens imateriais*, *créditos*, and all other *direitos patrimoniais*).

[71] *Pires de Lima*, BMJ 91 (1959) pp. 207, 208–09.

The concept of 'goods' has practically no meaning in the property law of Bulgaria, Germany, and Greece[72]—the term is used to describe, for example, the objects of certain commercial contracts as 'freight goods' or 'commission goods' or the interests protected by a delictual or criminal provision as 'legal goods'. The drafters of the Netherlands *Wetboek*, on the other hand, troubled themselves with a fundamental systemic exposition. Art. 3:1 Netherlands Civil Code uses *goed* and *registergoed* (Art. 3:10) as the general term for things [*zaken*] and rights in assets [*vermogensrechten*]. *Zaken* are, therefore, only one manifestation of goods [*goederen*]. *Zaken* are material objects capable of human control (Art. 3:2 Netherlands Civil Code). A *zaak* can be moveable [*roerend*] or immoveable [*onroerend*] (Art. 3:3 Netherlands Civil Code). The rules of the third book of the code apply to all *goederen*, those of the fifth book by way of contrast only deals with *zakelijke rechten*. They form a class of property rights to which belong, in addition to the 'real rights' [*zakelijke rechten*] namely ownership [*eigendom*] and limited property rights [*beperkte rechte op zaken*], also the rights set out in the third book of the civil code and the intellectual property rights originally intended for a ninth book. The third book has, as such, created a general property law which applies to all goods. The later books, in contrast, only deal with rights in certain classes of goods.[73] 5.14

3. Things

a. Things as the Point of Reference for *Erga Omnes* Property Rights

(1) Objects of Legal Transaction Capable of Being the Object of Property Rights

Interpreting 'things' as a sub-class of goods (or of objects of legal transaction)[74] was a step in the right direction. The question remains, however, which principle the distinction between these two categories is meant to serve. According to the view from the Netherlands, only material objects are simultaneously goods *and* things. We take the contrasting view that property rights as *erga omnes* rights create monopoly rights. They should therefore apply only to goods—but then to all such goods in which the creation of private rights of exclusion is (i) technically possible and (ii) desirable in the common interest, in a welfare economic sense. That, however, cannot only be the case for material objects. Moveable (corporeal) objects and land units are not 5.15

[72] *Αγαθό* is every product that meets the needs of a person, as well as everything which is produced for the consumer. The term for object (*Αντικείμενο/antikímeno*) describes an inanimate and perceptible object, as well as everyday economic resources. A thing (*Πράγμα*) is an inanimate material and tangible object which can independently count towards a person's possessions. *Papasteriou*, Empragmato Dikaio I, pp. 169–70 specifies: good → economic good → object → corporeal object = thing, and good → economic good → object → incorporeal object = right. Therefore, things are corporeal objects from the group of economic goods.

[73] *T.M.*, Parl. Geschiedenis III, p. 62. Whether there will ever come to a ninth book of the Netherlands Civil Code has become doubtful due to the progressive European and international legal unification in this area.

[74] Italy considers the opposite to be true. In Art. 810 Italian Civil Code, goods (*beni*) are a sub-class of things (*cose*). *Beni* are such *cose* which can be subject to rights.

the only objects which possess the potential for an exclusive assignment to persons. So much is now recognized everywhere in the European Union. Curiously, however, this is not brought to bear on the relevant definition. That could only happen if one (building on the Netherlands example) were to draw the line according not only to *material-physical* criteria but also (or primarily) according to *functional-juristic* criteria. On such a view, mere goods and objects of legal transaction (in contrast to 'things') are objects in which no *erga omnes* rights are possible, even though they are alienable by sale or gift.

5.16 The most important reason why not all objects of legal transaction (or goods) can be characterized as 'things' has to do with the exclusionary function of property rights. Their task—creating legal effects against third parties—cannot be realized in relation to all objects of legal transaction. Their fittingness as objects of property rights can falter on both superior law (e.g. constitutional law) and on the internal logic of a system of subjective monopoly rights. From this premise follows, for example, that objects which by their nature cannot be controlled are not capable of being the object of property rights. Something that cannot be controlled by reason of its physical nature cannot be assigned to the exclusive use of one human being. Any other conclusion would be illogical: for example, we can say that atmospheric air cannot be a 'thing' because it cannot be controlled, but also that the grant of a property right in the atmosphere would place all other human beings in the permanent danger of a trespass simply because they have to breathe. Ownership of the atmospheric air could also not be justified by reference to the common good; air is, from this perspective, not an appropriate object of property rights. Further, objects (although often saleable) that do not yet exist are generally not capable of being the object of property rights. The use of something that does not (yet) exist does not need (and cannot be prevented by) the grant of a property right. Besides, an object capable of being the object of property rights must be sufficiently ascertainable such that the creation of a private right of exclusionary use does not end up in emptiness or absurdity. One can, of course, sell a hundredweight of some sort of potatoes; if one gave the buyer a real right to one or the other 'hundredweight of potatoes of the sort X' before its separation from a larger mass (or even in some 'hundredweight of potatoes of the sort X, over which the seller can dispose'), the buyer would acquire a right of joint ownership in all of the then existing potatoes of the sort (or in all of the potatoes of the sort subject to the control of the seller). Both would shoot far beyond the aims of property law; in the result, it would make *all* the potatoes in the relevant mass *res extra commercium*. Property law therefore needs a principle of certainty or ascertainability.[75] In contrast to 'controllability',

[75] This can be found (with variations in the details) in all European property law systems. It can naturally also be found in those systems, e.g. in Spain, in which obligations can already transfer rights, and in which the criteria for determining which objects can be subject to property law were developed following contract law (for further detail see Bercovitz Rodríguez-Cano [-*Badenas Carpio*], Comentarios al Código Civil², p. 495, which says that the definition of *bien* was developed from Arts 1271 and 333 Spanish Civil Code). The reference point of a property right must be possible (Art. 1272 Spanish Civil Code), lawful (Art. 1271 Spanish Civil Code), certain (Art. 1273 Spanish Civil Code; within property law also by type and quantity: *Díez-Picazo*, Fundamentos III⁵, pp. 195–6), and already

however, the principle of ascertainability does not apply to corporeal objects only. For example, take the grant of a right to a local sports club to use land three times a year for a day-long football tournament which is transferable to other clubs. Such a right is indeed a (contractually relevant) object of legal transaction, but it is not an *erga omnes* property interest in the grantor's land. The club and its transferees do not get the power to exclude others from the use of the land (as a lessee would). The right (the supposed object of property rights) is much too imprecise for that. It leaves open, for example, on which days the tournament takes place, which areas exactly can be used for the purpose, and how many players and spectators are allowed to enter the land. For this reason, the concretization of what (or can be) objects of legal transaction are capable of being the object of property rights should not (or at least not only) be approached only from the perspective of the relevant object. The question must also be approached from the perspective of the functionality of the subjective rights with which property law is concerned. As our view flicks back and forth between these perspective, we see the whole picture more clearly. It becomes possible to rely less on criteria of external reality (corporeality, controllability, materiality, tangibility, asportability, etc.) and instead to rely on the *erga omnes* effect of the rights in question as the criterion for determining the ability of an object to be the object of property rights. An object of legal transaction that cannot be acquired to the exclusion of all others cannot be the point of reference of an *erga omnes* property right—and therefore cannot be a 'thing'. Besides this, a number of objects of legal transaction, particularly objects from the category of incorporeal normative things, can only be the point of reference for some, but not all, property rights. We argue, therefore, that an open definition of 'thing-ness' is needed, and that such a definition can be formulated as follows: *'Thing' includes every object of legal transaction in relation to which a legal system, which aims to serve the welfare-oriented principle of efficient resource allocation, can use the tool of* erga omnes *property rights.* All jurisdictions are committed to this framework definition; how exactly they give it content is a question of political value judgment.

(2) Information

Energy and information are examples of phenomena which can be disposed of by sale or gift, but cannot be grasped conceptually as legal objects to which a legal system can apply the tool of *erga omnes* property rights. Information or messages are (adopting Szpor's definition) are immaterial goods, which reduce (or are supposed to reduce) **5.17**

existent (a right cannot be created over prospective things: *Díez-Picazo* op. cit. p. 194). Further criteria to determine the reference point of a property right were derived from Art. 333 Spanish Civil Code. Accordingly, mobile or immobile property is everything which can be acquired. To avoid the circularity of such a definition, the possibility of 'acquisition' in this context only means that the object must in some way be useful to human beings (*Díez-Picazo and Gullón,* Sistema de Derecho Civil I^{12}, p. 384; *Badenas Carpio* op. cit. p. 495).

uncertainty.[76] It may sometimes appear that one can protect oneself against false information with the means provided by property law. A right to the correction of false entries in land registries is an example. This, however, serves to protect one's right of ownership in the relevant land unit, not one's right of ownership in the *information about* one's land unit. Private law protects information with obligational rights (especially personality rights) but not with property rights. No such right can be granted in information; information is not a fitting object of ownership.[77] The suitability of information for the type of protection afforded by property rights does not even depend on the distinction between publicly available and confidential information. Often, the former must remain accessible and reproducible for public law reasons. Viewed from within private law, however, the matter is no different. Information (e.g. that today is a certain day of the week, or that a war started on this day) may be sold, for example as part of a software package for a computer or smartphone. But nobody can be given such information for their truly exclusive use. That could not serve the welfare economic goals of property law; it would serve only the enrichment of the individual concerned.[78]

5.18 One could argue that matters are different in the case of confidential information. From the perspective of property law, however, the confidentiality of information makes no difference; confidential information cannot be exclusively given to one person *using the means of property law*. Information becomes, every time it is shared, a less-scarce good. True, many contracts and even general law provisions protect the confidentiality

[76] Szpor/Martysz/Wojsyk (-*Szpor*), Ustawa o informatyzacji działalności podmiotów realizujących zadania publiczne, pp. 39–40. In contrast to *Aleksandrowicz*, Komentarz do ustawy o dostępie do informacji publicznej[4], p. 95, *Szpor* only considers correct information to be information. However, this small distinction is inconsequential in property law.

[77] Correctly, in our opinion, *Phipps v Boardman* [1967] 2 AC 46, 127F-128B (Lord Upjohn) ('In general, information is not property at all. It is normally open to all who have eyes to read and ears to hear. The true test is to determine in what circumstances the information has been acquired. If it has been acquired in such circumstances that it would be a breach of confidence to disclose it to another then courts of equity will restrain the recipient from communicating it to another. In such cases such confidential information is often and for many years has been described as the property of the donor, the books of authority are full of such references; knowledge of secret processes, "know-how", confidential information as to the prospects of a company or of someone's intention or the expected results of some horse race based on stable or other confidential information. But in the end the real truth is that it is not property in any normal sense but equity will restrain its transmission to another if in breach of some confidential relationship'). On the legal characterization of information, see also *Philips v News Group Newspapers Ltd* [2010] EWHC 2952 (Ch) (Mann J) and *Philips v News Group Newspapers Ltd; Gray v News Group Newspapers Ltd; Coogan v News Group Newspapers Ltd* [2011] EWHC 349 (Ch); [2011] 2 WLR 1401 (Vos J). Both cases concerned an eavesdropping scandal. A newspaper had allegedly commissioned a private investigator to listen to messages in the voicemail of various celebrities. In the course of proceedings, the case also touched on the privilege against self-incrimination. Sec. 72 of the Senior Courts Act 1981 (the earlier Supreme Court Act) provides certain exceptions to this privilege, including an exception for 'technical and commercial information'. With this provision in view, Vos J in para. 76 explains that most forms of confidential information cannot, strictly speaking, be called property at all, even though they might have certain qualities usually associated with property. It is merely 'convenient' to speak of the protection of commercial (e.g. 'know-how' and 'trade secrets') as 'intellectual property claims'. In truth, however, 'technical and commercial information' is in no way intellectual property (para. 77). The view is similar in Hungarian law: *Menyhárd*, Dologi jog, pp. 134–5.

[78] It is unproblematic that any type of information and so-called 'apps' can be sold, both from a European point of view (Art. 2(j) and (m) Common European Sales Law), and from a national one. Consequently, information can be qualified as a thing where national sales law demands it. This does not mean that information constitutes a suitable reference point for a real right. This is not even the case under the far-reaching definition of a thing in Austrian law. (Confidential) information may be a legally protected interest and as such 'property' within the meaning of § 353 Austrian Civil Code, but not property within the meaning of § 354 Austrian Civil Code (for further detail see e.g. Klang [-*Bydlinski*], ABGB IV(2)[2], § 1053 p. 108 and Rummel [-*Aicher*], ABGB I[3], § 1053 no. 6).

of information in various ways,[79] even in ways that can be understood to be directed at effect against third parties.[80] Conceptually, however, this remains obligational—i.e. at its core, a matter of personality rights. The goal is always to protect the confidentiality of information, not to protect a right in information. As long as a secret remains a secret, it can only be used by the one who carries it insofar as he translates it into some kind of dealing. It is a part of the person who protects it. Nobody can grant ownership or even a limited real right (e.g. a right of use). When one is entrusted with a secret, it is not 'given away' or transferred; the discloser always retains the information himself. If he lifts the confidentiality of information that has been shared, he not only changes its character; he waives the protection of his private sphere on which he has, up to that point, insisted. So too, the espionage or unauthorized use of confidential information must remain a matter of the protection of personality rights under the criminal law or the law of obligations. When someone acquires insider information during an official meeting at a bank and uses it for a private trade on the stock market, for example, he does not interfere with a property right of the bank (or its informants), nor does he do so when he gives the information to a third party who uses it to enrich himself in turn. The third party does not violate anybody's right of ownership in the information. Whoever has received information can, according to the circumstances of the case, delete (or be forced to delete) the data from its storage medium or transfer (or be forced to transfer) the storage medium to someone else; he cannot, however, delete or transfer the information as such, not even when the information only appears from the organization of the symbols on their storage medium. Information is not only incapable of being owned, it is also incapable of being possessed, pledged, or even inherited.[81]

[79] Taking into account the law of unfair competition and the *culpa in contrahendo* (regarding the latter *inter alia* DCFR II.-3:302 [Breach of confidentiality]).

[80] Under breach of confidence, a third party who receives confidential information under circumstances which permit them to recognize its confidential character is treated as if they were the person to whom this information was originally confided (if a doctor or a priest disclose a secret to a third party, that third party is treated as if they themselves were the doctor or the priest).

[81] True, this is sometimes seen differently, but this seems without exception to rest either on considerations foreign to property law or on a divergent understanding of the meaning of 'information'. § 118(1) Slovakian Civil Code, for example, counts 'other assets' along with things and rights as objects of private law relations. Under this provision, perhaps information could also count as an 'other asset'? So much is conceivable for the law of contract, but not for property law. Even the confidentiality of information cannot be considered as a subjective property right that is transferable, heritable, capable of being pledged or enforced. The provisions seem not to have 'information' as such in mind so much as immaterial things of value such as trade secrets (see further *Horáček/Čada/Hajn*, Práva k průmyslovému vlastnictví², p. 309). Czech Nejvyšší soud České republiky 30 August 2011, 25 Cdo 3562/2009, Sbírka soudních rozhodnutí a stanovisek 2012 no. 22 confirms this view. The claimant demanded delivery of his patient file from a psychiatric institution on the basis of an action in vindication, in order to get access to the information held in the file. The court denied his claim on the basis that it was necessary to distinguish the information from the documents on which it was recorded. The patient had a claim to view his patient records under a special provision; the information in the records, however, was not a fitting object of property rights. The same result was reached in the criminal law context in CA Porto 15 July 2009, Processo 0816124 (Information entered in an electronic database including the addresses of an enterprise's customers was not a moveable thing, in contrast to the storage medium which could be stolen or misappropriated). A very broad definition of information is found, however, in sec. 1(4) of the US Uniform Trade Secrets Act 1985. This model law defines a 'trade secret' as 'information, including a formula, pattern, compilation, program, device, method, technique, or process, that (i) derives independent economic value, actual or potential, from not being generally known to, and not being readily ascertainable by proper means by, other persons who can obtain economic value from its disclosure or use, and (ii) is the subject of efforts that are reasonable under the circumstances to maintain its secrecy'. The concept of 'information' here is set out as a general term and the concept of 'trade secret' as a sub-set of information. If one adopted this terminology, however, one would have to distinguish between 'general or pure' information and

Every time information is shared, it becomes part of the person with whom it is shared. Where transfer (from one person to another) is impossible, so too is the creation of a real right. In contrast to the case of a right or even possession (which one no longer 'has' following a transfer) nothing is impinged upon when a message is transmitted. One who entrusts a secret to another increases the risk of betrayal, but he does not give the relevant information away. And one who obtains information illegally does not remove the authorized party from possession of the information. He violates the latter's personal right to the protection of confidentiality. Put the other way, one bound to keep information confidential (e.g. a banker or a pastor) is not thereby the victim of a property right violation.

5.19 It is important not to confuse information with other valuable goods, for example technical discoveries or personal intellectual creations. Patents are not granted for information as such, but rather for novel, reproducible, and commercializable solutions to a technical problem. Only this additional value, over and above mere information, creates a viable point of reference for a monopoly right; the added value is the object of protected, exclusive use. So too, one who sells his medical practice or business with its customer base does not just inform the purchaser about the counterparties with whom he has, hitherto, had contractual dealings. The business transaction is not concerned with this information, rather with the economic value that is connected to the sole and exclusive succession to a whole raft of relationships to clients, patients, or customers. This does not yet mean that a business sold with its client list is always an adequate point of reference for the creation of a property right, however that right is constructed; the latter, however, is at least in the realm of possibility.[82] The relationship between 'data' and 'databases' is similar. The (intellectual property law) protection of databases is conceptually possible (see Art. 7(4) of the Directive 96/9/EC of the European Parliament and of the Council of 11 March 1996 on the legal protection of databases). Such protection relates not to mere information, but rather to the art of compiling information

'special' information. What is decisive, in any case, is that only the added economic value of information, not the mere information itself, can be conceptualized as an object of property rights.

[82] Thus 'goodwill' can be encumbered with a charge in English and Irish law (sec. 860(7)(i) Companies Act 2006 and sec. 99(2)(i) Companies Act 1963, respectively). In a *fonds de commerce*, French law treats an aggregation of goods [*universalité de fait*] as a single good in accordance with the intention of the owner (*Carbonnier*, Droit civil II, p. 1623 no. 724). The *fonds de commerce* consists of corporeal and incorporeal goods including materials, wares, clientele, leases, trade names, trademarks, patents, etc. The *clientèle* is an important component of the *fonds de commerce* (*Terré and Simler*, Les biens[7], p. 63 no. 55). All of this taken together forms a single unit and can thus be treated as a single moveable thing—i.e. sold, leased, or pledged. Art. L142-2(1) of the Commercial Code provides expressly that a clientele—even the *achalandage* or the ability to acquire clientele—can be pledged. In Polish law, too, an 'enterprise' is said to be a fitting object of ownership (*Gniewek*, Prawo rzeczowe[8], p. 28 no. 68; Radwański and Dybowski [-*Stelmachowski*], System Prawa Prywatnego III[2], p. 216 no. 8; Radwański and Safjan [-*Katner*], System Prawa Prywatnego I, p. 1229 no. 152). Art. 55[1] p. 1 Polish Civil Code defines it as 'an organized aggregation of immaterial and material components, which are dedicated to the commercial activity.' In German law, clientele, know-how, and other forms of goodwill are only understood as objects of sale [*Kaufgegenstände*] under § 453 German Civil Code (BT-Drucks. 15/4060 p. 242), but not as objects of property rights or other special rights. The Spanish authorities, too, often treat the *fondo de comercio* not as an immaterial good, but as an aspect of a commercial establishment [*establecimiento mercantile*], which raises the value of the enterprise (TS 15 July 1985, RAJ 1985 no. 4055 p. 3407). Customer lists are, however, a suitable object for a contract of sale (*Menéndez*, Lecciones de derecho mercantil[5], p. 89). The position in Italian law is similar (*Galgano*, Trattato di diritto civile III, p. 471).

in an accessible form. The individual data (i.e. the symbols recorded on some storage device) are not objects of property rights. Nor are data transformed into 'things' when they are printed as letters on a page, compiled as numbers on a credit card, transformed into magnetic patterns, loaded onto a digital storage device—or any other alteration of the physical instantiation of their storage medium.[83] The fact that a PIN code is protected by criminal law and the law of obligations, but not by property law, is not due to the fact that it is not an independent corporeal object. Some rules of positive law suggest such a position,[84] but they only touch on the true reason. What is decisive, across all legal systems, is that one cannot grant real exclusive rights to pure information according to the internal logic of property law.

The same applies to the content of a telephone conversation.[85] Even if one were bold enough to characterize energy as an object of property rights,[86] listening in to a telephone conversation would not be problematic for its intrusion into this medium of communication (physically, the matter would not be fundamentally different to eavesdropping on a conversation in person) but rather for the unauthorized access to the content of the conversation.[87] Information is, nonetheless, sometimes characterized **5.20**

[83] Some think such a qualification should fail based on the principle that parts combined with a principal thing in such a way that they cannot be separated from it without damage to either, cannot be an independent reference point of property rights. If this is the case, it can be said that these partial things (components) are not things (any more). This can be seen with computer programs. For example, under Greek law a computer program is not a thing because it is not corporeal, and thereby only protected by copyright law. The situation is different however, if the program has been copied onto a material storage device and saved. In this case, the program is protected as a component of the storage device. If 'component' (or 'ingredient') in the technical sense is meant by Art. 953 Greek Civil Code, the program would still not be a thing if it were saved onto a digital storage device. This would no longer be due to the lack of corporeality, but to the lack of independence. In reality, it is the storage device which is protected, not its magnetic coating.

[84] CA Łódź 16 June 2009, II AKa 91/09, Lex-No. 582019, KZS 2010/2/52 does not qualify them as things for the purposes of criminal law. A PIN code cannot be stolen because it is not a thing within the meaning of Art. 45 Polish Civil Code; it is neither a component nor essential parts of the telephone. A PIN code does not have an 'independent material existence'. This conclusion is also reached in Sweden HD 1 June 2001, NJA 2001 p. 362 (the information in a customer database cannot be the object of the crime of *olovligt förfogande*, because the Law only protects the interests of owners and holders of security rights, not the exclusive rights over immaterial goods). The literature considers the possibility of recognizing information as a reference point to a right of ownership under Swedish law as very unlikely (*Wainikka*, SvJT 2003 p. 577).

[85] Likewise, but with a different justification Czech Nejvyšší soud České republiky 6 August 1998, 3 Tz 71/98, Sbírka soudních rozhodnutí a stanovisek 1999 no. 44. It concerned criminal proceedings, as so many cases which deal with questions of information and property law do. The court ruled that the content of a telephone conversation was not a thing within the meaning of § 89(13) Criminal Code (old version), although this provision also qualified 'controllable natural forces' and 'other assets' as things. Consequently, a conviction for theft was ruled out because, under § 247 Czech Civil Code, only 'things' can be stolen.

[86] In the Czech Republic, some authors even hold that electrical energy is a 'thing in the legal sense' (e.g. Švestka [-*Švestka*], Občanský zákoník I^2, p. 637 and *Švestka and Dvořák*, Občanské právo hmotné^5, p. 239). The term 'thing' in Czech law is in principle limited to *res corporales*. However, an exception had to be made for controllable energy.

[87] According to Hungarian jurisprudence (BH 2000/395, Legf. Bír. Pfv.II. 20.823/1998) 'telephone connection', i.e. a client's right to use the services provided by a telephone company, is merely a financially valuable right (of obligation), not an object which one can own. While this result appears plausible, it has nothing to do with the legal protection of information. It is not even indirectly related *via* the protection of a telephone number, which can be understood (like an address) as information about the telephonic availability of a person. A person who gives away a confidential telephone number is not infringing another person's property. It is not even an infringement of another person's property if a telephone company—in violation of the contract—removes a subjectively important telephone number from a client (e.g. the well-known number of a taxi service) and assigns it to a third party. The same applies if the telephone company does not allow the client to 'take the number with him' in the event of a change of service provider. These questions lie beyond the bounds of property law. (In property law, the taxi dispatch centre does not even have the option of injunction against the third party; it must solve this problem with the telephone company.) A telephone number is assigned to a client (like an address to

as a good or even as a thing, but one must look to the context of such decisions. When they are not concerned with the law of contract, they are concerned with criminal law, and in most cases with filling gaps in the criminal law which arose, or threatened to arise, in the way that criminal actions were defined for the protection of interests in property. The problem was the focus on corporeal objects. For example, in Cass. crim. 14 November 2000,[88] the manager of a mail order business had acquired knowledge of a customer's credit card number and misused it to charge her bank account for an order the delivery of which she had not accepted. The case turned on the question whether there was a criminally punishable act of deceit. The defendant had claimed that the definition of *bien* in Art. 314-1 French Civil Code was restricted to corporeal objects. The *Cour de cassation* rejected this argument; any object with an economic value was enough. The decisions of French criminal courts, in contrast, are not unified in their approach to the theft of information. Cass. 12 January 1989 confirmed the conviction of employees in a printing press for the theft of another's thing [*chose d'autrui*] under Art. 311-1 French Penal Code.[89] The defendants had copied valuable photosets and the customer cards of their employer onto private discs. In the same year, an employee who had copied the accounting documents of his employer and passed them on to a competitor was convicted of theft.[90] Information, according to the *Cour de cassation*, could be the object of a theft, because it could be the object of an exclusive property right. Cass. 3 April 1995,[91] on the other hand, acquitted two journalists who had published the income of a well-known manager in the Peugeot-Citroën concern in a French newspaper. The information came from an unknown tax official who had violated his official duties of secrecy. The journalists did not render themselves liable to criminal punishment because information was not a thing and therefore could neither be stolen nor 'fenced'. An appellate court in Paris, too, had denied the crime of incitement to theft in the case of a newspaper article that set out in detail how to build a decoder to access pay TV.[92] The court denied the charge of incitement on the basis that the decoder would not interfere directly in the *corpus* of the television producers' possession.

a resident or an email account to a user), therefore private law protects the right of a person in this case, not the right over a thing. A telephone number is no more a component of the telephone connection or device than a PIN code. The question of whether telephone numbers can be subject to ownership has not been widely discussed thus far. This is also the case in England and Ireland. In both countries, a client who changes service provider may 'take his number with him' owing to special laws. This is free of charge in Ireland. Under § 66 of the Austrian Telecommunications Act, the assignment of a telephone number does not constitute a temporary right to possession. This makes clear that telephone numbers cannot be owned in a property law sense. However, this idea does have supporters in the United States, who endorse this point from the perspective of the economic analysis of law. The question remains undecided. (For further detail, see *Gans/King/Woodbridge*, Information Economics and Policy 13 (2001) pp. 167–80 and *Haucap*, European Journal of Law and Economics 15 (2003) pp. 91–109.

[88] Bull. crim. 2000 Nr. 338 p. 10003.
[89] Bull. crim. 1989 Nr. 14 p. 38.
[90] Cass. 1 March 1989, Bull. crim. 1989 no. 100 p. 269.
[91] Bull. crim. 1995 no. 142 p. 397.
[92] CA Paris 24 June 1987, D. 1988 Somm. p. 226, note by *Marchi*; Gaz. Pal. 1987, II, p. 512, note by *Hassler*.

(3) Energy

5.21 Whatever one's attitude towards criminal law decisions of this type, the important point for present purposes is that they are cases of *criminal* law, not *property* law. They have nothing to do with the problematic of property law—despite the references to 'things' and 'ownership'—because none of the decisions were actually concerned with the transfer of either a good or rights in a good. A very similar phenomenon is encountered in the comprehensive European jurisprudence on electricity, heat, and other forms of energy. When not dealt with as a matter of criminal law, these too are almost always dealt with as matters of contract law. That is true even of jurisdictions in which the relevant statutory text (e.g. § 15 Austrian Consumer Protection Law,[93] 814 Italian Civil Code, Art. 947(2) Greek Civil Code, Art. 511-1(2) Catalonian Civil Code, Art. 15(2) Slovenian SPZ, § 5:14(2) Hungarian Civil Code [2014] (§ 94(2) Hungarian Civil Code [1959]), Art. 110(2) Bulgarian Property Law Statute, § 497 Czech Civil Code) or prevailing opinion treats electricity and other forms of energy as tantamount to things. Even an express legislative fiat cannot change the fact that electricity can only be considered as a thing for purposes *external to the law of property*. This is because forms of energy cannot be 'controlled' in a property-relevant sense. Light and heat (or other forms of kinetic energy) cannot *as such* be stored or made the object of a transfer. They can only be extracted from other forms of energy and transformed into another form again. Energy must 'flow' (which requires some change) in order to have utility (i.e. to be a 'good'). It is for this reason that energy cannot be assigned exclusively to one person's use and enjoyment. The electrical energy transported (through the movement of batteries) as electrical current constitutes no exception here. Electrical energy in batteries (condensers, coils, etc.) is not really kept ('stored'), but rather created on demand, and in household devices neither electrical current nor the electrical energy transported as current is 'consumed'. Electrons are, in a legal sense, not even 'objects': whether one thinks that they move 'in' the appliances or bounce around in them back and forth is legally meaningless. Household electrical appliances only transform electrical energy into light, motion, heat, sound, chemical energy, or similar.[94] When a surplus quantum

[93] OGH 28 December 1910, GlUNF 5281 claimed early on that energy within the meaning of Austrian law (§ 285 Austrian Civil Code) was a thing. The case concerned the lease of a workshop. The lease contract included a contract regarding the supply of steam power, which was necessary for the operation of the carpentry business. However, an adequate amount was not supplied. The OGH termed the contract for the supply of steam power as a sales contract, not a service contract, as steam is a thing within the meaning of the law. The thing in this case consequently has a material defect. This interpretation has been confirmed for contracts with consumers for all types of energy in § 15 Austrian Consumer Protection Law. This provision today defines all forms of energy as things. The scholarship is in agreement with this interpretation. It is occasionally claimed that 'electricity' is a physical thing and therefore subject to ownership (Schwimann and Kodek [-*Hofmann*], ABGB II^4, § 292 para. 2).

[94] Only a part of this is useful energy; however, this merely shows that (i) energy can be described as a good or object of transaction because of this useful part and (ii) by receiving energy one ultimately pays for a large amount of useless matter. This does not mean, however, that the useful part at least can be subject to ownership. The use and exchange value of the respective form of energy is only relevant in terms of economic pricing. Incidentally, Einstein's theory of mass–energy equivalence does not have any legal meaning, as (i) technology for the conversion of energy to mass as relevant to practical law does not exist and (ii) the terminology of mass and matter as used in physics is impractical in law. While a proton has a so-called 'point mass', it is not merely not a thing, but is not even an object in the legal sense.

of energy is available, what we colloquially refer to as 'storage' is similar. Electrical energy drives, for example, turbines, which pump water to a storage dam on higher ground; when one releases the water at a later point in time, one creates electrical energy again from the kinetic energy. The same basic pattern applies, for example, where electrical energy is used to heat salt to its molten state and so create a 'heat store'. Even such a device does not really 'keep' heat in custody. Energy, then, can be handled on the market and, in broad terms, its treatment on the market can be governed by the rules of contract law.[95] One can even squeeze the unilateral transformation of electrical energy into another form of energy into the criminal law category of 'theft'; but the notion that current or electrical energy can be possessed,[96] taken as a pledge, used under a usufruct,[97] or acquired as one's property *erga omnes* in any other way, appears absurd.

5.22 In fact, there is no judicial authority holding to the contrary, even under Art. 947(2) Greek Civil Code. CFI Athens 2832/2007[98] concerned 'contracts for the supply of electrical current' between a state-owned public limited company and the Greek state. The court upheld the company's claim for payment on the basis that the natural forces were treated, by way of legal fiction, as tantamount to things under Art. 947(2), and could therefore be the object of a contract of sale. CFI Athens 311/2005 concerned the claim for payment by the same public limited company against a private person that had bypassed their meter, 'tapped' current, and sold the same to others. The court confirmed that contracts for the supply of electrical current were to be characterized as contracts of sale which could, under certain circumstances, contain elements of a rental contract or contract for service.[99] The contract between the producer and consumer of electrical current, however, was generally a contract of sale. Protodikeio Thessaloniki 24446/1999 saw matters in the same way in a case in which electrical energy was marketed as a tradeable good.[100] The claimant could demand payment for electrical energy which, owing to a malfunctioning meter, had not yet been counted. Another raft of decisions

[95] This is the case for France, *inter alia* CA Nîmes 8 March 1990, Petites affiches 15 August 1990 no. 98 p. 8, note by *Leroy*, as well as *Collart Dutilleu and Delebecque*, Contrats civils et commerciaux[6], p. 120 para. 118; for Greece (along with the judgments cited in para. 115) Georgiades and Stathopoulos (-*Maggiva*), AK, Art. 513 para. 5, as well as *Kornilakis*, Edikó enochikó dikaio I, p. 159; for Poland Art. 555 Polish Civil Code; for Portugal STJ 22 February 2000, CJ(ST) VIII (2000-1) p. 110, as well as STJ 6 May 1998, BMJ 477 (1998) p. 451; for Spain AP Barcelona 14 June 2007, RAJ 2007 no. 1621 p. 408 and TS 3 June 2002, RAJ 2002 no. 4897 p. 8546, and for Germany Staudinger (-*Beckmann*), BGB (2004), § 453 para. 50). English law appears to qualify contracts regarding the supply of energy as service contracts (*Ball*, EJCL 10.3 (December 2006) pp. 1, 20; unfortunately, *Howard-Jones v Tate* [2011] EWCA Civ 1330; [2012] 2 All ER 369) is unclear.

[96] The Italian Court of Cassation, which previously drew on Art. 814 Italian Civil Code to affirm the possibility of possession of electricity and therefore also the protection of this possession, especially in the case of an interruption of the supply of electricity by the energy supplier, expressly corrected this. The more recent authorities (Cass. 3 September 1993, Nr. 9312, Foro it. 1995, I, p. 322 and Cass. 30 December 2004, Nr. 24182, Mass. Giust. civ. 2005, 1, 24182) explain the former confused the possession of electricity with the possession of the conductor (the cables 'behind' the electricity meter). The new argument (that the interruption of the electricity supply hinders the creation of possession of electricity) admittedly still misses the point.

[97] See also, and in turn for Italy, Cian and Trabucchi (-*Volpe*), Commentario breve[6], sub Art. 822 p. 798 (however, with the unconvincing argument that the use of energy does not allow for its conservation).

[98] All Greek judgments in this paragraph are cited according to the Isocrates database of the Athens Bar Association, unless otherwise indicated.

[99] See also CA Athens 105/1994, Arm. 1994 p. 1366.

[100] Arm. 53 (1999) p. 1530.

concern questions of criminal law. Areopag 1148/1999[101] convicted the manager of a residential complex with the serial theft of heat. He had 'tapped' the central heating system and supplied radiators in his dwelling and office. He was not, however, 'possessor' or 'owner' of the heat: rather, possession and ownership were in the residents of the complex; he had 'taken' heat from them. The decision was based on Art. 372(2) Greek Criminal Code and Art. 947(2) Greek Civil Code, according to which electricity, steam, and every other form of energy (e.g. heat) is to be treated the same as a moveable thing to the extent that the energy was subject to control within a certain space. Somewhat contradictory to this line of reasoning, on the other hand, is the decision of CFI Komotiní 85/200 in which (similar to the decisions of some Italian courts),[102] the right of a radio broadcaster to a particular frequency was held not to be a thing; the frequency could, accordingly, not be the point of reference for the protection of possession. A broadcasting frequency is naturally not a corporeal object, and, in principle, the protection of possession afforded by Greek law is limited to corporeal objects. Where energy is characterized, by way of legal fiction, as an object of property rights, the same should apply to radio frequencies as they can more straightforwardly be assigned to the exclusive use of a certain person. The court got the 'correct' answer under Greek law by holding that rights are not things. But this itself shows that Art. 947 Greek Civil Code traces the border between goods capable of protection with property rights and those incapable of protection with property rights in a problematic manner.

The French *Cour de cassation* also adopted the position early on that electrical current can be stolen.[103] This decision, however, was not readily reconcilable with the general prohibition of analogical reasoning in French criminal law, on the basis of which the German[104] (and in the end result also the English)[105] authorities denied the possibility of the theft of electrical current. The criminal law problem in both jurisdictions is (or appears) to have been solved through more precise statutory provision.[106] Swedish law, which labels the supply of electricity a 'transfer' [*överföring*] in the Electricity Statute (*Ellag* (1997:857)), has characterized unauthorized access to electricity (*olovlig* **5.23**

[101] NOMOS 294704; PoinChr. 2000 p. 594.

[102] Cass. 19 April 1991, no. 4243, NGCivil Code 1992, I, p. 386 affirmed the possibility to protect the possession of voice channels (frequencies, sometimes termed 'ether'), Cass. 28 April 1993, no. 4999, Mass. Giust. civ. 1993 no. 4999 p. 773 denied this possibility. Newer authorities deny the possibility of both possession and subjective property rights over energy (Cass. 3 September 1993, no. 9312; Foro it. 1995, I, p. 322, and Cass. 30 December 2004, no. 24182, Mass. Giust. civ. 2005 no. 24182 p. 1).

[103] Cass. 3 August 1912, D.P. 1913, 1, p. 439; p. 1913, 1, p. 337, note by *J.-A. Roux*, Extraction of energy undetected by the electricity meter; theft affirmed ('*Attendu, en effet, d'une part que l'électricité est livrée par celui qui la produit à l'abonné qui la reçoit pour l'utiliser; qu'elle passe, par l'effet d'une transmission qui peut être matériellement constatée, de la possession du premier dans la possession du second; qu'elle doit, dès lors, être considérée comme une chose, au sens de l'article 379 c. pén., pouvant faire l'objet d'une appréhension*'). Portuguese jurisprudence (Tribunal da Relação de Coimbra 24 February 1988, CJ XIII [1988-1] pp. 86–7; confirmed *inter alia* by Tribunal da Relação do Porto 29 April 2009, Processo 0847824) explicitly referenced this decision in order to claim, for their part, that the surreptitious theft of *energia eléctrica* constituted the criminal offence of theft of a moveable thing.

[104] RG 20 October 1896, RGSt 29 p. 111 and RG 1 May 1899, RGSt 32 p. 165.

[105] The criminal law there provides that 'electricity is not capable of ownership' (*Low v Blease* [1975] Crim. L. Rev. 513).

[106] See for Germany § 248c Criminal Code (which penalises the 'tapping' of 'another's' electrical energy however) and for France Art. 311-2 CP.

kraftavledning; Kap. 8 § 10 *Brottsbalk* (1962:700)) more plausibly—not as a taking, but as an unauthorized use of electricity. On this basis, the literature has properly concluded that electricity is not an appropriate object of property rights.[107] The same applies to the unauthorized use of heat. Neither electricity nor other forms of energy are things [*saken*].[108] Only in Italy has energy been argued, and accepted, to be an object of property law in the narrower sense—i.e. that one can possess energy and have property rights in it. These authorities were, however, overturned in 1993.

b. Real and Normative Things

(1) Real Things

5.24 Objects of legal transaction that are corporeal and controllable are particularly well suited to the creation of monopoly (or 'property') rights. The most obvious form of control over an object is physical control: what one can 'possess' in this sense is the ideal candidate for a fitting object of *erga omnes* property rights. Third parties can most easily recognize the suitability of these objects as objects of property rights. This explains why objects which can by nature (and not only pursuant to the intervention of a legal system) move from the 'factual control' (e.g. § 854 German Civil Code) of one person into the factual control of another person are straightforwardly 'things'. We call such things 'real'; one could also call them 'natural' things. What is decisive is that their existence and possession depend only on the facts of the external world. A legal system finds such things *realiter*, one need not 'make' them controllable (and therefore 'things') in order for legal system to create subjective rights in them. The division of things into 'real' and 'normative' categories is not precluded by the fact that legal (and not only factual) questions remain in the context of objects composed of multiple real things; such questions include whether the individual components remain independent objects of property rights. Rules which relegate certain things to the status of dependent 'components' of another, more complex thing do not create, *realiter*, non-existent things; rather, they establish what is to be regarded as the decisive (real or normative) reference point for the property right in question following the combination of several things into a more complex whole. A watch is composed of many parts, which before their combination were doubtless real things. Though they do not cease to exist physically as 'things' upon becoming parts of the finished whole, generally they do cease to exist legally as things. Their quality as cogs or screws is, to put it figuratively, suspended or supressed; they are now 'only (parts of) a watch'. If it were otherwise, the property law regime would run the danger of destroying the economic value of services. Cogs and screws do not, however, become normative things in this process; they are simply not

[107] *Hessler*, Allmän sakrätt, p. 44.

[108] The supply district heat through heated tap water is governed by the Swedish Fjärrvärmelag (2008:263). The unauthorized use of district heat (*olovlig avledning av värmeenergi*) is penalized by Kap. 8 § 10a *Brottsbalk* (1962:700). This offense consumes other criminal offenses, which may also be fulfilled. e.g. to 'channel off' this heated water is not separately penalized as theft (*Hessler*, Allmänn sakrätt, p. 44).

objects protected by property law or, to make the same point differently, they are not 'things' at all unless and until they are removed from the watch.[109]

(2) Normative Things

All other objects of legal transaction require a rule of positive law to gain the status of 'things'. This does not only stipulate the canon of property rights that may be held in them. Much more, they are creatures of the law in their nature as things. Because they are *legally constituted* things, we call them simply 'normative'. If the word did not have such a pejorative implication, one could also speak of 'fictive' things. A claim, for example, is not a feature of the external world. The existence of a pledge over a claim does only presuppose the decision, as a matter of positive law, that a claim can be pledged, but also (and more importantly) that there should exist such a thing as a 'claim' in the first place. Consequently, claims are 'normative' things in their role as the points of reference for security rights such as pledges. The same counts for a business undertaking, customer base, good will, and all choses in action that derive their value from the fact that having them entitles one to enforcement through the court system. **5.25**

The distinction between real and normative things is not identical with the distinction between corporeal and incorporeal things. This is illustrated by the case of land units. Land is, indeed, a corporeal object. As long as it has not been parcelled up, however, it remains an integral part of the earth; it is not (yet) a thing because the planet earth is not even an object for the purposes of private law. The surface of the earth and the soil are, by nature, not subject to human control without more. The relevant part of the earth's surface, which we call a land unit, only becomes an ownable 'thing' when it is, by means of legal rules, separated from other parts of the earth's surface. The law governing land units must, accordingly, always posit two distinct subject matters (which complement and complete each other, but which remain fundamentally distinguishable): one body of rules that determines which *erga omnes* rights are possible in land units, and another body of rules that determines what a land unit actually 'is', how it is identified, and how it is delimited (vertically and horizontally) from its surroundings.[110] The horizontal delimitation is typically provided today by land registries. The vertical delimitation, on the other hand, 'hides' itself—partly in the rules governing *res extra commercium*, but mainly directly in the concept of ownership that operates in the law governing land units. These rules decide not only what an owner is allowed to do with his land unit, but **5.26**

[109] This is also the case for 'total things' [*Gesamtsachen*], which are generally understood as autonomous things. Examples of this are a pile of grain or sand, a swarm of bees or a card game. It is correctly stated in Greece that it is the pile, not the individual grain (the swarm, not the individual bee, etc.) which constitutes a 'thing' within the meaning of Art. 947 Greek Civil Code (*Georgiades*, Empragmato Dikaio I, p. 80 no. 13).

[110] Correctly *Bohnert*, JZ 2011 p. 775, who differentiates rather divergently between (as termed by himself) 'intensional' and 'extensional' rights over land units.

also how far his prerogatives extend spatially—both upwards (into the air) and downwards (below the earth's surface).[111]

5.27 The distinction between real and normative things does not correlate to the common distinction between moveable and immoveable things, either. This is due firstly, but not only, to the fact that incorporeal objects (e.g. rights) cannot be understood straightforwardly as 'real' and that they can only be categorized as 'moveable' or 'immoveable' if the legal categorization completely divorces itself from its linguistic foundations.

Under Art. 202(1) Portuguese Civil Code, for example, 'a thing is anything that can be the object of legal relations'. According to this definition, rights are also things.[112] From Art. 204(1) Portuguese Civil Code, on the other hand, it follows that rights can be both moveable and immoveable things. Art. 204(1)(d), for example, classifies rights in immoveable things (e.g. land units, waters, trees fixed in the soil, etc) as immoveable things. This has been criticized as a somewhat unhappy strategy,[113] but remains the case, just as it remains the case that rights in moveable things must be understood as moveable things.[114] Claims are, incidentally, also 'moveable' things because, under Art. 205 Portuguese Civil Code, all things are 'moveable' that do not fall under the definition of 'immoveable' in Art. 204 Portuguese Civil Code. Art. 516 of the French, Belgian, and Luxembourgish Civil Codes also divide all objects into 'moveable' and 'immoveable'; *tertium non datur*. This applies equally to immaterial objects, i.e. rights. Because rights are 'abstract' (in our terminology: 'normative') creatures, they cannot be characterized as moveable or immoveable by reference to their own nature, but only by reference to the properties of the object to which they relate.[115] Rights, which have a moveable thing as their object, are accordingly moveable objects; rights, which have an immoveable thing as their object, are immoveable objects. Art. 526 of these respective codes name, as examples of the latter, rights of usufruct in immoveable things and servitudes over land. The list is, however, not exhaustive. For example, the claim of vindication of an immoveable thing is also counted as an immoveable object. Rights to claim some kind of 'giving' (*obligations de donner*, claims for an action or omission by the counterparty rather than a good), are qualified by reference to the object of the obligation: if the obligor is obligated to transfer ownership or another property right in an immoveable object, so too the corresponding claim is an immoveable object.[116] Practically, however, this only plays a role in exceptional cases

[111] See e.g. Art. 1344 Portuguese Civil Code and Art. 1001 Greek Civil Code.

[112] This clearly reflects the intention of the legislature: *Pires de Lima*, BMJ 91 (1959) pp. 207, 208 (*'Os direitos são, na verdade, coisas'*). See further *Carvalho Fernandes* op. cit. p. 545.

[113] *Carvalho Fernandes* op. cit. p. 561; *Cristas*, Transmissão contratual do direito de crédito, p. 526; *Menezes Cordeiro*, Direito civil português I(2)[2], p. 112 and Carvalho Fernandes and Brandão Proença (-*Sottomayor and Ribeiro*), Comentário ao Código Civil, note. 10.I to Art. 204, p. 461.

[114] *Carvalho Fernandes* op. cit. p. 563.

[115] *Terré and Simler*, Les biens[7], p. 42 no. 37; *Atias*, Les biens[10], p. 33 no. 51. Only the right of ownership takes a special position thus far. Because it merges with its object (in the French understanding), the right of ownership itself is, depending to the object in which it arises, a moveable or immoveable object (*Druffin-Bricca and Henry*, Droit des biens[3], p. 31).

[116] *Hansenne*, Les biens, p. 121; *De Page and Dekkers*, Traité élémentaire V[2], p. 635 no. 693; *Malaurie and Aynès*, Les biens[3], p. 33 no. 128 (*'Les obligations de faire ou de ne pas faire ne sont jamais immobilières, même si elles ont été*

because of the basic right-transferring effect of the obligation (Arts 1138 and 1583 French Civil Code)—particularly where the *obligation de donner* relates to a so-called *chose de genre immobilière*, for example '1000m^2 of a 10ha field, as yet unspecified'.[117]

In truth, most (but not all) objects qualified by the relevant legal system as corporeal moveable things are also real things—that is, things which move from one place to another and can be transferred in a physical sense. The overlaps are due to the fact that the (very common) category of moveable things implies that a thing so named can be separated from other things. If this were not the case, one could not move it. The German language, for example, began at an early stage to speak of a coffer (for example) as *Möbel* (from French *meuble*) because, in contrast to the castle in which it sat, a coffer could be taken on travels. Such a coffer is, of course, also a real thing. It is not connected to the land by anything except gravity acting on its own mass. For the same reason, the teapot sitting on a desk is (both) a 'moveable' and a 'real' thing. The differences between the concepts of 'moveable' and 'real', and between the 'immoveable' and the 'normative', therefore, rest on the fact that a legal system can determine arbitrarily what is meant by terms such as 'moveable' and 'immoveable'. A legal system can develop terminology more or less at will, whether or not it makes linguistic sense. 5.28

A building, for example—as a non-independent component of the land unit on which it is built—is not a 'thing' at all in the normal case. Its corporeal substance (the material out of which it is constructed) can be sold prior to demolition, but remains a so-called 'future thing', and therefore a mere object of legal transaction. Only when (and insofar as) the legal system recognizes a right of ownership in the building separate to the land, does it admit the building to the normative rank of 'thing'. That, however, does not change the fact that houses *per se* are in a very natural sense 'immoveable'. A pre-fabricated garage, freshly delivered by a heavy transport vehicle, is, on the other hand, a real as well as a moveable thing.[118] It stands there, in the first instance, only in virtue of gravity, and could be loaded up and transported away at any time. The various national legal systems, however, by no means stick to their own schemes of 'moveable' and 'immoveable' things. Rather, they make frequent exceptions in a number of very different and sometimes quite wonderful ways. Physical, immoveable things are transformed, in the eyes of the law, suddenly into moveable things, and physical moveable things are transformed legally into immoveable things. An example of the former in German law are the so-called 'apparent components' [*Scheinbestandteile*] of a land unit. Under § 95(1) German Civil Code, 'components of a land unit' do not include 5.29

> such things that are only connected with the surface and the soil for a transient purpose. The same applies to a building or other structure that is connected

contractées à propos d'un immeuble . . . L'obligation de donner a pour objet le transfert de la propriété. À la différence de l'obligation de faire, elle peut avoir une nature immobilière: il lui suffit d'être relative à un immeuble').

[117] *Malaurie and Aynès* op. cit. p. 33 no. 129; *Hansenne* op. cit. p. 122.

[118] Polish Sąd Najwyższy 11 February 1998, III CKN 358/97, LexPolonica-No. 2212138, Lex-No. 519925 (concerning a pavilion). A building is only a dependent part of a land unit if it is fundamentally connected to it.

with a land unit belonging to another through the exercise of a right over that land.[119]

Because German law only distinguishes between moveable and immoveable things, recognizing no third category between them, and because the abovenamed buildings and other structures are expressly not considered as components of a land unit, they were placed, out of necessity, into the category of 'moveable' things.[120] Even a monumental structure, then, is transformed by § 95 German Civil Code (despite all appearances) into a *Mobilie*. In truth, of course, it is as immoveable as an object can be; the classification leads to mysteries.

5.30 Examples of the opposite process—moveable things being transformed, by dint of law, into immoveable things *in toto* or in particular relationships[121]—are found particularly in the law of register goods,[122] that is, in the law of ships, aeroplanes, and (sometimes) automobiles. The most moveable among the moveable things are thereby treated as if they were immoveable.[123] Under Art. 205(2) Portuguese Civil Code, for example, moveables subject to registration (automobiles, ships, and aeroplanes) fall within the legal regime for moveable things, insofar as no special rules apply. A large number of special rules exist, however. They concern questions of publicity and, in virtue thereof, questions of granting and transferring rights in the named means of transport. They are not concerned with the transfer of possession (as in the case of other moveables) but rather with registration alone.[124] The alienation or encumbrance of these objects is only possible within the register (Art. 10(2) Portuguese DL 277/95).[125] Moreover, all registerable moveables can be encumbered (like immoveables) with a mortgage, but not (like other moveables) with an ordinary possessory pledge. Further, the provisions

[119] Art. 955 Greek Civil Code is almost identical to this provision. Art. 47 § 3 Polish Civil Code is very similar; however, this provision applies to immobile as well as mobile things. The question of what is a component of a land unit can, under Art. 49[1] Polish Civil Code, depend on the person (facilities for the delivery or disposal of liquids, steam, gas, or electrical energy and other facilities are not building components *insofar as they belong to an* undertaking': emphasis added).

[120] RG 19 September 1903, RGZ 55 pp. 281, 284 ('The Civil Code differentiates all things between mobile and immobile. Immobile things are only land units and its components. A special provision for non-components which are connected to the plot of land does not exist in the Civil Code. From this follows that things which are connected to the land unit for a merely temporary purpose are to be seen as mobile things. A third category does not exist'). Also RG 23 September 1904, RGZ 59 pp. 19, 21 and RG 2 June 1915, RGZ 87 pp. 43, 51.

[121] Sometimes only for purposes foreign to private law. For example, German tax law equates ships and airplanes with real estate for certain purposes (§ 21 EStG). This is justified by the claim that both are register goods (BFH 2 May 2000, BFHE 192 p. 84).

[122] An impressive example outside the law of register goods can be found in Hoge Raad 24 December 2010, LJN BO3644. The case concerned two port cranes, used for loading and unloading ships. The cranes ran on tracks, which allowed them to be moved back and forth over a distance of 600 to 800 metres. The *Hooge Raad* termed these cranes immobile things withing the meaning of Art. 3:3 Netherlands Civil Code. *Plank*, NTBR 2011 p. 202 is critical of this judgment. In Austria, it was decided that a company must 'generally be seen as a mobile thing' but must 'in individual relations be equated to immobile things' (OGH 1 June 1955, SZ 28/144, JBl 1956 p. 48).

[123] This is the case in Greece, see for further detail *Georgiades*, Empragmato Dikaio I, pp. 92–4 nos 13–24; *Kousoulas*, Empragmato Dikaio, p. 46; *Papasteriou*, Empragmato Dikaio I, pp.192–5 nos 13–23, and *Filios*, Empragmato Dikaio[3], p. 65.

[124] *Menezes Leitão*, Direitos reais, p. 73.

[125] The registration of mobile things is intended to be regulated by a *Código do Registo de Bens Móveis*.

governing the acquisition of immoveable property (including a binding agreement to make a final contract with real effect [Art. 413 Portuguese Civil Code] and the real pre-emptive right [a preference agreement with real effect: Art. 421 Portuguese Civil Code]) apply directly.[126] Arts 413 and 421 Portuguese Civil Code relate expressly to '*bens imóveis ou móveis sujeitos a registo*'. Thus one can say, with only mild exaggeration, that Portuguese law for the most part treats automobiles, ships, and airplanes as immoveable things.

This somewhat irritating regulatory approach has its origins in Italian law. Art. 815 Italian Civil Code provides that *beni mobili iscritti in pubblici registry*; that is, moveable goods inscribed in a public register, are subject to their own rules, and only subsidiarily to the rules governing moveable things generally. Registered goods thus remain moveable in principle, but approximate immoveable things in their legal treatment in many situations. *Beni mobili registrati* are automobiles, ships, and airplanes. Under Arts 249 and 864 *Codice della Navigazione*, ownership and other property rights in ships and aeroplanes are transferred subject to the rules that govern immoveable things. So, too, the possibility to encumber ships, airplanes, and even automobiles with a hypothec (see Art. 2810(2) and (3) Italian Civil Code) suggests a close relationship between registerable goods and immoveables. Only an ordinary pledge can be created over an 'ordinary' moveable thing (Art. 2784(2) Italian Civil Code). Further, the *mobili registrati* are not subject to the general provisions on good faith acquisition *a non domino* (Art. 1153 Italian Civil Code) as the true *beni mobili* are (Art. 1156 Italian Civil Code).[127] The technique of treating registerable things, especially seafaring ships, as tantamount to immoveables in different ways has been adopted quite widely. One encounters this approach, for example, in Bulgaria (Art. 46(1) Bulgarian Maritime Code), in Poland,[128] in Greece,[129] in Sweden,[130] and in France. Ships and aeroplanes are indeed moveable goods (Art. 531 French Civil Code). However, in virtue of registration and the applicability of the law of hypothecs, they are accorded a 'hybrid nature' between moveable and immoveable goods. Art. 2276 French Civil Code ('*en fait des meubles, la possession vaut titre*') does not apply to registerable goods. Possession here plays no role (although 5.31

[126] *Menezes Cordeiro*, Tratado de direito civil I(2)^2, p. 146.

[127] Tribunale Arezzo 8 February 2006, DVD Juris Data, Sistema di documentazione giuridica, Giuffrè 3/2011; Cass. 17 April 2001, Nr. 5600, Giur. it. 2001 p. 2020. A car can accordingly only be acquired in good faith *a non domino* before its registration or in the case of an incorrect registration. It is only a normal moveable thing until registration.

[128] Radwański and Safjan (-*Katner*), System Prawa Prywatnego I, p. 1208 no. 82.

[129] Art. 6 of the Greek Statute on Private Navigation provides that the transfer of ownership of ships requires registration; Arts 195 and following regulate hypothecs over ships. The situation for airplanes is similar under Statute 1815/1988. On the other hand, motor vehicles are subject to the ordinary possessory pledge. The same rules regarding transfer of ownership for moveable things also apply to them.

[130] Ships and aircraft are, according to the Swedish interpretation, *lösöre* (moveable things); however, they are still subject to a special regime. A buyer of larger ships (total length greater that 12 metres) is granted protection under property law upon submission of the application for registration (*ansökan om inskrivning*) in the shipping register (*skeppsregistret*) under Kap. 2 §§ 3 and 9 *Sjölag* (1994:1009). A buyer of a smaller ship is only granted protection upon gaining possession or completion of the registration in the register established for all moveable things by *Lag om handel med lösören, som köparen later i säljarens vård kvarbliva* (*1845:50 S.1*). The protection of property law for aeroplanes is also subject to a special registration regime (§§ 2c–e *Lagen om inskrivning av rätt till luftfartyg (1955:227)*).

it does in the case of automobiles).[131] Latvian law presents two surprises in this context. Statute law excludes trains from the moveable things (that is, generally, things than can be moved from one place to another without damaging their substance), but instead counts them as immoveable along with the whole railway apparatus (Art. 842 Latvian Civil Code). And Art. 843 Latvian Civil Code allows parties, by way of agreement, to apply the rules governing moveables to immoveables, and to apply the rules governing immoveables to moveables.

5.32 Courts operating within a legal framework that only permits them to distinguish between moveable and immoveable things do not just face linguistic difficulties. Sometimes they find themselves with a dire want of a conceptual basis on which to ground decisions. They then 'invent', for example, mixed concepts from novel forms of property and novel property rights; sometimes, they even grasp at the argument that the parties to a contract of sale can determine, with consequences for third parties, which things should be seen as moveable and which as immoveable. Such constructions are, in a body of law oriented around *erga omnes* effect, anything but unproblematic.

An illustration is found in Spanish TS 30 March 2000.[132] The Spanish Ministry of Education had purchased valuable historic tiles from a palace in private ownership, which were fully attached to the supporting wall. The owner was meant to keep the tiles for the ministry for a time, as a museum was being constructed for the works of the artist who had painted the tiles. The tiles therefore remained on the wall. The owner then sold the palace. The ministry brought a claim against the purchaser of the palace for delivery of the tiles. The claim was successful. The court held that the case was concerned with the sale of a future thing; the tiles would become moveable goods upon their separation from the palace wall. The latter is indeed correct, but it does not justify the decision. The claim for delivery (here, the right to separate the tiles from the wall) was based in a right of ownership in the tiles, but as long as the tiles were fixed on the wall, their character of moveable things was in suspense. Thus, the court allowed a claim for the *transformation* of an immoveable thing into a moveable thing, or, to put it another way, allowed a claim for the delivery of a moveable thing that did not 'actually' exist at all, and which was, for that reason, not capable of being the object of a vindicatory claim at the relevant time. In our view, the court would have had two possibilities to allow such a claim: it could (in violation of the *numerus clausus* principle which is not very rigorously enforced in Spanish law anyway) have accepted a new real right in immoveable property, namely a right to take something away;[133] or, it could have

[131] *Reboul-Maupin*, Droit des biens^2, p. 40 no. 73; *Malaurie and Aynès*, Les biens^3, p. 173 no. 574.

[132] RAJ 2000 Nr. 2431 p. 3772. cf. also Cass. civ. 15 April 1988, JCP 1988, II no. 21066, note by *Barbièri* (Sale of frescos from a church, over which the seller had private ownership. The church stood in Casenoves, an abandoned village near Perpignan. The frescos were originally by their nature immoveable things. However, they became moveable upon separation and therefore independent objects of ownership).

[133] By adhering to the *numerus clausus* principle, a right to remove the tiles under property law could come into question in the form of a servitude at best. In this event, however, a legal system must (i) permit personal servitudes and (ii) permit them to correspond to a single action. The second criterion is the reason why a 'removal servitude' would fail in Germany (RG, 24 March 1905, RGZ 60 p. 317; BayObLG 24 November 1965, DNotZ 1966,

apprehended the tiles as normative things separate to the land unit. A similar problem appeared in Austrian OGH 18 November 1993.[134] The parties disputed the ownership of a mural, which the defendant tenant had created in the leased premises. It was accepted between the parties that the mural could be removed by a properly qualified tradesman without damaging it. The OGH held, on the basis of § 297 Austrian Civil Code, that the theoretical possibility of removal was adequate to characterise the mural as a separate component of the premises (and of the land unit), capable of being the object of discrete rights. It was therefore the property of the tenant. CA Aix-en-Provence 15 February 1985 concerned a *cabanon*, a small wooden cabin.[135] The buyer had acquired it on the basis that he could demount and transport it away. The buyer then sold the cabin onto a third party, who duly demounted the cabin and loaded the frame and cladding onto a truck. The dispute arose from the fact that the first seller of the cabin had, in the meantime, sold the land unit to another third party, who did not feel himself bound by the agreement concerning the cabin; he brought a claim against the second buyer of the cabin for damages for violation of his property rights in it. The appellate court characterized the *cabanon*, in the first instance, as an immoveable good by nature (Art. 517 French Civil Code).[136] The parties to the first contract of sale had, however, treated the cabin in anticipation as a moveable good, and there was no legal problem with their approach. According to the court, the intention of the parties is, ultimately, dispositive of the classification of a thing as moveable or immoveable. When a contract is made concerning a '*per se*' immoveable thing, which concerns the thing in its future character as a moveable thing, the parties are allowed to treat the thing as moveable already at the time of contracting.[137]

c. Future Things

All of these decisions raise a problem, closely related to the concept of (in)dependent components and the *numerus clausus* principle, namely of the treatment of so-called 'future things'.[138] Future things are, with some limitations, already objects of (current) **5.33**

538). It would merely reproduce the content of a sales contract. This is different in Austria. So-called 'demolition servitudes' [*Abbruchdienstbarkeiten*] are permitted (OGH 21 November 2000, SZ 73/175).

134 Ecolex 1994 p. 228.

135 Gaz. Pal. 1985, I, p. 442, note by *Dureuil.*

136 According to this provision, '*les biens* (are) *immeubles, ou par leur nature, ou par leur destination, ou par l'objet auquel ils s'appliquent*'. The concept of a moveable good 'in virtue of anticipation' is not evident in the statutory text; it is a product of the scholarly literature and the abovenamed decision of the CA Aix.

137 *Terré and Simler*, Les biens[7], p. 35 no. 31.

138 We mean by 'future things' either things which do not yet exist at all (e.g. next year's harvest) or things whose quality as such is in suspense (e.g. the integral components of a machine; this year's harvest standing in the field). It appears that there is no consistency in Europe even regarding the definition of future things. e.g. Art. 211 Portuguese Civil Code defines *coisas futuras* not as things which do not yet exist, but as things over which a right-holder is not (or is not yet) entitled to dispone. *Menezes Cordeiro*, Tratado de direito civil I(2)[2], p. 159, however, distinguishes with the concurrence of Carvalho Fernandes and Brandão Proença (-*Sá Rebelo*), Comentário ao Código Civil, note 5 to Art. 211, p. 475 between future things in the objective or absolute sense (things which *in rerum natura* do not yet exist) and future things in a subjective or relative sense (things in existence, but which are not within the patrimony of the relevant person). In the Netherlands, it is important to distinguish between 'future

legal transaction; they can, as a rule, be sold and gifted in the present.[139] They are, however, certainly not real things, and as normative things they only come into existence when a legal system posits, by dint of legal fiction for some specific purpose, that they exist. This is only seldom the case, and presupposes that a future event will be given retrospective legal effect (not unlike a mirror image of the situation in which a declaration of avoidance undoes an earlier declaration of contractual intention *ex tunc*). In general, however, things must exist presently in order to be an object of subjective property rights. Only when the thing is present does a property right arise in it. It is only possible to make agreements today about a thing's future existence. When determining to whom a new thing belongs (or to whom some right in a new thing accrues), property law often has regard to past transactions and other circumstances that occurred before the creation of the thing; however, it does not recognize any present rights in future things. Even where it is possible to create a 'pledge over a future claim' and even to transfer such a pledge, as is the case in a number of legal systems, one is really dealing with an as yet inchoate property right. The same is true where one can deliver cloth to his tailor, and agree that the suit will belong to the customer, or where (as under §§ 3(1) and 8(1) German Statute on the Ownership of Apartments), separate ownership in a certain apartment can be granted in a building yet to be constructed on a land unit. If the pledged claim does not come into existence, if the suit is not tailored, or if the house is not built, these scenarios never lead to any kind of valuable property right.

An example of the exceptional case just mentioned is found in the English law rule that agreements concerning future claims made for the purposes of granting security can have retrospective effect.[140] The transfer of a not-yet-existing claim is invalid at common law; however, a transfer for value is valid in equity. Fundamentally, equity also regards the assignment as having occurred only when the claim actually arises.[141] However, an earlier assignment of a future claim has priority over all later dealings with the future claim that the assignor undertakes with third parties. This is understood by some authors to mean that the first assignment is retroactive.[142] Besides this, Art.

things' and 'future goods' (Art. 3:97 Netherlands Civil Code). Future goods reflect *coisas futuras* of Portuguese law. They are goods which do not yet exist at all, as well as goods, which do not yet belong to the person disposing of them (T.M., Parl. Geschiedenis III, p. 402). In certain cases, dealings with future goods are prohibited (e.g. Art. 4:4 Netherlands Civil Code prohibits dealings with rights of inheritance that have not yet vested).

139 See DCFR Art. IV.A.-1:201 (Goods): 'In this Part of Book IV: (a) the word "goods" includes goods which at the time of the conclusion of the contract do not yet exist.' A similar provision is also found in the law of gift (DCFR Art. IV.H.-1:102(1)). The latter, however, departs from several national gift regimes, for e.g. Art. 226(2) Bulgarian Statute on Obligational Relationships and Contracts and Art. 771(1) Italian Civil Code. According to these, the gift of a future thing is fundamentally void.

140 The problem only arises in the context of claims, because under the Bills of Sale Acts 1878 and 1882 no non-possessory real security in goods can be created against a natural person and because the practice in the context of legal persons tends towards the creation of a floating charge. See e.g. *Chapman (t/a Chapman & Co Solicitors) v Wilson* [2010] EWHC 1746 (Ch) (Vos J).

141 *Bell*, Modern Law of Personal Property, p. 380.

142 *Goode*, Commercial Law^3, p. 634. References to the authorities in von Bar and Drobnig (-*Swann*), The Interaction of Contract Law and Tort and Property Law in Europe, p. 377 no. 575. For a similar result, albeit with less clarity in the construction, see OGH 14 September 2004, 10 Ob 321/02g, RIS-Justiz and OGH 30 November 2006, JBl 2007 p. 379; ecolex 2007 p. 246. In both cases, the court asserts that 'by the assignment of future claims ... the assignee can only truly acquire the claim when it arises. Agreement over the assignment can,

1601-2 French Civil Cod and Arts 3:228 and 3:97 Netherlands Civil Code recognize a transfer of ownership, or rather creation of a pledge, with *ex tunc* effect.

Apart from such exceptional cases, future things fall outside the set of objects of legal transaction that are capable of being the object of property rights. The same applies to all objects which only exist in imagination at present as well as to objects which have some physical substrate (i.e. which are visible and tangible), but lack the character of a (real or normative) object because they are a non-independent component of another thing. A legal system can, in such cases, only extend the range of property rights in the main object. The general rule, however, remains unaffected by this. One can, in the present moment, guarantee rights in things that will exist in the future for the case that they successfully come into existence, but these rights are only effective upon the 'birth' of the thing in question. This formulation reflects the general position in the preponderance of European legal systems. **5.34**

Czech law, for example, takes the position that a future thing can only be the object of an obligational relationship (in which the parties have to decide which of them bears the risk of the thing never coming into existence).[143] Under Art. 1348 Italian Civil Code, 'the tender of future things can be the subject matter of a contract … subject to special statutory prohibitions'. Art. 1413 Latvian Civil Code is to the same effect; contracts over future things do not generally stumble on the principle that agreements with an impossible subject matter are void. Art. 1472 Italian Civil Code, however, expressly adds that, **5.35**

> in the case of a contract of sale of a future thing … ownership is acquired only when the thing is created. If the trees or fruits of a land unit are the subject matter of the sale, ownership is acquired when the trees are felled or the fruit is harvested.

Section 457 Sentence 2 Austrian Civil Code envisages that a pledge over the fruits of an already-pledged object only comes into existence in the separate(d) fruits. Above all, however, § 85(3) Sentence 1 Austrian Civil Code provides the rule that a pledge over fruits only ever arises when the fruits have been separated. Until that time, a pledge made over fruits can only be created in the form of a right in the main object. Under Austrian law, then, it has been held that a parcel of forest can be sold with the proviso that the seller retains the (relative) right (*vis-à-vis* the purchaser) to harvest the trees following the change of ownership, but not with the proviso that the seller retains ownership of the trees. Such an agreement has no effect against third parties.[144]

however, occur before this point in time.' Through such an assignment, 'a change in the legal responsibility for the claim' was effected, in virtue of which 'the transfer of the right occurred already at the time of the agreement'. See further OGH 23 February 2011, JBl 2011 p. 508.

[143] *Švestka and Dvořák*, Občanské právo hmotné[5], p. 275. Like many other legal systems, Czech law also draws a general distinction between the sale of a future thing under the condition that it arises and the so-called 'hopeful sale' (§ 2083 Czech Civil Code, e.g. the sale of a harvest). In the former case the risk in principle falls on the seller, in the latter on the buyer. Matters are similar under Art. 25 of the Bulgarian Statute on Obligational Relationships and Contracts.

[144] OGH 1 November 1980, EvBl 1981/48 (ÖJZ 1981 p. 160). See also the Scots case *Morison v A & DF Lockhart (A Firm)* [1912] SC 1017 (concerning the sale of wood from a tree trunk that the buyer was meant to fell; the seller died, and his heir, to whom property passed, refused to allow him to do so), and the French case Cass. civ. 23 May

Likewise under Ch. 2 § 7 of the Swedish JB, a purported right of ownership in trees can only be enforced against a third-party purchaser when they have already been separated from the land unit prior to the transfer of ownership in such a manner that they have lost their character as part of the land. A right of ownership in standing trees is only effective against third parties in connection with ownership in the land unit itself (Kap. 4 § 7 JB). However, the owner of the land unit can give another a right to fell the standing trees (Kap. 7 § 3 JB) that also binds his successor-in-title and, in virtue thereof, acquires third party effect (Kap. 7 § 11 and § 16 [Effectiveness against creditors of the acquirer] JB). The one disposing of the land unit must, however, draw attention to the existence of this right. Otherwise, the right is ineffective against the acquirer; the one entitled to fell the trees then has only an obligational right against his contractual partner (Kap. 7 §§ 18 and 19 JB). Portuguese law treats the sale of future things like the sale of the goods of a third party (Arts 893 and 892 Portuguese Civil Code; cf. Art. 467 Portuguese Commercial Code). As to the real effect (*eficácia real*) of a contract of sale over future things, Art. 408(2) Portuguese Civil Code provides that the transfer of rights occurs as soon as the seller acquires (ownership of) the thing. When a disposition concerns natural fruits or components of a thing, it only becomes effective at the moment of harvest or separation. The seller is only subject to an obligational duty to do everything necessary for the buyer to acquire the thing (Art. 880 Portuguese Civil Code). Art. 881 Portuguese Civil Code also operates with the category of 'goods of uncertain existence or title' (*bens de existência ou titularidade incertas*). The seller can, in principle, demand payment for such goods so long as the fact of uncertainty has been notified in the contract. Under Greek law, too, property in future things can only be transferred subsequent to their coming into existence. For example, under Arts 1064 to 1068 Greek Civil Code, one either acquires a property right (whether as outright owner or usufruct holder) in fruits *per separationem* (*με την αποχωρισμό*) or (as one entitled as a matter of the law of obligations) *per perceptionem* (*με τη συγκομιδή*, i.e. through picking).[145] Future things cannot be pledged (Art. 1209 Greek Civil Code). It is only possible to agree to a pledge contingently for the case that the thing arises and is delivered to the pledge creditor;[146] the same applies to the creation of a pledge over an expectancy right to the future acquisition of ownership.[147] The fruits of a thing are fundamentally (i.e. in default of any agreement to the contrary) free from a pledge encumbering the principal thing (Art. 1220 Greek Civil Code). In the framework of the antichresis, too, the creditor only acquires the fruits upon their separation (Art. 1221 Greek Civil Code). Under Art. 1130(1) French Civil Code, future things can be the

2012, D. 2012 p. 1934, note by *d'Avout* (the *Cour de cassation* accepted a proprietary *droit de crû et à croître*, a right to what has grown and what is to grow, in a forest, which since its inception in 1837 has been accorded *erga omnes* effect). In *Ellis v Noakes* [1932] 2 Ch. 98, the Court of Appeal accepted that standing trees could be bracketed out of a right to the surface and the soil by contractual agreement.

[145] See *Spyridakis*, Empragmato Dikaio I, p. 757.
[146] Areopag 408/1966, EEN 34 (1966) p. 158; *Triantos*, AK, Art. 1209 p. 1427 no. 2.
[147] CA Athens 6177/1998, EllDik 43 (2002) p. 203.

subject matter of an obligation. These include, according to Art. 1601-1 French Civil Code,[148] buildings yet to be constructed. In every case, however, it is clear that ownership of *choses futures* cannot be transferred at the time when the agreement is made, because in that moment the *choses* do not yet exist. When they come into existence, the contract then brings about (absent any other agreement) an acquisition of ownership by the party entitled; this ownership is 'originary', i.e. it does not pass derivatively to the buyer through the seller.[149] Things that are created in batches become, in principle, the property of the acquirer as they are finished. However, the parties can deviate from this position. They can structure their agreement such that acquisition of ownership in the newly created thing is deemed to vest retroactively at the moment of sale and purchase,[150] and the parties can agree under Art. 1601-3 French Civil Code that ownership should pass on a constant basis, consistent with the progress in construction. Pledges can validly be created over future things (Art. 2333 French Civil Code). This is because the procurement of possession is no longer a prerequisite for the creation of a pledge. However, the pledge itself only comes into existence in the moment that the *chose future* becomes real and becomes part of the patrimony of the pledge debtor. At that point in time, the thing is encumbered with the pledge 'automatically', without any further act of transfer and without any formality.[151] This position, again, reflects the construction in Art. 2(1) of the Greek Statute 2844/2000 on non-possessory pledges. This provision allows one to create a pledge over a future thing in the case that it is certain or at least ascertainable. Such a pledge, again, only comes into existence itself with the 'birth' of the thing it encumbers.

Sometimes, however, it seems that not only judicial decisions, but also special statutory regimes carve out exceptions from the rule that non-independent components of a composite thing cannot be the object of discrete property rights. In these cases, it appears as if future things were normatively equiparated with existing things—i.e. as if a new species of thing were being created. In German law, for example, the general rule is that the components of a land unit (including grain on the stalk) can only be pledged if the pledge creditor gets a right not only over the harvest but also over the entire land unit.[152] But there is another rule in the Statute on the Guarantee of Fertilizer and Seed Supply [*Gesetz zur Sicherung der Düngemittel- und Saatgutversorgung*].[153] Under § 1 of this Act, a statutory pledge encumbers the harvest to the benefit of one who has a **5.36**

[148] '*La vente d'immeubles à construire est celle par laquelle le vendeur s'oblige à édifier un immeuble dans un délai déterminé par le contrat. Elle peut être conclue à terme ou en l'état futur d'achèvement.*'

[149] *Zenati-Castaing and Revet*, Les biens[3], p. 168 no. 104.

[150] Art. 1601-2 French Civil Code provides expressly: '*La vente à terme est le contrat par lequel le vendeur s'engage à livrer l'immeuble à son achèvement, l'acheteur s'engage à en prendre livraison et à en payer le prix à la date de livraison.* Le transfert de propriété *s'opère de plein droit par la constatation par acte authentique de l'achèvement de l'immeuble;* il produit ses effets rétroactivement au jour de la vente' (emphasis added).

[151] *Aynès and Crocq*, Les sûretés[4], p. 226 no. 504.

[152] MünchKomm (-*Damrau*), BGB VI[5], § 1204 no. 11.

[153] The statute of 1949 and 1951 still applies today (in the version of 1 January 1964), although it was originally (as apparent from § 7) only intended to apply for a transitional period until 1951. It was conceived as a post-war emergency measure and was meant to bolster the willingness of industry to supply agriculturalists by providing a valuable real security interest.

claim arising from the supply of fertilizer or seed, even if the harvest has not yet been separated from the land on which it stands. This so-called 'harvest pledge' serves to give the supplier priority over other creditors of the agriculturalist, in that he can make good his claim against the 'fruits on the vine' in the course of enforcement proceedings (§ 810(1) German Civil Procedure Code; §§ 20, 21(1), and 148 German Statute on Court Auctions and Attachment Procedure).[154] This rule does not even require a connection between the seed or fertilizer delivered and of the agricultural fruits produced.[155] The pledge extinguishes *inter alia* when the farmer, with the knowledge of the pledge creditor, removes the harvest from the land unit in the course of ordinary agricultural practice, irrespective of the latter's permission.[156] Under § 810 German Civil Procedure Code other agricultural products still connected with the land unit can be encumbered by a pledge in the course of enforcement proceedings, as mentioned previously, but not earlier than one month before the crop can be usually expected to be ripe for harvest.

Under Art. 3:228 Netherlands Civil Code, all goods which can be transferred can be encumbered with a pledge. Art. 3:97 Netherlands Civil Code governs the supply of future goods (which is, along with agreement, a precondition for the transfer of ownership). This section provides:

> (1) Future goods can be delivered in advance, unless it is prohibited to make such goods the subject of an agreement or they are register goods. (2) A delivery in advance of future goods has no effect against someone who has obtained those future goods earlier on the basis of a prior delivery in advance. If [the delivery in advance] concerns a future tangible thing, then it will only have effect as from the moment at which the thing actually comes into the hands of the acquiring party.

Only a 'silent' (non-possessory) pledge, however, can be made over a future corporeal thing; further, only such a pledge is possible over a future claim until such time as the identification of the debtor occurs (Art. 3:237 Netherlands Civil Code).[157] Art. 3:237(4) Netherlands Civil Code, on the other hand, prescribes:

> If the pledgor or debtor does not properly perform his obligations towards a pledgee who has acquired a non-possessory pledge that is established in advance over fruits or crops standing in the field, then the court may authorize the pledgee to harvest those fruits or crops himself.

5.37 This provision works very well. It contains a plausible answer to the question what a pledge (or, in the case of the Spanish tiles, a right of ownership) in a legally not-yet-extant thing actually 'is'. One could interpret these rules as carving out an exception, in

[154] BGH 7 December 1992, BGHZ 120 pp. 368, 374.

[155] OLG Karlsruhe 18 March 1992, AgrarR 1993 p. 61.

[156] BGH 7 December 1992 op. cit. See further BGH 8 January 1964, BGHZ 41 p. 6; BGH 12 February 1959, BGHZ 29 p. 280. BGH 7 February 1992 op. cit. even opines that a pledge in such circumstances is extinguished when the pledge creditor was ignorant of the removal.

[157] *Hijma and Olthof*, Compendium van het Nederlands Vermogensrecht[9], p. 167 no. 263.

particular an exception to the general doctrine of components.[158] In that case, future things would appear to be a special sub-category of normative things. Alternatively, if one sticks to the principle that future things cannot be the object of present property rights, one must posit a somewhat clandestine relaxation of the *numerus clausus* principle—i.e. the creation of (one or more) novel property rights. Substantively, this approach would entail encumbrance of the main object (e.g. the house) with a right to the disaggregation of its respective components (e.g. the tiles). We are of the opinion that the second approach does better justice to the phenomenon at hand. It avoids the question why there is only a right of disaggregation and not other rights in a normative thing of this new type. The acceptance of a new property right in a currently existing (main) thing is a less dramatic break with the fundamental principles of property law than the recognition of a new normative thing that is potentially an object of all the various property rights. If the Spanish wall tiles were treated as a case in which a new normative thing is created, rather than as a case in which the land unit is encumbered with a right to remove the tiles, one would also have to provide comprehensive rules governing the relationship between the owner of the principal thing (the palace) and the tiles. Who, for example, would be entitled to deal with the tiles pending their separation? If one thinks that the tiles or the standing grain are a special type of normative things, one would also have to explain what is understood by a right of ownership or pledge in an object of legal transaction that may or may not exist in the future: the tiles could, for example, disappoint expectations and not survive to the moment of separation; the standing crop could be lost.

d. Development and Distribution of the Conceptual Definition of 'Thing' in the Legal Systems of Member States

(1) Ground, Legal Dispute, and Object

Sache ('thing') is, in many languages (and language families), an ambiguous word. It is **5.38**
particularly difficult to define because of the linguistic overlap between a legal dispute and the reason for which it arose, on the one hand, and the object on which the legal dispute about possession and right turns, on the other. Human beings dispute either 'in' a thing or 'over' a thing. In all languages, the second meaning of 'thing' developed out of the first (older) meaning, but never fully displaced it.[159] The state is concerned with public matters (*res publica*), the law of *zaakwarneming*[160] is concerned with the private matters of another. Public as well as private matters require disputation. Such disputes turn on something of substance, on the 'object' of the negotiation. They have generally concerned, from ancient times, something cognizable by the senses in which

[158] This view is arguably held by BeckOK (-*Sosnitza*), BGB^{20}, § 1204 no. 7; § 951(2) sentence 2 German Civil Code appears to indicate the contrary interpretation.

[159] See The Oxford English Dictionary (-*Simpson and Weiner*), Vol. XVII^{2} (Oxford 1989), p. 941.

[160] This is the Dutch expression for law of voluntary agency or *negotiorum gestio*.

ownership has arisen.[161] The person against whom one disputes is still called one's *Widersacher* (from German '*wider*' for 'contra'). A court in German-speaking countries decides, today as then, 'in the matter [*in der Sache*'] X *versus* Y', and its counterpart in England decides 'in re X' when dealing with an *ex parte* application. In Old High German, *Sahha,* from which both German '*Sache*' and English 'sake' (e.g. 'for the sake of') derive, already meant a dispute—often a legal dispute.[162]

5.39 Without some ground for disagreement, no dispute arises. This is reflected in the French term *chose*, Italian *cosa*, Spanish *cosa*, and Portuguese *coisa*. They are all derived from the Latin root *causa*.[163] In classical Latin, *causa* meant a matter, a debt—the 'point' of an argument.[164] The *causa* was, as such, the departure point for a legal dispute, and only later did the word come to be the expression for the legal dispute itself.[165] We call a case of importance for the development of the law a *cause célèbre* to the present day. The meaning of *causa* broadened in medieval vulgar Latin. A *causa* became any object of relevance, a *cose*,[166] and the jurists replaced *res* with *causa* for their purposes, too.[167] *Res judicata*, for example, transformed in Italian *cosa giudicata* (Art. 324 Italian Civil Code) and Portuguese *coisa julgada* (meanwhile however *caso julgado*: see Art. 497 and Art. 580 of the old and new versions of the Portuguese Civil Procedure Code, respectively[168]), Spanish *cosa juzgada*, and French *chose jugée*. *Causa* (French *cause*, Italian, Portuguese, and Spanish *causa*) itself, however, has remained ambiguous. The Romanic legal systems call the law of unjustified enrichment, for example, the law of *enrichissement sans cause*, *arricchimento senza causa*, *enriquecimento sem causa*, and *enriquecimiento sin causa*. It is concerned with the question whether a person has a 'legal ground' to retain an enrichment. *Chose* (*cose*), on the other hand, is a term that sometimes refers to a real object,[169] sometimes to everything that exists (i.e. an entity phenomenon),[170] sometimes to all spatial objects, and sometimes to everything that

[161] Jacob and Wilhelm Grimm (*-Heyne*), Deutsches Wörterbuch, Vol. VIII (Leipzig 1893), p. 1597 (with the remarkable comment, for the year 1893 at least, that the meaning of the German word *Sache* was limited to moveable objects; the use of this term for immoveable objects was said to be 'archaic'). This evidently had no impact on the formulation of § 90 German Civil Code, which was drafted about this time.

[162] Grimm op. cit. pp. 1592–94; Wissenschaftlicher Rat der Dudenredaktion (ed.), Duden: Das große Wörterbuch der deutschen Sprache, Vol. VII^3 (Mannheim 1999), p. 3261; *Johann Heinrich Campe*, Wörterbuch der Deutschen Sprache, Vol. IV (reprint Hildesheim and New York 1969), p. 4.

[163] *James H. Dee*, A Lexicon of Latin Derivatives in Italian, Spanish, French and English: A Synoptic Etymological Thesaurus With Full Indices for Each Language, Vol. I (Hildesheim, Zürich and New York 1997), p. 432.

[164] *Karl-Ernst Georges and Heinrich Georges*, Ausführliches Lateinisch-Deutsches Handwörterbuch, Vol. I (reprint Darmstadt 1995), p. 1040. '*Causa*' still had the meaning of 'chance' and 'opportunity' as well as connoting friendship and connection (*Carlton Lewis and Charles Short*, A Latin Dictionary: Based on Andrews edition of Freund's Latin Dictionary [reprint Oxford 1989] p. 303).

[165] *Georges and Georges* op. cit. p. 1043; *Lewis and Short* op. cit. p. 304. In Portuguese legal parlance, *causa* also has the meaning of *acção* ('claim'); *causa de pedir* (*causa petendi*) is the basis of a claim and the point of departure for a legal dispute (*fundamento do pedido* and *requisito da petição inicial*; see further *Prata, Dicionário jurídico I*^{5}, pp. 248–50).

[166] Paul Imbs (ed.), Trésor de la langue française: Dictionnaire de la langue française du XIXe et du XXe siècle (1789–1960), Vol. V (Paris 1997), p. 759.

[167] *Paul Robert*, Le Robert. Dictionnaire alphabétique et analogique de la langue française. Les Mots et les associations d'idées, Vol. I (Paris 1974), p. 763.

[168] So too Art. 2(1) Portuguese Civil Procedure Code (previous version) and Art. 2(1) Portuguese Civil Code (new version). In Brazilian usage, this has remained the *coisa julgada*: Arts 467 *et seq.* Brazilian Civil Code.

[169] Trésor V op. cit. pp. 758–9.

[170] *Robert* op. cit.

affects something or someone.[171] Even incorporeal objects and pure thoughts are called *choses*.[172] Mostly, however, according to the leading French dictionary, the modern meaning of *chose* is a physical object.[173] But that does not exclude the possibility of using *chose* to refer to the subject matter of a discussion, to the central question or for what has been said, nor, in a legal context, to refer to the core of a judicial decision—i.e. that which has been decided over.[174]

Causa is, of course, also couched within the universal terminology of 'causality' (in German '*Ursache*', cause, lit. 'original thing').[175] From this, the notion of *Bedingung* is not far ('condition', incorporating '*Ding*'). This term builds a bridge to the German folk court, the *Ding* or *Thing*, which is (*inter alia*) still reflected in the German terminology of the real [*dingliche*] rights of property law, as well as in the English *thing*, in the Icelandic *Alþingi* (parliament), and in the court of first instance in Sweden, the *Tingsrätt*.[176] Already the root word *Ding* (*Thing*) had the meaning of a legal matter or legal dealing.[177] Similar to the German *Sache*, the English *thing* later transformed into its current meaning of 'object of a process' or claim and then into 'object cognisable to the senses'.[178] That does not, however, necessarily mean that only physical objects, that objects which occupy space, can be called 'things'.[179] According to one American dictionary, it is only in legal parlance that the meaning of 'thing' is restricted to 'that which can be possessed or owned'.[180] The Czech word *věc* ('thing', from Old Slavonic *vešt*) is related to the Gothic *waihts* (which persists in Swedish *vätte* and German *Wicht*, the latter of which finds echoes in *Gewicht* or 'weight' but, incidentally, also in the German word for gnome!). The term *věc* is used in provisions of substantive law as a word for 'legal object' and 'matter' or 'case'; it is used in provisions of procedural law as a word for 'case', 'legal dispute', and 'legal norm'.[181] Such *Sachen* are, after all, *wichtig* ('important', lit. weighty). The Polish term *rzecz* (thing) has obvious roots in the Latin *res*. The Polish State (*Rzeczpospolita Polska*) is a 'public thing', as the *res publica*.[182] A person in ancient Greece is said to have even understood a statute as a 'thing' in this sense. Quite apart from the possibility that a few copies of a statute might be made, a statute was a unique document, drafted for eternity, written on durable and tamper-proof material and either stored in an archive or displayed in a public place.[183] 5.40

[171] Ibid. p. 755.
[172] Louis Guilbert, René Lagane and Georges Niobey (eds.), Grand Larousse de la langue française en six volumes, Vol. I (Paris 1971), p. 723.
[173] Ibid. (with the addition, that it is sometimes used to mean everything that is capable of possession).
[174] Ibid.
[175] See *inter alia Menezes Cordeiro*, Tratado de direito civil I(2)^2, pp. 9–10.
[176] See generally *Grimm*, Deutsches Wörterbuch II, p. 1152; on the various cognates see also Oxford English Dictionary op. cit. p. 941.
[177] Duden op. cit. p. 820; Oxford English Dictionary op. cit. pp. 941–2.
[178] Oxford English Dictionary op. cit. p. 942.
[179] Ibid. p. 943.
[180] The American Heritage Dictionary of the English Language^4 (Boston and New York 2006), p. 1797.
[181] *Štachová and Horák*, in Interakce českého a evropského práva, pp. 405, 409. See also *Václav Machek*, Etymologický slovník jazyka českého a slovenského (Prag 1957) p. 557.
[182] See further *Skrzydło/Grabowska/Grabowski*, Konstytucja Rzeczypospolitej Polskiej, p. 521.
[183] *McDowell*, To díkeo stin Athina ton klassikón Chrónon^5, p. 67.

(2) Property Law versus *Sachenrecht*

5.41 Against this linguistic background, it was an audacious move by the drafters of the German Civil Code (and the codes based on it later in the twentieth century) to define the word 'thing' [*Sache*] as a *terminus technicus* limited to 'corporeal objects'; to place this definition in the General Part of the Code (e.g. § 90 German Civil Code; Art. 947(1) Greek Civil Code) as if 'thing' could mean the same in the law of avoidance, the law of obligations, and the law of property; and, if this were not enough, to give this definition an importance that affects the entire system of the codified law. English law, which is fascinating for its much greater historical continuity, would never have allowed a similar move. A 'thing' has, in England and Ireland,[184] remained a colloquial term for the most part, and one to which jurists pay little attention. The common law does not use the term; to define it, therefore, was not and is not necessary.[185] One takes as one's point of departure not the objects in which *erga omnes* rights subsist, but rather the rights themselves, and therefore starts with the terminology and the concept of 'property'.

5.42 Blackstone's *Commentaries on the Laws of England*, published in 1765, still defined property as the single possible form of absolute control over things. 'Property', according to Blackstone, was 'that sole and despotic dominion which one man claims and exercises over the external things of the world, in total exclusion of the right of any other individual in the universe'.[186] More than a hundred years later, this was still the position taken by German law (§ 903 German Civil Code); English law had developed beyond this point by 1900. Blackstone did not only have an 'absolute', but also a 'physical' idea of property; he related his definition only to an 'external thing'.[187] The courts in Blackstone's time, however, had already recognized property in objects that were not features of the external world at all,[188] as well as forms of property that did not have an all-encompassing right (in Blackstone's sense of 'absolute') as their content.[189]

[184] Not, however, in Scotland: *Reid*, The Law of Property in Scotland, p. 8, explains that Scots property law is, at base, a 'law of things' (as German law). In Scotland, however, things are categorized as 'corporeal' and 'incorporeal' and all things are either 'heritable' or 'moveable'. Citing Bankton, Reid adds that 'natural philosophy examines things according to their properties and qualities, in order to discover their powers; physic considers them with respect to their medicinal virtues, and other arts and science in the respective views proper to them; and positive law regards them as the subject of rights; for only rights are the object of laws'. The English word 'thing', however, 'does not seem to be a sufficiently dignified word to carry the burden of having its own law. So the usual term is the law of "property". But "thing" is more accurate and the term "property" has the disadvantage that it is also sometimes used to mean the principal right that can exist in a thing, i.e. ownership'. The reformed Civil Code of Louisiana sets out Arts 448–476 under the rubric 'Things', apparently undisturbed by the word's lack of dignity.

[185] One of the few authors that has even engaged with the question on these terms is *Pollock*, LQR 10 (1894) pp. 318–22.

[186] *Blackstone*, Commentaries on the Laws of England II, p. 2.

[187] See further *Vandevelde*, (1980) 29 Buff. L. Rev. 325, 330.

[188] This concerned in particular incorporeal hereditaments (e.g. rent charges and certain offices) and this did not escape Blackstone. He labelled them as rights that flowed from corporeal things and were annexed to them, although they only existed as abstract ideas (*Blackstone* op. cit. p. 20).

[189] One example is provided by so-called 'qualified property' in animals *ferae naturae* (the right to capture wild animals and to own them for as long as they remain captive), another is provided by the so-called 'special property' of a pledgee in the pledged goods (*Blackstone* ibid. pp. 391–2 and 395–6).

Their character as things was, however, only posited in the case of certain objects, for example incorporeal hereditaments (rights in incorporeal objects that were originally subject to the special rules of real property law),[190] and later this method informed the entire system. This is evident above all in the rights in *choses in action*, which are furnished with *erga omnes* effect;[191] they implicitly posit that claims and other rights that can only be had in the course of an action have the nature of 'property'. The notion that property only referred to objects of the external world (physical objects) lost almost all practical importance in the course of the nineteenth century. From the notion of ownership of a physical object, a new meaning of 'property' developed, meaning some kind of *erga omnes* right in some kind of object. This process of de-physicalization naturally influenced the scope of 'property law', which expanded considerably. From this point, every valuable right could potentially ascend to the rank of a 'property right'.[192] At the same time, the idea consolidated that these rights were 'absolute' and both could be and had to be protected against third parties to the same extent as other property. As soon, however, as different forms of property arose, each protected to a different extent, it appeared impossible to define 'property' in the sense of Continental concept of 'ownership' as a mother or source of all property rights. Property had ceased to be a *terminus technicus* with the potential to stipulate the resolution of a legal dispute; it became a word that merely described the subject matter of the dispute.[193] Already at the beginning of the twentieth century, Blackstone's 1765 formulation of the notion of property was wholly abandoned. It was, as it has often (but inexactly and superficially) been said, replaced by a 'relative' view. Property concerns, since then, not neither only control

[190] For example, in the case of a freehold and leasehold interest in a right of way, the right of way itself was (and still is) considered as a thing (Law of Property Act 1925, sec. 1(2)(a): 'An easement . . . for an interest equivalent to an estate in fee simple absolute in possession or a term of years absolute'; see also *Pointon York Group Plc v Poulton* [2006] EWCA Civ 1001; [2007] 1 P & CR 6 (an incorporeal hereditament can include 'premises' and can be 'occupied' for the purposes of the Landlord and Tenant Act 1954, sec. 23(1)). If one looks closely, certain similarities to the Civilian legal systems appear. For example, a booth in the Prague Estates Theatre (*Stavovské Divadlo*) was understood in the early twentieth century as property and was even registered in the land registry (*Štachová and Horák*, in Interakce českého a evropského práva, pp. 99–112).

[191] It is, for example, possible to encumber a chose in action with an equitable charge or an equitable mortgage (*Werderman v Société Générale d'Électricité* (1881) 19 Ch D 246 (CA) [a charge on a patent for the purpose of securing a claim to a share in the profits of the patent's commercialization was also effective against a later holder of the patent]; *Bagot Pneumatic Tyre Co v Clipper Pneumatic Tyre Co* [1902] 1 Ch 146 (CA), and *Société Générale de Paris v Walker* (1885) 11 App Cas 20 (HL) [a transfer of shares by way of security was not perfected due to a lack of registration in the company's register of members; it nonetheless created an equitable mortgage in relation to these shares, and this mortgage was in turn given priority over a later equitable mortgage over the same shares]). A further example is found in the law of copyright. If a copyright owner gives someone a licence to copy his work, this licence will be effective against an assignee of the copyright, unless that assignee acquired the right as a 'good faith purchaser for valuable consideration and without notice' (sec. 90(4) Copyright, Designs and Patents Act 1988).

[192] An important reason for this could be the substantive poverty of the law of contract in the middle ages and the great importance of real actions for the effective protection of legal interests. Claims of performance (e.g. for the payment of interest) were thus interpreted as incorporeal hereditaments, as were other 'income sources' of the time (see *Holdsworth*, History of English Law II^4, p. 355 for the example of the 'assize of office'). The expansion of the concept of property was also connected with the tendency to fold all property rights not related to land into the category of choses in action. In this process, for example, intellectual property, claims and rights embodied in transferable paper instruments were put together in one group so that property rights in a part of them were carried over to the others (*Holdsworth* (1920) 33 Harv. L. Rev. pp. 997–1030). The trust, too, gained in importance in that almost every asset could become the subject matter of a trust, such that the claims of the beneficiary were furnished with effect against third parties—this had the result of extending the class of objects capable of being objects of 'property' rights.

[193] *Vandevelde* op. cit. pp. 329–33.

of physical objects nor control by one person that is to the exclusion of all others and therefore 'absolute'. In the end, it must be decided in every individual case what is meant by the term 'property'.[194]

(3) The Codified Definitions of 'Thing'

5.43 The word 'thing' is familiar in the codifications of Continental Europe; every one of them uses it. Every one of them has also—at least in principle—held fast to the concept of ownership in the sense of the 'mother right' of all real rights. This notwithstanding, the concept of a 'thing' by no means has the same content everywhere. Some codifications pay it little mind; in particular, they have not connected the concept of ownership to the concept of 'thing', or have done so only loosely. Others, again—often connected with the German Civil Code which was enacted on 1 January 1900—have taken exactly the opposite path. These are generally codifications that classify only corporeal objects as 'things', a step that today stands in the way of a common European understanding of property law no less than the concept of property in the modern common law.

5.44 The French Civil Code put (and still puts) worth neither on a separation nor on a definition of *biens* and *choses*. The terms *bien* and *chose* are used as synonyms, substituted for each other at will. Under Art. 543 French Civil Code, for example, '*On peut avoir sur les* biens, *ou un droit de propriété, ou un simple droit de jouissance, ou seulement des services fonciers à prétendre*'. The next provision, Art. 544 French Civil Code, on the other hand, provides that property is '*le droit de jouir et disposer des* choses *de la manière la plus absolue, pourvu qu'on n'en fasse pas un usage prohibé par les lois ou par les règlements*'. Under Art. 713 French Civil Code, ownerless *biens* belong to the public. Art. 714 French Civil Code, however, speaks of *choses* that no-one owns. The Dutch version of the Belgian Civil Code repeatedly translates *choses* with *goederen*.[195] If one considers any order or priority to be possible at all (a position with little support), then *bien* would appear to be the more important of the two terms. This is because it is *biens*, not *choses*, that are dealt within the second book of the *Code civil*. According to the classical view (which is not uncontested), *biens* are all *choses* that are useful for human beings and capable of appropriation.[196] Both terms embrace corporeal as well as incorporeal objects. Sometimes it is said that a *chose* becomes a *bien* when it is appropriated,[197] or, which tends in the same direction, that ownership itself makes it possible to

[194] Ibid. p. 330.

[195] e.g. Art. 526, in which *choses immobilières* became *onroerende goederen*, and Art. 1918, in which *choses* was also translated with *goederen*: see *Van Neste*, Zakenrecht I^2, p. 9 no. 2.

[196] *Atias*, Les biens^{10}, p. 1 no. 1 with reference to the older literature. See further *inter alia Zenati-Castaing and Revet*, Les biens^3, p. 18 no. 1; *Strickler*, Les biens, p. 6 no. 2; *Valette-Ercole*, Fiches de droit des biens, p. 5; *Planiol/Ripert/Picard*, Les biens^2, p. 58 no. 51, and *Reboul-Maupin*, Droit des biens^2, pp. 5 and 21.

[197] e.g. Brunet/Servais/Resteau (eds.), Répertoire pratique de droit belge I, p. 714 no. 26: '*Dès qu'une chose est appropriée, elle devient un "bien", élément du patrimoine de la personne qui se l'est appropriée. Les biens sont donc des choses appropriées.*'

transform a *chose* into a *bien*.[198] Others note that *bien* could have a broader meaning than *chose*; the latter is, according to this view, 'primarily' a *chose matérielle*.[199] This discussion is not really very productive, however. It is only marginally helpful to read, for example, that *choses* are 'in principle' corporeal objects, but can also be incorporeal.[200] And whenever *choses* are defined as objects that exist independently from a person,[201] it would appear that a conceptual definition of 'thing' is suddenly propounded that derives from Austrian law.

Section 285 Austrian Civil Code provides: 'Everything, which is distinct from the person, and which serves the use of human beings, is in a legal sense called a thing.' **5.45** Apart from animals,[202] everything that is not a human being is a thing. This definition reflects the natural law *summa divisio* between subjects of law and objects of law.[203] It has also been influenced by the reception of the writings of *Gaius*, from which the drafters of the Austrian Civil Code derived a strict division between the law of obligations and the law of things.[204] This is evident in the subtitles of the three Parts of the Austrian Civil Code (First Part: 'Of the Law of Persons', Second Part: 'Of the Law of Things', Third Part: 'Of the Provisions Common to the Law of Persons and the Law of Things'). According to contemporary understandings, however, this categorical dichotomy is too crude. The Second Part ('Of the Law of Things') also includes norms governing obligation and inheritance, and these areas have long been considered and analysed separately in Austria. Section 285 Austrian Civil Code is, for that reason, interpreted only as a 'programmatic provision' in the contemporary literature.[205] Indeed, only a few rules exist that are applicable to *all* 'things' in the sense of § 285 Austrian Civil Code.[206] The code rather moves swiftly to undertake a categorization of things according to various criteria. Section 291 Austrian Civil Code, for example, takes the criterion of 'nature' and divides things 'in corporeal and incorporeal; in moveable and immoveable, in consumable and non-consumable' things. The code returns to these terms often in later provisions, but does not by any means do so consistently; not infrequently, creative arts of interpretation are necessary in order to identify whether the norm (for example) applies to corporeal or incorporeal things. Already in § 293

[198] *Carbonnier*, Droit civil II, p. 1595 no. 707.

[199] *Bergel/Bruschi/Cimamonti*, Les biens², p. 1 no. 1; *Mazeaud and Chabas*, Biens⁸, p. 117 no. 1351; *Planiol/Ripert/Picard*, Les biens², p. 58 no. 51 ('*Le mot "biens" ne sut désigner que primitivement que des* choses, *c'est-à-dire des objets corporels, mobiliers ou immobiliers. Les progrès de la vie juridique l'ont fait sortir de ce sens étroit et primitif; on lui donne aujourd'hui une portée beaucoup plus large, comprenant tout ce qui est un élément de fortune ou de richesse susceptible d'appropriation au profit d'un individu ou d'une collectivité. Spécialement pour les particuliers, les biens ainsi entendus ne sont pas autre chose que l'actif de leurs patrimoines*'). See also *Villey*, Les biens et les choses en droit, p. 2 ('*Dans le livre II du Code civil, le Bien est Chose, une chose matérielle, sensible, corporelle*').

[200] *Druffin-Bricca and Henry*, Droit des biens³, p. 19.

[201] *Zenati-Castaing and Revet*, Les biens³, p. 18 no. 2 ('*Les choses peuvent se définir comme des objets qui existent indépendamment du sujet*'); *De Page and Dekkers*, Traité élémentaire V², p. 535 no. 531.

[202] Under § 285a Austrian Civil Code, animals are not things. However, the rules governing things are applied to them insofar as nothing is provided to the contrary (e.g. in § 1332a Austrian Civil Code).

[203] *Gschnitzer/Faistenberger/Barta*, Allgemeiner Teil des bürgerlichen Rechts², p. 395.

[204] *Iro*, Sachenrecht⁴, no. 1/1; Klang (-*Klang*), *ABGB II*², § 285 no. 1.

[205] Koziol/Bydlinski/Bollenberger (-*Eccher and Riss*), ABGB⁴, § 285 no. 1.

[206] Ibid.

Sentence 1 Austrian Civil Code, for example, moveable things are defined as 'things which can be moved from one place to another without damaging their substance; in the opposite case they are immoveable'. One perhaps ought to think that this provision applies only to corporeal things (incorporeal things have no substance that one could injure through 'movement'), but this is not the view that has been taken by the Supreme Court· It decided early on that an enterprise is generally to be seen as a thing, but at the same time, especially in the context of § 1070 Sentence 1 Austrian Civil Code (Retention of a right to repurchase is only possible in the case of immoveable things), that it had to be 'treated equivalent to the immovable things in certain constellations'.[207]

5.46 The Spanish Civil Code of 1889, too, retained the synonymous meaning of *cosa* and *bien*.[208] Italian law was the first Romanic legal system to at least define the concept of *beni* (but not that of *cose*). The *Codice civile* of 1942 provides in Art. 810: '*Sono beni le cose che possono formare oggetto di diritti*.'[209] Every 'thing' becomes a 'good' when it can be the object of a right. We agree with the basic logic of this proposition, but would suggest a terminological point only. We would not see goods as a subset of things, but rather the opposite; we would see things as a subset of goods (or, as we would prefer to call them, 'objects of legal transaction').

5.47 In the year 1900, after the coming into force of the Spanish Civil Code and a good forty years before the coming into force of the (second) Italian Civil Code,[210] the German Civil Code beat a wholly new path. In this code, the concept of a thing was defined for the first time as meaning 'only corporeal objects' (in § 90 German Civil Code). The drafters of the German Civil Code were of course also aware of Gaius' division of all things into *res corporales* (tangible objects, e.g. land units, garments, and also slaves) and *res incorporales* (intangible objects, e.g. an inheritance, usufruct, or claim).[211] In the eyes of those drafters, however, this classification was faulty because it put *objects* of rights and the rights themselves on the same level.[212] The root of this problem appeared to be that the corresponding definition of a thing (which, besides the Austrian Civil Code,[213] was also found in the General Land Law [*Allgemeines*

[207] OGH 1 June 1955, SZ 28/144, JBl 1956 p. 48.

[208] Terminologically, this equiparation is not very happy; as a matter of legal policy, however, it has proved itself to be rather successful. It has contributed to securing incorporeal objects an appropriate place in the law of property (*Díez-Picazo*, Fundamentos III^5, pp. 184, 186–7).

[209] Irritatingly, this text is translated in the official German language version of the Italian Civil Code (made for Bolzano) as follows: '*Sachen sind Dinge, die Gegenstand von Rechten sein können*', that is '*Sachen* are *Dinge* which can be the object of rights'. Italian *beni* has been translated here as *Sachen*, *cose* on the other hand has been translated as *Dinge*.

[210] Art. 406 Italian Civil Code of 1865 ('*Tutte le cose che possono formare oggetto di proprietà pubblica o privata sono beni immobili o mobili*' [All things, which can be objects of private or public ownership, are moveable or immoveable goods]) was hardly distinguishable from Art. 810 Italian Civil Code of 1942. *Cose* and *beni* were, already in 1865, virtually synonymous; the drafters of the first Italian Civil Code did not regard it as necessary to define the term *cosa*.

[211] *Gaius*, Institutionum Commentarius Secundus (cited in *Kniep*, Gai Institutionum Commentarius Secundus, p. 3 and Behrends/Knütel/Kupisch/Seiler (eds.), Corpus Iuris Civilis I^2, p. 60), 2.13 and 2.14.)

[212] HKK-BGB (-*Rüfner*), §§ 90–103 no. 4.

[213] § 285 Austrian Civil Code.

Landrecht] for the Prussian States[214]) applied both to corporeal and incorporeal objects. Already Kant had reacted to the categorical leap and defined a *Sache* as a *Ding* 'which is not capable of any imputation'; 'any object without free will, which lacks even freedom, is for that reason called a *Sache* (*res corporalis*)'.[215] Savigny adopted this narrowing of the conceptual definition of 'thing' to *res corporales* and elaborated on it thus:

> The unfree nature cannot be controlled by us as a whole, but only within defined spatial limits; we call such a limited piece of [unfree nature] a thing, and this is the object of the first kind of right that is possible: the right in a thing, which in its purest and freest form is called ownership.[216]

The thing-concept was restricted to components of the physical world.[217] The alternative view, expounded above all by *Gierke*, insisted that the definition of a thing also had to embrace incorporeal objects, which (e.g. the advantages of use or possibilities of action) arise from having a corporeal object.[218] Gierke and those that shared his view could, however, not convince the drafters of the German Civil Code. Already the first draft declined to consider rights as things in the legal sense.[219] The explanations distinguish between things 'in the narrow sense' and things 'in the wider sense'. A 'thing in the narrow sense' was said to be 'a spatially limited piece of the unfree nature', a 'thing in the wider sense' was said to everything that could be 'the object of a patrimonial right'.[220] This brings to mind the Gaian distinction between *res corporales* and *res incorporales*. The drafters had, however, already argued emphatically for a restriction of the definition to corporeal objects. By way of justification, they argued that this best reflected general linguistic usage. Besides this, it was argued necessary to prevent the expansion of 'property rights' through undesirable conclusions reached by analogical reasoning.[221] The German Civil Code was intended to distinguish itself expressly from the French *Code civil*.[222] The so-called 'First Commission', which was soon called, adopted this position in its advice on the formulation of the civil code, and warned

[214] ALR Teil I Titel 2 § 1: '*Sache* in general means, in this statute, everything that can be the object of a right or an obligation' [*Sache überhaupt heißt im Sinne des Gesetzes alles, was der Gegenstand eines Rechts oder einer Verbindlichkeit seyn kann*].'

[215] *Kant*, Metaphysik der Sitten I (cited here according to the edition by *Ludwig* 1986), p. 26.

[216] *von Savigny*, System des heutigen römischen Rechts I, § 53 p. 339. On the influence of Savigny's conceptual definition of *Sache* on the German Civil Code, see *inter alia Rüfner*, in Leible/Lehmann/Zech (eds.), Unkörperliche Güter im Zivilrecht, pp. 33–48.

[217] *Rüfner* op. cit. no. 6.

[218] *von Gierke*, Deutsches Privatrecht I, § 31 I, p. 270; in a similar vein Dernburg, *Lehrbuch des Preußischen Privatrechts I*[3], p. 125: 'Corporeal, spatially defined things are, according to this, by no means the only or even the main type of things. Above all, land counts as a unified thing ... and it is such a thing with its real subjective rights and encumbrances. Entitlements, for example mining rights, that are deemed equal to land units are not less things.'

[219] § 1 of this draft read: 'The provisions concerning things are to be applied to rights only by special provision [*Die über Sachen gegebenen Bestimmungen finden auf Rechte nur nach Maßgabe besonderer Vorschrift Anwendung*]' (*Johow*, Die Vorentwürfe der Redaktoren zum BGB. Sachenrecht I, pp. 15, 145).

[220] Ibid. p. 141.

[221] Ibid. p. 144.

[222] Ibid. p. 145.

of the danger of an ambiguous use of the word *Sache*. It was argued that the 'wider' definition of the Prussian and Austrian codifications should not, for this reason, be adopted.[223]

5.48 This radical step in the German *Bürgerliches Gesetzbuch* was resisted in whole by only a few of the codifications that followed, namely the Latvian Civil Code of 1937,[224] the Italian Civil Code of 1942, and the Romanian Civil Code of 2009/2011.[225] Under Art. 947(1) of the Greek Civil Code of 1940/1946, 'only corporeal objects are things within the meaning of the statute'.[226] In the literature, this definition is set out in more detail, namely that a thing is 'every independent, corporeal and incorporeal object of a controllable nature'.[227] An object is said to be corporeal when it exists by nature and can be perceived (with any of the senses, not only with the sense of touch). To be a thing, the object must be capable of being controlled and have a material content.[228] The criterion of corporeality excludes rights,[229] wealth, and enterprises from the ambit of 'things'. Portuguese law, superficially considered, takes a very different approach, but reaches, in the end, a very similar concept. Although Art. 202(1) Portuguese Civil Code provides that one can call 'everything that can be the object of legal relations' a 'thing', Art. 1302 Portuguese Civil Code leaves no doubt that 'only corporeal objects, moveables or immoveables, can be the object of the right of ownership'. That was an important development in the Civil Code of 1966, which replaced the *Código de Seabra* of 1867, which took a position in keeping with § 285 Austrian Civil Code.[230]

[223] *Jakobs and Schubert*, Beratung des BGB II(1), p. 426.

[224] Art. 841 of the Latvian Civil Code held (and holds) the older line of tradition; the law recognizes both corporeal and incorporeal things (*lieta*); the latter can also be the object of the right of ownership: Faber and Lurger (-*Klauberg and Kolomijceva*), National Reports VI, Latvia, p. 552.

[225] Arts 552 and 553 of the new Romanian Civil Code provide: 'Art. 552: Ownership is either public or private. Art 553: Objects of private ownership are all goods for use (*bunurile de uz*) and all goods of private interest (*bunurile de interes privat*), which belong to a natural person or a juristic person of public or private law, including the goods (*bunurile*) which find themselves in the private dominium (*domeniul privat*) of a public local administrative unit.'

[226] The concept of 'object' is also used in the Greek Civil Code but not defined; the details are simply unclear. It is certain, however, that the concept also includes incorporeal objects (such as claims and rights): *Georgiades*, Empragmato Dikaio I, p. 78.

[227] Ibid.; *Kousoulas*, Empragmato Dikaio, p. 32; *Papasteriou*, Empragmato Dikaio I, p. 169 no. 7.

[228] *Georgiades* op. cit.; *Papasteriou* op. cit. p. 170 no. 11.

[229] Greek law, however (as German law) recognizes numerous rights which, although they are not things, can be the object of property rights. The proposition can be formulated such that the legislature treats a number of rights, in a number of provisions (e.g. Art. 1178 [usufruct over rights and claims], Art. 1247 [pledge over rights and claims] and Art. 1259 Greek Civil Code [hypothec in a usufruct] as if they were things.

[230] Art. 369 Código de Seabra (the Portuguese Civil Code of 1867) provided: '*Cousa diz-se em direito tudo aquillo que carece de personalidade* [*Cousa* [the archaic form of *coisa*] means in law everything that does not have personality).' This text likely has its origins in Pascoal José de Melo Freire's 1789 edition of *Institutiones Iuris Civilis Lusitani*, which in turn drew on the systemic structure of Gaius' Institutes in the form of the Justinian *Institutes* (see *Menezes Cordeiro*, Direitos reais, pp. 21–3). *Pires de Lima*, who drafted Arts 202 and 1302 of the Portuguese Civil Code of 1966, expressly drew attention in BMJ 91 (1959) pp. 207–09 to the fact that Art. 369 Portuguese Civil Code of 1867 reflected § 285 Austrian Civil Code, and that § 90 German Civil Code and Art. 947 Greek Civil Code had narrowed the concept of things to corporeal objects; Art. 810 Italian Civil Code, he argued, only defined goods (*beni*) not things (*cose*). He opined that the General Part of the Portuguese Civil Code should adopt a broad concept of *coisa* but limit this concept for the particular needs of this or that sub-regime. This included the right of ownership. It was difficult, he argued, to conceptualize ownership in an incorporeal thing; it is possible, on the other hand, to imagine a usufruct over a claim (see Art. 1439 Portuguese Civil Code 1966).

Another intensive discussion, which sought its own path towards the 'correct' conceptual definition of things, took place in the late twentieth century in preparation for the new Netherlands Civil Code. Under Art. 555 of the old code, things [*zaken*] were 'all goods and rights, in which ownership can arise'.[231] For Art. 3:2 of the new code, a formulation was chosen in which 'things are material [*stoffelijke*] objects that can be controlled by humans'.[232] During the consultation process, it was claimed that many legal systems still suffered from a lack of clarity in the Roman law conception of property law, which attempted to govern the relationship between persons and things.[233] The drama was said to have begun when more and more *res incorporales* were shoehorned into a system tailored to *res corporales*. (This is particularly evident in Art. 814 Italian Civil Code, according to which energies with economic value 'count as moveable things'.) The distinction between *iura in re* and *iura in personam* did not solve the problem, either; both corporeal and incorporeal objects had been brought under the rubric of *iura in re*. The new Netherlands Civil Code thus attempted, with Art. 3:2, to bring developments to the point of a 'clean' separation between things and property rights.[234] § 90 German Civil Code was referred to—praised on the one hand, but also criticized for failing to depart fully from the concept of 'object' [*Gegenstand*] in which the concept of a *res* still subsisted. Besides this, § 90 German Civil Code was said to have given insufficient consideration to the fact that some property rights (for example pledges) are possible in objects other than corporeal objects.[235] The Netherlands legislature wished to clean up such inaccuracies (of which there are, in truth, even more than the drafters of the Netherlands Civil Code were aware).[236] It distinguished between a *goed* (any given asset) and *zaak* (a material object in the sense of Art. 3:2 Netherlands Civil Code). This basic dichotomy shapes the system of the new code to this day. Limited rights, which can exist in all *goederen*, are governed in Book 3 (*Vermogensrecht in het Algemeen*, 'Property Rights in General'); rights that can exist only in *zaken* are governed in Book 5 **5.49**

231 '*De wet verstaat door zaken alle goederen en regten welcke het voorwerp van eigendom kunnen zijn* [The law understands *zaken* as all goods and rights which can be the object of ownership].'

232 '*Zaken zijn voor de menselijke beheersing vatbare stoffelijke objecten* [*Zaken* are tangible, material objects that can be controlled by human beings].'

233 T.M., Parl. Geschiedenis III, p. 61.

234 Ibid. p. 62.

235 Ibid. p. 61. Here, on the basis of the norms of the German Civil Code applicable to pledges over rights, this complex of problems is given somewhat miserly treatment; it is said to be a kind of appendage to property law only.

236 In a series of provisions of the German Civil Code, the older conception of thing has crept back in largely unnoticed. e.g. in the section on 'Things and Animals' (§§ 90 and following), the code speaks often of rights, for example in § 99(2) ('Fruits of a Right') and § 100 (where use is defined as the fruits of a thing or of a right). § 119(2) allows the contestation of a declaration of will in the case of mistake 'concerning such characteristics of the person or of the thing, which is regarded as substantial in commercial dealings'. A 'thing' in the sense of this provision can be every object of a legal transaction, 'including an incorporeal object [*Gegenstand*], e.g., a right' (BGH 21 February 1952, LM § 779 no. 2, Bl. 316). § 243 German Civil Code provides an even more vivid illustration, which deals with obligations in kind [*Gattungsschuld*]. Under § 243(1), whoever 'owes an obligation in kind, is to supply a thing of average kind and quality'. A 'thing' in the meaning of this provision can, however, also be a right (e.g. a claim), and even a service; at least, the provision applies to them *mutatis mutandis* (e.g. contracts with travel agencies [BGH 12 March 1987, BGHZ 100 pp. 158, 174] and superficial renovations by a tenant [BGH 6 July 1988, BGHZ 105 pp. 71, 78]). A 'thing defined only by class' is, for property law, a contradiction in terms. The German Civil Code has thus made a logical error by placing its definition of 'thing' in the General Part, and not in the Property Law Part (as e.g. Art. 947(1) Greek Civil Code).

(*Zakelijke Rechten*, 'Rights in Things').[237] The *Raad van State* adopted this concept and welcomed the amendments as an improvement on the earlier position.[238]

5.50 Seen against the background of the political events of the twentieth century, the readiness of national legislatures in Central and Eastern Europe to adopt the approach developed in the German Civil Code, even after 1945, is quite astounding.

Art. 110(1) of the Bulgarian Property Statute of 1951 adopted the corporeal definition of things.[239] The Hungarian Civil Code of 1959 abstained from a general definition of things, but its § 94(1) restricted the class of objects capable of being owned (as in Bulgaria) to things which could be taken into possession. Under both codifications, an object had to be a corporeal one in order to be taken into possession.[240] Little has changed in the Hungarian Civil Code [2014].[241] Art. 45 of the Polish Civil Code of 1964 adopted § 90 German Civil Code almost word for word: 'Things within the meaning of the code are only corporeal objects.' Not only ownership, but also possession, is reserved for corporeal objects only (Art. 336 Polish Civil Code).[242] However, Art. 352 § 1 Polish Civil Code provides that 'one who in fact uses the land of another in the manner of a servitude ... is the possessor of a servitude', and Art. 352 § 2 Polish Civil Code adds that 'the provisions governing the possession of things apply to the possession of servitudes'. It is possible, then, at least to 'possess' such a right (see also § 1029 German Civil Code). The position is similar under the Czech Civil Code [2014], which was enacted just two months earlier. Here, the right of ownership (in contrast to possession) could only have a physical thing as its object. Under § 129(2) Czech Civil Code [1964], rights that allow a repeated or endurant exercise (such as a lease) could be the object of possession; one could also possess immaterial goods.[243] 'Things' were not, incidentally, defined *legaliter*; the definition implicit in the doctrine was, however, more or less coextensive with *res corporales*. This has changed under § 979 Czech Civil Code [2014]. Now it is the case that the provisions of property law apply to corporeal and incorporeal objects alike, however, they only apply to rights insofar as that is consistent with the right's character and no contrary provisions speak against it. At base, this reverts to the position, two hundred years older, of § 285 Austrian Civil Code. The General Part of the Estonian Civil Code (*Tsiviilseadustiku üldosa seadus* of 27 March 2002) uses 'object' as its general term.[244] Under § 48 of this statute, objects are things, rights, and other

[237] Under Art. 3:1 Netherlands Civil Code, *goederen* are 'all *zaken* and all property rights [*vermogensrechten*]'; under Art. 3:2, *zaken* are 'all material objects that subject to human control'.

[238] *Advies van de Raad van State*, Parl. Geschiedenis III, p. 62.

[239] See further Faber and Lurger (-*Stoimenov*), National Reports IV, Bulgaria, p. 403.

[240] *Menyhárd*, Dologi jog², pp. 46–7. § 433 of the Draft Private Law Code for Hungary of 1928 was formulated more clearly ('A thing is every corporeal object'). The main drafter had emphasized that so-called incorporeal things were, in truth, no things at all, but rather rights (*Kolosváry*, in Szladits (ed.), A magyar magánjog, p. 8).

[241] Under the heading 'Things', § 5:14 Hungarian Civil Code defines the subject matter as follows: '(1) Every corporeal object, which can be taken into possession, can be an object of the right of ownership. (2) The provisions applicable to things are applicable to money and securities as well as to natural forces that can be made use of as things. (3) The rules of property law are, insofar as no inconsistent provision applies, applicable to animals according to their nature' (see further Vékás [-*Menyhárd*], A Polgári Törvénykönyv magyarázatokkal, pp. 376–81).

[242] Radwański and Gniewek (-*Gołaczyński*), System Prawa Prywatnego IV², p. 28 no. 85.

[243] Švestka (-*Švestka*), Občanský zákoník I², p. 736.

[244] See further Faber and Lurger (-*Kullerkupp*), National Reports I, Estonia, p. 267.

economic assets, which can be the object of a right. The statute distinguishes between corporeal and incorporeal objects. Only corporeal objects are 'things' (§ 49(1); only they are objects of the right of ownership and other property rights under the Property Law Statute (*Asjaõigusseadus*) of 9 June 1993). The statute, however, provides for individual circumstances in which provisions applicable to 'things' are also applicable to rights (see § 49(2) General Part of the Estonian Civil Code; § 241(4) Property Law Statute). Art. 3(1) of the Slovenian Property Law Code of 17 October 2002, which came into force on 1 January 2003, provides that only 'things' can be the object of a real right, in principle. Things are defined as self-standing physical objects which can be controlled by human beings (Art. 15(1) Slovenian Property Law Code). Art. 3(2) Slovenian Property Law Code, however, immediately adds that rights can also be the object of a pledge and a usufruct. To the extent that rights can be the object of a property right, the provisions applicable to things are in principle applicable to rights as well (Art. 3(3) Slovenian Property Law Code).[245]

(4) Sweden

According to its modern self-conception, Swedish law puts great value in being a 'dynamic' property law (*dynamiska sakrätten*). Its traditional conception of a thing (*sak*) appears, however, not yet to have been displaced. It remains as it was when it was developed in answer to the question of what could be an object of the plenary (*fullgången*) right of ownership, i.e. of the most comprehensive right effective against everyone who might attempt to interfere with its exercise (*utövning*)?[246] By the term *sak* was (and is) understood a defined (*begränsat*) corporeal (*materiellt*) and physically perceptible (*fysiskt skönjbart*) object (*föremal*), over which one can exercise legal control. A *sak* can be moveable (*lösöre*) or immoveable.[247] The fact that the modern Swedish property law looks, at its core, to the priority of a claim (*anspråk*)—that is, to the better relative right in an object claimed by several persons—leads to unusual methods of analysis and also to some novel problems. (A 'dynamic' property law, for example, cannot on its own terms explain why an owner is able to demand his property back from a thief in the case that there is no third party making a competing claim). However, this point of view has not led to a specifically Swedish (or Scandinavian) concept of 'thing-ness'. Consider a shipment of oil to which three purchasers have claims, which cannot all be satisfied (the shipment consists of 100 units of oil, and every purchaser has a claim to fifty units). None of the purchasers has a better right to his claimed part so long as the relevant portion has not been separated from the rest.[248] If A has purchased the contents of 'ten tanks', B has purchased the content of five tanks that are already clearly 5.51

245 See further ibid., Slovenia, pp. 514 and 524.

246 *Hessler* op. cit. pp. 2–3 and 19 with reference to *Fehr*, Bidrag till läran om fordringspreskription, p. 139.

247 *Hessler* op. cit. pp. 19 and 44.

248 *Håstad*, Sakrätt[6], pp. 24 and 44.

ascertainable and labelled with his name, but there are not fifteen tanks on the ship, B's right would have priority over that of A. That is, however, just another way of saying that a new 'thing' only arises upon the separation of a quantity from the rest, and that, inversely, an admixed portion of a whole quantity is not a currently existing thing but a future thing—and, for this reason, not a suitable point of reference for an *erga omnes* property right.

e. National Taxonomies of 'Things' (and Other Objects)

(1) General

5.52 There is disagreement in Europe as to which objects of legal transaction should be recognized as objects of exclusive property rights. Further, differences of opinion exist both as to which criteria should be used to categorize them and as to the level of granularity that is desirable. One camp operates with long catalogues of 'things',[249] the other with little more than a clarification of the distinction between moveables and immoveables.[250] Besides this, civilian and common law approaches constantly irritate each other to the extent that both regard categorizations

[249] The German Civil Code, for example, stipulates under the title 'Things and Animals' what it defines as 'things' (§§ 90 and 90a), 'fungible things' (§ 91), 'consumable things' (§ 92), 'essential parts of a thing' (§§ 93–96), 'accessories' (§§ 97–98), 'fruits' (§ 99), and 'emoluments' (§ 100). Similar catalogues are found in the Greek Civil Code (apart from their placement in the structure of the code, Arts 947–965 Greek Civil Code largely reflect §§ 90–103 German Civil Code), Polish Civil Code (Arts 44–55³ Polish Civil Code) and Portuguese Civil Code (under Art. 203, 'things [are] moveable or immoveable, simple or compound, fungible or non-fungible, consumable or non-consumable, principal or accessorial, present or future'; Arts 204–216 then define these terms more closely and define fruits [Arts 212–215] and 'improvements' [Art. 216] as well). Still more detailed taxonomies of things are found in the introduction to the Second Part of the Austrian Civil Code ('Of the Law of Things') under the heading 'Of Things and their Legal Categorisation'. The definitions of 'thing' [*Sache*] (in §§ 285 and 285a Austrian Civil Code) distinguish according to the holder of the rights (e.g. § 286 Austrian Civil Code: 'state property' and 'private property'). § 291 Austrian Civil Code even provides: 'Things are categorised according to their nature in corporeal and incorporeal; in moveable and immoveable; in consumable and non-consumable; in ratable and non-ratable.' § 292 Austrian Civil Code and its following provisions build on this basis, and define these terms in turn. Rights are 'counted to' the moveable things by § 298 Austrian Civil Code, unless they are connected to the possession of an immoveable thing. Numerous other provisions deal with specific questions, including the theory of constituent parts [*Bestandteilslehre*] (§§ 294-297a Austrian Civil Code) and the concept of a 'whole thing' [*Gesamtsache*] (§ 302 Austrian Civil Code).

[250] The French (and Belgian and Luxembourgish) Civil Code, for example, uses legal definitions only to determine the content of certain property rights (e.g. in Art. 544 [*proriété*], Art. 578 [*usufruit*], and Art. 637 [*servitude*]). The points of reference of such property rights are, however, only roughly categorized into two main groups (Art. 516: '*Tous les biens sont meubles ou immeubles*'). Immoveable goods are then categorized into three groups; besides this, the Code resolves some single questions of definition and distinction (sometimes with very surprising results; e.g. under Art. 522 French Civil Code, cattle are, under certain circumstances, classified as 'immoveables'!). In other articles, the Code speaks repeatedly of *choses fongibles*, *fruits*, *produits*, *choses consomptibles*, and *accessoires*, but does not define these terms. The same approach is taken in the Bulgarian Property Statute (which concentrates entirely on the distinction between moveable and immoveable things) and in the Spanish Civil Code. The latter defines natural fruits, industrial fruits, and 'civil fruits', i.e. fruits that arise from legal relations (Art. 355 Spanish Civil Code). The former Czech Civil Code [1964] was also quite sparing with definitions. It divided, without defining the concept of a thing, all things into moveable and immoveable (§ 119) and then defined 'components' (§ 120) and 'accessories' (§ 121). This is still the law in force in Slovakia. The new Czech Civil Code [2014] made dramatic about-face in this respect. It introduced numerous definitions into the Fourth Title ('Things and their Categorisation') of its first book ('General Provisions') including 'things' (§ 489), 'public goods' (§ 490), 'fruits and uses' (§ 491), 'animals' (§ 494), 'patrimony' (§ 495), 'corporeal and incorporeal things' (§ 496), 'moveable and immoveable things' (§ 498), 'fungible and non-fungible things' (§§ 499 and 500), 'whole', 'components', and 'accessories' (§§ 501, 505, and 510).

common in the other system to be unusual; for this reason, they tend not to engage enthusiastically.

Not everything that a national legal system has to say about 'things' serves the purposes of property law as such. For the purposes of property law, objects can be grouped into a category either in order to allow particular property rights in those objects (but not in other objects of legal transaction), or in order to impose a different regime on the acquisition, encumbrance, and transfer of subjective rights that are otherwise identical in content (e.g. the right of ownership or a pledge). The problem is that only a few statutory schemes are really aimed clearly and consistently at these purposes. This observation even applies to the distinction between moveables and immoveables, which many European legal systems still regard as the *summa divisio* of all possible objects of property law. **5.53**

Only occasionally does a codification elevate the distinction between registerable goods and non-registerable goods to the rank of a higher-order taxonomic criterion. Under Art. 3:10 Netherlands Civil Code, *registergoederen* are goods for which inscription in the relevant public register is necessary for their acquisition, transfer, and encumbrance. *Registergoederen* can be either 'things' (*zaken*) or patrimonial rights. They include land units (Art. 3:89), seafaring and closed water ships (Arts 8:194 and 8:784), and airplanes. Further, all limited rights that are registered against a registerable good are in their turn registerable goods themselves (Art. 3:98) or shares in a registerable good (Art. 3:96).[251] Goods which can be transferred without an amendment of the register are not *registergoederen*, even if their registration is possible and practically advisable (e.g. as an aid to enforcement).[252] The category of *registergoederen* allows the Netherlands Civil Code to avoid having to equiparate the above-named valuable moveables with immoveables in order to fulfil the underlying policy. Transportability is irrelevant for categorization as registerable goods. However, the code has not really achieved a consistent application of this criterion. The third book presents the distinction between *goederen* and *registergoederen* in a prominent position right at the outset; however, quite surprisingly, it does not accord it any systemic importance later on—not even when providing how *goederen* are to be transferred. The relevant sections (Arts 3:89 and 3:90 Netherlands Civil Code) substantially rely again on the distinction

[251] *Hijma and Olthof*, Compendium Nederlands Vermogensrecht[9], p. 15; von Bar (-*Nieper and Ploeger*), Sachenrecht in Europa III, Niederlande, p. 160.

[252] Nieuwenhuis/Stolker/Valk (-*Huijgen*), BW[6], Art. 3:10 no. 1 and 2. A large number of such objects are also found in other legal systems. e.g. under Swedish *Lag om handel med lösören, som köparen låter i säljarens vård kvarbliva* (1845:50 S. 1) (LkL), the buyer of *lösöre* (moveable goods) can get protection against third parties in relation to the other creditors of a seller who remains in possession, through *kungörelse* (public notice) and entry in a register kept by a public authority (the *Kronfogdemyndigheten*). Registration replaces the *traditio*. The main purpose of registration consists in protecting the buyer from enforcement procedures against the assets of the seller (§ 1 LkL); besides this, the good faith acquisition of registered property is excluded (*Lag om godtrosförvärv av lösöre* (1986:796)). Registration can, besides this, be used for the transfer of security interests (*säkerhetsöverlåtelse*) (see further *Zetterström*, Sakrättens fyra huvudfall[2], p. 74). Under Art. 47(1) Bulgarian Maritime Code, the transfer of ownership in ships is only enforceable against third parties when it has been entered in the register of ships; for the creation of a hypothec over a ship, on the other hand, entry into the register is itself a constitutive (Art. 47(2) op. cit.).

between moveable and immoveable goods; Art. 3:89(4) Netherlands Civil Code provides somewhat incidentally that the transfer of *registergoederen* falls under the regime that governs immoveable goods.

5.54 Diverse other efforts to categorize things or goods according to some set of criteria in national legal systems are of little relevance to *erga omnes* property rights, even on their own terms. Many classifications first reveal their relevance in part or in whole in the context of the law of obligations. For example, the characterization of a thing as 'fungible' or 'non-fungible' is largely meaningless for the purposes of property law;[253] the relevant distinction usually only plays a role in the context of contract law.[254] Matters are similar with 'divisible',[255] 'commensurable',[256] and 'consumable' things;[257] in any case, there are only a few special rules that utilize these terms for purposes specific to

[253] See e.g. Art. 207 Portuguese Civil Code (fungible things are things that can be determined according to their type, quality, and volume when they are the object of legal relations). Similarly, § 91 German Civil Code, § 499 Czech Civil Code (a moveable thing that can be replaced by another thing of the same type is fungible; other things are not fungible; in case of doubt, judgment will be made according to some relevant custom), § 51(1) Estonian Civil Code (moveable goods that are specified by number, size, or weight in commerce and which lack characteristics by which they can be distinguished from other things of the same type; the parties may themselves determine under § 51(2) which things they treat as fungible), Art. 844 Latvian Civil Code (also with the rule that the parties can themselves determine that fungible things are to be treated as non-fungible and *vice versa*) and Art. 950 Greek Civil Code (fungible things are moveable things, which are generally determined by number, size, or weight in commerce). The Polish Civil Code, on the other hand, defines neither the concept of fungibility nor consumability (see further Radwański and Safjan [-*Katner*], System Prawa Prywatnego I, pp. 1188–90 nos 34–37). Further, the location of these definitions in the relevant codification differs. The German Civil Code places them in its General Part, the Greek Civil Code places them (less convincingly) in the beginning of its book on property law.

[254] e.g. correctly for German law Staudinger (-*Jickeli and Stieper*), BGB (2004), § 91 no. 8 and for Portuguese law (in which things are categorized as objects of so-called *obrigações genéricas* and where it is only suggested that such things require concretization in order to be transferred) *Vieira*, Direitos reais, p. 186, and *Pires de Lima and Antunes Varela*, Código Civil Anotado I[4], note 1 to Art. 207 p. 201. Provisions in which the concept of fungible goods crop up are still generally found in a purely obligational context (see e.g. Arts 1273, 1167, and 1096 Spanish Civil Code, and in § 2719 Czech Civil Code; see *Fiala and Kindl*, Občanské právo hmotné, p. 162). In French law, *choses fongibles* become important mainly in set-off and sales law. Under Art. 1291 French Civil Code, set-off [*compensation*] only occurs between '*deux dettes qui ont également pour objet une somme d'argent, ou une certaine quantité de choses fongibles de la même espèce et qui sont également liquides et exigibles*'. The risk of the innocent loss of the item is borne, for fungible things, by the seller (*Malaurie and Aynès*, Les biens[3], p. 46 no. 157). However, the concept of fungible things (more precisely: things of a type) does assume importance in property law to the extent that a *contrat translatif de propriété* (especially a contract of sale) only transfers ownership in the thing when the thing has been specified (*Malaurie and Aynès*, Les biens[3], p. 46 no. 157; *Carbonnier*, Droit civil II, p. 1610 no. 716). In Austrian law, the term 'fungible thing' [*vertretbare Sache*] is not to be found in the civil code, but it is common in the literature, and it is sometimes argued that fungibility is important in property law to the extent that vindication is only possible for non-fungible things, and the so-called 'vindication by quantity' [*Mengenvindikation*] is available for fungibles. A farmer, for example, who stores 10 tonnes of grain in a cooperative silo containing 100 tonnes of grain, can 'vindicate' 20 tonnes without having to prove *which* 20 tonnes belong to him (see *Barta*, Zivilrecht, pp. 545–7). However, that is only correct insofar as a so-called 'quantitative vindication' is restricted to fungibles; it does not mean that 'normal' vindication is excluded for fungibles. If only 20 tonnes were stored in the silo, there would be no problem of mixture in the first place.

[255] Art. 209 Portuguese Civil Code defines these as 'things that can be separated without any change to their substance, decrease in their value or damage'.

[256] § 303 Sentence 1 Austrian Civil Code: 'Commensurable things are those of which the commercial value can be determined by comparison with others; to these belong services, manual labour, and mental labour.'

[257] Art. 208 Portuguese Civil Code defines these as 'those things whose regular use results in their destruction or alienation'. Under § 92(1) German Civil Code, consumable things are moveable things, whose usual use consists in consumption or alienation. 'Consumption' here means the loss or degradation of the substance of the thing, as a rule through a physical or chemical process (MünchKomm [-*Holch*], BGB I(1)[5], § 92 no. 2). Art. 951 Greek Civil Code is formulated similarly, but does not include 'usual use through alienation'. See further § 52(1) Estonian Civil Code (General Part), § 301 Austrian Civil Code, and § 500 Czech Civil Code.

property law as such.[258] Legal terms of art such as 'components', 'accessories', 'aggregate objects', 'entire objects', 'fruits', 'uses', and 'improvements', on the other hand, that are used in the property law section of certain codifications generally concern, in their plural,[259] *all things*, or at least all things in a previously defined set.[260] They are concerned not with the attributes of objects capable of being the object of property rights, but rather with the question when a thing (with whatever attributes) is to be treated the same as another thing—i.e. whether it is to be regarded as discrete, as connected or, according to the context, partly discrete and partly connected.

The dichotomy between corporeal and incorporeal objects is found in many legal systems. Remarkably, however, this distinction does not correspond to the distinction between moveable and immoveable things, not even in legal systems that stipulate the corporeality of *all* 'things'. The attribute of corporeality is given greater importance in such legal systems than in the others, but it is not capable, in the end, of providing a *summa divisio* of all things; it is at best suited (and on closer inspection not even that) to distinguish between the different manifestations of *moveable* things. As far as one may try to stretch the concept of immoveable property, the heart of it, the soil, is simply a corporeal thing; the fact that certain rights (i.e. incorporeal objects) are repeatedly pushed into the category of immoveable property as a matter of doctrinal law does not change the fundamentally corporeal nature of the earth's surface. In other words, there 5.55

[258] For example, property law provisions that build on the category of 'consumable' things are often found in the law of usufruct, e.g. in § 1067 German Civil Code, Art. 1174 Greek Civil Code and Art. 1451 Portuguese Civil Code, which all provide for the acquisition of title by a usufructee in the case that a consumable thing is the object of a usufruct (the Portuguese Civil Code also distinguishes the usufruct of consumable and perishable things [*coisas consumíveis* and *coisas deterioráveis*]). In French law, the position is that the usufruct of a thing necessarily gives the one entitled a type of ownership right in a consumable thing, as does the loan of such a thing. Without the prerogatives of ownership, it would be impossible to make any use of consumables (*Carbonnier*, Droit civil II, p. 1607 no. 714; *Malaurie and Aynès*, Les biens[3], p. 42 no. 153). In Austrian law, the property law implications of the concept of consumable things (§ 301 Austrian Civil Code) is exhausted by the description of the usufruct [*Fruchtgenussrecht*]; this right can only be created in non-consumable objects (*Iro*, Sachenrecht[4], no. 1/16). It even sometimes occurs that a codification conflates consumable and fungible things, or at least combines them into the same category. Under Art. 337 Spanish Civil Code, all moveable goods are either fungible or non-fungible. The provision continues: 'To the first species belong those which cannot, by their nature, be used except in that they are consumed; to the second species belongs everything else.' Consumable goods thus appear to be a sub-category, at least, of fungible goods (for critical analysis see *Díez-Picazo and Gullón*, Sistema de Derecho Civil I[12], p. 394).

[259] This generally counts even for the legal systems that only consider corporeal objects 'really' to be things. Thus, § 99(2) German Civil Code and Art. 961(2) Greek Civil Code do not only define the fruits of a thing, but also the 'fruits' of a right; § 100 German Civil Code and Art. 962 Greek Civil Code (which define the concept of 'use') do the same. Under Art. 212(2) Portuguese Civil Code, 'fruits' are either 'natural or civil; those that come directly from a thing are said to be natural, and the rents or interests that a thing produces as a consequence of a legal relation are said to be civil'. Under Art. 54 Polish Civil Code, the uses of a right are the benefits which the right brings in accordance with its social and economic purpose. Further, the concept of 'fruits of a right' creates the risk of certain misunderstandings. Such provisions are not actually always concerned with the 'fruits' of a right, but rather with fruits (natural or civil) that are taken 'on the basis of a right', e.g. in Austrian law on the basis of a servitude over trees rooted in another's land (for critical analysis of this manner of speaking, see further *Gschnitzer/Faistenberger/Barta*, Allgemeiner Teil des bürgerlichen Rechts[2], p. 440).

[260] Under § 97 German Civil Code, Art. 956 Greek Civil Code, Arts 48, 50, and 191 Polish Civil Code, and Art. 210 Portuguese Civil Code, for example, moveable things can be the accessories of another thing, especially of a land unit, but the opposite is not possible—a land unit cannot be the accessory (or 'incident') of a moveable thing; a land unit is *always* the principal thing. This is also the case in the French right of *accession immobilière* (despite the fact that a general doctrine of accessories and components is not necessary under the general conception of the *Code civil*). Under the principle *superficies solo cedit*, the soil is always the bearer of anything connected with it, but never the other way around (*Malaurie and Aynès*, Les biens[3], p. 122 no. 442).

are no 'incorporeal immoveables' by nature, there are only (incorporeal) subjective rights that are placed under the law of immoveable property by particular legal systems for particular purposes.[261] Moreover, the legal systems in which the concept of an 'incorporeal thing' is regarded as a contradiction in terms place greater theoretical importance on the criterion of corporeality than the practical implication of this approach would justify. Even in such legal systems, more legal implications follow from the distinction between moveable and immoveable objects than from the exclusion of incorporeal objects from the definition of 'things'. Whether one is labelled the 'owner' or the 'holder' of a right seems, at first blush, to be nothing more than a *façon de parler*.[262] It is true that incorporeal objects cannot be 'delivered' in the same way as corporeal objects. That, however, is a blank fact confronting the legal system; a legal system must come to terms with it, even if that legal system requires a *traditio* for the conveyance of rights in corporeal objects. Besides this, to give one further example, the concept of the possession of rights [*Rechtsbesitz*] has not fully disappeared from those legal systems that supposedly only regard corporeal objects as things;[263] if one considers all the legal systems of the European Union together, the practical relevance of the distinction between corporeal and incorporeal things appears to be of much less importance anyway.[264] In some places, it plays a role only in tightly circumscribed parts of property law, for example in the law of good faith acquisition[265] or the loss of rights through prescription

[261] Examples are found *inter alia* in Art. 526 of the French, Belgian, and Luxembourgish Civil Codes (usufructs over an immoveable thing, real servitudes, and actions for the recovery of immoveables are themselves deemed immoveable goods), in Art. 204(1)(d) Portuguese Civil Code (rights bound up with land are deemed to be immoveable things along with land units, waters, plants connected to the soil and their fruits), and in a trio of provisions in the Czech Civil Code comprising § 496(2) ('Rights, whose nature allows it, and other things without physical substance are incorporeal things'), § 491(1) Sentence 1 ('Land units and subterranean constructions with an independent purpose are immoveable things, as are rights in such thing, and other rights that the law provides are immoveable things'), and § 1242 ('The building lease is an immoveable thing. The building to which this right relates is a component of that thing, but is also subject to the provisions governing immoveable things').

[262] In the French literature it has even been discussed, contentiously, whether rights in incorporeal goods are truly property rights or more rights of exclusive use. *Malaurie and Aynès*, Les biens[3], p. 58 no. 206 labels this debate as purely academic. Such rights are certainly transferable and effective against third parties, and that is really what counts in the final analysis.

[263] e.g. §§ 1029, 1090(2) German Civil Code (protection of the possessor of a land unit who has a basic servitude for the owner of the land unit, which the possessor is permitted to exert. The German Civil Code does not explicitly refer to a 'possessor of a servitude', but there can be no doubt that § 1029 German Civil Code protects the possession of a right) and Art. 352 Polish Civil Code (Possession of a servitude. Servitudes are the only right which one can possess under Polish law: Gniewek [-*Gołaczyński*], Kodeks cywilny[2], p. 494 no. 5). It is even more obvious in the Czech Republic. Under the Civil Code [1964], only controllable and useful corporeal objects were things 'as such' (for further detail see *Švestka and Dvořák*, Občanské právo hmotné[5], p. 239). Nevertheless, § 129 Czech Civil Code [1964] stated (and § 129 Slovak Civil Code states) that a 'possessor' is a person who uses a thing as if it were his own or exercises a right for himself, and that things can be 'possessed' as well as rights 'that allow a constant or repeated exercise'.

[264] E.g. from a Spanish perspective, the distinction between corporeal and incorporeal things (or between corporeal things, rights of use over these, and incorporeal things) appear foreign and not fit for purpose (*O'Callaghan Muñoz*, Compendio de derecho civil III[5], p. 31; *Castán Tobeñas*, Derecho Civil Español II[14], p. 61).

[265] Most legal systems rule out, for example, the good faith acquisition of claims. This is the case under Art. 2276 French Civil Code ('*En fait de meubles la possession vaut titre*'). This is because incorporeal moveable goods (claims, intellectual property, *fonds de commerce*, etc.) are unsuitable for possession according to the Court of Cassation. Cass. 7 March 2006, D. 2006 p. 2897, note by *Kuhn* as well as note by *Mallet-Bricout and Reboul-Maupin*, D. 2006 p. 2363 reaffirmed that '*l'article 2279* [Art. 2276 since 17 August 2006] *du code civil ne s'applique qu'aux seuls meubles corporels individualisés; que la licence d'exploitation d'un débit de boissons ayant la même nature de meuble incorporel que le fonds de commerce dont elle est un des éléments et ne se transmettant pas par simple tradition manuelle, c'est à bon droit que la cour d'appel a écarté pour la dite licence d'exploitation la présomption prévue par ce texte*'. This is occasionally criticized in the scholarship, as incorporeal objects are also *susceptibles de possession*

of time.[266] Even the law of vindication, on the other hand, can be applied to incorporeal objects (i.e. rights) as well as to corporeal objects.[267]

Art. 624-9 French Commercial Code, for example, provides for the *revendication* of moveable goods (*meubles*) in insolvency proceedings; this action is possible within three months since notice of the debt judgment initiating the proceedings. The provision has been applied to corporeal objects but also to 'incorporeal moveable things' (as conceived in the French jurisprudence) including *fonds de commerce*[268] and patents.[269] Under Art. 624-18 French Commercial Code, it is even possible in an insolvency proceeding to seek the vindication of rights that an insolvent buyer of goods subject to a reservation of title has acquired through the onward sale of the goods.[270] The seller can thus connect his right to the goods to the proceeds of their sale,[271] which effectively means that a claim can be the object of an action in *revendication*.[272] According to the French view, this is not even an unusual outcome. Already in the mid-nineteenth century, the Grenoble Court of Appeal recognized the *revendication* of a claim through the *cédant* against the *tiers cessionnaire*, after payment of the purchase price was missed for the first cession.[273] This accords, so far, with the view in Art. 2276 French Civil Code (previously Art. 2279 French Civil Code) that these provisions should only allow the good faith acquisition of moveable goods; the provision did not, therefore, stand in the way of a claim being the subject matter of a *vindicatio*. Moreover, Art. 1240 French Civil Code implicitly makes clear that a claim is an object capable of possession.[274]

(*Malaurie and Aynès*, Les biens[3], p. 171 no. 574; *Terré and Simler*, Les biens[7], p. 343 no. 431). Others maintain that this fact would not change the inapplicability of Art. 2276 French Civil Code to incorporeal goods (*Bergel/Bruschi/Cimamonti*, Les biens[2], p. 238 no. 221; *Larroumet*, Les biens[5], p. 571 no. 923; *Jourdain*, Les biens, p. 520). Moveable things are only corporeal moveable things within the meaning of this provision.

[266] e.g. *Malaurie and Aynès* op. cit. p. 58 no. 207 point out for France that ownership of corporeal objects is a perpetual right, while monopolies of use (copyright, patents, etc.) expire. The authors state that rights over incorporeal goods require the participation of third parties. A *fonds de commerce*, for example, cannot exist without clients, a trademark only has meaning if customers are aware of and pay attention to it. Ownership of corporeal goods, on the other hand, exists regardless of whether or not the good is used.

[267] The 'contrary' phenomenon of a legal system which rules out vindication despite its broad definition of a thing can be observed in Austria. The possibility of a vindication of rights is unanimously rejected by the scholarship of today. This despite the facts that the wording of § 366 Austrian Civil Code implies an applicability to all types of thing 'as such', and that the authors of the Austrian Civil Code intended the possibility of an action of ownership (vindication) for certain real rights (hunting rights, pledges, enjoyment of fruits) at least. However, the leading opinion of today is that the regulations regarding vindication must be tailored towards corporeal things. (For further detail see Klang [-*Kodek*], ABGB[3], § 366 no. 4).

[268] CA Caen 16 September 1993, D. 1994 p. 192, note by *Regnaut-Moutier*; confirmed by Cass. 21 November 1995, Bull. civ. 1995, IV, Nr. 266 p. 245; D. 1996 p. 211, note by *Regnaut-Moutier* ('*L'obligation de revendiquer dans le délai de trois mois imposée par l'art. 115 de la loi n°85-98 du 25 janvier 1985* [today Art. 624-9 Ccom] *à celui qui doit faire reconnaître son droit de propriété contre une personne soumise à une procédure de redressement judiciaire, n'est pas limitée aux meubles corporels*'). Equally Cass. 29 February 2000, no. 97-14575.

[269] Cass. 22 October 1996, Bull. civ. 1996, IV, no. 252 p. 217. See also Arts 611-8 and 712-6 Code de la propriété intellectuelle.

[270] In greater detail *Zenati-Castaing and Revet*, Les biens[3], p. 357 no. 218 and *Zenati-Castaing*, RTD civ. 1993 p. 305.

[271] Cass. 20 June 1989, *D.* 1989 p. 430, note by *Pérochon*.

[272] *Zenati-Castaing*, RTD civ. 1993 p. 305.

[273] CA Grenoble 15 April 1845, D. 1846 p. 208.

[274] *Zenati-Castaing and Revet* op. cit. p. 320 no. 198.

(2) Dividing 'Things' into Immoveables and Moveables

5.56 The notion that one can divide all things, even all *biens*, into 'immoveables' and 'moveables' rests on ideas that stretch back into classical antiquity.[275] It continues to influence many legal systems, despite deficits that have long been obvious; this is especially true of the Romanic legal systems. Art. 516 of the French, Belgian, and Luxembourgish Civil Codes provide: '*Tous les biens sont meubles ou immeubles*.' All goods are either moveable or immoveable; *tertium non datur*. Such a *summa divisio* of all goods (or things) employs a legal term of art; it purports to state a matter of physical reality, but is minded, in the end, only towards a legal ordering. This dichotomy also effects a certain regulatory technique. Nearly all Continental codifications work with a main category and a residual category.[276] They define the former, and put everything that remains into the latter. It is difficult to imagine a cruder method.

5.57 The distinction between immoveables and moveables has, to a large extent, developed from the perspective of immoveables. True, Art. 516 *Code Napoleón* provides that all goods are either moveable or immoveable. And, in France, the law determines whether a *bien* is moveable or immoveable: characterization is (at least according to the *Cour de cassation*) not a matter over which the parties can decide.[277] The civil code, however, lists all the immoveable goods exhaustively in Art. 517 *et seq* French Civil Code. This comprises a closed category.[278] *Meubles* serve the function of a residual class: everything that is not (listed as) an immoveable is moveable by definition.[279] In both groups—moveable and immoveable goods—are found corporeal and incorporeal objects. How one is meant to move an incorporeal object remains unclear; the language of the law has diverged widely from the ordinary meaning of the words it uses. The situation is the same in Spain and Italy. The Spanish and Italian Civil Codes copied the *Code*

[275] This division in turn replaced the division between *res mancipi* and *res nec mancipi*. *Res mancipi* (namely, land units located in Italy, slaves, four-legged animals) were subject to the control of the *pater familias* and were transferred according to a specific ritual, the *mancipatio*. *Res nec mancipi* fell into the residual category. Merely the *traditio* was required to transfer these (see *Díez-Picazo*, Fundamentos III[5], p. 207).

[276] One possible exception is Austria. § 293 Austrian Civil Code gives the impression, *prima facie*, that the statute considers a definition of moveables as its starting point and immoveables merely as a backup category. This can be interpreted to mean that everything that is not moveable is an immoveable. This notion is rejected by the Austrian literature. § 293 Austrian Civil Code is understood as a neutral distinction. Moveables and immoveables are seen as equal. Neither is a residual category. Rather, both categories are divided according to the criterion of a 'technically feasible change of location' (Koziol/Bydlinski/Bollenberger [-*Eccher and Riss*], ABGB[4], § 293 no. 1; likewise, Klang [-*Kisslinger*], ABGB[3], § 293 no. 4, and Schwimann and Kodek [-*Hofmann*], ABGB II[4], § 293 no. 1). 'Corporeal objects' *in toto* are divided along this line. The decisive factor is the possibility of a change of location. However, it must be conceded that this criterion is imprecise (*Kisslinger* op. cit. no. 5). Moveability as the rule and immoveability as the 'exception' (*Kisslinger* op. cit.; *Eccher and Riss* op. cit. § 298 no. 1) only applies to rights for which a change of location is obviously not applicable or appropriate (*Kisslinger* op. cit. § 298 no. 2).

[277] Cass. 26 June 1991, Bull. civ. 1991, III, no. 197 p. 115 ('*La nature, immobilière ou mobilière, d'un bien est définie par la loi, et la convention des parties ne peut avoir d'incidence à cet égard*'). This is criticized by the French literature (e.g. *Zenati-Castaing and Revet*, Les biens[3], p. 147 no. 90 and *Atias*, Les biens[10], p. 28 no. 46). Art. 843 Latvian Civil Code even states explicitly that the law or the parties may determine that rules which apply to immoveables can be transferred to moveable things. Art. 842 divides corporeal objects into moveable and immoveable. The decisive factor for this distinction is the question of whether the respective thing can be transported undamaged from one location to another. Surprisingly, trains are categorized as immoveables, while ships are categorized as moveables.

[278] *Malaurie and Aynès*, Les biens[3], p. 32.

[279] *Atias* op. cit. p. 33 no. 50; *Carbonnier*, Droit civil II, p. 1599 no. 709.

Napoléon quite faithfully. Under Art. 333 Spanish Civil Code, 'all things, which are or can be the object of appropriation are considered to be either moveable or immoveable goods'. Art. 334 Spanish Civil Code then lists which goods are immoveable and Art. 335 Spanish Civil Code ties the loose ends together: 'Those things capable of appropriation that are not named in the preceding section are moveable.' The drafters of this formulation appear, however, to have succumbed to fear in the face of their own boldness. The same section then adds that 'in general, anything that can be carried from one place to another without damaging the immoveable to which it is attached' is to be considered moveable, as well. Rights, on the other hand, are to be found in both groups; generally, however, they are aggregated to the category of moveables (Art. 336 Spanish Civil Code). Spanish law combined the French approach with that of Austrian law. Art. 812(1) Italian Civil Code remains noticeably closer to the literal meaning of the words *beni immobili* (the soil, springs and watercourses, trees, buildings, and other constructions, even when they are only connected to the soil with a transient purpose, and generally everything that is naturally or artificially connected to the soil); rights to *beni immobili* only accrue *erga omnes* effect through entry in a *pubblico registro immobiliare*. But it can also be said of Italian law that all things, which are not immoveable, are made into *beni mobili* (Art. 812(3) Civil Code: 'All other *beni* are *mobili*'), whether or not they are registered in a public register (Art. 815 Italian Civil Code). Art. 110(1) of the Bulgarian Property Statute follows this model with only small variations. The 'soil, buildings and other constructions, and generally everything that which is permanently connected to the soil by nature or by human conduct' are deemed to be immoveables. All other things remain moveables. The Polish Civil Code does not define its concept of moveables; from this omission it has been implied that every corporeal object that is not an immoveable or part of one is 'automatically' a moveable.[280] Matters are little different in Portugal either. Under the heading 'Classification of Things', Art. 203 Portuguese Civil Code provides (albeit combining very different classificatory criteria): 'Things are immovable or immovable, simple or composite, fungible or non-fungible, consumable or non-consumable, main or ancillary, present or future.' Art. 204 Portuguese Civil Code then lists comprehensively, but without a general definition, all the things deemed to be immoveables (which has led to debate about whether the list is exhaustive [*taxativa*] or illustrative [*exemplificativa*]),[281] and Art. 205(1) Portuguese Civil Code concludes with the (by now well-known) proposition that everything that is not an immoveable (in the sense of Art. 204 Portuguese Civil Code) is to be seen as a moveable. This '*classificação fundamental*' (which is complemented, as in the Netherlands, with the distinction between registerable and non-registerable goods) plays a particular role in Portuguese property law in relation to four points.[282] There are (i) property rights that can only

[280] *Piasecki*, Kodeks cywilny, Art. 45 note 2. Likewise, for Hungary *Menyhárd*, Dologi jog, p. 53.

[281] For a summary of the dispute see *Menezes Leitão*, Direitos reais, p. 65. The predominant opinion appears to be that the list in Art. 204 Portuguese Civil Code is not exhaustive (see, e.g. *Oliveira Ascensão*, Teoria Geral I^2, pp. 359–60; *Vieira*, Direitos reais, p. 145, and *Menezes Cordeiro*, Direito civil português I(2)^2, p. 120).

[282] See further *Menezes Leitão*, Direitos reais, pp. 63–4.

be held in immoveables,[283] (ii) property rights that can be held on immoveables and registerable goods,[284] and (iii) one property right (namely a pledge over goods [*penhor de coisas*]) that can only be held in moveables under Art. 668(1) Portuguese Civil Code. Besides these, the distinction plays a role in (iv) the rules governing the acquisition of real rights.[285] Even the more recent codifications tend to utilize the same schema. Art. 3:3(2) Netherlands Civil Code stipulates that only *zaken* and not *goederen* need to be divided into moveable and immoveable ('All *zaken* that are not immoveable are moveable'), and thereby overcomes at least the most obvious problem associated with the bifurcation of the world into moveables and immoveables. Besides this, everything has remained much as it was. The code divides all *zaken* into moveable (*roerende*) and immoveable (*onroerende*) categories by stipulating a definition of immoveables (Art. 3:3(1) Netherlands Civil Code)[286] and categorizing everything that remains as moveable (Art. 3:3(2) Netherlands Civil Code). § 498 Czech Civil Code, which falls under the title 'Immoveable and Moveable Things', provides the following definition:

> (1) Immovables are land units and subterranean constructions with an independent function, as well as real rights in such objects and rights that are provided to be immoveables by statute. If another legal provision stipulates that a certain object is not a part of a land unit, but if that object cannot be moved from one place to another without harm to its substance, that object is also immoveable. (2) All other objects, whether of a corporeal or incorporeal nature, are moveable.

A similar approach is taken even in Finland and in Sweden.[287] Everything that is not defined in the *Jordabalk* (JB) as an immoveable or part of an immoveable is *lös egendom*. The latter, however, embraces not only corporeal objects (*lösöre*) but also rights to immaterial property and various kinds of limited real rights.[288] Moreover, it is necessary to consider that the Swedish legal parlance does not always distinguish strictly between the subjective right and the object to which it refers. A pledged object itself becomes the pledge, an object in which one has a property right becomes his property, and so forth. 'Property', therefore, as in English, can mean both: the right and the object in which

[283] This includes *propriedade horizontal* (Art. 1414 Portuguese Civil Code), the *direito de habitação* (Art. 1484(2) Portuguese Civil Code), the *superfície* (Art. 1524 Portuguese Civil Code), basic servitudes (*servidões prediais*, Art. 1543 Portuguese Civil Code), and the real right of a timeshare (*direito real de habitação periódica*, Art. 1 DL 275/93 of 5 August 1993).

[284] Such as the escrow (*consignação de rendimentos*, Art. 656 (1) Portuguese Civil Code), hypothecs (*hipoteca*, Art. 668(1) Portuguese Civil Code), real promises (*promessa real*, Art. 413 Portuguese Civil Code), and the *preferência real* (Art. 421 Portuguese Civil Code).

[285] e.g. the right of acquisition (*ocupação*) only refers to moveables (Arts 1318 and 1345 Portuguese Civil Code) and the right of *acessão natural* only applies to immoveables (Art. 1327 Portuguese Civil Code). The time limit for an acquisition by prescription is longer for immoveables (Art. 1293 and following Portuguese Civil Code) than for moveables (Art. 1298 and following Portuguese Civil Code). The regime of *acessão industrial* also depends on whether moveables (Art. 1333 and following Portuguese Civil Code) or immoveables (Art. 1339 and following Portuguese Civil Code) are involved.

[286] Immoveables are *de grond* (the ground), *de nog niet gewonnen delfstoffen* (the as-yet unaccessed natural resources), *de met de grond verenigde beplantingen* (the plants which are connected to the ground), and *gebouwen en werken, die duurzaam met de grond zijn verenigd* (the buildings and structures which are, directly or in connection with others, permanently connected to the ground).

[287] Regarding Finland in further detail *Tepora*, Inledning till grunderna i sakrätten, p. 50.

[288] *Håstad*, Sakrätt[6], pp. 30 and 40–42.

one has the right.[289] The distinction between moveable and immoveable property also plays a role in sales law, but its main significance is in property law. So, for example, an immoveable can only be pledged through the delivery of a pledge instrument, whereas a moveable can only be pledged by delivery of the object. Moveable property can only be encumbered with a hypothec exceptionally, and in those cases only by an enterprise and not by an individual.[290]

The German Civil Code, on the other hand, has trodden its own path (and that, of course, within the framework of its conceptual definition of *Sachen* as limited to corporeal objects). This codification (i) contains numerous provisions concerning 'moveable' [*bewegliche*] things (e.g. §§ 929, 946, 947, 1204) but never their opposite, i.e. 'immoveable' [*unbewegliche*] things. It only provides for 'land units' [*Grundstücke*] (e.g. §§ 94, 311b(1), 873, 925, 946, 1191). And despite its clear tendency to provide a technical definition for its important terms, (ii) the code is silent on the definition of precisely the *Grundstück* and *bewegliche Sache*. It even refrains from providing that all *Sachen*, which are not *Grundstücke*, are *bewegliche Sachen*. This proposition, however, is regarded as expressing the valid law in Germany anyway. The literature adopts this as an iron principle;[291] the judicial authorities have not dared to question it. Thus, everything turns again on the content of the complementary term, this time '*Grundstück*'. A land unit is a defined portion of the earth's surface that has been cadastrally surveyed and entered into the land register [*Grundbuch*] as a land unit [*Grundstück*], whether on a particular folio or under a particular number of a common folio.[292] The position is substantially similar in Hungary.[293] **5.58**

The concept of the land unit in German law is not only unclear. It also raises an important secondary question: how does one justify defining the concept of moveable things negatively—i.e. as things for which no folio can be kept in the land register? Certainly, one remains ignorant concerning relation between the attribute of 'moveability' and the fact that such objects are not kept in the register. The German approach to the distinction between land units and moveable things is, further, only of limited comparative **5.59**

[289] *Undén*, Svensk sakrätt I[10], p. 12.

[290] *Håstad*, Sakrätt[6], pp. 29–30.

[291] See Staudinger (*-Jickeli and Stieper*), BGB (2004), Vorbem. zu §§ 90–103 no. 38; *Wieling*, Sachenrecht I[2], § 2 II 8; *Vieweg and Werner*, Sachenrecht[4], p. 578; *Wilhelm*, Sachenrecht[4], p. 23 no. 48.

[292] *Baur and Stürner*, Sachenrecht[18], § 15 no. 18. Besides this definition of land units, however, two further definitions exist, namely an 'economic' and a 'cadastral'. Under the 'economic' definition, a land unit is a portion of the earth's surface that is visibly bounded and exploited as a single asset (ibid. no. 16; Staudinger [-*Gursky*], BGB [2007], Vorbem. zu §§ 873 and following no. 13). Under the 'cadastral' definition, a land unit is a registered entity in the relevant cadastre (*Gursky* op. cit. nos 20–22). These terms are of importance in the public law context, and occasionally in the law of obligations (e.g. when it falls to be determined what the parties meant when they refer to 'land unit X' in a contract). But they play no role in the real property law of the German Civil Code.

[293] Here it is said that a statutory definition of land units would be superfluous, because every immoveable is registered discretely in the land register. To determine what is a land unit, it is sufficient to look at the rules governing registration in §§ 11–13 of the Statute of 1997 (*1997. évi CXLI. törvény az ingatlan-nyilvántartásról*). A definition of moveable things is equally unnecessary because everything that is not registered as a discrete immoveable in the land register is a moveable thing. The size and mobility of the object is irrelevant; even the furnace of a *steel* works is moveable, so long as it has not become a component of the immoveable on which it stands (*Menyhárd*, Dologi jog[2], p. 62).

value to the extent that it presupposes a specific registration system that embraces all land units—i.e. the *Grundbuch* of the German legal system.[294] This is the reason why Greek law, which has been otherwise so receptive of the German Civil Code, could not adopt its conception of the land unit. Art. 949 Greek Civil Code, which is limited to situations in which the assets of a person are treated as a whole but a distinction between moveable and immoveable property is made, says only that 'usufructs over land units and real servitudes are considered immoveable objects and all claims are considered moveable objects'. In cases of doubt, the limited personal servitudes, rights of use and claims sounding in damages by the owner of a land unit are considered as immoveable objects; within the scope of Art. 949 Greek Civil Code, pledges and hypothecs are, on the other hand, considered moveable objects.[295] Controllable natural forces and energy also fall within the moveable objects according to Arts 947(2) and 948 Greek Civil Code.

5.60 The division of all things into moveables and immoveables presents a difficult test for the European discussion of property law. This is not only because the *summa divisio* has little resonance in the common law, but also because subjective rights can neither be understood nor categorized according to the criterion of 'moveability'. The fiction that a claim is a moveable object borders on the absurd, as does the notion that servitudes are incapable of transportation. The classification of all things as either moveable or immoveable also makes a pan-European understanding of property law more difficult for other reasons. The border between moveable and immoveable is drawn, in different legal systems, according to different criteria. For contemporary purposes, there is not even uniformity on the question what should count as a corporeal object. This leads to the situation where the residual category of moveable objects becomes a miscellany of heterogenous objects whose content differs from legal system to legal system. Not least, this approach has led certain legislatures to further distinguish sub-types of both moveable and immoveable objects for various purposes. To the extent that one is only concerned

[294] Even where a land register exists, not all land registers necessarily include all land units (see for Poland e.g. Radwański and Gniewek [-*Gniewek*], System Prawa Prywatnego IV^2, p. 72 no. 13). European land registers differ especially according to what objects they register, and this in turn often leads to fundamental differences in the structure of the register. While the German and Polish land registry systems are structured around registerable land units, others, such as the Italian system, are structured around registerable dealings with land units. The Greek registers (of which there are seven!) are, again, structured around persons, not land units (the land unit cadastre, which the Statute 2308/1995 envisages, has not yet been realized). In England, by way of contrast, it is *rights* in land units that are registered (sec. 1(1) Land Registration Act 2002: register of title), namely 'legal freehold estates' and 'legal leasehold estates' with a remaining duration of more than seven years (sec. 3 and sec. 4(2)). Several estates of the same type can be bundled together in a single register, when they have the same proprietor (Land Registration Rules 2003, r. 3(1)). The registrar can create a separate register for every 'separate area of land' that is the object of an estate (r. 3(2)). In principle, however, a register will be kept for every estate under an individual title number (r. 2(2)). This comprises a 'property register', a 'proprietorship register', and (in the case that encumbrances exist) a 'charges register'. The property register describes the estate and refers, to the extent possible, to a 'title plan', i.e. an official map of the city or countryside. Details of the relevant lease agreement are registered to determine the content of a leasehold estate (Land Registration Rules 2003, r. 6(1)). The boundaries of a registered estate are, so long as the owner does not apply for a precise survey, the general boundaries (sec. 60 Land Registration Act 2002; Land Registration Rules 2003, r. 118(1)). The practice is to refer to the relevant plans in contracts of sale (e.g. 'The land shown edged in red on the Plan and known as Plot 1 St Giles Close Winchester': see *Chadwick v Abbotswood Properties* Ltd [2004] EWHC 1058 (Ch), [2005] 1 P & CR 10 para 45, where the parties disputed the exact boundary such that the estate could only be determined by reference to the extent of the land).

[295] *Triantos*, AK, Art. 949 p. 1161 no. 1.

with bundling certain moveables into one category for the purposes of family law or procedural law,[296] or with hiving off forested areas and agricultural land for special legal treatment,[297] such sub-categorization is understandable. But matters are more complicated when the construction of such sub-categories is due to the need to clarify which objects are 'moveable' as opposed to 'immoveable'. In such cases, this sub-categorization is given a much more fundamental task, namely of determining when the thing-ness of an object should be suspended (temporarily or permanently) in favour of another, 'main' object. This problem is addressed in other legal systems at a much more basic level. If a legal system recognizes only moveable and immoveable property, it might be seen as appropriate to work with double characterizations. Then the question becomes whether a particular object is 'mobile' or 'immobile' not in the abstract, once and for all, but on a case-by-case basis in the particular context. Animals, for example, appear in French law sometimes as moveable and sometimes as immoveable property;[298] it is impossible to say which they are *in abstracto*. Jurists more used to working with a distinct doctrine of components and accessories, and with a strictly defined concept of things, would never approach the problem in this way. For them, a right in a land unit is not an 'immoveable', nor are the moveable objects that fall within such a right (such as a pledge over land). The latter are 'accessories' [*Zubehör*] of a land unit, and the former is a 'component' [*Bestandteil*];[299] accessories remain moveable things, and components lose, to the extent they ever had it, the status of things completely.

Existing national sub-categorizations of 'immoveable things' do not follow any unified schema, either. Under Art. 46 § 1 Polish Civil Code, for example, **5.61**

> immoveable things ... [are] parts of the earth's surface that are the object of special ownership (land units), as well as buildings connected to the surface durably or parts

[296] e.g. Art. 3:5 Netherlands Civil Code adds the '*inboedel*' as a higher-order category of furniture and household objects. This concerns moveable things (according to the statutory definition) that belong to the appointment of a dwelling, with the exception of libraries and other culturally valuable collections.

[297] Under the Greek Statute 1734/1987 on Pastures and Forests and the Greek Statute 3208/2003 (FEK A'/ 24 December 2003) on the Protection of Forest Ecosystems, the creation of a forest registry and the governance of real rights in forests creates a rebuttable presumption of public ownership of forests. Special rules apply to forested land that came into private ownership before 11 September 1915 by way of prescription. Apart from such land, and land that is the special property of the churches and monasteries, forest is today state property. This, in turn, explains the rule in Art. 1149 Greek Civil Code, which created a special usufruct in forested land for the benefit of private individuals. Sweden, with Lag (1989:31) *om vissa samägda jordbruksfastigheter* created special rights for the management of agricultural land; further special provisions are found in Kap. 9 JB. Under Art. 46[1] Polish Civil Code. 'agricultural land' comprises land that is or could be used for the primary production of animals and plants, including market gardens, orchards and acquaculture. Art. 204(1)(a) Portuguese Civil Code counts 'agricultural and urban land' (*os prédios rústicos e urbanos*) as immoveables, and Art. 204(2) Portuguese Civil Code provides the following definition: 'By agricultural land [*prédio rústico*] is understood a bounded part of the earth's surface, and the buildings present on it, which are not economically independent; by urban land [*prédio urbano*] is understood every building, that is connected to the soil, with the land [*terrenos*], which serve them.' Spanish law distinguishes for the purposes of landlord and tenancy law between *predios rústicos* and *predios urbanos*. Within the ambit of the special regulations *Ley de Arrendamientos Urbanos* and *Ley de Arrendamientos Rústicos*, the Civil Code only has subsidiary importance.

[298] Under Art. 524 of the Napoléonic codes, for example, various animals are '*immeubles par destination*'. Art. 528 on the other hand provides: '*Sont meubles par leur nature les animaux*.'

[299] Under § 96 German Civil Code, only the 'rights, which are connected to ownership of a land unit ... [count as] components of the land unit'.

thereof, which are the object of special ownership rights separate to the land unit under some special provision.

Under § 498 Czech Civil Code [2014], immoveable things are divided into (i) land units, (ii) subterranean buildings that serve an independent purpose, and (iii) property rights that appertain to these immoveable things (§ 119(2) Czech Civil Code [1964], on the other hand, counted 'land units and buildings, which are connected to the soil with a solid foundation'). Under Art. 812(1) Italian Civil Code, 'immoveable things [are]... the soil, springs and waterways, trees, buildings and similar constructions, even when they are connected with the soil for a transitory purpose, and generally everything that is connected to the soil naturally or artificially.' In addition, under Art. 812(2) Italian Civil Code, mills, baths, and other swimming facilities are deemed to be immoveables, provided they are fixed in the riverbank or riverbed and are meant to remain so permanently for their use. The Napoleonic codes in France, Belgium, and Luxembourg approach matters quite differently. Art. 517 of all three Civil Codes distinguishes between goods, which are immoveable (i) by their nature, (ii) by virtue of their purpose, or (iii) by virtue of their connection with other objects. A good is immoveable by nature when it is fixed in the earth.[300] This includes the *fonds de terre* (i.e. land units: Art. 518),[301] which include the earth's surface, the soil beneath it, and mineral resources in the soil which are not the subject of another grant made by the state (in which case they are moveables), as well as plants and buildings. Plants are immoveable so long as they are fixed in the soil (Arts 520 and 521), and so are their fruits until they are harvested (Art. 520). The definition of 'buildings' in Art. 518 embraces houses and commercial buildings, as well as bridges, levies, and growing houses[302] that are anchored with metal ties. A tender reference is made in Art. 519 to 'wind and water mills, which rest on piles and comprise a part of a building'. Also considered to be immoveable by nature are installations that complement a building, such as electrical wires, lightning rods, elevators, and even wooden cladding,[303] as well as water pipes (Art. 523). Immoveable goods by virtue of their purpose are physically moveable things that form a single economic entity with an immoveable main object and are therefore said to share the same legal fate as the main object.[304] This fiction only applies in cases where both goods—the immoveable and the physically moveable—belong to the same owner. Besides this, the physically moveable goods must be necessary (and not merely convenient) for the economic use of the immoveable. The moveable thing must, without being 'fixed' in the sense of

[300] *Druffin-Bricca and Henry*, Droit des biens[3], p. 29 ('*Sont immeubles par nature tous les biens corporels répondant au critère de fixité et d'adhérence à la terre*').

[301] *Terré and Simler*, Les biens[7], p. 35 no. 31.

[302] Cass. civ. 1 February 1984, RTD civ. 1985 p. 738, note by *Giverdon and Salvage-Gerest*; Cass. 9 June 2004, D. 2004 p. 2405, note by *Reboul-Maupin*.

[303] *Terré and Simler* op. cit. p. 36 no. 31.

[304] von Bar (-*Beysen*), Sachenrecht in Europa IV, Belgien, p. 24; *Terré and Simler* op. cit. p. 37 no. 32; *De Page and Dekkers*, Traité élémentaire V[2], p. 607 no. 644.

Art. 534, serve the economic use of the land unit (as, for example, a cow does) or be permanently attached to it (*attaché à perpétuelle demeure*, Art. 525). This applies, for example, to the tables, stools, and tableware in a café and the bedding of a hotel business.[305] Art. 524 of these Civil Codes, which dates to 1804, is naturally directed towards agriculture but is also applied to industrial, commercial, and cultural purposes (e.g. the facilities in a theatre); Art. 524 itself refers to 'plant necessary for the running of forges, paper mills, and other works'.[306] A certain systemic inconsistency is found in Art. 527. In light of the categorization of all *biens* into moveable and immoveable, a more detailed definition of moveables would not actually have been necessary. However, the codes stipulate anyway that *biens* 'are either moveable by their nature or by force of legal provision'. Art. 528 continues that 'goods that can move themself from one place to another' are moveable by nature; Art. 529 then categorizes *obligations et actions* for the payment of money or the delivery of a good to the category of moveables *par détermination de la loi*. Again, we are concerned here with a fiction. What is necessary, however, is the implicit clarification that claims for the performance of a service do not qualify as 'goods', not even as moveable goods.

4. Of Rights and Objects: Contextual Thinking and Transformation in the Common Law

a. General

The common law in England and Ireland approaches many points quite differently. First, it is convenient to remember that the common law does not move from a definition of objects to the question what rights are possible in the object, but rather takes the exact opposite approach; it places subjective rights in the centre of the common law of property and pushes to the periphery the question in what objects those rights can arise. One of the many examples of this is provided by land registration. This embraces not only land units and the rights in land units, but registers all rights that relate to the use of the earth's surface. The common law of property only defines *en passant* what 'land' or any other given thing actually 'is',[307] and the notion that such a definition *in abstracto* for all objects would even be possible is somewhat 'un-English'. Of course, questions about the objects in which property rights can be had do not simply disappear, but they are answered in context, for example in the context of determining 5.62

[305] *Malaurie and Aynès*, Les biens³, p. 38 fn. 39.

[306] *Terré and Simler* op. cit. p. 39 no. 34.

[307] *Lawson and Rudden*, The Law of Property³, p. 5 observes correctly: 'Property lawyers take surprisingly little interest in land or ships or machinery or animals as such, but a great deal in abstract notions such as the "fee simple" in land, trust funds, stocks and shares, security interests, title, and documents of title. These are the instruments which relate the particular object to the rest of the economy. Thanks to them, assets . . . lead an invisible, parallel life alongside their material existence.'

the ambit of some specific statute (such as the Sale of Goods Act or the Law of Property Act 1925 [LPA]), or in the context of construing the intended meaning of 'property law terms' used in a contract or a will.[308]

The common law legal systems of the British Isles have not even produced a uniform definition of 'land'. Not seldom, common law judges and scholars make reference to Lord Coke's classical formulation:

> '"Land", "Terra" in the legal signification, comprehendeth any ground, soile, or earth whatsoever, as meadows, pastures, woods, moores, waters, marishes, furses and heath ... It legally includeth also all castles, houses and other buildings; for castles, houses etc., consist upon two things, viz., land or ground, as the foundation or structure thereupon; so as passing the land or ground, the structure or building thereupon passeth therewith.[309]

Statute law contains more technical definitions, which differ from statute to statute (and sometimes even from provision to provision within the same statute),[310] generally only with the ambition to provide a definition for the specific subject-matter of the statute. Besides this, the legislative preference is for exemplary rather than exhaustive lists (i.e. 'land includes'); true definitions are nowhere to be found. Under sec. 205(ix) LPA, for example, 'land' includes land of any tenure, and mines and minerals, whether or not held apart from the surface, buildings or parts of buildings (whether the division is horizontal, vertical or made in any other way) and other corporeal hereditaments; also a manor, an advowson, and a rent and other incorporeal hereditaments, and an easement, right, privilege, or benefit in, over, or derived from land; 'mines and minerals' include any strata or seam of minerals or substances in or under any land, and powers of working and getting the same; 'manor' includes a lordship, and reputed manor or lordship; 'hereditament' means any real property which on an intestacy occurring before the commencement of the Act might have devolved upon an heir. One is here dealing with *corporeal* and *incorporeal hereditaments*, that is with *real property*, which before the LPA would have passed on intestacy *ex lege* to a particular heir (which could not be extinguished nor be left to another person by testamentary disposition). Under sec. 132(1) Land Registration Act 2002, on the other hand, 'land' includes buildings, land covered with water, and mines and minerals.[311] Section 3 of the Interpretation Act 1889 prefaces its own definition with a rider, namely that 'land' as defined in other

[308] *Nokes v Doncaster Amalgamated Collieries Ltd* [1940] AC 1014, 1051 (HL) (Lord Porter: 'In truth the word "property" is not a term of art but takes its meaning from its context and from its collocation in the document or Act of Parliament in which it is found and from the mischief with which that Act or document is intended to deal'). Similar problems, of course, arise in the codified legal systems, see e.g. STJ 8 February 1974, BMJ 334 (1974) p. 293 (A testator used the term '*móveis*' and it was unclear, whether he meant moveables in the technical sense or only furniture, which uses the same word in Portuguese).

[309] *Coke* on Littleton, p. 4a (reproduced in *Garner* (1957) 21 Conv 141, 142).

[310] An example of this can be found in the various definitions of *land* in secs 61 and 68 Criminal Justice and Public Order Act 1994; see *DPP v Chivers* [2010] EWHC 1814 (Admin); [2011] WLR 2324 (DC).

[311] 'In this Act "land" includes (a) buildings and other structures, (b) land covered with water, and (c) mines and minerals, whether or not held with the surface.'

statutes can have a different meaning, and then provides that this expression includes 'messuages,[312] tenements[313] and hereditaments, houses and buildings of any tenure'. A different definition of land again is found in sec. 38(1) of the Limitation Act 1980. Here, 'land' is defined *not* to include incorporeal hereditaments. Under sec. 3 of the Irish Land and Conveyancing Law Reform Act 2009, 'land' includes a kaleidoscope of rights and things, namely

> (a) any estate or interest in or over land, whether corporeal or incorporeal, (b) mines, minerals and other substances in the substratum below the surface, whether or not owned in horizontal, vertical or other layers apart from the surface of the land, (c) land covered by water, (d) buildings or structures of any kind on land and any part of them, whether the division is made horizontally, vertically or in any other way, (e) the airspace above the surface of land or above any building or structure on land which is capable of being or was previously occupied by a building or structure and any part of such airspace, whether the division is made horizontally, vertically or in any other way, (f) any part of land.

The term 'property' does not describe objects with certain physical attributes (e.g. in the sense of a corporeal and either moveable or immoveable 'thing'). 'Property' describes rather the *status* of an object—that is, its attribution to a person in whole or in part for that person's exclusive use and therefore its belonging to that person.[314] Not the thing itself, but the legal relations that secure its use, have traditionally been the primary point of reference for the common law of property.[315] Such legal relations **5.63**

[312] 'Messuages' are practically identical to dwelling houses (*Fenn v Grafton* (1836) 2 Bing NC 617, 132 ER 238; *Kerslake v White* (1819) 2 Stark 508, 171 ER 719). The etymology is unclear; it is probably a medieval transcription error of the French *mesnage* (http://www.etymonline.com/index.php?term=messuage).

[313] A *tenement* is a physical thing which can be the object of tenure under common law (*Garner*, (1957) 21 Conv 141, 143). The term is derived from the Latin *tenere* (hold) or *tenementum*, and usually describes 'a large house constructed to be let to a number of tenants' (http://www.etymonline.com/index.php?term=tenement).

[314] *Gray*, CLJ 50 (1991), p. 252 ('Few other legal notions operate such gross or systematic deception. Before long I will have sold you a piece of thin air and you will have called it property. But the ultimate fact about property is that it does not really exist: it is mere illusion. It is a vacant concept—oddly enough rather like thin air . . . Of course, legal theorists have long sought to sidestep the unattainable quality inherent in the notion of private property by conceptualising property not as a thing but rather as a "bundle of rights" ').

[315] Elsewhere (Elements of Land Law, p. 8, reproduced in Worthington, *Personal Property Law*, p. 6) Gray observes: 'It is important at the outset to dispel one common lay notion concerning "property". Non-lawyers (and sometimes lawyers) speak loosely of property as the thing which is owned. While this usage is harmless enough in day-to-day speech, it has the effect of obscuring certain salient features of property as a legal phenomenon, for semantically "property" is the condition of being "proper" to (or belonging to) a particular person.' Gray adds to this: 'It was the philosopher, Jeremy Bentham, who had to remind lawyers that property is not a thing but a relationship. Bentham pointed out that in common speech in the phrase *the object of a man's property*, the words *the object of* are commonly left out; and by an ellipsis, which, violent as it is, is now become more familiar than the phrase at length, they have made that part of it which consists of the words *a man's property* perform the office of the whole.' The basis for this point of view apparently goes back to Locke's *Second Treatise of Government*, ch. V ('Of Property'), sec. 27 ('Though the earth, and all inferior creatures, be common to all men, yet every man has a property in his own person: this no body has any right to but himself. The labour of his body, and the work of his hands, we may say, are properly his. Whatsoever then he removes out of the state that nature hath provided, and left it in, he hath mixed his labour with, and joined to it something that is his own, and thereby makes it his property. It being by him removed from the common state nature hath placed it in, it hath by this labour something annexed to it, that excludes the

are varied and great in number. This is perhaps one of the reasons why the criteria which govern their categorization into groups are difficult to reduce to a single denominator. Besides this, in the vocabulary of the living law, historical categories compete with those derived 'merely' from legislative intervention. Both are used in parallel. Changes in English legal language occur slowly, and Anglophone jurists tend to avoid spending too much time on abstract systemic questions.[316] As a result, a number of inconsistencies have crept into the taxonomic schemata of the common law. It seems to have been forgotten, at certain points, that 'property' in this legal tradition is actually concerned with rights and legal relations; sometimes, at a lower level of the same taxonomy, the scheme seems to operate in a much more 'Contintental' fashion, that is, with *object-related* rather than *rights-related* criteria. It sometimes appears that even the ambition to avoid obvious logical inconsistencies is wanting.

'Property', as we explain in more detail below, is conventionally divided into 'real' and 'personal' property. It is said that real property concerns the rights and obligations of owners of land.[317] It includes corporeal and incorporeal 'hereditaments'; corporeal hereditaments include (or 'are') land. It is not seen as problematic that the LPA 1925 takes the exact opposite approach, using 'land' as the superordinate term, or that 'land' is still sub-divided into corporeal and incorporeal hereditaments. The term 'corporeal hereditament' itself therefore denotes, according to context, sometimes land as a physical object and other times a right or 'estate' in land. Estates and interests in land are *not* 'land' in general legal parlance or for the common law, but they *are* for the purposes of most statutes.[318] This terminological chaos is, however, not peculiar to the law governing land units; the term 'goods' fares little better. Goods (as 'choses in possession') form part of personal property and are thus obviously 'property'. But how one is meant to consider goods as property—even after one learns that the concept of property does not attach to the physical characteristics of an object but rather expresses that the object belongs to someone—remains a secret of English jurisprudence that remains well-hidden to the external observer.

common right of other men: for this labour being the unquestionable property of the labourer, no man but he can have a right to what that is once joined to, at least where there is enough, and as good, left in common for others').

[316] Explanations for this have always been ready to hand. e.g. in *Holmes*, The Common Law, p. 1 (see *Cao*, Translating Law, p. 23) one reads: 'The life of the law has not been logic: it has been experience. The felt necessities of the time, the prevalent moral and political theories, intuitions of public policy, avowed or unconscious, even the prejudices which judges share with their fellow-men, have a good deal more to do than the syllogism in determining the rules by which men should be governed. The law embodies the story of a nation's development through many centuries, and it cannot be dealt with as if it contained only the axioms and corollaries of a book of mathematics.'

[317] Megarry and Wade (*-Harpum/Bridge/Dixon*), The Law of Real Property[8], no. 1-002 ('Real property deals with the rights and liabilities of land owners').

[318] *Garner* op. cit. p. 143. See also *Commonwealth v New South Wales* (1923) 33 CLR 1 and *Trust Company Ltd v Chief Commissioner of State Revenue* [2007] NSWCA 255 (no. 49: 'In legal usage "land" is not confined to the physical thing, and can mean one of many legal constructs involving an estate in the land or an interest in the land').

b. The Historical Taxonomy

(1) Realty and Personalty

Property is divided historically into 'realty' and 'personalty' (or real and personal property). This dichotomy, which remains firmly anchored in the consciousness of English lawyers, naturally calls to mind the Romanic bifurcation of all goods into moveable and immoveable, but the two must not be confused.[319] The traditional *summa divisio* of the common law does not build on the question whether an object is moveable or immoveable, but rather on the question whether the 'property' in question gives its holder the legal power to demand possession that has been lost. That was (and is) the case for realty, but it was not for personalty until at least the mid-nineteenth century.[320] That had to do with the origins of English property law in the medieval system of feudal tenure.[321] The basis of this system was that absolute rights in land were held only by the Crown; its subjects could acquire and hold rights for the possession and use of land ('estates').[322] As rights derived from the radical title of the Crown, these rights had a particular rank. This status was expressed, for example, in an extended efficacy against third parties: certain estates (and only certain estates) give their holder the right to sue anyone for possession in the common law courts. In contrast, rights that did not derive from the system of feudal tenure and therefore fell under personalty were (and are) a perimeter against delictual interference with possession. Until the middle of the nineteenth century, this meant that the owner's remedies were limited to damages in money. A 'real action' was available to protect realty, only a 'personal action' was available to protect personalty. Real actions (claims for delivery of possession with particular procedural characteristics), however, were originally only available to the holder of 'freehold' land; for 'leasehold' land (i.e. temporally limited rights of use in land) an action for delivery only developed later—the 'action for ejectment', which produced the same outcome as a real action but was, technically speaking, an extended personal action.[323] 'Leases' ('leasehold land') came to occupy a kind of hybrid position; they transformed, 5.64

[319] The distinction between immoveables and moveables only informs English private international law, which can be explained by the fact that conflicts norms were, from the English point of view, generally formed in relation to the Civilian systems of the Continent.

[320] Reform was only effected with sec. 78 Common Law Procedure Act 1854. These new provisions are in force today; they are now found in sec. 3 Torts (Interference with Goods) Act 1977. The court can (a) order delivery of the thing and damages for the loss occasioned by deprivation of possession, (b) order delivery or (at the option of the defendant) damages for the value of the thing and for loss of possession, or (c) damages only. The claimant can choose between (b) and (c); an order for delivery is at the discretion of the court (sec. (3)(b)). (If the claimant chooses (b), he leaves the defendant the right to elect.) This is still some distance from a *vindicatio*, and to this day these limited rights to regain possession are seen as a part of the law of delict rather than of property law. In this, the late medieval procedural law lives on in the structure of modern property law (*Bell*, Modern Law of Personal Property, p. 19).

[321] *Williams*, Personal Property[18], p. 1.

[322] The *estate* (the 'status') determines, to be precise, the duration of *tenure* of a right of use in land (Megarry and Wade [-*Harpum/Bridge/Dixon*], The Law of Real Property[8], no. 2.005). It is in the best case unlimited and heritable, and is then called an *estate in fee simple* (or just *fee simple*).

[323] The 'action for ejectment' was, at base, nothing other than an offshoot of the writ of trespass. Apparently, the action quickly became even more popular than the old-fashioned real actions. English legal history holds certain examples of procedural tricks to make the benefits of this action available even to holders of a freehold estate (but not the opposite, i.e. the extension of real actions to holders of leasehold estates): *Bridge*, Personal Property Law[3], p. 2.

as so-called 'chattels real', into a sub-category of personal property. Only s. 1(1) LPA 1925 equiparated them with estates in land.

(2) Hereditaments

5.65 While personal property divided into chattels real and chattels personal (and while chattels personal divided further into choses in possession[324] and in choses in action[325]), the sub-division of realty was organized using categories taken from the laws of inheritance, namely 'hereditaments'.[326] The procedurally based taxonomy of property generally appears, at first blush, to be at odds with the technique of adding refinements from the law of succession. This unexplained change of categories begins to make sense when one considers that the paradigmatic hereditaments, so-called corporeal hereditaments, were subject to their own, peculiar succession regime. Corporeal hereditaments are, at base, nothing other than unlimited rights of use in land—i.e. 'freehold estates'. Both expressions describe the same phenomenon from different perspectives: a right to use land without a fixed end date is described as a freehold estate in the 'horizontal' relation to contemporaries; such a right is described as a hereditament in the 'vertical' relation to the next generation of right-holders. It is called corporeal because it is related to land. And it is called a hereditament because a freehold estate (not unlike the Continental *fideicommissum*) could not be transferred freely by testamentary disposition; a corporeal hereditament passed *ex lege* and without any action by the executor to a certain person, typically the eldest son of the deceased.

5.66 So-called 'incorporeal hereditaments' are even more mysterious. They consist, according to the common law understanding, of mere 'rights of property'. But so are the 'corporeal hereditaments', if one looks closely enough; even estates in fee simple are, according to the English doctrine, only rights in (or legal positions in relation to) land. In their characteristic as a complementary category to incorporeal hereditaments, however, corporeal hereditaments mutate from rights *in* an object to the physical object itself. The chameleon term changes colour again. Only in this manner is it possible to distinguish rights in land from rights in other objects and to sub-categorize those rights linguistically as 'incorporeal hereditaments', as property with no physical substrate.[327] That might sound impressive, but in substance it means nothing other than limited rights in land. Incorporeal hereditaments reveal themselves as limited real rights in land units; what distinguishes them from corporeal hereditaments is ultimately the fact that corporeal hereditaments give property rights in one's *own* land, whereas incorporeal

324 These are *goods*, i.e. corporeal moveable things.

325 Things without a physical substrate, i.e. incorporeal objects of legal transaction ('pure intangibles') and securities ('documentary intangibles').

326 From Latin *hereditatem* via French *hérédité*.

327 See further on the notion that we are dealing with 'incorporeal property', Megarry and Wade (-*Harpum/Bridge/Dixon*), The Law of Real Property[8], no. 31.001.

hereditaments give property rights in *another's* land.[328] The defining characteristic of corporeality is rather cosmetic. In truth, the one set of hereditaments are just as 'corporeal' as the other. The terminology, after all, serves no other goal. It is intended to express the fact that even certain 'minor' rights in land units were subject to the rules of real property. Incorporeal hereditaments were conceptualized as a part of the law of immoveable property early on, because they concerned land units.[329] In terms of legal policy, it was seen as desirable to afford them the privileges of the feudal system, particularly its idiosyncratic rules of succession. Incorporeal hereditaments should pass, just like a freehold estate, to the closest heirs of a decedent. With this goal in mind, however, another policy faded from view: that realty and personalty are, at the highest level of taxonomic ordering, organized according to procedural criteria. In the case of many incorporeal hereditaments, at least, it is unconceivable that their holder should have recourse to a real action against deprivation of possession. The holder of a right of way (an 'easement') has no right to demand possession of anything; nor does the bishop entitled to suggest a candidate for a local parish priest (an 'advowson'). The most that can be said is that 'realty' has been extended by the category of incorporeal hereditaments. The original touchstone of realty (the availability of a real action) was lost from view in that process, and the term itself transformed from a procedural category to a category in the law of succession.

Incorporeal hereditaments appear in many forms. A brief overview is sufficient for our present purposes. 'Rentcharges' have great practical importance, even following their substantial restriction in the Rentcharges Act 1977. A distinction is drawn between rentcharges and so-called 'rentservices'. Rental payments within a landlord–tenant relationship count to the latter group; only when a landlord–tenancy relationship is lacking do the annuities to be paid for the use of land count as rentcharges.[330] '*Profits a prendre*' include rights of appropriation, such as hunting and fishing rights.[331] 'Servitudes' are rights over another's land. They include 'easements' and 'restrictive covenants'.[332] Easements give the owner of a dominant land unit ('tenement') the right to undertake certain actions on the servient tenement. Exceptionally, they can also empower their holder to forbid certain actions on the servient land,[333] for example actions that would block natural light, air, or water movement, or undermine the foundations of a neighbouring structure. 'Restrictive covenants' resemble the latter category of easements in that they restrict the freedom of use of the tenement they encumber for the benefit of another, for example by prohibiting certain types of building construction **5.67**

[328] *Wylie*, Irish Land Law³, p. 352.

[329] This is evident in numerous rules, e.g. the rule that a deed (a specially sealed certificate) is necessary for the creation of an incorporeal hereditament (*Wylie* op. cit. p. 351).

[330] Megarry and Wade (-*Harpum/Bridge/Dixon*), The Law of Real Property⁸, no. 31-014.

[331] *Harpum/Bridge/Dixon* op. cit. p. 1316.

[332] *Lawson and Rudden*, The Law of Property³, p. 153.

[333] On the requirements of a valid easement, *Re Ellenborough Park* [1956] Ch 131, 163, 170 (CA); *Wylie*, Irish Land Law³, p 365. In contrast to English law, easements that demand a positive action from the owner of the servient tenement are possible in Irish law; see *Garner*, (1957) 21 Conv 141, 154.

or commercial use.[334] In contrast to the negative easements, however, restrictive covenants were only accepted in the law of property in the early nineteenth century, and then only in equity and not at common law.[335] The main consequence of this is that they are extinguished upon acquisition by a good faith purchaser of freehold land.[336] An 'advowson'[337] is the non-alienable (and today no longer registerable) right of the lord of a manor to suggest candidates for a local church office.[338] A 'manor' consisted of the mansion house, land in possession of feudal tenants, and common land accessible to all tenants for pasturing their livestock.[339]

(3) Personal Property

5.68 The point of departure for defining personal property (or 'personalty') is again familiar to the Continental jurist: personalty is all property that is not realty.[340] Personalty is not subject to any strict statutory *numerus clausus*. It is sub-divided into 'chattels real' and 'chattels personal'. Chattels real consist, for the most part, in leasehold interests in a land unit, that is in rights to use land based in a lease agreement. They are treated as personalty because they could, historically, only be enforced with a personal and not with a real action. Only in sec. 1(1) LPA 1925 were leaseholds finally recognized as interests in land. A leasehold has, in contrast to a freehold (or fee simple) a 'term of years absolute' and is, in this respect, one of the two forms of 'legal estate' recognized under the Act. A lease agreement gives rise to a real property right in land for the tenant (or 'lessee'), but is at the same time a 'personal' contract between him and the landlord (or 'lessor'). All other objects of personal property are chattels personal.[341] They are divided into choses (lit. 'things' from Anglo-Norman French *chose*) 'in possession' and 'in action'.[342] Choses in possession are tangible (i.e. corporeal) moveable objects. They belong to the absolute property of a person, which means that they are not counted as mere estates and cannot be parcelled and granted in sub-estates;[343] they are (excepting the lack of *vindicatio*)

[334] *Lawson and Rudden* op. cit. p. 156.

[335] In Ireland, this remained the case right up to the passage of the Land and Conveyancing Law Reform Act 2009.

[336] *Wylie* op. cit. p. 370.

[337] From Latin *advocatio* via archaic French *avouson*.

[338] Now subject to the Patronage (Benefices) Measure 1986 which imposes numerous limitations. The non-alienability of an advowson follows from sec. 3 and its non-registerability from sec. 3 Land Registration Act 2002.

[339] The term 'manor' crops up in statutes even today as a term of art (see *Harpum/Bridge/Dixon* op. cit. no. 2-011). The historical explanation in *Crown Estate Commissioners v Roberts* [2008] EWHC 1302 (Ch); [2008] 2 P & CR 15 (Lewison J) is instructive. The case concerned the acquisition of two manors (or 'lordships') on the Welsh coast and the question, which rights were connected with them (the 'right to a moiety of wreck' the 'right to estrays' and the statutory rights of a Lord of the Manor under the Game Act 1831' were confirmed).

[340] *Bridge*, Personal Property Law[3], p. 1.

[341] 'Chattel' is obviously related to 'cattle' and archaic French *chatel*. Cattle was personal, absolute property; it was not subject to the feudal system of tenure. An interesting linguistic parallel is found in Greek. *Prówato* (*Πρόβατο*), the modern Greek word for 'sheep', is derived from the verb 'to walk'. *Πρόβατα* are therefore things that walk or move themselves. In ancient Greek, this word denoted a 'herd' of any kind of animal (*Georgios Babiniotis*, Lexikon der griechischen Sprache, Athens 1998, p. 1487). Herds (cattle) are thus moveable wealth.

[342] This categorization is regarded as mutually exclusive: *chattels personal* can only ever be one or the other, but never both (*Colonial Bank v Whinney* (1885) 30 Ch D 261).

[343] Subordinated *interests* in chattels can, however, be created in equity (*Williams*, Personal Property[18], p. 47).

'property' in the Continental sense. When choses in possession appear as the subject matter of a contract or some other legal transaction, they are 'goods'[344] (earlier 'goods, wares and merchandise').[345] Future things, however, are not choses in possession; they are 'goods' for the purposes of sales law but not property law. Choses in action (in sec. 136 LPA 1925 and sec. 61 Sale of Goods Act 1979, 'things in action') are personal objects, the use of which consists in another's performance, which must be enforced by legal action (hence the name). The same, of course, can be said of all rights whose exercise is interrupted. What is specifically meant is that a chose in action differs from a chose in possession in that the latter's use and enjoyment is primarily guaranteed by the thing's factual, material possession. So-called 'pure intangibles' embrace immaterial objects such as claims based in contract, claims to damages, copyright, 'goodwill' and shares in a partnership, as well as testamentary claims. 'Documentary intangibles' are securitized rights, such as bills of lading, bills of exchange, and shares in a limited liability company.[346] Property in these rights depends on possession of the relevant certificate; often, it can only be transferred by delivery of the certificate.

c. Statutory Reforms

This evolved taxonomy informs the conceptual understanding and the terminology of the common law of property to this day. Real actions, however (such as the 'action for ejectment')[347] have long been abolished;[348] in the place of special actions for personalty and realty, a simplified, single action for possession (of land) has been available at least since 1875.[349] Since the reforms of 1922 (at the latest), the law of succession has not distinguished between real and personal property (chattels),[350] such that '*per se*' the positive legal basis of hereditaments has been removed.[351] Leaseholds transformed, in 5.69

344 Under sec. 61 Sale of Goods Act 1979, *goods* include 'all personal chattels other than things in action and money, and in Scotland all corporeal moveables except money'; 'and in particular "goods" includes emblements, industrial growing crops, 'and things attached to or forming part of the land which are agreed to be severed before sale or under the contract of sale'. Through sec. 2(c) Sale of Goods (Amendment) Act it was added that '*goods* includes an undivided share in goods'. For Ireland, the Sale of Goods Act 1893 continues in force, according to sec. 62 of which '*goods*' includes all chattels personal other than things in action and money, and in Scotland all corporeal moveables except money; and in particular "goods" includes emblements, industrial growing crops, and things attached to or forming part of the land which are agreed to be severed before sale or under the contract of sale'. The amendments introduced by the statute of 1995 only affect the laws of the United Kingdom.

345 *Bridge*, Personal Property Law³, p. 3.

346 sec. 181(2) Companies Act 1985.

347 Abolished by the Common Law Procedure Act 1852.

348 Namely in the Real Property Limitation Act 1833.

349 Supreme Court of Judicature Act 1875, Sched. 1, Order 48 (introduction of an action of a writ of possession that replaced the action of ejectment); today in Civil Procedure Rules 1998, Part 55, r. 55.1(a) ('a claim for the recovery of possession of land [including buildings or parts of buildings]').

350 The limitations for realty based in the law of succession were possibly already lifted by secs 4 and 5 of the Vendor and Purchaser Act 1874. The possibilities of testamentary disposition were substantially broadened by the Land Transfer Act 1897. The high point of modernization, however, was reached with Part 1 of the Administration of Estates Act 1925, in which the law governing the inheritance of personal property was extended wholesale to realty.

351 sec. 205(1)(ix) LPA 1925 uses the term *hereditaments* anyway, and defines it as 'any real property which on an intestacy ... before ... this Act might have devolved upon an heir'. This definition is, however, only relevant to the definition of *land* (found in the same section) for the purposes of LPA 1925.

the manner described above through sec. 1(1) LPA 1925, to real interests in land. They were (though still personalty)[352] often subjected to the same rules that applied to freehold estates. In consequence, the conventional distinction between real and personal property does not accurately reflect the current law in all respects. Sparkes has thus advanced the thesis that the objects of property law should, for this reason, be categorized as 'land' and 'not-land'.[353] He would further distinguish freehold from leasehold land, while 'not-land' would be divided into 'tangible' and 'intangible' property. This suggestion is, however, neither generally accepted nor particularly convincing. This is because it advances on the basis of a division of objects (land and not-land) but does not stick to this approach; it goes on to use a distinction between 'estates' and 'interests'—thereby effectively referring back to corporeal and incorporeal 'hereditaments', to which nothing, which is not land, corresponds. Besides this, one should not make too much of the distinction between property rights in land and property rights in 'other property'. Although these rights developed historically in partial isolation from one another,[354] there are many matters in which it hardly makes any difference whether land or personal property is at stake. The law of trusts and the concept of relativity of title provide two prominent examples. One could also remain with the conventional taxonomy adding only a proviso that land 'usually' includes chattels real. The addition of such a small inconsistency would, after all, not make that much of a difference.

d. The European Context

5.70 For all its imperfections, the common law sends an important message to the jurisdictions of the civil law: namely, the message that neither limiting 'things' to corporeal objects nor bifurcating the concept of property into 'immoveables' and 'moveables' will suffice. It would simplify the European discussion about property law considerably if the Civilians would lose their fixation with the *summa divisio* of all objects of property rights and if the common lawyers, for their part, would concede to a consistent categorization of the objects in which they think property rights can be held. Then it might be possible, from their respective points of view, to distinguish rationally between real things, land units, and incorporeal normative things. Pushing some peripheral questions to one side, the terms 'choses in possession', 'moveable things' (e.g. *bewegliche Sachen*), and *meubles par nature* all have practically the same meaning; they are all real objects. 'Land' would then correspond to land units [e.g. *Grundstücke*] insofar as one could separate the former from its feudal past and the latter from its register-based terminological inflection. 'Choses in action', on the other hand, are dealt with in this book as *incorporeal normative things*. The same counts for the assets of an undertaking (that

[352] *Bridge* op. cit. p. 2. The justification of this position is simply that the legislature did not change the historical characterization in the LPA 1925. Where the statute is silent, the old conceptual structure continues to operate. Its practical importance today, however, is probably just as a tool for the interpretation of testaments and contracts.

[353] *Sparkes*, A New Land Law, p. 25.

[354] *Murphy and Roberts*, Understanding Property Law^2, p. 25.

changes in its composition from time to time), insofar as it can be the object of a real security right (a 'floating charge'), and for certain incorporeal hereditaments, for example rights of pre-emption and the aforementioned advowson. Doubt only remains with respect to how real rights in things and in land units that are themselves the object of a real right (such as a pledge which can be the object of another pledge, or a hypothec that can be the object of a usufruct). The point of reference of the 'dominant' right is, in such a case, *itself* a right and therefore a normative thing; the point of reference of the 'servient' right is, on the other hand, a real thing or a land unit, respectively. As the economic purpose of the constellation is, in the end, to allow access to the corporeal asset that is the ultimate referent of the security arrangement, much speaks for the approach of characterizing the 'dominant' right by reference to this object, as well.

VI
Real Things

1. Real Things as the Objects of Property Rights

Real things are, comparatively speaking, the least problematic objects of property rights. Granted, no single thing can be found that can be the object of *all* the possible property rights found across the European Union, or even within the national property law of any one of its Member States. Real things are no exception to this general lack of uniformity. All around, legal systems are brimming with property rights that can *only* be held in land units or in incorporeal normative things, but not in the physically moveable things of the external world. The latter, however, are created in astronomical numbers every day, and destroyed in presumably the same volume. The soil, on the other hand, can neither be increased nor decreased,[1] and in this respect there is no phenomenon in it comparable to consumable or perishable goods.[2] The soil is more contested than real things; it has, for this reason, inspired more development of imaginative legal constructions than the familiar objects of trade and daily life. For incorporeal normative things, many of which became the object of *erga omnes* monopoly rights quite recently, unique solutions often had to be developed. Occasionally, one even stumbles upon property rights that have, as their reference point, an *aggregation* of assets of different types, for example the 'floating charge' of English law. 6.1

Property rights that can only arise in immoveables, but not in real things, include for example the Polish law heritable lease in state and municipal land units (Art. 232 Polish Civil Code), servitudes (Arts 296 § 1, 285 § 1, and 305 Polish Civil Code) and cooperative ownership.[3] With the exception of the servitudes, these rights can also be encumbered with a hypothec (Art. 65 GBHG), which moveable corporeal objects

[1] Isolated rules concerning the acquisition of alluvial soil (deposits on floodplains; see e.g. Arts 556–563 Belgian and French Civil Codes, Arts 1069–1072 Greek Civil Code, Arts 366–374 Spanish Civil Code, and Arts 1328–1332 Portuguese Civil Code) do not affect the general principle.

[2] The so-called *ususfructus irregularis* (§ 510 Austrian Civil Code), a usufruct in consumable things, is therefore necessarily a peculiarity of real things and rights. However, the Austrian Civil Code does not interpret this figure as a real right but as an obligational one similar to a loan in which the usufructee acquires title to the goods and then, following their consumption, is obligated to provide goods of the same type and quantity or their worth in money (Schwimann and Kodek [-*Spath*] ABGB II^4, § 510 no. 1; Klang [-*Klang*], ABGB II^2, p. 585). The difference to a loan consists in the fact that the *ususfructus irregularis* does not entail the payment of interest. § 510 Austrian Civil Code is reflected *inter alia* in § 1067 German Civil Code, which expressly provides that the usufruct of a consumable good entails transfer of title in the good to the usufructee; in German law, too, this is interpreted as an obligational transaction (Staudinger [-*Frank*], BGB [2009], § 1067 no. 1).

[3] Cooperative ownership can no longer be established; Art. 17^1(2) of the Statute on Residential Collectives was repealed with effect from 31 July 2007. All rights acquired before that date subsist, however, and can be transferred irrespective of this change in the law.

Foundations of Property Law. Christian von Bar and Jason Grant Allen, Oxford University Press. © Christian von Bar 2023.
DOI: 10.1093/oso/9780198885337.003.0006

cannot. An example provided by the law of the Czech Republic and Slovakia is the so-called real encumbrances. Under § 151n of the Slovakian Civil Code these are (as they were under § 151n Czech Civil Code [1964]) only permissible for immoveables, not for moveable things. (Under § 1257(1) Czech Civil Code [2014], servitudes can also be created over moveables.) The only (personal) servitude that is possible for moveable things, immoveable things, and rights found in German (§§ 1030, 1068, and 1085 German Civil Code), Greek (Art. 1142 Greek Civil Code), and Polish law (Arts 252 and 265 § 1 Polish Civil Code) is the usufruct; all other servitudes are limited to land units. The Common Law also confines the ambit of *restrictive covenants* and *easements* exclusively to land (the usufruct as such is not recognized; functional equivalents are possible with the lease and the trust).[4] The hypothec (§ 1113 German Civil Code, Art. 2393 French Civil Code, Art. 1257 Greek Civil Code) and the *Grundschuld* (§ 1191 German Civil Code), for example, are property rights that can only be created in land units or immoveables in Germany, France, and Greece; in some other jurisdictions they can be created in register goods,[5] but nowhere can they be created in regular, moveable things by ordinary dealings of private parties. In the Netherlands, property rights including the *erfdienstbaarheid* (real servitude, Art. 5:70 Netherlands Civil Code), the *erfpacht* (usufruct, Art. 5:85 Netherlands Civil Code) and the *recht van opstal* (heritable building right, Art. 5:101 Netherlands Civil Code) are reserved for immoveable *zaken*. In Austrian law and in numerous other jurisdictions (e.g. Art. 1058 Italian Civil Code [*servitù prediali*] and Art. 1543 Portuguese Civil Code [*servidões prediais*]), real servitudes (§§ 473, 474 Austrian Civil Code), *Wohnrecht* (*habitatio*, § 521 ABGB), and *Reallastberechtigung* (§§ 9 and 12 Austrian Civil Code) can only exist in land units, and the same applies to condominium property (§ 2(1) Austrian WEG) and ownership of parts of a shared cellar (§ 300 Austrian Civil Code). Apartment ownership (§ 1158 Czech Civil Code; Art. Portuguese Civil Code), condominium ownership (Arts 1002, 1117 Greek Civil Code; Art. 1414 Portuguese Civil Code), *Wohnrecht* (Art. 1183 Greek Civil Code; Art. 1022 Italian Civil Code [*abitazione*], Art. 1484(2) Portuguese Civil Code [*direito de habitação*], Art. 524(2) Spanish Civil Code [*habitación*]), real encumbrances (§ 1303 Czech Civil Code; Art. 1604 Spanish Civil COde [*censos*]), and building rights (Art. 952 Italian Civil Code; Art. 1524 Portuguese Civil Code [*superfície*]; § 1240 Czech Civil Code; Art. 40 Spanish Ley de Sueolo[6] [*derecho real de superficie*]) indicate in their very nomenclature their exclusive connection to immoveable property.

[4] Swedish law, too, recognizes only specific real use rights in land owned by another; the general usufruct (*avkomsträtt*) has no third party effects (*Hessler*, Allmänn Sakrätt, p. 314).

[5] e.g. in Italian law (Art. 2810(2) and (3) Italian Civil Code), in Netherlands law (Art. 3:227 Netherlands Civil Code), and in Portuguese law (Art. 688(1)(f) Portuguese Civil Code). Art. 106 Spanish LH permits hypothecs in real rights under specific conditions. Under Art. 12 *Ley de 16 de diciembre de 1954 sobre hipoteca mobiliaria y prenda sin desplazamiento de posesión* [LHMPSD] hypothecs in moveables are permitted for commercial entities (*establecimientos mercantiles*), automobiles, trams, and railway carriages in private ownership, aeroplanes, industrial plant, and intellectual and commercial property. Bulgarian law recognizes hypothecs in building rights that have been created but not yet realized, as well as hypothecs in moveables including ships and airplanes (Art. 47a Bulgarian Maritime Code; Art. 23(3) Bulgarian Civil Aviation Statute), under the Bulgarian Statute on Special Charges, Non-Possessory Charges in Commercial Undertakings, Industrial Plant and Goods.

[6] *Ley de Suelo* pursuant to the *Real Decreto Legislativo* 2/2008 of 20 June 2008.

The same can be said of leases over agricultural or commercial land and for rights to fell timber, at least where such rights are conceptualized as property rights (e.g. Kap. 7-11 Swedish JB).

It cannot even be said that all rights that can be held in real things can always be held in objects falling into the other two groups. Some legal systems come quite close to this position in practice,[7] especially when they interpret retention of title not as a special device for creating security interests in moveable things but as an expression of a more fundamental conceptual approach that allows the conditional transfer of ownership in moveables, but insists on the unconditional transfer of immoveables.[8] Even if a further step were taken—namely, to overlook the differences between pledge rights (derived from the law of moveable property and generally connected to possession) and the hypothec rights (which are derived from the law of immoveable property and are generally unconnected to possession)[9]—there are certain property rights that can only be held in real things but not (or not everywhere) in normative things. English law recognizes no absolute ownership in land units, and German law recognizes no absolute ownership in claims and other rights (§ 903 German Civil Code). The right of retention [*retentierecht*] of Art. 3:290 and the right of use [*recht van gebruik*] of Art. 3:226 Netherlands Civil Code are reserved for *zaken*; only the usufruct [*vruchtgebruik*] (Art. 3:201 Netherlands Civil Code) can be held in *goederen* generally. In Bulgarian, Czech, and Slovakian law, only a moveable thing can be encumbered with a right of retention 6.2

[7] In Austrian law, for example, even the law of pledges is in principle conceived for both moveable and immoveable things (§ 448 ABGB: 'A pledge can serve every thing that is in commerce. If moveable, it is a "hand pledge" [*Handpfand*] or a pledge in the narrower sense; if immoveable, it is a hypothec [*Hypothek*] or land pledge [*Grundpfand*]'); rules that distinguish the two really only concern the details of the creation of the pledge. Matters are similar in France and Belgium. A pledge can be created over both moveable and immoveable things. However, there are some specific rules for certain objects (see Arts 2333–2354 French Civil Code on the *gage de meubles corporels*; Arts 2355–2366 on the *nantissement de meubles incorporels*, and Arts 2387–2392 on the *gage immobilier*). The core of the rules concerning *gages immobiliers* (in Belgium, the *antichrèse*: Arts 2072, 2085–2091 Belgian Civil Code) comprises provisions on the hypothec (*Bourassin/Brémond/Jobard-Bachellier*, Droit des sûretés[2], p. 588 para. 2143). A wide range of objects are also covered by the non-possessory pledge (which is different to the moveable hypothec) under Arts 52–54 of the Spanish LHMPSD, including agricultural products (even those that have not yet been harvested), animals, plant and machinery, wares in storage and raw materials, art collections, licenses, concessions, and subsidies.

[8] The Austrian Land Registry Statute does not acknowledge conditional registration. At maximum, the narrow requirements of §§ 8 and 35 of the statute permit the registration of a priority notice (for further details see *Iro*, Sachenrecht[4], no. 8/5). Under German law, the agreement concerning the transfer of a land unit [*Auflassung*] under § 873 German Civil Code cannot, under § 925(2) German Civil Code, be made conditionally. This is also the case under Art. 1033 Greek Civil Code, as this requires transcription into the register, which is not fulfilled by a conditional transfer. On the other hand, Art. 409 Portuguese Civil Code permits the retention of ownership even for immoveables and moveable register goods. However, before this is valid *vis-à-vis* a third party, the condition precedent must be registered (*Pires de Lima and Antunes Varela*, Código Civil Anotado I[4], p. 376). Likewise, in Spain under Art. 23 LH, the validity *vis-à-vis* a third party of a *pacto de reserva de dominio* is dependent on its registration (*O'Callaghan Muñoz*, Compendio de derecho civil II(2)[2], p. 63). The details of this process are regulated in Art. 9(2) LH in conjunction wth Art. 51(6) RH (for details see López y López and Montés Penadés [-*Valpuesta Fernández*], Derechos reales, p. 817). The general admissibility of the retention of ownership over sold immoveables is derived from Art. 1255 Spanish Civil Code (*Amorós Guardiola*, RCDI 488 (1972) pp. 9–42).

[9] Under Art. 2784(2) Italian Civil Code, moveable things, aggregations of moveables, claims, and other rights can be given as pledges. In Germany and in Portugal, pledges are confined to moveables (§ 1204 German Civil Code; Art. 668(1) Portuguese Civil Code, *penhor de coisas*) and rights (§ 1273 German Civil Code; Art. 679 Portuguese Civil Code; however, Art. 680 Portuguese Civil Code states that this *penhor de direitos* must relate to a moveable). This is also the situation in Poland (Arts 306 §§ 1 and 327 Polish Civil Code) and Greece (Arts 1209 and 1247 Greek Civil Code).

(Art. 91 Bulgarian Statute on Obligations and Contracts; § 1395 Czech Civil Code; § 151s(1) Slovakian Civil Code),[10] and the sub-pledge (§ 1390 Czech Civil Code) is only provided for claims. In English law, pledges and 'charges' (non-possessory rights in equity) are rights in goods only. Besides the equity-based charge (and of course equitable mortgages), only the mortgage (which has evolved into a common law charge) is available for land.[11] Greek law only allows pledges (Art. 1209 Greek Civil Code), non-possessory registered pledges (Art. 1214 Greek Civil Code; Statute 2844/2000), the *antichrese* (Arts 1221 and 1222 Greek Civil Code), the floating charge (Arts 16–18 of Statute 2844/2000) and the so-called 'plant hypothec' over industrial machines (Statute 4112/1929) in moveables; the purchaser under a retention of title only gets an expectancy right in a moveable thing.[12] The ownership of land units cannot be transferred subject to a condition precedent of full payment of the purchase price (Art. 1033 Greek Civil Code), and at the present time no other real expectancy rights have been recognized except those arising from the conditional acquisition of moveable things.[13] In Swedish law, a commercial hypothec (*företagshypotek*) under Kap. 2 § 1 *Lag om företagshypotek* (2008:990) is restricted to moveable goods, as is the *retentionsrätt* (the right of retention in property of the debtor, which is in the possession of the creditor, where the latter has incurred expenses as a result)[14] and the *detentionsrätt* (the general right of retention in the case of failure of the other party's performance).[15] A retention of ownership with effect against third parties can, on the other hand, be created in all types of object.[16]

6.3 Although it is not possible to find a lowest common denominator of all property rights among the property rights that can be held in real things, it is true that physical, moveable things play a prominent role in the law of property—sometimes even a role that is characteristic of the law of property as a whole. Monopolization of the use of real things raises only relatively minor problems of legal policy. Absolute ownership and possession are possible in real things in every legal system; this cannot be said of any other class of objects of legal transaction. Their straightforward marketability gives the

[10] The right of retention is seldom interpreted as a real right. However, it is possible to have a right of retention over moveables (Art. 758 Portuguese Civil Code) as well as immoveables (Art. 759 Portuguese Civil Code).

[11] The 'legal mortgage' of an estate requires a *charge by deed expressed to be by way of legal mortgage* (secs 85(1) and 86(1) Law of Property Act 1925). In relation to registered land, a legal mortgage can no longer be created by the grant of a leasehold or sub-leasehold estate (sec. 23(1)(a) Land Registration Act 2002). This method of the creation of a legal mortgage only subsists for the estate owner of unregistered land (for details see Cheshire and Burn [*-Burn and Cartwright*], Modern Law of Real Property[17], p. 726). The same goes for the creation of a sub-mortgage, by which a security is used in turn as a security through the encumbrance of the secured claim (*Burn and Cartwright* op. cit. p. 727).

[12] See especially the case law of Areopag 1316/2010, NoB 59 (2011) p. 388; Areopag 2052/2006, NoB 55 (2007) p. 961; CA Athens 2748/1982, NoB 31 (1983) p. 511.

[13] Greek literature, in any event, consistently only discusses the expectancy right of a purchaser under retention of title, see e.g. *Georgiades*, E exasfálisi ton pistóseon, § 27 p. 562.

[14] For further details, see *Håstad*, Sakrätt[6], pp. 26–7.

[15] e.g. § 10 Köplag (1990:91).

[16] See e.g. *Håstad* op. cit. p. 183 and (*inter alia* regarding security papers) *Undén*, Svensk sakrätt I[10], p. 126, and the legislation regarding *äganderättsförbehåll*, the *Lag om avbetalningsköp mellan näringsidkare m.fl.* (1978:599), the *Konsumentkreditlag* (2010:1846) (ownership over moveables), as well as Kap. 4 §§ 4–6 JB (ownership over immoveables; see also *Hessler*, Allmänn sakrätt, p. 195).

more durable among them their status as the preferred objects of real security interests; even real use rights (such as usufruct and trust) are possible in such objects in every legal system (albeit to differing degrees). The capacity of real things to be the object of the right of ownership and of other property rights has few prerequisites. The only requirement is a corporeal, moveable object of legal transaction that exists objectively in the physical world. To determine whether such an object exists, one need only engage a little more closely with the criterion of corporeality and to enquire whether living creatures (animals) and money can be counted among those objects capable of assignment to a person for his exclusive use. No more complicated questions than this arise. The ownership of real things appears to be sensible and correct from the perspective of every European legal system; it enables human beings to direct their lives with autonomy and personal responsibility and underwrites a functional macro-economy.

The physical nature of real things also reveals an especially well-used point of reference in the rules governing the acquisition of ownership and the other property rights. **6.4** This is true both for acquisition *ex lege* and acquisition in virtue of intentional dealings, and, in this context, both for acquisition from the titleholder and (to the extent it is permitted in the relevant legal system) from one without title. For example, the right to appropriate *bona vacantia* to oneself[17] and (in some legal systems) prescriptive acquisition by possession is limited to moveable physical objects.[18] The same applies for the law of finding.[19] The acquisition of ownership in moveable (real) things

[17] The right to appropriate *bona vacantia* by private individuals is limited to moveables, e.g. in Germany (§§ 958, 928 German Civil Code; § 972(2) German Civil Code acknowledges the acquisition of ownership *via* registration upon obtaining a so-called exclusory order [*Ausschließungsbeschluss*]); Estonia (§ 96(1) LPA); Greece (Arts 1075 and 1076 Greek Civil Code); Italy (Art. 923 Italian Civil Code); Latvia (Art. 930 Latvian Civil Code); Poland (Art. 181 Polish Civil Code); Portugal (Arts 1318 and 1345 Portuguese Civil Code); Slovenia (Art. 50 Slovenian SPZ); Czechia (§ 1045(1) Czech Civil Code), and Spain (Art. 610 Spanish Civil Code, Arts 15(e) and 17 *Ley de Patrimonio de las Administraciones Públicas 33/2003 de 3 de noviembre*; *ocupación*). This also appears to be the case in France. The *Code civil* is missing regulations regarding *occupation*. However, it is considered impossible for immoveables because these would all already be acquired (*Malaurie and Aynès*, Les biens[4], p. 186 no. 590). Furthermore, immoveable *bona vacantia* fall to the public authorities (Arts 539 and 713 French Civil Code). However, some authors consider it possible to acquire intellectual creations (*créations de l'esprit*), meaning that their creation is to be understood as *occupation* (*Terré and Simler*, Les biens[8], p. 330 no. 414).

[18] § 937 German Civil Code; Art. 174 Polish Civil Code; § 134(1) Czech Civil Code [1964], and § 1091(1) Czech Civil Code [2014] respectively are only concerned with the acquisition by possession of moveable objects. § 900 German Civil Code acknowledges the acquisition by prescription following registration [*Buchersitzung*], which is bound to longer terms. Moveable as well as immoveable physical objects can be acquired by possession under Arts 1041 and 1045 Greek Civil Code. The terms here are also different lengths. The same applies in Bulgaria (land units ten, moveable things five years). In Austria (§ 1452 Austrian Civil Code), Spain (Art. 1940 Spanish Civil Code) and in Portugal (Art. 1287 Portuguese Civil Code), rights can also be acquired by possession, therefore rights over immoveables can be acquired by possession (Art. 1957 Spanish Civil Code; Arts 1293–1297 Portuguese Civil Code; *usucapião de imóveis*). The requirement for this, in Art. 1957 Spanish Civil Code, is ten years of good faith, lawful possession if the party is present, twenty years if they are absent. While ownership over immoveable physical objects is not acquired through its mere appropriation, this is not an obstacle to the acquisition by possession (*Sohst*, Das spanische Bürgerliche Gesetzbuch[2], note to Art. 610 pp. 134–5). In France (Art. 2272 French Civil Code) and Belgium (Art. 2265 Belgian Civil Code), the acquisition of immoveables by possession is equally possible. Art. 2258 French Civil Code defines acquisition by possession as a means to acquire a good or a right by the effect of possession. In Italy, moveables and immoveables can be acquired by possession. The only difference is the periods of time for this acquisition to take effect (the general rule in Arts 1158 and 1161 Italian Civil Code is twenty years for land units and ten years for moveables).

[19] e.g. in § 973 German Civil Code (Acquisition of ownership of the finder six months after report to the authorities); Art. 1081 in conjunction with Art. 1088 Greek Civil Code (Acquisition of ownership of the finder one year after report to the authorities); Arts 51 and 52 Slovenian SPZ (Acquisition of ownership one year after reporting the find to the police; acquisition of ownership by possession one year after the find if the thing is of low value),

from another often requires delivery,[20] as does the acquisition of a charge over such objects.[21] And the same applies further for the right of usufruct in moveable things.[22] The good faith acquisition of a thing as a result of the dealings of someone without good title to it is bundled, in practically all European legal systems, with physical delivery of the thing to the innocent acquiring party.[23] Conversely, good faith acquisition is often excluded entirely or for a limited period where the thing in question left the possession of its owner without his consent.[24] The same applies for good faith acquisition of clear title.[25] Even the abandonment of property (dereliction) usually requires the abandonment of possession.[26] Processing, connection, and mixture are all mechanisms for the statutory acquisition of title in moveable things.[27] Besides this, numerous

and § 1057(1) and (3) Czech Civil Code (duty to report the find to the municipality; after one-year authority to act as proprietary possessor; acquisition of ownership after three years). The finding of treasure (hidden or buried valuable things) also concerns moveable things (Art. 716 French Civil Code; Art. 932 Italian Civil Code; Art. 1324 Portuguese Civil Code; Art. 53 Slovenian SPZ; Arts 614 in conjunction with 351 Spanish Civil Code).

[20] This is the case, e.g. under § 929 German Civil Code; Art. 1034 Greek Civil Code; Art. 3:90 Netherlands Civil Code; § 426 Austrian Civil Code; Art. 60(1) Slovenian SPZ; Art. 1462 Spanish Civil Code; § 133(1) Czech Civil Code [1964] and § 1101 Czech Civil Code [2014] respectively (transfer of a generically determined moveable thing), and § 1102 Czech Civil Code [2014] (transfer of a registered moveable thing). Swedish law of transfer of ownership over moveable things (*lösöre*) has many variants, however it can be said that, as a rule, *traditio* is required. In some cases, this can be replaced with registration. If one of the parties is a consumer, a written contract can replace it (§ 49 *Konsumentköplag* (1990:932)). This is different in places in which the transfer of ownership is the direct consequence of the sales contract (e.g. Art. 1138(2) Belgian and French Civil Code, as well as Art. 879(a) Portuguese Civil Code). Here also are rules of contract law which directly follow from the physical and moveable qualities of the object. One example is a safekeeping contract. This contract can only concern moveable things (Art. 1918 Belgian and French Civil Code) and only be concluded with the real or fictitious transfer of the thing in question (Art. 1919 Belgian and French Civil Code: *tradition réelle ou feinte de la chose déposée* or *remise réelle ou fictive de la chose déposée*).

[21] This so-called *Faustpfandprinzip* can be found in § 1204 German Civil Code; Art. 1211 Greek Civil Code; Art. 2786 Italian Civil Code; Art. 3: 236 Netherlands Civil Code; § 451 Austrian Civil Code; Art. 669 Portuguese Civil Code; Arts 1863 and 1864 Spanish Civil Code; Kap. 10 § 2 Swedish *Handelsbalk* (1736:0123 2) (see: HD 4 December 1975, NJA 1975 p. 638), and § 1317(1) Czech Civil Code.

[22] e.g. § 1032 German Civil Code and § 1294 Czech Civil Code.

[23] This is the case under Art. 2279 Belgian Civil Code; § 932 German Civil Code; § 95 (1) Estonian LPA; Art. 2276 French Civil Code; Art. 1036 Greek Civil Code; Art. 1153 Italian Civil Code; Art. 169 § 1 Polish Civil Code, and Art. 464 (1) Sentence 1 Spanish Civil Code. The exceptions (e.g. § 934 Sentence 1 German Civil Code and Art. 1156 Italian Civil Code) are tightly bound to the general rules of transfer of ownership over moveables, and must therefore be discussed in that context.

[24] See e.g. Art. 2279 sentence 2 Belgian Civil Code; § 935 German Civil Code; § 95 (3) Estonian LPA; Art. 2276 sentence 2 French Civil Code; Art. 1038 Greek Civil Code; Art. 169 § 2 Polish Civil Code; Art. 464 (1) sentence 2 Spanish Civil Code.

[25] e.g. § 936 German Civil Code; Art. 1155 Italian Civil Code; Art. 1141 French Civil Code; Art. 170 Polish Civil Code.

[26] This is the case under § 959 German Civil Code; § 96(3) Estonian LPA; Art. 3:117 Netherlands Civil Code; Art. 180 Polish Civil Code, and Art. 460(1) Spanish Civil Code (*abandono de la cosa*; abandonment of possession). The French *Code civil* is missing such a regulation. The prevailing view appears to be that dereliction is a unilateral act. This means that its validity depends entirely on the will of the owner (*Terré and Simler* op. cit. p. 332 no. 417; *Larroumet*, Les biens[5], p. 136 no. 259 ['*Il y a abandon du droit de propriété, lorsqu'en vertu d'un acte unilatéral de sa volonté, le propriétaire d'une chose entend abdiquer son droit de propriété sur cette chose*']). In Portugal, the possibility of dereliction of moveables is derived from Art. 1318 Portuguese Civil Code. It is contested whether ownership over immoveables can be abandoned (*Pinto Duarte*, Direitos reais[2], pp. 54–5). If the abandonment of ownership over immoveables is attempted in Italy, the immoveable becomes property of the state (Art. 827 Italian Civil Code).

[27] §§ 946–948 German Civil Code; Arts 1057–1059, 1061 Greek Civil Code; Arts 566–576 French Civil Code (*adjonction*, *spécification*, and *mélange*); Arts 939 (*unione e commissione*) and 940 (*specificazione*) Italian Civil Code; Arts 5:14-16 Netherlands Civil Code; Arts 192 and 193 Polish Civil Code; § 135b(1) Czech Civil Code [1964] and §§ 1074 and 1078 Czech Civil Code [2014] respectively; § 5:65 Hungarian Civil Code [2014]. The law

provisions exist which specially provide for the protection of possession of moveable things.[28]

2. Spatiality, Tangibility, and Apprehensibility

Real things are those objects of legal transaction whose characteristic of 'ownability' arises solely in virtue of their corporeal nature. Corporeality gives them (and only them) 'moveability' and this, in turn, guarantees the necessary separation of a single, discrete real thing—not from an immoveable object, rather from *another* physically moveable object. When, from a stock of 100 identical glasses, one has been sold but not yet removed from the stock, the object of sale is only nominally a specified object. It is not yet corporeal or moveable. The same applies to fifty tonnes of potatoes that have been sold in a warehouse in which 1,000 tonnes of potatoes are stored. Until the point of separation for transport, the 'fifty tonnes of potatoes' is only a product of human belief and intention.[29] The relevant criterion of corporeality or moveability therefore consists, in the case of real things, in their individualization. That is the prerequisite for the acquisition of property rights in them and the prerequisite of transferring those property rights in turn. Provided of course that one is speaking of a fitting object of legal transaction, nothing more is required by the European legal systems for this purpose, and nothing more is in fact necessary. 6.5

Matters are different in the case of land units. Their uniqueness cannot be described adequately with the corporeality criterion, and their 'immoveability' is not the basis of their ownability, rather the opposite: their immoveable nature is a natural hurdle to ownership which the legal system must first remove by normative means. Land units comprise a part of the earth, and therefore possess a basically physical nature. But this does not, of itself, provide their corporeality. One must either conceive of a land unit 6.6

of connection is occasionally differentiated according to the principal thing. This can either be another moveable thing or a land unit (e.g. Arts 358–374 Spanish Civil Code, *derecho de accesión respecto a los bienes inmuebles*) and Arts 375–383 Spanish Civil Code, *derecho de accesión respecto a los bienes muebles*), as well as Arts 1333–1338 Portuguese Civil Code (*acessão industrial mobiliária*) and Arts 1339–1342 Portuguese Civil Code (*acessão industrial imobiliária*).

[28] e.g. Art. 75 Bulgarian LPA, § 859(2) German Civil Code, and Art. 343 § 2 Sentence 2 Polish Civil Code. By contrast, Portugal's right to self-help (Arts 1277 and 336 Portuguese Civil Code) does not differentiate between moveables and immoveables, while Spain decides this question entirely according to the right to self-defence in a criminal context (Art. 20(4) Spanish Penal Code).

[29] For example, under Section 16 of the English Sales of Goods Act 1979, the acquisition of ownership over identical things from a stock, which have been defined exclusively by amount, can only be excluded as long as these things have not been individually ascertained: 'Where there is a contract for the sale of unascertained goods no property in the goods is transferred to the buyer unless and until the goods are ascertained.' Before individualizing these goods, an undivided share, i.e. a non-material share of the specific stock corresponding to the amount owed, can be transferred to the purchaser (sec. 20A (1) and (2) Sale of Goods Act 1979). The purchaser thus becomes a co-owner of the stock. Until they are individualized, the goods are missing the physical separation required for their ability to be subject to property law; the only object of property rights is an incorporeal one, created by the legal system itself—an *imagined* portion of the whole.

(i) as a two-dimensional object (a mere surface without any spatial dimension upwards or downwards), or (ii) as a three-dimensional object which the projected boundaries of the land unit cut across horizontally. If a land unit were merely the two-dimensional surface, it would clearly be a geometrical construct, not a 'body', with the consequence that the legal system would lose any physical point of connection for the property rights it grants in land units. This appears to be neither fit for purposes nor indeed consistent with lived experience. Property law requires, rather, a three-dimensional concept of the land unit, according to which the land unit embraces part of the space above the land as well as the surface and a part of the invisible soil beneath it. This, however, is not a corporeal object. The 'land unit' that is the object of property rights, then, consists not *only* of something corporeal. The 'immoveability' specific to land units, on the other hand, does not assist with the land unit's individualization and limitation. In other words, that which 'moveability' provides for real things—i.e. making them fitting to be owned—is not provided for land by 'immoveability'. This task must be undertaken, in its entirety, by other criteria. Which criteria are up to the task (placement of boundary markers, boundary descriptions in public registers, etc.) is a decision that has to be taken on the basis of normative considerations; the relevant object itself has no 'natural' boundaries. One might object that all objects of legal transaction must be separated from the rest of reality in order to be owned—not only land units, but also the water in a tank from the water in the river from which it has been pumped.[30] The latter, one might add, is the same kind of factual process as the marking of a land unit's boundaries. In both cases, the legal system must express a normative decision, namely which criteria of individualization are to be used to determine the ownability of an object.[31] That is indeed true. But real things retain the special feature that their individualization proceeds from a different point of departure than that of land units. Real things are separated from each other in virtue of their physical properties, whereas the soil remains connected by its physical nature.

[30] River water is not a thing *per se*, it only becomes a thing when it has been bottled (*Menyhárd*, Dologi jog^2, p. 47; *Wieling*, Sachenrecht I^2, § 2 I 1 b). Damming does not turn river water into a thing. Cutting off a mill's water resource therefore does not constitute an infringement of the property of the mill owner; it is not 'his' water. However, the quality of running water as a thing is occasionally specially regulated. Art. 204(1)(b) Portuguese Civil Code names bodies of water as an autonomous subcategory of immoveables, however, they can also be relegated to being a part of a land unit (for further details, see *Pires de Lima and Antunes Varela*, Código Civil Anotado I^4, note 4 to Art. 204 p. 196 and *Menezes Cordeiro*, Tratado de direito civil I(2)^2, p. 130). Likewise, Art. 334(8) Spanish Civil Code and Art. 511-2(2)(b) Catalan Civil Code count bodies of water, both running and still, as immoveables (*O'Callaghan Muñoz*, Código Civil^6, Art. 407 p. 472). However, under Art. 339(1) Spanish Civil Code, rivers are public property and thus *res extra commercium*.

[31] As early as 1875, *Nasmith*, The Institutes of English Private Law II, p. 303, noted: 'Things are either *natural* or *artificial*. When thus used in antithesis to the term "natural", the word "artificial" imports two distinct classes of things—viz., those created immediately by the law, and those created by it mediately through individuals. It is with things *artificial*, the word being used in this sense, that the law is mainly concerned; for the first act of the law—if we may so express ourselves—when finding or coming in contact with any natural object, is to subjugate it, to take it out of the sphere of the *natural*, to place it within the pale of the *legal*, to label or to name it, and to assign to it legal attributes. The lawyer, as lawyer, does not regard the field, the horse, or the heirloom, as a thing of beauty or of pleasure, but as a subject of property, of which its peculiar characteristics are mere incidents. His attention is centred upon the means of acquiring legal interests in it, upon determining and defining what those interests are, and upon ascertaining in what way or ways they may be alienated or lost. As the merchant regards origin and quality solely as matters of value, so the lawyer considers them as mere elements of rights, duties, and obligations.'

The corporeality of an object of legal transaction depends, as Art. 3:2 Netherlands Civil Code formulates it,[32] on its materiality; this gives the object its spatial dimension.[33] Both of these criteria, however, refer to common sense concepts of everyday life, not to the concepts of corporeality and materiality as we might understand them in light of modern physics.[34] A chain of molecules, for example, or even an atom can be individuated and have mass; they do not, however, provide a proper object of property rights for the domain of legal reality. It is often said, for this reason, that the object in question must be 'perceptible', but it is contentious what exactly 'perceptible' means in the particular case. Originally, this meant that the object could be felt with the sense of touch (*res corporales sunt quae tangi possunt*);[35] this is evident in the English terminology of '(in)tangibles'.[36] But why should metal in its liquid state, held in a mould, not be a moveable (real) thing just because one had better not touch it? Others opine that this is not the kind of perception that is relevant; any one of the five senses will suffice.[37] Others again emphasize the senses of touch and sight, presumably on the basis that the corporeality of an object cannot be heard, tasted, or smelled. All of this seems a little pointless. What is important is that property law operates not on the aggregation but on the physical separation of the object.[38] In order for a person to obtain and maintain ownership in materials in their fluid and gaseous states, they must, therefore, be separated from the surrounding environment with some kind of container. Wine in the bottle is a corporeal object, wine spilt on the carpet is not one anymore. 6.7

3. Animals

Because Roman law considered even human slaves to be 'tangible things', it naturally never occurred to the Romans to exclude animals from the category of property. Animals have a body, and that was sufficient. Most legal systems have maintained this position into the present day. Animals belong to the choses in possession of English 6.8

[32] 'Things are material objects susceptible to human control.'

[33] Energies are already for this reason not real things. Even if they are equated with moveables by legislation, this does not mean they can be owned or otherwise subject to property law.

[34] In this sense, rightly, the unanimous Greek literature (*Georgiades*, Empragmato Dikaio I, p. 78 no. 6; *Kousoulas*, Empragmato Dikaio, p. 33; *Papasteriou*, Empragmato Dikaio I, p. 171 no. 11).

[35] See Gai. Inst. 2, 13 (complete and according to the translation of *Hausmaninger and Selb*, Römisches Privatrecht[9], p. 41: 'Corporeal things are such that can be touched, like land units, slaves, clothes, gold, silver and numerous other things').

[36] Art 2(h) CESL defines 'goods' and provides that the word means 'any *tangible* moveable items'. This has been translated into German (*Staudenmayer*, Vorschlag für eine Verordnung des Europäischen Parlaments und des Rates über ein Gemeinsames Europäisches Kaufrecht, S. 11) as 'for the purposes of this Regulation, the expression (h) 'goods' ['*Waren*'] means '*moveable corporeal objects* [*bewegliche körperliche Gegenstände*]' (emphasis added).

[37] In this sense and emphasizing the difference to Roman law, see *Georgiades*, Empragmato Dikaio I, p. 78; *Papasteriou*, Empragmato Dikaio I, p. 170 no. 11, also e.g. *Dekkers*, Précis I, p. 450 no. 731 ('*Sont corporels, les biens qui tombent sous les sens; incorporels, ceux qui ne tombent pas sous les sens*').

[38] In Scandinavia a *sak* has been traditionally understood as a separate (*begränsat*), corporeal (*materiellt*), and physically recognizable (*fysiskt skönjbart*) object (*föremal*), which can be the object of legal transactions (*Tepora*, Inledning till grunderna för sakrätten, p. 46; *Hessler*, Allmänn sakrätt, pp. 19 and 44).

law,[39] and are 'things' as defined in Bulgarian (Art. 110 Bulgarian Statute on Property), Greek,[40] Netherlands,[41] Portuguese,[42] Swedish,[43] Czech,[44] and Hungarian law.[45] They are 'goods' as defined in Spanish,[46] Belgian, and French law.[47] This has little meaning, however, for animals in the wild.[48] So long as they are not appropriated, they are not a fitting object of property rights,[49] and when that appropriation occurs through fishing or hunting, it is usually through the death of the animal. Hunting rights are not rights in animals, but rather rights in land units, and the fact that animal carcasses are real things is beyond doubt. Modern conceptions of animal protection have only raised the

[39] This has always been the case (*Blackstone*, Commentaries on the Laws of England II, p. 387: animals are chattels personal) and remains the case today (*Gablesfarm Dogs and Cats Home v HMRC* [2008] UKVAT V20519 nos 21 and 36: pets are indisputably personal and moveable chattels, goods, and possible objects of absolute property).

[40] *Georgiades*, Empragmato Dikaio I, p. 78; see also *Karakostas and Bredimas*, H prostasia ton zoon kai to dikaio.

[41] Animals are *zaken* within the meaning of Art. 3:2 Netherlands Civil Code. They are protected by criminal provisions (von Bar [-*Nieper and Ploeger*], Sachenrecht in Europa III, Niederlande, p. 163 with further references).

[42] Animals are considered things or objects of the law of ownership (Art. 202 and Art. 1302 Portuguese Civil Code respectively) and they are equated with moveables (e.g. in Arts 1318, 1323(1), and 1046(2) Portuguese Civil Code). This is confirmed by Art. 2, which concerns the trade of animals. The Portuguese Ministry of Justice considered a reception of § 90a German Civil Code (Ministério da Justiça, Reforma do Direito Civil [Coimbra 2005], p. 17), but did not receive a consistent answer from the law faculties which had been asked. The matter appears to have come to nothing.

[43] *Håstad*, Köprätt^6, p. 29. The rules of moveable (*lös egendom*) and corporeal, moveable property (*lösöre*) are consequently also applied to animals (e.g. those in the Köplag (1990:931) and in the Konsumentköplag (1990:931); see especially Kap. 1 § 1 Konsumentköplag).

[44] While the Czech Civil Code [1964] did not make any provisions for the quality of animals as things, this position was uncontested while the code was valid. Animals were considered things within the meaning of civil law (*Švestka/Spáčil/Škárová/Humák*, Občanský zákoník I^2, p. 641). § 494 Czech Civil Code [2014] now states that a living animal has a 'special meaning and value' as a sentient living being; a living animal is no thing, and the provisions concerning things are only to be applied to animals in measures that do not contradict its nature.

[45] Animals are undoubtedly things under the previous and the new Hungarian Civil Code (§ 5:14(3)). *Menyhárd*, Dologi jog^2, p. 53 believes it is not foreseeable whether animal protection laws will one day lead to a new category 'between' things and persons. The future effects of such a decision for the remaining aspects of law cannot currently be controlled in any event.

[46] In Spain as in France, animals are generally moveable goods. Art. 334(6) Spanish Civil Code permits an interpretation of these as immoveables under certain requirements (it mentions areas for stock breeding, pigeon lofts, beehives, and fishponds). However, under Art. 511-1(3) Catalan Civil Code animals do not count as things and stand under special statutory protection; provisions on goods only find application to animals when their nature so allows.

[47] *Carbonnier*, Droit civil II, p. 1865 no. 887; *Malaurie and Aynès*, Les biens^3, nos 5, 126, 138, and 591; *Reboul-Maupin*, Droit des biens^2, p. 39 nos 68–71; *Zenati-Castaing and Revet*, Les biens^3, p. 32 no. 8e. A draft law, approved by the *Assemblée nationale* on 30 October 2014 intends to create a new Art. 515-14 French Civil Code which qualifies animals as '*êtres vivants doués de sensibilité*', but which readily adds '*sous réserve des lois qui les protègent, les animaux sont soumis au régime des biens*'. Animals will therefore remain goods in the future. For further details, see *Mallet-Bricout and Reboul-Maupin*, *D.* 2014 pp. 1844–6.

[48] Their protection is predominantly aimed for conservation of the species, and at most secondarily concerned with the protection of the individual animal. Hence, most rules in France concerning the protection of pets are to be found in the *Code rural*, whereas the protection of animals in the wild is considered preservation of the *préservation du patrimoine biologique*, and consequently consigned to the *Code de l'environnement*.

[49] Wild animals are either property of the state (such as in Bulgaria, Poland, and in Italy) or are counted among the *res nullius* (such as in Portugal [Art. 1318 Portuguese Civil Code]), the Czech Republic [Prchalová, *Právní ochrana zvířat*, p. 16], Spain [Art. 465 Spanish Civil Code], and Germany [§ 960(1) Sentence 1 German Civil Code]). In the Czech Republic and in France (Art. 713 French Civil Code), the acquisition of these animals by hunting poses an exception to the rule that *bona vacantia* is the property of the municipality in which they are found. The Constitutional Court of the Czech Republic, 13 December 2006, Sbírka nálezů a usnesení 43 (2007) no. 226 p. 541 confirmed that Czech law does not acknowledge the possibility of *res nullius* acquisition. This is only different if the person in question has a legal title to purchase the free-ranging animals. It thus depends on whether a special statute explicitly permits the occupation. This has largely remained the case in § 1046(1) Czech Civil Code [2014]. A wild animal is thus *bona vacantia* while it is free ranging. An acquisition in line with the provisions in hunting law remains possible (Spáčil [-*Petr*], Občanský zákoník III, p. 258). Likewise, Art. 610 Spanish Civil Code only permits the procurement by acquisition of such animals which are subject to hunting and fishing.

question whether it is still appropriate today to regard animals as 'things'. Animals are, after all, living creatures, and more recently some legislatures have suggested that it is inappropriate to treat animals as *objects* at all. Section 285a Sentence 1 Austrian Civil Code, enacted in 1988, set the precedent with the provision: 'Animals are not things [*Sachen*]; they are protected through special provisions.' Section 90a Sentences 1 and 2 German Civil Code adopted an almost identical formulation in 1990. Poland followed in 1997 with Art. 1 Polish Statute on Animal Protection,[50] and § 494 Czech Civil Code has provided since 2014 expressly that an animal, as a sentient living creature, is 'no thing'. The position is similar in Art. 511-1(3) Catalonian Civil Code. Estonia, however, has rejected this trend and provided in § 49(3) Estonian Civil Code (General Part) that property law provisions apply to animals unless otherwise provided.

Section 285a Sentence 2 Austrian Civil Code and § 90a Sentence 3 German Civil Code, **6.9** however, immediately add that the provisions governing things are also to apply to animals, provided no special statutory provisions prevent this. Section 5:14(3) Hungarian Civil Code contains a similar provision. According to this, the rules of property law can be applied to animals only under due consideration of the statutory provisions that change the general position. Art. 1 Polish Statute on Animal Protection expresses the same idea, stating that matters not provided for in the statute are to be governed by the general rules applicable to things. Section 494 Czech Civil Code provides that the nature of an animal as a living creature does not prevent the application of property law rules to it. In truth, only the latter provision has any practical relevance, if at all; this provision might have implications more broadly, beyond the context of animal protection. Otherwise, these provisions are little more than token gestures; they do not change property rights in animals. Ownership of animals is anyway subject to special restrictions on their exercise based in public policy,[51] and the proposition that *lex specialis* has precedence over *lex generalis* is usually self-evident. Thus, provisions such as these only create new, hitherto unknown, problems.[52] If animals are not 'things', but the rules governing things should apply to them, it would have been desirable at the very least to make clear that the relevant rules are those governing moveable things.[53]

[50] Ustawa z dnia 21 sierpnia 1997 r. o ochronie zwierząt, Dz.U. 1997 no. 111 pos. 724 (As being capable of suffering, an animal is not a thing).

[51] This of course also includes animal protection (e.g. *Antoine*, D. 2003 p. 2652). (Art. L-214-1 *Code rural et de la pêche maritime* states: '*Tout animal étant un être sensible doit être placé par son propriétaire dans des conditions compatibles avec les impératifs biologiques de son espèce*').

[52] For example, in criminal law, the question whether or not animals could still be stolen, quickly arose. This was because the wording of the offence of theft requires moveable 'things'. German divorce law [*Scheidungsfolgenrecht*] discussed whether there should be a form of contact with a pet, in parallel to contact with a child (affirming AG Bad Mergentheim 19 December 1996, *NJW* 1997 pp. 3033, 3034; rejecting OLG Schleswig 21 April 1998, NJW 1998 p. 3127). Similar problems could arise in tax law, e.g. if the sales tax is linked to 'moveable things', if analogy is prohibited for taxation and if the object of the sale is an animal (see Administrative Court Warsaw 31 May 2011, II FSK 77/10, Lex-No. 1089026: a horse is a thing within the meaning of sales tax law. This is not impeded by the prohibition of analogy in tax law in Art. 217 Polish Constitution. Horses are also things within the meaning of sales law Art. 535 Polish Civil Code). Even the concept of animals as legal subjects is now being discussed (*Carbonnier*, Droit civil II, p. 1866 no. 887 even opines that the French jurisprudence vacillates between the personification and the reification of animals; Tribunal de grande instance Lille 23 March 1999, D. 1999 p. 350, note by *Xavier Labbée* is admittedly not particularly suitable evidence for this).

[53] French law shows that this does not go without saying. Art. 528 French Civil Code states that all animals which are kept by people are, in principle, moveable goods. However, due to their purpose and connection with a

Insofar as this much was taken for granted, these provisions effectively retained the old approach to thinking about animals. Indeed, otherwise the thesis would be remarkably lacking in consequences. If animals really did comprise their own group as objects of property rights, it would have been necessary to develop a truly animal-specific set of property rights, for example replacing the 'ownership' of animals with the right to 'keep' them.[54] But we are far from such a position. Not even the legal systems of Austria, Germany, Poland, and the Czech Republic have developed rules under which animals are excluded from being the object of property rights that can otherwise be had in real things (such as pledge rights). An animal-specific law of property remains to this day restricted to rules governing the acquisition and loss of property in animals. And in this context, animals are again treated as mundane objects of property rights—if, indeed, we are not in truth concerned with rights in land units owned by another.[55] The task in this context is, then, one of specifying rules for objects of property rights that can move about autonomously and must be fed and watered.

Often, the law is concerned with the finding of animals owned by another and the appropriation of ownerless animals. Art. 5:8(3) Netherlands Civil Code, for example, obliges the local mayor to attempt to sell an animal for two weeks following its finding and, if necessary, to have it slaughtered. Art. 1323 Portuguese Civil Code is concerned with the acquisition of ownership in animals that have wandered off. The finder generally acquires ownership one year from the date that he notified his find under Art. 1323 Portuguese Civil Code.[56] Under Art. 1125(2) Portuguese Civil Code, the partner of a so-called cattle breeding community (*parceiro pensador*) has protection of possession, even against the owner of an animal (*parceiro proprietário*) (Art. 1276 Portuguese Civil Code and following), in the case that the partner is hindered in his right to use (*utilização*) the animal. Art. 465 Spanish Civil Code engages at length with the conditions on which the possession of an animal is established. It is also common to find that ownership of certain types of animal is only permitted to zoological gardens and animal shelters (e.g. Art. 21 Bulgarian Statute on Animal Protection: Apes and Wild

land unit under Art. 524 French Civil Code, they become immoveable goods. Likewise, animals which their owner has transferred by way of lease are also considered immoveable under Art. 522 French Civil Code. This lasts for the length of time that the animals remain on the land unit due to the lease.

[54] *Antoine*, Rapport sur le régime juridique de l'animal, p. 29 suggested for France, in a report to the ministry of justice, to remove animals from the category of goods altogether and to classify them independently. This new category would not derive from the term *bien appropriable*, which may be acquired, but the term *être animé et sensible*. Alternatively, she suggested to introduce the term 'protected good' into property law, which would not be concerned with the protection of property, but instead with the interests of the animal.

[55] Apart from the aforementioned hunting law, this includes, e.g. the right of the owner of a swarm of bees, when engaged in their pursuit, to enter property which he does not own (e.g. § 962 German Civil Code; Art. 612 Spanish Civil Code; Art. 182 § 1 sentence 2 Polish Civil Code; Art. 1322(1) Portuguese Civil Code, and § 1014(1) Czech Civil Code). He is in need of this right in order to prevent the imminent loss of property if he does not pursue (§ 961 German Civil Code, Art. 612 sentence 3 Spanish Civil Code, Art. 182 § 1 sentence 1 Polish Civil Code; Art. 1322(2) Portuguese Civil Code).

[56] von Bar (*-de Seabra and Xavier*), Sachenrecht in Europa III, Portugal, p. 360. Art. 1323(4) Civil Code furnishes the finder with a retention right over the find, which is interpreted by Portuguese scholarship as a real security right (e.g. *Menezes Leitão*, Direitos reais[2], p. 473).

Cats). Frequently, bees play a special role (e.g. Art. 612 Spanish Civil Code; §§ 961–964 German Civil Code), and the ownership analysis in the case of mixing swarms is dealt with affectionately (§§ 963 and 964 German Civil Code; § 1014 Czech Civil Code). Occasionally, something analogous is found for doves, rabbits, and fish (Art. 613 Spanish Civil Code).

4. Money, Money Units, and Money Tokens

'Money' is an ambiguous term. One should distinguish not only between cash money, on the one hand, and 'book money' [*Buchgeld*], on the other,[57] but also between money, money units, and money tokens. In the case of book money (also called 'account money'), we are concerned neither with money nor with a physical object; the same counts for the fashionable appearance of so-called 'virtual money'. Book money is merely another word for a claim, typically a claim against a financial institution. This claim is directed towards the payment of money units or other units of value, but is not itself money.[58] With such a claim (i.e. book 'money'), one is admittedly able to make payments, depending on the agreement of the parties and the facts of the individual case, but that on its own does not create the quality of money. Quite apart from that, it has neither a physical substrate nor any commodity value of its own.[59] In more than a few European legal systems, it is no 'thing' for this reason alone. Cash, on the other hand, does not raise such questions. Banknotes and coins are objects with a spatial dimension and, as such, they are unproblematically real things capable of being owned. Banknotes and coins which are not (or are not any longer) legal tender display no special characteristics in comparison to other corporeal objects. Their transfer, and the 6.10

[57] *Larroumet*, Les biens[5], p. 7 no. 6 (Only state money [*monnaie étatique*], which is materialized through a coin or bank note, may be subject to a property right over the coin or bank note. This does not, however, apply to book money [*monnaie scripturale*]. Book money is merely the acknowledgement of a claim).

[58] Administrative Court Warsaw 30 April 2009, III SA/Wa 106/09, Lex-No. 508560 correctly emphasizes that while money tokens (coins and bank notes) have a physical existence and are thus similar to things, their value derives from their role as a means of payment. Money measures value. By contrast, 'bank money' is composed only of the right to make a certain sum of money accessible to the bearer. Bank money as a thing does not exist. STJ 13 January 2010, Processo 76/09.5YFLSB interprets the booking of an incoming transfer of money to a bank client's account as *depósito irregular* (Art. 1205 Portuguese Civil Code). The bank must therefore provide the sum in question to the account holder, even if the account was emptied by a fraudster. See also *Foley v Hill* (1848) 2 HL Cas 28, 9 ER 1002. The situation is more complicated in Spain, which acknowledges a regular pledge over titles, values and money (*dinero*) (TS 27 December 1985, RAJ 1985 n. 6654 p. 5690). *O'Callaghan Muñoz*, Compendio de derecho civil III[5], pp. 318–19 explains this using a peculiarity of money, which is such that its restitution does not cover the same amount in cash, merely its value. The irregular pledge (*prenda irregular*), which is often created as a result of rent deposits (*fianza arrendaticia*), is not a real right (*Díez-Picazo and Gullón*, Sistema de Derecho Civil III(2)[8], p. 144).

[59] From this follows, *inter alia*, that if too much is paid or if the payment is made to the wrong creditor, this stems from the law of obligations (which means, as a rule, unjust enrichment), and must be compensated accordingly (see for Hungary *Menyhárd*, Dologi jog[2], p. 49 and BH 1997/87). In Belgium and France, where some authors believe the vindication of claims is possible, there exists a discussion about the vindication of book money; however, these doctrines did not prevail (also *Beysen*, Die Kondiktion oder die Vindikation von Geld). However, in Austria judicial decisions have even recognized the vindication of book money. The OGH broadly equates cash and book money in the context of vindication by accepting the so-called 'quantity vindication' [*Quantitätsvindikation*], at least in cases in which cash has been converted to book money by way of payment into a (separated) account (OGH 10 April 1997, SZ 70/63; fundamentally as early as OGH 18 December 1929, SZ 10/356).

protection of ownership in them, follows the normal rules for physical moveable objects.[60] However, banknotes and coins imbued by law with the quality of a general medium of payment between all citizens (and not only within a bilateral relationship of debtor and creditor, as is the case with book money), can be equiparated with physical objects by express stipulation,[61] but not in every legal relation.[62] This is because they are units of money that are generally valid, which is to say that they direct *everyone* towards the abstraction of 'money'.[63] As real objects of external reality they have, as all banknotes and coins, their own commodity value; this can rise and fall. Money tokens of the types just named, however, also represent (and in fact first and foremost represent) a payment value that is independent of their commodity value, that remains constant and generally valid—the value of the money unit. The money unit to which money tokens refer, however, is emphatically not a commodity;[64] it is not even a fitting object of property rights. Units of value cannot be assigned to the exclusive use of any person. Every second, prices for goods and services are set, and such prices cannot be monopolized or 'transferred' in a property law relevant sense. It is not possible to acquire ownership in the value or price of '€100' (for example), with a property right effective *erga omnes*, such that no-one else can market his goods or services for this price without permission. In fact, one might even have to question the nature of money (NB: not of money units) as an object and therefore as an object of legal transaction. As the medium of exchange and measure of value, the transmission belt of the national economy as it were, money is created by public law and as a public good; money can also be altered, and even removed from the world, by force of law. That, however, affects only the aggregate sum of money and the legal concept of money.[65] Naturally, legal systems allow

[60] *Håstad*, Sakrätt[6], p. 249.

[61] Money (*pengar*) in the sense of money tokens is moveable property (*lös egendom*) in Swedish law (*Hessler*, Allmän sakrätt, p. 19). It is transferred and protected here, as everywhere, according to the ordinary provisions governing corporeal moveable things. In German law, BGH 14 July 2013, WM 2013 p. 1698 considered collectors' coins that are not suitable or intended for use as currency is only 'money' in the sense of § 935 Sentence 2 German Civil Code when they are recognized as an official means of payment. Accordingly, it is not possible to acquire ownership over stolen coins of this type in good faith under German law. They differ in this way from ordinary means of payment.

[62] This is different, for example, in criminal law, in which the offence of theft does not differentiate between the theft of real money tokens and the theft of other coins (e.g. Areopag 2222/2009, *NoB* 58 [2010] p. 1246: Theft of a gold coin worth 20,000 Euro).

[63] Money is today only an *abstractum* because the times are long gone in which coins as a means of payment were produced from precious metals. The purchasing power even of coins rests solely on the fact that they are recognized by the legal order, and no longer on the fact that the concrete piece of metal contained value (which could be realized, e.g. by smelting). The times are also past in which the central bank of a country was obliged to exchange the money units it issued for gold. Since the dissolution of the Bretton Woods system, this is true even of the US dollar. Since then, money only derives its value from the legal system and from the socio-political system in which it operates.

[64] e.g. sec. 14(1) Torts (Interference with Goods) Act 1977 and *Hessler*, Allmän sakrätt, p. 475 with reference to *Lag om handel med lösören, som köparen låter i säljarens vård kvarbliva* (1845:50) § 1. See also Administrative Court Katowice 15 April 2003, I SA/Ka 629/02, Lex-No. 102350 (The payment of money is not in itself a process which must be subject to sales tax. Under Art. 45 Polish Civil Code, only corporeal objects are 'things'. Money and securities must be distinct from this, as the value of money is not determined by trade, but by law. Cash is thus not a thing *sensu stricto* and therefore not a 'good' in the sense of the sales tax law).

[65] *Díez-Picazo and Gullón*, Sistema de Derecho Civil I[12], p. 393 rightly point out that money is merely a *concepto jurídico*. The concept of money (*dinero*) is embodied in coins (*moneda*) and bank notes (*papel moneda o billetes*). The latter are moveable and fungible things. A similar position is taken by Radwański and Safjan (-*Katner*), System Prawa Prywatnego I, p. 1218 no. 117 (money units must be distinguished from money tokens. Money units are immaterial and merely represent a value). In France, all authors emphasize that money is a mere instrument of

their subjects to divide the abstraction that is money into quantitatively certain money units; that is, after all, the very point of money as a creature of law. Money units become objects in this manner, and at the same time become objects of legal transaction. Through a contractual promise a claim arises, and this claim is directed to the creation of value denominated in the named money unit. It is a little like the obligation to deliver an object that the obligee, at the moment of promising, does not yet have. The point of reference of the contract is the possession of a monetary value, the object of the claim created by the contract is the creation of this monetary value, and the means of its creation are money tokens (or, in the case that the parties are satisfied with book money, the creation of a claim against a bank for the same monetary value). 'Money' *per se* can neither be sold, nor swapped, nor gifted. In the moment, however, in which it is determined, either as a sum or as a fraction ('X to receive half of my money'), or becomes determinable as such, an object of legal transaction arises in the relevant money unit or unit of value. What does not arise, however, is any *thing*, because even the money unit concretized in this manner remains a mere value and because values are not capable of being monopolized through the mechanisms of property law. They can be used by all the world and created, again and again, anew.

'Money' is, accordingly, not even an object; money units are objects of legal transaction; **6.11**
book money is only a fitting object of property rights insofar as claims are such; and only money *tokens* can be said to be fitting objects of ownership without qualification.[66] When a rule of private law speaks of 'money', what is generally meant is precisely this money token; only in the commercial and accounting context can the word 'money' also, sometimes, include book money. That, however, changes nothing of the fact that money and money units are not fitting objects of subjective property rights. An accounting unit and unit of value can be used by all subjects of a legal system, irrespective of whether it lacks a money token entirely (like the earlier European Currency Unit) or, as in the ordinary case, also takes material form of money tokens. If a given money unit is to be allotted to a person for his exclusive use, it is only through property law that this can be achieved, and for the purposes of property law everything depends on an

measurement (*instrument d'évaluation*) (e.g. *Larroumet*, Les biens[5], p. 8 no. 7; *Terré and Simler*, Les biens[8], p. 16 no. 12, and *Jourdain*, Les biens, p. 5 no. 3). Money enables the designation of rights or things as *biens*, but is not itself one of these (*Mathieu-Izorche*, Les biens, p. 30 no. 79).

[66] This would only be different if one were of the opinion that the so-called book money received a material element sufficient to qualify it as a corporeal good by virtue of the storage process on the respective data storage device (a position taken by *Libchaber*, Recherches sur la monnaie en droit privé, pp. 78–80 nos 90–93, and *Vanbelle*, Algemeen Juridisch Tijdschrift—Dossier Nr. 7, 1994–95, pp. 65–7 nos 21–31). However, this is not the case. While it is true that money transfers (being *instruments monétaires*) create money units (*unités monétaires*), a mere sequence of numbers on a piece of paper can no more be considered a material good which can be owned than the electric voltage on a computer. Both of these impart information, but neither are allocated to one person for their unique use. A bank account is, furthermore, not a data storage device as it lacks any physical reality; it is not possible to reclaim and transfer it (*Libchaber* op. cit. takes a contrary position). Only the claim for access to the denoted money unit can be transferred. The possibility of vindicating book money is also denied by French judicial opinion. The main significance of this is in insolvency law (Cass. 4 February 2003, JCP E 2003 n. 1363 p. 1536, note by *Robine* and Cass. civ, 22 May 2013, Bull. civ. 2013, IV, p. 99 no. 87 [claims of airlines against a bankrupt travel agent arising from the sale of flight licenses; no *action en revendication* concerning the money]).

appropriate point of reference for that person's monopoly rights. Claims are sufficient to this purpose only to a qualified extent, and by no means everywhere. Otherwise, money units must be embodied in some way, such that the real object can satisfy the legal requirements for a money token.[67] Money units become visible through money tokens, but money, money units, and money tokens are not identical.[68]

6.12 It is often said that 'money' belongs to the category of fungible,[69] consumable,[70] and even divisible things.[71] For the purposes of property law, such observations have barely any importance; they rather confuse more than they explain. It is often unclear what exactly is meant by 'money' in such statements.[72] Money is only divisible as an abstract unit of value, but an abstract unit of value is no thing. Consumability is a property that unites money tokens and money units, but cannot be attributed to 'money' itself. And the characterization of money as fungible is anyway not something of importance for the rules of property law *per se*;[73] this characterization remains for property law, even where 'money' is taken to mean money tokens,[74] without any real consequences. Even someone who takes a loan of a sum of money in cash, and promises thereby to repay

[67] Counterfeit money is not even a money token. Whether genuine banknotes that are later manipulated remain money tokens or become invalid is, to use a Continental turn of phrase, a matter of public law. Under the common law, a material alteration of a banknote causes it to lose its validity as the basis of a claim against the Bank of England (*Suffel v Bank of England* (1882) 9 QB 555 (CA) [change to the serial number]). Today, the same rule is found for banknotes as a special class in sec. 64(1) Bills of Exchange Act 1882. Special provisions relating to the Bank of England, however, have priority under sec. 97(3)(c). The alteration of banknotes is prohibited (sec. 12 Currency and Banknotes Act 1928).

[68] The distinction between money units and money tokens cannot be overcome by the fact that banknotes are, themselves, securities (e.g. promissory notes). True, in the case of securities, the recorded claim becomes a material part of the real object. Banknotes, however, do not embody any claim, not even a claim against the state. The relevant central bank must, it is true, replace an old banknote with a new one, but nothing more. It is not, in other words, a promise that has been transmuted into a thing (as in the case of a security). Rather, one has something like a debt security without a debt. A banknote has only the form, but not the content, of a debt security. Consistently with this fact (and with emphasis on the fact that nothing in the positive law depends on the characterization), *Bridge*, Personal Property Law[3], p. 10 characterizes money tokens as *choses in possession*, not *choses in action*.

[69] e.g. *Švestka and Dvořák*, Občanské právo hmotné[5], p. 243; *Torrente and Schlesinger*, Manuale di diritto privato[19], p. 175; *Bellante*, La caparra, p. 27 fn. 39; Cass. 15 July 1994, n. 6686, Giur. it. 1995, I, 1, p. 576; Staudinger (-*Jickeli and Stieper*), BGB (2004), § 91 no. 6; *Larroumet*, Les biens[5], p. 7 no. 6; *Carbonnier*, Droit civil II, p. 1571 no. 696; Bercovitz Rodríguez-Cano (-*Badenas Carpio*), Comentarios al Código Civil[2], p. 500 (money is the typical example of a fungible thing in Spain); *Torrente and Schlesinger* op. cit. p. 176; *Branca and Alpa*, Istituzioni di diritto privato[7], p. 157; *Pacilio*, Proprietà e diritti reali, p. 18, as well as *Pires de Lima and Antunes Varela*, Código Civil Anotado I[4], note. 1 to Art. 207 p. 201 (money is usually fungible, however it can be non-fungible, e.g. in the context of an exhibition of coins and banknotes). *Menezes Cordeiro*, Tratado de direito civil I(2)[2], pp. 149–50 by contrast differentiates between fungible things (*coisas fungíveis*; Art. 207 Portuguese Civil Code) and representative things (*coisas representativas*). Money is a representative thing, a thing which represents a value above its own material value, according to 'socio-juridical convention'.

[70] *Eliáš et al.*, Občanský zákoník. Velký akademický komentář I, § 1-487 p. 481; *Torrente and Schlesinger* op. cit. p. 176; MünchKomm (-*Holch*), BGB I(1)[5], § 92 no. 2; *Bercovitz Rodríguez-Cano* op. cit.; TS 14 November 1950, RAJ 1950 no. 1767 p. 1018); *Malaurie and Aynès*, Les biens[4], p. 46 no. 152 (money can only be consumed by spending it).

[71] *Thus Fiala and Kindl*, Občanské právo hmotné[2], p. 163.

[72] *Papasteriou*, Empragmato Dikaio I, pp. 193–5 nos 18–21 and *Spyridakis*, Epitomo Nomikó Lexikó, pp. 377–8 urge a distinction between money in the wider sense and money in the narrow sense. Money in the wider sense describes all fungible things which are used to barter and as a measurement and carrier of value. This includes currency, bank cheques, foreign money, banknotes and book money. Money in the narrow sense describes the coins and banknotes which function as legal tender in a given country.

[73] The law occasionally makes explicit reference only to the quality of money as a consumable thing. See e.g. Art. 1238 French Civil Code.

[74] However, not even this reduction to money tokens makes sense. Fungible things readily include coins which are not or no longer money tokens, but which are of interest to collectors by virtue of their particular series.

the debt in the same banknotes and coins and to leave them untouched in the meantime, is allowed to repay the borrowed sum in other banknotes and coins.[75] In contrast, someone who wrongfully takes a money token (e.g. a banknote), remains in possession and has not mixed it with other banknotes, must in principle deliver exactly that banknote. He cannot satisfy the obligation to deliver the other's property through the tender of other banknotes, because in such a context there is no regime analogous to the law of lending.[76] This becomes practically relevant when the claimant has a special interest in the delivery of some particular money token.[77] One example might be coins minted in a special edition that are primarily of interest to collectors, whose commercial value far exceeds their face value as legal tender, and whose inclusion in a collection might raise the value of the collection as a whole. Other cases are, however, conceivable in which a special interest in the delivery of an individual banknote might arise,[78] and even the possession of everyday coins, as corporeal things, is protected by property law, for example when they are required in certain denominations for the operation of a vending machine or a boom gate system.

Money tokens, on the other hand, stand in service of money and the exchange value of its units. Property law typically reacts to money tokens in that it governs the acquisition of ownership in money tokens with a more permissive regime than that which governs the acquisition of ownership in ordinary real things. This regime accords the existing **6.13**

[75] e.g. Art. 1893 French Civil Code; Art. 1814 Italian Civil Code and Art. 1753 Spanish Civil Code. Art. 1142 Portuguese Civil Code equates money given as loan with other fungible things. This is principally different with regard to safekeeping, including the safekeeping of money tokens (Cass. civ. 13 November 2001, JCP E 2002 no. 641 p. 666, note by *Barrière*; a theory of vindication of money units is not supported by this decision; *Martin*, D. 2002 pp. 3279, 3280 appears to hold a different view). Swedish HD 13 December 1989, NJA 1989 p. 768 concerned an unauthorized poker game. Several interested players had given the organizer money in cash. The organizer had stored this money separately. Had this game been conducted, the money would have been given to the winner. The money was (temporarily) recovered by the police prior to the start of the game. During this period of time, one of B's creditors was paid from this cash pursuant to a claim. The court ruled in favour of the aspiring players. They had not lost their separation right, as the money had been kept separately by B. This separation right could be enforced with regard to creditors of B, a bank.

[76] *Menyhárd*, Dologi jog^2, pp. 58–9; *Švestka/Spáčil/Škárová/Humák*, Občanský zákoník I^2, p. 692 (banknotes, in any event, which can be defined by identifying features, can be vindicated). Vindication of banknotes is possible under Art. 2279(3) Belgian Civil Code, under the condition that the possessor acts in bad faith and that the owner can prove his ownership right over the individual banknotes, for example because he noted the serial numbers of each respective banknote. Arrondissementsrechtbank Antwerp 23 January 1990, R.W. 1989–1990 p. 1268 dismissed a claim for vindication aimed at the restitution of 173 confiscated banknotes, as the plaintiff could not prove his claim. The identification of the banknotes based only on their amount (30 5,000 BEF notes and 143 1,000 BEF notes) was not deemed sufficient. However, Commercial Court Liège 9 April 1960, Jur. Liège 1959–1960 p. 292 upheld an *action en revendication* which was aimed at the restitution of money in cash, which had been kept in an envelope with a name written on it. The envelope had been found in the insolvency estate of a money changer. § 1041(2) Czech Civil Code and § 371 Austrian Civil Code correspond to this in their essential features. See also Czech Supreme Court 13 June 1923, Rv I 137/23, published in Vážný (ed.), Rozhodnutí nejvyššího soudu československé republiky ve věcech občanských V, no. 2720, and Swedish HD 27 May 1987, NJA 1987 p. 517 (cash in a cardboard box).

[77] An English court would also be able to order restitution of the money token. However, this would not be supported by sec. 3(2)(a) Torts (Interference with Goods) Act 1977 (order for delivery). This is because sec. 14(1) explicitly excludes money from the term 'goods'.

[78] Even banknotes which are still legal tender can, in some cases, have a high collector's value. They could carry handwritten notes of a celebrated public figure, they could be difficult to acquire within the borders of the respective country, etc. *Goode*, Commercial Law^3, p. 451 n. 7 while referencing a publication in *The Times* from 9 March 1983, gives the example of a £1,000 banknote, issued in 1933, which was sold on 8 March 1983 for £6,800, despite still only allowing the holder to withdraw the nominal amount from the Bank of England.

interest of the current owner less weight than it accords the acquisitive interest of the recipient. This is evident from the numerous provisions that govern the good faith acquisition of money tokens from a transferor without title.[79]

Under § 117(1) Hungarian Civil Code [1959], the fundamental principle was that the right of ownership could only be acquired from the owner of a thing. Ownership could be acquired in good faith from a non-owner in commercial transactions (§ 118(1) Hungarian Civil Code [1959]) and from persons entrusted with a thing by the owner (§ 118(2) Hungarian Civil Code). Section 119 Hungarian Civil Code [1959], however, provided that 'the transferee of money or bearer securities becomes their owner, [even] where the transferor was not their owner'. This provision totally excluded the '*nemo dat*' rule that no-one can transfer more rights than he himself has; ownership in money tokens was even acquired when the transferee was *mala fides* in respect of the legal position of the transferor.[80] Section 5:39(2) and (3) Hungarian Civil Code [2014] have retained the old rule, but have defined when a transaction occurs in 'commerce'. German law does not go quite so far as Hungarian law in this regard. A transferee who has notice or is grossly negligent in failing to notice that the money tokens he is receiving do not belong to the transferor does not acquire ownership in them. However, the origin of coins cannot, as a rule, be determined at all, and the origin of banknotes only in highly exceptional circumstances. Section 935(2) German Civil Code immediately excludes 'money' (what is meant is money *tokens*) from the general bar in § 935(1) German Civil Code to the good faith acquisition of objects that left the possession of their owner unintentionally. This leads, in most cases, to the same result as the Hungarian rule. One must have actually observed the theft of money to be disqualified from acquiring ownership.[81] The rules in § 935(2) German Civil Code reflect, in all relevant senses, the rule in § 95(3) Sentence 3 Estonian LPA, Art. 169 § 2 Sentence 2 Polish Civil Code,

[79] These special provisions are typically only not necessary in countries (such as Italy, Arts 1153 and 1154 Italian Civil Code) in which stolen things can be acquired in good faith (meaning without knowledge of the theft and the lack of ownership of the transferor). In these cases, the good faith acquisition of money tokens is subject to the same rules as the good faith acquisition of other real things (*Ascarelli*, Obbligazioni Pecuniarie, p. 16). While *Mengoni*, Gli acquisti a non domino[3], p. 88 attempted to limit the possibility of good faith acquisitions of stolen things to objects which, like cash, must circulate quickly and securely, this argumentation could not prevail in the face of the text of the Italian Civil Code. There are also no special provisions for cash in Sweden. The conditions for an acquisition with an effect against third parties (especially the conditions for *tradition*: see *Håstad*, Sakrätt[6], p. 171) are determined *e contrario* from § 1 *Lag om handel med lösören, som köparen låter i säljarens vård kvarbliva* (LkL) (1845:50 p. 1) (*Henriksson*, Sakrättsliga moment och deras ekonomiska konsekvenser, p. 71). § 2 Lag (1936:83) *angående vissa utfästelser om gåva* maintains the requirement of transfer for gifts within the meaning of property law.

[80] This at least (and with further references) according to Faber and Lurger (-*Szilágyi*), National Reports III, Hungary, pp. 616–17.

[81] If the object in question is a collector's item, which is only legal tender 'by the way', then the view that the basic principle of § 935(1) German Civil Code should be applied is the correct one. Such coins are not stolen from their owner because they represent money units, but because they themselves are valuable (like jewellery, silver, or gold) (correctly BGH 14 June 2013, WM 2013 p. 1698). Running counter to this, albeit in the context of the rules of free movement of goods, is the judgment of the CJEU of 23 November 1978, Rs. 7/78 (*Thompson*), NJW 1979 p. 485. The CJEU ruled that silver coins are always to be declared legal tender, not goods, if they are legal tender in a member state. The same applies to *Krugerrand* gold coins. While it is not quite clear whether these are legal tender in South Africa, they are treated as such by most member states and are thus to be classified as such in EU law.

Art. 3:86(3)(b) Netherlands Civil Code, and Art. 1039 Sentence 1 Greek Civil Code.[82] Under Art. 78(1) Bulgarian Property Law Statute, and Art. 464(1) Spanish Civil Code, the good faith acquirer of moveable goods is deemed to occupy the same legal position as a *título* (title-holder), but one who lost such a good or had it taken from him unlawfully can demand delivery from anyone in possession. Astonishingly, no exemption is found here for money. Matters are similar under Art. 2276 French Civil Code. Art. 2279(3) Belgian Civil Code, on the other hand, excludes the *vindication* of stolen banknotes from a good faith acquirer expressly, and a similar provision is found in § 371 Austrian Civil Code. Section 367 Austrian Civil Code provides for good faith acquisition of real things in only three cases (public auction, acquisition from an authorized commercial agent, and acquisition for value from a person entrusted with the thing by its owner). But § 371 provides that money tokens (putting the case of comingling to one side) can become the property of a good faith acquirer, even when the money tokens were unintentionally lost by their true owner.[83]

Special rules for cash are found in other areas of property law. However, none of them have the goal of enhancing the currency of money tokens; they are, therefore, only phenotypically part of 'the law of property in money'. Parts of the law of finding fall in this category. Arts 184 and 187 Polish Civil Code, for example, generally serve to vest ownership of lost and found cash in the state. Art. 5:9 Netherlands Civil Code suggests the reason for this sort of policy. 'Where a found object given to the Municipality for safe keeping is cash, the Municipality is only obligated to pay out an equal amount to the one entitled to claim it.' The point of this is to enable the municipal authority to deposit the cash into a bank account; the authority would otherwise have to secure, at its expense, the stock of lost and found banknotes on some premises.[84] 'Money' also crops up occasionally in the definitions of a 'trove' (e.g. in Art. 352 Spanish Civil Code). In Austria, an ordinary pledge can be created over cash, such that specific banknotes are handed over and that the self-same banknotes have to be delivered on the discharge of the debt.[85] However, a so-called 'sum' or 'aggregate' pledge [*Summenpfand* or *Sammelpfand*] can also be created, in which the pledgee must hold the relevant money tokens only according to their value; the pledgor retains *pro rata* ownership in them. In the case of an irregular pledge (*pignus irregularis*: see e.g. Art. 1851 Italian Civil Code), the pledgor is only entitled to payment of an appropriate sum; the transaction is, somewhat artificially, couched as one in which the demand for payment of the pledged sum 6.14

[82] 'Money' in the sense of this provision is domestic as well as foreign money tokens, whether they are banknotes or coins. By contrast, coins and banknotes which are no longer legal tender are not money (*Triantos*, AK, Art. 1039 p. 1262 no. 2).

[83] Klang (-*Leupold*), ABGB[3], § 371 no. 33.

[84] If the finder does not deposit cash with the municipal authority, but keeps it in order to discover the owner himself, the decision depends on the individual case. If the found property is a wallet containing a low sum of money, the finder is obligated to keep and give out the wallet with the specific banknotes. Greater amounts of cash can require the finder, in accordance with the requirement to keep it safe, to deposit the money with a bank (Nieuwenhuis/Stolker/Valk [-*Stolker*], BW[6], Art. 5:9 no. 1).

[85] For more details regarding this and the following see *Gschnitzer/Faistenberger/Barta/Call/Eccher*, Sachenrecht[2], p. 195.

were itself pledged,[86] such that the pledgee can get satisfaction by setting off this demand. In contrast, Art. 347 Spanish Civil Code only provides a rule of interpretation. It provides: 'When in any sale, legacy, gift or other disposition in which there is a reference to moveable or immoveable property, possession or ownership thereof should be transferred with everything located therein', but 'any cash, securities, credits, and shares whose documents' are deemed not, without express intention, to be so transferred. The rules governing ownership of confused things are also unrelated to the currency of money tokens. These provisions are, it is true, generally applicable to money tokens, but they present a more general problem of categorization that extends far beyond money tokens—one that is, in the last instance, a purely technical problem. The application of the general rules governing confusion to cash is, however, often irritatingly complicated. It concerns the question of who should be seen as the owner of banknotes and coins that have been added to a quantity of cash that was already aggregated by another. This type of dealing does not affect the ownership position of the new money tokens in the case that they became the property of the owner of the existing stock of money tokens (e.g. if he acquired ownership of them before depositing them in the cash register),[87] or in the case that the new money tokens added to an existing stock can still be identified (e.g. because they are enclosed in a marked envelope, or because they are the only banknotes of that type in the cash register at the time).[88] In all other cases, however, a change does occur in the ownership constellation, and in many cases this change does not only affect the new money tokens but also the existing stock. A great variety of scenarios is conceivable. A child might mistakenly deposit a number of different coins in the piggy bank of a friend; a thief might hide a stolen €50 note in a box together with some of his own, or together with others that he stole from third parties, or he might slip the stolen banknote secretly into his girlfriend's wallet. He might simply, over time, combine thousands of stolen banknotes with his own stock of cash. A cashier might find a banknote lost by a supermarket customer and, without putting it in an envelope, simply add it to the notes in the cash register.

6.15 Under § 948 German Civil Code, the rules that govern the connection [*Verbindung*] of moveable goods are to be applied analogously when 'moveable things are mixed [*vermischt*] or combined [*vermengt*]'. Under § 947(1) German Civil Code, on the other hand, when moveable things of such a type are joined such that 'they become components of a single thing', the erstwhile owners of the components become the co-owners of the new thing; 'their shares are to be determined by reference to the proportional value of the things at the point of their combination'. When, however, one of those things

[86] OGH 24 April 1923, SZ 5/100.

[87] This was possibly overlooked by Tribunale Cagliari 15 March 1993, Riv. giur. Sarda 1994 p. 346 (the court states that the bank acquires ownership of the money which an account holder pays into his account in cash according to Art. 939 Italian Civil Code. However, in case of doubt in these cases, ownership of the money is already transferred transactionally, not as a consequence of comingling with the bank's cash reserves).

[88] Example: Upon leaving the church, an excited groom mistakenly places a €500 note, instead of a 50 Euro note, into the collection box. As long as there is not a second €500note in the collection box, the groom can take it back because it has not yet comingled with the rest of the money in the box.

is properly seen as the 'principal thing', the owner of that object becomes the sole owner of the new thing under § 947(2) German Civil Code. What this entails for cash is not completely clear; however, it seems to be generally accepted *that* these provisions also apply to money tokens.[89] In the first instance, one would have to investigate what is to be regarded as the relevant quantity. If only one or more banknotes or coins of the same value have been mixed (one or more €50 banknotes, one or more €2 coins) the 'mixture' would only occur in respect of banknotes and coins of this value; only in the case that a mixture of money tokens of different denominations are mixed would the whole stock of cash be regarded as 'connected' [*verbunden*].[90] The next question that would arise is whether there is a 'principal thing'. This would only be the case in highly exceptional circumstances in the case of cash—for example, in the case of a cash register or in the case that the values in question are very different. (However, in such a case one can probably also deny that anything was meaningful 'mixed' in the first place.)[91] In general, the outcome of such cases is not sole ownership but co-ownership. What *exactly* is the point of reference for the co-owners' rights, however, remains to be determined. The correct view is that we are dealing with co-ownership of each individual banknote and coin (and not with co-ownership of the whole 'aggregate quantity', e.g. the contents of the cash register). Every co-owner can thus avail himself of every remedy provided by property law to protect his interests in every banknote and coin against third parties. For the relations between the co-owners, on the other hand, property law itself is largely meaningless; the community of co-owners [*Miteigentümergemeinschaft*] must be dissolved (§ 749 German Civil Code) and the combined goods must be divided according to the provisions in § 752 German Civil Code. What arises is thus an obligational claim against the party in possession of the money tokens for the delivery of however many units of value (e.g. 'euros') make up the owner's share—represented, as usual, in money tokens denominated in that money unit. The original sole ownership of the combined money tokens thus extinguishes upon their admixture, and co-ownership extinguishes on their division. In Austrian law, it follows from § 371 Austrian Civil Code that ownership of money tokens can be acquired *ex lege* as a result of combination [*Vermengung*].

[89] Judicial opinion from the superior courts, however, is still lacking; BGH 14 January 1993, NJW 1993 p. 535 deals with *Krugerrands* and other gold coins.

[90] It is, however, contentious what happens in case of doubt regarding the composition or the number of the money tokens added to the stock. BGH 3 June 1958, NJW 1958 p. 1534 note *Hoche* assumes (albeit not in relation to money tokens—the court was concerned with metal bars) that co-ownership should not be prevented from arising in the aggregate because of doubts concerning the respective shares. That is only a question of proof and of burden of proof. However, § 742 German Civil Code (presumption of equal shares per head) is thought not to apply. It is an open question whether a minimum sum is certain enough (i.e. 'there was at least €200 in my wallet before the theft'), and whether the burden of proof can be allocated differently depending on whether the party in possession of the aggregate has acted in good or bad faith.

[91] This is according to an early decision of the Supreme Court of the First Czech Republic of 4 October 1921, Rv I 415/21 (under § 371 Austrian Civil Code), reported in Vážný (ed.), Rozhodnutí nejvyššího soudu československé republiky ve věcech občanských III, no. 1215, also in *Rouček Sedláček, et al.*, Komentář k československému obecnému zákoníku občanskému a občanské právo platné na Slovensku a v Podkarpatské Rusi II, p. 340) ('One cannot speak of the mixture of money in the sense of § 371 Austrian Civil Code, when a person in possession of a small sum (50 CZK) admixes a large sum (12,200 CZK), especially not when the latter sum was composed of banknotes with a higher individual face value than the total value of the money tokens first in possession of that person.' His own 50 CZK were so small in relation to the aggregated value that the cash of the other party was still seen as separated from it. However, it was also the case that only one 50 CZK note was found in the whole stock of cash).

The relationship between this provision and the general rule § 415 Austrian Civil Code is, however, again not completely clear.[92] It is clear that, as a rule, co-ownership arises. But judicial decisions on the combination of money tokens appears to be completely absent in Austria; the Austrian Supreme Court has only dealt with the question of the so-called 'quantitative vindication' [*Quantitätsvindikation*] in the case of the combination of cash and book money. Co-ownership in the 'whole' arises under Art. 193 § 1 Polish Civil Code and under § 5:66(1) Hungarian Civil Code [2014] (earlier § 134 Hungarian Civil Code [1959]); only when one of the things now joined together has a significantly higher value than the others do the things of lesser value become component parts of the more valuable thing (Art. 193 § 2 Polish Civil Code). The dissolution of the community of ownership follows largely similar rules to those found in German law (Art. 210 Polish Civil Code; §§ 5:83 and 5:84(1)–(4) Hungarian Civil Code [2014], earlier §§ 147 and 148 Hungarian Civil Code [1959]). Under Art. 56 Slovenian Civil Code, the same rules govern combination and the unification of moveables into a new thing (Art. 55 Slovenian Civil Code). Co-ownership arises in the combined stock, provided that none of the erstwhile things is to be seen as a 'main' thing; if such is the case, the owner of *that* thing becomes owner of the new thing created through combination (Art. 55 Slovenian Civil Code). Art. 939 Italian Civil Code provides the point of departure for Italian law. Under Art. 939(1) Italian Civil Code, one remains the owner of his things so long as they can be separated from the 'unified whole' without any material damage; otherwise, community ownership arises in proportion to the value of each person's property.

> However, if something can be regarded as the principal thing or is of a much greater value than the others, even if it only serves to decorate them, the owner of the principal thing acquires property in all of them. (Art. 939(2) Italian Civil Code)

For example, imagine that someone has several sets of all the Euro coins currently in circulation, and that one of those sets came into the collection under mysterious circumstances. As a matter of the law of obligations, that would give rise only to a set-off of the face value of the coins. In the Netherlands, the legal consequences of the combination [*vermenging*] of money tokens is subject to Art. 5:15 and Art. 5:14 Netherlands Civil Code. Here, by way of contrast, arises a rule of common ownership. From its literal meaning, Art. 5:15 Netherlands Civil Code only applies to methods of mixture that lead to the creation of a single thing. But the provision is applied to money tokens that cannot be individualized in their current state as well. However, it is assumed (because a claim for the delivery almost always fails on procedural grounds by reason of the lack of certainty of the thing to be vindicated) that the person in whose hands the mixture occurs generally becomes the sole owner. Besides this, the requirements of legal certainty are said to militate for this result. Not only is the concept of 'delivery' said to be unclear in the context of cash. Further, the extent of the confusion is said to be unclear: is it only the money tokens in the person's wallet at the time, all the cash that the

[92] Schwimann and Kodek (-*Klicka and Reidlinger*), ABGB II^4, § 371 nos 1 and 5.

person later puts in his wallet, or all the cash that the person has generally?[93] Sole ownership in the person of the one mixing should, as a rule, also arise under Czech law[94] (§ 1079 Czech Civil Code [2014] however follows § 415 Austrian Civil Code and provides for co-ownership in shares), and the situation is the same according to current opinion in French law.[95]

[93] N.v.W., Parl. Geschiedenis V, p. 108.

[94] Švestka (-*Spáčil*), Občanský zákoník I[2], p.788. (In case of the mixture of another's money with one's one, the traditional point of departure was that the person mixing the money would become owner so long as the banknotes could not be identified by their serial numbers. Whoever lost ownership in this way would have an obligational claim to compensation.) From the perspective of criminal law, this could only have the consequence that a theft would occur in the case that the victim of a fraud resorted to self-help and took the appropriate sum from the possession of a fraudster; the defrauded party in such a situation was said to be taking another's property (Czech Supreme Court 18 February 1976, St 1/75, Sbírka soudních rozhodnutí a stanovisek 1976 no. 13).

[95] Cass. civ. 6 May 1930, p. 1930, I, p. 248 (the mixture of cash money leads to the loss of ownership; the erstwhile owner is left with a claim to compensation that has no special priority); Cass. 17 July 1929, p. 1929, I, p. 378; Cass. civ. 8 February 1928, p. 1928, I, p. 135. Also Cass. civ. 25 March 1997, *D.* 1997 p. 481, note by *Martin*; JCP E 1997, II n. 991 p. 199, note by *Pétel*, and CA Paris 14 October 1997, D. 1998 p. 91, note by *Larroumet*. Following this line of authority, Cass. civ. 10 May 2000, D. 2000 p. 277, note by *Lienhard* (the owner of a shop had promised to pay the income from a butchery in the shop, minus her wages, to a company on a weekly basis; she became insolvent, and there was held to be *revendication* in favour of the company because it was not owner of the money taken into the register).

VII
Normative Things with a Physical Substrate: Land Units

1. The Purpose of Forming Land Units

Next to real things, we find normative things. They do not exist by nature, rather, they are capable of being the point of reference of property rights in virtue of a legal system. Normative things can, in turn, be classified as (i) normative things with a physical substrate and (ii) purely normative things. There is currently no satisfactory pan-European term that can be used for either category. We will call the things that belong to the first category 'land units' (from German *Grundstück*, plural *Grundstücke*). We have to stipulate at the outset that neither the English of the common law, nor indeed the languages of many other legal systems, have a true equivalent for '*Grundstück*',[1] and that even those legal systems that use this term as a term of art give it a different meaning to the term as used in this book.[2] What appears to be of importance to us, in the first instance, is this: legal systems, when they create land units (more precisely: the entities that we call 'land units') create objects in landscapes that are capable of being owned. Although **7.1**

[1] 'Estate' would be a suitable word, but it no longer describes the *object* of rights in land, rather, those rights themselves. '*Grundstück*' could probably best be translated as 'tenement'. It has the advantage that, in contrast to 'estate' in its modern meaning, 'tenement' actually describes a thing (something that is 'held' from French *tenir*—not *how long* it is held). Today, however, the term is often (especially in Scotland) restricted to apartments. Besides, it is broader than the concept of *Grundstück* as we define it, because tenements (like 'hereditaments' and indeed '*Grundstücke*' as defined in German law under § 96 German Civil Code) also includes certain *rights* in land.

[2] Art. 46 § 1 Polish Civil Code defines land units [*Nieruchomości*] as 'parts of the earth's surface, which are the object of special property'. The existence of a land register is, therefore, not unconditionally necessary for the existence of a land unit. § 2(a) of the Czech Cadastral Statute No. 256/2013 distinguishes between 'land units' and 'parcels'. Only parcels can be transferred, that is, parcels of the surface or rooms which are recorded in the cadastre. A land unit, however, even when it is only a part of a parcel, can be leased and acquired through prescription (*Spáčil and Spáčil*, Přehled judikatury ve věcech občanskoprávních vztahů k pozemkům, p. 85). The possession of a part of a parcel (a 'land unit' in this terminological scheme) requires its real separation from the rest of the world, but such separation is also sufficient (a land unit must only 'show' itself: Nejvyšší soud České republiky 23 January 2002, 22 Cdo 96/2000, Soubor civilních rozhodnutí Nejvyššího soudu C 987, and Nejvyšší soud České republiky 30 April 2006, 22 Cdo 806/2006). The most neutral term in Austrian law is that of 'land' [*Land*]. A piece of *Land* becomes a *Grundstück* when it becomes part of a cadastral municipality with its own number in the boundary cadastre or land tax cadastre (§ 7a Austrian *Vermessungsgesetz*; § 5(1) Austrian AllgGAG). § 7a(1) Austrian *Vermessungsgesetz* provides the following definition: 'A *Grundstück* is such a part of a cadastral municipality which is marked as such with its own number in the boundary cadastre or land tax cadastre.' Sometimes, the terms 'parcel' or 'land parcel' [*Parzelle, Grundparzelle*] are used synonymously (*Rassi*, Grundbuchsrecht, no. 1). The cadastres mentioned form the basis of the land register [*Grundbuch*] and the data in them regarding location, boundaries, and the use of the land unit are used in the land register. (§ 2(2) Sentence 1 Austrian GUG). In Spanish law, TS 10 December 1960, RAJ 1960 no. 4095 pp. 2664, 2666 defines an estate [*finca*] as 'a part of the earth's surface' that 'is enclosed by a polygonal line and is an object of ownership'. Portuguese law refers to the 'soil' [*solo*], not to the 'surface' [*superfície*]. Under Art. 204(2) Portuguese Civil Code, an agricultural land unit is a limited part of the soil, and an urban land unit is a building that is connected to the soil.

Foundations of Property Law. Christian von Bar and Jason Grant Allen, Oxford University Press. © Christian von Bar 2023.
DOI: 10.1093/oso/9780198885337.003.0007

it is perceptible to the senses, and therefore often called 'corporeal', a landscape is not, without more, a thing. Things—that is, fitting objects of property rights—are only created in a landscape with the act of parcelling. Only when a parcel is determined pursuant to the rules of the relevant legal system[3] do actual or potential[4] objects of property rights arise in a landscape—namely, *land units*. In other words, in order to understand what a land unit 'is', one must first answer the preliminary question why the concept of a land unit is needed at all. The answer varies from legal system to legal system. There are important areas of law that require the concept of 'moveable thing' but do not require the concept of 'land unit'; criminal law, for example, is such a category.[5] And it is by no means given that property law has to have the same concept of 'land unit' as, for example, the law of surveying, construction law or tax law. Property law and the law of obligations do not even necessarily deal with 'land units' with the same purpose in mind, and for that reason they give the term quite different meanings.[6] One must,

[3] *Spyridakis*, Epitomo Nomikó Lexikó, p. 9 is of the opinion that a land unit is said to arise as soon as the different parts of the earth's surface are bounded from each other with natural or artificial markets. That is, however, only the case where a legal system requires nothing further than these factual dealings, and that time—if there ever was such a time—is long since passed. An interesting view in earlier states of affairs is afforded by Swedish law. There, the boundaries of a land unit (*fastighet*) follow the markers on the ground made pursuant to law (*laga ordning*), so long as they have been lawfully determined (*lagligen bestämd*). If these markers cannot be determined any more with certainty (*fastställa med säkerhet*), they are to be determined with the help of cadastral plans (*förrättningskarta*), purchase documentation, relations between possessors and other criteria. If legally recognized boundary markers are entirely absent, the land unit is to be determined with the help of a plan (*karta*) and documents (Kap. 1 § 3 JB). If necessary, old boundary markers (so-called *rå* and *rör*) and other ancient boundary markers can be referred to Kap. 1 § 4 JB).

[4] A 'landscape' is not even an ownerless thing. Ownerless things must still be 'things', i.e. at least potentially fitting objects of property rights. As a result, only real things and land units (according to the national terminology immoveables) can be ownerless—not 'land' itself. § 928 German Civil Code, for example, provides for the dereliction of a land unit. The latter becomes ownerless, until the public *fiscus* exercises its right of appropriation through registration in the land register. Under Art. 1345 Portuguese Civil Code, however (which draws on the nearly identical Art. 827 Italian Civil Code), 'immoveable objects [*coisas imóveis*] without a known owner can be seen as state property'. In Italy and Portugal, therefore, state property arises automatically *ex lege*. Immoveables are thus never ownerless; an act of appropriation is not necessary. Matters are similar in Spain. *Inmuebles* (or *bienes inmuebles*) are automatically state property when they have no other owner (Art. 17 *Ley del Patrimonio de las Administraciones Públicas*); see further *Díez-Picazo and Gullón*, Sistema de Derecho Civil III(1)[8], pp. 176–7.

[5] In the German Criminal Code, the word '*Grundstück*' is found only in § 106b (Disruption of the activity of a legislative organ in its building 'or on the *Grundstück* belonging thereto'). Section 287 German Criminal Code makes the lottery of 'immoveable things' punishable. These provisions obviously have nothing to do with the protection of property rights; land units can neither be stolen (§ 242 German Criminal Code) nor misappropriated (§ 246 German Criminal Code). Portuguese and Spanish law, however, treat the 'usurpation' of property rights (*usurpação de coisa imóvel* and *usurpación de derecho real inmobiliario* respectively) as a crime (along with the alteration of boundary markers) (Art. 215 Portuguese Criminal Code; Art. 245 Spanish Criminal Code). The concept of 'immoveable' in Art. 215 Portuguese Criminal Code is coterminous with that of Art. 204 Portuguese Civil Code (Figueiredo Dias [-*Damião da Cunha*], Comentário Conimbricense do Código Penal II, pp. 261–2, 270). The fact that buildings are also 'land' in the Criminal Justice and Public Order Act was confirmed in *DPP v Chivers* [2010] EWHC 1814 (Admin), [2011] WLR 2324 (DC).

[6] For example, under German law, the term 'leases of land units' (§ 578 German Civil Code) includes the lease of a part of a campsite (OLG Frankfurt 20 June 1985, NJW-RR 1986 p. 108) and the lease of the outside wall of a house to install a vending machine (Palandt [-*Weidenkaff*], BGB[71], introductory note to § 535 no. 97). The situation is similar in Portugal. Portuguese law differentiates between the lease (*contrato de locação*) of immoveable things (*arrendamento*) and moveable things (*aluguer*). The *arrendamento* concerns all immoveable things within the meaning of Art. 204(2) Portuguese Civil Code, e.g. urban and agricultural land units (*Pires de Lima and Antunes Varela*, Código Civil Anotado II[4], note 2 to Art. 1023 p. 344). The tenancy can relate to the whole land unit or only a part. Regarding urban land units, outside walls and terraces can be leased for the purpose of advertising. Windows can be leased to persons who want to watch a parade (*Menezes Leitão*, Direito das obrigações III[4], pp. 308–09). In England, a distinction must be made between rights, especially between security rights derived from common law and those derived from equity. At common law, a registered charge or mortgage refers to an undivided, entire freehold, whereas these charges can refer to a part of a freehold in equity, e.g. one of two apartments

therefore, be content, in the first instance, with a 'property law based' conception of 'land units' and with the modest claim that the formation of land units serves to create property rights in the useable parts of the planet Earth. Without land units, this would not be possible. Without these normative objects, we would lack any controllable object at all; we would not know to which part of the planet any given property right relates.

Land units, in the sense so defined, are indeed things with a physical substrate, like the landscape out of which they are carved by the legal system. The so-called 'law of immoveable things' expresses so much in numerous places. A non-negligible number of the property rights that can be acquired under this branch of the law would be impossible if this were not the case; one need only think of condominium rights or rights of way. But this does not mean that land units owe their nature as 'things' to the materiality of the soil that belongs to them. The opposite is the case. Their soil component does not, properly seen, even give them the property of corporeality. True, one can stand on a field and get one's shoes dirty; in this sense it can be said that one is dealing with a 'corporeal' thing. But this is not the concept of corporeality which is of importance to the concept of a land unit. For the purposes of property law, the first task is to create a 'thing' in the first place, which means the *normative* creation of a spatial entity that is a fitting object of property rights. Real things are delineated from other real things by their corporeality, and that is what conditions their suitability as objects of property rights. The case is different for land units. Land units must first be created by the legal system—from all sides, i.e. in the air, in the soil, and on the surface—as a thing (as a *corpus*). Their natural properties in and of themselves, as a matter of fact, speak *against* their characterization as things. This challenge can only be overcome by the legal system itself. Land units therefore have property law alone to thank for their existence and for their ability to be the object of property rights. Land units are things with a physical substrate, but are at base normative things. They are like the geometric figures that would appear if one traced a grid pattern over the surface of the earth with a computer programme. Land units in property law are, in the last instance, products of imagination. They are not naturally existing, that is, separated from each other by their physical properties. Their individualization is the consequence of legal intervention. Land units are used wherever—but only where—humans monopolize use of the environment, as well as goods and rights, by means of property rights. Hunter and gatherer societies do not create land units, planned economies only create them in a limited scope,[7] and the concept is inutile to govern the use of the oceans and the ocean floor. The creation of land units by property law serves to monopolize resources in the hand 7.2

of a legally undivided house (*Garwood v Bank of Scotland Plc* [2012] EWHC 415 (Ch); [2013] BPIR 450 [Norris J]). For the Netherlands, *Bartels*, NTBR 2013 pp. 124–5 supports the thesis that an object cannot only be a 'thing' or a mere 'good' depending on the context (e.g. under Art. 7:5 Netherlands Civil Code energy is counted among moveable things). Instead, *Bartels* supports that a thing can be immoveable under Art. 3:3(1) Netherlands Civil Code and moveable under European law (p. 125). In that case, both Art. 7:2 (sale of immoveable things) and Art. 7:5 Netherlands Civil Code (sale of moveable things) would be applicable.

[7] A significant example can be found in Art. 142 of the Civil Code of Tajikistan. According to this, only buildings and technical installations come under the term 'immoveables'. This is because land belongs to the state exclusively

of private individuals. Monopolization of this type is prohibited in regions that belong, or should belong, to all. In case these regions are found in the sovereign territory of a state, then they are usually positioned *extra commercium* (whether *de facto* or *de jure*);[8] in case they are found outside of such territory, they are assigned to the community of states (and their citizens) generally and are immune to the formation of land units, at least so long as states respect international law and refrain from the forceful colonization of these increasingly attractive, but still relatively untouched, regions. At present, only public (and public international) law concessionary rights (allowing use but not ownership) are possible in such places.

7.3 For example, the use of the oceans and the ocean beds is generally subject to the United Nations Convention on the Law of the Sea (UNCLOS), which came into force in 1994.[9] This distinguishes between the Territorial Waters (Art. 3 UNCLOS: up to 12 nautical miles from the so-called 'baseline'), the Contiguous Zone (Art. 33 UNCLOS: up to 24 nautical miles from the baseline), the Exclusive Economic Zone (Art. 57 UNCLOS: up to 200 nautical miles from the baseline), the Continental Shelf (insofar as this is found beyond the 200 nautical mile line), and International Waters or the high seas (Art. 86 UNCLOS). The Territorial Waters are subject to the sovereignty of the coastal state (Art. 2 UNCLOS). In the Contiguous Zone, the coastal state retains certain powers of control. In the Exclusive Economic Zone, the coastal state has sovereign rights 'for the purpose of exploring and exploiting, conserving and managing the natural resources, whether living or non-living, of the waters superjacent to the seabed and of the seabed and its subsoil' (Art. 56 UNCLOS). Under Arts 76 and 77 UNCLOS, a coastal state can also claim similar rights in relation to the Continental Shelf. In relation to International Waters, under Art. 87 UNCLOS all states enjoy the freedom of navigation and overflight, the freedom to lay undersea cables and pipelines, the freedom to create artificial islands and other installations, and the freedom of fishing and scientific research. Art. 133 UNCLOS distinguishes 'the Area' from the International

and is not in the realm of private legal transaction (*Knieper/Chanturia/Schramm*, Das Privatrecht im Kaukasus und in Zentralasien, p. 339).

[8] Good examples can be found in Arts 822(1) and 823 Italian Civil Code and Art. 927 Greek Civil Code (according to which the coasts, beaches, bays, and harbours are things for public use and thus belong to the treasury). The actual coastline (not the outside border of territorial waters) can be up to 500 metres away from land (Areopag 735/1976, Isokrates-Database). For marine areas which belong to it, the treasury can generally use private law to protect and defend its property (*Triantos*, AK, Art. 968 nos 2 and 3). Likewise, Art. L2111-4 French *Code général de la propriété des personnes publiques* public and natural marine territory (*domaine public maritime naturel*) covers, *inter alia*, the soil and the subsoil of the sea between the outside border of territorial waters and the coastline. The same applies to the soil and subsoil of saltwater ponds, which are directly, naturally, and permanently connected to the sea, as well as land which has been washed ashore or abandoned by the sea (*lais et relais de la mer*; for details see *Auby/Bon/Auby/Terneyre*, Droit Administratif des biens[5], p. 53 no. 63). The situation is similar in Sweden. Water areas (*vattenområden*) in the sea (*havet*) are generally public waters (*allmänt vatten*). The threshold between public and private waters (*enskilt vatten*) is determined according to the rules of the *Lag om gräns mot allmänt vattenområde* (1950:595). In the inland, only the four largest Swedish lakes (Vänern, Vättern, Hjälmaren, and Storsjön) are public waters (§§ 1 and 5 op. cit.). Under Art. 132(2) of the Spanish Constitution, the coastal zone, beaches, territorial waters, and natural aides of the economic area and the continental shelf belong to the state. Details can be found in Art. 3 ff *Ley de Costas*.

[9] UNTS 1833 p. 3.

Waters. The Area means all solid, fluid, and gaseous mineral resources *in situ* 'at or beneath the seabed, including polymetallic nodules'. Art. 136 UNCLOS assigns the Area to the 'common heritage of mankind'. Property law questions concerning use of the oceans must be examined against this background of public international law. The Territorial Waters are generally in the ownership of the relevant coastal state. Here, national property law also applies; whether, and to what extent, this is also the case in the Exclusive Economic Zone is less clear.[10] Wind energy installations do not stand on land units in either case, however, and therefore cannot be seen as part of a land unit; under German law, for example, they would be seen as moveable things pursuant to the rules governing so-called 'apparent components' [*Scheinbestandteile*] (§ 95(1) German Civil Code). Mining activities in the Territorial Waters and in the Exclusive Economic Zone are subject to the relevant national law. The appropriation of resources in the 'Area' is governed by Arts 150 and following UNCLOS. These resources are inalienable (Art. 137(2) UNCLOS), but states and private actors can claim, acquire, or exercise rights in minerals recovered from the Area (though not in the Area itself) (Art. 137(3) UNCLOS). Mining in the Area is subject to the approval and monitoring of the International Seabed Authority.[11]

Because land units are creatures of law, they can only be divided and combined according to its rules.[12] The *division* of land units is an everyday process; their *merger* is not. However, it remains true that land units can be increased and decreased in quantity. A land unit need not even comprise a single, physically contiguous part of the earth's surface—but here the European legal systems diverge.[13] From the perspective of property law, there is nothing necessarily opposed to treating parcels of land separated by large distances as dependent parts of one and the same land unit. Land units need not meet on the same level of the earth's surface, either; the surface of one property on a slope might shoot over a lower-lying land unit in a direct horizontal level. Such situations arise often in artificially manufactured urban spaces as a result of widespread 7.4

[10] For details, see e.g. *Hofmann and Baumann*, RdE 2012 pp. 53, 55, 58, and *Böttcher*, RNotZ 2011 pp. 589, 591.

[11] In this regard, and concerning the details of the prospection process, see *Jenisch*, NordÖR 2010 p. 379.

[12] Depending on the quality of a landscape's surface, the division of land units can be limited with the purpose of ensuring adequate cultivation. For example, under Art. 1376(1) Portuguese Civil Code the areas of cultivable agriculture (*terrenos aptos para a cultura*) may not fall under a certain minimum. Under Art. 1376(2) Portuguese Civil Code, the division of rural areas is not permitted in cases in which a plot would become an enclave as a consequence of the division. The legislators wished, with this ruling (and with Art. 1552 Portuguese Civil Code), to prevent the creation of new servitudes (rights of way, *servidão de passagem*), which were deemed one of the most problematic consequences of small, fragmented land units (*Pires de Lima and Antunes Varela*, Código Civil Anotado III², note 5 to Art. 1376 p. 259). Under Art. 1377 Portuguese Civil Code, the base areas (*terrenos*), which serve a purpose other than agriculture or are parts of an urban land unit, can be divided virtually arbitrarily. Art. 1382 Portuguese Civil Code concerns the merging of agricultural land units, which belong to the same rights holder.

[13] The situation is different in Greece. Estates which do not share a border or a connection cannot constitute one and the same land unit, see e.g. Areopag 1623/2001, Isokrates-Database (a land unit sold was not connected to its other part on the opposite side of the street. It was therefore not transferred, because both parts were separated by a public street. Public streets serve the purpose of individualizing land units and differentiating them from one another. Admittedly, in this case, it was to be assumed that the defendant acquired ownership of the other part by prescription). Likewise, Areopag 1100/1998, Isokrates-Database in a criminal case and Areopag 215/1996, Dioikitiki Diki 8 (1996) p. 724 in a case involving state liability (dispossession when dividing a land unit by building a street).

construction on boundaries. The land itself, however, which a land unit requires for its normative creation, cannot be increased. The existence of land is, moreover, only imperilled in coastal regions (in contemporary Europe, this is highly exceptional). This makes 'interests in land' a prized possession. Their monopolization requires stable relations; stable relations require a high degree of legal certainty. This explains, for example, why rights in land units can generally only be acquired or transferred pursuant to some special form, and why the prescriptive acquisition of land is generally subject to longer time periods than the prescriptive acquisition of real things. The comparative perspective shows that something highly prized is often subject to considerable variations in the normative regimes devised to govern it. The law governing the formation of land units and the law governing the use of land units confirms this. The former is concerned with striking the difficult balance between party autonomy, which militates for diversity, and the imperative to protect third parties from too much complexity. The latter is concerned to allocate optimally organized rights over land to the maximum possible number of legal subjects.

2. Corporeality, Spatiality, Normativity

a. Firm Connection with the Soil

7.5 It is often claimed that land units are surfaces, namely 'parts of the surface of the earth'. This is correct only to the extent that an object of legal transaction can only be characterized as a 'land unit' when it has a solid connection with the soil, with the *fonds de terre* (Art. 518 French Civil Code).[14] It is not correct, however, that the mere plane of the earth's surface is a land unit. This follows as a matter of necessity in those legal systems that only permit property rights in corporeal objects, because two-dimensional planes have no spatial dimension and cannot, in such legal systems, be 'things' at all. The reason is somewhat more succinct in other legal systems: no-one can really walk, plant, or build on a two-dimensional plane; very little of relevance to property law and its purposes can be done with such an object at all.

7.6 Although its physical substrate (i.e. the soil) does not adequately describe it, the soil is a necessary pre-requisite for the formation of a land unit. Without a solid connection to the ground, no fitting object of property rights in the nature of a land unit could be formed. The volume of space above the surface of a parking space, or the airspace above a house, are not fitting objects of a separate right of ownership, even if permission for

[14] Irritatingly, there does not even seem to be a consensus in Europe about this term. For example, in the Netherlands, the term *grond* ('ground') in Art. 3:3 Netherlands Civil Code is interpreted by recourse to Art. 5:20 Netherlands Civil Code (which details which objects are included in ownership rights over *grond*). This also includes the surface of the earth. The surface of the earth is in turn understood to be the upper limit of ownership of immoveable things (Asser [-*Mijnssen/van Velten/Bartels*], Zakenrecht[15], p. 108 n. 81) and is itself the object of ownership rights (T.M., Parl. Geschiedenis V, p. 120).

their use (e.g. for the construction of a skyscraper that projects into the space) is extremely valuable and is described as a 'sale'.[15]

Across Europe, the position in Ireland is unique. Under sec. 3(e) of the Irish Land and Conveyancing Law Reform Act 2009, 'land' includes

> the airspace above the surface of land or above any building or structure on land which is capable of being or was previously occupied by a building or structure and any part of such airspace, whether the division is made horizontally, vertically or in any other way.

It appears as if Irish law wanted to take a self-consciously 'modern' approach in departing from the traditional position at common law. But the idea given expression in sec. 3(e), that different strata of air can have different owners,[16] is not ultimately convincing. This is unchanged by the imposition of conditions—i.e. that it must be possible to use the relevant stratum of air through the construction of a building and that, if no building yet exists, the location and dimension of the stratum must be determined precisely. Otherwise, the relevant transaction would have to fail for uncertainty. Even after the destruction of a building, ownership is said to subsist in the air strata previously occupied by it.[17] This concept, however, must be the result of a miscomprehension, because without a solid connection to the ground no spatial thing in the sense of property law can exist. A stratum of air remains nothing but air: even if it possesses length, height, and breadth, it does not constitute any kind of *corpus*. Thus, numerous risks loom for the development of cities as well as for the clarity and certainty of Irish law. One need only consider the question of property rights in air strata, and how those property relations would behave in case of a natural or artificial depression of the surface of the soil surface below.

The open spaces for playgrounds or parking spaces[18] found beneath a modern high-rise building on pillars are also best seen as non-independent parts of the relevant land unit, which are in the common ownership of all apartment owners in the building. In

[15] Rightly decided in *Rolfe (Inspector of Taxes) v Wimpey Waste Management Ltd* [1988] STC 329, 357 (*Harman* J, *obiter*: the airspace separated from the soil beneath it is no 'item of property'); this, however, does not exclude the proposition that a land unit can be encumbered by a real right of use of the airspace above it or that such a right can be registered, e.g. in the form of a servitude (*Sohst*, Das spanische Bürgerliche Gesetzbuch^2, note to Art. 350 p. 88 with examples from the Spanish jurisprudence). See also the Belgian Cass. 13 September 2013, RCJB 2014 S. 288 (the volume of a marked parking space is not a fitting object of separate ownership).

[16] *Wylie*, Land and Conveyancing Law Reform Act, p. 39 no. 33 with fn. 51 and 54.

[17] Ibid. fn. 52 and 53.

[18] Whether and under which circumstances parking spots, especially parking spots in larger buildings, can be independent objects of ownership is assessed with a surprising degree of diversity in Europe. Many jurisdictions require interior space at the least. In Czech law, in which the *superficies solo cedit* principle was not in force prior to 1 January 2014, the assessment depended on whether the parking spot constituted an independent building. This was denied by Nejvyšší soud České republiky 26 October 1999, 2 Cdon 1414/97, Právní rozhledy no. 1/2000. A parking spot on a land unit, the surface of which has been fixed for the purposes of parking, is not a building within the meaning of civil law. Such a parking spot cannot be legally separated from the land unit to which it belongs. Cass. civ. 6 June 2007, Bull. civ. 2007, III, no. 98; *D.* 2007, p. 2356, note by *Atias* possibly reaches a different conclusion. The case concerned the validity of a right to the *jouissance exclusive sur une partie commune*, this being the parking spot.

order to comprise its own land unit, and to become an independent thing, this space would have to be built up differently; at least, its construction would have to be agreed upon in advance in a contract between all the apartment owners.[19] Even then, one who builds a dwelling on a houseboat[20] or on the upper story of a double decker bus cannot claim to own a land unit. Boats and buses have no solid connection to the water or the ground on which they sit or stand.[21]

b. Spatiality

7.7 A land unit occupies space.[22] This space arises through its conceptual separation from other spaces. Property law traces its horizontal boundaries, extending somewhat into the soil and somewhat into the air, in the first instance conceptually parallel to the surveyor's lines projected onto the surface of the earth. The latter occurs, insofar as one is available,[23] by reference to a cadastre—i.e. to an official description of the land parcels of an administrative region. The vertical lines run up and down from the two-dimensional boundary lines on the surface. Both lines, the horizontal and the vertical, delimit a land unit from other land units and from spaces that are not land units at all. In the ordinary case, the former task is performed by horizontal boundaries and the latter task by vertical boundaries. But there are also cases in which the horizontal

[19] This is the case in Greek law, see Areopag 635/2010, EfAD 3 (2010) p. 930, note by *Danilatou*, and very similar in Polish law, see Bieniek and Rudnicki *(-Bieniek)*, Nieruchomości. Problematyka prawna[5], p. 473 no. 3 (A parking space in a large garage cannot be a separate 'room' because it is not separated from other parking spaces by walls. A parking space is furthermore not a 'room' belonging to an apartment [Polish Sąd Najwyższy 19 May 2004, I CK 696/03, OSP 2005/5/61, Lex-No. 147749]). On the other hand, Art. 5:106(2) Netherlands Civil Code has created the possibility of a so-called *appartementsrecht* even over an unbuilt land unit. This made it possible to obtain a real and exclusive right of use over a parking spot (*Hijma and Olthof*, Compendium van het Nederlands Vermogensrecht[9], no. 232a).

[20] Hoge Raad 15 January 2010, NJB 2010 no. 189 (A houseboat is a moveable thing even if it cannot move on its own and can only be towed a few metres away from its berth because nearby bridges are too low to allow access. A boat is not even qualified as an immoveable if it is connected to the municipal water and electricity supplies).

[21] What exactly is sufficient to constitute a 'solid connection' can become problematic on an individual, case-by-case basis. In general, one should agree with, e.g. Czech Constitutional Court 6 May 2003, ÚS 483/01, Sbírka nálezů a usnesení 30 (2003) no. 60 p. 107, and require that the object cannot be removed from the ground without damage and that the connection to the ground can withstand exposure to the elements. This is formulated similarly in Art. 334(3) Spanish Civil Code (everything with a solid connection to an immoveable thing, such that it cannot be removed without damage, is an immoveable thing).

[22] The French literature correctly states that ownership of a land unit has as its object a part of the country's territory, namely the ground and the elements connected to the ground (*Bergel/Bruschi/Cimamonti*, Les biens[2], p. 188 no. 154). However, this right of ownership is not limited to the ground. Differentiation of the assets can occur not only on a surface, rather it presupposes a spatial representation of the volume taken up by the land unit. The plot of land is merely a horizontal cut through this space (*Bergel/Bruschi/Cimamonti*, Les biens, p. 191 n o. 156; likewise *Savatier*, D. 1965, I, p. 213 ['*La surface ne peut servir qu'à porter et à soutenir un volume* [. . .] *l'immeuble ayant découpé la surface sur laquelle repose sa propriété doit nécessairement achever la représentation de celle-ci, en découpant, dans l'espace, le volume qu'il assoit sur cette surface*']).

[23] Greece is currently working on the finalization of a land register. Separate land registers exist on the Ionian Islands and in the Dodecanese. For the time being, legal relationships surrounding a land unit arise from the so-called transcription book. It is structured according to the names of the owners of the land units, and essentially contains no more than authenticated copies of the respective sales or gift contracts. In order to prove his claim for restitution, an owner must precisely delineate the borders of the land unit. This is usually done by including a topographical plan from which the form, exact location, direction, and area of the land unit can be ascertained (Areopag 1170/2011, Isokrates-Database).

boundaries of a land unit border onto a public beach, some other area that has been placed *extra commercium*, or on a national border. Likewise, a land unit, properly seen, can be framed in the vertical plane by other land units (e.g. in an apartment building), which is to say it can be truncated in its vertical extension. Everything that *comprises* the space sketched out by these boundaries (not: everything which is *found within* that space) 'is' the land unit.

The image of a land unit as a cube extending up from a square footprint is, however, an oversimplified model. This is not because the earth has contours, which can usually be ignored safely for the purposes of property law, nor is it because land units have to follow some set geometric forms; land units are not generally required to have straight boundaries on the surface of the land, either.[24] Rather, it is because the distance of the upper and lower horizontal limits of a land unit cannot be meaningfully stated by reference to the surface in numerically quantified terms. In no jurisdiction are land units said generally to end (for example) 200 metres above and 30 metres below the surface.[25] Such a rule would not make sense from the perspective of property law, because it would be too inflexible. Monopoly rights over the environment in which human beings live must be effective enough to incentivize investment in land units; however, this monopoly must not extend beyond limits consistent with the common weal. This means that every legal system must necessarily engage in a difficult balancing of interests. How far the boundaries of property rights in land units should extend in the vertical plane, in contrast to the horizontal plane, can only be determined sensibly in relation to the nature of the soil, the categories of permitted use, the location, and the interests of the broader community in using the space in question. The consequence of this is that land units become 'thinner' in their heights and depths. They can, as it were, have 'different height and depth' depending on their purpose, location, and nature;[26] we are, after all, dealing with normative and not with real things. **7.8**

[24] For example, this is the case in Greece. The side boundaries of a land unit may be determined by straight or curved lines, cf. e.g. *Symboulio tes Epikrateias* 159/1999, Isokrates-Database, and Upper Administrative Court Piraeus 614/2007, Isokrates-Database. Besides this, the mathematical area of a two-dimensional, drawn land unit is usually smaller than the 'real' surface of the land unit in any event, because a two-dimensional representation can usually not exactly depict the area's increase due to height and depth (*Trajer and Trajerová*, Katastr nemovitostí^{2}, p. 10).

[25] This is unchanged by national regulations regarding permitted flight altitudes over a land unit. These do not contain any general statements regarding the volume of land units, instead focusing in this respect on a small detail. For example, in the United Kingdom the rules of air traffic control (S.I. 1985/1714, Reg. 5(1)(e)) state that no aircraft may fly closer than about 150 metres from a person, a lake, a vehicle, or a building. Special regulations exist for take-off and landing. See also *Bernstein of Leigh (Baron) v Skyviews & General Ltd.* [1978] QB 479, 487 (Griffiths J) (the absurd result that every aircraft and every satellite commits trespass by flying over a land unit must be avoided). Incidentally, the common law has always acknowledged immunities favouring aircraft operators. These date back to the operation of hot air balloons (*Pickering v Rudd* (1815) 4 Camp. 219, 220; 171 ER 70, 71) and are today contained in sec. 76(1) Civil Aviation Act 1982. Incidentally occasions also arise in which the owner of a land unit attempts to argue, in his favour, that an object is so far below the surface that he, the owner, is not responsible for it. VG Braunschweig 08 December 2010, 2 A 295/09, Juris-Database concerned an air-raid shelter from the Second World War, which had to be backfilled for safety reasons. The owner of the land unit relied unsuccessfully on the defence that, as the shelter lay 27 metres below the surface, it was no longer his and he was not responsible for it.

[26] One of thousands of examples is a number of land units in the Ymittros, a suburb of Athens. In order to prevent any impairment of the air supply to Athens, the residents of Ymittros may only build houses with a maximum of two storeys. A land unit in Ymittros therefore takes up less space than a land unit in other districts of Athens.

7.9 This peculiarity of land units is more readily articulated and dealt with when one thinks not of the object itself, but of the property rights allowed in it. This is, indeed, how it is generally done. European legal systems shift their point of view whenever it comes to the definition of land units in space. They displace the description of 'land units' as objects with a description of the content of the property rights allowed in that type of object. To provide a frame of reference, they often define the most comprehensive right recognized in land units by the relevant system—i.e. on the Continent, the civil law concept of the right of 'ownership'. In this manner, they implicitly answer in the affirmative the question whether the same concept of a land unit is really suitable for *all* property rights; the efficaciousness of so-called 'limited real rights' is specified according to their content, not according to the volume of the object to which they refer. A hypothec has the same land unit as *its* object as the right of ownership or any other real right.[27] The holder of the hypothec, however, can only prevent certain specified dealings by the owner or by a third party, namely against such actions as would cause some deterioration in the land unit and thereby a reduction in the value of the hypothec as a security interest (e.g. § 1134(1) German Civil Code, Art. 117 Spanish LH; cf. Art. 701 Portuguese Civil Code). The holder of a servitude such as a right of way can, even though his right relates to an entire land unit, only prevent dealings that somehow detriment his right of way.[28] If matters were otherwise—if every property right, concretized in the facts of each set of circumstances formed a unique land unit—the legal position would become dramatically more complicated. Possession, however, takes on a special role. Insofar as a system of property law recognizes 'partial possession' [*Teilbesitz*], it also recognizes an object that is separate to the object in which ownership and other 'genuine' property rights are held; where land units are subject to a regime of acquisition through prescriptive possession, it is thus possible so to acquire part of a land unit.[29] But this only confirms that possession oscillates between 'fact' and 'right' in any case.

[27] Some jurisdictions have a different interpretation. If land units are 'combined', a charge on one of the original land units does not automatically extend to the new (larger) land unit. However, this legal position can also be interpreted to mean that the 'combination' of land units in such cases is a contradiction in terms. By contrast, if a land unit is divided, then whether or not the charge remains attached to the new land units depends on the type of charge. An analogous problem can be seen within the context of the question of whether a usufruct can exclude not only certain uses, but also certain spatially, but not legally, separated components of the land unit (such as an apartment, a lawn, etc.). This case is judged very differently in various European countries. For example, Art. 253 § 2 Polish Civil Code states that while a usufruct always applies to a whole land unit, the exercise of the right to usufruct may be limited to a certain part of the land unit. It would be consistent if the usufruct always applied to the whole usufruct. If the usufruct does not include certain parts, then these parts should themselves be qualified as land units.

[28] e.g. CFI Thessaloniki 14609/2007, Arm. 10 (2007) p. 1505 (Injunction against placing steel poles onto the surface subject to a right of way. The poles were intended to support a balcony yet to be constructed, which would have been covered by the defendant's planning permission. The building plan and planning permission did not interfere with the right of way by themselves, however constructing the support poles certainly did).

[29] See, for common law, *Zarb v Parry* [2011] EWCA Civ 1306; [2012] 1 WLR 1240, and from the extensive Italian case law, see e.g. Cass. 27 February 2008, no. 5134, Riv. notariato 2008 p. 1069; Cass. 13 December 2005, no. 27413, Juris data DVD; TribunaleNapoli 19 October 2005, Giur. Merito 2006 p. 1696; Cass. 24 May 2004, no. 9913, Juris data DVD; Cass. 11 June 1998, no. 5809, Mass. Giust. civ. 1998 p. 1287, and Cass. 01 March 1995, no. 2332, Mass. Giust. civ. 1995 p. 480. German law acknowledges the possibility of partial possession [*Teilbesitz*] of things in § 865 German Civil Code. Any spatially separated component of the thing can be the object of *Teilbesitz*, even, e.g. a garden or a parking spot on another person's land unit (MünchKomm [*-Joost*], BGB VI^5, § 865 no. 3).

Because 'estates', rather than 'land units', are registered in English law, some questions are posed in rather different terms there. Certain property rights, such as rights of way and hunting rights, define their spatial reference as it were by themselves. Their extent is determined according to the same rules that determine the extent of an estate. They are, in other words, not given over one or more land units, rather, they appear as independent entities in and of themselves.

The shift in the plane of description—from the object itself to property in the object—is 'only' pragmatic, but it is not theoretically invalid because the existence of a thing is inseparable from its ability to be an object of property rights; it is a general feature of the concept of property law presented in this book that the concept of a 'thing' is in part determined by the content of property rights. For this reason, one may say that a land unit ends where its owner's rights of use end. Earlier, it was often said that *la propriété du sol emporte la propriété du dessus et du dessous* (Art. 552(1) French Civil Code), i.e. that ownership of the soil extended up into the air and down into the earth (see e.g. Art. 840 Italian Civil Code, Art. 350 Spanish Civil Code, and Arts 1042 and 1043 Latvian Civil Code). Section 297 Austrian Civil Code goes too far when it says that the airspace above the soil belongs to the owner of the soil; the Austrian literature itself gives this formulation little importance and contains references to numerous exceptions that limit it.[30] Already in Art. 552(2) and (3) French Civil Code it becomes apparent that the drafters of the *Code Napoléon* were not really thinking about unlimited ownership upwards and downwards; they were mainly concerned with the space needed for ordinary construction activities on and below the surface. In this respect, the formulation chosen in Art. 1344 Portuguese Civil Code appears happier. Art. 1344(1) also starts by stating that ownership in immoveables embraces the airspace above the surface as well as the subsoil and everything that is held in it and has not been separated by law or contractual dealings. Art. 1344(2), however, immediately adds that the owner cannot prohibit the dealings of a third party in the prevention of which he has no interest by reason of their height or depth. This can be generalized: a land unit ends where an owner has no further interest worthy of protection. 7.10

Ways of formulating this proposition differ, but in the end they all point to the same core concept. Under Art. 143 Polish Civil Code, property in a land unit stretches 'above and below the surface according to the socio-economic purpose of the land unit's defined boundaries'. The spatial extent of a land unit is thus functionally determined by reference to 'socio-economic' considerations—namely, the purposes of the law of property itself. It is generally accepted that the vertical extent of a property right can differ according to the function and use of a land unit.[31] The Spanish Civil Code refers the question to Art. 1 of a statute on aerospace navigation (*Ley 48/1960, de 21 de julio, sobre* 7.11

[30] *Gschnitzer/Faistenberger/Barta/Call/Eccher*, Sachenrecht², p. 63. These exceptions include the regulations regarding mineral raw materials, § 2 *Luftfahrtgesetz* (concerning flyover rights of aircraft) and § 86 *Luftfahrtgesetz* (limitations of the height of buildings in safety zones, see OGH 26 June 1979, SZ 52/102).

[31] *Gniewek*, Prawo rzeczowe⁸, p. 70 no. 196.

Navegación Aérea), according to which 'the soil ends where the airspace begins, which belongs to the state'. Art. 5:21(1) Netherlands Civil Code formulates thus: 'The right of the owner to use the surface includes the right to use the space over and below the surface.' Art. 5:21(2) Netherlands Civil Code, however, qualifies this immediately: 'The use of the space over or under the earth's surface is permitted to another, when it is so high above or so deep below the surface that the owner has no interest in preventing it.' This expresses more elegantly the idea found also in § 905 German Civil Code:

> The right of the owner of a land unit extend into the space above the earth's surface and into the body of the earth below the surface. The owner can, however, not prohibit actions that occur at such a height or such a depth that he has no interest in their exclusion.

Art. 1001 Greek Civil Code adopts this formulation, and something similar is found in Art. 840 Italian Civil Code, as well:

> Property in the soil extends into the area below the surface, and everything it contains, and the owner can undertake whatever excavations and other works that do not harm his neighbour. The owner of the soil, however, cannot oppose the actions of third parties that occur at such a depth or at such a height that he has no interest in excluding them.

In the Czech Republic, the legal categorization of an area of space (a 'nothing') already posed riddles during the time of the First Republic (i.e. under § 297 of the then-applicable Austrian Civil Code). A space was said not to be part of a land unit; the law only provided that the master of a land unit was also the master of the space above it.[32] The idea elaborated in the middle of the nineteenth century by *von Jhering*, that property rights of a land unit owner should be limited above and below by reference to the practical needs of the owner,[33] was not adopted in the strongly Romanist-influenced literature. *Randa*, for example, was satisfied with the application of a general prohibition of arbitrary abuse of rights.[34] The Czech Civil Code [1964] contained no formulation reflective of those found in other European jurisdictions. In the literature, aid was sought from the principle that things must, in order to be fitting objects of ownership, be useful and subject to human control.[35] Under § 506(1) Czech Civil Code [2014], the space above a land unit is now recognized as a component of the land unit. The owner must, however, tolerate third party use of this space and of the deeper strata of the soil

[32] *Rouček/Sedláček et al.*, Komentář k československému obecnému zákoníku občanskému a občanské právo platné na Slovensku a v Podkarpatské Rusi II, p. 44.

[33] *von Jhering*, JhJb 6 (1863) pp. 81, 90.

[34] *Randa*, Právo vlastnické dle rakouského práva v pořádku systematickém II, p. 24 n. 34. Bulgaria is also missing an explicit provision for the vertical extent of the right of ownership of immoveables. It has been suggested, for building land, to refer to the respective planning permissions, or otherwise to refer to what is necessary for the ordinary use of the land unit (*Stavrou*, Veshtno pravo, p. 80).

[35] *Eliáš et al.*, Občanský zákoník. Velký akademický komentář I, p. 495. Nejvyšší soud České republiky 19 December 2011, 22 Cdo 1000/2010, Právní rozhledy 7 (2012) p. 263 ruled that it was unlawful to intrude into a neighbouring land unit with a part of one's own building (such as a balcony or an extension of the insulation).

below 'for important reasons', on the basis that he himself has no 'reasonable' basis on which to prevent such use. In the common law, too, the nineteenth-century authorities took their point of departure from the Latin maxim *cuius est solum, eius est usque ad caelum et ad inferos*.[36] In the meantime, a more pragmatic approach has come to prominence, and one distinguishes between two strata of the airspace, the 'upper' and 'lower'. The *cuius est solum* principle has no relevance for the former; property rights in land are limited to the lower stratum,[37] i.e. to the space necessary for the usual use and enjoyment of land. *Cuius est solum* is just a 'colourful' turn of phrase;[38] in truth, the formula is inexact and 'mainly serviceable as dispensing with analysis'.[39]

Because land units are conceived as (normatively) bounded *spaces*, minerals and other subterranean resources are not themselves land units, even when they are clearly differentiated from other strata of the soil like coal seams.[40] A right to extract mineral resources might either be a right of appropriation in relation to the land unit concerned (like a hunting or fishing right), or it might be a concession from the state over a part of the earth that belongs to the state but is not the object of a private property right. The latter are often called 'mining "property"'. Such minerals are, so long as they have not been extracted, objects of (public law) legal transaction, but not yet things in the form of 'land units'. They become real things (in our conceptual scheme) following their extraction. **7.12**

Under Art. 84(1)(c) of the Portuguese Constitution, for example, mineral resources (with the exception of common stone, earth, and other materials that are conventionally used for building) are part of the public patrimony. Exploration rights in mineral resources can only be granted pursuant to so-called 'administrative contracts' [*contratos administrativos*].[41] Art. 1457 Portuguese Civil Code governs the relationship between the usufructor and the land unit owner in relation to the conduct of mining activities. The provision has, however, barely any importance today; the extraction of

[36] e.g. James VC in *Corbett v Hill* (1870) LR 9 Eq 671: 'The ordinary rule of law is that whoever has got the *solum*, whoever has got the site, is the owner of everything up to the sky and down to the centre of the earth.' Jessel MR was more moderate in *Newcomer v Coulson* (1877) 5 Ch D 133: 'Now "land" according to English law includes everything on or under the soil; all buildings that you may erect on it; all mines that you may sink under it.'

[37] *Bernstein of Leigh (Baron) v Skyviews & General Ltd.* [1978] QB 479. The defendant had taken aerial photographs of the plaintiff's house and offered these to him for sale. The plaintiff considered this to be trespass on his land and claimed damages. He referred to the principle of *cuius est solum, eius est usque ad caelum et ad inferos* and to *Gifford v Dent* [1926] W.N. 336 (this judgment, however, had merely stated that if a person erects a sign in such a way that it intrudes into the air space of the neighbouring land unit at a height of 1.5 metres, this constitutes trespass; see also *Kelsen v Imperial Tobacco Co. (of Great Britain and Ireland) Ltd.* [1957] 2 QB 334). Griffiths J dismissed the action on the grounds that he could not find a precedent which supported the interpretation that the rights of an owner over his land's air space extend to an unlimited height.

[38] *Griffiths* J op. cit. p. 485C.

[39] *Commissioner for Railways et al v Valuer-General* [1974] AC 328, 351–2 (Lord Wilberforce).

[40] They are immoveables at best. e.g. Art. 3:3 Netherlands Civil Code defines vertical layers when considering immoveable things [*onroerende zaken*]. If a gold seam lies under a land unit with a house on it, there are three immoveable things: the ground, the natural resources, and the building. At the same time, Art. 3:3 Netherlands Civil Code does not establish vertically divided property. Art. 5:20 Netherlands Civil Code determines that the ownership of the ground also includes the gold occurrence and the house. Deviation from this is possible by law (especially those laws which pertain to ownership of mines), but not through an agreement of the parties.

[41] Art. 9 DL 90/90 from 16 March 1990; *Menezes Cordeiro*, Tratado de Direito Civil I(2)^2, pp. 68–9.

minerals without a government concession is generally prohibited. Even the landowner himself must acquire a concession.[42] Art. 840(1) Sentence 2 Italian Civil Code excludes everything that is 'an object of the statutes on mines, quarries, and peat fields' from the right of ownership of a land unit. In France, a mine can only be the object of a concession (Art. L131-1 *Code minier*); mines that are not merely quarries [*carriers*] belong to the state.[43] The concession, however, is interpreted as immoveable property, even where it is granted to the owner of the surface land. It may not, however be encumbered with a hypothec (Art. L132-8 *Code minier*). The holder of the concession owes the owner of the surface land a payment called a '*redevance tréfoncière*' (Art. L132-15 *Code minier*). The Swedish system follows the same principles. Minerals [*mineraliska ämnen*] may only be extracted on the basis of a state concession; the holder of such a concession becomes owner of the minerals as they are extracted (Kap. 1 §§ 1 and 4 *Minerallagen* (1991:45)). The surface owner can only extract minerals for his domestic use [*för husbehov*] (Kap. 5 § 2 *Minerallagen*); he is entitled, along with the state, to a compensation payment by the holder of the concession (Kap. 7 § 7 *Minerallagen*). Under § 17 of the German Mining Statute, a 'mining property' right arises with the creation of a certificate of entitlement [*Berechtigungsurkunde*]; this is entered into the land registry. Under § 8 of the statute, this right entitles its holder to acquire ownership in the minerals. However, it is not 'ownership' in the sense of § 903 German Civil Code, rather a right of appropriation and use. It cannot be sold or otherwise transferred without official consent. The surface owner retains ownership only of such minerals as are 'proper to the land' [*grundeigen*]; the 'mineable' [*bergfreie*] minerals do not belong to him. The same concept operates in Austrian law. Extraction of mineral resources contained in the Austrian Mineral Resources Statute occurs on the basis of so-called 'mining authorizations' [*Bergwerksberechtigungen*]. These are rights granted by the state that are treated like immoveable things (§ 40). In the 'mining registry' [*Bergbuch*], however, no land units are listed—only *Bergwerksberechtigungen*, their amendments, and transfers.[44] Mining authorizations only resemble land units insofar as they are both characterized as immoveable things and they are both created through a decision of the legal order. The same story is repeated in the Czech Republic. The owner of a mining operation there does not own a separate land unit; his rights of appropriation relate to a so-called 'deposit' [*ložisko*], i.e. 'a natural collection of minerals' (§ 4 Czech Statute No. 44/1988 on the Protection and Use of Minerals). The Republic is the owner of so-called 'reserved minerals' (under § 3 these include oil, magnesite, radioactive minerals, and halite) and their deposits (Art. 11(2) of the Charter of Fundamental Rights and Freedoms 2/1993 and § 5(2) Czech Statute No. 44/1988 on the Protection and Use of Minerals); only non-reserved minerals belong to the owner of the land unit in which they are found (§ 7 Czech Statute No. 44/1988 on the Protection and Use of Minerals).

[42] *Pires de Lima and Antunes Varela*, Código Civil Anotado III[2], note 2 to Art. 1457 p. 496.
[43] *Bergel/Bruschi/Cimamonti*, Les biens[2], p. 208 no. 173.
[44] Kodek (-*Höller*), Grundbuchsrecht, preface to § 1 no. 41; *Rassi*, Grundbuchsrecht, no. 61.

The same applies for mines as appropriate.[45] Greek law interprets so-called 'mining property' as a stand-alone real right of exploration, extraction, and use. It does not flow from the ownership of the surface land. Art. 1001 Greek Civil Code provides expressly that the general rule (according to which ownership in a land unit extends upwards and downwards) only applies 'insofar as the law does not provide otherwise'. The law provides otherwise in the Mining Code.[46] Under Art. 3 of this code, ownership of a land unit does not embrace 'ores', whether they are subterranean or on the surface. The right to extract and use ores is an independent real right, the so-called 'ore ownership [Δικαίωμα Μεταλλειοκτησίας, *dikéoma metalioktisías*]'. Ores themselves belong exclusively to the state; the state as owner can grant rights of 'ore ownership' which are, in turn, transferable and heritable.[47] Art. 350 Spanish Civil Code presents its description of the content of property rights in immoveables with the express proviso of separate 'provisions in the statutes governing mining and water'. Property in mining operations inures in the state. Mineral resources can be exploited by the state directly or through the granting of mining concessions (Art. 2(1) *Ley de Minas 22/1973* of 21 July 1973 in connection with Art. 132(2) of the Spanish Constitution). Bulgarian mining law enables the holder of a mining concession or exploration license to agree contractually on compensation for the loss of use of the surface land with the surface owner (Art. 75(1) Bulgarian Mineral Resources Statute). If the parties do not reach an agreement, the state can impose compulsory acquisition measures as necessary at the request of either party. Even in this case, however, a concession does not establish any independent property right in the (surface) land unit. In English law, the principle that all mines and minerals belong to the holder of the relevant fee simple estate does no more than providing a point of departure that simplifies the analysis. Gold and silver in mines belong to the Crown at common law. Sections 1 and 2 of the Petroleum Act 1998 allot all rights in oil in subterranean strata to the Crown as well. Under the Coal Act 1938, rights to extract coal were granted by the Coal Commission against royalties; in due course, the Coal Industry Nationalisation Act 1946 vested these rights in the National Coal Board, then (under the Coal Industry Act 1987) in the British Coal Corporation and finally (under the Coal Industry Act 1994) in the Coal Authority. These bodies grant authorizations to extract coal.[48] Section 4 of the Treasure Act 1996 also vests every treasure trove in the Crown. The statute defines the term 'treasure' in great detail; essentially, the concept embraces cultural and historical artifacts that have been buried in the soil for a long period of time.

[45] Czech Nejvyšší soud České republiky 29 January 1997, 3 Cdon 265/96, Právní rozhledy 6 (1997) p. 325 (a mine is a location, from which metal is extracted. It is therefore not an independent object of civil relations, but rather a component of a repository of reserved stone. Should the case concern unreserved stone, then the mine is a component of the land unit on or in which it is located).

[46] Statute 210/1973 (Official Journal A' 5 October 1973).

[47] *Georgiades*, Empragmato Dikaio I, p. 51 nos 13–14.

[48] Megarry and Wade (-*Harpum/Bridge/Dixon*), The Law of Real Property[8], no. 3-044.

c. Forming Land Units Above and Below the Surface

7.13 A *Grundstück* is, in its literal meaning, a surface, a 'piece of ground'; in its legal meaning, however, a land unit is a *space*. For the purposes of property law, understanding a land unit as an area of the surface encourages misconceptions about the 'corporeality' of land units. This, and the fact that 'ground' and 'building' are not necessarily owned by the same person in all legal systems today, makes it possible to conceptualize spaces above and below the surface of the earth as land units in the relevant sense—i.e. when a national property law treats them as (independent) objects of property rights. What is absolutely essential is that all things called 'land units' have a solid connection to the surface. Everything besides this is a question of the adequacy of existing juristic concepts. In contrast to certain national legal traditions, we think that a strict and coherent spatial conception of land units would tidy up the conceptual and lexical household of property law considerably. Such a reorganization would also have a salutary effect on discourse at the European level. The leaner the terminological apparatus, the easier it is to find mutual intelligibility and understanding.

7.14 Since all the legal systems of Europe have come (back) to the position that certain parts of buildings should be seen as independent objects of property rights—sometimes even whole buildings and other constructions—they have, in effect, realized the separate formation of land units in the space above and below the earth's surface. Apartments and other artificial spaces are thus, normatively, made into stand-alone things. From there, it is only a small step to recognize them as land units, provided that they are separated from the other apartments in the building under the relevant law (e.g. with their own folio in the land registry). The same applies for houses, floors, cellars, and even for natural subterranean spaces.

7.15 Arts 840(2) and 934 Italian Civil Code qualify the principle of *superficies solo cedit* as being subject to special provisions; nothing else can follow 'from legal title or statute'. For this reason, not even subterranean caves are automatically included in the property of the surface owner.[49] The Court of Cassation has, rather, held the line that ownership of land units is capable of vertical as well as horizontal separation. When the use of the surface land does not require the use of caves beneath, separate ownership of the latter is possible.[50] The Italian judicial opinions have repeatedly underlined the autonomy of possession of spaces above and below the surface.[51] Property in each of these spaces can be acquired through possession, independently of the other.[52] The Court of Cassation

[49] See the extensive Italian jurisdiction in this regard, e.g. Tribunale Bari 23 January 2007, no. 156, Juris Data DVD; Cass. 15 November 2006, no. 24302, Juris Data DVD; Cass. 27 July 2006, no. 17091, Juris Data DVD; Cass. 21 April 2004, no. 7655, Giust. civ. 2005, I, p. 2754; Cass. 6 September 2002, no. 12983, Giur. it. 2003 p. 429; Cass. 20 March 2001, no. 3989, Juris Data DVD; Cass. 6 April 1987, no. 3318, Juris Data DVD, and Cass. 16 September 1981, no. 5130, Juris Data DVD.

[50] Cass. 6 September 2002, no. 12983 op. cit. and Cass. 20 March 2001, no. 3989 op. cit.

[51] Tribunale Bari 23 January 2007, no. 156 op. cit.; Cass. 15 November 2006, no. 24302 op. cit., and Cass. 16 September 1981, no. 5130 op. cit.

[52] Cass. 2 April 2004, no. 7655 op. cit.

has not declared what *exactly* the object of ownership in a 'cave' is meant to be; it has deemed it sufficient to speak of this object as an 'immoveable'.[53] To the extent that the Court of Cassation has based its reasoning on Art. 840 Italian Civil Code, which is the first provision in the Part of the code dealing with land ownership (*proprietà fondiaria*), it would appear that the court treats caves at least like land units. Similarly, cellars and other subterranean facilities that do not extend above the surface are entered separately into the cadastral records, and can have their own land registry entry as independent land registry entities (§ 300 Austrian Civil Code). Such cellars are not only entered into the land register, they are also equiparated with other land register entities.[54] The underground constructions in question therefore bear all the characteristics of an independent land unit in the legal sense.[55] Of the Slovenian law of building floor ownership (*etažna lastnina*)[56] which governs apartments, commercial spaces, and other standalone spaces that form a functional unit, it is said that the law creates a special type of division of the right of ownership in immoveable things.[57] In contrast to the position in German law, common ownership of the soil is said not to play a decisive role; the emphasis is instead on separate ownership of the relevant spaces.[58]

The Spanish Civil Code does not operate with a strictly developed conceptual definition of the land unit.[59] In special statutes, however, which have been amended through Art. 396 Spanish Civil Code,[60] so-called 'horizontal ownership' has introduced a new and more precise concept into Spanish law (although the term itself is, here and elsewhere, somewhat unhappy).[61] In substance, this refers back to the so-called *legislación* **7.16**

[53] This applies accordingly to the qualification of subterranean buildings, such as cellars or boiler rooms. These are defined in law as immoveables, not as land units (*terreni*), because they are characterized as buildings. They are thus registered in the cadastre for immoveables, not land units. However, if a boiler room is not the common property of all apartment owners, it is merely an accessory of an apartment or house (Art. 817(1) Italian Civil Code). As such, it is only sold with the apartment as a rule (Art. 818(1) Italian Civil Code). If the parties reach a different agreement, this room can be 'the object of a separate legal transaction' (Art. 818(2) Italian Civil Code). In this case, it becomes an 'autonomous fraction' of the immoveable, which is nothing more than a separate land unit within the meaning of the terminology proposed here.

[54] OGH 13 December 1966, SZ 39/212.

[55] OGH 19 March 1964, ÖJZ 1964 p. 390 (EvBl 1964 p. 260) showed restraint in answering the question of whether one should speak of 'ownership' of cellars, or whether the term 'servitude' is more appropriate. However, since then these misgivings have been made obsolete by the unambiguous wording of § 300 Austrian Civil Code.

[56] *Etažna* = storey or floor, *lastnina* = ownership. It is regulated in the *Zakon o poslovnih stavbah in poslovnih prostorih* (Ur.l. SRS 18/1974) as well as in the Arts 105–127 Slovenian SPZ.

[57] Frank and Wachter (*-Ferčič and Tratnik*), Handbuch Immobilienrecht in Europa, Slowenien, pp. 1343, 1351.

[58] Tratnik, WGO-MfOR 45 (2003) pp. 94, 104.

[59] e.g. Arts 368, 388, and 390 Spanish Civil Code equate *finca* and *heredad*, Arts 573, 581, and 582 Spanish Civil Code equate *finca* and *propriedad*, Art. 1471 Spanish Civil Code equates *finca* and *inmueble*, and Art. 530 Spanish Civil Code even appears to equate *finca*, *predio*, and *inmueble*. Art. 530 Spanish Civil Code can be found under the heading of '*De las diferentes clases de servidumbres que pueden establecerse sobre las* fincas' and states '*La servidumbre es un gravamen impuesto sobre un* predio *en beneficio de otro perteneciente a distinto dueño. El* inmueble *a cuyo favor esté constituida la servidumbre se llama* predio *dominante*; *el que la sufre*, predio *sirviente*' (emphases added).

[60] The current formulation of Art. 396 Spanish Civil Code is based on statutes of 26 October 1939, of 21 July 1960, and most recently of 6 April 1999.

[61] The widespread term of 'horizontal' (and occasionally of 'vertical') ownership draws on rather problematic imagery. Ownership does not have a direction; it is thus neither horizonal nor vertical. Furthermore, land unit ownership exists for spaces, which are limited horizontally as well as vertically by nature. Therefore, if one intends to differentiate between horizontal and vertical ownership, one's choice of adjective must meet the more important axis for the picture in question. Whether the horizontal or the vertical axis is more important is, in turn, the subject of persistent disagreement. While apartments, etc. are located in the 'vertical' above a surface area's space,

hipotecaria.[62] This governs *inter alia* the registration of *fincas* (land units) in the land register. It is now possible to create independent land units (*fincas independientes*) in the sense of Art. 44(1) *Reglamento Hipotecario* with Art. 8 *Ley Hipotecario* out of 'objects of special property' (Art. 396 Spanish Civil Code). This concerns apartment and building floor ownership as well as the other '*entidades hipotecarias*' of Art. 8 *Ley Hipotecario*.

7.17 Art. 44(1) *Reglamento Hipotecario* provides an exception to the general rule. It provides that, when a building or a row of (attached) buildings is subject to the regime of 'horizontal ownership' (*propiedad horizontal*) or 'building floor ownership' (*propiedad por pisos*), a register folio will be created. As a consequence of this, whole buildings and the surface on which they rest (connected to the building parts that belong to all owners in community) constitute an independent land unit; further, so do individual floors, levels that can be used independently, as well as business premises. The latter are independent land units in their own right, for which register folios are created.[63] Spanish law has thus retreated from the principle of the unity of the register folio (*folia registral*) and has replaced it with a principle of plurality; Spanish law has, accordingly, enabled the creation of *fincas independientes*.[64] *Fincas* and *bienes inmuebles* are by no means one and the same. This is evident from a comparison of Art. 334 Spanish Civil Code and Art. 8 *Ley Hipotecario*. Trees, plants, and hanging fruits for example are *bienes inmuebles*, but obviously not *fincas*. Conversely, agricultural enterprises are *fincas*, but not *bienes inmuebles*.[65] A *finca* has been described by the Tribunal Supremo as 'a part

they also cut this space's vertical axis horizontally. There is no compelling reason to base this terminology on the apartment's vertical rather than the horizontal limits. 'Vertically', such property lies above and below the property of other apartment owners; however, it is also separated from this by 'horizontal' lines. Nonetheless, the terminology of 'horizontal ownership' has become widespread vernacular not only in Spain, but also in Portugal (Arts 1414–1438-A Portuguese Civil Code [*regime de propriedade horizontal*]; for further details on the development of the Portuguese terminology, see *Cunha Gonçalves*, Da propriedade horizontal ou por andares, pp. 18–23 and *Henrique Mesquita*, Direitos reais, pp. 272–5). Greek law acknowledges both 'horizontal' as well as 'vertical' ownership. Horizontal ownership (Statute 3741/1929) is apartment ownership, which is composed of the exclusive ownership of an apartment or a floor and co-ownership of the ground as well as the common rooms. 'Vertical' ownership (Statutory Order 1024/1971 and Arts 1002, 1117 Greek Civil Code) is the separate and autonomous ownership of a building (in contrast to the ownership of an *apartment* in a building), which has been constructed alongside one or more buildings on the same land unit. It comprises co-ownership of the whole common land unit and individual ownership of the building. An agreement to establish vertical ownership must be notarized and registered. The vertical ownership may be separately charged with a hypothec, if the register discloses the corresponding limit of the hypothec (Arts 480, 480a, 486, and 492 Greek CPC). The holder of 'vertical' ownership may (notwithstanding restrictions from building law) extend the height of his building, while the holder of apartment ownership may not do this. There exist amalgamations of horizontal and vertical ownership, namely when at least two multi-storey buildings are located on the same land unit and are divided into storeys. Thus, in this sense, Greek law is based on the same images as Portuguese and Spanish law. Finally, the Italian Civil Code does not acknowledge *proprietà orizzontale*, however jurisdiction has acknowledged a *condominio orizzontale* (also known as *super condominio*: Cass. 4 November 2010, no. 22466, Giust. civ. 2011 p. 168; App. Milan 24 June 2006, Giur. Merito 2007 p. 1008). This refers to the co-ownership of buildings (termed 'vertical' in Greek law). This applies especially to terraced houses, for which common areas such as gardens, pools, heating installations, etc. are in co-ownership. The *super condominio* is not regulated by statute, it is subject to the general rules of co-ownership.

[62] Composed predominantly of the *Ley Hipotecaria* (LH) and the *Reglamento Hipotecario* (RH).

[63] *Díez-Picazo*, Fundamentos III^5, p. 244.

[64] Of course, this has received criticism in the Spanish literature: see, e.g. *Roca Sastre et al.*, Derecho hipotecario V^9, pp. 10–11.

[65] Under Art. 334(5) Spanish Civil Code, only such machines and facilities as are necessary for the enterprise count as immoveables, not the enterprise itself. However, the term 'immoveable' is not used in a uniform way by

of the earth's surface that is enclosed by a polygonal line and is an object of property', by way of reference to then-current definitions in the literature.[66] But this description was not wholly apt. At least in the formal sense, a *finca* is rather 'everything for which a register folio is created'.[67] This is follows from Art. 243 *Ley Hipotecario* and Art. 378 *Reglamento Hipotecario*. Spanish doctrine distinguishes, against this background, between so-called '*fincas materiales*' and land units that are capable of registration (*fincas registrales*) as forms of *entidades hipotecarias*. Such hypothecary entities are recognized in their own, single *folio registral*.[68] Everything that is listed in Art. 8 *Ley Hipotecario* forms, in the system of Spanish law, a *finca*, an independent land unit.[69] This position is reflected in Portuguese law with the so-called 'autonomous fractions of urban property' (*fracções autónomas dos prédios urbanos*). They are also immoveables.[70] Even if one were minded to understand them as a part of an immoveable only, that would not alter their fittingness as independent objects of property rights,[71] and accordingly of their quality as land units.

The Spanish concept of land units might display peculiar features related to the relevant law of registration, which are specific to the Spanish legal system; its approach, however, sets out in the right direction. The same can be said of more recent considerations in French law. In Art. 562 of a draft for the reform of French property law prepared by the *Association Henri Capitant*, there is a proposal for the civil code to state clearly that a *fonds* (land unit) can be the object of a spatial division, which would have the result of creating 'volumes'.[72] A *fonds*, on this view, could be divided such that a third party could acquire such a part of the *fonds* as determined by contractually agreed spatial boundaries. The current text of the French Civil Code **7.18**

the Spanish legislature. Art. 6(1) *Ley del Catastro Inmobiliario* uses *bien inmueble* exclusively for cadastral purposes (and here to mean 'plot' or 'parcel' [*parcela*] or 'piece of ground' [*porción del suelo*]). Under Art. 6(2) (in conjunction with Art. 8 *Ley del Catastro*) *bienes inmuebles* include, *inter alia*, (i) the different, separate elements of buildings, which are accessible for independent use and which are subject to the specific regulation of partial or apartment ownership, as well as the total, which forms a total using different, separate, mutually bound elements which have been obtained in one single legal act, as well as storage rooms and leisure areas (ii) the space covered by an administrative concession over *bienes inmuebles* or public institutions affected by the same, and *bienes inmuebles de características especiales*, meaning complex totals for a specific use.

[66] TS 10 December 1960, RAJ 1960 no. 4095 pp. 2664, 2666 ('*trozo de la superficie terrestre cerrado por una línea poligonal y objeto de propiedad*'). This older definition is perhaps too narrow for some situations, precisely because it is limited to the earth's surface. That such a limitation is outdated can be inferred from Art. 17(1) *Ley de Suelo*; in this regard, see *Tamayo Haya*, in: Orduña Moreno (ed.), Los sistemas de transmisión de la propiedad inmobiliaria en el derecho europeo, pp. 412–13). There is no comprehensive statutory definition of the *finca* to date.

[67] *Díez-Picazo and Gullón*, Sistema de Derecho Civil III(1)[8], p. 237. cf. *Díez-Picazo*, Fundamentos III[5], p. 242.

[68] Regarding the overall concept, see *Roca Sastre et al.*, Derecho hipotecario III[9], pp. 164–76 and 211–36.

[69] *Díez-Picazo*, Fundamentos III[5], pp. 242–5 (even administrative concessions [*concesiones administrativas*] within the meaning of Art. 44(6) *Reglamento Hipotecario* can be *fincas*).

[70] *Menezes Leitão*, Direitos reais[2], pp. 65–6

[71] Art. 1415 Portuguese Civil Code and regarding this *Carvalho Fernandes*, Teoria geral do direito civil I[2], p. 556.

[72] Périnet-Marquet (ed.), Propositions de l'Association Henri Capitant pour une réforme du droit des biens, p. 124 Art. 562: '*Un fonds peut faire l'objet d'une division visant à conférer à un tiers la propriété d'une partie de ce fonds situé au-dessus ou au-dessous d'une limite conventionnellement fixée. La propriété du dessus est appelée propriété superficiaire, celle du dessous propriété tréfoncière. Un fonds peut également, moyennant établissement d'un état descriptif de division, faire l'objet d'une division spatiale portant création de volumes.*'

recognizes neither 'ownership of volume' nor the *droit de superficie*. The proposal resembles the concept of 'strata property',[73] which is used in other parts of the world to describe the notion that property rights in buildings can be divided one the horizontal as well as vertical plane. English law has always seen matters thus, even if not in so many words, and this position was fixed by statute in 1925. Section 205(1)(ix) of the Law of Property Act 1925 provides that '*Land* includes land of any tenure, and mines and minerals, whether or not held apart from the surface, buildings or parts of buildings (whether the division is horizontal, vertical or made in any other way)'. The legislature has, in this manner, built on older layers of the common law. The latter had for some time followed the rule that a freehold estate can be created in one of the upper stories of a building, even when the lower stories and the surface are held in freehold by another.[74]

7.19 Just how complicated the terminology of property law becomes when rights in parts of buildings capable of separate ownership are still conceptualized in relation to the surface land is illustrated by German legislation governing the ownership of apartments. Section 1 of the German Apartment Ownership Statute establishes ownership in 'apartments' [*Wohnungen*] and co-ownership in 'spaces of a building not dedicated to a dwelling'. But what apartments and spaces actually 'are' is not addressed unambiguously in either the statute itself nor in the literature on it. The alternatives are, however, ready to hand. Either one sees 'apartments' as a third category of things in German law,[75] or one assigns them to the existing categories—i.e. *either* as moveable things *or* as land units casting apartments (much like 'apparent components' [*Scheinbestandteile*] under § 95 German Civil Code). Only the latter warrants serious consideration. Apartments do not, as a result of §§ 2 and 3 of the German Apartment Ownership Statute enabling 'special property' [*Sondereigentum*], become an independent category of things. This 'special' property is not special because it is a 'special right of ownership in apartments', but because its object is not part of the property owned by the community of apartment owners. The point of reference for this community property, without which the special property cannot be had and to which it 'belongs' (§§ 1 and 6 German Apartment Ownership Statute), is, as the statute expressly provides, a land unit (§ 3(1) German Apartment Ownership Statute). The

[73] Sec. 3(1) and (2) Conveyancing (Strata Titles) Act 1961 of the Australian state of New South Wales provides: 'Land may be subdivided into lots by registering a strata plan in the manner provided by or under this Act. When a plan has been so registered, the lots comprised therein, or any one or more thereof, may devolve or be transferred, leased, mortgaged, or otherwise dealt with in the same manner and form as any land held under the provisions of the Real Property Act, 1900, as amended by subsequent Acts.' Common ownership arises in shared facilities (sec. 9). Easements are created over the load-bearing structures and the roof of the building in favour of the apartments (secs 5–8). This further confirms that the individual apartments are to be seen as independent land units.

[74] *Coke* on Liddleton, p. 48b.

[75] Czech law appears to be developing in this direction. A house thus once again becomes a component of an immoveable thing, however, since 2014, there exists only one object of ownership, namely the 'unit'. The former differentiation between co-ownership of the common thing (house, land unit) and the individual ownership of the unit was abolished (*Eliáš et al.*, Nový občanský zákoník s aktualizovanou důvodovou zprávou a rejstříkem, pp. 499–500). The unit is composed of the apartment and of the fraction of the common part of the house. As such, it is an immoveable thing (§§ 1158(1) and 1159 Czech Civil Code).

point of reference of the special property, however, remains foggy. The statute only explains that it is a 'restriction' of the co-ownership rights of all the co-owners. But that sounds like a limited real right in land units (of one's own and of others) that is just *called* 'ownership' (but does not actually reflect the German concept of ownership itself).[76] However, precisely this point is vehemently contested in the German cases and literature (and elsewhere):[77] apartment ownership, it is said, is 'true ownership'.[78] But if this is so—if one refuses to recognizes the remarkable concept of common ownership encumbered with rights of sole ownership—the only remaining option is to conceptualize apartments as land units in their own right. They are surely things, but just as surely they are not moveable things. They are, rather, normative things with a physical substrate—namely, land units. The fact that the land 'surface' and the parts of the building without an independent status (such as stairwells)[79] also constitute an independent land unit (*ex lege* in the co-ownership of all apartment owners) is nothing to the point.

[76] Such as under Art. 5:106 Netherlands Civil Code and § 2(1) Sentence 1 Austrian Apartment Ownership Statute. The latter provision defines apartment ownership as the right of a co-owner of an estate to exclusively use the 'object of apartment ownership' [*Wohnungseigentumsobjekt*]. Objects of apartment ownership can be apartments, other autonomous spaces, and parking areas for cars. Every apartment owner is a co-owner of the 'land unit' on which the apartment is situated. Apartment ownership thus becomes common ownership 'of the land unit' in combination with a real right of use of the object of apartment ownership (*Feil/Marent/Preisl*, Grundbuchsrecht[2], § 2 Wohnungseigentumsgesetz no. 2). It is thus a *limited* real right in its own way, which is merely called 'ownership'. However, its formation and acquisition necessitate registration in the land registry (as in Germany: §§ 4 and 7 German Apartment Ownership Statute). Registration occurs by determining the land unit, on which the object of apartment ownership is located, and registering the apartment ownership in the corresponding *folio*; for further details, see *Feil/Marent/Preisl* op. cit., § 5 Wohnungseigentumsgesetz no. 5).

[77] Italian law consistently treats apartment ownership as true ownership. Ownership cannot be 'chopped up' under Italian law; Italian law follows a 'unitarian' concept of ownership (this, at least, is the prevailing opinion, e.g. *Bianca*, Diritto civile VI, p. 205). Ownership of land (*proprietà fondiaria*) and ownership of immoveables are essentially the same thing. While a variety of specific regulations exist for ownership of immoveables, these do not affect the general concept of ownership.

[78] BGH 19 December 1991, NJW 1992 pp. 978, 979; *Baur and Stürner*, Sachenrecht[18], § 29 no. 10; Staudinger (-*Spiegelberger*), BGB (2005), § 31 Wohnungseigentumsgesetz no. 15; Bärmann (-*Pick*), WEG[11], Introduction no. 64 ('Special ownership is true ownership within the meaning of § 903 German Civil Code'). Criticism has been expressed by Bärmann and Seuß (-*Drasdo*), Praxis des Wohnungseigentums[5], Section A I nos 60–61 (who sees the possibility to contractually influence apartment ownership as contrary to the Civilian concept of ownership) and *Merle*, Das Wohnungseigentum im System des bürgerlichen Rechts, p. 172 (who does not consider apartment ownership true ownership because its object is not a 'thing'). A judgment remarkable for its concept of a land unit in German law is BGH 10 February 2012, NJW 2012 p. 2343. Co-owners of a house had granted each other exclusive rights of use of their respective apartments through contractual obligation. The house accrued moisture damage from water which had flowed from the upper apartment into the apartment below it. The BGH rejected compensation regardless of fault (analogous application of § 906(2) Sentence 2 German Civil Code, the so-called 'neighbour law compensation claim'), because the provision is focused on emissions from one land unit to another. This case concerned one single land unit. By contrast, the BGH did not clarify whether the legal situation would have been different if the apartments had fallen under the regime of apartment ownership. It merely confirmed that a compensation claim could not be considered if the emissions originate from an institution of common ownership.

[79] What belongs to the apartment and what are to the parts of the building without independent status may of course be subject to contention. One example is balconies. CFI Hradec Králové 5. September 2003, 52 Ca 25/2003-107, Sbírka rozhodnutí Nejvyššího správního soudu 3 (2004) no. 136 counted them among the non-independent parts of a building, while Polish Sąd Najwyższy 3 October 2002, III RN 153/01, MP 2006/12 p. 654, OSNP 2003/18 Pos. 423, Lex-No. 80436 counted them as belonging to the apartment. As a balcony belongs to the apartment, thus the court, only the owner of the apartment (not the sum of all apartment owners) are liable for its renovation.

d. Forming Land Units by Partitioning Land

7.20 A land unit must be individualized in order to perform the functions of a thing. This individualization occurs through the division of land according to rules of the legal system. Everywhere, these rules refer to the geometrical figure of a surface. To determine a surface, data about its square meterage alone is insufficient.[80] It is also necessary to have an outline and fixed points of orientation;[81] the less requirements a legal system imposes on the form of a land unit, and the more irregular its outline can be, the more points of orientation are required. The area projected onto the surface of the earth by this outline against the relevant landmarks, however, remains a purely conceptual (and thus incorporeal) construct. This is barely evident in the everyday usage of certain languages; in rural areas, one often speaks of his 'area' when referring to his land unit. A spatial connotation is implicit in the word 'area'. But this connotation finds no resonance in the law. If one knows the outline and the location of a land unit, one can begin to determine the space that it occupies. The circumstances in which land units are created across Europe, however, do not appear to be understood in all the relevant details; the task of illuminating them is one for scholars of comparative legal history.[82] Two models fall for consideration. It is conceivable that, in the beginning, occupants and immigrants took possession of parcels of land and announced this to the outside world—in whatever way, but, in any case, in a manner later accepted by the legal system. Alternatively, and more realistically, we could presuppose that, at the dawn of the period of time in which our current law was formed, land had been assigned to its users under some feudal system of concessions: private in form, but sovereign in substance. In England, the implications of this model are palpable to the present day.[83] With

[80] Aptly put in TS 1 May 2010, RAJ 2010 Nr. 3692 p. 10570 (a claim for vindication from Art. 348 Spanish Civil Code can only be filed if the thing in question is individualized, namely with the aid of an exact determination of the surface area using compass directions, so the location of the thing is certain. This therefore necessitates a site plan. It is not sufficient for the purposes of Art. 348 Spanish Civil Code to claim ownership of a surface area of an amount of square metres). See also Czech Nejvyšší soud České republiky 23 January 2002, 22, Cdo 96/2000, Soubor civilních rozhodnutí Nejvyššího soudu C 987 (Even for the purposes of acquisition by prescription, a land unit must at least 'show itself') and OLG Frankfurt/Main 28 January 1985, MittRhNotK 1985 pp. 43, 44 (one cannot imagine ownership of a land unit in any other way but a specific surface area).

[81] e.g. Areopag 1170/2011, Isokrates-Database (Contracts about land units must contain the precise dimensions, the borders of the land unit and the names of the neighbouring owners, and must be notarized. Furthermore, a notarized topographic plan of the land unit, showing it in relation to neighbouring land units and the streets, and not merely its shape, but also its exact location, direction and area, is required) and *Bergel/Bruschi/Cimamonti*, Les biens^2, p. 193 no. 157 (the separation of immoveable property) begins with the demarcation of borders to neighbouring land units). The English system uses so-called title plans, meaning an outline on the basis of Ordinance Survey maps. Such a plan is required for registration (Land Registration Rules 2003 SI No. 1417, r. 5(a)). An official example can be found in http://eservices.landregistry.gov.uk/www/wps/QDMPS-Portlet/resources/example_title_plan.pdf; details can be found in the Practice Guide 40 of the Land Registry and its supplements (http://www.landregistry.gov.uk/professional/guides/practice-guide-40), especially Supplement 5—Title plan.

[82] To some extent in *Grossi*, Quaderni fiorentini XVII (1988) p. 359, 394 et seq. See also *Castronovo and Mazzamuto*, Manuale di diritto privato europeo II, pp. 28–31.

[83] Traces of this can certainly also be found in other legal systems. The Greek state, for example, remains a kind of super-owner of the so-called *Vakúfia*. These are areas which were not private property in the Ottoman Empire, but rather served religious purposes or belonged to the community. Greece, when newly created, accepted the rights of usufruct and administration of the Muslim population over these areas with the London Protocol of 3 February/22 January 1830. The state thus became their super-owner (see from Greek jurisdiction Areopag 454/2011, NoB 59 (2011) p. 2177 and CA Larissa 384/2011, Isokrates-Database).

the allotment of lands for personal (proper) use, the first step in the formation of land units was achieved. The smaller the sub-units were, the more precisely their boundaries had to be determined. One recognized a land unit in a portion of land as soon as the legal system afforded the private rights in it with *erga omnes* effect and allowed its transfer to other persons. The formation of land units, and the formation of property in the land went (and go) hand in hand: the recognition of ownership in land creates land units, and the creation of land units enables ownership in land. But the formation of land units and the *content* of ownership are not woven together in this way: the creation of land units does not require a concept of 'ownership' on the Civilian model—i.e. a concept of ownership that is eternal and indivisible.[84] Nothing in the internal logic of property law demands an identical concept of ownership for all types of thing; what is necessary is only that every right of 'ownership' clearly identifies the point of reference in which it entails subjective property rights.

e. Altering the Composition of a Land Unit

Leaving special limits on alienability to one side for the moment, the formation of land units is bundled up with the possibility of transferring and acquiring ownership in them. Land units are, however, not entities that are fixed once and forever. Their aggregate number can be increased through division and even reduced through consolidation. Such legal operations are, however, much more complicated than in the case of real things. In order to achieve such an outcome in the case of a real thing, one need only break it, take it apart, or compose it in such a way that a new economic good results. In all cases, a purely factual dealing is sufficient to create a new object that is the fitting object of property rights. Land units, on the other hand, are normative things, and for this reason their division and consolidation requires normative dealings. The mere act of planting a hedge, digging a trench, or raising a wall does not make one land unit into two; the removal of a hedge, trench, or wall does not make two land units into one—not even when they both belong to the same owner.[85] 7.21

[84] The distinction between possession and ownership is a recent one in any event. This distinction was unknown to many ancient legal systems, despite the fact that these had a conception of land units (tellingly, e.g. classic Greek law, see *McDowell*, To díkeo stin Athina ton klassikón chronon[5], p. 207). This shows that even the question of whom the land unit 'belongs to'—usually not a specific person, but rather a whole family—can be clearly separated from the question of what a land unit 'is'.

[85] It is, admittedly, sometimes contentious whether two land units belonging to the same owner and sharing a border are not, in fact, one land unit. Polish Sąd Najwyższy 30 October 2003, IV CK 114/2002, OSNC 2004 no. 12 Pos. 201, Biul.SN 2004 no. 12 Pos. 6 answered this question in the negative. Neighbouring land units, which may be the property of a single individual, but have different land register entries, are separate immoveables until they are joined in one entry. However, Polish Sąd Najwyższy 27 December 1994, III CZP 158/94, OSNC 1995 no. 4 Pos. 59 ruled in contrast that an immoveable is an area which is subject to the ownership of one legal subject and is surrounded externally by the land units of other legal subjects. The relation to the land registers would thus be meaningless.

(1) Merger of Land Units

7.22 The consolidation of land units is a relatively uncommon procedure. It is typically motivated by reasons outside of property law and, for this reason, it is often effected with mechanisms outside of property law. The most well-known example is the consolidation of land units in the course of a sovereign intervention, colourfully known in German as 'cleansing' the cadastral district [*Flurbereinigung*]. Such a process is necessary, for example, where too-frequent division of land units has led to small parcels insufficient for the purposes of modern agriculture. It is then in the public interest to consolidate land units to provide the agricultural sector with a more adequate basis for its subsistence. Property rights in the new land units arise *ex lege*; the formation of land units and the acquisition of ownership thus remain, in such a process, relational processes. The legal basis for such a procedure, however, is generally found in special legislation; among the civil codes, only Art. 1382 Portuguese Civil Code provides for this kind of consolidation of land units.[86]

In France, the terminology is of *remembrement*. The *remembrement* of land units is aimed at bringing to an end the fragmentation, scattering, or poor division of land, where and to the extent to which such developments hinder or prevent its rational use.[87] This affects both agricultural and rural land units. The *remembrement rural* is intended to enable the use of large, modern agricultural plant and machinery (Arts 121-1 and 123-1 *Code rural et de la pêche maritime*). The *remembrement urbain*, on the other hand, serves the purposes of city planning. It has been the object of numerous legislative instruments. The older ones concerned land units laid waste in the Second World War; today, the legislative purpose is rather the *exécution des plans d'urbanisme* (Art. L322-1 and following *Code de l'urbanisme*). One distinguishes, in turn, between *remembrement forcé* and the consensual consolidation, called *remembrement amiable*. Under Art. L123-13(1) *Code rural et de la pêche maritime*, which concerns the *remembrement rural*, encumbrances on the affected land units are carried over (with the exception of servitudes). A similar rule is also provided for the *remembrement urbain*.[88] The Polish equivalent of these rules is found in the Statute of 26 March 1982 On the Consolidation and Exchange of Immoveables.[89] Art. 1 of this statute establishes that the consolidation of land units serves the purpose of creating favourable conditions for agriculture and forestry. In Greek law, too, the consolidation of land units rests on

[86] In fact, the Portuguese Civil Code contains several different provisions to guarantee a sufficient size for agricultural areas. Art. 1376 Portuguese Civil Code prohibits the division of agricultural fields (*terrenos aptos para a cultura*) into plots which would fall below the minimum size determined for the by the law. Art. 1382 Portuguese Civil Code concerns the merging (*emparcelamento*) of agricultural land units which belong to the same owner. The idea contained in this provision is to combat the fragmentation and scattering of agricultural land units and thereby improving the technological and financial conditions for agriculture. The details are provided in DL 103/90 of 22 March 1990 (*Regime de Emparcelamento e Fraccionamento de Prédios Rústicos*). Measures for the consolidation through sovereign intervention can be initiated by the state as well as privately.

[87] *Jourdain*, Les biens, p. 425 no. 341.

[88] Ibid., p. 432 no. 348. Details are discussed in JClCiv Code (-*Peignot*), Aménagement foncier agricole et forestier, Annex I, Fasc. 40, nos 136–137.

[89] Dz.U. 1982 no. 11 Pos. 80, rewritten in Dz.U. 2003 no. 178 Pos. 1749.

a ministerial decision; this leads not only to an originary acquisition of title, but also to the clearance of all existing encumbrances. The latter are transformed into obligational claims to damages against the new owner.[90] Spanish law organizes the *concentración parcelaria* on the basis of the national Statute on Agricultural Reform and Agricultural Development (*Ley de Reforma y Desarollo Agrario*—LRDA, Decree 118/1973 of 12 January 1973) and several regional statutes of the autonomous communities. What results from this framework is *fincas de reemplazo* or *fincas resultantes de la concentración* (Art. 222 LRDA). They, along with the real rights relating to them, are entered into the land registry (Arts 235–239 LRDA).[91]

The more difficult question is whether land units can also be consolidated through the exercise of private property rights. This question does not turn on whether the right in question requires the cooperation of a land registry office or some other public body. Even the transfer of land units requires the action of such bodies. If this were the case, one would remain within the framework of the relevant system of property law (in contrast to the sovereign procedures outlined above). But the consolidation of land units through the private exercise of their owner's property rights is only unproblematic in the case that the land units in question are wholly unencumbered—and in such a case, their consolidation would be, from the point of view of the owner, quite pointless.[92] One generally desires to effect such a procedure in order to clear away registered relationships that have become unwieldy or to satisfy the public law conditions of a development application, for example a rule that requires a certain minimum size for the construction of a building.[93] We could thus say that the consolidation of two land units by their common owner is *always* a procedure motivated from outside; it always follows the logic of 'cleansing', not the internal logic of property law. The process can, however, bring the latter into substantial difficulty in cases where it is sought to acquire a building permit and the land units in question are already encumbered with rights in **7.23**

[90] More details in Areopag 689/1992, EEN 35 (1993) p. 520 and EllDik 1994 p. 99, as well as Protodikeio Athens 2749/2010, Isokrates-Database (both cited while emphasizing the fact that these cases concern originary acquisition of ownership).

[91] Details in *Sánchez Hernández*, Redur 4/2006, pp. 75–85.

[92] It is conceivable that the land units should be consolidated with the purpose of allowing the owner of several smaller land units to take up and secure a high loan. However, in many countries this aim can be achieved more easily and more cost-effectively by creating an 'indivisible' hypothec (e.g. Art. 2809(2) Italian Code Civil; Art. 696 Portuguese Code Civil; Art. 2393(2) French Code Civil; § 1132(1) German Code Civil) (*Müller-Bromley*, Modernisierung des portugiesischen Hypothekenrechts, p. 122).

[93] These are the two main reasons given in the German literature for the 'consolidation' of land units. As consolidations improve the clarity of the land register, thus making land unit transactions easier, they are free of charge as a rule (BeckOK [*-Kral*], GBO, § 5 no. 7). This also confirms that the interest in the consolidation of land units is, at its core, a public one. If a land unit is too small and thus does not fulfil the requirements of the Greek Construction Statute (Statute No. 1577/1985), then Greek law (under the statutory direction 690/1948 [Gazette A'133/8 May 1948] or under Art. 7 § 10 of the new Greek Construction Ordinance [Statute 4067/2012, Gazette A' 79/ 9 April 2012]) stipulates that the land unit must be consolidated with a neighbouring land unit on which construction is possible. Multiple neighbouring land units, on which construction is not possible, must thus be consolidated in such a way that they constitute one or more land units on which construction is permitted (Arts 301–303 Code for the Construction Authorities [*Kódikas basikís poleodomikís nomothesías*]). The situation is very similar under Bulgarian law (Art. 17(2) Nos 2 and 3 of the Bulgarian Statute on Territory and Spatial Planning). The consolidation of land units leads to originary acquisition. While keeping in mind the different system of registration, English law also acknowledges the consolidation of registered estates by the registrar if multiple similar estates have the same owner (Land Registration Rules 2003, r. 3(4)).

favour of third parties. Unless the union of two land units is expressly prohibited on this basis (or at least made condition on a satisfactory agreement between the owner and the rights-holders),[94] the legal system itself must embody a judgment about what should happen to existing encumbrances. The answer to this question, however, differs across legal systems.

If one were dealing with real things rather than land units, matters would be no different. Often, there are no detailed rules for real things either. The civil codes of Portugal, Spain, and the Czech Republic, for example, have not developed an express answer to the question what happens in cases of connection, combination, or processing when the relevant thing is encumbered with a pledge; one must rely on the general principle that originary acquisition of ownership extinguishes previous encumbrances. The situation is the same in Italian law. *Accessione* (Art. 934 Italian Civil Code), *unione* (Art. 939 Italian Civil Code), *commistione* (Art. 939 Italian Civil Code), and *specificazione* (Art. 940 Italian Civil Code) are elements of the acquisition of ownership *ex lege*,[95] for which pre-existing encumbrances are in turn extinguished.[96] Only hypothecs subsist (and extend to the new thing in its entirety) under Art. 2811 Italian Civil Code. The answer given in the abovementioned § 949 German Civil Code is more complex. If the owner of the encumbered thing (the pledge debtor) is sole owner of the second thing (with which the first thing is united) the pledge extends to the new thing in its entirety; if he is only a part owner of the first thing, his partial ownership right stands in the place of the first thing and the new thing does not even fall to him in part—all prior encumbrances are extinguished. The latter rule also applies in case that the encumbered first thing is a material component of a new principal thing [*Hauptsache*], whether that thing is a real thing or a land unit.[97] The creditors' erstwhile rights are transformed, in the best case, to (obligational) claims to compensation. With the extinction of their point of reference, the encumbrances themselves cease to exist.

7.24 These rules, however, cannot be carried over to land units without adjustment—not least, because a land unit cannot be the 'material component' [*wesentlicher Bestandteil*] of another land unit. Moreover, the general principle applies that encumbrances subsist following the consolidation of two land units. In and of itself, this is compatible with the rule provided in § 949 German Civil Code for moveable things. This is because a land unit, consolidated with another land unit, remains in the sole ownership

[94] Under Art. 22(2) Polish Land Registry Act, properties charged which limited real rights can only be consolidated if the entitled parties agree on the position of these rights over the property created through consolidation. In Czech law, almost every consolidation (and every division) of land units requires the approval of the local building authority. Upon the application of all concerned land unit owners under § 77 in conjunction with § 82(2) Building Statute No. 183/2006, a planning decision [*územní rozhodnutí*] is issued. Only land units of the same nature can be consolidated (one cannot, e.g. consolidate a garden and an agricultural field). Special attention must be paid to § 35(7) Cadastral Ordinance No. 357/2013, which provides that it is not permissible to consolidate parcels or parts of parcels which are the subject of different information pertaining to rights; an exception applies to parcels and their parts over which a real encumbrance is registered, the extent of which is set out in the geometric plan.

[95] *Torrente and Schlesinger*, Manuale di diritto privato[19], p. 273.

[96] *Bianca*, Diritto civile VI, p. 324.

[97] Correctly decided in BGH 23 October 1953, NJW 1954 p. 265.

of the person that initiated the process of consolidation. There is no other person involved; the old owner of the first land unit is also the sole owner of the new land unit. In consequence, all existing encumbrances subsist; there is no reason for their extinction. A question, however, remains to be answered, concerning the object to which these encumbrances refer following the creation of the new (consolidated) land unit: only to the part to which they first referred, or to the new land unit as a whole? If one opts for the latter option—which is consistent with the basic principles of property law—it remains only to determine the hierarchy of encumbrances of the same type, and in this task one can choose (as a matter of legal policy) whether to develop a rule (mandatory or default, for example, governing the priority of register entries) or to leave the matter to the agreement of the parties in question. In the event, legal systems that carry prior encumbrances over to the new land unit as a whole often decide for the latter option.[98] In Austria, for example, the rule of 'joint liability of the "land register entity" [*Grundbuchskörper*]' (under which liability always attaches to the registered 'entity', which may comprise multiple land units, not the registered land unit)[99] has the consequence that the consolidation of land units always results in the liability attaching to the new land unit as a whole without qualification. A precondition of consolidation is that both the affected land units demonstrate an economic connection and belong to the same owner (§ 5(2) AllgGAG). It makes no difference what kind of encumbrances are involved; with the consent of the owner, even land units with greatly different levels of encumbrance can be consolidated into a *Grundbuchskörper* (§ 5(3) AllgGAG). However, this all remains conditional on the requirement that the priority of the encumbrances concerned is organized such that nothing changes for the creditors apart from an increase in the funds available to satisfy them (§ 5(3) AllgGAG). In Czech law,[100] in Netherlands law,[101] and in German law, judicial opinion and the

[98] For example, Art. 22 Polish Land Registry Act provides that limited property rights encumbering one of the connected land units encumber all of them. This, however, does not affect established exercise of a usufruct or servitude. Encumbered land units can only be connected when the beneficiaries of the encumbrances agree to the relative priority of their rights. The provisions of this section are also to be applied to the priority of certain rights and claims listed in Art. 16, as well. Swedish law also provides that a hypothec which charges one of the original land units also charges the new land unit after its consolidation with another (Kap. 6 § 16 JB). If the consolidation threatens to impair one of the hypothecs, then whether a consolidation occurs will depend on the consent of the hypothec creditor concerned (Kap. 10 § 2(2) Fastighetsbildningslag (1970:988)]).

[99] Regarding this and the following, *Rassi*, Grundbuchsrecht, no. 513.

[100] Under Czech law, real rights relate to that part of the earth's surface which is surrounded by the boundaries of the land unit in the moment in which the real right is created. Pledges over land therefore do not extend to parts of the land unit which are added at a later date (*Baudyš*, Katastr nemovitostí^{2}, p. 158).

[101] Under Art. 3:227(2) Netherlands Civil Code, pledge rights and hypothec rights to a thing extend to everything encompassed by the ownership right to the thing. The components of a land unit are available to satisfy a hypothec (after all, they lose their character as objects of separate rights under Art. 5:20 Netherlands Civil Code), and so is the accretion [*aanwas*], for example new land on a mudflat or a riperian land unit. When a land unit grows through the drying out of a body of water, the relevant hypothec grows to extend over the new land, too (Asser [-*van Mierlo and van Velten*], Vermogensrecht algemeen III^{14}, p. 290 no. 279; see also M.v.A. II, Parl. Geschiedenis III, p. 734). The question of what happens in the case of the legal unification of land units is not answered in Art. 3:227 Netherlands Civil Code. *Van Mierlo and van Velten* op. cit. gives the example of an owner of an encumbered land unit purchasing an unencumbered adjacent land unit and combining them. In such a case, although both land units are joined in the ownership of a single owner, two parcels remain as legally independent objects and a hypothec over one does not extend to the other.

preponderance of the scholarly literature follows an alternate thesis,[102] namely that encumbrances (i.e. hypothecs, *Grundschulden*, real servitudes) do not 'automatically' extend to the new land unit that results from a consolidation. Following a consolidation, a hypothec only extends to that part of the new land unit to which it originally referred.[103] The result of this approach is an internal parcelling of land units that is quite difficult to reconcile dogmatically: land units are created within land units. It is inconsistent to treat the consolidated land units as simple (non-independent) components of the 'new' land unit, on the one hand, and to treat them as capable of being the objects of 'special rights', on the other.[104] They are only capable of being objects of specific rights when they are characterized as (independent) land units. What else should they be, after all? At the same time, the relevant literature treats the 'new' land unit as an independent patrimony and object of legal dealings. New hypothecs (and so forth) can, after all, be created over the new land unit as a whole. Granted, it is no longer possible to encumber the erstwhile land units with new (separate) pledges (§ 7(1) German GBO), but this rule does not exclude servitudes and *Reallasten* (§ 7(2) German GBO). Thus, land units within land units remain; the remarkable construction is reminiscent of Russian dolls (*matryoshkas*)—one opens a doll and a new, smaller doll appears.

(2) Division of Land Units

7.25 The division of land units can be interpreted coherently within the framework of property law more easily. A division is based, insofar as it is not the consequence of a sovereign intervention (i.e. a taking), either on the fulfilment of the elements of a statutory provision that enables the division of land units or on the exercise of the property rights of the owner of the land unit, which requires the cooperation of others. The law of statutory acquisition of ownership effects the creation of new land units primarily through rules governing prescriptive possession. Some legal systems also count the law of good faith acquisition in this category. In any case, provided an appropriate land registry system exists, this body of law can certainly create new land units.[105] In German law, for

[102] A different (and, in our view, correct) position is taken by Staudinger (*-Jickeli and Stieper*), BGB (2004), § 93 no. 40.

[103] BGH 21 October 1977, NJW 1978 p. 320. Real rights already vested in the land unit remain according to their old boundaries; this is even the case when land units are united in the cadastre (BGH 24 November 2005, NJW 2006 pp. 1000, 1001). This is similar for servitudes if the main land unit is merged with another (BayObLG 05 December .2002, NJW-RR 2003 pp. 451, 452): in the case of a dominant land unit that is joined with another land unit, the entitlement formally extends to the owner from time to time of the new 'whole' land unit. The exercise of the rights concerned, however, is limited to the benefit of the part that used to be the dominant land unit.

[104] However, this appears to be the prevailing view in the scholarship: for details see Staudinger (*-Gursky*), BGB (2008), § 890 nos 3 and 33.

[105] For example, in France the publicity of the register (*publicité foncière*) permits the identification of a land unit. The *fichier immobilier*, established in 1955, facilitates the search for existing land units via multiple charts, namely a personal chart for every holder of a right over an immoveable, a chart for every immoveable, and a parcel card, which records multiple combined parcels on the basis of the cadastre. However, this publicity in the matter of land units has a merely declaratory function under French law. It is meaningless for relations between a buyer and a seller, as well as for the question of transfer of ownership between them. The information in the register merely serves the protection of third parties, who may have acquired competing rights from the same seller (*Aynès and Crocq*, Les sûretés[5], p. 287 no. 634). This follows from Art. 30(1) Décret n° 55-22 portant réforme de la publicité

example, the principle of 'public confidence in the registry' (§ 892 German Civil Code) extends not only to the property rights registered in land units but also to the existence of the relevant land units.[106] This becomes especially important in cases involving acquisition of part of a land unit that has been incorrectly registered as an independent land unit (e.g. because the absence of the necessary planning permit was overlooked). Acquisition of ownership and formation of the land unit fall, in this case, into a single operation.

The position would appear to be the same in Austrian law (unfortunately, authority on the point is lacking). The Austrian land register enjoys public confidence (at least where such operates in favour of acquiring for value). The point of reference is the existence of a 'land register entity' [*Grundbuchskörper*]. If a land unit is deregistered with one entity and registered (incorrectly) with another, that is registered with a person other than the true owner, this mis-registration nonetheless enjoys public confidence. As a result, a third party that acquires the entity in good faith also becomes owner of the land unit in question.[107] From this, one could draw the conclusion that even an entity that does not actually exist could be brought into being through good faith acquisition. This conclusion would be supported by the fact that registration generally has a constitutive effect (§ 4 Austrian Land Register Statute).

The law of prescriptive acquisition leads to the creation of a new land unit when it goes beyond moving the boundary between two neighbouring land units (which often occurs), and projects stand-alone objects of ownership. This is the case when a legal system provides that an area lying completely within a land unit belonging to another can be acquired through prescription, that is without enlarging an existing, neighbouring land unit.[108] But the provisions that allow for ownership in land to be taken away from a person differ from legal system to legal system. 7.26

foncière. Unpublicized disposals over land units *inter vivos* are only invalid *vis-à-vis* such third parties as have acquired competing rights, from the same seller, on the grounds of processes for which publication is mandatory. Publicity also has the function of informing the public administration about land units. The legal situation is very much the same in Belgium. Registration is not a requirement of validity for the transaction with regard to the parties among each other. The registration (*transcription*) is only necessary in order to validate the transaction with regard to third parties (Art. 1 Loi sur la révision du régime hypothécaire): for further details, see *Grégoire*, Publicité foncière, p. 40 no. 125. This is also the case under Art. 2644 Italian Civil Code.

[106] BayObLG 6 February 1981, MittBayNot 1981 pp. 125, 126 and BayObLG 11 May 1995, MittBayNot 1995 pp. 291, 293 ('Public confidence in the registry also extends to the legal existence of the registered land unit as such'), as well as OLG Frankfurt 28 January 1985, MittRhNotK 1985 pp. 43, 44 ('As one cannot conceive ownership over a land unit other than in relation to a certain area, the registration of the land unit's area belongs to that part of the registry's contents which is covered by public confidence in the registry'). See also Staudinger (-*Gursky*), BGB (2008), § 892 no. 33.

[107] *Feil/Marent/Preisl*, Grundbuchsrecht^2, § 7 GBG no. 16.

[108] The situation is equivalent where co-owned shares of a formerly common land unit are transformed into individual property through prescriptive acquisition. cf. Areopag 696/2009, NoB 57 (2009) p. 2159: It is assumed of a co-owner, who possesses the common thing, that he possesses it in the name of the other co-owners; he can thus not raise the objections of extraordinary prescriptive acquisition or limitation as long as he has not notified the other owners of his decision to possess the common thing, either in part or as a whole, for himself. Such a notification is, however, not necessary—and prescriptive acquisition is possible—if an informal division of the common land unit has occurred among the co-owners. From this point onwards, every co-owner possesses 'his' part of the land unit exclusively for himself.

In Greek law, for example, Areopag 1134/2011 held that nothing stands in the way of acquiring ownership of part of a land unit in the course of ordinary and extraordinary prescriptive possession,[109] and that in this manner a land unit is created—albeit one that cannot be developed. The defendant in possession had not fenced in the part of the land unit in question (fencing was, by reason of the stony ground, not feasible) but he had manifested the intention, through his own conduct and through the conduct of his employees in patrolling the land, to possess it as if it belonged to him. However, the possession of parts of land units in this way is prohibited by statute for the very small agricultural land units distributed to landless farmers by way of lottery in Emergency Statute 431/1968.[110] Under Polish law, on the other hand, any immoveable (land units, buildings, and premises) can be acquired through prescriptive possession regardless of the identity of its owner.[111] This is the case for immoveables owned by the state since 1 October 1990 (when Art. 177 Polish Civil Code was repealed). The only exceptions are buildings owned by productive cooperatives, because these are treated as part of an inalienable usufruct in the relevant land unit (Arts 272 and 254 Polish Civil Code). Other than this, the legal position seems relatively unclear. It appears (in contrast to Greece) that with the exception of the soil itself, non-independent components of an immoveable object cannot, in principle, be acquired by prescriptive possession.[112] The Supreme Court, however, held in a judgment of 6 June 1973 that possession is only possible in the case of things in which a real right can be acquired. In consequence, possession *animo domini* of components of a thing (buildings, premises) would appear to be excluded in principle; under Art. 47 § 1 Polish Civil Code, a component of a thing cannot be the object of a separate right of ownership or other real rights. Only buildings and premises that can be objects of separate property rights can be objects of possession *animo domini* and be acquired by prescription.[113] The court, however, did not follow this reasoning exactly in its later judgments. It later held that occupation of a *de facto* (but not *de jure*) delineated part of a premises that was already the object of separate rights could result in prescriptive acquisition, and thus created smaller premises within the premises.[114] However, it also decided that one could not acquire ownership over a single room in this manner.[115] Italian law, too, recognizes prescriptive possession of

[109] NoB 60 (2012) p. 646.

[110] Areopag 220/2010, NoB 58 (2010) p. 1744.

[111] Gniewek (-*Nadler*), Kodeks cywilny^2, p. 312 no. 2.

[112] Thus, with reservations, Radwański and Dybowski (-*Stelmachowski*), System Prawa Prywatnego III^2, p. 394 no. 163. It is possible to acquire a land unit strip by prescription (*Gniewek*, Prawo rzeczowe^8, p. 91 no. 262), not however a building which is a component of the land unit (Gniewek [-*Nadler*], Kodeks cywilny^2, Art. 172, p. 313 no. 5).

[113] Polish Sąd Najwyższy 6 June 1973, I CR 413/73, Lex-No. 7265 (it is not possible to acquire a part of a building by prescription, thus acquiring ownership, if this would lead to the partitioning of a building which is not the object of separate ownership).

[114] Polish Sąd Najwyższy 15 March 1989, III CZP 14/89, OSNC 1990 no. 2 Pos. 27, Lex-No. 3523. Polish Sąd Najwyższy 17 February 2011, III CSK 147/10, Lex-No. 818558 also points in this direction (concerning the prescriptive acquisition of an area of land, which was originally an essential component of a state-owned river; land which is only covered by water at high tide [oxbow lakes] can be acquired by prescription).

[115] Polish Sąd Najwyższy 15 March 1989 op. cit. Likewise, if on occasionally different grounds Czech Nejvyšší soud České republiky 25 November 2003, 22 Cdo 296/2002 and 3 April 2007, 22 Cdo 781/2006, Právní rozhledy no. 15/2007 p. 568 (no prescriptive acquisition of a room which, while located in the neighbouring house, can only be accessed through the house whose owner claimed prescriptive acquisition).

parts of a land unit; the surface area of the new land unit that arises is determined by the judgment that grants the claim; cadastral plans are not dispositive but serve as an aid.[116] Matters are very different in Austrian law. There, entry into the cadastre already produces legal effects. Under § 8(1) Austrian *Vermessungsgesetz*, the boundaries set down in the cadastre are binding. The natural boundaries of the property cannot be enforced against someone who acquires a land unit in reliance upon the cadastral boundaries (§ 49 Austrian *Vermessungsgesetz*). Acquisition in reliance on the cadastre leads, in other words, to a good faith acquisition of the corresponding surface land, even when the natural boundaries (hedges, streams, etc.) diverge. But the priority of the cadastral boundaries also excludes the prescriptive acquisition of individual parts of a land unit (§ 50 Austrian *Vermessungsgesetz*). Someone who uses a part of his neighbour's land by reason of a misplaced fence does not so acquire it.

The division of a land unit against the will of its owner is not generally possible; but the owner himself cannot generally effect a division in the unilateral exercise of his property rights, either. Naturally, he can build a wall clear across his land, plant a hedge, or dig a trench. But he thereby only divides his land unit in a physical, not a legal sense.[117] Not even the surveyor's marks that accompany such a factual dealing (e.g. *bornage*) would necessarily change this result.[118] The division of a land unit is generally dependent on the bilateral cooperation of a contractual partner (generally a purchaser) or the prior decision of the authority that keeps the land register, which is generally made **7.27**

[116] Art. 950(2) Italian Civil Code; see in this regard Cass. 23 January 1995, no. 739, Mass. Giust. civ. 1995 p. 135.

[117] For this reason, a variety of formulations in the French literature are, in our view, imprecise, e.g. *Jourdain*, Les biens, p. 415 no. 331 ('*Normalement, le propriétaire d'un fonds a le droit de diviser celui-ci en plusieurs parcelles pour aliéner chacune d'entre elles à un acquéreur différent; le droit de lotir fait partie des attributs de propriété tel que celui-ci est compris par le Code civil*') and Bergel/Bruschi/Cimamonti, *Les biens*[2], p. 700 no. 623 ('*Le droit de diviser librement son fonds et d'en céder des parcelles à des personnes différentes est normalement inhérent au droit de propriété et ne relève que du droit du propriétaire de disposer de son bien*'), also *Terré and Simler*, Les biens[8], p. 309 no. 377. The *lotissement* is defined more precisely in Cass. 8 July 1987, Bull. civ. 1987, III, p. 83 no. 142 ('*constituent un lotissement l'opération et le résultat de l'opération ayant pour objet ou ayant eu pour effet la division volontaire en lots d'une ou plusieurs propriétés foncières par vente ou locations simultanées ou successives en vue de la création d'habitations, de jardins ou d'établissements industriels ou commerciaux*'). *Lotissement* thus necessitates the sale or lease of a land unit.

[118] The French legal opinion holds that *bornage* is merely the basis for assessment of immoveables. *Périnet-Marquet*, Propositions de l'Association Henri Capitant pour une réforme du droit des biens, Art. 651 defines it as the '*opération qui a pour effet de reconnaître et fixer, de façon contradictoire et définitive, les limites séparatives des propriétés privées appartenant ou destinées à appartenir à des propriétaires différents*'. Its administrative basis is the cadastre. The *bornage* determines the dividing line between two land units with the aid of *bornes* (border markers: see *Terré and Simler*, Les biens[8], p. 236 no. 277). They materialize the graphic outline of the land unit. The cadastre in turn is composed of documents created by the municipalities responsible, which assign numbers to parcels (*Bergel/Bruschi/Cimamonti*, Les biens[2], p. 197 no. 161). *Bornage* thus represents parcels, not ownership statuses. The cadastral documents thus only have administrative and fiscal significance. The main function of the cadastre remains to facilitate an estimation of the value of land units, and to levy taxes on this basis. Cadastral registrations thus cannot establish a title, nor can they be used to verify ownership, as they have a merely indicative effect even in such cases in which the border is contested (*Bergel/Bruschi/Cimamonti* op. cit. p. 198 no. 162). The situation is similar under Italian law. While it is customary, upon the sale of a partial area of a land unit, to mark the new borders with boundary stones, this only has a clarifying function, and is not the basis of ownership (and does not create a land unit in the legal sense) (*Bianca*, Diritto civile VI, p. 440). In Czech law, the borders of a land unit are determined by a committee of employees of the land registry, the municipality and other public institutions. The owners of the land unit and other rights-holders are summoned to this event (§ 42(1) Czech Katastrální zákon no. 256/2013 Gbl.). However, the improvement of the information in the cadastre does not affect the legal positions over the land unit (§ 50(2) Czech Katastrální zákon).

on the application of the vendor or with his permission. What is common to both systems is only that the division of a land unit can be conditional on the granting of some administrative permission. They differ, however, in the following respect: in the first model, the sale and division of a land unit proceed in a single operation, while in the second model the formation of a new land unit is made prior to a dealing with property rights in it.

7.28 In French law, the division of a land unit is seen in principle as an exercise of the private autonomy of a rights-holder. The division itself is brought about through an agreement (a 'contract') between the disponor and the disponee; the creation of a (new) land unit and the acquisition of ownership are not seen as cumulative, either temporally or legally. In the nineteenth century, the *lotissement* (the distribution of a land unit by lot) occurred purely through a contractual process. Only at the beginning of the twentieth century did the legislature intervene in pursuit of a policy to discourage the creation of excessively small parcels. At least, statute made the most important *lotissements* subject to an instance of administrative approval (today Art. R. 421-19 *Code de l'urbanisme*). The contractual core of the division remains, however, unaffected by this instance. The same can be said for the Italian system. The purchaser acquires, upon execution of the contract of sale, ownership in the relevant land unit. The erstwhile land unit is thereupon divided into two different land units. However, this dealing only acquires *erga omnes* effect if the contract of sale satisfies requirements of written formality and if it is entered in a public register (*trascrizione nei pubblici registri immobiliari*). The latter occurs, in turn, either on the basis of an *atto pubblico* or of a *scrittura privata autenticata* (Art. 2657 Italian Civil Code). A plan of the new land unit is appended to the contract of sale and forwarded to the cadastral office, which updates its information on the basis of these data. If the new land unit has no access to a public street, a servitude over the other land unit arises *ex lege* and *ipso iure* (Art 1062 Italian Civil Code; so-called *destinazione del padre di famiglia*[119]). In Greek law, a land unit is created by a valid, notarized legal dealing and its subsequent entry into the so-called 'transcription book', i.e. through submission of the contract of sale to the land registry. In English law, too, the owner of a land unit can alienate his freehold estate by way of sale. The contract of sale must describe the object in adequate detail. Generally, this occurs through a linguistic description of the land unit and reference to a plan.[120] Such a plan is, in practice, also required when the object of sale belongs to a freehold estate that is already registered.[121] Matters proceed accordingly in the subsequent transfer of ownership ('conveyance') of a part of a land unit.[122] In the case of an unregistered freehold, the conveyance may occur by means of Form TP1 at the Land Registry, and this formal process is mandatory

[119] Details in *Torrente and Schlesinger*, Manuale di diritto privato[19], p. 299 as well as *Branca and Alpa*, Istituzioni di diritto privato[7], p. 207.

[120] In case of a sale of a land unit, a plan drawn to an appropriate scale is especially desirable, cf. *Lloyd v Stanbury* [1971] 2 All ER 267, 273 (Brightman J); *Scarfe v Adams* [1981] 1 All ER 843, 845 (Cumming-Bruce LJ) (stating that a plan drawn to a scale of 1:2500 is useless when it comes to the partition of a building).

[121] Barnsley (-*Thompson*), Conveyancing Law and Practice[4], pp. 151–2.

[122] Ibid. pp. 527ff and p. 542.

in the case of a registered freehold.[123] If it remains unclear what part of the land unit is to be alienated, despite the description and the plan, reference will be made to information outside the contract of sale.[124] The conveyance then occurs through Form AP1, which is an application to change the register according to a description of the land.[125] The purchaser, however, acquires a conditional ownership of the land in equity already upon execution of the contract,[126] such that he is protected by sec. 29(2)(a)(i) Land Registration Act 2002 against later purchasers. Parts of an estate can also be registered separately, for example when they are to be encumbered with a registerable charge (Land Registration Rules 2003, r. 3(3)). In consequence, a real security interest is also possible over just a part of a registered estate.[127] In exceptional cases, an application can also be made to the court to 'clean up' a set of legal relations that have become too complex.[128]

In Germany, on the other hand, the formation of land units precedes the creation of new rights of ownership; these are two discrete legal processes. The expression 'land unit division' [*Grundstücksteilung*] describes the division of one land unit into several independent registered land units.[129] In contrast to the consolidation or 'adscription' of land units, the process of division is not even provided for in the relevant land register regulations, the *Grundbuchordnung*; express provision on division are only found in the (public law) Construction Code (especially § 19(1) German Construction Code). Nevertheless, there is general agreement on the requirements of the substantive law concerning division.[130] The object divided must be (i) a land unit in the legal sense, a right similar to a land unit, or a so-called right of 'apartment ownership' [*Wohnungseigentum*]. The owner of the land unit must (ii) make a declaration concerning the division to the land registry and deliver the necessary planning permissions. Finally, the division must (iii) be published in the land register. The division is made legally effective by the publication of new, independent land units based on the updated technical survey data from the cadastral records.[131] Registration is the constitutive act for the creation of a new land unit. The land unit parts [*Grundstückteile*] that were previously part of one land unit acquire their own registration number in the course of this process.[132] In Austria, the division of a land unit is governed by the Land **7.29**

[123] Land Registration Rules 2003 (SI No. 1417), r. 13(1); see also Land Registry, Practice Guide 21—Using transfer forms for less straightforward transactions (February 2011), section 1.2 (http://www.landregistry.gov.uk/professional/guides/practice-guide-21).

[124] *Scarfe v Adams* [1981] 1 All ER 843 (CA) (recourse to architectural designs contained within the auction catalogue).

[125] Land Registration Act 2002, sec. 27(1) and (regarding the formalities) Land Registration Rules 2003 (SI No. 1417), r. 58.

[126] *Thompson* op. cit. pp. 243ff.

[127] *Slessinger* (2011) 75 Conv 92–95.

[128] e.g. see *Ellison v Cleghorn* [2013] EWHC 5; 2013] All ER (D) 49 no. 47 (Briggs J (Ch): 'Where the parties are already co-owners of land which they intended at the outset should eventually be divided between them, then partition is the direct and natural means of achieving that objective, with recourse to the court if the beneficiaries will not all consent.' The legal basis for a partition by court order is Section 14 Trustees Act 1996.

[129] Staudinger (-*Mayer*), BGB (2009), § 1026 no. 5.

[130] For further details, see BeckOK (-*Kral*), GBO[15], § 7 nos 8 ff.

[131] *Mayer* op. cit.

[132] *Kral* op. cit. § 7 no. 24.

Subdivision Act [*Liegenschaftsteilungsgesetz*]. Additional provisions are found in the Survey Act [*Vermessungsgesetz*]. A land unit division plan, issued by the responsible public authority under § 1 *Liegenschaftsteilungsgesetz*, is a prerequisite; this plan rests in turn on a prior survey (§ 36 *Vermessungsgesetz*). The owner then has to apply for the entry of the division in the survey court [*Vermessungsgericht*] (§ 39 *Vermessungsgesetz*). The division is first entered into the cadastre and only then, with constitutive force, in the land register (§ 11(1) *Vermessungsgesetz*). Entries in the cadastre do not, even to the extent they are adopted in the land register, enjoy public confidence.[133] A land unit only becomes accessible to legal transactions when it is published as a 'land register body' [*Grundbuchkörper*] or part of a *Grundbuchkörper* in the land register; this conclusion is drawn by way of analogy to §§ 431, 444, and 445 Austrian Civil Code. Prior to publication in the land register, a land unit only exists under the narrow provisions of §§ 433 and 435 Austrian Civil Code.[134]

Under § 23(2) of the Hungarian Statute LXXVIII of 1997 on the Development and Protection of the Build Environment, the division of a land unit is an administrative process that begins with the application for an amendment in the land register. Polish law adopts a kind of hybrid system. This characterization relates to the fact that the division of a land unit follows as the result of an administrative decision, which occurs on the application of a person who has a legal interest in the division and bears the costs arising therefrom. On the other hand, the definition of a land unit in Polish law is not complete in the sense that it is not possible to say with certainty whether a decision of this type (at least) creates a new land unit. The definition in Art. 46 § 1 Polish Civil Code does not determine what meaning the land register has for the conceptual definition of a land unit. As such, it remained contentious whether the presence of multiple land register entries for a single area automatically led to the existence of multiple land units.[135] The Supreme Court confirmed this in a decision of 2003.[136] Neighbouring land units, which belong to the same owner but are registered in different entries remain discrete land units until they are united in one land register entry. In 1994, the same court had adopted the exact opposite position. A land unit is an area in the ownership of one person, which is framed in its external perimeter by the land units of other persons. The relationship to the land register, according to this approach, was meaningless; what was determinative was the separation of the surface such that it could be identified as an independent object of ownership.[137] Following this approach, it is not relevant whether a land unit comprises one or several (sub-)parcels or whether a land register entry exists for each or for all together.[138] It is important to remember that not all land rights in Poland are registered in a single system. This cannot, however, be taken to mean that a

[133] OGH 24 March 2004, 2 Ob 12/03h.

[134] For further details, see *Feil/Marent/Preisl*, Grundbuchsrecht², § 4 no. 5.

[135] Radwański and Safjan (-*Katner*), System Prawa Prywatnego I, p. 1181 no. 17.

[136] Polish Sąd Najwyższy 30 October 2003, IV CK 114/2002, OSNC 2004 no. 12 Pos. 201, Biul.SN 2004 no. 12 Pos. 6, Lex-No. 131941.

[137] Polish Sąd Najwyższy 27 December 1994, III CZP 158/94, OSNC 1995 no. 4 Pos. 59, Lex-No. 4156.

[138] Bieniek and Rudnicki (-*Bieniek*), Nieruchomości. Problematyka prawna¹, p. 350.

land unit that is not entered in a land register cannot be divided. The division of land units is, to complicate matters further, not defined in any Polish statute.

The problem of the continued existence of pre-existing encumbrances is less acute in the context of division than in the context of the consolidation of land units. The basic principle is the same in all legal systems: encumbrances on the original land unit carry over to the new land unit(s). In Czech law, for example, the Supreme Court has decided that the division of a land unit with a 'real encumbrance' (a kind of servitude that has its origins in the Soviet period) has no effect on the encumbrance; every new land unit remains subject to the encumbrance, provided that it falls within the encumbrance's spatial extent. If, however, a dominant land unit is divided, the servitude subsists for the benefit of the owner of each new land unit.[139] The Supreme Administrative Court affirmed this approach: when a land unit is divided into parcels in a geomatic such that new objects of property rights arise, the right of ownership in the sense of tax law subsists unaffected.[140] In other words, a property right does not change in scope because its point of reference gets a new parcel number.[141] Only in the case of certain servitudes such as rights of way can a newly created parcel be freed of encumbrances, for example when the right of way only even encumbered part of the original land unit.[142] If, by way of contrast, a dominant land unit is divided, § 1299(2) Czech Civil Code[143] calls for a consideration of whether the division works disproportionately to the advantage of those entitled (e.g. because the number of those entitled to use the right of way rises excessively). The French jurisprudence and literature are clear that the division of a land unit does not affect the content of a hypothec.[144] This follows Art. 2393(2) French Civil Code, under which a hypothec is essentially indivisible. It subsists, under this provision, over all the encumbered land units—'*sur chacun et sur chaque portion des ces immeubles*'. If a land unit is sold in parcels or divided, each '*lot*' is encumbered with the whole hypothec. Art. 123 Spanish *Ley Hipotecaria* takes the same approach. If a land unit encumbered with a hypothec is divided into two or more land units, the claim of the hypothec holder is not divided unless this has been agreed between the relevant parties. The creditor can choose any of the new land units for the satisfaction of his claim, or indeed all of them. In Germany and in Austria, land unit divisions generally require some administrative approval, but not the approval of creditors with limited property rights. These rights carry over (again with the usual 7.30

139 Czech Nejvyšší soud České republiky 14 August 2008, 22 Cdo 2016/2007, Soubor civilních rozhodnutí Nejvyššího soudu, C 6523.

140 Czech Supreme Administrative Court 16 May 2008, 2 Afs 70/2007-55, Sbírka rozhodnutí Nejvyššího správního soudu, 2008 no. 1631.

141 *Baudyš*, Katastr nemovitostí[2], p. 158.

142 *Bradáč*, Věcná břemena od A do Z[4], p. 83.

143 For further details, see *Baudyš* op. cit. p. 160 (regarding the virtually identically formulated previous provision in § 151p(3) Czech Civil Code [1964]).

144 Cass. civ. 6 March 1996, Bull. civ. 1996 no. 63 p. 42. '*L'hypothèque étant indivisible, la division de l'immeuble par suite d'un partage n'entraîne pas division de l'hypothèque*'. *Aynès and Crocq*, Les sûretés[5], p. 321 no. 680; *Bourassin/Brémond/Jobard-Bachellier*, Droit des sûretés[2], p. 535 no. 2015; *Albiges and Dumont-Lefrand*, Droit des sûretés[3], p. 341 no. 559.

exceptions for certain types of servitude: §§ 1025 and 1026 German Civil Code; § 3 Austrian *Liegenschaftsteilungsgesetz*) to the new land units.

3. The Creation of Land Units and the Nature of the Surface

a. Particular Rights in Particular Land Units

7.31 The substantive features of the surface of the earth associated with a land unit are, as a rule, irrelevant for the latter's formation. The object can be an urban or a rural area; a land unit can consist of building land, agricultural land, field, forest, or waste land, mountainous or flat topography—it can even be covered in water. The surface of a landscape is only inconsistent with the formation of a land unit when its properties lead the legislature to reserve land of a certain type for public ownership or otherwise being *extra commercium*. The same consequence follows from legislative provisions that prohibit the division of certain types of land into (overly) small units. Such prohibitions generally take the form of a rule that agricultural land or forest must maintain a certain minimum size in order to qualify as a point of reference for property rights. Otherwise, the classification of land units according to the features of the surface is only relevant for the types of property rights that can be held.[145] Where particular modalities of acquisition have to be accounted for, this is usually not a question of property law but

[145] While Art. 204(1) Portuguese Civil Code explicitly counts agricultural and urban land units, as well as waters, as immoveables (and Art. 204(2) Portuguese Civil Code elucidates what is meant by agricultural or urban land units), this terminology, taken from Art. 374 Portuguese Civil Code [1867], was only retained for the purposes of tenancy and fiscal law (*Pires de Lima*, BMJ 91 (1959) pp. 207, 211; *Pires de Lima and Antunes Varela*, Código Civil Anotado I[4], note 3 to Art. 204 p. 196). To avoid difficulties differentiating between *prédio rústico* and *prédio urbano*, Portuguese fiscal law has recently incorporated the concept of mixed land units (*prédio misto*). However, this is meaningless in private law (*Vieira*, Direitos reais, p. 160). This is no different in Italian law, although the Italian Civil Code also discerns between agricultural (Arts 846 and following Italian Civil Code) and urban (Arts 869 ff. Italian Civil Code) immoveables. The reasons for this distinction are always rooted in public law (for further details, see *Gambaro*, Proprietà privata e disciplina urbanistica). While the Spanish Civil Code does not acknowledge a corresponding distinction between *fincas rústicas* and *fincas urbanas*, it is discussed in the scholarship. It is said that it depends on the site on which the land unit is located, as well as the population density in the area, existing building development and the current usage (*Sohst*, Das spanische Bürgerliche Gesetzbuch[2], note to Art. 1523 pp. 263–4). Not all land units in rural areas are *fincas rústicas*, and not all land units in cities are *fincas urbanas* (*Roca Sastre et al.*, Derecho hipotecario III[9], pp. 203–10). The differentiation in Roman law between field ground (*praedia rustica*) and city ground (*praedia urbana*) continues to have an effect in some provisions of the Greek Civil Code (e.g. Arts 619, 620, 1024, 1029, 1162, and 1163 Greek Civil Code). 'City ground' is such ground which is understood or provided by law to be intended for redevelopment, regardless of whether or not it is already developed (Areopag 498/1953, NoB (A) 1953 p. 855; Areopag 632/1967, NoB 16 [1968] p. 239; Areopag 1793/2006, ArchN 2007 p. 582), and also independent of the public urban land-use plan. 'Field ground' serves the cultivation of fruits (Areopag 534/1956, NoB 5 [1957] p. 184; Areopag 632/1967 op. cit.; Areopag 506/1965, NoB 14 [1966] p. 425). This differentiation is only of minor value in a purely property law sense. For example, it is significant when it must be decided who is the immediate possessor of the land unit. Whether he has natural authority over the land unit depends on whether he takes such actions which correspond to the nature of this authority (*Kousoulas*, Empragmato Dikaio, p. 138). An interesting judgment was made in Czech Nejvyšší soud České republiky 22 April 2004, 22 Cdo 1274/2003, Soubor civilních rozhodnutí a stanovisek Nejvyššího soudu, C 2672 (garages, which bordered the land unit of the defendant, could only be accessed by passing through an arch with a lockable gate, which was formed by the ground floor of the plaintiff's house. The court dismissed the establishment of a servitude in the form of a right of way because the Czech Civil Code only provides the possibility of a right of way over a land unit, not 'through' a building. A sustainable solution to this case could only be found by way of public building law).

of administrative requirements relating to application and approval.[146] Provisions that (like Art. 869 Italian Civil Code) require the owner of a land unit to conform to local planning schemes are addressed to the owner of an urban land unit, but express at base a public law encumbrance on him. Otherwise, encumbrances of rights in land units vary according to their use. There is, it is true, a difference between the owner of a residential suburban land unit preventing others from picking his roses and the owner of a forested land unit preventing others from gathering berries and other forest products.[147] This does not, however, mean that the right of ownership (a usufruct, etc.) in a residential land unit is a different property right to that held in a piece of forest. Ownership remains ownership, however strong or weak the exclusivity connected with the right of ownership may be in the concrete circumstances of a given case.[148]

There are not very many examples to support the proposition that a certain type of property right is restricted to land units with particular substantive features only. Most of them are found in the realm of real rights of use. **7.32**

The perpetual usufruct provided for by Arts 1 and 12 of the Polish Statute of 14 July 1961 on the Development of Areas in Cities and Settlements,[149] and the later Art. 232 § 1 Polish Civil Code,[150] could, originally, only be created over urban (not rural) land units. (Prior to the change of the political regime, it could only be created over state owned land units; later, it could be created over land units owned by a municipal authority too.)[151] The specific legislation governing the perpetual usufruct was, however, frequently amended. Under Arts 1, 10, and 13 of the current statute (the *Ustawa o gospodarce nieruchomościami*), since 1 January 1998 a perpetual usufruct can be created over public land units of all kinds.[152] The only exceptions that have been preserved are

146 Regulations which prohibit foreign nationals (sometimes even EU citizens) from acquiring domestic agricultural and forestry areas, or tie it to specific administrative authorization, also belong into this group (e.g. for Hungary *Kozma*, WiRO 2012 pp. 221–32).

147 See strikingly Swedish HD 17 September 1986, NJA 1986 p. 637. Lars and Britt had cut lichen in a community forest and within one week had removed a total of 1300 15-litre containers. The issue in question was whether this action constituted a crime. Swedish law names the felling of living trees, the cutting of branches, and the harvesting of grass on another's ground as criminal offences. Berries, fungi, free-growing flowers, and game are not objects of the ownership of forest land units (Kap. 12 § 2(2) BrB; *Håstad*, Sakrätt[6], p. 44). The court characterized the lichen as a product of nature which could only be harvested with the consent of the owner of the land unit. While the collection of small amounts was permitted, this massive harvest was definitely too large.

148 The Swedish rights of commons (*allemansrätt*), which allow persons to enter other persons' land units under certain circumstances in order to pick berries, camp etc. was thus formulated as a limit on the protection of ownership (*egendomsskydd*) (Kap. 2 § 18 *Regeringsformen*: '*alla ska ha tillgång till naturen enligt allemansrätten oberoende av vad som föreskrivits ovan*.') This so-called 'right to nature' essentially has its roots in customary law, but is also expressed in criminal law provisions (for further details, see *Bengtsson*, Speciell Fastighetsrätt[10], p. 145). A variety of land units are exempt from this *allemansrätt* to nature. This includes developed land units, gardens, and agricultural fields, which would sustain damage should people set foot in them (Kap. 12 § 4 BrB; details in *Bengtsson* ibid. p. 149). Art.145 of the Bulgarian Forestry Statute provides that the access to forests for people and animals may only be limited if this is explicitly intended by law or by administrative acts.

149 Dz.U. 1961 no. 32 Pos. 159.

150 To this day, the text states: 'Land units belonging to the *fiscus* within the administrative boundaries of cities and land units of the *fiscus* outside of those boundaries that are part of the planning scheme of a city and serve the realisation of its economic objectives, as well as land units of the divisions of territorial self administration and their associations can be given in perpetual usufruct to natural and juristic persons.'

151 For further details, see Radwański and Gniewek (-*Cisek*), System Prawa Prywatnego IV[2], p. 152 no. 40, and Gniewek (-*Cisek*), Kodeks cywilny[2], p. 375 f nos 4–6.

152 *Gniewek*, Prawo rzeczowe[8], p. 167 no. 509.

land units that are 'in the stock of agricultural property of the *fiscus*'.[153] The 'cooperative ownership' [*własność spółdzielcza*] is a special property right in land units developed with buildings, but following the entry into force of the Statute of 14 June 2007,[154] this right can no longer be created. Czech law has a rule against 'real encumbrances' (servitudes) over agricultural property for the purposes of providing a public network (§ 4 of the Statute on the Protection of Agricultural Land Stock).[155] Such networks must use land other than agricultural land. Agricultural land units should, presumably, not be encumbered with real encumbrances that do not serve agricultural purposes. The 'agricultural pledge' (which has since been abolished) found in Statute 2184/1920, by way of contrast, related to agricultural land units only. German (§ 1038 German Civil Law) and Greek (Art. 1149 Greek Civil Code) law recognize 'usufruct in forests and mines', which is an imprecise manner of expression. A 'forest' is not an object that is capable of being the object of property rights as such; what is meant is a land unit covered with forest. By way of contrast, the so-called 'proprietary servitudes' of Art. 13 of the Greek Statute 3741/1929 can only be created over developed land. Industrial land units (i.e. land units owned by an undertaking with permanent machinery and other plant) can, according to Statute 4112/1929, be the object of a special security right, and an *antichrese* is only permissible under Art. 1221 Greek Civil Code in things that, by their nature, bear fruits. Under Art. 8 of the Statute of 26 May 1965, No. 590, the leaseholder of an agricultural land unit holds a pre-emption right. The emphyteusis of Italian law (*enfiteusi*, a 'perpetual lease') is also limited to agricultural land, but appears not to have any contemporary importance in practice.[156] Land units can be encumbered with servitudes of all kinds, even though jurists commonly speak of agricultural, industrial, and urban servitudes and even though this usage is reflected in Art. 1033 Italian Civil Code. Matters are similar in Austria. Section 474 Austrian Civil Code distinguishes between servitudes in agricultural land units (so-called *Feldservituten* or 'field servitudes') and servitudes in other land units (so-called *Hausservituten* or 'house servitudes'). This provision is followed by catalogues of typical field (§§ 475 and 476 Austrian Civil Code) and house servitudes (§ 477 Austrian Civil Code), and by some special provisions (§§ 487 and following Austrian Civil Code). Most of these catalogued servitudes are restricted by their nature to certain categories of land unit (§ 496 Austrian Civil Code, for example, deals with a right to take water from another's land; there must, accordingly, exist water on the servient land unit). At both the federal and provincial level, statutes provide for forest and pasture servitudes with special rules for field servitudes. However, these provisions all have less to do with the character of the right concerned and more to do with the concrete use of the land unit in the given case; § 474 Austrian Civil Code has been interpreted by the Austrian Supreme Court in this

[153] Gniewek (-*Cisek*), Kodeks cywilny^{2}, p. 376 no. 6.

[154] Dz.U. 2007 no. 125 Pos. 873.

[155] Statute No. 334/1992 Gbl. According to § 1(2) op. cit., the stock agricultural land encompasses farmland, hops fields, vineyards, gardens, orchards, meadows and pastures, meaning 'agricultural ground'.

[156] *Torrente and Schlesinger*, Manuale di diritto privato^{19}, p. 285.

way.[157] The whole range of property rights relating to habitation can only meaningfully relate to residentially developed land units. To these rights belong so-called timesharing, unless of course a national legislature has opted to transpose Regulation 94/47/EC in a purely obligational legal framework, or the legal system in question allows timesharing in all types of land unit (regardless of whether real rights should follow from the parties' agreement or not). The latter is the case in England.[158]

b. Water and Land Units with Water

(1) Naturally Flowing Waters

Areas of land wholly or partly covered with water demand somewhat closer examination. In this context, one must draw distinctions across various axes, in particular according to whether the water is flowing or still,[159] and in both cases according to whether the water is subject to a public law or a private law regime. A naturally flowing water (water as sea, river, or stream, as opposed to water in a man-made system of channels or containers) is *per se* not an object of property rights, and is therefore not capable of constituting a land unit. Only surfaces covered with a pond[160] or lake are capable of 7.33

[157] OGH 13 April 1983, SZ 56/60.

[158] Timeshare is not a technical term in common law. The word merely has a fixed meaning in the context of statutes which transpose the Directive. The possibility of timeshare outside of its scope of application is not limited. Disregarding consumer rights, it should be possible to timeshare, e.g. hunting and fishing rights. This is implied by a publication by the United Kingdom tax authority HMRC, titled the Stamp Duty Land Tax Manual: SDLTM10022 (http://www.hmrc.gov.uk/manuals/sdltmanual/sdltm10022.htm). Despite changes in the meantime to the relevant laws regarding holiday homes, it has remained unchanged. Section 1(1)(a) of the Timeshare Act 1992 (since repealed) defined 'timeshare accommodation' as 'living accommodation' used for leisure purposes. The use must be temporally limited. 'Accommodation' according to this Act meant accommodation in a building or in a caravan (Section 1(2)(a)). The current Timeshare, Holiday Products, Resale and Exchange Contracts Regulations 2010 SI Nr. 2960 defines 'timeshare contracts' for its purposes as a contract between a trader and a consumer which has a duration of more than one year. The consumer acquires, for consideration, the right to use overnight accommodation for at least two periods of time (reg. 7(1)). The type of accommodation is left undefined. Under common law, a right of use is normally grounds for a lease (e.g. *Smallwood v Sheppards* [1895] 2 QB 627 [lease of a meadow for three (non-consecutive) public holidays] and *Cottage Holiday Associates Ltd v Customs & Excise Commissioners* [1983] 1 QB 734 [one-week leases of a cottage spanning eighty years]), and sometimes for a licence. There are also timeshare models which make use of trusts or a corporate structure (details in *Edmonds*, International Timesharing[2], Kap. 2). In practice, it is more an exception than a rule that a timeshare contract forms the basis for a property right (a right with an unambiguous third-party effect). This also applies to the establishment of tenancy or lease with a third-party effect (SDLTM10022 op. cit.).

[159] The distinction is made either according to the predominant impression of the exterior (a castle which is surrounded by a moat, which itself has an inflow and outflow, does not constitute flowing waters) or according to legal rules. However, § 43(1) Czech Statute No. 254/2001 Gbl. defines watercourses (flowing waters) as surface waters running by gravity in their channel either permanently or for the prevailing part of the year, which includes waters which are artificially dammed. The aforementioned moated castle would be located in a 'watercourse' by this definition.

[160] Czech Nejvyšší soud České republiky 16 July 2008, 22 Cdo 1121/2008, Stavebně správní praxe XII (2009) no. 3 p. 5 is, for these purposes, rather irritating. While applying provisions of the Czech Fisheries Act (Statute No. 99/2004 Gbl.), the court determined that a 'pond' should be seen as a separate, individual object of ownership, but did not state whether the pond itself was a land unit or an immoveable. A 'pond' within the meaning of the relevant statute should not be seen as a body of water itself, but also the various works and installations needed for fish farming. Such a 'pond' is said to be an object which is not comprised only of itself, but which is also created by the flooded land unit. This caused the court to view the owner of the land as a co-owner of the pond. Whether the owner of the pond is also conversely co-owner of the land unit was not stated. It was also unclear how the court was able to determine the legal positions of the parties as co-owners based on the autonomous 'ownability' of the pond, as the principle of *superficies solo cedit* was not part of Czech law at this time.

being so-called 'water land units'. This is because flowing water is not a controllable object. Granted, a legal order can coherently ascribe certain rights to private persons or to the state itself, and can even call these rights 'ownership'; however, the nomenclature does not alter the basic fact that these are not private property rights *in the body of water itself* (even including private property rights that fall into the patrimony of the public fiscus). The same can be said of other use rights in flowing waters. Such rights of use really only require one to think 'from the land to the water' and not 'from the water to the land'. Where the latter is indeed the case, one is generally in the territory of rights in water more accurately characterized as 'public', and most legal systems tend in such contexts to subject the soil concerned (i.e. the bed of the body of water and the soil below it) to the public law regime that governs the body of water. We have already seen that the law of the sea floor follows exactly this pattern.

7.34 The proposition that naturally flowing water *per se* is withheld from the ownership of private persons and that flowing waters can, in consequence, not be independent (water) land units, appears to be a robust proposition of common European law. That waters are here and there characterized as immoveables does not affect the generality of this basic proposition.

In English law, a landowner has no property in water that seeps through his land or that flows through it in a certain course.[161] Under Art. 822(1) Italian Civil Code, rivers, streams, and lakes 'belong to the state' and are '*demanio pubblico*' along with the sea coasts, beaches, roadsteads, and harbours. Under Art. 10(1) Polish Water Act,[162] waters are either property of the *fiscus* or another legal or natural person, but Art. 10(2) counts the waters of the territorial sea, the coastal seas (including those of the Gulf of Gdansk), all inland flowing surface and ground waters to the fiscus. Waters belonging to the fiscus are public waters under this section, and as such they remain (subject to any contrary provision) *extra commercium*. In the Czech Republic, the proposition that rivers are not objects subject to control is taken to the conclusion that they cannot be the property even of the state; natural waters are seen as ownerless. They are neither a component nor an accessory to a land unit on or under which they happen to be found (§ 3(1) Water Act; Statute No. 254/2001 Gbl.). The position is similar in Slovakia (§ 120(2) Slovakian Civil Code; drawing water is permitted for household use without any special permission: § 18(1) Slovakian Water Act). Art. 967 Greek Civil Code deems 'large lakes and their banks as well as freely and continuously flowing waters' to be objects of common usage and, in so doing, places them *extra commercium*. In France, the water of rivers and streams are considered *res communes*, which are *extra commercium*.[163] By virtue of § 1 Austrian *Wasserrechtsgesetz*, all waters are divided into 'public' and 'private'. Public ownership is prescribed in § 2(1)(a) of that statute for all waters listed in a schedule. Under § 2(1)(b) and (c), a rebuttable presumption is

[161] Megarry and Wade (-*Harpum/Bridge/Dixon*), The Law of Real Property[7], no. 3-047.
[162] Ustawa z dn. 18 July 2001 Prawo wodne (Dz.U. 2012 no. 0 Pos. 145).
[163] *Bergel/Bruschi/Cimamonti*, Les biens[2], p. 218 no. 183.

established that all water is public property. What is meant is, however, only ownership of the water *body* (this follows § 4 which is concerned with ownership of the riverbed). Art. 334(8) Spanish Civil Code characterizes flowing and resting waters as immoveable goods, but ownership in them is understood not just in the normal sense but as a form of '*propiedad especial*' (this follows from Arts 407–425 Spanish Civil Code as well as several special provisions). Waters in the sense of *Ley de Aguas* are, further, as a matter of principle in public ownership;[164] their characterization as immoveables therefore holds little practical importance. Artesian water and other subterranean waters were generally removed from private ownership in 1973.[165] Art. 204(1)(b) Portuguese Civil Code also counts waters expressly to the category of immoveable things (albeit not to land units). In the Portuguese literature, it is said that waters acquire the status of independent immoveables only after their separation [*desintegração*]; up to that point, they are mere components of land units.[166] That does not undermine the practical relevance of treating waters as immoveables completely, however—not least as it is argued that river water is an 'immoveable' because it is contained by the river bed.[167] The operative element of this approach is a rather fuzzy doctrine of components that has been woven into the concept of 'immoveables'. Flowing water that is not public (Art. 1385 Portuguese Civil Code) can, under Arts 1386–1402 Portuguese Civil Code, be an object of private water property rights [*propriedade das águas*] (public waters are subject to their own special provisions). This private 'water property', however, should not be seen as a right in the water but as a right, derivative of the right in the soil, to use the so-called *águas particulares* listed in Art. 1386 Portuguese Civil Code. The list includes, e.g. waters that flow from a spring on a private land unit, rainwater that falls on a land unit, or lakes that are located on a private land unit and are fed from ground water. Under Art. 1387 Portuguese Civil Code, plants for the storage of water (wells, dams, aqueducts, etc.) as well as the bed of non-navigable rivers that flow over private land are possible objects of private property rights.

Public ownership of water can also extend to constructions in water. In Italy, all constructions over rivers and public lakes (bridges, harbours, levies) belong to the public domain; private persons can, at most, acquire a *superficie* in such works. In Polish law, the point of departure is similar but, according to a decision of the Warsaw Administrative Court of 2009, a distinction is made according to the purpose of the construction.[168] The court had to decide who has responsible for the maintenance of a river levy—the state, as owner, or the aquaculturist whose interests the levy served most directly. The court decided for the aquaculturist. The public ownership arising 7.35

164 For exceptions to the so-called *dominio público hidráulico*, see *Díez-Picazo and Gullón*, Sistema de Derecho Civil III(1)[8], pp. 198–9. Registered still waters (which can be autonomous land units under Art. 66 RH) are subject to a transition period of fifty years. They become public property in 2035. The previous owners will then receive concessions for use (*Lasarte Álvarez*, Derechos reales y derecho hipotecario[7], p. 267).

165 Mining Act of 21 July 1973 (*Ley 22/1973, de 21 de julio de Minas*).

166 *Pires de Lima and Antunes Varela*, Código Civil Anotado I[4], note 4 to Art. 204 p. 196.

167 *Menezes Cordeiro*, Tratado de Direito Civil I(2)[2], p. 130.

168 Judgment of 16 January 2009, II OSK 1874/07, Lex-No. 515978.

from water law could not be conflated with private law ownership (Art. 140 Polish Civil Code); water is not a thing in the sense of Art. 45 Polish Civil Code.[169] Standing water and water in channels on a land unit were non-independent components of the land unit. Such water therefore belonged to the land unit owner. Flowing water, on the other hand, was a public good. It was affirmed that the public ownership of water extends, according to Arts 14, 17, and 18 of the Polish Water Law, to the soil beneath and the banks around public waters. From this, however, it was not possible to derive the position that public water rights 'automatically' extend to works around the water; the provisions of the water law did not prevent a divergence of ownership between the water itself and the works around it, and these provisions had priority over the general provisions of private law (Art. 143 Polish Civil Code). The levy in this case was not in the register of water works for the improvement of water quality, but for the purposes of a private aquaculture undertaking. This, and the other circumstances of the case, showed that the levy served only private purposes. Under Art. 64 of the Polish Water Law, every person who draws a benefit from a piece of water infrastructure could be required to contribute to the costs of its maintenance. In this case, the aquaculturist was certainly the owner of the levy and therefore responsible for these costs, not the state.

7.36 The bracketing out of flowing waters from the concept of the land unit means that no private property rights can be established in them. However, as noticed previously, private use rights remain possible (e.g. rights of drawing or damming water). Such rights can be understood, insofar as no additional provisions of public law prevent such an approach, as part of the ownership of a land unit by a private party.[170] In principle, the situation is similar to a hunting right. Properly seen, hunting rights are not rights in the wild animal but rights to use the land unit on which the hunting is undertaken; the point of reference for a right to draw or dam water is not the flowing waters, but the land unit on which the activity is undertaken. Further, just as a hunting right does not entitle its holder to take all types of game, the rights of an occupier of the land unit concerned is limited to certain flows of water. Thus, for example, Art. 644 French Civil Code only gives the occupant the right to draw water for the irrigation of his land unit when the

[169] With the exception, naturally, of water in a water pipeline or in a container. These are things within the meaning of Art. 45 Polish Civil Code; accordingly, the provisions of water law do not apply (Radwański and Safjan [-*Katner*], System Prawa Prywatnego I, p. 1207 no. 79).

[170] In Portuguese law, rights to use of water for public waters are the subject of specific statutes (Arts 59 ff. Water Law [*Lei da Água*, Statute 58/2005 of 29 December 2005] and DL 226-A/2007 of 31 May 2007). Rights to use of public waters are only granted administratively. Depending on their content, these rights take the form of either concessions (*concessão*), licences (*licença*), authorizations (*autorização*), or by way of prior communication (*mera comunicação prévia*). An in-depth discussion can be found in *Mendes*, in Tratato de direito administrativo especial II, pp. 108–12. Furthermore, notice must be taken of Art. 1386(1)(a) Portuguese Civil Code. In Austria, there are so-called 'water books' [*Wasserbücher*] which serve as a public registry (§ 124 Austrian Water Law). However, this registration serves a merely declaratory purpose, and does not have a constitutive effect (§§ 22(2), 26(4) op. cit.; OGH 11 October 1978, SZ 51/135; *Rassi*, Grundbuchsrecht, no. 62). In Czech law, the use of river water (removal, damming, pisciculture, etc.) is dependent on previous governmental or municipal consent (§ 8 Czech Water Law). In common law, too, a landowner has a right of use of waters, for example the right to remove leachate and, in the case of flowing water, the right to fish (details can be found in Megarry and Wade [-*Harpum/Bridge/Dixon*], The Law of Real Property[7], no. 3-048). However, these rights are severely restricted by the public law regulations in secs 24ff Water Resources Act 1991.

river in question is not a classified public watercourse.[171] Fundamentally, he is allowed (subject to any special environmental protection provisions under Art. 215-1 *Code de l'environnement*) to use it as he likes, provided he returns it to its ordinary course. Similar rules are found elsewhere, too, for example in Ch. 2 § 2 of the Swedish *Lag med särskilda bestämmelser om vattenverksamhet* (1998:812) (under which the right to use flowing waters [*flytande vatten*] accrues to all surrounding land units in equal parts, even when a greater part of the water flows over one of the land units. Similarly, Art. 5:40 Netherlands Civil Code provides the conditions under which the owner of a land unit bordering on flowing, public waters can use water. The provision names, by way of example, the irrigation of fields and the watering of animals. Other uses are possible, however, provided they do not count as prohibited dealings in relation to the other landowners roundabout (Art. 6:162 Netherlands Civil Code).

The fact that a flowing body of water constitutes neither a land unit itself nor a component of a land unit over which it flows does not, however, mean that the bed of the watercourse and the layers of soil beneath this bed remain privately owned, i.e. an integral component of the land unit seen as a whole. Generally, the riverbed and the soil below it are only attributed to the state when the watercourse is characterized as public. The difference, from the perspective of property law, is apparent: in the first case, the private occupant is allowed to tunnel beneath the watercourse, in the latter he is not. **7.37**

For French law, Art. L215-2 *Code de l'environnement* leaves no doubt that the bed of a non-public watercourse is part of the land unit over which it flows. The relevant owners own the ground below, to the middle of the watercourse. The same applies to the so-called mixed watercourses. These are not, strictly speaking, public, but a specific public interest subsists in them with the consequence that their bed remains in private ownership but the rights to use the water (Arts 644 and 645 French Civil Code) accrue to the state (and further to those to whom it grants concessions).[172] In Italian law, Art. 1(1) of the *Regolamento recante norme per l´attuzione di talune disposizioni della legge 5 gennaio 1994* makes it clear that the surface waters (*acque superficiali*) belong to the state.[173] This term refers *prima facie* only to the body of water itself. The superior courts, however, have left no doubt that the riverbed, riverbanks, and all submerged surfaces also belong to the state.[174] The riverbed itself is conceptualized as a land unit under state ownership. This approach corresponds with Art. 942(1) Italian Civil Code. According to this provision, land that is left by flowing waters (i.e. when they move

[171] A watercourse only becomes a public watercourse by an administrative *décision de classement*. Under Art. L2111-7 Code général de la propriété des personnes publiques, natural fluvial public territory (*domaine public fluvial naturel*) is composed of the watercourses and lakes which belong to the state and its regional authority, meaning they have been entered into the *domaine public fluvial*. This entry occurs if there is a corresponding public interest (Art. L2111-12 Code général de la propriété des personnes publiques). This is generally preceded by an *enquête publique* (Art. L2111-12(2) Code général de la propriété des personnes publiques).

[172] *Bergel/Bruschi/Cimamonti*, Les biens², p. 220 no. 183-1.

[173] D.P.R. no. 238 of 18 February 1999, Regolamento recante norme per l´attuzione di talune disposizioni della legge 5 gennaio 1994 n. 36 in materia di risorse idriche, Gazz. Uff. no. 173 of 26 July 1999.

[174] Cass. sez. un. 18 December 1998, no. 12701, Riv. giur. edilizia 1999, I, p. 937.

from one bank toward the other) remains in public ownership; the landowner on the other bank, by way of contrast, loses some of his land. Art. 942(2) Italian Civil Code adds that 'flowing waters' include rivers, streams, and other waters designated as public by relevant statutes. Further, Art. 945 Italian Civil Code stipulates that islands that form in the bed of rivers and streams are public, and that land left when a river or stream finds a new course remains subject to the legal regime applicable to public land (Art. 946 Italian Civil Code).[175] The same applies to interventions in the natural flow of a river (Art. 947 Italian Civil Code). Art. 14(1) of the Polish Water Statute, which has already been mentioned, is to this extent consistent with the Italian approach, attributing the soil beneath surface waters to the ownership of the so-called 'water owner'—i.e. the state.[176] The same approach is taken in many of the German federal states [*Länder*]. According to § 5 of the Baden-Württemberg *Wassergesetz*, for example, the ordinary civil law provisions on land ownership only apply to publicly owned riverbeds to the extent that those provisions are reconcilable with the restrictions inherent in dedication of a given river to a certain use, and with other restrictions arising from water law. Fundamentally, private law dealings cannot be performed with public property. Czech law, by way of contrast, distinguishes between watercourses and land units. The riverbed is not a component of 'its' river and is, for this reason, a fitting object of the right of ownership. The Netherlands Civil Code suffices itself (as does English law)[177] with a few special provisions which ascribe the soil under bodies of water to the state: e.g. Art. 5:25 Netherlands Civil Code (Floor of the territorial sea and the Wadden Sea area), Art. 5:26 Netherlands Civil Code (Ocean beaches to the foot of the dunes), and Art. 5:27(1) Netherlands Civil Code (land units on which public waterways are located). From these provisions, one can deduce that riverbeds and lakebeds are, in principle, capable of private ownership. Under Art. 84(1)(a) and (c) of the Portuguese Constitution, lakes,

[175] Arts 942 and 946 Italian Civil Code were changed by Arts 1 and 3 of Statute of 5 January 1994, No. 37 (Gazz. Uff. no. 14 of 19 January 1994, Suppl. Ord. no. 11). Before then, the owner of the adjoining land unit was entitled to the *alveus derelictus*. The basic principle is that the new version of Art. 946 Italian Civil Code does not have a retroactive effect (*inter alia* Cass. 14 January 1997, no. 300, Giust. civ. 1997 p. 1312; Cass. 31 January 2008, no. 2314, Mass. Giust. civ. 2008 p. 127, and Cass. 6 February 2007, no. 2608, Mass. Giust. civ. p. 2).

[176] See, from more recent times, Polish Sąd Najwyższy 17 February 2011, III CSK 147/10, Lex-No. 818558. In connection with the creation of a reservoir, the supplying river was adjusted, which caused it to change its course. An area of land which was previously covered by the river was thus exposed. This area has not been flooded in almost eighty years. The court confirmed the starting point, that the land unit within the limits of the riverbank had been the property of the water owner, meaning the state. However, as the land unit was no longer flooded, this rule was no longer applicable. The relations of ownership over the land unit had not changed *ipso iure* upon withdrawal of the water; however, it had since then become an object which could be acquired by prescription. *In casu*, due to the fact that the plaintiff had made use of it *animo domini* (by building a well from which she obtained water for her house), it had become property of the plaintiff. Likewise, for Greek law, see Areopag 867/2007, NoB 55 (2007) p. 2072. Non-navigable but freely and constantly flowing rivers are *res extra commercium*. They belong either to the tax authorities or the relevant municipality. If a river leaves its bed, the bed belongs to the owners of those land units which border the riverbank. This, however, requires a complete and general departure from the old bank and the creation of a new bank, which was missing *in casu*. The stretch of shore from which the water had withdrawn thus remained the property of the tax authorities. However, the original defendant and his heirs had planted an orange grove there, and continuously maintained it since 1940. They had prescriptively acquired this area in good faith and thus acquired ownership of it.

[177] For a river which is subject to tides, the riverbed belongs to the Crown up to the point to which the water regularly rises, unless the Crown has not exercised its right to dispose over it: *AG v Earl of Lonsdale* (1868) LR 7 Eq 377, 389 (Malins VC).

lagoons, and navigable watercourses 'together with their beds' are in public ownership (the list is not exhaustive).[178] The Bulgarian state owns all riverbeds and riverbanks (Art. 11 Bulgarian Water Statute). In Austria, where most waters are public, a strict distinction is drawn between rights of ownership in the body of water and rights of ownership in the bed, bank, and substrate. It is thus conceivable that a private person might remain the owner of the bed and banks of a public watercourse (§ 2(2) Austrian *Wasserrechtsgesetz*). This private owner can, accordingly, prevent the exploitation of the bed of the body of water.[179] All that is required is that a private right of ownership does, in fact, exist, such that the presumption in § 4(1) Sentence 2 of that statute can be rebutted—i.e. that the substrate of a public body of water is also in the public domain. In the Czech Republic, too, the riverbed is considered as a component of the river; it can accordingly be held in private hands.[180]

(2) Still Water

Standing waters can also be in exclusive public ownership and thus (as *res extra commercium*) fall outside the rules governing the creation of land units for purposes of property law. Generally, this is the legal position only for lakes and lagoons that are designated as public *ex lege* or have been expressly so designated by a public authority on some statutory basis. In other cases, they are generally part of the land unit on which they are found, which we might call a 'water' land unit [*Wassergrundstück*]. There is no distinction to be made, in principle, between a lake, canal, or pond that is wholly situated on one person's land unit and one that stretches over several land units, nor is it relevant that a private land unit borders on a publicly owned part of the substrate.[181] The borders of the land unit extend, in straight lines, over the land beneath the water. The land unit continues into the body of water, not the other way around (i.e. that ownership of the water extends to the soil beneath).[182] The water of a lake, a canal, or a pond 7.38

[178] STJ 5 June 1996, BMJ 458 (1996) p. 237.

[179] OGH 30 September 1959, SZ 32/115 (reduction of shingle in the riverbed).

[180] Czech Nejvyšší soud České republiky 5 November 2007, Cdo 2903/2006, Právní rozhledy 2008 no. 10 (a land unit with a discrete parcel number, which forms the riverbed of a watercourse, can be an object of private law relations) and Czech Supreme Administrative Court 24 February 2004, no. 7 A 33/2002, Sbírka rozhodnutí Nejvyššího správního soudu 9 (2004) no. 316 (the owners of land units in which watercourses flow, must tolerate this and, under § 50 Water Law [Statute No. 254/2001 Gbl.] also for example the plants on the river bank. They must also maintain the riverbed in a condition which allows the water to continue flowing. A network of ditches is also a part of the land unit: Czech Nejvyšší soud České republiky 28 January 1998, 3 Cdon 1305/96, Soudní rozhledy 1998 vol. 8).

[181] For some examples, see Hoge Raad 15 January 2010, NJB 2010 no. 189; Arrondissementsrechtbank Zwolle 9 February 2011, HA ZA 09-1386, LJNNr. BQ4126 (A water parcel, privately owned by a municipality, bordered a water parcel with land in private ownership. The dispute concerned a berth for a houseboat) and Arrondissementsrechtbank Leeuwaarden 29 September 2010, 98573; HA-ZA 09/707. The case concerned two land units, separated by a branch canal. This was not a public waterway. The canal was the property of the defendant. The court denied that the plaintiff had prescriptively acquired a servitude which allowed him to navigate the canal. The court also found that under Art. 5:21 BW the land unit owner has an exclusive right of use over the water located on the land unit. Hof Leeuwaarden 6 November 2012, 200.089.178/01 confirmed this decision.

[182] In Swedish law, Kap. 1 §§ 3 and 4 JB determine the borders between two privately owned areas of water primarily according to charts and documents (*karta och handlingar*), alternatively according to *rå*, *rör* and other

is no more a land unit than the water flowing in a riverbed. The inverse proposition (that the soil is part of the water standing on it) is disingenuous for the reason that changes in the water level would constantly alter property rights relations.[183]

7.39 Art. 5:20(1)(d) of the Netherlands Civil Code thus stipulates that, insofar as no contrary provision exists, ownership of the soil embraces not only groundwater that comes to the surface via a well, spring, or pump, but also water that is found on the relevant land unit and is not connected with water on another land unit. (In the latter case, the water—like the air above the surface of a land unit—is *res nullius*.[184]) Art. 5:29 Netherlands Civil Code adds that the borders of a land unit follow the line of the banks, and Art. 5:31 Netherlands Civil Code envisages a procedure by which the 'owners of land and water' can agree on a border that diverges from the waterline. The distinction between land units and 'water land units' is based on practical, rather than specifically property law motivations. So much is confirmed by Art. 5:36 Netherlands Civil Code, according to which the border between two land units runs in the middle of small waterways (such as ditches and drains). Water land units are, so to speak, just 'normal' land units. Under § 3 Austrian *Wasserrechtsgesetz*, for example, private ownership subsists in enclosed ponds, wells, and lakes; the law characterizes such waters consistently as an accessory to the land (§ 3(3) Austrian *Wasserrechtsgesetz*).[185] Art. 12(1) of the Polish *Prawo Wodne* ascribes still water and water in ditches to the owner of the relevant land unit. A 'ditch' is defined as an artificial channel which leads water permanently or periodically and whose surface area at the mouth is no wider than one and a half metres (Art. 9(1) point 13 Polish *Prawo Wodne*). Still waters and well waters are components of the relevant immoveable.[186] The same applies to water systems that are permanently connected to the immoveable.[187] Groundwater, on the other hand, is neither a thing in its own right nor a non-independent component of the land unit.[188] In French law, non-public waters (*les eaux non domaniales*) are subject to private law. Besides precipitation (Art.

traditional markers. The land unit owner can dispose over the still water (*råda*) (Kap. 2 § 2 *Lag med särskilda bestämmelser om vattenverksamhet* (1998:812)).

[183] It appears that Art. 943 Italian Civil Code struggles with this problem. The provision states that water-covered land, which is located at the point of the outflow of a lake or pond, also belongs to the owner of the lake or pond, even when the water level is low. Conversely, the owner does not acquire a right to the land along the river-bank, which is covered when the water is exceptionally high. The authors of this regulation were clearly thinking 'from the water to the land', instead of, more plausibly, thinking from the land below to the water standing on it. Czech Nejvyšší soud České republiky 16 July 2008, 22 Cdo 1121/2008, Stavebně správní praxe (supplement to Urbanismus a územní rozvoj) XII (2009) no. 3 p. 5 is hardly convincing in its statement that the owner of a pond and the owner of the ground below it are co-owners of the pond—and presumably also co-owners of the ground, but this does not become clear.

[184] Nieuwenhuis/Stolker/Valk (-*Stolker*), BW[6], Art. 5:20 no. 1.

[185] The tax authority can also be a private owner. Thus, not all public waters are common commodities. OGH 15 October 1970, EvBl 1971/124, ÖJZ 1971 p. 212 demonstrated this for the Hallstätter See. While the lake constituted state property, it has long been acknowledged that it is an accessory of the Upper Austrian *Salzkammergut*, and the previous ruling landowner had not permitted use by the general public. This was also the case for its legal successor, the Republic of Austria. Therefore, while the lake was a state asset, it was not a public commodity.

[186] Radwański and Safjan (-*Katner*), System Prawa Prywatnego I, p. 1204 no. 69.

[187] Ibid. p. 1205 no. 72.

[188] Ibid. p. 1204 no. 70.

641 French Civil Code) and spring water (Art. 642 French Civil Code),[189] fresh water ponds and lakes belong to the land unit owner, at least when they are fed by rainwater or spring water rather than by water from a watercourse (in which case they are seen as part of that watercourse and are subject to the rules that govern it).[190] As noticed earlier, Art. 967 Greek Civil Code categorizes only 'large lakes and their shores' as things in common use. 'Small lakes', in particular those enclosed within a land unit, remain straightforward objects of private ownership. The owner of such a land unit is simply permitted to use water that percolates to the surface; he is not even required to let it flow.[191] Bulgarian law contains almost identical rules (Art. 24(1)–(3) Bulgarian Water Act). In Czech law, ponds are entered in the land register as land units under the label 'water areas', whereas dykes are registered as constructions.[192] Conversely, however, a pond—'as a land unit covered with water'—is not a standalone object of private law relations because 'one cannot deal with the pond without its bed and banks'.[193] However, according to the jurisprudence of the Supreme Court, the 'pond as a whole', which is formed of the land units and any facilities built around it to enable its effective use, can constitute an object of private law dealings.[194] Czech Nejvyšší soud České republiky 16 July 2008 reflects this position. The owner or leaseholder of a pond is entitled to use it for fishing and aquaculture: 'The owner of the land unit, on whose surface the pond is formed, cannot be excluded from his part of ownership in the pond.'[195] In England, a pond or lake is 'part of the land', such that they belong to the owner of the land on which they stand. In the case of multiple landowners around the shores of a lake, the border is drawn in case of doubt to the middle of the body of water.[196] Strictly speaking, it is not a question of ownership of the water in English law. The claim of possession arose historically not from a claim to the water itself, but to the land on which it stands. One could never, and cannot now, demand the return of water than flows from a pond onto the land of another.[197]

4. Land Units, Not 'Immoveables'

The question remains of how 'land units' relate to 'immoveables' (i.e. to 'immoveable things'). It could be argued that it makes no difference what term one uses to describe 7.40

[189] Cass. civ. 25 April 1928, D.H. 1928 p. 269 permitted the sale not only of spring water, but also of the spring itself. This points to the possibility of interpreting a spring itself as a land unit, if a corresponding division of land units has taken place.

[190] *Bergel/Bruschi/Cimamonti*, Les biens[2], p. 216 no. 180; *Terré and Simler*, Les biens[8], p. 208 no. 225.

[191] CA Athens 8099/1977, Arm. 32 (1978) p. 446.

[192] *Trajer and Trajerová*, Katastr nemovitostí[2], p. 5.

[193] Czech Nejvyšší soud České republiky 28 May 1998, 2 Cdo 1192/97, Soudní rozhledy 9 (1998) pp. 476–7.

[194] Czech Nejvyšší soud České republiky 28 February 2006, 22 Cdo 1118/2005, Soubor civilních rozhodnutí a stanovisek Nejvyššího soudu, C 4004.

[195] Czech Nejvyšší soud České republiky 16 July 2008, 22 Cdo 1121/2008, Sbírka soudních rozhodnutí a stanovisek 2009 no. 65.

[196] Cheshire and Burn (*-Burn and Cartwright*), Modern Law of Real Property[17], p. 177.

[197] *Coke* on Liddleton, p. 4a; *Blackstone*, Commentaries on the Laws of England II, p. 18.

the parts of the planet Earth that are fitting objects of property rights: land unit, immoveable, immoveable thing—or, in reference to Alf Ross' classical contribution to legal realism, simply *tû-tû*.[198] Indeed, many consider 'land unit' (or, to be more precise, the relevant national terminology for a patch of soil) and 'immoveable' to be one and the same.[199] That is the case even in Germany, where the civil code carefully avoids the terminology of 'immoveable things' [*unbewegliche Sachen*] and speaks only of 'land units' [*Grundstücke*]. On one view, insofar as the code recognizes the existence of *bewegliche Sachen*, it implies their counterpart, i.e. *unbewegliche Sachen*, and just chooses to call them *Grundstücke*.[200] That may be the case, but it does not solve the real problem. An initial difficulty arises from the fact that some legal systems characterize the *fonds de terre*, *tierras*, and so forth merely as a part of the immoveable (such that every patch of soil is an immoveable, but not every immoveable is a patch of soil) while the common law avoids both terms and speaks only of 'land'. But the deeper problem is that *all* of these approaches classify objects according to a criterion that, for property law at least, only arises in the second instance; in other words, they put the cart before the horse. The primary question, to which this section has been dedicated, is: What *exactly* is the concrete point of reference for an exclusive right of use in an area of the earth's surface? None of the conventional terms—neither 'land', nor *immeubles*, nor *unbewegliche Sache* will do. (Nor will it do if we equate the terminology of 'land unit' with one of these inadequate conventional concepts.) A legislature could plausibly characterize the earth's surface,[201] a house, a body of water,[202] an agricultural animal,[203] an

[198] This essay, originally in the Danish language, was published at least three times, namely in the commemorative publication for Henry Ussing (Copenhagen 1951) pp. 468–84, in the Scandinavian Studies in Law 1957 pp. 138–53, and in Harv. L. Rev. 1956–57 pp. 812–25.

[199] This is the case in § 50(1) Estonian Civil Code, in Art. 18(1) Slovenian SPZ (see *Tratnik*, WGO-MfOR 45 [2003] pp. 94, 99), in § 119(2) Czech Civil Code [1964] or § 498(1) Czech Civil Code [2014] and in various other countries. For example, in Sweden, *fastighet* and *jord* are only rarely differentiated with precision. §§ 292 and 293 Austrian Civil Gode differentiate between moveable things ('*bewegliche Sachen*') and immoveable things ('*unbewegliche Sachen*'). This differentiation is taken up in multiple places in the statute, e.g. in § 431 Austrian Civil Code (forms of transfer of ownership of 'immoveable things'). However, § 433 Austrian Civil Code uses the term 'land with its ... components' ('*Liegenschaft ... mit ihren Bestandteilen*'). The *Grundbuchgesetz* in turn refers to *Grundbuchskörper*, which always includes a *Liegenschaft*. According to § 7a(1) Austrian *Grundbuchgesetz*, 'land unit' [*Grundstück*] is the technical term for a piece of the earth's surface registered in the cadastre. In the literature, the terms 'immoveable thing', 'land unit', and '*Liegenschaft*' are frequently used interchangeably (e.g. in Schwimann and Kodek [-*Hofmann*], ABGB II^4, § 297 no. 1). For Hungarian law see *Menyhárd*, Dologi jog, p. 52.

[200] e.g. Staudinger (-*Jickeli and Stieper*), BGB (2004), Vorbem. to §§ 90–103 no. 37 ('Immoveable things are land units including their essential components').

[201] e.g. Art. 948 sentence 1 Greek Civil Code (the ground and its components are immoveable things); Art. 812(1) Italian Civil Code (*sono beni immobili il suolo* [...]); Art. 518 French, Belgian, and Luxembourgish Civil Code (*les fonds de terre et les bâtiments* are *immeubles par leur nature*); Art. 334 Spanish Civil Code (among others, *tierras*, buildings, paths, and other structures, trees and even statues, reliefs, paintings, and other utilitarian or decorative objects, which are installed in buildings or land by the owner of the land unit in a way which shows intent to permanently bind them to the soil, are *bienes inmuebles*); Art. 204(1)(a) Portuguese Civil Code (which characterizes *prédios* as a subgroup of *coisas imóveis*). *Grond* ('ground') within the meaning of Art. 3:3 Netherlands Civil Code includes the earth's surface. The earth's surface is in turn seen as the upper limit of ownership of immoveable things. If structures stand on the ground and are combined with it in such a way that ownership of the soil would follow from ownership of the structure, then the surface of the land unit changes according to the nature of the structures (Asser [-*Mijnssen/van Velten/Bartels*], Zakenrecht^{15}, p. 108 no. 81).

[202] Under Art. 204(1)(b) Portuguese Civil Code, waters are immoveable things (although not land units); see, moreover, Art. 812(1) Italian Civil Code: '*Sono beni immobili ... i corsi d'acqua*'.

[203] e.g. Art. 524 French, Belgian and Luxembourgeois Civil Codes. See, moreover, Art. 334(6) Spanish Civil Code (in which animal breeding facilities and beehives which are combined with a *finca* are counted among the immoveables, but not the animals themselves).

enterprise,[204] or a right to another's piece of ground[205] as 'land' or 'an immoveable'. It is less plausible, however, to characterize them as 'land units' in the sense that is important for a proper conceptual understanding of property law.

The concept of an immoveable is significantly wider than the concept of a land unit. There is an almost endless array of objects that, without being land units, are classified as immoveables by national legal systems.[206] With terms like *unbewegliche Sache*, *immeuble*, or even 'land', national legal terminologies generally do not convey the sense that the object is a possible point of reference for *erga omnes* property rights. For this characteristic, remarkably, there is no term currently in usage that would be suitable for a pan-European approach. We think that 'land unit' can close this gap insofar as it describes the object, which is individuated by the legal system, in which one claims a right when one says that he is owner of a piece of the earth's surface. No different to 'fungible things' or 'consumable things', 'immoveables' (and 'immoveable things') are general categories.[207] A national legal system (and its doctrinal scholarship) uses such terms for different purposes to those that motivate our proposed terminology of 'land unit'. The concept of an immoveable in most legal systems is concerned with specific consequences of the formation of a land unit, for example, the mode of acquisition and the transfer of registered rights,[208] or the term is used to express the idea that one who has a right of use over the land unit of another is able to access those goods of the owner that are implicated in his use of it. Such rules, however, differ from specific property right to property right; in the European context, they must be developed separately.[209] Further, they are rather concerned with the distinction between registered and non-registered things than with that between moveable and immoveable things (e.g. Art. 3:10 Netherlands Civil Code). Of greater importance is the fact that rules like this always presuppose another type of rule—namely, that the legal system in question allows and enables the resection of bodies of land and characterizes them as fitting objects 7.41

[204] In Art. 1:98(3) Lithuanian Civil Code, the legislator explicitly reserved the right to designate certain objects as immoveable, although this is factually not the case. Art. 1:110(2) sentence 2 Lithuanian Civil Code made use of this by stating that a company should be regarded as an immoveable thing.

[205] e.g. Arts 526 French, Belgian and Luxembourgish Civil Code, Art. 50 Polish Civil Code, Art. 334(10) Spanish Civil Code, and also § 96 German Civil Code ('rights which are combined with the ownership of a land unit count among the components of this land unit').

[206] Under Art. 334(7) Spanish Civil Code, to provide a further example, even the fertilizers meant to cultivate farmland are immoveables, as long as they are located on the premises on which they are to be used.

[207] Admittedly, analysis of this is hindered by language. It is possible that authors mean the same thing, but by using different words they formulate exactly opposing theses. It is, however, just as possible that the theses are different in their substance.

[208] For example, in Italian law all legal acts pertaining to immoveables within the meaning of Art. 812(1) and (2) Italian Civil Code must be indiscriminately entered into the *pubblico registro immobiliare* by way of *trascrizione* (Arts 2643–2696 Italian Civil Code). There is a broad kaleidoscope of fourteen different categories of legal acts which must be registered.

[209] First, it is not guaranteed that the distinction between moveables and immoveables follows the same rules everywhere; further, it is not guaranteed that the distinction serves same purposes. For example, the Spanish Civil Code's systematic basis attributes far less meaning to the distinction than the German or Italian codes (*Díez-Picazo*, Fundamentos III[5], pp. 203 and 206). Moreover, careless application of the definition of immoveables leads to irritation, even in one and the same legal system. *Díez-Picazo*, Fundamentos III[5], 212 notes drily that court approval is mandatory if a minor seeks to sell a dovecote, and that even an adult may only sell a dovecote by way of notarial certification (*escritura pública*), merely because Art. 334(6) Spanish Civil Code qualifies a dovecote on a land unit as an 'immoveable'.

of property rights. The terminology of 'moveable/immoveable' does not speak to this all-important question at all.[210] A 'moveable' is not a fitting object of property rights because the object is moveable (water and driveable shipyard cranes are moveable, too),[211] but because they are *spatially separated* from other objects and as such—i.e. being real objects—they are capable of exclusive allocation to one person. An 'immoveable' is, in contrast, not a 'thing' by nature; it only becomes a thing when it takes the form of a *land unit*. The characterization of things as 'moveable' rests on a fuzzy concept, but seldom has disruptive consequences. When one adds 'immoveables' to the picture, however, and elevates the latter to the status of an independent legal category, the lack of clarity grows into a grave conceptual problem.

[210] This is can be seen by the fact that one and the same thing can be a moveable and an immoveable at the same time in some legal systems. This is the case not only in France, but also in Spain. For example, TS 21 December 1990, RAJ 1990 no. 10359 p. 13270 concerned a dispute over the irrigation systems of a land unit. The irrigation systems had been sold, but were charged with a hypothec. The court assumed that the hypothec extended to the irrigation systems by virtue of agreement between the parties. These were moveable goods under Art. 111 *Ley Hipotecaria*, while at the same time being (as accessories) *inmuebles por destinación* or *pertenencias*. In view of such double qualifications, the scholarship finds itself forced to differentiate between 'regular' and 'irregular' immoveables. It points out that the Spanish Civil Code, in contrast to the French Civil Code, does not state that all things 'are' either moveables or immoveables, but rather that they are to 'be regarded' as moveables or immoveables (*Díez-Picazo*, Fundamentos III[5], p. 210). This, admittedly, does little to clarify the matter.

[211] Nevertheless, the Netherlands and Belgian judicial authorities qualifies these as 'immoveable' things (HR 24 December 2010, NJB 2011 no. 199; Cass. 14 February 2008, Pas. belge 2008 no. 110 p. 440).

VIII
Purely Normative Things

1. Immaterial Objects Protected by Property Law

a. Regulatory Approaches in Continental Legal Systems

The third group of objects of property rights are purely normative things. This is a kaleidoscope of objects of legal transaction, difficult to organize, that are neither real (corporeal) objects nor have a physical substrate (like land units). Claims, shares in a business, enterprises, business relationships and goodwill, intellectual creations, discoveries, marks, and other similar objects are often of appreciable economic value. They are, however, not something one can see or touch; they are immaterial creatures of the law.[1] That such immaterial goods fall within the circle of objects protected by property rights is neither a novel idea, nor one unique to those legal systems that have extended the concept of a 'thing' beyond corporeal objects.[2] All European legal systems—even those with an intentionally narrow definition of 'things'—recognize property rights in purely normative objects.[3] What differs among them is the number of such rights and the number of the normative objects in which they can be held. From the European perspective, no fundamental or irreconcilable problems arise, but there are some non-trivial questions. It is certainly fair to say that all European legal systems have, for a long time, paid relatively little attention to purely normative objects.[4] Their current importance is based on fairly recent economic and technical developments, including new markets created on the basis of the Internet. Activity on the Internet demands not only a sale of goods law enriched with elements of the law of service contracts (think of the market in so-called mobile 'apps'), it also shows that customers are interested in purchasing more than just the things of physical reality. Some objects of today's fast-paced commerce were simply unknown to the drafters of the codifications 8.1

[1] *Carbonnier*, Droit civil II, p. 1603 no. 712 names goods which exist because of a right and are rights themselves. This admittedly only concerns a sub-set of the entirety of 'normative things'.

[2] Spanish law even goes so far as to say that the distinction between corporeal and incorporeal objects has no fundamental relevance to property law. A variety of authors consider the differentiation of property rights, depending on whether they pertain to corporeal objects, real rights to corporeal objects, or incorporeal objects, to have no bearing (e.g. *O'Callaghan Muñoz*, Compendio de derecho civil III[5], p. 31 and *Castán Tobeñas*, Derecho Civil Español II[14], p. 61). However, it is noted that the legal system only recognizes a limited number of incorporeal objects as suitable for property rights (*Díez-Picazo*, Fundamentos III[5], 186–7).

[3] It is a different matter *where* a Civil Code regulates rights to rights (whether in the law of obligations or the law of property, or to put it differently: whether it *names* these rights property rights).

[4] e.g. for France, *Reboul-Maupin*, Droit des biens[2], p. 44 no. 94.

Foundations of Property Law. Christian von Bar and Jason Grant Allen, Oxford University Press. © Christian von Bar 2023.
DOI: 10.1093/oso/9780198885337.003.0008

of the nineteenth and twentieth centuries.[5] Further, among those 'immaterial goods' that they did know were many that they believed could be handled simply *as if* they were land units or goods, even though it was clear to everyone that they were 'technically' rights. In this group we find rights in rights in physically existing things. The main example is, of course, rights which encumber another's right of ownership in a thing—that is, rights in the right of ownership in a physically existing thing.[6] Further examples include a pledge right in a pledge over a jewel,[7] a pledge right in a usufruct in some corporeal object (e.g. Art. 3:236(1) Netherlands Civil Code), a hypothec in a usufruct in a land unit,[8] or a usufruct in a hypothec (or land charge) in a land unit.[9] Such

[5] A good example of the amendment of codifications required by modern forms of economics and modern information technology is the comparison between the Czech Civil Code [1964] and the Czech Civil Code [2014]. While only *res corporales* were recognized as 'things' under the Code of 1964 (without being obligated to do so by the text) (*Švestka and Dvořák*, Občanské právo hmotné[5], p. 273), § 489 Czech Civil Code [2014] states, fifty years later, that a thing in the legal sense is everything which can be distinguished from a person and whose purpose is to be used by people. § 489 Czech Civil Code [2014] adds that the provisions of the section concerning absolute property rights may be applied to corporeal and incorporeal things, and to rights only insofar as their character allows and nothing else is provided for by the law.

[6] If someone transfers ownership of his bicycle to another person, he does not transfer 'the bicycle' as a thing, but rather the *right* of ownership in this thing. If someone grants another person a pledge, he does not provide a pledge over the bicycle, but rather he charges his right of ownership in the bicycle with the pledge to the benefit of the creditor. This is not always expressed clearly by some civil codes. e.g. while § 929 German Civil Code (correctly) refers to the 'transfer of ownership in a thing', § 1204 German Civil Code refers (inaccurately) to charging 'a moveable thing' instead of charging the *right of ownership* in that moveable thing. The so-called 'limited real rights' are therefore ultimately invariably rights to rights. Art. 3:8 Netherlands Civil Code expresses this clearly.

[7] e.g. § 1273(1) German Civil Code ('a right can also be the object of a pledge'; 'rights' within the meaning of this provision also encompass pledges to moveable things as well as to land units); Art. 680 Portuguese Civil Code (which permits pledges over rights if these rights have a moveable thing as their object and if they can be transferred), and § 173(1) Slovak Civil Code and § 1390 Czech Civil Code (concerning the so-called sub-pledge or *subpignus*; this is created by pledging a claim secured by a pledge if the object of the pledge is a corporeal thing). Under Art. 1861 Spanish Civil Code, pledge and hypothec contracts can secure every type of obligation. The pledge to rights and claims counts as a special type of pledge (*prenda especial*). It is permitted if the pledged right can be qualified as a moveable thing (*Díez-Picazo and Gullón*, Sistema de Derecho Civil III(2)[8], p. 144; TS 26 September 2002, RAJ 2002 Nr. 7873 p. 14321 For English law, *Donald v Suckling* (1866) LR 1 QB 585 (QB) confirms that a pledge can be charged with a pledge ('sub-pledge' to debentures). This is also confirmed by *Halliday v Holgate* (1868) LR 3 Ex 299 (Ex Ch). For the Netherlands, Art. 3:228 Netherlands Civil Code states that all goods, which can be transferred, can be charged with a pledge or with a hypothec.

[8] A hypothec over a usufruct over a land unit is impossible under German law (§ 1113(1) German Civil Code). However, in Greek law (Art. 1259 Greek Civil Code; in further detail Areopag 280/2011, NoB 59 [2011] p. 1891; Ca Athens 7567/1991, EllDni 34 [1993] p. 641), in Italian law (Art. 2810 Italian Civil Code), and in French law (Art. 2397 French Civil Code), hypothecs over a usufruct are permitted. (Both provisions permit charging not only immoveable goods with a hypothec, but also a usufruct, which has such goods as its object. A hypothec can also relate to a *droit de superficie*, a *bail emphythéotique* [*Cabrillac/Mouly/Cabrillac/Pétel*, Droit des sûretés[9], p. 648 no. 857], and a *bail à construction* [Art. L 251-3 *Code de la construction et de l'habitation*].) The case is similar in Portuguese law (Art. 688(1)(e) Portuguese Civil Code). The acquisition of a pledge over a usufruct over a thing or a negotiable instrument is governed in Art. 3:236(1) Netherlands Civil Code. Polish law acknowledges hypothecs over a perpetual usufruct, but not over a 'normal' usufruct (Art. 65(2) No. 1 Polish Land Registry Act), as well as the hypothec over a hypothec to secure a claim (Nos 2 and 3 op. cit.).

[9] A usufruct over another person's hypothec is possible under § 1068 German Civil Code (see also § 1080 German Civil Code: Usufruct in a land charge or annuity land charge) and under Art. 1178 Greek Civil Code (*Triantos*, AK, Art. 1178 no. 2: a pledge and a hypothec can be the object of a usufruct if the usufruct is acquired for the claim secured by the pledge or hypothec). This is apparently not possible under Italian law (a usufruct over a hypothec is held here to be inconceivable, as the hypothec cannot produce fruits), or under French law. However, a usufruct under French law can be acquired not only for corporeal things, but also claims, copyrights, patents, a *fonds de commerce*, and other incorporeal goods (*Terré and Simler*, Les biens[8], p. 705 no. 788). Usufructs over usufructs are also possible (*Terré and Simler* op. cit.; the authors give the example of the statutory right of use of parents [legal usufruct, *droit de jouissance légal*] over a usufruct gifted to or inherited by their children), as are rights of use over a usufruct (Cass. 14 January 1997, Bull. civ. 1997, I, p. 13 Nr. 22; RTD civ. 1998 p. 414, note by *Zénati*). Austrian law, too, appears to exclude a hypothec over a usufruct. While real usufructs (*Fruchtnießung* under § 509 Austrian Civil Code) can pertain to claims, this is only as long as the exercise of the usufruct does not lead to

pyramid-shaped constructions conceal *rights in rights* (rather than in real things and land units), but do not change the basic fact that the actual object of value—the object of ultimate importance in the constellation—is either a real thing or a land unit. The layering of use rights and rights of exploitation merely results in a marginal, ultimately negligible, expansion of the category of property law's objects. We will not concern ourselves with this category here. The only exception is where the ultimate object of value is a purely normative thing—for example, a pledge over a pledge over a claim.[10]

To assert that purely normative objects are protected by property rights in all legal systems of the European Union is one thing; to gather and categorize them is another. For this, we need appropriate taxonomic criteria, but the European dialogue necessary for their development has not even started.[11] In many parts of the European Union, a coherent terminological apparatus is missing—even for a purely internal description and classification of economic objects that are often (and again imprecisely)[12] called 'immaterial'.[13] That is obviously the case in systems where the concept **8.2**

consumption (Klang [-*Klang*], ABGB II², p. 583). This would appear to be the case for a hypothec, because it entitles the holder to satisfaction out of the land unit.

[10] A pledge over a pledge over a claim is possible, e.g. under Austrian law (§§ 454, 455 Austrian Civil Code; so-called *Afterpfandrecht*; Koziol/Bydlinski/Bollenberger [-*Koch*], ABGB⁴, § 454 no. 4 even considers it to be possible that such an *Afterpfand* can be established separately—i.e. it must not necessarily include the claim secured by the original pledge; however Klang [-*Klang*], ABGB II², p. 448 holds a different view). It may be the case that pledges to rights are only ever permitted if these rights in their turn have a moveable thing as their object (and are transferable). This is the case under Art. 680 Portuguese Civil Code and Art. 1864 Spanish Civil Code. A pledge over a pledge cannot be acquired separately if the pledge and the claim cannot be separated (compare § 1274(2) German Civil Code); however, pledged claims and security rights created in them remain pledgeable.

[11] Even in the literature of the 'great' European legal systems, attempts are seldom made to categorize and order purely normative things. Spanish authors, who do not hold the distinction between corporeal and incorporeal objects to be very important, include a variety of heterogenous entries under the heading of 'incorporeal objects', such as energy or intellectual or industrial property (*Díez-Picazo*, Fundamentos III⁵, 186–9). For French law, *Carbonnier*, Droit civil II, pp. 1603–05 no. 712 (followed by *Reboul-Maupin*, Droit des biens³, p. 57 no. 105) differentiates between two types of incorporeal goods: rights which have a corporeal good as their object and rights which do not. The first group is composed of rights which are moveable or immoveable under Arts 526 and 529 French Civil code, depending on the object to which they pertain. He counts among these all real rights (excepting ownership), claim rights and causes of action (regarding these, see JClCiv Code [-*Loiseau*], Biens, Arts 527–532 Fasc. 20 nos 6–11). The second group consolidates the 'absolute incorporeal goods'. These are rights which are detached from any material carrier, such as stocks and shares, public offices, a client base, companies (*fonds de commerce*), property of works of literature, science, and art, and industrial property. For Portuguese law, *Menezes Cordeiro*, Tratado de Direito Civil I(2)², pp. 108–12 differentiates between three types of *coisas incorpóreas*: intellectual goods (*bens intelectuais*), services (*prestações*), and juristic *quia* or realities (*quia jurídicos*). Intellectual goods encompass literary and artistic works, inventions and marks, which may as a rule have a corporeal carrier, but are outside the scope of application of real rights. Performance consist of human conduct (*conduta humana*). The legal system authorizes the creditor to demand the performance of an act. *Prestações* correspond to services in economics, and can be understood as incorporeal things. The author counts technological and social figurations among the juristic *quia*. This concerns empowerments, authorizations, and expectations. A differentiation between rights which are qualified as things (Art. 204(1)(d) Portuguese Civil Code: rights which pertain to immoveable things are for their part already immoveable things) and rights over rights (e.g. a usufruct over claims, the *usufruto de créditos* or *usufruto de capitais postos a juro* under Art. 1464 Portuguese Civil Code) is to take place.

[12] Imprecise because the issue in question is not whether something has a monetary value (whether it concerns a material or immaterial interest), but rather how to distinguish between objects which are composed of matter and those which are not. If we take 'material' to mean 'holding monetary value', it also applies to the so-called 'immaterial' goods.

[13] Some authors believe that 'immaterial' goods or things are 'actually' incorporeal rights (e.g. *Zenati-Castaing and Revet*, Les biens³, p. 92 no. 45). Others speak of incorporeal goods, incorporeal property, *meubles incorporels, propriétés intellectuelles, droits de clientèle*, or of use monopolies (for further detail, see *Malaurie and Aynès*, Les biens³, pp. 58–60 nos 206–208).

of a thing is restricted to corporeal objects; such an approach invites the assignment of everything incorporeal into a vague, residual category, usually described by means of an arbitrary list of examples in the belief that such a list effectively removes the need to give the matter closer thought.[14] But the terminological deficit pokes one more offensively in the eye in systems where jurists (as, e.g. under Art. 516 French Civil Code and the codes based on it[15]) are effectively forced into assigning purely normative things into the category of moveables or immoveables.[16] Linguistically, at least, it is impossible to move a claim or another type of right or to let them rest.[17] Material-less objects cannot validly be assigned to either the moveable or the immoveable objects; an analogous question would be to ask whether automobiles should be classified as animals or plants (or whether they should be sometimes the one and sometimes the other, depending on the manner and purpose of their use).

[14] See for Poland Radwański and Dybowski (-*Machnikowski*), System Prawa Prywatnego III[2], p. 27 no. 60, who believes it is impossible to organize property rights to rights in a coherent system, and that it must therefore suffice to merely list them. According to *Gniewek*, Prawo rzeczowe[8], p. 2 no. 4 the basis for the creation of a property right to a right is only a corresponding decision by the sovereign legislator. The passages in which the author expands on the foundations of Polish property law do not mention rights as objects of property rights any further. In Austrian law, too, attempts to expand the division between corporeal and incorporeal things, established in § 291 Austrian Civil Code and consolidated in § 292 Austrian Civil Code, into an efficient system of 'incorporeal things' have proved unsuccessful. There is instead an erratic variety of individual observations. Thus, for example, all waves and rays, but also data, formulas, codes and information are included among incorporeal things (Koziol/Bydlinski/Bollenberger [-*Eccher and Riss*], ABGB[2], § 292 no. 1). 'Incorporeal things' are ultimately nothing more than a residual category. Everything that is neither a corporeal thing nor a land unit is an incorporeal thing. Incorporeal things are sometimes conflated with 'all other rights' within the meaning of § 285 Austrian Civil Code (Klang [-*Kisslinger*], ABGB[3], § 292 no. 4). These include all claims, immaterial rights and other property rights, as well as services (§ 303 Austrian Civil Code), Internet domains (*Eccher* op. cit. § 285 no. 4) and company shares (Schwimann and Kodek [-*Hofmann*], ABGB II[4], § 292 no. 5). Strangely, only the ownership right itself is not to be regarded as an 'incorporeal thing' (Rummel [-*Spielbüchler*], ABGB I[3], § 292 no. 1).

[15] The long-range effect of French law's *summa divisio* can be felt to this day where a civil code (such as the Latvian Civil Code in § 841) primarily differentiates between corporeal and incorporeal objects of property law. Under this provision, incorporeal things are personal and real rights, as well as the right to claims insofar as they are components of a patrimony. However, § 846 Latvian Civil Code subsequently counts all real rights, depending on the type of things to which they relate, among moveable or immoveable property. Latvian law categorizes claims as 'moveable property', even when the object of the claim is an immoveable thing.

[16] Under Art. 526 French Civil Code (similar to Art. 813 Italian Civil Code), 'immoveable due to the object to which it relates' is true for a usufruct to an immoveable thing, servitudes, and actions which serve the purpose of vindicating an immoveable thing. Under Art. 529 French Civil Code, 'moveable by dint of law' are, by way of contrast, obligations and actions which have liquidated sums as their object. A claim to transfer an immoveable only defined by type is thus immoveable, while a claim to transfer a thing sold under a retention of title is moveable. Art. 949 Greek Civil Code provides that in cases in which a difference is made between a person's immoveable property as a whole and the moveable property, a usufruct to a land unit as well as a real servitude will fall under immoveable objects and claims will fall under moveable objects. While Swedish law does not carve world into moveable and immoveable things, it is nevertheless divided into 'land possession' on the one hand and 'moveable property' on the other. Moveable property is not identical to 'moveable things' (*lösöre*). Pledges, shares, intellectual property rights and claims are examples of moveable property, but not moveable things (*Håstad*, Sakrätt[6], pp. 41–2).

[17] Under Art. 202 Portuguese Civil Code, a thing is everything which can be an object of legal relations. Rights can therefore also be 'things' within the meaning of this provision (which we consider to be entirely correct and which would correspond to the concept of the author of this provision [*Pires de Lima*, BMJ 91 [1959] pp. 207, 208: '*Os direitos são, na verdade, coisas*'; see in this regard *Carvalho Fernandes*, Teoria geral do direito civil I[2], p. 545]). However, Art. 204(1)(d) Portuguese Civil Code then classifies rights, which are inherent in immoveable things, as immoveable things in turn. Rights which are inherent in moveable things are therefore to be understood as moveable things (*Carvalho Fernandes* op. cit. p. 563). This is considered an imperfect technique for regulation, as is sometimes drily noted ('*Trata-se de técnica manifestamente imperfeita*': *Carvalho Fernandes* op. cit. p. 551). In France, *Carbonnier*, Droit civil II, p. 1605 no. 713 leaves no room for doubt that the need neatly to cleave even completely incorporeal goods into the categories of 'moveable' and 'immoveable' things is merely the result of an arbitrary decision by the legislator.

European private law should finally take up the yoke of searching for a more rational system of classification.[18]

b. *Choses In Action*

The approach that prevails in the British Isles is not much more convincing; in any case, it is not the kind of approach that could be adopted as a 'European' one because it is based on the category of *choses in action*, which is too bound up in the history of English procedural law and is only comprehensible against that idiosyncratic background. The common law uses this term as the general term for *choses* or 'things' that one can, in case of impingement by another, only demand back or realize by way of a legal action. At first blush, that sounds like a distinction between goods, which one can recover oneself (in the last instance by force) and objects whose protection entails recourse to the courts. That is not quite what is meant, however, because in a modern state under the rule of law the protection of *every* object of legal transaction entails recourse to the courts. What is rather meant is objects that cannot be factually possessed nor *realiter* 'used'. The expression 'choses in action' originally (i.e. before the sixteenth century) stood for actionable private rights to money.[19] These included payable contractual claims for payment of money and rights to payment of damages in tort.[20] In the course of the following centuries, the category was broadened to include contractual rights and claims which (in contrast to the claim in damages arising from non-performance of a contractual obligation) were not (yet) actionable as such. For example, shares in a company and insurance are often listed as choses in action, and, following its statutory recognition so is intellectual property.[21] Choses in action formed (and form) a part of the 'personal property' of a person.[22] This category is often called simply 'personalty' and has always included goods. Goods, however, could traditionally not be sought *in natura* by way of a legal action. The default remedy remained a money claim—even against a thief. A person's right of ownership in the goods was lost as soon 8.3

[18] More recent legislative projects have shown that such effort is present. Admittedly, the results may be contentious. For example, in Czech law, as in many other countries, certificated securities are regarded as moveable, corporeal and fungible things ((§§ 514 and 516(1) Czech Civil Code). Register securities by contrast are seen as moveable(!) incorporeal things. It is rightfully complained of that the scholarship was unable to classify this new form of security papers appropriately (*Telec*, Právní rozhledy 12 (2011) pp. 444, 445).

[19] *Sweet*, LQR 10 (1894) pp. 303, 304; *Smith*, Assignment, para. 2.16 and (for a distinction from public law) para. 2.30 ff.

[20] *Elphinstone*, LQR 9 (1893) pp. 311, 313. The law of restitution had not yet become detached from the doctrine of quasi-contract. 'Contractual' claims thus included claims from unjust enrichment. Both were (and are) *choses in action*.

[21] *Smith* op. cit. paras 2.17–2.18.

[22] See *Ser Vaas Inc v Rafidian Bank* [2012] UKSC 40, [2013] AC 595 in confirmation of [2011] EWCA Civ 1256 and [2010] EWHC 3287 (Ch) (Arnold J). This case concerned the question of whether a claim of the state of Iraq should be considered 'property ... intended for use for commercial purposes' within the meaning of sec. 13(4) State Immunity Act 1978, which demanded the clarification of the term 'property' in sec. 13(2)(b). ('Subject to subsections (3) and (4) below (b) the property of a State shall not be subject to any process for the enforcement of a judgment or arbitration award or, in an action in rem, for its arrest, detention or sale'). Lord Clarke said: 'It is common ground ... that the monies payable under the Scheme to Iraq are a debt and a chose in action and as such property within the meaning of section 13(2)(b) of the Act' (para. 10).

as the defendant paid his debt. Goods were, accordingly, personalty (i.e. they belonged to private persons and did not belong, ultimately, to the Crown as did estates in land) but they were no choses in action. Ownership in goods entitled the owner to a claim for monetary compensation but not for physical delivery. Only the right to damages was both at once—i.e. personal property *and* a chose in action. And so it remains in the modern law, the justification appearing to be that the owner of a corporeal object (a 'corporeal chattel' or a 'chose in possesion') which finds itself in the possession of another by reason of a bailment or a tort holds more than a mere chose in action because his property right is not exhausted by a mere claim. It has, for example, always been recognized that the bailor (and not the bailee) of a thing should be seen as its owner.[23] In the case that the thing is damaged, the bailor has a cause of action against the third-party tortfeasor, not the bailee.[24] If the bailor only had a chose in action, he would not have any claim against the third-party at all.[25] The distinction between *things in possession* and *things in action* also played a role in matrimonial law: things in possession passed into the exclusive possession of the husband, but to deal with a thing in action he needed the active cooperation of the wife.

8.4 The right to the payment of money pursuant to a legal action could only be definitively classified as a chose in action, however, once an exception to the basic non-transferability of claims was achieved.[26] Objects that are not *transferable* can only be considered as 'property' in a very limited sense; they 'belong' to me, but I cannot exploit them by way of alienation.[27] In the conceptual schematic of the common law, the non-transferability of most claims—which persisted into the nineteenth century—was a consequence of the 'personal relation' between a creditor and a debtor. A way to avoid this conclusion was found in the idea that a debt could be extinguished and subsequently replaced by a newly created debt (with the same content) against a third party. The transfer or assignment of a chose in action was thus achieved indirectly, by way of replacement of the original obligation of the assignor with a new obligation of the assignee.[28] Working from the basis of the Roman law concept, the English lawyers reasoned that a 'novation' was achieved when A's obligation to pay B a certain sum of money was replaced (with the consent of all parties) by A's obligation to pay C. This

[23] *Williams*, Personal Property[18], p. 30.

[24] In depth *Tettenborn*, CLJ 53 (1994) p. 326.

[25] cf. *Leigh & Sullivan Ltd v Aliakmon Shipping Co. Ltd (The Aliakmon)* [1986] AC 785 (HL) (A buyer cannot claim restitution from a third party, who is culpable for damages sustained by the thing, if he is neither owner nor possessor of the thing).

[26] *Williams* op. cit. p. 32.

[27] Claims arising in tort held an exceptional position insofar as their transferability was limited further (this was connected to the doctrines of 'maintenance' and 'champerty', whose purposes were to prevent the purchase of rights to claims). Claims in tort were, by way of exception, at least partially transferable and could therefore be counted among the choses in action from the beginning. They were transferable if the right to the thing, which was the object of the claim, was also transferred. The main case for this was the transfer of ownership of a damaged moveable thing. In this case, the corresponding claim could also be transferred (*Williams v Protheroe* (1829) 5 Bing 309, 130 ER 1080; 3 Y & J 129, 148 ER 1122 (Ex Ch); *Dawson v Great Northern & City Railway Co* [1905] 1 KB 260, 271 (Stirling LJ); *Sparham-Souter v Town and Country Developments (Essex) Ltd* [1976] QB 858, 868, and *Trendtex Trading Corpn v Credit Suisse* [1980] QB 629, 654–55 (respectively Lord Denning MR).

[28] *Guest*, Guest on the Law of Assignment, paras 1-05 and 1-62 ff.

construction suffered from the complication that the debtor (A) had to consent to the 'assignment' camouflaged as a novation; in practice, however, the problem was solved by the contractual device of a declaration by the debtor at the outset that he was obliging himself to either his contractual partner or any other person to whom the claim was later assigned. This practice, which was originally only intended for use of claims arising from bills of exchange, was extended by means of a power of attorney granted to the assignee to all things in action. It was even extended to the so-called 'equitable choses in action'—i.e. objects that could only be realized by means of a claim in the courts' *equitable* jurisdiction.[29] This led to a further extension. Under the rules of equity, however, not only equitable choses in action but also legal choses in action could be directly assigned from one person to another; the assignee could then sue the debtor in his own name (without a power of attorney). Thus, where the assignee had to sue the debtor in the name of the assignor at common law, he could sue the debtor in his own name in the equitable jurisdiction—even under a common law right, i.e. a 'legal' chose in action.

The concept of choses in action found its way into statutory language only gradually. **8.5**
The first statute that adopted this terminology (and, with its help, consolidated the legal position which had become somewhat complex) was the Judicature Act 1873. Section 25(6) determined that, henceforth, every 'absolute' assignment of a debt (by which was meant an assignment that was not conditional nor solely for the purposes of granting security) or of another *legal* chose in action should be effective at common law as well as in equity. The assignee thereby acquired the right of the assignor directly, and could sue on the debt in his own name (see Law of Property Act 1925 sec. 136, which reproduces and replaces sec. 25(6) of the Judicature Act 1873). A valid assignment is conditional on the written form and the written notice to the debtor; if these conditions are not satisfied, the assignment remains today effective only in equity and not at common law, and is enforceable only according to equity's special rules.[30]

The most important examples of choses in action that belong to the property of a **8.6**
person today are debts (particularly those arising from insurance contracts), goodwill (the immaterial value of a business), company shares, bills of exchange, and intellectual property rights (including patents, copyright, trademarks, trade secrets and know-how).[31] Choses in action are generally divided into 'pure intangibles' und 'documentary intangibles'. The former include, in particular, ordinary claims (not necessarily claims for money), copyright, and goodwill. (The registerable rights of intellectual property law fall somewhat through the cracks; they are choses in action

[29] *Williams* op. cit. pp. 36–7.

[30] At common law, notice to the debtor is a requirement of validity; in equity, notice is merely a requirement for the validity of an assignment pertaining to third parties (it protects the assignee under the rule in *Dearle v Hall* (1828) 3 Russ 1; 38 ER 475 *vis-à-vis* those who assert that they themselves have acquired a chose in action or a right from the assignor, for example through a 'second' assignment). In equity, the assignment is already complete upon execution of the assignment contract (*Holt v Heatherfield Trust Ltd* [1942] 2 KB 1, 4–5 (Atkinson J); *Re City Life Assurance Co Ltd* [1926] 1 Ch 191, 215–16 (Pollock MR) and 220 (Warrington LJ)).

[31] *Bridge*, Personal Property Law^3, pp. 4–5.

but are neither pure intangibles nor documentary intangibles—they are 'semi-pure' intangibles.) Claims (called 'debts' in English legal parlance) can be transferred or given as security; they are, for example, fitting points of reference for a mortgage or a charge. Assets of a personal nature are not choses in action under sec. 136 of the Law of Property Act 1925, regardless of their value. Examples include rights to sue for damages[32] arising from a personal injury, injury to reputation,[33] or interference in the personal correspondence of another.[34] The characterization of an object as a chose in action has, ultimately, a descriptive rather than a normative function. It expresses the fact that one is dealing with a *transferable object of legal transaction*, which can be the point of reference for security rights or a trust. An object is, however, not transferable or encumberable *because* it is a chose in action—it is a chose in action because it is transferable or encumberable.

2. Normative Things Assigned Independently of Ownership

8.7 Within the category of purely normative objects of legal transaction (i.e. 'incorporeal things', 'immaterial goods', 'choses in action'), it is helpful to remember that being a fitting object of property rights *in general* is not to mean that something is a fitting object of the right of *ownership*;[35] even though they are sometime treated as such in the literature, the two are not the same. Not everything that is a proper point of reference of 'a property right' is necessarily and for that reason a fitting object of the *right of ownership*.[36] So much becomes apparent if one looks at the matter closely. In answering the

[32] *Bridge* op. cit. p. 7.

[33] *Ord v Upton* [2000] Ch 352 (CA).

[34] *Haig v Aitken* [2001] Ch 110 (concerning the personal correspondence of a bankrupt).

[35] For example, this is traditionally the case in Portuguese law. Under Art. 1302 Portuguese Civil Code, only corporeal things can be objects of ownership. While Art. 1302 Portuguese Civil Code is a provision regulating ownership rights (it is found in Book III, Title II, Chapter I—Ownership in General), it is nevertheless interpreted as pertaining to general property law. This has the consequence, that generally only corporeal things can be objects of a real right. While this legislative technique has been criticized as 'technically questionable', its purpose is clearly to exclusively determine the objects of real rights (*Vieira*, Direitos reais, p. 131). Incorporeal things are not subject to property law (*Vieira*, op. cit. p. 132). §§ 489 in conjunction with 496(2), 979, and 1011 Czech Civil Code take an exactly inverse route by accepting ownership and co-ownership of claims. In Austrian law, intellectual property rights are counted among the things (Klang [-*Kisslinger*], ABGB^3, § 292 no. 6).

[36] This is different with regard to the constitutional guarantee of property rights. It is apparent that even claims or shares must be protected from being forcibly transferred to the state. Private law does not have this problem. It is therefore hardly mandatory to refer to constitutional rulings when establishing a foundation for the 'ownability' of claims and other non-material goods in private law, as the French literature does (such as *Revet*, RTD civ. 2010 p. 584). The French *Conseil constitutionnel* (Cons. Const. 10 June 2010, JO 16 June 2010, p. 10988 ['*exercice du droit de propriété des créanciers garanti par les articles 2 et 4 de la Déclaration des droits de l'homme et du citoyen de 1789*']; Cons. Const. 29 December 1999, JO 31 December 1999, p. 20012 ['*droit de propriété des titulaires de créances*']), and the European Court of Human Rights (e.g. ECtHR 9 December 1994, *Raffineries Grecques Stran et Stratis Andreadis c. Grèce*, No. 13427/87, http://hudoc.echr.coe.int/sites/fra/pages/search.aspx?i=001-62469, no. 59) have qualified claims as property, or as goods protected by the respective guarantee of property, on multiple occasions. However, this has no direct bearing on private law. This must even apply to decisions such as *SerVaas Incorporated v Rafidian Bank* [2012] UKSC 40, [2013] AC 595, in confirmation of [2011] EWCA Civ 1256, [2012] 1 All ER (Comm) 527 and [2010] EWHC 3287 (Ch) (Arnold J), which qualified claims (*choses in action*) as property as a matter of course. This occurred in the course of a determination of whether another state may cite its immunity with regard to its 'property', or whether it was merely an issue of property in use for commercial purposes. The latter is also unproblematic from the point of view of English private law.

question which objects can be 'owned', lumping together all purely normative things simply will not do. This has been attempted, repeatedly, but the basic problem has not been solved; in particular, the distinction developed by Gaius for Roman law[37] between corporeal and incorporeal things, which is still characteristic of several legal systems, falls short in this context.

One of the most renowned proponents of the 'ownability' of incorporeal objects was Franz von Zeiller. In his 1812 commentary, von Zeiller wrote in the style of an apology for (his drafting of) § 353 Austrian Civil Code:

> If I am owner of a corporeal thing, e.g. a clock, I can alienate, use, degrade, or destroy it. But in the case that I hold only a right in the clock such as a right of use, pledge, possession, or an obligational claim, the entitlements that flow to me directly over this corporeal thing are much less extensive than those that flow to the owner. The difference lies only, however, in the difference of the object. In the latter case, the clock does not belong to me, rather, the right of possession, or use, or pledge is my property. With these rights I can deal freely and exclusively to the extent that their nature allows, as can a creditor over his credit; I can use my right wholly or partially or not at all; I can transfer it to another, or disclaim it unconditionally; I can (in a possessory or petitory sense) enforce it. Here, too, we find the characteristic features of ownership; whether it is applied to things animate or inanimate, moveable or immoveable, the concept is not displaced. The concept of ownership is, accordingly, to be extended to incorporeal things, or rights.[38]

This set the tone, as it were. In the nineteenth century, virtually every author in the jurisdiction of the Austrian Civil Code adopted this simple 'yes/no' dichotomy and got passionately involved in the dispute about whether ownership was truly possible in incorporeal things, or whether it indeed had to be limited to corporeal things.[39] Many

[37] This distinction between corporeal and incorporeal things appears always to have been problematic. It is especially apparent that this was foreign to the tradition of older German law (in further detail *Kocher and Steppan*, Grundzüge der Privatrechtsentwicklung und der Geschichte der Rechtswissenschaft in Österreich, p. 106).

[38] *von Zeiller*, Commentar über das allgemeine bürgerliche Gesetzbuch für die gesammten Deutschen Erbländer der Österreichischen Monarchie, vol. II/1, pp. 110–11. The question whether incorporeal things are fitting objects of the right ownership, to which *Zeiller* pointedly assumes a position, is of course much older and has been discussed extensively in the literature of previous centuries.

[39] In the latter sense, e.g. *v. Winiwarter*, Sachenrecht I^2, p. 107 (Ownership is limited to corporeal things, because 'if one understands ownership, as per the legal definition, as the right with which to handle the substance and uses of a thing at will, then it already follows that the term ownership cannot be applied to rights at all, as a specific right to their substance and a specific right to their uses are not always conceivable'); *Unger*, System des österreichischen allgemeinen Privatrechts I^5, p. 526 ('thus ownership in the technical sense, as well as according to the common law, must also be limited to the total legal control of corporeal things in our Austrian law, unless one wants to fall into complete corruption and disintegration of the terms, as well as into immeasurable confusion'), and *Krainz*, System des österreichischen allgemeinen Privatrechts I^3, p. 97 ('Notwithstanding, the idea of ownership of rights, especially of claims, must be dismissed as a logical impossibility. Ownership of one's rights would be a power over one's own power—which is absurd'). A different view was taken by *v. Stubenrauch*, Commentar zum ABGB I^8, p. 428 fn. 2 ('Objects of ownership are, according to the vision of our Civil Code (§ 353) and according to the older doctrines, not only corporeal, but also incorporeal things (rights) such as a claim, a pledge, a servitude, etc. However, the word ownership is used here in the common meaning, and is intended to express only the control of a subject of a patrimonial right over the same, which means that the subject can take what action he will with this right') and *Randa*, Právo vlastnické dle rakouského práva v pořádku systematickém, p. 22.

later statutory drafters also felt compelled to express a position on this question. What kept Austrian jurists occupied then thus continues to exercise European jurists to the present day.

8.8 Not a few codifications became fixed on the idea that the right of ownership is only possible in 'corporeal objects'—more precisely, objects to which those codifications attribute corporeality; in the relevant national terminology, such objects are generally 'moveable' and 'immoveable' things. Germany (§ 903 German Civil Code), Greece (Art. 999 Greek Civil Code),[40] and Portugal (Art. 1302 Portuguese Civil Code)[41] belong to this group, as do for example the Netherlands (Art. 5:1(1) Netherlands Civil Code), Hungary (§ 5:13 Hungarian Civil Code), and Poland (Art. 140 Polish Civil Code). The legal systems of the common law, on the other hand, distinguish between 'realty' and 'personalty', and distinguish in the latter category between choses in possession and choses in action (as set out above), but do not connect this with the proposition that 'incorporeal things' are unfitting objects of ownership. They rather approach the question as one of *property rights*; the abstract question, in which *objects* those rights can be held, is hardly ever posed independently. By way of contrast, § 353 Austrian Civil Code puts it very clearly: 'Everything that belongs to someone, all his corporeal and incorporeal things, are his property [*Eigentum*].' Finally, in a third group of legal systems, the question of ownership in 'immaterial' goods continues to be debated intensely.[42] Contemporary debates within French jurisprudence, for example, are barely distinguishable from those in Austrian jurisprudence of 150 years ago.[43]

[40] The provision itself is more cautious in its wording, stating that only things or what are *viewed as things* by the law can be the object of ownership.

[41] Art. 1303 Portuguese Civil Code explicitly states that copyright law and industrial property are subject to special provisions. The provisions in the Civil Code, however, enjoy a subsidiary application if they correspond to the nature of these rights, and if the regulation, which is specifically established for them, does not contradict the application. It follows, at least indirectly, from Art. 1303 Portuguese Civil Code, that incorporeal things of all types (literary and artistic works, inventions, models, symbols, marks, logos) are not subject to property law, but to other regimes (*Menezes Leitão*, Direitos reais[2], pp. 60–61; *Oliveira Ascensão*, Direito civil—Direito de autor e direitos conexos, p. 673 fn. 2). Incidentally, when Portuguese judgments occasionally speak of 'ownership' of money stored in a bank account, this is merely inaccurate terminology. It refers to the claim against the bank: STJ 15 March 2012, Processo 492/07.TBTNV.C2.S1.

[42] For Czech law, *Stuna and Švestka*, Právní rozhledy 2011 pp. 366, 367 n. 3, comment that a claim is not a thing in the legal sense; it is a right not capable of being owned (and because this is the case, it can lapse). *Eliáš*, Právní rozhledy 2011 pp. 410, 411 maintains that it is not a problem under the provisions of the Czech Civil Code [2014] to regard a claim as a thing in the legal sense. The law of obligations regulates the reciprocal legal relationship between the creditor and the debtor. It also determines how a claim is created and how and when the debtor should fulfil his obligation. However, a claim is also an asset and a thing in the legal sense, and as such an object of the right to ownership. Thus, the creditor is protected against interferences from third parties. A lapse is thus not a problem, as it does not cause a claim to extinguish.

[43] *Carbonnier*, Droit civil II, p. 1642 no. 730 fn. 1 states that there can be no real ownership of an incorporeal good; one can only be the holder of a claim or a share, as these are rights and not things ('*Se dire propriétaire d'une créance, d'une part sociale, d'un patrimoine, n'est pas une langue juridique correcte; on est titulaire, non pas propriétaire, parce que ce sont des droits, non des choses*'). *Zenati-Castaing and Revet*, Les biens[3], p. 93 no. 47 maintain that a right to claim is only a personal right on the part of the debtor, but not necessarily on the part of the creditor. There is nothing to hinder the creditor from viewing his right as a thing and taking whatever action he desires with it. For this reason, the law (in Art. 529 French Civil Code) could regard rights to claims as moveable things and enable their surrender and even possession (Art. 1240 French Civil Code). For *Fabre-Magnan*, RTD civ. 1997 pp. 583, 601 no. 22, all assets, be they corporeal or incorporeal, are objects of ownership. A good is a thing which is acquirable, ownership thus pertains to an aggregate of assets which includes property rights as well as rights to claims. Claims are said to be goods, whose owner is the holder of the aggregation (*Fabre-Magnan* op. cit. p. 603 no. 24). To support this thesis, authors frequently refer to Art. L 111-1 *Code de la propriété intellectuelle*,

In all of this, the question itself has been framed incorrectly. A preliminary question must be answered before one can meaningfully engage with the question whether non-physical objects of legal transaction are fitting objects of the right of ownership. Does a purely normative object even *need* to be owned, or be capable of ownership, in order for a legal system to ascribe it exclusively to a person? This is certainly not the case for many immaterial assets. Thus, a sensible first step would be to determine which purely normative things can be ascribed to a person even without the right of ownership.[44] The criterion that enables us to determine this class of objects emerges, in turn, from a simple test. Can the object conceivably exist without one knowing to whom it belongs? To put it the other way around, is its ascription to a person an intrinsic criterion of its existence? This is the case, for example, with claims. A claim only arises because there exist a creditor and a debtor; a creditor-less claim is not conceptually possible. A real thing or a land unit, on the other hand, must be *ascribed* to the exclusive use of a person; the right to its use is not immanent within its existence. Precisely for this reason, such things need the legal concept of ownership, and claims do not. Claims, in other words, are not unfitting objects of ownership because they are not 'corporeal objects'. It is true that they are not, but this feature only leads one accidentally to the true answer. Claims are not fitting objects of the right of absolute ownership because they cannot even be imagined without legal attribution to some person.[45] 8.9

which grants the creator of an intellectual work an exclusive incorporeal right of ownership, which is valid against all persons. Finally, *Malaurie and Aynès*, Les biens[4], p. 61 no. 204 state that the concept of ownership is not suited to incorporeal goods. For example, a *fonds de commerce* is not only composed of the real assets and the wares intended for sale, but also of the possibility to gain and retain customers. This 'custom' cannot be acquired, as the customers are free to migrate to a different provider.

[44] The issue of whether 'possession' of purely normative things is possible must be separate from this. This question has different answers in the legal systems of the various member states. For example, German law only acknowledges possession of corporeal objects (§ 854 German Civil Code). Despite some confusion due to the wording of § 1029 German Civil Code, incorporeal objects cannot be objects of possession (Staudinger [-*Bund*], BGB (2007), preface to §§ 854–872 no. 44 with further references). For all *goederen* (things and property rights), Art. 3:107 Netherlands Civil Code acknowledges both possession (*bezit*) and 'holdership' (*houderschap*); accordingly, claims can be objects of possession (Nieuwenhuis/Stolker/Valk [-*Rank-Berenschot*], BW[6], preface to Art. 3:107 no. 2). In Spanish law, 'rights' are suitable objects of possession (Arts 430–432 Spanish Civil Code; for further detail, see *Díez-Picazo*, Fundamentos III[5], pp. 678–9). In Bulgarian law, servitudes to a certain part of another person's thing are available for *quasi possessio* (*Venedikov*, Novo veshtno pravo, p. 37). However, answering the question of what, exactly, is a fitting object of possession does not contribute to the classification of purely normative things. This is because the answer is the same for all incorporeal things, and moreover because the role of possession in the creation of *erga omnes* enforceable legal positions is always more varied and nebulous than the role of ownership.

[45] Therefore, STJ 15 March 2012, Processo 492/07.TBTN.C2.S1 (the question of entitlement to banking transactions must not be confused with the question of 'right to ownership' of the money) is imprecise. Claims can neither be nor become *bona vacantia*. A *contrato de remissão* (a debt settlement agreement under Art. 863(1) Portuguese Civil Code) extinguishes the obligation. By contrast, the *remissão* in property law follows unilaterally from the holder of the ownership right. Depending on whether a moveable or immoveable thing is concerned, this is called either abandonment (*abandono*) or renunciation (*renúncia*) (*Menezes Cordeiro*, Tratado de Direito Civil II(4), pp. 373–5). Abandonment has no effect on real things. The same is the case for land units. Various provisions on a national level ensure that the state has a subsidiary ownership position with regard to land units. Art. 827 Italian Civil Code (distinctively titled '*beni immobili vacanti*') notes that immoveable things, which are in nobody's ownership, belong to the patrimony of the state. Netherlands law also assumes that a piece of land always belongs to somebody (Asser [-*Mijnssen/van Velten/Bartels*], Zakenrecht[15], no. 110). There is no corresponding provision to Art. 5:18 Netherlands Civil Code (abandonment of rights) for land units. Among others, the purpose of this is to avoid burdening the state (which would otherwise gain ownership automatically: Art. 5:25 Netherlands Civil Code) with the costs of disposal of contaminated ground (*Mijnssen/van Velten/Bartels* op. cit. no. 111a). Regulations like this thus originate from mainly public law concerns. They do not change the fact that a claim may extinguish as soon as it no longer has a holder, but

8.10 The situation is the same for company shares,[46] and indeed for whole businesses.[47] If we adopt a certain legal policy, these appear (like claims) to be fitting objects of property

this does not apply to a land unit which is no longer in anybody's ownership. Instead, provisions such as Art. 827 Italian Civil Code confirm the theoretically (and in other legal systems, the practically) possible existence of land units without ownership. On this approach, the very fact that land units continue to exist in *rerum naturam* even without an owner means that a rule could be created allowing land units without owners to fall *ex lege* into the ownership of the state (or a rule prohibiting the abandonment of ownership of land units). An analogous provision for claims is inconceivable. As previously stated, Austrian law principally views claims as things (§ 292 Austrian Civil Code), over which ownership is possible (§ 1424 Austrian Civil Code names an 'owner of the claim [*Eigentümer der Forderung*]'). However, upon closer inspection it becomes clear that a number of provisions regarding ownership in Austrian law cannot, in fact, be applied to claims. This especially concerns provisions which require qualified possession of the thing. This in turn can only exist for corporeal things. This rightly includes the right of vindication (§ 366 Austrian Civil Code) and the law governing the relationship between owners and possessors. For example, it does not find application when a person disposes of a claim to A and then purports to dispose of it to B; A has no ownership-based right against B, a good faith subsequent acquirer (OGH 3 July 1979, SZ 52/110). § 633 Austrian Civil Code, with remarkable imprecision, refers to 'things, rights, works, and other deeds', thus differentiating between things and rights—even though, according to the approach taken, rights 'actually' are things. For Hungarian law, *Menyhárd*, Dologi jog, p. 40 argues correctly that rights and claims can be the object of a limited real right, but not the object of ownership, however he also fails to give the critical reason—claims are always already attributed to a person.

[46] This is no different from bearer shares. e.g. Art. 2354 Italian Civil Code acknowledges two types of shares. These can be either *nominative* (registered shares) or *al portatore* (bearer shares), at the discretion of the shareholder (*Cendon*, Commentario al Codice Civile, Arts 2325–2362, Società per azioni, p. 566). Registered shares are tied strictly to the shareholder's person and their transfer requires notarization (Art. 2355(3) Italian Civil Code). By contrast, bearer shares are nameless and are transferred by a simple handing over of the paper (Art. 2355(2) Italian Civil Code). This does not mean, however, that these shares can exist without a bearer. Only the physical piece of paper titled 'share' can be 'bearerless'. The French legal scholarship is divided over the question of whether the so-called *valeurs mobilières*, which include shares, can be objects of ownership (answering in the affirmative is *Lassalas*, L'inscription en compte des valeurs, no. 354; answering in the negative is *Causse*, JCP E 1992, I, 194 p. 533 no. 18). For an overview of this contentious issue, see *Pélissier*, Possession et meubles incorporels, p. 147 no. 309 nn. 644–647. The author qualifies *valeurs mobilières* as moveable incorporeal things which could be the object of an exclusive right (*droit privatif*). Securities in a company law sense were deemed as moveable corporeal goods until their dematerialization through the French law of 30 December 1981. Since then, these *valeurs mobilières* are qualified as incorporeal moveable goods, which may be a reference point for an exclusive right (*Terré and Simler*, Les biens[8], p. 354 no. 447). However, Arts L228-1(9) Ccom and L211-17(1) Code monétaire et financier refer to a transfer of ownership of *valeurs mobilières* and *titres financiers* by registering in the buyer's securities deposit, Cass. 19 May 1998, Bull. civ. 1998, IV, p. 130 no. 161; D. 1998 p. 551, note by *Martin* ruled that the rules of manual gifts (*don manuel*) are also applicable to dematerialized bearer instruments, and Cass. 5 May 2009, Bull. civ. 2009, IV, no. 66 (see *Martin*, D. 2009 p. 2444, *d'Avout*, D. 2010 p. 123 and *Revet*, RTD civ. 2010 p. 136 no. 9) not only refers to 'ownership' of dematerialized shares, but considers it possible that 'possession' of shares in good faith justifies an assumption of ownership if the shares are not registered at time of transfer. In Netherlands law, neither 'ownership' not 'abandonment of ownership' of shares should be possible, as Art. 5:18 Netherlands Civil Code only acknowledges the dereliction of moveable things. In German law, BGH 10 May 2007, NJW 2007, pp. 2254, 2255 states: 'the law only associates the term *bona vacantia* with the renunciation of ownership of land units or moveable things (or things equated with these) (§§ 928, 958 ff German Civil Code)'. By this interpretation, rights do not become *bona vacantia*, but are extinguished. Greek law differentiates between nominal and non-nominal titles, to which the person who holds the paper is entitled. A nominal title would fall to the tax authority in the event of an estate without heir, in the absence of any other regulations. Stocks and shares without bearers do not exist in Greece.

[47] Ownership in companies is very contentious. Especially in Czech and Polish law, this question is answered in the positive. As early as § 153(1) Czech Civil Code [1964] in conjunction with § 5(2) Czech Commercial Code (old version), a company could not only be the object of a pledge, but also of ownership and co-ownership. A company is regarded as *universitas iuris* (§ 501 Czech Civil Code [2014]), to which the provisions regarding things in the legal sense must be applied. Even the 'client base' is said to have an 'owner' (§ 489 Czech Civil Code [2014]). For Hungarian law, *Menyhárd*, Dologi jog[2], pp. 44–7, 152–3, states that it is not necessary to view corporeal objects only as objects of ownership. He considers the fundamental difference between corporeal and incorporeal objects to be the different required modes of transfer. § 5:14(2) Hungarian Civil Code abandons the earlier idea of assigning financial market instruments and shares to the 'objects of ownership rights', and instead limits the definition of a 'thing' to corporeal objects. In Polish law, a widespread view remains that 'companies' (definition in Art. 55[1] sentence 1 Polish Civil Code) and agricultural businesses (Art. 55[3] Polish Civil Code) constitute objects of ownership (e.g. *Gniewek*, Prawo rzeczowe[8], pp. 28–9 nos 68–71; Radwański and Dybowski [-*Stelmachowski*], System Prawa Prywatnego III[2], p. 216 no. 8, as well as Radwański and Safjan [-*Katner*], System Prawa Prywatnego I, p. 1229 no. 152; differentiating are *Ignatowicz and Stefaniuk*, Prawo rzeczowe[2], p. 72 no. 2 [references to 'ownership of a company' do not mean ownership in the technical legal sense of the Polish civil code]). Polish Sąd

rights, but not of the right of ownership. In order to exist, they must be attributed to a person. They become fitting objects of property rights when and insofar the holder of such a right can encumber it, typically such that someone else can look to the object for satisfaction and can defend this interest against all others. The situation is somewhat different for scientific texts, poems, novels, melodies, product designations, and solutions to technical problems. They all have a conceptual existence even in the absence of legal attribution to a person; they must not belong to a person in order to exist. For this reason, the terminology of intellectual 'property' [*Eigentum*] is entirely correct. It also reflects the position in European Union private law. Art. 19(1) of Regulation (EC) Nr. 40/94, for example, makes it clear that Community trademarks can be the object of all property rights, and very similar drafting is found in Art. 29(1) of Council Regulation (EC) No. 6/2002 on Community designs. The fact that many legal systems ascribe the relevant objects of property ownership[48] to the 'creator', 'inventor', or their employer[49] not through the general law of property (e.g. found in the civil code) but through special statutory ownership regimes does not alter the fundamental appropriateness of the right of ownership for these 'immaterial' goods .[50] It merely shows that the ownership

Najwyższy 6 April 2005, III CK 656/04, Biul.SN 2005/10/12, Lex-No. 156996 likewise refers to the 'owner of a company'.

[48] Which objects specifically belong to this category must be clarified by the laws of intellectual property, which we cannot analyse in detail. Alongside the classic reference points of this area of law (intellectual creations, industrial inventions, marks) can be found a variety of further objects. e.g. in French law, under Art. L-112-2 *Code de la propriété intellectuelle*, the *nom de domaine* is named alongside computer programs (*Malaurie and Aynès*, Les biens[4], p. 69 no. 216). By contrast, Czech Nejvyšší soud České republiky 19 April 2012, 23 Cdo 3407/2010, Právní rozhledy 19/2012, p. 678 considers the right to a domain name to be a (relative) obligation, not an ownership right, as it does not refer to a thing in a legal sense. In the context of Art. 4(2) of the so-called Computer Programs Directive (Directive 2009/24), ECJ 3 July 2012, C-128/11, CR 2012 p. 498 also refers to the 'ownership' of a user over the copy of the respective computer program.

[49] It is certainly not uncommon for the general law of ownership to be given a subsidiary (filler) function. Art. 1303(2) Portuguese Civil Code explicitly stipulates this; argumentation to this effect is common practice in French courts (e.g. Cass. 24 March 1993, Bull. civ. 1993, I, no. 126 p. 84, JCP 1993, II, 22085 p. 272, note by *Greffe*: acquisition of incorporeal ownership of stereotypes by *actes de possession*). Spanish law also regards intellectual property as a property right *sui generis* and follows from this that the Código Civil can be applied in a subsidiary, supplementary manner (*Díez-Picazo*, Fundamentos III[5], p. 188). For example, the object of a copyright is not the corporeal object which shapes it, but rather the intellectual creation as such (López y López and Montés Penadés [-*López Beltrán de Heredia*], Derechos reales, pp. 317, 325). The ownership of a painting (corporeal object) may be held by someone other than the creator of the picture (likewise for French law, e.g. Cass. civ. 1 December 2011, Bull. civ. 2011, I, no. 208 p. 201, RTD civ. 2012 p. 131, note by *Revet*, JCP 2012 p. 1650, note by *Caron*: the creator of illustrations engraved on zinc plates for the purpose of producing lithographs is not necessarily entitled to ownership of the zinc plates). The ownership regime applicable to corporeal things is thus contained in the Civil Code, while the ownership regime of the creation is contained in a special law. The different types of intellectual property are said to be artificial creations of the law. For this reason, the law only connects certain intellectual achievements, limited according to their type, with the creation of real rights (*Díez-Picazo* op. cit. pp. 186–7). This is also endorsed by *Ahrens and McGuire*, Modellgesetz für Geistiges Eigentum, pp. 21–2, by their conception of a *numerus clausus* of intellectual property rights. They differentiate between an absolute protective right (which is intended to protect, *inter alia*, works of literature, science and art, computer programmes, scientific publications, and photographs) and other protective positions (to which they assign, for example, trade and business secrets).

[50] *Terré and Simler*, Les biens[8], p. 329 no. 412 remark: '*Mais il n'en demeure pas moins que les créations de l'esprit ne découlent généralement d'aucun bien préexistant et que l'occupation se présente alors comme le seul mode d'appropriation de ces meubles incorporels. En d'autres termes la création est une occupation.*' Intellectual creations are thus, in general, *res nullius*. Intellectual creations are interpreted as a form of 'occupation' and are, to this extent, at the same level as the acquisition of game and fishery products, as well as *res derelictae*; although creation and occupation take place in a single step (p. 330 no. 414). *Pélissier*, Possession et meubles incorporels, p. 229 no. 431 counters: '*la création littéraire et artistique n'est pas une res nullius puisque le droit privatif et l'œuvre naissent*

regime applicable to real things and land units is not well adapted to the peculiarities of copyright, patent rights, and trademark rights.[51]

8.11 Ownership has a double function. It allocates objects of legal transaction to the exclusive use of a single person, and it enables dealings with the right so allocated—in particular, its transfer and encumbrance. The first function shoots wide of the mark in the context of claims, company shares, and a whole raft of other 'immaterial' goods. This leads one to ask whether ownership is necessary, after all, for the second function, namely the transfer and encumbrance-enabling aspect of ownership. If one answers this question in the affirmative, the disposition of a claim becomes a part of the law of ownership; if one answers it in the negative, the disposition of a claim remains an aspect of the law of obligations, and the creation of a security interest in this right (such as a pledge) becomes a part of the 'law of property' (broadly construed), not the 'law of ownership' as such. One's answer depends, in turn, on where the emphasis should lie; on the 'ascription aspect' of ownership or on the fact that ownership serves as a vehicle for the transfer of objects. We think that emphasis *must* remain on the ascription function, as long as European private law uses the word 'ownership' as a term with more than purely descriptive content. To interpret the assignment of a claim as a transfer of ownership would not, in our view, add anything. Such a view rather leaves the term 'ownership' wanting independent content; one could not distinguish 'ownership' from any of the other property rights. That, however, would have regrettable consequences—including the impoverishment of the legal lexicon and loss of the explanatory power of one of its central concepts. Besides, one would lack a word for the person who is able to set a chain of encumbrances in motion. If we say that A transfers not the claim itself,

simultanément. En revanche, l'invention préexiste à l'attribution du brevet. Tant que le droit de brevet n'a pas été accordé, l'invention est un bien sans maître, susceptible d'être acquis par occupation.' She does not, however, question the ownership of literary and artistic creations. She also endorses the idea that an abandoned *fonds de commerce* ceases to exist, as it no longer has a clientele, and that a claim without a creditor lapses. This, in her view, is different for an artwork. The author demonstrates this by citing Tribunal civil Seine 15 November 1927, D.P. 1928, 2, p. 89, note by *Nast*; p. 1928, 2, p. 137, note by *Chavegrin*, and Paris 6 March 1931, D.P. 1931, 2, p. 88, note by *Nast*; p. 1932, 2, p. 145, note by *Geny*: An artist had disfigured his painting by stabbing it with a knife and had subsequently thrown it into the dustbin. A passer-by had then taken possession of it. The abandonment of the ownership of the material carrier and the carrier's subsequent possession were said to be possible, but not possession of the *droit moral*. The creator remains entitled to this. The passer-by had thus acquired ownership of the painting's material carrier, but not intellectual ownership of the artwork.

[51] *Vojčík*, Práva priemyselného vlastníctva, p. 17 aptly states that 'normal' and intellectual or industrial property both have an *effect erga* omnes. Both owners are permitted to exclude everyone from the use of the object concerned and both are permitted to grant other persons rights to their things. The immaterial and 'ownable' objects of intellectual and industrial property can, however, be used by a greater number of persons than real things and land units, anywhere and independently from one another. Intellectual property is thus more vulnerable than real property. The objects of intellectual property are removed from factual possession; they must first be presented in a manner accessible to the human senses. The objects of intellectual property cannot be lost. Additionally, ownership in private law does not usually lapse, while the intellectual and industrial property rights are constrained to a time limit. See, for Italian law, the impressive studies of the difference between the general private law ownership and intellectual property by *Sena*, Riv. dir. ind. 2010 pp. 164–72, and by *Vanzetti*, Riv. dir. ind. 2010 pp. 173–84. From a Spanish point of view, *Díez-Picazo*, Fundamentos III^{5}, pp. 188–9 considers all immaterial goods to be suitable objects of real rights. From a theoretical standpoint, there would be nothing against speaking of *derechos reales sobre bienes inmateriales*, as long as it is clear that these are only real rights *sui generis*. The application of rules of classic real rights to intellectual property rights ultimately take place by way of analogy.

but rather (as in the case of a corporeal thing) *ownership* of the claim, we would have to describe the transfer of any other right in the same way—i.e. as a matter of the transfer of ownership in the relevant right. One would, according to this view, not transfer the pledge in a corporeal thing or in a claim, but would transfer ownership in pledge (ownership in a hypothec, not the hypothec, etc.). The consequence would be that one could not even say what 'ownership' actually comprises; it would be indistinguishable from the other property rights. 'Ownership in a claim' would be as non-expressive a verbal construct as 'ownership in a pledge over a claim' or 'ownership in a pledge over a real thing'. A pledge right, after all, cannot exist without someone to hold it. The notion of a right-holder is an intrinsic element of the right itself, and for this reason, its transferability arises directly from its own nature, not from some 'ownership' that is superimposed onto it. But nowhere do we find the proposition that only what is owned can be transferred (or be the object of any other legal dealing).

3. Points of Reference of Special Property Rights

a. Factors in the Instrumental Equiparation with Other Things

The task remains to identify which normative objects of legal transaction cannot be owned, but are nevertheless fitting objects of other property rights. The attempt to compile an exhaustive list of such objects is attended by non-trivial difficulties. The broad spectrum of legal policy and the diversity of the juristic concepts in which these policy judgments are given expression across Europe are considerable, even today. Nevertheless, in the first instance, what can be said from a non-parochial perspective is that a purely normative object of legal transaction can be characterized as a 'thing' when the potential for exclusive attribution to a person is intrinsic within it. This is absent in the case of many objects that the modern economy deems to have a money value, such as information, energy, future things, and money units themselves.[52] Objects of this kind are, admittedly, fitting objects of contractual obligations, but they are unfitting not only as objects of the right of ownership but also of property rights generally. No conceivable property right would enable their exclusive allocation to a given person—not ownership, nor any tailored, more limited, property right. An object of legal transaction only has the potential for exclusive allocation to a person (however that be constructed) when it is *controllable*, *ascertainable*, and of economic value; the latter is usually expressed in the *transferability* of one's holding of the object.[53] 8.12

[52] Above, paras 108 ff and paras 173 ff. Some codes count as among 'things', and others maintain the same for information. For example, the Lithuanian Civil Code operates with the category of 'objects of civil law relations' and explicitly counts information among them (Art. 1:97(1) Lithuanian Civil Code). This stands to reason in the context of law of obligations, but not in a property law context.

[53] Art. 333 Spanish Civil Code condenses similar criteria by stating that every thing (*cosa*) that is or can be an 'object of acquisition' is to be regarded as a moveable or immoveable good (*bien*). Here, the continued effect of the unhappy *summa divisio* of things into moveable and immoveable goods can be observed, and the category of 'things suitable for acquisition' has a certain circularity. The underlying idea behind this is, at base, merely the

No national law can ignore these factors when determining whether an object is to be considered a 'thing'. Everything beyond these factors is a question of legal policy (and therefore of value judgment). The considerations that guide that value judgment, however, are not just economic. Whether (and which) rights of exclusion are deemed appropriate for (which) purely normative objects is also related to a legal system's aspiration for internal coherence.

8.13 If the characteristic of most purely normative things is that they can be the point of reference of special property rights, but not of the right of ownership, it can be said that they can only be equated with 'things, properly so called' for specific purposes. This observation, in turn, permits an assessment of which purely normative things might be *partially* equated with conventional things. These are claims, company shares, undertakings (with their client relationships), and goodwill, and a residual group of rights that could be described as privileges or concessions. The objects of intellectual and industrial property law are, by way of contrast, not only fitting objects of property rights generally but also of the right of ownership in particular. They do not fall within this group, and we will bracket them out of further discussion because intellectual and industrial property law has long since coalesced into an independent body of law, the details of which cannot be dealt with adequately in the course of a general enquiry into the general law of property. Subjective rights in real things and land units that are endowed with *erga omnes* effects by a legal system are excluded from this list for a different reason. Admittedly, such rights can (as we have seen) become the point of reference for another property right, but ultimately there is a real thing or a land unit that gives the primary right, at the base of the inverted pyramid, lasting value. In the context of real things and land units, therefore, one is still concerned with the law of things, properly so called, even when one moves through the intermediated layers of that pyramid—i.e. between the primary right and the proximate point of reference of other property rights in that right.[54]

b. Claims

8.14 Every European legal system—whether it limits the concept of 'thing' to corporeal objects or not—also recognizes specific property rights in a raft of claims (and/or causes

conviction that the thing must be useful for a human and must have an economic value (*Díez-Picazo and Gullón*, Sistema de Derecho Civil I[12], p. 384; Bercovitz Rodríguez-Cano [-*Badenas Carpio*], Comentarios al Código Civil[2], p. 495).

[54] The Portuguese scholarship tends to negate the concept of rights in rights, reasoning that a subjective right cannot have another right as its object, only a thing (a good) (*Vieira*, Direitos reais, pp. 132–3). However, it is added that the usufruct to rights and the pledge to claims do not really relate to a right, but to the object of this intermediary right. If this object takes the form of a corporeal thing, then the usufruct and the pledge over the right is of a real nature. If the object is not a corporeal thing, then this is not the case. A usufruct over equities (stocks, shares: see Art. 1467 Portuguese Civil Code), a usufruct over copyrights (Art. 45 Portuguese CDADC), a pledge over copyrights (Art. 46 CDADC), and a pledge over stocks all constitute positions in the law of obligations (*Vieira* loc. cit.).

of action) directed towards the performance of some obligation. We shall refer to this category in the following as 'claims' [*Forderungen*].[55] The most common property right in a claim is the pledge; sometimes it also appears as a hypothec[56] or a sub-pledge. The possibility of creating a pledge over a claim exists in every European legal system.[57] The fact that the terminology of 'investment funds' is sometimes used,[58] or that different statutory language[59] is used for pledges of things and pledges of rights,[60] does not undermine the basic observation that claims can be subject to property rights in the nature of a pledge; nor does the fact that codifications often locate the law of pledges in very different places—sometimes within the law of obligations rather than property law.[61] In some legal systems, although admittedly not everywhere, claims are also

[55] There do not seem to exist statutory definitions of the term 'claim' (*crédito, créance, Forderung*, etc.). § 241 German Civil Code provides that the creditor is entitled 'by force of the obligational relationship' to 'claim [*fordern*] a performance from the debtor', but this provision at most states that obligational demands are *Forderungen*—but does not state that non-obligational (i.e. property law-based) demands are not *Forderungen*. Art. 397 Portuguese Civil Code defines an 'obligation' (*obrigação*) as the legal relation in virtue of which one person is bound to the performance of some benefit to another. *Crédito* or *direito de crédito* stand on the 'active' side of an obligational relation, i.e. the right to demand some kind of performance of another (*Prata*, Dicionário jurídico I[5], p. 406).

[56] A hypothec over a claim (e.g. in the form of a hypothec over moveables under §§ 2387–2419 Romanian Civil Code: see *Alunaru*, ERCL 2010 pp. 197, 215) is, at its core, merely another name for a pledge to a claim.

[57] English law distinguishes between a 'charge' (a security interest cognizable in equity) and a 'mortgage' (assignment of collateral). An English law 'pledge' can only exist in relation to real things.

[58] § 489 Czech Civil Code states that a 'thing' in the legal sense is any object that is not a person that is of use to humans. According to the supporting materials, things include so-called 'investment funds'. It explicitly names forward contracts (sales contracts about future things at a price already fixed at the time of contract) and swap contracts (contracts about the exchange of future assets under agreement of multiple payments) (*Eliáš et al.*, Nový občanský zákoník s aktualizovanou důvodovou zprávou a rejstříkem, p. 224). The object of these contracts is said to be the right or the obligation to sell or buy assets, by which is meant claims. § 979 Czech Civil Code confirms that investment funds are objects of property law.

[59] e.g. in Germany a distinction is drawn between a pledge over a thing [*Sachpfand*] and a pledge over a claim [*Forderungspfand*]. Distinctions like this, drawn by *content* between different pledges, only cause problems when applied to securities: see Cass. 27 December 2011, no. 28900, Mass. Giust. civ. 2011 p. 1862 (it cannot be generally said whether shares of an investment fund are embodied in securities or not; the question of whether they can only be pledged by transferring the relevant document must be decided on a case-by-case basis).

[60] French law has recently begun to differentiate between *nantissement* (a pledge to incorporeal goods, Art. 2355 French Civil Code) and *gage* (a pledge to a *bien mobilier ou un ensemble de biens mobiliers corporels*, Art. 2333 French Civil Code); for further detail, see *Albiges and Dumont-Lefrand*, Droit des sûretés[3], p. 299). In the Belgian and Luxembourgish Civil Code, *nantissement* remains a generic term. Under Art. 2071(1) Belgian and Luxembourgish Civil Code, *nantissement* is a contract in which a debtor transmits the thing to his creditor as a security for the obligation. Art. 2072 adds '*le nantissement d'une chose mobilière s'appelle gage. Celui d'une chose immobilière s'appelle antichrèse*.' *Gage* is thus the *nantissement* of a moveable thing; *antichrèse* is the use-pledge [*Nutzungspfand*] of an immoveable thing. The *gage* in Belgian law can relate to corporeal as well as incorporeal moveable goods (*Grégoire*, Publicité foncière, p. 436 no. 1019). This terminology was also used in France until the 2006 reform of the *droit des sûretés*. Most civil codes use a single word for the pledge; the technique followed by Art. 328 Polish Civil Code, which is to apply the rules of pledge over a thing (*zastaw na rzeczach*) to pledge over a right (*zastaw na prawach*) by way of a legally mandated analogy is also prevalent.

[61] This is also the case in Portuguese and Italian law. Arts 666–685 Portuguese Civil Code are found in Book II (Law of Obligations/ *Direito das Obrigações*), Title I (Of obligations in general/*Das obrigações em geral*), Chapter VI (*Garantias especiais das obrigações*), Part IV (pledges/*penhor*). Areas of the Portuguese scholarship therefore deny that pledges and usufructs to claims (*créditos*) are real in nature, for example, *Pinto Duarte*, Direitos reais[2], p. 32. *Vieira*, Direitos reais, pp. 132–3 takes a nuanced view. He opines that it depends whether the ultimate reference point of the pledge or usufruct is a corporeal thing (such as in the case of a right to a right to a thing), or merely an obligation (such as in the case of pledges or usufructs to claims [Arts 679, 1463 Portuguese Civil Code]). In the latter case, pledges and usufructs are an obligation. Otherwise, they are a property right. The Italian Civil Code does not set out the rules for pledges and hypothecs with the other property rights (in Book III). Rather, these are found in Book IV (about the 'protection of rights'). It is the prevailing view that pledges and hypothecs are property rights (e.g. *Cendon*, Proprietà e diritti reali I, p. 26 and *Comporti*, Diritti reali in generale[2], p. 249). However, a claim is merely the object of a *pegno irregolare* and not a *bene*. For this reason, the legal nature of such a pledge is highly controversial (an overview of this discussion can be found in *Gabrielli*, Il pegno, pp. 200 ff). In any event, factoring contracts owe their dogmatic legitimation to pledges to claims (*Tucci*, Garanzie sui crediti dell'impresa e tutela dei

recognized as fitting points of reference for a usufruct,[62] a trust (which is for present purposes functionally equivalent), and a lien.[63] Retention of title rights in claims, on the other hand, as retention of title rights generally, are only rarely characterized as property rights.[64] Where whole undertakings (and their claims) are elevated to the status of objects of property rights, on the other hand, claims come indirectly into the field of vision of 'property law'.

8.15 Claims generally are not fitting points of reference for all property rights; moreover, not every claim is a fitting point of reference for the property rights currently under discussion—i.e. the pledge, usufruct, trust, and lien.[65] In order to be itself encumbered with a use right or security right, a claim must satisfy a number of conditions. The most important of these is that the claim must be *transferable*.

finanziamenti, p. 162). French law sees the previously mentioned Art. 2355 French Civil Code (*nantissement de meubles incorporels*) inserted into Book IV Civil Code (*Des sûretés*), thus passing over Book II, dedicated mainly to property law (*Des biens et des différentes modifications de la propriété*), and Book III, dedicated mainly to the law of obligations (*Des différentes manières dont on acquiert la propriété*). Belgian and Luxembourgeois law leaves Art. 2072 of their respective codes (concerning the *gage*) in Title XVII of the third book (*Du nantissement*), where it precedes regulations concerning *privilèges* and *hypothèques*. However, in French as in Belgian law, the law of credit securities (*droit des sûretés*) constitutes a separate field of law not integrated into the law of things. Netherlands law, in turn, has an entirely different approach. Pledges to claims are there found in Art. 3:227 Netherlands Civil Code, a provision of the general law of property. Claims are goods within the meaning of Art. 3:1 Netherlands Civil Code.

[62] While *Terré and Simler*, Les biens[8], p. 710 no. 796 emphasize for French law that the usufruct to incorporeal goods cannot be easily constructed (the law acknowledges it in Art. 588 French Civil Code only for life annuities), it is generally accepted in the scholarship. The same is true of the usufruct to claims (*Malaurie and Aynès*, Les biens[4], p. 267 no. 814 p. 267 ['*Bien que le Code ne l'ai pas prévu, le domaine de l'usufruit s'est étendu aux biens incorporels, tels que fonds de commerce, valeurs mobilières, propriétés intellectuelles, créances ou sommes d'argent, etc.*'], see furthermore *Françon*, RTD civ. 1957 p. 1 and *Bergel/Bruschi/Cimamonti*, Les biens[2], p. 298 no. 251). For a discussion of the usufruct over claims in German and Netherlands law, see e.g. *Wilhelm*, Sachenrecht[4], p. 774 no. 1942 and Nieuwenhuis/Stolker/Valk (*-Mellema-Kranenburg*), BW[6], preface to Art. 3:201 no. 1; for a similar discussion in Greek law (Art. 1179 Greek Civil Code), see *Triantos*, AK, Art 1178 p. 1393 no. 2 (while it not a property right in the technical sense, it is a subjective right which confers a direct and absolute power over another's subjective right). Art. 265 § 1 Polish Civil Code provides for a usufruct over rights.

[63] While the lien in common law is only applicable to real corporeal objects in principle (including security papers), a lien could also be created for a claim *ex lege* in equity (see *Goode*, Commercial Law[3], p. 619).

[64] Retention rights are regularly restricted to real things. cf. Art. 3:290(1) Netherlands Civil Code (the holder must be in possession of the thing), § 175(1) Czech Civil Code [1964] and § 1395(1) Czech Civil Code [2014], and for Spanish law *Carrasco Perera/Cordero Lobato/Marín López*, Tratado de los derechos de garantía II[2], pp. 158–9 (no retention rights to claims). Even their nature as 'real' is highly contentious (for example, *Díez-Picazo*, Fundamentos III[5], p. 119 rejects the Spanish *derecho de retención*). It is difficult in any case to determine a standard interpretation of 'the' retention right, as retention rights exist in many forms (e.g. under Art. 1866(1) Spanish Civil Code, a pledge contract grants the creditor the right to retain the thing in his own possession or the possession of a third person to whom the thing was conferred until his claim has been offset). In Portuguese law, the *direito de retenção* is regarded as a real right. It relates to moveables (Art. 758 Portuguese Civil Code) as well as immoveables (Art. 759 Portuguese Civil Code). It is furthermore correct that the term 'moveable thing' includes claims (Arts 202 in conjunction with 205 Portuguese Civil Code). The French *Cour de cassation* has qualified the *droit de rétention* to a thing as a *droit réel* on multiple occasions (Cass. civ. 7 January 1992, Bull. civ. 1992, I no. 4 p. 3, RTD civ. 1992 p. 586, note by *Gautier*; Cass. 3 May 2006, Bull. civ. 2006, IV no. 106 p. 107; Cass. 24 September 2009, Bull. civ. 2009, I no. 178 p. 160, D. 2010 p. 302, note by *Borga*, JCP 2009 p. 380, note by *Aynès*). Cass. 26 May 2010, Bull. civ. 2010 no. 94 p. 116 subsequently acknowledged that the creditor of a pledge to a claim (the *créancier nanti*) has a *droit de rétention* as soon as the debtor receives news of the *nantissement*. In this case, a loanee had assigned a claim to the loaner to secure his loan, and had informed the tenant of this in accordance with Art. 1690 French Civil Code. As early as Cass. civ. 7 April 1998, Bull. civ. 1998, IV p. 99 no. 123, JCP E 1998 p. 1143, note by *Stoufflet* (and arguably also Dijon 3 September 1986, Banque 1987 p. 304, note by *Rives-Lange* [cited according to *Parance*, La possession des biens incorporels, p. 400 no. 579 fn. 10]), courts acknowledged implicitly that a bank may have a *droit de rétention* to the credit balance of a current account it manages.

[65] In English law, claims which cannot be assigned can become objects of a disposition in certain circumstances, such as their inclusion in a trust.

In Austrian law, the transferability of an object belongs to the necessary conditions for the existence of a 'thing' (as defined in Austrian law) (see § 285 Austrian Civil Code) and therefore also to the preconditions for the creation of a pledge right over a claim. Rights that are persistent through time (in German, so-called *Bestandrechte* including the lease-type rights of *Miete* and *Pacht*) are thus only pledgeable when they are alienable, i.e. when there is neither a prohibition on the lessee sub-leasing nor a lessor's right of termination triggered by disposal (see § 11 and § 30(2) Nr. 4 of the Austrian *Mietrechtsgesetz*). In many cases, the right to re-purchase an object is a highly personal right; while the claim to delivery of the object that arises from the exercise of such right is, the right itself is not a fitting object for a pledge.[66] Under Art. 3:228 Netherlands Civil Code, all goods that are transferable can be encumbered with a pledge (and/or a hypothec). These are identified in Art. 3:83 Netherlands Civil Code, which expressly stipulates the rights of ownership, the limited real rights, and claim rights to be transferable—the latter insofar as transfer is not excluded by contract or a contrary legal provision, or contraindicated by the nature of the claim itself. All other rights, on the other hand, are non-transferable unless expressly provided. Non-transferable claims in Netherlands law include, for example, the right to compensation for immaterial damage (in contrast to Austrian law[67]). In German law, § 1274(2) German Civil Code stipulates that a pledge cannot be created over a right that is non-transferable, and a similar approach is taken in Art. 265 Polish Civil Code and § 1069(2) German Civil Code to usufructs over rights. The same approach is found in Art. 1247(1) Greek Civil Code. In Greek law, non-transferable (and therefore non-pledgeable) rights include the right of habitation (Art. 1183 Greek Civil Code), usufruct (Art. 1166 Greek Civil Code) and the claim for delivery of an owner against one in possession (Art. 1094 Greek Civil Code). Under Art. 327 Polish Civil Code, only alienable (i.e. transferable) rights can be the object of a pledge; for example, a pledge right (such as a hypothec) cannot be transferred without the secured claim (Art. 323 § 2 Polish Civil Code). The assignment of a claim is not possible when excluded by contractual provision, the general law, or the special features of the parties' obligational relationship (Art. 509 § 1 Polish Civil Code). In Belgian law, Art. 2071(2) Belgian Civil Code has provided since 1999 that goods designated by law to be non-transferable cannot be pledged.[68] A *créance d'aliments* (i.e. alimony) can be pledged by contractual agreement under Belgian law; the fact that such a right is not subject to all the normal methods of enforcement is not regarded as sufficient to make this right non-transferable (in contrast to the approach taken in § 400 German Civil Code).[69] A first-instance decision from Ghent notices that

[66] OGH 24 March 1971, JBl 1971 p. 569.

[67] Schwimann and Kodek (-*Hinteregger*), ABGB II^4, § 448 no. 17.

[68] Art. 2071(2) Belgian Civil Code was only introduced in 1999. The background of this was a difference of opinion between the *Cour de cassation* and the *Cour constitutionnel* over the 'pledgeability' of doctors' claims against their patients' health insurers (for further details, see http://www.dekamer.be/kvvcr/showpage.cfm?section=/flwb&language=nl&rightmenu=right&cfm=/site/wwwcfm/flwb/flwbn.cfm?lang=N&legislat=49&dossierID=1287).

[69] Lüttich 13 March 1923, Pas. belge 1923, II p. 123. For Greek law, see CA Patras 389/2007, AchNom 2008 p. 228. In Bulgarian law, it is said that an assignment is economically pointless if the creditor cannot enforce his claim. Such claims can thus not be charged with a security right (*Pavlova*, Grazdansko pravo, Obshta Chast I, p. 174).

a pledge can be created over 'all sums' and 'all claims' which arise from a legal relationship provided they are sufficiently certain or ascertainable.[70] A comparable provision to Art. 2071(2) Belgian Civil Code is absent in the French version of the *Code civil*. Under the 2006 reforms of the *droit des sûretés*, however, every corporeal thing that is not designated as *extra commercium* or as non-disponible can be pledged.[71] This provision bites, in principle, on moveable incorporeal things rather than on claims (Art. 2355(4) and (5) French Civil Code). In the absence of specific provisions to the contrary in the third chapter of the code (*Du nantissement de meubles incorporels*), the pledge of a claim is subject to the second sub-part (*Des sûretés sur les meubles*) of the second part (*Des sûretés réelles*) of the new fourth book (*Des sûretés*). The law, however, is silent on the question whether a non-transferable claim can be pledged. The question has barely been raised in the literature. The authors that have engaged with the topic, however, confirm that French law also follows the principle that a claim must be *disponible* to be pledged.[72] The approach in the newer Member States of the European Union is similar. Art. 128(3) Slovenian Civil Code expressly provides that a pledge over rights (*pignus nominis*) and securities require an object of value that can be dealt with in relevant ways. The position under Art. 4:201 Lithuanian Civil Code is not completely clear; according to the literal meaning of the provision, only corporeal objects and real rights (illustrated by a non-exhaustive list in Art. 4.204(1)) can be pledged; however, these rights too must be transferable. In §§ 277, 314(1) Estonian *Asjaõigusseadus*and Art. 1294 Latvian Civil Code one finds the familiar rule that all incorporeal things (rights) can be the object of a pledge insofar as they are transferable. This is also the approach in Hungarian and Swedish law.[73]

8.16 The requirement of transferability is surprising at first blush, but appears justified when one considers that the encumbrance of a claim with a property right would, in case of its alienation, always amount to a partial assignment of the encumbered right (from an economic perspective, at least).[74] The requirement of transferability is meant to prevent the circumvention of prohibitions on assignment. For the same reason, claims that extinguish upon the creditor's death, which are of a highly personal nature, are not pledgeable;[75] nor are other rights whose content would change with a change of creditor.[76] Further, claims whose transfer is effectively precluded by contractual agreement

[70] Tribunal de première instance Gent 1 December 1999, R.W. 2000–2001 p. 487.

[71] *Cabrillac/Mouly/Cabrillac/Pétel*, Droit des sûretés[9], p. 555 no. 742.

[72] *Mignot*, Droit des sûretés, p. 423 no. 1556 and *Stoufflet*, JCP, supplement to no. 20 of 17 May 2006 pp. 19, 20 (*'Est reconnu par les articles 2355 et suivants du Code civil le nantissement de tous les types de créances de somme d'argent, commerciales aussi bien que civiles, contractuelles ou non contractuelles. Ne sont exclues que les créances légalement indisponibles ou soumises à une indisponibilité contractuelle dans la mesure où la loi ne s'y oppose pas'*).

[73] Petrik (-*Pomeisl*), Polgári jog. Kommentár II, p. 130; *Hessler*, Allmän sakrätt, pp. 6, 21.

[74] A pledge is close to an assignment both in structure and in effect (Staudinger [-*Wiegand*], BGB (2009), § 1274 no. 23).

[75] MünchKomm (-*Roth*), BGB II[6], § 398 no. 62; Klang (-*Kisslinger*), ABGB[3], § 292 no. 5.

[76] See e.g. for Czech Republic *Švestka and Dvořák*, Občanské právo hmotné[5], p. 393; for Germany § 399 German Civil Code; for Portugal Art. 577 Portuguese Civil Code, and for Spain *Díez-Picazo and Gullón*, Sistema de Derecho Civil II(1)[10], p. 240 with reference to Art. 1112 Spanish Civil Code (which states that all rights acquired through an obligation can be transferred according to the laws, unless the opposite was agreed).

are generally not pledgeable.[77] Beyond this, many claims are placed *extra commercium* for reasons of public policy or humanitarian considerations.[78] This group might include, by way of example, public welfare entitlements (e.g. expectancy of a state old-age pension), certain claims to maintenance,[79] or insurance claims (e.g. arising from fire damage to a building).[80]

Claims arising from a contractual relationship or a statutory obligational relationship are not, however, the only fitting objects of a pledge (or of a usufruct, trust, or lien). The source of the obligation is not dispositive.[81] Nor is it necessary for the claim to be for the payment of money;[82] the claim *secured* by the pledge, not the *pledged asset* itself, has to be a money claim. Further, claims to the production of some physical object can generally be pledged, as can many claims that have some positive act—a *facere*—as their content.[83] Generally, all that is required is that the object of the claim has some valuation that can be expressed as a market value in money,[84] and sometimes that the claim arises from a 'written instrument' (as in Arts 2800 and 2801 Italian Civil Code, which **8.17**

[77] Through a contractional preclusion of transferability (§ 399 German Civil Code, Art. 3:83(2) Netherlands Civil Code), claims are removed from legal transactions according to the prevailing French, Netherlands (Art. 3:228 Netherlands Civil Code), and German scholarship (BGH 11 March 1997, NJW 1997 pp. 3434, 3435; Staudinger [-*Busche*], BGB (2012), § 399 no. 65). They can thus no longer be pledged according to § 1274(2) German Civil Code, or charged with a usufruct according to § 1069(2) German Civil Code (Staudinger-[*Wiegand*], BGB (2009), § 1274 no. 30; a different position is taken in part by *Wagner*, JZ 1994 pp. 227–33). However, the parties are free contractually to exclude the cession of a claim without excluding pledging it, as §§ 1069(2) and 1274(2) German Civil Code are merely rules for interpretation (correctly for § 1069(2) German Civil Code MünchKomm [-*Pohlmann*], BGB VI[5], § 1069 no. 15). Under § 364c Austrian Civil Code, a contractual exclusion of dispositions or charges is only effective with regard to third parties if it originates in certain familial relationships and is entered into the land registry, otherwise dispositions and charges which are contrary to the agreement are effective (*Iro*, Sachenrecht[4], no. 4/32; Rummel [-*Spielbüchler*], ABGB I[3], § 364c no. 6).

[78] *T'Kint*, Sûretés[4], p. 34 no. 49 with reference to Arts 1408 ff Belgian *Code judiciaire*.

[79] e.g. Art. 14(2) French Loi No. 91-650 of 9 July 1991 concerning the *réforme des procédures civiles d'exécution*.

[80] e.g. § 317(1) Czech CPC.

[81] e.g. see for France *Albiges and Dumont-Lefrand*, Droit des sûretés[3], p. 300 no. 490 (*'Le législateur ne fixe aucune limite particulière dans la détermination de la créance nantie. Bien au contraire, il semble laisser toute latitude aux parties. ... Ensuite parce que l'origine de la créance nantie importe peu: il n'est pas précisé que cette créance nantie doive avoir une origine particulière'*) and for Spain *Carrasco Perera/Cordero Lobato/Marín López*, Tratado de los derechos de garantía II[2], p. 266 (claims of all kinds may be pledged, regardless of whether they are monetary in nature or not, including claims which stem from a real or absolute right, such as claims from contracts and from tort, even including future claims).

[82] This is stated explicitly in Art. 1179 sentence 2 Greek Civil Code (which states that if the claim is not a monetary claim then the usufructuary is entitled to collect it). Art. 1180 Greek Civil Code even considers the usufruct to a monetary claim to be a special case, stating that if the claim over which the usufruct exists is a monetary claim, then the creditor and the usufructuary are jointly entitled and obligated to collect the claim. Instead of or subsequent to the collection, both are entitled to request the secure and interest-bearing investment of the capital with the usufructuary's rights reserved. The usufructuary determines the type of investment. The French Civil Code does not contain specific provisions regarding the usufruct to claims, aside from Arts 584 and 586. There is, however, consensus within the legal scholarship that any claim can be the object of a *nantissement* (e.g. *Cabrillac/Mouly/Cabrillac/Pétel*, Droit des sûretés[9], p. 583 no. 778). The *nantissement* can also have a prospective claim as its object (Art. 2355(1) French Civil Code).

[83] However, under Arts 679–685 Portuguese Civil Code, rights can also be the object of a pledge if they are directed at the delivery of a moveable thing, can be transferred (Art. 680 Portuguese Civil Code), and cannot be charged with a hypothec (Art. 666(1) Portuguese Civil Code). From this follows that claims which are directed at the transfer of an immoveable thing or the performance of an action (so-called *prestações de facto*) can *not* be the object of a claim (*Pires de Lima and Antunes Varela*, Código Civil Anotado I[4], Art. 680 p. 699 and *Pestana de Vasconcelos*, Direito das garantias, p. 247). It is possible to have a pledge over hypothec claims, as the object is not the land unit itself, but rather the claim secured by it. This is confirmed by *Ramos Alves*, Penhor, pp. 142, 146.

[84] *Švestka/Spáčil/Škárová/Humák*, Občanský zákoník I[2], p. 1085: The object of the claim must be saleable, as the creditor can only then be satisfied by the proceeds.

refer to an '*atto scritto*'). The price criterion is satisfied in Greek law, for example, by claims for maintenance[85] but not for claims for compensation for pain and suffering.[86] If the claim is oriented toward delivery of a real thing, the pledge creditor acquires on delivery a pledge over the thing that is to be realized according to the normal rules; contemporaneously, the pledge over the claim (to delivery of the thing) extinguishes.[87] By way of contrast, a pledge over a claim to the transfer of a land unit is not possible where such a pledge would breach the *numerus clausus* principle—i.e. because the applicable law does not allow land units to be pledged,[88] and does not provide for an automatic transformation of the 'immanent' pledge into a 'permissible' property right in an immoveable.[89] If the claim is for a positive action, it must be some reasonable performance.[90] The idea of a usufruct over a claim other than a claim for money causes some authors consternation, because this type of claim has no type of 'fruits' (i.e. interest) and cannot therefore be 'enjoyed'.[91] A usufruct over a claim to delivery of a real thing, however, only has value when the creditor acquires ownership of the thing on delivery and the usufructor acquires the usufruct *ex lege*. This occurs, for example, under § 1075 German Civil Code. Besides this, a right encumbered by a usufruct can be a use right (if only a relative one), for example the right of a lessee.[92]

c. Company Shares

8.18 Company shares (rights of membership) are distinguishable from 'normal' claims in that they generally give a person not just a single right, but a whole bundle of rights in relation to the corporation and his fellow shareholder-members. These are concerned with profit participation, participation in the formation and expression of the corporate will, and participation in the assets of the corporation, even if the latter are generally realizable only in the case of its dissolution. A company share need not, however, always give its holder all of these rights; according to the applicable law and the constitution of the corporation in question, a given class of shares might only afford their holders one of them. Company shares can be distinguished according to the

[85] CA Patras 389/2007 AchNom 2008 p. 228.

[86] Protodikeio Athens 6340/2005, Isokrates-Database.

[87] See e.g. § 167(2) Czech Civil Code [1964] and § 1337 Czech Civil Code [2014], and Art. 1254 Greek Civil Code (see *Papasteriou*, Emprágmato Díkeo III, pp. 265–6 nos 16 and 19, as well as Protodikeio Thessaloniki 159/2009, Isokrates-Database).

[88] See for Greek law *Georgiades*, Emprágmato Díkeo, p. 1153.

[89] This is the solution under § 1287 Sentence 2 German Civil Code (creation of a security hypothec).

[90] Galgano (-*Gorla and Zanelli*), Commentario del Codice Civile Scialoja-Branca, Pegno e Ipoteche, Arts 2784–2899 p. 147.

[91] See *Cervelli*, I diritti reali^{2}, p. 167 (assuming a position taken by *Ferrara*, Riv. it. per le scienze giur. 1904, pp. 325, 400). cf. for French law the discussions in *Libchaber*, RTD civ. 1997 pp. 615, 623 no. 12 and *Françon*, RTD civ. 1957 p. 2 no. 1 (who admittedly both assume that not only monetary claims can be objects of a usufruct).

[92] This position is correctly taken by *Libchaber*. It has long been the case in French case law that a usufruct to the right of use of the lessee can exist (Montpellier 13 March 1856, D.P. 1857, II, p. 160; confirmed by Cass. 19 January 1857, D.P. 1859, I, p. 279). In more recent years, Cass. 25 April 1974, D. 1974 p. 644, note by *Cozian*, accepted a usufruct over a lease. A widow had inherited the usufruct to the whole of her deceased husband's goods. The deceased had been a lessee of multiple buildings, which he had sub-let.

type of company concerned. Here we can distinguish between a 'company of persons' [*Personengesellschaft*] and a 'capital corporation' [*Kapitalgesellschaft*]. The latter can be further distinguished according to whether the shares take the form of written instruments or not. The holder of a share in a 'company of persons'—a 'partnership'—is typically (but not necessarily) a co-owner of its patrimony, regardless of the type of object that patrimony comprises. The details depend, as always, on the organizational form in question, the applicable law, and on the provisions of its constitutive documents. In the internal relation of the members *inter se*, the scope of every member's rights is limited by the identical rights of every other member. In relation to the 'company' itself, the scope of every member's rights is limited by the administrative powers granted to its managers. Every share in such an organizational form embraces all the individual assets of the association, like a lasso. Thus, the individual member's powers of disposition over associational assets are limited, even where the member is properly characterized as their co-owner. As long as the association subsists, the most he can do is to deal with his share as a whole. His share gives him no power to deal with the individual assets that give it value; ultimately, those assets are not only the point of reference for his share but also for every other member's share. So long as a thing that is part of the association's joint patrimony has not been transferred to a single member, it remains within the power of disposition of the competent representative organ of the association. The holder of a share in a 'capital corporation', on the other hand, has neither a right to its assets nor to the corporation itself; persons, even juristic persons, are not fitting objects of property rights. Beyond any rights to vote and receive dividends, holding a share in a corporation means only the right to receive a *pro rata* share of corporate assets on dissolution; as long as the corporation exists, *it* is the only subject to which the legal system attributes rights in the corporate patrimony.

Like claims, shares are fitting objects of some property rights.[93] Again, the rights of pledge,[94] usufruct,[95] and trust[96] come into consideration, as do hypothec, mortgage, and charge. Pledges and usufructs over shares are sometimes even provided for together in a special statute.[97] In jurisdictions where hypothecs can only be created over **8.19**

[93] In French law, stocks and shares are thus qualified as moveable things by dint of law (Art. 529 French Civil Code). These are, so it is said, rights which can be analysed as rights to claims of the shareholders against the juristic person on the one hand, and as rights to a part of the profits on the other hand (*Carbonnier*, Droit civil II, p. 1605 no. 713; JClCiv Code [-*Loiseau*], Biens, Art. 527 à 532 Fasc. 10 no. 9).

[94] e.g. for Austrian law OGH 18 June 1997, SZ 70/115; for Slovenian law Art. 22 Slovenian SPZ; for Italian law the judgments cited in *Orsingher and Salomone*, Manuale del pegno e delle ipoteche, p. 279, and for French law, where *droits sociaux* are considered rights to claims, the differing regulations depending on whether the title is or is not an *instrument financier* within the meaning of Art. L211-1 *Code monétaire et financier*. If it is, one is presented with a *nantissement de compte-titres* (Art. L211-20 *Code monétaire et financier*), otherwise with a *nantissement de parts sociales* (Arts 1866 ff. Civil Code).

[95] e.g. Art. 1177 Greek Civil Code (usufruct over company shares entitle one to participation in the shareholder meeting), Art. 2:201 ff Netherlands Civil Code (usufruct over company assets), and Art. 1467 Portuguese Civil Code (usufruct over equity securities). In French law, the possibility of a usufruct to *valeurs mobilières* at least is entirely uncontested (see *Prieur/Schiller/Revet/Mortier*, JCP N 2011, 1221 p. 32 and Cass. civ. 4 April 1991, Bull. civ. 1991, I, no. 129 p. 86 (concerning the usufruct to *titres au porteur*).

[96] e.g. *Hunter v Moss* [1994] 1 WLR 452 (CA).

[97] This is the case in Spanish law (Arts 126–133 *Ley de Sociedades de Capital, Real decreto legislativo* 1/2010 of 2 July 2010) and in Portuguese law (Art. 23 *Código das Sociedades Comerciais*, DL 262/86 of 2 September 1986, concerning the *usufruto e penhor de participações*). See also Art. 2352 Italian Civil Code and Art. 1467 Portuguese Civil

land units, rights tantamount to land units,[98] and registered vehicles (ships, airplanes, and sometimes automobiles), the encumbrance of a share with a hypothec is of course excluded.[99] But even in the Netherlands, where Art. 3:228 Netherlands Civil Code uses a relatively ambiguous formulation ('all goods, which are susceptible of transfer, can be encumbered with a pledge *or* a hypothec'[100]), parties do not really have the freedom to choose between a pledge or a hypothec. Rather, it depends on the point of reference of the security right: 'If the right is established on a registered good, it is a right of hypothec; if the right is established on another type of good, it is a right of pledge': Art. 3:227(1) second sentence Netherlands Civil Code. There is no pledge over registered goods, and there is no hypothec over non-registered goods.[101] Under Art. 2:198 Netherlands Civil Code, shares in a private limited company (*besloten vennootschap met beperkte aansprakelijkheid* or 'BV'), for example, can (only) be encumbered with a pledge; they are not *registergoeden* as defined in Art. 3:10 Netherlands Civil Code. The same counts for shares in a 'nameless company' (*naamlozen vennootschap* or 'NV', the equivalent of the *Société Anonyme* or a public limited company); they, too, can be encumbered with a pledge but not with a hypothec (Art. 2:89 Netherlands Civil Code). Substantively, however, hypothecs and pledges over company shares barely differ. The common law systems allow a mortgage as well as a charge over company shares; Scots law allows only a mortgage.[102] The holder of a usufruct over company shares (e.g. *usufruto de títulos de participação*) has, as Art. 1467(1) Portuguese Civil Code stipulates, the right to dividends paid out of the company, the right to voting on corporate affairs short of changes to the constitution or dissolution, and the right to *pro rata* participation in the assets of an insolvent company.

8.20 Putting the peculiarities of trust law to one side,[103] a company share (like all other purely normative objects of legal transaction) must generally be *transferable* in order to

Code (usufruct to stocks and shares; there is no corresponding provision for rights to claims in the Portuguese Civil Code).

[98] e.g. a hypothec over a usufruct over a land unit is usually possible, see A.P. 280/2011, NoB 59 (2011) p. 1891 and CA Athens 7567/1991, EllDni 34 (1993) p. 641. Polish law acknowledges a hypothec over a perpetual usufruct and over a special communal right of ownership (Art. 65(2) Polish *Ustawa r. o księgach wieczystych i hipotece*).

[99] This is the case, e.g. under § 1113 German Civil Code, Art. 2393 French Civil Code (for exceptions for ships and airplanes, see *Albiges and Dumont-Lefrand*, Droit des sûretés[3], p. 340 no. 557), Art. 1259 Greek Civil Code, and Art. 65 Polish *Ustawa r. o księgach wieczystych i hipotece*.

[100] Emphasis added.

[101] Things are similar under Arts 666, 688–691 Portuguese Civil Code, as well as the Spanish *Ley de 16 de diciembre de 1954 sobre hipoteca mobiliaria y prenda sin desplazamiento de posesión* or Art. 132 *Real decreto legislativo 1/2010*. Under Art. 666 Portuguese Civil Code, a right to claims can only be created for rights which cannot be charged with a hypothec (details in von Bar [-*de Seabra and Xavier*], Sachenrecht in Europa III, Portugal, pp. 387–8; comparatively examined and with further references in *Menéres Campos*, Hipoteca, pp. 55 ff.). Art. 2389 Romanian Civil Code permits the existence of a hypothec over moveables, including over credit and deposits with banks and other financial institutions, as well as over stocks, shares, claims, intellectual property, and other incorporeal goods (for further details, see *Sacalschi*, Grundeigentum und Sicherheiten in Rumänien[2], pp. 73–4).

[102] *Enviroco Ltd v Farstad Supply A/S* [2011] UKSC 16, [4] and [59]; [2011] 1 WLR 921, 924 and 935 (Lord Collins and Lord Hope). Scottish law misleadingly speaks of a 'share pledge'. This is misleading because this 'pledge' contains a *fiducia cum creditore*, exactly like the English mortgage. Both grant ownership, not (only) possession.

[103] Under English trust law, the holder of company shares can also convert his share into a trust and name himself the trustee, if the share 'as such' is not transferable. This is explained legally and politically with the fact that a trust, in principle, merely creates a relationship between the beneficiary and the trustee, which does not change the

be a point of reference of property rights at all. The details of acquisition vary, as always, but this diversity does not affect the basic question of shares' property status. This applies as well to the special methods of transfer that govern shares embodied in a written certificate as to the register-based rules of good faith acquisition[104] and the prescriptive acquisition of company shares.[105] However, it is important not to confuse the creation of a pledge over a share through agreement with attachment in the course of enforcement proceedings. The latter must (allowing for the specificities of the relevant organizational form) remain available to ensure that a debtor cannot defeat his creditors by contributing his assets to a company in exchange for shares.

As for the transferability of claims, statute or contractual provision can exclude the transfer of company shares or make it conditional on the consent of the other shareholders, as, for example, §§ 717, 719 German Civil Code and Art. 863 § 1 Polish Civil Code. Austrian law allows pledges over shares in a partnership only where the governing documents allow, or where all partners consent unanimously.[106] Only claims to the payment of dividends and to a *pro rata* share of assets on liquidation can be pledged without qualification.[107] The possibility of creating a pledge over shares in a juristic person is the subject of special provisions; § 76(3) of the Austrian *Gesetz über Gesellschaften mit beschränkter Haftung*, for example, confirms so much expressly. The shares in a French law *société civile* are also transferable only subject to the consent of all members of the association (Art. 1861(1) French Civil Code); the same rule applies to the *société en nom collectif*, another kind of partnership (Art. L221-13 French *Code de commerce*). Without their release, the members of such an association remain 'captive'.[108] In Czech law, it has long been accepted that the shares in partnership are not transferable;[109] § 116 of the Czech Statute on Trading Corporations and Cooperatives (Statute No. 90/2012) has confirmed the line taken in the previous authorities. By way of contrast, with the consent of the members' meeting and in default of any contrary provision in the governing documents, shares in a limited partnership and in a limited liability company can be transferred to non-members and are accordingly also pledgeable (see §§ 123 and 208(2) of Statute No. 90/2012). In Swedish law, not only shares in a public corporation but also shares in a non-registered trading company are objects of

legal position of the trustee in relation to the company and does not grant the beneficiary any direct rights against the company. While the beneficiary can force the trustee to behave in a certain way to the beneficiary's favour, he cannot replace the trustee with the aid of the court. The company share itself thus remains non-transferable.

[104] e.g. for German law BGH 20 September 2011, BGHZ 191 p. 84 (concerning the requirements of good-faith acquisition of a company share to a limited liability company [*GmbH*] under § 16(3) Germany GmbHG).

[105] e.g. for Italian law Art. 1994 Italian Civil Code (effects of good-faith possession of certificated securities), Cass. 5 September 1995, no. 9314, Giur. it. 1996, I, 1, p. 948 (acquisition only of the title, not the status of membership, if the buyer does not meet the requirements for the latter) and for Czech law Nejvyšší soud České republiky 28 August 2007, 29 Odo 1216/2005, Sbírka soudních rozhodnutí a stanovisek 2008 no. 50 (a company share can be acquired by prescription).

[106] OGH 5 October 1999, 2Ob250/99z.

[107] Schwimann and Kodek (-*Hinteregger*), ABGB II[4], § 448 no. 14; however, a different view is taken by *Reich-Rohrwig*, ecolex 2011 pp. 4, 6–7.

[108] *Cozian/Viandier/Deboissy*, Droit des sociétés[20], S. 498 no. 1145.

[109] Czech Nejvyšší soud České republiky 23 September 2008, 29 Cdo 646/2008.

'ownership' and 'pledge',[110] but they cannot be the point of reference for a *floating charge* (Kap. 2 § 1 *Lag (2008:990) om företagshypotek*).

d. Business Undertakings

8.21 European legal systems take rather different approaches to the question whether whole enterprises can be the object of property rights, in particular security rights. An 'enterprise' (or, in the idiom of European Union law, 'undertaking') could be defined (as in Art. 55[1] Sentence 1 Polish Civil Code) as an organized whole of material and immaterial components dedicated to the pursuit of an economic activity. The material components of the 'whole undertaking' include real things and land units, and the immaterial components include claims and rights, especially intellectual and industrial property rights, that belong to the undertaking. Other valuable objects of legal transaction include things like customer base and goodwill.

8.22 Customer base and goodwill are considered to be independent objects of property rights in several legal systems. To the extent they are, they cannot be considered as components of the 'whole undertaking' for the purposes of property law.[111] For example, under § 489 Czech Civil Code, an undertaking's customer base is treated not merely as a fitting object of property rights, but as a fitting object of the right of ownership.[112] However, it is not completely clear what either 'customer base' and 'goodwill' actually are, nor how one differs the one from the other. In English law, for example, it has been said that:

> Goodwill regarded as property has no meaning except in connection with some trade, business, or calling . . . The word [includes] whatever adds value to a business by reason of situation, name and reputation, connection, introduction to old customers, and agreed absence from competition, or any of these things.[113]

Goodwill and customer base are thus not only closely connected with the undertaking, but also with each other; if one is taken to be 'property' (in the English law sense) in its own right, so must the others.[114] Perhaps it could be said that the 'customer base' can more easily be separated from the undertaking itself than goodwill. The transfer of an undertaking transfers, all else being equal, both its customer base *and* goodwill. Not

[110] *Håstad*, Sakrätt[6], p. 41.

[111] It is irrelevant for private law that the customer base can be 'property' in constitutional law (e.g. within the meaning of Art. 1 of the first Additional Protocol to the ECHR: ECtHR 26 June 1986, *van Marle u.a. vs. Nederlanden*, Application nos 8543/79; 8674/79; 8675/79 and 8685/79, §§ 41–42 of the judgment).

[112] Under § 489 Czech Civil Code, a thing in the legal sense is everything which is distinct from a person and serves the use of humans, and under § 979 the provisions of the part on 'absolute property rights' are applied to all corporeal and incorporeal things; however, they are applied to rights only insofar as their character allows and the law does not determine otherwise.

[113] Lord Lindley in *Inland Revenue Commissioners v Muller and Co's Margarine Ltd* [1901] AC 217, 235.

[114] What can be used to secure a loan and transferred independently of an undertaking's building is shown impressively, for English law, in *Chapman (t/a Chapman & Co Solicitors) v Wilson* [2010] EWHC 1746 (Ch) (e.g. the case files of a law firm alongside goodwill and future claims).

infrequently, however, the customer base in some sector (in the form of information about customers) is transferred independently; the transferring undertaking henceforth refrains from doing business in that sector. Goodwill, on the other hand, 'sticks' to the undertaking, at least when 'goodwill' is used to denote the market reputation of the undertaking and, thereby, the fact that it is able to acquire and retain customers in the future. In this sense, 'goodwill' and 'undertaking' cannot sensibly be separated; one cannot simultaneously stop trading but retain one's goodwill in that sector as an independent object that can be held or alienated. In any case, characterizing goodwill and customer relationships as fitting objects of property rights often hits against insurmountable problems. That is obviously the case in jurisdictions with a corporeal concept of things, but problems arise in other systems as well. Swedish law, for example, has declined to characterize the goodwill of an undertaking as a point of reference for ordinary property rights; it treats goodwill instead as an object of intellectual property rights.[115] The protection of goodwill guarantees the right against unlawful competition (§§ 4 and 8 *Marknadsföringslag* (2008:486)), not property rights as such. In Swedish law, the notion of goodwill is most important in the context of calculating the purchase price of an undertaking and for the purposes of tax law.[116] That is consistent with the view that a customer register is not seen as an object of property rights. Its content can, under § 1 *Lag (1990:409) om skydd för företagshemligheter*, be protected as a trade secret, but the list itself is not an object of property rights.[117] In French law, a distinction appears between *clientèles commerciales* and *clientèles civiles*. Of the former, one reads that they are an important component of a *fonds de commerce*. *Clientèles civiles* (e.g. the clients of a lawyer or the patients of a doctor) are mentioned more often in the standard property law literature; they are generally characterized today as incorporeal goods.[118] The judicial decisions have vacillated. For a long time, primary emphasis was put on the personal character of the relationship resting on the special trust between the professional and his client or patient. A *clientèle civile* was said to be non-marketable (i.e. not a *bien*) in order to protect clients' freedom of choice.[119] To maintain the value of a clientele, however, judges began quite early to accept the idea of a '*contrat de présentation*'.[120] A professional was said to have the right to introduce and recommend his successor to his clientele and, further, to promise not to compete with him.[121] In a judgment of 7 November 2000, the *Cour de cassation* finally recognized the transferability of the

[115] *Koktvedgaard and Levin*, Lärobok i Immaterialrätt[7], pp. 22–3.

[116] If an undertaking is sold not through the sale of company shares but through the sale of assets, and if the purchase price is higher or lower than the value of the individual assets, there exists a positive or negative goodwill for the purposes of tax law under Kap. 18 *Inkomstskattelag* (1999:1229).

[117] HD 1 June 2001, NJA 2001 p 362.

[118] e.g. *Malaurie and Aynès*, Les biens[3], p. 60 no. 212; *Carbonnier*, Droit civil II, p. 1900 no. 912; *Zenati-Castaing and Revet*, Les biens[3], p. 105 no. 59.

[119] e.g. Cass. 7 February 1990, D. 1991, somm. P. 354, note by *Penneau*, and Cass. 3 July 1996, D. 1997 p. 531, note by *Descamps-Dubaele*. See also JClCiv Code (*-Loiseau*), Art. 527 à 532, Fasc. 20, no. 16.

[120] This was held as early as Cass. civ. 13 May 1861, p. 1861 p. 638.

[121] For further detail, see *Loiseau* op. cit. See also Cass. civ. 7 June 1995, D. 1995, Jur. p. 560 note by *Beigner* ('*si la clientèle d'un médecin ou d'un chirurgien-dentiste n'est pas dans le commerce, le droit pour ce médecin ou ce chirurgien-dentiste, de présenter un confrère à sa clientèle, constitue un droit patrimonial qui peut faire l'objet d'une convention régie par le droit privé*').

clientèles civiles subject to the condition that the freedom of choice of the patients is guaranteed.[122] *Clientèles civiles* thereby became marketable incorporeal goods in French law.

8.23 Undertakings, 'organized totalities for the pursuit of an economic activity' as explained above, have never risen to the rank of objects of property rights in a number of European legal systems. Granted, one can everywhere buy and sell undertakings. They are considered to be objects of legal transaction in every legal system. But they are not considered to be 'things'. Only the individual assets that belong to the totality are considered fitting objects of property rights; not even a security right can be created over the undertaking *per se*. Rather, ownership or title in every individual object must be encumbered separately. This process is often simplified by party agreement on some kind of collective designation to identify the objects in question in their contractual documentation; this does not change the basic fact that, in such systems, as many individual property rights arise as there are individual assets. This is the case *inter alia* in Germany,[123] Portugal,[124] and Austria. That an undertaking is a 'whole thing' [*Gesamtsache*[125]] that must be 'considered as a whole' (§ 302 Austrian Civil Code), is irrelevant from the perspective of property law. An undertaking can be 'a whole' as the object of a contract of sale, but cannot 'as a whole' be an object of a pledge (for example). This is because it cannot, according to the Austrian jurisprudence, be entered into the land register nor otherwise transferred 'as a whole'.[126]

8.24 This approach, however, is fading increasingly into the background when we look at matters from a pan-European perspective. Jurisdictions such as Bulgaria, Romania, the Czech Republic, Hungary, and Poland go particularly far; in these jurisdictions, the prevailing opinion seems to be that undertakings are objects fitting even for the right of ownership.[127] The modern approach is exemplified in a statement by the highest court

[122] Cass. 7 November 2000, D. 2001, p. 2400, note by *Yvan Auguet*: '*que si la cession de la clientèle médicale, à l'occasion de la constitution ou de la cession d'un fonds libéral d'exercice de la profession n'est pas illicite, c'est à la condition que soit sauvegardée la liberté de choix du patient*.'

[123] See *Vieweg and Werner*, Sachenrecht^{4}, p. 289 no. 10.

[124] The prevailing view in the Portuguese literature does not qualify an undertaking as a corporeal thing and concludes from this that property rights cannot relate to an undertaking as a whole. Only the individual things which make up the undertaking can be subject to property rights (*Vieira*, Direitos reais, pp. 133–6; *Oliveira Ascensão*, Direito Civil—Reais^{5}, p. 41). The question of whether customer relations can be subject to a property right is not even raised in the Portuguese property law literature. Tribunal da Relação do Porto 15 July 2009, Processo 0816124 ruled that customer data, stored on a computer database, was not a 'moveable thing' and could thus neither be stolen nor embezzled in the context of criminal law. The generic definition of 'things' in Art. 202(1) Portuguese Civil Code (i.e. 'everything which can be the object of legal relations') could not be applied in criminal law.

[125] Schwimann and Kodek (-*Hofmann*), ABGB II^{4}, § 302 no. 3.

[126] OGH 19 January 1966, ÖJZ 1966, 290 (EvBl 1966/232). The OGH corrected a misleading expression used in OGH 3 November 1925, SZ 7/351. The issue at hand in that case had been whether an engine situated on an undertaking's land fell within the scope of the hypothec over the relevant land unit. The engine had been described as an 'accessory of the undertaking'. The later judgment in OGH 19 January 1966 corrected this; while the undertaking could be an 'accessory' of the land unit, it could not be the reference point of a hypothec; this only ever has a land unit as its object. Thus, ordering a hypothec over the land unit would be the only way to (indirectly) create a pledge over the undertaking 'as a whole'. Without such measures, only the creation of pledges over the individual assets of the undertaking would be possible.

[127] An undertaking can thus also be the object of a pledge under § 1310(1) Czech Civil Code. Naturally, an undertaking always remains an object of legal relations (as a 'whole thing'); it is not a legal subject itself. Under Art. 15 Bulgarian Ccom and § 2175(1) Czech Obchodní zákoník the buyer acquires everything through the purchase

in Poland, for example, which speaks of the 'owner of an undertaking'.[128] The view that an undertaking (including an agricultural concern)[129] is a fitting object of the right of ownership is widely held in Poland.[130] We think, however, that such an approach shoots past the mark. The proposition that an undertaking—a constantly changing body of physical and normative things—can be the object of the right of 'ownership' must surely be read down as a proposition that it is a fitting object of property rights more broadly. It is inherent in the concept of an 'undertaking' that it has a kind of proprietor; without such a person, the assets in question could not be organized into a system and directed towards an economic goal. Thus, the Polish courts are surely right to deny the remedy of vindication over an undertaking. The thesis that Art. 55² Polish Civil Code[131] applies to obligational as well as property rights[132] does not change the fact that Art. 140 Polish Civil Code only recognizes 'ownership' in corporeal things. With the expression 'ownership of an undertaking', therefore, the Polish courts cannot be taken to mean 'ownership' in the technical legal meaning stipulated by the code. At most, such formulations can be taken to mean 'a *sui generis* kind of ownership', i.e. 'ownership' of a special type of object of property rights. One obviously uses 'ownership' to refer to this right by way of shorthand, because no more fitting term has yet been found.[133]

In the Netherlands, an undertaking (including its goodwill) can be pledged or (as under Art. 2561 Italian Civil Code) encumbered with a usufruct. In a case involving a bank, the result would be a security interest akin to the floating charge of English law. Rights arising from the encumbrance of individual objects, however, have priority over rights arising from the encumbrance of the undertaking as a whole.[134] In Spain, an undertaking ('*empresa*' or '*establecimiento mercantil*') can be the object of a *hipoteca mobiliaria* (Arts 19–33 *Ley de 16 de diciembre de 1954 sobre hipoteca mobiliaria y prenda sin desplazamiento de posesión*) and of a usufruct (Arts 160, 834, and 1375 Spanish Civil Code contain family law inflected special rules on usufructs over undertakings in the relationship between parents and minor children as well as between marital partners). Granted, the characterization of an undertaking as a 'thing' is intensely debated

of an undertaking which belongs to the business as a whole. The transaction is still a purchase of a business, even when the parties exclude the purchase of an individual post, as long as the whole does not lose its business character.

[128] Polish Sąd Najwyższy 6 April 2005, III CK 656/04, Biul.SN 2005/10/12, Lex-No. 156996.

[129] Art. 55³ Polish Kodeks cywilny defines an agricultural business as farmland including its forest land units, its buildings or parts thereof, its equipment and its inventory, if these form an organizational unit with all rights which are related to the maintenance of an agricultural business.

[130] *Gniewek*, Prawo rzeczowe⁸, pp. 28–9 nos 68–71. See also Radwański and Dybowski (*-Stelmachowski*), System Prawa Prywatnego III², p. 216 no. 8 (objects of ownership can also be companies and agricultural businesses), and Radwański and Safjan (*-Katner*), System Prawa Prywatnego I, p. 1229 no. 152 (the rules of property law are applicable to a company; it is an object of ownership).

[131] This states that, in case of doubt, a legal transaction which has a company as its object extends to everything which is included in the company.

[132] Sąd Najwyższy 21 October 2010, IV CSK 118/10, Lex-No. 688489, OSNC-ZD 2011/2/41, Biul.SN 2011/1/11.

[133] See *Ignatowicz and Stefaniuk*, Prawo rzeczowe², p. 20 no. 2, p. 43 no. 4, p. 44 no. 6 and p. 72 no. 2 (though they propose the rather unconvincing theory that the so-called company property can conceptually be compared to 'intellectual property' and the water use rights, colloquially called 'water property').

[134] *Raaijmakers*, Ondernemingsrecht, p. 64.

by certain authors; *hipotecas mobiliarias* and usufructs, it is said, can in truth only be created over individual objects of the undertaking. Such a position, however, is difficult to reconcile with the statutory language.[135] The *pegno rotativo* of Italian law was developed for the practice of the banking industry; it is characterized as something extraordinary, a '*pegno anomalo*'.[136] The relevant contract provides for the exchange of the objects originally pledged with new ones. The original pledge subsists, such that no new right has to be created. A number of cases in which a rotating pledge can be used have been specially provided by statute;[137] the judicial decisions generally treat its application even beyond these categories as valid.[138] Another variant is the *pegno omnibus*. This is a pledge to secure a particular debt against all present and future claims and goods of the debtor. The agreement creating a *pegno omnibus* also reflects common banking practice.[139] The Italian literature attributes the *pegno omnibus* and the *pegno rotativo* functions that are thought to reflect an English law 'floating charge'.[140] Under Art. 8(1) of the Greek Statute 4332/1929, the Agricultural Bank of Greece (which was created in that year) acquires *ipso iure* a so-called 'agricultural pledge' to secure its loans. This pledge extends to the whole agricultural business of the debtor (see Art. 8(1)(b) of Statute 4332/1929).[141] Special rules allow non-possessory pledges over the plant and equipment of certain commercial undertakings.[142] Most importantly, Arts 16–18 of Statute 2844/2000 created the possibility of a Greek law floating charge (called 'κυμαινόμενη ασφάλεια'). This is understood to be a non-possessory, proprietary security right that leaves the debtor with all the normal powers of dealing with the object charged but obligates him to replace things he has disposed of with other things of like value. The object of the security right can change; what remains is the value of the security. A precondition for the creation of such a 'floating' debt, however, is its registration in a public register. Swedish law, too, allows a business hypothec (*företagshypotek*) under Kap. 2 § 1 *Lag (2008:990) om företagshypotek*. This, too, is likened to the English law floating charge. It can only be created by the proprietor of the undertaking; it is not

[135] See, in detail, *Broseta Pont and Martínez Sanz*, Manual de derecho mercantil I[11], pp. 136–7, 147–8; see also *Fischer and Fischer*, Spanisches Handels- und Wirtschaftsrecht[2], pp.158–60.

[136] *Gabrielli*, Il pegno anomalo, especially p. 181; Martuccelli and Pescatore (-*Gabrielli*), Dizionario di diritto civile, Pegno, p. 1258; Valentino (-*Maimeri*), Commentario al Codice Civile III, p. 797; Lipari and Rescigno (-*Macario*), Diritto civile IV, p. 253.

[137] See especially Art. 34 Decreto legge No. 213 of 24 June 1998 und Art. 9 Decreto legge no. 170 of 21 May 2004 (concerning the *contratti di garanzia finanziaria*; the debtor retains the right to dispose over the pledged thing according to the contract, but remains obligated to offer a security of equal value in its place).

[138] Cass. 26 January 2010, no. 1526, Riv. notariato 2011, 1, p. 162; Cass. 1 February 2008, no. 2456, Mass. Giust. civ. 2008, 2, p. 145; Cass. 5 March 2004, no. 4520, Fallimento 2005 p. 547, and Cass. 5 March 2004, no. 4507, Mass. Giust. civ. 2004, p. 3.

[139] For further details, see *Volanti*, Obbligazioni e contratti 4 (2010) pp. 280, 282, as well as *Gambaro and Morello*, Lezioni di diritto civile, p. 518.

[140] *Rescigno*, Banca, Borsa e titoli di credito 1999, p. 583 fn. 3; *Rescigno*, Banca, Borsa e titoli di credito 2001, p. 1 fn. 4.

[141] See Areopag 1125/2010, NoB 59 (2011) p. 115; Areopag 404/2007, Isokrates-Database; Areopag 1053/2004, Isokrates-Database; Areopag 2001/2002, NoB 51 (2003) p. 896; Areopag 1156/2001, Isokrates-Database, and Areopag 549/2001, Isokrates-Database.

[142] This includes the pledge to industrial equipment (see CA Thessaloniki 80/1996, Harm. 50 p. 367), the pledge to mining equipment and the pledge to cinema equipment. The creation of these rights requires not only a private record with a secure date, but also the registration in a public book kept by the *Protodikeio*. Also of note is the pledge without possession over tour buses.

possible to encumber it further with a security right. The creditor, however, can assign his claim and where he does so the security right follows the claim.[143]

In its home jurisdiction of England (from whence it has also been introduced in Cypriot law),[144] the floating charge has—remarkably—never been defined by statute. The Companies Act 2006 uses the term in several places, but never defines it. Section 251 of the Insolvency Act 1986 defines the term, but does so only by saying that a 'floating charge' is a 'charge which, as created, was a floating charge'! This definition also expressly embraces Scottish floating charges (under sec. 462 Companies Act 1985)—but that does not say much, either. The drafters obviously took the meaning of the term to be self-evident and simply accorded it the common law meaning developed by the judges.[145] Under the express caveat that he was not thereby advancing an 'exact definition', Romer LJ in suggested three characteristics of a floating charge in an early twentieth-century case. According to this formulation, a floating charge is (i) a charge on a class of the present and future assets of a company, (ii) that class is one which, in the ordinary course of the business of the company, would change from time to time, and (iii) until some future step is taken by or on behalf of the chargee, the company may carry on its business in the ordinary way and deal with the assets within the particular class of assets.[146] More recent authorities have adopted these characteristics and developed them further, for example noting that the first two of these characteristics are common in practice but do not assist in the differentiation of a fixed from a floating charge.[147] A floating charge can, for example, also extend to the whole assets of a business (and not just one class)[148] and can be created by juristic persons other than companies.[149] Besides, the crystallization of a floating charge (i.e. its concretization over certain objects) need not necessarily rest on a measure of the charge—it can also be triggered automatically by the occurrence of some stipulated state of affairs.[150] Against this background, Goode has described the floating charge as one of the most 'subtle' of equity's creations; it has remained, despite numerous judicial decisions and extensive scholarly treatment, difficult to define. The floating charge is an 'interest' that operates *in rem*, relating not to specific assets but to a fund which in turn comprises a constantly changing set of assets.[151] It is a further development of the idea of a (fixed) charge over future things (e.g. not-yet-acquired trading stock). The agreement that creates a floating charge, however, leaves the debtor the power to dispose of his goods in the ordinary course of business; after all, he should ultimately use the profits from this 8.25

[143] *Håstad*, Sakrätt[6], pp. 355–6.

[144] *Neocleous and Kyriacou*, Restructuring and Insolvency 2009/10, p. 51.

[145] *National Westminster Bank Plc v Spectrum Plus Ltd (Re Spectrum Plus Ltd)* [2005] UKHL 41 no. 98; [2005] 2 AC 680, 717 (Lord Scott).

[146] *Illingworth v Houldsworth (Re Yorkshire Woolcombers Association Ltd)* [1903] 2 Ch 284, 295.

[147] *National Westminster Bank Plc v Spectrum Plus Ltd (in Liquidation) (Re Spectrum Plus Ltd)* [2005] UKHL 41; [2005] 2 AC 680, 720 (Lord Scott).

[148] This also follows implicitly from sec. 876(1)(b) Companies Act 2006 (registration of all floating charges on the whole or part of the company's property or undertaking).

[149] Thus, e.g. sec. 1 Industrial and Provident Societies Act 1967.

[150] *Goode*, Legal Problems of Credit and Security[3], no. 4-31.

[151] Ibid. no. 4-01 (English law struggles with the concept of 'funds' or 'patrimony').

trading to repay the secured loan. The image is of a charge 'hovering' over the current and future pool of assets; they are 'attached' only when the debtor's power to dispose of the assets ends, according to the terms of the relevant agreement, usually as a result of a default. The charge then 'crystallizes' and becomes a fixed charge over the specific assets then in the pool. One could thus say that a floating charge is a charge whose attachment is contractually delayed.[152] A floating charge can be over a whole undertaking, embracing goodwill as well as the 'other property' and 'all assets' of a company.[153] The floating charge is, moreover, a *presently existing* security, not a future security, because the chargee may have priority, in the case of crystallization, even over third parties with earlier charges over the same assets. This is only the case, of course, where the debtor has dealt with the assets outside of the ordinary course of business in the favour of that third party,[154] or when the third party was *mala fides*—i.e. knew or ought to have known that the debtor was dealing in an impermissible manner.[155] Goode thus defines a floating charge as an existing security in a pool of assets that the debtor can freely administer in the course of his business.[156]

8.26 French law belongs to the group of legal systems which have long recognized undertakings *per se* as fitting objects of real security rights. French law uses the term *fonds de commerce* to describe a totality of goods, a *universalité de fait*, that is treated by its holder *qua* single good.[157] A *fonds de commerce* consists of corporeal goods (materials and wares) and incorporeal goods (clientele, rights of use arising from rental contracts, trade names, marks, patents, etc.). A *fonds de commerce* can be sold, leased, or pledged *in toto*.[158] One even speaks of 'transfer of ownership' in this context; the transfer of a *fonds de commerce* generally requires a formal writing (Art. L-141-1 French *Code de commerce*).[159] The pledge (*nantissement*) of a *fonds de commerce* is comprehensively regulated in Arts L142-1 to L142-5 French *Code de commerce*. Points of reference for a pledge under Art. L-142-2(1) *French Code de commerce* are commercial signs and names, leases, clientele and goodwill ('*achalandage*'), furniture, 'material' which serves the commercialization of the *fonds*, patents, licences, marks, and all other intellectual property rights. Art. L-142-2(3) *French Code de commerce* provides a default rule that, in the absence of agreement to contrary, a pledge over a *fonds de commerce* relates to the commercial sign and name, leases, clientele, and goodwill. The French law *nantissement du fonds de commerce* does not affect the undertaking's stock or any claims it holds.[160]

152 Ibid. no. 4-02.

153 *Evans v Rival Granite Quarries Ltd* [1910] 2 KB 979, 999 (Buckley LJ).

154 *Taylor v M'Keand* (1880) 5 CPD 358 (Divisional Court); *Payne v Fern* (1881) 6 QBD 620 (Field J).

155 *English & Scottish Mercantile Investment Co Ltd v Brunton* [1892] 2 QB 700, 707 (Lord Esher MR).

156 *Goode* op. cit. no. 4-03.

157 *Carbonnier*, Les biens, p. 1623 no. 724.

158 Ibid. p. 1901 no. 912; *Malaurie and Aynès*, Les biens^3, p. 71 no. 218.

159 For further detail, see *Malaurie and Aynès*, Les biens, p. 82 no. 229; *Jourdain*, Les biens, p. 521 no. 436 and JClCiv Code (-*Loiseau*), Biens, Art. 527 à 532, Fasc. 20 no. 25.

160 See also Cass. civ. 1 December 2011, Bull. civ. I, no. 208, o. 201; RTD civ. 2012 p. 131, note by *Revet*; JCP 2012 p. 1650, note by *Caron* (purchase of a *fonds de commerce* by a printing company specialized in the production of lithographs. The court denied that the purchase had also effected the acquisition of two zinc plates which had been used in 1954 to produce thirty lithographs by Giacometti).

These are meant to remain an independent (additional) source of collateral for the trader.[161]

e. Privileges

The inclusion of privileges in the list of 'objects of legal transaction fitting as objects of property rights' appears foreign from the perspective of some legal systems, and familiar from the perspective of others. In this context, divergences appear that are not often noticed. We are mostly concerned with concessions and permissions to participate in some market; besides this, we are also concerned with particular prerogatives, particularly rights (which possess some value) of proposing candidates for the occupation of some office or other position.[162] Individual examples of the latter group are provided by both English law and French law. English law is well-known for relics such as the 'advowson'—the power, traditionally characterized as 'property' (i.e. an 'incorporeal hereditament'), of a landowner to 'present' a candidate to fill an empty position in the Anglican clergy. (Today, advowsons may not be transferred for value and are not registerable). In French law, we find the *offices ministériels*—specific public offices (e.g. that of an *avocat à la Cour de Cassation*, a notary, or a publicly auctioneer) have a monetary value, in the sense that the right to suggest a successor inures in them. Not the office itself, but the right of proposal is the object of value.[163] The French literature concludes from this that the *offices ministériels* are an example of *biens incorporels*.[164] The judicial *dicta* characterized them as objects of the right of ownership quite early,[165] at least of a 'special type' of ownership.[166] In the modern literature, on the other hand, it is often argued that such rights appurtenant to a public office cannot be 'ownership properly so called' because they inure in a *public* office.[167] There seems to be agreement only on the fact that the right to present a successor to the competent appointing authority is what constitutes a *droit patrimonial* that can, in turn, be the subject of private law dealings—not the office itself.[168] **8.27**

Our understanding of property law is not really assisted by the characterization of a right of presentation as an 'asset' or 'incorporeal good'. The fact that an object has a *de facto* monetary value and is heritable does not necessarily entail that it is a fitting **8.28**

[161] *Simler and Delebecque*, Droit civil: les sûretés, la publicité foncière[5], p. 626 no. 717; *Albiges and Dumont-Lefrand*, Droit des sûretés[3], p. 310 no. 533.

[162] The *privilèges* in French law are subjective property rights. These are therefore not meant here; this concerns privileges which form a reference point for subjective property rights.

[163] Cass. civ. 28 May 1946, S. 1947, 1, p. 9, note by *Béguet*.

[164] JClCiv Code (-*Loiseau*), Biens, Art. 527 à 532, Fasc. 20 no. 14.

[165] Cass. 11 November 1857, S. 1858, 1, p. 55.

[166] Cass. 6 January 1880, DP 1880, 1, p. 361, note by *Dutruc*; S. 1881, 1, p. 49, note by *Labbé*.

[167] *Malaurie and Aynès*, Les biens[4], p. 67 no. 212.

[168] Cass. 21 October 1959, JCP G 1959, II, 11353, note by *Becqué*. See also Cass. civ. 16 July 1985, RTD civ. 1987 p. 91, note by *Mestre*; JCP G 1986, II, 20595, note by *Dagot* ('*que, si l'office notarial et le titre de notaire ne sont pas dans le commerce, le droit, pour le notaire, de présenter un successeur à l'autorité publique constitue un droit patrimonial qui peut faire l'objet d'une convention régie par le droit privé*').

object of property rights, and the description of such a right of presentation as 'property' just equates the concept of 'property' with the concept of 'asset'. First, questions arise whether one is still in the domain of private law at all, and whether administrative authorizations to exercise a particular profession or occupation, with which the *offices ministériels* are sometimes compared,[169] have even the constitutional protections afforded to 'property'.[170] What is more decisive, however, is the question whether a particular right can be encumbered or otherwise transferred. That is no more the case for an *office ministériel* than for a taxi licence. An *office ministériel* cannot be pledged, and a taxi licence is inseparably connected with the person of the licensee.[171] It is necessary to examine each case closely. The situation is very different, for example, in the case of a *licence de débit de boisson* (a licence to sell beverages). In this case, French law faces the problem that such a licence forms a crucial part of the *fonds de commerce* that is a food and drink business. This leads some to opine that the *fonds de commerce* cannot be transferred without the *licence de débit de boisson*. But that position has been rejected by many authors; a licence can be pledged,[172] and, what is more, subsists even when the *fonds de commerce* ceases to exist; even in this case the licence can still be transferred.[173] If one adopts this analysis, the status of concessions as objects of property rights is established. The 'ownability' of concessions, however, falters on the fact that there is no such thing as a concession without a concession-holder. A further, more marginal point can also be marshalled, which is that the *Cour de cassation* has recently confirmed that a *licence de débit de boisson* cannot be acquired on the basis of Art. 2276 French Civil Code ('*En fait de meubles, la possession vaut titre*').[174] This decision—which has not received a unanimous reception in the literature[175]—was, however, made in a different context and must be read together with similar *dicta* in relation to claims,[176] identification documents,[177] a *fonds de commerce*,[178] sums of money,[179] and patents.[180] In all

[169] *Loiseau* op. cit.

[170] Denying this for a taxi concession is Cons. const. 30 December 1982, J.O. 31 December 1982 p. 4033 ('*Considérant que les autorisations d'exploiter des services de transports publics réguliers de personnes accordées à des fins d'intérêt général par l'autorité administrative à des entreprises de transports ne sauraient être assimilées à des biens objets pour leurs titulaires d'un droit de propriété et comme tels garantis, en cas d'expropriation pour utilité publique, par l'article 17 de la déclaration des droits de l'homme*').

[171] *Zenati-Castaing and Revet*, Les biens[3], pp. 196–7 no. 51.

[172] *Delebecque*, note under Rapp. CA Paris 9 April 1996, JCP G 1997, I, 4033, no. 22. See also Cass. avis, 8 February 1999, Bull. 1999 Avis, no. 1, p. 1 ('*La licence d'exploitation d'un débit de boissons de 4e catégorie constitue un droit incorporel saisissable*').

[173] *Loiseau* op. cit. no. 15.

[174] Cass. civ. 7 March 2006, Bull. civ. 2006, IV, no. 62, p. 62; D. 2006 p. 2897, note by *Kuhn*; RTD civ. 2006 p. 350 note by *Revet*; D. 2006 p. 2363, note by *Mallet-Bricout and Reboul-Maupin*; JCP G 2006, II, 10143 p. 1655, note by *Loiseau* ('*l'article 2279* [since 17 August 2006 Art. 2276] *du code civil ne s'applique qu'aux seuls meubles corporels individualisés; que la licence d'exploitation d'un débit de boissons ayant la même nature de meuble incorporel que le fonds de commerce dont elle est un des éléments et ne se transmettant pas par simple tradition manuelle, c'est à bon droit que la cour d'appel a écarté pour la dite licence d'exploitation la présomption prévue par ce texte*').

[175] In support of the application of Art. 2276 Civil Code are, *inter alia*, *Malaurie and Aynès*, Les biens[3], p. 171 no. 574, as well as *Terré and Simler*, Les biens[7], p. 343 no. 431; against its application are *Bergel/Bruschi/Cimamonti*, Les biens, p. 238 no. 221; *Larroumet*, Les biens[5], p. 571 no. 923 and *Jourdain*, Les biens, p. 520.

[176] Cass. 2 December 1856, DP 1856, I, p. 443; Cass. 25 November 1929, DH 1930 p. 3.

[177] Cass. 4 July 1876, DP 1877, I, p. 33.

[178] Cass. civ. 2 March 1960, Bull. civ. 1960, I, no. 141 p. 112.

[179] Cass. civ. 6 May 1997, Bull. civ. 1997, I, no. 144, p. 96.

[180] Paris 17 February 1988, D. 1989 somm. p. 50, note by *Colombet*.

these cases, the *Cour de cassation* has based its decision on the reasoning that Art. 2276 French Civil Code only applies to *meubles corporels individualisés*, not on the basis that these objects do not need the concept of ownership for their allocation (under the law of property) to a person.

The beverage concessions of French law are, of course, just one example of a category of entitlements that sit between public law and private law, and, within the latter, between relative and absolute private law rights. Another type of permission or authorization with candidature for 'property status' is a resource mining concession.[181] English law treats the private right to gather beach debris and the right to convene a market as a 'private property right'. That is consistent. Both rights can, at least in theory, be transferred and used as collateral.[182] Even a licence to pollute the environment has recently been held to be property by an English court,[183] as has a waste management licence,[184] a textile export quota,[185] and (at least for the purposes of the Insolvency Act 1986) the so-called 'milk quota', the right of a farmer to sell milk without paying taxes. The fact that the transfer of a milk quota is subject to complicated conditions did not prevent the court from treating this right as a form of property. It was sufficient that there existed a market for milk quotas and that their transfer implied the active involvement of voluntary counterparties (i.e. buyer and seller).[186] Under Art. 688(1) Portuguese Civil Code, not only immoveables but some moveables and also some rights can be encumbered with a hypothec; the latter category includes rights arising from a concession over public goods. Examples include ordinary concessions for the exploitation of resources (*recursos minerais*) and administrative authorizations to operate a port, beach, or parking facility.[187] In each case, there is a private right in a public good arising from some administrative decision, not in goods that the concession-holder himself contributes to his business.[188] Art. 333 Spanish Civil Code categorizes all 'things' that are capable of appropriation into moveable and immoveable goods. Art. 334(10) Spanish Civil Code includes concessions over public buildings, servitudes, and real rights in land units as 'immoveable goods'. These rights are characterized as immoveable goods by way of analogy in order to apply the legal regime applicable to immoveables to them.[189] **8.29**

[181] For example, under Art. L131-1 French Code minier, mines may only be exploited on the basis of a concession or directly by the state. The concession is explicitly qualified by Art. 132-8 French Code minier as an immoveable property right, even though it may not be charged with a hypothec ('*L'institution d'une concession, même au profit du propriétaire de la surface, crée un droit immobilier distinct de la propriété de la surface. Ce droit n'est pas susceptible d'hypothèque*').

[182] Cheshire and Burn (*-Burn and Cartwright*), Modern Law of Real Property[17], p. 84.

[183] *Armstrong DLW GmbH v Winnington Networks Ltd* [2012] EWHC 10 (Ch), [2013] Ch 156 ('An EUA [a European Union Allowance in the form of a Carbon Emission Allowance] could be classified as intangible property at common law'. It is 'neither a chattel [chose in possession] nor a chose in action. Rather it is a form of "other intangible property"'; Morris QC at [35]).

[184] *Re Celtic Extradition Ltd (in liq); Re Bluestone Chemicals Ltd (in liq)* [2001] Ch 475 (CA).

[185] *A-G of Hong Kong v Chan Nai-Keung* [1987] 1 WLR 1339.

[186] *Swift v Dairywise Farms Ltd* [2000] 1 WLR 1177, confirmed in [2001] EWCA Civ 145; [2003] 2 All ER 304.

[187] *Andrade da Silva*, Código dos Contratos Públicos comentado e anotado[3], note to Art. 408 DL 18/2008, pp. 1021–2. Art. 408 op. cit. concerns the so-called *contratos de concessão de exploração de bens do domínio público*.

[188] STJ 23 September 2008, Processo 08A2245 (concerning a private vessel which was used to transport passengers for a public shipping line; Art. 688(1)(d) Portuguese Civil Code could not be applied to this vessel).

[189] *Díez-Picazo*, Fundamentos III[5], p. 222.

Concesiones administrativas that affect or encumber land units are entered into the land register (Art. 31 *Reglamento Hipotecaria*); one example is the concession for a private person to use the soil in a communal cemetery.[190] The Austrian judicial decisions have generally been concerned with public licences (e.g. beverage licences or authorizations to practice a manual trade) in the context of enforcement proceedings, particularly in so-called 'executive enforcement'. Under § 341 Austrian *Exekutionsordnung* an enforcement proceeding can generally only be brought against an undertaking *per se*. Thus, as we have seen, while undertaking cannot be the object of a pledge, it can be the object of enforcement measures. Where the undertaking, however, has been abandoned and all that remains is a concession, the concession itself can become the direct object of the enforcement proceedings.[191] As no specific 'enforcement law' considerations explain this state of affairs, it would seem that at least *certain* licences are fitting objects of *certain* property rights in Austrian law. Generally, these licences are bound up with the so-called 'real trades' [*Realgewerbe*], for which a transferable licence exists. Licences bound to a named person, on the other hand, can generally not be transferred to another; they are, as such, not able to be pledged.[192] This notwithstanding they, too, are subject to attachment in the course of enforcement proceedings under § 341 Austrian *Exekutionsordnung*, insofar as they can be used for the satisfaction of a creditor. Thus, we can say that when a licence is non-transferable (e.g. because tied to a particular qualification of the licensee), the creation of a pledge is excluded but not attachment in the course of 'executive' enforcement proceedings.[193]

8.30 Greek law, by way of contrast, approaches concessions from a purely public law perspective. Admittedly, Art. 970 Greek Civil Code provides for the acquisition of 'private rights' in public goods through a concession of the competent public authority, insofar as such a course of action promotes or is consistent with the public interest. According to the prevailing opinion, however, concessions themselves are the product of a purely public administrative act[194] in favour of a particular person or undertaking.[195] Further, and more importantly, this provision is said (without prejudice to the ambiguous

[190] TS 25 October 1993, RAJ 1993 no. 7654 p. 9720.

[191] OGH 4 May 1926, SZ 8/144.

[192] There are certain particularities for location-bound licences. They can be pledged alongside the land unit as 'accessories' if the land unit is charged with a hypothec (Klang [-*Klang*], ABGB II^2, p. 404).

[193] Therefore, the law permits, for example, the attachment of a kindergarten licence. This does not entitle the holder to operate a kindergarten business, but it does consist of a 'business-adjacent' right within the meaning of § 341 Austrian EO. The licence as such is not transferable because it requires the head of the kindergarten to have certain qualifications. However, the holder of the licence and the head of the kindergarten need not be the same person; the holder must merely prove that they have employed suitable staff. Thus, the licensee can grant permission to a (qualified) third party, and by the same token use of the licence by way of, e.g. attachment or pledge would also seem possible. Even in the case of a concession that cannot be pledged, the business in question can still be leased and the lease payments can be attached (OGH 8 July 1938, SZ 20/162). In some cases, it is possible to relinquish the concession in favour of a creditor (OGH 19 December 1934, SZ 16/248). In such cases, one's own concession is given up with the purpose of granting another person an identical concession. This ultimately bypasses the prohibition of transfer.

[194] Areopag 1033/2000, EllDni 42 (2001) p. 435; Areopag 1256/2005, EllDni 48 (2007) p. 1098.

[195] CFI Thessaloniki 3502/2005, Harm. 59 (2005) p. 1578; Areopag 1033/2000, EllDni op. cit. The concession may only be extended to the contractor's legal successor in certain special cases (*Triantos*, AK, Art. 970 p. 1183 no. 2).

wording of the section itself) to create only a public law legal relationship, and from this premise the conclusion is drawn that the rights of the concession-holder are not rights of a private law nature.[196] They are said to be neither obligational nor property rights, but subjective rights *sui generis* with roots in public law. Apart from the possibility of the possessory remedies available to a detentor under Art. 887 Greek Civil Code, they are said only to acquire *erga omnes* effect in virtue of public law rules.[197]

[196] CFI Kozani 1/1996, Harm. 51 (1997) p. 904; CFI Lefkada 64/1999, ArchN 2000 p. 707.
[197] CFI Kozani op. cit. and CFI Lefkada op. cit.

IX
Objects of Legal Transaction Connected to Things

1. Overview

Most 'things' consist of a plurality of 'objects of legal transaction'. A clock, a land unit with a building on it, an undertaking, or (according to some points of view at least) even a company share (which comprises a claim to a capital fund, a claim to dividends from profits, and a claim to participate in corporate governance) are *constellations of objects* that are shaped into 'things'. This leads to the question of the relation of a whole to its parts. It must ultimately be determined whether any given combination of objects becomes a 'thing' that eclipses the individual objects that make it up. Do objects that were 'things' in their own right before they were combined with each other keep that status after their combination, or do they sink to the status of 'mere' objects that can be sold and gifted, but no longer transferred or encumbered? The question has to be posed on its own terms. If we can only describe what a 'thing' is in the abstract, we lack the means to determine what is *a* thing and what is a *new* thing. A screw, for example, is just as obviously a 'thing' (a 'moveable') as the clock in which it is put to work; which object is the relevant target of legal attention remains unclear. That determination, however, has wide-ranging implications. If we are concerned only with the clock, property rights can only be held in the clock as a whole and not in the components from which it was built.[1] Physically speaking, the components and materials from which the clock was made still subsist; legally speaking, however, they have lost their quality as (independent) 'things'.[2] Property law does not take cognizance of them anymore, we might say; it sees only the clock (in contrast to the law of obligations). The components of a clock are nobody's things, nor are they 'ownerless' things. The only thing that exists is the clock. Screws, hands, and face only become things (again) when they are separated 9.1

[1] Real rights of third parties to the new thing extend to the related (former) things; property rights to the related (former) things are extinguished; see CA Athens 3205/1986, EllDni 27 (1986) p. 1178 and STJ 31 January 1996, BMJ 453 (1996) p. 46 (a retention of title, which had been negotiated in a contract for the delivery and installation of elevators in urban land units, became invalid as soon the required installation had taken place). Only the idea that relative rights and obligations with relation to components remain unchanged is now conceivable (e.g. Czech Nejvyšší soud České republiky 31 October 2001, 20 Cdo 2369/99, Soubor rozhodnutí Nejvyššího soudu 22 (2008) no. C 1055: A judgment concerning the principal thing, in which an obligation is established or *vis-à-vis* which the existence or nonexistence of a legal relationship is determined, generally also concerns components of the principal thing. A component may also be excluded, but this must be explicitly stated in the judgment).

[2] For the philosophical and historical origins of this point of view, which remains indispensable for property law to this day, and for the concept of a 'new' thing, see *Dolezalek*, AcP 195 (1995) pp. 392, 394–405.

Foundations of Property Law. Christian von Bar and Jason Grant Allen, Oxford University Press. © Christian von Bar 2023.
DOI: 10.1093/oso/9780198885337.003.0009

from the clock. One might be tempted to say that their 'thing-ness' is in a kind of temporary suspense. But even that proposition would not be entirely accurate. When they come into existence again, the law will not ascribe them to the person who once owned them. They will belong to the person that owned the clock (so long as the clock existed). The 'old' screw is, legally, a 'new' thing.[3] Granted, the value and significance of a component (e.g. a housing made of gold) might have been such that its owner became the sole or joint owner of the clock, such that the remaining components became his sole or joint property in turn (once they reappeared).[4] But that confirms rather than contradicts the idea that new, self-standing things arise in the sequence 'component-clock-component'. According to the same principle, even a totally functional clock could lose its quality as a thing. Consider, for example, a clock that is made specially for a tower clock on a building like a castle or church. Such a clock would become, on installation, (a part of a) 'building' and would generally undergo, in the same 'juristic moment', a further metamorphosis. A 'building' is, in most legal systems, (a part of a) 'land unit'. In those legal systems that operate with the *superficies solo cedit* rule, the land unit is the only 'thing' that exists, in a legal sense, once the clock is installed.

9.2 Determining what is to be seen as one thing and what as two or more things is complicated—for a whole raft of reasons. The question rests on a combination of factual observations and legal considerations. Further, there is no single answer for all types of object. What comprises one *real* thing cannot be determined according to the same criteria as what comprises one *land unit* or one purely *normative* thing. In the case of real things, the primary consideration will be physical connections between components; in the case of land units, the primary consideration will be conditions of use and the regulation of land in the public interest;[5] in the case of purely normative things, the primary consideration will be purely normative criteria. What is to be seen as *one* claim and what as *two* claims (company shares, undertakings, etc.) cannot be answered by

[3] There is thus no suspended or 'resting' ownership. In contrast to Roman law, separated components do not return to the ownership of their former owner (see, implicitly, e.g. Art. 554 French Civil Code and, explicitly, BGH 21 December 1956, BGHZ 23 p. 57).

[4] See e.g. § 947 German Civil Code; §§ 414–416 Austrian Civil Code (owners generally remain owners of their things, but only as long as they exist as autonomous things. If this is no longer the case, then generally co-ownership of the new thing results. Exceptions to this are made when one component has a much greater value); Art. 1333 Portuguese Civil Code and Art. 375 Spanish Civil Code.

[5] Admittedly, the question of what *a* land unit 'is' has more facets. One need only think, for example, of the *accessione di immobile a immobile*, which is common in a variety of legal systems, including Italy and the Czech Republic (detailed regulations in §§ 1068–1071 Czech Civil Code). This concept concerns the right of accrual in relation to immoveable things (for further details, see *Torrente and Schlesinger*, Manuale di diritto privato[14], p. 275). Art. 941 Italian Civil Code is concerned with alluvial soil (*alluvione*), stating that the combination of earth and the accretion of soil, which is constantly and imperceptibly formed on land units which are located along the banks of rivers or streams, belong to the owner of the land unit, subject to any other special provisions. A further example comes from rights of habitation (see, e.g. Administrative Court Gdańsk 19 February 2009, III SA/Gd 434/2008, LexPolonica-No. 2263653, Lex-No. 545838 [a toilet, for the exclusive use of the occupant of a dwelling, but situated outside the walls of this dwelling, is a room belonging to it] and Polish Sąd Najwyższy 3 October 2002, III RN 153/01, Monitor Prawniczy 2006/12 str. 654, OSNP 2003/18 poz. 423, Prokuratura i Prawo- dodatek 2003/6 poz. 36, Rejent 2003/12 str. 212, OSNP 2003/18/423, LexPolonica-No. 357141, Lex-No. 80436 [a balcony which serves the exclusive use of a dwelling's owner is a component of the dwelling. Thus, the owner is solely responsible for its upkeep]).

reference to ontological criteria only; these are exclusively legal questions.[6] A second complication arises from the fact that connections between things (or objects) have their basis in very different factual processes. Liquids are mixed, mass-produced goods combined, metal components and plastic-wrapped cables are assembled into machines, walls are built on foundations to make houses. The legal systems of Europe apprehend these processes sometimes with the 'law of *things*' and sometimes with the 'law of *ownership* in things', and thereby (often without any obvious reason) with very different parts of their civil law—as well as adopting very different solutions to the proverbial 'devil in the detail'. A third complication arises when the manipulation or processing of a thing legally brings a new thing into existence: if a random stranger, for example, paints another's canvas, the situation is a simple one of damage to property—in any case, the canvas would remain 'just' a canvas. If a renowned artist were to do the same, however, the vandalized canvas would become an 'artwork'. The new label indicates the creation of a new thing; the task is to decide to whom that thing should be ascribed for the purposes of property law.

The phenomenon of connected objects has another facet, as well. There exist certain **9.3**
objects with a double nature, that is, they are 'objects of legal transaction' that have the status of (independent) 'things' in some but not in all combinations. Often, it can only be determined on the facts of the case whether one is dealing with a single thing (formed of several objects of legal transaction) or with several things, after all. An object of legal transaction only remains a 'thing' to the extent that the legal system affords it the quality of an object that can be dealt with independently. It loses some of its nature as a thing when and insofar as it shares the fate of another thing—the main thing [*Hauptsache*] or 'principal thing'. Only land units[7] are (nearly) always 'principal

[6] Whether the rules of mixture can also be applied to incorporeal objects, such as companies, has occasionally been discussed, but this does not impact the statement made in the above text. The Austrian OGH 19 January 1965, SZ 38/5 ruled that the creation of an index of a customer's addresses does not lead to a mixture in the sense of § 414 Austrian Civil Code, as this provision is only applicable to corporeal things. However, OGH 10 December 1952, SZ 25/327 partially contradicts this. Here, the court ruled in the case of a merger of two carpentry businesses (pursuant to an invalid contract) that a 'mixture' had taken place. Due to the broad definition of things in Austrian law, it was said to be possible to apply § 414 Austrian Civil Code to companies. The difference between the two judgments can be explained thus: the carpentry businesses as whole things are incorporeal, but are (also) composed of corporeal things, so, in contrast to the addresses, a physical mixture can be assumed.

[7] The issue of distinguishing the principal thing from the accessory thing, as indicated by *Malaurie and Aynès*, Les biens[3], p. 126 no. 442, only appears in relation to the *accession mobilière*, not the *accession immobilière*. This is correct. It is, however, doubtful that this situation arises from the rule of *superficies solo cedit*, as the authors claim. This rule equates soil with 'land unit', which seems to us not precise enough, as we interpret land units to be spaces or normative things with a physical substrate. The rule that land units are always main, never (contingent) secondary things, also carries weight where houses, apartments, and storeys are separate objects of ownership. Apartments (etc.), which can be separate objects of ownership, also do not share the legal fate of the objects needed to construct them or that are built into them. Rather, these objects share the legal fate of the apartment. That the prevalent rules of the so-called 'reverse accession' should bring an exception to the rule that land units are always the principal thing, as is frequently claimed, does not appear correct. These rules do not, in truth, assign the ownership of the soil to the ownership of the building, rather they lead to a change of ownership of a developed land unit. Under Art. 1340(1) Portuguese Civil Code, the following applies for the *acessão industrial imobiliária* (for further details to this, see *Vieira*, Direitos reais, pp. 696–7): a person who builds a product on the land unit of another in good faith, sows or cultivates on this, and thereby doubles the value of the whole land unit, becomes the author of the 'incorporation' (*autor da incorporação*) and acquires ownership by paying the value that the land unit had before its value increase. This is a form of 'potestative' acquisition of ownership (for further details and to distinguish Art. 1340 from Art. 1343 Portuguese Civil Code, see STJ 7 April 2011, Processo 108/1999.P1.S1 and STJ 19

things'.[8] Real things and purely normative things, on the other hand, can descend to the status of dependent things (adjunct things [*Nebensachen*] or 'accessory things'),[9] whether that be in relation to one another (automobile papers and automobile;[10] debt claim and bond certificate), or in relation to a land unit (cattle and agricultural undertaking), according to the facts of the case at hand. A distinction can be drawn between things that are 'strongly' and 'weakly' dependent. By their nature, for example, 'rights connected with the ownership of a land unit' (§ 96 German Civil Code) are 'strongly'

April 2012, Processo 34/09.0T2AVR.C1. S1). Under Art. 376 Spanish Civil Code, if two things are unified, then the principal thing is taken as the thing with which another has been connected for its decoration, use, or completion. Spanish law has similar rules to Portuguese law in the event of an 'author' building partially on his own, partially on a neighbouring land unit in good faith. Applying the doctrine of 'reverse accession' (*accesión invertida*) to this *construcción extralimitada*, the building can be interpreted as the principal thing, the neighbouring land unit as the secondary thing. In these situations, under Spanish law, the rule of *superficies solo cedit* is replaced by the rule of *accessorium sequitur principale*. The court can grant the 'author' of the building ownership of the (neighbouring) land unit in return for compensation (TS 31 May 1949, RAJ 1949 no. 721 p. 436; TS 17 July 1971, RAJ 1971 No. 1044 p. 739). The situation is similar under § 418 sentence 3 Austrian Civil Code. This states that if a landowner recognizes that a third party is constructing on his land unit while honestly believing to be entitled to do this, then the builder becomes owner of the land unit *ex lege*. Art. 938 Italian Civil Code (instructive in this matter are Cass. 5 June 2012, no. 9052, DVD Juris Data; Cass. 16 March 2011, no. 6177, Mass. Giust. civ. 2011 p. 420, and Cass 10 January 2011, no. 345, Mass. Giust. civ. 2011 p. 28) contains a further variant of the *accessione invertita*, stating that if a part of the bordering land unit is taken into possession by the construction of a building in good faith, and if its owner does not object within three months of the commencement of construction, then a judicial authority can grant the builder the ownership of the building and the possessed ground, with regard to the individual circumstances. The builder is then obligated to pay the owner of this land twice the value of the area taken into possession, as well as compensation for damages. Only the ground which lies immediately under the building is subject to the reverse accession (*Galgano*, Trattato di diritto civile I^2, p. 445). The judicial decisions have even created the concept of *accessione invertita della pubblica amministrazione* (laying the groundwork are Cass. 10.June 1988, nos 3940, 3941, 3942, 3943, 3945, and 3946, FA 1988 p. 1973; Foro it. 1988, I, 2262; Giust. civ. 1988, I, 2242). This has the consequence that, in the case of an unlawful occupation of a private land unit by the state (i.e. without the due process of a lawful taking; often in the course of roadworks), the citizen loses his ownership and maintains a right to compensation instead (for further details, see *Diana*, La proprietà immobiliare urbana I, p. 480 and *Invernizzi*, Riv. giur. edilizia 2000 p. 595). However, this doctrine violates human rights (ECtHR 17 May 2005, *Pasculli v Italy*, see *Conti*, La proprietà e i diritti reali minori, p. 267).

[8] Compare, e.g. § 97 German Civil Code (only moveable things can be an accessory) and § 946 German Civil Code (connection of moveable things with a land unit); Arts 956, 959, and 960 Greek Civil Code (accessories of a land unit, a building or estate); Art. 852 Latvian Civil Code (moveable accessories of an immoveable are subject to the provisions of immoveable things); Art. 5:20 Netherlands Civil Code (ownership of the soil also includes buildings and works; this rule precludes that a land unit can become a component of a considerably more valuable building); Art. 48 in combination with Art. 191 Polish Civil Code (components of a land unit). See also, for Italian law, Cass. 12 March 2001, n. 3610, Giur. it. 2002, 1384 (a fresco, categorized as a cultural good, is a part of an apartment even if the fresco is much more valuable than the whole apartment).

[9] A similar idea is conceivable for those parts of buildings, which extend over the borders of the land unit, but remain components of the part of the building, which stands on the neighbouring land unit; cf. Hof Amsterdam 23 August 2011, 200.073.345, LJN BR6841, concerning a bunker from the Second World War, which German occupying troops had constructed across several land units. The court considered whether to regard the smaller part of the bunker, situated on one land unit, as the secondary thing, and the other, larger part of the bunker situated on another land unit as the principal thing, but ultimately did not accept this. The basic principle of apportionment by lot subsisted, because the bunker had long ago lost its original function and was now used only as a storage room.

[10] Czech Nejvyšší soud České republiky 11 April 2007, 21 Cdo 694/2006, Soubor rozhodnutí Nejvyššího soudu, no. C. 5024 (the vehicle registration document is a component of the vehicle for which it is issued; it can thus not be the object of a retention right as such) and Czech Nejvyšší soud České republiky 26 May 2007, 25 Cdo 1999/2005, Soubor rozhodnutí Nejvyššího soudu, no. 5250 (a vehicle without the vehicle registration document is not fully functional; to withhold it without justification is thus a violation of ownership to the detriment of the vehicle's owner). A comparable example from the law of land units are title documents. While they 'should' be qualified as chattels in the form of choses in possession, they are understood as accessories of the land for which they are issued *Harrington v Price* (1832) 3 B & Ad 170, 110 ER 63).

dependent on the land unit.[11] Real servitudes (i.e. rights of use that accrue to the owner of the dominant land unit over the land unit of another) provide a convenient example. These rights are, admittedly, fitting objects of property rights *per se*. But a real servitude (such as a right of way) 'sticks' to the dominant land unit such that it cannot be transferred or encumbered independently; indeed, ownership of the dominant land unit cannot be transferred or encumbered without the right of way, either. The right of way remains, however, an independent object in at least one relationship: the owner of the dominant land unit can always renounce his right of way without, at the same time, renouncing his right of ownership. On the other hand, claims, for example, have only a 'weak' (i.e. contingent rather than necessary) relation to their certificated form; the destruction of the paper instrument does not lead to the destruction of the claim, even though the claim cannot be transferred without (i.e. except by) a transfer of property rights in the written instrument.[12] The same applies to the type of things that are

[11] Likewise, Art. 50 Polish Civil Code and § 54(4) Estonian Civil Code (rights connected to ownership also count as components of an immoveable), furthermore §§ 498 and 1241 Czech Civil Code. Similarly, under § 298 Austrian Civil Code, rights are numbered among moveable things unless they are connected to the possession of an immoveable thing or declared as an immoveable thing by the constitution. Immoveable rights through the allocation to an immoveable thing, then, are the rights to which the owner or other real title-holder is legally entitled, e.g. a real servitude (OGH 29 March 1990, JBl 1991 p. 727), not, however personal servitudes, lease, or a water right to the benefit of a specific person (OGH 19 October 1993, ecolex 1994 p. 224; Klang [-*Kisslinger*], ABGB³, § 294 nos 40–41). The same result is achieved in Portuguese and Spanish law, albeit through different terminological (and conceptual) means, by qualifying implicit rights in immoveables as immoveables *themselves* (Art. 204(1)(d) Portuguese Civil Code; Art. 334(10) Spanish Civil Code). This method is modelled on French law. There, rights which have an immoveable thing as their object are themselves qualified as immoveable goods. Art. 526 French Civil Code mentions, by way of example, the usufruct to immoveable things and real servitudes. This enumeration is not exhaustive, as the right of habitation, right of use, *superficie*, the hypothec to immoveable things, and the claim for delivery of an immoveable thing are all classified as immoveable goods (*Druffin-Bricca and Henry*, Droit des biens³, p. 31). The Greek Civil Code and the Netherlands Civil Code do not contain a comparable provision to § 96 German Civil Code. Art. 3:4 Netherlands Civil Code merely mentions that everything is to be regarded as a component of a thing that is generally regarded as 'part' of a thing. The judicial *dicta* and the literature only ever speak of moveable components; rights as components are never explored. One must pay attention to Art. 3:7 Netherlands Civil Code, which states generally that a dependent right is a right that is connected to another right in such a way that it cannot exist without this right. The chief example of this is the real servitude. This right is connected to the right of ownership of the land unit (Nieuwenhuis/Stolker/Valk [-*Huijgen*], BW⁶, Art. 3:7 Nr. 1).

[12] If the document in which the claim is embodied is lost or destroyed, then the conditions under which the claim can be raised (again) are dependent on the type of document and the applicable securities law. Belgian law regulates these details in a separate statute, the *Loi relative à la dépossession involontaire des titres au porteur*. This concerns the loss, theft, and destruction of bearer instruments. The statute organizes a motion of '*opposition*' against the further use of the paper instrument (Art. 2). The *opposition* is published in the *bulletin des oppositions*. Every disposition transaction occurring after the publication is void *ex lege* (Art. 16). The Luxembourgish *Loi du 3 septembre 1996 concernant la dépossession involontaire de titres au porteur* follows similar rules. The corresponding provisions in French law (*Décret n°56-27 du 11 janvier 1956 relatif à la procédure à suivre en cas de dépossession de titres au porteur ou de coupons* and *Décret n°64-1183 du 27 novembre 1964 relatif au remplacement ou au remboursement des titres d'emprunts émis par l'Etat, détériorés, détruits, perdus ou volés*) have lost much of their earlier meaning since 1988, when registration became obligatory for many securities, which lose their materiality with the *inscription en compte*, thereby are not at risk of loss (*Carbonnier*, Droit civil II, p. 1874 no. 893). In German law, under §§ 466, 483 FamFG, a 'bidding process' can be conducted for bearer papers. Its most important effect is that the document can be declared invalid. It then does not have any legal effects (§ 478(1) FamFG). Once the process has been submitted successfully, the rights from the document may be enforced by the applicant without having to present the (now invalid) document (§ 479(1) FamFG). It is possible to have certain securities, particularly shares, declared invalid out of court (§§ 64, 73, 226 German *Aktiengesetz*). The Austrian *Kraftloserklärungsgesetz* of 1951 follows very similar principles. Once the document has been declared invalid, the applicant can request payment or, bit by bit with delivery of the relevant court orders, the issue of a new document from the obligated party (§ 13 *Kraftloserklärungsgesetz*). Under Art. 1110 Greek Civil Code, the holder of the document is assumed to be the lawful holder of the document, thereby also the lawful holder of the claim. However, possession of the document is merely a (refutable) indication that the bearer holds the rights concerned, not a constitutive requirement. The rights arising from the document cannot be exercised so long as a replacement

typically called accessories. Consider the clock once again, but this time a valuable standing clock in the panelled library of an ancient building. The clock is, surely, an independent, real thing. It could be carried out and transferred individually. But it is also a dependent accessory of the land unit (which means it is a mere 'object of legal transaction' as we have defined that term); as such, it is subject to the legal regime governing land units. If two parties agreed to the transfer of 'the land unit' in the absence of some contractual stipulation to the contrary, most legal systems would envisage the clock going with the land unit.[13] This legal consequence is not always just the product of the ordinary rules of contractual interpretation, either. In many legal systems, the applicable property rights regime changes as well; ownership of the clock is governed not by the rules on 'moveable real things' but by the rules on land units. German law, for example, would be concerned, in the first instance, not with the transfer of the clock but with the *Grundbuch* registration of the acquisition of the right of ownership in the land unit. But this means that the clock can be, according to the context, *either* an independent thing *or* an object of legal transaction bound up in a land unit—without independent existence as a thing.

has not been found in the case of its loss. Swedish law counts securities ('*värdepapper*') among *lös egendom*, but not among *lösöre*. The protection of third parties is dependent on the type of right, either by registration (thus for financial instruments in the sense of Kap. 1 § 1 *Lag (1991:80) om handel med finansiella instrument* under the law *Lag* (1998:1479) *om kontoföring av finansiella instrument*) or possession of the document (*Zetterström*, Sakrättens fyra huvudfall[2], p. 75). As a rule, the holder of a 'running debt certificate' (*löpande skuldebrev*) is assumed to be entitled to the right to claim (Kap. 2 § 13(1) *Lag (1936:81) om skuldebrev*). This assumption is an active right to payment (*aktiv betalningslegitimation*) (*Mellqvist and Persson*, Fordran & Skuld[6], p. 156). If a bond (*skuldbrev*) is lost, it must be replaced by a new document and the original one declared invalid. This procedure is laid out in *Lag (2011:900) om dödande av förekommen handling*, which also lists the documents which may be declared invalid by the court (§ 2). Flight tickets, train tickets, and entrance tickets are precluded from being declared invalid (HD 4 October 1967, NJA 1967: 90; this judgment was reached under a previous statute). The debtor is obligated to issue a new document (§ 12 *Lag om dödande av förkommen handlingen*).

[13] e.g. §§ 311c (purchase of land units), 926(1) (transfer of land units), 1120 (hypothec), and 1096 (real preference right) German Civil Code; Art. 958 Greek Civil Code (in doubt, a real legal transaction concerning a principal thing also extends to accessories); Art. 818(1) Italian Civil Code; Art. 853 Latvian Civil Code (ownership of adjunct things belonging to the principal thing is transferred with the sale of the principal thing; *accessorium sequitur principale*); Art. 4.14(1) and (2) Lithuanian Civil Code (accessory things share the fate of the principal thing; should it come to dispute with regard to the secondary things they are to be transferred to the purchaser together with the principal thing, unless a differing agreement can be proved), and Arts 347 and 449 Spanish Civil Code. Art. 449 Spanish Civil Code adds that the assumption of possession follows from the possession of the immoveable thing for furniture and objects on or in the immoveable thing, unless it is established or proved that these objects are excepted). However, Art. 210(2) Portuguese Civil Code clarifies that as long as nothing to the contrary is decided, legal transactions which have the principal thing as their object do not include the accessory things. Principal things (*coisas principais*) are all things that are not subordinate to another thing, while accessory things (Art. 210(1) Portuguese Civil Code) (*coisas acessórias ou pertenças*) are moveable things which, without being a component (*parte integrante*), are intended to serve or decorate the principal thing. Art. 210(2) Portuguese Civil Code thus gives up the traditional rule of *accessorium sequitur principale*. This was branded by the literature as a 'historical error' on the part of drafter Pires de Lima. *Menezes Cordeiro*, Tratado de Direito Civil I(2)[2], p. 170 notes that the provision in Art. 210(2) is applicable law, so one must live with it. He adds that in the normal societal life, the transaction over the principal thing should include the secondary things, at least those secondary things which are obviously recognizable as such, and it is thus unthinkable that, having sold a pair of shoes, an assistant in a shoe shop should refer to Art. 210(2) and remove the shoelaces. Also counted among the many critics of this provision is *Menezes Leitão*, Direitos reais, p. 80, who adds that the problems of Art. 210(2) must be solved by a restrictive interpretation. This provision should only be applied to accessory things which have an independent value in relation to the principal thing and are not essential for its use.

2. Connections Between Objects

a. Combination and Mixture

In order to be fitting objects of property law, materials in liquid and gaseous form must be confined in some kind of container (a bottle, tank, or closed piping system). Only then are they delimited; only then can they be 'things'. If some quantity of the liquid held in a container escapes or is poured into another container, an additional (new) thing is created. This is the case, for example, when a publican serves his guest a glass of red wine. The volume of wine in the glass is a new thing, separate from the volume of wine remaining in the bottle. The glass and its contents, however, remain separate things. The wine belongs to the guest, and the glass remains the property of the publican. The vernacular usage reflects this fundamental difference—i.e. when we speak of the 'glass of wine' and the 'wine glass'. The relationship between the liquid and its container is, however, not fully described with this language. In the commercial context, one who acquires 'a bottle of wine' thereby acquires *one* thing, namely the combination of wine bottle, liquid contents, labels, and sealing materials. Bottles, wine, paper, and corks are, in this case, so many objects of legal transaction bound up into one 'thing'. One who orders 'a bottle of wine' in a restaurant, on the other hand, which is de-corked and placed on the table, finds himself in much the same position as his more modest neighbour (who ordered only a glass); the contents of the bottle belong to the guest, but the 'wine bottle' belongs to the restaurant—the composite 'bottle of wine' that was in the cellar does not exist, as such, any more. The fact that a liquid requires a container to be a thing does not mean that the liquid and its container *always* form one single thing. The same quantity (of wine) could be individuated by means of another bottle. Conceptually, however, it is entirely possible to treat wine and bottle as one unified thing. 9.4

The legal concept of 'mixture' [*Vermischung*] is of particular relevance to gases and liquids,[14] which can be mixed with other materials of the same type and state. The precondition for mixture in the legal sense is that the *new* quantity that arises through 9.5

[14] Not even these expressions are used consistently across the European legal systems. In German, the terms are *Vermischung* (from *mischen*, the German verb 'to mix') and *Vermengung* (from *Menge*, which is used in mathematics to describe both the combination of geometrical parts and the concept of quantity, from the same root as English 'many'). According to the German usage, liquids are *vermischt* and solids (grain, herding animals, cash) are *vermengt* (see, e.g. *Wilhelm*, Sachenrecht[4], p. 452 no. 1072). The Greek usage appears to be the exact opposite with respect to liquids and solids and the equivalent Greek terms. The Dutch term *vermenging* (see Art. 5:15 Netherlands Civil Code), which is clearly the etymological cognate of the German *Vermengung*, appears to mean both: von Bar [-*Nieper and Ploeger*], Sachenrecht in Europa III, p. 285 translate *vermenging* with *Vermischung*. In Swedish, *sammanblandning* also applies to both 'mixture' and 'combination'. The decisive factor would seem to be that the objects in question lack an individual character—for example, cash, oil, or grain (*Håstad*, Sakrätt[6], p. 25, 168 and *Millqvist*, Sakrättens grunder[5], p. 79). That shows only that no legal consequences follow from classification. Wood in a timber yard, for example, can validly be said to be '*vermischt*' or '*vermengt*' (see Austrian OGH 30 October 1979, *SZ* 52/154). Both 'mixture' and 'combination' are, in any case, factual rather than legal operations. Neither the intention of the one who mixes/combines, nor his *bona* or *mala fides*, is relevant (*Triantos*, AK, Art. 1059 p. 1284 no. 1). This translation will generally follow the German usage, insofar as it is idiomatic in English, but will not draw any strict or technical distinction between combination and mixture.

mixture acquires the property of 'thing-ness' at the cost of the quantities that were mixed. A simple example is the volume of liquid that fills a carafe, into which the contents of two bottles have been poured (whether the bottles belonged to the same or different persons); another example is quantity of petrol that has been put into a tank that was already half-full (whether the person filling intended to pay for it or not). The effect is in both cases the same, and is no different to the consequences of building a clock from a set of parts. The only object of property rights at the end of these processes is the contents of the carafe or fuel tank. The same analysis applies to the mixture of things like grain in a silo (again, whether the grain comes from the same or different farmers). Quantities of grain delivered in containers do not exist as objects of property rights following their combination or mixture in the silo; because this is the case, erstwhile property rights in them must not survive, either (e.g. see Art. 1060 Greek Civil Code). A single grain of corn in the silo or in the container is not a 'thing' either; it becomes a thing, like any other object, only through individuation or delimitation, for example when someone takes it in their hand or (e.g. in a laboratory) marks it with some kind of identifier. In other words, one can sell a smaller quantity from a hundred thousand litres or a hundred thousand tonnes of some mass commodity in a tank or silo, but one cannot acquire *ownership* in the quantity sold until it is clear *which sub-quantity exactly* has been sold. Conceivably, one could have (sole or joint) ownership of the (whole) quantity in the silo, but one cannot have (either sole or joint) ownership of some not-yet-delimited quantity.[15] The problem is, at base, always the same.[16] It also arises when

[15] This is true even despite a so-called 'quantity vindication' [*Quantitätvindikation* or *Mengenvindikation*] being recognized in a few legal systems. Under Austrian law, the (former) owner of part of a mixed quantity can demand the delivery ('*Ausfolgung*') of his portion (see, e.g. OGH 31 August 1994, *ecolex* 1994 p. 812), provided he can still prove the volume or quantity (e.g. 100 tonnes; 100 litres). While the recourse to the right of vindication follows from the position of the entitled party as co-owner, it is, at its core, nothing more than the 'reification' [*Verdinglichung*] of an essentially obligational *inter partes* claim. Admittedly, this amounts to a violation of the *numerus clausus* principle of property rights. Ultimately, the right to delivery of one's part of a mixed quantity is an *erga omnes* right to the whole, namely the encumbrance of the right of ownership in the whole (which is the only thing conceivably capable of being owned) with a real right to separation. It resembles the right to the separation of fruits known in some legal systems (e.g. Arts 1064–1068 Greek Civil Code), and the use rights which some European systems created upon implementation of the Timeshare Directive. The 'quantity vindication' also exists in French law. For example, if A has supplied B with '100,000 special construction nails' under a retention of ownership device, A has priority to 100,000 nails of that type in the case of B's insolvency even though the insolvent B is in possession of more nails and it is unclear which nails were supplied by which supplier (*Sliwka*, Herausgabeansprüche als Teil des zivilrechtlichen Eigentumsrechts? p. 138). This follows from Art. L624-16(3) French *Code de commerce*. Under this provision, in the case of insolvency, even moveable things that are incorporated into another thing can be vindicated, as long as the separation of both things is possible without damage. The same applies for the vindication of fungible things, if the debtor has things of a similar type and condition and the delivered things were sold subject to a retention of title. Swedish law follows the principle that rights with *erga omnes* effects are not possible in objects without individual characteristics as long as they have not been separated (*Millqvist*, Sakrättens grunder[5], p. 79). However, exceptions are discussed for cases in which the person who is in possession of the quantity is obligated to render accounts under *Lag (1944:181) om redovisningsmedel* and in which acts to the contrary would be punishable as fraudulent dealing (*Millqvist* op. cit. p. 94). See also HD 1 September 1994, NJA 1994 p. 506: *erga omnes* effect with regard to the creditors of a grain storage facility, in which the grain of the owner was also stored, was affirmed; admittedly this conclusion could also be justified by reference to the applicant's position as co-owner of the whole quantity (*Håstad*, Sakrätt[6], p. 174).

[16] For this reason, § 414 Austrian Civil Code and following, for example, regulate the complex of connections between things in a few provisions, beginning with the following statement of the basic rule of ownership: 'Who processes the things of another; who unites, mixes, or combines them with his own, has thereby no claim to the property of another.'

one paints the walls of a house with paint.[17] The paint ceases to be a 'thing' *per se*, once it cannot be separated from the walls again. The paint (wine, petrol, etc.) could just as well have been spilled and soaked into the soil.

As processes, mixture and combination always touch both the law of things and the right of ownership in things. Most European codifications, however, tend to neglect the first and to approach the phenomenon only from the second aspect. They go directly to the question: to whom should ownership in the newly minted thing be allocated? One thus finds oneself in the middle of the law on *acquisition* of ownership *ex lege*. The shortcut that legislative drafters gain by adopting this approach, however, has a price; not all statutory formulations reach the degree of clarity that would have been achievable had they intentionally chosen to separate the 'law of things' from the 'right of ownership in things'. **9.6**

The Austrian Civil Code, for example, chooses a (not unproblematic) point of departure in the rule that mixture and combination leave ownership relations in principle unaffected. Mixed or combined things that can be separated again should be 'replaced' [*zurückgestellt*] to their owners. When, however, separation is not possible, then 'the thing belongs to the stakeholders in common' (§ 415 Austrian Civil Code). This is consistent with § 371 Austrian Civil Code, under which things that cannot be distinguished generally present no object for a claim based on ownership (however, the so-called 'quantity vindication' is not consistent with § 371 Austrian Civil Code). The French civil code deals with mixture and combination (*mélange*) along with connection (*adjonction*) and processing (*spécification*) in Arts 565–577 French Civil Code, which govern *accession mobilière* (the right to increases of moveable things). These rules are, however, considered to be dead law,[18] not least because they have been overlaid and, in practical terms, displaced by Art. 2276(1) French Civil Code.[19] The basic principle of the law of *accession* is that the owner of a principal thing also acquires ownership in the accessory thing (*accessoire*), and has to compensate the accessory's erstwhile owner for his loss of ownership. Details concerning the determination of what is a principal thing and what is accessory are left wholly to the precepts of 'natural equity'. These provisions do not apply to incorporeal goods at all (e.g. the merger of two *fonds de commerce*). The *mélange* of two things leads, in principle, to co-ownership of the jumbled-up quantity *pro rata*, according to relations pre-mixture, unless one of the things is substantially more valuable than the other. Art. 939(1) Italian Civil Code is not particularly clear, either. Where several things with different owners have been 'unified or mixed' to form a single whole ('*sol tutto*'), but can be separated without substantial damage, each retains his right in his (original) **9.7**

[17] Example taken from Staudinger (*-Jickeli and Stieper*), BGB (2004), preface 13 to §§ 90–103 German Civil Code.

[18] *Malaurie and Aynès*, Les biens[3], p. 125 no. 441 ('*droit mort, jamais appliqué*').

[19] *Terré and Simler*, Les biens[8], p.17 no. 246.

thing and has the right to demand its delivery. However, where the *sol tutto* cannot be separated without substantial damage, common ownership arises in proportion to the value of each (original) object. This approach is not entirely happy, however, because the things that were combined actually ceased to exist when a 'single whole' was created. Under Art. 1325 Portuguese Civil Code, 'accession' occurs when something owned by one person is connected with something that person does not own. Combination ('*união*'), mixture ('*confusão*' or '*mistura*'), and processing ('*especificação*) are regulated in Arts 1333–1338 Portuguese Civil Code (*acessão industrial mobiliária*). Portuguese law determines the property law and obligational consequences of mixture according to whether the mixture was *bona fides* (Art. 1333), *mala fides* (Art. 1334), or accidental (Art. 1335).[20] German law, in §§ 947 and 948 German Civil Code, looks to whether a thing is to be regarded as the principal thing [*Hauptsache*]. If this is not the case, co-ownership arises from mixture, otherwise the owner of the principal thing becomes sole owner. The former Czech Civil Code [1964] (and its sister code, the Slovakian Civil Code) by way of contrast, is silent on the question; these legal systems deal with mixture as a kind of hybrid between accession (§ 135a Czech Civil Code [1964]) and specification (§ 135b Czech Civil Code [1964]). These provisions, however, recognize that in the case of accession, the principal thing receives an increase, where mixture does not necessarily require a 'principal thing'; further, in the case of specification (i.e. processing), there is always an intentional act, where mixture might be the result of a purely factual events. Granted, when things are really mixed intentionally by their (erstwhile) owners, each of them becomes a co-owner of the new thing. Otherwise, an application of the doctrine of accession would not be possible in this context. But here again we encounter the unclear proposition that no change in the ownership position occurs where the things mixed can be separated again. If, however, the mixture has created a new material or the constituent parts can only be separated with great difficulty, § 135b Czech Civil Code [1964] is to be applied by way of analogy.[21] The new law (§§ 1078 and 1079 Czech Civil Code [2014]) distinguishes between two situations. Where things of a different type (e.g. different aggregate materials) are mixed, every owner gets a proportionate share in the new whole). If, on the other hand, things of the same type are mixed, every owner becomes an owner of a fraction of the new quantity. In Polish law (Arts 193 and 47 Polish Civil Code) and Estonian law, the doctrine of 'components' (i.e. the connection of moveable things in such a manner that one thing becomes a material component of another) is applied to cases of mixture. The owners of the original things become owners of the new thing, unless the one of the things in question is to be regarded as a 'principal thing' (§ 107(1) and (4) Estonian LPA). All prior rights in the mixed thing are generally extinguished; they subsist, however, when one

[20] *Vieira*, Direitos reais, pp. 691 ff.

[21] *Eliáš et al.*, Občanský zákoník. Velký akademický komentář I, p. 606.

of the things was encumbered with a third party right and the owner of that encumbered thing retains (or rather, acquires) an ownership interest in the new thing (§ 107(5) Estonian LPA). Art. 56 Slovenian Civil Code, too, governs cases of mixture with the rules applicable to the connection of moveable things. If someone loses his right of ownership in a thing through mixture, combination, or processing, prior rights in that thing are also extinguished (Arts 57 and 58 Slovenian Civil Code) unless the relevant owner acquires the right of ownership (sole or joint) in the new thing (Art. 58(2) Slovenian Civil Code). Art. 93 Bulgarian LPA and Art. 1059 Greek Civil Code take the same approach. Again, the provisions applicable to the connection of moveable things are to be applied *mutatis mutandis* to mixture. If the things mixed cannot be separated, or can be separated only with disproportionate expense, their owners acquire sole or co-ownership of the newly created quantity—according to whether there is a 'principal thing' in the mix or not.[22] A familiar pattern is found also in Art. 5:15 Netherlands Civil Code, which provides for the application of the rules on the connection of moveable things in Art. 5:14 Netherlands Civil Code to cases of mixture. The relationship between the two is said to be evident in the fact that human effort only plays a subordinate role in both.[23] When one of the mixed materials is properly regarded as a 'principal thing', sole ownership of the product arises in its owner. If, for example, oil belonging to different owners is mixed in a tank, generally a co-ownership situation would arise in Netherlands law because none of the oil quantities could be seen as the 'main' one. If, however, a certain amount of preservative is added to a substance, the right of ownership in the preservative is thought to be lost, as the base material (e.g. vegetable oil) is properly to be regarded as the principal thing.[24] The situation is regarded differently in the case where independent 'things' can no longer be distinguished. If, for example, two herds of sheep 'mixed' together, no co-ownership would arise because a herd of sheep is not a 'thing'.[25] This, however, is not consistent with the fact that Art. 5:15 Netherlands Civil Code is meant to apply to the mixture of cash;[26] the 'mixed' banknotes in a wallet do not form a *single* thing, either. In consequence, one must operate with a presumption of ownership in favour of the owner of the wallet and an obligational claim on the part of the person who can no longer prove ownership in 'his' banknote.[27] It has even been suggested that Netherlands law should adopt a provision reflective of § 963 German Civil Code (on the unification of bee swarms, under which the person who pursues his swarm acquires ownership of the whole swarm); ultimately, however, this approach did not meet with approval for want of practical relevance.[28]

22 For further details, see *Triantos*, AK, Art. 1059 p. 1284 no. 2 and *Venedikov*, Novo veshtno pravo, p. 213.
23 Asser (-*Mijnssen/van Velten/Bartels*), Zakenrecht[15], no. 71.
24 *Mijnssen/van Velten/Bartels* op. cit.
25 Ibid. no. 72.
26 N.v.W., Parl. Geschiedenis V, p. 108.
27 Ibid.
28 M.v.A. II, Parl. Geschiedenis V, p. 112.

b. Creation of New Real Things through Connection of Extant Things

9.8 A phenomenon very similar to mixture and combination (and, as we have seen, one often dealt with in the same sweep in European codifications) is the 'connection' [*Verbindung*] of so many single things into a new (real) thing.[29] However, this raises an even greater need for regulation. When quantities should be treated as 'mixed' hardly ever raises jurisprudential problems; usually, this question could be answered by any child. The 'connection' of real things is often different. Here, the objects in question generally remain optically distinguishable. It is 'only' the preservation of their functional connection that is important, because property law is meant to avoid the destruction of economic value.[30] What should be seen as 'belonging together' in this sense, and what should not, is not always straightforward. One need only consider whether a replacement motor, installed into an automobile, is legally 'still just' a motor or is 'already just' part of a car. The answer to this question is not inconsequential. In the first case, the mechanic could retain ownership in the motor pending payment in full and could, if necessary, vindicate this right (i.e. get his hands on the motor); in the second case, the mechanic could only get a security interest over a property right in the whole car (generally connected with possession).[31] We can trace the policy implications of this decision: in the first case, the interests of the mechanic would be well-served, but not the general interest in the maintenance of the (maximal stock of) roadworthy vehicles.

[29] If a liquid substance and a solid substance are combined to a homogeneous new thing, it is not a 'mixture' in the literal sense, however, this is legally meaningless. One need only think of a battery, which cannot produce a current without the acid contained within it. Alternatively, in the case of a perfume bottle, even if it is opened, the liquid contained within it can only fulfil its function as perfume if the atomizer belonging to the bottle serves its purpose. (By contrast, the dispersed perfume ceases to be a thing as it can no longer be separated from its environment.)

[30] German BGH 3 March 1956, NJW 1956, 788 (the purpose of § 93 German Civil Code is to prevent economic values from being destroyed without justification, thus causing damage to the economy), and for Greek law, see *Georgiades*, Empragmato Dikaio I, p. 100 no. 1. This idea makes, at best, a marginal appearance in other legal systems. See e.g. for Polish law Radwański and Safjan (-*Katner*), System Prawa Prywatnego I, p. 1191 no. 41 (the component is what is needed for the realization of the thing's economic function); Polish Sąd Najwyższy 28 June 2002, I CK 5/02, Glosa 2003/3 str. 47, Prawo Bankowe 2002/12 str. 17, LexPolonica-No. 358693, Lex-No. 56604 (the new thing must form a unit in the economic sense; the separation must lead to a clear change in the possible uses of the separated element or the remaining thing; whether an element is a component of a thing is determined by an objective judgment based on economic merits) and Polish Sąd Najwyższy 11 January 2006, II CKS 65/05, Lex-No. 191130 (a traffic light and the street form an economic whole and thus the traffic light is a component of the street).

[31] Separate ownership in the engine is possible under German law (BGH 8 October 1955, NJW 1955 p. 1793 [a serially manufactured engine is not an essential component of a tractor]; BGH 27 June 1973, BGHZ 61 p. 80 [the same applies to a serially manufactured reconditioned engine in a used car]; BGH 11 November 2011, BGHZ 191 p. 285 [module of a power plant; a summary of the previous jurisdiction can be found in no. 18]), Spanish law (TS 13 December 1949, RAJ 1949 no. 1472 pp.875, 876) is to the same effect. On the other hand, separate ownership of the engine is not possible under Greek law (Protodikeio Athens 385/1975, NoB 20 [1972] p. 945; see also Protodikeio Heraklion 310/1962, NoB 10 [1963] p. 1066 [tyres are components of the vehicle]), Polish law (*Gniewek*, Prawo rzeczowe[8], p. 10 no. 24; *Dmowski and Rudnicki*, Komentarz do kodeksu cywilnego I[9], Art. 47 p. 215), Portuguese law (von Bar [-*de Seabra and Xavier*], Sachenrecht in Europa III, Portugal, p. 361), and Czech law (the engine is only an independent thing once it is separate from the vehicle: *Eliáš*, Občanský zákoník. Velký akademický komentář I, p. 493). This should also be the case in the Netherlands under Art. 3:4(1), however there has hitherto been no judgment in this matter.

The legal systems of Europe approach this question, too, in very different ways. These differences are manifest both in the methodological and conceptual framework they adopt and in the practical results.[32] The French Civil Code bridles the horse by its tail, as it were. It begins with the stipulation that all goods are *either* moveable or immoveable (Art. 516 French Civil Code) and then sets out a whole raft of rules that are meant to help judges to distinguish between these two categories. The reader feels himself transported to a grand bourgeois apartment, in which he is instructed regarding the details of artworks, wallpaper, and porcelain. However, he only learns what is 'a *moveable*', and not what is '*a* moveable'. The drafters appear not to have come upon the second question; at best, they tacitly left it over to custom. The rules on *accession mobilière* and *adjonction* (Arts 566–569 French Civil Code) are of no assistance in this regard. They approach the phenomenon of connection from a purely ownership-oriented point of departure (and, this being the case, those provisions have generally been superseded in practice by Art. 2276(1) French Civil Code[33]). '*Tout ce qui s'unit et s'incorpore à la chose appartient au propriétaire*', declares Art. 551 French Civil Code—and nothing more. The following provisions, to which this provision refers, do not reveal what is understood by 'unification' or 'incorporation'; the only matter on which they shed some light is when a moveable becomes an immoveable. The ownership-based approach, interwoven with obligational elements, follows through to Arts 567 and 568 French Civil Code (and, incidentally, § 415 Austrian Civil Code). According to these provisions, a '*partie principale*' exists where some accessory has been 'unified' with it only for the use, ornament, or complement of the principal object. If, however, the accessory is of much greater value than the principal object, and has been connected without the knowledge of its owner, the owner can demand separation and return—even when this would cause damage to the *partie principale*. Moreover, Art. 569 French Civil Code stipulates that when two things have been 'unified' such that one cannot be seen as an accessory of the other, the object of greater value or volume is deemed to be the principal object. 9.9

[32] This also includes the question of the role of party autonomy in a legal system. While this question is also a factor in the law of connection of several real things, it has its emphasis in the law of connection of real things with land units. For French law, *Dross*, Droit des biens, p. 340 no. 412, states that the fact that an engine can be vindicated by itself is due to the fact that in cases in which a contract is focused on the use of a moveable thing, the thing's separation can and must still be provided, despite Art. 566 French Civil Code. This is because the owner of the *accessoire* specifically declines to lose his ownership through *accession mobilière* in these cases. Thus, the connection is legally impossible, which is equal to factual impossibility. This analysis is stated to be in accordance with the rule in Art. 2370 French Civil Code ('*L'incorporation d'un meuble faisant l'objet d'une réserve de propriété à un autre bien ne fait pas obstacle aux droits du créancier lorsque ces biens peuvent être séparés sans subir de dommage*'), as well as the rule in Art. L 624-16(3) *Code de commerce* ('*La revendication en nature peut s'exercer dans les mêmes conditions sur les biens mobiliers incorporés dans un autre bien lorsque la séparation de ces biens peut être effectuée sans qu'ils en subissent un dommage. La revendication en nature peut également s'exercer sur des biens fongibles lorsque des biens de même nature et de même qualité se trouvent entre les mains du débiteur ou de toute personne les détenant pour son compte*').

[33] See also *Mazeaud and Chabas*, Biens[8], p. 338 no. 1609 ('*Quant à la 'jonction' de deux choses mobilières, elle ne présente guère d'intérêt pratique. En effet, si les propriétaires de deux choses mobilières qui se trouvent unies étaient liés par un contrat, ce contrat détermine leurs droits; sinon le propriétaire qui a uni à sa chose une chose mobilière accessoire, peut le plus souvent—sa bonne foi étant présumée—invoquer l'article 2279 C. civ.* [now Art. 2276], *en vertu duquel il est devenu propriétaire de ce meuble avant toute accession*').

9.10 English,[34] Spanish, and Italian law follow this model to the present day. A 'doctrine of components' in such terms has not been established in these legal systems. Arts 375–383 Spanish Civil Code, which govern the connection of moveable goods (*derecho de accesión respecto a los bienes muebles*) embrace *unión* (and *adjunción*), *mezcla*, and *confusion* as well as specification (*especificación*). Art. 375 Spanish Civil Code provides that where two moveables belonging to different owners are connected with each other in such a way that they form one thing, in the absence of bad faith, the owner of the principal thing acquires the accessory thing and has to compensate the owner of the latter for its value. From this, two basic rules are derived for the whole law of accession: (i) ownership in the new thing is ascribed to the owner of the principal thing, and (ii) the owner of the accessory thing is given compensation in money. This principle of *accessorium sequitur principale* is taken to entail the so-called *relación de principalidad y accesoriedad* in the case of an inseparable thing. The *cosa accesoria* is whatever is connected to the *cosa principal* for the purposes of the latter's ornamentation, use, or completion (Art. 376 Spanish Civil Code). In other cases, the object of higher value or with the greater volume counts as the *cosa principal* (Art. 377 Spanish Civil Code). If the objects can be separated without damage, the respective owners can demand their separation (Art. 378 sentence 1 Spanish Civil Code). A motor can be removed from an automobile in which it is installed, for example, under this provision.[35] In Italian law, too, the case of a motor would be resolved by application of the accessory principle (*principio di accessorietà*);[36] however, in Italian law this principle yields a different result. An acquisition of ownership only occurs by way of *accessione* where two complementary goods belonging to different owners are united. In this case, the principle of *accessorium sequitur principale* applies; the owner of the *cosa principale* acquires ownership in the *accessoria*. In the case of an *accessione di mobile a mobile* (Art. 939(2) Italian Civil Code), the owner of the principal thing acquires ownership in the accessory thing, but must compensate the latter's erstwhile owner according to rules that distinguish between good faith and bad faith scenarios. No more detailed provisions are to be found. The owner of the automobile thus becomes owner of the motor.

9.11 The 'doctrine of components' [*Bestandteilslehre*] developed in the German Civil Code takes a different approach. This doctrine, which was understood by the drafters of the *Bürgerliches Gesetzbuch* as a counterpoint to the accession doctrine of the Romanic legal systems set out above, happily distinguishes between two questions: (i) when and

[34] A comprehensive theory of components is lacking. The decisive cases so far have rather concerned the efficacy of retentions of title. A general rule is that if an object is incorporated into a different chattel, the title to it subsists as long as the thing retains its separate identity and can be removed (*Hendy Lennox (Industrial Engines) Ltd v Grahame Puttick Ltd* [1984] 1 WLR 485, 494 (*Staughton* J) concerned delivery of diesel engines which had been built into generator sets and secured with bolts; they remained identifiable by their serial numbers, were not changed fundamentally, or indeed destroyed, by the installation and could be removed within hours; retention of title under these circumstances was effective). See, regarding this ruling, *Chaigley Farms Ltd v Crawford, Kaye & Grayshire Ltd* [1996] BCivil Code 957, 961 (*Garland* J, obiter).

[35] See, for further details, Bercovitz Rodríguez-Cano (*-Bercovitz Álvarez*), Comentarios al Código Civil², pp. 538–9, as well as *Díez-Picazo*, Fundamentos III⁵, pp. 287–8.

[36] Foundations provided by *Dell'Aquila*, L'acquisto della proprieta per accessione, unione, commistione e specificazione (1979) and (for accession in the context of immoveables) *Paradiso*, L'accessione al suolo (1994).

how a thing loses its independence in favour of a new thing and (ii) to whom ownership in the new thing should be ascribed (which latter question pervades the field in the Romanic approach). The German approach, which has been followed in the Netherlands, Portuguese, and Estonian codifications, follows this distinction so far, in fact, that the two questions are addressed in totally different parts of the code. Other codifications place them in different sections of a single part, and do so clearly enough. On the whole, one gets the impression that the legal systems of Europe are more harmonized in their approach to the ownership *implications* of connection than in their approach to the *preconditions* for such a connection coming about.

Section 93 German Civil Code, which is contained in the general (first) part [*Allgemeiner Teil*] provides that 'components of a thing that cannot be separated from each other without destroying or changing the nature of one or the other' cannot be 'objects of separate rights'. What cannot be the 'object of separate rights' is no thing; the only 'thing' is the composite 'whole object'. The question *who* is to be regarded as the owner of the composite (new) thing is not a question of the 'law of things' [*Sachenrecht*] in the German idiom, but of the 'law of ownership' [*Eigentumsrecht*]. Under §§ 947 and 948 German Civil Code the answer is given, namely that it depends on whether any of the connected objects (the code uses the term 'things' [*Sachen*], for better or worse) is to be regarded as the principal thing [*Hauptsache*]. If that is the case, its owner acquires sole ownership in the new thing that has been created from the connection; in other cases, a co-ownership situation arises. The Netherlands Civil Code also adopts this approach. A thing can only be the object of a property right in its entirety—i.e. as a unified whole. Under Art. 5:3 Netherlands Civil Code, then, the owner of a thing is also the owner of its components (*bestanddeelen*)] unless the law otherwise provides. Art. 5:14 Netherlands Civil Code then stipulates three fundamental principles:

> (1) If a movable thing becomes a component of another movable thing, which has to be regarded as the principal thing, then the ownership of the movable thing passes over to the owner of the principal thing. (2) If none of the movable things can be identified as the principal thing, and they belong to different owners, then these owners will become co-owners of the new thing, each of them for a share proportionally to the value of the movable thing he owned before. (3) The principal thing is the thing of which the value exceeds the value of the other thing considerably or the thing that is regarded by generally accepted views (common opinion) as the principal thing.

The question *whether* a connected object can be the component of something (else) is determined by the provisions contained in Book Three (Property Law in General). The provisions of Book Five (Property Rights) only apply to objects that are attributed 'thing status' in Book Three, and Art. 3:2 Netherlands Civil Code in particular. Under Art. 3:4(1) Netherlands Civil Code, 'common opinion' (*verkeersopvatting*) is decisive. Everything that forms part of a thing according to generally accepted views is a 'component' of that thing. This is said to be a 'social' criterion. Art. 3:4(2) Netherlands Civil Code quickly adds a 'physical' criterion, however, providing that a thing that is attached to another (principal) thing in such a way that it cannot be separated from it without substantial damage becomes a 'component' of the principal thing. The most important question is whether a 'thing' would be incomplete without one of its components.[37]

9.12 Aside from their terminology,[38] German and Netherlands law differ in that German law does not have the flexibility provided by the latter's 'social' criterion. However, even in Netherlands law the 'social' criterion is subordinate to the 'physical' one.[39] When an object (as defined in Art. 3:4(2) Netherlands Civil Code) is firmly connected with a thing, it no longer matters whether 'common' opinion would also regard it as being a component. Moreover, § 93 German Civil Code is by no means only concerned with 'physical' states of affairs; rather, it also asks whether the components of a thing can be separated from the thing without substantially changing its nature. However, the approach taken in these neighbouring jurisdictions does sometimes produce different outcomes. According to the judicial decisions of the *Hoge Raad* in the Netherlands, for example, the fact that a thing can generally only be used pursuant to a contractual licence is said to speak against its character as a component.[40] By way of contrast, 'component status' is said to follow from constructive agreement in relation to another thing,[41] and the fact that it would be incomplete without the connected, complementary object.[42] For this reason, the mass-produced motor would be a 'component' of the automobile under Dutch law. It could be a 'component' under German law, too, but (as we have seen) this is determined solely by reference to whether it is an 'essential' component, and the German judicial decisions have denied that this is the case. A motor is just a 'simple' component. It can easily be removed and installed in another automobile. Its 'nature' is not changed through this process, and the automobile could be rendered usable again by the installation of a new motor.[43]

37 Nieuwenhuis/Stolker/Valk (*-Huijgen*), BW[6], Art. 3:4 no. 3 p. 1287.

38 The Netherlands Civil Code (like the Greek Civil Code), rightly acknowledges only 'components'. These correspond to 'essential' or 'substantial' components [*wesentliche Bestandteile*] in German law. The German judicial decisions and literature continue to operate with the terms 'simple' and 'essential' components. However, this causes more confusion than clarification, and certainly endangers the intellectual coherence of the doctrine itself. For example, one may read that a 'unified, but composite thing' is composed of components. Accordingly, 'components' are characterized by their physical connection to the thing (MünchKomm [*-Holch*], BGB I(1)[5], § 93 no. 5); they form an 'economic unit' with it (*Baur and Stürner*, Sachenrecht[18], § 3 no. 14). If, however, everything which is not an essential component (§ 93 German Civil Code), 'apparent' component (§ 95 German Civil Code), or accessory (§ 97 German Civil Code) is a 'non-essential component', then the separation into 'essential' and 'simple' ('non-essential') has a function in obligational law at best, but certainly not in property law. It is thoroughly sufficient in Netherlands law to separate independent things from components. This is also, rightly, the prevailing view in Greek law. Attempts to differentiate between essential (inseparable, not independent) and non-essential (separable, independent) components have been decidedly rejected in the scholarship (e.g. *Georgiades*, Empragmato Dikaio I, pp. 101–02 no. 4). 'Non-essential' components would be practically indistinguishable from accessories (Arts 956–960 Greek Civil Code), and there would be no need for a third category between 'components' and 'accessories' (Areopag 399/1981, EEN 49 [1982] p. 132; Protodikeio Athens 385/1972, NoB 20 [1972] p. 945 note by *Spyridakis*; Protodikeio Lamia 45/1966, NoB 14 [1966] p. 455).

39 Von Bar (*-Nieper and Ploeger*), Sachenrecht in Europa III, p. 165.

40 Hoge Raad 16 March 1980, NedJur 1980 no. 600 pp. 1957, 1962.

41 Hoge Raad 15 November 1991, NedJur 1993 no. 316 pp. 1154, 1163. The Hoge Raad and the BGH agree on this point, cf. BGH 11 November 2011, BGHZ 191 p. 285 (no. 18).

42 Hoge Raad 27 November 1992, NJ 1993 no. 317 pp. 1163, 1168. The cap of a marker pen which prevents it from drying out should thus be a component of a single thing.

43 This is also a good example to illustrate the effect of Art. 5:14(3) Netherlands Civil Code. Consider a new car, where the coachwork is the principal thing and the engine merely a component. When a used car of low value

The *Bestandteilslehre* of German law has not only been received into Netherlands law with the abovementioned modifications. It has left visible traces in other jurisdictions, too: in Austrian law[44] (even though the Austrian Civil Code only recognizes 'accessories' [*Zugehör*] in § 294 Austrian Civil Code), Slovenian law,[45] Czech law,[46] Polish law,[47] Hungarian law,[48] Greek law, Portuguese law, and the legal systems of the Baltic states. Under Art. 953 Greek Civil Code, for example, a component is defined as part of a composite thing from which the principal thing cannot be separated without damage or a change to its essence or function.[49] The similarity to § 93 German Civil Code is unmistakable. The components of a thing form, in their sum, the 'thing' in the legal sense (see also Art. 954 Greek Civil Code). What is decisive (in the terms discussed above) is the 'physical' criterion, i.e. whether the component and principal thing can be separated without damage to either. The judicial decisions under Art. 953 Greek Civil Code have, for example, confirmed the 'component status' of a coolroom,[50] automobile tyres,[51] an automobile motor,[52] and the motor of a ship.[53] Time and again, reference **9.13**

receives a new engine, the oppose appears *prima facie* to be the case. However, the commentary allows an interpretation based on usage in cases like the one described. The engine would remain a component in this case (the *Nota van Wijzigingen* explicitly mention the example of an old car with a new engine, as well as a silver or gold ring with a diamond set into it [N.v.W., Parl. Geschiedenis V, p. 1]; in each case the less valuable thing is the principal thing).

44 See, for examples from an extensive jurisdiction, on the one hand OGH 1 April 1959, ZVR 1960 p. 38 (a car battery is not an independent component of the car) and on the other hand OGH 25 September 1997, *SZ* 70/188 (installing cables into a television system is legally a connection, because the cables become components of the system).

45 Under Art. 16(1) Slovenian Civil Code, a component is everything which is regarded as part of a thing by general consensus. A component must be separated from the thing to become an independent reference point of property rights (Art. 16(2) Slovenian Civil Code). The former owners of the connected objects acquire *pro rata* co-ownership of the new thing (Art. 55(1) Slovenian Civil Code), unless the thing is regarded as a principal thing by general opinion (Art. 55(3) Slovenian Civil Code), in which case its owner becomes the sole owner of the new thing (Art. 55(2) Slovenian Civil Code).

46 Under § 120(1) Czech Civil Code [1964] and § 120(1) Slovak Civil Code, a component of a thing is everything which naturally belongs to it and cannot be separated from a thing without devaluing it. The component is not a legally independent thing, therefore all legal acts concerning the thing also concern its components (*Švestka and Dvořák*, Občanské právo hmotné[5], p. 246). What exactly has the character of a component depends on its nature and on the risk of devaluing the thing in the event of separation. The devaluation can be estimated according to economic and aesthetic criteria (*Eliáš*, Občanský zákoník. Velký akademický komentář I, p. 493). § 505 Czech Civil Code [2014] retained the former rules with regard to components of moveable things, stating that a component of a thing is everything which naturally belongs to it and cannot be separated from it without devaluing it.

47 Under Art. 47 § 2 Polish Civil Code, everything which cannot be removed from the thing without damage or fundamental change to its or the thing's being is a component of the thing. Polish Sąd Najwyższy 28 June 2002, I CK 5/02, Glosa 2003/3 str. 47, Prawo Bankowe 2002/12 str. 17, LexPolonica-No. 358693, Lex-No. 56604 focuses on whether the new thing constitutes a unit in the economic sense and mentions *obiter* (as the facts of the case concerned a wagon-weighing machine) the example of a desk drawer. This, they say, is a component of the desk, as their separation would lead to a fundamental change in the usability of the drawer and the desk. It is also, but not only, a matter of physical connection between two things. A loose, gravity-based connection can be sufficient, if the whole constitutes a material and economic unit.

48 Under § 5:15 Hungarian Civil Code, the right to ownership includes everything which is connected with the thing in such a way that separation would result in the destruction of the thing or of the separated part, or if separation would significantly reduce the value or usability.

49 To the following in more detail, see *Georgiades*, Empragmato Dikaio I, pp. 100–08; *Kousoulas*, Empragmato Dikaio, pp. 52–4; *Papasteriou*, Empragmato Dikaio I, pp. 226–47, and *Filios*, Empragmato Dikaio[3], pp. 70–76.

50 CA Athens 7636/1975, NoB 24 (1976) p. 633.

51 Protodikeio Herakleion 310/1962, NoB 10 (1962) p. 1066.

52 Protodikeio Athens 385/1975, NoB 20 (1972) p. 945.

53 CA Athens 4815/1982, EEmpD 33 (1982) p. 605 (an auxiliary engine is also a component of a ship).

is made to general opinion.[54] Components share the legal fate of the composite thing. Every disposition over a composite thing embraces all its components, even when their composition is effected at a point of time *after* the disposition itself.[55] Property rights in components are extinguished.[56] A component can no longer be vindicated,[57] nor can it be divided independently of the principal thing.[58] Possession *animo domini* over a component is conceptually possible, but this does not entail the possibility of acquiring ownership in a component by prescription.[59] The general consequences of connection are governed according to a well-worn pattern. Under Art. 1058 Greek Civil Code, co-ownership arises in a new thing in relation to the value of the (former) things that comprise it. If, however, one of them is properly to be seen as the principal thing, its owner acquires ownership in the new, composite thing. Art. 1058 Greek Civil Code thus provides a form of acquisition of ownership by force of law.[60] The mere fact of connection is sufficient; there is no mention of good faith or capacity; an agreement that every owner of a component should retain ownership in 'his' thing would be ineffective.[61] The Portuguese civil code provides a definition of 'things' in its first, general book (Art. 202 Portuguese Civil Code). According to Art. 203 Portuguese Civil Code, 'things' are divided *inter alia* between moveable and immoveable, principal and accessory. Under Art. 204(1)(d) Portuguese Civil Code, rural and urban land units, and things belonging to them, are counted as immoveable things. 'Components' (*parte integrante*) include, for example, moveable things that are materially connected to the land unit on a permanent basis. 'Accessories' (*coisas acessórias*) and appurtenances (*pertenças*) are, according to Art. 210(1) Portuguese Civil Code, moveable things that are in the ongoing service of another thing without being a *parte integrante* of it. The right of accession (i.e. acquisition of ownership in a thing in virtue of its connection with another thing of which it is not a component), by way of contrast, is set out in the third book (Arts 1325–1343 Portuguese Civil Code). This form of increase is a self-standing pathway for the acquisition of ownership (Art. 1316 Portuguese Civil Code); the moment in which the connection or incorporation occurs is decisive (Art. 1317(d) Portuguese Civil Code). Portuguese law, like Italian law, thus comprehends 'accession' to include every process by which things lose their autonomous existence through integration in another thing,[62] but diverges to the extent that acquisition of ownership and characterization

[54] Areopag 35/1961 NoB 9 (1961) p. 715; CA Athens 671/1974, NoB 22 (1974) p. 1077; CA Patras 204/1953, *NoB* 1 (1953) p. 546 (bus coachwork).

[55] CA Patras 45/1973, NoB 21 (1973) p. 1488; CA Patras 204/1953, NoB 1 (1953) p. 546.

[56] See Arts 1057, 1058, 1060 Greek Civil Code, and in this respect, CA Athens 7636/1975, NoB 24 (1976) p. 633; Areopag 298/1963, NoB 11 (1963) p. 1191. The engine continues to belong to the car's owner, even once it has been removed from the car. Rights which existed to the engine before its installation into the car remain expired and are not recreated 'automatically'.

[57] CA Patras 204/1953, NoB 1 (1953) p. 546; Protodikeio Athens 385/1972, NoB 20 (1972) p. 945.

[58] Areopag 35/1961, NoB 9 (1961) p. 715; Areopag 426/1961, *NoB* 10 (1961) p. 158.

[59] CA Athens 7483/1978, NoB 28 (1980) p. 76; Areopag 579/1982, NoB 31 (1983) p. 366 note by *Spyridakis*; Areopag 1705/1981, NoB 30 (1982) p. 1060; CA Patras 195/1982, NoB 31 (1983) p. 386 note by *Georgiades*.

[60] Protodikeio Thessaloniki (in chamber) 12815/2002, Harm. 2002 p. 1610.

[61] Areopag 298/1963, NoB 11 (1963) p. 1191.

[62] *Vieira*, Direitos reais, p. 681. See also *Mota Pinto*, Teoria geral do direito civil[4], p. 342, according to which a thing only becomes a thing in the legal sense (Art. 202 Portuguese Civil Code) if it has an '*existência autónoma ou separada*'.

as a component are clearly delineated. Further, the prevailing view in Portuguese law is that accession generally works in the favour of the person whose part has the highest value. The *acessoriedade* is said to find its justification in the value relations of the things concerned; what is more valuable is the *coisa principal*. If, then, the motor is worth more than the automobile, its owner becomes owner of the automobile too, but must naturally compensate its value in money (Art. 1333(1) Portuguese Civil Code). However, the 'author of the connection' can also be made to take the principal thing, if the relevant owners themselves prefer compensation in money (Art. 1333(4) Portuguese Civil Code).[63] If the things have the same value and complement each other such that their separation is impossible or would occasion disproportionate costs,[64] the doctrine of accession fails. If the parties concerned cannot reach agreement, Portuguese law resorts to emergency responses such as an auction for the (new, composite) thing between the owners (Art. 1333(2) Portuguese Civil Code) or, in the case that none of them are interested, sale to a third party (Art. 1333(3) Portuguese Civil Code). The same basic pattern is found in Estonian law. A 'substantial component' of a thing is every part that cannot be separated from it without destruction or significant change (§ 53(1) Estonian Civil Code, General Part). A component, insofar as the law does not provide otherwise, cannot be separately encumbered with a real right. Art. 850 Latvian Civil Code distinguishes, in the first instance, between principal and accessory things. Principal things are independent legal objects, (unseparated) accessories are not. They are 'things' (the word here loses its technical meaning) that only exist in virtue of the principal thing, belong to a principal thing, or are connected with a principal thing in some other way. Art. 851 Latvian Civil Code distinguishes between substantial components, fruits, accessories, uses made of the principal thing and encumbrances over the principal thing. A 'substantial component' is everything that stands in an inseparable relation to a principal thing, such that it the component either cannot come into existence without the principal thing or would not be recognized as a thing of this type (Art. 854 Latvian Civil Code). Arts 4.12–4.15 Lithuanian Civil Code adopt the same approach with small variations. A component is a substantial part of a principal thing when it is inseparably connected with it or installed within it in such a way that it cannot, according to its nature, be used without it or would be seen as incomplete without it (Art. 4.15 Lithuanian Civil Code). The consequences in terms of ownership relations are found in Arts 980–981 Latvian Civil Code and Art. 4.54(1) Lithuanian Civil Code, respectively. They give subjective criteria an unusual amount of weight. Granted, *pro rata* co-ownership arises when moveable things belonging to so many owners are connected (to form a new, single thing) in the absence of prior agreement, and cannot be separated without disproportionate costs. In other cases, however, the things are to be separated at the cost of the party who brought about the connection (Art. 981 Latvian Civil Code, Art. 54.4(2)

[63] For further details (and comparative references to Italian law), see *Pires de Lima and Antunes Varela*, Código Civil Anotado III², note 4 to Art. 1333 p. 152; *Carvalho Martins*, Acessão, pp. 77–8 and von Bar [*-de Seabra and Xavier*], Sachenrecht in Europa III, Portugal, p. 361.

[64] If the parts are separable, every party can demand separation and vindicate their thing (*Vieira* op. cit. p. 682).

Lithuanian Civil Code). Besides this, owners can demand transfer of ownership or compensation in money under a certain, unusually detailed set of conditions (see Arts 982–986 Latvian Civil Code).

9.14 The leading case in Swedish law is, at the same time, a classic of Sweden's so-called 'dynamic' property law. The facts of HD 16 February 1960[65] were that A had sold and delivered a lorry to B subject to a retention of title. Subsequently, C sold and delivered new tyres to B, also subject to a retention of title. B installed these on the lorry. In the insolvency of B, A took possession of the (largely unpaid) lorry and disposed of it. C sued A for compensation for the tyres; A was argued to have known that they were only supplied subject to a retention of title and that they, too, had not been paid for. The court took the determinative question to be whether the retention of title clause between C and B[66] could have *erga omnes* effect even following installation of the tyres. A 3:2 majority answered this question in the negative, albeit not without encouraging express legislative intervention. The court distinguished between the protection of commerce (*omsättningskyddet*) as between C and B and creditor protection (*borgenärsskyddet*) as between A and C. In the relationship between C and B, the retention of title clause was effective, but not between C and A. The questions of 'creditor protection' as between C and A were not governed by any statutory provision. Fundamentally, then, a 'right to delivery of possession' (i.e. the retention of title clause) has *erga omnes* effect.[67] It had, however, been settled law since 1955[68] that this effect can be lost when the thing is incorporated (*infogat*) into another moveable thing and its removal would cause the latter a significant loss of value. The court based its creditor protection reasoning *inter alia* on the fact that standard tyres had been negotiated that would be easy to replace. But it was true that an automobile without tyres could not function as intended.[69] Automobile and tyres are, on the facts, generally regarded as a single object. That was not, however, treated as determinative of the question. Rather, a comprehensive assessment of the competing interests was necessary. In the literature, it is emphasized against this background that an *erga omnes* right to delivery of possession must logically mean that a person can demand his thing back even when it serves the improvement (*förbättring*) and individualization (*individualisationen*) of another thing. That is generally regarded, however, as unacceptable.[70] Above all, it is argued that such acceptance of the *erga omnes* effect would entail the recognition of a secret (or 'silent') hypothec over moveables. Such a right, however, would violate the publicity principle expressed in the requirement for delivery (*tradition*) for the transfer of ownership under chap. 10 § 2 *Handelsbalk* (1736:0123 2), the requirement for registration for the transfer of a security

[65] NJA 1960 p. 9.

[66] The agreement between A and B was valid under the provisions of *Lag (1978:599) om avbetalningsköp mellan näringsidkare* (*inter alia*—for contracts between companies and consumers, the *Konsumentkreditlag* (1992:830) [KkrL] is applicable). There would thus not have been a question of 'creditor protection', as C had not even claimed to have a right to the lorry.

[67] *Håstad*, Sakrätt[6], p. 188.

[68] HD 8 January 1955, NJA 1955 p.1.

[69] See as early as HD NJA 1935 p. 416.

[70] *Håstad* op. cit. pp. 45–6.

right (*säkerhetsöverlåtelse*) under *Lag (1845:50 S. 1) om handel med lösören* and the requirement for notice (*denuntiation*) under *Lag (1904:48 S. 1) om samäganderätt.*[71] In insolvency law, too, creditor interests are said to be served by the requirement that things be kept together that form an economic unit.[72] There are no judicial decisions yet on the scenario where the thing in question is not supplied on credit. It has been suggested that the owner of the more valuable thing should get ownership, and that co-ownership should result where the things are of equal value.[73]

c. Loss of 'Thing Status' in Favour of a Land Unit

(1) Lines of Connection between Real Things and Land Units

Nearly every real thing finds itself within the four corners of some land unit.[74] To treat real things as non-independent components of the land unit simply in virtue of their location, however, would not do. If that approach were taken, trade would be the privilege of landowners exclusively; besides this, everyone who found himself on the soil of another or indeed on a public way would lose all the property he carried with him *ex lege*. Delineation of land units and real things is therefore required by both reason and justice. From this, a number of freedom-enhancing general rules can be derived to the effect that something is, in case of doubt, *not* part of a land unit (but rather a real or purely normative thing). The second main objective of the law governing connections between things consists, in part, of setting out the exceptions to this basic rule.[75] In other words, the core question is when (and by what process) real things lose their character as such and become (part of) a land unit. **9.15**

This is only conceivable when a real thing becomes connected with a land unit along one of two axes; the real thing must (i) sit directly on or in the soil of a land unit, or (ii) be connected to a building (in exceptional cases, possibly a tree[76]).[77] If connected **9.16**

[71] Ibid. pp. 296–7.

[72] *Undén*, Svensk sakrätt I[10], pp. 105–06.

[73] *Håstad* op. cit. p. 47.

[74] In cases (e.g. seafaring vessels) where this is not the rule, the respective things are often subjected to a system similar to that of land units. The rules concerning the components of land units are not infrequently used to determine the components of a ship by analogy (see e.g. for Greek law *Spyridakis*, NoB 20 [1972] pp. 948–54 in a note to Protodikeio Athens 358/1972).

[75] A third series of questions, which will not be further analysed here, is concerned with the connection (or combination) of real things, land units, and purely normative things to a new purely normative thing, such as a company. The Greek judicial decisions (Protodikeio Syros 276/1964, NoB 13 [1965] p. 848; Protodikeio Chalkida 691/1971, NoB 20 [1972] p. 109; CA Athens 5523/1984, EEN 51 [1984] p. 846; CA Athens 3205/1986, EllDni 27 [1986] p. 1178; CA Thessaloniki 1634/1990, EllDni 35 [1994] p. 159; CA Thessaloniki 2863/1990, Harm. 46 [1992] p. 44) for example, characterize the machines of a company as fictitious components of the company's land unit charged with a hypothec. CA Athens 355/1975, Harm. 29 (1975) p. 586 interprets this to mean that the machines of a company should be understood as its components, however only in relation to the mortgagee. The literature has a more nuanced view for the period of time before the hypothec creation. It is only after this point that the accessories are fictitiously equated with components *ipso iure* (for further details, see *Adamopoulou*, Ypothíki se michanímata katá ton N. 4112/1929, pp. 69–74).

[76] One example is a treehouse. OVG Lüneburg 8 September 2010, DVBl 2010 p. 1381 considers a treehouse an essential land unit component (not merely an 'apparent' component) when it has not been constructed with the intention of removing it after temporary use. A child's swing and a sandbox on the land unit of an apartment building are even more so permanent land unit components, as they are typically used by multiple generations of children.

[77] These two basic situations are a theme in a variety of statutory regulations. An example can be found in § 506(1) Czech Civil Code (which states that the component of a land unit is the area above and below its surface,

to a building (stones and other objects are laid upon a foundation to form a building; a satellite dish is installed on a roof), it is common to look first towards the criterion of the connection's solidity and fixture. This criterion is found, albeit with differences at the level of detail[78] and a number of exceptions,[79] in almost all the European legal systems.[80] The problem is only that the criterion must not be elevated to the rank of

the buildings on the land unit and other installations, with the exception of temporary buildings, and including everything *which is sunk into the land unit or fixed into the walls*). Another example can be found in Kap. 2 §§ 1 and 2 JB. Under Kap. 2 § 1 JB, buildings, pipes, fences, and other installations which are secured in or on the ground for permanent use, as well as trees and other plants with roots, and natural fertilizer, all belong to the land unit. By contrast, the following belong to the land unit as accessories under Kap. 2 § 2 JB: the permanent fittings and other objects fixed to the building, if these are suitable for the permanent use of the building or a part of the building, such as partitions, lifts, banisters, pipes and conduits for water, heat, light, or other things with taps, switches, or similar equipment, boilers, heaters, chimneys, tiled stoves, interior windows, window blinds, fire prevention devices, security equipment, and keys. As a rule, the bath and other sanitation, the stove, the drying cabinet, the refrigerator, washing machines, and mangles belong to buildings if they are for housing. Parts of sales buildings are the shelves, counter, and window displays. Parts of event venues are the stage and seating area. Parts of agricultural buildings are the feeding devices and milking systems; and parts of factory buildings are the cooling and ventilation systems. Replacement parts and duplicate parts of the named objects do not belong to the building.

[78] The aforementioned satellite dishes are a good example. CA Lisbon 19 March 2009, Processo 67/08.3TVLSB. L1-6 considers them components of the building (*equipamento (parabólica) a integrar o edifício*), and as such components of the common part (*parte comum*) of the land unit or the building in the sense of Art. 1421 Portuguese Civil Code, which belong to the apartment owner. The same view is taken in Sweden. It is important to determine that the building has been equipped (*försedd*) with a real thing. The statute (previous fn.) uses this expression to denote an evident external connection (*påtagligt yttre samband*). According to an expression in the legislative materials, the object must be connected to the building in such a way that they constitute a functional 'community' ('*anbringats i sådant samband med denna, som motsvarar föremålets ändamålsgemenskap med byggnaden*': SOU 1947:38 p. 95). The object, such as a parabolic antenna, does not necessarily have to be 'fixed' to the building (HD 16 October 1997, NJA 1997 p. 699); rather, it depends entirely on the character of the object (*Håstad*, Sakrätt[6], p. 31). In fact, for German law, LG Nürnberg-Fürth 5 May 1993, DGVZ 1996 p. 124 even states that a permanent satellite attachment merely constitutes an accessory (*Zubehör*), thus precluding it from being a component (§ 97(1) German Civil Code). Admittedly, this judgment's relevance is limited. The attachment had been replaced and the judgment only concerned the delivery of the dismantled attachment in connection with sales law.

[79] It is not always important to have a fixed connection, as is shown for Swedish law in the aforementioned case of the parabolic antenna in the attic but under the roof. (Rather, it is important in accordance with the conception there, to have a functional community of the real thing and the land unit.) Under French law, the *destination* of the antenna, either control or husbandry of the land unit, is sufficient; a fixed connection is not necessary (Art. 524(1) and (2) French Civil Code). A satellite dish must necessarily also count among the fixtures in English law (*Fairgate International Ltd v Citibank International Plc* [2005] EWCA Civ 569, [19]; [2006] 1 P & CR 17, 23). This judgment is, however, not entirely clear, as it concerns the undisputed assertion of a party. Furthermore, both fixtures and fittings are discussed; however, fittings can also include chattels in English law. That a satellite dish (as opposed to a transmitter) is a fixture was decided for Australian law in *Macrocom v City West Centre* [2001] NSWSC 374 (*Windeyer* J).

[80] e.g. Art. 110(1) Bulgarian LPA (anything that is securely connected to the ground or a building becomes an immoveable); § 94(1) German Civil Code (the essential components of a land unit include the things which are securely connected to the ground); Art. 954 Greek Civil Code (components of a land unit are also things which are securely connected to the ground, especially the buildings); Art. 48 Polish Civil Code (unless provided otherwise in statutes, the components of a land unit above all include buildings and other permanently connected installations as well as trees and other plants from the moment of their planting or sowing); see also Art. 191 Polish Civil Code and Art. 204(3) Portuguese Civil Code (a component is every moveable thing which is permanently materially connected to the land unit). Art. 334 Spanish Civil Code occasionally refers to 'connection' but also to 'fixed connection' in places (e.g. immoveable goods are said to be (1) land units, buildings, pathways, and all types of structures that are connected to the ground; (2) trees, plants, and hanging fruits, as long as they are connected to the earth or are an essential component [*parte integrante*] of an immoveable; (3) everything which is firmly connected to the immoveable, so that it cannot be separated from it without breaking the material or damaging the object; (4) the statues, reliefs, paintings, and other objects for use or decoration, which are installed in buildings or country seats by the owner of the land unit in a way which makes the intention to connect them permanently to the ground clear; (6) animal breeding facilities, dovecotes, apiaries, fish ponds, or similar breeding facilities, if the owner installs or maintains them with the intention of permanently connecting them to the land unit and they form a permanent part of the land unit; (8) mines, quarries, and waste dips, as long as their material is connected to the strike, as well as flowing and stagnant waters; (9) dikes and structures whose intended purpose is to remain at a fixed point on the river, in the sea or on a coast, even if the structures float in the water). The French Civil Code acknowledges neither

a general doctrine that governs the doctrine of components (or indeed accession) for land units. Such an approach would risk putting the cart before the horse.[81] To determine whether a real thing 'belongs' to a building only makes sense once it has been determined whether a building 'belongs' to the land unit it sits on. If a real thing is brought into direct contact with the soil of a land unit, however, then the criterion of 'fixture' (whatever its substantive merits) has little descriptive power. In purely physical terms, a trench lined with concrete and covered with a steel grate is no more 'fixed' to the soil than a statue or even a garden chair. In all three cases, it is only gravity that holds the object and the soil together. Nonetheless, the concrete in the trench is always counted as part of the land unit, and the garden chair is not; the status of the statue would require a case-by-case analysis.[82] Because the distinction cannot sensibly rest only on whether a thing is wholly, partly, or not at all visible above the soil,[83] the law has no other choice

the criterion of the 'fixed connection' nor (as § 94 German Civil Code does) 'things connected firmly to the soil'. However, in the context of the *immeubles par destination*, Arts 524(3), 525 French Civil Code (much like Art. 810 Italian Civil Code) mention the phrase *attaché à perpétuelle demeure*. Moveable things, which the owner has permanently connected to the land unit, are thus immoveable by their 'determination'. The scholarship also uses the criteria of *attache*, *adhérence*, or *incorporation* to define the *immeubles par nature*. For example, *Terré and Simler*, Les biens[8], p. 38 no. 33 consider *immeubles par nature* to be the ground and everything adhering to the ground (*tout ce qui adhère au sol*). This means the *fonds de terre* and everything, that is connected to the ground (*ce qui est fixé au sol*), meaning plants and structures that 'adhere' to the ground. A similar view is taken by *Malaurie and Aynès*, Les biens[4], p. 34 no. 126 (*immeubles par nature* are the ground and everything connected to it (*tout ce qui s'y attache*), meaning buildings and plants). Under § 498(1) Czech Civil Code, immoveable things are land units and subterranean structures with their own purpose, as well as real rights to these, and rights which are declared real by law. If a legal provision determines that a thing is not a component of the land unit, and if the thing cannot be moved from place to place without destroying its essence, then this too is an immoveable thing.

[81] The authors of the German Civil Code appear to have succumbed to this. § 94(1) German Civil Code determines the 'firm connection' [*feste Verbindung*] of an object with the ground to be important, and, in this context, gives the example 'especially buildings'. § 94(2) German Civil Code then states that the things used to construct the building are its essential components. § 95 German Civil Code names as an important factor for 'apparent' components [*Scheinbestandteile*] that they must be only temporarily connected to the ground. The authors of Arts 954 and 955 Greek Civil Code proceeded in a similar manner, although 'buildings' are explicitly not a component of the land unit in this provision.

[82] In German law, the answer depends on whether the statue has been set up for a temporary purpose (§ 95 German Civil Code) on a solid foundation (§ 94(1) German Civil Code). French law (Art. 525(4) French Civil Code) even specifically provides for these: '*Quant aux statues, elles sont immeubles lorsqu'elles sont placées dans une niche pratiquée exprès pour les recevoir*'. A statue is usually an *immeuble par destination*. The basis for *destination* is either that the moveable thing is designated for service or husbandry of the land unit without being fixed to it (Art. 524(1) and (2) French Civil Code) or that it is permanently connected to the land unit (*attaché à perpétuelle demeure*; Arts 524(3) and 525 French Civil Code). In the case of a statue in a garden, the *destination* would be based on the permanent connection to the land unit (for further details, see *Terré and Simler*, Les biens[8], p. 40 no. 34). If a statue is a part of a park's plan, then it is seen as a fixture in English law, even if the statue is only connected to the land unit by its own weight (*Berkley v Poulett* [1977] 1 EGLR 86; *Hamp v Bygrave* [1983] 1 EGLR 174).

[83] A transportable shooting stick, which is inserted into the earth, naturally remains a real thing. This is also the case if the hunter, to prevent theft, completely hides it under the topsoil until his return the next morning. A drainpipe, which totally lies on the ground, is considered by many to be an essential component of the building from which it removes waste (thus, e.g. Kap. 2 § 2 Swedish JB and Art. 523 French Civil Code [pipes, which serve to conduct water in a house or another land unit, are immoveable and constitute a part of the land unit to which they are connected; whether the pipes lie on or under the topsoil does not matter], and Areopag 1136/1980, NoB 29 [1981] p. 522; a different view is taken by Czech Nejvyšší soud České republiky 4 November 2003, 22 Cdo 1308/2003, Právní rozhledy 4/2004, p. 192 and § 509 Czech Civil Code). A more recent example from the Netherlands (HR 6 December 2012, NedJur 2013 no. 2, LJN BX7474) concerns rock bolts used in tunnel construction, which were rammed deep into the ground. The claimant's land unit partially contained the bolts. Originally, upon completion of the train tunnel, the claimant had consented to the bolts in the ground of his land unit. He demanded their removal ten years later, as he wished to construct an underground car park. The *Hoge Raad* annulled the decision of the appellate court on the grounds that it had neither been sufficiently explained why the bolts were tunnel components, nor why they should have lost this quality upon completion of the tunnel. Whether the bolts in the ground had become components of the claimant's land unit remained open, but the court considered it possible.

than to make reference to the purpose(s) of the connection. The question when a real thing loses its independent quality cannot be answered by reference to purely factual (or 'physical') criteria alone. It cannot even be said that a real thing always becomes a component of the land unit to whose soil it is (ultimately) attached. A heating oil tank, for example, is not always a component of the land unit in which it is submerged;[84] the tank can be or become a component of *another* (neighbouring) land unit, for example when it is meant to provide the neighbouring house with energy, and the same goes for other facilities such as utilities connections.[85]

(2) Connection to the Soil

9.17 Under the influence of some rather unhappy statutory formulations, it is easy to overlook the fact that houses and other constructions[86] (in contrast to the statute and the

[84] That an oil tank belongs to the land unit is affirmed, e.g. for Swedish law by *Håstad*, Sakrätt[6], p. 31, even if the tank is connected to the ground only by its own weight. See also, for Cypriot law, Supreme Court 15 July 1999, *Ambrosia Oils Ltd. v Kypriakí Demokratia meso Ypourgoú Ekonomikón*, Appeal no. 2204/1999 (1999) 3 AAD 457, CyLaw database (the oil tank is a part of the real estate) and for German law OLG Munich 24 November 2011, BauR 2012 p. 550 and BGH 19 October 2012 (see the following note).

[85] A good example is BGH 19 October 2012, MDR 2013 p. 329 (Following the division of a land unit, it transpired that the subterranean oil tank for one house's central heating now lay in a different land unit. The tank was an essential component of the house. In the court's view, the tank was a building material installed for the construction (§ 94(2) German Civil Code). The subdivision of the property did not change this basic characterization of the tank; it became a component of the building, and was part of the land unit to which the relevant building belonged. Whether the subsequent shutdown of the oil tank and the dissolution of the 'component connection' between the tank and the house led to ownership of the tank falling to the claimant according to § 94(1) German Civil Code was left open by the court. However, in any event, the claimant no longer had to tolerate the tank on his land unit following this event). Under Swedish law, the dominant land unit also includes buildings and facilities which, though installed outside this land unit, serve the permanent exercise of a servitude, and thus do not belong to the servient land unit, on which they are located. The same applies to pipes and conduits, for which an easement has been obtained, provided that on creation pursuant to the *Ledningsrättslagen* (1973:1144) it was stipulated that the right should belong to the land unit (Kap. 2 § 1 Swedish JB). The land unit being discussed here is usually a factory or other site belonging to the company that manages the power mains, cf. HD 16 November 1982, NJA 1982 p. 700. § 506(2) Czech Civil Code clarifies explicitly that a subterranean structure, that is not itself an immoveable thing, is a component of the land unit, even if it extends to below a different land unit. Under the previous legislation, Czech Nejvyšší soud České republiky 30 September 2002, 22 Cdo 2125/2000, Soubor rozhodnutí Nejvyššího soudu, C 1468 ruled that a wall, which had remained standing after the demolition of a house and which was connected to the neighbouring house, remains a component of the land unit on which it was constructed, (only) as long as it fulfils some economic purpose. An interesting case for comparison to BGH 19 October 2012 op. cit. is Areopag 1349/2010, Isokrates-Database (A father had transferred two separate vertical titles in his land unit to his son and his daughter. A well and a cistern were located on the part belonging to the daughter. The son attempted to claim them for himself. His complaint was rejected as the well and the cistern belonged to the whole land unit, thus the well and the cistern were co-owned by the parties). Areopag 1476/2008, NoB 57 (2009) p. 428 concerned irrigation systems, which ran through another person's land unit, but were indispensable for the supply of the claimant's land unit. This was not, according to the court, sufficient reason for an analogous application of Art. 1010 Greek Civil Code (partial superstructure over another's land), as there was no aboveground structure. There was no superstructure within the meaning of Art. 1010 Greek Civil Code over the surface in question.

[86] This applies, accordingly, to trees. These, too, are only rarely (e.g. to decorate a garden) planted when they are fully grown (then, as is stated in Art. 973 Latvian Civil Code, they become the property of the land unit owner as soon as they have struck root in the land unit). If it is not a case of natural regeneration (flight of seeds), then trees are usually planted into the earth as seedlings or saplings. The question at hand is thus almost never whether a 'tree' has become a part of the land unit, but whether the seed, seedling, or sapling has. If this is the case, then the fully grown tree naturally also continues to be a land unit component (a good example can be found in BGH 27 January 2006, NJW 2006 p. 1424: no damages for the minimum market value of a land unit if a tree is felled illicitly; the tree as such is not an autonomous thing). There is a clear difference in the case of plants which are for sale, but temporarily planted in a nursery. The correct interpretation is that they do not lose their quality as

oil tank discussed above) are not actually 'connected' with the soil at all, let alone in a 'fixed' manner. Houses are built *in situ*; living and office containers (and other transportable structures) are placed in their finished condition on the soil. Typically, they remain independent things.[87] In other words, the numerous rules stipulating that buildings are components of a land unit satisfy themselves with the determination of one thing only. They are not concerned with the actual process of connection.[88] Only in the case of seeds and plants is that sometimes different.[89] Moreover, these rules stem from a time when the technical possibilities were much more restricted than they are today. Looking at the requirement for a 'fixed connection', however, already points

autonomous things (*Triantos*, AK, Art. 954 p. 1166 no. 6; Austrian OGH 28 November 1933, SZ 15/240 [plants set into a leased nursery do not become the property of the ground owner, as the contractual agreement between the parties shows that the plants are only temporarily connected to this ground]; § 507 Czech Civil Code [only the plants *grown* on the land unit are its components]). These plants are not yet located in their final destination. A weeping willow, whose trunk became so wide over the years that the trunk stood partially on the neighbouring land unit, and whose upper part also reached over to the neighbouring land unit, was co-owned by both land unit owners according to Hoge Raad 20 May 2011, 10/00077, LJN-Nr. BP9997. The court reached this surprising decision on the grounds of the different wordings of Art. 5:20(1)(f) (the ownership of the ground also covers the plants) and Art. 5:20(1)(e) Netherlands Civil Code. This provision states that buildings must be examined to determine whether they are a component of another building. If ninety per cent of a building is located on one land unit and ten per cent on another, then the building is usually exclusively owned by the land unit owner on whose land unit the major part of the building is located. However, Art. 5:20(1)(f) does not contain a similar provision for plants. The rule in these cases must therefore be the creation of co-ownership; the size of the parts is not important. The application of Art. 5:44(2) Netherlands Civil Code, which states that the roots of a plant located on a neighbouring land unit and which extend to one's own may be capped and acquired, does not lead to a different conclusion. While the court states that the roots remain the property of the plant's owner until their separation, this does not relate to the relation of exclusive ownership and co-ownership. Art. 5:20(1)(f) Netherlands Civil Code concerns the vertical expansion of a plant, while Art. 5:44(2) Netherlands Civil Code concerns its horizontal expansion.

[87] See Polish Sąd Najwyższy 11 February 1998, III CKN 358/97, LexPolonica-No. 2212138, Lex-No. 519925, as well as Swedish HD 1 March 1996, NJA 1996 p. 139 (a portable shed is not a land unit accessory within the meaning of the term in Kap. 2 §§ 1 and 2 Swedish JB).

[88] This can be clearly seen in Art. 334 Spanish Civil Code, which lists immoveables but neither defines nor qualifies them. *Díez-Picazo*, Fundamentos III[5], p. 213 divides them into four groups in accordance with the traditions of French law: the *inmuebles por naturaleza*, the *inmuebles por incorporación* (which most closely resemble components [*Bestandteile*] in German law), the *inmuebles por destino/destinación y las pertenencias* and the *inmuebles por analogía*.

[89] Under § 94(1) sentence 2 German Civil Code, Art. 954(1) no. 4 Greek Civil Code and Art. 48 Polish Civil Code, seeds become an (essential) component of the land unit when they are sowed, likewise for plants when they are planted. This is more precise than, e.g. Art. 812 Italian Civil Code, which states that immoveable things are the soil, springs and watercourses, trees, buildings and other structures, even if they are only temporarily connected to the ground, as well as everything which has been naturally or artificially incorporated (*incorporato*) into the ground generally. In the case of trees, Art. 956 Italian Civil Code (prohibition of the separate ownership of cultivations) must be taken into consideration (the ownership of cultivations can neither be created nor transferred separately from the ownership of the ground). Under Kap. 2 § 1 Swedish JB, trees and other plants with roots are land unit components. The same applies in Czech law (*Eliáš et al.*, Občanský zákoník. Velký akademický komentář I, p. 494), Estonian law (§ 54(1) Estonian Civil Code), and Hungarian law (§ 5:15 Hungarian Civil Code [2014] and § 95(1) Hungarian Civil Code [1959]; *Menyhárd*, Dologi jog[2], p. 62). Conversely, Cypriot law acknowledges a dual ownership of land units (*Διαδική ή πολλαπλή ιδιοκτησία*). The soil and the trees located thereon can thus belong to different persons. These legal rules originate in the Ottoman Empire. The Ottoman administration could grant private persons the right to plant trees on public ground (*Arazi Mirie*). The private persons then became the detentors of the trees. The ground was often left to another private person to cultivate. Thus emerged the problem of dual ownership. Until 1946, the ground owner could sell the ground and the trees to different persons. Countless olive trees are still subject to this system to this day. Under Scots law, even previously sowed crops can be interpreted as moveable things (as *fructus industriales*). This means that the vendor of the land remains the owner of the crops even after the land's transfer, unless there has been an agreement to the contrary (*Boskabelle Ltd v Laird* [2006] CSOH 173; [2006] SLT 1079 [Outer House, Lord Turnbull]).

to the energy expenditure necessary to move an object and transport it (without destroying it). The lower this cost is, the more likely it is that one is dealing with an object that is (still) a real thing; the higher it is, the more likely it is that the land unit should be seen as the relevant thing. Of course, it is all a matter of proportion rather than absolute measurements. Even when modern technology could allow the transportation of a whole building (with its foundations), the owner would presumably shy away from the costs involved; they would virtually never stand in a reasonable relation to the value of the objects to be moved.[90] A building is virtually safe against loss (as opposed to destruction); whoever constructs a building has expended effort to make its location permanent.[91] The effort to secure a building's location indicates a specific purpose, and this purpose is ultimately decisive: an object becomes a non-independent part of a land unit when its connection to the latter's soil is the expression of its dedication to a specific use. The erstwhile real thing must either serve the construction of a building, or it must be required for the final use of the ground to which it is attached (e.g. its fertility). Granted, a legal system can determine the component quality of a thing according to other criteria as well.[92] And granted, a legal system can at a later point in time revoke the legal recognition given to a composite entity, for example separating house and land unit into separate objects of property rights.[93] Neither of these propositions, however,

[90] e.g. CA Athens 464/2005, EllDni 2005 p. 1522 emphasizes that the test for the degree of 'fastness' of a connection must be carried out in relation to the value of the object in question. CA Crete 36/1963, NoB (11) 1963 p. 951 and Protodikeio Thessaloniki 2637/1975, Harm. (30) 1976, p. 45 also consider the necessary type and degree of connection to mean that the separation is disproportionately arduous or expensive.

[91] In light of this, Czech law, which only considers a building as an immoveable if it is connected to the ground by a solid foundation, asks whether the building can withstand natural forces (Czech Constitutional Court 6 May 2003, ÚS 483/01, Sbírka nálezů a usnesení Ústavního soudu ČR, vol. 30 no. 60 p. 107: a requirement of the connection by a solid foundation is that the thing cannot be separated from the land unit without damage. The solid connection to the land unit must be able to withstand the effects of nature which are present in the relevant locations. Besides this, the connection must survive the natural 'impacts' of the thing itself; what this means is not entirely clear; presumably that gravity alone should not be sufficient. From the position of a building, a solid foundation is a geometrical, spatial construction and physically clearly defined, namely for a precise building, in a precise location and in precise internal and external conditions.

[92] e.g. under Kap. 2 § 3 Swedish JB, industrial plant [*Industritillbehör*] falls to the property of an industrial company as an essential component (*tillbehör* embraces 'essential components' as well as 'accessories' as those concepts are defined in, e.g. German law). The land unit must be either wholly or partially equipped for industrial enterprise, machines or other equipment must be 'introduced' to the land unit, and they must have been actually used for industrial enterprise. The provision is not concerned with the degree of fixation. The only circumstance under which the aforementioned things do not belong to the land unit, is if the owner registers a declaration to this effect pursuant to Kap. 24 JB in the cadastral records (*Fastighetsregistrets inskrivningsdel*). Art. 812 Italian Civil Code even states generally that buildings and other structures become land unit components even if they are only connected to the ground for a temporary purpose. This is relevant for, e.g. barracks and kiosks. The connection to the ground here is of a purely economic quality. Likewise, under the Greek Statute 4112/1929, the permanent machines and facilities of a company are treated like immoveable things. They are viewed as stand-alone things and are thus compulsorily auctioned independently from the building (Protodikeio Trikala 349/1997, Harm. 51 [1997] p. 1502). However, in contrast to Art. 1282 Greek Civil Code (extension of the hypothec to accessories), Statute 4112/1929 does not test whether the land unit owner acquired the machines through a transaction. The right of ownership, like every other property right of third parties to the machines, lapses permanently. The land unit owner acquires the ownership of the machines originally and *ipso iure*, even if they were bought under a retention of title or merely leased or borrowed. A counter-exception only exists in the case of a leasing contract (Art. 4(2) Greek Statute 1665/1986).

[93] e.g. Czech law only reintroduced the rule of *superficies solo cedit* in § 506(1) Czech Civil Code [2014]. This rule does not apply in Lithuania (see, for further details, *Rozenfelds*, Juridica International 6/2001, pp. 108, 109, and *CLC/Baltmane&Bitans*, Grundeigentum and Sicherheiten in Lettland, p. 3 [the problem is solved thus: the building owner is granted the right *ex lege* to lease the used land unit in exchange for compensation; § 3056 Czech Civil Code grants the building owner a right of first refusal]) or Slovakia (§ 120 Slovakian Civil Code) to this day.

is concerned with the property law of connection *per se*; rather, they are extra-legal interventions (based on economic or social policy considerations).[94] Ultimately, the relegation of a thing to the status of a non-independent part of a land unit, in the absence of some dedication to a specific use, is a matter of the law of mixture. Think, for example, of fallen leaves and windfall that rots down into humus, of fertilizer and pesticide,[95] and of liquids that—intentionally or unintentionally—seep into the soil.

The loss of 'thing status' in favour of a land unit in virtue of dedication to a certain use is often evident in the vernacular used to describe things. 'Concrete' in an excavation only becomes a 'foundation' because it was brought to the site in order for a building to be constructed upon it; concrete that spills from a cement truck onto someone's lawn remains a lump of concrete, and only becomes a piece of that land unit when it is inseparably mixed with the soil.[96] 'Seeds' need the soil to develop into grain; they accordingly become part of the land unit and pass into the ownership of the land unit owner as soon as they are sown. 'Seed stock' stored in a silo, on the other hand, remains an independent thing, and a tradable commodity. Borderline cases, however, can only be determined on a case-by-case basis, taking all the circumstances into consideration and with reference to the jurisprudence of the relevant legal system. In general, one asks first whether the connection with the soil is permanent or only temporary,[97] whether **9.18**

The previous Czech law and the current Slovakian law consider only what is solidly connected to the land unit and is not a 'building' as an essential land unit component (*Eliáš et al.*, Občanský zákoník. Velký akademický komentář I, p. 494). Thus, it frequently had to be decided at which point in the construction or under which other circumstances a 'building' existed. Tennis courts and other sports fields were not 'buildings', but land units or land unit components (CFI Hradec Králové, 19 Co 82/2004, Soudní rozhledy, no. 8/2005); the same applied to a terrace (Czech Nejvyšší soud České republiky 17 September 2002, 22 Cdo 2918/2000, Soudní rozhledy, no. 3/2003).

[94] This can be clearly seen in Latvian law. Under Art. 968 Latvian Civil Code, firmly connected buildings are viewed as part of the ground. *Rozenfelds*, Journ. Univ. Latvia: Law 5 (2013) pp. 120–36 expands on this. However, this does not apply if the land was returned to its original owner. It was obviously expected that the rules of restitution of the reinstated right to ownership would lead to a continual 'pruning' of the legal relationships concerned; Rozenfelds explains, however, that the amount of 'divided' ownership actually increased over time. In the Czech Republic, and in other countries of the former Eastern Bloc, the abolition of the principle of *superficies solo cedit* led to agricultural production cooperatives and other collectives becoming the owners of the buildings located on the farmers' land.

[95] Czech Nejvyšší soud České republiky 24 March 2004, 29 Odo 207/2002, Soubor rozhodnutí Nejvyššího soudu 2007, C 2902.

[96] If the required dedication to a specific use is lacking, then not even the fixed connection causes a moveable thing to lose its quality as a thing under Italian law (Cian and Trabucchi [*-Pellegrini*], Commentario breve[8], p. 779). This is no different under the doctrine of 'apparent' components.

[97] e.g. under Kap. 2 § 1 Swedish JB, buildings, conduits, fences, and other facilities which were *fixed into or onto the ground for lasting use* belong to a land unit. Under § 95 German Civil Code, things which are only connected to the soil for a temporary purpose do not count among components of a land unit. Art. 8 Slovenian SPZ states that 'everything which by intention is permanently affixed to or is permanently on an immoveable, above it or below it, is an element of the immoveable, except where the law provides otherwise'. By contrast, a general rule regarding the connection of real things and land units is absent in the Austrian Civil Code, as it was in all previous codifications. It was left at a series of individual provisions. At their core, they amount to the same principle: if it is permanently connected to the land unit, it becomes the land unit's dependent component. § 297 Austrian Civil Code provides that buildings count as immoveable things. Nothing follows from this in the issue of the building ownership, but it is uncontested that the principle of *superficie solo cedit* effects that no separate ownership of buildings is created (*Ostheim*, ÖJZ 1975 p. 202). It remains important that the building or the thing connected to the land unit is fixed to it for a permanent purpose (OGH 17 December 1980, JBl 1981 p. 479; *Ostheim* op. cit. p. 205). See also OGH 22 March 1993, SZ 68/33 (Itan air raid bunker [*Luftschutzstollen*], which the German occupying force had constructed in the Second World War. The OGH decided that the bunker had not been constructed with a permanent purpose. It was thus a temporary building capable of being the object of separate rights [*Superädifikat*],

the (economic or aesthetic) purpose of the object can only be realized through interaction with the soil of a land unit (and perhaps even the soil of a *specific* land unit), and whether the chosen method of connection is such that it would be taken by an objective bystander to be directed to the construction or maintenance of a building on the land.

9.19 Presentation of the details on this point would require an independent commentary. The judicial decisions of the European jurisdictions have addressed an almost endless variety of questions; the results diverge considerably, as one might expect. One cannot, however, place too much importance on this fact. The factual scenarios are almost never completely the same. The category of light constructions—including greenhouses,[98] wooden modular buildings,[99] pre-fabricated garages,[100]

which should be treated as a moveable thing according to established judicial opinion [e.g. OGH 28 June 2011, JBl 2011 p. 788]. The bunker was thus the property of the builder [*in casu* this was the state of Austria], not the property of the land unit owner. Thus, the latter could demand the removal of the *Superädifikat*).

[98] There exists extensive jurisdiction pertaining to glass greenhouses. It Italian law, it is a question of whether they are (permanently) fixed to the ground (e.g. T.A.R. Lombardia Brescia 19 November 2009, n. 2223, Foro amm. Tribunale amministrativo regionale 2009, p. 3069 and Pretura S.Remo 1 October 1987, Riv. pen. 1988, p. 286). In Cypriot law, less attention is paid to the permanence of the connection (e.g. Supreme Court 31 August 1999, *Rosary Gardens Ltd. v Υπουργού Οικονομικών* (Minister for the Economy), Case no. 805/1998 , CyLaw Database). In German law, BGH 16 November 1973, MDR 1974 p. 298 states, applying § 94(2) German Civil Code (things introduced in the construction of a building become land unit components), that it is sufficient for a greenhouse to be set on a foundation constructed for this purpose. Arrondissementsrechtbank 's-Gravenhage, 12 September 2012, HA ZA 11-2004, NJF 2012 p. 453 concerned a growing system (not a greenhouse) for tomatoes. The court rejected the argument that this was not a component of the greenhouse within the meaning of Art. 3:4(2) Netherlands Civil Code on doubtful grounds. It was said that, while the open-topped pipes had been specifically constructed for the greenhouse in one long piece and rolled out on location to prevent leakage, they could still be easily cut and taken away. They would lose value and functionality this way, but this was deemed unimportant.

[99] There is a clear tendency to qualify these as belonging to the land unit. For example, Administrative Court Bydgoszcz 15 March 2006, I SA/Bd 26/06, Lex-No. 521525 states that while buildings must have a foundation, not every permitted type of building fulfils this requirement. The building must not be able to be removed without destroying it, and it cannot have been constructed for a merely temporary purpose. The court affirmed that a wooden holiday home, located on several foundation bases which were sunk into the ground and which were themselves connected to the wooden construction with bricks, was subject to land tax obligations. The house was also connected to the public supply network. The German BFH 4 October 1978, NJW 1979 p. 392 emphasizes that the statute does not explicitly state how strongly the structure must be embedded into the ground to qualify as a fixed connection within the meaning of § 94(1) German Civil Code. As a result, every connection which grants the structure the stability it needs for its purpose must suffice. It is therefore sufficient for a prefabricated wooden house to have wooden stakes in the ground as its foundation. LG Konstanz 20 March 1981, ZIP 1981 p. 512 (confirmed by OLG Karlsruhe 11 November 1982, Justiz 1983 p. 13) ruled that a prefabricated wooden house, which is constructed on top of a concrete foundation created for this purpose as well as one with piles and wooden joists, becomes an essential land unit component. BGH 10 February 1978, NJW 1978 p. 1311 stated that a prefabricated wooden house that does not have a fixed connection with the foundation becomes an essential land unit component, if it rests on the foundation due to its own high weight. This is why a retention of title in a prefabricated house loses its effect. A fixed connection is present if the structure is merely held to the land unit by its own weight, as long as this weight is equivalent to being 'anchored'. A differing view would have the unsatisfactory result that prefabricated houses could not be financed by types of finance for immoveables. The Supreme Court of Cyprus reached the same conclusion in Supreme Court 8 March 2000, *China Wanbao Engineering Corporation & A. Panayides Contracting Ltd. v Κυπριακής Δημοκρατίας, μέσω Εφόρου Προστιθέμενης Αξίας* (Republic of Cyprus), Case no. 518/1999, CyLaw Database. See for Greek law, *Triantos*, AK, Art. 954 no. 3.

[100] Polish Sąd Najwyższy 11 February 1998, III CKN 358/97, LexPolonica-No. 2212138, Lex-No. 519925 rejected their quality as components because they do not have foundations. In contrast, German BFH 4 October 1978, NJW 1979 p. 392 affirmed it even without a foundation or other form of anchoring. Likewise OLG Düsseldorf 26 May 1981, BauR 1982 p. 164 (concerning a garage which had been mounted on a sill which in turn had been laid on a level plane without an anchor; the connection must be intended to be permanent) and BayObLG 11 November 1988, WuM 1989 p. 93 (prefabricated garages, which are set up on the soil without a foundation, are essential land unit components in virtue of their own weight. The constructive parts of the prefabricated garages was therefore communal property). The Bulgarian Court of Cassation 29 April 2009, no. 266, III. civil chamber considers

tents,[101] huts, kiosks, pavilions, and barracks—is particularly important. Huts, kiosks, pavilions, and barracks have often been held to be components of the land unit on which they stand even when they do not rest on a foundation.[102] It is occasionally suggested that the 'ground' on which they rest can include the surface of a body of water, a firmly anchored pontoon bridge has thus been held to form part of a land unit with water.[103] Another point of emphasis in the judicial decisions is technical constructions (e.g. wind power installations,[104] driveable harbour cranes,[105] traffic lights,[106] irrigation equipment,[107] weighbridges,[108] and so

pavilions and garages which can be transported using a crane to be moveable things. The same applies to all structures which can be transported from one location to another without dismantling them into their individual parts.

[101] e.g. Supreme Court of Cyprus 4 April 2013, *Σαββάκης Αριστείδης v Δήμου Γερμασογειας* (*Savvakis Aristides v Council of Yermosoyia*), Case no. 115/2011, CyLaw Database (The construction in question was deemed to be a building due to its size and shape, the materials used and because it was attached to the ground as well as to the neighbouring structure).

[102] See for Italian law also Cian and Trabucchi (*-Pellegrini*), Commentario breve[8], p. 779 and the judgments of the Court of Cassation cited therein, and for Swedish law HD 1 March 1996, NJA 1996 p. 139 (a shed or storehouse is not land unit *tillbehör*). For German law, BGH 10 February 1978, NJW 1978 p. 1311; JZ 1978 p. 396 states that a prefabricated pavilion set on purpose-built concrete pilings becomes an essential land unit component. It is sufficient that the pavilion and the base form an integrated structure. It was said to be insignificant that the stakes or pilings could be removed from the ground with a more or less great technical effort. Polish law has a tendency to be more cautious. The requirement is, on principle, for masts, billboards (Administrative Court in Warsaw 9 April 2014, VIII SA/Wa 1035/13, Lex-No. 1468420 stated that the frame of a billboard is not a component of the land unit) and also for barracks, pavilions, and similar structures, a solid connection to a foundation under Art. 48 Polish Civil Code (Polish Sąd Najwyższy 11 February 1998, III CKN 358/97, LexPolonica-No. 2212138, Lex-No. 519925). An interesting historical observation is made by *Stutz*, FS Gierke, pp. 1187, 1250. Despite the fact that churches in the Middle Ages, typically made only of wood, should have been considered moveable things (what can burn is a moveable; '*was die Fackel verzehrt, ist Fahrnis*'), they were apparently never considered as such. This is explained by the fact that the altar at least would have had a solid connection to the ground and would have been considered the principal thing.

[103] Under Art. 812(2) Italian Civil Code, mills, baths, and other floating structures count among immoveables, if they are permanently and solidly anchored to the shore or riverbed for their use. Art. 334(9) Spanish Civil Code counts as immoveables structures, even those which float on water, which are intended to remain in a fixed point of a river, lake, or coast. See also, for Swedish law, *Håstad*, Sakrätt[6], p. 31, as well as (regarding a pontoon bridge) Hovrätten för Västra Sverige 30 December 1985, RH 1986:84. Swedish HD 10 October 1997, NJA 1997 p. 660 concerned a floating dock. It was, according to the court, an essential component of an industrial company (*Industritillbehör*) if it is included in a land unit that is entirely or partially equipped for industrial enterprise and is mainly used for this enterprise. These things only do not belong to the land unit if a declaration to that effect from the land unit owner has been registered in the relevant part of the cadastral records (Kap. 13 § 9,Kap. 24 §§ 1 and 3 JB). In Netherlands law, Hoge Raad 15 January 2010, NJB 2010 no. 189 concerned a houseboat. This was ruled a moveable thing, even if it cannot move by itself and can only be towed a few metres from its berth as the surrounding bridges are too low. The boat would not even become an immoveable if it were connected to the communal water and electricity network. *Chelsea Yacht and Boat Co. Ltd. v Pope* [2000] 1 WLR 1941 (CA) takes the same approach.

[104] These are typically land unit components if they are located within the territory of a state and do not belong to the category of 'apparent components'; cf. Supreme Court of Cyprus 10 June 2011, *D.K. Windsupply Ltd. v Κυπριακή Δημοκρατία*, Case no. 1387/2009, CyLaw Database (The judgment mainly concerned the generator's and wind gauge's quality as components. While their service life was shorter and their value higher than the remaining facility, they formed an essential component of a structure within the meaning of the law).

[105] Hoge Raad 24 December 2010, LJN BO3644 (affirmed as an immoveable).

[106] Polish Sąd Najwyższy 11 January 2006, II CKS 65/05, Lex-No. 191130 (a traffic light constitutes a land unit component; an agreed retention of title over it and the corresponding claim for delivery based in Art. 222 § 1 Polish Civil Code thus lapse).

[107] See, for a so-called 'improvement facility', Czech Nejvyšší soud České republiky 28 January 1998, 3 Cdon 1305/96, Soudní rozhledy no. 8/1998, as well as Czech Constitutional Court 24 May 1994, Pl. ÚS 16/93, Sbírka nálezů a usnesení Ústavního soudu České republiky, vol. 1 p. 189 no. 25, and for a drainage system in a moor Czech Nejvyšší soud České republiky 28 January 1998, 3 Cdon 1305/96, Soudní rozhledy no. 8/1998 (both were affirmed as immoveables).

[108] Polish Sąd Najwyższy 28 June 2002, Glosa 2003/3 str. 47, Prawo Bankowe 2002/12 str. 17 (LexPolonica-No. 358693, Lex-No. 56604) (To decide the question of whether certain elements constitute parts of a composite thing,

forth).[109] Gravestones and burial sites are also the subject of a very diverse set of judicial decisions, often unusually complex in virtue of the public law considerations that intersect with property law in this context.[110]

(3) Connection with Buildings

9.20 If real things are connected to a building, the question arises intuitively (as it does in the context of the mixture of real things) whether the object can be removed from the building without physical damage to either.[111] The test often works unproblematically. Stones cannot be removed from a wall and a wall cannot be removed from its foundation without causing damage. Joists cannot be removed from between the stories of a building; the floor of one storey (and ceiling of the storey below it) would collapse. As a result, any attempted retention of title in such objects will be extinguished upon installation; they form a '*partie intégrante*' of the building.[112] By way of contrast, a rotary press does not become part of the land unit (*immeuble par nature*) simply in virtue of being installed (even if screwed down) onto a concrete surface. They remain subject to a retention of title by the supplier. According to the French

both the physical and the functional connections between the things must be taken into account. If the things constitute an economic whole, then they are components of a composite thing, even if this whole can be easily dismantled. The case in question had apparently concerned such a whole, so a separate security interest in the form of an ownership right in the weighbridge could not be created. The scale in question was composed of numerous physically and functionally connected parts. Its steering elements were located in a particular building, which had been expressly constructed for it in consideration of special construction law provisions; without this building the steering elements could not have functioned properly).

[109] According to the interpretations of Czech law, a heat exchanger (Nejvyšší soud České republiky 25 June 2002, 28 Cdo 990/2002, Soubor civilních rozhodnutí a stanovisek 2002 no. C 1379) and a transformer (Nejvyšší soud České republiky 26 February 2008, 22 Cdo 1118/2007, Soubor civilních rozhodnutí a stanovisek, 2007 no. C 6035) are not land unit components. CA Debrecen, Gf. II. 30371/2013/4; BDT2014.19, Bírósági Döntések Tára 2/2014, 7-10 rejected an industrial plant as a component, CA Poznan 18 January 2013, I ACa 736/12, Lex-No. 1283363 likewise rejected a mechanical ventilator mounted above a fireplace exit. By contrast, a gravity ventilator, like heating and sewer pipes, are a component of the immoveable. See also Cass. 17 November 2004, no. 21730, Mass. Giust. civ. 2011, 1, p. 32. The case concerned large silos for olive oil, whose stability largely hinged on their own weight. The Court of Cassation nevertheless applied the doctrine of accession and held the silos to be components of the immoveable (whose value they surpassed). The decisive factor was that the physical connection brought about a 'complex good'. The purpose of the connection was thus crucial. A good consequently remains a moveable thing under Art. 812 Italian Civil Code if it is only provisionally connected with the ground or required this for its own functionality.

[110] A good example can be found in Polish Sąd Najwyższy 29 September 1978, III CZP 56/78, OSNCP 1979/4 poz. 68, OSNPG 1979/2 poz. 13 str. 36, LexPolonica-No. 301283, Lex-No. 2309. The case concerned a walled burial place. The court held that this was not an object of separate ownership withing the meaning of Art. 47 §§ 1 and 2 Polish Civil Code. The decision of who was to be buried in this family burial place must thus be taken jointly by the persons who paid the costs of the construction, the persons who had paid the fee, and the persons who, as close family members, certainly had a claim to be buried there. If they could not agree (*in casu*, the son from a first marriage resisted the burial of his deceased father's second wife, who had only been married to his father in church), then the court must decide. Areopag 100/2011, NoB 59 (2011) p. 1603 ruled that while the graves as well as the cafeteria (for a traditional post-funeral coffee) were land unit components, they belonged to the public domain. This has the consequence that the graves and the cafeteria are *extra commercium*. Private parties could only be granted a separate right of use.

[111] For two examples, see Art. 110(1) Bulgarian LPA and § 55(1) Estonian Civil Code. The latter provision states that all things from which the building was constructed and which are permanently connected to it and cannot be separated from it without damage to itself or the building are essential components of a building.

[112] Paris 30 April 1993, D. 1993, Somm. p. 291, note by *Pérochon*.

Cour de cassation, there is no 'incorporation' of the type required by the doctrine of accession. The attachment of the plant was simply '*destiné à permettre à la machine de fonctionner normalement, ce système de fixation n'avait pas eu pour conséquence de la rendre indissociable de son support en béton de manière définitive et irrémédiable et ne pouvait donc empêcher son démontage*'. The machine could, without further ado, be removed from the floor.[113] Rugs simply resting on the floor do not lose their independence as objects of property rights; a carpet that is attached to the floor, on the other hand, is subsumed within the right of ownership in a land unit. Rugs that are not glued to the surface of the floor but are attached by means of corner mouldings present a borderline case;[114] some courts have been inspired by such cases to rarefied heights of theory.[115] A balcony is part of the external envelope of a building, insofar as (and because) its construction is integrated into the external cladding of the building. Its parts (but, according the judicial dicta of certain German first instance courts, not the 'space' they form) are thus objects of the right of ownership of *all* the apartment owners in a building, even when the balcony is accessible only from one apartment (unless there is some specific statutory rule to the contrary).[116] By way of contrast, agricultural sprinkler systems, pumps, fuel supply systems, car wash facilities, and illuminated signs remain separate objects of the right of ownership insofar as they can be disassembled and removed at will.[117]

[113] Cass. civ. 12 February 1991, Bull. civ. 1991, IV, no. 69, p. 47; D. 1993, Somm. p. 291, note by *Pérochon*.

[114] See, from the (not entirely consistent) German judicial decisions, e.g. LG Hamburg 19 December 1978, NJW 1979 p. 721; LG Köln 15 June 1979, NJW 1979 p. 1608, and KG 8 December 1998, VersR 1999 p. 617.

[115] OLG Köln 1 April 2003, VersR 2004 p. 105, e.g. developed a term for the component in accordance with insurance law—apparently expressly for carpeted floors. The reason given for this was that the question had only been posed from the perspective of insurance law. The court stated that a consideration only in property law in accordance with §§ 93 and following German Civil Code would be insufficient in the majority of cases. Thus, a definition of the building components from the perspective of insurance law were required. This was based on the intended distinction between the areas of house contents insurance and home insurance. An average insured party would concentrate on this point. The home insurance would typically cover the risk of substance damage to the building, while the house contents insurance covered damage to the furniture or and things for use or consumption. Fitting a carpet supported its characterization as a building component. The carpet typically could not be reused after this. This circumstance alone was, however, not decisive. A fitted carpet could become a building component if the building was not ready for occupancy without it. The fitted carpet would then be included in the building to make it habitable. This should be assumed if the fitted carpet is placed directly on the floor. In the presence of flooring underneath the carpet which made the building habitable, such as parquetry or tiles, this decision would have to rest on the manner of fastening of the carpet to the floor. Were the carpet only loosely placed on the floor or fastened in such a way that its possible and indeed intended removal would not cause damage to the floor, then the carpet would be furniture and thus house contents. Were the carpet fastened to the floor in a way that, upon its removal, would necessarily damage the floor, then the carpet would be a building component.

[116] CFI Hradec Králové 5 September 2003, 52 Ca 25/2003-107, Sbírka rozhodnutí Nejvyššího správního soudu 3/2004, no. 136; Cass. civ. 27 March 2008, Bull. civ. III, no. 59, p. 54, and Cass. 29 January 2003, Bull. civ. III, No. 19, p. 18 (a balcony were a part of common ownership [*partie commune*], not separate property [*partie privative*]; a special right of use would not change this [*Bergel/Bruschi/Cimamonti*, Les biens[2], p. 624 no. 556; *Terré and Simler*, Les biens[8], p. 533 no. 636]). Areopag 731/2001, EllDni 42 (2001) p. 939 was concerned with a similar problem (this time the case concerned a cellar which could only be accessed through one apartment). The court ruled that with the contract of sale in question, an ownership interest in the stairwell concerned was also acquired. Since the establishment of horizontal ownership, the stairwell, and with it the cellar which it opened, was exclusively owned by the plaintiff. The stairwell only served the property of the plaintiff, and also represented the only access to the cellar.

[117] Areopag 1013/2004, Isokrates-Database; OLG Celle 18 March 2003, OLGR Celle 2003 p. 299. See also, regarding this differentiation, Austrian OGH 15 March 1972, SZ 45/29 (pipes laid within the brickwork are a component of the building).

9.21 It is not possible, however, simply to apply the rules governing the mixture of real things to the connection of real things with land units; the results would be unsatisfactory in several respects. Roofing tiles,[118] installed windows and doors,[119] heating and cooling equipment,[120] and elevators[121] would not necessarily form part of the property of the building and land unit owner. That would be unacceptable because it would prevent any sensible use and management of, let alone commerce in, land units. Besides this, proceedings to enforce security rights in building components would leave real estate as a veritable ruin and in so doing quickly render rural and urban landscapes alike unliveable. There must therefore exist rules that allow such objects as can be removed from buildings *without* physical damage to be characterized as non-independent building components. Some European legal systems stipulate that the decisive criterion is whether the (erstwhile) real thing was installed in the building in the course of its 'construction',[122] but then hasten to add that things serving the 'completion' (i.e. 'finishing') of a building also serve its 'construction'.[123] In any case, what is really operative

[118] e.g. in the case of Swedish HD 25 September 1986, NJA 1986 p. 513, A had lived with his girlfriend (B), had paid for a fence, a terrace, and roof tiles for her house, and had connected them to the ground or to the house. A and B ended their relationship. The court rejected A's claim for delivery. While objects that a usufructuary (*nyttjanderättshavare*) or some other person includes in a land unit generally become a part of the land unit only when ownership of the land unit and of the separate object coalesce in the same person (Kap. 2 § 4 JB), this case concerned building and land unit components (*fastighetstillbehör* and *byggnadstillbehör*) within the meaning of Kap. 2 §§ 1 and 2 JB. The objects had been fitted to a specific immoveable. Such objects are intended to remain on the land unit almost without exception. It would thus be the natural approach to qualify them as a part of the right of ownership in the land unit. In other words: the case must be viewed as if A had transferred the ownership to the objects to B. Special circumstances (*särskilda omständigheter*) which would speak against this were not given.

[119] e.g. see Czech Nejvyšší soud České republiky 14 September 2006, 28 Cdo 2628/2005, ECLI CZ:NS:2006:28.CDO.2628.2005.1. A fire door is a component of the building, as its removal would disturb the functionality of the building and would devalue it. The devaluation was ruled to consist of the danger to the building's safety. See also CA Piräus 1426/1995, ArchN 47 (1996) p. 697, as well as Areopag 560/1992, EllDni 34 (1993) p. 1481 (components of a building were said to be all things that were fixed to the building so it could function as intended, meaning the building materials used for the foundations, the walls and the roof, as well as the stairs, window wings, window panes, doors, fitted carpets, the boiler, wash basins, baths, electric and hydraulic installations, central heating, heaters, the telephones, and the elevators).

[120] Their quality as components is confirmed by Czech Nejvyšší soud České republiky 16 February 2011, 21 Cdo 230/2010, ECLI CZ:NS:2011:21.CDO.230.2010.1 and Cass. civ. 2 March 1999, JCP 1999, II, 10180, p. 1841, note by *Cutajar* (The plaintiff had delivered and installed, subject to a retention of title, heating and ventilation equipment, as well as the water pipes and sanitary facilities for the immoveable of a company which later became insolvent. An application for recognition of its right of ownership in the goods, made after the opening of settlement proceedings, was rejected. The goods in question had been incorporated into the immoveable; they thus ceased to exist in nature. Therefore, the retention of title did not have any effect for the remaining creditors, notwithstanding its validity between the plaintiff and the company). cf. also BGH 13 March 1970, BGHZ 53 pp. 324, 325 (a heating installation is an essential component of a residential building) and Swedish HD 1 March 1996, NJA 1996 p. 139 (the conduits of a central vacuum system are general land unit *tillbehör*, likewise the necessary engine).

[121] e.g. see STJ 31 January 1996, BMJ 453 (1996) p. 46 (an elevator is a building component; a retention of title clause expires upon its installation). The same conclusion is reached by CA Thessaloniki 339/1968, Harm. (23) 1969 p. 36 and TS 22 December 2010, RAJ 2011 no. 17 p. 59 (a condominium owners' association could not decide, against the will of a shop owner, to install an elevator if the elevator shaft would lead through the shop; this would be a violation of his property).

[122] Thus, approximately, Art. 954(2) Greek Civil Code, § 94(2) German Civil Code, and § 55(1) Estonian Civil Code.

[123] This was ruled as early as RG 14 November 1938, RGZ 158 pp. 362, 367. See also, in this context, § 416 Austrian Civil Code, according to which things brought in for repair become the ownership of the owner of the principal thing.

is the purpose for which a thing is *used*, not the manner in which it is *connected* to a building. Everything that is dedicated permanently to the creation of a unique building is part of the building, and by default therefore also part of the land unit.[124]

The English law doctrine of 'fixtures' also works with both criteria—the factual and the purposive. Objects that are 'fixed' to land are, in principle, part of that land. The law of fixtures determines the situations in which a corporeal moveable thing (in English legal parlance, a 'chattel') passes into the 'property' of a landowner or mortgagee in virtue of the creation of some firm connection. Since *Hellawell v Eastwood*,[125] the test comprises two limbs. The first limb of the test looks at the manner in which the chattel is 'annexed' to the soil or to the structure of the building, how firm the annexation is, and whether it can be removed without causing damage to either the chattel itself or the structure of the building. The second limb looks to the purpose of the annexation, that is, whether it serves the permanent and material improvement of the building, is merely for a temporary purpose, or whether the annexation is in fact for the realization of the use of the object itself as a chattel.[126] A high degree of physical attachment might offset the fact that it cannot be proved that the chattel was brought to the land unit in order permanently to improve a building (and *vice versa*). With the same result as a recent French *Cour de cassation* decision,[127] certain machines were characterized in *Hellawell v Eastwood* as 'fixtures' on the basis that their attachment to the floor only served to make them stationary and thus functional *as chattels*. According to Bridge, the position would be no different in the case of a rug nailed to the floor in order to keep it spanned, or in the case of curtains, mirrors, pictures and other objects of a decorative nature nailed to the walls. A chattel that rests on the floor solely by its own weight is, in case of doubt, no fixture. The position is different, however, when the chattel is material to the use of land[128] or can only be removed from the soil on which it rests by demolition.[129] In *Holland v Hodgson*, Blackburn J explained the difference with the example of stones. If they are laid on top of each other to form a dry stone wall, they are 'fixtures'; if the same stones are stacked in the same way only for the purposes of storage on a 9.22

[124] CA Piräus 1426/1995, EllDni 38 p. 1669. The supporting materials for the Swedish JB state that something must be fastened in such a way that a 'community of purpose' between the object and the building becomes clear (*Anbringats i sådant samband med denna, som motsvarar föremålets ändamålsgemenskap med byggnaden*) (SOU 1947:38 p. 95; see also *Håstad*, Sakrätt[6], p. 31 and HD 16 October 1997, NJA 1997 p. 699). Cass. 17 November 2004, no. 21730, DVD Juris Data is also clear in this regard. The case concerned the turbines of a hydroelectric power station, which had been integrated into a building. The court qualified the turbines as immoveable things, as they were a component of a uniform structure. Without the turbine, the building would not have been a hydraulic power station, and without the building the turbine would not have been able to generate power.

[125] (1851) 6 Ex 295; 155 ER 554. See from more recent times *Berkley v Poulett* [1977] 1 EGLR 86 (CA) and *Elitestone Ltd v Morris* [1997] 2 All ER 513; [1997] 1 WLR 687 (*Lord Lloyd of Berwick*).

[126] *Bridge*, Personal Property Law[3], p. 104.

[127] Cass. civ. 12 February 1991, Bull. civ. 1991, IV, no. 69, p. 47; D. 1993, Somm. p. 291, note by *Pérochon*.

[128] *Bishop v Elliot* (1855) 11 Ex 113; 156 ER 766 left open, whether a house key was a fixture by this principle, but it is probable that no one would seriously answer this question in the affirmative.

[129] Such as a chalet which lies on concrete pillars (*Bridge* op. cit. with reference to *Elitestone Ltd v Morris* [1997] 2 All ER 513; [1997] 1 WLR 687).

construction site, they remain 'chattels'.[130] The dedication of chattels to a given purpose implicit in bringing them onto a land unit, however, must also be reflected objectively in the manner of connection—that is, it must be recognizable to third parties.[131] The concept of 'fittings', however, that is common in the usage of real estate agents has no technical meaning in English law.[132]

9.23 Always relevant is the creation and maintenance of the purposive function of a particular type of building, often indeed of a particular building itself. Different considerations apply to a modest detached home[133] and a manorial estate building,[134] a research institute and an industrial plant, a hotel and a museum,[135] a house in the warmer climes of a country and a house in its temperate zones.[136] The particular features of a particular building may also reveal whether an object found within it is merely being stored there temporarily or not. If so, it is not a component of the building, and does not affect its characterization.[137] If, on the other hand, certain wares have been brought to a place for the construction of a new building and are actually used for that, the right of ownership in them passes naturally to the land unit owner—even when the supplier has (attempted to) retain his title pending full payment of the purchase price.[138]

[130] (1872) LR 7 CP 328.

[131] *Melluish (Inspector of Taxes) v BMI (No 3) Ltd* [1996] AC 454, 473 (Lord Browne Wilkinson).

[132] *Haydon-Baillie v Bank Julius Baer & Co Ltd* [2007] EWHC 1609 (Ch) (Morgan J) (The case concerned complicated real security rights in a castle complex. The question was, among others, what exactly was the subject of the mortgage? Morgan J doubted at para. 35 'if the word "fittings" has a sufficiently precise general meaning so as to exclude things which are in law chattels' and added at para. 105: 'In my judgment, the word does not have a precise legal meaning.' He then clarified at para. 198: 'Whether the protected fittings became fixtures depends upon whether they were sufficiently annexed to the land to become part of the land. The question as to "sufficient annexation" depends upon the extent and also the purpose or object of the annexation').

[133] e.g. BGH 13 March 1970, BGHZ 53 pp. 324, 325 (a heating installation is an essential building component of a residential building). For Swedish law, HD 1 March 1996, NJA 1996 p. 139 ruled that a built-in dishwasher was land unit *tillbehör*. Even though this position would not have been taken at the time of the JB's drafting, a built-in dishwasher were so frequent today that it must be intended for the building's permanent use.

[134] e.g. RG 14 November 1938, RGZ 158 p. 362 (the so-called *Wolfenbüttler Zimmer* in the Braunschweiger Schloss; the wood panelling was judged an essential component of the castle).

[135] CA Nafplion 8/1959, NoB (7) 1959 p. 840, rightly stated that it depends if it is the thing which makes the building a hotel, a factory, or a residential building (for which reason the court *in casu* qualified the machines in question as building components).

[136] e.g. BGH 21 May 1953, NJW 1953 p. 1180 worded it cautiously, stating that at any rate, in Northern Germany, a finished residential building must be furnished with a complete heating system and a cooking area in the kitchen; in this case they were thus essential building components within the meaning of § 94(2) German Civil Code. (On the other hand, a fitted kitchen composed of serially manufactured parts is usually neither an essential component, nor an accessory according to the usage current in the relevant district: see OLG Düsseldorf 19 January 1994, NJW-RR 1994 p. 1039.)

[137] See the materials reproduced in NJA II 1972 p. 23 on the Swedish JB.

[138] Austrian OGH 17 December 1980, JBl 1981 p. 479 (The case concerned the ownership of building materials, which had been delivered and installed with a retention of title. The OGH decided that the installation was clearly intended to remain permanently. The owner of the land unit had thus acquired ownership of the things according to § 297 or § 417 Austrian Civil Code. The retention of title clause did not hinder this, as parties are not permitted to diverge from the principle of *superficie solo cedit* in the case of a permanent connection). See also Paris 30 April 1993, D. 1993, Somm. p. 291, note by *Pérochon*.

(4) Property Law Protection of Investment in the Context of Temporally Limited Rights of Use

Persons that have been authorized to use the land of another for the construction of a building[139] require special protection.[140] Without it, the end of the period of authorized use would be attended by the alternate threats of unjustified enrichment of the land unit owner or the neglect of the land unit.[141] Lessees, usufructuariess, and those with other use rights in another's land find themselves in a different position to that of a vendor who supplies building materials and machinery for construction. Such vendors want to turn over goods; their interest is not in the land unit but in the consideration paid for the delivery of their wares. If they want to secure their claim for the purchase price with an (*erga omnes* effective) right in the land unit of another, they have to obtain such a right expressly. Lessees and usufructuaries, by way of contrast, already have rights of use in another's land unit. If those rights include the right to construct a building, conflict of values threatens to arise. The law of accession has the tendency to treat the building and the land as unit, the law governing rights of use has the tendency to treat the building and the use right as unit. After all, the person in question paid for the right to build. Of course, a legal system could resolve this conflict with a (law of obligations 9.24

[139] Corresponding problems occasionally occur with plantations; see, e.g. *Venedikov*, Novo veshtno parvo, p. 211 and Austrian OGH 28 November 1933, SZ 15/240 (plants planted in a leased tree nursery did not become the property of the land unit owner, as the contractual agreement of the parties showed that the plants were not intended to be permanently connected to the ground).

[140] A good example of this nuance is TS 27 January 2011, RAJ 2011 no. 300 p. 805. The case concerned the gift of a land unit which contained a reversion clause (*cláusula de reversion*). The defendant had been gifted a land unit with the purpose of constructing a tree nursery there, but had used the land unit for another purpose and had thus been obligated to its return (*devolución*). Compensation (Art. 361 Spanish Civil Code) or a so-called *liquidación del estado posesorio* were both eliminated by the court, as was the application of the rules of 'reverse accession' (by which the building owner can become land owner). One who builds on his own land, but must later transfer that land to another because he has not respected the conditions stipulated by the party from whom he acquired it, has no claim to the legal protection of his investment. In fact, he must return the land in the condition in which he acquired it—even if this requires demolition.

[141] Thus, see the valid criticism by *Terré and Simler*, Les biens[8], p.751 no. 856 of Art. 599(2) French Civil Code. This provision does not allow a usufructuary to claim compensation for the improvements he claims to have made, even if the value of the thing were increased. Cass. 4 November 1885, *S.* 1886, 1, p. 113 and Paris 2 May 1994, D. 1994, IR 177 applied Art. 599(2) French Civil Code to buildings constructed by the usufructuary. These are categorized as improvements, even if they are new buildings, which excludes compensation. The authors also indicate that it is inconsistent to place the usufructuary in a worse position than a possessor in bad faith, especially as the judicial *dicta* have, in the past, applied the Art. 555 French Civil Code to buildings constructed by a tenant who has failed to reach an agreement as to property relations with the owner first (e.g. Cass. Civ. 6 November 1970, Bull. Civ. 1970, III, no. 592 p. 432 and Cass. Civ. 10 November 1999, Bull. Civ. 1999, III, no. 211 p. 149). *Terré and Simler* op. cit., as well as *Dross*, Droit des biens, p. 337 no. 408 make a case to apply Art. 555 French Civil Code to all persons who construct a building on another's land. Admittedly, this does not really solve the problem. Art. 555 French Civil Code applies to *accession immobilière*, and differentiates between builders in good and bad faith. Builders who believe themselves to be the land unit owner in good faith cannot be subject to a claim to remove the facilities, plant and constructions in question by the actual owner (Art. 555(4) French Civil Code) and may claim compensation. Bad faith builders can. The land unit owner has the right to either prevent construction or to demand that the person who used the land unit in bad faith (this includes the tenant) remove buildings (Art. 555(1) French Civil Code). In the first instance, the owner must pay compensation to the builder. In the event of a heritable building right (*emphytéose*), the *emphytéote* does not have a right either to removal or to compensation at the end of the period of use (*Terré and Simler* op. cit. p. 822 no. 934). The same applies for the *bail à construction*. The land unit owner acquires ownership of all constructions upon termination of the contract, unless it has been otherwise agreed (Art. L 251-2 *Code de la construction et de l'habitation*), and does not owe compensation. The legislator thereby sought to make this kind of arrangement attractive to land unit owners (*Terré and Simler* op. cit. p. 825 no. 940).

based) compromise. Without prejudice to the *superficies solo cedit* principle (i.e. that *every* planting, construction, or other work above or below the soil belongs to the land owner: e.g. Art. 934 Italian Civil Code), this approach leaves the question of what is to occur with the building at the end of the specified period to the relevant area of law (i.e. tenancy law, law of usufruct, etc.) and addresses the remaining difficulties as a problem for the law of restitution—i.e. a matter of monetary compensation. This is the approach taken by Italian law, for example.[142] Many legal systems are not, however, satisfied with such an approach. They instead rely on the law of property itself, operating with an *erga omnes* protection that extends to the case where the land unit itself has been alienated. The same basic approach, however, produces considerable differences in translation. These arise from the manifold variables that compound in this context across the European jurisdictions. These include the uneven distribution (and different content) of use rights over the land of another,[143] the divergent borders between the 'obligations' and 'property' law,[144] the different degrees of readiness to apply, by analogy, rules from the law governing property rights acquired by way of voluntary transaction to situations involving constructions built with permission or excuse,[145] and of course

[142] The tenancy law provisions, applicable *per analogiam legis* to other rights of use, are based on three fundamental rules: (i) upon termination of the contract, the tenant must return the thing to the landlord in the state in which the tenant received it (Art. 1590(1) Italian Civil Code); (ii) *miglioramenti* (improvements, Art. 1592(1) Italian Civil Code) must be compensated by the landlord if he consented to them—the tenant can then claim either the compensation for his costs or the increase in value of the land unit, depending on which amount is lesser; (iii) If improvements were made without the consent of the land unit owner, then the tenant can remove the *addizioni*, as long as this is possible without damaging the thing and the owner does not want to keep them. In this case, he must pay the lesser of the aforementioned amounts (for details, see *Torrente and Schlesinger*, Manuale di diritto privato[14], p. 691, as well as *Benincasa and Genovese*, Locazione e affitto, pp. 983–4). The right to usufruct (Arts 985 and 986 Italian Civil Code) follows the same basic rules (*Torrente and Schlesinger* op. cit. p. 291). Under Art. 986, the usufructuary can include additions, if they do not change the economic purpose of the thing.

[143] These interactions can be seen even within one and the same legal system. For example, what § 95(1) sentence 2 German Civil Code means in practice depends on whether one accepts that a usufructuary has the right to construct a building on a land unit he does not own. This was rejected by KG 23 July 1991, DNotZ 1992 p. 675 under § 1037(1) German Civil Code (which does not grant the usufructuary the right to alter or substantially change the thing); however, this matter is contested (e.g. a different result was found by OLG Celle 21 December 1951, MDR 1952 p. 744).

[144] A license to use a land unit that is structured as a real right is a much more efficient way to grant third party protection than the doctrine of 'apparent components' [*Scheinbestandteilslehre*]. This is clearly demonstrated in OLG Bamberg 18 March 2010, 1 U 142/09, Juris-Database. The case concerned rose bushes, which a lessee had planted in order to gain rose leaves to sell. The court did not qualify them as apparent components. They were thus not intended for the sale of the whole plant, but rather to gain fruits, comparable to a winegrower's vineyard. The leased land unit was auctioned following the lessor's insolvency. The new owner legally ended his contract and let the land unit to a new lessee, whose incorrect treatment of the roses rendered them essentially unusable. The first lessee's claim for damages was rejected for lack of a real right to the roses. The first lessee thereby lost any protection of his investment.

[145] Thus, for German law RG 11 May 1942, RGZ 169 pp. 172, 175 (authorized construction), as well as BGH 30 April 1958, BGHZ 27 pp. 197, 199, and BGH 26 February 1964, BGHZ 41 pp. 177, 179 ('excused' construction). By contrast, in Austrian law the general rules for building on another's land (§ 418 Austrian Civil Code) are applied (OGH 19 October 1978, SZ 51/143; OGH 13 June 1990, SZ 63/100). According to this, the neighbour generally acquires ownership of the part of the building which extends to his land unit. This is different if the neighbour does not intervene, even though he recognizes that his property is being utilized and the builder is operating in good faith (not even mere negligence). In this event, the builder acquires ownership of the built-upon area and the neighbour can only claim compensation for its value. If the extension is only slight, then § 416 Austrian Civil Code (governing connection of a real thing with a principal thing) is applied by analogy. This has the consequence that the extended part of the building becomes the property of the builder, but the builder does not acquire ownership of the built-upon area (OGH 4 December 1984, SZ 57/192).

the degree of flexibility which different codes have incorporated into their general governing accession provisions.[146]

Property law, however, has a number of alternatives ready to hand. One alternative is to accept that a 'solid' connection with the soil of another results in loss of ownership and correct this later with a real right of removal in favour of the land unit user. This is the model adopted in Italian law and by the common law systems.[147] **9.25**

The point of reference of these so-called rights of removal in English law is always a 'fixture', which belongs to the category of 'corporeal hereditaments'—i.e. non-independent components of 'land' that are upon separation transformed (back) into 'chattels' thereby become independent objects of property rights (again). The tenant of residential premises is allowed to remove things connected to the building for living amenity during or after expiration of the tenancy period (so-called 'tenant's fixtures'). A similar rule operates in commercial premises for so-called 'trade fixtures'. They admittedly become components of the land unit during their attachment, but the land unit is encumbered at the latest upon expiration of the tenant's rights to use the property with a right of removal. The right of removal is, in such cases, a subsidiary property right that flows from the tenancy, but it remains enforceable as such even against the landlord's successor-in-title. By the same token, the tenant can transfer his 'estate' (i.e. his title to use the property) for the purposes of granting a security interest to a third party.[148] Rights of removal can also form the subject matter (and even the sole subject matter) of a property right to take fruits (a so-called '*profit à prendre*'). Whether, and under what circumstances, a right of removal itself can be created as a stand-alone property right (e.g. in favour of a vendor in a retention of title clause) remains unsettled. At common law, such a property right in a legal estate (besides the *profit à prendre*) is possible in the form of a right of entry, which is created in a deed and is accompanied by an 'estate rentcharge' secured with a claim to the removal of the fixture.[149] Other than this, such rights are generally excluded.[150] In equity, a standalone right of removal is certainly conceivable—but under circumstances which the cases have not yet made entirely clear. Leaving questions of form to one side, the *erga omnes* effect of such a right would depend on (i) the land unit purchaser's knowledge of the contract of sale between the

146 For example, under Netherlands law the general provisions governing mixture support the notion that the thing which is generally only made available by a rent contract does not become a land unit component (H.R. 16 March 1980, NedJur 1980 no. 600 pp. 1957, 1962).

147 For further details, see *Rieländer*, Sachenrechtliche Erwerbsrechte, pp. 479–89.

148 e.g. see *Re Samuel Allen & Sons Ltd* [1907] 1 Ch 575 (Parker J) (Machines had been bought from a supplier for a business subject to a retention of title clause and installed by the buyer into the building leased by her as intended; the transfer of the right to garnish the goods was agreed with the seller. The court ruled that his claim took priority over the equitable mortgage to the leasehold estate which the buyer had granted a bank) and previously *The London and Westminster Loan and Discount Company Ltd v Drake* (1859) 6 CB NS 798; 141 ER 664.

149 *Melluish (Inspector of Taxes) v B.M.I. (No. 3) Ltd.* [1996] AC 454 (HL); see also *Michael Gerson (Leasing) Ltd v Greatsunny Ltd* [2010] EWHC 1887 (Ch); [2010] Ch 558.

150 This is also followed by sec. 1(2) LPA 1925. Rights to take things away are not explicitly named here as possible charges of a legal estate, but the wording in sec. 1(2)(a) LPA 1925 ('right, or privilege') leaves room for interpretation.

land unit vendor and the supplier of the goods in question, and (ii) the terms of the contract of sale over the land unit itself.[151]

9.26 The second alternative is to ensure, in violation of the *superficies solo cedit* principle, that no change of ownership in the goods occurs in the first place. Rules to that effect are found either in provisions governing the right of ownership or in provisions governing the law of things. The former approach is found in the Austrian Civil Code.[152] The latter approach is found in the doctrine of 'apparent components' [*Scheinbestandteilslehre*]. Section 95 of the German civil code introduced a particularly broad version of this doctrine into the European discourse in 1900. Numerous other jurisdictions have adopted it, for example Poland (see Art. 47 § 3 Polish Civil Code),[153] which even contains a special provision for 'facilities' that belong to an 'undertaking' that, in light of the public interest in utilities provision, must be bracketed out of a land unit owner's private property (Art. 49 Polish Civil Code).[154] This problem is known in all jurisdictions; only a few codifications address it expressly, including Estonian and Czech law.[155] The Swedish statute law uses the concept of 'apparent components' for constructions of all kinds, but generally requires a particular use right, namely the Swedish understanding of usufruct. In any case, a usufructuary retains ownership in the things he connects to the land unit.[156] Where one entitled to the use of a land unit does not lose ownership of the building on it, he can at any time dismantle it (including before the termination of his period of use) or otherwise deal with it. It does not only have the status merely as a 'moveable thing'—with all the consequences that entails.[157] In those systems that adopt this doctrine, the 'moveable things' in question do not even lapse into the land unit after the conclusion of the period of authorized use.

[151] e.g. see *Gough v Wood & Co.* [1894] 1 Q.B. 713 (CA).

[152] § 297 Austrian Civil Code states that things which are '*fest verbunden*' with the land unit should be viewed as its components. However, it follows from § 435 Austrian Civil Code that this does not apply for things which are not intended for permanent transfer. While, strictly speaking, this provision only regulates the question of ownership transfer to these things, the term '*Scheinbestandteil*' has become common for them in Austria.

[153] According to this, an object which is connected with a thing for temporary use does not become a component of the thing and even remains a separate property if it would be destroyed by the separation, such as an oven in a bakery (Polish Sąd Najwyższy 4 November 1963, I CR 855/62, OSNC 1964/10/209, Lex-No. 105481). Temporary does not mean short-lived. The time of use can be substantial. The critical factor is only that the circumstances show that the connection is not intended to be permanent (Polish Sąd Najwyższy 28 June 2002, I CK 5/02, Glosa 2003/3 p. 47, Prawo Bankowe 2002/12 p. 17, LexPolonica-No. 358693, Lex-No. 56604).

[154] These include facilities like water and sewerage.

[155] § 509 Czech Civil Code (engineering networks, water conduits or sewerage are not components of the land unit in which or on which they are located) and § 54(2) Estonian Civil Code.

[156] Under Kap. 2 § 4 Swedish JB, things which a usufructuary (*nyttjanderättshavare*) includes in a land unit only become the land unit property if the land ownership and the ownership of the thing are united in one person.

[157] Austrian law corresponds to this. There, also, such structures are regularly held to be moveable things capable of being the object of special rights (OGH 11 April 1958, SZ 31/57); their transactional acquisition is thereby subject to § 367 Austrian Civil Code, which applies to moveable things (OGH 13 June 1990, JBl 1991 p. 238). The same applies to the owner's rights to exclude (OGH 18 April 1951, *SZ* 24/104). The lack of intention to permanently retain the thing on the land unit can result from the nature of the thing (OGH 22 February 1956, EvBl 1956/148; ÖJZ 1956 p. 296 [barracks]; OGH 1 April 1953, SZ 26/83 [wooden shed]), as well as from the builder's possibly limited time of use (OGH 24 June 1971, SZ 44/101 [lease]). The burden of proof is on the party who claims that there was no intention to retain the thing (OGH 13 June 1990, JBl 1991 p. 238). Cellar buildings are a special case, as § 300 Austrian Civil Code allows separate (land) ownership to be created for them (OGH 9 September 1980, *SZ* 53/109 [underground car park]). Here, ownership of the land and of the structure are separated; on the other hand, the structure becomes a land unit in its own right.

On this point, too, the German law doctrine of components differs from the French law doctrine of accession—even though the two approaches converge in other respects in surprising ways. In Cass. 19 September 2012,[158] a father gifted a land unit to his daughter but retained a usufruct over it, and ultimately constructed dwellings on it. The case turned on the question whether the dwellings triggered any tax liability for the daughter. The tax authorities argued that they did, in reliance on Art. 551 French Civil Code. An acquisition of ownership occurred *ex lege* at the point in time of construction, through the doctrine of accession. The daughter argued that the father, as usufructuary, remained owner of the buildings that he had constructed, and that no transfer of ownership occurred. Surprisingly, the *Cour de cassation* decided in favour of the daughter. She had not been enriched through the construction of the buildings, because no accession to her property occurred at the time of construction—that would only occur when the usufruct came to an end.[159] The decision has been criticized sharply in the literature,[160] but at its core it is consistent with a line of earlier authorities. Cass. 27 September 2006 provides one example.[161] X leased a land unit to Y in 1972 to run a campground; Y proceeded to build a number of structures on it. The lease was renewed once. In 2001, Y sought a second renewal of the lease. X was in principle willing to extend, but sought a higher rent in virtue of the structures, which had increased the value of the property. The appellate court applied Art. 555 French Civil Code, holding that the owner of a land unit who does not insist on the removal of buildings at the end of a lease period becomes their owner. They remained, on the other hand, in the ownership of the tenant during the period of the tenancy, such that their value could not be included in the valuation of the land unit. The *Cour de cassation* quashed this decision. The first 'renewal' was in fact a new lease,[162] by reason of which the landlord was allowed to include the value of the buildings. The important aspect for present purposes is the court's confirmation of the rule that an accession occurs only at the end of a tenancy period—a rule that has been confirmed over and over[163] since the decision in Cass. civ. 1 December 1964.[164] It appears necessary to include (in alignment with the German law doctrine of components) that the tenant remains sole owner of the buildings he erects during the period of his tenancy.[165] What that means in practical **9.27**

[158] Bull. civ. 2012, III, no. 128 p. 117.

[159] The court did not decide whether the acquisition was then liable to taxation. *Dross*, RTD civ. 2013 pp. 141, 148 no. 5 states that such a liability is doubtful, as under Art. 599 French Civil Code the usufructuary cannot claim compensation for improvements he made or claims to have made upon termination of the usufruct, even if they increased the value of the thing. From this could be derived that there was no intention to gift the houses. The usufructuary would not relinquish his compensation, rather he is not entitled to compensation by law.

[160] For example, by *Tardos*, D. 2012 p. 2871, who criticized that the judgment implicitly conferred a *droit de superficie* to the usufructuary and thereby vertically divided the property for the duration of the usufruct.

[161] Bull. civ. 2006, III, no. 183 p. 152. See, also, Cass. 14 November 2012, in *Dross*, RTD civ. 2013 pp. 141, 149 no. 6.

[162] This is different in the case of a rent contract which was not terminated, but rather tacitly extended, Cass. civ. 4 October 1972, Bull. civ. 1972, III, no. 493 p. 360.

[163] e.g. Cass. civ. 26 November 1985, Bull. civ. 1985, III, no. 154 p. 117; Cass. Ass. Pl. 7 May 2004, Bull. Ass. Pl. 2004 no. 9 p. 19. See also *Lardeux*, RDC 2007 pp. 371–5.

[164] Cass. civ. 1 December 1964, Bull. civ. I, no. 535. The court departed from the previous authorities, which had stated that the landlord acquires ownership of the structures built by the tenant at the point of their *creation* (Cass. 14 December 1921, D.P. 1925, I, p. 111).

[165] *Dross*, Les choses, p. 755 no. 410.

terms, however, is not clear for every situation. Granted, the tenant might be permitted to demolish the house, (sub)let it, and even encumber it with a hypothec.[166] Further, in the case of damage caused to the building by a third party, he alone is entitled to compensation and bears the risk of diminution in value.[167] But it is contentious under what circumstances he may sell such a building. Some opine that sale would entail alienation of the tenancy, which would only be possible if the relevant agreement allowed this or there were some exceptional statutory right.[168] Others opine, in reliance on older authorities,[169] that property under a deferred right of accession can be sold without anything further;[170] it is said also to be subject to immoveable pledges.[171]

9.28 The doctrine of apparent components can be understood as a concretization of the fundamental principle that all things which 'permanently' inform the character of a land unit or building—but only such things—share its legal destiny. This principle derives, as mentioned earlier, from § 95 German Civil Code and is found today in Art. 955 Greek Civil Code, Art. 47 § 3 Polish Civil Code and § 55(2) Estonian Civil Code.[172] Objects that are 'only connected to the soil for a temporary purpose', as § 95(1) Sentence 1 German Civil Code formulates it, are not components of the land unit—not even when the connection is completely 'solid'. According to § 95(1) Sentence 2 German Civil Code, the same counts for a building or other structure that has been connected with the land unit of another pursuant to a right, and § 95(2) German Civil Code stipulates further that things that are only 'installed in a building' for a temporary purpose do not belong to the components of the building. § 95(1) Sentence 1 applies, first and foremost, to tenants under a lease,[173] but not to suppliers who utilize a retention of title

[166] Thus, as early as Cass. 13 December 1872, S. 1872, I, p. 104.

[167] Cass. civ. 1 December 1964 op. cit. (the case in question concerned compensation for damages incurred during the war) and Cass. civ. 02 April 2003, Bull. civ. 2003, III, no.76 p. 69.

[168] *Dross* op. cit.

[169] See, especially, Cass. 11 August 1884, S. 1885, I, p. 231 (The sale of buildings constructed by the tenant during his tenancy is subject to land tax, even if the contract provides that the tenant would remove the buildings upon termination of the contract).

[170] *Planiol/Ripert/Picard*, Les biens², p. 275 no. 279, as well as Rép. civ. Dalloz (-*Cohet-Cordey*), V° Accession, p. 10 no. 68.

[171] This position was taken as early as Rouen 20 August 1859, S. 1859, II, p. 647, as well as implicitly in Cass. 19 July 1893, S. 1894, I, p. 241.

[172] Under Art. 955 Greek Civil Code, things which are only temporarily connected to the ground do not count as land unit components. The same counts for buildings and other works generally that are connected with the land unit of another in which the builder has a real right of some kind. § 55(2) Estonian Civil Code has this wording in the English translation: 'A thing attached to a building for a temporary purpose is not a part of the building', and Art. 47 § 3 Polish Civil Code states that objects which are only connected to the thing for temporary use are not its components.

[173] In German law, *Mieter* and *Pächter*. In the case of a connection with the soil formed under a tenancy relationship for a period of time, the rebuttable presumption is that the tenant has only done so in his own interest and did intend the building to fall to the land unit owner at the end of the period (BGH 31 October 1952, BGHZ 8 pp. 1, 5). The connection is only intended for the duration of the lease, therefore for a temporary purpose (RG 19 September 1903, RGZ 55 pp. 281, 284; RG 2 June 1915, RGZ 87 pp. 43, 51; BGH 20 May 1988, BGHZ 104 pp. 298, 301; BGH 15 May 1998, NZM 1998 pp. 679, 680). This presumption does not only apply to buildings constructed by the lightweight construction method (such as a hunting box constructed by a holder of a hunting right [*Jagdpächter*]: LG Landau (Pfalz) 12 July 2002, GuT 2003 p. 227 and LG Arnsberg 19 July 1938, DJ 1939 p. 668), but also substantial constructions, which cannot be removed without destroying them (BGH 31 October 1952 op. cit.). A substantial building does not, in any case, lapse into the land unit where the relevant agreement envisages the tenant removing it on termination and restoring the land unit to its original condition (RG 23 September 1904, RGZ 59 pp. 19, 20; BGH 31 October 1952, BGHZ 8 pp. 1, 6). This can be different if the tenant and the landlord did not come to a

(whose admitted goal is the final alienation of the things in question). When tenants connect things (of their own or of a third party)[174] with a land unit in the exercise of a right in that land unit, the connection is, in case of doubt, not taken to be a permanent one but one planned for the duration of the tenancy. Section 95(1) Sentence 2, on the other hand, provides for cases where a person undertakes works on another's land unit pursuant to a real right. Here, too, the builder has ownership in the thing connected to the soil, up to and including ownership in massive buildings.

The position in Greek law accords with that in German law in almost every detail. Under Art. 955(1) Greek Civil Code, buildings and other works incorporated into a land unit pursuant to a real right remain apparent components and therefore the property of the builder. Examples include a usufructuary who has built a warehouse on the encumbered land, or the holder of a real servitude who has laid irrigation pipes in another's land. Art. 955 Greek Civil Code also applies in cases where the holder of a real right cedes his right to a third party and that third party undertakes a construction.[175] The text of Art. 955 Greek Civil Code mentions only the holders of real rights expressly, however, the provision has been applied by way of analogy to users of land units with (only) an obligational right, too (in Greek law, these include tenants, developers, and licensees).[176] The unifying criterion is, in all cases, the temporary purpose of the construction. This is determined according to commercial usage.[177] Moveable things which are only incorporated into a building for a temporary purpose, do not count as components of the building, either (Art. 955(2) Greek Civil Code). Examples include the fixtures of a usufructuary or a rental tenant.

In all legal systems, a special problem is presented by ownership relations pertaining to public utility pipelines. 'Installations for the supply and removal of liquids, steam, gas or energy, and similar installations' under Art. 49 Polish Civil Code do not become components of the buildings they serve when they belong to an undertaking. That makes sense, because the security of the population's utility supply is dependent on such provisions.[178] Electricity, television and telephone cables, water pipelines, and community heating networks are entities on whose secure functioning everyone depends; they **9.29**

specific agreement regarding the fate of the building; its solid construction thus allowing for the conclusion that the building is intended by its builder to fall to the landlord (lessor) (BGH 31 October 1952 op. cit.).

[174] The connection originator is not necessarily the owner of the things which he incorporates into the land unit, as argued (correctly) by Staudinger (*-Jickeli and Stieper*), BGB (2004), § 95 no. 23.

[175] *Triantos*, AK, Art. 955 no. 3 p. 1168; Areopag 221/2001, EllDni 42 (2001) p. 1628.

[176] *Georgiades*, Emprágmato Díkaio I, p. 108 and *Triantos* op. cit. *Georgiades* emphasizes, in accordance with Protodikeio Volos 242/1967, EllDni 8 (1967) p. 431, that Art. 955 Greek Civil Code can also be applied to use rights based in a public law provision.

[177] e.g. CA Thessaloniki 734/1973, Harm. (27) 1973 p. 686 and Areopag 1376/1978, NoB 26 (1978) p. 1063.

[178] This purpose is also served by provisions like Art. 1031 Greek Civil Code, which obligates the land unit owner to tolerate utility pipes and cables for the neighbouring land unit passing through his own. The land unit owner receives compensation in this event. This provision refers to lines for electricity, gas, and clean water, but not sewer pipes, lines for irrigation, or installations to channel sea water into a swimming pool (Areopag 1752/2001, EllDni 43 (2002) p. 1418; Areopag 4/1995, EllDni 36 (1995) p. 587; Areopag 1492/1982, EllDni 24 (1983) p. 782; CA Athens 179/1978, NoB 26 (1978) p. 12299; Areopag 1476/2008, NoB 57 (2009) p. 428).

should not be subject to the particular interests of individual land unit owners or jeopardized by the vagaries of changing ownership in land units.[179] In contrast to many legal systems, which place their reliance on the general rules of the 'apparent component' doctrine[180] or on special rules governing individual networks,[181] as the case may be (Swedish law is particularly detailed[182]), Art. 49 Polish Civil Code brings these considerations to the fore in an express provision in the codification itself.[183] This represents an exception from the general rule in Art. 48 Polish Civil Code, under which buildings and other installations permanently connected to the soil become components of the relevant land unit. A comprehensive body of judicial dicta exists on Art. 49 Polish Civil Code. Water pipelines, for example, are 'installations' in the sense of this provision,[184] as are electricity cables[185] and installations that transmit television signals.[186] A transformer housing is a component of the electricity network, not of the

[179] See e.g. for Polish law Bieniek and Rudnicki (*-Bieniek*), Nieruchomości. Problematyka prawna[5], p. 883 no. 1, as well as Polish Sąd Najwyższy 13 January 2011, III CSK 85/10, Lex-No. 686143, G.Prawna TPwF 2011/16/8 (The case concerned a privatized land unit which had previously been the property of the state. Electricity pylons and a static transformer were located on the land unit. The court rejected the lower court's construct of a 'real obligation', holding that it violated the *numerus clausus* principle of property rights. Instead, the Supreme Court made use of Art. 49 Polish Civil Code. Registering a servitude had not been necessary). By contrast, as the important factor is the security and functionality of these public networks, the owner does not have to tolerate the installation of cables in a building standing on his land unit as well (e.g. BGH 26 September 2003, NJW-RR 2004 p. 231). For further details regarding high frequency carrier cables, see *Schmittmann*, MMR 2009 pp. 520–25. Even utility lines (water, electricity) which only supply the immediately adjacent land unit, are not the property of the utility company; they are not a part of the public distribution network (BGH 10 June 2011, NJW-RR 2011 p. 1458; Bulgarian Court of Cassation 19 April 2012, 882/2011, I. Civil Chamber).

[180] See, for German law, OLG Stuttgart 1 October 2012, CR 2012 p. 783 (It is acknowledged by the courts [e.g. BGH 27 April 1994, BGHZ 126 p. 56] that communication cables—like other utility lines—are not connected with ownership of the land unit. Rather, they can be the object of certain special rights under § 95 German Civil Code. The same must also apply for the optical fibres used in telecommunications, even in the event that the applicable German telecommunication statute does not contain a corresponding provision. The construction and maintenance of a network is said to be possible only when ownership of the cables is attributed to a single entity rather than to every land unit owner [no. 30]). The quality of utility lines as apparent components is typically explained by the state's obligation to provide basic services, to which a 'right' within the meaning of § 95(1) Sentence 2 German Civil Code corresponds.

[181] This is the case, e.g. in France (Arts 649 and 650 French Civil Code explicitly refer to special provisions with regard to servitudes established for the public use). It is, however, doubtful whether the *servitudes d'utilité publiques* are really 'servitudes', as they are missing a dominant land unit (*Terré and Simler*, Les biens[8], p. 282 no. 340). They resemble the *charges réelles* which charge a land unit in the public interest much more closely (*de Bertier-Lestrade*, D. 2003 p. 587). Examples can be found in Art. L 45-9 *Code des postes et des communications électroniques* and Art. L152-1 *Code rural et de la pêche maritime* (concerning public water and sewerage lines; the licensee has a right to lay permanent underground pipes, the so-called *droit d'établir à demeure*). The question of ownership of the utility lines is not explicitly provided anywhere; furthermore, there does not appear to exist any jurisdiction in this matter.

[182] The modernized 'cable right statute' (*Ledningsrättslag* (1973:1144)), which authorizes the right-holder to lay or use lines and other installations on another's property, is especially pertinent. Public wireless communication networks and their base stations are also included (the impetus for this was HD 7 June 2004, NJA 2004 p. 336; however, the decision not to qualify base stations for mobile phone networks as 'line components' is outdated owing to § 2 no. 4 lit. (c) *Ledningsrättslag*). Furthermore, installations of line-based telecommunication, wireless and radio broadcasting (including antennae mounted on houses and aerial masts) and, of course, electricity lines (there are special statutes for high and low voltage lines) and data transfer lines also fall into this category. Water and sewerage lines are regulated separately (among others, in Kap. 2 § 1 *Ellag* (1997:857)) (for these, see HD 16 November 1982, NJA p. 700: sludge removal and other water purification plant were parts of the network), as well as heat energy supply lines and lines for the underground disposal of carbon dioxide. The statute also concerns, in § 2a, tunnels and other underground passages, if they are necessary to lay lines through a particular area.

[183] This is supplemented by the regulations in Arts 305[1]–305[4] Polish Civil Code, which concern the so-called 'plant operation servitude'.

[184] Pietrzykowski (*-Skowrońska-Bocian*), Kodeks cywilny I[4], Art. 49 no. 4, p. 202.

[185] Polish Sąd Najwyższy 13 January 2011 op. cit. (fn. 1259).

[186] Polish Sąd Najwyższy 3 December 1998, II CKN 216/98, Lex-No. 82290.

land unit on which it stands.[187] 'Installations' covered by Art. 49 § 1 Polish Civil Code are, however, only 'external installations'. Cables internal to a house are 'internal installations'.[188] Ground water wells are not subject to these provisions; they serve to access water, not distribute it, and therefore remain a component of the relevant land unit.[189] The undertaking to which a pipeline belongs is also its possessor *animo domini* (Art. 336 Polish Civil Code). The decisive factor is that the pipeline in question is connected to the network run by the undertaking.[190] The alternate opinion, that pipelines remain components of the undertaking itself,[191] has not been adopted. According to a whole line of authorities, they remain independent moveable things,[192] which can be sold and leased (in whole or in part).[193]

(5) Private Autonomy?

The question arises whether the owner of a principal thing can agree with a counterparty, with *erga omnes* effect, that something connected to a principal thing (or still a component *in situ*) should be treated as a thing in its own right in circumstances where the default statutory position casts it as a component. This question arises generally for the law governing the connection of things, but it is particularly important where real things are connected with land units. This is because, as we have seen, the connection of a real thing with a land unit is determined first and foremost by the *purpose* of the connection, and this purpose is generally determined by the parties in question (i.e. the one doing the connection and the land unit owner). To conclude (on that basis, or any other) that the law of connection was dispositive in this context,[194] however, would be **9.30**

[187] Polish Sąd Najwyższy 18 June 2004, II CK 359/2003, LexPolonica-No. 389555.

[188] Bieniek and Rudnicki (-*Bieniek*), Nieruchomości. Problematyka prawna[5], p. 886 no. 4.

[189] Polish Sąd Najwyższy 1 February 1973, II CR 673/72, LexPolonica-No. 329205, Biul. Inf. SN 1973/7 poz. 123.

[190] Polish Sąd Najwyższy 13 January 2011 op. cit.

[191] *Skowrońska-Bocian* op. cit.

[192] CA Poznań 14 July 2010, I Aca 397/09, Lex-No. 756573. The conclusion reached should also implicitly result from Art. 49 § 2 Polish Civil Code, added in the year 2008, which states that the owner of the facilities is the person who carried the costs of their construction. If this person was not the undertaking, the undertaking can request the transfer of ownership against compensation. The court concluded from this that Art. 49 Polish Civil Code did not contain a statutory acquisition of ownership mechanism.

[193] Polish Sąd Najwyższy 22 January 2010, V CSK 206/09, Lex-No. 578047.

[194] However, this appears to be the dominant view in Portuguese law. Art. 1316 Portuguese Civil Code counts accession (*acessão*) among the mechanisms of ownership acquisition. The legislative policy seems to have been that, if the relevant facts are present at the time of incorporation, the ownership acquisition should be completed *ex lege* and *ipso jure* (Art. 1317(d) Portuguese Civil Code) (*Pires de Lima and Antunes Varela*, Código Civil Anotado III[2], note 7 to Art. 1340, p. 165). Today, the industrial (but not the 'natural' accession under Art. 1327 Portuguese Civil Code: *Carvalho Martins*, Acessão, p. 24) is widely interpreted as an intentional acquisition (*Oliveira Ascensão*, Direito Civil—Reais[5], pp. 306–09; von Bar [-*de Seabra and Xavier*], Sachenrecht in Europa III, Portugal, p. 361; Tribunal da Relação do Porto 14 February 1980, CJ (1980-1) 40; STJ 5 March 1996, CJ(ST) IV (1996-1) 129, 131). In this context, there is a theory that the persons involved can settle the conflict between their ownership rights through intentional dealings, meaning that they can find solutions which differ from the statutory default position. If a structure is built on a land unit, the land unit owner may reach an agreement with the builder to the effect that the latter could benefit from accession, even if the owner is entitled to the right of accession under Art. 1340(1) or Art. 1341 Portuguese Civil Code. A usufructuary (who is the holder of the right of accession under Art. 1449 Portuguese Civil Code) could also reach an agreement with the owner that the latter should obtain the right (*Vieira*, Direitos reais, p. 711). The rules of the law of accession are not applicable if the parties concerned wanted to agree the connection of their respective things contractually in accordance with the *princípio da autonomia*

unconvincing—both for the connection of real things with a new real thing and for the connection of real things with the soil or a building. Consider the tenant of a land unit who operates a nursery on it. His trees do not remain his property because he and the landlord have so decided; they remain his because the legal system stipulates, on the basis of the existence of a lease agreement, that the plants are not intended to remain connected to the soil permanently. The decision that a connected thing is a component of the relevant land unit is made, in other words, by the law itself. The parties to a contract of sale or a licence agreement are entitled to use all the design options that the law of connections makes available to them—but they cannot break outside the framework provided to them entirely. The laws of connection and accession are, properly seen, *jus cogens.* Third parties, for example the acquiror of a land unit or a creditor with a security interest in a land unit, must know what they are getting. A higher degree of private autonomy in the context of the law of components or accession would jeopardize the necessary legal certainty. It would result in a substantial dilution of the principle that there is a *numerus clausus* of property rights. Investment in land units would be burdened by an intolerable informational cost. The stability of the real estate market, which is meant to promote the just distribution of land units, would suffer; land units would lose value because their buyers and secured creditors could never be sure of the value of what they were getting. The contrary position is, in our view, difficult to defend from a property law perspective, and contradicts the preponderance of views across the European legal systems.

9.31 The Austrian case OGH 17 December 1980,[195] for example, concerned a dispute over building materials. These were supplied subject to a retention of title provision and were installed on a permanent basis in the relevant building. The land unit owner thus, according to the court, became owner of the building materials pursuant to §§ 297 and 417 Austrian Civil Code. The retention of title clause agreed between the parties did not stand in the way, because the parties could not contract around the *superficies solo cedit* principle. The English case of *Lictor Anstalt v Mir Steel UK Ltd* concerned a hot strip mill.[196] The court determined that the agreement of the parties that the plant was not a 'fixture' was irrelevant to its legal characterization; this was a matter for the objective law. Almost at the same time, *Michael Gerson (Leasing) Ltd v Greatsunny Ltd* held that installed plant becomes a 'fixture' even when the parties have expressly agreed to the contrary.[197] The Netherlands Civil Code follows the 'unity principle' (also found in the German Civil Code), according to which a thing

privada (*Vieira* op. cit. pp. 683–4 with references to the Italian doctrine). To what extent such agreements affect third parties in reality does not appear to be clear in every detail.

[195] JBl 1981 p. 479. See, for the imperative nature of the doctrine of components, OGH 12 December 1984, JBl 1985 p. 741.

[196] [2011] EWHC 3310 (Ch); [2012] Bus LR D 84 (David Richards J). The court was not compelled to decide whether the thing in question was actually a fixture.

[197] [2010] EWHC 1887 (Ch); [2010] Ch 558 (Strauss QC); confirmed in [2011] EWCA Civ 416. The same conclusion is reached in *Melluish (Inspector of Taxes) v B.M.I. (No. 3) Ltd.* [1996] AC 454, 473 (Lord Browne-Wilkinson).

can only be an object of property rights in its entirety. Art. 5:3 Netherlands Civil Code provides that, insofar as the law does not determine otherwise, the owner of a thing is also the owner of its components. The principle of the fundamental indivisibility of property rights can thus only be derogated by law, and not by party agreement. Art. 1057 Greek Civil Code is also *jus cogens*. This provides that ownership in a land unit extends to its essential components. Agreement to the contrary (especially a retention of title clause concerning an erstwhile moveable thing) is unenforceable under this provision.[198] If, for example, the occupier of a land unit erects a structure on land owned by another or plants trees on it, the dispositive question is whether the requirements of Art. 955 Greek Civil Code (on apparent components) are fulfilled.[199] Czech Nejvyšší soud České republiky 11 August 2009 adopted equally express language.[200] Under this ruling, only a factual separation of the components, accompanied by a devaluation of the principal thing, has the legal consequence that a component becomes a thing independent from the principal thing; party agreement is insufficient. As long as a component is connected to the principal thing, the intention of the owner cannot change the fact that it is a single thing that is transferred, with all its components, unless they are named expressly in the contract of sale. The Czech Civil Code [2014] has not changed this position.[201] Granted, § 508 of the new code has created the possibility of registering a caveat in the cadastral records, which is meant to have *erga omnes* effect for the protection of all lessors and vendors that have made use of a retention of title clause. However, not even this approach demotes the *superficies solo cedit* rule to the status of a default statutory rule. The provision rather reinforces the basic premise that the purchaser of a land unit must be able, without much effort, to determine what he is buying—in this case, by looking in the register. It is undeniable, of course, that the delineation between the components of a thing and its accessories occasionally raises borderline questions; the border between mandatory and default rules can accordingly be quite 'thin'. Under Art. 817 Italian Civil Code, for example, all things that are permanently dedicated to the function or ornamentation of another thing are accessories. All the legal dealings with and legal relations concerning the principal thing extend to the accessories automatically (Art. 818(1) Italian Civil Code). The parties are, however, able to change this position by agreement. In that case, the accessories become the object of independent dealings and relations (Art. 818(2) Italian Civil Code). However, the termination of accessory status by agreement cannot affect pre-existing rights in the principal thing held by third parties (Art. 819 Italian Civil Code).

[198] Areopag 298/1963, NoB 11 (1963) p. 1191.

[199] CA Thessaloniki 2996/2005, Harm. 60 (2006) p. 876, Areopag 1882/1999, EllDni 41 (2000) p. 1629, CA Athens 8749/2004, EllDni 46 (2005) p. 840.

[200] 21 Cdo 2366/2008. In this sense also Bulgarian Court of Cassation, fist Civil Chamber, No. 386/1965 (the law of connection is mandatory law. In consequence, the owner of material lost the right of ownership permanently *ex lege*). However, *Venedikov*, Novo Veshtno pravo, p. 221 believes that the thing, which has become a moveable thing again upon separation, returns to the ownership of its former owner.

[201] *Eliáš et al.*, Nový občanský zákoník s aktualizovanou důvodovou zprávou a rejstříkem, p. 236.

9.32 The position in French law is a little unclear, because contested. It is increasingly argued that the owner of a moveable thing is able to prevent his thing becoming immoveable through the operation of the doctrine of *accession immobilière*. If, for example, a good were supplied for the construction of a building subject to a retention of title clause, it is said that the land unit owner can waive his right of accession. The waiver would be valid because the rules of accession are alterable by consent. The waiver would also work, without any register publicity, against the creditors of the land unit owner. Questions of *ergo omnes* effect are said to be exaggerated.[202] This position cannot, however, be completely reconciled with the judicial decisions of the superior courts. The *Cour de cassation* did indeed decide in 1970 that Art. 551 French Civil Code—according to which everything that is incorporated into a thing belongs to that thing's owner—is not *d'ordre public* and can be displaced by express waiver of the owner.[203] More recently, in 2002, the *Cour de cassation* held that the right of accession followed *ex lege* subject to contrary agreement.[204] This certainly gave momentum to the notion that accession may be waived.[205] The case of Cass. civ. 26 June 1991,[206] however, held that verandas sold subject to a retention of title lost their moveable nature at the point in time at which they were connected to the *fonds de terre*; the parties could not determine by agreement whether a thing is moveable or immoveable.[207] Cass. civ. 02 March 1999,[208] in turn, concerned a contract for the delivery and installation of heating equipment, ventilation ducts, and plumbing for a building. The contract stipulated that the supplier would remain owner of the installations until payment had been made in full. The supplier argued that, technically, the clause was not a retention of title but a waiver of the right of accession under Art. 551 French Civil Code.[209] Be that as it may, the *Cour de cassation* emphasized that the goods in question had been incorporated into the building and for that reason no longer existed as independent things. As a result, the supplier could

[202] Thus argues, e.g. *Zenati-Castaing and Revet*, Les biens[3], p. 152 no. 95.

[203] Cass. civ. 6 November 1970, Bull. civ. 1970, III, no. 592 p. 432 ('*Les dispositions de l'article 551 du code civil suivant lesquelles tout ce qui s'incorpore a la chose appartient au propriétaire ne sont pas d'ordre public et peuvent être écartées par la renonciation expresse de celui-ci*').

[204] Cass. civ. 27 March 2002, Bull. civ. 2002, III, no. 78 p. 68 ('*Qu'en statuant ainsi, alors que, sauf convention contraire, l'accession opère de plein droit*').

[205] *Zenati-Castaing and Revet* op. cit. p. 219 no. 142; *Malaurie and Aynès*, Les biens[4], p. 131 no. 451.

[206] Bull. civ. 1991, III, no. 197 p. 115; D. 1993 p. 93; JCP 1992, II, 21825, p. 107, note by *Barbiéri*; RTD civ. 1992 p. 144, note by *Zenati* ('*alors que la nature, immobilière ou mobilière, d'un bien est définie par la loi, et que la convention des parties ne peut avoir d'incidence à cet égard*').

[207] It is true that this judgment was met with firm resistance in the legal scholarship. The qualification of *immeubles par destination* and *immeubles par anticipation* at least is entirely dependent on the will of the parties: note by *Zenati* op. cit. p. 145 ('*Les meubles par anticipation ne sont rien d'autre que des immeubles déclarés meubles par convention*') and *Freij-Dalloz* op. cit. p. 94 no. 8 ('*Le recours à la volonté des parties pour déterminer la nature d'un bien n'est donc pas une innovation.... Le code civil l'a autorisé aux art. 524 et s. pour la détermination des immeubles par destination et la jurisprudence l'a utilisé pour forger la catégorie des immeubles par anticipation*').

[208] JCP 1999, II, 10180, p. 1841, note by *Cutajar*.

[209] This argument, in turn, has its own history. After Cass. civ. 23 April 1974, D. 1975 p. 287, note by *Jean Mazeaud*, had decided '*que l'immeuble en construction sur le terrain d'autrui auquel il s'incorpore, et qui est édifié en exécution d'un contrat de louage d'ouvrage, n'était pas la propriété de l'entrepreneur, même avant la réception des travaux par le maître de l'ouvrage*', commercial practice had applied waiver clauses to the doctrine of accession and had even convinced a first instance commercial court of the approach (Tribunal de grande instance Nanterre 16 December 1994, Petites affiches 1997 p. 19; for further details, see note by *Cutajar* op. cit.).

assert the right he claimed against his contractual partner, but not against the other creditors in the insolvency of the land unit owner.

The (inverse) question has also been posed whether a '*per se*' still immoveable thing can be made 'moveable' by force of a contractual agreement to the effect that its future moveability is assumed. The core problem has already arisen in the context of future things. The theory of *meubles par anticipation*, for example, has been presented in the context of the sale of grain standing in the field or the sale of standing trees as *meubles*,[210] but has also been applied to a wooden hut by an appellate court in Aix-en-Provence.[211] One doctrinal school in French law holds that the will of the contractual parties takes priority. Where a contract is made concerning immoveable things in terms that concern their future, moveable, condition, the things in question can be characterized as moveable as from the point in time of the contract's formation.[212] Conversely, however, the purported *erga omnes* effect of such an agreement poses a problem, particularly in relation to (i) a future acquiror of the land unit that (still) incorporates the *meubles par anticipation* and (ii) a creditor with a registered hypothec over the land unit. The judicial *dicta* have vacillated on this point. Initially, the courts held that the *mobilisation par anticipation* was effective against third parties where the buyer can take possession of the newly mobilized moveable through separation prior to the sale.[213] More recently, the *Cour de cassation* has opined that Art. 2276 French Civil Code cannot be applied to anticipated moveable goods because the acquiror of such things is able to check the entitlement of the seller through inspection of the public register.[214] An appellate court in Reims has decided that the rights of the acquiror over 'anticipated' moveable goods only enjoys priority over the rights of the new land unit owner when the sale was recorded in the register prior to the sale of the land unit.[215] The purchase of standing trees could, relative to the (genuine) land unit purchaser, at best be treated as the earlier sale of the land to the buyer of the trees. Two more recent decisions have made the *erga omnes* effect of an 'anticipated mobilization' dependent on the land unit acquiror's knowledge of the *mobilisation par anticipation*.[216] An appellate court in Agen has opined that the 9.33

210 *Terré and Simler*, Les biens[8], p. 48 no. 41.

211 Aix-en-Provence 15 February 1985, Gaz. Pal. 1985,1, p. 443, note by *Dureuil.*

212 *Terré and Simler* op. cit. p. 47 no. 41; *Atias*, Les biens[11], p. 44 no. 57.

213 The foundations for this were laid in Cass. 30 March 1868, D. 1868, I, p. 147; and Cass. civ. 02 June 1934, DP 1935, I, p. 65, note by *Fréjaville* ('*le droit du créancier hypothécaire ne pourrait être paralysé que par le jeu de l'article 2279* [now 2276] *c. civ., si l'acheteur était déjà entré de bonne foi en possession des arbres coupés*'); Amiens 24 October 1922, RTD civ. 1923 p. 180; Tribunal civil Marmande 13 July 1931, RTD civ. 1931 p. 920; Tribunal civil Chambéry 12 July 1951, Gaz. Pal. 1951, 2, p. 266 (possession by marking the trees is sufficient). This view is supported by *Terré and Simler* op. cit. p. 48 no. 41 and by *Malaurie and Aynès*, Les biens[4], p. 38 no. 135.

214 Cass. civ. 04 July 1968, Bull. civ. 1968, III, p. 247, no. 321; RTD civ. 1969, p. 144, note by *Bredin* ('*Mais attendu que l'article 2279 du Code civil est inapplicable aux meubles par anticipation, qu'en effet, l'acquéreur de ceux-ci est en mesure de vérifier la qualité du vendeur en consultant les titres de la propriété immobilière dont ces biens font partie jusqu'à la vente*') (The buyer had acquired the land unit ownership by private deed on 1 April and had sold 161 trees to a company from this ownership on 4 April. Later, the land unit sale was found to be void. The original owner and the company subsequently came into dispute. The company invoked Art. 2276 French Civil Code and claimed an acquisition of moveable things by anticipation and possession (marking the trees). However, even this would not have helped in this case, as the company acted in bad faith).

215 Reims 10 May 1982, JCP G 1982, II, 20225, note by *Dagot.*

216 This approach is supported by *Dross*, Droit des biens, p. 281 no. 342.

sale of *meubles par anticipation* is not subject to the rules of the *publicité foncière*. But, it continued, it is not effective against the subsequent acquiror of the land unit without knowledge of the sale of the *meubles par anticipation* at the time of the notarial conveyance.[217] This result has also been reached by an appellate court in Nancy. Even though, in principle, a dispute between the buyer of *meubles par anticipation* and the buyer of the land unit could be resolved by reference to the rules concerning *publicité foncière*, matters are different when the buyer of the land unit that relies on the publication of his title had knowledge of the prior sale of the *meubles par anticipation*—even when these moveables have not been removed from the land unit at the time of the second sale.[218] The supposedly dispositive force of the doctrine of accession is thus not beyond doubt in French law, either; at least a good faith purchaser without notice has good prospects of being protected.

3. Creation of New Things through Separation

a. Temporarily Separated Parts

9.34 Assuming that the act of separation does not cause the destruction of the newly individuated thing, a new object of property rights is created where connected things are separated. If a page is torn from this book, it can be dealt with separately,[219] and the same principle applies to materials derived from the demolition of a building.[220] That is almost trite. A more precise examination is required, however, for (i) things that are only separated from a principal thing temporarily and (ii) so-called 'fruits'. It is sometimes said that temporary separation—for example, for purposes such as transport or repair—does not negate the characterization of a thing as a component. A (new) independent thing only arises when the separation is permanent.[221] The principle stated so

[217] Agen 09 December 1992, JCP G 1993, IV, 1772, p. 211.

[218] Nancy 13 December 1989, unpublished.

[219] The passage of ownership follows the separation (or the transfer upon separation) in the 'consensus systems' as well, even if the sale contract was finalized beforehand (e.g. Art. 155 § 2 Polish Civil Code and relating to this Polish Sąd Najwyższy 28 June 2002, I CK 5/02, Glosa 2003/3 str. 47, Prawo Bankowe 2002/12 str. 17, LexPolonica-No. 358693, Lex-No. 56604 and Art. 880 in conjunction with Art. 408(2) Portuguese Civil Code [for this, see STJ 23 November 1976, BMJ 261 (1976) 165] and Art. 1472(1) Italian Civil Code) (sale or transfer of future things).

[220] Thus, Art. 532 French Civil Code (according to which materials, which stem from the demolition of a building, as well as those which are assembled to construct a new one, are moveable things until they are used in the construction. See, for this, Cass. civ. 10 June 1981, Bull. civ. 1981, III, no. 119; RTD civ. 1982 p. 164, note by *Giverdon*. A builder had been ordered to remove certain buildings he had constructed on another's land. Although the buildings had not yet been demolished, the land unit owner desired a pledge over moveables. He argued that the buildings consisted of a collection of things (bricks, tiles, etc.), which were already 'conceptually separate' and therefore should be viewed legally as moveable things. This was rejected by the Cour de cassation. The buildings were still immoveable things as they had not been demolished at the time of the pledge. (Incidentally, this decision is incompatible with the doctrine of *mobilisation par anticipation*.)

[221] Thus, e.g. Staudinger (*-Jickeli and Stieper*), BGB (2004), § 93 no. 12 with reference to RG 2 July 1919, Gruchot 64 (1920) pp. 95, 97 (using, albeit only *illustrandi causa*, the example of windows removed for repair, which would not negate their character as essential components of a building); *Eliáš et al.*, Občanský zákoník. Velký akademický komentář I, p. 493 and *Švestka (-Spáčil/Škárová/Hulmák)*, Občanský zákoník I^2, p. 658. The preparatory works of the Swedish *Jordabalk* (1970:994) contain the remark that an object, which is to be seen as *byggnadstillbehör* and

broadly cannot, however, be true; at least, the problem that this doctrine is meant to solve remains unclear. When, for example, the door of a dwelling is removed for repairs and is taken by a tradesman to his workshop with permission, the house owner remains the owner of the door. This follows, however, from the self-evident rule that the owner of a thing is the owner of things that are separated from it—at least those things that are not 'fruits' or other products subject to a special acquisition regime.[222]

A rule that the door remains (a legally unseparated part of) a land unit is not, when we look at things this way, strictly necessary. It would actually be incorrect, because it would deny the tradesman the ability to acquire a security right (such as a pledge or lien) in the door; moreover, it would not explain why he is able to avail himself of all the usual legal instruments that protect possession.[223] Nor is it generally necessary, for the protection of any other property right in the land unit, that components separated temporarily remain (essential) components of the land unit.[224] It would appear almost absurd, in fact, to subject a good faith purchaser of the above-mentioned door to the rules governing the rules of innocent acquisition of land units (which presuppose registration) rather than to the rules governing innocent acquisition of moveable things. Of course, one could argue that one who comes into possession *animo domini* **9.35**

only temporarily—e.g. for repairs—removed from the building, does not lose its quality as *byggnadstillbehör* (NJA II 1966 p. 36). Admittedly, the boundaries between components and accessories in Swedish law is fluid.

[222] e.g. Art. 546 (which states that the ownership of the thing, moveable or immoveable, grants a right to everything it brings forth) and Art. 547 French Civil Code (according to which fruits of the earth brought forth naturally or through effort belong to the owner by virtue of the doctrine of accession); the applicable principle is that of *accession par production* (*Dross*, Les choses, p. 22 no. 16-1; *Terré and Simler*, Les biens[8], p. 240 no. 242). More general provisions include § 953 German Civil Code (the ownership of the principal thing continues for the separated components; it is not newly created, and for this reason the encumbrances on the principal thing subsist [Soergel (-*Henssler*), BGB XIV[13], § 953 no. 3]; earlier third party rights are not revived [MünchKomm (-*Stresemann*), BGB I(1)[6], § 93 no. 14a]) and Art. 1064 Greek Civil Code (the owner of the thing is, as a rule, entitled to the ownership of products or other components of the thing upon their separation from the thing). A provision corresponding to § 953 German Civil Code or Art. 1064 Greek Civil Code is missing from the Portuguese Civil Code. This can have consequences in practice. For example, while STJ 23 November 1976, BMJ 261 (1976) p. 165 ruled that the acquiror of an as yet unseparated component of a land unit only acquires an obligational claim against the seller; the buyer could vindicate the component neither as against him nor as against an innocent third party. A widespread view is that this should be different upon separation. The buyer is then entitled to vindication under Art. 1311 Portuguese Civil Code, as he becomes the owner of the former component upon separation under Art. 408(2) Portuguese Civil Code (*Menezes Cordeiro*, Tratado de Direito Civil I(2)[2], p. 135).

[223] e.g. Areopag 1748/2005, EllDni 48 (2007) p. 1692; CA Athens 464/2005, EllDni 46 (2005) p. 1539 and *Triantos*, AK, Art. 954 p. 1167 no. 8.

[224] The rights and procedures available to the holder of a security right against the possessor or detentor of a temporarily separated thing must be determined on a case by case basis according to the exact right he has and according to the legal system in which he has it—in particular, whether or not he can demand the physical re-incorporation of the thing in the principal thing. For example, Art. 1283 Greek Civil Code provides that if a moveable thing, which constitutes a component or accessory of the land unit subject to a hypothec, has been removed from the land unit and its ownership transferred to a third party, then the hypothec creditor is not entitled to claim this thing from the third party. Components and land unit accessories are not subject to the hypothec if the owner transfers the newly moveable thing to a third party. This is because Art. 1283 Greek Civil Code refers to the ownership transfer according to Art. 1034 Greek Civil Code, which in turn is reliant on the transfer of the thing (*Triantos*, AK, Art. 1283 p. 1485 no. 1). In English law, the mortgage usually includes all fixtures. As a rule, the mortgagor does not have the right to remove them. This is only different if the removal occurs within the limitations of the normal business dealings and the mortgagee would have consented to this given knowledge of the circumstances (Cheshire and Burn [-*Burn and Cartwright*], Modern Law of Real Property[17], pp. 160–61). If 'fixtures' have been removed without permission, the mortgagee has no claim to their replacement. He is entitled only to compensation (*Gough v Wood & Co.* [1894] 1 Q.B. 713).

of a temporarily separated thing thereby terminates the thing's component status: if copper plates or gutters are stolen from a roof, for example, they are from that point not 'permanently' connected with the building.[225] In the case of the tradesman in our example, who sells the door, the situation would be no different. The doctrine that a temporary separation does not affect the component quality of a thing can thus only be determinative in the case that the principal thing (in our case, the land unit on which the house stands) rather than the component is alienated or encumbered in such a way that a component is temporarily separated. One who disposes of a land unit disposes of its parts as well. That, however, can be more easily and coherently justified when one characterizes those parts from the time of their separation onwards simply as accessories rather than as (essential) components.[226] Accessories have a double nature, and that double nature is relevant here. Accessories follow only 'by default' the fate of their principal thing; a thing's (essential) components, on the other hand, are bound to it always.[227] Ultimately, however, this is just a semantic disagreement in any case. When the owner of a principal thing expressly excludes a separated thing from the relevant legal transaction, the separation transforms *ipso jure* from a temporary to a permanent one.

b. Fruits, Accession, Products, and Uses

9.36 So-called 'fruits' present a special category of new things created through separation from a principal thing. The concept derives from the Latin tradition; it is to this day a peculiarity of the Civilian systems. The common law has no use for a term of art of this kind (i.e. 'fruits').[228] This is related, among other things, to the fact that leaseholders are understood to have a property right that provides them with rights to use things

[225] Like connection, separation is a brute act, not a legal transaction. Therefore, who undertook the separation and whether it occurred with or without permission is meaningless for the question of whether a new autonomous thing was created. For example, see RG 20 January 1923, RGZ 106, 149, 151 (in times of crisis, the local authority seized business premises to convert it into living space. In the course of this measure, the shop windows were removed and replaced with windows suitable for a residence. The shop windows were sold. They had lost their quality as essential building components upon their removal (which, incidentally, the court did not deem necessary), as they were permanently separated from the building).

[226] A temporary spatial separation (usually for repairs) is not significant for accessory status; this does not end the quality of the real thing as accessory (e.g. § 97(2) sentence 2 German Civil Code; Art. 957(2) Greek Civil Code; Art. 51 § 3 Polish Civil Code). A similar view is taken in Austrian law. While the permanent separation of an object from the principal thing can indicate the end of its character as an accessory (OGH 27 November 1991, ecolex 1992 p. 409; JBl 1992 p. 515); the same cannot be said for a merely temporary separation (OGH 8 September 1964, SZ 37/115; JBl 1965 p. 422: the case concerned the removal of a tractor from a farm for repairs). Not even the mere closure of a business is sufficient; the land unit must be redesignated with the consequence that nobody needs the objects located there (OGH 27 November 1991 op. cit.).

[227] Of course, this does not rule out that there can be essential components of accessory parts, cf. e.g. RG 2 July 1919, Gruchot 64 (1920) p. 95 (the boiler was ruled to be an essential component of a locomotive, which was an accessory of the land in itself until its dismantlement and removal).

[228] All *emblements* are 'fruits' within the meaning of the civil law tradition, but not all 'fruits' are *emblements*. The latter comprises the yearly harvest (Cheshire and Burn [-*Burn and Cartwright*], Modern Law of Real Property[17], p. 504). At common law, a tenant for life retained the right to the imminent harvest of his terminated estate, and retains this right in equity (e.g. A's life estate was arranged according to B's life span; B dies). While *Burn and Cartwright* ibid. mention all types of fruits to which the tenant for life has a claim, this term is only descriptive; there is no definition of 'profits' or of 'fruits' in statutory property law.

that are tantamount to ownership.[229] These rights include, in particular, the right to acquire and use the inherent productivity of a thing, its so-called 'profits'. The focus of the common law thus looks past question of what does *not* belong to the owner, and looks to exact opposite question of what *remains his*. To this it must be added that the modern common law treats the 'freehold life estate' no longer as an 'estate' (though it remains such in equity). The legal figure of the usufruct (the Continental equivalent of the freehold life estate, for example the German law *Nießbauch*), which rests on the concept of 'use' and its most important sub-category, 'fruits', appeared to the common law eye as somewhat crude; the right to use a land unit as a 'tenant for life' was much more flexible. The allocation of the right to exploit a thing, in particular to exploit land, is realized in a manner tailored to each individual case, not with a legal 'one size fits all'. The allocation of the product of a thing's exploitation follows either the contractual agreement between landlord and tenant or the terms of the relevant trust deed.[230] Without a trust, a freehold life estate cannot be created. One who appropriates the productive output of a thing that should, according to the governing document, belong to another, engages in a violation of duty known as 'waste'.[231] (The standard example is a lease agreement or trust deed that allows a person to pick apples, but not cut down the apple tree[232]).[233] A collective term for the objects so put out of reach, however, does not exist.

229 The rights of use of a tenant for life at common law (and thus, also in equity) do not differ from the rights of a lessee (*Sweet*, Challis's Law of Real Property³, p. 340).

230 The rights of a tenant for life have long been explicitly defined in the respective documentation (*Sweet* op. cit. p. 340). For this reason, it was never thought necessary to establish a general legal rule for the use rights of a tenant for life. While the second part of the Settled Land Act 1925 provided for the rights of disposition of a tenant for life, it did not provide for the rights of use. The Settled Land Act was repealed for future trusts by sec. 2(1) Trusts of Land and Appointment of Trustees Act 1996. For trusts established since 1996, secs 12 and 13 provide that the beneficiary for life has the right to the profits of the trust property, but does not have the unlimited right to live on the land unit.

231 The rights of use of a tenant for life were originally primarily defined 'in the negative', meaning *via* his liability for waste. Waste is damage to buildings or the ground through which the successor to the right of use risks permanent loss (*Burn and Cartwright* op. cit. p. 505).

232 The situation regarding the use of trees is unusually complicated. The tenant was liable for the felling of timber, as the trees were traditionally seen as a part of the inheritance, not the yearly product, unless the use of the land unit consisted of the periodic felling of trees (*Burn and Cartwright* op. cit. p. 506). Which trees did and do constitute timber was (and, under common law for lease contracts and under equity for freehold life estates, still is) a complicated question, which is occasionally overshadowed by local customary law (*Honywood v Honywood* (1874) LR 18 Eq 306, 309, Jessel MR). On the one hand, it had become customary to free the tenant for life from his liability for waste in the relevant instrument (*Sweet* op. cit. p. 340). This freedom was limited in equity to avoid wasteful clear felling, so their limitations had and have to be explicitly included in the exclusion of liability (Sec. 135 LPA). On the other hand, the tenant for life was legally authorized to fell and sell timber with the consent of the trustees or the court, even if he were liable without this consent (sec. 66 Settled Land Act 1925; according to this one quarter of the proceeds counted as profits, the rest counted as capital money to the benefit of the successor in possession). Furthermore, the tenant for life was permitted to fell trees which were not timber according to the local customary law nor the general rules, and did not serve the protection or decoration of the land unit (*Re Harker's Will Trusts* [1938] Ch 323). A further exception, called 'estover', permits the felling of trees for repairs to the land unit or to gain heating fuel for the house (*Burn and Cartwright* op. cit.). As far as that, the rights of use of the tenant for life extended beyond the yearly land unit products; this is a further reason not to operate with the term 'fruits'.

233 *Burn and Cartwright* op. cit. p. 504 summarizes the rights and obligations of a tenant for life in common law to the effect that the tenant for life may draw the annual profits, but may not take or destroy anything that constitutes a permanent part of the inheritance. 'Inheritance' describes the land unit (hereditament) in the condition in which it passes to the successor in the right of use ('remainderman' or 'reversioner'). What this condition is, is by no means certain in the abstract; the answer, which is now only relevant in equity, must be gained from the extensive case law regarding waste.

9.37 For the civil law jurisdictions, on the other hand, 'fruits' is a conventional category of private law. The codifications of Continental Europe use it in a panoply of individual provisions, including those regulating law of contract, the law of restitution and the law of succession. The meaning of the term 'fruits' for property law itself, however, is relatively narrow. It is used to refer to things (real or normative—land units are never 'fruits') that property law apportions, upon their creation, to a person other than the owner of the principal thing from which they arise. This occurs when (and because) a person has a contractual or statutory right of use in the property of another, particularly in the land unit of another, which embraces the statutory acquisition of objects that only acquire 'thing-ness' through separation.

9.38 A distinction is generally drawn between fruits in the form of *things* and fruits in the form of *rights*. Irrespective of small variations in the details of the terminology, one finds a broadly similar approach in all the legal systems concerned.

Art. 3:9(1) Netherlands Civil Code, for example, juxtaposes so-called *natuurlijke vruchten* and *burgerlijke vruchten* ('natural' and 'civil' fruits) in Art. 3:9(2). The former are produced by *zaken* (corporeal objects), the latter are also 'produced' by rights. Art. 3:9(4) Netherlands Civil Code stipulates that natural fruits become independent things upon separation and that civil fruits become independent rights at the point in time of their maturity (*opeisbaarheid*). This is largely consistent with the approach in § 99(1) and (2) German Civil Code. However, § 99(3) German Civil Code also distinguishes between 'direct' and 'indirect' fruits. In particular, the products of a thing [*Sache*] are 'direct thing-fruits' [*unmittelbare Sachfrüchte*] (fruits in the ordinary sense, including milk, wool, young animals) as are corporeal objects that are won from the exploitation of a principal thing (e.g. mineral resources).[234] The produce that a usufructuary gains through work, on the other hand, are considered as 'direct right-fruits' [*unmittelbare Rechtsfrüchte*], as are wild animals (as understood by German law) captured under a hunting right.[235] Under Art. 3:9(1) Netherlands Civil Code, on the other hand, only things that are the fruits of another thing are 'natural fruits'. The 'civil fruits' of Art. 3:9(2) Netherlands Civil Code arise from rights that, according to commercial usage are the fruits of goods [*goederen*], which means fruits of both rights *and* things. Game caught pursuant to a hunting right is, in Netherlands law, no 'fruit' at all. This is because the hunting right is no 'thing' and the game is no 'right'. A typical indirect thing-fruit [*mittelbare Sachfrucht*] in the sense of § 99(3) German Civil Code is rental income; an 'indirect right-fruit' [*mittelbare Rechtsfrucht*] is interest payable by reason of default.[236] Italian law, too, contrasts *frutti naturali* and *frutti civili*. Under Art. 820(1) Italian Civil Code, natural fruits are those that arise directly from a thing [*cosa*] whether with or without human intervention, e.g. agricultural products, wood, young animals, and the products of mines, quarries and peat reserves.[237] Civil fruits

[234] MünchKomm (-*Holch*), BGB I(1)^5, § 99 no. 4.
[235] Ibid. no. 9.
[236] e.g. BGH 3 June 1981, *BGHZ* 81 pp. 8, 13.
[237] *Bianca*, Diritto civile VI, p. 101.

consist of the consideration given for the transfer of a use right, including in particular interest on a debt or rental income (Art. 820(3) Italian Civil Code). Civil fruits arise periodically; they do not require a 'separation' from the principal thing (Art. 821(3) Italian Civil Code). In Portuguese law, a 'fruit' is anything that a thing produces regularly without 'affecting its substance' (Art. 212(1) Portuguese Civil Code). Objects of 'periodical production' include agricultural produce, with the exception of young animals that maintain the 'capital'—i.e. the headcount of the herd (Art. 212(3) Portuguese Civil Code). The ongoing exploitation of mines and quarries is considered to generate 'fruits' rather than not one-off yields.[238] Besides this, Art. 212(2) Portuguese Civil Code distinguishes between *frutos naturais* and *frutos civis*. The former arise directly from a thing; the latter comprise the income or products that a thing produces in virtue of some legal relationship. The Czech legal terminology distinguishes between 'fruits' (*plody*) and 'benefits' (*užitky*). Already under the Czech Civil Code [1964], however, the basic distinction between *fructus naturales* and *fructus civiles* was common.[239] In § 491 of the Czech Civil Code [2014], *fructus naturales* now appear as *plody* and *fructus civiles* appear as *užitky*.[240] The substantive content of the latter is only the claim to some performance on the basis of an obligational relationship, not ownership in that relationship.[241] Section 404 Austrian Civil Code speaks of 'growth' [*Zuwachs*], not 'fruits',[242] but for all intents and purposes that is not considered to make any difference.[243] It has rightly been pointed out that §§ 414 and following, which fall under the rubric of 'artificial growth' has nothing to do with the law of fruits at all—those provisions are concerned with the law of combination.[244] French law distinguishes between *fruits* and *produits*. A *fruit* is every *bien accessoire* that a principal thing brings forth regularly without loss to its substance. A *produit* (e.g. the products of a mine or quarry) are, on the other hand, only won from the capital stock irregularly, and reduce the substance of the principal thing.[245] The law distinguishes (*inter alia* in Arts 547 and 582–584 French Civil Code) between 'natural', 'industrial', and 'civil' fruits; civil fruits include, for example, rental income and dividends.[246] Arts 354 and 355 Spanish Civil Code adopt the same tri-partite classification. *Frutos naturales* are the products of the earth that arise of themselves, including young animals and other animal products. *Frutos industriales* are products of all sorts that arise from a land unit as a result of cultivation or other labour. *Frutos civiles* include rental income from a building or

[238] *Pires de Lima and Antunes Varela*, Código Civil Anotado I^4, Art. 212 pp. 204–05.

[239] *Eliáš et al.*, Občanský zákoník. Velký akademický komentář I, p. 526.

[240] § 491(1) Czech Civil Code states that '[a] fruit is what a thing regularly provides by its inherent nature, as follows from and is appropriate to its usual intended purpose, whether or not as a result of the endeavour of man' and that '[b]enefits are what a thing regularly provides by its legal nature.'

[241] *Švestka (-Spáčil/Škárová/Humák)*, Občanský zákoník I^2, p. 784.

[242] *Zuwachs* means everything that arises from a thing, or accrues to a thing, without being given to the owner by another person. *Zuwachs* is caused by nature or by art or by both alike. The 'natural fruits of the land, namely such benefits as it creates without being worked' are first discusses in § 404 Austrian Civil Code. They 'grow to [the benefit of] the owner of the land'.

[243] Schwimann and Kodek (-*Klicka and Reidlinger*), ABGB II^4, § 404 no. 1.

[244] *Gschnitzer/Faistenberger/Barta/Call/Eccher*, Sachenrecht^2, p. 90.

[245] *Carbonnier*, Droit civil II, p. 1620 no. 722.

[246] Cass. civ. 28 November 2006, *D.* 2006, Cahier de droit des affaires, p. 3055, note by *Lienhard*.

tract of land and things like pension rights. Art. 53 § 1 Polish Civil Code refers to the 'natural benefits of a thing' and counts to this category its fruits and other components separated from it, insofar as they are its ordinary products. 'Civil benefits' are the products of a thing by reason of a legal relationship (Art. 53 § 2 Polish Civil Code) and the benefits of a right are the products, that the right guarantees in accordance with its socio-economic purpose (Art. 54 Polish Civil Code). The position taken in Art. 93 of the Bulgarian Property law is very similar.

9.39 The policy sought with the concept of fruits (or 'benefits') is made very clear in many of the Continental legal systems. Art. 55 § 1 Polish Civil Code, for example, stipulates that the person entitled to the use of a thing becomes the owner of the fruits (or benefits) that are separated from it during his entitlement. The civil benefits accrue to him according to the period of his title. The person entitled to draw the benefits of a thing becomes their owner upon the act of separation (Art. 190 Polish Civil Code). The basic rule in Art. 5:1(3) Netherlands Civil Code, that the owner of a thing becomes the owner of its fruits,[247] is followed by an exception in Art. 5:17 Netherlands Civil Code, according to which the ownership right of the thing-owner is displaced in case another person has been given a use-right in the thing. According to the Spanish approach, a *fruto* is a new *cosa*, which accrues to the holder of the right in the thing (*titular de la cosa*) which has brought the fruit forth.[248] The preponderance of the French literature interprets both *fruits* and *produits* as *accessoires*.[249] The principle of *accessorium sequitur principale* applies: an *accessoire* generally follows the fate of the principal thing. In consequence, the owner of the capital object generally becomes *ex lege* the owner of its fruits and products (Arts 546, 547, and 1614 French Civil Code). Matters are different, however, where a usufruct has been created. The usufructuary has the right to *fruits* (Art. 582 French Civil Code). *Produits*, on the other hand, only accrue to the usufructuary under special circumstances, for example when a mine or quarry was already in production at the time the usufruct was created (Art. 598 French Civil Code) or when the usufruct relates to a forest that was planned for harvesting (Art. 591 French Civil Code). Section 405 Austrian Civil Code is formulated against the assumptions of an agricultural society, and begins with the trusty, basic principle that natural fruits are the property of the owner of the thing that produces them. The exceptions to this rule concern the good faith possessor of a thing (§ 330 Austrian Civil Code) and persons that are entitled to

[247] There is not explicit provision for the ownership conditions of separated components which are not fruits. In the Netherlands, the principle that the owner of the principal thing is also the owner of the separated new thing also applies (*Snijders and Rank-Berenschot*, Goederenrecht[1], p. 36 no. 44, while indicating that the ownership of fruits can fall to a usufructuary). This can be substantiated by Art. 5:3 Netherlands Civil Code, according to which the owner of the thing is also the owner of the thing's (unseparated) components. There is no indication that a separation would have an effect on the ownership conditions.

[248] *O'Callaghan Muñoz*, Código Civil[6], Art. 354 Civil Code p. 418.

[249] *Carbonnier* op. cit.; *Zenati-Castaing and Revet*, Les biens[3], p. 187 no. 122 also describe fruits as '*des accessoires, des biens dépendant génétiquement d'un autre bien*' with the consequence that the *bien accessoire* follows the *bien principal* (see also p. 178 no. 112). Thus, as a rule, fruits belong to the owner of the principal thing (p. 192 no. 126). On the other hand, *Malaurie and Aynès*, Les biens[4], p. 51 no. 160 and *Terré and Simler*, Les biens[8], p. 129 no. 123 define fruits and benefits without recourse to the term *accessoire*. They merely emphasize that fruits and benefits generally belong to the owner of the principal thing on the basis of the *droit d'accession*.

fruits on the basis of a real servitude or a lease agreement [*Pachtvertrag*] entitling them to take fruits.[250] A contractual agreement concerning the ownership position after separation of the fruits is considered to be possible.[251] Section 130(2) Czech Civil Code [1964] brought it crisply to the point: fundamentally, the lawful possessor had the rights of an owner, in particular the right to the fruits and benefits of a thing.[252] Sections 1066 and 1073 Czech Civil Code [2014], by way of contrast, proceed from the basic principle that the fruits of a land unit belong to the land unit owner and the fruits of an animal belong to the owner of the animal. The right of usufruct, however, gives its holder the right to take the fruits and benefits of another's thing (§§ 1285(1), 1346(1) Czech Civil Code [2014]; also Art. 56 Bulgarian Property Law), and the beneficiary of a trust can be given the same right under § 1457(3) Czech Civil Code [2014]. In Italy, the doctrine is propounded that fruits connected to the 'mother' thing are *frutti pendent*, that is, non-independent components.[253] Granted, as 'future things' one can gift and sell them (Art. 820(2) Italian Civil Code), but they only become *frutti naturali*, and thus independent objects of property rights, upon physical separation (Art. 1472 Italian Civil Code). They fall into the ownership of the owner of the thing that has produced them unless a usufruct right and the *ius separandi* that accompanies it reposes in another person. The same approach is taken in Arts 1065–1068 Greek Civil Code, with some modifications of the details. In the appropriation of fruits, foremost priority is given to the holder of the so-called right of taking fruits (*dikéoma karpolipsías* or *karpoktisías*); an obligational right (such as the obligational rights to use a field under Arts 641–647 Greek Civil Code) is sufficient, even when it has been acquired in good faith from someone with defective title (Arts 1067 and 1068 Greek Civil Code).[254] The second order of priority is given to the non-entitled but good faith possessor—that is, someone who acts on the assumption that he is the owner of the principal thing or holder of a usufruct right (Art. 1066 Greek Civil Code). Next in line are the holders of limited property rights (Art. 1065 Greek Civil Code), again the usufruct (Arts 1142, 1150 Greek Civil Code), real servitudes, and limited personal servitudes for the appropriation of products (harvesting of timber, excavation of sand, Arts 1118, 1120, 1188 Greek Civil Code), and the pledge, provided that the pledgee has been granted by contract the right to take fruits (Art. 1221 Greek Civil Code). (A hypothec only affects fruits as security; ownership of fruits does not pass to the hypothec creditor.) The owner of the principal thing stands last in the order of priority (Art. 1064 Greek Civil Code). The actual acquisition of ownership occurs either *per separationem* (*με τον αποχωρισμό*) or *per perceptionem*

250 *Klicka and Reidlinger* op. cit. § 405 no. 1.

251 LG Wien 31 March 1950, EvBl 1950/294, *ÖJZ* 1950 p. 280 (Horse manure belongs to the owner of the horses. There was no contract to the effect that it became the property of the owner of the stables). Unseparated fruits, on the other hand, are not fitting objects of separate rights; they can only be the object of obligational agreements (OGH 1 October 1980, EvBl 1981/48, ÖJZ 1980 p. 160: no *erga omnes* effective retention of title in standing timber resources).

252 Under § 131(1) Slovakian Civil Code and Czech Civil Code [1964] (now § 1000 Czech Civil Code [2014]), e.g. the possessor without title had (has) to deliver the thing and its fruits and benefits to the owner.

253 *Bianca*, Diritto civile VI, p. 101.

254 For further details, see Areopag 1233/1993, EEN 61 (1994) p. 749.

(*με τη συγκομιδή*) (i.e. through a rightful or a good faith act of harvesting and taking into possession).

9.40 The many anecdotes concerning fruits on branches hanging on or over a land unit boundary reflect a surprisingly diverse legal position. As long as the branch and its fruits remain attached to the tree, they are essential components of the same and they belong to the owner of the land unit on which the tree stands.[255] On this point, at least, there seems to be little disagreement (perhaps because it is not a very important problem in and of itself). Differences of opinion emerge, however, when it comes to the question of who is allowed to cut what, under which conditions, from the tree, and proliferate when it comes to ownership of the severed parts and of fruits that fall naturally from the branch. In some legal systems, distinctions are even drawn between branches, on the one hand, and roots, bramble shoots, and twigs on the other. Under Art. 673 French Civil Code, for example, the owner of an 'invaded' land unit is only permitted to cut the latter group unilaterally; he must leave the shortening of overhanging branches to their owner and, if needs be, obtain a court order to force him to do what is necessary. That is also the approach taken in Art. 37 of the Belgian *Code rural*. Art. 672-1 Luxembourgish Civil Code reflects Art. 673 French Civil Code in many respects but gives the neighbour at least the right to pick the fruit and so appropriate short of going to the court. § 149(2) Estonian *Asjaõigusseadus* and Art. 1099 Latvian Civil Code also grant such a right. Other legal systems make a general choice for the more practical approach of self-help. Some allow it without any advance notice,[256] others seem to insist on advance notice without exception,[257] and others again impose a reasonable notice period in the case of branches, if not of roots.[258] In Luxembourg, a neighbour is allowed to pick the fruits but not cut the overhanging branch; in England, one is allowed to cut the branch but not pick the fruits, and in Germany one is allowed to do both. Under English law, a severed branch and the fruit hanging on it become chattels, and continue to belong to the owner of the tree. If the 'abator' (of the nuisance of an invading branch) cuts branches and fruit for his own purposes (e.g. to sell them), he commits the tort

[255] If a tree is located exactly on the boundary line, there will be conflict about the ownership of the tree itself. For some, the land ownership continues vertically for the corresponding 'half' of the tree. Others maintain that the tree is co-owned by the land unit neighbours (such as § 150 Estonian *Asjaõigusseadus* and for the Netherlands H.R. 20 May 2011, 10/00077, LJN-No. BP9997). The latter creates new things, and also has the effect that the fruits of such a tree, as well as the tree's timber should it be felled, belong to the land unit owners equally (§ 149(4) Estonian *Asjaõigusseadus*).

[256] This is the situation under the English right of abatement of nuisance (*Mills v Brooker* [1919] 1 KB 555 (DC)) and also under Kap. 3 § 2 Swedish JB (*Ljungman*, Om skada och olägenhet på grannfastighet, pp. 25, 190, 193).

[257] See Art. 1366(1) Portuguese Civil Code and § 127(1) Slovakian Civil Code. After this period, the neighbour is allowed to remove the branches or roots of the tree, albeit in a responsible manner and at an appropriate time of year. The requirement of consideration includes a prior warning. § 1016(2) Czech Civil Code now explicitly relies on an appropriate time limit, upon the expiration of which the neighbour affected can resort to self-help. § 149(1) Estonian *Asjaõigusseadus* and Art. 4.42(1) Lithuanian Civil Code create the right to cut off roots, branches, fruits, and bushes and to acquire them, without exception after an appropriate time limit has expired fruitlessly.

[258] This is the case under, e.g. § 910 German Civil Code, Art. 5:44(1) and (2) Netherlands Civil Code, and Art. 150 Polish Civil Code. Where self-help follows advance notice, the latter implies the right of the owner of the offending plant to enter his neighbour's property and rectify the matter himself. This right is express in, e.g. Art. 149 Polish Civil Code, Art. 1367 Portuguese Civil Code, and § 127(3) Slovakian Civil Code.

of conversion.[259] The situation is the same in Sweden. Picking fruit from overhanging branches is not a permitted action.[260] Under § 910 German Civil Code,[261] Art. 150 Polish Civil Code and numerous other provisions,[262] the neighbour is allowed to keep both the severed branches and the fruit on them. The position is the same regarding fruits that fall from a branch across the boundary line. They fall, in almost every legal system, into the ownership of the land unit owner,[263] albeit sometimes with the proviso that the land unit in question must not be a land unit that serves some public use (§ 911 German Civil Code; Arts 148 and 207 Polish Civil Code; § 1016(1) Czech Civil Code). Under English law, however, even such fallen fruits remain the property of the owner (or entitled occupier) of the land unit on which the tree stands.[264]

4. Transformation of Things

a. Creation of New Things through the Manipulation or Processing of Several Inputs

If the concept of 'fruits' is of peculiar importance for the whole of the law applicable to land units, doctrines concerning the transformation of things is of peculiar importance to the law of real things.[265] Our concern is with products that acquire a new identity in the course of being processed and which must, accordingly, be recognized as new things. As such, new things raise the question of ownership: should they belong to the 9.41

[259] *Mills v Brooker* op. cit. This is also the case in Swedish law. The right to self-help does not provide the foundation for a right of appropriation (Kap. 2 § 1 and Kap. 3 § 2 JB).

[260] HD 23 October 1907, NJA 1907 p. 471 (*in casu*, however, a criminal delict was not found because the neighbour was honestly mistaken about the legality of his actions).

[261] Under Art. 122 German EGBGB, fruit trees can be subject to divergent laws in the respective federal states: Staudinger (-*Roth*), BGB (2001), § 910 no. 25.

[262] If a neighbour is entitled to cut off the roots and branches that extend to his land unit, he becomes their owner by separation (this is the case in Czech and Slovakian law: *Holub*, Sousedská práva², p. 134, in § 149(1) Estonian LPA and in Art. 1099 Lithuanian Civil Code). If a tree extends over the land unit border and poses a threat to the neighbour's house, then the neighbour may demand that the tree be felled. If this does not occur, then the building owner may resort to self-help and keep the wood (Art. 1098 Latvian Civil Code).

[263] e.g. Art. 37 sentence 2 Belgian *Code rural*; § 911 German Civil Code; § 149(3) Estonian *Asjaõigusseadus*; Art. 673 French Civil Code; Art. 672-1 Luxembourgish Civil Code; Art. 4.42 (3) Lithuanian Civil Code; Art. 5:45 Netherlands Civil Code, and for Swedish law, see *Ljungman*, Om skada och olägenhet på grannfastighet, p. 193 (who remarks that this question was purposefully not addressed by the legislature in order to prevent querulous litigants from using this banal pretext to take legal action; *Ljungman* op. cit. refers to Lagberedningens förslag till jordabalk III [Stockholm 1905–09] p. 109, which I cannot access).

[264] If the fruit naturally falls onto a neighbouring land unit, this does not change the ownership over the fruit. However, the owner does not have the right to enter the neighbour's land unit to collect this fruit (*Mills v Brooker* op. cit.).

[265] e.g. § 950 German Civil Code; Arts 570–572 French Civil Code; Art. 1061 Greek Civil Code; Art. 5:16 Netherlands Civil Code; Arts 192 and 193 Polish Civil Code, as well as § 1074 Czech Civil Code [2014] state this explicitly (for the Czech Civil Code [1964], Czech Nejvyšší soud České republiky 5 November 2002, 22 Cdo 761/ 2001, Soubor rozhodnutí Nejvyššího soudu, C 1524 had rejected the idea of the possibility of a 'processing' of an immoveable thing. The restoration of a building does not defer ownership to the restorer while the original building continues to exist. Restoration does not create a new thing in a legal sense). Art. 940 Italian Civil Code speaks of someone who uses another person's material (*materia*) from which to create a new thing. Incidentally, this appears to have been different in Roman law, as a usufruct of a swamp or forest expired if it was turned into farmland: *Dolozalek*, AcP 192 (1995) pp. 392, 402.

owner(s) of the original thing, from which they were created, or the person(s) who transformed them into one or more new things? In the case of land units, no similar problem arises because land units cannot be 'processed' to create 'new' land units. Certain land unit components, typically the soil, can be 'processed', but not the land unit *per se* (understood correctly as a normatively defined space). The transformation of a heath into a pasture, the removal of a hedge separating two fields, or the construction of a house (on one's own or another's property) all leave the existence of the land unit unaffected (subject of course to possible prescriptive consequences). All of these changes can, in the long-term, be reversed; the dispositive factor, however, is that these processes do not lead legally to the creation of new land units. The notion that a builder should become the owner of a land unit in virtue of work he has invested in its improvement does not even arise; the investment of work *cannot* change the identity of a land unit by reason of its normative character. A land unit is always an independent, principal thing and never a dependent, accessory thing, for the very reason that labour and effort do not affect its normatively determined space; that space lies outside their reach. Even when the surface of a land unit is built upon, it remains the same land unit. Likewise, when fruit is picked, it is not the investment of effort by the pickers, but the physical separation of the fruit from the tree that presents a legal question—one oriented towards the produce rather than the land unit. The land unit subsists even after the plucking of the fruit; the land unit and the produce are clearly identifiable, separate entities. As such, there is no reason for property law to separate the land unit owner from his land unit *as well as* from his apples, and to place the picker in his stead—not even when the picker, as lessee or usufructuary, is entitled to carry out the separation of the fruit from the trees.

9.42 In the case of real things, however, matters lie quite differently. If they are processed in some way, the law will often see them, irreversibly, as having a new identity. A new product arises from various processes. Sometimes, processing even a single raw element will suffice, for example where a rough diamond is worked into one or more cut diamonds, or a where a copper ingot is heated, drawn into wire and spooled. In other cases, the original things are destroyed (e.g. grapes are pressed and turned into wine, eggs are hatched in an incubator), or disassembled (e.g. animal bodies are butchered, metal billets are cut with high-precision lasers). Processes that take a real thing apart cannot be equiparated with the separation of moveable things from a land unit. In the case of land units, the original and principal thing (i.e. the land unit) is preserved. In the case of real things, one of two questions arises. In one set of cases, it is obviously not the case that the original thing subsists—for example, a slaughtered and butchered animal. In another set of cases, the existence of the original thing is, itself, the question—for example, does the law of property see 'olives' or only 'pitted olives' and 'olive pits'? If only pitted olives and olive pits remain, the question arises: who owns the *new* biomass, considered as a whole? If property law characterizes the mass of pitted olive flesh as 'the (original) olives', a different question arises—namely, who should be given ownership of the (newly created) pits? 'Processing', however, quite often (perhaps usually) only consists in the *connection* of objects. In such cases, the question is one of the joinder of things, for example the preparation of a product from various elements. Here, a transformation takes place insofar as none of the (erstwhile independent) things can still be seen as the principal thing—i.e. as a thing in favour of which the others have been relegated to the status of mere 'components'. If a defective cable is swapped in an automobile, for example, the replacement part will, indeed, generally cease to be an independent thing and will fall into the ownership of the owner of the automobile. The 'thing quality' of the automobile, however, and therefore his position as 'owner' remain fully unaffected by this operation. If a raw steak is seasoned with salt and pepper, it remains a steak. If paint is applied to a canvas, it becomes part of the canvas, and if milk is poured into tea, it is still 'tea' in the cup. In both common sense and in the logic of the law, an 'original thing' subsists (regardless of the fact that certain changes in the state of affairs might be relevant from the perspective of a physicist). In other words, certain physical operations that (admittedly) occur are of no relevance to ownership of the principal thing; all that they effectuate is the destruction of accessory things and, accordingly, the destruction of the ownership rights that existed in *them*. If, on the other hand, raw meat is processed with the salt and pepper (and other ingredients) into 'sausage', or if cables, metal parts, plastic, rubber, and glass are made into a 'car' (and not just repaired: see, e.g. § 416 Austrian Civil Code), then, according to the applicable doctrine of components or accession, most or all of these materials cease to exist as 'things'. The situation is generally similar where a painter creates a 'painting' from a canvas and paints,[266] or when tea and milk are mixed with rice to make a 'pudding'. A principal thing, which has incorporated the other things as accessories, is no longer to be found; *all* of the erstwhile things have ceased to exist. In their place exists a new thing, and it is by no means obvious to whom that new thing belongs.

It is not always straightforward to distinguish the rules concerning *processing* from those concerning the *connection*, *combination*, and *mixture* of real things. In place of the ancient example of the miller who takes grain from numerous farmers and stores it in a single silo, let us take the example of a medium-sized enterprise that manufactures copper electrical wires. Customers deliver copper ingots to the company, which smelts them in a single batch and then draws the metal into wire which is then, in the course of an involved process, insulated, cut to length, and spooled according to the needs of the market. The first question to arise is whether the act of smelting *itself* is a process that creates a new thing. Even if one is minded to answer this question in the negative (e.g. on the basis that the wire-drawing and insulation, not the smelting, is the really important process) the smelting does, in fact, create a new thing. The copper ingots

[266] e.g. OLG Stuttgart 20 March 2001, NJW 2001 p. 2889. It is not sufficient to *pose* a hodgepodge of objects as an artwork. Cass. 12 December 1991, no. 13399, DVD Juris Data, was concerned with Joseph Beuys' 'Olive Stones'. These were composed of a simple 'installation', meaning the side-by-side placement of five sandstone tubs which had been used to decant olive oil in the eighteenth century. Beuys had discovered them in the Palazzo Durini and had filled them with stone monoliths and olive oil. That was all. A 'new thing' was not created by this action; the owners of the tubs retained their ownership.

do not survive this process as such—all that subsists is the volume of mixed molten copper. The owners of the ingots lose their right of ownership upon destruction of the ingots and acquire a right of co-ownership in the fluid, and therefore mixed, volume of copper. 'Processing' begins at this point (at the latest), even if one is not prepared to recognize the smelting as the relevant point in time. Equally, new things are created whatever view one takes—first the single length of wire, then the insulated, measured, cut, and spooled electrical cable. Disagreement might arise on who should be seen as the 'creator', but the result is clear in the end: it is the manufacturer, not the customers. If this is accepted and the value creating work embodied in the cables exceeds the value of the copper ingots, the manufacturer becomes owner of the cable rolls, subject of course to whatever contractual arrangements he has made to transfer ownership in them to his customers.

9.43 The proposition that a 'new' thing can be created from one or more objects is only plausible if it is first accepted that normative considerations flow also into the concept of 'real' things. However, this recognition does not undermine the validity of the basic proposition. The distinction between 'real' and 'normative' things is only of relevance insofar as it helps to determine which objects are fitting objects of property rights for what reasons; it does not help to determine what should be regarded as a single object and what should be regarded as two objects. The legal rules that stipulate the prerequisites (and consequences) of the transformation of real things into *new* real things no more exceed this framework than the rules of law governing accession and components. What is more difficult to articulate is the reason for which private law operates with the idea that new objects arise from processing in the first place. The answer could run that it does so in order to avoid undue divergence from common sense and the customs of the market. The law has to be comprehensible in everyday speech and habits of thought.[267] In other words, no legal system can afford to deny that 'sausage', 'copper wire', 'mobile telephones', and 'television screens' are bought and sold (as opposed to a sum of resources and intermediate products whose present condition and interactions cannot be described in a manner fitting of the needs of the market or permitting of the formulation of rules of property law). The central concern is convenience and efficiency, not physics. The acquiror of a product should not need to concern himself with its history; he should, wherever possible, only need to negotiate with *one* owner and acquire *one* thing. If that were not the case, no manufactured product could be apprehended as a unitary object of property rights, with the implication that the market could not fulfil its function of facilitating the ordered distribution of things among a community of persons.

9.44 Most European legal systems reflect this imperative of simplification in their legislative provisions, in which a recurring feature is the creation of a 'new thing' following investment of effort. The theme is present even in traditional codifications that concern

[267] *Dolezalek*, AcP 195 (1995) pp. 392, 398.

themselves little with the categorization of 'things' and, for this reason, contain no detailed provisions (or even general principles) on the creation of 'new' things. When it is accepted that an object can change its owner through processing or transformation (which is the case in both common law and Civilian systems),[268] it follows implicitly that the new right of ownership arises in a new thing. Otherwise, the loss of ownership in the original material could not be justified. For this reason, no objections could really be made from the English point of view against the relevant explanations in the Continental codifications. Take, for example, *spécification* in Arts 570–572 French Civil Code. The theme of these articles is the ownership relations concerning a *chose nouvelle* that has arisen through the processing of some moveable material that belongs in whole or part to another.[269] It would be insufficient to concentrate only on the *spécification* of materials belonging to another;[270] equally, it would not do to exclude the unification of two things from the scope of *spécification* and to interpret that law by reference to the idea, as found in the *Code civil*, that the investment of effort 'reifies' the things—i.e. makes it proper to consider them as 'thing'.[271] The *spécification* is, regardless of its

[268] See, especially, *Borden (UK) Ltd v Scottish Timber Products Ltd* [1981] Ch 25 (CA), esp. p. 35 (*Bridge* LJ), 44 (Templeman LJ), 46 (*Buckley* LJ), 43 and 44 (Templeman LJ) (if resin is used in the production of wood chipboards with the result that the resin no longer exists, then the ownership of the resin expires); *Clough Mill Ltd v Martin* [1985] 1 WLR 111, 123 (Oliver LJ: Yarn is spun into cloth; the cloth is a new thing, the retention of title in the yarn expires); *Re Peachdart Ltd* [1984] Ch 131, 142 (Vinelott J: if leather is cut to produce handbags, the ownership of the leather expires) and *Chaigley Farms Ltd v Crawford, Kaye & Grayshire Ltd* [1996] BCC 957, 963 (Garland J: if animals are delivered to a slaughterhouse and slaughtered there, the ownership of the animals expires).

[269] *Terré and Simler*, Les biens[8], p. 218 no. 247. The term *spécification* expresses the idea that a thing is 'new' when it belongs to a new type or category (*Dolezalek* op. cit. p. 396). The German word '*Verarbeitung*' has its core in the added '*Arbeit*' (lit. 'work'), *spécification* in *especie*. Likewise, *especificación* in Spanish is an alteration of the type (*mutación de la especie*); one is concerned with a *speciem mutare* or *speciem facere* (*Díez-Picazo*, Fundamentos III[5], p. 315). For Swedish law, von Bar (*-Westermann and Herrmann*), Sachenrecht in Europa I, p. 505 maintain that the decisive factor is whether the processing or assembly of things includes an alteration of *identity*, meaning that a new thing must be created in relation to the original objects.

[270] One view correctly states that it is not only the ownership rights to the original materials which expire following the process, but all the limited real rights which encumber the right of ownership, too. According to a widely held view, this applies even if it is the owner of the original materials who does the processing: see § 950(2) German Civil Code (bad faith or loss of the original materials do not hinder this: OLG Köln 23 August 1996, NJW 1997 p. 2187); § 107(5) Estonian Asjaõigusseadus; Art. 1061(2) Greek Civil Code (which diverges by requiring the owner not to add in bad faith: Art. 1062 Greek Civil Code, see further *Triantos*, AK, Art. 1061 p. 1285 no. 6); Art. 58 Slovenian SPZ, and for Czech and Slovakian law *Eliáš et al.*, Občanský zákoník. Velký akademický komentář I, p. 608. Austrian law is more nuanced. The rights of third parties to a thing expire if it is installed as a dependent component of another thing (OGH 4 December 1984, SZ 57/192 concerning retention of title). In the case of processing, however, a retention of title in the original materials is held to give rise to co-ownership in the product (OGH 16 November 1976, SZ 49/138: retention of title in the fabric continues as co-ownership of the blouses). Rights of third parties should only expire if the thing is intended for processing (OGH 12 April 1961, ÖJZ 1961 p. 323). For Spanish law, *Díez-Picazo*, Fundamentos III[5], p. 317 emphasizes that Art. 383 Spanish Civil Code only includes the owner of the material (*dueño de la materia*) and the author of the processing (*especificante*). The question of ownership usually arises between the author of the process and the former owner of the materials. Nevertheless, a situation can arise in which the processor is already the owner of the original materials, but these were charged with the rights of third parties. In this case, Art. 383 Spanish Civil Code should be applied by analogy: if the *especificante* acted in good faith, the real rights should expire; if the *especificante* acted in bad faith they should continue. In the latter case the holder of these rights could be contented with a claim in damages. Art. 94 of the Bulgarian Property Law Statute distinguishes according to whether the processor acted *bona fides* or *mala fides*; if the latter, ownership falls to the owner of the materials subject to an obligation to restitute any unjustified enrichment.

[271] This position is taken by *Dross*, Les choses, p. 730 no. 396. Cass. civ. 1 December 2011, Bull. civ. 2011, I, p. 201 no. 208; JCP 2012 p. 1650, note by *Caron* concerned a work by the artist Giacometti, which had been engraved in zinc plates. The Giacometti Foundation had claimed that it had become the owner of the plates by 'accession'. The *Cour de Cassation* rejected this, however only with the argument that customs in the profession contradicted an *accession mobilière*. See also *Terré and Simler* op. cit., who attempt to distinguish *spécification* from *adjonction* by

placement in the code, not an accident of accretion but effects the creation of a completely new thing.[272] Nor is it helpful to claim that the *spécification* creates, rather than a new thing, a 'complex thing' (*chose complex*).[273] This does not, after all, answer the true question: is one looking at one *chose* or several *choses*? In Austria, the civil code does not adopt a more conceptually clear approach, but the judicial opinions do, insofar as they define 'processing' [*Verarbeitung*] in §§ 414 and 415 Austrian Civil Code (which is set out in the context of 'accession') as the 'transformation [*Umgestaltung*] of a new thing'—i.e. a change of its external form, dedication to purpose, usability or application, which according to commercial use creates a thing of a new kind.[274] True, nowhere in the code is a 'new thing' mentioned expressly, but the position of the Austrian courts is nevertheless supported by reference to § 416 Austrian Civil Code, which allocates third party materials applied only to the 'improvement of a thing' to the 'owner of the principal thing.' With the exception of the Portuguese Civil Code, all the later codifications operate with the criterion of a 'new thing' or a work of a 'new kind' (e.g. Art. 383 Spanish Civil Code, which speaks of an *obra de nueve especie*). However, surprisingly, they apply this criterion not in their provisions on things but in those governing the circumstances of *ex lege* acquisition of ownership in moveables (e.g. Art. 94 Bulgarian Property Law; § 950 German Civil Code, § 106 Estonian LPA; Art. 1061 Greek Civil Code; Art. 940 Italian Civil Code; Art. 985 Latvian Civil Code; Art. 4.55 Lithuanian Civil Code; Art. 5:16(1) Netherlands Civil Code; Art. 192 Polish Civil Code; § 135b Slovakian Civil Code; Art. 57 Slovenian Civil Code; § 135b Czech Civil Code [1964]); § 1074 Czech Civil Code [2014]). Art. 1336 Portuguese Civil Code speaks of *coisa transformada* and Art. 1337 Portuguese Civil Code of *coisa especificada*).

stating, with reference to Art. 566 French Civil Coded, that in the case of the latter, two things which are owned by different people are unified to create a new thing in such a way that the two original things can be separated. This does not touch the core of the matter, particularly as a *mélange* is characterized by the original things not being separable using a justifiable effort.

[272] Accurately stated in *Zenati-Castaing and Revet*, Les biens[3], p. 215 no. 140 ('*La spécification n'est pas intrinsèquement un cas d'accession*'). This view is also taken in Portuguese law, in which the legislator was likewise imprecise when regulating manipulation and transformation in the context of the law of accession (Arts 1336–1338 Portuguese Civil Code). The characterization as an 'accession' within the meaning of Art. 1325 Portuguese Civil Code would have the equally unavoidable and unacceptable consequence of having to characterize work as a thing (*Oliveira Ascensão*, Direito civil—Reais[5], p. 303). This is repeated in Spanish law. Arts 375–383 Spanish Civil Code, dedicated to the law of accession (*derecho de accesión*), again include *especificación*. Art. 377(2) Spanish Civil Code considers the worked material (the metal, the canvas, the stone which a sculptor transforms into a statue, etc) as a subsidiary. *Díez-Picazo*, Fundamentos III[5], p. 315 and *Díez-Picazo*, Ensayos jurídicos III, pp. 3237, 3255 clarifies that as *accesión* means the connection of one thing with another (Art. 375 Spanish Civil Code), '*en la especificación no puede haber accesión*'. The *especificación* is thus the use of another's material to produce a work of a different type (Art. 383 Spanish Civil Code).

[273] This position is taken by *Dross* op. cit. p. 731 no. 396-2 ('*L'article 570 se réfère certes à la formation "d'une chose nouvelle", mais la place de la spécification au sein des dispositions relatives à l'accession et le fait que son attribution ne s'opère pas selon les principes de l'occupation... mais balance entre le maître de la matière et le spécificateur, montre suffisamment qu'il n'y a pas chose nouvelle mais bien complexe*').

[274] OGH 12 April 1961, ÖJZ 1961 p. 323 ('In any case, there must be a transformation of the thing, in a change in its external form, dedication to a [different] purpose, and application. What is decisive is the commercial consensus on whether a 'new' thing arises or whether one is dealing with the same thing, which has merely experienced a minimal change') and OGH 15 September 1967, ÖJZ 1968 p. 293 (*Verarbeitung* requires the 'transformation' of a thing that changes its dedication to purpose and useability. What is said to be determinative is whether the thing belongs to a different category following the work, whether it now serves a different purpose, or whether it has been made useless for the original purpose).

How one determines whether (and from what point in time)[275] a new thing has really been created depends on a value judgment based on consideration of a whole range of criteria. Those criteria must, accordingly, reflect the reason for asking such a question—namely, the idea that it can be reasonable to extinguish the right of ownership in an 'old' thing (along with all the lesser rights that encumber that right) and to allocate ownership in the 'new' things that have been created from it *either* to the owner of the old thing *or* to the creator of the new things. This allocation of ownership proceeds *ex lege*, and does not depend on the idea that processing brings about an ownerless thing—not even for a 'juristic instant'. Intuitively, one looks to whether a processed object is given a new name in commercial usage (e.g. from 'grain' to 'wholegrain bread').[276] The new name indicates that the original thing has been assigned to a new 'species' by the market, and that is, historically, the core idea of 'specification'.[277] One must also bear in mind, a further range of considerations: common parlance is often imprecise and technical lexicons too precise; the relevant domain of transaction is often difficult to define exactly; intermediate products within a single process are often seen differently to intermediate products that are sold on to a third party for further processing;[278] a legal system need not be bound by linguistic accidents (e.g. German distinguishes between a (raw) *Diamant* and a (cut) *Brilliant* but English refers to both simply as 'diamonds'[279]). It is also possible for a new thing to exist at the end of some manufacturing process that is called exactly the same as the material from which it was made (e.g. a 'ring' can be melted down and cast into new 'ring' in a different style).[280] Some of these problems 9.45

[275] One coincides with the other on the abstract-terminological level. However, there can be slightly differences in the legal appraisal of facts in practice, as it is sometimes said (inconsistently) that a new thing is only created upon completion of the process of alteration (thus e.g. BGH 12 January 1972, JZ 1972 p. 165 [sale of cabbage under a retention of title; the defendant had not acquired ownership of the resulting sauerkraut through processing it, but rather, at best, acquired ownership of the final product, the tinned sauerkraut; even the latter was rejected *in casu*, as the value of the processing was too low], as well as OLG Bremen 4 May 2006, OLGR Bremen 2006 p. 728 [started, but not yet finished, armouring of a limousine had not yet created a new thing]), while others bring the time forward and focus on the irreversibility of the measures (*Re Peachdart Ltd* [1984] Ch 131, 142 [Vinelott J: cutting of leather for a handbag; a new thing is created upon the cutting, not the completion of the handbag]).

[276] The 'new name' can be found repeatedly in the judgments of German courts (e.g. OLG Köln 10 May 1991, NJW 1991 p. 2570; OLG Köln 23 August 1996, NJW 1997 p. 2187 [stating that the requirements of § 950(1) German Civil Code are fulfilled particularly if the newly produced thing is put into circulation under a new name and the economic significance of the produced thing is a different one in relation to the original material]; KG 30 September 1960, NJW 1961 pp. 1026, 1027 ['linguistic usage'] and OLG Düsseldorf 13 August 1998, OLGR 1999 p. 219); however, the BGH has never, it seems, used the 'new name' as a dispositive criterion. For Spanish law, *Aymerich Renteria*, ADC 40 (1987) p. 1194, states that the name of the product is on the same level with the other criteria (form, quality, purpose), which play a role in the assessment of novelty; after all, the product of labour which is presented with a new name would almost always count as new. The grain example stems, with alteration, from *Triantos*, AK, Art. 1061 Greek Civil Code p. 1285 no. 4.

[277] e.g. *Becquet*, Le bien industriel, p. 110 no. 47 (*spécification* is the transformation of a thing of a certain type to a thing of a different type. The thing is 'new' if it differs from the old thing by its name, its form or chemical composition. If an object obtains a different name in common parlance, then one can be 'certain' that it is a new thing).

[278] 'Sauerkraut', for example, could be seen as a new product even when the processing enterprise does nothing more than fermenting the cabbage and then sends it off for packaging by a specialist third party. When, on the other hand, the whole process is completed under the auspices of a single enterprise, from cabbage to cans, then according to BGH 12 January 1972, JZ 1972 p. 165 a 'new' thing only arises through the act of canning and not fermentation.

[279] Example taken from *Aymerich Renteria*, ADC 40 (1987) pp. 1149, 1195.

[280] Example taken from *Eliáš et al.*, Občanský zákoník. Velký akademický komentář I, p. 607.

can be resolved by the popular method of referring to 'usage in the market',[281] but many of them cannot. A criterion often found in the older literature,[282] albeit one which has long been recognized as insufficient on its own,[283] is the concept of added value. This criterion is more relevant to the question of ownership than to the characterization of 'things'. In the Netherlands, one finds a modernized form of this criterion in the proposition that a new thing (as defined in Art. 5:16 Netherlands Civil Code) is 'new' when its value is due in large part to the relevant process itself.[284] The test, whether the economic function of the erstwhile things has changed or, as in Italian law, whether they have a new 'socio-economic individuality', is helpful even if it is not always incisive.[285] A new thing is certainly present where the materials from which it was made cannot be recovered any longer, at least not with reasonable effort. 'Soap' is thus a new thing,[286] regardless of whether it was made with materials belonging to the manufacturer, materials belonging to a third party, or with a mix of the two.[287] A further indicium for the existence of a new thing is the change of form of the materials used.[288] The chemical treatment of lumber against pest infestation no more creates a new thing than feeding or training an animal[289] or spray-painting an automobile;[290] by way of contrast, processing leather into a handbag[291] or processing limestone into quicklime does.[292]

[281] e.g. Palandt (*-Bassenge*), BGB[74], § 950 no. 3; Nieuwenhuis/Stolker/Valk (*-Stolker*), BW[6], Art. 5:16 no. 3b; Austrian OGH 12 April 1961, ÖJZ 1961 p. 323.

[282] e.g. *Rouček, Sedláček, et al.*, Komentář k československému obecnému zákoníku občanskému a občanské právo platné na Slovensku a v Podkarpatské Rusi II, p. 438. See also Art. 94 Bulgarian LPA.

[283] Processing barley into malt creates a new thing (BGH 28 June 1954, BGHZ 14 p. 114), likewise according to OLG Stuttgart 20 March 2001, NJW 2001 p. 2889 for the alteration of an artwork to a new stage of development (e.g. colouring a pencil sketch), but this also applies if the malt or the finished artwork achieves a lower market value (due to a collapse of prices or a change in aesthetic perceptions) than the barley or the draft sketch. Incidentally, the question of whether a new thing was created by an increase in value should not be conflated with the question of to whom the new thing should belong. For example, under Art. 192 § 1 Polish Civil Code a person who has created a new moveable thing from another person's materials acquires ownership of the thing if the value of the amount of work involved exceeds the value of the materials; in this case the value only plays a role for the allocation of ownership, but not for the decision of whether a 'new' thing exists.

[284] *Stolker* op. cit.

[285] *Gambaro and Morello*, Trattato dei diritti reali I, p. 801.

[286] Example taken from *Torrente and Schlesinger*, Manuale di diritto privato[20], p. 289.

[287] *Borden (UK) Ltd v Scottish Timber Products Ltd* [1981] Ch 25 (CA).

[288] See, *inter alia*, Art. 983 Latvian Civil Code. A change in the form appears also to be indicative in Art. 940 Italian Civil Code, itself modelled on Art. 570 French Civil Code. Art. 940 Italian Civil Code states that a person who has used a material which did not belong to him to create a new thing acquires ownership of the new thing *regardless of whether the material can regain its original form or not.* While he must pay the owner the price of the material, this is not the case if the value of the material greatly exceeds the value of the work involved. In the latter case, the thing belongs to the owner of the material, who must pay for the work. The emphasized wording merely means that a transformation can be present even if the material's original form can be recreated. *Ourliac and de Malafosse*, Histoire du droit privé. Les biens[2], p. 171 no. 145 confirm this by defining specification as the alteration of a raw material through human effort, either by changing its chemical composition or its physical structure.

[289] Swedish HD 1 December 1959, NJA 1959 p. 590 (piglets had been sold subject to a retention of title and on an instalment plan to a fattener who later became insolvent; the buyer was permitted to select the [now adult] pigs, despite the main increase in value being due to the fattening); *Westermann/Gursky/Eickmann*, Sachenrecht[8], § 53 no. 6 (training an animal).

[290] However, OLG Bremen 4 May 2006, OLGR Bremen 2006 p. 728, considers it possible that the armouring of a limousine (as protection against assassins) creates a new thing in comparison to the standard model.

[291] *Re Peachdart Ltd* [1984] Ch 131 (*Vinelott* J).

[292] *Thorogood v Robinson* (1845) 6 QB 769, 115 ER 290.

b. Allocation of Property Rights in New Things

(1) Material Owner and Manufacturer

The question of ownership arises as soon as a transformative process creates one or more new things. The person who owned the thing(s) used as material and the person who did the processing are the only conceivable candidates. If the circumstances implicate several such persons, the question is one of co-ownership rather than sole ownership; however, although multiple *material owners* are readily conceivable, there seems to be no support for the idea that co-ownership arises in the case that multiple persons are involved in *processing* those materials into something new.[293] In any case, the internal logic of the law of processing seems to exclude any further persons, beyond material owner and processor, from being considered. If some other person held a lesser property right in the materials (i.e. a right encumbering the right of ownership in certain materials), the best he could hope for is for his right to subsist and encumber the right of ownership in the *new* thing. He cannot expect to have his right elevated to a right of ownership *per se*.[294] The processor, on the other hand, cannot 'transfer' the productive capacity of his enterprise, nor encumber it by way of security—not even in an anticipatory manner. In contrast to the enterprise as a whole, 'labour' and the organization of productive capacity is not a fitting object of property rights itself. In consequence, it appears impossible for a third party to stipulate (with *erga omnes* effect by agreement with the processor) that the latter should work on its behalf, such that *it* be seen as the 'processor' of the new thing and acquire ownership *ex lege*. (Consider, for example, a bank that has extended credit to a manufacturing firm.) Nor can the material owner and the (*de facto*) processor stipulate by agreement that a third party is to count as the (*de jure*) processor—neither a creditor nor anyone else.[295] Any other 9.46

[293] A similar constellation is not unthinkable (*Vieira*, Direitos reais, p. 364; *Fiala and Kindl*, Občanský zákoník komentář I, p. 351), but unlikely, as a cooperation of multiple fabricants is usually a company and thus only one manufacturer or 'specificant', as companies which operate on different levels of a process are typically each the manufacturer of a semi-finished product and, as sub-contractors are typically employees under the organizational control of another, are excluded from being potential owners of the product (e.g. BGH 20 January 1988, BGHZ 103 p. 108).

[294] Sometimes, the question even arises whether a limited real right subsists not only to encumber the right of ownership in materials in the case that ownership of the new thing vests in the material owner, but also whether it could subsist to encumber the processor's right of ownership in the newly created thing, which arises and displaces the (encumbered) right of ownership of the materials owner. The situation is as follows according to the wording of Art. 8(1) and (2) Polish Law on Registered Pledges: if a registered pledge existed over the materials, the product of the relevant process is subject to the pledge. An economy with a weak credit system has a strong imperative to provide robust creditor protection. From the property law perspective, however, it is unconvincing. The materials, after all, do not survive the kind of process we are concerned with (potatoes are made into chips, sugar into sweets ['a typical situation': *Mojak and Widło*, Zastaw Rejestrowy i rejestr zastawów[3], p. 109 no. 3]); a register cannot say anything about things that do not exist, so it cannot prevent their unencumbered good faith acquisition by a third party (Art. 13 op. cit.) either.

[295] Admittedly, not even this appears to be completely certain. This question has not yet been decided in English law. It is conceivable that the acquisition of ownership by the manufacturer must be correctly interpreted as arising through possession, not processing. This might lead to direct acquisition by a bank through the manufacturer as intermediary. However, thus far, this is mere speculation. Likewise, in French law, this question is never specifically addressed. However, there are voices in the literature that would interpret the provisions on *spécification* to mean that 'labour' should be declared as the principal thing. Further, there seems to be agreement that the law of *accession mobilière* (to which the French Civil Code also counts *spécification*) can be avoided by agreement (e.g. Rép. civ. Dalloz [-*Cohet-Cordey*], V° Accession, p. 3 no. 11 and *Larroumet*, Les biens[5], p. 609 no. 968; with certain caveats also *Becquet*, Le bien industriel, p. 351 no. 145). If one takes this point of departure literally, it would still seem

approach would not only bring about a 'reification' of *activity*, but also a circumvention of the *numerus clausus* principle that limits the objects and type of property rights. Creditors are not implicated in the conflict of rights (of ownership) brought about by a process of 'specification'. Banks must, accordingly, get by with the conventional means at their disposal, subject to the preconditions of validity governing acquisition of the right of ownership between parties pursuant to contract—even and especially when the relevant security arrangements were established before the thing in question existed. Theoretically, it would be possible to allocate ownership to the material owner *and* processor jointly as a matter of principle. Fortunately, however, this finds little support as a basic approach.[296] Co-ownership vesting in material owner and processor remains an exceptional solution, used if at all to resolve exceptional cases.[297] To treat the

conceivable that a court could arrive at the position that material owner and *spécificant* could accord the newly created thing to a third party by way of a direct acquisition. In German (*Dolezalek*, AcP 195 [1995] pp. 392, 413 while admittedly being unclear), Portuguese, and Czech law, on the other hand, this conclusion would be impossible. Processing is a state of affairs that triggers acquisition of ownership *ex lege*; the provisions of § 950 German Civil Code and Arts 1336–1338 Portuguese Civil Code are thus consistently interpreted to be mandatory law. Czech law arrives at the same position under § 135b Czech [1964] and § 1074(1) in connection with § 978 Czech Civil Code [2014]. In Italian law, an agreement regarding the ownership of a future thing only acquires *erga omnes* effect when the thing actually arises (Art. 1472 Italian Civil Code). The thing must have been created, before it can be conveyed to third parties; a deeming 'processing clause' in favour of a third party is thus excluded. In the end, the situation under Austrian law is the same. In the case that A processes things on behalf of B, which things belong to C, A is said to become the owner by force of law (Klang [-*Klang*], ABGB II^2, p. 287). How this result is reconciled with the generally accepted principle of party autonomy, however, is unclear. It would seem that A and B ought to have the freedom to stipulate which of them becomes owner at the end of the process. The solution, in Austrian law at least, could be C's role in the relevant process—i.e. as a precondition to the effectiveness of the relevant contractual agreement. Even agreements between the person ordering (B) and the person processing (A) are possible under limited circumstances only; for example, a person who commissions another to process his materials can retain ownership in the products that result up to the value of the materials, but no further (Klang [-*Bydlinski*], ABGB IV(2)^2, p. 626); anything above this would violate the principle against non-possessory pledges (Rummel [-*Spielbüchler*], ABGB I^3, § 415 no. 7). If, on the other hand, the processor is also owner of the processed materials, an acquisition of ownership by another can only occur as a result of a legal transaction under §§ 425 and following Austrian Civil Code (*Gschnitzer/Faistenberger/Barta/Call/Eccher*, Sachenrecht^2, p. 92). A valid agreement to the effect that a non-involved third party can become owner by way of direct acquisition thus appears impossible: see also BGH 27 September 1990, BGHZ 112 p. 243.

[296] The Austrian OGH supports this position. It states that the basic idea [*Grundgedanke*] of §§ 414 and following Austrian Civil Code is that the owner of the original materials and the processor acquire co-ownership of the product, namely of the 'new' thing (thus, renouncing previous jurisdiction, OGH 15 November 1976, SZ 49/138 in the case of delivery with retention of title. OGH 22 September 1927, SZ 9/175 had decided that retention of title in a 'new' thing *yet to be manufactured* could not exist; such an agreement would be inconsistent with the principle of legal certainty. OGH 15 November 1976 no longer considered this argument convincing. The legislature only provided for the acquisition of sole ownership if one of the original things was the principal thing or if the value of either the original materials or the process greatly exceeded the other).

[297] Under Art. 572 French Civil Code, co-ownership arises when someone uses their own and someone else's materials to create a thing of a new kind, even if the materials are not completely destroyed as things in their own right, so long as they could not be (re)separated without some loss. In the latter case, the new thing belongs to both owners in common and in relation to the materials that belonged to each of them and in consideration of the nature of those materials and the cost of the relevant procedure. That is a complicated solution, when one considers a textbook example such as the cabinetmaker that makes a wardrobe from his customer's wood and his own fasteners and fittings. It is also adopted in Art. 192 Polish Civil Code for the case that the value of labour and materials are equal (Radwański and Dybowski [-*Stelmachowski*], System Prawa Prywatnego III^2, p. 414 no. 200). BGH 19 October 1966, BGHZ 43, 117, NJW 1967 ü. 34 holds that it is possible to stipulate in a so-called 'processing clause', that the supplier of raw materials acquires a right of ownership in the finished product in proportion to the value of the materials he supplies. Under Arts 1336–1338 Portuguese Civil Code the creation of co-ownership in favour of material owner and processor is generally excluded. Under § 135b(1) Sentence 2 Czech Civil Code [1964], parity of value between labour and material gave rise to co-ownership, but the court could alter the proportions of ownership on the application of one of the parties with constitutive effect *Švestka (-Spáčil/Škárová/Hulmák)*, Občanský zákoník I^2, p. 789). Under § 1076 Czech [2014], co-ownership is possible between multiple material owners, but

material owner and processor as co-owners by default would be a lazy compromise. The law adopts the category of 'new things', after all, precisely in order to enable persons to alienate and acquire products without having to concern themselves with the chain of title throughout the stages of its production. Ideally, a single person should be able to determine the subsequent fate of a thing at any given point in time.

The proposition that the owner of materials from which a new thing is made is one candidate for the ownership of the new thing requires no special justification from the perspective of property law. Section 414 Austrian Civil Code even avows the fundamental principle that whoever processes the materials of another has no claim to the own them. The same proposition is found in other codifications, too, including Art. 570 French Civil Code and Art. 5:16(1) Netherlands Civil Code.[298] What is rule and what is exception is sometimes less than clear, but it is never in doubt that the owner of raw materials is presumed to be a candidate for ownership. This is evident in the fact that things can transmute into a new thing through natural events, destructive anger, or negligent damage.[299] The mere fact that a vase is shattered raises no question of ownership in the shards. The owner of the destroyed vase becomes *ex lege* owner of the newly created shards. One can justify this either on the basis of a state of affairs triggering some rule of acquisition (i.e. provisions allotting newly separated components of a thing to the owner of a thing such as § 953 German Civil Code, Art. 1064 Greek Civil Code and Art. 408(2) Portuguese Civil Code), or on the basis that the shards of a vase stand in lieu as a kind of surrogate.[300] Only the owner of the (erstwhile) vase has, in consequence, the right to take the shards to a ceramic workshop for reconstruction. As soon as a 'vase' exists (again), the whole game begins anew; now, however, the owner of the workshop enters into play as a candidate for ownership (so much is implicit, whether intentionally or not, in the literal meaning of many codifications)—it is he, after all, who transformed so many worthless shards into a vase again. 9.47

not between the material owner(s) and the processor. The position is the same in Italian law. Art. 940 Italian Civil Code envisions only the creation of sole ownership according to the relative value of material and labour. Co-ownership is a peculiarity of the law of mixture (Art. 939 Italian Civil Code).

[298] Art. 5:16(1) Netherlands Civil Code is the 'basic idea' (N.v.W., Parl. Geschiedenis V, p. 110; Nieuwenhuis/Stolker/Valk [-*Stolker*], BW[6], Art. 5:16 no. 2). Art. 570 French Civil Code states that if a workman uses material which does not belong to him to create a thing of a new type, whether that material can regain its original form or not, then the owner of the material has the right to demand the newly created thing in exchange for the estimated pay. The structure of the legislation means this too is a fundamental principle.

[299] If a thing is destroyed (like the vase in the following example), one can only argue that no 'new' thing exists only if one assumes that 'new' requires an increase in value or even an increase in value brought about by labour. This is not convincing; an increase in value presents a reason to allocate the newly created thing to the person whose labour created it from something old, but has no bearing on the question whether a new thing has been created distinct from its input materials.

[300] Naturally, there are situations in which one cannot speak of a surrogate, but in this case, one is almost always in the thought pattern of the doctrine of mixture, meaning situations in which the original material is combined with other objects or contaminated by them. Only in such cases can a direct acquisition of ownership by way of possession come into consideration. In cases of processing, the manufacturer will always be in possession of the thing. Thus, there is no reason to differentiate between acquisition of ownership by way of possession and by way of processing—not even when thinking of the acquisition scenarios recognized by the common law.

9.48 Against this discussion, one must ask why the European legal systems consider the processor as a candidate for ownership at all. This question, however, has nothing to do with theories about the appropriate social and moral value accorded to capital and labour, which tend to be ideologically loaded.[301] Rather, the question is one completely internal to property law—it is a purely 'capitalist' policy choice that falls to be taken, as it were, and so much is evident from the fact that the *employee* who does the relevant work is never considered, as such, in the role of the 'processor' or 'manufacturer'. This role is reserved for the owner of the relevant enterprise. Property law often privileges the person who creates the increase in value inherent in the new object; in the Continental systems, at least, the creation of value generally leads the allocation of ownership.[302] That, in turn, bears obvious resemblance to an 'insolvency law' type of justification: because the resources of the processor enable this value creation, those resources (in the form of ownership in the product) should remain in the patrimony of the processor—and, accordingly, accessible to his creditors. The erstwhile owner of the materials (and, in case of insolvency, *his* creditors) should not be enriched with value created by another. This justification falls short, however, to the extent that some adjustment is generally presupposed, in the form of payment of money, to balance the relative enrichment between them.[303] It thus remains unexplained why the processor's creditors (but not the material owner's creditors) should be privileged, in insolvency and enforcement proceedings, with a right to the newly created thing rather than a claim for money to compensate the loss of property rights. Even if one does not want to discount it completely, the creation of value as a criterion of ownership allocation must be interpreted as a market-oriented criterion. Ownership in a new product accrues to the producer, when it does so, not in the interests of the producer *per se*, nor even in the interests of his creditors. Rather, it accrues to him in the interests of *customers*. The customers of a manufacturer ('the market') have an interest to acquire products without running the risk of their rights being subordinated to an outsider by operation of good faith acquisition rules. Customers should be able to see the manufacturer as the owner of newly created goods; if the case were otherwise, they would be required to enquire after the provenance of goods produced from multiple components, which can be an endless enquiry. A person should be able to go to a bakery and buy a 'cake', without thinking about whether the baker has duly paid his supplier of flour (and eggs, and sugar). Where, however, the 'baker' is merely a trader who procures his cakes in a marketable state from a wholesale bakery, customer protection is rather subordinate to the law of good faith acquisition. The formal justification for this is that the cake in question is no 'new thing' *vis-à-vis* the final consumer; substantively, we are concerned with

[301] This can be, and is frequently, viewed differently in light of theories from the world of law and economics (e.g. *Demsetz*, AmEconRev 57 [1967] p. 347).

[302] This view is taken in almost all Civilian systems; see e.g. for Italian law *Torrente and Schlesinger*, Manuale di diritto privato[14], p. 277 and *Mattei*, La proprietà, p. 186 (the legislature decided as a matter of policy that the value of work should find expression in property rights).

[303] See e.g. Art. 94 Bulgarian LPA; § 95(1) German Civil Code; Art. 571 French Civil Code; Art. 1063 Greek Civil Code; Art. 940 Italian Civil Code; Artikel 983 Latvian Civil Code; Art. 4:55(1) Lithuanian Civil Code; Art. 383(1) and (2) Spanish Civil Code; § 1074(2) Czech Civil Code, and § 5:65 Hungarian Civil Code.

a problem that arises in every trading business. The risk that a trader is not the owner of his stock in trade is a general one, present every time any person acquires any thing. We are here concerned with a much more specific risk. The purchaser of a newly created thing should, at the very least, be able to proceed on the assumption that he is acquiring *one* thing; he should not be exposed to the risk that his act of purchase itself is already a violation of another's right of ownership because one of the components from which the thing was made is the property of a third party. (Take, for example, a raisin baked in a cake.) That the *whole* cake is not really the property of the (apparent) 'baker' is a problem that has nothing to do with the law of processed goods. The latter is concerned only to exclude the problems that would arise if the third-party materials used to create a new thing were considered as 'things' that survived the manufacturing process. It is exponentially more difficult to recognize third party rights in processed materials than to recognize third party rights in the new thing considered as a whole—quite apart from the fact that one would simply never know where and when one could draw the line around an enquiry into provenance. The law of good faith acquisition thus extends a good step beyond the law of processed goods; without it, however, the latter would not function.

The core question is, accordingly, under which circumstances the customer's interest in allocation of the right of ownership to the producer is legitimate and, therefore, worthy of protection. The criterion of substantial value-creation by the manufacturer, which is used in many legal systems, makes sense only in *this* context. However, it does not express the true reason for which ownership accrues to the manufacturer. If it did, it would be impossible to explain why someone who creates a new thing on commission—often using another's materials, and typically, but not always, for consideration—does not become owner in any European legal system.[304] The owner of the ceramic workshop in **9.49**

[304] Different legal constructs are used to justify this result. Some claim that a person who manufactures a thing for another on the basis of a contract is not the thing's 'manufacturer' in the legal sense. Many consider the provisions or legal rules of specification to be modifiable despite their nature as property law provisions; they are not applicable if the parties had agreed something else. To support this claim, reference is frequently made to provisions from the law governing contracts for services, from which unreflecting conclusions are often drawn regarding the allocation of property rights. For example, in Italian law, reference is made to Art. 2223 Italian Civil Code, whereby the provisions regarding the *contratto d'opera* are also applicable where the manufacturer provides the materials—in such a case, the producer does not even acquire ownership where he owns the original materials. In Spanish law, too, the law of processing is held not to apply between the parties of a *contrato de obra*. A relevant manufacturing process is held only to exist in the case that the materials belong to a third party to the contract (Bercovitz Rodríguez-Cano [-*Bercovitz Álvarez*], Comentarios al Código Civil[2], p. 545). Under Art. 1212(1) Portuguese Civil Code, the decisive factor is the time of the acceptance of the work: if the work to be performed is the production of a moveable good, and if the materials concerned were provided wholly or substantially by the manufacturer, ownership in the materials passes, at the point in time of *acceptance* of the work, to the one who commissioned it; if the materials were provided by that party, on the other hand, they remain his property and he remains the owner of the finished product. Sometimes, reference is even made to the law of treasure trove(!) in order to bring about the desired result. In Austrian law, for example, it is generally assumed in the context of contracts for services [*Dienst- und Werkverträge*] that a manufacturing process is undertaken in the interests of the customer and that the customer 'remains' the owner of the products (*Iro*, Sachenrecht[4], § 6 no. 18; correctly and more extensively *Gschnitzer/Faistenberger/Barta/Call/Eccher*, Sachenrecht[2], p. 92). Reference is made, by way of justification, to § 401 Sentence 2 Austrian Civil Code (according to which, when a contractor is engaged expressly to search for a certain treasure, the client becomes sole owner if it is found and the contractor does not even get the co-ownership that would normally follow under § 401 Sentence 1 Austrian Civil Code). (Against the prevailing opinion, see *Holzner*, JBl 2009 pp. 684, 685, who interprets § 415 Austrian Civil Code to reach the result that

our example, above, acquires no ownership in the newly repaired vase, even though it is worth much more than the shards from which it was (re)constructed. This result has nothing to do with the 'value of the work' performed; it is, rather, explained by reference to the fact that a repair business *per se* produces new things that are generally recognizable and not for its own purposes—if it (unlawfully) puts those things on the market, then (but only then) is the purchaser's legal position governed by the law of good faith acquisition from a seller without title. A 'manufacturer' remains—as Art. 5:16(2) Netherlands Civil Code and § 5:65 Hungarian Civil Code expressly recognize[305]—someone who creates *for himself*, i.e. for his own stock, even where he uses the materials of another for that purpose and even where he knows that it does not belong to him.[306] The defining characteristic of value-creation, to which many Continental legal systems refer in order to distinguish the materials owner from the manufacturer, has the advantage of being relatively easy to incorporate into statutory language. But it does not express clearly the idea of greatest importance. Value-creation is only a helpful criterion when it expresses the complexity of the relevant manufacturing process. The more effort and materials are required for the production of a new thing, the more harmful it would be to commerce if the thing ever had to be deconstructed into its constituent parts; by the same token, the more easily recognizable the constituent materials remain, the less speaks for a change of ownership relations brought about through the manufacturing process. If a gold bar is crafted into an elegant necklace, no participant in the market should have to think about the provenance of the raw materials used; on the other hand, if boards are simply stacked in the yard of a sawmill, the purchaser cannot be entirely sure that the sawlogs belonged to the sawmiller. It is only probable, however, and by no means certain, that the value of the product is higher than the value of the raw materials in one case but lower in the other.

9.50 English law deals with the question of manipulation of things in a remarkably relaxed manner; a fixed rule to the effect that a manufacturer acquires ownership in a new thing only when he adds significant value to its constituent materials is foreign to the common law. An elaborate system in the manner of the Civilian tradition has not, to date, been developed in English law; the legal position is, accordingly, less than certain in some circumstances.[307] The general principle is that B becomes the owner at least in the case that B lawfully uses materials belonging to A for the purpose of

contract for services leads to a situation of co-ownership and that the situation differs only in the case of a contract of employment.)

[305] Where a person manufactures a new thing at the request of another, 5:16(2) Netherlands Civil Code provides that the manufacturer does not acquire ownership (N.v.W., Parl. Geschiedenis Boek V, pp. 110–11), and § 5:65(1) Hungarian Civil Code states that a person who has created a new thing through processing in good faith *for themselves* then they are obligated to refund the value of the thing or transfer title in the new thing depending on the choice of the original thing's owner (emphasis added).

[306] Certain legal systems reject an acquisition of ownership if the manufacturer is aware of the fact that the materials do not belong to him. This is the case under Art. 94 Bulgarian LPA and Art. 383 Spanish Civil Code. These provisions differentiate between good and bad faith.

[307] *Clough Mill Ltd v Martin* [1985] 1 WLR 111, 124 (Oliver LJ).

creating new goods when those materials cannot be individuated without unreasonable effort.[308] If materials are used for the production of another chattel, existing rights of ownership in them are extinguished.[309] A and B can, however, agree contractually that the materials owner (A) becomes owner of the goods upon their creation rather than the manufacturer (B).[310] This is also the position in Italian law. Beyond this, Art. 940 Italian Civil Code provides that someone who uses the materials of another to create a new thing becomes that thing's owner unless the value of the materials is significantly greater than the value of the new thing. In that case, the new thing belongs to the owner of the materials used to create it, who is obligated to pay the price of the work involved. A similar formulation is found in § 1074(1) Czech Civil Code[311] and § 950(1) German Civil Code,[312] and in numerous other civil codifications.[313] Art. 571 French and Belgian Civil Code go so far as to speak of a 'principal thing'.[314] Art. 5:16(2) Netherlands Civil Code gets closer to the effective point. Granted, the code treats manufacturing (rather unfortunately) as a sub-category of mixture.[315] But it

[308] Ibid., 119 (Goff LJ).

[309] *Chaigley Farms Ltd v Crawford, Kaye & Grayshire Ltd* [1996] BCivil Code 957, 961 (Garland J).

[310] *Clough Mill Ltd v Martin* op. cit. 119 (Goff LJ), 124 (Oliver LJ).

[311] According to this provision, a new thing created by the manipulation of moveable things belonging to several owners belongs to the person who contributed most to its creation with new materials or labour, provided that its earlier condition cannot be recreated at all or without unreasonable loss.

[312] The manufacturer acquires ownership of the thing as long as the value of the effort involved is not 'far less' than the value of the material.

[313] e.g. Art. 1061 sentence 1 Greek Civil Code (one who creates a new moveable thing through the manipulation of another's material acquires ownership in the new thing only when the value of the work required is obviously higher than the value of the materials); Art. 383(2) Spanish Civil Code (if the material is more precious than the work in which it was used, or is higher in value, its owner can elect between keeping the new thing subject to compensation or demanding compensation himself for loss of the material); Art. 192 § 1 Polish Civil Code (one who creates a new moveable thing from the materials of another acquires ownership in it if the value of the effort invested exceeds the value of the materials). In Austrian law, an extensive interpretation of § 416 Austrian Civil Code led to the same conclusion (Rummel [-*Spielbüchler*], ABGB I³, § 416 no. 2). Occasionally, it appears that users have been tangled up in the many constellations in which one can use the criterion of value creation. Under § 106(1) Estonian *Asjaõigusseadus*, the person who has manipulated another person's moveable thing into a new thing becomes the owner of this new thing if his work is worth more than the original thing. If the original thing has a higher value, then the new thing belongs to the owner of the original thing. However, if the manufacturer acted in bad faith, then the owner of the materials can demand the ownership of the new thing even if the work is worth more than the material. Also, under Art. 4:55(1) Lithuanian Civil Code, if a person manipulates another person's material in good faith, then the former becomes the owner of the new thing, as long as the work is worth more than the material. If the material is worth more than the work, then the owner of the material becomes the owner of the new thing. He can, however, renounce this acquisition of ownership and demand monetary compensation for his material. Further special provisions concern themselves with the different value relations, in case the manufacturer uses his own materials, the other person's, or a third party's (Art. 4:56 Lithuanian Civil Code). Art. 383 Latvian Civil Code speaks of the creation of a new thing by artistic or professional manipulation of another person's material. If this occurs in good faith and if the material has lost its original form, then the manufacturer becomes the owner of the new thing, even if the original materials can still be separated from the new thing. He must compensate the owner of the materials either with things of a like type and value, or with money; the monetary value is based on the highest achievable market price at the time of the process concerned (Art. 985 Latvian Civil Code). If things belonging to multiple persons were manipulated or connected, then the rules of the law of mixture (Arts 980–985) are applied. Conflicts between multiple persons about the exercise of a right of election are resolved according to the majority; the weight of each vote is determined by the respective share in the value; if necessary, lots will be drawn (Art. 986 Latvian Civil Code).

[314] If the work was so significant as to greatly exceed the value of the materials used, then the work would count as the principal thing and the manufacturer would have the right to retain the new thing by paying the owner the estimated price of the material at the time of the repayment.

[315] See T.M., Parl. Geschiedenis V, p. 109.

makes ownership by the manufacturer conditional on the question whether someone creates a new thing 'for himself',[316] regardless of whether the new thing is created from one or more moveable things that do not belong to him in whole or in part. The manufacturer becomes owner of the new thing unless the costs of doing so are too trivial to justify this result. Art. 5:16(2) Netherlands Civil Code is relevant above all in cases where goods are delivered conditional to a retention of title; the provision is intended to prevail over such a retention of title.[317] In Sweden, it is necessary to consult several different statutes to gain an overview of the applicable law; the result, however, falls within the broad parameters of the traditional rules of the Civilian tradition. If a new thing is produced on order from materials mainly at the manufacturer's own disposal, Swedish law sees a contract of sale (§ 2 Swedish Contract Law); in consequence, the buyer only acquires enforceable property rights with possession or registration (*Lag (1845:50 S.1) om handel med lösören, som köparen later i säljarens vård kvarbliva*). If, on the other hand, the buyer also provides the preponderance of the materials necessary for the commission, Swedish law sees a contract for services; the buyer retains a right to separate mixed property (*separationsrätt*) during the whole process.[318] Special rules exist for boats. A buyer who orders a boat that is yet to be build can retain a *separationsrätt* over his materials through registration (*Lag (1975:605) om registrering av batbyggnadsförskott*), and, when he has paid in advance, even in the whole boat.[319] If materials belonging to another have been implicated, the manufacturer acquires ownership in the new thing regardless of his good or bad faith, provided its value significantly exceeds the value of the materials in question.[320]

(2) Private Autonomy

9.51 As in doctrines governing the connection of objects, the law governing the transformation of things raises the question of whether the applicable rules can be contracted away or not. At first blush, a cleavage appears to run through the European legal systems. For some, the property law rules governing changes made to things are evidently a default rather than a mandatory regime and is for this reason factually[321] as well as

[316] Whether a person manufactures a thing (or has it manufactured) 'for themselves', depends largely, but not totally, on commercial usage according to H.R. 5 October 1990, NedJur 1992 no. 226 p. 869. A manufacturer still produces the thing for himself despite a client's commission if he (the manufacturer) has a decisive influence over the manner of the production, the final form of the product and carries the risks of loss, usability and price changes. Thus, tables from an industrial furniture production are the property of the manufacturer. However, if the client gives precise instructions to a carpenter to create a table from his own wood, then the client remains the owner of the table.

[317] N.v.W., Parl. Geschiedenis V, p. 111.

[318] *Håstad*, Sakrätt, pp. 44–5 (including a critique of the derivation of the *separationsrätt* from obligational categories); von Bar (-*Westermann and Herrmann*), Sachenrecht in Europa I, p. 505.

[319] This is criticized with reference to the legal position under § 950 German Civil Code by *Håstad* op. cit. p. 45. He doubts that it is genuinely justified to differentiate whether the manufacturer uses the client's wood or uses wood which he has bought using money the client has paid in advance.

[320] *Håstad* op. cit. p. 47.

[321] While German jurisprudence has an extravagant amount of cases regarding manufacturing processes, there are almost no decisions on this matter in French law (one of the very rare exceptions can be found in Cass. civ. 1

legally of subordinate importance;[322] for others, those rules are taken as self-evidently mandatory.[323] If one looks closer, however, these differences quickly diminish. Nowhere does the principle of private autonomy enable the material owner and the manufacturer to agree contractually, either between themselves or with a third party, that any given person becomes the owner of the new thing;[324] it always turns on whether they can agree (with *erga omnes* effect) that the materials owner should be seen as the owner of the new thing in circumstances where the law would otherwise allocate ownership to the manufacturer. This question, however, is answered in the positive almost everywhere, and this result is justified. Such a limited recognition of contractual autonomy does not undermine the consumer interest which underlies the legal regime for allocation of property rights in new manufactures. Where such a clause is given effect, the customer is subject to the general risk of acquiring a thing from someone without good title, but he is not subject to the specific risk that the components of a thing each have their own chain of title that must be investigated, on pain of standing only with whatever rights the law of good faith acquisition provide. An agreement between materials owner and manufacturer that imposed such a risk onto consumers would be unacceptable. Ultimately, the law of good faith acquisition only protects consumers from the risk that a new thing *in its entirety* belongs not to the person who produced it, but to some other (single) person; this is, however, a risk that everyone who acquires a thing has to run. As such, it is appropriate to permit a material owner and a manufacturer to structure their ownership relations *inter se* so long as the thing's status as a single object of property rights is not jeopardized.

December 2011, Bull. civ. 2011, I, p. 201 no. 208). The rules of the *Code civil* regarding *accession mobilière* are held to be basically useless. First, Art. 2276 French Civil Code almost always prevents the vindication of moveable things. Besides this, the allocation of the new thing generally follows the contract between the parties (seen in *Planiol/Ripert/Picard*, Les biens², p. 278 no. 284).

[322] e.g. see for Austrian law OGH 15 November 1976, SZ 49/138 and Rummel (-*Spielbüchler*), ABGB I³, § 415 no. 7; for Italian law Ruperto (-*Servello*), La giurisprudenza sul codice civile III, p. 763 (the rules governing processing should only be applied if the parties had not agreed anything else), and for Czech law *Švestka (-Spáčil/Škárová/Humák)*, Občanský zákoník Komentář I², p. 786 (§ 135b Czech Civil Code [1964] and § 1074(1) Czech Civil Code [2014] only concern cases in which a person manipulates the thing without a prior agreement with its owner; an agreement between the parties would be prioritized. It is admittedly not entirely clear how this position stands in relation to § 978 Czech Civil Code [2014], which provides that the parties may only diverge from the provisions of property law, if the legislation explicitly provides this. Such a provision cannot be found).

[323] The law governing manufacturing processes is mandatory law because of its nature as property law, according to the predominant view in German law (BGH 12 January 1972, JZ 1972 p. 165; BGH 15 June 1989, NJW 1989 p. 3213; indirectly in BGH 28 June 1954, BGHZ 14 pp. 114, 117) and in Hungarian law (Vékás [-*Menyhárd*], A Polgári Törvénykönyv magyarázatokkal, p. 407). In Spanish law, the acquisition of ownership by an *especificante* (Art. 383 Spanish Civil Code) in good faith is interpreted as a form of originary acquisition. The manufacturer obtains ownership by force of law; he is unable to renounce the acquisition. Even if he reaches a different contractual agreement with the owner of the materials, it is technically a renunciation of previously acquired ownership, not of the acquisition (*Lacruz Berdejo*, Elementos III(1)³, p. 152).

[324] For French law, *Becquet*, Le bien industriel, p. 155 no. 155 elucidates with reference to a decision reached in the context of landlord and tenant law, Cass. civ. 19 December 1972, Bull. civ. IV, no. 339 p. 314 that the mere fact that the manufacturer and the owner of the original thing had a contract was not sufficient. In order to be able to deviate from the rules concerning *accession mobilière*, the parties' desired result must be the creation of a new good.

9.52 Two alternatives are posited in legal systems that restrict contractual freedom to allocate ownership freely (and refrain from achieving the same result under cover of the proposition that the relevant provisions should not be *applied* in scenarios framed by a contractual agreement).[325] Each alternative leads, from the perspective of contractual autonomy, to very similar results. The first is to give one or the other party, according to the good or bad faith of the manufacturer, the option to elect between ownership in the thing of increased value or monetary compensation (this is the approach, e.g. taken by § 5:65 Hungarian Civil Code). The second is to tweak the concept of a 'manufacturer': a manufacturer 'in the legal sense' is said to be whoever the parties declare the manufacturer to be (where the parties are the 'factual' manufacturer and the materials owner). This is the approach taken in the German judicial authorities. 'It can be taken as uncontroversial on the basis of the authorities and doctrinal literature', said the *Bundesgerichtshof* in 1966,

> that the supplier who provides raw materials to a manufacturer subject to a retention of title can, through a contractual clause known as a 'manufacturing clause' [*Verarbeitungsklausel*], enforce his proprietary claim despite § 950 German Civil Code, through to the final manufactures.[326]

The court thus treated the law of manufacturing processes as mandatory on the one hand, but, on the other, permitted a contractual stipulation of the manufacturer that it described somewhat nebulously as 'a legal dealing of property law classification'.[327] The consequence is that the supplier of raw materials who avails himself of a retention of title clause becomes the owner *without* there occurring a derivative acquisition through the person of the factual manufacturer. It is even said to be possible to agree to a certain proportion of shared ownership in favour of the materials supplier.[328] In the framework of contracts for work, the party ordering the work is in any case characterized as the 'manufacturer'.[329] Effectively, one can observe the same result in Greek law as well.[330]

[325] See also, for Polish law, *Dmowski and Rudnicki*, Komentarz do kodeksu cywilnego I[6], p. 227 no. 1.

[326] BGH 19 October 1966, BGHZ 46 pp. 117, 118. This result is not nearly as uncontested in the literature as the BGH claimed. Some unreservedly hold to the mandatory nature of § 950 German Civil Code. They demand that the manufacturer should be determined only according to objective criteria, so there cannot be an objective transfer of the function as a manufacturer (e.g. *Westermann/Gursky/Eickmann*, Sachenrecht[8], § 53 III 2d, p. 484 no. 17). Others opine that the role of 'manufacturer' can be transferred to another party only where an industrial concern is *in fact* controlled by a third party and thus no longer really produces 'for itself' (*Medicus and Petersen*, Bürgerliches Recht[24], p. 258 no. 518–19). According to these views, the buyer with a retention of title is generally the 'manufacturer', with the consequence that a derivative acquisition occurs *via* the person who performs the manufacturing process. This gives the creditor an advantage, but is unfavourable to the material supplier, which is why this idea was unsuccessful in practice.

[327] BGH op. cit. p. 121.

[328] Ibid.

[329] BGH 28 June 1954, BGHZ 14 pp. 114, 117; BGH 3 March 1956, BGHZ 20 pp. 159, 163. This view was already taken by the legislators: Mot. III p. 361; Prot. III p. 243.

[330] *Triantos*, AK, Art. 1061 p. 1285 no. 2.

5. Objects with a Double Nature

a. Ontologically Dependent Things

In a final category of objects are found objects of legal transaction whose character as 'things' depends on the *context* in which they are subjected to analysis. These are objects with a kind of 'double nature'. They appear, depending on the perspective from which they are viewed, sometimes as dependent components of another thing and sometimes as independent objects of property rights. Such objects can, in other words, be both at once—mere 'objects of legal transaction' *and* 'things'. Looking at matters more closely, one can also distinguish according to whether the objects of legal transaction/ things in question are dependent in a 'strong' or ontological sense or in a 'weak' or contingent sense—that is, for some purposive or instrumental reason only. An object is ontologically dependent on another thing when it shares the latter's legal fate (with one exception), which is to say it only maintains its own 'thingness' (in virtue of remaining an object of separate dealings) because some person abstains from exercising a right. Ontologically dependent objects thus only occur in the form of ('reified') rights. Moreover, the category only contains real rights,[331] which for their own part are either components of a land unit (especially real servitudes) or have their own definition in the relevant catalogue as '*immeubles*' and 'land' (to the extent a doctrine of components does not form a part of the relevant legal system).[332] To characterize such rights as land unit components or immoveables is not an expression of legislative arbitrariness; we are not concerned with a violation of the internal logic of property law. Land units are, after all, not real but normative things; they are creatures of the legal system. As such, the category is certainly capable of embracing rights;[333] only the category of real things cannot do that. Such an approach would be in principle available in the case of purely normative things,[334] but legal systems typically reach for the concept of the accessory 9.53

[331] Obligational rights can, despite Austrian OGH 2 October 1963, SZ 36/125 possibly ruling differently, at best be accessories of the thing and thereby also of a land unit, but cannot be components. To view this differently is to ignore the difference between the component and the accessory (in a similar vein, see Klang [-*Kisslinger*], ABGB^3, § 294 no. 40). The court assumed that rights could, in general, be 'components' of the thing for whose use they are intended. *In casu*, the plaintiff had entered into a contract with the defendant concerning the inheritance of their father. The plaintiff had received half share of the land unit '*Ecke K/H Straße*'. She now demanded half of a sum of money located on a bank account belonging to the estate, and which was denoted '*Ecke K.-H.-Straße*'. She claimed the bank account was an accessory of the land unit. The OGH rejected this. A bank account did not serve a land unit permanently, not even if the means therein were intended to reconstruct the house belonging to the land unit.

[332] e.g. Art. 526 French Civil Code, Art. 334(10) Spanish Civil Code, and § 498 Czech Civil Code; slightly differing in the regulatory practice but identical in the idea is Art. 813 Italian Civil Code.

[333] Common law even acknowledges situations in which the land, to which a servitude is connected, is itself composed of a servitude. English law acknowledges profits in gross, meaning *profits à prendre*, which are not connected to a land unit, but purely to a right. It follows that, for example, the right of X to fish on Y's land unit (profit of piscary) may be connected with a right of way over Z's land unit to ease the exercise of the fishery. This applies even if X does not have possession of the land unit (*Buckley* J in *Hanbury v Jenkins* [1901] 2 Ch 401, 422–3).

[334] Still, under Art. 1692 French and Belgian Civil Code (and similarly Art. 1263 Italian Civil Code and Art. 1528 Spanish Civil Code), the sale or assignment of a claim is extended to its accessories (*les accessoires de la créance*), such as guarantees, pre-emption rights, and hypothecs. With the assignment, all *accessoires* pass to the assignee by force of law (for further detail, see *Terré/Simler/Lequette*, Les Obligations^9, p. 1228 no. 1290). Likewise, § 524(2) Czech Civil Code [1964] and § 524(2) Slovakian Civil Code (which is worded identically) formulate(d) that accessories and all connected rights are transferred with the assigned claim. Czech Nejvyšší soud České republiky

joinder of security rights with claims.[335] With the assignment of a claim, for example, a guarantee also follows to the benefit of the assignee without any great to-do.[336] Matters differ only when the assignee waives or disclaims that acquisition; in that case, the guarantee extinguishes.[337] One does not express this form of dependency between a right and another right by saying that a guarantee is a 'component' of a secured claim (as one would do in the case of a real servitude and a land unit). The contract of guarantee is made with a person other than the debtor of the secured claim. Claims are, after all, only points of reference for a limited number of property rights and are not a point of reference for the right of ownership. Besides this, the historical approach to the concept of real servitudes, with which we are generally (and sometimes exclusively)[338] concerned in this context, is very specific. Real servitudes have not been interpreted as an expression of legal relations between persons (i.e. land unit owners) but as an expression of legal relations between land units themselves, namely a 'dominant' and a 'servient' one.[339]

9.54 This conventional understanding continues to operate in many legal systems, at least on a subliminal level—in the common law[340] as well as Civilian systems. Clear examples are provided by Art. 50 Polish Civil Code[341] and § 96 German Civil Code.

24 June 2003, 21 Cdo 306/2003, Sbírka soudních rozhodnutí a stanovisek no. R 31/2004 states that a contract concerning the assignment of a claim is a legal state of affairs to which the provisions governing assignment of a pledge refer, because all accessories and all related rights follow a claim assigned by one person to another, including a pledge right, which secure the assigned claim. § 1881(1) Czech Civil Code [2014] essentially kept this approach.

[335] While the real servitude (Art. 1118 Greek Civil Code) is interpreted as an 'accessory real right', as always, transfer of the dominant land unit also transfers the servitude *ipso iure* (Areopag 329/1996, EllDni 37 [1996] p. 677; Areopag 817/1993, EllDni 36 [1995] p. 152), and as agreements between the transferring person and the acquirer only have obligational effect *inter partes* (see also Protodikeio Thessaloniki 17391/2002, Harm. 57 [2003] p. 215). The idea of an accessory real right is an unhappy one: claims can only be extinguished through partial or whole performance and no equivalent exists in the law applicable to land units; further, accessory obligations may have a different person as debtor to the primary claim, which they secure.

[336] See DCFR III.-5:115 and the references to comparative law there.

[337] Guarantee and primary claim cannot be owed to different creditors: see Areopag 797/1999, EEmpD 2000 p. 80; RG 22 October 1914, RGZ 85 pp. 363, 364, and BGH 19 September 1991, BGHZ 115 p. 177 (the assignment of a primary claim without the rights of a guarantee lead to extinction of the guarantee). The guarantee is also accessory in Austria (this follows from § 1351 Austrian Civil Code: *Gschnitzer/Faistenberger/Barta/Eccher*, Österreichisches Schuldrecht Allgemeiner Teil^2, p. 270); thus, it cannot be transferred separately (§ 1394 Austrian Civil Code). Exceptions to this accessory nature can be made in cases of a guarantee with knowledge for the debts of an incapacitated person (§ 1352 Austrian Civil Code), in insolvency law (§§ 151 Austrian IO, 48 Austrian AO), under § 7(1) Austrian WucherG and for some special situations derived from the fundamental principle of good faith (for further details, see Schwimann [-*Mader and Faber*], ABGB VI^3, § 1351 no. 2).

[338] e.g. in Italian law. There is no polished doctrine of components, so rights cannot be interpreted as components of land units. However, real servitudes (*servitù prediale*) belong to a category clearly defined as being different from other property rights. According to the conventional Latin understanding, and thus also the Italian, the *servitu prediali* (and this only) is an encumbrance on a land unit for the benefit of another land unit (Art. 1027 Italian Civil Code). The continued effect of the *utilitas fundi*, 'use of the land' can be seen here; it is seen as indispensable to this day (*Caruso and Spanò*, Le servitù prediali, p. 175). By contrast, all other property rights are conceived for the use of their holder. This can be clearly seen in their wording, which differs significantly from Art. 1227 Italian Civil Code (e.g. Arts 1021(1) [use right] and 1022 [habitation right] Italian Civil Code).

[339] *Caruso and Spanò* op. cit. p. 11.

[340] e.g. sec. 187 LPA 1925 states that a servitude is 'annexed' to the relevant land, and under sec. 205(1)(ix) LPA 'land' includes servitudes. sec. 62(1)–(3) LPA follow this line by saying that servitudes 'appertain' to the land (which is, of course, ambiguous; servitudes may 'belong' to the land unit, but also be 'connected' to it or 'concern' it).

[341] Which states that the rights connected to the ownership are also components of the immoveable.

Both use the language of (their respective) doctrine of components to classify rights that are 'connected with a land unit' as 'components' of that land unit. The German commentary compiles a remarkably long list of such rights;[342] of practical importance under § 96 German Civil Code are also real servitudes, real rights of pre-emption, and such other encumbrances that are entered into the land register 'for the benefit of the owner from time to time of a land unit' (§§ 1094(2) and 1105(2) German Civil Code). It is not completely clear, however, what exactly is 'connected' in either the Polish or German provisions. Linguistically, there are two possibilities: a connection with the right of ownership in the dominant land unit, or a connection with the land unit itself. Only one of these can be correct; in our view, it is the second. The property rights embraced by these provisions are neither appendages or extensions to the scope of the *right of ownership*, they are rather integral components of a land unit *itself* (and for this very reason objects with a double nature). They form a part of the 'land unit' as a normative thing. The habit of speaking of rights 'connected with ownership' used in such provisions cannot be intended to 'stretch' the meaning of 'ownership' itself. This would contradict the basic notion of ownership as the best possible right in a thing (a 'better' right than the 'best' is impossible). It seems rather intended to be descriptive of the situation, without implying any normative proposition, that real servitudes and other rights do not accrue to the possessor of a dominant land unit but to its owner in Polish and German law. That, however, is a second order question; these provisions deal with the object (i.e. land unit) itself, not with holding rights in it. From the point of view of the servient land unit, the relevant feature is an encumbrance of the rights in it; from the point of view of the dominant land unit, of relevance is the concretization of what the dominant land unit itself 'is'. Not only buildings and plants are part of the land unit; so too is its legal 'bracing' with the neighbouring land unit(s). As such, the right of ownership in the dominant land unit cannot be transferred or encumbered without also transferring or encumbering the relevant rights in the servient land unit. The owner of the dominant land unit is only free to alter the extent of his land unit by surrendering these rights. That is no different, in principle, to demolishing a house or excavating soil.

The practical consequences of this approach—which is contentious in Europe **9.55**
generally[343]—are not very great; they manifest, for example, in cases involving disclaimer of ownership by one person and appropriation by another person under some

[342] Palandt (-*Grüneberg*), BGB[74], § 96 no. 2 names (with further references), real pre-emption rights and real encumbrances (including rights of expectation concerning the entry of the relevant rights in the land register), reversion claims regarding a heritable building lease, hunting rights, and rights concerning overhanging constructions (§ 912 German Civil Code) alongside real servitudes.

[343] For example, Swedish law operates on the principle that everything is 'land property' that is also an accessory to a land unit (von Bar [-*Westermann and Herrmann*], Sachenrecht in Europa I, pp. 502–03). What counts as accessories (according to the terminology of Swedish law, this includes components), follows from Kap. 2 Swedish JB. Rights are not listed here, they are thus not a characteristic which constitutes a land unit (land pledges, among others, count as moveable things: *Håstad*, Sakrätt[6], p. 41). For this reason, rights of this type, especially servitudes, are connected with ownership of the dominant land unit but not with ownership of the servient land unit. They cannot be transferred separately (Kap. 14 § 3 Swedish JB). This also applies for the fishing rights in private waters (§ 9 Fiskelag [1993:787]) and hunting rights (§ 10 Jaktlag [1987:259]: the land unit owner has the hunting rights for the ground which belongs to the land unit).

claim of title. Not only does such a waiver leave the right of ownership in the land unit untouched; it leaves the land unit *itself* untouched. As such, the rights inherent in the land unit subsist. They can, following acquisition of ownership by the new owner, be exercised by that new owner; in the meantime, they subsist as rights without a holder.[344] Only when one of the land units as such is extinguished is the servitude destroyed (e.g. Art. 1135 Greek Civil Code).[345]

Of greater relevance is the question whether servitudes attach to the right of ownership or to the land unit itself in the common law. This is of relevance for two reasons. First, the conceptual approach taken by the common law to land units and servitudes—'land' and 'easements' in English legal parlance—is not fully compatible with the Continental approach. Secondly, the common law conceptualizes a lease over land as a real right (rather than an obligational one). Despite these differences, however, the legislative point of departure rather confirms our proposition that servitudes in land should be understood as elements of the relevant land unit. Reference should again be made to sec. 62 LPA 1925 (earlier, sec. 6 Conveyancing Act 1881), according to which dealings with land by default extend to buildings, hedges, fences, and so forth, without the need for express agreement. That has been interpreted to mean that dealings with land may, in certain circumstances, lead to the creation of 'new' servitudes. In *Graham v Philcox*,[346] for example, the owner (M) of a land unit with two houses on it granted a lease in one of the houses to B, who later transferred his rights to D. The tenant (first B, later D) was granted a right of way over the part of the land unit on which the larger house was situated. M later transferred his 'freehold estate' (i.e. the common law's closest equivalent to Continental 'ownership' in land) in the leased part of the land unit to W, who in turn transferred it to the complainant. The part of the land unit not subject to a lease (on which the larger house stood) was later transferred to the defendant. The complainant had acquired a right of way over the defendant's land *via* the default mechanism in sec. 62 LPA 1925, because the tenant at the operative time had one. This, too, supports the proposition that servitudes become part of the dominant land unit. *MRA Engineering Ltd v Trimster Company Ltd*,[347] however, concerned a 'red' and a 'green' parcel both in the ownership of the complainant. The complainant leased the 'red' parcel to S and granted him a right of way over the 'green' parcel. The latter was subsequently sold to the defendant. Following this, the lease with S was terminated. The defendant, who had also acquired an option to purchase the 'red' parcel, wanted to exercise the option

[344] e.g. Staudinger (-*Pfeifer*), BGB (2004), § 928 no. 27 and Palandt (-*Bassenge*), BGB^{72}, § 928 no. 3. A land charge over a land unit that has become ownerless is extinguished; it can be removed from the land register without the permission of the earlier owner (BGH 10 May 2012, NJW-RR 2012 p. 1105, FGPrax 2012 p. 145).

[345] However, the requirement for this is that using the land unit becomes totally impossible, for example because agricultural land has been permanently flooded. If a building belonging to a dominant land unit is completely destroyed, a real servitude that pertains exclusively to the use of that building is said to expire—in contrast to servitudes that relate to other buildings as well, or that were acquired by prescription (CA Larissa 542/1978, EllDni 20 [1979] p. 72; CFI Lamia 171/1980, ArchN 34 p. 37). The mere redesign of a dominant land unit leaves the servitude unaffected, as does the factual narrowing of a right of way on the servient land unit (*Triantos*, AK, Art. 1135 nos 1–2 pp. 1351–2).

[346] [1984] QB 747 (CA).

[347] (1988) 56 P & CR 1 (CA).

but could not agree on a purchase price with the complainant. This turned *inter alia* on the continued existence of the right of way over the 'green' parcel. The court held that the servitude was extinguished with the termination of the lease agreement. Dillon J held that the right of way was 'appurtenant to his lease'.[348] In other words, the servitude here was annexed to the leasehold right—it was not part of the land unit. The Law Commission adopted a similar approach: 'Appurtenance is to an estate in land, and so it is possible, for example, for the lessee... to have an easement over adjoining land and for that easement to be appurtenant to the lease without benefiting the freeholder.'[349] In *Barrett v Morgan*,[350] Lord Millett distinguished between cases where the relevant leasehold and freehold are united in the same person and cases in which a leasehold is forfeited or terminated. A servitude would subsist in the former but not in the latter. In *Wall v Collins*,[351] on the other hand, Carnwarth LJ opined that an easement must be 'appurtenant to a dominant tenement' but 'not necessarily to any particular interest for the time being'. Here, the servitude appears to be connected to the 'land' and not to the 'estate' of the 'dominant tenement'. A leaseholder has, for the duration of his lease, a right of way—which, according to the court, was not extinguished by the fact that the leaseholder acquired ownership in 'his' tenement. *MRA Engineering Ltd v Trimster Company Ltd*, in which the servitude was extinguished upon termination of the lease, was not discussed. The Law Commission in turn welcomed the result in *Wall v Collins*, but held its reasoning to be faulty. An English law easement is connected to the right, not to the land.[352] The scholarship is beginning to give up. Neither the proposition that easements are connected to the land nor the proposition that easements are connected with an estate can be defended consistently.[353]

b. Purposively Dependent Things

'Weakly' or contingently dependent things remain to be discussed. In this context, the relationship between rule and exception is effectively reversed. Things that are dependent for some specific purpose are, in principle, independent objects of property rights.[354] They only descend to the status of (dependent) objects of legal transaction in a specific context. This occurs when, and to the extent that, a legal system 'stretches' dealings that transfer or encumber the right of ownership in a thing to objects or **9.56**

[348] Ibid. p. 5.

[349] Law Com Rep no. 327: Making Land Work: Easements, Covenants and Profits à Prendre (2011), para. 2.2, para. 3.232, and following state that if an easement or profit is conceded in favour of the tenant, or if the tenant concedes a servitude as a charge, this only applies for the duration of the contract. If an encumbered leasehold is forfeited, the easement is also extinguished. If an encumbered lease is surrendered, the easement subsists and encumbers the freehold estate.

[350] [2000] 2 AC 264, 270.

[351] [2007] EWCA Civ 444; [2007] Ch 390, 395.

[352] Law Com Rep no. 327 op. cit. nos 3.252–3.255.

[353] *Lyall* (2010) 74 Conv 300.

[354] This is expressly emphasized for accessories in various legal provisions. An example among many is Art. 818(2) Italian Civil Code (accessories can be the subject of separate legal dealings and relations).

things that have not been expressly named by the parties. Two basic scenarios can be identified. The first concerns real things that, although they both possess a delimited corporeal existence, are perceived as equally important parts of an imagined whole. Standard examples are books in a library or stock in a warehouse. The connection is much clearer where a real thing is, in practical terms, not even functional on its own—consider a single card in a card game. Such aggregate things (*universalità*) raise the question whether it is possible to deal with them in a single legal act. An affirmative answer would mean that they would (together) be characterized as 'a thing'. It would also mean that a single dealing would touch every single thing within the aggregate.[355] Every single card would be, in the case of an affirmative answer, a dependent thing *vis-à-vis* the game, but not *vis-à-vis* any other single card. This, however, would not change the fact that, because the single cards remain to this extent independent things, their owner could (for example) gift each card individually to a different person. The second group of contingently dependent things, with which we will deal first in the text that follows, are so-called accessory things [*Nebensachen*] that are not physically connected to a principal thing but are functionally so closely connected that dealings with the principal thing are deemed, by default, to be dealings with them. This assumption makes sense at least in situations where one thing is in close physical proximity to another and ordinary commercial understanding subordinates one because it serves the use of the other. A retailer customer who buys a pair of shoes should not have to lead separate negotiations to acquire ownership in the shoelaces, too.[356] The situation may be different, however, where a wholesaler imports thousands of shoes; in such a scenario, it is entirely conceivable that the shoelaces might be negotiated separately.

(1) So-Called Accessories

9.57 The law of accessory things—*accesoires*, *pertinenze*, *accessoires*, *accesorios*, *przynależności*, *Zubehör*, and similar—displays an unusual richness of variety across contemporary European legal systems. Every translation of the relevant national term threatens to distort its meaning; it nearly always bears different connotations in the language of translation to those it bore in the original linguistic context. The concept only developed in the Middle Ages;[357] it never gained a foothold in some legal systems and already belongs to legal history in others. The Netherlands Civil Code, for

[355] e.g. this is the case in Italian law (for further details, see *Trimarchi*, Universalità di cose, Enc. dir. XLV, p. 801 and *Rascio*, Universalità patrimoniali, Novissimo Digesto italiano XX, p. 94).

[356] This example is taken from *Menezes Cordeiro*, Tratado de Direito Civil I(2)^2, p. 170. It shows well that the wording of Art. 210 Portuguese Civil Code is problematic: *coisas acessórias* or *pertenças* are moveable things that, without being *partes integrantes* of another thing, serve the use or decoration of another thing. Insofar as no inconsistent provision exists, legal dealings that touch the principal thing do not embrace the accessories. Art. 210(2) Portuguese Civil Code is seen today as a historical error by the legislature; see also *Menezes Leitão*, Direitos reais^2, p. 79.

[357] Roman law appears to not have acknowledged accessories as a category (*Marrone*, Istituzioni di diritto romano, p. 285).

example, abolished it some years ago.[358] Most other legal systems in the Civilian tradition have retained the category, but approach 'accessories' from different perspectives. The most easily recognizable fault line runs along the external borders of the doctrine of components [*Bestandteilslehre*]. Where this doctrine is defined by statute, 'components' and 'accessories' are defined as mutually exclusive categories; a 'component' (sometimes an 'integral' or 'essential' component) is, in such codifications, never an 'accessory', and an accessory is never a component.[359] Swedish law, on the other hand, has largely demolished the distinction between these two categories. In Swedish law, many things that count as 'integral components' of a land unit in German, Estonian, Greek, Polish, or Hungarian law count as accessories (*tillbehör*), whether general or pertaining to a building.[360] The distinction between *partes integrantes* and *pertenecias* only caught on in Spain as its cognate was being abandoned in the Netherlands. In Spanish law, the terminological distinction is purely descriptive without any textual anchor in the civil code.[361] The same can be said for the distinction that has been suggested in the Italian literature between *pertinenza* and *res composita*.[362] The notion of 'components' is also absent from the French Civil Code, which recognizes *accessoires*

[358] The *hulpzaken* ('helpthings') of Art. 653 Netherlands Civil Code (old version) no longer appear in the new version as *terminus technicus*. Only Art. 3:254 Netherlands Civil Code (new version) is reminiscent of them. The provision deals with the enforcement of a hypothec over immoveables extending to moveable things that are, according to commercial opinion, dedicated to the permanent service of the relevant immoveable and are recognizable as such from their form. Removing the category of accessory things also had considerable consequences in the law of secured credit, as a number of this which were previously automatically included in the asset pool of a hypothec as *hulpzaken* could no longer be used. In practice, this is remedied by an agreement, called a *hulpzakenbeding*, by which the creditor is granted a pledge in the accessories in question (*Snijders and Rank-Berenschot*, Goederenrecht[4], p. 35 no. 43).

[359] For example, this is the case under the practically identical § 57(1) Estonian Civil Code, Art. 956 Greek Civil Code and § 97(1) sentence 1 German Civil Code (stating that accessories are moveable things which are determined to serve the principal thing's economic purpose *without being a component of the principal thing*, and are in a corresponding spatial relation to it: emphasis added). § 5:16 Hungarian Civil Code follows this line: In doubt, the ownership right extends to anything which is not a component, but which is necessary or beneficial to its regular use or maintenance. The Portuguese civil code also differentiates between components on the one hand and subsidiary things or accessories on the other. Under Art. 204(3) Portuguese Civil Code, every moveable thing, which is materially connected to the land unit with a lasting effect, is a *parte integrante*. On the other hand, under Art. 210 Portuguese Civil Code, subsidiary things (*coisas acessórias*) or accessories (*pertenças*) are moveable things which permanently serve or decorate another thing without being *partes integrantes*. Subsidiary things (*coisas acessórias*) and accessories (*pertenças*) are used synonymously. Accessories are connected to the principal thing economically, a component materially (*Pires de Lima and Antunes Varela*, Código Civil Anotado I[4], note 1 to Art. 210 p. 203).

[360] Kap. 2 § 1(1) Swedish JB also counts trees, other plants, fertilizer, buildings, and other structures among the accessories. Conduits, fences, and structures which are fastened into or onto the ground for permanent use also belong to the land unit. Under Kap. 2 § 2 Swedish JB, fixtures and other objects with which the building is equipped count among the building's accessories if they are suitable for the permanent use of the building or one of its parts. Examples of these are partition walls, elevators, banisters, pipes or conduits for water, heat, lighting or other things which have faucets, switches, or similar equipment, boilers, heaters, chimneys, tiled stoves, interior windows, window blinds, fire safety devices, protective devices, and keys. For apartments, the same applies for bathtubs and other sanitary facilities, stoves, airing cupboards, refrigerators, as well as washing machines, and mangles. Whether floors, stairs, doors, and windows are accessories is not hypothesized, as they are components of the building (for further details, see von Bar [-*Westermann and Herrmann*], Sachenrecht in Europa I, pp. 518–22).

[361] For further details, see *Díez-Picazo*, Fundamentos III[5], pp. 197–9 (*Pertenencias* are said to be a softer manner of creating land ownership than *partes integrantes*. *Pertenencias* may be separated from the principal by a simple act of will, while *partes integrantes* must be physically removed from it).

[362] For further details, see *Gazzoni*, Manuale di diritto privato[13], p. 206 (Accessories are a relationship between the principal thing and the subsidiary thing, not, as in the case of *res composita*, a unification of two things; a principal thing does not exist here). It is only this distinction which allows the proposition that, for example, pages of a book are not 'accessories' of the book. There can be no book without pages; thus, the book is a *res composita* with regard to the pages, not the principal thing.

but does not define them. The reader is referred to the general definitions of moveables and immoveables.[363] From them, in combination with a few other provisions,[364] the importance of the maxim *accessorium sequitur principale*[365] can be inferred. In this way, it is possible to describe an *accessoire* as a *bien* that is, on the one hand, dependent on another *bien*, but remains, on the other hand, a (moveable or immoveable) *bien* in its own right.[366] However, this dependence is said to result not only from the fact that one good is dedicated *to the use* of another, but also from the fact that one good is *produced from* another.[367] In consequence, one school of opinion even posits (albeit not without controversy) *fruits* as *accessoires*.[368] However, one must avoid confusing *accessoire* and *accession*. Through *accession* a single good arises in the world; accessory and principal thing are two distinct goods.[369] English, Irish, and Cypriot[370] jurists, 'get' what their Continental counterparts mean when they speak of accessories. But in strict terms, the common law recognizes only what it calls 'fixtures' and 'chattels'. However, in the context of land, the concept of fixtures has been 'stretched'. A house key, for example, is not 'annexed' to the house, but is counted as a fixture rather than as a chattel.[371] Thus, the position is reached that ownership in the key passes with ownership in the house. Fixtures, on the other hand, are beyond the purview of 'land law'; the key to a filing

[363] e.g. Arts 522 and 524(1) and (2) French and Belgian Civil Codes, which state that moveable things, which serve the economic purpose of the land unit, are immoveable things 'by determination'. Moveable things can therefore be 'immobilized' as a result of their use; they become *immeubles par destination*. Among these are the animals and objects which the owner of a land unit has brought to it for the use of a land unit. If, for example, pigeons, rabbits or fish find their way into another loft, enclosure, or reservoir (Art. 564), then the *destination* favouring the first land unit ends and is created anew in favour of the second land unit; the animals then become its *accessoires*. The owner of an *immeuble par destination* can end its immobilization simply by a separate sale. Admittedly, under certain circumstances, this sale would be invalid relative to the good faith of the creditor of a hypothec (for further details, see *Zenati-Castaing and Revet*, Les biens[3], p. 184 no. 119 and p. 186 no. 121).

[364] Especially Arts 546 and 566 (accession), 1018 (legacy), 1615 (sale), and 1692 (assignment) French Civil Code.

[365] 'The accessory follows the principal thing.' This, of course, is a simplification. What is meant (as clearly expressed in e.g. Art. 52 Polish Civil Code), is that so long as something is an 'accessory', legal dealings and relations that touch the principal thing also extend to the accessory unless the parties or some legal provision determine otherwise.

[366] *Zenati-Castaing and Revet*, Les biens[3], p. 177 no. 112.

[367] Ibid.

[368] This is argued by *Carbonnier*, Droit Civil II, p. 1620 no. 722 and *Zenati-Castaing and Revet* op. cit. p. 187 no. 122. *Malaurie and Aynès*, Les biens[3], p. 48 no. 160, and *Terré and Simler*, Les biens[7], p. 123 no. 123 (rightly) manage to define fruits and products without using the term *accessoire*. They content themselves with the statement that the owner is entitled to the fruits and products under the rules of the *droit d'accession*. This is also the opinion in Spanish law. *Díez-Picazo*, Ensayos jurídicos III, p. 3406 clarifies that fruits and products belong to the owner of the 'mother thing' under the rules of the *derecho de accesión*, and *O'Callaghan Muñoz*, Código Civil[6], Art. 354 Civil Code p. 418 emphasizes that fruits are new things. In light of this, a part of the Portuguese scholarship proposes to distinguish subsidiary things in the narrow sense (*coisa acessória 'stricto sensu'* within the meaning of Art. 210(1) Portuguese Civil Code) from subsidiary things in the broad sense (*coisa acessória 'lato sensu'*). Besides the 'actual' accessories (*pertenças*), the latter also includes fruits (*frutos*), products (*produtos*), and improvements (*benfeitorias*). *Menezes Leitão*, Direitos reais[2], pp. 78–9 considers this idea unfounded or, at least, outdated, as Art. 210(1) Portuguese Civil Code equates subsidiary things (*coisa acessória*) with accessories (*pertenças*). He emphasizes that *partes integrantes* are not autonomous things. The same applies for *benfeitorias* and for fruits which have not yet been selected (Art. 204(1)(c) Portuguese Civil Code); they become autonomous things upon separation, without then being the principal thing's accessory.

[369] *Zenati-Castaing and Revet* op. cit. p. 177 no. 112.

[370] Art. 2 Kap. 224 lit. (b) of the Cypriot LPA differentiates, like English and Irish law, between fixtures and chattels. The main criterion for this differentiation is the solid connection.

[371] 'Everybody knows that a key, although in its nature a chattel, belongs to the house, and passes with the freehold': *Moody v Steggles* (1879) 12 Ch. D. 261 (Fry J). See also *Botham v TSB Bank Ltd* [1996] EWCA Civ 547 (1997) 73 P & CR D1 (The hypothec extends to the furnishings of the charged house).

cabinet or a cupboard cannot pass with the same trick. For this reason, the law governing the construction of contracts has to do the heavy lifting.[372] The fact that an identical problem is solved using legally such very different approaches has a historical explanation. The modern law of contract had not evolved when the doctrine of fixtures emerged. To the present day, however, a special category of chattels continues to exist—so-called 'heirlooms'. These are moveable things that fall into an estate although the estate 'actually' only consists of 'land'. Someone who inherits a castle, for example, also inherits the pictures in it even though they are not fixtures.[373]

Looking more closely, we discover two conceptual differences. There is no consensus in contemporary Europe concerning which things can be classified as accessories at all and, in the case of an affirmative answer, which principal things they can be attributed to. Both lists—the list of accessories and the list of principal things—contain many different entries; moreover, there are considerably different possibilities envisaged for the connection between them. Some legal systems accept only moveable corporeal things as accessories,[374] while others do not hesitate to categorize rights,[375] particularly security rights and even claims[376] as accessories under the relevant national concept of accessories or at least to stipulate that with the transfer of a moveable thing a claim in damages for prior damage to that thing also passes.[377] Even immoveables sometimes slip into the role of accessories,[378] albeit only in relation to other immoveables but not in relation to real things.[379] The game is repeated when we ask which things come into **9.58**

[372] This is not exclusive to the common law. The provisions of German law concerning the transfer of ownership of moveable things make no statement regarding the fate of accessories.

[373] e.g. *Parker v Parkin (Re Parker)* [1910] 1 Ch 581. A precondition of this approach is that there is a relevant custom in commerce (*Williams*, Personal Property[18], p. 150) or a connection of the moveable thing to the land via a settlement (e.g. sec. 67 Settled Land Act 1925; for further details, see Megarry and Wade [-*Harpum/Bridge/Dixon*], The Law of Real Property[8], no. 10-004). Since sec. 2 Trusts of Land and Appointment of Trustees Act 1996 came into effect, such settlements can no longer be newly created. However, the term 'heirlooms' is often used in a wider sense for all objects of value, which are intended to remain with the family for multiple generations. In this sense, it is a colloquial expression without a specific legal meaning (*Viscount Hill v Dowager Viscountess Hill* [1897] 1 QB 483).

[374] Thus, among others, § 97(1) German Civil Code, § 57(1) Estonian Civil Code, Art. 956 Greek Civil Code, Art. 51 § 1 Polish Civil Code and Art. 17(1) Slovenian *Stvarnopravni zakonik*. As it is not a thing in its own right, a telephone number (for example) is not an accessory of the telephone (CA Łódź 16 June 2009, II AKa 91/09, Lex-No. 582019, KZS 2010/2/52).

[375] Under § 121(3) Czech Civil Code [1964] and § 513 Czech Civil Code [2014], e.g. interest, interest for late payment, late payment fees, and costs related to enforcement are 'accessories of a claim'.

[376] e.g. under French law claims directed to the recovery of an immoveable good (Art. 526 French Civil Code) are counted among the *accessoires* of a *droit réel*; they are therefore characterized as immoveable things (*Zenati-Castaing and Revet* op. cit. p. 179 no. 114).

[377] Claims in damages for conversion and trespass to goods require that the claimant either had possession or a right to immediate possession at the time of the event that caused the damage (Street [-*Murphy*], on Torts[13], p. 278; Palmer and McKendrick [-*Palmer*], Interests in Goods[2], pp. 63, 71–81). If a thing is transferred, which is connected to a potential claim in conversion, the acquiror can demand delivery or damages from the offending party (*Williams*, Personal Property[18], pp. 168–70).

[378] For example, this is the case in Italian law (in which the garden and the garage are used as typical examples of accessory things, see *Torrente and Schlesinger*, Manuale di diritto privato[19], p. 182 and Cian and Trabbucchi [-*Pellegrini*], Commentario al codice civile[8], p. 781), as well as in Spanish law (one ploughed field could thus be the *accesorio* of another: Bercovitz Rodríguez-Cano [-*Sánchez Aristi*], Comentarios al Código Civil[2], p. 1308). The jurisprudence in Bulgarian law also occasionally qualifies basements and rooms below the roof as accessories of an apartment (Court of Cassation 4 May 2010, no. 108, I. Civil Chamber).

[379] *La Torre*, Cinquant'anni col diritto, p. 529 states, regarding Italian law, that a land unit could theoretically be the accessory of a moveable thing. He mentions the keeping of livestock, in which the livestock far exceed the value

consideration as a principal thing. Some legal systems take the position that a principal thing must always be an immoveable,[380] others also envisage a real thing in this role.[381] Others again even consider purely normative things as appropriate candidates for the status of principal things. Swedish law distinguishes between 'general', 'building', and 'industrial' accessories.[382] The Swedish legislature has placed particular importance on the latter for the purposes of secured credit.

9.59 Naturally, many other details of the national definitions of accessories vary. For example, one can only speak of 'accessories of a building' coherently (§ 98 No. 1 German Civil Code) when and insofar as buildings are conceptualized as independent real things; in other cases, they are necessarily land unit accessories. Matters are the same in the case of so-called *Landgut* (lit., 'estate': § 98 No. 2 German Civil Code), hence also an agricultural business. Insofar as such a business is not elevated to the rank of a (purely normative) 'thing', from the perspective of property law only the relevant land unit can be considered as a principal thing; there is no other thing in sight. A further example is provided by the characteristic of 'spatial relationship'. Spatial proximity between an accessory and a principal thing can only be required by legal systems that stipulate that the principal thing must either be a real thing or a land unit; purely normative things cannot stand in spatial relationships.[383] Matters are further complicated by the fact that the same concept of 'accessories' is often not even used consistently within one and the same legal system, for example because it is considered necessary to distinguish between the law of obligations and the law of property. From the perspective of contract law, for example, it seems less necessary to characterize only 'things' (in the property law sense) that belong to the seller as the 'accessories' of the object of a sale

of the land unit. He states that this theoretical possibility is not followed in practice, as transactions concerning immoveable things are subject to certain formal requirements.

380 Among these is Spanish law. *Pertenencias* only occur as subsidiary things to an immoveable thing (*Díez-Picazo*, Fundamentos III^5, p. 198). Among the examples for such subsidiary things are building plans (TS 18 March 2002, RAJ 2002 no. 2848 p. 4917). (Estonian and Latvian law have specific provisions for these. Under § 58 Estonian Civil Code and Art. 862 Latvian Civil Code, certificates, maps, and plans, and, in the case of land also documents relating to construction, are accessories of the land unit, to the extent they concern its transfer and the possession. In Lithuanian law, the same applies to ships.)

381 e.g. in German, Estonian, Greek, Polish, Slovenian, and Portuguese law (a *coisa principal* can be a moveable thing: *Menezes Cordeiro*, Direito civil português I(2)^2, p. 170 gives the example of the spare wheel and floor jack in relation to the vehicle). For Italian law, *Albano*, Pertinenze, Enc. giur. XXIII, p. 194, notes that accessories are distinct from a '*de facto* whole thing', as the principal thing can be moveable or immoveable, as well as the subsidiary thing, in the case of accessories.

382 For further details (including in relation to industrial plant) von Bar (-*Westermann and Herrmann*), Sachenrecht in Europa I, pp. 518–22.

383 'Spatial proximity' is only (and at best) one of the characteristics used in the definition of 'accessory', if rights are excluded from the circle of the subsidiary, as well as the circle of the principal things: see, e.g. § 97 German Civil Code, § 57(1) Estonian Civil Code, Art. 956 Greek Civil Code, Art. 51 § 1 Polish Civil Code, and Art. 210 Portuguese Civil Code. In Austrian law, if proximity as well as economic dependence is demanded for characterization as an accessory (Klang [-*Kisslinger*], ABGB^3, § 294 no. 21), this only applies to real things. Under Kap. 2 §§ 1 to 3 Swedish JB, the presumption of accessory status only applies to objects in one of the external relations to the land unit there described. By contrast, industrial accessory retains its character as accessory even when it is employed outside of the business premises (e.g. the scaffolding which a business sets up on a client's land unit to complete a job there: von Bar [-*Westermann and Herrmann*], Sachenrecht in Europa I, pp. 518–22).

agreement.[384] From the perspective of property law, on the other hand, in case of doubt one would only count objects that the seller is entitled to dispose of as 'accessories' (allowing for the applicable regime of good faith acquisition).[385] Finally, it is necessary to consider very different national forms of secured credit. A Civilian hypothec draws much of its distinctiveness from the fact that it extends to the accessories of the land unit it encumbers;[386] for a common law mortgage (but not a common law charge), by way of contrast, a separate agreement concerning the chattels to be covered is practically advisable where the debtor is a natural person.[387]

Besides this, the characteristic of 'functional dependence' that distinguishes between accessory and principal thing is described in different terms. For § 97(1) German Civil Code and Art. 956 Greek Civil Code, for example, a thing only becomes an accessory insofar as it is dedicated to the 'economic purpose of the principal thing'[388] but the concept of 'economic purpose' is not precise. A sauna installed in the basement of a dwelling house has been characterized as an accessory,[389] as have the organ[390] and bells[391] of a church. Section 121(1) Slovakian Civil Code and Czech Civil Code [1964] **9.60**

[384] This is different, e.g. under Art. 51 § 2 Polish Civil Code (accessories can only be the property of the owner of the principal thing), and § 121(1) Czech Civil Code [1964] and § 510(1) Czech Civil Code (2014); in Austrian law, the question of whether the owner of the principal thing and the accessory must be identical is contested (for further details, see Klang [-*Kisslinger*], ABGB^3, § 294 no. 21). For contract law, little speaks for such a requirement (Art. 155 Polish Civil Code). A bicycle pump affixed to the bicycle can be considered sold with the bicycle, even if it does not belong to the seller or the owner of the bicycle.

[385] This can be shown in more detail only by examining the law of good faith acquisition and the individual security rights in question. E.g. in Swedish law (von Bar [-*Westermann and Herrmann*], Sachenrecht in Europa I, pp. 518–22), if a land unit is sold as a whole, then the buyer obtains the land unit accessories (unless otherwise agreed), even if he knows that the seller has previously sold them to a third party. Under Kap. 2 § 4 JB, this does not apply to things which were brought to the land unit without becoming the property of the land unit's owner. Kap. 4 § 17(2) JB only entitles the land unit's buyer, who acted in good faith with regard to the quality as accessories, to a right of price reduction or a right to rescind. Things which a third party has brought to the land unit only attain the quality of land unit accessories from the moment the land unit owner becomes the owner of these things (HD 9 October 2007, NJA 2007 p. 652). Under Art. 818(2) Italian Civil Code, a thing stops being an accessory with a change in the purpose to which the thing is dedicated or with a separate disposition over it. The termination of accessory status can, however, not affect the legal position of third parties who have already acquired rights in the principal thing (Art. 812(3) Civil Code).

[386] e.g. Art. 2397 French Civil Code, Art. 45(2) Belgian Hypothec Law, Art. 2118(1) Luxembourgish Civil Code, § 1120 German Civil Code, Art. 84 Polish *Ustawa r. o księgach wieczystych I hipotece*, and § 5:103(1) sentence 2 Hungarian Civil Code [2014] (a pledge extends, in case of doubt, to the accessories of the thing in question).

[387] A mortgage in the form of a deed (secs 85(1) and 86(1) LPA 1925) is required at common law in order to charge a legal freehold or a legal leasehold. If it is unregistered land, then one must also pay attention to sec. 52(1) (mortgage by way of lease or sub-lease). This also requires a deed (see sec. 205(1)(ii) LPA 1925). If this process concerns registered land, then sec. 23(1)(a) Land Registration Act 2002 qualifies it as a charge by way of legal mortgage; the real legal transaction here requires the form of a deed (Land Registration Rules 2003 SI no. 1417, r. 103 and Land Registration Act 2002, sec. 25(1)). In relation to goods, a mortgage must be in writing but not necessarily in the form of a deed where the thing is not delivered (which is the normal case) (*Calnan*, Proprietary Rights and Insolvency, no. 5.32). If the debtor remains in possession of the thing and if he is a natural person, an inventory is necessary (secs. 4 and 8 Bills of Sale Act (1878) Amendment Act 1882).

[388] Under which circumstances this is the case is specified with the help of *ex lege* accessories (§ 98 German Civil Code; Arts 959, 960 Greek Civil Code). These are moveable things which serve the economic purpose of an industrial enterprise or agricultural concern. Here, the law positions itself above the will of the parties and bindingly decides that the things concerned serve the relevant economic purpose. e.g. Art. 959 Greek Civil Code applies to all commercial undertakings concerning oil presses (CA Crete 37/1959, EEN 26 [1959] p. 717), bakeries (Protodikeio Athens 5169/1976, EEN 43 [1976] p. 888), and tobacco stores (Areopag 1165/1974, *NoB* 23 [1975] p. 714), among others.

[389] AG Aschaffenburg 7 July 1998, DGVZ 1998 p. 158.

[390] RG 14 March 1910, JW 1910 p. 466; *Triantos*, AK, Art. 956 Greek Civil Code, p. 1169 no. 3.

[391] BGH 25 May 1984, *NJW* 1984 pp. 2277, 2278.

look to whether an accessory has been dedicated by its owner to the 'constant' use of a principal thing; § 510(1) Czech Civil Code [2014], on the other hand, looks to whether the accessory is to be 'permanently' used with the principal thing towards the latter's economic purpose. Art. 51 § 1 Polish Civil Code takes the position that an accessory must be 'necessary' for the use of the principal thing as intended. Sometimes, a distinction is drawn between agricultural and urban land units.[392] Art. 817(1) Italian Civil Code looks to whether the dedication of a thing is to the service or decoration of another thing, whether by the owner of the thing or by one who has a real right in it. In Greek law, it is thought to be possible for one and the same accessory to serve two principal things simultaneously (e.g. a pump that supplies two land units with water).[393] Moreover, an accessory is said to be able to have accessories itself, in which case the first accessory is pulled into the role of a principal thing.[394] A subsidiary thing is only an 'accessory' if it is dedicated to serving the economic purpose of the principal thing 'permanently'; hard cases are to be resolved by reference to market custom (Art. 957(1) Greek Civil Code), from which it has been derived (for example) that a telephone is not an accessory of an apartment.[395] Some legislatures deal tenderly with further details. Art. 4.19(2) Lithuanian Civil Code—after stipulating that a subsidiary thing must serve the principal thing and must, in virtue of its nature, be permanently connected to it—places evident importance on clarifying that the 'mere' placement of two things together does not establish a such relation. Art. 857 Latvian Civil Code provides that a subsidiary thing cannot be seen as an accessory against the will of its owner. Accessories of a building must make the building more 'fit for purpose' and more 'pleasant' rather than just serving the use of the building for personal or commercial purposes. Construction materials are not accessories (Art. 859 Latvian Civil Code). Nor are material stocks, products already destined for sale (Art. 860 Latvian Civil Code), or agricultural inventory (equipment, seed stock, livestock); fertilizer, straw, and animal feed on the other hand may be accessories. Even the food stores of a ship are considered individually; they do not become accessories of the ship (Art. 861 Latvian Civil Code).

9.61 The concept of 'accessories' appears, after all of this, as a widely distributed but ambiguous one with a more or less common core but a diffuse outer border. It defies any precise definition in the pan-European context. 'Property law' itself can be properly determined correctly without the concept at all. For this reason alone, however, one need not dismiss 'accessories' as an inutile term of art. In our view, it is helpful (despite its ambiguities) to formulate a rebuttable presumption that can, in practice, reduce the burden of proof necessary to answer the truly fundamental question: where one thing ends and the next thing begins. Provisions under which a real right extends

[392] e.g. *Pires de Lima and Antunes Varela*, Código Civil Anotado I^4, note 2 to Art. 210 p. 203 (animals and agricultural equipment or furniture, decorations, and other utensils which belong to an urban land unit).

[393] Georgiades and Stathopoulos (*-Dimakou-Kiaou*), AK, Art. 956, pp. 68–69 no. 12 and *Triantos*, AK, Art. 956, S. 1169 para. 2. If one of the land units is disposed of, there also occurs a disposal of the water pump to the relevant notional fraction (*Dimakou-Kiaou* aaO; *Spyridakis and Perakis*, AK, Art. 956 para. 2).

[394] CA Athens 32/1956, EEN 23 (1956) p. 543.

[395] CA Thessaloniki 356/1979, NoB 29 (1981) p. 571.

to accessories by default (see Art. 958 Greek Civil Code), prove themselves as helpful norms of interpretation for day-to-day commerce (and they are sorely missed by some in those jurisdictions where they are lacking). Moreover, they help to minimize the dangers of conflicting publicity requirements in dualist transfer systems.[396] The category of 'accessory' is an instrument with which a legal system is able to give a name to those things which (within the relevant framework) reasonable parties could be said to have intended the transfer if they had not provided otherwise expressly.[397] Accessories are, accordingly, generally less important things—things that the parties did not 'think of'. The category enables, besides this, a distinction between objects that can only *ever* be allocated to one person and objects that are, in principle, separate things that can be seen as a unit for certain purposes. It thus allows parties to conclude more streamlined agreements. They need only name expressly those subsidiary things that should *not* pass to the person acquiring the principal thing; they need not concern themselves with the rest, because the legal system provides for these by default. This is particularly important in the context of land units, and in this context generates significant cost savings in light of the widespread formalism of dealings with land. In the context of moveable things, by way of contrast, a tacit reference to the general law of contractual interpretation is generally sufficient.[398] Someone who sells a picture generally wants to transfer its frame, too;[399] a statute does not need to provide this expressly. In the case of land units, the need for legal certainty is noticeably higher because significantly more complex economic units often coalesce in this context.

The concept of 'accessories' therefore presents a domain of property law that is subject to contractual derogation. Fundamentally, this counts both for the law of moveable things and for the law of immoveables. Granted, it is sometimes argued that statutory **9.62**

[396] For example, land units are transferred by registration, but moveable things by possession, land unit accessories can also be transferred by possession. Which manner of regulation is used to accomplish this goal is essentially meaningless. A rule like § 926 German Civil Code (in case of doubt, the transfer of ownership in a land unit extends to land unit accessories) achieves the same effect as, e.g. § 294 Austrian Civil Code and the corresponding constructions in French and English law, which characterize the accessories of an immoveable thing as immoveable in their own right (Klang [-*Kisslinger*], ABGB^3, § 294 no. 42).

[397] The presumptive effect of the definition of 'accessory' is rightly limited to 'legal dealings' with the principal thing in Art. 52 Polish Civil Code (albeit without prejudice to contrary statutory provisions), for example. This does not apply for other 'legal events' (Gniewek [-*Gniewek*], Kodeks cywilny^2, p. 118 no. 6; while Pietrzykowski [-*Skowrońska-Bocian*], Kodeks cywilny I^4, p. 206 no. 4 differs in some points, no. 7 emphasizes that the expropriation does not extend to the accessories of the expropriated thing). The (correct) view is that prescriptive possession does not extend to the accessories of the principal thing. However, this question is seldom discussed. For German law, the answer should lie in §§ 97 and 937 German Civil Code, as § 937 only concerns the prescriptive possession of the moveable thing, and accessories are autonomous moveable things under § 97. In consequence, accessories can be the object of an independent prescriptive process, but cannot be the object of a 'dependent' prescription (likewise for Polish law: *Skowrońska-Bocian* op. cit.). The presumption in § 926(1) German Civil Code (in case of doubt, the transfer of a land unit also means the transfer of its accessories) is only concerned with acquisition through voluntary legal dealings.

[398] On closer inspection, the European civil codes differ even on this point. Some apply their general rule (i.e. that legal dealings with a thing also cover its accessories) to all principal things (such as § 57(3) Estonian Civil Code; Art. 818(1) Italian Civil Code; Art. 17(2) Slovenian SPZ; § 510(2) Czech Civil Code), while others express this principle only for the relevant contractual agreement and the transfer of land unit ownership, but remain silent on the fate of accessories of moveable things (e.g. §§ 311c and 926 German Civil Code; there is no explicit provision regarding accessories of a transferred moveable thing, so one generally adopts a broad construction of the so-called 'real agreement' [*dingliche Einigung*]: MünchKomm [-*Holch*], BGB I(1)^5, § 97 no. 46).

[399] Example taken from *Liserre*, Lezioni di diritto privato^2, p. 390.

arrangements which extend hypothecs and (where they exist) land charges to land unit accessories are mandatory law. A hypothec, it is said, could not be conceived differently.[400] That does not seem very convincing.[401] It does not address the basic problem which the law of accessories is directed at solving, and it leads to difficult restrictions on competition. The machinery associated with a large agricultural business, for example, is not accounted for in the price of the relevant land unit. Why, then, should a legal system deny the owner of the business the possibility to agree with a bank that certain machines do not fall within the scope of a hypothec over the land unit, such that this inventory can be used as a security for another creditor? Only when the business as a whole is disposed of do matters lie differently.[402] It always depends on what, exactly, the object of the relevant transaction is. Against this background, the idea that one can categorize purely normative things as 'accessories' appears inconsistent. To speak of a guarantee as an 'accessory' of a claim is wide of the core idea of accessories because a guarantee is not an object that can be dealt with separately to the claim. Claims to

[400] This is the prevailing view in Polish and in German law. Art. 84 Polish Land Registry Act, from which cannot be derogated by contract, overrides Art. 52 Polish Civil Code (Radwański and Safjan [-*Katner*], System Prawa Prywatnego I, p. 1194 no. 45; Dmowski and Rudnicki [-*Rudnicki*], Kometarz do Kodeksu cywilnego I^9, pp. 230–31), especially to the extent that enforcement proceedings concerning an immoveable also embraces its accessories (Art. 947 § 1(2) Polish Civil CodeP). This is largely viewed in the same way in German law. It is not permitted to determine conditions differing from § 1120 German Civil Code (which delineate the assets covered by a hypothec) (RG 12 June 1906, RGZ 63 pp. 371, 373; RG 3 October 1929, RGZ 125 pp. 362, 365; BGH 30 November 1995, NJW 1996 pp. 835, 836), as this would be incompatible with commercial interests and with the *numerus clausus* principle of limited types of property rights. The parties may only limit the liability under a hypothec on the level of the law of obligations (RG 3 October 1929 op. cit.; BGH 30 November 1995 op. cit.) and in this manner help the debtor with a plea, within the constraints of § 1157 German Civil Code. The rule that a pledge charging a land unit also extends to the accessories is regarded as imperative in Swedish law. In the case of industrial accessories, Kap. 2 § 3 Sentence 2 JB provides that a retention of title in delivered goods can be protected with registration against third parties' attempts to furnish the goods under a hypothec (for further details, see von Bar [-*Westermann and Herrmann*], Sachenrecht in Europa I, pp. 518–22).

[401] Criticism of the prevailing view in German law can be found in Staudinger (-*Wolfsteiner*), BGB (2009), § 1120 no. 2. A number of European legal systems leave significantly more room for contractual freedom in the law of hypothecs. For example, § 457 Austrian Civil Code is taken to mean that, in doubt, a pledge only extends to the accessories of the respective principal thing. However, even this only applies to accessories which were already present at the time of the creation of the pledge; the parties' intentions determine what applies to accessories which arrive later (OGH 28 August 1991, SZ 64/109). Art. 857 Latvian Civil Code and § 5:103 Hungarian Civil Code (pledges—to which registered pledges in immoveables equivalent to a hypothec also count—only extend to the accessories of the relevant thing in case of doubt) commit themselves further to contractual freedom. § 153(2) Czech Civil Code [1964] and § 1346(1) Czech Civil Code [2014] are default rules only. The parties can determine that a pledge, contrary to a statutory presumption, does not extend to accessories *Švestka (-Spáčil/Škárová/Humák)*, Občanský zákoník I^2, p. 1087). § 151d(2) Slovakian Civil Code explicitly states that accessories are only included if the contract does not state anything to the contrary. Art. 4.171(2) and (3) Lithuanian Civil Code should also be read in this manner. The situation is unclear under Art. 140(2) Slovenian SPZ and Art. 2356 Romanian Civil Code. Both provide only for the extension of a relevant pledge over land to accessories. In Netherlands law, accessories do not fall into the scope of a hypothec in any event, as the new Netherlands Civil Code no longer acknowledges the category of accessories. Art. 3:254 Netherlands Civil Code states that the rules governing hypothecs can be applied to moveable things which are judged by commercial use to serve an immoveable thing permanently, where a non-possessory pledge over the moveable and a hypothec over the immoveable have been created. Such a rule had not previously been necessary, as the old Netherlands Civil Code classified the respective accessory thing as an immoveable in its own right and thus was automatically included in the scope of the hypothec (Nieuwenhuis/Stolker/Valk [-*Huijgen*], BW^6, Art. 3:254 no. 5).

[402] Under Art. 55^3 Polish Civil Code, agricultural businesses, for example, are farmland, including forested land units, buildings and their parts, furniture and equipment if they form or can form an organizational unit, with all rights which are connected to the direction of agriculture. However, it is contested whether such businesses can be objects of ownership (Radwański and Dybowski [-*Stelmachowski*], System Prawa Prywatnego III^2, p. 216 no. 8 answer in the affirmative).

interest payment can be characterized either as independent claims or, according to the applicable law of assignment, the fruits of another claim. They are, however, not 'accessories'. Interest payments are not, after all, dedicated to 'serve' another claim. The assets of an undertaking are, insofar as they are granted independent status as objects of property rights by the applicable law, components of the undertaking—not independent assets that are allocated to the undertaking but remain separate. For the same reason, it appears to be of no great importance to discuss buildings and surface area as 'accessories'. In the context of a concept of immoveables that lacks specificity, it is possible to say that a garage or basement belongs to a particular apartment,[403] or to say that a courtyard and garden belong to a house. But the concept of land unit presented in this book (namely: a land unit is a normative thing with a physical substrate) prohibits such language. A 'garage' is, on this view, only an accessory when it remains a separate, independent (real) thing—otherwise, a garage is a component of the land unit on which it stands and is, accordingly, legally non-existent. A garden, too, is only a dependent part of a land unit; like the basement and the courtyard, it only acquires the quality of a 'thing' in and of itself when the relevant statute (as in Austria,[404] the Czech Republic, and Slovakia[405]) expressly so envisages.

(2) Individual Things and Indivisible Things

The last 'problem group' is the category of collections of things that are considered, in their totality, to comprise a whole.[406] These are normative entities that some legal **9.63**

[403] Thus Cass. civ. 21 June 2000, 98-14045 ('*que dans la mesure où l'offre portait nécessairement sur un logement dont le locataire avait une parfaite connaissance puisqu'il l'occupait, aucun texte n'imposait au bailleur de préciser les accessoires de la chose vendue telle qu'une cave*'—a cellar is an *accessoire* of the apartment sold).

[404] Under § 300 Austrian Civil Code, cellars can be registered as land units in their own right (for further details, see, e.g. Klang [-*Klang*], ABGB II^2, pp. 27–8).

[405] Under § 121(2) Slovak and Czech Civil Code [1964] (the new Czech Civil Code does not contain this provision), the auxiliary rooms and areas dedicated use with the apartment are (were) considered accessories. This provision has led to an extensive and rather counterintuitive jurisprudence. Czech Nejvyšší soud České republiky 2 July 2008, 22 Cdo 1455/2008, Právní rozhledy 3/ 2009 concerned a lease which had been agreed in 1961 with a building cooperative about a first-floor apartment (kitchen, three rooms 'with accessories'). From the documents of the apartment, it could be inferred that a cellar belonged to it. In 1998, the plaintiffs bought the apartment, comprised of a kitchen, three rooms, a closet, a bathroom, a pantry, a toilet, a hallway, and a cellar with an area of 4.8m^2. In the declaration required for the division of apartments into provide property, it is mentioned that the apartment also consists of 'an area in cellar No. 9 with an area of 4.8m^2'. The declaration, however, designated this cellar as 'common area'. The complainant took issue with this. The 'auxiliary rooms' [*vedlejší místnosti*] and 'auxiliary premises' [*vedlejší prostory*] were argued to be accessories. The court took the approach that auxiliary 'rooms' included non-habitable rooms within the apartment (kitchen, hallway, bathroom, etc.) whereas 'premises' were rooms (cellar, shed) that were outside the apartment but dedicated to its use. Auxiliary rooms were 'components' of the apartment, and auxiliary premises its 'accessories'. The latter were integral components of the building, not the apartment. They belonged to the owner of the building (the owner of the principal thing) and had been determined by him to be used along with the apartment. The claim had to be rejected, as the cellar was not a component of the apartment, but at best an accessory. This result is difficult to comprehend terminologically, as it amounts to a distinction between accessories which are components and accessories which are 'really' accessories. The cellar was allocated to the second category. A garage, on the other hand, is not an 'auxiliary premises' and therefore not an accessory of an apartment; it does not serve needs of habitation (Czech Nejvyšší soud České republiky 4 April 2001, 26 Cdo 2340/99, Soudní rozhledy under C 395).

[406] This concept has its origin in Roman law. Roman law differentiated, as demonstrated by *Wieling*, Sachenrecht I^2, pp. 55–60, between (i) *res unitae, corpora unita*, (ii) *res compositae sive connexae, universitas rerum cohaerentium* (mechanically connected things), and (iii) *universitas rerum distantium*, things notionally considered as an entity.

systems invoke to serve a temporary purpose. Insofar as they elevate notional collective entities to the rank of objects of property rights, they spare the market the need to deal separately with so many individual objects; it is sufficient to effect one legal dealing with the totality. A notional *universitas* of this sort only exists for the period of time in which this need subsists—thereafter, it disintegrates back into its constituent parts. Within this period of time, separate things become components of an imaginary whole. Take the well-worn example of books in a library: to the extent they are elevated to the rank of an object of property rights, one can dispose of a library as such and the individual books that comprise it are counted to the library just as an individual page is counted to the book. They are components of a single, larger unity rather than individual accessories. Further examples include card and board games, which have already been mentioned, a set of porcelain wares, a construction kit, the volumes of an encyclopaedia, a warehouse inventory, valuable collections, or—of increasing importance—the assembly of software and user handbooks.[407] Earlier, standard examples were herds of livestock and bee swarms (which are to this day provided for in national codifications in considerable detail).[408] Whether an undertaking or agricultural business should be seen as a single (collective) entity, which is often the case, sometimes expressly in statute,[409] appears doubtful. Admittedly, there are undeniable parallels. But there are also important differences. Undertakings, even when they are relevant to the rank of fitting objects of property rights *per se*, are not fitting objects of the right of ownership; from the perspective of property law, they display the peculiarity that security arrangements (such as the floating charge) concerning undertakings are often oriented towards a 'collective thing' that only becomes concrete in the future. Above all, however, undertakings also comprise separate objects that lack the double nature that is essential for the existence of a *universitas*. So-called 'goodwill' and, in some legal systems, a 'firm' itself, for example, exists *only* as the component of an undertaking, not as an object that can be dealt with separately.[410] An undertaking is thus at best a non-genuine 'collective thing'. Genuine collective things consist of separate things that are in principle each in and of themselves objects of separate dealing.

The latter were subdivided into (a) *universitas rerum sive facti* (corporeal things) and (b) *universitas iuris* (incorporeal things, such as an inheritance).

[407] e.g. albeit in the context of a law of guarantee which cannot distinguish between accessories and collections of things: BGH 1 October 1992, NJW 1992 pp. 3224, 3225; possibly also BGH 4 November 1992, NJW 1993 pp. 461, 462, and later BGH 22 December 1999, NJW 2000 pp. 1415, 1416.

[408] Radwański and Dybowski (*-Stelmachowski*), System Prawa Prywatnego III^2, p. 219 no. 11 (which held that a swarm of bees was an exception to the rule in Polish law that there can be no ownership of collections of things, and was an autonomous object of ownership).

[409] Art. 55^1 Polish Civil Code, e.g. defines an 'undertaking' as an *organized whole* of immaterial and material components, which are applied to the performance of an economic activity, and Art. 55 Polish Civil Code defines an agricultural undertaking as an *organizational entity* composed of the discrete individual things described in that provision.

[410] Koziol and Welser (*-Kletečka*), Bürgerliches Recht I^{13}, 255 overlook this point, arguing that a collective object 'above all' embraces the incorporeal things and other objects that belong with it, for example the customer list and goodwill of an enterprise.

In legal systems that only accept corporeal objects as things, however, collective entities are excluded at the outset as objects of separate legal dealings. This does not follow, even though it is often said otherwise, from the so-called 'fundamental principle of specialty' [*Spezialitätsgrundsatz*].[411] This principle limits what can be created under it. What is rather decisive is that a notional collection of things has no real existence. One can sell such an 'object' in the relevant legal systems, but one cannot convey ownership in them or encumber them; they are, simply stated, not 'things'.[412] Admittedly, multiple things can be disposed of under a collective name, but that is simply a convenient (abbreviated) manner of speaking. The mere fact that the parties call the object to be transferred a 'library', 'warehouse', or similar does not provide the relevant legal system with an adequate basis on which to invalidate the transaction. But this type of language only achieves its purpose when it is sufficient to create a valid claim to the conveyance of property rights in every individual thing concerned. Ownership, in other words, only moves from one person to another when the parties have satisfied the applicable national rules for the transfer of every single real thing in question. That means that the contract must clearly establish that the relevant individual thing should be transferred with the rest; otherwise, the legal dealing is (to the relevant extent) ineffective. The relevant legal act must, for example, list the individual objects or otherwise describe them precisely[413]—how precisely is the subject of an extensive German jurisprudence.[414] Besides this, the relevant requirements of the law of possession must of course be met for every single item, to the extent that possession is involved in the relevant transfer 9.64

[411] This principle is explained at length in many textbooks and commentaries in the Civilian tradition. *Menyhárd*, Dologi jog, p. 85, e.g. mentions the principle of specialty in the context of collective things. It means that a property right can only be in (relate to) a single, individuated thing but not in aggregations of things.

[412] This is the position *inter alia* in Germany (Staudinger [-*Jickeli and Stieper*], BGB [2004], comments 17–19 to §§ 90–103); in Greece (Protodikeio Náfplio 90/1968 NoB 16 (1968) p. 428 makes clear, that a vindication over an aggregation of things is technically, according to Art. 218 Greek Civil Code, a plurality of individual claims for delivery relating to each separate thing); in Poland (*Piasecki*, Kodeks cywilny, Art. 45 Anm. 2), and in Hungary (see previous fn.).

[413] e.g. Austrian OGH 27 April 1994, SZ 67/78 (pledge over a warehouse; erection of notice signs was sufficient; see also OGH 19 December 1984, JBl 1985 p. 541).

[414] In relation to claims for possession pursuant to security arrangements over a warehouse (see BGH 24 June 1958, BGHZ 28 p. 16) there is a useful summary in OLG Düsseldorf 17 January 2012, NJW-RR 2012 p. 689. What is decisive is whoever sees the relevant agreement can recognize which things are to be transferred and which not (BGH 12 February 1992, NJW 1992 p. 1156; BGH 13 January 1992, NJW 1992 p. 1161). A pledge over material and product stock is invalid when an objective party, looking only at the relevant clause, is not able to identify the things affected—i.e. without reference to further documentation such as inventories (BGH 11 December 1997, BGHZ 137 p. 267; BGH 13 June 1956, BGHZ 21 p. 52, 56). It is possible to transfer possession of all stores of raw materials, intermediate products, and finished products that appear from a storage plan annexed to the relevant agreement (BGH 24 June 1958; s. also BGH 26 June 2008, ZIP 2008 p. 1437), but not to transfer simply 'all stocks and claims' (Schimansky/Bunte/Lwowsky [-*Ganter*], Bankrechts-Handbuch[4], § 95 no. 28). The German courts have upheld a transfer of a named book collection of a named firm on an identified floor of a business premises (BGH 13 January 1992, NJW 1992 p. 1161 and BGH 19 September 1994, NJW-RR 1994 p. 1537) especially when books not owned by the transferor are expressly marked as such. On the other hand, attempts to transfer simply a named book collection (without any indication of where it sits) were held to be invalid. The transfer of possession of a collection of porcelain samples was held to be valid where sufficient indications of the owner company's records (including financial records) were made (BGH 3 July 2000, NJW 2000 p. 2898). The relevant collection was stored in rooms that were made accessible to the secured creditor and parts of it found elsewhere were specially marked with stickers. Reference to an inventory list may also be sufficient, provided it clearly identifies the object of the agreement (BGH 20 December 1978, WM 1979 p. 300, 301), but not contractual references to an inventory that, although annexed to the agreement, simply described the materials according to their type and weight (BGH 18 April 1991, NJW 1991 p. 2144, 2146).

mechanism; otherwise, the item in question (although it belongs to a collective thing) will not be transferred. If, for example, a 'library' is transferred, the dealing is effective *vis-à-vis* any single book when the parties have named and numbered every volume held at a specific location in an appropriate electronic database and the transferee is put into possession of the collection as far as the relevant law requires. If, at the relevant point in time, some of the books are on loan to third parties, some legal systems stipulate that ownership only pass to the transferee when the required possessory relations are satisfied, for example through assignment of the right to demand delivery of the books (§ 931 German Civil Code) or through some specific possessory construction (Art. 1034 in connection with Art. 977 sec. 2 Greek Civil Code). At most, the category of 'collective things treated as a whole' has, in these legal systems, relevance for the law of obligations or the law of succession; for property law, it is not a functional category.[415] One need not even know exactly what a collective thing actually 'is' or into which sub-categories the category can be divided.[416]

9.65 Italian law approaches this question—in theory at least—differently.[417] Art. 816(1) Italian Civil Code defines a collective thing (*universalità di mobile*) as a 'plurality of moveables that belong to a single person and have a unitary purpose'. An *universalità* thus arises from the intentions of the owner of the individual *cosi* that make it up.[418] They lose their legal individuality and only get it back through a relevant *actus contrarius*. Such an act occurs when a single thing is made the object of separate legal acts and relationships. Until that occurs, all legal acts (including, e.g. the creation of a pledge) touch the *universalità* as a whole. The concept of a collective thing is created in virtue of its simplifying role for the parties. However, it demands higher effort on the part of the legislature. It felt itself bound, for example, to stipulate that the rules of innocent acquisition, which rest on possession, do not apply to collective things (see Arts 1153 and 1856 Italian Civil Code). The buyer of an *universalità* must exercise special

[415] This is sometimes even the case in legal systems where the codification not only provides a definition of 'collective things' but also (§ 302 Austrian Civil Code) expressly provides that a collective thing [*Gesamtsache*] is 'thought of as a whole' [*als Ganzes betrachtet wird*]. Even in Austria, this definition is of greatest importance for obligations law. An undertaking that is understood as a 'whole' can be, as a whole, the object of a contract of sale. For property law, however, the characterization of an object of legal transaction as a *Gesamtsache* is of no importance. It is sometimes argued that undertakings can be transferred as a whole in violation of the *Spezialitätsgrundsatz* (*Zankl*, Bürgerliches Recht, para. 303; *Bydlinski*, Privatrecht[6], para. 309), but this is not convincing. The principle is one of individuated transfer, even in the case of undertakings. Matters are only different where components of the undertaking appear in the guise of land unit accessories or a wholesale transfer is simplified in some other way. The latter can be said, in particular, of warehouse stock under § 427 Austrian Civil Code, where the stock can be delivered 'by sign'. It does not follow from this provision, however, that *Gesamtsachen* are generally impracticable to transfer individually (see *contra* Klang [-*Kisslinger*], ABGB[3], § 302 para. 10). In any case, an undertaking cannot 'as a whole' be the point of reference for a pledge (OGH 19 January 1966, EvBl 1966/232, ÖJZ 1966, 290, which also makes clear that an undertaking cannot fall into the scope of a hypothec independently of the undertaking's land unit).

[416] Polish Sąd Najwyższy 7 February 2002, I CKN 572/00, Lex-No. 53159 divides collective things, e.g. into 'organized' and 'unorganized' totalities, and considers a cassette in a video library to belong to the second category. However, this has no relevance for property law.

[417] In judicial practice, Art. 816 Italian Civil Code is of minimal significance. Modern databases and commentary reveal very few decisions on it, which is particularly surprising given that in Italy an undertaking is considered a *universitas iuris*.

[418] *Bianca*, Diritto civile VI, p. 83. *Trimarchi*, Istituzioni[16], p. 91 also considers the possessor to be entitled to effect such a dedication to purpose.

caution. The law of usufruct refers, in Art. 994 Italian Civil Code, to the classic example of a collective thing—the herd. One may doubt whether the creation of a usufruct over a herd of livestock retains much practical importance today.[419] However, the Italian legislature felt it was necessary to stipulate that the usufructuary of a herd must replace animals that perish without natural replacement; the usufruct over a single animal, on the other hand, extinguishes upon its death. French law deals with the characterization of *universalités* more easily because it works with a very open-textured concept of *biens*. An *universalité* is, in French law too, interpreted as a collection of goods that forms a totality.[420] As soon as this totality accrues sufficient coherence to be administrated as a whole, it becomes a *bien* in its own right on the basis that the owner would want it that way.[421] That is true of both the 'de facto' *universalités de fait* as well as the 'de jure' *universalités de droit*. Both of these categories are said to be able to gather goods of different kinds (e.g. the *fonds de commerce* is an important example of an *universalité de fait*).[422] The *universalité de droit* consists not only of goods but also debts (inheritances and the community property of marital partners); their autonomy is protected, in particular, by provisions on 'real subrogation' (*subrogation réelle*).[423]

Matters are peculiarly unclear in Spain,[424] Portugal, and Slovakia. Modelled on Art. 816 Italian Civil Code,[425] Art. 206 Portuguese Civil Code provides that a plurality of things that belong to a single person and are dedicated to a single purpose is a 'composite thing' (*coisa composta*) or a '*de facto* totality' (*universalidade de facto*). The *coisas singulars* that comprise the *universalidade* can, however, be objects of separate legal relations. Defining 'composite' and 'collective' things in a single category may seem like an unhappy approach, but this provision at least makes clear that collective things consist of moveable objects. That must be correct, but it leads immediately to the question whether a 'collective thing' as understood by Portuguese law is really a 'thing' at all, and this question remains unanswered. In our view, the answer must be in the negative.[426] Slovakian law (and, earlier, Czech law in § 153(1) Czech Civil Code [1964]) refers to collective things in § 151d(1) Slovakian Civil Code, which provides that a pledge can be created over a moveable or immoveable thing, claim, undertaking, or 'any other collective thing'. This seems to have collections in mind, but also things of different kinds **9.66**

[419] The origin of this rule in Roman law is unmistakable: *Bonfante*, Istituzioni di diritto romano[10], p. 337. A less antiquated variant is found in Art. 257 Polish Civil Code on usufructs over means of production.

[420] *Carbonnier*, Droit civil II, p. 1623 no. 724.

[421] *Zenati-Castaing and Revet*, Les biens[3], pp. 202–03 no. 132.

[422] *Carbonnier* op. cit.

[423] Ibid. p. 203 ('*L'autonomie de l'universalité de droit (autrement dit sa qualité de bien) a pour conséquence que l'aliénation d'un de ses composants n'affecte pas sa permanence laquelle est assurée par la substitution au bien sortant de sa contrepartie, en vertu de la subrogation réelle*').

[424] The *universalidad de hecho* is seldom the subject of scholarly analysis. *Díez-Picazo*, Fundamentos III[5], p. 186 explains that it becomes itself an object of legal relations. This text cites, by way of example, the various facilities listed in Art. 334(6) Spanish Civil Code—animal raising facilities, dovecotes, beehives, fish ponds, and similar, as well as cattle herds (see here also the usufruct provisions in Art. 499 Spanish Civil Code), animal teams (see also the sales law provisions in Art. 1491 Spanish Civil Code), and paintings, sculptures, ceramics, and book collections (in which Art. 54(1) LHMPSD enables the creation of a pledge).

[425] *Vieira*, Direitos reais, p. 218.

[426] See also, albeit not in agreement with the prevailing opinion, *Vieira*, Direitos reais, pp. 663–4.

(such as the furnishings in a legal practice). Such a 'thing-complex' is, in other parts of the provision, obviously taken to be a single (unified) thing. It is clear that simple dealings can be performed concerning art galleries, shops, libraries, and so forth in the law of obligations. However, irritatingly, separate legal dealings are necessary to change the parties real (i.e. property law) position.[427] Czech Nejvyšší soud České republiky 28 February 2006[428] describes a collective thing (*věc hromadná*, lit. 'mass thing') as things that have a similar or identical character or are dedicated to the same purpose. The subject matter of that decision, however, was only an obligational and not a property law problem, namely the rescission of a sale concerning bathroom furnishings (cupboards, sinks, mirror) on the basis one of them (a cupboard) was defective. The Supreme Court allowed the claim. The contract was concerned with a purpose-bound, stylistic whole. Only the subsequent commentary approached the property law aspects of this proposition, and took the approach that a charge over an undertaking had the character of a so-called 'general hypothec'. Not only could the undertaking be sold as a whole; further, it could be pledged as such.[429] The Czech Commercial Code (*Obchodní zákoník*) in its old version, however, distinguished carefully between the sale of an undertaking (§ 476(1) Czech Commercial Code), the transfer of claims and debts (§ 477), the transfer of intellectual property (§ 479 Czech Commercial Code), and the transfer of moveable and immoveable things (§ 483(1) Czech Commercial Code). Only some years later was more clarity brought to this obvious contradiction in Czech Nejvyšší soud České republiky 20 January 2011.[430] This case concerned a pledge over a warehouse. The court decided that a warehouse was a fitting object of property rights in the form of a pledge; moreover, the question whether it was a 'collective thing' or a collection of (separate) things was not important. The only case in which an object could be pledged was when the pledge creditor would have no appropriate means by which to get satisfaction from liquidation of the relevant object. A warehouse, it was said, is apprehended as a single thing in commercial usage, and that was what the law should look to. The pledge related to the warehouse as such, not to the individual things taken from it in the normal course of business. The object of the pledge was the things which were, at the relevant point in time, present in the warehouse. In this case, the parties had satisfied the principle of certainty of object with a reference to 'medical supplies in the warehouse of the pharmacy at [address XYZ]'. That the expression 'medical supplies' is fuzzy at the margins was said not to stand in the way of such an approach. The legal position has changed to a certain degree, at least, in the meantime. § 501 Czech Civil Code [2014] now provides that a complex of individual things belonging to a single person that are treated as an object and bear a common name are considered to be a collective thing. The provisions of the old version of the Commercial Code were adopted, with minimal modifications, in §§ 2175–2183 Czech Civil Code [2014].

[427] *Fiala and Kindl*, Občanské právo hmotné², pp. 164–5; *Vassilev*, Bulgarsko veshtno pravo, p. 19.
[428] 33 Odo 447/2004, Soubor rozhodnutí Nejvyššího soudu, no. C 4200.
[429] *Švestka (-Spáčil/Škárová/Humák)*, Občanský zákoník I², p.1083.
[430] 21 Cdo 3757/2009, Soudní judikatura, no. 10-11/2011.

X

Things and Rights

Why is it the case that one can acquire a wristwatch as his 'property'? An important part of the answer is because property law recognizes the watch as a 'thing'—in a way it no longer recognizes the watch's hands, movement, or face. Although they can still be objects of certain independent legal dealings, the latter have ceased to be *things* in the sense meant in property law. If matters were any different, separate property rights would be possible in them, including (for example) retention of title in favour of the suppliers of the watch components. Anyone acquiring the watch would have to enquire into the history not only of the watch itself but also of all the components from which it was made. He could never be sure of his property. Property law, as the law of rights in things, therefore not only has to answer the question what a *thing* 'is' and why one needs the concept of 'thing-ness', but also what *a* thing is (i.e. what is to be seen as 'a' thing and what as several things). The screws and hands of a watch only become separate things again when the watch is destroyed and its parts lose their functional organization. Although they have in fact been used, from the legal point of view they are, from this moment, new things. And because they are newly created things, ownership in them accrues to the owner of the (former) watch and not to the suppliers of the materials from which it was first made. Ownership in the watch as such, on the other hand, is thereby extinguished. The thing in which that right was fixed exists no more. Compare this case, however, to the case of a standing clock integrated into the wall of a hall. Such a clock is not even a thing at all. It is a part of the castle of which the hall is a part, which is in turn part of the land unit on which the castle sits. Clock, hall, and castle are given no more recognition by property law than the hands, movement, and face of the wristwatch. There is only a single thing—namely, the land unit. At most, a legal system can (exceptionally) allow the parties to a contract to anticipate the thingness of the clock at a time when it is still connected to the wall, in a manner which generates legal effects for third parties. However, in such cases it is necessary to consider whether the clock is to be seen as a thing for all purposes in the law of property *per se*, or 'only' in the context of a real right of separation. Even in a 'causal' transfer regime that operates independently of possession, the clock would only pass into the ownership of the buyer in the former case. 10.1

The question what a thing 'is' can never be answered in a blanket fashion; 'thing' is a relative term. In the sense we mean it in *property law*, a thing is everything, but only such things, that can be the point of reference of some person's *property right*. Things are conceptually necessary to imagine rights, and rights are conceptually necessary to describe things. The concept of a thing in the law of possession is different to the 10.2

Foundations of Property Law. Christian von Bar and Jason Grant Allen, Oxford University Press. © Christian von Bar 2023.
DOI: 10.1093/oso/9780198885337.003.0010

concept of a thing in the law of rights. A rental apartment is a thing in both the law of obligations and also in the law of possession: the rental tenant enjoys protection against breaches of his household peace. But an apartment is only a thing in the sense of the law of rights when the right to use it bears a 'real' character. In the legal systems of the civil law, this is only the case where the apartment is a so-called 'proprietary apartment' [*Eigentumswohnung*], that is, when the law grants its owner both 'horizontal' and 'vertical' ownership in it. Because one needs 'things' both to describe and guarantee rights, the conceptual definition of a thing is bound integrally together with the content of the relevant subjective rights. A 'thing' in the sense we mean it in the context of the right of ownership is not necessarily the same as a 'thing' in the context of a pledge, a hypothec, a usufruct, or (to the extent it is endowed with *erga omnes* effect) a retention of title. The narrowing of the concept of a thing to corporeal objects that we have observed in some European legal systems only makes sense once it is recognized that they are concerned with a definition that is necessary in the context of the right of ownership—or, more precisely, for describing the point of reference of the right of ownership in so-called 'moveable' things or 'chattels'.

10.3 To define 'things' in property law as 'everything that can be the point of reference of a person's property right' is neither circular nor arbitrary. It is not circular because the number of property rights recognized by any given legal system is limited and closed. One speaks of the *numerus clausus* of property rights. True, there are questions at the margin, because the courts of many European countries have always deemed it necessary to expand the repertoire of property rights given to them by statute or tradition. In the English legal tradition, it is also quite possible that common law and equity are not completely unanimous on the point. But that generally concerns only *marginalia*; where the development of the law (as in the case of expectancy rights) has strayed beyond conventional limits, it has led to efforts to derive novel innovations directly from statutory text—rather bolstering than undermining the *numerus clausus* concept.

10.4 To define 'things' in property law as everything that can be the point of reference of a subjective property right is not arbitrary, either. This conceptual definition sharpens the concept of the right in question. All property rights have a spatial, temporal, and substantive dimension. None of them is unlimited. The right known as 'ownership', for example, can only last as long as the thing to which it relates continues in existence; it is an 'eternal' right. Ownership also secures its holder a larger sphere of freedom of action than any other right. But ownership can only sensibly be applied to corporeal objects. Ownership is needed to allocate objects that are not by their very nature ascribed to a particular person for his exclusive use. Possession alone cannot achieve this, because possession has no content. Claims, for example, may be 'things' within the context of certain property rights, such as the right of pledge. But they stand, for this reason, outside the scope of the right of ownership. Ownership is just not necessary for them: there simply *is* no claim without a creditor and a debtor. If the attributes of 'creditor' and 'debtor' meet in one and the same person (as can happen, for example, in the case of an inheritance), the claim itself extinguishes. The object and its 'holding' are inextricably woven together; the right is oriented to the object and the object to the right. Only with the creation of a pledge does the claim become a 'thing', because the claim is thereupon allocated to someone other than the creditor.

The decisive criterion for an object's suitability as an object of the right of ownership is corporeality. This has two substantive grounds. Corporeality enables delimitation, and ownership enables permanent allocation. Without delimitation, such an allocation is impossible. Electricity, for example, must be consumed in the moment in which it is created. For this reason—even though matters are seen differently in some legal systems—electricity does not satisfy the basic prerequisites for the creation of property. Nor is it very helpful to distinguish systematically between 'moveable' and 'immoveable' things. Many moveable objects are not in fact things—take flowing waters, or a crane on rails in a working port. Something wholly immoveable, on the other hand, can crop up in the category of 'moveables' when it is the object of a separate right of use. For example, consider an underground garage constructed beneath a neighbouring land unit on the basis of a real right. Not 'moveability' or 'immoveability' but *delimitability* is the dispositive criterion. 10.5

Because property rights grant monopoly rights of use, their objects must be capable of human control. Moreover, the legal system must allow their monopolization by persons. Where no rights exist, no legal 'things' exist either. Where ownership in land is excluded, there are no land units. This applies, for example, to the ocean bed. The ocean is, itself, incapable of being controlled by persons and it is for this reason not a fitting object of property rights. What cannot be controlled can be an 'object' [*Gegenstand*] but not a 'thing' in the sense of property law. Many objects belong to this category—not least the planet on which we live. All 'things' are objects, but not all objects are 'things'—not by a long way. The concept of an 'object' provides a second useful service in our conceptual schema. It also excludes persons from the concept of 'things'. No-one 'belongs' in the property law sense—either to himself or to any other person. Persons are definitionally beyond the purview of property rights. This applies to juristic as well as 'natural' persons. They do not belong to anybody. The only conceivable property rights are real use rights over shares in a corporation, not the corporation itself. 10.6

Between the category of 'things' and the category of 'objects' stands a third category, which in this book has been labelled *objects of legal transaction*. Objects of legal transaction are all objects that can be sold, swapped, or gifted. Not everything that can be sold, swapped, or gifted can be monopolized. Future objects, for example, belong to this category—such as the harvest of the coming season, quantities that have not yet been concretized such as '1000 tonnes of potatoes of the variety *x*', or indeed so-called 'cryptocurrencies'. Every 'thing' is an object of legal transaction, but not every object of legal transaction is a 'thing'. Further, many objects exist that are not objects of legal transaction because they have been designated as *extra commercium* or because they cannot be made the subject matter of a 'translative' (from *translatio*) dealing. For example, trade in human organs is *per se* prohibited. Human organs are 'objects' following 10.7

their extraction from the body of a donor pending their transplantation, but they are not objects of legal transaction (they are not 'goods') and they should not be understood as 'things', either.

10.8 It is difficult to categorize things, because their categorization requires one to hold the reflexivity of right and object squarely in view. Against this background, we suggest a basic distinction between *real* and *normative* things. A thing is 'real' (assuming it fulfils the other criteria of the definition) when it is perceptible with the senses and does, in fact, exist. Its existence is not dependent on whether a person holds rights in it. A normative thing, by way of contrast, is a product of the law. Real things are straightforward objects of property rights. The monopolization of physically delimited, transportable things of the external world presents legal policy but relatively minor problems. Everywhere in Europe, real things are subject to both 'ownership' and 'possession'. The suitability of real things for ownership and the other rights of property law demands little by way of prerequisites. It only requires an object of legal transaction individuated by its corporeal nature. Real things are those objects of legal transaction whose suitability as objects of the right of ownership follows from their corporeality itself. Corporeality gives them (and only them) 'moveability', and this characteristic in turn guarantees the necessary delimitation of a single real thing (not from an immoveable, but rather) from another real, physical thing. Proper characterization requires one only to determine which *corpus* is the intended target in cases where several physical objects are connected into something that could comprise an independent object of ownership in its own right—as, for example, the wristwatch in our example above.

10.9 Normative things, by way of contrast, are pure creatures of juristic imagination. No-one can see them or touch them; they can only be 'thought'. Land units, too, belong to this category. They present the peculiarity that they have what we have called a physical substrate—they are rooted in the soil. The soil, however, 'is' not the land unit; it is only an (integral, which is to say non-independent) part of it. If one were to define a 'land unit' by reference to its physical attributes, it would not be a 'thing' at all—in fact, as an unseparated part of the surface of planet Earth, it would not even be an 'object'. A land unit is not just a 'surface area' of the earth, even though efforts are frequently made (in many legal systems) to define land units precisely with this term. A surface area is something two-dimensional, and two-dimensional objects are not suitable as points of reference of property rights: one can, unfortunately, do nothing with them. Land units, however, exist precisely to enable ownership (or ownership-like rights of use such as English law 'estates') of delimited parts of the outermost layer of Earth's crust. For this, it is necessary to create spaces above and below the surface that follow an outline sketched on the two-dimensional plane. A land unit owes its corporeal nature—and its quality as a 'thing'—exclusively to rules of law. Real things derive their corporeality from their individuation from other things. In the case of land units, the situation is quite different. They must first be formed as a thing (a *corpus*) by the legal system—and that on all sides, i.e. up in the air, down into the soil, and out across the surface. Land units do not exist by nature. Their individuation is a consequence of legal intervention projected onto nature. For this reason, the number of land units can be increased and decreased while the landscape onto which these units are projected subsists unchanged. The proliferation of land units is an everyday procedure; the reduction of extant land units, however, is a less common and more involved process. The sheer number of subjective property rights that are possible to hold in land units has no parallel in any other class of thing. At the same time, land units exist in a range of different forms. On the correct view, apartments in a building are properly seen as 'land units' in their own right, too.

Purely normative things lack any physical substrate. They have no reflection in the external world. They are a rich kaleidoscope of immaterial objects that are protected in **10.10**
some way or another by property law. To date, their categorization and classification has not been achieved convincingly—a circumstance that relates to the inadequate state of our general appreciation of the *reflexivity of things and rights*. The preponderance of purely normative things is characterized by the fact that their allocation to a person does not require the concept of 'ownership'. Their allocation to a legal subject is an intrinsic part of their existence as legal objects. This applies, as we have seen, to claims. But it also applies to shares in corporations, and indeed entire undertakings. Counterexamples that prove the rule are scientific texts, poems, novels, melodies, and so forth. They have a conceptual existence even without legal allocation to a person. For this reason, we speak of them as 'intellectual property', and this parlance is fundamentally correct; talk of 'ownership of an undertaking' (or similar) is, by way of contrast, false. In other words, it is possible to classify purely normative objects in the first instance according to whether they are fitting objects of the right of ownership. Being a suitable object for property rights generally, of course, is not necessarily the same as being a suitable object for the right of ownership specifically. Most purely normative things are only a fitting object of special (or 'smaller') property rights, but not the right of ownership.

Purely normative objects of legal transaction can only step up to the rank of 'things' **10.11**
when they possess the inherent potential for exclusive allocation to a person. This is often lacking even for objects to which the market ascribes very significant economic value—for example, information, energy, future things, and money units. They are not only not fitting objects of the right of ownership; they are not fitting objects for any property rights at all. To put the point differently, they cannot be allocated exclusively to a single person by means of any conceivable property right. An object of legal transaction only has the potential for exclusive allocation when it is controllable, ascertainable, and transferable. The latter is (for example) inapplicable in the case of information because the number of people with knowledge of information increases when information is shared, which in turn excludes the idea of a 'transfer' in the sense of a legal dealing. Purely normative things are only ever equiparated with 'genuine' things (i.e. things with some inherent physical *characteristica* of delimitation) for specific purposes; they are for this very reason only fitting objects for specific property rights, not all property rights. This observation in turn allows us to predict which purely normative things might come into consideration as being tantamount to other things. At the

current time, this catalogue would include only claims, shares in corporations, undertakings with customer relationships and goodwill, and a residual group of rights that are best described as privileges. To these belong (at least according to the judgment of most European legal systems) concessions and market access permissions, in addition to a handful of (sometimes valuable) rights to propose the occupant of an office or other position.

Further Reading

Andreas Abegg, Die Evolution des Verwaltungsvertrags zwischen Staatsverwaltung und Privaten: Der kontrahierende Staat in Deutschland, Frankreich und der Schweiz seit dem 18. Jahrhundert (Berne 2010)
Maria G. Adamopoulou, Ypothíki se michanímata katá ton N. 4112/1929 (hypothecs in plant machinery according to G. 4112/1929) (Athens and Komotiní 2007)
Thomas Adlercreutz, Äganderatten till kroppen, SvJT 2004 pp. 809–17
Jorge Manuel Afonso Alves, Bens de domínio público: classificação, avaliação e contabilização em Portugal (Braga 2004)
Hans-Jürgen Ahrens and Mary-Rose McGuire, Modellgesetz für Geistiges Eigentum (Munich 2012)
Bram Akkermans, The Principle of Numerus Clausus in European Property Law (Antwerp 2008)
Raffaele Albano, Pertinenze, in: Enc. giur. vol. XXIII (Rome 1990)
Tomasz Aleksandrowicz, Komentarz do ustawy o dostępie do informacji publicznej (4th edn, Warsaw 2008)
Antal Almási, Dologi jog. vol. I: *kötet* (Budapest 1928)
Christian Alunaru, Zum neuen Rumänischen Zivilgesetzbuch—Vertragsrechtlicher Teil, ERCL 2010 pp. 197–216
Christian Alunaru, 'Das Rumänische Sachenrecht zwischen zwei Gesetzbüchern' (2011/2012) IJVO 17 pp. 29–59
Manuel Amorós Guardiola, El pacto de reserva de dominio en los bienes inmuebles, RCDI 488 (1972) pp. 9–42
Jorge Andrade da Silva, Código dos Contratos Públicos comentado e anotado (3rd edn., Coimbra 2010)
Suzanne Antoine, L'animal et le droit des biens, D. 2003 pp. 2651–4
Tullio Ascarelli, Obbligazioni Pecuniarie, in: Antonio Scialoja, Giuseppe Branca (founder), Francesco Galgano (ed.), Commentario del codice civile. vol. IV: Delle obbligazioni. Art. 1277–1284 (Bologna and Rome 1959)
Jean-Marie Auby, Pierre Bon, Jean-Bernard Auby, and Philippe Terneyre, Droit Administratif des biens (5th edn, Paris 2008)
John Austin (Robert Campbell ed.), Lectures on Jurisprudence or the Philosophy of Positive Law (5th edn, London 1885)
Louis d'Avout, De l'utilitité résiduelle du droit commun en matière de transfert d'actions et autres titres financiers, D. 2010 pp. 123–7
Louis d'Avout and Blandine Mallet-Bricout, La liberté de création des droits réels aujourd'hui, D. 2013 pp. 53–61
Regina Aymerich Renteria, La especificación en el Código civil, ADC 40 (1987) pp. 1149–232
Johannes Bärmann, Zur Dogmatik des gemeinen Raumeigentums, AcP 155 (1956) pp. 1–27
Johannes Bärmann, Wohnungseigentumsgesetz. Kommentar (11th edn, Munich 2010)
Johannes Bärmann and Hanns Seuß (eds), Praxis des Wohnungseigentums (5th edn, Munich 2010)
Christian von Bar and Ulrich Drobnig, The Interaction of Contract Law and Tort and Property Law in Europe (Munich 2004)
Christian von Bar, Principles of European Law. Non-Contractual Liability Arising out of Damage Caused to Another (PEL Liab.Dam) (Munich, Brussels, Berne, Oxford 2009)
Christian von Bar and Stephen Swann, Principles of European Law. Unjustified Enrichment (PEL Unj. Enr.) (Munich, Brussels, Berne, Oxford 2010)
António Barreto Menezes Cordeiro, Do trust no direito civil (Coimbra 2014)
Heinz Barta, with the cooperation of *Reinhold Beiser, Martin Binder et al.*, Zivilrecht: Grundriss und Einführung in das Rechtsdenken (Vienna 2004)

S. E. Bartels, Een hermafrodiet in het zakenrecht, NTBR 2013 pp. 124–5

Diogo Bártolo, Venda de bens alheios, in: António Menezes Cordeiro et al. (eds), Estudos em Homenagem ao Prof. Doutor Inocêncio Galvão Telles. vol. IV: Novos Estudos de Direito Privado (Coimbra 2003), pp. 383–436

Petr Baudyš, Katastr nemovitostí (2nd edn, Prague 2010)

Samuel Becquet, Le bien industriel (Paris 2005)

Hubert Beer, Die relative Unwirksamkeit (Berlin 1975)

Okko Behrends, Rolf Knütel, Berthold Kupisch, and Hans Hermann Seiler (trans.), Corpus Iuris Civilis. Text und Übersetzung. Vol. I: Institutionen (2nd edn, Heidelberg 1997)

Marco Bellante, La caparra (Milan 2008)

Brigitte Belloir-Caux, Dictionnaire de droit des biens (Paris 2013)

Bertil Bengtsson, Om fastighetsbesittning och besittningsrubbning, in: Festskrift till Hans Thornstedt (Stockholm 1983), pp. 75–122

Bertil Bengtsson, Speciell Fastighetsrätt. Miljöbalken (10th edn, Uppsala 2010)

Maurizio Benincasa and Andrea Genovese, Locazione e affitto, in: Dizionario di diritto privato (edited by Silvio Martucelli and Valerio Pescatore) (Milan 2012) pp. 982–95

Matthias Berberich, Virtuelles Eigentum (Tübingen 2010)

Pierre Berlioz, La notion de bien (Paris 2007)

Bérénice de Bertier-Lestrade, Utilisation normale de la propriété privée et servitudes d'utilité publique, D. 2003 pp. 587, note to Cass. 19 June 2002

Erwin Beysen, Die Kondiktion oder die Vindikation von Geld (unpublished Master's thesis, University of Osnabrück 2000)

Cesare Massimo Bianca, La vendita e la permuta, in: Filippo Vassalli (ed.), Trattato di diritto civile italiano. Vol. 7.1 (2nd edn, Turin 1993)

Cesare Massimo Bianca, Diritto civile. Vol. VI: La proprietà (Milan 1999, reprint 2004)

Gerard Bieniek and Stanisław Rudnicki, Nieruchomości. Problematyka prawna (Warsaw 2004)

Lina Bigliazzi Geri, Oneri reali e obbligazioni propter rem, in: Antonio Cicu and Francesco Messineo (eds), Trattato di diritto civile e commercial. Vol. 11.3 (Milan 1984)

Marc Billiau, L'opposabilité des contrats ayant pour objet un droit eel, in: Marcel Fontaine and Jacques Ghestin (eds), Les effets du contrat à l'égard des tiers, comparaisons franco-belges (Paris 1992), pp. 190–221

Jean-René Binet, Protection de la personne. Le corps humain, in: JclCiv Code, Art. 16 à 16-13, Fasc. 12 (Paris 2009)

Peter Birks, Six Questions in Search of a Subject: Unjust Enrichment in a Crisis of Identity, Jurid.Rev. 1985 pp. 227–52

William Blackstone, Commentaries on the Laws of England. Vol. II: Of the Rights of Things (Oxford 1766, reprint Chicago 1979)

Michał Bobrzyński, Das Verfügungsrecht über den Gegenstand des Finanzpfandrechts, in: Marc Liebscher (ed.), Harmonisierung des Wirtschaftsrechts in Deutschland, Österreich und Polen. Jahrbuch des Krakauer Forums der Rechtswissenschaften der Jagiellonen Universität (Baden-Baden 2008), pp. 255–76

Hans-Jürgen Bocianiak, Ausgewählte Probleme der Tierhalterhaftung im Lichte der Rechtsprechung, VersR 2011 pp. 981–5

Leif Böttcher, Das Meer als Rechtsraum—Anwendbarkeit deutschen Sachenrechts auf Offshore-Windkraftanlagen und Möglichkeiten der Kreditsicherung, RnotZ 2011 pp. 589–601

Joachim Bohnert, Der Kataster im System des Sachenrechts, JZ 2011 pp. 775–80

Pietro Bonfante, Istituzioni di diritto romano (reprint of the 10thedn, Turin 1966)

José Luís Bonifácio Ramos, Domínio público e domínio privado: mitos e sombras, O direito 141 (2009) pp. 815–52

José Luís Bonifácio Ramos, O animal: coisa ou tertium genus? O direito 141 (2009) pp. 1071–1104

Manuella Bourassin, Vincent Brémond, and Marie-Noëlle Jobard-Bachellier, Droit des sûretés (2nd edn, Paris 2010)

Albert Bradáč, Věcná břemena od A do Z (4th edn, Prague 2009)

Manuel Broseta Pont and Fernando Martínez Sanz, Manual de derecho mercantil Bd. I (11th edn, Madrid 2002)

Dörte Busch, Eigentum und Verfügungsbefugnisse am menschlichen Körper und seinen Teilen (Frankfurt am Main et al. 2012)

Peter Bydlinski, Der Sachbegriff im elektronischen Zeitalter: zeitlos oder anpassungsbedürftig? AcP 198 (1998) pp. 287–328

Peter Bydlinski, Grundzüge des Privatrechts für Ausbildung und Praxis (6th edn, Vienna 2005);

Richard Calnan, Proprietary Rights and Insolvency (Oxford 2010)

Claus-Wilhelm Canaris, Die Verdinglichung obligatorischer Rechte, in: Horst Heinrich Jakobs (ed.), Festschrift für Werner Flume zum 70. Geburtstag. vol. I (Cologne 1978), pp. 371–428

Albina Candian, La notion de biens, EJCL 2007, vol. 11.3 pp. 1–15

Deborah Cao, Translating Law, Multilingual Matters (Clevedon 2007)

Simona Caruso and Giuseppe Spanò, Le servitù prediali (Milan 2013)

António Carvalho Martins, Acessão (Coimbra 1992)

Orlando de Carvalho, Princípios e características do Direito das coisas, BFD 87 (2011) pp. 1–20

Orlando de Carvalho, Direito das coisas—do direito das coisas em geral (Coimbra 2012)

Carlo Castronovo and Salvatore Mazzamuto, Manuale di diritto privato europeo. vol. II: Proprietà obbligazioni contratti (Milan 2007)

Raffaele Caterina, Il possesso, in: Antonio Gambaro (ed.), Trattato dei diritti reali. vol. 1: Proprietà e possesso (Milan 2008) pp. 357–488

Hervé Causse, Principe, nature et logique de la « dématérialisation », JCP E 1992, I, 194 pp. 530–34

Stefania Cervelli, I diritti reali. Manuale e applicazioni pratiche dalle lezioni di Guido Capozzi (2nd edn, Milan 2007)

CLC/Baltmane&Bitans, Grundeigentum und Sicherheiten in Lettland (Schriftenreihe des CLC, Bd. 8, Vienna and Graz 2003)

Giovanni Cattaneo, Riserva della proprietà e aspettativa reale, Riv.trim.dir. e proc.civ. 1965 pp. 945–1004

Angelo Chianale, L'ipoteca, in: Rodolfo Sacco (ed.), Trattato di diritto civile, I diritti reali. vol. 6 (Turin 2005)

Edward Coke, The First Part of the Institutes of the Laws of England. A Commentary on Littleton (19th edn, London, 1st americ. edn, Philadelphia 1853)

Ambroise Colin and Henri Capitant, Cours élémentaire de droit civil français (vol. I, 7th edn, Paris 1931)

François Collart Dutilleul and Philippe Delebecque, Contrats civils et commerciaux (6th edn, Paris 2002)

Marco Comporti, Contributo allo studio del diritto reale (Milan 1997)

Marco Comporti, Diritti reali in generale, in: Antonio Cicu and Franco Messineo (eds), Trattato di diritto civile e commercial. vol. 8, part 1 (Milan 1980)

Marco Comporti, La proprietà europea e la proprietà italiana, Riv. dir. civ. 2008, I, pp. 189–206

Maria Costanza, Numerus clausus dei diritti reali e autonomia contrattuale, in: Studi in onore di Cesare Grassetti. vol. I (Milan 1980), pp. 421–51

Roberto Conti, La proprietà e i diritti reali minori (Milan 2009)

Gérard Cornu, Vocabulaire juridique (8th edn, Paris 2009)

Maurice Cozian, Alain Viandier, Florence Deboissy, Droit des sociétés (20th edn, Paris 2007)

Damien Cremean and Sandy Thompson, Actions in Rem; Arrest of Ships; Maritime Liens, in: Michael William Duckett White (ed.), Australian Maritime Law (2nd edn, Sydney 2000)

Maria de Assunção Oliveira Cristas, Transmissão contratual do direito de crédito—do carácter real do direito de crédito (Coimbra 2005)

Luís da Cunha Gonçalves, Da propriedade horizontal ou por andares (Lisbon 1956)

Nicholas Curwen, General and Special Property in Goods, Legal Studies 20 (2000) pp. 181–97

Brian Davenport, End of an Admiralty Belief, LQR 114 (1998) pp. 169–72

Hilary Delany, Equity and the Law of Trusts in Ireland (4th edn, Dublin 2007)

Ioannis Deliyiannis, Oikogeneiako Dikaio. vol. II (Athens 1987)

Enrico Dell'Aquila, L'acquisto della proprietà per accessione, unione, commistione e specificazione (Milan 1979)

Heinrich Demelius, Österreichisches Grundbuchsrecht: Entwicklung und Eigenart (Vienna 1948)

Harold Demsetz, Toward a Theory of Property Rights, The American Economic Review 57 (1967) 347–59

Heinrich Dernburg, Lehrbuch des Preußischen Privatrechts und der Privatrechtsnormen des Reichs. vol. I (3rd edn, Halle 1881)

Sarah C. Derrington, The Continuing Utility of the Action in Rem, LQR 123 (2007) pp. 358–61

Sarah C. Derrington and James M. Turner, The Law and Practice of Admiralty Matters (Oxford 2007)

Luis Díez-Picazo, Autonomía privada y derechos reales, RCDI 1976, pp. 299–330

Luis Díez-Picazo, La modificación de las relaciones jurídico-reales y la teoría de la accesión, in: Luis Díez-Picazo, Ensayos jurídicos, vol. III Derechos reales, derecho registral, derecho de sucesiones, derecho mercantil, varia (Madrid 2011), pp. 3237–60

Luis Díez-Picazo, Producción de los bienes y rendimiento económico, in: Luis Díez-Picazo, Ensayos jurídicos, vol. III Derechos reales, derecho registral, derecho de sucesiones, derecho mercantil, varia (Madrid 2011), pp. 3406–14

Gerardo Diana, La proprietà immobiliare urbana, vol. I (Milan 2007)

Gero Dolezalek, Plädoyer für Einschränkung des § 950 BGB (Verarbeitung), AcP 195 (1995) pp. 392–444

Filippos Doris, Emprágmati Asfália (Athens 1986)

Ondřej Dostál, Komu patří mé tělo: Několik úvah o právním statutu oddělených částí těla a mrtvoly, Zdravotnictví a právo 10 (2003) pp. 8–14

William Dross, L'ordre public permet-il que soit créé un droit réel perpétuel? RTD civ. 2013 pp. 141–59

William Dross, Propriété et droits réels, RTD civ. 2013 pp. 141–59

Gerhard Dulckeit, Die Verdinglichung obligatorischer Rechte (Tübingen 1951)

Carsten Thomas Ebenroth, Karlheinz Boujong, Detlev Joost, and Lutz Strohn (eds), Handelsgesetzbuch. vol. II: §§ 343–475h (2nd edn, Munich 2009)

James Edmonds, International Timesharing (3rd edn, London 1991)

Karel Eliáš, Nový občanský zákoník ve Sbírce zákonů, Právní rozhledy 7 (2012) pp. 229–34

Karel Eliáš, Objekt vlastnického práva a návrh občanského zákoníku (Také o abstrakci v juristickém myšlení), Právní rozhledy 11 (2011) pp. 410–12

Karel Eliáš, Věc jako pojem soukromého práva, Právní rozhledy IV (2007) pp. 119–26

Karel Eliáš et al., Nový občanský zákoník s aktualizovanou důvodovou zprávou a rejstříkem (Ostrava 2012)

Howard W. Elphinstone, What Is a Chose in Action? LQR 9 (1893) pp. 311–15

Wolfgang Ernst, Der zweifache Verkauf derselben Sache—Betrachtungen zu einem Rechtsproblem in seiner europäischen Überlieferung, in: Eva Jakab and Wolfgang Ernst (eds), Kaufen nach römischem Recht: antikes Erbe in den europäischen Rechtsordnungen (Berlin 2008) pp. 83–103

Wolfgang Ernst, Eigenbesitz und Mobiliarerwerb (Tübingen 1992)

Sjef van Erp, European Property Law: A Methodology for the Future, in: Reiner Schulze and Hans Schulte-Nölke (eds), European Private Law: Current Status and Perspectives (Munich 2011), pp. 227–48

Muriel Fabre-Magnan, Propriété, patrimoine et lien social, RTD civ. 1997 pp. 583–613

Murad Ferid and Hans Jürgen Sonnenberger, Das Französische Zivilrecht. vol. 2: Schuldrecht, Die einzelnen Schuldverhältnisse. Sachenrecht (2nd edn, Heidelberg 1986)

Francesco Ferrara, L'usufrutto dei crediti nel diritto civile italiano, Riv. it. per le scienze giur. 1904, p. 325 ff (=L'usufrutto dei crediti nel diritto civile italiano, Turin 1905)

Martin Fehr, Bidrag till läran om fordringspreskription enligt svensk rätt (Stockholm 1913)

Jorge de Figueiredo Dias (ed.), Comentário Conimbricense do Código Penal, Parte Especial. vol. II: Artigos 202 a 307 (Coimbra 1999)

Pavlos Filios, Empragmato Dikaio (3rd edn, Athens 2009)

Thomas Finkenauer, Zum Begriff der Rechtsnachfolge in § 221 BGB, JZ 2000 pp. 241–7

Klaus-Bernd Fischer and Ana-Katharina Fischer, Spanisches Handels- und Wirtschaftsrecht (2nd edn, Heidelberg 1995)

Ursula Floßmann, Österreichische Privatrechtsgeschichte (6th edn, Vienna and New York 2008)
Werner Flume, Vom Beruf unserer Zeit für die Gesetzgebung, ZIP 2000 pp. 1427–30
André Françon, L'usufruit des créances, RTD civ. 1957 pp. 1–27
Jens Thomas Füller, Eigenständiges Sachenrecht? (Tübingen 2006)
Andrea Fusaro, Oneri reali e obbligazioni «propter rem», in: Digesto delle discipline privatistiche—Sezione civile. vol. XIII (Turin 1995)
Enrico Gabrielli, Diritti reali, Il pegno (Trattato di diritto civile; edited by Rodolfo Sacco) (Turin 2005)
Enrico Gabrielli, Il pegno anomalo (Padua 1990)
Paolo Gallo, Arricchimento senza causa e quasi contratti (i rimedi restitutori), in: Rodolfo Sacco (ed.), Trattato di diritto civile, Le fonti delle obbligazioni. vol. 2, pp. XIV–276 (Turin 1996)
Antonio Gambaro, La proprietà, in: Giovanni Iudica and Paolo Zatti (eds), Trattato di diritto privato (Milan 1990)
Antonio Gambaro, Proprietà privata e disciplina urbanistica (Bologna 1977)
Antonio Gambaro and Umberto Morello, Lezioni di diritto civile (Milan 2012)
Giuseppe Gandolfi, Onere reale, in: Enciclopedia del diritto. vol. XXX (Milan 1980)
Joshua S. Gans, Stephen S. King, and Graeme Woodbridge, Numbers to the People: Regulation, Ownership and Local Number Portability, Information Economics and Policy 13 (2001) pp. 167–80
Maria Olinda Garcia, O arrendamento plural—quadro normativo e natureza jurídica (Coimbra 2009)
J. F. Garner, Meaning of 'Land' in Administrative Statutes (1957) 21 Conv 141–51
Francesco Gazzoni, La trascrizione immobiliare. vol. I (2nd edn, Milan 1998)
F. Gény, Une théorie nouvelle sur les rapports juridiques issus du contrat de travail, RTD civ. 1902 pp. 333–43
Apostolos S. Georgiades, Empragmato Dikaio. vol. I (Athens 1991)
Apostolos S. Georgiades, E exasfálisi ton pistóseon (Athens 2001)
Otto von Gierke, Deutsches Privatrecht. vol. I: Allgemeiner Teil und Personenrecht (Leipzig 1895)
Richard Giesen, Scheinbestandteil—Beginn und Ende, AcP 202 (2002) pp. 689–721
Shalev Ginossar, Rights in rem—A New Approach, Israel L Rev 14 (1979), pp. 286–336
Michele Giorgianni, Diritti reali, in: Novissimo Digesto italiano. vol. V (Turin 1960)
Bernard Glansdorff, Chronique de jurisprudence. Les droits réels (1965–66), J.T. 1968 pp. 1–5
J. J. Gomes Canotilho and Vital Moreira, Constituição da República Portuguesa Anotada. vol. I (Coimbra 2007)
Pedro González Poveda, Acciones protectoras del dominio y de la posesión (Barcelona 2002)
Roy Goode, Commercial Law (3rd edn, London 2004)
Barbara Graham-Siegenthaler, Kreditsicherungsrechte im internationalen Rechtsverkehr: Eine rechtsvergleichende und international-privatrechtliche Untersuchung (Berne 2005)
Kevin Gray, Elements of Land Law (London 1987)
Kevin Gray, Property in Thin Air, CLJ 50 (1991) pp. 252–307
Paolo Greco and Gastone Cottino, Della vendita: Arts. 1470–1547, in: Antonio Scialoja and Giuseppe Branca (eds), Commentario del codice civile (2nd edn, Rome and Bologna 1981)
George Gretton, Trusts Without Equity, ICLQ 49 (2000) pp. 599–620
Paolo Grossi, La proprietà e le proprietà nell'officina dello storico, Quaderni fiorentini XVII (1988) pp. 359–422
Giuseppe Grosso, Corso di diritto romano. Le cose. Con una 'nota di lettura' di Filippo Gallo (Turin 1941, reprint 2001)
Hugo Grotius, De jure belli ac pacis libri tres. Drei Bücher vom Recht des Krieges und des Friedens: Paris 1625. New German Translation and Introduction by Walter Schätzel (Tübingen 1950)
A. G. Guest, Guest on the Law of Assignment (London 2012)
Birke Häcker, Proprietary Restitution after Impaired Consent Transfers: A Generalized Power Model CLJ [2009] 324–60
Henry Hansmann, Property, Contract, and Verification: The Numerus Clausus Problem and the Divisibility of Rights, Journ. Leg. Stud. XXXI (2002) pp. 373–420
John Hare, Shipping Law & Admiralty Jurisdiction in South Africa (Cape Town 1999)
Justus Haucap, Telephone Number Allocation: A Property Rights Approach, European Journal of Law and Economics 15 (2003) pp. 91–109

Ronny Hauck, Die Verdinglichung obligatorischer Rechte am Beispiel einfacher immaterialgüterrechtlicher Lizenzen, AcP 211 (2011) pp. 626–64

Petr Havlan, Veřejné vlastnictví v právu a společnosti (Prague 2008)

Herbert Hausmaninger and Walter Selb, Römisches Privatrecht (9th edn, Vienna 2001)

Cynthia Hawes, Property Interests in Body Parts: Yearworth v North Bristol NHS Trust, MLR 73 (2010), pp. 130–40

Silvia Tamayo Haya, El principio de especialidad o de determinación, in: Orduña Moreno et al. (eds), Los sistemas de transmisión de la propiedad inmobiliaria en el derecho europeo (Pamplona 2009), pp. 537–64

Philipp Heck, Grundriß des Sachenrechts (2nd reprint of the edition Tübingen 1930, Aalen 1970)

Jan Hellner, Metodproblem i rättsvetenskapen studier i förmögenhetsrätten (Visby 2001)

Per Henriksson, Sakrättsliga moment och deras ekonomiska konsekvenser (Stockholm 2009)

Henrik Hessler, Allmän Sakrätt. Om det förmögenhetsrättsliga tredjemansskyddets principer (Stockholm 1973)

Manuel Henrique Mesquita, Direitos reais—sumário das lições ao curso de 1966–1967 (Coimbra 1967)

Henrik Hessler, Allmän Sakrätt. Om det förmögenhetsrättsliga tredjemansskyddets principer (Stockholm 1973)

Sten Hillert, Servitut (3rd edn, Uppsala 1991)

Ruben A. Hofmann and Hendrik Baumann, Die zivilrechtliche Behandlung von Hochseekabeln in der Nordsee, RdE 2012 pp. 53–8

W. S. Holdsworth, History of English Law. vol. II (4th edn, London 1936)

W. S. Holdsworth, The History of the Treatment of Choses In Action by the Common Law Harv. L. Rev. 33 (1920) 997–1030

Oliver Wendell Holmes, The Common Law (Boston 1881, reprint 1990)

Heinrich Ewald Hörster, Zum Erwerb vom Nichtberechtigten im System des portugiesischen bürgerlichen Gesetzbuchs (Coimbra 1988)

Christian Holzner, Zur Anwendbarkeit der gesetzlichen Verarbeitungsregeln auf den Werkvertrag, JBl 2009 pp. 684–90

Anthony M. Honoré, Ownership, in: Anthony Gordon Guest (ed.), Oxford Essays in Jurisprudence (Oxford 1961), pp. 107–46

Roman Horáček, Karel Čada and Petr Hajn, Práva k průmyslovému vlastnictví (2nd edn, Prague 2011)

Heinz Hübner, Der Rechtsverlust im Mobiliarsachenrecht (Erlangen 1955)

Roberto Invernizzi, Accessione invertita e CEDU, Riv. giur. edilizia 2000 pp. 595–6

J. E. Jansen, Over de ontzakelijking van dieren en de grenzen van het zaaksbegrip, R.M. Themis 2011 pp. 187–201

Uwe Jenisch, Renaissance des Meeresbodens, NordÖR 2010 pp. 373–82 and pp. 429–33

Ulf Jensen, 36 lektioner i sakrätt (Uppsala 1991)

Rudolf von Jhering, Zur Lehre von den Beschränkungen des Grundeigenthümers im Interesse der Nachbarn, JhJb 6 (1863) pp. 81–130

Reinhold Johow, Die Vorentwürfe der Redaktoren zum BGB. Sachenrecht. Teil I: Allgemeine Bestimmungen, Besitz und Eigentum, in: Werner Schubert (ed.), Die Vorlagen der Redaktoren für die erste Kommission zur Ausarbeitung des Entwurfs eines Bürgerlichen Gesetzbuches (Berlin 1982)

Immanuel Kant, Metaphysik der Sitten. Teil 1: Metaphysische Anfangsgründe der Rechtslehre (neu hrsg. von Bernd Ludwig Hamburg 1986)

I. Karakostas and A. Bredimas, H prostasia ton zoon kai to dikaio (Tierschutz und Recht) (Athens and Komotini 2004)

Alina Kilian, Wörterbuch der Rechts- und Wirtschaftssprache. vol. II: Deutsch-Polnisch (Warsaw 2002)

George William Keeton and Lionel Astor Sheridan, The Law of Trusts (12th edn, London 1993)

András Kisfaludi, Ötödik könyv. Harmadik rész I. cím, in: Lajos Vékás (ed.), Szakértői Javaslat az új Polgári Törvénykönyv tervezetéhez (Budapest 2008)

Carl Friedrich Ferdinand Kniep (trans.), Gai Institutionum Commentarius Secundus. §§ 1–96 (Sachenrecht) (Jena 1912)

Rolf Knieper, Lado Chanturia, and Hans-Joachim Schramm, Das Privatrecht im Kaukasus und in Zentralasien (Berlin 2010)

Gernot Kocher and Markus Steppan, Grundzüge der Privatrechtsentwicklung und der Geschichte der Rechtswissenschaft in Österreich (2nd edn, Vienna 1997)

Georg E. Kodek, Grundbuchsrecht (Vienna 2007)

Mogens Koktvedgaard and Marianne Levin, Lärobok i Immaterialrätt (7th edn, Stockholm 2003)

Bálint Kolosváry, A dologi jog általános tanai; A birtok és birtokvédelem; A tulajdonjog, in: Károly Szladits (ed.), A magyar magánjog, Ötödik kötet, Dologi jog (Budapest 1942), pp. 1–321

Christian Kopetzki, Die Verwendung menschlicher Körpersubstanzen zu Forschungszwecken, in: Festschrift für Manfred Burgstaller (Vienna 2004) pp. 601–18

Panos Kornilakis, Katapisteftikí ekhórisi ton apetiseon (Thessaloniki 1978)

Efi Kounougeri-Manoledaki, Techniti gonimopoiisi kai Oikogeneiako Dikaio (Athens 2005)

Efi Kounougeri-Manoledaki, Oario kai gonimopoiimeno oario pou vriskontai exo apo to anthropino soma—H nomiki tous fusi kai metaxeirisi kata to astiko dikaio, Arm. 53 (1999) pp. 465–79

Marinos Kourtis, Astikó Díkeo metamoschéfseon, símfona me ton N. 2737/1999 (Athens 2002)

Ágota Kozma, Einschränkungen für EU-Bürger beim Erwerb landwirtschaftlich genutzter Flächen in Ungarn, WiRO 2012 pp. 221–32

Josef Krainz, System des österreichischen allgemeinen Privatrechts. vol. I (Der allgemeine Theil und das Sachenrecht) (3rd edn, Vienna 1899)

Peter Krebs and Maximilian Becker, Die Teilverdinglichung und ihre Anwendung auf Internetdomains, JZ 2009 pp. 932–43

Antonio La Torre, Cinquant'anni col diritto (Milan 2008)

Tamás Lábady, A forgalomképtelen törzsvagyon és az „aláépítés" jogi kérdése, BDT 2009 p. 83

Xavier Labbée, Respect et protection du corps humain. L'enfant conçu. Généralités, in: JClCiv Code, Art. 16 à 16-13, Fasc. 50 (Paris 2006)

Gwendoline Lardeux, Constructions nouvelles édifiées par le preneur sur le terrain loué: droit commun de l'accession et particularisme de bail commercial, RDC 2007 pp. 371–5

Christine Lassalas, L'inscription en compte des valeurs: la notion de propriété scripturale (Clermont-Ferrand 1997)

Adolf Laufs and Emil Reiling, Schmerzensgeld wegen schuldhafter Vernichtung deponierten Spermas? NJW 1994 pp. 775–6

Ján Lazar, Über die Entwicklung des slowakischen Privatrechts, ZEuP 2013 pp. 789–811

Pey-Woan Lee, Inducing breach of contract, conversion and contract as property, OxJLegStud 29 (2009) pp. 511–33

Barnabás Lenkovics, A dologi jog vázlata. Hetedik átdolgozott kiadás (7th edn, Budapest 2006)

Rémy Libchaber, La recodification du droit des biens, in: Le Code civil 1804–2004. Livre du bicentenaire (Paris 2004), pp. 297–372

Rémy Libchaber, Recherches sur la monnaie en droit privé (Paris 1992)

Rémy Libchaber, L'usufruit des créances existe-t-il? RTD civ. 1997 pp. 615–29

Marc Liebscher and Fryderyk Zoll, Einführung in das polnische Recht (Munich 2005)

Mario Lipari, Vendita con riserva di proprietà, in: Enciclopedia del diritto. vol. XLVI (Milan 1993)

Antonio Liserre, Lezioni di diritto privato (2nd edn, Milan 2009)

Seve Ljungman, Om skada och olägenhet på grannfastighet—Ett bidrag till läran om immisionernas rättsliga behandling (Uppsala 1943)

Grégoire Loiseau, Biens. Biens meubles par nature ou meuble corporels, in: JClCiv Code, Art. 527 à 532, Fasc. 10 (Paris 2011)

Grégoire Loiseau, Biens. Biens meubles par détermination de la loi ou meuble incorporels, in: JClCiv Code, Art. 527 à 532, Fasc. 20 (Paris 2011)

Carmen López Beltrán de Heredia, La propiedad intelectual, in: Angel M. López y López and Vicente L. Montés Penedés, Derechos reales y derecho inmobiliario registral (Valencia 1994), pp. 317–40

Stephan Lorenz, § 241a BGB und das Bereicherungsrecht: Zum Begriff der Bestellung im Schuldrecht, in: Thomas Rauscher (ed.), Festschrift für Werner Lorenz zum 80. Geburtstag (Munich 2001), pp. 193–214

Kevin F. K. Low, Equitable Title and Economic Loss (2010) 126 LQR pp. 507–12

Andrew Lyall, What are Easements Attached or Appurtenant to? (2010) 74 Conv 300–07
Geo Magri, Archeologia e proprietà, Riv. crit. dir. priv. 2009 pp. 73–106
Frederic William Maitland, The Unincorporated Body, in H.D. Hazeltine, G. Lapsley and P.H. Winfield (eds), Selected Essays (Cambridge 1936), pp. 128–40
Blandine Mallet-Bricout and Nadège Reboul-Maupin, Droit des biens (juin 2005/juillet 2006), D. 2006 pp. 2363–72
Didier Martin, De la revendication des sommes d'argent, D. 2002 pp. 3279–84
Didier Martin, Usufruit et propriété de droits sociaux, D. 2009 pp. 2444–7
Matteo Marrone, Istituzioni di diritto romano (Palermo 2006)
D. M. McDowell, To díkeo stin Athina ton klassikón Chrónon (5th edn, Athens 2009)
Mary-Rose McGuire, Die Lizenz. Eine Einordnung in die Systemzusammenhänge des BGB und des Zivilprozessrechts (Tübingen 2012)
Gerhard Mehrtens, Das gesetzliche Veräußerungsverbot (Göttingen 1974)
Mikael Mellqvist and Ingemar Persson, Fordran & Skuld (6th edn, Uppsala 2001)
Joana Mendes, Direito administrativo da água, in: Paulo Otero and Pedro Gonçalves (eds), Tratato de direito administrativo especial. vol. II (Coimbra 2009), pp. 11–134
Maria Isabel Helbling Menéres Campos, Da hipoteca—caracterização, constituição e efeitos (Coimbra 2003)
António Menezes Cordeiro, A posse: perspectivas dogmáticas actuais (3rd edn, Coimbra 2000)
Luís Manuel Teles de Menezes Leitão, Direito das obrigações. vol. III: Contratos em especial (4th edn, Coimbra 2006)
Luigi Mengoni, Gli acquisti a non domino (3rd edn, Milan 1994)
Aurelio Menéndez, Lecciones de derecho mercantil (5th edn, Madrid 2007)
Luís Manuel Teles de Menezes Leitão, Garantias das obrigações. Relatório sobre o programa, conteúdos e métodos de ensino (Coimbra 2006)
Attila Menyhárd, A Legfelsőbb Bíróság ítélete a soproni mélygarázs ügyében. Forgalomképtelen ingatlan felszínén, felszíne alatti vagy feletti részén emelt épület tulajdonjogának megszerzése, Jogesetek Magyarázata 4/2010 pp. 19–27
Werner Merle, Das Wohnungseigentum im System des bürgerlichen Rechts (Berlin 1979)
Thomas W. Merrill and Henry E. Smith, Optimal Standardization in the Law of Property: 'The *Numerus Clausus* Principle', 110 Yale L.J. 2000–01, pp. 1–70
Dietrich Meyer-Ravenstein, Ist das Urteil des Europäischen Gerichtshofs für Menschenrechte vom 26. 6. 2012 über die Zwangsmitgliedschaft in Jagdgenossenschaften verfassungsmäßig? AUR 2013 pp. 124–30
Ralf Michaels, Eigentum, in: Jürgen Basedow, Klaus J. Hopt and Reinhard Zimmermann (eds), Handwörterbuch des Europäischen Privatrechts vol. I, pp. 358–62 (Tübingen 2009)
Marc Mignot, Droit des sûretés (Paris 2010)
Jan Mojak and Jacek Widło, Zastaw Rejestrowy i rejestr zastawów. Komentarz praktyczny (3rd edn, Warsaw 2009)
Jens Müller, Der Allgemeine Teil im portugiesischen Zivilgesetzbuch—Entstehungsgeschichte und ausgewählte Einzelprobleme (Hamburg 2008)
Stephanie Müller-Bromley, Die Modernisierung des portugiesischen Hypothekenrechts (Baden-Baden 2004)
W. T. Murphy and S. Roberts, Understanding Property Law (2nd edn, London 1994)
Hans Joachim Musielak, Der Rückerwerb des Eigentums durch den nichtberechtigten Veräußerer, JuS 2010 pp. 377–82
David Nasmith, The Institutes of English Private Law: Embracing an Outline of the Substantive Branch of the Law of Persons and Things. vol. II: Things (London 1875)
Alessandro Natucci, La tipicità dei diritti reali. vol. I (Padua 1982)
Alessandro Natucci, Numerus clausus e analisi economica del diritto, NGCivil Code 2011, II, pp. 319–33
Zoltán Navratyil, A varázsló eltöri pálcáját (Budapest 2012)

Vytautas Nekrošius, Grundzüge der Reform des Zivilrechts in der Republik Litauen (unter besonderer Berücksichtigung des Sachenrechts), in: Helmut Heiss (ed.), Zivilrechtsreform im Baltikum (Tübingen 2006) pp. 83–98

Endre Nizsalovszky, Korlátolt dologi jogok, in: Károly Szladits (ed.), A magyar magánjog. vol. V: Dologi jog (Budapest 1942, reprint 1999), pp. 321–834

Endre Nizsalovszky, Magyar magánjog mai érvényében, II. kötet, Dologi jog (Budapest 1931)

José Carlos de Medeiros Nóbrega, Der rechtsgeschäftliche Eigentumserwerb an beweglichen Sachen in Deutschland und Portugal (2nd edn, Norderstedt 2010)

Franz Novak, Das Stockwerkseigentum im Wiener Rechte des Mittelalters, ZRG GA 54 (1934) pp. 89–115

A. J. Oakley, Parker and Mellows: The Modern Law of Trusts (8th edn, London 2003)

José de Oliveira Ascensão, Direito civil—Direito de autor e direitos conexos (Coimbra 1992)

José de Oliveira Ascensão, Direito Civil—Reais (5th edn, Coimbra 1993, reprint 2000)

Lucia Orsingher and Luigi Salomone, Manuale del pegno e delle ipoteche (Macerata 2007)

Sebastian Omlor, Verkehrsschutz im Kapitalgesellschaftsrecht—das System des gutgläubigen Erwerbs von GmbH-Geschäftsanteilen, WM 2009 pp. 2105–12

N. C. van Oostrom-Streep, Zakelijke werking van huurbepalingen: de Hoge Raad stelt grenzen, WPNR 2010 p. 469

Rolf Ostheim, Superädifikate auf eigenem Grund, ÖJZ 1975 pp. 202–09

Paul Ourliac and J. De Malafosse, Histoire du droit privé. Les biens (2nd edn, Paris 1971)

Pedro Pais de Vasconcelos, Contratos atípicos (Coimbra 1995)

Thanasis K. Papachristou, I technití anaparagogí ston Astikó Kódika, in: Festschrift für I. Manoledakis. vol. III (Athens 2007), pp. 915–26

Massimo Paradiso, L'accessione al suolo (Milan 1994)

Béatrice Parance, La possession des biens incorporels (Paris 2008)

Sandra Passinhas, Os animais e o regime português da propriedade horizontal, ROA 66 (2006-II) pp. 833–73

Maria Pavlova, Grazdansko pravo, Obshta Chast, vol. I (Sofia 1996)

Mark Pawlowski, Estoppel, Constructive Trusts and Unconscionability Trusts & Trustees 12 (2006) pp. 10–15

Susanna Peichl, Der Embryo in vitro—seine rechtliche Qualifikation und die Alternative der 'Embryoannahme', ÖJZ 2003 pp. 581–92

Anne Pélissier, Possession et meubles incorporels (Paris 2001)

Hugues Périnet-Marquet (ed.), Propositions de l'Association Henri Capitant pour une réforme du droit des biens (Paris 2009)

Steven Perrick, Carel Asser's handleiding tot de beoefening van het Nederlands burgerlijk recht. vol. VI: Erfrecht. Erfrecht en schenking (12th edn, Deventer 1996)

L. Miguel Pestana de Vasconcelos, Direito das garantias (Coimbra 2011)

Ferenc Petrik, Tulajdonjogunk ma—A dologi jog mai érvényében (Budapest 2007)

Marietta Pietrek, Konsens über Tradition? Eine Studie zur Eigentumsübertragung in Brasilien, Deutschland und Portugal (Tübingen 2015)

Fernando Andrade Pires de Lima, Das coisas, BMJ 91 (1959) pp. 207–22

P.J. van der Plank, Havenkranen onreorend? Over het verschil tussen rijden an drijven, NTBR 2011 pp. 202–06

Frederick Pollock, 'What Is a Thing?' LQR 10 (1894) pp. 318–22

Frederick Pollock and Robert Samuel Wright, An Essay on Possession in the Common Law (Oxford 1888)

András József Pomeisl, A forgalomképtelen ingatlanokkal való rendelkezésről, Gazdaság és Jog 2009/5 pp. 14–19

Ana Prata, Dicionário jurídico. vol. I: Direito civil, processo civil, organização judiciária (5th edn, Coimbra 2008)

Jesko Preuß, Rechtlich geschützte Interessen an virtuellen Gütern (Berlin 2009)

Jean Prieur, Sophie Schiller, Thierry Revet and Renaud Mortier, L'usufruit de droits sociaux. Quelle place pour la liberté contractuelle? JCP N 2011, 1221 pp. 32–43

William L. Prosser, The Nature of Conversion (1957) 42 Cornell LQ 168–84
Athanasios K. Pouliadis, Η δικαστική ρύθμιση της χρήσης της οικογενειακής στέγης επί διακοπής της συμβιώσεως των συζύγων (A.K. 1393), Arm. 1995 pp. 589–604
Muireann Quigley, Propertisation and Commercialisation: On Controlling the Use of Human Biomaterials, Mod.L.Rev. 2014 pp. 677–702
M. J. G. C. Raaijmakers, Ondernemingsrecht (Deventer 2006)
Leo Raape, Das gesetzliche Veräußerungsverbot des Bürgerlichen Gesetzbuchs (Berlin 1908)
Raffaele Rascio, Universalità patrimoniali, Novissimo Digesto italiano, vol. XX (Turin 1975) pp. 94–112
Jürgen C. T. Rassi, Grundbuchsrecht (Vienna 2010)
Hugo Ramos Alves, Do penhor (Coimbra 2010)
Antonín Randa, Držba dle rakouského práva v pořádku systematickém (vol. I) (Prague 1890) and Právo vlastnické dle rakouského práva v pořádku systematickém (vol. II) (Prague 1922, reprint vol. I and II edited by Jiří Spáčil, Prague 2008)
Johannes Reich-Rohrwig, Verpfändung und Pfändung von OG- und KG-Anteilen, ecolex 2011 pp. 4–10
Matteo Rescigno, Le garanzie 'rotative' convenzionali: fattispecie e problemi di disciplina, Banca, Borsa e titoli di credito 2001 pp. 1–29
Matteo Rescigno, Il privilegio per i finanziamenti bancari a medio e lungo termine a favore delle imprese, con particolare riguardo alla rotatività del suo oggetto, Banca, Borsa e titoli di credito 1999 pp. 583–607
Rép. civ. Dalloz (*-Cohet-Cordey*), V° Accession (Paris 2009)
Thierry Revet, La consécration de la propriété des créances par le Conseil constitutionnel, RTD civ. 2010 pp. 584–7
Thierry Revet, Propriété et droits réels, RTD civ. 2010 pp. 133–40
Frederick Rieländer, Sachenrechtliche Erwerbsrechte (Munich 2014)
Knut Rodhe, Handbok i sakrätt (Lund 1985)
Alf Ross, Tû-tû, in: Festschrift für Henry Ussing (Kopenhagen 1951) pp. 468–84
Carsten Roth, Eigentum an Körperteilen (Heidelberg 2009)
František Rouček, Jaromír Sedláček et al., Komentář k československému obecnému zákoníku občanskému a občanské právo platné na Slovensku a v Podkarpatské Rusi. vol. II: §§ 285–530 (Prague 1935)
Jānis Rozenfelds, Latvian Property and Collateral Law and Protection of Foreign Investments, Juridica International 6 (2001) pp. 108–13
Jānis Rozenfelds, Superficies Solo Cedit in Latvian Law, Journ. Univ. Latvia: Law 5 (2013) pp. 120–36
Thomas Rüfner, Savigny und der Sachbegriff des BGB, in: Stefan Leible, Matthias Lehmann and Herbert Zech (eds), Unkörperliche Güter im Zivilrecht (Tübingen 2011), pp. 33–48
Domenico Rubino, La compravendita, in: Antonio Cicu and Francesco Messineo (eds), Trattato di diritto civile e commerciale. vol. 23 (2nd edn, Milan 1962)
Domenico Rubino, L'ipoteca immobiliare e mobiliare, in: Antonio Cicu and Francesco Messineo (eds), Trattato di diritto civile e commerciale. vol. 19 (Milan 1956)
Bernard Rudden, Economic Theory v. Property Law: The *Numerus Clausus* Problem, in: John Eekelaar and John Bell (eds), Oxford Essays in Jurisprudence. Third series (1987), pp. 239–63
Cesare Ruperto (ed.), La giurisprudenza sul codice civile. Coordinata con la dottrina, Libro III (Artt. 810–951) Della proprietà, (Milan 2011)
Paloma Saborido Sánchez, Reflexiones sobre el tercero hipotecario (Madrid 2008)
Adrian Ştefan Sacalschi, Grundeigentum und Sicherheiten in Rumänien (Verband Deutscher Pfandbriefbanken, vol. 47, 2nd edn, Berlin 2011)
Ángel Sánchez Hernández, La concentración parcelaria y sus fases, Redur 4/2006 pp. 75–85 (http://www.unirioja.es/dptos/dd/redur/numero4/sanchez.pdf)
Johan Sandstedt, Sakrätten, Norden och europeiseringen—Nordisk funktionalism möter kontinental substantialism (Stockholm 2013)
Joaquim Sarrate i Pou, Formprobleme bei Grundstücksveräußerungen im deutsch-spanischen Rechtsverkehr (Frankfurt on the Main 1998)

René Savatier, La propriété de l'espace, D. 1965, I, pp. 213–18

Friedrich Carl von Savigny, Das Recht des Besitzes (7th edn, Vienna 1865)

Friedrich Carl von Savigny, System des heutigen römischen Rechts. vol. 1 (Berlin 1840, 2nd reprint Aalen 1981)

Fabio Massimo Scaramuzzino, Die Zusendung unbestellter Ware. Vertrag, Rückgabe und Schadensersatz (Regensburg 2010)

Alexander Schall, Die Pfändung von Anteilen an einer englischen Kapitalgesellschaft (private/public company limited by shares), WM 2011 pp. 2249–53

Herbert Schimansky, Josef Bunte, and Hans-Jürgen Lwowsky, Bankrechts-Handbuch (4th edn, Munich 2011)

Peter Schlechtriem and Ingeborg Schwenzer (eds), Commentary of the UN Convention on the International Sale of Goods (CISG) (3rd edn, Oxford 2010)

Peter Schlechtriem and Ingeborg Schwenzer (eds), Kommentar zum Einheitlichen UN-Kaufrecht (5th edn, Munich 2008)

G. K. Schmelzeisen, Die Relativität des Besitzbegriffs, AcP 136 (1932) 38–87 and 129–209

Holger Schmidt, Auf dem Weg zur vollen Anerkennung immaterieller Vermögenswerte als Kreditsicherheit? WM 2012 pp. 721–31

Karsten Schmidt (ed.), Münchener Kommentar zum Handelsgesetzbuch. vol. VII: Handelsgeschäfte (§§ 407–475h) (2nd edn, Munich 2009)

Martin Schmidt-Kessel and Silvan Schubmehl (eds), Lauterkeitsrecht in Europa. Eine Sammlung von Länderberichten zum Recht gegen unlauteren Wettbewerb (Munich 2011)

Schmittmann, Wem gehört das Inhouse-Telefonkabel? Die Rechtsstellung des Gebäudeeigentümers gegenüber TK-Unternehmen, MMR 2009 pp. 520–25

Klaus Ulrich Schmolke, Das Servitutenrecht des BGB aus rechtsökonomischer Sicht, WM 2010 pp. 740–48

Peter Schneiderhan, Der Quasi-Contract im schottischen und englischen Recht (Düsseldorf 1996)

Klaus Schreiber, Die Grundprinzipien des Sachenrechts, Jura 2010 pp. 272–5

Günter Christian Schwarz, § 241a BGB als Störfall für die Zivilrechtsdogmatik—Zu den systemwidrigen Folgen der Umsetzung der EG-Fernabsatz-Richtlinie, NJW 2001 pp. 1449–54

J. de Seabra Lopes, Direito dos registos e do notariado (6th edn, Coimbra 2011)

Giuseppe Sena, Note critiche sul procedimento di mediazione e conciliazione—Sua disapplicazione alla proprietà industriale e intellettuale, Riv. dir. ind. 2010 pp. 164–72

Philippe Simler, La réforme du droit des sûretés—Un livre IV nouveau du Code civil, JCP 2006, I, 13, no. 124, pp. 597–600

Wiesław Skrzydło, Sabina Grabowska, and Radosław Grabowski, Konstytucja Rzeczypospolitej Polskiej. Komentarz encyklopedyczny (Warsaw 2009)

Radosław Skwarło, Ustawa o przekształceniu prawa użytkowania wieczystego w prawo własności nieruchomości. Komentarz (Warsaw 2008)

Emma Slessinger, Who's in Charge Here? (2011) 75 Conv 92–95

Christoph-Karl Sliwka, Herausgabeansprüche als Teil des zivilrechtlichen Eigentumsrechts? Die *rei vindicatio* und funktionsäquivalente Ansprüche des Eigentümers gegen den Besitzer im französischen, englischen und deutschen Recht (Berlin 2012)

Marcus Smith, The Law of Assignment (Oxford 2007)

Rudolph Sohm, Eduard Hölder, and Emil Strohal, Drei Beiträge zum bürgerlichen Recht (Leipzig 1905)

Wolfgang Sohst, Das spanische Bürgerliche Gesetzbuch. Text und Kommentar (2nd edn, Berlin 2003)

Olaf Sosnitza, Besitz und Besitzschutz (Tübingen 2003)

Jiří Spáčil and Michal Spáčil, Přehled judikatury ve věcech občanskoprávních vztahů k pozemkům (Prague 2011)

Peter Sparkes, A New Land Law (Oxford 1999)

Peter Sparkes, Certainty of Property: Numerus Clausus or the Rule with No Name? ERPL 2012 pp. 769–804

Ioannis Spyridakis, Genikes Arches. vol. I and II (Athens 2007)

Ioannis Spyridakis, Note under CA Athens 236/1976, NoB 24 (1976) pp. 638–40

Ioannis Spyridakis, Zur Problematik der Sachbestandteile (Tübingen 1966)

M. I. Spyridakis, Epitomo Nomikó Lexikó (Athens and Komotini 2008)
Naďa Štachová and Ondřej Horák, Věc v právním smyslu: historicko-srovnávací úvaha, in: Interakce českého a evropského práva (Brünn 2009) pp. 405–35
Astrid Stadler, Die Vorschläge des Gemeinsamen Referenzrahmens für ein europäisches Sachenrecht—Grundprinzipien und Eigentumserwerb, JZ 2010 pp. 380–92
Pasquale Stanzione, Manuale di Diritto Privato (3rd edn, Turin, 2013)
Liviu Stănciulescu, Drept Civil. Contracte Speciale. Succesiuni (Bukarest 2002)
Dirk Staudenmayer (ed.), Vorschlag für eine Verordnung des Europäischen Parlaments und des Rates über ein Gemeinsames Europäisches Kaufrecht (Munich 2012)
Stoyan Stavrou, Vaprosi na balgarskoto veshtno pravo (Sofia 2008)
P. A. Stein, Note under HR 5. March 2004, NedJur 2004, no. 316, pp. 2706–07
William J. Stewart, The Law of Restitution in Scotland (Edinburgh 1992)
Jean Stoufflet, Le nantissement de meubles corporels, JCP, Beilage zu Nr. 20 vom 17 May 2006 pp. 19–22
J.C. van Straaten, Economische eigendom—bezit—verjaring—overdrachtsbelastning (I), WPNR 2011 pp. 980–4
Moritz von Stubenrauch, Commentar zum österreichischen Allgemeinen bürgerlichen Gesetzbuche. vol. I (8th edn, Vienna 1902)
Ulrich Stutz, Das Eigenkirchenvermögen, Festschrift für Otto Gierke (Weimar 1911) pp. 1187–1268
Stanislav Stuna and Jiří Švestka, K pojmu věc v právním smyslu návrhu nového občanského zákoníku, Právní rozhledy 10 (2011) pp. 366–73
Thorsten Süß, Von Meteoriten, Skeletten und anderen Kostbarkeiten, Jura 2011 pp. 332–5
Charles Sweet, Challis's Law of Real Property (3rd edn, London 1911)
Jiří Švestka et al., Ochrana osobnosti (Prague 1996)
Jiří Švestka and Jan Dvořák, Občanské právo hmotné (5th edn, Prague 2009)
Károly Szladits, Dologi jog és kötelmi jog, Jogtudományi Közlöny 42 (1895) pp. 334–5
Károly Szladits, in: József Ginyovszky (ed.), Az Osztrák Polgári Törvénykönyv hatásában a magyar magánjogra (Budapest, no year)
William Swadling, in: Peter Birks (ed.), English Private Law. vol. I: Sources of law, law of persons, law of property (Oxford 2000)
Charles Sweet, Choses In Action, LQR 10 (1894) pp. 303–17
Ferenc Szilágyi, Wind Power under Hungarian Private Law, ERPL 21 (2013) pp. 371–86
Grażyna Szpor, Czesław Martysz and Kajetan Wojsyk, Ustawa o informatyzacji działalności podmiotów realizujących zadania publiczne. Komentarz (Warsaw 2007)
Antoine Tardos, L'accession différée en matière d'usufruit: vers la qualité de propriétaire de l'usufruitier constructeur? D. 2012 pp. 2871–5
Antoine Tardos, Création de droit réel: consécration de l'autonomie de la volonté, D. 2012 p. 2596
Nigel Teare, The Admiralty Action in rem and the House of Lords [1998] LMCLQ pp. 33–42
Ivo Telec, Duševní vlastnictví a jeho vliv na věc v právním smyslu, Právní rozhledy 12 (2011) pp. 444–50
François Terré, Introduction générale au droit (Paris 1998)
François Terré and Yves Lequette, Henri Capitant, Les grands arrêts de la jurisprudence civile (10th edn, Paris 1994)
François Xavier Testu, L'autonomie de la volonté, source de droits réels principaux, JCP G 2012, 1400, pp. 2352–7
Andrew Tettenborn, Reversionary Damage to Chattels, 53 (1994) CLJ 326–42
Hans-Wolf Thümmel, Abschied vom Stockwerkseigentum, JZ 1980 pp. 125–34
Andrea Torrente and Piero Schlesinger, Manuale di diritto privato (19th edn, Milan 2009)
Andrea Torrente and Piero Schlesinger, Manuale di diritto privato (21st edn, Milan 2013)
Václav Trajer and Pavlína Trajerová, Katastr nemovitostí (2nd edn, Prague 2010)
Matjaž Tratnik, Das neue slowenische Sachenrecht, WGO-MfOR 45 (2003) pp. 94–108
Mario Trimarchi, Universalità di cose, Enc. dir. vol. XLV (Milan 1992) pp. 801–22
Giuseppe Tucci, Garanzie sui crediti dell'impresa e tutela dei finanziamenti (Milan 1974)
P. G. Turner, Consequential Economic Loss and the Trust Beneficiary CLJ 69 (2010) pp. 445–7

Joseph Unger, System des österreichischen allgemeinen Privatrechts. vol. I (5th edn, Leipzig 1892)
Jo Vanbelle, Geld juridisch bekeken, Algemeen Juridisch Tijdschrift-Dossier Nr. 7, 1994–95, pp. 65–7
Kenneth J. Vandevelde, The New Property of the Nineteenth Century: The Development of the Modern Concept of Property Buff. L. Rev. 29 (1980) 325–67
Adriano Vanzetti, Diritti reali e proprietà industriale (e mediazione obbligatoria), Riv. dir. ind. 2010 pp. 173–84
Maria João Romão Carreiro Vaz Tomé and Diogo Leite de Campos, Propriedade fiduciária (trust)—estudo para a sua consagração no direito português (Coimbra 1999)
František Vážný (ed.), Rozhodnutí nejvyššího soudu československé republiky ve věcech občanských. vol. III, no. 838–1393 (Prague 1921) and vol. V, no. 2136–749 (Prague 1923)
Lajos Vékás, Érvénytelen szerződés és jogalap nélküli gazdagodás, Magyar Jog 7/2003, pp. 385–400
Giacomo Venezian, Dell'usufrutto, dell'uso e dell'abitazione (Naples and Turin 1931)
José Alberto C. Vieira, Direitos reais (Coimbra 2008)
Michel Villey, Les biens et les choses en droit (Paris 1979)
Peter Vojčík, Práva priemyselného vlastníctva (Bratislava 1998)
Antonio Volanti, Pegno omnibus, credito garantito e prelazione, Obbligazioni e contratti 4 (2010) pp. 280–88
Emmanuil Vouzikas, Metavívasi kuriótitas pros exasfálisi apetíseos, EEN 18 (1951) pp. 657–8
Emmanuil Vouzikas, Note under CA Athens 1142/1957, NoB 6 (1957) p. 557
Spyridon Vrellis, Díkaio Allodapón (Athens 2003)
Eberhard Wagner, Absolute Wirkung vertraglicher Abtretungsverbote gleich absolute Unwirksamkeit verbotswidriger Abtretung? JZ 1994 pp. 227–33
Christina Wainikka, Information som självständigt objekt, SvJT 2003 pp. 577–86
Peter Watts, The Tort of Conversion and Equity's Rules against Merger: Campbell v Dominion Breweries Ltd NZ Recent L. Rev. (1994) pp. 336–43
Amalie Weidner, Kulturgüter als res extra commercium im internationalen Sachenrecht (Berlin 2001)
Amédéo Wermelinger, Das Stockwerkeigentum: Art. 712a–712t ZGB (Zurich 2010)
Franz Wieacker, Sachbegriff, Sacheinheit und Sachzuordnung, AcP 148 (1943) pp. 57–104
Joseph Max von Winiwarter, Des dinglichen Sachenrechtes erste Abtheilung: Nach dem österreichischen allgemeinen bürgerl. Gesetzbuche. vol. I (2nd edn, Vienna 1839)
Sarah Worthington, Personal Property Law. Text, Cases and Materials (Oxford 2000)
Wolfgang Zankl, Bürgerliches Recht (5th edn, Vienna 2010)
Frédéric Zenati, Propriété et droits réels, RTD civ. 1992 pp. 791–9 and 1993 pp. 162–71
Frédéric Zenati-Castaing, Pour une rénovation de la théorie de la propriété, RTD civ. 1993 pp. 305–23
Stefan Zetterström, Sakrättens fyra huvudfall (2nd edn, Uppsala 2008)

Index